'A timely, innovative and insightful book that addresses a wide range of vitally important contemporary concerns of global reach ranging from climate change to food security to China's role in Africa through the lens of non-trade issues. The editors and contributors are to be congratulated for cutting edge scholarship with real world significance.'

Randy Peerenboom, La Trobe University Melbourne, Australia

'China's growing role in the WTO, both because of its involvement in numerous disputes and as a full participant to its overall activities, and China's active engagement in multilateral and regional law making concerning environmental, social and economic matters generally makes this volume quite timely. The contributors cover a wide spectrum of issues making this publication an indispensable tool for all those concerned in current problems of the global economy.'

Giorgio Sacerdoti, Bocconi University, Italy, and former Chairman of the WTO Appellate Body

'*China's Influence on Non-Trade Concerns in International Economic Law*, edited by Paolo Davide Farah and Elena Cima, is a most timely book on an important issue. This book is impressive both because of the breadth and depth of the topics addressed. For anyone interested in the future of the multilateral trading system, this book will be a very interesting and at times provocative read.'

Peter Van den Bossche, World Trade Institute (WTI), Switzerland and Member, Appellate Body, World Trade Organization

'This is really a "masterwork" which has appeared at the "right time" on the "right topic". The book assesses China's development on non-trade concerns within the context of the WTO by use of global justice and sustainable development principles. It is a great collection which critically examines China from multiple perspectives.'

Minyou Yu, Wuhan University, China

China's Influence on Non-Trade Concerns in International Economic Law

This volume examines the range of Non-Trade Concerns (NTCs) that may conflict with international economic rules and proposes ways to protect them within international law and international economic law. Globalization without local concerns can endanger relevant issues such as good governance, human rights, right to water, right to food, social, economic, cultural and environmental rights, labor rights, access to knowledge, public health, social welfare, consumer interests and animal welfare, climate change, energy, environmental protection and sustainable development, product safety, food safety and security. Focusing on China, the book shows the current trends of Chinese law and policy towards international standards. The authors argue that China can play a leading role in this context: not only has China adopted several reforms and new regulations to address NTCs; but it has started to play a very relevant role in international negotiations on NTCs such as climate change, energy, and culture, among others. While China is still considered a developing country, in particular from the NTCs' point of view, it promises to be a key actor in international law in general and, more specifically, in international economic law in this respect. This volume assesses, taking into consideration its special context, China's behavior internally and externally to understand its role and influence in shaping NTCs in the context of international economic law.

Paolo Davide Farah teaches climate change, trade, energy, and environmental law and policy at West Virginia University, USA. He has variously taught classes on public international law, international economic law and WTO law, European law, Comparative law, and Chinese law in Italy, United Kingdom, USA, China, and other countries. He was a Visiting Scholar for the academic year 2011–2012 at Harvard Law School, East Asian Legal Studies Program and a Senior Fellow at the Institute of International Economic Law (IIEL), Georgetown University Law Center, Washington DC, USA. He is Director of Research of gLAWcal – Global Law Initiatives for Sustainable Development (www.glawcal.org.uk) and is Principal Investigator for EU Commission research projects in collaboration with European, Chinese, Russian, and Japanese universities. He is an expert in the interaction between trade, economic globalization, and NTCs, such as sustainable development, energy, environment, and human rights, with a special focus on China and other Asian countries. He has previously worked as an intern at the Legal Affairs Division of the World Trade Organization in Geneva and was an Associate Lawyer of Baker and McKenzie Law Firm, Milan, Italy. He graduated with a Maitrise in International and European Law from Paris Ouest La Defense Nanterre University (France), LLM in European Legal Studies from the College of Europe in Bruges (Belgium) and a Dual PhD in international law from Aix-Marseille University (France), and University of Milan (Italy).

Elena Cima, PhD candidate in international law at the Graduate Institute of International Law and Development Studies in Geneva, where she also works for the LLM Program in International Law. Her research interests include public international law, international trade law, international environmental law, energy law, and Chinese law. She is a member of the American branch of the International Law Association (ILA), for which she served as reporter. Her publications have focused on international trade law, energy law, and Chinese law and policy. She holds an LLB, honored summa cum laude, from the University of Milan and an LLM degree from Yale Law School.

Global Law and Sustainable Development

Series editor: Paolo Davide Farah

West Virginia University, USA and gLAWcal – Global Law Initiatives for Sustainable Development, UK

This series provides a new focus on the relationship between international law, economy and trade, with special attention to what are commonly referred to as non-trade-related values and concerns. Through research and policy analysis the series sheds new light on a range of issues relating to good governance and human rights in the widest sense. It is held that the values supporting these issues are directly affected by the global expansion of world trade and need to be upheld in order to balance the excesses of globalization. Multidisciplinary in approach, the series integrates studies from scholars and researchers with a range of different backgrounds and interdisciplinary expertise from law, economics, political science, and sociology through to history, philosophy, and natural science.

Other titles in this series:

The Reform of International Economic Governance, Antonio Segura Serrano (2016)

China's Influence on Non-Trade Concerns in International Economic Law

Edited by
Paolo Davide Farah

WEST VIRGINIA UNIVERSITY (USA)
and
GLAWCAL – GLOBAL LAW INITIATIVES FOR SUSTAINABLE DEVELOPMENT (UK)

Elena Cima

GRADUATE INSTITUTE OF INTERNATIONAL AND DEVELOPMENT STUDIES (SWITZERLAND)

Routledge
Taylor & Francis Group
LONDON AND NEW YORK

First published 2016
by Routledge

2 Park Square, Milton Park, Abingdon, Oxfordshire OX14 4RN
52 Vanderbilt Avenue, New York, NY 10017

Routledge is an imprint of the Taylor and Francis Group, an informa business

First issued in paperback 2019

British Library Cataloguing in Publication Data
A catalogue record for this book is available from the British Library

Library of Congress Cataloging in Publication Data
A catalog record for this title has been requested

ISBN: 978-1-4094-4848-8 (hbk)
ISBN: 978-0-367-43989-7 (pbk)

Typeset in Galliard
by Apex CoVantage, LLC

Contents

Figures

Tables

Abbreviations

AANZFTA	Australia–New Zealand Free Trade Agreement
AB	Appellate Body
ABA	American Bar Association
ACFTU	All China Federation of Trade Unions
ACLA	All China Lawyers Association
ADP	Ad Hoc Working Group on the Durban Platform for Enhanced Action
AFTA	ASEAN Free Trade Area
AGOA	African Growth and Opportunity Act
AJFTA	ASEAN–Japan Free Trade Agreement
AMS	ASEAN Member States
AoA	Agreement on Agriculture
AOSIS	Alliance of Small Island States
ASEAN	Association of South-East Asian Nations
BAP	Bali Action Plan
BIT	Bilateral Investment Treaty
BSE	Bovine Spongiform Encephalitis
CA	Corporate Accountability
CAA	Consumer Affairs Authority
CAC	Codex Alimentarius Commission
CAFTA	China–ASEAN Free Trade Agreement
CAP	Common Agricultural Policy
CASE	Consumer Association of Singapore
CBD	Convention on Biological Diversity
CBDR	Common But Differentiated Responsibilities
CBDRRC	Common But Differentiated Responsibilities and Respective Capabilities
CBHD	China Blue High Definition
CBM	Coalbed Methane
CCA	China Consumers' Association
CCAN	China Civil Climate Action Network
CCP	Chinese Communist Party
CCTV	China Central Television
CDM	Clean Development Mechanism
CEDAW	Convention on the Elimination of All Forms of Discrimination against Women
CEPT	Common Effective Preferential Tariff
CERs	Certified Emission Reductions
CESCR	Committee on Economic, Social, and Cultural Rights
CIT	Corporate Income Tax
CLB	China Labour Bulletin

CLS	Core Labor Standards
CNOOC	China National Offshore Oil Corporation
CNPC	China National Petroleum Corporation
CNY	Chinese Yuan
COD	Chemical Oxygen Demand
COP	Conference of the Parties
CP	Crude Protein
CPD	Central Propaganda Department
CPI	Intellectual Property Code
CPCC	Chinese People's Political Consultative Conference
CRC	Convention on the Rights of the Child
CSR	Corporate Social Responsibility
CUJ	Consumers Union of Japan
CVMA	Canadian Veterinary Medical Association
CYCAN	China Youth Climate Action Network
DC	Developing Country
DDA	Doha Development Agenda
DFO	Department of Fisheries and Oceans
DNA	Designated National Authority
DOE	Designated Operational Entity
DSB	Dispute Settlement Body
DSU	Dispute Settlement Understanding
EB	Executive Board
EBA	Everything But Arms
EC	European Commission
EIA	Environmental Impact Assessment
EPC	European Patent Convention
EPO	European Patent Office
ETS	Emission Trading System
EU	European Union
FAO	Food and Agriculture Organization
FDI	Foreign Direct Investment
FET	Fair and Equitable Treatment
FON	Friends of Nature
FTA	Free Trade Agreement
GAPP	General Administration of Press and Publications
GATS	General Agreement on Trade in Services
GATT	General Agreement on Tariffs and Trade
GCC	Gulf Cooperation Council
GDP	Gross Domestic Product
GECF	Gas Exporting Countries Forum
GHG	Greenhouse Gas
GOFA	Global Online Freedom Act
GONGO	Government-Organized Non-Governmental Organization
GR	Genetic Resources
GSGI	Global Shale Gas Resource Initiative
HBV	Hepatitis B virus
IC	Inuit Community
ICCPR	International Covenant on Civil and Political Rights
ICESCR	International Covenant on Economic, Social and Cultural Rights
ICH	Intangible Cultural Heritage
ICJ	International Court of Justice

ICSID	International Centre for Settlement of Investment Disputes
ICT	Information and Communication Technologies
IEC	International Electro Technical Commission
IGC	Intergovernmental Committee on Intellectual Property and Genetic Resources, Traditional Knowledge and Folklore
IIPA	International Intellectual Property Alliance
ILC	International Law Commission
ILO	International Labour Organization
IMF	International Monetary Fund
INC	Intergovernmental Negotiating Committee
INDCs	Intended Nationally Determined Contributions
INGO	International Non-Governmental Organization
IPCC	Intergovernmental Panel on Climate Change
IPPC	International Plant Protection Convention
IPRs	Intellectual Property Rights
ISO	International Organization for Standardization
ITO	International Trade Organization
IVWG	Independent Veterinarians' Working Group
LDC	Least-Developed Country
LNG	Liquefied Natural Gas
ME	Metabolizable Energy
MEA	Multilateral Environmental Agreement
MEP	Ministry of Environmental Protection of the People's Republic of China
MFN	Most Favored Nation
MIGA	Multilateral Investment Guarantee Agency
MLR	Ministry of Land Resources
MMR	Marine Mammal Regulations
MNC	Multinational Corporation
MNE	Multinational Enterprise
MOF	Ministry of Finance
MOFTEC	Ministry of Foreign Trade and Cooperation
MOP	Meeting of the Parties
MOST	Ministry of Science and Technology
MPAA	Motion Pictures Association of America
MRL	Maximum Residue Level
MRV	Measurement, Reporting and Verification
NCCCC	National Coordination Committee on Climate Change
NCFR	Non-Conventional Feed Resources
NDRC	National Development and Reform Commission
NEC	National Energy Commission
NFIDC	Net Food-Importing Developing Country
NGO	Non-Governmental Organization
NIC	Newly Industrialized Country
NPC	National People's Congress
NT	National Treatment
NTC	Non-Trade Concern
OBFM	Objective-Based Fisheries Management
ODF	Open Document Format
ODS	Ozone Depleting Substances
OECD	Organization for Economic Co-operation and Development
OFDI	Outward Foreign Direct Investment
OGEC	Organization of Gas Exporting Countries

OIE	International Office of Epizootics
OOXML	Open XML
OPEC	Organization of the Petroleum Exporting Countries
PCT	Patent Cooperation Treaty
PDD	Project Design Document
PIL	Public Interest Litigation
POP	Persistent Organic Pollutant
PRC	People's Republic of China
PSA	Product Sharing Agreement
PTA	Preferential Trade Agreement
PVC	Plant Variety Certificate
QIP	Quarantine Inspection Permit
R&D	Research and Development
RA	Risk Assessment
RIL	Rights Interest Litigation
RTA	Regional Trade Agreement
RSC	Regional Supervision Center
SACU	South African Custom Union
SAL	Social Action Litigation
SAQSIQ	State Administration of Quality Supervision, Inspection and Quarantine
SARFT	State Administration of Radio, Film, and Television
SASAC	State-Owned Assets Supervision and Administration Commission of the State Council
SAT	State Administration of Taxation
SBR	Seal Ban Regulation
SEE	Society of Entrepreneurs and Ecology
SEZ	Special Economic Zone
SGSR	Secretary-General Special Representative
SIPO	China's State Intellectual Property Office
SME	Small and Medium Enterprise
SOE	State-Owned Enterprise
SPS	Sanitary and Phytosanitary
SSA	Sub-Saharan Africa
SWF	Sovereign Wealth Fund
TBT	Technical Barriers to Trade
TCE	Traditional Cultural Expressions
TCM	Traditional Chinese Medicine
TIPR	Traditional Intellectual Property Rights
TK	Traditional Knowledge
TNC	Transnational Corporation
TRI	Toxics Release Inventory
TRIPS	Trade-Related Aspects of Intellectual Property Rights
UK	United Kingdom
UN	United Nations
UNCHE	United Nations Conference on the Human Environment
UNCITRAL	United Nations Commission on International Trade Law
UNDP	United Nations Development Program
UNEP	United Nations Environment Program
UNFCCC	United Nations Framework Convention on Climate Change
UPOV	Protection of New Varieties of Plants
US	United States
USD	US Dollar

USTR	United States Trade Representative
VAT	Value-Added Tax
VCLT	Vienna Convention on the Law of Treaties
WHO	World Health Organization
WIPO	World Intellectual Property Organization
WIR	World Investment Report
WHO	World Health Organization
WMO	World Meteorological Organization
WTO	World Trade Organization

Notes on Editors

Paolo Davide Farah teaches climate change, trade, energy, and environmental law and policy at West Virginia University, John D. Rockefeller IV School of Policy and Politics, Department of Public Administration and College of Law, USA. He has variously taught classes on public international law, international economic law and WTO law, European law, Comparative law, and Chinese law in Italy, in the UK (as Senior Lecturer), USA, and China (as Visiting Professor).

He was a Visiting Scholar (2011–2012) at Harvard Law School, East Asian Legal Studies Program, a Fellow (2004–2005) at the Institute of International Economic Law (IIEL), Georgetown University Law Center, Washington DC, USA.

He is Director of Research of gLAWcal – Global Law Initiatives for Sustainable Development (www.glawcal.org.uk) and is Principal Investigator for EU Commission research projects in collaboration with Russian, Japanese, and Chinese Universities such as Tsinghua University, Peking University, Beijing Normal University (BNU), Wuhan University, China–EU School of Law (CESL), Beijing Foreign Studies University (BFSU), East China University of Political Sciences and Law (ECUPL), Shanghai JiaoTong University (SJTU), Tongji University.

He was individually awarded of the Science and Technology Fellowship (STF) Program in China funded by the European Union and the European Commission Delegation to China and Mongolia. He was also EU Commission Marie Curie Fellow at Tsinghua University School of Law, THCEREL – Center for Environmental, Natural Resources and Energy Law in Beijing (China) and at the Department of Philosophy, at the CRAES – Chinese Research Academy on Environmental Sciences in Beijing (China), at Peking University School of Government and at Beijing Normal University Department of Business and Economics.

As Scientific Director, since 2006, he has been coordinating the Summer Law Institute in China – Executive Education Training Program (www.summerlawinstitute.com) held in China.

He was an International Consultant and Legal Advisor for projects implemented for the United Nations Development Program, for the Italian Ministry of Economic Development and Commerce and for the OECD.

He is an Appointed Member of the International Law Association – ILA Committee on Sustainable Development and the Green Economy in International Trade Law and of the ILA Committee on the Role of International Law in Sustainable Natural Resource Management for Development.

He has previously worked at the Legal Affairs Division of the World Trade Organization in Geneva and was an Associate Lawyer of Baker and McKenzie Law Firm, Milan, Italy.

He is an expert in the interaction between trade, economic globalization, and NTCs, such as sustainable development, energy, environment, and human rights, with a special focus on China and other Asian countries.

He graduated with a Maitrise in International and European Law from Paris Ouest La Defense Nanterre University (France), LLM in European Legal Studies from the College of Europe in Bruges (Belgium), and a Dual PhD in international law from Aix-Marseille University (France) and University of Milan (Italy).

Elena Cima is a PhD candidate in international law at the Graduate Institute of International Law and Development Studies in Geneva, where she also works for the LLM Program in International Law. Her research interests include public international law, international trade law, international environmental law, energy law, and Chinese law.

Prior to starting her doctoral studies, she worked at Yale Law School as a research scholar and teaching assistant. Previously, she spent a year as a visiting scholar at Harvard Law School, at the Department of East Asian Legal Studies, where she first started working on Chinese law. Later, she moved to Beijing, where she was Marie Curie Fellow at Tsinghua University and Beijing Normal University and worked as a researcher for over two years on projects funded by the European Commission on energy trade and investment. In Beijing, she was part of the team managing the Summer Law Institute in China – Executive Education Training Program held in Beijing, while being a research associate for gLAWcal – Global Law Initiatives for Sustainable Development (United Kingdom). She is a member of the American branch of the International Law Association (ILA), for which she served as reporter. Her publications have focused on international trade law, energy law, and Chinese law and policy. She holds a Bachelor of Laws LLB, honored summa cum laude, from the University of Milan and an LLM degree from Yale Law School.

Notes on Contributors

Angelica Bonfanti, Associate Professor of International Law (University of Milan); PhD (University of Milan).

Julien Chaisse, Professor, Faculty of Law and Director of the Centre for Financial Regulation and Economic Development (CFRED), The Chinese University of Hong Kong; PhD in Law (University of Aix-Marseilles III, France); LLM in European Law (University of Tubingen, Germany).

Leïla Choukroune, Director (Research Professor) of Centre for Social Sciences and Humanities (CSH), New Delhi (India), the French National Research Center (CNRS) multidisciplinary Research Unit on South Asia. When Associate Professor of international economic law with the Faculty of Law of the University of Maastricht in the Netherlands, she was Deputy Director of the Institute for Globalization and International Regulation (IGIR) and Director of the Advanced Master in international economic law. She holds a Doctorate in international law (magna cum laude) from the University Paris I Pantheon-Sorbonne and is a qualified lawyer to the Paris bar.

Nadia Coggiola, Assistant Professor of Private Law (University of Torino, Italy); Fellow of Centro di Diritto Comparato e Transnazionale (CDCT); PhD in Comparative, Private and European Law (University of Ferrara, Italy); LLM (University of Torino, Italy); Post-MA in International, European and Comparative Law (University of Torino, Italy); MA in International and Comparative Law (University of Trento, Italy).

Rogier Creemers, Lecturer in the Politics and History of China, Department for Politics and International Relations, University of Oxford (United Kingdom); Fellow, Institute for Globalization and International Regulation, Maastricht University (Netherlands); PhD in Law (Maastricht University, 2012); Master's degrees in Sinology and International Relations (Leuven, 2004; 2006). Currently, he works at the University of Oxford, where he researches China's information technology policy and regulation. His work has been published in prestigious journals including *The China Journal* and the *Chinese Journal of Communication*. He also edits *China Copyright and Media*, an authoritative database of translated Chinese regulatory and policy documents.

Thomas Deleuil, PhD in Public law (CERIC, Aix-Marseille University, France). He focuses his research on international environmental law, global governance, and indigenous issues. He has been legal adviser on climate change negotiations and environmental law at the French Ministry of Foreign Affairs from 2014 to 2016.

Lorenzo Di Masi, Lawyer at Crowell and Moring LLP Brussels (Belgium); LLM (University College London, United Kingdom); JD (University of Milan, Italy).

Claudio Di Turi, Associate Professor of Public International Law and European Union Law, Dipartimento di Scienze Aziendali e Giuridiche, Università della Calabria (Italy); DES in Public International Law (The Graduate Institute of International Law, Geneva, Switzerland); law degree (Bologna University, Faculty of Law, Italy).

Shujie Feng, Associate Professor, Tsinghua University, School of Law, Director of Innovation and Competition Law Center; PhD (University Paris I Pantheon-Sorbonne); LLM (Remin University of China); LLB (Shandong University).

Andrea Filippetti, EU Commission Marie Curie Fellow, London School of Economics and Political Science (United Kingdom), and Researcher at the at National Research Council – CNR (Italy); Visiting Fellow at the Birkbeck Centre for Innovation Management Research, University of London. He has been Fulbright-Schuman Post Doc at Harvard University, Center for European Studies, and Visiting Fellow at Columbia University, Department of Political Science. He has published on innovation, the globalization of intellectual property rights, technological change and productivity growth.

Danny Friedmann, Research Associate (The Chinese University of Hong Kong); PhD (The Chinese University of Hong Kong); LLM (University of Hong Kong); BBA (Nyenrode Business University).

Christophe Germann, PhD (University of Berne) and DEA (Master, European Institute of the University of Geneva); Attorney at law in Geneva and Visiting FNS Research Fellow at the Law Schools of the University of Oxford and of Birkbeck College, University of London (2011).

Julie Gibson obtained her LLB from the University of Aberdeen in 2012 and her LLM in International Law and Sustainable Development (with distinction) from the University of Strathclyde in 2016. Her specific areas of interest lie within the role of law in international development; having worked voluntarily within the sector in Kenya, Bangladesh, China and Zambia. While studying she worked closely with the Strathclyde Centre for Environmental Law and Governance on the Climate and Sustainability Project, mapping the legal and policy links between sustainable development and climate change in the lead up to the formulation of the Sustainable Development Goals and the COP21 negotiations. She has been involved in a number of research projects, most recently focussing on the promotion of sustainable development within small islands in Europe.

Lukasz Gruszczynski, Assistant Professor, Institute of Legal Studies, Polish Academy of Sciences, Poland; PhD (European University Institute); LLM (Central European University); MA (Jagiellonian University).

Weidong He, Professor of Environmental Law, Law Institute, Shanghai Academy of Social Sciences – SASS (China); Academic Director of Research Centre of Environment and Resources Law, Shanghai Academy of Social Sciences – SASS (China); PhD and LLM, Wuhan University (China).

Jean Yves Heurtebise, Assistant Professor, FuJen Catholic University, Department of French Language and Culture, Taipei (Taiwan); Associate Member of the Research Center for Comparative Epistemology and Ergology (CEPERC) at Aix-Marseille University (France); Affiliated Scholar of the Kozmetsky Global Collaboratory in Stanford University (KGC, US); PhD (summa cum laude) in History of Philosophy and Continental Epistemology, MA, MSc (magna cum laude) at Aix-Marseille University (France).

Junhong Hu, Associate Professor of Economic Law at Beijing Normal University (China); Admitted to the Beijing Bar (China); PhD in Law and Economics (Università degli Studi di Roma Tre, Italy).

Zhixiong Huang, Professor of International Law, Wuhan University (China); PhD (Wuhan University, China); MILE (World Trade Institute, Berne, Switzerland).

Imad Ibrahim, Research Associate at gLAWcal – Global Law Initiatives for Sustainable Development (United Kingdom), EU Commission Marie Curie Fellow at Tsinghua University in Beijing (China) and at Beijing Normal University (China). Lawyer admitted to the Lebanese Bar. Master in European Interdisciplinary Studies (College of Europe); LLB (Lebanese University, Beirut) with a specialization in European, French, and Lebanese Law.

Anselm Kamperman Sanders, Professor of Intellectual Property Law, Maastricht University (Netherlands); Director Institute for Globalisation and International Regulation (IGIR), Director Advanced Masters Intellectual Property Law and Knowledge Management (LLM/MSc), Academic Director IEEM Intellectual Property Law School, IEEM Macao SAR, China, Professeur Invité a l'Université de Liège.

Mark Klaver, LLM (Harvard Law School, USA); JD (University of Toronto, Faculty of Law, Canada).

Marion Lemoine, CNRS Researcher, IODE, Faculty of Law and Politic Sciences, Rennes 1 University (France).

Luo Li, Professor of Law, Beijing Institute of Technology, School of Law. Research Associate at Tsinghua University School of Law, Center for Environmental, Natural Resources and Energy Law (THCEREL). Member of the EPSEI project.

Xinjie Luan, Guest Professor in Hochschule für Wirtschaft und Recht Berlin (Germany); Professor and Director of the International Trade Institute, China Jiliang University, Hangzhou (China); Guest Senior Researcher at China's World Trade Organization Institute, University of International Business and Economics, Beijing (China).

Jianqiang Nie, *Doctor Iuris*, Professor of Law, Wuhan University, China; Vice-director, Wuhan University Institute of International Law; PhD (University of Berne, Switzerland).

Libiao Ning, Professor of Jurisprudence and Human Rights Law, Guizhou University (China); PhD (Jilin University, China); LLM (Hunan Normal University, China).

Tivadar Ötvös, Research Associate at gLAWcal – Global Law Initiatives for Sustainable Development (United Kingdom), EU Commission Marie Curie Fellow at Tsinghua University in Beijing (China) and at Beijing Normal University (China). PhD in Civil Law (Pavol Jozef Šafárik University in Košice, Slovakia) LLM and LLB (Pavol Jozef Šafárik University in Košice, Slovakia)

Carla Peng, Research Professor, Institute of Law, Shanghai Academy of Social Sciences – SASS, Shanghai (China).

A. Rajendra Prasad, Professor of Law, Chairman, Faculty of Law and former Principal, Andhra University, Visakhapatnam, India has 30 years of teaching and research experience. He obtained his PhD in Consumer Law from Andhra University, India. He headed the School of Corporate Law, Indian Institute of Corporate Affairs, Ministry of Corporate Affairs, Government of India. He is the recipient of 'Best Thesis' Award (1996), 'Best

Researcher Award' (2001) and 'Best Academician Award' (2008) from Andhra University. He is also the recipient of prestigious Commonwealth Fellowship and worked as Commonwealth Academic Fellow in the Faculty of Law, University of Sheffield, UK. He published many papers on consumer law in reputed national and international journals and attended many national and international conferences on consumer law including those held in Malaysia, New Zealand, Canada, the US, South Africa and the Netherlands.

Denise Prévost, Associate Professor of International Economic Law at Maastricht University (Netherlands); PhD (Maastricht University, Netherlands), LLM (University of South Africa), LLM (Maastricht University, Netherlands); BLC and LLB (University of Pretoria); Visiting Professor, China–EU School of Law (CESL); Member of the Editorial Board, *Netherlands Journal of International Law*.

Piercarlo Rossi, Aggregate Professor at University of Piemonte Orientale (Italy); PhD in Comparative Law (University of Florence, Italy); Visiting Scholar at University Jean Moulin Lyon 3 (France) and at University of Muenster (Germany); Research Unit Coordinator at University of Piemonte Orientale (Italy) for the Project EPSEI.

Xin Shu, Legal Counsel at Baidu Online Network Technology; Trader at Bank of Beijing; Master (Tsinghua University, School of Law).

James R. Simpson, Affiliate Professor, Thomas S. Foley Institute for Public Policy and Public Service, Washington State University; PhD (Texas AandM University, USA), BS and MS (University of Arizona, USA).

Francesco Sindico, Reader in International Environmental Law at the University of Strathclyde Law School in Glasgow, Scotland, UK and Director of the Strathclyde Centre for Environmental Law and Governance; PhD (Universitat Jaume I, Castellon de la Plana, Spain); LLM (Universidad Autonoma de Madrid, Spain); LLB (Università degli Studi di Torino, Italy).

Roberto Soprano, PhD (University of Salerno, Italy); MILE (World Trade Institute, Berne, Switzerland); MA and BA (University of Milan, Italy).

Francesca Spigarelli, Assistant Professor of Economics and Director of China Center at University of Macerata (Italy); PhD at University of Ancona (Italy).

Michael Trebilcock, Professor of Law and Economics, University of Toronto, Faculty of Law (Canada); LLM (University of Adelaide, Australia); LLB (University of Canterbury, New Zealand).

Riccardo Tremolada, PhD Candidate at University of Naples Federico II (Italy); SJD Candidate at Shanghai JiaoTong University (China); LLB, Università degli Studi di Milano, School of Law; Research Associate at gLAWcal – Global Law Initiatives for Sustainable Development (United Kingdom); Research Fellow (2013), Università degli Studi del Piemonte Orientale, DiSEI – Dipartimento di Studi per l'Economia e l'Impresa (Italy); EU Commission Marie Curie Fellow (2013) at the CRAES – Chinese Research Academy on Environmental Sciences in Beijing (China) and at Tsinghua University School of Law, THCEREL – Center for Environmental, Natural Resources and Energy Law in Beijing (China).

Valentina Sara Vadi, Professor of International Economic Law (Lancaster University, United Kingdom); Avvocato (Florence Bar, Italy); PhD (European University Institute), MJur (Oxford, United Kingdom), MRes (EUI), M Pol Sc and JD (Siena, Italy).

Jayashree Watal, Counsellor in the Intellectual Property Division of the WTO since 2001 and represented India in TRIPS negotiations from May to December 1990 (the drafting stage).

Ningning Zhang, Principal Staff Member, Department of Policies, Laws and Regulations, Ministry of Industry and Information Technology of The PRC.

Flavia Zorzi Giustiniani, Assistant Professor of International Law, Uninettuno University (Italy); PhD in International Law (University of Teramo, Italy), Diploma in International Humanitarian Law (ICRC), political science degree and law degree (University of Florence, Italy).

Foreword

It took a long time for Nation-States to realize that the citizens' happiness does not depend solely on the economic growth. The ongoing process of establishing policies integrating non-trade matters into the government's strategies reflects the increasing awareness of the importance of non-economic values in guaranteeing the stability of the regime in place, in addition to contributing to the achievement of sustainable development objectives.

Since the adoption of the "Open Door Policy" in 1978 by President Deng Xiaoping, to the implementation of the "Go West" strategy in 2000 by President Jiang Zemin, and finally the "Leap East" plan embraced by President Xi Jinping, China's top priorities have been to ensure the economic welfare of the State and its citizens. Despite the Chinese miracle that has occurred over the past few decades and the astonishing economic growth that was witnessed, China still needs to find appropriate solutions to realize the social and economic rights and lift out of poverty a large part of the Chinese population that has not yet benefited from this industrial and economic revolution. According to the current Premier of the State Council of the People's Republic of China, Li Keqiang, the recent slowdown reflects a shift in the growth from "High Speed to Medium-to-High Speed".

Yet, this reality led to an imbalanced situation, whereby the economic sector took primacy over other essential matters that concern Chinese society, which resulted in new social problems and started to threaten the miraculous achievements that were made. In response, President Hu Jintao introduced the concept of "Harmonious society" in 2002, in order to balance economic and non-economic values. In fact, the concept of harmonious society has deep roots in the country, since Confucius promoted the concept in ancient China. President Hu Jintao established the basics of the harmonious society while stating that: "We must focus on economic development as our central task, making development our top priority and facilitating and all-round progress in economic, political and cultural aspects and in the building of a harmonious society. We must stick to the direction of reform for a socialist market economy, step up institutional innovation, deepen reforms aimed at galvanizing creative vitality of society and increase the inherent dynamics for economic and social development." Therefore, the Chinese Government initiated a reform process in 2002, whereby it progressively integrated Non-Trade Concerns (NTCs) at the central and local level.

This book arrives at a significant moment in the Chinese political context. The increased importance of NTCs in shaping Chinese politics is happening simultaneously with declining economic growth in the country also due to the financial crisis that shocked the world and affected the Chinese economy. This juxtaposition highlights the significance the Chinese government is giving to solve some of the disharmonies that have occurred in the past as a result of the disproportionately strong focus on economic development.

In fact, the book aims to provide an overview of trade and NTCs in China, taking into consideration all the abovementioned factors, which have already affected the government's position when it comes to the adoption of policies that try to balance economic growth and sustainable development. The reader will possess a clear understanding of the situation governing the relation between trade and NTCs in international trade and the World Trade Organization (WTO) system as well as how this relationship materializes in the Chinese legal system and society.

This text covers different Chinese laws and policies established by the government related to international trade, foreign direct investment, and sustainable development as well as environmental protection and climate change in addition to fundamental rights and cultural diversity. It also takes a close look at public health along with food and product safety and consumer protection.

In order to attract foreign direct investments and to compete at the global level, since Deng Xiaoping's Open Door Policy of 1978, China has been establishing friendly market regulations toward corporations, but sometimes at the expense of labor rights. Section One further elaborates on the current reforms made to tackle the problems of corporate social responsibility and labor rights in the People's Republic of China.

Additionally, China has taken major steps toward respecting the environment by adopting new environmental laws to better regulate industrial activity and encourage sustainable development. The Chinese government has also fostered the role of civil society through non-governmental organizations (NGOs) by giving them more freedom in order to provide further suggestions to improve the existing environmental laws. However, when it comes to the international landscape, China still considers itself a developing country that has the right to development, even if it means polluting the environment. Despite the effects of climate change on the country, Beijing still argues that the developed countries must assume greater responsibility based on the pollution that they caused in the last century. However, the historic US–China Joint Announcement on Climate Change confirmed President Xi's commitment to reaching a successful climate agreement in Paris as well as to China's involvement in the international arena and to better support sustainable development.

In the second section, the authors have described these issues in detail while focusing on the critical role that the country can play in the environmental field on the national and international level. The third section of the book focuses on fundamental rights in the country, mainly the right to food and water but also several controversial issues such as China's domestic censorship and media control policies and the interplay between trade and audiovisuals in the context of the WTO, where the Chinese regime has tried to use the issue of morality to justify restricting the importation of certain products. The last section offers an overview of Chinese public health regulations and the debate at the WTO concerning China's claim to the transfer of technology to developing countries.

Thus, the discussion about further integrating NTCs in the Chinese legal system is only expected to grow in the light of the legal reforms that are taking place mainly under President Xi Jinping, who made the fight against corruption the official objective of his mandate. Therefore, this book is relevant to the debate because the distinguished authors have not only provided an overview of the problems related to each issue, but have also suggested appropriate policy solutions. Such policies should be implemented with a comparative approach to avoid halting or further decreasing growth.

This matter is also relevant for numerous developing and developed countries that seek to balance trade and NTCs. However, considering the size of the Chinese economy, the second-largest in the world, a sudden shift of economic policies in any direction would directly influence the world economy. As such, this book not only sheds light on potential solutions to the problem, but also suggests some strategies for integrating the non-economic values without actually hindering the economic growth of the People's Republic of China. On the one hand, it offers further insights for the government to improve the current regulations, and for Chinese civil society to move toward the adoption of better rules, on the other.

Professor Gianmaria Ajani
Professor of Comparative Law and Chinese Law
President of University of Turin, Italy and Former
Coordinator of EU Commission Marie Curie IRSES
– Project EPSEI

Foreword

Italy and China: Allies for the Environment

With respect to the environment, Italy and China have cultivated a relationship that looks towards the future. Their alliance is comprised of robust roots, which have grown and strengthened over the last few decades.

While China and Italy have cooperated in a variety of sectors, they have focused heavily on environmental issues. Of utmost strategic importance, they have taken actions in areas such as sustainable architecture, reduction of urban pollution, and production of renewable energies. In the near future, the global economy will revolve around these very types of technologies.

A new world order will arise to face the challenges posed by climate change, built around a circular and sustainable economy. China will inevitably play a leading role in such a global endeavour, while Italy will necessarily retain major relevance as an economic and technological partner.

China's involvement in the realisation of a new global economic system will be critical. Indeed, although China contributes enormously to global greenhouse gas emissions, it is also the biggest investor in renewable energies and in technologies fostering energy efficiency. China is currently the greatest laboratory for sustainability on the planet: it is the most populated country in the world, it has the fastest-growing economy, and it devotes an extraordinary drive to improve living conditions for hundreds of millions of people.

Unlike Europe, which is essentially stable in both demographic and economic terms, China continues to grow at a fast pace, both from a qualitative and a quantitative perspective. China is thus the arena where the struggle for sustainable socio-economic development is unravelling. This crucial challenge will involve a great number of people, who now finally have the ability and the technologies required to harmonize growth with environmental needs.

The US and China, which together account for 45 per cent of global greenhouse emissions, had clearly and repeatedly stated that they were intending to pursue an ambitious, binding and effective agreement at the UN Climate Conference which was held in Paris.

In September 2015 the UN approved the 17 Sustainable Development Goals for the planet, which replace the Millennium Development Goals. Notably, they indicate even by their name that the Earth's future must be a sustainable one.

The words of Pope Francis's encyclical "Laudato Sì" gave another extraordinary push towards "integral ecology", an environmental aim that is also a social and economic objective.

It appears, therefore, that the political, cultural, and ethnic conditions needed to build a new development model are finally in place. Italy and China intend to share and foster this model to build a better future for our planet.

H. E. the Minister Gian Luca Galletti
Minister of the Environment and Protection of Land and Sea of Italy

Foreword

With globalization advancing on all fronts, trade matters can no longer remain isolated from other concerns. This is evident in the WTO context, where many joint activities between the WTO and other international organizations, such as UNEP, WIPO or WHO, are helping to better frame the interactions between trade and Non-Trade Concerns (NTCs). The WTO preamble explicitly recognizes the need for respecting sustainable development, which also contributes to enhancing coherence between the WTO and NTCs in areas such as development and environmental protection. It is also clear from the WTO jurisprudence that WTO Members have the right to give priority to NTCs – so long as they respect WTO rules, notably avoiding unjustifiable or arbitrary discrimination, as well as disguised restrictions on international trade. WTO Members have understood this well. In that regard, the role and impact of China in the international economic legal order, in the WTO in general and in the WTO dispute settlement system can only be said to be impressive. This is true with regard to trade matters and NTCs. This book provides a fascinating appraisal of China's actions relating to NTCs and its influence on shaping these concerns through its active participation in the WTO, including in the WTO dispute settlement system.

Professor Gabrielle Marceau
WTO Legal Affairs Division, Professor at University of Geneva,
President of the Society of International Economic Law (SIEL)

Foreword

Due to the growing intensity of international trade in goods and services, "Non-Trade Concerns" have gradually acquired major influence in international trade negotiations. In particular, the fact that productive processes not only deliver goods that can be traded on the market, but are also increasingly functional to non-commercial objectives, is especially relevant for trade in agricultural and food products.

Expo 2015 provided an extraordinary chance to reflect on the importance of public goods linked to food production. At the global level it was a remarkable opportunity to share the idea that agriculture not only produces food, fibres, energy and fuels, but also social and environmental impacts that determine the future of our planet. Indeed, several matters intertwine in the field of agriculture, spanning from food security to environmental protection and regional development, just to mention the most relevant ones. These issues involve the planet at all of its latitudes, though with diverse intensity and modalities depending on the degree of economic development and the different socio-economic contexts that have matured at the national or regional level. Europe, for example, shows a stronger drive towards certain ethical standards than other trade partners, and has adopted a much more cautious approach in evaluating certain risks. Indeed, the EU Common Agricultural Policy itself can be deemed an integral part of European welfare, thanks to its provisions on animal well-being, environmental good practices (both obligatory and optional), rural development and all other requirements that sectorial operators must satisfy to guarantee food healthiness.

Certainly, as different approaches and understandings compete in the arena of international trade, it is hard to define a framework to combine diverse reasons and previsions with the objectives of trade liberalization. This complex diversity is not only manifest between developed and developing countries, but also paramount within the former (or at least perceived as such). Thus has been, at least, the course of history until now, but the world is changing rapidly and so is the weight of economic and trade actors. Trade routes and geopolitical balances are then constantly adapting to the rising protagonists of the world stage, the so-called emerging economies. Among them, China best represents this changing landscape. Its remarkable growth in wealth, territorial expansion and availability of resources place this giant in a key position for the world economy. Therefore, China naturally influences the scope of NTCs with its external policies. In fact, this issue has always been the object of passionate debate. Traditionally, it is a matter of claim for less developed countries, which accuse the most developed ones of using non-commercial objectives as protectionist instruments. More recently, however, it has also been a concern in most advanced contexts, where certain prerogatives and guarantees once taken for granted might be gradually waning.

This complex combination of divergent visions and relevant economic interests has recently brought many actors to prioritize bilateral relations instead of the multilateral system. Many countries thereby increasingly renounce negotiations on a global scale, including the ones at the World Trade Organization. This has implied a fragmentation of conditions and values presiding over commercial exchanges, which in turn inevitably had a negative impact on the international sharing of instruments and approaches aimed at global development. Conversely, the launched Sustainable Development Agenda contains many ambitious goals. It enshrines the aspiration to create the structural conditions needed for a sustainable and enduring development, and there is no doubt that the role of trade will be decisive for this endeavour. Taking once again the example of agriculture and food, everyone agrees that markets work properly, favouring an efficient and balanced distribution of resources, including food. Easier said than done, of course, first, because these issues have traditionally been part of the national security agendas in virtually every country in the world, and thus they are treated with extreme caution; and second, since behind food and agriculture lie profoundly different cultures, sensitivities and infrastructural possibilities (both material and immaterial).

This volume offers a broad perspective on the above-outlined issue, hence serving as an absolutely critical reference for policy-makers. The analysis of the Chinese context and its peculiarities, as well as its interpretation from the perspective of trade relations, offers important insights to fully understand the main keys for the future of international trade relations.

H. E. the Minister Maurizio Martina
Minister of Agriculture, Food and Forestry Policies of Italy

Acknowledgements

The moment of writing the book acknowledgements is very important. It is the opportunity to endorse those institutions and people that have helped facilitate this achievement.

When I decided to prepare this research proposal, I was based in Beijing, China, as part of the Science and Technology Fellowship (STF) Program funded by the European Union and the European Commission Delegation to China and Mongolia (EuropeAid/127024/L/ACT/CN_STF/08), which permitted me to spend 2 years of research in China.

As an Associate Researcher at the Center of Advanced Studies on Contemporary China (CASCC) in Turin, Italy and at University of Turin, Department of Law, associate partners of the consortium which established the China–EU School of Law (CESL), I applied for one of the CESL Grant 2011–2012 with a research project on "Current Trends of Chinese Law towards Non-Trade Concerns such as Sustainable Development, Energy and the Protection of Environment, Public Health, Product and Food Safety, Consumer Protection, Food Security, Right to Food, Right to Water, Social and Economic Rights, Labor Rights from the Perspective of International Law and WTO Law" (Short name: *China and Non-Trade Concerns*).

The objective of this study was to combine different perspectives on Non-Trade Concerns that have raised diverging opinions amongst both scholars and practitioners. This project offers a multifaceted approach to the research topic, as it draws upon a broad research group. This diverse range of expertise favors academic debate and offers the possibility of covering a wider range of aspects of the specific topic.

My research proposal received endorsements and included scholars from other CESL partner institutions: such as Maastricht University Faculty of Law, Department of International and European Law and the Institute for Globalisation and International Regulation (IGIR) of the Netherlands; and Tsinghua University, School of Law, Institute of Public International Law and the Center for Research on Intellectual Property Law in Beijing, China.

As part of the research proposal, three CESL Conferences "China's Influence on Non-Trade Concerns in International Economic Law" were organized under this same topic and framework. The first conference was hosted at the Center for Advanced Studies on Contemporary China (CASCC) in Turin, Italy and at University of Turin, Department of Law on November 23–24, 2011. The second was hosted at Tsinghua University, School of Law on January 14–15, 2012, and the third at Maastricht University, Faculty of Law on January 19–20, 2012.

There are milestones and turnouts in the academic life of each academic that shapes the scholarship and the research towards new long-term visions and the future. The Science and

Technology Fellowship (STF) Program in China and, later, this CESL Grant research project, were of such importance to shape my academic career and scholarship.

The lively academic conversations during these three CESL conferences and also the exchange with some of the STF researchers and fellows have developed along these years resulting in an incredible path of research and outcomes.

In particular, beyond the specific results of the three CESL Conferences and the books in three languages, these research projects have created the scientific basis and roots for the emergence of new scholarship and vision which brought to the founding of gLAWcal - Global Law Initiatives for Sustainable Development of the United Kingdom. gLAWcal is an independent non-profit research organization that aims at providing a new focus on issues related to economic law, globalization, and development; namely, the relationship between international economy and trade, with special attention to a number of non-trade-related values and concerns.

Furthermore, among the other most relevant follow-ups and research spin-offs of this CESL research project, it is significant to mention that these topics have been further developed in parallel to the preparation of these books and reciprocally nourished in three supplementary EU commission funded projects (EPSEI, LIBEAC and POREEN) that I have proposed in collaboration with other colleagues which are producing many more results. These results are periodically posted at www.glawcal.org.uk.

The objective was twofold. First, to obtain further funding for the research, beyond the costs of the publication of the three books and of the organization of the three CESL Conferences partially covered by the CESL Grant and second, to achieve many more scientific results of such broad research areas and topics which I could only start to address through the CESL Grant period.

At the same time of the preparation of this CESL Grant research proposal and during the evaluation period, along with Piercarlo Rossi of University of Piemonte Orientale and University of Turin, STF colleague Jean-Yves Heurtebise of Aix-Marseille University, both contributors to this CESL book, and several colleagues from other Universities including Mingyuan Wang and Haifeng Deng of Tsinghua Law School, we decided to submit a broader collaborative research proposal to the EU commission.

The "Evaluating Policies for Sustainable Energy Investments: Towards an Integrated Approach on National and International Stage" (EPSEI) project was funded by the Marie Curie IRSES of the European Union's Seventh Framework Programme (FP7/2007–2013) under REA grant agreement n° 269327, in consortium with several European, Chinese and Russian Universities and was implemented from April 2011 to April 2015. The Chinese partner institutions were Tsinghua University School of Law, Center for Environmental, Natural Resources and Energy Law (THCEREL) and the Chinese Research Academy of Environmental Sciences (CRAES).

The research of some of the contributors to the CESL Grant Conferences and to the book which lead to their results and Session Three of the First CESL Conference held at the CASCC in Turin, Italy, was partially funded by the EPSEI Project and it is included in Part II of the Book, "Sustainable Development, Environmental Protection, and Climate Change." In the framework of the EPSEI and CESL projects, a special acknowledgement should be addressed to University of Piemonte Orientale, Dipartimento di Studi per l'Impresa e il Territorio (DiSEI) in Italy that, through the project "GOING EAST. Enhancing Asian Research Cooperation in Higher Education for the Challenges of Global Markets" (Id. 2011/1410) funded by Fondazione Cariplo, had contributed to co-sponsor few researchers seconded for their research period in China.

After the success with the EPSEI proposal, I decided, along with Jean-Yves Heurtebise, to submit a second project proposal. The "Liberalism in Between Europe And China" (LIBEAC) project was funded by the Marie Curie IRSES of the European Union's Seventh Framework Programme (FP7/2007–2013) under REA grant agreement n° 317767 and it is currently ongoing from January 2013 to December 2016. The Chinese partner institutions are Peking University, School of Government and Law School and Tsinghua University, Department of Philosophy, School of Law and School of Public Policy and Management.

In fact, the Second CESL Conference held at Tsinghua University School of Law, Beijing, China has also been participated in by researchers of the LIBEAC project, in particular, the Session One dedicated to "Multiculturalism, Liberalism, Right to Development and International Trade" had the contribution of Li Qiang of Peking University School of Government, Daniel Bell of Tsinghua University, Department of Philosophy. Session Three "Public Health, Product and Food Safety, Consumers Protection" had the contribution of Shujie Feng of Tsinghua University School of Law.

The research of some of the contributors to the CESL Grant Conferences and to the book publications, which lead to their results, was partially funded by the LIBEAC project and it is included in Part III of the Book, "Fundamental Rights and Cultural Diversity."

With other partner institutions in Europe and China, we have submitted another project proposal. The "Partnering Opportunities between Europe and China in the Renewable Energies and Environmental Industries" (POREEN) project was funded by the Marie Curie IRSES of the European Union's Seventh Framework Programme (FP7/2007–2013) under REA grant agreement n° 318908 and it is currently ongoing from January 2013 to December 2016. The Chinese partner institutions are Beijing Normal University, Shanghai Jiao-Tong University, East-China University of Political Sciences and Law in Shanghai and Tongji University in Shanghai.

The research of some of the contributors to the CESL Grant Conferences and to the book publications which lead to their results, was partially funded by the POREEN project and it is included in Part I of the Book, "Public Policy, International Trade, and Foreign Direct Investment. The Role of States and Non-State Actors in Economic Globalization."

The greatness of the institutions is done by the array of personalities, so it is also essential for me to mention the people who were of importance in the different stages of the project.

First of all, I would like to thank Gianmaria Ajani, who was Vice-Director of the Center of Advanced Studies on Contemporary China (CASCC) at the time I was a Research Fellow there and later at University of Turin, Department of Law, and who is currently Professor of Comparative Law and Chinese Law and Rector at University of Turin, for his vision and for making the participation of the CASCC to the CESL consortium and activities along with Marina Timoteo at University of Bologne; Peter Van Den Bossche who has greatly supported this project from the very first moment with the participation of Maastricht University, Department of International and European Law and IGIR – Institute for Globalisation and International Regulation, inviting other colleagues to contribute and join the research proposal such as Anselm Kamperman Sanders, Valentina Vadi, Denise Prevost, Leila Choukroune, Rogier Creemers and to host the Third CESL Conference; Haifeng Deng, Shujie Feng, Bing Bing Jia and Mingyuan Wang for the participation of Tsinghua University School of Law and to host the Second CESL Conference. Finally, special thanks and acknowledgements should be addressed to Valentina Vadi for her invaluable support all along the implementation of the CESL Grant.

Besides this book publication in English within the gLAWcal Book Series on "Global Law and Sustainable Development" with Routledge Publishing in the United Kingdom, the results of this CESL Grant will be published in Italian and in Mandarin Chinese. Beside this first gLAWcal Book series, a second one was later established on "Transnational Law and Governance" also with Routledge Publishing.

The publication of these three books and the three CESL Conferences have been partially sponsored by China–EU School of Law (CESL) at the China University of Political Science and Law (CUPL). The activities of CESL at CUPL are supported by the European Union and the People's Republic of China.

This book was able to be published thanks also to the funding and support of gLAWcal – Global Law Initiatives for Sustainable Development (United Kingdom) and West Virginia University, John D. Rockefeller IV School of Policy and Politics, Department of Public Administration (USA).

Professor Paolo Davide Farah
July 2016

1 Introduction and Overview

Paolo Davide Farah

The motivating idea for this project is to explore the range of Non-Trade Concerns (NTCs) that may conflict with international economic rules with a specific focus on how China can play a decisive role in these matters. If, on the one hand, this volume looks at the tensions between trade and non-trade values through the Chinese experience, on the other, it contextualizes this analysis within the broader framework of public international law.

Public international law appears highly fragmented, as different treaties and rules, which often express different values, increasingly overlap. Although the goal of multilateral trade agreements and that of the treaties and institutions promoting different values do not inherently conflict, the norms adopted to achieve them might come into conflict, and, in practice, tensions do exist. In particular, norms with distinct objectives – such as sustainable development, environmental protection, public health, product safety, food security, consumer protection, the right to food, and the right to water – might affect trade patterns, or, conversely, changes in trade flows influence and possibly jeopardize the realization of such norms.

Tensions do exist not only between each state's conflicting obligations, but among states as well, since their priorities differ considerably. With regard to NTCs, developing countries do not have the same approach as developed ones. Public opinion and policy-makers in industrialized nations fear that a further liberalization of international trade may undermine or jeopardize policies and measures protecting a variety of non-trade values and react by increasingly resorting to trade restrictions. On the other hand, developing countries and, even more so, the least-developed ones have more pressing concerns to address, and tend to look at many of the trade measures introduced by developed countries to address NTCs with distrust if not with resistance or dissent, because they suspect such measures often hide protectionist goals. Moreover, developing countries see these measures as an attempt by developed countries to impose their social, ethical, or cultural values and preferences. The key challenge is finding ways to satisfy the right of developed nations to grant social values the degree of protection they consider appropriate, while minimizing the negative effects in terms of market distortion for their trading partners.

Prior to China's accession to the World Trade Organization (WTO), many cautioned that its integration would not only be long and difficult, but possibly damaging to the Organization itself as well as its Members. In view of preventing this outcome, some experts decided to tackle the challenge of integrating China in the world trading system by focusing on the country's market access concessions, tariff reductions, and liberalization requirements. A second group of scholars placed more emphasis on transparency issues instead, such as legal and administrative policies that China should adopt to ensure equitable and efficient resolution of trade disputes. *Per contra*, the issue of the potential influence of China's WTO accession on NTCs has rarely been addressed in a comprehensive manner. Interestingly, though, the country's influence in this area is now becoming more and more evident in the geopolitical context, considering the impact that China has had not only at the WTO but in other international fora as well, often in combination with the BRICS countries (Brazil, Russia, India, China and South Africa) and other developing countries.

This volume is organized into four parts. Each part deals with a different area or cluster of areas where non-trade values somehow intersect with international rules governing world trade. Given the key role China is playing in drawing new rules of the game in many of these areas, the authors in each part have tried to evaluate the country's internal and external strategies, always keeping in mind its distinctive and unique characteristics.

In his introductory chapter, **Paolo Davide Farah** sets out a reliable analysis of the key issues in international economic law, which are then further analyzed in the subsequent contributions in this volume. The author first examines the role China plays at the crossroads between its right to development and its essential role in taking into account NTCs while pursuing a sustainable model of development. The author then offers a non-exhaustive, yet insightful, overview of NTCs – such as environmental protection, public health, food security, human rights, and the interplay between cultural products and public morals – exploring their integration in the multilateral trading regime of the WTO.

Part I Public policy, international trade, and foreign direct investment: The role of states and non-state actors in economic globalization

Part I looks at the links between public policy, international trade, and foreign investment, focusing on the roles played by both the state and non-state actors in China in the context of economic globalization.

Claudio Di Turi addresses the highly debated issue of the relevance of the fundamental principles and rights concerning labor in the context of the globalization of the economy. The author focuses on the practice of the ILO and the WTO showing that, although the two legal subsystems of international trade and human rights evolved in reciprocal indifference, they both pursue the same goal, i.e. the promotion of social justice. Ultimately, neither human rights law nor trade law can completely foster human dignity on their own. Against the backdrop of a comprehensive analysis of the law and practice of the WTO, as well as the difficulties surrounding the WTO Doha Round of negotiations, the author defends the thesis that WTO Agreements should be interpreted in coherence with human rights rules.

Angelica Bonfanti explores whether and how corporate social responsibility contributes to ensuring that multinational corporations (MNCs) that operate in China comply with human and social rights and environmental protection laws. Since an international treaty specifically regulating MNCs' activities has never been adopted, in order to assess Chinese international obligations in this field, the author chooses to examine the framework of the main international obligations binding China with regard to human rights, as well as environmental and social rights protection. In evaluating whether China has correctly adapted its domestic law to accommodate the international obligations undertaken and has put in place the necessary measures to ensure compliance with such obligations, the author emphasizes the notion of the "harmonious society" (*hexie shehui*).

Leïla Choukroune investigates the development of a China-specific public interest litigation (PIL) that illustrates, and simultaneously challenges, the justiciability of socio-economic rights in an authoritarian regime. After exploring the roots of the recent Chinese movement, the author addresses its limitations, which are inherent to the Chinese legal system: the lack of an independent judiciary, a legislative process that does not reflect the will of the people, the frequent and arbitrary repression of rights defenders, and the systematic promotion of mediation as the best alternative to dispute settlement. The author argues that, despite these limitations, the emergence of the Chinese PIL shows that Chinese citizens have exercised their legal tools at the right time, with the result of having generated innovative judicial activity fostered by novel civil society activism.

Valentina Sara Vadi adopts an international investment law approach to explain the rise of Chinese bilateral investment treaties (BITs) while investigating the social, cultural, and environmental consequences of China's investment treaty–making program. The latter has become a key component of China's development policy, and, like other emerging economies, China has gone from a mere recipient of investment flows to a leading source of FDIs. The emerging role of China as a capital exporter contributes to the current debate about the interplay between international investment law and non-economic issues. If China wishes to become a great global power, it must take non-economic concerns into account, and therefore it is in the country's best interest to negotiate more equitable BITs. Against this backdrop, the author questions whether or not Chinese BITs can provide a new paradigm and promote sustainable development.

China's investment strategy is taken on by **Mark Klaver** and **Michael Trebilcock**, who argue that Chinese investment presents African states with a major opportunity for sustainable economic growth. China's main motivation for investing in Africa is to access the country's natural resources, but Chinese investors also seek market access. Despite serving China's own interests, Chinese investment in Africa has expedited economic growth in various African countries. Nevertheless, it still presents a number of major drawbacks. As to the correct response to such drawbacks, the authors suggest that African states have varying levels of good governance, and while no policies are one-size-fits-all, economic development is ultimately best achieved by cultivating Africa's manufacturing sector.

Part II Sustainable development, environmental protection, and climate change

Part II of the volume addresses the delicate intersection between trade regulations and measures adopted in the name of sustainable development, environmental protection, and climate change mitigation, exploring the role China plays in shaping these relations.

Francesco Sindico and **Julie Gibson** explore the evolution of international climate change practice and its repercussions on trade relations among countries. The authors argue that three key trends can be identified in the development of the international climate change regime: the prevalence of soft commitments, the fragmentation of international efforts in relation to climate change, and an increasing complexity within the relevant adopted instruments. After analyzing the trends in the development of the overall international climate change efforts, the authors focus on the specific nature of the climate-trade relationship within the broader debate on trade and environment, and assesses whether softer, more fragmented, and more complex international climate change practice may increase trade tensions.

Imad Ibrahim, Thomas Deleuil and **Paolo Davide Farah** investigate the place and practice of the principle of common but differentiated responsibilities (CBDR) in the ongoing international climate negotiations. In their analysis, the authors study the regime's evolving role and understanding of the principle during the recent developments. After the adoption of the Bali Action Plan, new issues have appeared in negotiations and the centrality of CBDR appears to be fading. As a result, recent decisions refer more and more often to contextual norms of differentiations rather than making direct reference to CBDR. Yet, the Paris agreement has proved that the latter principle will always constitute an essential element in the international climate change negotiations. The authors thoroughly explores these developments, keeping in mind that the CBDR represents only *one* expression of differential treatment and, irrespective of what expression might eventually prevail, it is the parties' actual obligations that will matter.

Marion Lemoine assesses the current functioning of the Clean Development Mechanism (CDM) from a developing-country perspective. The author provides an analysis of the regional distribution of CDM projects and evaluates the content of the sustainable development input within the projects to investigate whether developing countries are the effective beneficiaries of the mechanism in terms of sustainable development. The effective implementation of sustainable development through CDM remains one of its main problems, and technology transfer has been effective only in less-industrialized states.

Elena Cima examines the international framework regulating the process of technology transfer in the renewable energy sector and identifies the obstacles that prevent the transfer from being more successful. Without denying the relevance of all the efforts at the international level to facilitate such transfer, the author draws from the Chinese experience to argue that the most effective way to address the *real* obstacles to technology transfer is to enact comprehensive domestic policies in the recipient country. The author further argues that the creation of a strong legal structure and a suitable investment scenario in the host country is a main driver of technology transfer, while contributing to the country's development. Besides, it enables the host country to develop its own technology and become an active part of the process.

Weidong He explores the relationship between China's recent rapid economic growth and environmental protection, as he formulates suggestions for improving the implementation of China's environmental laws to cope with the issues plaguing the effectiveness of the system. China's pattern of development, which is the main cause of the country's environmental issues – together with the international environmental movement – pushed the Chinese government to pay increasing attention to environmental issues. After a detailed description of China's environmental protection framework, the author analyzes the fundamental principles and institutions of the Chinese environmental legal system, as well as the degree of China's international environmental cooperation.

Luo Li, who formulates proposals for improving the judicial relief system for environmental disputes in China, takes on a different aspect of China's environmental legal framework. Presently, China has developed a system of judicial relief for environmental disputes that integrates administrative, criminal, and civil litigation. Although this system has generated discernible positive effects, there is still considerable room for improvement. The author argues that China lacks an effective way to protect the environment and the environmental interests of the general public, and, therefore, improving the legislation behind procedural law and regulating environmental public interest litigation more clearly is a pressing matter.

Carla Peng explores the recent reforms of the Chinese legislative framework as a reaction to the implementation of the results of the climate negotiations, and especially of the UNFCCC and the Kyoto Protocol. As one of the major international environmental issues, climate change plays a direct role in national energy security and affects the country's strategy for national economic growth. By implementing the UNFCCC and the Kyoto Protocol, China has made great legislative achievements, but its legal system continues to face serious problems, such as incomplete climate and energy policies, lack of supporting regulations, and difficulties in implementation and enforcement. The author argues that a new reform breakthrough is necessary if China intends to complete its transition to a low-carbon economy.

Zhixiong Huang explores the evolving role played by Chinese Non-Governmental Organizations (NGOs) in the ongoing climate change debate. Climate change is an area of extreme political sensitivity and technical complexity, which may produce substantial obstacles to the participation of NGOs. China's unique situation as both the largest developing country and one of the largest greenhouse gas emitters would seemingly provide an additional obstacle to Chinese NGOs' involvement in China's climate politics. Despite being latecomers to the game, as international consensus about the need to mitigate climate change continues to increase, the stimulus for Chinese NGOs to get involved has also escalated. Judging by the domestic and international presence of Chinese NGOs, climate change has now become one of the most dynamic areas for Chinese NGOs.

Paolo Davide Farah and **Riccardo Tremolada** carry out an in-depth analysis of the current shale gas regulatory framework, moving from previous experiences of unconventional gas exploitation in the US to evaluating their possible applications in China, where regulatory and enforcement hurdles are exacerbated by an energy sector characterized by technological deficiencies, barriers to market access, and a limited liberalization of gas prices. Shale gas has been defined as a revolution in the global energy landscape. This is even truer in China, whose large shale gas reserves are likely to have a crucial effect on the regional gas market and on China's energy mix. Nonetheless, this advance does not come without risks, because shale gas exploitation poses a number of legal, regulatory and environmental challenges, which could negatively impact future exploitation and commercialization, not only in China.

Part III Fundamental rights and cultural diversity

Part III of this book turns to the issues of fundamental rights and cultural diversity, and their relationship with international economic law from a Chinese perspective.

Jean Yves Heurtebise explores the role played by NTCs in the transfer of legitimacy from nation-states to international institutions, necessary to cope with the globalized nature of the contemporary world economy. The challenge brought by NTCs not only requires overcoming national selfishness, but it also calls for universal recognition of some fundamental rights, implying the constitution of a legal-ethical platform, potentially superseding national sovereignties and bridging cultural differences. To help understand China's reluctance to embrace NTCs, the author conducts a comparative analysis of Chinese and Western legal cultures, comparing the debate between "Confucians" and "Legalists" in ancient China to the one between natural law theorists and legal positivists in contemporary Europe.

Flavia Zorzi Giustiniani analyzes the way the WTO deals with the right to food and demonstrates the negative impact that WTO obligations, and in particular those deriving from the Agreement on Agriculture, have on the right to food, stressing the fact that this negative impact is not inevitable. In principle, WTO and human rights obligations are not incompatible. The Agreement establishing the WTO envisages that states should conduct their trade relations with a view towards raising standards of living, and Members should refrain from supporting any WTO measure or decision that could harm the enjoyment of the right to food.

Libiao Ning also centers his chapter around the right to food, drawing the reader's attention to China. By doing so, the author explores the cultural basis behind ensuring the right to food in China and then analyzes the government's political inclination as well as the measures taken to protect such right, showing the remarkable progress made in China. After providing a precise and detailed overview of the existing problems, the author concludes with some proposals for the improved protection of this right.

James R. Simpson addresses the highly debated question of China's ability to feed itself over the next few decades. The author uses science-based research to project China's food security up to 2030, using the calculation of all-animal and aquaculture feedstuffs requirements and availabilities as a starting point and factoring in a series of other elements, such as constraints on China's natural resources and the potential of biotechnology in relation to crop production. Although China's animal and crop productivity is quite low, the research reveals that China will most likely maintain its agricultural superpower status, further investigating *how* the country will use its agricultural powerhouse.

Roberto Soprano explores China's attitude towards the protection of the human right to water. China's awareness of the country's water scarcity problems has pushed the government to invest widely in the sector, although investments have been disproportionate between rural and urban areas. In order to comply with international obligations and protect, promote, and fulfill the right to water, China must rethink its policies and projects to reduce the inequitable access to water and make further efforts to diminish the pollution of water resources to provide safe drinking water for people in both urban and rural areas.

Christophe Germann revisits the idea that the promotion of cultural diversity combined with the freedom of expression in authoritarian regimes might change the international law paradigm on intellectual property protection. In the absence of other capable international fora, the author argues that the WTO could play a pivotal role in the elaboration and implementation of new rules aimed at materializing equitable access, openness, and balance. However, so far, the WTO has not succeeded in encouraging such "equitable trade" and the litigation between the US and China on cultural goods and services clearly illustrates some of the causes of this failure. As a solution, the author introduces the idea of variable geometry for the duration of copyright protection as a novel remedy against excessive intellectual property protection eroding and damaging both cultural diversity and equitable trade.

Rogier Creemers looks at the nexus between media control and international trade in China. Since media plays a crucial role in Chinese politics and is closely monitored by a complex web of institutional and regulatory measures, understanding how the censorship system operates helps better gauge the impact of international trade law on this important aspect of Chinese domestic regulation. Against this background, the author proceeds to analyze the tensions between the media control system and the expectations of the international trade regime, paying particular attention to the WTO dispute between China and the US on *Publications and Audiovisual Products*, looking both at the substantive impact of the decisions and at the political dimension of implementation and retaliation.

The WTO *China – Publications and Audiovisual Products* dispute is at the core of another chapter within this volume. **Anselm Kamperman Sanders** presents an innovative analysis of this dispute, exploring the way in which trade in cultural works has led to discussions on NTCs in the context of free trade agreements and WTO obligations. The author offers a comprehensive overview of the relevant case law and demonstrates that China is characterized by the convergence of measures that are all subservient to the desire to exercise full political and cultural control over the media market, addressing whether the moral exception argument raised successfully by China to defend its policies will be sustainable in the long run.

Danny Friedmann argues that the Chinese government uses social media as an instrument to censor and guide its population. The author examines the Chinese attitude towards social media and the way it relates to international trade law, especially through the analysis of BITs, which might be used by other countries to oblige China to meet its commitments and give foreign social media companies market access. Although China has obligations towards the global community via international treaties, the freedom of expression provisions in both the Universal Declaration of Human Rights and the International Covenant on Civil and Political Rights are not equipped to help foreign companies gain access to the Chinese market.

Julien Chaisse and **Xinjie Luan** revisit the high-profile WTO dispute on the EU seal import ban that has captivated the attention of the international community for over five years, from a legal and economic perspective. Instead of commenting on the merits of the WTO decision, the authors return to the facts and the law to provide a novel analysis of the dispute, with a view to shed light on some of the arguments that the WTO Panel and Appellate Body ignored, such as, among others, the differences between the risk assessment mechanism in the WTO Agreement on Technical Barriers to Trade and the Agreement on the Application of Sanitary and Phytosanitary Measures.

Part IV Public health, product and food safety, consumer protection

Part IV of the volume addresses the complex and highly debated intersection between trade regulation and the protection of public health, product safety, and consumers' rights, adopting once again a very unique perspective based on China's experience.

Denise Prévost examines the most relevant provisions of the WTO Agreement on the Application of Sanitary and Phytosanitary Measures (SPS) to establish the extent to which it permits China to pursue its NTCs in the area of food safety, as well as plant and animal health. The analysis of the WTO rules that discipline the trade-restrictive effect of such health regulations and conformity assessment procedures will also determine the possibilities for the EU to pursue its trade interests by using the rules of the SPS Agreement to challenge China's SPS measures.

Lorenzo Di Masi looks at the presence of NTCs in Regional Trade Agreements (RTAs) signed by the Association of South-East Asian Nations (ASEAN) and by China, in order to evaluate their possible contribution to the evolution of international economic law in a "sustainable development oriented" direction. The author first discusses the reasons that have led China and ASEAN to pursue an intensive regional policy during the last ten years and argues that the Chinese government has always entered into RTAs for geopolitical and economic reasons, which explains why it has given only partial attention to sustainable development issues. However, China's continued display of flexibility in negotiations, combined with the fact that sustainable development has become an essential part of the country's economic planning, leaves open the possibility of new unexpected scenarios.

Lukasz Gruszczynski, Tivadar Ötvös and **Paolo Davide Farah** discuss the basic obligations for national product safety regulations imposed by the WTO Agreement on Technical Barriers to Trade (TBT) and look at the rules on technical standards that are applicable in the relations between China and its trading partners. In recent decades, the problem of product safety has become one of the main issues on the agenda of national regulators. Although the TBT Agreement constitutes an important part of the WTO legal regime, it seems to be somewhat unappreciated by WTO Members, as TBT disputes have been rare. The authors argue that, as a consequence, the scope of the Members' obligations and rights flowing from TBT provisions is uncertain, affecting the predictability of the whole system and further discouraging Members from initiating disputes under the agreement.

Piercarlo Rossi examines China's provisions aimed at consumer protection within a broader analysis of how consumer protection laws may create an exception, if not even an obstacle, to the principles of international trade. Studying the provisions aimed at protecting consumers in different jurisdictions from a strictly legal point of view, the author finds that there are no consistent doctrines concerning the balance between provisions directed at protecting competition and markets and those solely designed to protect consumers. Turning to the study of Chinese consumer laws, the author remarks on the importance of conducting such analysis, taking into account the specific features of the Asian region China belongs to.

The issue of consumers' legal protection is subsequently taken up by **A. Rajendra Prasad**, who focuses on developing countries. Consumers exist throughout the globe but encounter distinct problems depending on their country of residence. Taking into account the specific problems of developing countries as far as consumer protection is concerned, the author examines the legislative attempts of various Asian countries to protect consumers' interests. The author uses the Indian experience as a case study to show how consumer protection has been able to trigger a new legal revolution with informal dispute resolution.

Junhong Hu examines the innovative legislative principles introduced with the adoption of the Chinese Tort Liability Law, as well as their effects on the system of product liability and legal regulations of product safety, especially in the light of the product safety accidents that recently occurred in China. The author investigates the reasons why, even though China has enacted strict laws on product safety, including administrative laws on product supervision and punishment and tough civil and criminal laws on product liability, consumer safety cases in which serious damage occurs constantly arise.

Nadia Coggiola addresses the issue of compensation of damages caused by environmental pollution, aiming to identify the reasons and meanings of the discrepancies between the rich and comprehensive Chinese legislation and the poor litigation records on compensation for damages caused by exposure to dangerous substances. The very essence of this controversial issue can only be grasped by inquiring how formal rules are actually implemented in Chinese courts and, as a result, the author investigates beyond the narrow borders of Chinese black-letter law to unveil the judicial and extrajudicial hurdles that undermine an effective implementation of the existing laws and regulations.

Shujie Feng, **Xin Shu** and **Ningning Zhang** explore the contribution of the WTO Agreement on Trade-Related Aspects of Intellectual Property Rights (TRIPS) in solving one of the most controversial problems raised by biotechnology, namely the patentability of biotechnological inventions. Since all WTO Members experience different levels of technological and economic development, and since they do not share the same morals and ethics, divergences are unavoidable. Against this background, and taking into account the role of the TRIPS Agreement in harmonizing national laws, the authors conduct a comparative evaluation of TRIPS implementation in the field of biotechnology, focusing on China, the US, and the EU.

Jayashree Watal addresses the need to find a balance in the protection of intellectual property rights (IPR) between the short-term interest in maximizing access to medicines and the long-term interest in promoting creativity and innovation. This task has been made more difficult at the international level on account of IPR treaties that may not take account of differing levels of economic, technological, and social development. The author further explores whether the flexibilities provided for in the TRIPS Agreement, as well as in subsequent instruments adopted by WTO Members, such as the Doha Declaration on TRIPS and Public Health and the Paragraph 6 Decision, are sufficient to solve the problem of access to medicines and medical technologies.

Jianqiang Nie explores the intersection between intellectual property, genetic resources, traditional knowledge, and traditional cultural expression from a Chinese perspective. The author investigates two fundamental issues related to the relationship between the TRIPS Agreement and the Convention on Biological Diversity: how to clarify legal requirements or conditions under IP legislation to prevent the unlawful or unjustifiable approval of IP rights over genetic resources, traditional knowledge, and traditional cultural expression (defensive protection), and how to make use of the IP legal system to protect genetic resources, traditional knowledge, and traditional cultural expression (positive protection).

Francesca Spigarelli and **Andrea Filippetti** address the emerging issues related to the infringement of IPRs of indigenous people by foreign multinational enterprises (MNEs). By settling their branches in the developing world, MNEs are able to capture traditional knowledge, register patents based on such principles, and incorporate them into their products. The industrialized countries win in this game. The authors analyze the pharmaceutical sector in China, focusing on traditional Chinese medicine and the growing presence of foreign pharmaceutical companies in the country.

2 The Development of Global Justice and Sustainable Development Principles in the WTO Multilateral Trading System through the Lens of Non-Trade Concerns: An Appraisal on China's Progress*

Paolo Davide Farah

I Introduction: Resorting to "Non-Trade Concerns" to stem the excesses of globalization

From the WTO protests in Seattle in 1999 to Occupy Wall Street in 2011, civil society has continued to express dismay and anger towards human, social, and environmental consequences of the global expansion of world trade and of the monetary and commercial translation of all interpersonal transactions. The ongoing economic instability in several countries and regions throughout the world, along with the volatility of the market and job losses, has lead to an increase in protests that are currently reaching the highest possible levels of conflict against the so-called establishment.

Additionally, the growing of political discourse and public opinion regarding the migration crisis and the global fight against terrorism are also providing momentum to some relevant segments of this variegated movement.

* This chapter is part of the results of the Research Project on "*Current Trends of Chinese Law towards Non-Trade Concerns such as Sustainable Development and the Protection of Environment, Public Health, Food Safety, Cultural, Social and Economic Rights, Labor Rights and the Reduction of Poverty from the Perspective of International Law and WTO Law*" coordinated by Professor Paolo Davide Farah at gLAWcal – Global Law Initiatives for Sustainable Development (United Kingdom) and at West Virginia University John D. Rockefeller IV School of Policy and Politics, Department of Public Administration, in partnership with the Center of Advanced Studies on Contemporary China (CASCC) in Turin (Italy), Maastricht University Faculty of Law, Department of International and European Law and IGIR – Institute for Globalisation and International Regulation (Netherlands) and Tsinghua University, School of Law, Institute of Public International Law and the Center for Research on Intellectual Property Law in Beijing (China). Three different parts of the early draft of this paper were presented at Conferences Series on *"China's Influence on Non-Trade Concerns in International Economic Law"*, First Conference held at the Center of Advanced Studies on Contemporary China (CASCC) in Turin (Italy) on November 23–24, 2011; Second Conference held at Tsinghua University, School of Law on January 14–15, 2012; Third Conference held at Maastricht University, Faculty of Law on January 19–20, 2012. The most recent versions of this paper were presented at the American Society of International Law (ASIL) International Economic Law Interest Group (IEcLIG) 2014 Biennial Research Conference in partnership with the University of Denver Sturm College of Law Sutton Colloquium: *"Reassessing International Economic Law and Development: New challenges for Law and Policy"*, University of Denver Sturm College of Law, Denver, CO, USA, November 13–15, 2014 and at the International Conference *"Consumer Policy in China: New Trends and Challenges"*, held at the Faculty of Law of University of Macau (China) on December 15–16, 2015. This publication and the Conference Series on "China's Influence on Non-Trade Concerns in International Economic Law" were sponsored by China–EU School of Law (CESL) at the China University of Political Science and Law (CUPL) in Beijing (China). The activities of CESL at CUPL are supported by the European Union and the People's Republic of China. An extended version of this paper appeared at 30 (1) Columbia Journal of Asian Law 2016.

Majority votes favoring Brexit and other political turmoil happening around European countries, in the United States, and in different parts of the world are just some of the most critical examples on how the existing systems are failing. Specifically, global governance and law with borderless globalization are to blame for the inability to find appropriate solutions to face the challenges of a constantly changing society. Unfortunately, this inability creates a risk that leaves behind an increasing part of the population who are unable to benefit from such globalization.

For example, more and more political leaders are trying to use this discontent among the society for obtaining an easy consensus, without truly having a real program to improve the life of the people. More importantly, without endorsing the intrinsic dangers, a strong shift back towards nationalism might come to fruition in the long-term as a result.

The related fear of the people toward the risks of a world without barriers are very real and concrete. Moreover, the proposed solutions to face these problems are certainly influenced by the negative visions on globalization and liberalism, which neglect to take into account the positive effects of the free trade and liberalization of the markets.

Since the beginning of the Industrial Revolution, the success of the capitalist mode of production is marked by its results in terms of demographic, economic, and technological development. Between 1810 and 2010, the total income per capita multiplied by nine, the world population by six, and the pace of technological innovation grew exponentially.

However, one needs to bear in mind two important caveats regarding the effectiveness and legitimacy of the industrial mode of production of goods and the commercial mode of wealth distribution during their global expansion. The first caveat is that the global development of the industrial mode of production of goods caused a perturbation in the balance that regulates the interaction between man and the environment: climate change,[1] depletion of fisheries, soil erosion, and pollution are the flip side of the global triumph of the Industrial Revolution.

As stated in the report *Limits to Growth,* issued by the Club of Rome in 1972, and as rephrased more recently in the 2005 *Millennium Ecosystem Assessment*, "Human activity is putting such strain on the natural functions of Earth that the ability of the planet's ecosystems to sustain future generations can no longer be taken for granted."[2] The fact that the current mode of development is not sustainable means that its persistence will soon result in its own end: human development has exhausted the Earth's production, absorption, and recycling capacity. The second caveat is that the inequalities between rich and poor countries have increased paradoxically due to the global development of the commercial wealth distribution. This process has taken place since 1820 and throughout the twentieth century with the exception of the "golden age of capitalism" from 1950–1973.[3]

Therefore, the idea of limiting the excesses of globalization while controlling the international institutions that create them – such as the International Monetary Fund (IMF) or the World Trade Organization (WTO) – may be, to a certain extent, justified. As Former Director-General of the WTO Pascal Lamy once stated: "For better and for worse,

1 Gabrielle Marceau & Mireille Cossy, *Institutional Challenges to Enhance Policy Coordination – How WTO Rules Could Be Utilized to Meet Climate Objectives?* 371–394 (Proceedings of the World Trade Forum 2007, International Trade on a Warming Globe: The Role of the WTO in the Climate Change Debate, 2008). See also Paolo Davide Farah & Riccardo Tremolada, *Global Governance & Intangible Cultural Heritage in the Information Society: At the Crossroads of IPRs & Innovation*, in The Handbook of Global Science, Technology, and Innovation (Daniele Archibugi & Andrea Fillipetti eds, 2015).

2 Millennium Ecosystem Assessment Board, *Millennium Ecosystem Assessment, Living Beyond Our Means* 3 (United Nations, 2005).

3 Andrés Solimano, The Evolution of World Income Inequality: Assessing the Impact of Globalization (Economic Commission for Latin America and the Caribbean (ECLAC), December 2001).

globalization of the issues increases, on a daily basis, the need to organize democratic, global forms of governance that are both legitimate and efficient. In other words: democratic."[4]

In fact, for many years, the General Agreement on Tariffs and Trade (GATT) and the WTO have been highly criticized and portrayed as the least transparent and democratic of all international organizations. Indeed, most of the meetings and debates are held *in camera*, and agreements are reached at the intergovernmental level without any public participation.[5] The lack of civil society participation in the ongoing negotiation rounds at the WTO affects the rights to both information and participation of all parties, as these fundamental rights were made clear by the 1998 Aarhus Convention (*Access to Justice*),[6] Article 21 of the Universal Declaration of Human Rights,[7] as well as Principle 10 of the Rio Declaration on Environment and Development.

However, the WTO has gradually begun to open up to civil society, both through the participation of Non-Governmental Organizations (NGOs) in the plenary sessions of the most important ministerial conferences and through the establishment of a contact group dedicated to NGOs within the WTO secretariat. Additionally, the WTO website provides access to a wide range of highly detailed information on trade issues and the relevant committees. Moreover, the WTO's Appellate Body (AB) has authorized the submission of *amicus curiae* briefs as well as the opening of public hearings.[8] Thus, as trade institutions expand their competence, the role of civil society in the institutions that govern international trade is becoming more and more substantial.[9]

Hence, the right approach is not to oppose the global sovereignty of certain international organizations, but rather to propose concrete reforms[10] to provide such institutions with the democratic legitimacy they now lack. In addition to the increasing democratic transparency of their decisions, it is mostly the outer frame of analysis which should be amended.[11]

Democratic legitimacy and social justice based on human rights principles should be used as the regulatory framework to structure global expansion of economic welfare as well as

4 Pascal Lamy, La Démocratie-Monde – Pour une autre Gouvernance Globale 20 (Seuil, 2004).

5 For a general overview of the WTO rules, *see* Peter Van Den Bossche, The Law and Policy of the World Trade Organization 917 (2 ed., Cambridge University Press, 2008); Mitsuo Matsushita, Thomas Schoenbaum & Petros C. Mavroidis, The World Trade Organization: Law, Practice and Policy 989 (Oxford University Press, 2003); David Luff, Le Droit de l'Organisation Mondiale du Commerce. Analyse Critique 771 (Bruylant, 2004); Paolo Picone, Aldo Ligustro, Diritto dell'Organizzazione Mondiale del Commercio 505 (CEDAM, 2002).

6 Convention on Access to Information, Public Participation in Decision-Making and Access to Justice in Environmental Matters, 2161 UNTS 447; 38 ILM 517 (1999).

7 UN General Assembly, Universal Declaration of Human Rights, December 10, 1948, 217 A (III), http://www.unhcr.org/refworld/docid/3ae6b3712c.html (last visited August 6, 2016).

8 Gabrielle Marceau & Matthew Stilwell, *Practical Suggestions for the Administration of Amicus Curiae Briefs by WTO Adjudicating Bodies*, 4(1) J. Int'l Econ. L. 155, 155 (2001).

9 Heidi k. Ullrich, *Expanding the Trade Debate: The Role of Information in WTO and Civil Society Interaction, Information and Communication Technologies and Human Rights Advocacy: the Case of Amnesty International*, in Civil Society in The Information Age 19, 19–36 (Peter Hajnal ed., Ashgate, 2002); Elisabeth Tuerk, *The Role of NGOs on International Governance NGOs and Developing Country WTO Members: Is there Potential for Alliance?*, in International Economic Governance and Non Economic Concerns 169, 169–210 (Griller Stefan ed., Springer, 2003).

10 Thomas D. Zweifel, International Organizations and Democracy: Accountability, Politics, and Power 14 (Lynne Rienner Publishers, 2006).

11 Meinhard Hilf & Goetz J. Goettsche, *The Relation of Economic and Non-Economic Principles in International Law*, in International Economic Governance and Non-Economic Concerns, *supra* note 9, at 5–46; Robert Howse, *How to Begin to Think about the "Democratic Deficit" at the WTO*, in International Economic Governance and Non-Economic Concerns, *supra* note 9, at 79–102.

WTO rules.[12] However, the difficulty and limit of this approach lies in the fact that it affirms both that human rights should guide the process of global legal integration and that the WTO should implement such process.[13] Suggesting that WTO law guarantees respect for fundamental human rights implies a refusal to evaluate the practices of organizations such as the WTO itself and the IMF.[14]

Indeed, WTO rules and principles not only prevent Members from discriminating against other Members in general, but also severely restrain their ability to adopt trade measures against another Member whose practices do not respect human rights. Likewise, accession to the WTO is not subject to any criterion related to respect for human rights, and its rules require that each Member – following accession to the WTO – can enjoy the same commercial benefits as the others, thus preventing Member States from discriminating based on the protection of human rights.[15] Nevertheless, GATT exceptions allow Members to adopt measures that restrict trade in goods manufactured by prisoners. Another interesting example is the waiver granted to all countries that are parties to the *Kimberley Process*,[16] which is designed to certify the origin of rough diamonds[17] from sources that are free of conflict fueled by diamond production (so-called *blood diamonds*).[18] Some WTO provisions might be interpreted so as to give Members the opportunity to pursue human rights objectives. For example, the exceptions set out in GATT Article XX could provide a viable framework for action. On the other hand, the recent trend of signing Regional Trade Agreements (RTAs) where States often choose carefully with which other States they wish to engage in such a partnership[19] can give more importance to the influence of human rights in trade policy decisions and have consequences in terms of legal empowerment.

This debate also looks at the idea of resituating the notion of Non-Trade Concerns (NTCs). The integration of NTCs within the WTO decision-making process should add a regulatory reference to certain non-economic values and fundamental rights to the economic criteria

12 Ernst-Ulrich Petersmann, *Time for a United Nations "Global Compact" for Integrating Human Rights into the Law of Worldwide Organizations: Lessons from European Integration*, 13(3) Eur. J. Int'l L. 621, 621–650 (2002). *See*, also, Gabrielle Marceau & Aline Doussin, *Le Droit du Commerce Internationale et les Droits Fondamentaux et Considérations Sociales*, 27(2) L'Observateur des Nations Unies 241, 241–47 (2010).

13 Ernst-Ulrich Petersmann, *From "Negative" to "Positive" Integration in the WTO: Time for "Mainstreaming Human Rights" into WTO Law?*, 37 Common Mkt. L. Rev. 1363, 1363–382 (2000).

14 Philip Alston, *Resisting the Merger and Acquisition of Human Rights by Trade Law: A Reply to Petersmann*, 13(4) Eur. J. Int'l L. 815, 815–84 (2002).

15 There is, of course, a possibility to opt out of commercial relations with a new Member (so-called cause of non-compliance), but it has never been used by the Members.

16 The Parties of the Kimberley Process are listed at the following address: http://www.kimberleyprocess.com/site/participants.html (last visited August 6, 2016). They include Angola, Armenia, Australia, Bangladesh, Belarus, Botswana, Brazil, Canada, Central African Rep., China, Côte d'Ivoire, Croatia, Dem. Rep. of Congo, European Community, Ghana, Guinea, Guyana, India, Indonesia, Israel, Japan, Laos, Lebanon, Lesotho, Malaysia, Mauritius, Namibia, Norway, New Zealand, Russia, Separate customs territory of Taiwan, Sierra Leone, Singapore, S. Africa, S. Korea, Sri Lanka, Switzerland, Tanzania, Thailand, Togo, Ukraine, the US, Venezuela, Vietnam, and Zimbabwe.

17 Rough diamonds are diamonds that are unworked or simply sawn, cleaved, or bruted and fall under the Relevant Harmonised Commodity Description and Coding System 7102.10, 7102.21, and 7102.31. Kimberley Process Certification Scheme § 1 (August 2003). Margo Kaplan, *Note, Carats and Sticks: Pursuing War and Peace through the Diamond Trade*, 35 N.Y.U. J. Int'l L. & Pol. 559, 587 (2003).

18 Daniel Feldman, *Conflict Diamonds, International Trade Regulation, and the Nature of Law*, 24 U. Pa. J. Int'l Econ. L. 835, 840 (2003).

19 This is, of course, subject to negotiation and depends on negotiating power of the different parties involved.

that have defined globalization so far.[20] From this perspective, according to the author, the current standby and the eventual success of the Doha Round depends on the ability to integrate all the different partners in joint discussions on non-economic values and parameters.

The right to development and other associated rights, such as the right to food, shelter, water, and so on,[21] are all, to some extent, directly affected by international trade. To elucidate, international trade law, both within and outside the WTO, determines how global trade evolves and limits the ways in which trade policy can be used to encourage domestic policies, which, in developing countries, allow greater legal empowerment. Allowing more substantial participation of developing countries within the WTO and promoting the opening up of trade and custom barriers, such as for agricultural products, might have an extremely important impact on the issues connected to NTCs. While furthering this assertion, rights of disadvantaged farmers in developing countries could be positively, though indirectly, affected. This is precisely why some experts call for the expansion of the concept of NTCs to the dissemination and production of agricultural products, qualifying them as global public goods.[22]

With regard to NTCs, the main issue is that developing countries do not have the same concerns as developed ones. When a country still faces problems related to basic health care and hygiene, fewer resources remain to deal with issues like animal welfare and food safety. Developing countries will try to achieve a high level of protection for NTCs, primarily in those areas where the same level of protection is granted by industrialized countries whose market they want to access. The key challenge is how to satisfy the right of developed nations to grant social values the degree of protection they consider appropriate, while minimizing the negative effects in terms of market distortion for their trading partners. This is exactly where the WTO can prove itself very useful. For example, the regulation of investments and protection of intellectual property rights on product and production processes as well as issues related to patents derived from traditional knowledge or traditional medicine, fall within both the international legal system (Agreement on Trade-Related Aspects of Intellectual Property Rights or TRIPS[23] and Patent Cooperation Treaty or PCT[24]) and the European one (European Patent Convention).

The following section of this chapter examines the particularities of China at a crossroads between the "Right to Development" and "NTCs," given that China still seeks to grow its economy and expand industry to bring millions of more people out of poverty. Simultaneously, it plays an essential role (together with other BRICS countries) in creating a model

20 James R. Simpson & Thomas J. Schoenbaum, *Non-Trade Concerns in WTO Trade Negotiations: Legal and Legitimate Reasons for Revising the "Box" System?*, 2(3/4) Int'l J. Agric. Resources, Governance & Ecology 399, 399–410 (2003).

21 Ludivine Tamiotti, Trade and Climate Change. A Report (United Nations Environment Programme & the World Trade Organization, WTO Publications: World Trade Organization, 2009); Patricia Birnie, Alan Boyle & Catherine Redgwell, International Law and the Environment (Oxford University Press, 2008); Christine Breining-Kaufmann, *The Right to Food and Trade in Agriculture*, in Human Rights and International Trade 341, 381 (Thomas Cottier, Joost Pauwelyn & Elisabeth Bürgi Bonanomi eds, Oxford University Press, 2005); Rebecca Bates, *The Road to the Well: An Evaluation of the Customary Right to Water*, 19(3) Rev. Eur. Cmty. & Int'l Envtl. L. 282, 293 (2010). Joanne Scott, *Integrating Environmental Concerns into International Economic Law*, in International Economic Governance and Non Economic Concerns, *supra* note 9, at 371–88; Upendra Baxi, *The Human Right to Water: Policies and Rights*, in Water and the Laws in India 149, 166 (Ramaswamy R. Iyer ed., Sage, 2009).

22 Simpson & Schoenbaum, *supra* note 20, at 399–410.

23 *Agreement on Trade-Related Aspects of Intellectual Property Rights*, 1869 U.N.T.S. 299; 33 ILM 1197 (1994).

24 *Patent Cooperation Treaty*, TIAS 8733; 28 UST 7645; 9 ILM 978 (1970).

to "develop" sustainably, with a view towards tackling climate change, avoiding the increasing environmental risks and damages, and balancing the attractions of foreign investments with labor rights, human rights, and public health.

The subsequent section titled "Non-Trade Concerns status in the WTO multilateral system" develops a non-exhaustive overview and explores the integration of NTCs in the WTO. In particular, the interplay between environment and trade[25] is examined and the prospects for the new acceding Members, taking China as a case study and its accession to the WTO in 2001, the change in the attitude of the WTO DSB while ranking public health issues over trade, the relations between food security and international trade regulations, the difficult balance of the right to access essential medicines and the protection of their IPRs, the respect of other human rights in the multilateral trading system, and the relations between cultural products and public morals.

II China at a crossroads: From "right to development" to "Non-Trade Concerns" in the global context

In recent years, the world has confronted an incredible critical depletion of natural resources, with increasing risks and disruption to the environment, overpopulation as a major environmental issue, extremely deteriorating public health, economic depression at the global level, a massive increase in commodities pricing (even the most essential ones in view of guaranteeing the right to food), global famine in poor countries as well as the reappearance of hunger in growing areas of the developed world, international tensions, and the eventual adoption or re-adoption of martial law.

In this evolving and constantly changing context, China successfully developed over the last 30 years without completely overcoming its internal disparities. However, the tension between the national regime and international influences has never been completely resolved.[26] On the one hand, the Chinese government keeps encouraging vertical integration of the production system within its borders in order to build an independent industrial system. On the other, China has become a global economic player, contributing massively to economic globalization: not only has it received an enormous amount of foreign direct investment, but it also actively engages in global trade and capital exports.

It is arguable whether China's accession to and integration in the WTO had beneficial consequences for world trade as a whole or had only negatively affected its trading partners while at the same time stressed the limits of the WTO and the trading system in an

25 One of the examples will be examined in the following analysis is the *US – Shrimp* case. If we can justify restricting importation of shrimp to comply with the societal objective to protect turtles, we certainly can bend economic laws to protect NTCs and related fundamental social and environmental rights. *See* Gabrielle Marceau, *Trade and the Environment: The WTO's Efforts to Balance Economic and Sustainable Development, in* Economie Environnement: Ethique, de la Responsabilité Sociale et Sociétale 225, 225–35 (C. Bovet, H. Peter & R. Trindade Trigo eds, Schulthess, 2009). *See*, also, Appellate Body Report, *United States – Import Prohibition of Certain Shrimp and Shrimp Products*, WT/DS58/AB/R (October 12, 1998); Report of the Panel, *United States – Import Prohibition of Certain Shrimp and Shrimp Products*, WT/DS58/RW (June 15, 2001); Appellate Body Report, *United States – Import Prohibition of Certain Shrimp and Shrimp Products Recourse to Article 21.5 of The DSU by Malaysia*, WT/DS58/AB/RW (October 22, 2001).

26 Gianmaria Ajani, *Legal Change and Economic Performance: an Assessment*, in Asian Constitutionalism in Transition: A Comparative Perspective 281, 281–305 (Tania Groppi, Valeria Piergigli & Angelo Rinello eds, Giuffrè Editore, 2008).

irreparable way. Probably, neither of these two options is totally correct. China's accession to the WTO has been a milestone[27] for the country itself, for world trade, and for all the other emerging economies and developing countries that have acquired more negotiating power over the years, and has established new geopolitical relations through the BRICS' influence in the international trade and non-trade arenas.

China achieved accession to the WTO following a nearly 15-year negotiation process which had many legal, political, and social implications for all parties.[28] China's accession surely presented the world trading system with opportunities, but also posed the challenge of integrating an economy with strong structural, behavioral and cultural constraints.[29] Many of the effects of this process are now evident throughout the world after nearly 15 supplementary years, but China's role in world trade has merely added complexity to the preexisting puzzle created by globalization.

At the time of its accession, the other WTO Members endorsed and acknowledged that China's participation was necessary to further expand the global market liberalization and integration, which are fundamental principles of the WTO. It has been clearly understood that, even though the challenges and implications were many, without China the WTO would have been only a partial *worldwide* trade organization.[30] However, in the years that followed China's accession to the WTO, other factors revealed that the rules set by Western countries to regulate their interests could not be simply applied to non-Western countries without producing friction. Within the WTO system, the best example of these evident disharmonies is the complete standstill of the Doha Round.

The road to the signature of China's Accession Protocol was long,[31] but these difficulties pale in comparison to those that have not yet been tackled in terms of achieving real implementation of its provisions throughout the People's Republic of China (PRC)[32] and those still need to be solved at the global level to integrate China and other countries that have acceded to the WTO in the last 10 years. Globalization and expansion of trade have created an interconnected world with the result that some countries have benefited from an increase in their economic development while others have seen a gradual reduction in their growth rates and employability of their citizens. However, these challenges are even more relevant

27 Robert Herzstein, *Is China Ready to WTO Rigors?*, 99 Center for Security Policy Publications F-33 (1999).

28 *See*, generally, Karen Halverson, *China's WTO Accession: Economic, Legal, and Political Implications*, 27(2) B.C. Int'l & Comp. L. Rev. 319, 319–23 (2004); Alan Alexandroff, *Concluding China's Accession to the WTO: the U.S. Congress and Permanent Most Favored Nation Status for China*, 3(1) UCLA J. Int'l L. & Foreign Aff. III 23, 25 (1998–1999).

29 *See* John H. Jackson, *The Institutional Ramifications of China's Accession to the WTO*, in China in the World Trading System: Defining the Principles of Engagement (Frederick M. Abbott ed., Kluwer Law International, 1998).

30 *See* WTO, *WTO Ministerial Conference Approves China's Accession*, Press Release (November 10, 2001), http://www.wto.org/english/news_e/pres01_e/pr252_e.htm (last visited August 6, 2016); *see* James Feinerman, *China's Quest to Enter the GATT/WTO*, 90 Am. Soc'y Int'l L. Procedure 401, 402 (1996). *See*, also, Maria Weber, Il Miracolo Cinese: Perché Bisogna Prendere la Cina sul Serio 83–84 (Il Mulino, 2003). Leila Choukroune, *Chine et OMC: l'Etat de Droit par l'Ouverture au Commerce International?* 6 Revue de Droit des Affaires Internationales 655 (2002).

31 Raj Bhala, *Enter the Dragon: An Essay on China's WTO Accession Saga*, 15(6) Am. U. Int'l L. Rev. 1469, 1471 (1999–2000).

32 *See* Paolo Davide Farah, *Five Years of China's WTO Membership. EU and US Perspectives about China's Compliance with Transparency Commitments and the Transitional Review Mechanism*, 33 Legal Issues of Economic Integration 3, 263–304 (2006); Donald C. Clarke, *China's Legal System and the WTO: Prospects for Compliance*, 2 Wash. U. Global Stud. L. Rev. 97, 97 (Winter 2003).

considering the impact of the economic crisis in 2008. Following the crisis, the system had to integrate the increasing number of petitions from developing countries and emerging economies in many different areas and, on the other side, to account for the requests from civil society in the developed world to protect non-economic values that were under stress due to the increasing growth of many poor and developing countries and the contraction in growth (and its social impact) of the industrialized world. Somehow, globalization is finally bringing more prosperity, wealth, and opportunities to the developing world with the need to duly monitor the actions of multinational companies located and operating in those countries to limit their incredible power and influence. At the same time, the developed world is not growing as before because lower-cost products from developing countries have taken the market share previously belonging to the products from the industrialized countries.

Prior to China's accession to the WTO and the subsequent debates on implementation, a great number of analysts have argued that not only will China's integration be long and difficult,[33] but it could also damage the WTO and its Members. In view of overcoming these challenges, some experts decided to focus on the analysis of the market access concessions, tariff reductions, or liberalization requirements for China's integration in the world trading system. A second group of scholars, researchers, and analysts placed more emphasis on transparency issues, such as legal and administrative policies, that China must establish to ensure equitable and efficient resolution of commercial and trade disputes.[34] However, the issue of the consequences and influence of China's WTO accession on NTCs has rarely been addressed,[35] which is now becoming even more evident in the geopolitical context, considering the impact that China along with the other BRICS and developing countries has, not only at the WTO, but also in other international fora.

The intersection of the NTCs and China's participation in the WTO is manifested in the social and environmental consequences of the competition between economies with different levels of development as well as different levels of social protection and implementation of health and environmental standards. Still, the relocation of production seems to have been the only answer to the increasing economic pressure exercised on European companies by

33 Paolo Davide Farah & Elena Cima, *China's Participation in the World Trade Organization*, in El Comercio con China. Oportunidades Empresariales, Incertidumbres Juridicas 83, 87 (Aurelio Lòpez-Tarruella Martìnez ed.,Tirant lo Blanch, 2010). *See*, in general, *China and the WTO: Compliance and Monitoring*, Hearing before the U.S. – China Economic and Security Review Commission, One Hundred Eight Congress, Second Session, February 5, 2004, US Government Printing Office, Washington, 2004.

34 United States Government Accountability Office (GAO), *Report to Congressional Committees: U.S.-China Trade, Opportunities to Improve U.S Government Efforts to Ensure China's Compliance with World Trade Organization Commitments*, GAO-05–53, October 6, 2004, Washington, 2004, at 6, http://www.gao.gov/new.items/d0553.pdf (last visited August 6, 2016); Karen Halverson, *supra* note 28, at 346; Jiangyu Wang, *The Rule of Law in China: A Realistic View of the Jurisprudence, the Impact of the WTO, and the Prospects for Future Development*, Singapore J. Legal Stud. 374, 374–89 (2004); Alan Alexandroff, *The WTO's China Problem*, 21(4) Policy Options 64 (2000).

35 Paolo Davide Farah, *Influence des Considérations 'Autres que D'Ordre Commercial' en Droit International et OMC sur les Transformations de la Loi Chinoise: une Perspective Européenne*, in Market Economy, Rights, Freedoms and Commun Values in Europe and Asia, Europe-Asia International Conference, University Paul Verlaine-Metz, Metz, France, March 18, 2011; Parikshit K. Basu & Yapa M. W. Y. Bandara, *Introduction: Socio-Economic Development in China – WTO Accession and Related Issues*, in WTO Accession and Socio-Economic Development in China 1, 1–18 (Parikshit K. Basu & Yapa M. W. Y. Bandara eds, Chandos Publishing, 2009); Parikshit K. Basu, John Hicks & Richard Sappey, *Socio-Cultural Challenges to Economic Growth in China-Looking Ahead*, in WTO Accession and Socio-Economic Development in China, at 165–84.

"low-cost" producers. However, such relocation has resulted in job losses for European citizens within the European Union and could have a corrosive influence on fundamental social values in Europe as well as in the host countries. Both public opinion and political leaders, as well as policy-makers, fear that international trade – and, in particular, its further liberalization – may endanger public policies at different levels: environmental protection and sustainable development, good governance, cultural rights, labor rights, public health, social welfare, national security, food security, access to knowledge, interests of consumers, and animal welfare.[36] A global consensus has emerged on the necessity to integrate NTCs – which reflect different social aspirations and fears – into the external policy of the European Union and the United States to adopt measures related to international trade and foreign investment. Moreover, the European Union and the United States strongly demand the possibility to act in all international areas to defend and preserve these values by giving them a high degree of protection.

Nevertheless, many of the measures that developed countries introduced to address NTCs were received by developing countries with suspicion, resistance, and even hostility.[37] Developing countries, including China, doubt the authenticity of such considerations and think they might actually hide protectionist purposes. Moreover, developing countries see these measures as a means the industrialized world uses to impose its own social, ethical, and cultural values on developing country exporters. Nonetheless, not only has China undergone serious reforms and adopted new regulations to address the issue of NTCs, but the country has even begun to play an important role in the international negotiations on NTCs – such as those on climate change, energy, culture, and so on.

In fact, China could play a leading role in this field for both cultural and geostrategic reasons. China is trying more and more to develop its soft power and to harmonize its commercial power with its strong cultural beliefs. From this perspective, the discourse on "Asian values" launched by the conservative government of Singapore – and which was then silenced by the Asian crisis during the 1990s – can be rearticulated in terms of international law. The goal is to both minimize the value of the critics towards human rights by qualifying them as Western, and promote fundamental rights as closer to the "Asian" thought:[38] "First of all, in many countries in Asia and South East Asia, the sense of human rights is very weak and foreign, and they have no theoretical background for the concept of human rights. Rather they are concerned with overcoming starvation and poverty, not by means of promoting human rights but by increasing national wealth and mutual aid."[39]

Today, China's dependence on energy has become the main obstacle to the development of its power.[40] To tackle this issue, China has entered into a global redefinition of power strategy, which has two main features: the regionalization of power as a means and energy security as an end.[41] On the one hand, the creation of international organizations like the

36 *See*, in general, Robert Howse & Joanna Langille, ***Permitting Pluralism: The Seal Products Dispute and Why Should Permit Trade Restrictions Justified by Non-Instrumental Moral Values***, 37 YALE J. INT'L L. (2012).

37 Han Sung-Joo, ***Forward & Asian Values: An Asset or a Liability***, in CHANGING VALUES in ASIA: THEIR IMPACT ON GOVERNANCE AND DEVELOPMENT 3, 9 (Han Sung-Joo ed., Japan Center for International Exchange, 2003): "To many Asian leaders, Western concern for areas such as human rights and the environment is often seen as unwarranted interference at best and as revealing ulterior motives at worst."

38 *Id.*

39 Hyakudai Sakamoto, ***Foundations of East Asian Bioethics***, 6 EUBIOS J. ASIAN & INT'L BIOETHICS 31, 31–32 (1996).

40 Gabrielle Marceau, ***The WTO in the Emerging Energy Governance Debate***, 5(3) GLOBAL TRADE & CUSTOMS J. 83, 83 (2010).

41 *See* Paolo Davide Farah & Piercarlo Rossi, CONNECTING ENERGY, SECURITY AND SUSTAINABILITY BETWEEN EUROPE AND ASIA: POLICY, LEGAL AND SOCIAL-ECONOMIC DIMENSION (Eurasia-Pacific Rim Book Series, Imperial College University Press/World Scientific, 2015).

United Nations (UN), WTO, and IMF seems to mark the end of the Nation-States or at least partially question their sovereignty. On the other, however, the formation of regional powers – Brazil in South America, the France-Germany axis in Europe, Russia in Eastern Europe, South Africa in Southern Africa, India in Southeast Asia, China in East Asia, and so on – has introduced new actors, thus questioning the *status* of the ultimate decision-maker and of international bodies themselves, while facilitating negotiations within smaller groups of actors sharing a similar history and culture, which could help take over the impasse faced by both trade (GATT) and environmental (Kyoto Protocol)[42] multilateral consultations. Because of the shortcomings of multilateral agreements, RTAs have become defining features of the globalization process over the last few years. The need for further trade and economic development between States is evident in the developing country regions in particular, but it is arguable whether the RTAs will risk jeopardizing the multilateral trading system leaving the bittersweet residue of success of such regional negotiations, including further protection of NTCs, without having reached an effective and real worldwide minimum consensus on such important matters that globalization affects so dramatically. In short, the perspective on the integration of world regions through RTAs is Janus-faced. Particularly when negotiations are between countries with disproportionate levels of economic power, trade agreements can have a powerful effect on political stability and increase the risk of inter-state conflict as well as intra-state conflict because of the economic adjustments involved in pursuing regional trade integration. Conversely, regional blocks with like-minded countries that have similar economies or socio-cultural similarities serve as powerful tools to negotiate based on common interests both within and outside the WTO.[43]

However, the paradox of China's potential to be a new global regional player promoting the recognition and protection of NTCs – for example through the recognition of the right to water[44] – is based on certain conditions that conflict with the very reasons that motivate its implementation.

At the cultural level, the quest for Chinese soft power is motivated by the will to retrieve its qualification of "Asian culture," which China should represent on the front line. However, China promotes an antagonistic vision, based on the defense of the East Asian culture threatened by the West, which, in the short term, can prove unifying at the national and regional levels, but is extremely risky in the long term: "[former] President Hu Jintao has said China must strengthen its cultural production to defend against the West's assault on the country's culture and ideology, according to an essay in a Communist Party policy magazine [. . .]: 'We must clearly see that international hostile forces are intensifying the strategic plot of Westernizing and dividing China, and ideological and cultural fields are the focal areas of their long-term infiltration,' Mr. Hu said, according to a translation by The Associated Press."[45] The risk is that of approaching any conflict in cultural terms, so as to make it impossible to find a consensus between different civilization areas.

42 *Kyoto Protocol to the United Nations Framework Convention on Climate Change*, UN Doc FCCC/CP/1997/7/Add.1, December 10, 1997; 37 ILM 22 (1998).

43 Paolo Davide Farah & Piercarlo Rossi, *National Energy Policies and Energy Security in the Context of Climate Change and Global Environmental Risks: A Theoretical Framework for Reconciling Domestic and International Law Through a Multiscalar and Multilevel Approach*, 20(6) Eur. Energy & Envtl. L. Rev. 232, 232–44 (2011).

44 China voted in favor of the right to water in the 64th plenary session of the General Assembly, 108th meeting (Am), resolution recognizing access to clean water, sanitation as a human right, accepted with 122 votes in favor, none against, and 41 abstentions.

45 Edward Wong, *China's President Lashes Out at Western Culture*, New York Times (January 4, 2012).

On the other hand, in terms of international law, the integration of NTCs in the text of WTO agreements requires the creation of a global constitutionalization of the law,[46] which would allow a limitation of the WTO's power even within its scope of action – in the same way in which the constitution restrains the authority of the laws.[47] This limitation reflects a set of principles that are not just economic. However, this raises two problems from China's perspective: on the one hand, China has the tendency to invoke a right to development, which should prevail over any form of international legal regulation – human rights, environmental rights, right to water, right to food, and so on – whenever its commercial freedom is threatened, risking to reproduce the West's unsustainable mode of economic development. On the other, China cannot be yet qualified as a constitutional law regime, not only because some of the provisions of the constitution of the PRC are subject to flexible implementation – a suitable example is the third line of paragraph 33 ("The State respects and preserves human rights"), which was added in 2004 – but even more because China's notion of the ***rule of law*** dodges the fundamental principle of accountability[48] in order to highlight the concept of sovereignty.[49] However, the principle of a global constitutionalization of the right to food, water, education, health, and so on requires the local[50] regime of national sovereignty to submit to an evaluation which is both external and reciprocal.

In conclusion, it can be discussed whether it is up to the European Union and the other social actors to foster integration of NTCs in the WTO, so to ensure democratic and egalitarian participation of all parties to sustainable and global trade: resorting to the "Stiglitz proposals" – namely extending the anti-dumping legislation[51] in order to adopt legal measures that set trade to social and environmental standards whose overall non-compliance amounts to a disguised subsidy – could be a solution to "constitutionalize" NTCs within the WTO.

III Non-Trade Concerns status in the WTO multilateral system

1 Integrating NTCs in the WTO

At the outset it should be noted that NTCs have no clear definition. Even the WTO Doha Ministerial Declaration did not provide an official definition of NTCs. The conference only

46 *See* Chapter 17 (Heurtebise) in this volume.

47 Kaarlo Tuory, *Fundamental Rights Principles: Disciplining the Instrumentalism Policies*, in ARGUING FUNDAMENTAL RIGHTS 33, 33–52 (A.J. Menéndez & E.O. Eriksen eds, Springer, 2006): "Constitutions contains provisions on institutional practices which have been expressly specialized in the task of law self's limitation."

48 Report of the Secretary-General, *The Rule of Law and Transitional Justice in Conflict and Post-Conflict Societies*, UN Doc. S/2004/616, para. 6: "[The rule of law] refers to a principle of governance in which all persons, institutions and entities, public and private, including the State itself, are accountable to laws that are publicly promulgated, equally enforced and independently adjudicated, and which are consistent with international human rights norms and standards."

49 Bing Bing Jia, *A Synthesis of the Notion of Sovereignty and the Ideal of the Rule of Law : Reflections on the Contemporary Chinese Approach to International Law*, 53 GERMAN Y.B. INT'L L. 11, 11–64 (2010).

50 On this point, *see* Björn Ahl, Exploring Ways of Implementing International Human Rights Treaties in China, 20(3) NETHERLANDS Q. HUMAN RIGHTS 361, 361–403 (2010). *See*, also, by the same author, *Statements of the Chinese Government before Human Rights Treaty Bodies: Doctrine and Practice of Treaty Implementation*, 12(1) AUSTRALIAN J. ASIAN L. 82, 82–105 (2010).

51 Joseph Stiglitz, *A New Agenda for Global Warming*, in THE ECONOMISTS' VOICE: TOP ECONOMISTS TAKE ON TODAY'S PROBLEMS 22, 22–27 (Joseph E. Stiglitz, Aaron S. Edlin & J. Bradford Delong eds, Columbia University Press, 2008); *see*, also, PAOLO DAVIDE FARAH & ROBERTO SOPRANO, DUMPING E ANTIDUMPING 3–7 (Ilsole24ore, 2009).

stated that[52] "[they] take note of the non-trade concerns reflected in the negotiating proposals submitted by Members and confirm that non-trade concerns will be taken into account in the negotiations as provided for in the Agreement on Agriculture."[53] In theory, "defining NTCs and adopting clear criteria would be the best way even for the most ardent free trader or export minded country"[54] since the latter country will know the rule of the game and the balance that must be made between trade issues and NTCs. However, as a matter of fact, NTCs are difficult to specify and, considering the extremely different domestic conditions and large number of WTO Member States, they cannot readily be shaped with models aimed at assessing the economic effects of alternative scenarios.[55] Moreover, several countries have an interest in maintaining this undefined context and refuse any attempt to regulate the many different aspects of NTCs to avoid the potentially high costs for their economies of a binding set of rules adopted at the WTO. Yet, "a balance must be established in the WTO between trade liberalization and NTCs where the economic dimension of trade will be balanced with non-economic values."[56]

However, the Agreement on Agriculture[57] allows governments to pursue NTCs such as food security, poverty alleviation, environmental protection, and rural development through the use of domestic support measures.[58] Some countries have questioned the way that other States may pursue objectives related to NTCs if their doing so will cause trade distortion. The agreement allows all WTO Members to maintain some support measures to achieve the abovementioned objectives.[59] Developing countries asked for a degree of flexibility in the area of domestic support in order to address their NTCs issues.[60] That is why, for instance, they demanded stronger provisions on NTCs as well as special and differential treatment.[61] NTCs matters seem to be accepted to a large degree; nevertheless, a problem occurs when discussing the extent of their application and the instruments necessary to support these NTCs in both developed and developing countries.[62]

Recently, Members have filed disputes before the WTO regarding matters related to the interplay between trade and NTCs, especially following the accession of new Members to the WTO multilateral system. Generally speaking, the AB is qualified to interpret the rights

52 Simpson & Schoenbaum, *supra* note 20, at 401.

53 World Trade Organisation, *Agriculture: Negotiations, Modalities Phase: Chairperson's Overview Paper*, https://www.wto.org/english/tratop_e/agric_e/negoti_modoverview_e.htm (last visited August 6, 2016).

54 Simpson & Schoenbaum, *supra* note 20, at 403.

55 Ralf Peters & David Vanzetti, Shifting Sands, Searching for a Compromise in the WTO Negotiations on Agriculture: Policy Issues in International Trade and Commodities Study Series. 23, 10 (United Nations, 2004).

56 Simpson & Schoenbaum, *supra* note 20, at 400.

57 Uruguay Round Agreement, Agreement on Agriculture, https://www.wto.org/english/docs_e/legal_e/14-ag_01_e.htm (last visited August 6, 2016).

58 Josef Schmidhuber et al., *Agricultural Trade, Trade Policies and the Global Food System*, in World Agriculture: Towards 2015/2030: an FAO Perspective 232, 245 (Jelle Bruinsma ed., Routledge, 2003).

59 Susan Ariel Aaronson & Jamie M. Zimmerman, Trade Imbalance: The Struggle to Weigh Human Rights Concerns in Trade 56 (Cambridge University Press, 2007).

60 Joseph A. McMahon, The Negotiations for a New Agreement on Agriculture 45 (Martinus Nijhoff Publishers, 2011).

61 Miho Shirotori, *Notes on the Implementation of the Agreement on Agriculture*, in A Positive Agenda for Developing Countries: Issues for Future Trade Negotiations 125, 156 (United Nations Conference on Trade and Development, 2000).

62 Susette Biber-Klemm & Michael Burkard, *The Impact of Agriculture Subsidies*, in Rights to Plant Genetic Resources and Traditional Knowledge: Basic Issues and Perspectives 324, 354 (Susette Biber-Klemm & Thomas Cottier ed., CABI Publishing, 2006).

of Members as set out in the WTO covered agreements. The AB in *China – Raw Materials*,[63] in response to Chinese claims that a State has the right to regulate trade, stated the following: "[. . .] we understand the WTO Agreement, as a whole, to reflect the balance struck by WTO members between trade and non-trade related concerns."[64] The AB considered that a Member joining the WTO has abandoned all rights to regulate NTCs in exercising its sovereignty and the rights to regulate trade. Yet, certain questions remain unanswered such as, "is the AB qualified to determine and to interpret the rights of Members to regulate non-trade-related-concerns that are not set out in the WTO Agreement?"[65]

The following sections analyze the mechanism by which NTCs matters were integrated in the WTO multilateral system while focusing on the existing legal provisions related to every NTC, as well as the case law before the Dispute Settlement Body (DSB) that played an essential role in opening the door for the integration of these concepts with a balance of free trade.

2 *The interplay among environment, health, and trade, and the prospects for the new acceding Members: China as a case study*

China, like other Member States, has joined the WTO on the basis of Accession Protocols and has benefited from the Dispute Settlement Understanding (DSU) which became applicable to disputes.[66] The Accession Protocol is considered an "integral part of the WTO Agreement."[67] However, a country aiming to participate in an established international organization will have more obligations and criteria to fulfill and integrate in its own internal legal system compared to the founders of such organization, which actively created and decided how to shape and develop the rules of the system.[68] Moreover, the alteration of the obligations of an existing Member State in case of an accession of a new Member is not consistent with the WTO rules.[69] Additionally, existing WTO Members have a willingness to use their bargaining power to obtain further commitments and economic policy changes from States seeking to join the WTO.[70] As a consequence, there is the impression that recently acceded Members became second-class citizenry without having the capacity to fully exploit the rights under WTO law, while being burdened by additional negotiated obligations.[71]

In the case of the Protocol of Accession of China, such obligations "exceed[ed] the existing requirements of the WTO agreements,"[72] and China was considered the country with

63 Report of the Panel, *China – Measures Related to the Exportation of Various Raw Materials*, WT/DS394/R, WT/DS395/R, WT/DS398/R (July 5, 2011); Appellate Body Report, *China – Measures Related to the Exportation of Various Raw Materials*, WT/DS394/AB/R, WT/DS395/AB/R, WT/DS398/AB/R (January 30, 2012). Asif H. Qureshi, *Distinguished Essay: Reflections on the Global Trading Order Twenty Years After Marrakesh: A Development Perspective*, in Eur. Y.B. Int'l Econ. L. 2014.

64 Appellate Body Report, *China – Measures Related to the Exportation of Various Raw Materials*, *supra* note 63.

65 Asif H. Qureshi, *supra* note 63, at 104.

66 Matthew Kennedy, *The Integration of Accession Protocols into the WTO Agreement*, 47(1) J. World Trade 45, 48 (2013).

67 Report of the Panel, *China – Measures Related to the Exportation of Rare Earths, Tungsten, and Molybdenum*, WT/DS431/R, WT/DS432/R, WT/DS433/R (March 26, 2014).

68 Antonio Parenti, *Accession to the World Trade Organisation: A Legal Analysis*, 27(2) Legal Issues of Economic Integration 141, 155 (2000).

69 *Id.* at 156.

70 Mitali Tyagi, *Flesh on a Legal Fiction: Early Practice in the WTO on Accession Protocols*, 15(2) J. Int'l Econ. L. 391, 395 (2012).

71 *Id.* at 397.

72 Julia Ya Qin, *"WTO-Plus" Obligations and Their Implications for the World Trade Organization Legal System – An Appraisal of the China Accession Protocol*, 37 (3) J. World Trade 483, 483 (2003).

the most of "WTO Plus" obligations among the current Member States.[73] However, since China's accession in 2001, other new Member States, such as Vietnam, were obliged to accept even more WTO Plus commitments than China.

China's commitments cover "areas ranging from the administration of China's trade regime (transparency, judicial review, [. . .]), to the Chinese economic system (market economy commitments), to new WTO disciplines on investment (such as investment measure [. . .])."[74] Simultaneously, China has obtained significant concessions, in particular extensions that allow China to postpone the termination of some of its WTO-inconsistent measures which might be offset by some of the incumbent Members' more stringent obligations.[75]

China recently made use of the notion of NTCs in its disputes to justify mainly measures to protect the environment.[76] Its attempts to define the role of international trade in determining environmental outcomes and the effects of trade on the environment have generated some controversy.[77]

From the beginning, the WTO has almost exclusively prioritized free trade over environmental protection when it comes to the trade–environment conflict.[78] That is why the WTO was called "GATT-zilla," which describes a trade monster that was intent on eating its way through the global ecosystem.[79] In fact, coherence among WTO rules and existing multilateral treaties regarding the environment has often been lacking.[80] Moreover, the WTO initially gave little attention to climate change.[81] Principles such as the Polluter Pays[82] leave it to the parties to determine the means by which to implement their obligations.[83]

73 Handbook on Accession to the WTO: Chapter 5, Substance of Accession Negotiations, https://www.wto.org/english/thewto_e/acc_e/cbt_course_e/c5s1p1_e.htm.

74 Julia Ya Qin, *supra* note 72, at 483.

75 Tokio Yamaoka, *Analysis of China's Accession Commitments in the WTO: New Taxonomy of More and Less Stringent Commitments, and the Struggle for Mitigation by China*, 47(1) J. World Trade 105, 155 (2013).

76 Bill Butcher, *WTO Open Trade Rules and Domestic Environmental Protection Policies: A Balancing Approach*, in Environmental Taxation and Green Fiscal Reform: Theory and Impact 69, 71–77 (Larry Kreiser et al. ed., Edward Elgar, 2014).

77 Werner Antweiler, Brian R. Copeland & M. Scott Taylor, *Is Free Trade Good for the Environment?*, 91(4) Am. Econ. Rev. 877, 877 (2001).

78 David Coates, Kathy Smith & Will (C. William) Walldorf, The Oxford Companion to American Politics 440 (David Coates ed., Oxford University Press, 2012). On the fragmentation of international law, the lack of coherence, and the need of a multiscalar and multilevel approach to face the challanges of climate change, *see* Farah & Rossi, *supra* note 43.

79 J. Samuel Barkin, *The Environment, Trade and International Organizations*, in Handbook of Global Environmental Politics 334, 335 (Peter Dauvergne ed., Edward Elgar, 2005). *See*, also, Andrew L. Strauss, *From GATTzilla to the Green Giant: Winning the Environmental Battle for the Soul of the World Trade Organization*, 19(3) U. Pa. J. Int'l Econ. L. Vol. 769, 769 (1998).

80 Johanne Muller, *Strengthing Development Politics and Global Partnership*, in Climate Change, Justice and Sustainability: Linking Climate and Development Policy 331, 333 (Ottmar Edenhofer et al. ed., Springer, 2014).

81 David Satterthwaite et al., *Adapting to Climate Change in Urban Areas, The Possibilities and Constraints in Low- and Middle-Income Nations* 91 (International Institute for Environment and Development, Human Settlements Discussion Paper Series, 2007), http://pubs.iied.org/10549IIED.html (last visited August 6, 2016).

82 According to the principle, "the polluter should bear the expenses of carrying out the (pollution prevention and control measures decided by public authorities to ensure that the environment is in an aceptable state." *See*, Jean-Philippe Barde, *Economic Instruments in Environmental Policy: Lessons From the OECD Experience and Their Relevance to Developing Economies* 5–6 (OECD Development Centre, Working Paper No. 92, 1994), http://www.oecd.org/dev/1919252.pdf (last visited August 6, 2016).

83 Bradly J. Condon & Tapen Sinha, The Role of Climate Change in Global Economic Governance 38 (Oxford University Press, 2013).

Additionally, because of climate change, some Members have begun to debate the transfer of low-carbon technologies to States in need.[84] Broadly speaking, energy issues did not get much prominence at the WTO, yet the landscape started to change as many oil producing countries have joined the WTO.[85] Energy trade is one of the most significant trade sectors and constitutes the largest primary commodity of global trade in terms of volume and value.[86] It is worth mentioning that WTO rules are relevant to the energy sector, while energy security and climate mitigation constitute priorities on the global agenda.[87]

The first generation of GATT/WTO cases invoking environmental concerns through GATT Article XX highlighted a negative approach from the adjudicatory bodies for considering environmental matters under Article XX[88] of the GATT. In the *United States – Tuna and Tuna Products from Canada* case,[89] an import prohibition on tuna and tuna products imposed by the United States against Canada was found discriminatory by the Panel and could not be justified under Article XX(g) of the GATT since no equivalent restrictions on domestic production and consumption of tuna were imposed as well.[90] In the *Tuna/Dolphin I* case,[91] the United States imposed a ban on the import of Tuna from countries whose *"incidental kill ration"* of dolphins was greater than its own on the basis of Article XX(b) or (g) of the GATT.[92] Mexico challenged the US measure claiming that the latter violated article XI of the GATT. The Panel decided that the restrictive measure could not be justified under Article XX(b) or (g) of the GATT.[93] The main criticism in both *Tuna/Dolphin* cases was that the national coercion was used through trade restrictions to force foreign countries to protect dolphins with an extraterritorial effect of the US domestic measures in view of affecting environmental policies of other States. In this situation, the United States employed unilateral trade restrictions to encourage a number of nations to abandon

84 Ramgopal Agarwala, *Towards a Global Compact for Managing Climate Change*, in Post-Kyoto International Climate Policy: Implementing Architectures for Agreement 179, 195 (Joseph E. Aldy & Robert N. Stavins, Cambridge University Press, 2010). *See* Chapters 10 (Lemoine) and 11 (Cima) in this volume.

85 Paolo Davide Farah & Elena Cima, *Energy Trade and the WTO: Implications for Renewable Energy and the OPEC Cartel*, 16 (3) J. Int'l Econ. L. 707, 707–40 (2013); Paolo Davide Farah & Elena Cima, *L'Energia nel Contesto Degli Accordi dell'OMC: Sovvenzioni per le Energie Rinnovabili e Pratiche OPEC di Controllo dei Prezzi*, 2 Diritto Del Commercio Internazionale 343, 343–81(2013); Sajal Mathur & Preeti Mann, *GATT/WTO Accessions and Energy Security*, in Trade, the WTO and Energy Security: Mapping the Linkages for India 73, 74 (Sajal Mathur ed., Springer, 2014).

86 Rafael Leal-Arcas, Andrew Filis, & Ehab S. Abu Gos, International Energy Governance: Selected Legal Issues 138 (Edward Elgar, 2015).

87 Alan Yanovich, *WTO Rules and the Energy Sector*, in Regulation of Energy in International Trade Law: WTO, NAFTA and Energy Charter 1, 42 (Yulia Selivanova ed., Kluwer Law International, 2011).

88 *See* GATT Article XX, Legal Texts: GATT 1947, The General Agreement on Tariffs and Trade (GATT 1947), https://www.wto.org/english/docs_e/legal_e/gatt47_01_e.htm (last visited August 6, 2016).

89 Report of the Panel, *United States – Prohibition of Imports of Tuna and Tuna Products from Canada*, L/5198–29S/91 (February 27, 1982).

90 Nathalie Bernasconi-Osterwalder, Environment and Trade: A Guide to WTO Jurisprudence 87 (Routledge, 2005).

91 Report of the Panel, *United States – Restrictions on Imports of Tuna*, DS21/R (September 3, 1991).

92 Paul Ekins & Robin Vanner, *Reducing the Impacts of the Production and Trade of Commodities*, in Trade, Globalization and Sustainability Impact Assessment: A Critical Look at Methods and Outcomes 277, 281 (Paul Ekins & Tancrede Voituriez eds, Routledge, 2009).

93 Andreas F. Lowenfeld, International Economic Law 389–91 (2d, OUP Oxford, 2008).

tuna fishing techniques that killed dolphins.[94] Before adopting these trade-distorting measures, however, the United States should have tried to make use of other means to obtain similar results in favor of the values they aimed to protect (the environment) with less trade-restrictive effects. The ruling in the 1994 *Tuna/Dolphin* case,[95] brought by the Netherlands and the European Union (formerly EC – European Communities), which was affected as secondary exporters of tuna imported from primary producing countries, confirmed that Article XX cannot be interpreted in such a way to permit the application of trade measures with extraterritorial effects within the jurisdiction of other Member States with the objective of forcing those countries to change their polices.[96] Thus, also in this case, the measure could not be justified under Article XX of the GATT signaling that the WTO is giving primacy of trade over the environment.[97]

In the *United States – Superfund* case,[98] the environmental aspects of toxic waste formed the background of the dispute rather than having a direct influence on the result.[99] In this case, the European Union, Canada, and Mexico claimed that a US excise tax, a corporate income tax and appropriations on petroleum, and a tax on certain imported substances produced or manufactured from taxable feedstock chemicals may have breached Article III.2 of the GATT.[100] The Panel established that the first set of measures on petroleum constituted a violation of Article III.2 of the GATT because there was a tax differential applied to imported products compared to domestic ones.[101] The US government did not argue about the existence of this differential, but stated that the measure's trade effects were irrelevant and, for this reason, no violation of the GATT/WTO agreements should be found. However, the Panel rejected this argument because the sole violation of the provision's letter is sufficient. Regarding the second measure on certain imported substances produced or manufactured from taxable feedstock chemicals, the Panel recognized that the tax applied was perfectly aligned with the WTO rules since it was a licit border tax adjustment.[102] The revenue of this tax was used to sponsor environmental programs in favor of the domestic US producers. However, the Panel's interpretation adopted in this case, unfortunately, does not seem to be supported by subsequent case law. In fact, it took time for the DSB to recover from the past, the positive provisions and thoughts included in the opinions of the

94 David M. Driesen, ***What is Free Trade?: The Real Issue Lurking Behind the Trade and Environment Debate***, in TRADE DISPUTES AND THE DISPUTE SETTLEMENT UNDERSTANDING OF THE WTO: AN INTERDISCIPLINARY ASSESSMENT 5, 11 (James C. Hartigan, Hamid Beladi & Kwan Choi eds, Emerald Group Publishing Limited, 2009).

95 Report of the Panel, ***United States – Restrictions on Imports of Tuna***, DS29/R (June 16, 1994).

96 PETER R. GARDINER & K. KUPERAN VISWANATHAN, ECOLABELLING AND FISHERIES MANAGEMENT 20–21 (WorldFish Center, 2004).

97 KATI KULOVESI, THE WTO DISPUTE SETTLEMENT SYSTEM: CHALLENGES OF THE ENVIRONMENT, LEGITIMACY 85 (Kluwer Law International, 2001).

98 Report of the Panel, ***United States – Taxes on Petroleum and Certain Imported Substances***, L/6175–34S/136 (June 17, 1987).

99 KRISTA NADAKAVUKAREN SCHEFER, SOCIAL REGULATION IN THE WTO: TRADE POLICY AND INTERNATIONAL LEGAL DEVELOPMENT 159 (Edward Elgar, 2010).

100 FEDERICO ORTINO, BASIC LEGAL INSTRUMENTS FOR THE LIBERALISATION OF TRADE: A COMPARATIVE ANALYSIS OF EC AND WTO LAW 128 (Hart Publishing, 2004).

101 GARY CLYDE HUFBAUER, STEVE CHARNOVITZ & JISUN KIM, GLOBAL WARMING AND THE WORLD TRADING SYSTEM 41 (Peterson Institute for International Economics, 2009).

102 Yulia Selivanova, ***Managing the Patchwork of Agreementsin Trade and Investment, in*** GLOBAL ENERGY GOVERNANCE: THE NEW RULES OF THE GAME 49, 59 (Andreas Goldthau & Jan Martin Witte eds, Brookings Institution, 2009).

adjudicatory bodies of this case and develop, in more recent cases, such similar environmental friendly interpretations of the WTO agreements. Far from being perfect, those interpretations in favor of the environment in the *United States – Superfund* case are even more relevant if we remember that this case was ruled in 1987.

In the *Thailand – Cigarettes* case,[103] Thailand decided to permit the importation and exportation of tobacco seeds, tobacco plants, tobacco leaves, plug tobacco, shredded tobacco, and tobacco only by license on the basis of public health concerns.[104] The US challenged Thailand's decision under Article XI of the GATT to apply quantitative restrictions on the importation of cigarettes, claiming that the Thai government permitted the sale of domestic cigarettes. Moreover, in the event the cigarette imports were permitted, Thailand applied higher internal excise taxes on the imported cigarettes compared to the taxes applied to domestic like products. Thailand argued that these restrictions were justified by the exception contained in Article XI:2(c) because cigarettes should be classified as agricultural or fisheries products within the meaning of Article XI. Furthermore, the Thai government did not have to apply these measures to the domestic production because, as observed by the Panel, the US cigarettes were not considered like products, since they contained additives and flavorings that make them easier to smoke than their Thai counterparts. Hence, public health concerns affirmed by the World Health Organization (WHO) seem to arise from the ease of access factor attached to western cigarettes and the consequent increase in smoking. Further, the WHO submitted expressly that there was a lack of scientific evidence to prove as to which cigarette was more harmful than the other. Then, the Panel considered such measures to control or reduce the consumption of cigarettes to fall within the scope of Article XX (b) but nevertheless found Thailand's measure on license and quantitative restrictions unnecessary since less trade-restrictive alternatives existed, such as warning labels or ingredients lists.[105] To the contrary, the Panel did not consider the higher internal excise taxes for imported cigarettes in violation of Article III of the GATT because the legislation did not mandate the State authorities to apply these higher taxes to the imported products, but rather left it as an option. It is relevant to stress that the Panel rejected the use of Article XX(b) to justify Thailand's measures[106] despite the fact that in the 1990s the World Health Organization heavily criticized the US government and cigarette companies while aiming to reduce tobacco-related mortality.[107]

In the *Canada – Herring Salmon* case,[108] a Canadian national measure made it compulsory for herring and salmon caught in Canadian waters to be processed in Canada before being exported. Canada attempted to justify the measure on the basis of Article XX(g) for

103 Report of the Panel, *Thailand – Restrictions on Importation of and Internal Taxes on Cigarettes*, DS10/R- 37S/200 (November 7, 1990).

104 Obijiofor Aginam, Global Health Governance: International Law and Public Health in a Divided World 84 (University of Toronto Press, 2005).

105 Lawrence O. Gostin, Public Health Law: Power, Duty, Restraint 264 (2d, University of California Press, 2008).

106 Fabio Costa Morosini, The Mercosur and WTO Retreaded Tires Dispute: Rehabilitating Regulatory Competition in International Trade and Environmental Regulation 17 (ProQuest Information and Learning Company, 2007).

107 Report of the Panel, *Thailand – Restrictions on Importation of and Internal Taxes on Cigarettes, supra* note 103, at Page 14–16, Paragraphs 50–57. *See*, also, David P. Fidler & Martin S. Certon, *International Considerations*, in Law in Public Health Practice 93, 116 (2d, Richard A. Goodman et al. ed., OUP USA, 2007).

108 Report of the Panel, *Canada – Measures Affecting Exports of Unprocessed Herring and Salmon*, L/6268–35S/98 (March 22, 1988).

the conservation of natural resources.[109] When it came to the interpretation and application of Article XX(g), the Panel limited itself to a restrictive interpretation of the text of Article XX(g), reducing the possible scope of the application of the exception.[110]

The outcome of the disputes demonstrates that all the environmental questions pivoted, to a large extent, on GATT Article XX. With the intention of saving the trading system, the adjudicatory bodies have sometimes used unreasonable legal justifications and at other times very restrictive interpretations and reasoning as to why Article XX could not be used. However, these claims threatened the trading system by causing concerns about its hostile attitude towards the environment.[111] The AB corrected the Panels' errant holdings made in the *US – Gasoline*, *US – Shrimp*, and *EC – Asbestos* cases, signaling to the public that the era of runaway Panels on environmental matters had ended.[112] It is worth mentioning that the *CAFE* case was the first to open the new era for balancing trade and environment before the abovementioned cases created a shift in the dispute settlement rulings.[113] In this case, the EU challenged the US corporate average fuel economy standard, the "gas guzzler" tax and the luxury tax on cars over USD30,000. The Panel decided that these measures were discriminatory. At the same time, it did not confirm the restrictive interpretation of the "necessity" test by the EU in its statement and found, according to the US argument, that the measure to be justified under Article XX needed to be "primarily aimed at" the conservation of exhaustible natural resources and at rendering effective restrictions imposed on domestic production and consumption. Therefore, the United States was not obliged to take the least-restrictive measures to serve environmental goals[114] because, as determined by the Panel, if no requirement was placed on imported cars, the CAFE program's objectives would be prejudiced since large imported cars would not be subject to any restriction on fuel consumption. Thus, the application of fleet averaging to imported cars in a similar manner as its application to domestic cars clearly served the purpose of fuel conservation, and served to render effective the conservation measure. In these respects, fleet averaging met two of the key requirements of Article XX(g).

Paragraph 5.66 of the *CAFE* dispute states:

> This analysis suggested to the Panel that in the absence of separate foreign fleet accounting it would be possible to include in a revised CAFE regulation an averaging method that would render the CAFE regulation consistent with the General Agreement. As such a revised method was only hypothetical at this time (since fleet averaging did not exist independently of separate foreign fleet accounting), and since the CAFE regulation would in the view of the Panel require substantial change if separate foreign fleet accounting were removed, the Panel did not consider that it could or should make a finding on the consistency of a revised regulation. This could only be determined on the basis of the actual elements of a revised CAFE scheme.

109 Massimiliano Montini, *The Neccessity Principle as an Instrument to Balance Trade and the Protection of the Environment*, in Environment, Human Rights and International Trade 135, 148 (Francesco Francioni ed., Hart Publishing, 2001).

110 *Id.* at 148–49.

111 Steve Charnovitz, *Trade and the Environment in the WTO*, 10(1) J. Int'l Econ. L.(2007), http://papers.ssrn.com/sol3/papers.cfm?abstract_id=1007028 (last visited August 6, 2016).

112 *Id.* at 14–15.

113 Report of the Panel, *United States – Taxes on Automobiles*, DS31/R (October 11, 1994).

114 Linda A. Malone, International Law 185, 205 (Emanuel Law Outlines, 1995). *See* Paragraphs 5.64, 5.65 and 5.66 of the Report of the Panel, *United States – Taxes on Automobiles*, *supra* note 113.

For that reason, the decision confirmed the inconsistency of the US measures with the WTO Agreements.

When it comes to the cases that highlight the shift in the dispute settlement reasoning, the Panel in *US – Gasoline*[115] weighed a US measure on air quality establishing one scheme to regulate the content of imported gasoline and another to regulate the content of US gasoline. The AB under the newly created WTO modified the Panel reasoning by stating that the interpretation of GATT Article XX requires a two-step analysis, verifying first whether the measure at stake falls under one of the provision's subparagraphs and, second, whether it complies with the *chapeau*. Here, the AB found that the US measure was indeed covered by paragraph (g) of Article XX,[116] but it could not be justified under the *chapeau* because of the discriminatory element of the measure.

Similarly, in the *US – Shrimp* dispute,[117] although the AB declared that the US import ban applied to shrimp for protecting endangered turtles on the high seas and in foreign jurisdictions was related to the conservation of exhaustible natural resources and thus covered by Article XX(g), the exception was not applicable because the measure was not justifiable under the *chapeau* of Article XX.[118] In paragraph 184 of its report, the AB stated:

> In reaching these conclusions, we wish to underscore ***what we have not decided in this appeal.*** We have not decided that the protection and preservation of the environment is of no significance to the Members of the WTO. Clearly, it is. We have not decided that the sovereign nations that are Members of the WTO cannot adopt effective measures to protect endangered species, such as sea turtles. Clearly, they can and should. And we have not decided that sovereign States should not act together bilaterally, plurilaterally or multilaterally, either within the WTO or in other international fora, to protect endangered species or to otherwise protect the environment. Clearly, they should and do.

115 Report of the Panel, *United States – Standards for Reformulated and Conventional Gasoline*, WT/DS2/R (January 29, 1996) and Report of the Appelate Body, *United States – Standards for Reformulated and Conventional Gasoline*, WT/DS2/9 (May 20, 1996).

116 W.J. Davey, *WTO Dispute Settlement Practice Relating to GATT 1994*, in The WTO Dispute Settlement System 1995–2003 (Studies in Transnational Economic Law Set) 191, 204 (Federico Ortino & Ernst-Ulrich Petersmann eds, Kluwer Law International, 2004); Sophie Nappert & Federico Ortino, *International Resolution of Energy Trade and Investment Disputes*, in Regulation of Energy in International Trade Law: WTO, NAFTA and Energy Charter 303, 313 (Julia Selivanova ed., Kluwer Law International, 2011); Ben Saul, David Kinley & Jaqueline Mowbray, The International Covenant on Economic, Social and Cultural Rights 1081 (OUP Oxford, 2014); Robert Read, *Process and Production Methods and the Regulation of International Trade*, in The WTO and the Regulation of International Trade: Recent Trade Disputes 239, 259 (Nicholas Perdikis & Robert Read eds, Edward Elgar, 2005); M. Kent Ranson et al., *The Public Health Implications of Multilatreal Trade Agreements*, in Health Policy in a Globalising World 18, 21 (Kelley Lee, Kent Buse & Suzanne Fustukian eds, Cambridge University Press, 2002).

117 Appelate Body Report, and Report of the Panel, *United States – Import Prohibition of Certain Shrimp And Shrimp Products*, *supra* note 25; Appellate Body Report, *United States – Import Prohibition of Certain Shrimp and Shrimp Products Recourse to Article 21.5 of The DSU by Malaysia*, *supra* note 25.

118 Ernst-Ulrich Petersmann, *From "Member-Driven Governance" to Constitutionally Limited "Multilevel-Trade Governance" in the WTO*, in The WTO at Ten: The Contribution of the Dispute Settlement System 86, 101 (Giorgio Sacerdoti et al. ed., Cambridge University Press, 2006).

This is an important statement to support the protection of the environment and an advice to the WTO Member States to find proactively and jointly a balance and an agreement between trade and environment in the WTO and in other international contexts.

In the *Asbestos* case,[119] banning asbestos on the basis of protecting public health[120] was ultimately found to be justified under Article XX(b) and the *chapeau* of Article XX[121] because no discrimination was found between the domestic and imported products. As such, the WTO agreements support the Members' ability to protect human health and safety at the level of protection they deem appropriate. The same argument was applied a few years later, in the *Brazil – Retreaded Tyres* dispute,[122] where the Panel and the AB held that the ban of European tyres was necessary to protect health and the environment, but it was applied inconsistently with the WTO requirement because the restrictive measures did not include all exporting countries.[123] Brazil imposed restrictions on EU retreaded tyres, justifying the measure under Article XX as necessary for the protection of human health since the accumulation of waste tyres constitutes a breeding ground for mosquitoes which spread malaria and dengue fever while causing long-term toxic leaching. The Panel accepted Brazil's claims.[124] However, Brazil excluded MERCOSUR from these restrictive measures,[125] so the AB reversed the Panel's ruling with respect to the analysis under the chapeau of Article XX due to the violation of the non-discrimination principles within the meaning of the chapeau of the Article XX and requested that Brazil apply and extend these provisions to all countries.[126] Despite the importance of the WTO Panels' and AB's rulings for the protection of public health and the environment, some critics alleged that the settlement created a narrow construction of the public health exception to GATT. Scholars lamented the loss of national control over health risks due to these decisions while indicating that the WTO favors the markets over other values.[127] However, despite the criticism, it is clear from these cases that the WTO DSB has struck a balance between the

119 Report of the Panel, *European Communities – Measures Affecting Asbestos and Asbestos-Containing Products*, WT/DS135/R (September 18, 2000) and Appellate Body Report, *European Communities – Measures Affecting Asbestos and Asbestos-Containing Products*, WT/DS135/AB/R (March 12, 2001).

120 Helen Walls et al., *Trade and Gloal Health*, in Globalization and Health 100, 107 (2d, Johanna Hanefeld ed., Open University Press, 2014); Geoffrey Cockerham & William Cockerham, Health and Globalization 119, 134 (Polity Press, 2010).

121 Kulovesi, *supra* note 97, at 102.

122 Report of the Panel, *Brazil, Measures Affecting Imports of Retreaded Tyres*, WT/DS332/R (June 12, 2007) and Report of the Appelate Body, *Brazil – Measures Affecting Imports of Retreaded Tyres*, WT/DS332/AB/R (December 3, 2007).

123 Julia Ya Qin, *Managing Conflicts Between Rulings of the World Trade Organization and Regional Trade Tribunals: Reflections on the Brazil-Tyres Case*, in Making Transnational Law Work in the Global Economy: Essays in Honour of Detlev Vagts 601, 607 (Peiter H. F. Bekker, Rudolf Dolzer & Dr. Michael Waibel eds, Cambridge University Press, 2010); Mohammad F. A. Nsour, Rethinking the World Trade Order: Towards a Better Legal Understanding of the Role of Regionalism in the Multilateral Trade Regime 45, 79 (Sidestone Press, 2009).

124 Tracey Epps, International Trade and Health Protection: A Critical Assessment of the WTO, 230, 233 (Edward Elgar, 2008).

125 Mohammad F. A. Nsour, *supra* note 123, at 79.

126 Qin, *supra* note 123, at 607.

127 Cockerham & Cockerham, *supra* note 120, at 134.

protection of public health and trade, while prioritizing the former in case of a serious public health matter.

In spite of some court decisions that were not aligned with the protection of health, the environment and the principles of sustainable development, the relevant case law together with the work of other international organizations and negotiations beyond the WTO strongly influenced the passage from the GATT to the WTO in 1995 to embrace a new trade dimension that takes NTCs into due consideration. Indeed, the WTO's Preamble recognizes among the listed objectives: "allowing for the optimal use of the world's resources in accordance with the objective of sustainable development, seeking both to protect and preserve the environment and to enhance the means for doing so in a manner consistent with their respective needs and concerns at different levels of development."[128] In fact, the protection of NTCs in the following case law has grown increasingly robust since January 1, 1995, when the WTO officially commenced.

As a matter of fact, a relevant shift in the dispute settlement ruling can be seen in the *Tuna/Dolphin Case II* of 2011.[129] In this case, Mexico claimed that the US measures establishing the conditions for the use of a "dolphin-safe" label on tuna products, which may vary depending on the geographical area and location where the tuna is caught and the type of vessel and fishing method by which it is harvested, breached Articles I:1 and III:4 of the GATT, as well as other articles related to the TBT Agreement.[130]

As stated in the AB Report at Paragraph 172, tuna caught by "setting on" dolphins is currently not eligible for a "dolphin-safe" label in the United States, regardless of whether this fishing method is used inside or outside the Eastern Tropical Pacific Ocean (ETP).[131] As described in footnote 355 of the AB Report, "the fishing technique of 'setting on' dolphins takes advantage of the fact that tuna tend to swim beneath schools of dolphins in the ETP. The fishing method involves chasing and encircling the dolphins with a purse seine net in order to catch the tuna swimming beneath the dolphins."[132]

Even according to the recent compliance Panel Report requested under Article 21.5 of the DSU, following the Panel and AB Reports, tuna caught in the Eastern Tropical Pacific large purse seine fishery, where most of Mexico's fleet fishes, could be labeled as dolphin-safe only if both the captain and an independent observer certified that the tuna was caught without harming dolphins. Tuna caught in all other fisheries would require only a captain certification with a lower level of costs for the final product. These relevant differences

128 WTO Analytical Index: Marrakesh Agreement Marrakesh Agreement Establishing the World Trade Organization, Preamble, https://www.wto.org/ENGLISH/res_e/booksp_e/analytic_index_e/wto_agree_01_e.htm (last visited August 6, 2016).

129 Report of the Panel, *United States – Measures Concerning the Importation, Marketing and Sale of Tuna and Tuna Products*, WT/DS381/R, (September 11, 2011), Appellate Body Report, *United States – Measures Concerning the Importation, Marketing and Sale of Tuna and Tuna Products*, WT/DS381/AB/R (May 16, 2012) and Report of the Panel, *United States – Measures Concerning the Importation, Marketing and Sale of Tuna and Tuna Products, Recourse to Article 21.5 of the DSU by Mexico*, WT/DS381/RW, (April 14, 2015).

130 Vicki Waye, *International Trade Law, Climate Change and Carbon Footprinting*, in SUSTAINABLE BUSINESS: THEORY AND PRACTICE OF BUSINESS UNDER SUSTAINABILITY PRINCIPLES 251, 255–56 (Geoffrey Wells ed., Edward Elgar, 2013).

131 Appellate Body Report, *supra* note 129, at Page 69, Paragraph 172.

132 *Id.* at Page 69.

amounted to *de facto* discrimination against Mexican tuna and tuna products because such tuna were subjected to additional burdens and costs not faced by tuna caught by other WTO Members.

The WTO Panel started addressing the question of whether a voluntary labeling requirement can be conceived of as a technical regulation that must comply with the TBT Agreement where a legal test will then be conducted to check if the measures are applied in a discriminatory manner and, if so, whether they are more trade-restrictive than necessary to fulfill a legitimate objective.[133] In this situation the Panel did not find the US measures discriminatory since they applied to capture method rather than the national origin of the products. However, the AB reversed the Panel's finding and judged these measures as discriminatory, considering that the US measures *de facto* granted most US products and like products from other WTO Members better conditions and corresponding, relevant competitive advantages to access the US market that did not apply to Mexican tuna products.[134] The AB further developed this reasoning and noted that "the US measure does not address mortality (observed or unobserved) arising from fishing methods other than setting on dolphins outside the ETP, and that tuna caught in this area would be eligible for the US official label."[135]

Moreover, the AB reversed the Panel's findings that Mexico had demonstrated that the US "dolphin-safe" labeling provisions are more trade-restrictive than necessary to fulfill the legitimate objectives of the United States. The AB considered that the Panel's analysis and its comparison between the challenged measure and Mexico's proposed alternative measure was imprecise and inconsistent and that "the Panel erred in concluding, in paragraphs 7.620 and 8.1(b) of the Panel Report, that it has been demonstrated that the measure at issue is more trade-restrictive than necessary to fulfil the United States' legitimate objectives, taking account of the risks non-fulfilment would create."[136] For this reason, the AB reversed the Panel's findings that the measure at issue is inconsistent with Article 2.2 of the TBT Agreement.[137]

This case shows the WTO's clear shift from favoring trade openness over environmental concerns. Compared with the decision in the previous GATT/WTO tuna cases, the decision in the *Tuna/Dolphin Case II* of 2011, recognizing the protection of the environment and sustainable development in the TBT Agreement as a means of derogation from the provisions (when applied in a non-discriminatory way) and against the principle of territoriality (that was strictly applied in *Tuna/Dolphin Case I*),[138] clearly demonstrates an attempt to reconcile trade rules with NTCs.[139]

133 Sofya Matteotti & Olga Nartova, *Implementation and Monitoring of Process and Production Methods*, in Trade Agreements at the Crossroads 167, 171–72 (Susy Frankel & Meredith Lewis eds, Routledge, 2013).

134 Waye, *supra* note 130, at 256.

135 Appellate Body Report, *supra* note 129, at Paragraph 251.

136 *Id.* at 127–28, Paragraph 331.

137 Rafael Leal-Arcas, Climate Change and International Trade 131 (Edward Elgar, 2013).

138 Report of the Panel, *United States – Restrictions on Imports of Tuna*, *supra* note 91.

139 James K. R. Watson, The WTO and the Environment: Development of Competence Beyond Trade 181, 190 (Routledge, 2012).

The *EU Seals* case, in which the "public morals" exception contained in Article XX(a) of the GATT was raised related to an "environmental issue" like the inhuman method of hunting seals, also demonstrates the emergence of environmental concerns in WTO case law.[140] However, in *EU Seals*, the result was different because the respondent could not successfully verify the *chapeau* of Article XX. Still, the AB upheld the Panel's finding that the EU Seal Regime is "necessary to protect public morals" within the meaning of Article XX(a) of the GATT 1994. Nevertheless, it is Article XX of the GATT that represents a deliberate determination to grant WTO Member States the decision on the scope of a domestic measure regarding NTCs.[141] One might say that Article XX of the GATT provides the last bit of sovereignty left to the Member States in the WTO system. It allows a country to impose trade restrictions when requirements under Article XX are met. Likewise, quantitative restrictions on trade and discriminatory regulation of foreign commerce under some circumstances which also include environmental laws could be applied.[142] Yet, some States employ trade-restrictive measures to protect domestic industry. Furthermore, some countries tried to benefit from the exceptions mentioned in Article XX to alter other states' trade policies within their own jurisdiction.

Most scholars agreed that it was impossible for China to maintain a perfect implementation record following its accession to the WTO (as has happened to all WTO Member States), and disputes over the correct implementation of China's WTO obligations were certain to arise.[143] The high risk of China's non-compliance with WTO rules meant that China had to accept the instruments, procedures and multilateral (opposed to bilateral) framework of the WTO dispute settlement system despite China's legal culture and past resistant attitude towards international adjudication.[144]

Among the WTO's many challenges, environmental protection is one of the most debated NTCs within the organization. Certainly, Multilateral Environmental Agreements (MEAs), the ongoing international negotiations on climate change, and the increasing number of countries with sophisticated environmental laws and regulations have pushed the WTO to gradually open its door to environmental concerns. However, considering the high diversity of interests and needs of the Member States, when States attempt to justify trade barriers or different treatment based on environmental issues, the majority of developing countries interpret these NTCs as a form of green protectionism.[145] China, like many other developing countries, has prioritized economic growth over environmental concerns, which has caused an incredibly high level of air and water pollution and produced many other environmental

140 Report of the Panel, *European Communities – Measures Prohibiting the Importation and Marketing of Seal Products*, WT/DS400/R; WT/DS401/R (November 25, 2013). Appellate Body Report, *European Communities – Measures Prohibiting the Importation and Marketing of Seal Products*, WT/DS400/AB/R, WT/DS401/AB/R (May 22, 2014). *See* Chapter 26 (Chaisse & Luan) in this volume.

141 Driesen, *supra* note 94, at 11.

142 *Id.* at 18–19.

143 Craig Pouncey et al., *China as a WTO Member: Systemic Issues*, in DOING BUSINESS WITH CHINA 19–20 (Jonathan Reuvid & Li Yong eds, Routledge, 2008).

144 Marcia Don Harpaz, *Sense and Sensibilities of China and WTO Settlement*, in CHINA AND GLOBAL TRADE GOVERNANCE: CHINA'S FIRST DECADE IN THE WORLD TRADE ORGANIZATION 233, 240 (Ka Zeng & Wei Liang eds, Routledge, 2013). *See*, also, Paolo Davide Farah, *L'Influenza della Concezione Confuciana sulla Costruzione del Sistema Giuridico e Politico Cinese*, in IDENTITÀ EUROPEA E POLITICHE MIGRATORIE 193–226 (Giovanni Bombelli & Bruno Montanari eds, Vita e Pensiero, 2008).

145 Urs P. Thomas, *Trade and the Environment: Stuck in a Political Impasse at the WTO after the Doha and Cancun Ministerial Conferences*, 4(3) GLOBAL ENVIRONMENTAL POLITICS 9, 18 (2004).

and health impacts on the population.[146] On the other hand, it has to be recognized that China's accession to the WTO (and its participation in other international organizations and fora, such as the climate change negotiations) has positively influenced the country's internal environmental regulations which it has strengthened to comply with international standards.[147] While it is disputable that China fully complies with the positive environmental laws and regulations that it has adopted throughout its entire territory, it has also adopted discriminatory laws and regulations in other fields by disguising their justifications based on environmental concerns and sustainable development to secure governmental control and adopt discriminatory trade measures in order to boost its internal market and favor its domestic industry.

The mining sector offers an excellent example of the extent to which such governmental control can push itself. State ownership over mineral resources is exercised by the State Council and is not affected by the alteration of ownership of the land where the resources are found. According to the Mineral Resource Law of the People's Republic of China,[148] "[m]ineral resources belong to the State"[149] and there is actually a straightforward reason to which the Chinese government might root its claims. Such reason is to be found in public international law, where ownership of natural resources – and hence all kinds of raw materials– rests upon the legal concept of sovereignty.[150] The latter evolved through a series of Resolutions adopted by the UN General Assembly starting in 1952, establishing the "rights of peoples and Nations to permanent sovereignty over their natural wealth and resources."[151] Sovereignty over natural resources derives from sovereignty over a State's territory, which implies control of such resources as well as sovereignty over all the activities that take place within that territory. However, such doctrine might seem unfair if we consider the so-called resource curse: since natural resources are unevenly distributed throughout the world, it would not be entirely fair to grant States such exclusive rights. This concern led to

146 Regarding the water management in China and how the EU Water Framework Directive might be an excellent model for China, *see* Deng Yixiang et al., *China's Water Environmental Management Towards Institutional Integration. A Review of Current Progress and Constraints vis-a-vis the European Experience* 113, J. Cleaner Production, 285, 285–98 (2016).

147 Xingle Long et al., *Are Stronger Environmental Regulations Effective in Practice? The Case of China's Accession to the WTO,* 39 J. Cleaner Production 161, 161–62 (2013). *See*, also, Malin Song et al., *Statistical Analysis and Combination Forecasting of Environmental Efficiency and its Influential Factors since China Entered the WTO: 2002–2010–2012*, 42 J. Cleaner Production 42, 42–51 (2013). *See* Chapters 12 (He), 13 (Li), 14 (Peng) and 15 (Huang) in this volume.

148 Mineral Resource Law of the People's Republic of China (March 19, 1986, as amended on August 29, 1996).

149 Mineral Resource Law of the People's Republic of China, Article 3.

150 See Jorge E Viñuales, *The 'Resource Curse' – A Legal Perspective,* 17 Global Governance 197 (2011). *See*, also, James N. Hyde, *Permanent Sovereignty over Natural Health and Resources*, 50(4) Am. J. Int'l L. 854 (1956); Nico Schrijver, Sovereignty over Natural Resources (Cambridge, 1997); Thomas Dietz, Elinor Ostrom, & Paul C. Stern, *The Struggle to Govern the Commons*, 302 Science 1907 (2003); Lynton K. Caldwell, *Concepts in Development of International Environmental Policies*, 13 Natural Resources J. 190 (1973); Julia Ya Qin, *Reforming WTO Discipline on Export Duties: Sovereignty over Natural Resources, Economic Development and Environmental Protection*, 46(5) J. World Trade 1147, 1163–65 (2012).

151 General Assembly Resolution 626 (VII), December 21, 1952. The UN General Assembly based this important document on two previous resolutions: resolutions 523 (VI) of January 12, 1952 and 626 (VII) of December 21, 1952. The idea expressed here was then confirmed and further explored by the two 1966 International Human Rights Covenants as well as two resolutions – resolution 3201 (S.VI) of May 1, 1974, and resolution 3281 (XXIX) of December 12, 1974.

the emergence of the doctrine of the environment as a common concern of mankind.[152] According to such principle, the domestic use and exploitation of natural resources is elevated beyond exclusive national jurisdiction to become an international concern, therefore subjected to international regulation.[153]

Given its rich broad variety of raw materials, China chose to stick to the first principle and exercised strict control over its resources. This principle perfectly suited China's development agenda and, through its power over natural resources, the country managed to lift hundreds of millions of people out of poverty, sustaining an average Gross Domestic Product (GDP) annual growth rate of 9.3 during the past 20 years.[154] Such principle is even enshrined in the Constitution;[155] Article 6 states that "The basis of the socialist economic system of the PRC is socialist public ownership of [the means of production]," where "means of production" certainly includes raw materials and natural resources.[156]

The State control over the country's resources takes different forms and can be seen as the root cause of the two main strategies adopted by China to support, boost, and foster its domestic industry: on the one hand, the limitation of the quantity of raw materials that can be exported (export restraints) and, on the other, of the possibility for foreign firms to access the Chinese market. Under both strategies, the government plays a crucial role.

In fact, when it comes to NTCs, the main WTO disputes involving China and concerning NTCs related to environmental matters specifically are *China – Raw Materials*[157] and *China – Rare Earths*.

In the first dispute, Beijing imposed restrictive measures on the export of nine types of raw materials, in particular various forms of bauxite, coke, fluorspar, magnesium, manganese, silicon carbide, silicon metal, yellow phosphorus, and zinc. The United States, the European Union, and Mexico challenged these measures claiming that they breached China's commitments under China's Accession Protocol Part I, paras 1.2, 5.1, 5.2, 8.2, and 11.3[158] and GATT Articles VIII, VIII:1, VIII:4 X:1, X:3 (a), XI:1[159] since the new regulations constituted export duties, export quotas, export licensing, and minimum export-price requirements.[160]

152 The "common concern of mankind" principle replaced the earlier "common heritage of mankind" concept, first introduced by Arvid Pardo in 1968 but adopted by the international community only two decades later. *See* Patricia Birnie & Alan Boyle, International Law and the Environment 97–99 (2d, Oxford University Press, 2002); Edith Brown Weiss, Environmental Change and International Law: New Challenges and Dimensions (United Nations University Press, 1992); Philippe Sands, Greening International Law (Earthscan, 1993); Philippe Sands, Richard Tarasofsky & Mary Weiss, Principles of International Environmental Law (Manchester University Press ND, 1994); Laurence Boisson de Chazournes, Ethique Environnementale et Droit International (Ed. scientifica, 2003); Keman Baslar, The Concept of the Common Heritage of Mankind in International Law 306 (Martinus Nijhoff Publishers, 1998).

153 Ben Saul, *China, Resources, and International Law* (Sydney Law School, Legal Studies Research Paper No. 11/82, November 2011), at 9.

154 *Id.*

155 Constitution of the People's Republic of China.

156 Xu Xuelei & Xu Xin, *Information Disclosure of State-Owned Enterprises in China* 4(1) Tsinghua China Law Review 14 (2012).

157 Report of the Panel and Appellate Body Report, *China – Measures Related to the Exportation of Various Raw Materials*, *supra* note 63.

158 Accession of the People's Republic of China, WT/L/432 (November 23, 2001), Para. 11.3.

159 Legal Texts: GATT 1947 The General Agreement on Tariffs and Trade (GATT 1947), articles VIII:1(a), X: 1, X:3(a), VI:1, https://www.wto.org/english/docs_e/legal_e/gatt47_01_e.htm.

160 Butcher, *supra* note 76, at 72–73.

These exports restraints increased the prices of raw materials at the global markets and, as a consequence, the Chinese domestic industries gained advantage through sufficient supply and lower prices. The Chinese government claimed that these measures were justified under Article XX of the GATT.

In fact, China had stated among its arguments that some of its export duties and quotas were justified because they were measures "relating to the conservation of exhaustible natural resources" for some of the raw materials. However, China was unable to provide evidence that it adopted these restrictions in conjunction with measures applicable to domestic production or consumption of the raw materials so as to conserve the raw materials. It is important to highlight here that even though the decision did not favor China, the Panel acknowledged that China appeared to be on the path to adopting a legal framework to justify its quotas under WTO rules, but that the framework was not yet WTO-consistent because it still needed to be put into effect for domestic producers to avoid any accusation of violating the WTO non-discrimination principles.

As to the other raw materials, China claimed that its export quotas and duties were fundamental and necessary in view of protecting the public health and its people. Unfortunately, China could not produce evidence that the adopted measures, such as export duties and quotas, would reduce pollution, in the short or long term, and therefore improve the health of its citizens.

The Panel and AB had to examine whether China could use Article XX to justify its failure to comply with its commitments under Paragraph 11.3 of China's Accession Protocol. In *China – Publications and Audiovisuals Products*, China's defence based on Article XX was allowed as the language of paragraph 5.1 of China's Accession Protocol granted China the right to regulate trade.[161] Taking the note of the same, the AB in the present case stated that the language of Paragraph 11.3 being in contrast to paragraph 5.1, does not suggest that China may have recourse to Article XX to justify a violation of its obligation to eliminate export duties.[162]

Thus, the debate over the place of the Accession Protocols in the WTO multilateral system continues since the basis on which WTO Accession Protocols take legal effect has not been raised in the DSB.[163] That is why, for instance, the AB had the opportunity to take a different reasoning concerning the application of Article XX to the Accession Protocols. Moreover, the AB confirmed the Panel's position that even if Article XX was applicable in this case, China has failed to provide a link between the measures taken and the objective of protecting the environment and public health.[164] Thus, the NTCs argument was rejected.

The second dispute, *China – Rare Earths*, concerned export restriction measures that Beijing adopted on rare earths, tungsten, and molybdenum (which are raw materials used in the production of various kinds of electronic goods),[165] with the justification of protecting the environment, preserving resources, reducing pollution caused by mining, and promoting

161 Report of the Panel, *China – Measures Affecting Trading Rights and Distribution Services for Certain Publications and Audiovisual Entertainment Products*, WT/DS363/R (August 12, 2009) and Appellate Body Report, *China – Measures Affecting Trading Rights and Distribution Services for Certain Publications and Audiovisual Entertainment Products*, WT/DS363/AB/R (December 21, 2009).

162 Butcher, *supra* note 76, at 72–73.

163 Kennedy, *supra* note 66, at 46–47.

164 Butcher, *supra* note 76, at 73.

165 Report of the Panel, *China – Measures Related to the Exportation of Rare Earths, Tungsten, and Molybdenum*, *supra* note 67 and Appellate Body Report, *China – Measures Related to the Exportation of Rare Earths, Tungsten, and Molybdenum*, WT/DS431/AB/R, WT/DS432/AB/R, WT/DS433/AB/R (August 7, 2014). *See*, also, Butcher, *supra* note 76, at 74.

sustainable development.[166] According to China's Accession Protocol, China must eliminate all export duties except for those included in Annex 6. With the exception of tungsten ores and concentrates, which are not included in the claim's terms of reference, none of the other products at issue are included in Annex 6. Therefore, China is not entitled to adopt any export duties on them.

Once more, China tried to invoke Article XX of the GATT to justify its measures which were "necessary to protect human, animal and plant life and health" from the pollution caused by mining the products at issue. Yet again, both the Panel[167] and the AB found that Article XX did not justify the breach of Paragraph 11.3 of China's Accession Protocol. It is relevant to note that, although China was not successful in its claim, the Panel agreed with China that the term "conservation" in Article XX(g) does not have to be read simply as meaning "preservation" of natural resources. The Panel stated that, in accordance with the general public international law principles of sovereignty over natural resources in line with various UN and other international instruments as described above in this section, each WTO Member may take into consideration its own internal conditions and may decide autonomously on how to reach the needs and objectives of sustainable development when preparing or adopting laws or regulations related to the conservation of exhaustible natural resources. However, the Panel clarified that "conservation" does not allow Members to adopt measures to control or manipulate the international market for a specific natural resource, which is what the challenged export quotas were designed to do. In particular, the main objective of the measures adopted by the Chinese government was to favor domestic extraction and secure preferential use of those raw materials by Chinese domestic industries.

Another relevant issue that was examined at the AB level relates to China's claim of "intrinsic relationship" between Article XII:1 of the Marrakesh Agreement[168] and Paragraph 1.2 of China's Accession Protocol. The AB stated that "the Marrakesh Agreement, the Multilateral Trade Agreements, and China's Accession Protocol form a single package of

166 *See* Butcher, *supra* note 76, at 76.

167 It is relevant to note that in the Section 7.3.2.1.8 of the Report of the Panel, *China – Measures Related to the Exportation of Rare Earths, Tungsten, and Molybdenum, supra* note 67, at Paragraphs 7.118–7.120, Page 66, there is a "*Separate Opinion by One Panelist.*" This panelist "is unable to agree with some of the findings and conclusions contained in Paragraphs 7.63 to 7.117 above. This section reflects the views of that panelist. I agree with the ultimate conclusion reached by this Panel that, in this dispute, China cannot justify its export duties on rare earths, tungsten, and molybdenum products pursuant to Article XX(b) of the GATT 1994 (GATT Article XX(b))." So, even if Article XX(b) was applicable to justify China's export duties, those duties were not "necessary to protect human, animal, or plant life or health", as required under Article XX(b). Under the concrete circumstances, China's imposition of the export duties in question was considered to be inconsistent with China's WTO obligations. Then, the Panel: "However, contrary to the finding made by the Panel's majority, I believe that a proper interpretation of the relevant provisions at issue leads to the conclusion that the obligations in Paragraph 11.3 of China's Accession Protocol are subject to the general exceptions in Article XX of the GATT 1994. I am well aware of the findings of the Panel and the Appellate Body in the China – Raw Materials dispute regarding the availability of Article XX of the GATT 1994 (GATT Article XX) to justify violations of Paragraph 11.3 of China's Accession Protocol. In my view, China has submitted new arguments in this dispute that have helped the Panel to appreciate the legal complexity of this issue. The Panel's majority has undertaken a long and careful evaluation of the parties' arguments concerning this matter. I agree with many parts of the Panel's majority's analysis of this issue and I respect this Panel's majority decision. Nonetheless, I respectfully disagree with certain key aspects of its reasoning and findings [. . .]." This was an important statement and clarification may be used as reference point in future cases, but under the concrete circumstances, terms, and conditions of the Chinese measures at issue in this case.

168 Marrakesh Agreement Establishing the World Trade Organization, https://www.wto.org/ENGLISH/res_e/booksp_e/analytic_index_e/wto_agree_01_e.htm.

rights and obligations that must be read together."[169] The AB found that Paragraph 1.2 of China's Accession Protocol, which provides that the Protocol "shall be an integral part of the WTO Agreement", builds a bridge between the package of Protocol provisions and the package of existing WTO rights and obligations.

However, this statement does not provide an answer to whether there is an objective link between ***an individual provision*** in China's Accession Protocol and China's existing obligations under the Marrakesh Agreements and the Multilateral Trade Agreement and whether China can rely on the existing general exceptions in these Agreements to justify a breach of its commitments under China's Accession Protocol for NTCs, in general, and environmental concerns, in particular.[170]

The WTO has crossed a long road when it comes to balancing the relation between trade and NTCs where the Panels' and AB's jurisprudence has ensured respect for NTCs, including environmental matters on the expense of trade in several cases, as shown above. However, the accession of new WTO Members resulted in new obligations (WTO Plus Obligations) upon the acceding countries (most of them developing or emerging economies) which were stipulated in their Accession Protocols.

There is an ongoing debate as to whether such an increase of WTO Plus Obligations is fair and, as described through the case law above, whether the WTO commitments included in the Accession Protocols can be violated on the basis of expectations stated in the GATT, mainly Article XX, since they should represent "a single package of rights and obligations that must be read together." It is arguable that these potential limitations on the use of Article XX of the GATT may be considered a new form of unfair discrimination perpetuated against developing countries which are gradually entering the WTO. This is even less justifiable if it may impede the adoption of reasonable and non-discriminatory measures that have the sole objective of protecting the environment and facilitating sustainable development.

This paradigm is yet to be clarified either through supplementary WTO multilateral negotiations or the Panel or AB case law to avoid the risk of revitalized limitations on the applications of NTCs in the near future on the basis of the WTO Plus Obligations imposed on newly acceding WTO Members.

So far, the decisions of the Panels and AB in the different cases which were filed against China adopted different attitudes and/or different justifications in their rulings, but generally it seems that their legal reasoning and clarifications (including the use of dissenting opinions among the Panelists), even when the final decisions were not in favor of the specific measures at issue which were consequently not justified under Article XX of the GATT, showed that the Panels and AB are more and more willing to carefully consider the environment and sustainable development.

3 *Ensuring respect for human rights matters in the multilateral trade system*

In recent decades, the WTO has increasingly come under pressure for reconciling the requirements of free trade with requests for protecting NTCs related to public health.[171]

169 Appellate Body Report, *China – Measures Related To The Exportation of Rare Earths, Tungsten, and Molybdenum*, *supra* note 165, at Parargraph 5.70.

170 Report of the Panel and Appellate Body Report, *China – Measures Related To The Exportation of Rare Earths, Tungsten, and Molybdenum*, *supra* note 67 & *supra* note 165.

171 Sieglinde Gstohl, *Blurring Regime Boundaries: Uneven Legalization of Non-Trade Concerns in the WTO*, 9(3) J. Int'l Trade L. & Pol'y 275, 275 (2010).

The conflict between trade and public health is multifaceted, spanning the clash between trade-related intellectual property rights and human rights, investments in research and development, the right to health and access to medicine,[172] and the protection of tangible and intangible cultural heritage.[173]

In particular, the TRIPS Agreement sets international minimum standards for the protection and enforcement of intellectual property rights, and allows WTO Members to insert public health concerns into their national intellectual property laws.[174] The Doha Declaration concerning the TRIPS Agreement and Public Health includes seven paragraphs, and indicates the importance that WTO Members ascribe to effectively addressing public health concerns.

The modern multilateral trade regime and the international human rights movement constitute products of post–World War II phenomena. Since the States have committed to liberalize trade in goods and services under international economic law, there is the potential for conflict between a State's obligations under international human rights law and its obligations under international economic law.[175]

172 Frederick M. Abbott, *WTO TRIPS Agreement and its Implications for Access to Medicines in Developing Countries*, Study Paper 2a, United Kingdom Commission on Intellectual Property Rights 8–10 (February 14, 2002), http://papers.ssrn.com/sol3/papers.cfm?abstract_id=1924420; PAUL HUNT et al., NEGLECTED DISEASES: A HUMAN RIGHTS ANALYSIS 35 (World Health Organisation, 2007); DOHA WTO Ministerial 2001: TRIPS WT/MIN(01)/DEC/2, Declaration on the TRIPS Agreement and public health, adopted on 14 November 2001, https://www.wto.org/english/thewto_e/minist_e/min01_e/mindecl_trips_e.htm; Alexandra G. Watson, ***International Intellectual Property Rights: Do TRIPS' Flexibilities Permit Sufficient Access to Affordable HIV/AIDS Medicines in Developing Countries?***, 32(1) BOSTON COLLEGE INT'L & COMP. L. REV. 143, 145–48 (2009); Jakkrit Kuanpoth, ***TRIPS-Plus under Free Trade Agreements, in*** INTELLECTUAL PROPERTY & FREE TRADE AGREEMENTS 27, 30 (Christopher Heath & Anselm Kamperman Sanders eds, Hart Publishing, 2007); Peter Drahos, ***Four Lessons For Developing Countries From The Trade Negotiations Over Access To Medicines***, 28(1) LIVERPOOL L. REV. 11, 14 (2007); Rochelle Cooper Dreyfuss & César Rodríguez-Garavito, ***The Battle over Intellectual Property Laws and Access to Medicines in Latin America: A Primer on Global Administrative Law, Intellectual Property and Political Contestation***, in BALANCING WEALTH AND HEALTH: THE BATTLE OVER INTELLECTUAL PROPERTY AND ACCESS TO MEDICINES IN LATIN AMERICA 1, 17 (Rochelle Dreyfuss & César Rodríguez-Garavito ed., OUP Oxford, 2014); DILIP K. DAS, 'The Doha Round of Multilateral Trade Negotiations: Causal Factors Behind the Failure in Cancún', (Research Paper, Toronto, 2003) at 12; UNITED NATION COMMISSION ON TRADE AND DEVELOPMENT & INTERNATIONAL CENTER FOR TRADE AND SUSTAINABLE DEVELOPMENT, RESOURCE BOOK ON TRIPS AND DEVELOPMENT 484 (Cambridge University Press, 2005); CYNTHIA HO, ACCESS TO MEDICINE IN THE GLOBAL ECONOMY: INTERNATIONAL AGREEMENTS ON PATENTS AND RELATED RIGHTS 218 (OUP USA, 2011); Andrew D. Mitchel & Tania Voon, ***The TRIPS Waiver as a Recognition of Public Health Concerns in the WTO, in*** INCENTIVES FOR GLOBAL PUBLIC HEALTH: PATENT LAW AND ACCESS TO ESSENTIAL MEDICINES 56, 75–76 (Thomas Pogge, Matthew Rimmer & Kim Rubenstein eds, Cambridge University Press, 2010). *See also* Chapters 34 (Feng, Shu & Zhang), 35 (Watal), and 36 (Nie) in this volume.

173 Paolo Davide Farah & Riccardo Tremolada, ***Diritti di Proprietà Intellettuale, Diritti Umani e Patrimonio Culturale Immateriale***, 2, 1 RIVISTA DI DIRITTO INDUSTRIALE, 21, 21–47 (2014); Paolo Davide Farah & Riccardo Tremolada, ***Conflict between Intellectual Property Rights and Human Rights: A Case Study on Intangible Cultural Heritage***, 94, 1 OREGON LAW REVIEW (2015).

174 HUNT et al., ***supra*** note 172, at 35.

175 Koen De Feyter, ***Introduction***, in ECONOMIC GLOBALISATION AND HUMAN RIGHTS: EIUC STUDIES ON HUMAN RIGHTS AND DEMOCRATIZATION 1, 7–8 (Wolfgang Benedek, Koen De Feyter & Fabrizio Marrella eds, Cambridge University Press, 2007).

Each of these regimes has a strong impact on the respective area of competences and they are closely interconnected, but unfortunately they did not develop instruments for solving problems between the two systems and conflicts of overlapping jurisdiction. Yet, human rights violations have increased in quantity and sometimes become more sophisticated (e.g. abuses connected to the respect of a State contract signed with a multinational company). For these reasons, the international community must rethink the instruments used to protect human rights.

Since it is not possible to determine conclusively whether globalization has had a positive or negative effect on human rights, the international community, including governments, international organizations, civil society, policy-makers, and scholars, must isolate the negative effects of globalization so they can be reframed to protect human rights without foregoing economic development. If the sole term of reference for a successful private enterprise is to decrease the prices of products as much as possible and increase company profits without considering the impact on the wealth and health of society, the endeavor will be unsustainable in the long term. This is also the direct effect on the behavior of producers who are less and less inclined to spend more resources to provide adequate protections for their workers.[176] However, we cannot overlook the fact that globalization and increased trade may improve conditions for a larger share of the population to come out from poverty. In this way, globalization may improve human welfare and indirectly create the basis for the formation of a middle class that, after having reached an independent economic status and achieving a degree of stability, will demand political freedoms.[177]

As described above, trade liberalization has been criticized for its emphasis on economic outcomes and GDP growth at the expense of human rights and other societal values.[178] The WTO is accused of having, among the provisions of the agreements, requirements that may conflict with a State's human rights obligations and societal objectives, while limiting the ability of WTO Members to retaliate against other States for breaching human rights obligations through the use of trade sanctions.[179] In addition, the elimination of quantitative restrictions and the application of non-discrimination principles between domestic and imported products might encourage States to boost the competitiveness of their own industries by adopting new laws and regulations for limiting or watering down human rights, such as the labor rights of the workers permitting the private companies to apply for new contractual conditions that reduce the minimum wage or other rights.[180] Nevertheless, defendants of the WTO state explicitly that the rationale behind the WTO approach is that, in case of human rights violations, trade sanctions may conceal a disguised form of protectionism where the measure taken strictly for protectionism purposes is not motivated by human rights concerns.[181] Furthermore, the WTO would govern trade and not issues such as human

176 *Id.*, at 7–8.

177 Jessica M. Karbowski, *Grocery Store Activism: A WTO Compliant Means to Incentivize Social Responsibility,* 49(3) VA. J. INT'L L. 727, 734 (2009).

178 Rebecca Bates, *The Trade in Water Services: How Does GATS Apply to the Water and Sanitation Services Sector?*, 31 SYDNEY L. REV. 121, 133–35 (2009).

179 Karbowski, *supra* note 177, at 734–35.

180 SARAH JOSEPH, BLAME IT ON THE WTO?: A HUMAN RIGHTS CRITIQUE 3–4 (OUP Oxford, 2013).

181 Michael J. Trebilcock, *Trade Policy and Labour Standards: Objectives, Instruments And Institutions* 18–24 (Law And Economics Research Paper NO. 02–01, Faculty of Law, University of Toronto, Conference on "International Economic Governance and Non-Economic Concerns," Vienna, Austria, European Community Studies Association, December 10 and 11, 2001).

rights, and some of them even argue that the WTO indirectly promotes human rights through stimulation of trade and an improved global governance of international trade and international economic law, not to mention that the substantive rules and practices of the organization are increasingly incorporating human rights issues within its framework.[182]

As a matter of fact, Article XX of the GATT allows human rights protection through its general exceptions for measures necessary to protect public morals (XX(a)), to protect human life (XX(b)), and for measures relating to the products of prison labor (XX(e)).[183] Article XX(g) is primarily an economic and environmental provision since it relates to natural resources, but it has human rights ramifications in some circumstances.[184] Moreover, Article XX(a), (b), and (e) require that a measure satisfy a "necessity" test to justify non-economic objectives which implies that trade issues are prioritized over other objectives.[185] The jurisprudence of the Panel and AB in several WTO cases related to either environmental or health concerns, such as the *US – Shrimp* case,[186] highlights the fact that Article XX offers a significant mechanism, and room for State sovereignty, for justifying discriminatory treatment to respond to measures from other Member States that affect NTCs. It was shown through the *US – Shrimp* case that Article XX imposes limitations on the use of trade measures for non-trade policy purposes, but those measures may find justification under Article XX.[187] Yet, Member States have rarely mentioned the reference to ***human rights*** in their petitions or arguments developed before the WTO, and they are not present in the Panel or AB findings.[188] This is due to the restrictive interpretation of Article XX applied in the Panels' decisions and reasoning based on their views about the very deep meaning and purposes of the GATT, while the AB's decisions regarding Article XX show that an exception, in particular a general exception like the ones included in Article XX, should be treated like any other treaty provision which must be interpreted according to its terms, context, and in light of the core object and purpose of such a treaty.[189]

Furthermore, the GATT 1979 Agreement on Technical Barriers to Trade (TBT),[190] also called Tokyo Round Standards Code, adopted the notion of Non-Product-Related (NPR) Process

182 Olufemi Amao, Corporate Social Responsibility, Human Rights and the Law: Multinational Corporations in Developing Countries 218–19 (Routledge, 2011).

183 Sarah H. Cleveland, ***Human Rights Sanctions and the World Trade Organisation***, in Environment, Human Rights and International Trade 199, 233 (Francesco Francioni ed., Hart Publishing, 2001).

184 Adam McBeth, International Economic Actors and Human Rights 85, 119 (Routledge, 2011).

185 Amao, ***supra*** note 182, at 224.

186 Report of the Panel, and Appellate Body Report, ***United States – Import Prohibition of Certain Shrimp and Shrimp Products, supra*** note 25; Report of the Panel, ***United States – Import Prohibition of Certain Shrimp and Shrimp Products, Recourse to Article 21.5 of the DSU***, WT/DS58/RW (June 15, 2001); Appellate Body Report, ***United States – Import Prohibition of Certain Shrimp and Shrimp Products Recourse to Article 21.5 of the DSU by Malaysia, supra*** note 25.

187 Anthony Cassimatis, Human Rights Related Trade Measures under International Law 336 (Brill, 2007).

188 Niels Beisinghoff, Corporations and Human Rights: An Analysis of ATCA Litigation against Corporations 57 (Peter Lang GmbH, Internationaler Verlag der Wissenschaften, 2009).

189 Andrew Newcombe, ***General Exceptions in International Investments Agreements***, in Sustainable Development in World Investment Law 351, 363–64 (Marie-Claire Cordonier Segger, Markus W. Gehring & Andrew Paul Newcomb eds, Kluwer Law International, 2010).

190 At the end of the Tokyo Round in 1979, after several years of negotiations since 1947, 32 GATT Contracting Parties signed the plurilateral Agreement on Technical Barriers to Trade (TBT) which was called the Tokyo Round Standards Code. Its provisions were further expanded through the adoption of the

and Production Methods (PPM). The NPR PPM requirements refer to measures that target the production methods of goods, starting from the consideration that not all the processes are in themselves equivalent in terms of the societal effects to obtain a specific final product.[191] PPM measures are divided into two categories: Product-Related measures that may have detectable and identifiable leftovers in the final product and Non-Product-Related measures that do not have any visible or verifiable leftovers in the final product, but may still have effects beyond the product itself.[192] The GATT 1947 or WTO Panel and AB reports have not adopted any cases with a leading ruling, which clarified in a definitive or at least clear way the treatment to be granted to the NPR PPMs under general trade liberalization rules.[193] Nevertheless, it appears that exceptions in GATT Article XX have the capacity to protect unilateral NPR PPM measures, as the *Tuna/Dolphin Case II* of 2011 ("dolphin-safe" labeling), where consumers' choice was based on the method of production rather than the product itself, previously showed.[194] The further relevant step in this legal reasoning is the application of the NPR PPMs to human rights issues. It has to be highlighted that the Panel and AB cases have developed and clarified the conditions for evaluating the "likeness" of two products through the use of the four criteria analysis (set by the Border Tax Adjustments) which do not need to be cumulative: (i) the properties, nature, and quality of the products; (ii) the end-uses of the products; (iii) consumers' tastes and habits – more comprehensively termed consumers' perceptions and behaviors – in respect of the products; and (iv) the tariff classification of the products.[195] If the NPR PPMs would become, for example, a fifth criteria in this list, it would be more possible for countries to adopt trade-related human rights measures despite their inconsistency with the WTO system, because these measures would be covered under Article XX.

Additionally, another subject that remains unsolved and highly relevant for NTCs is the concept of extraterritoriality that we already examined in this chapter; however, we focused our reasoning and evaluation on environmental concerns, when we compared the *United*

TBT Agreement in 1995 with the creation of the WTO. *See* Technical Barriers To Trade: Technical Explanation – Technical Information on Technical Barriers to Trade, https://www.wto.org/english/tratop_e/tbt_e/tbt_info_e.htm.

191 OECD, *Processes and Production Methods (PPMs): Conceptual Framework and Considerations on Use of PPM-Based Trade Measures* 15–16 (OCDE/GD(97)137, 1997).

192 Kateryna Holzer, Carbon-Related Border Adjustment and WTO Law 91, 93 (Edward Elgar, 2014).

193 Ilona Cheyne, *Consumer Labelling in EU and WTO Law*, in Liberalising Trade in the EU and the WTO: A Legal Comparison 309, 319 (Birgitte Egelund Olsen, Karsten Engsig & Sanford E. Gaines Sørensen eds, Cambridge University Press, 2014).

194 *Id. See* Report of the Panel and of the Appellate Body, *United States – Measures Concerning the Importation, Marketing and Sale of Tuna and Tuna Products, supra* note 129; Report of the Panel, *United States – Measures Concerning the Importation, Marketing and Sale of Tuna and Tuna Products Recourse to Article 21.5 of the DSU by Mexico, supra* note 129.

195 Appellate Body Report, *European Communities – Measures Affecting Asbestos and Asbestos-Containing Products, supra* note 119, at Paragraph 101. *See* also Report of the Panel, *Japan – Taxes on Alcoholic Beverages* ("*Japan – Alcoholic Beverages*"), WT/DS8/R, WT/DS10/R, WT/DS11/R, adopted November 1, 1996, as modified by the Appellate Body Report, WT/DS8/AB/R, WT/DS10/AB/R, WT/DS11/AB/R, DSR 1996:I, 125 (Article III:2 of the GATT 1994); Appellate Body Report, *Japan – Alcoholic Beverages*, WT/DS8/AB/R, WT/DS10/AB/R, WT/DS11/AB/R, adopted November 1, 1996, DSR 1996:I, 97.

States – Tuna and Tuna Products from Canada case,[196] the *Tuna/Dolphin Case I*[197] and the *Tuna/Dolphin Case II* of 2011 ("dolphin-safe" labeling).[198] In those cases, this issue was gradually addressed with an evolution that started in the first two disputes with a very narrow interpretation stating that a given State's regulations cannot be enforced in another State's jurisdiction on the basis of international trade rules under the auspices of the expectations of Article XX (b) and (g). In the last dispute, which was actually adopted after the creation of the WTO and inclusion of the WTO Preamble, the interpretation favored measures that have the sole objective of protecting the environment and promoting sustainable development. Whether this last interpretation of the extraterritoriality principles will be consistently applied to trade measures adopted for the protection of human rights or other areas of NTCs in the future remains to be seen.[199]

Along with Article XX, Article XXI(c) provides proof of the willingness to consider human rights concerns when the WTO assesses compliance with trade measures. Article XXI(c) states the following: "Nothing in this Agreement shall be construed [. . .] (c) to prevent any contracting party from taking any action in pursuance of its obligations under the United Nations Charter for the maintenance of international peace and security."[200] Likewise, the Panels and the AB have made use of general principles of international law to support their interpretations based on the ordinary meaning of the terms of the WTO Agreement as was proved in the *US – Standards for Reformulated Gasoline and Conventional Gasoline*[201] where the AB held that the WTO Agreement should not be read in "clinical isolation from Public International Law."[202]

The abovementioned matters create additional challenges for the WTO legal system that strives for trade openness, however, while taking NTCs into consideration. If the WTO succeeds in fully integrating human rights issues into the system through the adoption of further provisions in the WTO agreements and/or thanks to a more straightforward and solid case law, it would constitute a further tool to protect and guarantee human rights even when trade is concerned, recognizing the existing (and necessary) interdependence between the two systems. As a matter of fact, a completely different analysis should be dedicated to the indirect impact that the accession to the WTO may produce in terms of domestic legal reforms of the WTO-acceding Member States, including new regulations that would strengthen the protection of human rights. It has to be noted that following China's

196 Report of the Panel, *United States – Prohibition of Imports of Tuna and Tuna Products from Canada*, *supra* note 89.

197 Report of the Panel, *United States – Restrictions on Imports of Tuna*, *supra* note 91.

198 Report of the Panel and Appellate Body Report, *United States – Measures Concerning the Importation, Marketing and Sale of Tuna and Tuna Products*, *supra* note 129 and Report of the Panel, *United States – Measures Concerning the Importation, Marketing and Sale of Tuna and Tuna Products, Recourse to Article 21.5 of the DSU by Mexico*, *supra* note 129.

199 Sandra L. Walker, Environmental Protection Versus Trade Liberalization: Finding The Balance: An Examination Of The Legality Of Environmental Regulation Under International Trade Law Regimes 91, 97–98 (Facultés Universitaires Saint-Louis, Brussels, 1993).

200 GATT 1994 General Agreement on Tariffs and Trade 1994, XXIII. Article XXI, https://www.wto.org/ENGLISH/res_e/booksp_e/analytic_index_e/gatt1994_08_e.htm.

201 Report of the Panel and Appellate Body Report, *United States – Standards for Reformulated and Conventional Gasoline*, *supra* note 115.

202 Chien-Huei Wu, WTO and the Greater China: Economic Integration and Dispute Resolution 99 (Martinus Nijhoff, 2012).

accession to the WTO in 2001, the 10th National People's Congress (NPC) at its 2nd Session on March 14, 2004, approved important amendments to the Chinese Constitution[203] relevant to the discussion. While the WTO accession was not the sole reason for this move towards reforms, it is to be noted that several internal political concerns played an essential role in fastening and creating the political consensus for the adoption of those amendments in the Chinese Constitution, even as an *internal response* to WTO membership and consequent liberalization.

The leftist intellectuals in China sharply contested China's WTO accession because of the impact it would have had on a country that still describes itself in Article 1 of its Constitution as "a socialist State under the People's democratic dictatorship led by the working class and based on the alliance of workers and peasants." Those intellectuals considered globalization, free trade, and liberalistic principles, which are intrinsic parts of the WTO, to be disruptive for the interests of the Chinese people.

If we carefully analyze the amendments to the Chinese Constitution, we can find many relevant and interesting changes. In particular, a third paragraph has been added to Article 33: "The State respects and preserves human rights." After the adoption of this amendment, the question which arose was whether the Chinese government would take actions and implement reforms to respect the spirit of the law or whether Article 33 would remain hollow. It seems that the Labor Contract Law of the People's Republic of China,[204] which went into effect on January 1, 2008, is one of the first relevant consequences of the human rights amendment to implement the Chinese Constitution in the Chinese legal system, followed by the Law of the People's Republic of China on the Prevention and Control of Occupational Diseases[205] and by the Work Safety Law of the People's Republic of China.[206] Then, it is also significant to highlight the clear reference in the Chinese Constitution to the protection of private property ("Citizens' lawful private property is inviolable")[207] and the obligation to compensate in case of expropriation or requisition.[208] Furthermore, the second paragraph of Article 11 of the Chinese Constitution states that the "State protects the lawful rights and interests of the non-public sectors of the economy such as the individual and private sectors of the economy. The State encourages, supports and guides the development of the non-public sectors of the economy and, in accordance with law, exercises supervision

203 Constitution of the People's Republic of China (PRC), adopted on December 4, 1982 and amended by the 10th NPC at its 2nd Session on March 14, 2004, *See*, also, Chen Jianfu, *The Revision of the Constitution in the PRC*, 53 China perspectives (Online) 1, 4–9 (May–June 2004).

204 Zhōnghuá Rénmín Gònghéguó Láodòng Hétóng Fǎ (中华人民共和国劳动合同法) [Labor Contract Law of the People's Republic of China] (promulgated by the Standing Comm. Nat'l People's Cong., June 29, 2007, effective January 1, 2008, amended December 28, 2012).

205 Zhōnghuá Rénmín Gònghéguó Zhíyèbìng Fángzhì Fǎ (中华人民共和国职业病防治法) [Law of the People's Republic of China on the Prevention and Treatment of Occupational Diseases] (promulgated by the Standing Comm. Nat'l People's Cong., October 27, 2001, amended December 31, 2011).

206 Zhōnghuá Rénmín Gònghéguó Ānquán Shēngchǎn Fǎ (中华人民共和国安全生产法) [Work Safety Law of the People's Republic of China] (promulgated by the Standing Comm. Nat'l People's Cong., June 29, 2002, amended August 27, 2009).

207 Article 13 of the Constitution of the People's Republic of China (PRC), adopted on December 4, 1982 and amended by the 10th NPC at its 2nd Session on March 14, 2004.

208 *Id.*

and control over the non-public sectors of the economy."[209] A fourth paragraph was added to Article 14: "The State establishes a sound social security system compatible with the level of economic development." This article further develops the meaning of Article 33 of "the respect and preservation of human rights" calling for a concrete change in the life of the Chinese citizens by establishing a "sound social security system." The Chinese Government has adopted several different laws to implement this principle in the Chinese legal system, such as the Law of the People's Republic of China on Protection of the Rights and Interests of the Elderly,[210] the Mental Health Law of the People's Republic of China,[211] and, to a certain extent, also the Resolution of the Standing Committee of the National People's Congress on Adjusting and Improving the Family Planning Policy. Of course, beyond the letter of all these laws and regulations, the Chinese authorities and officials need to effectively implement the spirit of these laws in day-to-day practice to meet the relevant and overreaching objectives to improve the Chinese population's quality of life.[212]

Having taken into consideration all these issues, in the author's opinion, the WTO has indirectly contributed to these Chinese legal reforms, which better protect the rights of Chinese workers and citizens as a whole and balance the effects that globalization and free trade would have had in the Chinese internal legal system. In sum, when the link between trade and human rights is taken into account, we need to carefully evaluate, from a comparative law perspective, the new Member States' internal legal reforms to protect human rights, following their WTO accession, and not only those reforms that are specifically addressed by the WTO agreements and practice.

4 *Guaranteeing food security at the national level while embracing international trade regulations*

The UN established the Food and Agriculture Organization (FAO) in 1945 as a specialized agency during the First Session of the FAO Conference held in Quebec City, Canada. The FAO is certainly the international organization designed to cover most of the issues related to food security, food safety, and agricultural products, but the relations and conflicting areas among these relevant issues and international trade regulations are quite evident. Since GATT 1947, NTCs have been included in agriculture trade policy and negotiations, mainly for the important role they play in this specific field for the national security and stability of the countries. During the ongoing negotiations and in particular during the Uruguay Round, this definition has evolved such that the NTCs include "food security, food safety and quality, rural development and animal welfare."[213] Food security emerged as a NTC that shall be

209 Second paragraph of Article 11 of the Constitution of the People's Republic of China (PRC), adopted on December 4, 1982 and amended by the 10th NPC at its 2nd Session on March 14, 2004.

210 Zhōnghuá Rénmín Gònghéguó Lǎonián Rén Quányì Bǎozhàng Fǎ (2012 Nián Xiūdìng) (中华人民共和国老年人权益保障法(2012年修订) [Law of the People's Republic of China on Protection of the Rights and Interests of the Elderly] (Promulgated by the Standing Comm. Nat'l People's Cong., December 28, 2012).

211 Zhōnghuá Rénmín Gònghéguó Jīngshén Wèishēng Fǎ (中华人民共和国精神卫生法) [Mental Health Law of the People's Republic of China] (Promulgated by the Standing Comm. Nat'l People's Cong., June 26, 2012).

212 *See* Chapters 4 (Bonfanti), 5 (Choukroune), 29 (Gruszczynski, Ötvös & Farah), 30 (Rossi), 31 (Prasad), 32 (Hu), and 33 (Coggiola) in this volume.

213 Simpson & Schoenbaum, *supra* note 20, at 402.

taken into account in the reform of agricultural trade.[214] Food security was, for the first time, defined at the global level during the 1974 World Food Summit as the "availability at all times of adequate world food supplies of basic foodstuffs to sustain a steady expansion of food consumption and to offset fluctuations in production and prices".[215] This definition gives us the idea that when the issue started to appear as a global concern, States mainly considered food security in terms of volume and stability of food supplies. Throughout the years this concept has evolved and has been redefined at various World Summits, Conferences and FAO Reports such as those in 1983, 1996, and 2001[216] and reports from other international organizations and fora such as the 1986 World Bank (WB) Report on "Poverty and Hunger" and the 1994 United Nations Development Program (UNDP) Human Development Report, including a definition of food security as "access to vulnerable people," with attention to the relevant differences between chronic and temporary food insecurity connected to natural disasters and armed conflicts. This characterization has expanded to also cover the need of food safety and better quality of food in terms of nutritional balance. The link between food security and food safety became a focal point to construct so-called human security.[217]

The definition adopted in Rome in 2001 in *The State of Food Insecurity in the World 2001* gave more importance to consumption and the right of individuals to have access to food: "Food security [is] a situation that exists when all people, at all times, have physical, social and economic access to sufficient, safe and nutritious food that meets their dietary needs and food preferences for an active and healthy life."[218]

On a different level, national food security was described as the "ability of a country to secure an adequate total supply of food to meet the nutritional needs of its population at all times, through domestic production, food imports and/or the temporary use of national food stocks."[219] We are living in a more and more interconnected world, but each Nation-State needs to attain or preserve food security for its population within its borders as independently as possible from external intervention or even, in certain circumstances, a foreign country's efforts to protect its national security and sovereignty.[220] In order to achieve a sufficient level of independence, governments need to have a clear food security plan, in particular with a balance among internal production, food reserves, and availability for the most vulnerable people.[221]

214 Michael Blakeney, Intellectual Property Rights and Food Security 10 (CABI, 2009).

215 United Nations,. *Report of the World Food Conference, Rome 5–16 November 1974* (New York, 1975).

216 FAO, *World Food Security: a Reappraisal of the Concepts and Approaches*, Director General's Report, Rome, 1983; FAO, *Rome Declaration on World Food Security and World Food Summit Plan of Action*, World Food Summit, November 13–17, 1996; FAO, *The State of Food Insecurity in the World 2001*, Rome, 2002.

217 *Id. See*, also, Patricia Bonnard, *Improving the Nutrition Impacts of Agriculture Interventions: Strategy and Policy Brief* 6 (Food and Nutrition Technical Assistance Project, 2001); Carmen G. Gonzalez, *Institutionalizing Inequality: The WTO Agreement on Agriculture, Food Security, and Developing Countries*, 27(2) Colum. J. Envtl. L. 431, 466–67 (2002).

218 FAO, *The State of Food Insecurity in the World 2001*, Rome, 2002.

219 FAO, *Report of the Expert Consultation on International Fish Trade and Food Security* 65 (Casablanca, Morocco, January 27–30, 2003).

220 George Kent, Freedom from Want: The Human Right to Adequate Food 200 (Georgetown University Press, 2005).

221 Dr. V. P. Raghavan, *Food Security Concern for India under WTO Regime: An Analysis*, in WTO, India, and Emerging Areas of Trade: Challenges and Strategies 95, 96 (P. Rameshan ed., Excel Books, 2008).

The concept of national sovereignty in the food security field is also very aligned with the principles and objectives of sustainable development. If a country is able to produce internally what it needs to satisfy the subsistence rights of its population, it also means less use of transportation to transfer goods from one country to another and less impact and consequences for the environment and climate change.

Unfortunately, we do not live in a perfect world, but rather in one with incredible disharmonies and conflicting interests in which the lack of truly enlightened *global governance* means that most actions have not been based on global justice and sustainable development. Many sovereign States are not able to produce independently what they need or, even when they could, are not able to fully exercise their own decisions. Free trade, liberalism, and neoliberal economic reforms have certainly improved the situation in many developing countries, reducing poverty and increasing wealth for quite some time and for a growing part of the population. However, too much room has been given merely to "economics," and the lack of robust laws and regulations to balance economic analysis and objectives with sustainable development[222] has left the global governance, and indirectly the decision-making process, in the hands of a handful of multinational companies or, even worse, groups that exercise control beyond the borders, operating without any transparent legal identity.

Most multinational corporations are not interested in sovereignty, national security, and food security issues other than to protect and profit from their business investments. Actually, they benefit from the fragmentation of international law,[223] and they operate more easily in countries where the rules are less stringent, generally in developing countries.[224] The limited presence of laws and regulations eases the environment for corporations because they can operate more freely. Multinational corporations are generally profit-driven and may implement their objectives more thoroughly when deep liberalism is adopted, which gives individuals and private initiatives wide latitude as opposed to the invasive involvement of the State. However, it is now clear that strong liberalist principles do not create a fairer world on their own, but they risk facilitating a world ruled by unelected, authoritarian and profit-driven (opposed to human development oriented) organizations such as some (not all) multinationals. They do what they are supposed to do to make a profit and otherwise benefit their shareholders. It is not formally and institutionally their role to auto-regulate their actions if they are not requested to do so or if the rules of the game do not directly

222 Regarding the risks posed by neoliberalism for food security and sustainable development, *see* Carmen G. Gonzalez, *Trade Liberalization, Food Security and the Environment: The Neoliberal Threat to Sustainable Rural Development*, 14 Transnational Law & Contemporary Problems 419, 465–69 (2004).

223 On the fragmentation of international law, *see* Patrick Daillier & Alain Pellet, Droit International Public 642–728 (7th, L.G.D.J, 2002); Mireille Delmas-Marty, Les Forces Imaginantes Du Droit (II). Le Pluralisme Ordonné 7–8 (Seuil, 2006): "Ce qui domine le paysage, loin de l'ordre juridique au sens traditionnel, c'est le grand désordre d'un monde tout à la fois fragmenté à l'excès, comme disloqué par une mondialisation anarchique, et trop unifié, voire uniformisé par l'integration hégemonique qui se realise simultanéament dans le silente du marché et le fracas des armes". *See*, also, Francis Snyder, *Governing Economic Globalisation: Global Legal Pluralism and European Law*, 5(4) Eur. L. J. 334–35 (1999).

224 Laurence Boy, *Le Décifit Démocratique de la Mondialisation du Droit Économique et le Rôle de la Société Civile*, 3(4) Revue Internationale de Droit Économique 479–82 (2003); Civil Society, International Courts and Compliance Bodies (Tullio Treves et al. eds, T.M.C. Asser Press, 2005).

(laws and regulations) or indirectly (corporate social responsibility – CSR and accountability for the good public imagine of the company) impose to act accordingly.[225]

Moreover, the view that liberalism has enabled many countries to reduce poverty is correct, but at the same time and to a certain extent, it is an assumption because what has to be examined is at what costs, in the long term, has this wealth been achieved. The negative production externalities of industrialization are enormous; the externalities of the excesses of globalization, free trade and neoliberal thoughts are even more dramatic, in terms of loss of quality of life, water and air pollution, climate change, environmental risks and natural disasters, health problems, and new diseases connected to industrialization without control and rules.

This long excursus is essential to highlight the pivotal role that food security[226] and food safety may have in the paradigm shift which is envisageable from an import-export-oriented model to the need to reestablish more locally oriented production. This change would allow communities to reappropriate control of local production including cultural components and choice of domestic production and consumption. At the same time, this more local community criterion is already being adopted from the bottom, within a growing number of societies, through civil society involvement in creating new and innovative ways for product commercialization like exchanges that allow communities to trade without the use of common currency (with the use of alternative currency) or similar other methods or metrics to measure progress.

In the author's opinion, achieving food security by establishing local independence has become increasingly urgent considering the current economic crisis, the systemic problems created by the exacerbated import-export model and a debit and credit system that is not sustainable and has brought our society down a dead-end street of defaults, unemployment, and social unrest, as seen in the recent examples of Argentina and Greece and as the incredible financial turmoil underway in China may indicate.

To try to solve or find constructive solutions to some of the problems discussed above, in the context of the Doha Development Agenda (DDA), the European Union promoted the establishment of a "Food Security Box" to enhance the trading capacities of developing countries. Among the different objectives was a proposal to include special provisions to support the agriculture sector.[227] It has been proposed that any future WTO agreement must grant the right to any other WTO Member State to produce domestically a certain

225 Patrizio Merciai, Les Entreprises Multinationales en Droit International 37 (Bruylant, 1993); Francesco Francioni, Imprese Multinazionali, Protezione Diplomatica e Responsabilità Internazionale 13 (Giuffrè, Milano, 1979); Alberto Santa Maria, Diritto Commerciale Comunitario 245 ff. (Giuffrè, 2008); Angelica Bonfanti, *Le Imprese Multinazionali tra Responsabilità e Accountability nel Diritto Internazionale* (Doctoral thesis, Università di Milano, 2007); Pia Acconci, *Responsabilità Sociale d'Impresa, Imprese Multinazionali e Diritto Internazionale*, in Emilio d'Orazio, La Responsabilità Sociale d'impresa: Teorie, Strumenti, Casi, Politeia, XIX, 72, 71–80 (Notizie di Politeia, 2003); Stefano Zamagni, *L'Impresa Socialmente Responsabile nell'Epoca della Globalizzazione*, in Emilio d'Orazio, at 28–42.

226 Matias E. Margulis, *The World Trade Organisation and Food Security After the Global Food Crises*, in Linking Global Trade and Human Rights: New Policy Space in Hard Economic Times 236, 249 (Daniel Drache & Lesley A. Jacobs eds, Cambridge University Press, 2014).

227 Michael John Westlake, *Addressing Marketing and Processing Constraints that Inhibit Agrifood Exports A Guide For Policy Analysts And Planners* 12 (FAO Agricultural Services Bulletin 160, 2005), http://www.fao.org/ag/ags/ags-division/publications/publication/en/c/38656/ (last visited August 6, 2016).

percentage of agricultural production to feed the population and with a minimum measure, in terms of calories consumed or some other objective measure without any possibility for other countries to forbid these practices.[228] This measure would be particularly important for developed countries to counterbalance the potential strong negative effects of tariff reductions on their agricultural sector.

When it comes to evaluating WTO case law involving food security issues, one must immediately look at the *Hormones* case[229] in which the European Union imposed a ban on the domestic sale and import of meat or meat products from cattle that were treated with six kinds of natural or synthetic hormones for the purpose of growth promotion. The United States and Canada challenged the measure on the basis of the Agreement on Sanitary and Phytosanitary Measures (SPS),[230] while the European Union justified it on the basis of the precautionary principle.[231] The AB upheld the Panel's finding that the EU import prohibition was inconsistent with Articles 3.3 and 5.1 of the SPS Agreement, but rejected the Panel's interpretation, stating that the requirement that SPS measures be "based on" international standards, guidelines or recommendations under Article 3.1 is not equivalent to requiring that SPS measures must "conform to" such standards. In particular, under Article 3.3 of the SPS Agreement, "Members may introduce or maintain sanitary or phytosanitary measures which result in a higher level of sanitary or phytosanitary protection than would be achieved by measures based on the relevant international standards, guidelines or recommendations, if there is a scientific justification, or as a consequence of the level of sanitary or phytosanitary protection a Member determines to be appropriate in accordance with the relevant provisions of paragraphs 1 through 8 of Article 5." According to Article 5.1: "Members shall ensure that their sanitary or phytosanitary measures are based on an assessment, as appropriate to the circumstances, of the risks to human, animal or plant life or health, taking into account risk assessment techniques developed by the relevant international organizations." Both the Panel and the AB stated that the EU measures did not comply with the WTO agreements because the EU measures were not based on a risk assessment as required under Articles 5.1 and 5.2 of the SPS Agreement in order to prove its claims;[232] however, the AB reversed the Panel's finding where it stated that Article 5.1 requires that there should be a "rational relationship" between the measure at issue and the risk assessment.[233]

228 Simpson & Schoenbaum, *supra* note 20, at 406–08.

229 Report of the Panel, *EC Measures Concerning Meat and Meat Products (Hormones) Complaint by the United States*, WT/DS26/R/USA (August 18, 1997) and Appellate Body Report, *EC Measures Concerning Meat and Meat Products (Hormones)*, WT/DS26/AB/R, WT/DS48/AB/R (January 16, 1998).

230 Understanding the WTO Agreement on Sanitary and Phytosanitary Measures, https://www.wto.org/english/tratop_e/sps_e/spsund_e.htm.

231 This principle means that precautionary action must be taken before scientific certainty of cause and effect is established. *See* Lucy Emerton et al., *Economics, the Precautionary Principle and Natural Resource Management: Key Issues, Tools and Practices*, in Biodiversity and the Precautionary Principle: Risk, Uncertainty and Practice in Conservation and Sustainable Use 253, 254 (Rosie Cooney & Barney Dickson eds, Routledge, 2005).

232 Veena Jha, *Environmetal and Health Regulations*, in Environmental Regulation and Food Safety: Studies of Protection and Protectionism 14, 19 (Veena Jha ed., Edward Elgar, 2006).

233 Mitsuo Matsushita, *WTO Dispute Cases Relating to Food Safety Issues*, in Trade Disputes and the Dispute Settlement Understanding of the WTO: An Interdisciplinary Assessment 283, 288 (James C. Hartigan, Hamid Beladi & Kwan Choi eds, Emerald Group Publishing Limited, 2009).

It is relevant to note that the AB had also reversed the Panel's finding that the EU import prohibition was inconsistent with Articles 3.1 and 5.5 of the SPS Agreement because, as stated by the AB, the EU measure did not apply arbitrary or unjustifiable treatments and differences in protection levels in respect of added hormones in treated meat and naturally occurring hormones in food.[234] In fact, the AB found that the European Union demonstrated enough evidence that there were genuine anxieties concerning the safety of those added hormones in treated meat instead of the naturally occurring hormones in food;[235] the necessity for harmonizing the internal regulations of its Member States was part of the effort and mandate to establish a common internal market for beef;[236] and the Panel's finding was not supported by the "architecture and structure" of the measures to consider them in violation of the WTO. Furthermore, the AB clarified that the SPS Agreement does not allocate the "evidentiary burden" on the WTO Member State imposing the SPS measure.

The AB's reversals of the Panel's finding and its related reasoning clearly demonstrate to WTO Member States how to design their policies in a way that is justifiable under the provisions of the SPS Agreement.

Following the AB ruling in 1998, the EU Commission funded 17 scientific studies concerning the impact that hormone residues in meat have on human health.[237] In this dispute, the GATT and the WTO were unable to achieve compliance since the European Union maintained the ban,[238] but the ruling discouraged other WTO Members from banning the hormones in question.[239]

Another relevant case for our analysis is *Japan – Measures Affecting Agricultural Products.*[240] In this case, both the WTO Panel and AB found the Japanese government's requirement to test and confirm the efficacy of a particular quarantine treatment for each variety of eight agriculture products coming from the US to be inconsistent with the SPS Agreement.[241] The United States challenged the Japanese restrictions on imports of apples, cherries, peaches (including nectarines), walnuts, apricots, pears, plums, and quince in order to prevent the infestation of Japanese orchards with the parasitic codling moth, an insect that can damage fruits.[242] In such a case, the Member State must be able to show a "rational or objective relationship" between the SPS measure and the scientific evidence,[243] which was unsuccessful

234 Appellate Body Report, *EC Measures Concerning Meat and Meat Products (Hormones)*, *supra* note 229, at Paragraphs 219–226.

235 *Id.*

236 *Id.*, at Paragraphs 245–46.

237 Bernard Hoekman & Joel Trachtman, *Continued Suspense: EC-Hormones and WTO Disciplines on Descrimination and Domestic Regulation*, in The WTO Case Law of 2008, 151, 157 (Henrik Horn & Petros C. Mavroidis eds, Cambridge University Press, 2010).

238 For further information please see Proceedings under Article 22 of the DSU (remedies), https://www.wto.org/english/tratop_e/dispu_e/cases_e/ds26_e.htm.

239 Charan Devereaux, Robert Z. Lawrence & Michael D. Watkins, Case Studies in US Trade Negotiation, Volume 2: Resolving Disputes 31, 83 (Institute for International Economics, 2006).

240 Report of the Panel, *Japan – Measures Affecting Agricultural Products*, WT/DS76/R (October 27, 1998); Appellate Body Report, *Japan – Measures Affecting Agricultural Products*, WT/DS76/AB/R (February 22, 1999).

241 Catherine Button, The Power to Protect: Trade, Health and Uncertainty in the WTO 5 (Hart Publishing, 2004).

242 Schefer, *supra* note 99, at 199.

243 Appellate Body Report, *Japan – Measures Affecting Agricultural Products*, *supra* note 240, at Paragraphs 79–85.

and thus the measures had to be eliminated.[244] The AB upheld the Panel's finding under Article 5.7 according to the fact that a measure may be provisionally adopted in respect of a situation where relevant scientific information is insufficient and on the basis of available pertinent information, and may be maintained unless the Member which adopted the measure "seek[s] to obtain the additional information necessary for a more objective assessment of risk" and "review[s] the [. . .] measure accordingly within a reasonable period of time."[245]

The *EC – Approval and Marketing of Biotech Products*[246] dispute concerns two distinct matters: (1) the operation and application by the European Union (formerly EC – European Communities) of its regime for the approval of biotech products, and (2) certain measures adopted and maintained by EU Member States prohibiting or restricting the marketing of biotech products. "Biotech products" in this dispute refers to plant cultivars that have been developed through recombinant deoxyribonucleic acid (recombinant DNA) technology. The European Union adopted a regime to control the release into the environment of genetically modified organisms and to conduct a case-by-case evaluation of the potential risks biotech products may have, with the objective of protecting human health and the environment. On the basis of that evaluation, the marketing of a particular biotech product is either approved or not, and individual EU Member States may provisionally restrict or prohibit the use and commercialization of these products. The WTO Panel did not consider the EU's general moratorium to be a valid SPS measure, because the European Union did not adopt a transparent risk-assessment procedure and, instead, consisted only in a procedural decision to delay the final substantive approval decision in breach of SPS Annex C(1)(a) and Article 8. Furthermore, besides the undue delay, the safeguard measures should have been adopted only in case sufficient evidence to conduct a risk assessment was not a viable option, which was not actually proved and therefore violated the provisions of Article 2.2.

The abovementioned disputes highlight a lack of WTO cases concerning food security matters other than health concerns, and therefore Member States may be willing to challenge unjustifiable, discriminatory, or disguised food security practices, other than those related to health, allowing the dispute settlement body to contribute through its case law to the ongoing debate concerning global food security governance via the WTO.

As stated in the above analysis, food security constitutes a national security concern in many developing countries such as China.[247] For instance, prior to China's accession to the WTO, the Member States raised questions about the impact of WTO accession on China's long-term food security as well as the implications on its agricultural policy and agricultural sector.[248] The general view is that the Chinese government has adopted new laws and

244 *Id.*, at Paragraphs 86 – 91. Epps, *supra* note 124, at 233.

245 Terry Marsden et al., The New Regulation and Governance of Food: Beyond the Food Crisis? 250 (Routledge, 2012).

246 Report of the Panel, *European Communities – Measures Affecting the Approval and Marketing of Biotech Products*, WT/DS291/R (September 29, 2006).

247 Baris Karapinar, *"Sustainability" in Chinese Agriculture: Stakeholders' Perceptions and Policy Trade-offs* 10 (NCCR Trade Regulation, Swiss National Center of Competence in Research, Working Paper No 2009/43). *See* Chapter 20 (Simpson) in this volume.

248 Fen Lu, *China's WTO Accession: The Impact on its Agriculture Sector and Grain Policy*, in Agriculture and Food Security in China: What Effect WTO Accession and Regional Trade Arrangements? 55, 69 (Chunlai Chen & Ron Duncan eds, ANU E Press and Asia Pacific Press, 2010). *See*, also, Chunlai

regulations in the agricultural sector to comply with its WTO requirements, but at the same time it has also adopted policies to control the immediate or long-term negative effects that those liberalization measures would have produced against the interests of the Chinese farmers and of the population in general. In particular, the Chinese government tried to move towards policies which favored the modernization of the agricultural sector to be able to face globalization and world competition.[249]

As already pointed out, food security is certainly closely linked to the right to food.[250] China is not so willing to publicly discuss its human rights records, and it is of particular interest to note China's general behavior towards UN Special Rapporteurs, which is far from supportive, as it has shown reluctance to accept their pending requests to visit.[251] The Special Rapporteurs' roles are quite important both for raising relevant questions but also for conducting fact-finding processes in target countries through their missions and country visits. However, China decided to invite the UN Special Rapporteur on the right to food, Olivier De Schutter, to visit China from December 15 to 23, 2010.[252] China considers the human right to adequate food (and, to some extent, also the other trade-related human rights to water and sanitation) a less political and sensitive topic on which the government has established a growing set of policies and the political will to improve the internal context in favor of the Chinese population. The UN Special Rapporteur on the right to food had indeed recognized China's advances on food availability and in the programs to reach self-sufficiency in basic food supply and challenges in ensuring the sustainability of agricultural production. He also examined the remaining challenges affecting access to adequate food, in particular among poor rural and urban households, including increasing land degradation, pollution and climate change.

All these matters cannot avoid, of course, raising the need for scrutiny and monitoring of the general context of the Chinese legal and political framework which may affect the right to adequate food. For these reasons, the list of recommendations to the Chinese government included in the Final Report of the UN Special Rapporteur on the right to food, following his mission and country visit, in regards to the support of small agricultural producers, includes the need to:

Chen & Ron Duncan, *Achieving Food Security in China: Implications of WTO Accession*, in Agriculture and Food Security in China: What Effect WTO Accession and Regional Trade Arrangements? 55, 69 (Chunlai Chen & Ron Duncan eds, ANU E Press and Asia Pacific Press, 2010); Jikun Huang & Scott Rozelle, *Agricultural Development and Policy Before and After China's WTO Accession*, in Agriculture and Food Security in China: What Effect WTO Accession and Regional Trade Arrangements? 55, 69.

249 Huang & Rozelle, *supra* note 248, at 69.

250 *See* Chapters 18 (Zorzi Giustiniani) and 19 (Ning) in this volume.

251 Katrin Kinzelbach, The EU's Human Rights Dialogue With China: Quiet Diplomacy And Its Limits 190 (Routledge Research in Human Rights, 2015).

252 Olivier De Schutter, *Mandate of the Special Rapporteur of the Right to Food, Preliminary Observations and Conclusions, Mission to the People's Republic of China from 15 to 23 December 2010*, Beijing, China, 23 December 2010, http://www.srfood.org/images/stories/pdf/officialreports/de-schutter-china-statement.pdf (last visited August 6, 2016); Olivier De Schutter, *Report of the Special Rapporteur on the Right to Food, Addendum*, Mission to China, Human Rights Council, 19th Session, Agenda Item 3, A/HRC/19/59/Add.1, 20 January 2012, http://www.srfood.org/images/stories/pdf/officialreports/20120306_china_en.pdf (last visited August 6, 2016).

> *[i]mprove transparency* and *limit the risks of corruption of local officials* in land deals, thus ensuring effective compliance with the 2007 Property Law, for example by creating a system whereby the buyers authorized to develop land would pay the compensation due into a trust fund, which in turn would compensate the land-losing farmer, ***without the amount transiting through the local public officials.***[253]

Another recommendation in favor of small agricultural producers included in Paragraph 41 suggests that the Chinese government "[b]etter circumscribe the possibility for the collective to impose readjustments, as well as the possibility for the State to evict land users in the public interest, including by allowing courts to apply much stricter scrutiny to the authorities' reliance on these exceptions to the security of tenure of the land user."[254] Both recommendations perfectly align with the amendments to the Chinese Constitution adopted in 2004 that were described in the previous section, i.e. the added third paragraph of Article 33 for the respect and preservation of human rights,[255] the second paragraph of Article 11 ("Citizens' lawful private property is inviolable"),[256] and the obligation to compensate in case of expropriation or requisition.[257] It is necessary to stress that land as real property is treated differently than other properties. According to Article 10 of the Chinese Constitution:

> [l]and in the cities is owned by the State. Land in the rural and suburban areas is owned by collectives except for those portions which belong to the State in accordance with the law; house sites and private plots of cropland and hilly land are also owned by collectives. The State may in the public interest take over land for its use in accordance with the law. No organization or individual may appropriate, buy, sell or lease land, or unlawfully transfer land in other ways. All organizations and individuals who use land must make rational use of the land.[258]

Although individuals cannot privately own land, they may obtain transferable land-use rights for a number of years for a fee. In this sense, the UN Special Rapporteur recommended to "[e]nsure a greater security of land use rights, including by automatically extending such rights beyond the current 30-year term, unless no member of the household to whom the land has been contracted still lives on the land."[259]

The agricultural sector and the connected land ownership and rights are of course very sensitive issues from a political, cultural, and historical point of view. Nevertheless, in his report, the UN Special Rapporteur stressed that the special legal and political treatment of

253 De Schutter, *supra* note 252, at Paragraph 41, Letter b, Page 17.
254 *Id.*, Paragraph 41, Letter c, Page 17.
255 Article 33 of the Constitution of the People's Republic of China (PRC), adopted on December 4, 1982 and amended by the 10th NPC at its 2nd Session on March 14, 2004.
256 Article 13 of the Constitution of the People's Republic of China (PRC), adopted on December 4, 1982 and amended by the 10th NPC at its 2nd Session on March 14, 2004.
257 *Id.*
258 Article 10 of the Constitution of the People's Republic of China (PRC), adopted on December 4, 1982 and amended by the 10th NPC at its 2nd Session on March 14, 2004.
259 De Schutter, *supra* note 252, at Paragraph 41, Letter a, Page 17.

the land and connected land rights in China are substantially affecting the right to adequate food. He also suggested specific options and solutions to the Chinese government like "allowing courts to apply much stricter scrutiny to the authorities' reliance on these exceptions to the security of tenure of the land user."[260] Then it is left to China to find appropriate solutions ("Better circumscribe the possibility for the collective to impose readjustments, as well as the possibility for the State to evict land users in the public interest")[261] that are compatible with the specific cultural and historical context to protect the right to adequate food, following the recommendations.

In Paragraph 43, letter d, the UN Special Rapporteur on the right to food also referred to social security as a human right. There he suggested to the Chinese government to "[d]efine the right to social security as a human right, which beneficiaries may claim before courts or administrative tribunals, and inform beneficiaries about their rights, which is essential to ensuring respect for the right to social security and reducing the risks of corruption or favoritism at the local level."[262]

Again, this recommendation aligned with the 2004 Amendment to the Chinese Constitution which added a fourth paragraph to Article 14: "The State establishes a sound social security system compatible with the level of economic development." Of course, assuming that the Chinese government follows the recommendation and implements a law establishing social security as a human right compatible with the "level of economic development," it is unknown whether the measure will be considered sufficient by the UN or other international standards.

As this short analysis shows, the issue of food security and the related human right to food implies many more legal and political reforms that go beyond issues strictly related to food security and safety. These topics raise issues of transparency, independence, administrative, procedural and judicial fairness, access to knowledge and information, property and land rights that are all critical for the real and full achievement of food security and safety, and the right to food in the territory of the PRC.

5 *Restriction of trade openness on cultural products on the basis of public morals*

The concept of public morals includes a wide range of cultural, social, and ethical values.[263] It is clear that morals, ethics, beliefs, ideals, and dogmas may vary depending on the different communities and the national or regional context.

As a matter of fact, WTO rules impact culture in many different ways, and it is not possible to create a universal, commonsense instrument to handle all the aspects related to public morals.[264] So, through case law, the WTO must try to find a balance between free trade and

260 *Id.*

261 *Id.*, Paragraph 41, Letter c, Page 17.

262 *Id.*, Paragraph 43, Letter d, Page 18.

263 MATTHIAS HERDEGEN, PRINCIPLES OF INTERNATIONAL ECONOMIC LAW 206 (Oxford University Press, 2013).

264 Nicola Wenzel, *Article XX lit.a GATT*, in WTO: TECHNICAL BARRIERS AND SPS MEASURES 2, 82 (Rüdiger Wolfrum, Peter-Tobias Stoll & Anja Seibert-Fohr eds, Brill, 2007).

relevant national or regional characteristics like public morals and public order, forbidding any means of arbitrary and unjustifiable discrimination among domestic and imported products. ***Cultural products*** are the tangible or intangible creations from a specific culture or societal practice,[265] like audiovisual products (film, video, television radio, etc.) and printed publications (magazines, books, periodicals, etc.). The failure of the United States and the European Union to agree on the definition of cultural products by the end of the Uruguay Round resulted in the establishment of WTO rules that contain little explicit guidance on how WTO law applies to cultural products.[266]

Article XX(a) of the GATT states that "[. . .] nothing in this Agreement shall be construed to prevent the adoption or enforcement by any contracting party of measures [. . .] necessary to protect public morals" which is also included in Article XIV GATS,[267] together with the reference to the maintenance of public order.[268]

In the *US – Gambling* case,[269] Antigua and Barbuda (hereinafter also "Antigua") requested consultations regarding measures applied by central, regional, and local authorities in the United States that affected the cross-border supply of gambling and betting services. According to Antigua, those US Federal and State measures, including federal laws such as the Wire Act, the Travel Act, and the Illegal Gambling Business Act (IGBA), whose cumulative impact resulted in making unlawful the supply of gambling and betting services on a cross-border basis, had dramatically affected Antigua's market and economy. Following implementation of the US measures, the Antiguan market registered a tremendous loss of 24 billion USD in one year (and corresponding loss of GDP) and a loss of employment caused by the rapid reduction from 119 gambling companies registered in Antigua down to 28 companies.

In this case, the Panel considered the term "public morals" to denote standards of right and wrong conduct maintained by or on behalf of a community or nation. The dictionary (*Shorter Oxford English Dictionary, 2002*) definition of the word "order" that appears to be relevant in the context of Article XIV(a) reads as follows: "A condition in which the laws regulating the public conduct of members of a community are maintained and observed; the rule of law or constituted authority; absence of violence or violent crimes."[270]

The drafters of the GATS clarified in footnote 5 that "[t]he public order exception may be invoked only where a genuine and sufficiently serious threat is posed to one of the

265 Farah & Tremolada, *supra* note 173, 21–47.

266 Tania Voon, *Culture, Human Rights and the WTO*, in The Cultural Dimension of Human Rights 186, 187 (Ana Vrdoljak ed., Oxford University Press, 2014); David J. Bederman, Globalization and International Law 126–27 (Palgrave Macmillan, 2008).

267 Services: GATS The General Agreement on Trade in Services (GATS): Objectives, Coverage and Disciplines, https://www.wto.org/english/tratop_e/serv_e/gatsqa_e.htm.

268 Uruguay Round Agreement General Agreement on Trade in Services, Article XIV, https://www.wto.org/english/docs_e/legal_e/26-gats_01_e.htm. *See*, also, Rolf H. Weber & Mira Burri, Classification of Services in the Digital Economy 125, 131 (Springer, 2012).

269 Report of the Panel, *United States – Measures Affecting the Cross-Border Supply of Gambling and Betting Services*, WT/DS285/R, (November 10, 2004) and Appellate Body Report, *United States – Measures Affecting the Cross-Border Supply of Gambling and Betting Services*, WT/DS285/AB/R, (April 7, 2005).

270 Report of the Panel, *United States – Measures Affecting the Cross-Border Supply of Gambling and Betting Services*, *supra* note 269, at Paragraphs 6.465–6.467, Page 238. *See*, also, Mirina Grosz, Sustainable Waste Trade under WTO Law 440 (Brill, 2011).

fundamental interests of society." Hence, in the author's view, the dictionary definition of the word "order," read together with footnote 5, suggests that "public order" refers to the preservation of the fundamental interests of a society, as reflected in public policy and law. These fundamental interests can relate, *inter alia*, to standards of law, security and morality.[271]

The Antiguan Government declared that it has taken steps since the mid-1990s to build up a primarily Internet-based, "remote-access" gaming industry as part of its economic development strategy. Additionally, it has established a very solid set of laws and regulations to avoid foreign or domestic companies using this flourishing industry to hide other illicit objectives, such as money laundering or any other forms of financial or organized crime.

In fact, the United States stated that the close enforcement cooperation between federal and state authorities with an overreaching set of laws and regulations was essential to taking action against criminal organizations that use interstate commerce and interstate communications with impunity in the conduct of their unlawful activities. As such, the US legislation was mainly concerned with effectively curtailing gambling operations because the profits from illegal gambling are huge and they are the primary source of the funds which finance organized crime.[272]

Moreover, Antigua listed a vast array of gambling and betting games and services which are offered on a commercial basis in the United States (and elsewhere) and which had clearly showed that the United States was also strongly exploiting the market opportunities that this sector may provide to the domestic economy in terms of employment and taxes that US federal and state authorities could collect. For these reasons, Antigua considered unacceptable or unjustifiable similar statements like the ones that the United States reported at the DSB meeting of June 24, 2003 that cross-border gambling and betting services are prohibited because of "the social, psychological dangers and law enforcement problems that they created, particularly with respect to Internet gambling and betting."[273] The United States also expressed its "grave concerns over the financial and social risks posed by such activities to its citizens, particularly but not exclusively children."[274] In the opinion of Antigua, those arguments had to be rejected, considering that these concerns should have been applied by the US authorities against their domestic market as well and not only foreign providers.

The AB decided that the US GATS Schedule included specific commitments on gambling and betting services and that the entry of "other recreational services (except sporting)" in the US Schedule must be interpreted as including "gambling and betting services" within its scope. Reversing the decision of the Panel, the AB also found that:

> the United States has demonstrated that the Wire Act, the Travel Act, and the Illegal Gambling Business Act are measures *necessary to protect public morals or maintain public order*, in accordance with paragraph (a) of Article XIV, but that the United States has

271 *Id.*

272 *Id.*, Paragraph 3.262, Page 102.

273 *Id.*, Paragraph 3.253, Page 99. *See*, also, the Minutes of the DSB meeting, June 24, 2003, WT/DSB/M/151, Paragraph 47.

274 Chrisitine Kaufmann & Rolf H. Weber, *Reconcilaing Liberlized Trade in Financial Services and Domestic Regulation*, in The World Trade Organization and Trade in Services 411, 418 (Kern Alexander & Mads Tønnesson Andenæs eds, Martinus Nijhoff, 2008).

> not shown, in the light of the Interstate Horseracing Act, that the prohibitions embodied in those measures are applied to both foreign and domestic service suppliers of remote betting services for horse racing and, therefore, has not established that these measures satisfy the requirements of the chapeau [of Article XIV].[275]

Even though the final decision went partially against the United States, it is relevant to stress its application to the Wire Act, the Travel Act, and the Illegal Gambling Business Act of the exception under Article XIV(a) to protect public morals and to maintain public order.

The public morals exceptions under Article XX(a) and its relation to cultural products was considered in the *China – Publications and Audiovisual Products* case,[276] in which the United States challenged several Chinese measures that limited the number of entities having the right to import and distribute reading materials, audiovisual home entertainment products, sound recordings, and film for theatrical release. All these products may qualify as "cultural goods and services" under the legal definition contained in the UNESCO Convention.[277]

China claimed that these measures and mechanisms for selecting those private and business entities were essential for avoiding the importation into China of reading materials and finished audiovisual products with inappropriate content. This Chinese provision was a necessary means to protect public morals within the country, according to the meaning of Article XX(a) of the GATT.[278] The United States claimed that the Chinese laws and regulations provided preferential treatment to Chinese-sourced products over foreign publications and entertainment products in addition to the fact that the Chinese regulations restricted market access to foreign material in contrast with trade commitments included in its Accession Protocol, the GATS, and the GATT.[279] In this case, the Panel decided in favor of the United States, but left the door open to consider cultural concerns as it interpreted broadly the public moral exception under Article XX(a) GATT.

The *US – Gambling*, *China – Publications and Audiovisual Products*, and the *EU – Seals* decisions constitute important and relevant landmarks concerning the possible clash between

275 Appellate Body Report, *United States – Measures Affecting the Cross-Border Supply of Gambling and Betting Services, supra* note 269, at Paragraph 173, Page 126. *See*, also, Schefer, *supra* note 99, at 238. Berta Esperanza Hernández-Truyol & Stephen Joseph Powell, Just Trade: A New Covenant Linking Trade and Human Rights 147 (NYU Press, 2012).

276 Report of the Panel and Appellate Body Report, *China – Measures Affecting Trading Rights and Distribution Services for Certain Publications and Audiovisual Entertainment Products, supra* note 161.

277 William J. Davey, Non-discrimination in the World Trade Organization: The Rules and Exceptions 258 (Martinus Nijhoff, 2012). *See* Chapters 22 (Germann), 23 (Creemers), 24 (Kamperman Sanders), and 25 (Friedmann) in this volume.

278 Angelica Bonfanti, *Public Morals in International Trade: WTO Faces Censorship*, in International Courts and the Development of International Law: Essays in Honour of Tullio Treves 687, 695 (Nerina Boschiero, Tullio Scovazzi, Cesare Pitea & Chiara Ragni eds, T.M.C. Asser Press, 2013). *See*, also, Julia Qin, *Pushing the Limit of Global Governance*, 10 Chinese J. Int'l L. 271–322 (2011).

279 Bryan Mercurio & Mitali Tyagi, *China's Evolving Role in WTO Dispute Settlment: Acceptance, Consolidation and Activation*, in European Yearbook of International Economic Law 2012, 89, 104 (Christoph Herrmann & Jörg Philipp Terhechte eds, Springer, 2011); Mira Burri, *The Trade Versus Cultural Discourse: Tracing Its Evolution in Global Law*, in Culture and International Economic Law 104, 115 (Valentina Vadi & Bruno de Witte eds, Routledge, 2015); Frieder Roessler, *Comment: Appellate Body Ruling in China-Publications and Audiovisual Products*, in The WTO Case Law of 2009: Legal and Economic Analysis 119, 119 (Henrik Horn & Petros C. Mavroidis eds, Cambridge University Press, 2011).

trade expansion and the protection of public morals in the WTO case law.[280] Through these cases, the dispute settlement jurisprudence confirmed that WTO Member States have the right to determine the level of protection that they consider appropriate, and as such States should receive "some scope to define and apply for themselves the concepts of public morals and public orders in their respective territories, according to their own systems and scales of values."[281]

6 *Conclusion*

Globalization has transformed and shaped the contemporary world, which is increasingly interconnected without borders. Globalization is the result of a combination of factors, which include the role of technology, the improvement of telecommunications such as the Internet, and advances in transport for the movement of goods and services.

But globalization is not only limited to trade in goods, and society has to face challenges and risks such as environmental crises, energy security, terrorism, and the role of multinational companies in the production chain and the effects on society.

The idea of limiting the excesses of globalization may be, to a certain extent, justified. There is an increasing need to establish innovative instruments, new forms of global governance, and democratic control to limit the risk that important societal values, which should be upheld to balance the excesses of globalization, are directly or indirectly affected by the global expansion of world trade. Globalization without local concerns can endanger relevant issues such as good governance, human rights, right to water, right to food, social, economic and cultural rights, labor rights, access to knowledge, public health, social welfare, consumer interests and animal welfare, climate change, energy, environmental protection and sustainable development, product safety, food safety, and security.

This chapter explored the legal reasoning and clarifications of the Panels and the AB (including the use of dissenting opinions among the Panelists) following the passage from GATT to the WTO. Even when the final decisions were not in favor of the specific measures at issue (which were therefore not justified under Article XX of the GATT), the adjudicatory bodies were increasingly willing to carefully consider the environment, sustainable development, and other NTCs.

Furthermore, in the author's opinion, the WTO has indirectly contributed to some of the Chinese legal reforms, even outside the areas of WTO and international trade law. These reforms aim to better protect the rights of Chinese workers and citizens as a whole and balance the negative effects that globalization and free trade would have had on the Chinese internal legal system.

The increase of WTO Plus Obligations for new WTO Member States and the potential limitation on the use of Article XX of the GATT is raising concerns. In particular, they might be considered new forms of unfair discrimination perpetuated by those who until now had the power against developing countries which are gradually entering the WTO.

280 Panagiotis Delimatsis, *The Puzzling Interaction of Trade and Public Morals in the Digital Era*, in TRADE GOVERNANCE IN THE DIGITAL AGE: WORLD TRADE FORUM 276, 277 (Mira Burri & Thomas Cottier eds, Cambridge University Press, 2012).

281 Report of the Panel, *United States – Measures Affecting the Cross-Border Supply of Gambling and Betting Services, supra* note 269, at Paragraph 6.461, Page 237. *See*, also, MIRINA GROSZ, WTO LAW, SUSTAINABLE WASTE TRADE UNDER WTO LAW 441 (Brill, 2011).

This is even less justifiable if it may impede the adoption of reasonable and non-discriminatory measures that have the sole objective of protecting the environment and facilitating sustainable development.

Therefore, these matters must be clarified either through supplementary WTO multilateral negotiations or the Panel or AB case law. China is having a leading role in these issues.

It is also expected that the WTO and other international economic organizations will have to find a balance between globalization, sustainable development and local concerns. The inclusion of more and more developing countries and emerging economies in the international economic system is making this necessity very urgent. It is also revealing the potential unfairness and inconsistencies in the system. What will be seen in the years to come is whether China, and other emerging economies, will represent a solution to find a balance between globalization and sustainable development or will become the means to rupture a system.

Keeping in mind the stepping stones of the WTO environmentally friendly case law, and the ongoing WTO negotiations, one can be positive of the need for the WTO to continue on the path towards sustainable development.

Part I

Public Policy, International Trade, and Foreign Direct Investment

The Role of States and Non-State Actors in Economic Globalization*

* This Book Part I "Public Policy, International Trade, and Foreign Direct Investment: The Role of States and Non-State Actors in Economic Globalization" is participated by researchers funded by the Marie Curie IRSES of the European Union's Seventh Framework Programme (FP7/2007–2013) under REA grant agreement n° 318908 Acronym of the Project: POREEN (2013–2016) entitled "Partnering Opportunities between Europe and China in the Renewable Energies and Environmental Industries", within the results coordinated by gLAWcal – Global Law Initiatives for Sustainable Development (United Kingdom).

3 Economic Globalization and Social Rights

The Role of the International Labor Organization and the WTO*

Claudio Di Turi

Introductory remarks

This chapter purports to make some remarks on a highly debated issue among public international law scholars: that is, the relevance of the fundamental principles and rights concerning labor in the context of the globalization[1] of the economy. I chose to approach the subject matter in the light of the practice of certain international organizations that appear competent *ratione materiae* – the International Labor Organization (ILO) – or whose aims and statutory objectives can eventually interfere with the enjoyment of human rights in the social field – the World Trade Organization (WTO).[2] While the practices of the ILO appear to be

* This chapter is part of the results of the Research Project on "*Current Trends of Chinese Law towards Non-Trade Concerns such as Sustainable Development and the Protection of Environment, Public Health, Food Safety, Cultural, Social and Economic Rights, Labor Rights and the Reduction of Poverty from the Perspective of International Law and WTO Law*" coordinated by Professor Paolo Davide Farah at gLAWcal – Global Law Initiatives for Sustainable Development (United Kingdom) and at West Virginia University John D. Rockefeller IV School of Policy and Politics, Department of Public Administration, in partnership with the Center of Advanced Studies on Contemporary China (CASCC) in Turin (Italy), Maastricht University Faculty of Law, Department of International and European Law and IGIR - Institute for Globalization and International Regulation (Netherlands) and Tsinghua University, School of Law, Institute of Public International Law and the Center for Research on Intellectual Property Law in Beijing (China). This publication and the Conference Series were sponsored by China–EU School of Law (CESL) at the China University of Political Science and Law (CUPL). The activities of CESL at CUPL are supported by the European Union and the P.R. of China.

1 The term "globalization" is usually understood as a complex economic phenomenon, in which it is possible to distinguish different components such as the increase in international commercial exchange, the application in the production sectors of information and computer technology, the intensification of international competition, the increase in number and strength of transnational business groupings and worldwide strategies, the planet-wide financing dominated by the necessity to maximise the yield of invested capital, and the phenomenon of volatility of the markets connected to them. *See* Economic Globalization and Human Rights (W. Benedek, K. De Feyter & F. Marrella eds, Cambridge University Press, 2007). For an ILO approach, *see* Globalizing Social Rights: The International Labour Organization and Beyond (S. Kott, J. Droux eds, Palgrave Macmillan, 2013). *See* also *Workers Rights in a Globalizing World: the Role of Labour Provisions in Free Trade Agreements*, ILO Conference, May 8, 2014, Toronto (Canada).

2 There are obviously also other international *fora* dealing with trade and human rights, such as United Nations and the High Commissioner for Human Rights: UNGA, *Globalization and its Full Impact on the Full Enjoyment of all Human Rights*, Doc. A/RES/64/160 (March 12, 2010); *Globalization and its Impact on the Full Enjoyment of Human Rights*, Doc. E/CN.4/2002/54 (January 13, 2002); *The Impact of the Agreement on Trade-related Aspects of Intellectual Property Rights on Human Rights*, Doc. E/CN.4/Sub2/2001/13 (June 27, 2001); *Human Rights, Trade and Investment*, Doc. E/CN.4/Sub.2/2003/9 (July 2, 2003); *Liberalization of Trade and Services and Human Rights*, Doc. E/CN.4/Sub2/2002/9 (June 25, 2002). *See* also the Report of the UN General Secretary, *Globalization and Interdependence:*

very sensitive towards the impact of globalization, since their actions aim towards the achievement of the goals set forth in the "Decent Work Agenda," on the other hand, within the WTO, the establishment of a link between human rights and trade has long been treated as a Non-Trade Concern.[3] Is this variance, which is certainly due to the different scope of respective activities of the aforementioned organizations, likely to undermine human rights in the social field? I will provide an answer to this question after examining some relevant aspects of both ILO and WTO recent law and practice.

Is globalization a threat to human rights in the social field?

The recognition of globalization's influence on the structure and conduct of international relations and the rules related thereto justifies the choice of setting the legal analysis of fundamental labor rights within the economic phenomenon – globalization. Globalization might as well have contributed to the so-called fragmentation of international law into distinct subsystems that "threaten its unity,"[4] and of which the legal order of the WTO could represent an example. This approach could bring the provisions and principles of human rights, and those concerning international trade, to a unity that allows the satisfaction of the objectives established in Article 28 of the Universal Declaration of Human Rights, according to which "everyone is entitled to a social [. . .] order in which the rights and freedoms set forth in this Declaration can be fully realized."[5] The main reason for this is that globalization constitutes one of the multiple aspects related to the creation of the "social order" mentioned thereto.[6]

In the context of globalization, several Western countries with advanced economies and numerous union associations, concerned about the growing commercial penetration of developing countries (DC) in their markets, blame the latter and the companies operating within their territories for tolerating and deliberately facilitating forms of unfair competition – the so-called race to the bottom. Such practice consists of the lowering of costs of production as a result of the lack of respect for international laws concerning social rights, which gives rise to the phenomenon of social dumping including the disadvantageous consequences on employment within their territories. Developing countries object that their high levels of productivity arise from their relative abundance of labor as a production factor. Therefore, the lower cost of goods in the international markets should not be seen as the result of a dumping measure since the economic law of "comparative advantages" justifies the price.[7]

Sustained, Inclusive and Equitable Economic Growth for a Fair and More Equitable Economic Growth for all, Including Job Creation, Doc.A/66/223 (August 1, 2011).

3 *See* in general, Lorand Bartels, *Trade and Human Rights,* in OXFORD HANDBOOK OF INTERNATIONAL TRADE LAW chapter XXI (D. Bethlehem et al. eds, Oxford University Press, 2009); Wolfgang Benedek, *The World Trade Organization and Human Rights,* in ECONOMIC GLOBALIZATION AND HUMAN RIGHTS 143 (W. Benedek et al. eds, Cambridge University Press, 2007); Susan Ariel Aaronson, *Sleeping in slowly: how human rights concerns are penetrating the WTO,* WORLD TRADE REV. 413 (2007); INTERNATIONAL TRADE AND HUMAN RIGHTS: FOUNDATIONS AND CONCEPTUAL ISSUES (Frederick Abbott, Christine Breining- Kaufmann & Thomas Cottier eds, University of Michigan Press, 2006); HUMAN RIGHTS AND INTERNATIONAL TRADE (Thomas Cottier, Joost Pauwelyn & Elisabeth Burgi eds, University of Michigan Press 2005).

4 International Law Commission, *Fragmentation of International Law: Difficulties Arising from the Diversification and Expansion of International Law,* Doc. A/CN.4/L.682 (April 13, 2006).

5 Universal Declaration of Human Rights, GA res. 217A (III), UN Doc A/810 at 71 (1948), Article 28.

6 *See* also Ernst-Ulrich Petersmann, *Human Rights and the Law of the World Trade Organization,* 37 (2) J. WORLD TRADE 241, 243 (2003).

7 For a presentation of those arguments, *see* PHILIP ALSTON, LABOUR RIGHTS AS HUMAN RIGHTS (Oxford University Press, 2005).

However, this heated debate mainly revolves around the issue of respective commitments to liberalism rather than on those of development and human rights protection. The High Commissioner for Human Rights, in a number of reports,[8] has repeatedly called for a "human rights approach to international trade,"[9] which establishes the promotion and the protection of human rights as part of the objectives of trade liberalization, and examines the effect of trade liberalization on individuals. Moreover, the human rights approach would seek coherence between trade rules and human dignity, promoting international cooperation for the fulfillment of human dignity in the context of trade liberalization. Is such an approach likely to preserve individual social rights? I think so, but since cooperation is required, it involves not only states but all subjects of international law with special regard to intergovernmental organizations. Among them, the ILO, as I will show below, is probably the best equipped to deal with globalization and human rights relations.

The "social dimension of international trade" and the role of the ILO

With the creation of the ILO, a United Nations (UN) specialized agency (Article 57 of the Charter), in 1919, the international community attempted to establish a "social dimension of international trade," in which trade could be reconciled with labor. The ILO's institutional apparatus is modeled on the principle of "tripartism," which means that the interests of member states, employers, and workers are granted on an equal footing.[10] As stated in its Constitution and in the Declaration of Philadelphia (1944) annexed to it, the ILO aims at the pursuit of "social justice;" however, the normative contents differ in the two legal instruments. In fact, while the preamble to the Constitution identifies social justice with better working conditions and indicates the areas falling into the ILO's field of competence, the prospective of the Declaration of Philadelphia reaches more widely. Article I*a* of the Declaration affirms the principle that "labor is not a commodity,"[11] and Article II*a* gives to "all human beings the right to pursue both their material and spiritual well-being in conditions of freedom and dignity, of economic security, and equal opportunity."[12] Therefore, the Declaration focuses on the human person and individual dignity. It is interesting to compare both the ILO Constitution and the

8 *Supra* note 2.

9 The "Human Rights Approach" to international trade advocated thereto includes two essential aspects: on the one hand, the liberalization of international trade flows must be "consistent" with the evolution of all conditions necessary to the enjoyment of human rights; this way the adoption of trade measures even only potentially restrictive in the area of fundamental social rights represents a violation of the latter. On the other hand, and as far as this method is concerned, the High Commissioner requires from UN member states a "constant examination of trade and policy" with the aim of evaluating the impact of the effective enjoyment of fundamental human rights in the social field. *See Analytical study of the High Commissioner for Human Rights on the Fundamental Principle of Non-Discrimination in the Context of Globalization*, Doc E/CN.4/2004/40 (January 15, 2004) ¶¶ 11–12.

10 Francis Maupain, *L'OIT, la Justice Sociale et la Mondialisation*, 278 RCADI 205 (1999).

11 Universal Declaration of Human Rights, *supra* note 5, Article I*a*. For the purposes of this contribution, labor can be understood by making reference to ILO's preamble, which calls for an international action aimed at "the regulation of the hours of work [. . .] of the labor supply, the prevention of unemployment, the provision of an adequate living wage, the protection of workers against sickness, disease and injury arising out of this employment, the protection of children, young persons and women, provision for old age and injury, protection of the interests of workers when employed in countries other than their own, recognition of the principle of equal remuneration for work of equal value, recognition of the principle of freedom of association, the organization of vocational and technical education and other measures."

12 Universal Declaration of Human Rights, *supra* note 5, Article II*a*.

Declaration with Article 6 of the International Covenant on Economic, Social, and Cultural Rights (ICESCR), according to which member states recognize "the right to work, which includes the right of everyone to the opportunity to gain his living by work which he freely chooses or accept [. . .];"[13] "the steps to be taken by a state party [. . .] shall include technical and vocational guidance and training programs, policies to achieve [. . .] economic, social and cultural development and full and productive employment under conditions safeguarding fundamental political and economic freedoms to the individual."[14]

As a result of the ILO's normative function, the "international labor code" includes norms contained in the two main instruments adopted: *recommendations* (acts used to elaborate the principles set forth in the conventions that should be followed by the adoption of a corresponding internal state law), and *binding conventions* (acts open to ratification by the member states). The streams of economic globalization have had great repercussions both on the ability of the ILO to assure a parallelism between economic growth and social progress, as well as on the member states' capabilities to respect the obligations flowing from the conventions and recommendations adopted, thus undermining the statutory purpose of achieving social justice. In this respect, the ILO, in its practice over the last decade, has tried to establish a connection between international trade and social standards using certain rules of its Charter as a legal basis.

The ILO Charter, in fact, aims to prevent international competition from taking place at the expense of workers' interests. For example, according to the third *considering* of the preamble, "the failure of any nation to adopt humane conditions of labor is an obstacle in the way of other nations which desire to improve the conditions in their own countries." According to the ILO, a "social dimension of international trade" is possible through a strict coordination with the WTO[15] at the *institutional* (reciprocal participation as *observateur*), *material* (by harmonizing the respective norms), and *procedural* (through the identification of suitable mechanisms to assure the reciprocal participation of the procedures aimed at the assessment of violations of norms and the consequent reactions) levels. A first step in this direction was made by taking into consideration the provisions of the GATT/WTO system concerning dumping, public subsidies, and the Dispute Settlement Understanding (DSU)[16] in order to determine whether unfair trade practices could lead to forms of social dumping because of their presumed incompatibility with a "normal" level of social protection. However, the WTO did not engage in such a stance, because of the difficulty of determining the "exact value" of the imported goods, as required by GATT rules on dumping. Most significantly, the WTO still refuses to grant "observer" status to ILO bodies, thus preventing any potential for effective cooperation between them.

In creating the normative content of the social dimension within trade relations, ILO practice has identified a narrow group of labor principles and rules contained in binding conventions as well as non-binding recommendations adopted by the International Labor Conference. The so-called core labor standards (CLS) include principles and rules that aim to safeguard certain basic human rights: Conventions Nos. 29/1930 (Forced Labor), 98/1949 (Right to Organize and Collective Bargaining), 100/1951 (Equal Remuneration), 111/1958 (Discrimination in Employment and Occupation), 105/1957 (Abolition of

13 International Covenant on Economic, Social and Cultural Rights, 993 UNTS 3, Article 6, ¶ 1.

14 *Id.*, Article 6, ¶ 2.

15 Unlike the ILO, the WTO is not a Specialized UN Agency. It is an international organization that succeeded GATT as a permanent forum for the discussion of trade, services, and agricultural issues, as part of multilateral agreements. *See* the Final Act Embodying the Results of the Uruguay Round of Multilateral Trade Organization, Marrakesh 1994.

16 ILO Doc. GB. 261/WP/SLD/1, November 1994, ¶ 26.

Forced Labor), 138/1973 (Minimum Age for Admission at Work), 87/1948 (Freedom of Association and Protection of the Right to Organize), and 182/1999 (Abolition of Worst Forms of Child Labor). The ILO Declaration on Fundamentals Principles and Rights at Work[17] makes the CLS even more "visible." This Declaration incorporates the CLS into a single instrument that establishes their legally binding character without requiring new obligations from the member states and, also, provides and employs a control instrument (*suivi*; *follow up*), strongly connected to the Declaration. The Declaration commits ILO members to "respect, promote, and realize," in good faith, the principles concerning the fundamental rights that are the subject of the aforementioned conventions, namely: a) the freedom of association and the effective recognition of the right to collective bargaining; b) the elimination of all forms of forced or compulsory labor; c) the effective abolition of child labor; and d) the elimination of discrimination in employment and occupation. According to the document, these principles and rights have been expressed and developed in the form of specific rights and obligations in conventions recognized as fundamental both inside and outside the organization.[18] The binding nature of such a commitment does not flow from the document, which remains a manifestation of international soft law, but rather from the ILO membership, which includes the voluntary acceptance of the principles and rights set out in its Constitution and in the Declaration of Philadelphia. Moreover, it is worth mentioning that the members' obligation to ensure CLS arises "from the very fact of membership in the organization [. . .] even if they have not ratified the Conventions in question."[19] I have argued elsewhere whether CLS belongs to customary or *jus cogens* law.[20] If one divides the abovementioned principles into two categories, some may be considered rooted in the legal conscience of the vast majority of states that have ratified the instruments that sanction them while the second category of principles can instead be traced to the level of economic development of each country. The level of universality of the relative provisions is therefore inferior. Principles pertaining to union freedom, prohibition of forced labor, and non-discrimination in employment often fall into the first category because they exist at the intersection of civil rights, political freedom, and economic rights, and include the individual as well as the collective dimension. The international regulation on child labor seems different in that it is possible to distinguish two aspects: the definition of the minimum age to start working on the one hand, and the exploitation of child labor on the other.

As far as the second case is concerned, the obligation against child labor seems to have *jus cogens* nature. It is not possible here to dwell on the ILO standards, in general. Most of them are flexible and promotional, and these characteristics often prevent them from being interpreted as "core" labor standards (for instance, the ILO conventions on working time, minimum wage, health, and security of the workplace, or the right to equal pay for men and women).[21]

17 The document was adopted by the International Labor Conference in June 1998, with 273 votes in favor and 43 abstentions. *See* Francis Maupain, *The Liberalization of International Trade and the Universal Recognition of Workers' Fundamental Rights: the New ILO Declaration on Fundamental Principles and Rights at Work and its Follow-up*, in Scientific And Technological Development and Human Rights 35 (Linos Sicilianos ed., ILO, 2001).

18 *See* Article 1(b) of the Declaration, www.ilo.org.

19 Article 2 of the Declaration. *See* Philip Alston, *"Core Labour Standards" and the Transformation of the International Labour Rights Regime*, 15 (3) Eur. J. Int'l L. 457–521 (2004).

20 Claudio Di Turi, Globalizzazione dell'Economia e Diritti Umani Fondamentali in Materia di Lavoro: il Ruolo dell'OIL e dell'OMC (Giuffré 2007).

21 *Id.*, at 81–110.

The WTO and human rights: Conflict or convergence? The role of public international law

Although the creation of the WTO renewed faith in multilateral trade, it also raised anxieties throughout wide sectors of civil society, which fear that the organization sacrifices state sovereignty in favor of interests not subject to popular scrutiny.[22] Moreover, allegations are often made that WTO law does not support a legal environment that protects social rights[23] even though trade rules aiming at liberalization in a number of different areas could likely have a strong impact on human rights. Undoubtedly, the agreement establishing the WTO does not mention human dignity,[24] even if some wording of the preamble to the agreement itself may pave the way for a more human rights oriented interpretation of the covered agreements. The preamble calls for trade relations "[to] be conducted with a view to raising standards of living, ensuring full employment and a large and steadily growing volume of real income [. . .] in accordance with the objective of sustainable development", thus promoting trade as a means to obtain greater individual well-being and development through rights. Multilateral trade should therefore also take into account the needs of private persons.

The two legal subsystems of international trade and human rights were born and evolved in reciprocal indifference, at least until the intensification of trade began to highlight its potential repercussions on the enjoyment of fundamental rights. This point calls for a more precise analysis, in order to call attention to similarities and differences between trade law and human rights law. As liberal systems, in their essence, both pursue the same goal, that is the promotion of social justice. Moreover, trade rules strengthen human rights since they generate more openness, transparency, lower prices, and technology transfer which, in turn, support the right to development.[25] Both subsystems, in fact, set the principle of non-discrimination as their foundation, even if the principle plays a different functional role within each separate legal order. On the other hand, international trade rules cannot play the role of human rights rules because they address states, not individuals, and apply to a legal order in which the private person has no legal status.

Besides analyzing the WTO's conceptual foundations, in order to better assess the relevance of the human being within its legal system, it should be mentioned that the WTO is a proper subject of international law, since the treaty establishing it is a source of public international law. Moreover, the WTO itself is an international organization, and, as such, it must conduct itself, e.g. creating and interpreting rules, with respect for certain rules of international law.[26] This is an important point since, for the limited purposes of this short

22 Sarah Joseph, Blame it on the WTO? A Human Rights Critique 265–266 (Oxford University Press, 2011).

23 Joost Pauwelyn, Conflict of Norms in Public International Law: How WTO Relates to Other Rules of International Law 20 (Cambridge University Press, 2003).

24 WTO law and practice have shown, since the establishment of the Organization, strong pressures coming from both civil society and legal scholars to take in due consideration the so-called Non-Trade Concerns, that is (*inter alia*) democratic deficit within WTO organs, the role of public opinion, development issues, health, labor rights, and the protection of the environment. WTO case law has sometimes given relevance to some of these interests (public health and environment protection, for instance). This suggests the importance of WTO judiciary in giving progressive relevance to topics well-rooted in the civil society. The willingness of WTO judicial bodies to foster an interpretation of WTO agreements in line with values shared worldwide, even if not formally enshrined in legal texts, should be welcomed.

25 Ernst-Ulrich Petersmann, *Theories of Justice, Human Rights and the Constitution of International Markets*, European University Institute working paper No. 2003/17, 14, 20–23.

26 In *US – Gasoline*, the Appellate Body has said that the WTO "cannot be read in clinical isolation from public international law." Appellate Body Report, *United States – Standard for Reformulated and*

contribution, the analysis will discuss some WTO/human rights profiles relevant to public international law. The first issue to deal with is the jurisdiction of WTO organs whose competence is established by the WTO Dispute Settlement Understanding (DSU) Articles 1.1, 3.2, 7, 11, and 19.2. The WTO case law suggests that, when determining the law applicable to disputes arising in the context of the covered agreements, WTO panels and the Appellate Body may not use human rights law to settle such disputes; however, surely *all rules of public international law* – not only the Vienna Convention on the Law of Treaties (VCLT) – can be applied in the interpretation of those agreements.[27] This latter interpretation acknowledges the power of the DSU to deal, albeit indirectly, with human rights issues so long as political organs refuse to amend the existing agreements to explicitly bring human rights within the general WTO jurisdiction or to engage in negotiations with the same goal. This understanding of the DSU allows for an interpretation of the WTO system in line with the more general values enshrined in public international law and, for our purposes, with the ILO's social goals. In fact, such interpretation does not arbitrarily widen the jurisdiction of WTO adjudicative organs, since past DSU practice has not shown reluctance to adjudicate cases where non-trade allegations regarding the environment or public health were under scrutiny (*Shrimp* and *Asbestos* cases, *see infra*). Even though, at present, parties have rarely raised human rights concerns before the WTO, legal grounds do not exist to prohibit WTO panels and the Appellate Body from dealing with such issues in the future.

Raising human rights issues through GATT: Non-discrimination principles and general exceptions

A state may raise human rights objections through GATT if another state adopts trade-restrictive measures that violate human rights in its own territory and these measures,[28] *prima facie*, infringe the fundamental GATT principle of non-discrimination enshrined in Articles I (Most Favored Nation Clause, which prohibits states from treating the products of one member state less favorably than the *like products* of other member states) and III (National Treatment Clause: the imported product may not be subject to regulations less favorable than those applied to *like products* of other member state). In other words, a state that allows child labor or slave practices could not successfully challenge another state for imposing unilateral trade sanctions against it on the basis of violating GATT principles. Such a trade-restrictive measure would be permitted based on the assumption that forced labor made the products in violation of a fundamental human rights principle: the products prompting the sanction are not "like" any other goods manufactured by adults in countries that do not exploit child labor and, in contrast, respect workers' rights.

Conventional Gasoline [hereinafter *US – Gasoline*], WT/DS2/AB/R (April 29, 1996), ¶ 18. *See* Gabrielle Marceau, *WTO Dispute Settlement and Human Rights*, 13(4) EUR. J. INT'L L. 753, 766 (2002).

27 In *Korea – Measures Affecting Government Procurement*, WT/DS163/R, (May 1, 2000) ¶ 7.96, the Panel said that "we take note that art. 3.2 of the DSU requires that we seek [. . .] to clarify the existing provisions of WTO Agreements in accordance with customary rules of interpretation of public international law. However, the relationship of the WTO Agreements to customary international law is broader than this. Customary international law applies [. . .] to the extent that there is no conflict or inconsistency [. . .]; (it) applies to the WTO treaties and to the process of treaty formation under the WTO."

28 Various examples of trade sanctions are given by JAMES HARRISON, THE HUMAN RIGHTS IMPACT OF THE WORLD TRADE ORGANIZATION 60–63 (Oxford and Portland, Hart Publishing, 2007). For a general discussion, *see* ANTHONY CASSIMATIS, HUMAN RIGHTS RELATED TRADE MEASURES UNDER INTERNATIONAL LAW (Leiden, Brill, 2007).

The question to be answered is the following: can goods be differentiated on the basis of their production or process methods? The distinction between "product requirements" – which relate to the physical characteristics of the products – and "production/process methods" – which take into account the way exported goods are produced – is at the heart of both GATT and WTO case law when determining the "likeness" of two products in order to ascertain whether an imported product has been treated differently from domestic ***like products***. In the two ***Tuna*** cases, the United States (US) measures at stake prohibited the import of tuna from a state unless that state complied with US rules on dolphin-safe fishing practices. However, GATT panels held that tuna caught according to US prescriptions could not be distinguished from tuna caught in other ways.[29] As far as WTO case law is concerned, in ***US – Import Prohibition of Certain Shrimp and Shrimp Products*** (Shrimp/Turtle I),[30] the US had treated differently imported shrimp (caught with techniques that, according to US legislation, endangered turtles' lives) from shrimp caught in conformity with US legislation, and therefore, distinguished shrimp in a manner other than its purely physical nature. According to the Appellate Body, the determination of the "likeness" of two products depends on the degree of competitiveness and substitutability between them, taking into account the following criteria: the properties, nature, and quality of the products; the end-uses of the products; the consumers' tastes and habits; and the tariff classification of the products.[31] Thus, the GATT non-discrimination principle does not take into account factors other than the "physical" characteristics of the product. Therefore, national measures restricting the import of goods produced in violation of human rights would likely be successfully challenged by the exporting state that argues the measures' non-conformity with GATT.

If a state measure is found to be inconsistent with the GATT non-discrimination principle because it discriminates between ***like products***, it might still be justified under Article XX, which contains a list of exceptions to the main GATT principles and provides a mechanism which allows a state to protect domestic interests for public policy reasons,[32] if specific requirements are met. For a measure to comply with Article XX, it must fall within the substantive scope of one of the Article's subparagraphs as well as satisfy the requirements of the ***chapeau***,[33] which commands that the state measure cause neither an "arbitrary or unjustifiable discrimination" nor a "disguised restriction on international trade."[34] GATT panels and the Appellate Body have invalidated state measures, though consistent with Article XX,

29 Report of the Panel, ***United States – Prohibition of Imports of Tuna and Tuna Products from Canada*** [hereinafter ***Tuna/ Dolphin I***], BISD 29S/91 (September 3, 1991).

30 WTO Doc. WT/DS58/R (May 15, 1998).

31 Appellate Body report, ***European Communities – Measures Affecting Asbestos and Products Containing Asbestos,*** WT/DS/135/AB/R (March 12, 2001) ¶¶ 98, 101, and 115. It is important to take note, however, that the Appellate Body said that the aforementioned criteria are "simply tools to assist in the task of sorting and examining the relevant evidence [. . .]; they are neither a treaty-mandated nor a closed list of criteria that will determine the legal characterization of products." Therefore, other factors could be taken into account in the future, in order to assess the legality of human rights measures.

32 Article XX provides as follows (only the part relevant to this work has been quoted): "Subject to the requirement that such measures are not applied in a manner which would constitute a means of arbitrary or unjustifiable discrimination between countries where the same conditions prevail, or a disguised restriction on international trade, nothing in this Agreement shall be construed to prevent the adoption or enforcement by any contracting party of measures: a) necessary to protect public morals; b) necessary to protect human, animal, or plant life or health; or e) relating to products of prison labor." From a Human Rights perspective, ***see*** UNHCHR, ***Human Rights and World Trade Agreements: Using General Exception Clauses to Protect Human Rights,*** 2005, www.ohchr.org/Documents/Publications/WTOen.pdf (last visited July 13, 2016).

33 Appellate Body Report, ***US – Gasoline, supra*** note 26, ¶ 6.20.

34 General Agreement on Tariffs and Trade, October 30, 1947, 61 Stat. A-11, 55 UNTS 194 [hereinafter GATT], Article XX.

that were deemed to be disproportionate[35] or non-transparent.[36] Moreover, the WTO system always prefers the adoption of multilateral solutions.[37] Article XX lists specific exceptions and does not permit broad justifications for deviating from GATT obligations.[38] A party cannot invoke the Article in support of any measure intending to protect human rights, and GATT/WTO case law seems to confirm that unilateral sanctions are certainly not the best way to promote or protect human rights abroad.[39]

However, many scholars argue that measures aimed at protecting public morals,[40] life, or health, may be adopted, while the debate about measures relating to prison labor remains more controversial,[41] since it might be impossible to separate the objective, which is to protect human rights by means which might be discriminatory. Unfortunately, this short contribution does not permit us to dwell on important issues such as the "necessity" of the measure for safeguarding public morals and health;[42] the "relation" to prison labor;[43] the extraterritorial effects of the measures;[44] and, finally, the most suitable way to interpret GATT/WTO provisions in order to integrate human rights concerns with the system.[45] However, one should wonder whether Article XX is actually a suitable mechanism to advance human rights within

35 Appellate Body Report, *United States – Import Prohibition of Certain Shrimp and Shrimp Products* [hereinafter *Shrimp/Turtle I*], WT/DS58/AB/R (November 6, 1998), 161–184. The so called proportionality test weighs the state non-commercial interest, its effectiveness in fostering it, and impact on multilateral trade. It is debatable whether this test can really be suitable to enhance and protect human rights.

36 *Ibid.*, 180.

37 In both *US – Gasoline* (631–632) and *Shrimp Turtle I* (166–171), the measures were invalidated under the *chapeau* because of US refusal to negotiate international agreements; however, in *Shrimp/Turtle II*, the AB stated that, even if an agreement could not be reached, the US had to make at least "serious good faith efforts to reach international agreements," WT//DS58/AB/RW (October 22, 2001), at 122.

38 Report of the Panel, *Tuna/ Dolphin I*, *supra* note 29, at 197.

39 The "multilateral" approach clearly undermines the feasibility of unilateral actions.

40 In the recent case *EC – Measures Prohibiting the Importation and Marketing of Seal Products*, WT/DS400/AB/R, WT/DS401AB/R (June 18, 2014), the Appellate Body upheld Panel conclusion that the EU Seal Regime does not violate Article 2.2 of the TBT Agreement because it fulfills the objective of addressing EU public moral concerns on seal welfare to a certain extent, and no alternative measure was demonstrated to make an equivalent or greater contribution to the fulfillment of the objective. In particular, AB said that EU Seal Regime is "necessary to protect public morals" within the meaning of Article XX(a) of the GATT 1994.

41 Can the exception be used with regard to products made using forced labor, or is it rather an economic provision aiming at preventing states from gaining unfair advantages through the exporting of goods made with unpaid work? *See* Sarah H. Cleveland, *Human Rights Sanctions and International Trade: A Theory of Compatibility,* 5 JOURNAL OF INTERNATIONAL ECONOMIC LAW 133, 162 (2002); ADAM MC BETH, INTERNATIONAL ECONOMIC ACTORS AND HUMAN RIGHTS 119 (Routledge, 2010).

42 STEVE CHARNOVITZ, THE MORAL EXCEPTION IN TRADE POLICY, IN TRADE LAW AND GLOBAL GOVERNANCE 325–376 (Cameron May, 2002). In the *Asbestos* case, the AB stated that a State "cannot justify a measure inconsistent with [. . .] GATT provision as necessary [. . .] if an alternative measure which it could be reasonably expected to employ and which is not inconsistent with other GATT provisions, is available to it" (¶ 170). *See* Carlos M. Vazquez, *Trade Sanctions and Human Rights-Past, Present, and Future,* 6(4) J. INT'L ECON. L. 797, 819–820. According to Vazquez, "An inquiry into whether a human rights based trade measure is necessary to protect morals or health in the exporting State implicates the debate about whether economic sanctions are at all effective in achieving their asserted goals."

43 In *Shrimp/Turtle I*, the Appellate Body said that the measure at stake was not "disproportionately wide in its scope and in relation to the policy objective [. . .]. The means (were) in principle reasonably related to the ends" (¶ 141). There should be a relation between the restriction to international trade and the state interest, and such relation should be an "observably close and real one."

44 Francesco Francioni, *Environment, Human Rights and the Limits of Free Trade,* in ENVIRONMENT, HUMAN RIGHTS AND INTERNATIONAL TRADE 1, 19 (Hart, 2001).

45 *See* DSU Article 3.2, stating that WTO Agreements need to be "interpreted in the light of customary rules of interpretation;" Vienna Convention on the Law of Treaties Articles 31–32.

the WTO, with special attention on social rights, for example when goods are made by children through forced labor. I personally do not think so, and I will try here to briefly explain why. WTO members are for the most part signatories of human rights treaties. During the Uruguay Round, no member raised reservations concerning the compatibility between WTO rules and existing human rights treaties, and the WTO is an international organization which must respect *jus cogens* rules, as well as its member states. Therefore, in order to advance human rights in the WTO most efficaciously, the WTO system should be interpreted in harmony and coherence with the "international public order of human rights."[46]

The WTO and the social clause

In order to promote a social dimension to international trade, proposals have been advanced to include "social clauses" in WTO agreements.[47] Such proposals flow from the existence of a relevant precedent, dating back to the post-war project to build an International Trade Organization (ITO), which included a provision aimed at establishing a link between fair trade and workers' rights (Article 7 of the Havana Charter). However, while human rights advocates and ILO circles have repeatedly claimed that the introduction of a social clause could serve social rights, the WTO strongly refused to engage in discussions to establish a formal link between trade and human rights rules. The first WTO Ministerial Conference held in Singapore in 1996 affirmed "the commitment to the observance of internationally recognized CLS," but it rejected "the use of labor standards for protectionist purposes and agree[d] that the comparative advantage of countries, particularly low-wage countries must in no way be put in question."[48] As stated in paragraph 4, for the Ministers, the ILO was the competent forum to establish and deal with CLS. A recent book[49] linking social clauses to the problem of the labor legislation flexibility demonstrates the constant attention that the ILO pays to these clauses. Moreover, commodity agreements often contain social clauses.

Social clauses, or provisions aiming at promoting respect for ILO standards, are set often in some bilateral and multilateral trade and investment treaties[50] or the General System of Preferences Schemes of States or groups of States.[51] By doing so, WTO law allows the

46 *See* also the important International Law Association resolution (No. 5/2008) adopted during the Rio meeting where it was agreed, "WTO members and bodies are legally required to interpret and apply WTO rules in conformity with the human rights obligations of WTO members under international law."

47 According to a concise definition, a social clause consists of "garanties ou règles [. . .] établissant un lien entre le commerce international et le respected certaines norms de travail [. . .] prévoyant le recours à des measures de réaction telles que le restrictions commerciales or retrait de préferences commerciales." Claudio Di Turi & Anne-Marie La Rosa, *Clause sociale*, in Dictionnaire de Droit International Public 186 (J. Salmon ed., Collectif, 2001).

48 1996 Singapore Ministerial Declaration, ¶ 4.

49 Jean-Michel Servais, International Labour Law 34 (Kluwer Law International, 2009).

50 *See* Free Trade Agreements between USA and Morocco, the North American Free Trade Agreement (NAFTA), or the Central American Free Trade Agreement (CAFTA). European Union has recently signed a number of bilateral trade agreements of a new generation with South Korea (2011), Central America (2012), Colombia and Peru (2013), and Singapore (2014), all including adherence to international labour standards. See C. DI TURI, ***La strategia commerciale dell'Unione europea tra regionalismo economico e multilateralismo: quale ruolo per gli accordi di libero scambio di nuova generazione?*** in ***Studi sull'integrazione europea***, 2014, p. 81: For an evaluation of the ILO's influence on this new kind of free trade agreements, see Jordi Agustì-Panareda, Franz Chrstian Ebert, Desirée LeClerq, ***Labour Provisions in Free Trade Agreements:Fostering their Consistency with the ILO Standards System***, ILO, Geneva, 2014.

51 European Union Council Regulation No. 978/2012 of October 25, 2012, applying a scheme of generalised tariff preferences and repealing Council Regulation (EC) No 732/2008, http://eur-lex.europa.eu/legal-content/en/ALL/?uri=CELEX%3A32012R0978 (last visited July 13, 2016). *See* Robert Howse,

inclusion of such clauses within preferential trade agreements. As such, the WTO itself seems more willing today than in the past to cooperate with the ILO, at least at a study group level.[52] It is difficult to imagine a more favorable WTO attitude towards social clauses, given the darkness surrounding the Doha development agenda and maybe even the future of the WTO itself.

Concluding remarks

In this chapter, I attempted to highlight challenges and opportunities for social rights posed by globalization, a multifaceted economic process whose impact on human rights is monitored both at the ILO and the WTO within the scope of their respective statutory goals and means of action. Therefore, while the ILO's practice still focuses on its normative function to advance social rights,[53] the difficulties surrounding the WTO Doha Round of negotiations do not permit any optimism about amending some of the WTO's agreements in order to make human rights protection a statutory goal.[54]

Through my analysis of the law and practice of both the ILO and the WTO, I have emphasized various institutional, normative, and jurisprudential tools. Neither human rights law nor trade law can completely foster human dignity on its own. In order to progress towards widespread recognition of human dignity, WTO agreements should be interpreted in coherence with human rights, customary, cogent, and conventional rules. Finally, it is worth considering that new challenges concerning the promotion and the protection of social rights are emerging: one may think, for instance, to negotiations surrounding the Transatlantic Trade and Investment Partnership between EU and USA, with attempts at inserting a Trade and Sustainable Development Chapter, containing relevant ILO provisions, into the final Agreement.[55] It is maybe no time to formulate judgments about the ongoing negotiations, but the attention showed by the European Parliament, that is the European institutions representing citizens interests, make European peoples aware of ILO's social rights being in good hands.[56]

Brian Langille & Julien Burda, *The WTO and Labor Rights: Man Bites Dog*, in SOCIAL ISSUES, GLOBALIZATION AND INTERNATIONAL INSTITUTIONS 157, 198 (Virginia Leary & David Warner eds, Brill, 2006).

52 ILO-WTO, MAKING GLOBALIZATION SOCIALLY SUSTAINABLE (M. Bacchetta. M. Jansen eds, ILO-WTO, 2011); *Trade and Employment: Challenges for Policy Research*, WTO Secretariat Geneva 2007.

53 In its landmark *Declaration on Social Justice for a Fair Globalization* (2007), the ILO emphasized its key role in achieving progress and social justice through the Decent Work Agenda, a concept developed in 1999, placing it at the core of the Organization's policies to reach its constitutional objectives, www.ilo.org. In its 325th session, ILO Governing Body (Geneva 29 Oct./12 Nov. 2015, doc. GB 325 PV, paras. 37–64)) decided to appoint a Committee of the Whole in order to evaluate the impact of the 2007 Declaration on the Member States domestic legal order, while supporting the mobilization of resources with regard to assisting them in their efforts to respect, promote and realize principles enshrined in 1998 Declaration on Fundamental Principles and Rights at Work. This document confirms how principles enshrined in the two Declarations are still relevant for ILO practice as being regularly monitored by ILO's supervision machinery.

54 However, *see* WTO's former Director General Lamy speeches: *Lamy Calls for Mindset Change to Align Trade and Human Rights* (January 23, 2010); *Trade and Human Rights Go Hand in Hand* (September 26, 2010), www.wto.org.

55 See the EU position at: http://trade.ec.europa.eu/doclib/docs/2013/july/tradoc_151626.pdf; or at: http://trade.ec.europa.eu/doclib/docs/2015/november/tradoc_153923.pdf (last visited July 13, 2016).

56 See the European Parliament resolution of 8 July 2015 containing the European Parliament's recommendations to the European Commission on the negotiations for the Transatlantic Trade and Investment Partnership (TTIP) (2014/2228(INI), doc. P8_TA(2015)252, *Negotiations for the Transatlantic Trade and Investment Partnership*, in http://www.europarl.europa.eu/plenary/it/home.htm (last visited July 13, 2016).

4 Multinational Corporations and Corporate Social Responsibility in a Chinese Context

An International Law Perspective*

Angelica Bonfanti

Introduction

The use of cutting-edge technologies and the improvement of telecommunications and transport in the last few decades have led to the development of new production models based on the relocation of some phases of the production process to different countries around the world. Multinational corporations (MNCs) have replaced states as the main actors in this new international economic scenario. This phenomenon, together with its accession to the World Trade Organization (WTO), has contributed to transforming China into one of the main economic actors operating in the global market. In this scenario, China plays a dual role: it receives foreign investment and, simultaneously, behaves as an international investor itself.[1]

This chapter aims at analyzing two sets of issues linked to this broad theme: on the one hand, it focuses on China's international responsibility for wrongful acts connected with business activities; on the other hand, it focuses on corporate social responsibility (CSR), with the aim of assessing whether and how CSR contributes to ensuring that MNCs that operate in China comply with human and social rights and environmental protection.

Corporate activities in a Chinese context: International law issues

From a methodological point of view, this chapter embraces the international law perspective. Accordingly, it takes Chinese law into consideration with the sole purpose of assessing

* This chapter is part of the results of the Research Project on "*Current Trends of Chinese Law towards Non-Trade Concerns such as Sustainable Development and the Protection of Environment, Public Health, Food Safety, Cultural, Social and Economic Rights, Labor Rights and the Reduction of Poverty from the Perspective of International Law and WTO Law*" coordinated by Professor Paolo Davide Farah at gLAWcal – Global Law Initiatives for Sustainable Development (United Kingdom) and at West Virginia University John D. Rockefeller IV School of Policy and Politics, Department of Public Administration, in partnership with the Center of Advanced Studies on Contemporary China (CASCC) in Turin (Italy), Maastricht University Faculty of Law, Department of International and European Law and IGIR - Institute for Globalisation and International Regulation (Netherlands) and Tsinghua University, School of Law, Institute of Public international law and the Center for Research on Intellectual Property Law in Beijing (China). An early draft of this paper was presented at Conferences Series on "*China's Influence on Non-Trade Concerns in International Economic Law*", First Conference held at the Center of Advanced Studies on Contemporary China (CASCC) in Turin on November 23-24, 2011. This publication and the Conference Series were sponsored by China–EU School of Law (CESL) at the China University of Political Science and Law (CUPL). The activities of CESL at CUPL are supported by the European Union and the P.R. of China.

1 UNCTAD, *World Investment Report 2011, China*.

its compliance with international law. Given their relevance in terms of international law, the chapter will first deal with the structure of MNCs and the role of the Chinese state.

As far as the former is concerned, two specific elements characterize the structure of MNCs: the delocalization of the production process – carried out through either the incorporation/constitution of "subsidiaries" in the so-called host states or the institution of contractual relationships with local corporations – and the subordination of MNCs' activities to the direction of the "home corporation," located in the so-called state of origin. Taking into consideration the definitions provided by the main international instruments dealing with the regulation of MNCs' activities since the 1970s, MNCs qualify as "economic entit[ies] operating in more than one country or a cluster of economic entities operating in two or more countries,"[2] characterized by "public, mixed or private ownership, which own or control production, distribution, services, or other facilities outside the country in which they are based."[3] Pursuant to the same definitions, they are composed of "a decision-making center located in one country, and of operating centers, with or without legal personality, situated in one or more other countries,"[4] "so linked that they may co-ordinate their operations in various ways."[5]

Therefore, a dichotomy exists between the plurality of legal persons composing the MNC – each of which is incorporated as an autonomous entity, under the national law of the state of incorporation – and the entirety of the MNC from the economic point of view that behaves as a single entity on the market. This dichotomy gives the MNCs the chance to delocalize the production to those countries where favorable treatment is offered, and to take advantage of the *lacunae* existing among the national laws and jurisdictions of the states in which they operate.[6] Such a dichotomy produces significant consequences in international law. Indeed, it is questionable which domestic law governs the MNCs' activities, how the forum-shopping phenomenon could be avoided in order to guarantee better protection to values essential to the international community, such as the protection of fundamental human rights, which states should ensure that the conduct of MNCs complies with law, and which courts are competent to decide the relevant disputes.[7]

2 UN Sub-Commission for the Promotion and Protection of Human Rights, *Norms on the Responsibilities of Transnational Corporations and Other Business Enterprises with Regard to Human Rights*, August 26, 2003, UN Doc. E/CN.4/Sub.2/2003/12/Rev.2. [hereinafter UN Norms].

3 ILO, *ILO Tripartite Declaration of Principles Concerning Multinational Enterprises and Social Policy*, November 16, 1977, No. 6 [hereinafter ILO Tripartite Declaration].

4 Institut de Droit International, *Les Enterprises Multinationales*, Oslo, September 7, 1977, Rapporteur Berthold Goldman, www.idi-iil.org.

5 OECD, *OECD Guidelines for Multinational Enterprises. Recommendations for Responsible Business Conduct in a Global Context*, May 25, 2011, No. I.3 [hereinafter OECD Guidelines].

6 *See* Philip Blumberg, *Accountability of Multinational Corporations: The Barriers Presented by Concepts of the Corporate Juridical Entity*, 24 Hastings Int'l & Comp. L. Rev. 297 (2001); Peter Muchlinski, Multinational Enterprises and the Law (Wiley-Blackwell, 1999); François Rigaux, *Transnational Corporations*, in International Law: Achievements and Prospects 121 (Mohammed Bedjaoui ed., Martinus Nijhoff Publishers, 1991); Celia Wells & Juanita Elias, *Catching the Coscience of the King: Corporate Players on the International Stage*, in Non-State Actors and Human Rights 141 (Philip Alston ed., Bloomsbury, 2005).

7 *See* generally Economic Globalisation and Human Rights (Wolfgang Benedek, Koen De Feyter & Fabrizio Marrella eds, Cambridge, 2011); Corporate Responsibility for Human Rights Impacts: New Expectations and Paradigms (Lara Blecher, Nancy Kaymar Stafford, Gretchen C. Bellamy eds, American Bar Association, 2014); Transnational Corporations and Human Rights (Olivier De Schutter ed., Hart Publishing, 2006); Just Business: Multinational Corporations and Human Rights (John Gerard Ruggie ed., W. W. Norton & Company, 2013); Beth Stephens, *The Amorality of Profit: Transnational Corporations and Human Rights*, 20 Berkeley J. Int'l L. 45 (2002).

With specific reference to China, it should be noted that the state still plays a primary – or, at the least, fundamental – role in the economy.[8] This produces significant effects under international law. Indeed, international law regulates the attribution of obligations and the imputation of international responsibility differently, depending on whether the misconduct is ascribable to state organs or to private persons. While the conduct of the former is considered a state act, giving rise to the state's international responsibility, private persons' conduct can be simply qualified as "*catalyseur*"[9] of the state's international responsibility. In the light of the conclusions reached by the International Court of Justice in the *Hostages Case*,[10] in similar circumstances the responsibility of the state arises only from its own unlawful omission, such as for not having taken the measures required to prevent and repress such private conduct.[11]

As far as China is concerned, private MNCs' conduct – such as the activities put in place by MNCs originating from Western countries and operating, through their subsidiaries, in China – must be distinguished from those of the Chinese state-owned enterprises (SOEs). The latter are business entities established by central and local government, owned – totally or mostly – by the state, and whose supervisors are governmental officials.[12] SOEs account for about one-third of production in the Chinese economy[13] and, today, are frequently involved in Chinese outward investment,[14] especially to African countries in the extractive and infrastructure sectors.[15] While in the case of private Western MNCs, China is only bound to guarantee that the MNCs operating in its territory do not violate human rights and do not harm the environment, in the latter case – should the SOEs be considered as state organs or should their conduct be attributed to the state on the basis of the criteria set out by the International Law Commission (ILC) Articles on Responsibility of States for Internationally Wrongful Acts[16] – then China could be held responsible for their misconduct. Among the criteria upon which such attribution of responsibility could be based, pursuant to Article 8, the state shall be considered

8 On this topic, *see* OECD Working Group on Privatisation and Corporate Governance of State Owned Assets, *State Owned Enterprises in China: Reviewing the Evidence*, January 26, 2009, www.oecd.org/daf/ca/corporategovernanceofstate-ownedenterprises/42095493.pdf (last visited July 14, 2016).

9 The expression is quoted from Luigi Condorelli, *L'imputation à l'Etat d'un fait internationalement illicite: solutions classiques et nouvelles tendances*, in Recueil des Cours – Hague Academy of International Law 96 (Martinus Nijhoff Publishers, 1984-VI).

10 ICJ, *Case concerning United States Diplomatic and Consular Staff in Tehran, United States v Iran*, Judgement, May 24, 1980, ICJ Rep., 1980, at 3, ¶ 58.

11 On this international law issue, *see* Art. 11, Draft Articles on State Responsibility, adopted by the International Law Commission on First Reading, Yearbook of the International Law Commission Vol. II, Part II 58 (United Nations, 1996). Among others, *see* also Roberto Ago, *Quatrième rapport sur la responsabilité des Etats*, in Roberto Ago, Scritti sulla Responsabilità Internazionale degli Stati (Vol. II, Jovene, 1986), ¶¶ 61–146; Condorelli, *supra* note 9, at 93, 156; Jimenez de Arechaga & Attila Tanzi, *International State Responsibility*, in International Law: Achievements and Prospects 359–361 (Mohammed Bedjaoui ed., Martinus Nijhoff Publishers, 1991); Franck Latty, *Actions and Omissions*, in The Law of International Responsibility 355 (James Crawford, Alain Pellet & Simon Olleson eds, OUP Oxford, 2010).

12 *See State Owned Enterprises in China: Reviewing the Evidence, supra* note 8.

13 *Ibid.*

14 *See* Chapter 6 (Vadi) in this volume.

15 *See* Chapter 7 (Klaver & Trebilcock) in this volume.

16 ILC, *Draft Articles on Responsibility of States for Internationally Wrongful Acts*, November 2001, in *Yearbook of the International Law Commission*, 2001, Vol. II, Part Two, "ILC Articles".

responsible for those private acts carried out under its control, direction or instructions,[17] while, pursuant to Article 5, it shall be attributed the conduct of private persons that exercise "elements of governmental authority."[18]

In case the conduct of SOEs is attributed to the state, it is questionable which states, if any, could, should, or would have an interest in invoking the international responsibility of China. In this regard, it must be stressed that, pursuant to Article 41 of the ILC Articles, if serious violations of human rights and massive environmental damage occur, the other states are bound by solidarity duties. On this basis, the states shall not recognize the situation as lawful, they shall cooperate to bring the violation to an end, and they shall not aid or assist its author in maintaining such a situation. Additionally, if China breaches an obligation owed to the international community as a whole, pursuant to Article 48, any state of the international community – other than the injured state – could invoke China's international responsibility and demand the cessation of the internationally wrongful act, assurances of non-repetition, and reparation in the interest of the injured state or of the beneficiaries of the breached obligation.[19]

CSR in international law

When a MNC's conduct is at stake, one must consider an additional concept: corporate social responsibility. CSR is strongly connected with another concept whose function in this field must be emphasized: corporate accountability (CA). CSR and CA refer to the role played by MNCs in protecting human rights and the environment as a result of their activities. Their legal model and basis can be found in various soft law instruments providing for standards of conduct for MNCs, such as the Organization for Economic Co-operation and Development Guidelines for Multinational Enterprises (OECD Guidelines),[20] the International Labour Organization Tripartite Declaration of Principles Concerning Multinational Enterprises and Social Policy (ILO Tripartite Declaration),[21] the United Nations (UN)

17 ILC, *supra* note 16, art. 8. Frédéric Dopagne, *La Responsabilité de l'État du Fait des Particuliers: les Causes d'Imputation Revisitées par les Articles sur la Responsabilité de l'État pour Fait Internationalement Illicite,* 34 REVUE BELGE DE DROIT INTERNATIONAL 492 (2001); Claus Kress, *L'organe de Facto en Droit International Public. Réflections sur l'Imputation à l'Etat de l'Acte d'un Particulier à la Lumière des Développements Récents,* 105 REVUE GENERALE DE DROIT INTERNATIONAL PUBLIC 93 (2001).

18 Djamchid Momtaz, *Attribution of Conduct to the State: State Organs and Entities Empowered to Exercise Elements of Governmental Authority*, in Crawford, Pellet & Olleson, *supra* note 11, at 244.

19 ILC, *supra* note 16, arts 41, 48. *See* Annie Bird, *Third State Responsibility for Human Rights Violations,* 21 EUR. J. INT'L L. 883 (2009); Martin Davidowicz, *The Obligation of Non-Recognition of an Unlawful Situation*, in Crawford, Pellet, Olleson, *supra* note 11, at 677; Giorgio Gaja, *States Having an Interest in Compliance with the Obligation Breached*, in Crawford, Pellet, Olleson, *supra* note 11, at 956; Andrea Gattini, *Les obligations des Etats en droit d'invoquer la responsabilité d'un autre Etat pour violations graves d'obligations découlant de normes impératives du droit international général*, in OBLIGATIONS MULTILATÉRALES, DROIT IMPÉRATIF ET RESPONSABILITÉ INTERNATIONALE DES ETATS 150–151 (Pierre-Marie Dupuy ed., Pedone, 2003); Nina H. B. Jørgensen, *The Obligation of Non-Assistance to the Responsible State*, in Crawford, Pellet, Olleson, *supra* note 11, at 686; *Id.*, *The Obligation of Cooperation*, in Crawford, Pellet, Olleson, *supra* note 11, at 695.

20 *Supra*, note 5.

21 *Supra*, note 3.

Global Compact,[22] the UN Norms on the Responsibilities of Transnational Corporations and Other Business Enterprises with Regard to Human Rights (UN Norms),[23] and the Secretary-General Special Representative (SGSR) Guiding Principles on Business and Human Rights (Guiding Principles).[24] Through their subjection to these non-binding standards of conduct, corporations – even if not, or not unanimously, considered as international subjects – are increasingly held accountable to international law.[25]

Standards of conduct established by each legal instrument have different fields of subjective and objective application and different levels of effectiveness. While the ILO Tripartite Declaration deals only with social rights protection and the Guiding Principles with human rights protection, the other instruments have a broader field of application, which generally refers to all areas affected by MNCs' conduct. Among these areas are the following: environment, human and social rights protection, and the fight against corruption.[26] Moreover, while some instruments – such as the ILO Tripartite Declaration, the UN Norms, the Guiding Principles and the Global Compact – have a universal scope, others – like the OECD Guidelines – have only a regional one. Nonetheless, with regard to the regional scope, it should be noted that even if China has not adhered to the OECD Guidelines, they still apply to the Chinese subsidiaries of Western MNCs because they reach MNCs of adhering countries, wherever they operate.

CSR and CA refer to two different stages of the same process; they provide standards of conduct to MNCs, and influence or control their observance, respectively. CSR is

22 UN Global Compact, www.unglobalcompact.org.

23 *Supra*, note 2.

24 Special Representative of the Secretary-General on the Issue of Human Rights and Transnational Corporations and Other Business Enterprises, *Guiding Principles on Business and Human Rights: Implementing the United Nations "Protect, Respect and Remedy" Framework*, UN Doc. A/HRC/17/31, March 21, 2011 [hereinafter Guiding Principles].

25 *See* generally Pierre-Marie Dupuy, *Retour sur la théorie des sujets du droit international*, in MAN'S INHUMANITY TO MAN: ESSAYS ON INTERNATIONAL LAW IN HONOUR OF ANTONIO CASSESE 77 (Lal Chand Vohrah, Fausto Pocar, Yvonne Featherstone, Olivier Fourmy, Christine Graham, John Hocking & Nicholas Robson eds, Kluwer Law International, 2003). On the international subjectivity of MNCs, *see* also Vincent Chetail, *The Legal Personality of Multinational Corporations, State Responsibility and Due Diligence: the Way Forward*, in UNITÉ ET DIVERSITÉ DU DROIT INTERNATIONAL: ÉCRITS EN L'HONNEUR DU PROFESSEUR PIERRE-MARIE DUPUY 105 (Denis Alland, Vincent Chetail, Olivier de Frouville & Jorge E. Viñuales eds, Martinus Nijhoff Publishers, 2014); Patrick Dumberry, *L'entreprise, sujet de droit international. Retour sur la question a la lumière des devoloppements récents du droit international des investissements*, 108 REVUE GENÉRALE DROIT INTERNATIONAL PRIVÉ 104 (2004); Argyrios Fatouros, *Transnational Enterprise in the Law of State Responsibility*, in INTERNATIONAL LAW OF STATE RESPONSIBILITY FOR INJURIES TO ALIENS 383 (Richard Bonnet Lillich ed., American Bar Association, 1983); ROSALYN HIGGINS, PROBLEMS AND PROCESS. INTERNATIONAL LAW AND HOW WE USE IT 49–50 (Clarendon Press, 1994); Karsten Nowrot, *New Approaches to the International Legal Personality of Multinational Corporations. Towards a Rebuttable Presumption of Normative Responsibilities*, www.esil-sedi.eu/fichiers/en/Nowrot_513.pdf (last visited July 14, 2016).

26 UN Norms cover the mentioned fields, even if they expressly refer only to human rights; the OECD Guidelines provide standards on corruption, transparency, consumer protection, scientific and technological innovation, competition, and tax regulation, too. *See* David Weissbrodt & Muria Kruger, *Norms on the Responsibility of Transnational Corporations and Other Business Enterprises with Regard to Human Rights*, 97 AM. J. INT'L L. 901 (2003); Elisa Morgera, *OECD Guidelines for Multinational Enterprises*, in HANDBOOK OF TRANSNATIONAL GOVERNANCE: INSTITUTIONS AND INNOVATIONS 314 (Thomas Hale & David Held eds, Polity, 2011); Scott Robinson, *International Obligations, State Responsibility and Judicial Review Under the OECD Guidelines for Multinational Enterprises Regime*, in 30 UTRECHT J. INT'L EUR. L. 68 (2014).

the phenomenon according to which "private companies should no longer base their actions on the needs of their shareholders alone, but rather have obligations towards the society in which the company operates."[27] When effectuating decision processes, it compels corporations to consider the interests of all those stakeholders affected by the activities of the MNC. CSR is legally founded in the Universal Declaration of Human Rights, which provides that "organs of society" must respect human rights,[28] and, among others, in the Stockholm Declaration,[29] Agenda 21,[30] and the Johannesburg Declaration.[31]

In this context, the "corporate responsibility to respect human rights," one of the pillars of the SGSR normative framework, acquires importance.[32] The Guiding Principles perceive the corporate responsibility to respect human rights as a moral prescription, quasi-universally recognized by corporations themselves and the other actors in civil society. As regards its content, the Guiding Principles call on corporations not only to abstain from violating human rights, but also to put in place measures necessary to ensure compliance.[33] Therefore, corporations are called upon to respect the entire catalogue of human rights, as listed in the UN Covenants,[34] the Universal Declaration,[35] and the ILO Declaration on Core Labor Standards.[36] In order to comply with such norms, corporations should follow due diligence processes, proportional to the specific characteristics, structure, and size of the corporation, aimed at avoiding or mitigating human rights risks, both actual and potential.[37] Nonetheless,

27 Elisa Morgera, Corporate Accountability in International Environmental Law 11–12 (Oxford University Press, 2009). *See* also André Nollkaemper, ***Responsibility of Transnational Corporation in International Environmental Law: Three Perspectives***, in Multilevel Governance of Global Environmental Change. Perspectives from Science, Sociology and the Law 181 (Gerd Winter ed., Cambridge, 2006); Ramon Mullerat, Corporate Social Responsibility: the Corporate Governance of the 21st Century (Kluwer Law International, 2005).

28 Universal Declaration of Human Rights, GA res. 217A (III), UN Doc. A/810 at 71 (1948), preamble.

29 Declaration of the United Nations Conference on the Human Environment, UN Doc. A/Conf.48/14/Rev. 1(1973), June 16, 1972 (in ILM, 1972, p. 1416 ss.), preamble.

30 Agenda 21: Programme of Action for Sustainable Development, UN Doc. A/Conf.151/26 (1992), June 14, 1992, ch. 30, Strengthening the Role of Business and Industry.

31 Johannesburg Declaration on Sustainable Development, September 4, 2002, ¶¶ 27 and 29; Johannesburg Plan of Implementation, No. 9, 17, 19(t), 24 (g), 45ter, 79(d), 100(c), 122(f).

32 Guiding Principles, ***supra*** note 24, No. 11. *See* also ***Protect, Respect and Remedy: a Framework for Business and Human Rights***, Report of the Special Representative of the Secretary-General on the issue of human rights and transnational corporations and other business enterprises, John Ruggie, UN Doc. A/HRC/8/5, April 7, 2008; ***Business and human rights: Towards operationalizing the "protect, respect and remedy" framework***, Report of the Special Representative of the Secretary-General on the issue of human rights and transnational corporations and other business enterprises, UN Doc. A/HRC/11/13, April 22, 2009. On the latter, *see* Angelica Bonfanti, ***L'attuazione del quadro operativo "protect, respect, remedy" nei lavori del Rappresentante speciale delle Nazioni Unite sui diritti umani e le imprese multinazionali***, 3 Diritti umani e diritto internazionale 626 (2009); Peter Muchlinski, ***Implementing the New UN Corporate Human Rights Framework: Implications for Corporate Law, Governance and Regulation***, 22 Business Ethics Quarterly 145 (2012).

33 Guiding Principles, ***supra*** note 24, No. 12.

34 International Covenant on Economic, Social and Cultural Rights, 993 UNTS 3; International Covenant on Civil and Political Rights, 999 UNTS 171.

35 Universal Declaration of Human Rights, ***supra*** note 28.

36 ILO Declaration on Fundamental Principles and Rights at Work, 37 ILM 1233 (1998).

37 Erika R. George, ***Influencing the Impact of Business on Human Rights: Corporate Social Responsibility through Transparency and Reporting***, in Corporate responsibility for human rights impacts: new expectations and paradigms 253 (American Bar Association, 2014); Peter Muchlinski, ***Rethinking CSR:***

pursuant to Guiding Principle No. 12, "the responsibility of business enterprises to respect human rights is distinct from issues of legal liability and enforcement, which remain defined largely by national law provisions in relevant jurisdictions."[38]

This last issue is strongly connected to the theme of "corporate accountability." CA refers to corporations being subject to the monitoring and control carried out by the stakeholders involved in, and affected by, their activities.[39] Scholarly writings underscore the nature of CA as a "'quasi-juridical' answerability based on standards that are internationally defined and implemented."[40] The parameters according to which CA is implemented differ according to the circumstances[41] and to the specific international instruments taken into account.

The realization of CA is strongly connected with the implementation of the SGSR normative framework's third pillar, according to which states must take appropriate steps to ensure, through judicial, administrative, legislative, or other appropriate means, that when such abuses occur within their territory and/or jurisdiction, those affected have access to effective remedy.[42] Therefore, MNCs are accountable only as far as their conduct is monitored, their abuses punished, and their victims compensated.

MNCs within the framework of China's international obligations

Soft law instruments addressing MNCs embody principles established by international treaties and customary law and adapt their content to their addressees. Since an international treaty specifically regulating MNCs' activities has never been adopted,[43] in order to assess Chinese international obligations in this field, it is necessary to examine the framework of the main international obligations binding China with regard to human rights, environmental rights, and social rights protection.

As far as environmental protection is concerned, China has ratified the most significant international conventions. They include the Conventions on Biological Diversity,[44] the UN

Developing a General Principle of Due Diligence in National and International Economic Law, XXXVIII (106) NOTIZIE DI POLITEIA (2012).

38 Guiding Principles, *supra* note 24, No. 12.

39 Craig Forcese, *Regulating Multinational Corporations and International Trade Law*, in THE OXFORD HANDBOOK OF INTERNATIONAL TRADE LAW 723 (Daniel L. Bethlehem ed., Oxford University Press, 2009); Elisa Morgera, *From Corporate Social Responsibility to Accountability Mechanisms*, in HARNESSING FOREIGN INVESTMENT TO PROMOTE ENVIRONMENTAL PROTECTION: INCENTIVES AND SAFEGUARDS 321 (Pierre-Marie Dupuy and Jorge E. Viñuales eds, Cambridge University Press, 2013).

40 MORGERA, *supra* note 27, at 20, recalling Nazli Choucri, *Corporate Strategy Toward Sustainability*, in SUSTAINABLE DEVELOPMENT AND INTERNATIONAL LAW 193 (Winfried Lang ed., Martinus Nijhoff, 1995).

41 Nollkaemper, *supra* note 27, at 9–14.

42 Guiding Principles, *supra* note 24, No. 26. *See* Angelica Bonfanti, *Access to Remedy for Victims of Business-Related Abuse?:Some Reflections*, in BUSINESS AND HUMAN RIGHTS 131 (M.K. Sinah ed., Sage, 2013).

43 Negotiations for a binding instrument are currently ongoing. See Report on the first session of the open-ended intergovernmental working group on transnational corporations and other business enterprises with respect to human rights, with the mandate of elaborating an international legally binding instrument, A/HRC/31/50, 5 February 2016.

44 Convention on Biological Diversity, 1760 UNTS 79. *See* Chapter 34 (Feng, Zhang & Shu) in this volume.

Framework Convention on Climate Change,[45] the Convention for the Protection of the Ozone Layer,[46] the Montreal Protocol,[47] the Stockholm Convention,[48] the Rotterdam Convention,[49] and the Basel Convention.[50] Therefore, China's ratifications imply that it has accepted environmental obligations in line with its Western trade partners.

On the contrary, the treaty obligations binding China in the field of human and social rights protection are not as numerous or complete as the environmental ones. Indeed, China has not ratified some of the most significant conventions in both fields. As far as human rights are concerned, even though China has ratified the conventions against genocide,[51] torture,[52] and discrimination,[53] as well as the Convention on the Rights of the Child[54] and the International Covenant on Economic, Social and Cultural Rights,[55] it has abstained from agreeing to be bound – even after having signed it in 1998 – by the International Covenant on Civil and Political Rights.[56] However, this *lacuna* does not have the effect of exempting China from the observance – at least – of those fundamental human rights set out by the Universal Declaration, the content of which has evolved into customary international law, thus binding also those states that have refused to accept the corresponding treaty obligations.

The protection of social rights shows some significant *lacunae* too. China has ratified only 12 per cent of all ILO conventions,[57] including the conventions on the prohibition

45 United Nations Framework Convention on Climate Change, 1771 UNTS 107. *See* Chapter 10 (Lemoine) and Chapter 14 (Peng) in this volume.

46 Convention for the Protection of the Ozone Layer, 1513 UNTS 323.

47 Montreal Protocol on Substances that Deplete the Ozone Layer, 26 ILM 1550 (1987).

48 Stockholm Convention on Persistent Organic Pollutants, 40 ILM 532 (2001).

49 Convention on the Prior Informed Consent Procedure for Certain Hazardous Chemicals and Pesticides in International Trade, 38 ILM 1 (1999).

50 Basel Convention on the Control of Transboundary Movements of Hazardous Wastes and Their Disposal, 1673 UNTS 126.

51 Convention on the Prevention and Punishment of the Crime of Genocide, 78 UNTS 277.

52 Convention against Torture and Other Cruel, Inhuman or Degrading Treatment or Punishment, 1465 UNTS 85.

53 International Convention on the Elimination of All Forms of Racial Discrimination, 660 UNTS 195; Convention on the Elimination of All Forms of Discrimination Against Women, 1249 UNTS 13.

54 Convention on the Rights of the Child, 1577 UNTS 3.

55 International Covenant on Economic, Social and Cultural Rights, *supra* note 34. *See* Chapters 3 (Di Turi) and 5 (Choukroune) in this volume.

56 International Covenant on Civil and Political Rights, *supra* note 34. *See* Jacques deLisle, ***From Economic Development to What – and Why?: China's Evolving Legal and Political Engagement with International Human Rights Norms***, in Rethinking Law and Development: the Chinese experience 107 (Guanghua Yu ed., Routledge, 2013); Na Jiang, China and International Human Rights: Harsh Punishments in the Context of the International Covenant on Civil and Political Rights (Springer, 2014); Shiyan Sun, ***The Understanding and Interpretation of the ICCPR in the Context of China's Possible Ratification***, 6 Chinese J. Int'l L. 17 (2007). *See* also Sanzhuan Guo, ***Implementation of Human Rights by Chinese Courts: Problems and Prospects***, 8 Chinese J. Int'l L. 161 (2009).

57 Qiu Yang, ***ILO Fundamental Conventions and Chinese Labor Law: From a Comparative Perspective***, 2 Chinese L. & Pol. Rev. 18 (2006). *See* Chapter 3 (Di Turi) in this volume.

of child labor[58] and against discrimination,[59] while it has not ratified the conventions on freedom of association,[60] on collective bargaining,[61] and on prohibition of forced labor.[62] However, in assessing the framework of China's international obligations in this field, one must consider that the fundamental principles on the protection of social rights – including the prohibition of forced labor, as well as on freedom of association and collective bargaining – are defined as core labor standards, which all states, "even if they have not ratified the conventions in question, have [. . .] to respect, to promote and to realize, in good faith."[63] Therefore, China's position should be considered from this perspective.

CSR in harmonious society: Concluding remarks

In evaluating whether China has correctly adapted its domestic law to accommodate the international obligations undertaken and has put in place the necessary measures to ensure compliance with such obligations, strong emphasis should be placed on the notion of "harmonious society" (*hexie shehui*).

As prescribed by President Hu Jintao in 2005, China intends to pursue a "harmonious society" that is "democratic and ruled by law, fair and just, trustworthy and fraternal, full of vitality," and a society which "maintains harmony between man and nature."[64] The concept of a "harmonious society" requires the introduction of Non-Trade Concerns, such as poverty reduction, income distribution, and environmental protection, into the path of economic development. It codifies a goal, which, in international law, might be assimilated to "sustainable development:" "a harmonious society advocates an overall, coordinated and sustainable development concept, making the interests of different sectors balanced," calling to "pay attention to the relationship between humanity and nature; properly protect natural resources; reduce pollution; and make efforts to raise the quality of the environment in order to realize sustainable development."[65]

58 Worst Forms of Child Labour Convention, C182; Minimum Age Convention, 1973, C138.

59 Discrimination (Employment and Occupation) Convention, 1958, C111; Equal Remuneration Convention, 1951, C100.

60 Freedom of Association and Protection of the Right to Organise Convention, 1948, C87.

61 Right to Organise and Collective Bargaining Convention, 1949, C98.

62 Abolition of Forced Labour Convention, 1957, C105; Forced Labour Convention, 1930, C29.

63 ILO Declaration on Fundamental Principles and Rights at Work, *supra* note 36. On its legal value, Philip Alston, *"Core Labour Standards" and the Transformation of the International Labour Rights Regime*, 15 Eur. J. Int'l L. 457 (2004). *See* Chapter 5 (Choukroune) in this volume.

64 Kin-Man Chan, *Harmonious Society*, in International Encyclopedia of Civil Society 821 (Springer, 2009); Paolo Davide Farah, *L'Influenza della Concezione Confuciana sulla Costruzione del Sistema Giuridico e Politico Cinese*, in Identità Europea e Politiche Migratorie 193 (Giovanni Bombelli & Bruno Montanari eds, Vita e Pensiero, 2008).

65 *Harmonious Society*, The 17th National Congress of the Communist Party of China, September 29, 2007, english.peopledaily.com.cn/90002/92169/92211/6274603.html (last visited July 14, 2016).

Legislative reforms recently adopted in the areas of Chinese corporate,[66] environmental,[67] labor,[68] human rights,[69] and consumer rights[70] law should be read in this light. Among them, it is important to mention the introduction into corporate law of the provision, according to which a corporation must "comply with laws and administrative

66 Zhōnghuá Rénmín Gònghéguó Gōngsī Fǎ (2013 Xiūzhèng) (中华人民共和国公司法(2013修正) [Company Law of the People's Republic of China] (Promulgated by the Standing Comm. Nat'l People's Cong., December 29, 1993, amended October 27, 2005, and December 28, 2013).

67 Zhōnghuá Rénmín Gònghéguó Huánjìng Bǎohù Fǎ (中华人民共和国环境保护法) [Environmental Protection Law of the People's Republic of China] (promulgated by the Standing Comm. Of the Nat'l People's Cong., December 26, 1989); Zhōnghuá Rénmín Gònghéguó Gùtǐ Fèiwù Wūrǎn Huánjìng Fángzhì Fǎ (2013 Xiūzhèng) (中华人民共和国固体废物污染环境防治法(2013修正) [Law of the People's Republic of China on the Prevention and Control of Environmental Pollution by Solid Wastes] (Promulgated by the Standing Comm. Nat'l People's Cong., June 29, 2013); Zhōnghuá Rénmín Gònghéguó Hǎiyáng Huánjìng Bǎohù Fǎ (中华人民共和国海洋环境保护法) [Marine Environmental Protection Law of the People's Republic of China] (promulgated by the Standing Comm. Of the Nat'l People's Cong., August 23, 1982, amended December 28, 2013); Zhōnghuá Rénmín Gònghéguó Qīngjié Shēngchǎn Cùjìn Fǎ (2012 Xiūzhèng) (中华人民共和国清洁生产促进法(2012修正) [Cleaner Production Promotion Law of the People's Republic of China] (Promulgated by the Standing Comm. Nat'l People's Cong., February 29, 2012). *See* Richard J. Ferris, Jr. & Hongjun Zhang, ***The Challenges of Reforming an Environmental Legal Culture: Assessing the Status Quo and Looking at Post-WTO Admission Challenges for the People's Republic of China,*** 14 Geo. Int'l Envtl. L.Rev. 429 (2002); Aldo Chircop, ***Regional Cooperation in Marine Environmental Protection in the South China Sea: a Reflection on New Directions for Marine Conservation***, in Maritime Issues in the South China Sea: Troubled Waters or a Sea Of Opportunity 87 (Nien-Tsu Alfred Hu & Ted L. McDorman eds, Routledge, 2013); Joanna I. Lewis & Kelly Sims Gallagher, ***Energy and Environment in China: Achievements and Enduring Challenges***, in The Global Environment: Institutions, Law, and Policy 259 (Regina S. Axelrod, Stacy D. VanDeveer & David Leonard Downie eds, CQ Press, 2011).

68 Zhōnghuá rénmín gònghéguó láodòng hétóng fǎ (中华人民共和国劳动合同法) [Labor Contract Law of the People's Republic of China] (promulgated by the Standing Comm. Nat'l People's Cong., June 29, 2007, effective January 1, 2008, amended December 28, 2012); Zhōnghuá rénmín gònghéguó zhíyèbìng fángzhì fǎ (中华人民共和国职业病防治法) [Law of the People's Republic of China on the Prevention and Treatment of Occupational Diseases] (promulgated by the Standing Comm. Nat'l People's Cong., October 27, 2001, amended December 31, 2011); Zhōnghuá rénmín gònghéguó ānquán shēngchǎn fǎ (中华人民共和国安全生产法) [Work Safety Law of the People's Republic of China] (promulgated by the Standing Comm. Nat'l People's Cong., Jun 29, 2002, amended August 27, 2009). Comments available in: Li Jing, ***China's New Labor Contract Law and Protection of Workers***, 32 Fordham Int'l L.J. 1083 (2009); Hilary K. Josephs, ***Measuring Progress under China's Labor Law: Goals, Processes, Outcomes***, in Obligations and Property Rights in China 91 (Perry Keller ed., Ashgate, 2011); Yunqiu Zhang, ***Labor Law Reforms: China's Response to Challenges of Globalization,*** in Modern Chinese Legal Reform: New Perspectives 131 (Xiaobing Li & Qiang Fang eds, University Press of Kentucky, 2013).

69 Zhōnghuá Rénmín Gònghéguó Lǎonián Rén Quányì Bǎozhàng Fǎ (2012 Nián Xiūdìng) (中华人民共和国老年人权益保障法(2012年修订) [Law of the People's Republic of China on Protection of the Rights and Interests of the Elderly] (Promulgated by the Standing Comm. Nat'l People's Cong., December 28, 2012); Zhōnghuá Rénmín Gònghéguó Jīngshén Wèishēng Fǎ (中华人民共和国精神卫生法) [Mental Health Law of the People's Republic of China] (Promulgated by the Standing Comm. Nat'l People's Cong., June 26, 2012); Zhōnghuá Rénmín Gònghéguó Jiānyù Fǎ (中华人民共和国监狱法) [Prison Law of the People's Republic of China] (Promulgated by the Standing Comm. Nat'l People's Cong., December 29, 1994, amended October 26, 2012); Zhōnghuá Rénmín Gònghéguó Wèi Chéngnián Rén Bǎohù Fǎ (2012 Nián Xiūdìng) (中华人民共和国未成年人保护法(2012年修订) [Law of the People's Republic of China on the Protection of Minors] (Promulgated by the Standing Comm. Nat'l People's Cong., September 4, 1991, amended October 26, 2012).

70 Zhōnghuá Rénmín Gònghéguó Xiāofèi Zhě Quányì Bǎohù Fǎ (中华人民共和国消费者权益保护法) [Law of the People's Republic of China on Protection of Consumer Rights and Interests] (Promulgated by the Standing Comm. Nat'l People's Cong., October 31, 1993, amended October 25, 2013).

regulations, social morality and business ethics, act in good faith, subject itself to government and public supervision; and undertake social responsibility."[71] Therefore, Chinese law now explicitly establishes CSR as law. Other legislative initiatives have followed a similar direction and provide CSR with specific contents: among them, the guidelines,[72] certification schemes,[73] and codes of conduct for listed companies,[74] as well as the standards for overseas investment,[75] all of which charge corporations with the duty to comply with certain standards of conduct and procedures.

In light of this analysis, it is possible to conclude that the legislative measures passed in the field of environmental, human, and social rights protection contribute to adapting the domestic legal system to the international obligations binding China and to the international soft law principles on CSR. In so doing, they operate, at least theoretically, within Chinese law as a means for making corporations accountable, and sustainable development viable.

71 Company Law of the People's Republic of China, *supra* note 66, art. 5. Virginia Harper Ho, *Beyond Regulation: Comparative Look at State-Centric Corporate Social Responsibility and the Law in China*, 46 VAND. J.TRANS'L L. 375 (2013); Li-Wen Lin, *Corporate Social Responsibility in China: Window Dressing or Structural Change?*, 28 BERKELEY J. INT'L L. 68 (2010; Jingchen Zhao, *Promoting Stakeholders' Interest in the Unique Chinese Corporate Governance Model: More Socially Responsible Corporations?*, 21 INT'L CO. & COM. L.REV. 373 (2010); *Id.*, CORPORATE SOCIAL RESPONSIBILITY IN CONTEMPORARY CHINA (Edward Elgar, 2014).

72 SASAC, Guidelines to the State-owned Enterprises Directly under the Central Government on Fulfilling Corporate Social Responsibilities (2008); SEPA, Regulation on Environmental Information Disclosure (2007). *See* Li-wen Lin, *Corporate Social Accountability Standards in the Global Supply Chain: Resistance, Reconsideration, and Resolution in China*, 15 CARDOZO J. INT'L & COMP. L. 321 (2007).

73 China National and Textile and Apparel Council, CSC9000T, China Social Compliance 9000 for Textile and Apparel Industry.

74 Shanghai Stock Exchange, Guide on Environmental Information Disclosure for Companies Listed on the Shanghai Stock Exchange; Shenzhen Stock Exchange, Guide on Listed Companies' Social Responsibility (2006); Guide on Social Responsibility of Listed Companies, Securities and Futures Management Institutions, and Securities and Futures Services Institutions (Fujian Guide, 2008).

75 State Council's Nine Principles on Overseas Investment (2006); China Export-Import Bank's Environmental Policy (2007); SASAC Statement on Overseas State-owned Companies (2008); State Council Regulations on International Contracts (2008); Guide on Sustainable Overseas Silviculture by Chinese Enterprises, State Forestry Admin. (2008); Guidelines for Environmental and Social Impact Assessments of the China Export and Import Bank's Loan Projects (2009); Environmental Policies on China's Investment Overseas (2010); Guidelines on Environmental Protection for China's Outbound Investment and Cooperation (2013); Guidelines for Social Responsibility in Outbound Mining Investments (2014). *See* Mary Lynne Calkins, *Make Friends First, Certify Later: China and ISO 14000*, 9 GEO. INT'L ENVTL. L. REV. (1997); Kirk Herbertson, *Leading While Catching Up?: Emerging Standards for China's Overseas Investments*, 11 SUSTAINABLE DEV. L. & POL. 22 (2011); Wojtek Mackiewicz Wolfe & Annette S. Leung Evans, *China's Energy Investments and the Corporate Social Responsibility Imperative*, 6 J. INT'L L. & INT'L REL. 83; Timothy Webster, *China's Human Rights Footprint in Africa*, 51 COLUMBIA J. TRANSN'L L. 626 (2013). *See* also Chapter 6 (Vadi) in this volume.

5 Rights Interest Litigation, Socio-Economic Rights, and Chinese Labor Law Reform*

*Leïla Choukroune***

> *I don't care if they come to arrest me, I have nothing to lose: I am only asking for what I am entitled to, what I earn with my blood and sweat.****
>
> *Improving workers rights is a crucial step to a better and more just China.*****

With the global economic slowdown unveiling the systemic limits of its foundations, the Chinese miracle is deeply questioned by popular unrest and publicly voiced aspirations. Strikes and protests are indeed erupting at an unprecedented rate everywhere in China. This wave of revolts against an economic system and a political regime perceived both as unjust and repressive is taken very seriously by Chinese leaders who fear this popular dissent could undermine the much-needed social stability. Unwilling to turn towards a different political

* This paper is part of the results of the Research Project on *"Current Trends of Chinese Law towards Non-Trade Concerns such as Sustainable Development and the Protection of Environment, Public Health, Food Safety, Cultural, Social and Economic Rights, Labor Rights and the Reduction of Poverty from the Perspective of International Law and WTO Law"* coordinated by Professor Paolo Davide Farah at gLAWcal – Global Law Initiatives for Sustainable Development (United Kingdom) and at West Virginia University John D. Rockefeller IV School of Policy and Politics, Department of Public Administration, in partnership with the Center of Advanced Studies on Contemporary China (CASCC) in Turin (Italy), Maastricht University Faculty of Law, Department of International and European Law and IGIR - Institute for Globalisation and International Regulation (Netherlands) and Tsinghua University, School of Law, Institute of Public international law and the Center for Research on Intellectual Property Law in Beijing (China). This publication and the Conference Series were sponsored by China–EU School of Law (CESL) at the China University of Political Science and Law (CUPL). The activities of CESL at CUPL are supported by the European Union and the P.R. of China.

** Parts of this contribution are based on fieldwork and interviews performed in China and Hong Kong. I hereby would like to thank the NGOs, lawyers, and workers who have answered my questions and provided me with invaluable comments and insights. For complementary research on related issues, please see: Leïla Choukroune, "The Language of Rights and the Politics of Law: Perspectives on China's Last Legal Ditch Struggle", *International Journal for the Semiotic of Law*, 2015, pp. 1–25; Leïla Choukroune, "India-China Labour Public Interest Litigation (PIL), in Surya Deva (ed.), *Socio-Economic Rights in Emerging Free Markets: Comparative Insights from India and China*, Routledge, 2016, pp. 147–165.

*** *See China Labour Strikes Gain Momentum*, a documentary from Al Jazeera, October 1, 2010, http://www.youtube.com/watch?v=-3UY6oaKPRg. The quote is from a Chinese worker of the Guangzhou region interviewed in the context of the many protests that have erupted after the Honda factory strike of May 31, 2010. As developed below, this particular strike has been analyzed as a turning point in the Chinese workers' movement. The discourse of rights and the legitimate expectations deriving from these rights indeed reached a certain level of sophistication and clarity while the workers' determination seemed unequalled. *See* in particular, China Labor Bulletin's Research Report, *The Workers Movement in China – 2009–2011*, October 2011.

**** Quote from a Chinese labor lawyer, *see China Labour Strikes Gain Momentum*, *supra* note**. These testimonies and declarations are similar to those I could gather myself when doing fieldwork in the regions of Shenzhen, Dongguan, and Canton. As explained below, one striking feature of the workers discourse is the strategic and conscious use of a rights-based discourse.

model, Beijing has resorted to a variety of governing techniques, mixing brutal repression with the gradual introduction of greater socio-economic rights. This cynical combination has taken a variety of shapes – from the adoption of more protective labor regulations to the prevention of free labor unions and the organization of massive crack-down campaigns on rights defenders. Among these contradictory trends, one recent phenomenon deserves particular attention: the apparition, development, and limitation of a rights-based movement often referred to as public interest litigation (PIL).

PIL emerged as a rights advocacy strategy in the United States (US) civil rights movement of the 1960s, and the term has been broadly used worldwide to describe the many ways general grievances relating to the enforcement of socio-economic rights have been litigated by the courts. The term includes the remedies awarded to the victims of the state. However, PIL as well as "public interest lawyering" are too often used as catchall phrases covering quite legal processes from the legal aid services offered to the poor to various types of procedures employed in either public or private law to redress specific or general wrongs with the aim of advancing broader socio-political objectives.

An original incarnation of PIL is progressively appearing in China. The nascent Chinese approach, referring to general grievances litigated in relation to the complicated implementation of social and economic rights, is neither judge-led nor judge-induced. Within an authoritarian one-party state, the nonexistence of a truly independent Chinese judiciary partly explains this key difference, but other Chinese idiosyncrasies contribute to the disparity. As developed below, in the absence of a genuine democratization movement, and without the unanimous support of independent administrative and judicial institutions,[1] a number of elements have, however, permitted the emergence of a unique Chinese collective litigation movement that shows some similarities with PIL and, to some extent, finds its inspiration in its American or Asian predecessors. For the past ten years, indeed, Chinese legal scholars and China watchers have observed the birth, development, and logical limitations of a rights-based and civil society-led movement deploying the law and existing judicial avenues as powerful tools for social emancipation to further the basic legal regime provided by the Chinese Constitution and other legislative developments. Interestingly, this sinicization (中国化 *Zhōngguóhuà*) of PIL finds its roots and strength through the use of rights-based tools themselves, which has been reinforced by a language of rights largely disseminated by the media – including official channels – and ambiguously tolerated by a state that both generates and limits rights. While this grassroots-led movement concerns itself with a number of rights,[2] China is developing its most interesting and, as we will see, most controversial variation of PIL within the field of labor law.[3] In this context, it emerges what I would designate a China-specific *Rights Interest Litigation* (RIL), that illustrates, while challenging,

1 In their work on PIL in Asia, Po Jen Yap and Holing Lau identify three main engines for the development of PIL: "*democratization, transnational migration of norms and ideals, judicial recognition of the institutional role of courts in shaping public law discourse within their jurisdiction.*" *See* PUBLIC INTEREST LITIGATION IN ASIA 2 (Po Jen Yap & Holning Lau eds, Taylor & Francis, 2010).

2 *See* Chapters 2 (Farah), 15 (Huang), 17 (Heurtebise), 19 (Ning), 21 (Soprano), 23 (Creemers), 30 (Rossi), and 32 (Hu) in this volume.

3 Environmental cases also provide an interesting basis for discussion, but they have not, as in other Asian countries such as India or even Hong Kong, involved the same innovative uses of law as labor law cases do.

the justiciability of socio-economic rights[4] in an authoritarian regime.[5] RIL, moreover, questions the intentions of China's legal reforms and the Chinese leadership's true interest in confronting the current regime with the objective of establishing a genuine rule of law.

The following discussion demonstrates why and how Chinese citizens have exercised their legal tools at the right time, with the result of having generated innovative judicial activity fostered by novel, civil society activism, but also how this has led to political disenchantment, which may last indefinitely.

The right time to exercise the legal tools

The constitutional promise of a rights-based China

China has made undeniable progress throughout the last 30 years of institutional and legislative reform. The constant flow of norms is certainly impressive in terms of vigor and political will. The legal revolutions of 1972–1982, 1992–1999, and 2001 have resulted in the following normative landscape transformations: the adoption of a constitution detached from its revolutionary legacy, the promotion of a "socialist market economy" and "socialist rule of law," the accession to the World Trade Organization (WTO), and a complete overhaul of "economic law" to bring about greater uniformity and improved legislative transparency.[6] Despite the persistence of many elements inherited from the revolutionary period, one may no longer ignore the relative institutionalization of Chinese norms and practices. Moreover, whatever the political system that will eventually emerge from China, it will likely base itself on the institutional foundations established by a non-democratic[7] constitutional order. In this sense, the recent constitutional developments, although limited, bear interest.

Adopted on 4 December 1982, the Constitution of the People's Republic of China[8] (Constitution) has been amended a number of times (1988, 1993, 1999, and 2004) to integrate the new objectives of the regime and celebrate Chinese leaders' thought. Largely modeled after the 1936 Constitution of the Soviet Union, the Chinese Constitution has evolved towards a more modern, yet hybrid instrument. In 1999 the National People's Congress (NPC) amended the Constitution in order to introduce the concept of the "rule of law" as a guiding principle. However, this *yifa zhiguo (*依法治国 rule *by* law) mostly refers to the need for the country to be governed by law and coexists in the constitutional text with Marxism–Leninism, Mao Zedong Thought, and Deng Xiaoping theory – all doctrines

4 Since February 2001, China is a party to the International Covenant on Economic, Social and Cultural Rights and, as such, has been examined by the UN Committee reviewing the implementation of its obligations. *See* Leïla Choukroune, *Justiciability of Economic, Social, and Cultural Rights: The UN Committee on Economic, Social and Cultural Rights' Review of China's First Implementation of the International Covenant on Economic, Social and Cultural Rights, 19(1)* Colum. J. Asian L. *(2005).*

5 As discussed below, a number of authors have interrogated the politics and practices of courts in authoritarian regimes hence providing a better view of the functions of the judiciary in non-democratic countries. *See* Tom Ginsburg and Tamir Moustafa, Rule By Law: The Politics of Courts in Authoritarian Regimes (Cambridge University Press, 2008).

6 For an analysis of theses reforms, *see* Leïla Chourkoune & Stanley B. Lubman, *Chine: l'Incomplète Réforme par le Droit,* Esprit (February 2004).

7 For a positive overview of recent constitutional developments, *see* Michael William Dowdle, *Of Parliaments, Pragmatism, and the Dynamics of Constitutional Developments: the Curious Case of China*, N.Y.U. J. Int'l L. & Pol. (Fall 2002).

8 Zhōnghuá Rénmín Gònghéguó Xiànfǎ (Xianfa).

insisting on the "leadership" of the Party. Interestingly, the 2004 constitutional amendments carried this ambiguous modernizing trend further by recognizing "private property" and stressing the state's intention to "respect and protect human rights."[9] While the interpretation and application of these general promises remain rather limited, this language of rights has, however, penetrated Chinese society from the Supreme People's Court to the Chinese workers who now point to the Constitution as an instrument to protect and develop their rights. In this regard, one cannot analyze the Chinese Constitution solely as a pure political instrument serving the ambitions of the one-party state; the Constitution must also be viewed as one of the paradoxical engines of reform and development of rights-conscious discourse and actions in a variety of legal fields in relation to socio-economic and political expectations.

Labor law and corporate social responsibility: How to discipline contradictory forces at work

Contract as emancipation

In the context of corporate social responsibility (CSR), labor law appears as one, if not the key, area of possible emancipation. While acceptance of international standards and practices remains selective,[10] modernization of Chinese employment rules also faces resistance from national and multinational enterprises. As the recent debate on the passing of the new Labor Contract Law of the People's Republic of China (Labor Contract Law) showed, the reform and modernization of Chinese law, in general, has a specific positive effect on Chinese labor law.

Since the laws on labor and trade unions entered into force in 1995[11] and 2002, Chinese workers have received theoretical protection and, although this may not yet fully comply with international standards – China has ratified only four of the eight Fundamental Conventions of the International Labour Organization (ILO) –[12] this protection is not negligible. Several other rules and regulations adopted at the national and local levels, such as the Work Safety Law of the People's Republic of China[13] of June 29, 2002 and the Law on the

9 For a general appraisal of the different phases of China's legal reforms, *see* The China Quarterly's special issue on China's Legal System, Vol.191, September 2007. *See* Chapter 2 (Farah) in this volume.

10 The selective nature of this internationalisation was pointed out several years ago by Pitman Potter. For a recent analysis of these trends and China's emergence on the international scene, *see* Pitman Potter, *China and the International Legal System: Challenges of Participation,* 191 The China Quarterly 699–715 (September 2007).

11 The Labor Law, which came into effect in January 1995, still remains the foundation of China's modern labor system. It required all enterprises to sign employment contracts with all full-time employees and to grant these employees special rights-based protection vis-à-vis their employers on a wide range of issues such as working hours, overtime payments, health and safety at work and, very importantly, termination of contracts. Once again, the real issue has been the implementation of this quite complete set of norms. *See* Chapters 3 (Di Turi) and 4 (Bonfanti) in this volume.

12 *See* http://www.ilo.org/ilolex/english/docs/declworld.htm (last visited July 16, 2016).

13 Zhōnghuá Rénmín Gònghéguó Ānquán Shēngchǎn Fǎ (中华人民共和国安全生产法) [Work Safety Law of the People's Republic of China] (promulgated by the Standing Comm. Nat'l People's Cong., Jun 29, 2002, amended August 27, 2009).

Prevention and Treatment of Occupational Illnesses of the People's Republic of China[14] of October 27, 2001, represent real normative advances. However, proclaiming rights does not necessarily guarantee their implementation, and these rights lack guarantees since many extrajudicial factors prevent their application. The granting of labor rights, for instance, remains highly selective. Almost two-thirds of the population has yet to receive protection from labor rights established in the 1995 Labor Law of the People's Republic of China[15] (Labor Law). It should also be noted that some categories of workers are inadequately protected and are indeed victims of abject discrimination, such as through the residence permit system (*hukou* 戶口), and job discrimination on the basis of gender or disability, among others. Lastly, forced or obligatory labor, which is almost universally banned, plays a dark role in this general picture. Most countries adhere to ILO Conventions 29 (1930) and 105 (1957);[16] however, China has not ratified either convention and has taken a highly ambiguous position. The state continues to use forced labor on a large scale and does so illegally, while condemning the crime of forced labor within private enterprises. There is no clear indication today of a legislative reappraisal of the policies of "reform through labor" (*Laogai* or *laodong gaizao* 勞動 改造) or "re-education through labor" (*Laojiao* or *laodong jiaoyang* 勞動教養所). These relatively profitable activities maintain a virtual underground economy, aided and supervised by the state. Moreover, although the central government prohibits worker strikes, local authorities that are generally more responsive to the demands of workers do not always frown upon them. Finally, and very importantly, the absence of independent union representation severely curbs Chinese workers' collective exercise of their fundamental rights and freedoms.[17]

Nonetheless, workers have started to organize themselves, and, with the help of legal advisers from Non-Governmental Organizations (NGOs) and private law firms, they have formulated claims against private businesses and local governments. Some reactions have resulted in violence. In November 2008, for example, hired thugs assaulted and seriously injured a labor activist working for the Dagong People Centre, a non-profit organization providing library services and legal advice to the migrant workers of Shenzhen. The victim had promoted the new Labor Contract Law. The Chinese press gave an unusual amount of attention to this incident, signaling the significant recent shift in the mindset of China's people and leaders. The *Nafang Dushibao* (Southern Metropolitan Daily), a popular and prestigious newspaper, reported the case with the utmost empathy, speculating that the instigators of the assault acted on behalf of businessmen in collusion with corrupted local government officials. The journalist concluded his article by musing about the well-known risk that in countries which lack effective legal recourses, the relationship between workers,

14 Zhōnghuá Rénmín Gònghéguó Zhíyèbìng Fángzhì Fǎ (中华人民共和国职业病防治法) [Law of the People's Republic of China on the Prevention and Treatment of Occupational Diseases] (promulgated by the Standing Comm. Nat'l People's Cong., October 27, 2001, amended December 31, 2011).

15 Zhōnghuá Rénmín Gònghéguó Láodòng Fǎ (中华人民共和国劳动法) [Labor Law of the People's Republic of China] (promulgated by the Standing Comm. Nat'l People's Cong., July 5, 1994).

16 *See* http://www.ilo.org/ilolex/english/newratframeE.htm (last visited July 16, 2016). *See* also Chapter 3 (Di Turi) in this volume.

17 While China has ratified the 1966 UN Covenant on Economic, Social and Cultural Rights in 2001, it has also made a clear reservation to Article 8 (*right of everyone to form trade unions and join the trade union of his choice*): "The application of Article 8.1 (a) of the Covenant to the People's Republic of China shall be consistent with the relevant provisions of the Constitution of the People's Republic of China, Trade Union Law of the People's Republic of China and Labor Law of the People's Republic of China."

employers, and government can devolve into anarchic violence. The Chinese central government worries about that exact scenario. These steps of rightful resistance challenge not only the development model based partly on cheap labor, but also the opacity of the many unethical managerial practices so often denounced by Western companies. This growing legal discontent functions as one of the Chinese government's main motivations to rethink its social policies. It is now time to prevent labor conflicts by choosing a more sustainable path.

Indeed, China's relative legal rationality did not lead to the integration of the main international standards the country has ratified – starting with the International Covenant on Economic, Social and Cultural Rights (ICESCR). Instead, foreign companies based in China have adopted voluntary codes of conduct, giving rise to much doubt about the benefits of a volunteer system, as evidenced by the recent debate on the adoption of a new Labor Contract Law. In March 2006, the NPC Standing Committee approved a first draft law on labor contract and sought public comment. By April, the congress had received 191,849 comments, mostly from workers, according to official sources. The responses from foreign firms, especially their representative bodies, such as the American Chamber of Commerce in Shanghai and the European Chamber of Commerce, were the most surprising. After years of criticizing the loopholes in China's legal system, the multinationals rejected a document that would give greater protection to labor rights because it would delay economic reforms and thus have a negative effect on investment.[18] Seeking to maintain the advantage of low-cost labor, these multinationals prioritized their economic ambitions over supporting progress in Chinese labor law.[19]

Despite external pressure, the new Labor Contract Law[20] took effect on January 1, 2008, and its Implementing Regulations, which were promulgated by the State Council, entered into effect on September 18, 2008. These texts contain some advances and clarify several legal concepts. Among the most significant changes brought by this law are specific penalties for not signing employment contracts,[21] limitations to the use of fixed-term contracts, consultation procedures, and, very interestingly, several measures to strengthen employees' representation through collective contracts and collective bargaining. Indeed, pursuant to the Labor Law and the new Labor Contract Law, an enterprise "may" enter into a collective contract with its employees. The collective negotiations are generally conducted at the company level between the official union's representatives (The All China Federation of Trade Unions or ACFTU), and the company's management. However, the new Labor

18 *See* the reports of the American Chamber of Commerce of Shanghai and the European Chamber of Commerce, http://www.business-humanrights.org/Links/Repository/785039 (last visited July 16, 2016).

19 This much-publicized debate obliged some companies to answer for their attitude and to reveal their Chinese labor policy. *See* the ***Business and Human Rights*** site that provided a summary of the main arguments and documents at http://www.business-humanrights.org/Documents/Chinalabourlawreform (last visited July 16, 2016).

20 Zhōnghuá Rénmín Gònghéguó Láodòng Hétóng Fǎ (中华人民共和国劳动合同法) [Labor Contract Law of the People's Republic of China] (promulgated by the Standing Comm. Nat'l People's Cong., June 29, 2007, effective January 1, 2008, amended December 28, 2012).

21 Article 10 para. 1 of the new ***Labor Contract Law*** reads as follows: "To establish an employment relationship, a written employment contract shall be conducted," and para. 3 specifies: "In the event that an employer fails to conclude a written employment contract with a worker at the time it starts to use him, and it is not clear what labor compensation was agreed upon with the worker, the labor compensation of the new worker shall be decided pursuant to the rate specified in the collective contract; where there is no collective contract or the collective contract is silent in the matter, equal pay shall be given for equal work."

Contract Law also allows regional collective bargaining within a certain industry, and in areas below the county level.[22] The collective contracts thus negotiated, and submitted to the local labor bureau for examination and verification, become binding legal instruments for the company and its employees.[23] This, of course, poses the questions of the Chinese workers' representation in the absence of freedom of association, and of the many local interpretations and applications of the law.[24] Nevertheless, this new type of collective bargaining generates certain promises, as if the contract could play the role of an emancipator, leading the socialist harmonious society towards a contract-based society where the government would eventually assume responsibility in front of the people.

A laboratory for social change

In July 2008, Walmart's decision to sign collective contracts with the employees of one of its more than 100 stores in China made worldwide headlines. This first deal concluded with Walmart's trade union in the northern industrial city of Shenyang mandated an 8 per cent salary increase for all workers in 2008, an additional 8 per cent increase due in 2009, paid holidays, a social security scheme, remuneration for overtime, and the promise to receive higher pay than the local minimum wage. Similar collective contracts were to be signed with every Walmart store. Was this too good to be true? Between 2009 and 2011, discussions with the Chinese workers of the Pearl River Delta and Shanghai regions created doubts about the effectiveness of the global CSR policies and other codes of conduct that a wide range of multinational corporations proudly developed over ten years.[25] However, the Walmart collective contracts were not the result of an unexpected change in favor of a philanthropic approach of twenty-first-century management. They were the consequence of a high-level campaign run by the Chinese government and the ACFTU. If China has not exactly had the past reputation as a paradise for workers' rights, as demonstrated above, the

22 The first regional collective contract was reached in Shenzhen between 49 enterprises (with 2,500 employees) on September 6, 2006, after more than four months of negotiation. According to the contract, employees would be paid 910 Chinese Yuan (CNY) per month – more than 100 CNY over the local minimum wage. *See* Andreas Lauff, Employment Law and Practice in China 297 (Sweet and Maxwell Asia, 2008). From field work and interviews conducted between 2009 and 2011, the practice seems however relatively limited.

23 A positive example of a potentially robust local application has been given by the *Shenzhen Labor Regulations*. *See* http://www.clb.org.hk/en/node/100292 (last visited July 16, 2016). But local governments do not necessarily take the same implementation path, which, of course, creates many gaps in the general legal regime.

24 In China, the first set of regulations recognizing the legal status of unions was promulgated in Guangzhou in 1922. On May 1, 1925, the All China Federation of Trade Unions (ACFTU) was officially created but remained quasi-inactive during the first years of the People's Republic of China and ceased its work during the Cultural Revolution. It was not until October 1978 when Deng Xiaoping endorsed the positive role of unions, allowing the rebirth of the ACFTU, that it began to be fully active. Eventually, on October 23, 1983, the New Labor Union Charter was signed and still serves today as a reference document. The ACFTU works under the principle of "democratic centralism" and all "grass-root" unions need to evolve under its supervision. Highly dependent on the State-Party system, the ACFTU acts at best as a bridge between workers and management. *See* http://www.acftu.org.cn/template/10002/index.jsp (last visited July 16, 2016). With the new *Labor Contract Law* and its 130 million members, some observers expected the ACFTU to gain a new legitimacy. *See* generally China Labor Bulletin.

25 *See* Chapter 4 (Bonfanti) in this volume.

new political line of the Chinese Communist Party, on the contrary, envisages smoother labor relations as a key for economic stability.

Major national and international businesses are concerned about this legal and social revolution because the social and economic consequences are unprecedented. In any event, this legally binding approach seems much more effective than any voluntary system of reporting since it also produces hopes for new social developments and paves the way towards the long-awaited democratization phase.[26] Indeed, the long-term trend remains relatively clear: to avoid severe consequences, the Chinese government needs to empower Chinese employees with new rights and to ensure that these rights are justiciable. Of course, one should not be too naïve about the consequences of such a transformation within the global economic downturn and accompanying delay of profound political reforms.[27] Nonetheless, a business argument in favor of new labor laws persists,[28] and the Chinese government – no matter what the business lobbies say at the national and local levels – has the will to implement certain crucial reforms on which the future of its economy could depend.[29] In this sense, the social transformations that have empowered Chinese workers serves as a laboratory for future political developments.

Civil society: Articulating the hopes

These positive changes are supported by the emergence of a dynamic civil society that encompasses many different manifestations of independent activism and articulates the hopes of the Chinese population in a variety of socio-economic fields. Among this group of activists, three key actors play a distinctive role: rights defenders, NGOs,[30] and media.

26 Generally speaking, *see* the excellent reports of China Labor Bulletin, http://www.china-labour.org.hk/en/ (last visited July 16, 2016). *See* WHAT WILL DRIVE CHINA'S FUTURE LEGAL DEVELOPMENT? REPORT FROM THE FIELD (U.S. G.P.O., 2008). In June 2008, several human rights activists testified before the American Congressional Executive Commission. Their contributions, including Han DongFang's talk, are available at http://www.cecc.gov/pages/hearings/2008/20080618/index.php (last visited July 16, 2016).

27 According to official sources, 20 million Chinese migrant workers have lost their jobs due to the global economic crisis. *See* http://news.xinhuanet.com/english/2009–02/02/content_10750749.htm (last visited July 16, 2016).

28 *See* Anita Chan, ***Between Blood, Tears, Toys and NGOs***, Yale Global Online (December 13, 2007), http://yaleglobal.yale.edu/content/blood-tears-toys-and-ngos (last visited July 16, 2016). After the China Toy crisis, Anita Chan and Jonathan Unger analyze why brand-name multinationals can't afford a lawless labor environment in China. In another paper, Anita Chan, one of the best international experts of the Chinese labor movement, analyzes the transformation of China's trade unions from a historical perspective. Anita Chan, ***China's Trade Unions in Corporatist Transition***, in JONATHAN UNGER, ASSOCIATIONS AND THE CHINESE STATE: CONTESTED SPACES 69–85 (M. E. Sharpe, 2008). *See* http://rspas.anu.edu.au/ccc/pubs/chan_a.php (last visited July 16, 2016).

29 *See* JINGLIAN WU, UNDERSTANDING AND INTERPRETING CHINESE ECONOMIC REFORM (Thomson, 2005). This book provides a comprehensive, scholarly-credible, yet readable approach to the Chinese economy. The social aspects of this long-term transformation are well-explained by this respected Professor of the Chinese Academy of Social Sciences. *See* as well ALEXANDRA HARNEY, THE CHINA PRICE: THE TRUE COST OF CHINA'S COMPARATIVE ADVANTAGE (The Peguin Press, 2008). This insightful book cleverly captures the dark side of the Chinese economic miracle in exploring the real factory life of thousands of exploited workers. The inconvenient truth and ineffectiveness of social audits and the failure of short-term CSR policies are systematically documented by workers' interviews. Signs of hope nevertheless appear from a legal perspective. Chinese workers are gradually winning more rights to the benefits of both social progress and long-term quality business relations. The reader does not find scholarly-based analysis of the comparative advantage theory here, but it is worth reading for a better understanding of the local reality.

30 *See* Chapter 15 (Huang) in this volume.

The rights defenders, from academics to professional attorneys and "barefoot lawyers" (*weiquan renshi* 維權人士), gained tremendous importance from the second half of the 1990s onwards, with the furtherance of legal reforms, and the separation of these legal professions from direct public administration. Banned between 1957 and 1977, the 1978 Constitution gradually reinstated the lawyer's role in society, and the new criminal rules passed in 1979 restored the right of defense. However, lawyers remained "legal agents of the state," a type of official with special status, whose activities were fully overseen by public bodies. While the "All China Lawyers Association" (ACLA) and its local branches took increasing charge of managing these professionals, it did not ensure their independence, as they reported to the Ministry of Justice. Independence did not arrive until the adoption of the 1996 Law on Lawyers of the People's Republic of China[31] (Law on Lawyers) envisaged as the professional charter for a burgeoning profession. Lawyers finally gained a right to work outside the state system, and private firms mushroomed. Among the successful – yet always monitored, if not repressed – lawyers are many famous practitioners from the Chinese University of Political Sciences and Law, such as Mo Shaoping for criminal defense, Zhou Litai for migrant workers, Tong Lihua, who mostly concentrates on labor law, and Wang Canfa, who works in the context of the Center for Legal Assistance to victims of pollution.

At the same time, encouraged by foreign donors such as the European Union (EU) or US and private bodies such as the Ford Foundation or the American Bar Association (ABA), a number of NGOs appeared all over China. Among them one could mention the well-known Wuhan University Center for Protection of Rights of the Disadvantaged Citizens, created by Wang Exiang, a Supreme People's Court Justice, or Beijing Children's Research and Legal Aid Center, or the Peking's University Center for Women's Law and Legal Services, founded by Guo Jianmei.

Simultaneous to the progressive organization/institutionalization of the work of the lawyers and the NGOs, the media developed a keen interest in social-related subjects, hence forming an implicit alliance with rights activists. With the surge in publicity, the rights abuses and cases made by the Chinese rights defenders attracted public support and the government's sympathy, not to mention the attention of many blogs and websites created by the lawyers and NGOs themselves.[32] For example, the Chinese media, which had direct access to the workers during the dramatic 2010 auto industry strikes, reported heavily throughout most of the protests.[33] Confronted with the need to tackle new forms of social protest that could develop into larger problematic movements, the Chinese government often relaxed

31 Zhōnghuá Rénmín Gònghéguó Lǜshī Fǎ (中华人民共和国律师法) [Law on Lawyers of the People's Republic of China] (promulgated by the Standing Comm. Nat'l People's Cong., May 15, 1996).

32 For an interesting English-language account of the many Chinese web publications, *see*, for instance, China Labor News Translation at http://www.clntranslations.org/ (last visited July 16, 2016). The China Labor Bulletin regularly reports on the latest labor news and activists' projects, see http://www.clb.org.hk/en/ (last visited July 16, 2016). Lastly, as will be explained below, the work of the NGO *Yirenping* is absolutely fascinating; they have indeed assisted no less than 200 antidiscrimination lawsuits and are particularly successful in the area of Hepatitis B virus discrimination cases. *See* as well the excellent work of Fu Hualing, *From online Mobilization to offline Action: Yireping and Public Interest Litigation*, http://papers.ssrn.com/sol3/papers.cfm?abstract_id=1730122 (last visited July 16, 2016). *See* as well the China Collective Bargaining Forum where the work of activists, lawyers and academics is easily accessible at http://www.jttp.cn/ (last visited July 16, 2016).

33 *See*, for instance, Wang Kan, *Collective Awakening and Action of Chinese Workers: the 2010 Workers' Strikes and Their Effects*, SOZIAL GESCHICHTE ONLINE 6 (2011).

its restrictions on freedom of information to allow a relatively broad coverage of these protests. While this pragmatism does not put an end to the infinite capacity of the Beijing leadership to arbitrarily deploy repressive techniques, it helps rights defenders reach their visibility objective and certainly plays a role in the dissemination of the rights-based discourses.

Innovative judicial activity and novel activism

This more favorable legal and social context, together with the maintenance – if not development – of numerous labor-related infringements and abuses, led to the progressive development of a China-specific RIL. Differing from the Indian Social Action Litigation (SAL), the Chinese RIL is neither judge-led nor judge-induced and does not blossom in a democratic regime, where the separation of powers limits the arbitrariness of the state. Rather, it appeared in an authoritarian one-party state, where the judiciary does not have independence and the lawmaking process does not reflect the will of the people. The Chinese RIL is rights-led, and the system relies on the active engagement of civil society to promote and defend the minimal rights base guaranteed by the Chinese Constitution and other legislative accomplishments. Permitted by the authoritarian state, the Chinese RIL does not *a priori* question the regime or challenge the legitimacy of the judicial power, and it believes in the capacity of the current judicial system to enforce the rights claimed by the Chinese population. The Chinese RIL is largely, although not exclusively, concerned with economic and social rights, and has reached a certain level of sophistication and effectiveness in the fields of environment, health,[34] and labor.[35] Oriented towards the working class and not only the poorest strata of Chinese society, the Chinese RIL tends to focus on broad interests, hence participating in the protection of all citizens' rights. Original in its aspirations and manifestations, the Chinese RIL has developed a unique form in the area of labor rights and discrimination. A closer look at the recent labor context offers a first explanation of this unpredictable development.

Broadening the locus standi

To maintain economic growth and social stability, local and national authorities have turned a blind eye to some obvious violations of the law and tried to handle the corresponding increase in labor disputes. Labor disputes have indeed proliferated as a direct result of deep changes in China's economy, and novel methods of settling disputes have arisen. In 1995, China's court handled 28,285 labor disputes. By 2004, this number had multiplied by four to reach 114,997 cases with a 47 per cent chance for workers to win their case, and only a 13 per cent chance for employers. While a shift had occurred from mediation to court actions, there is little cause for drawing any encouraging conclusions since it is hardly a general trend. Only a limited number of disputes may be subject to the courts, and, with the adoption of the Labor Dispute Mediation and Arbitration Law of the People's Republic

34 *See* Chapters 30 (Rossi), 31 (Prasad), and 32 (Hu) in this volume.

35 In this regard, we tend to disagree with Fu Hualing and Richard Cullen who seem to view the Chinese PIL as an instrument to foster the emerging middle class well-being. *See* Fu Hualing & Richard Cullen, *The Development of Public Interest Litigation in China*, in PUBLIC INTEREST LITIGATION IN ASIA, *supra* note 1, at 9.

of China[36] (the Labor Dispute Mediation and Arbitration Law) in May 2008, the government now encourages a return to mediation and arbitration. The already overwhelmed labor bureaus thus face unprecedented difficulties. In Shanghai, the Pudong Labor Dispute Arbitration Commission reveals that complainants filed 744 disputes in the area of Pudong alone by May 2008, representing a year-on-year rise of 330 per cent. In the first three quarters of 2008, China's Labor Dispute Arbitration Committees had accepted 520,000 new cases on the basis of the Labor Dispute Mediation and Arbitration Law, a 50 per cent increase over the same period in 2007.[37] Recent studies also reveal a sharp increase in the number of labor disputes entering Chinese courts. In 2008, after the passage of the Labor Contract Law and the Labor Dispute Mediation and Arbitration Law, the number of labor dispute cases almost doubled to reach 693,000.[38] In this context, the China Labour Bulletin (CLB) program on labor rights litigation provides an excellent example of these developments. Since 2003, the CLB has created cooperative links with law firms and NGOs across China, as well as with hundreds of individual lawyers, to provide workers who cannot afford legal and court fees, and who have a legitimate grievance, with effective legal defense in court and/or determined representation in mediation or arbitration proceedings.[39] Among these cases, discrimination issues and Hepatitis B cases in particular have proven to be quite successful.

The case of HBV

The recent developments of hepatitis B virus (HBV) cases provide an interesting and impressive illustration of the use of RIL. HBV carriers have used the 2007 Employment Promotion Law of the People's Republic of China[40] (Employment Promotion Law) to bring legal claims against a variety of employers for the discrimination they suffered throughout their recruitment processes. As described above, this evolution took place within the context of improved legislative protection of rights holders and a more vast dissemination of these cases by the Chinese media.[41] In 2003, for instance, the cases of Zhou Yichao and Zhang Xianzhu, two carriers of HBV and victims of employment discrimination, made the headlines. A website was created to support their fight and functioned as a law-reviewing and lawmaking proposal center. Warning the government to take the societal importance of HBV seriously (about 10 per cent of the Chinese population carries the disease), and invoking national and international human rights provisions, the supporters of Zhou and Zhang petitioned the Chinese state (by asking the State Council) to remove HBV from the list of disqualifying diseases for civil service examinations and recruitment procedures and requiring the

36 Zhōnghuá Rénmín Gònghéguó Láodòng Zhēngyì Tiáojiě Zhòngcái Fǎ (中华人民共和国劳动争议调解仲裁法) [Labor Dispute Mediation and Arbitration Law of the People's Republic of China] (promulgated by the Standing Comm. Nat'l People's Cong., December 29, 2007, effective May 1, 2008).

37 *See* China Ministry of Labor and Social Securityì and China Labor Net.

38 Although it is always difficult to gauge the exact number of disputes, the Chinese Supreme People's Court has recently published a number of interesting figures. *See* http://en.chinacourt.org/ (last visited July 16, 2016).

39 *See* http://www.clb.org.hk/en/node/100020 (last visited July 16, 2016).

40 Zhōnghuá Rénmín Gònghéguó Jiùyè Cùjìn Fǎ (中华人民共和国就业促进法) [Employment Promotion Law of the People's Republic of China] (promulgated by the Standing Comm. Nat'l People's Cong., August 30, 2007, effective January 1, 2008).

41 The *China Daily* itself features HBV stories and supports the antidiscrimination movement. *See*, for instance, *A Woman's Battle Against HBV Discrimination*, China Daily (August 7, 2011), http://www.chinadaily.com.cn/china/2011–08/07/content_13064556.htm (last visited July 16, 2016).

protection of privacy rights for the carriers of HBV. These claims settled in 2007 with the passage of the Employment Promotion Law and in 2010 when a new regulation, jointly issued by the Ministry of Health and the Ministry of Human Resources and Social Security, stated that compulsory tests for HBV must be removed from pre-employment physical exams for civil servants. Simultaneously, a significant number of lawsuits took place all over China, and most of them resulted in compensation to the HBV victims.[42]

The disenchanted citizen

Although extremely encouraging and promising, this RIL trend is also challenged by the inherent limitations of the current Chinese legal and judicial system. As observed by Fu Hualing and Richard Cullen:

> The reliability of courts as a forum for PIL can no longer be taken for granted. Courts were a comparatively reliable forum for PIL in the 1990s. Under Xiao Yang's terms as Chief Justice, the courts were more receptive to challenging lawsuits and lawyers enjoyed some breathing space in the court room in advocating rights. Since 2003, unfortunately, more constraints (not least via the courts themselves) have been placed on legal activism and PIL.[43]

In stabilizing and disciplining the Chinese population, Chinese harmonious society may reveal the true nature and limitations of the government's objective as it sheds an unpleasant light on the possible (mis)use of RIL to support the regime.

Harmonious authoritarianism and the dependent judge

The Chinese RIL system suffers from the lack of a truly professional and independent judiciary. During the years of reform, the courts were reorganized according to a four-tier hierarchy, with the Supreme People's Court (*Zuigao renmin fayuan* 最高人民法院) at the top.[44] Around 200,000 judges preside over approximately 3,000 Basic People's Courts. The judges' level of professionalism jumped considerably in 2002 with the establishment of the standard national exam, which has a success rate of around 10 per cent. The vast majority of practicing judges have, nevertheless, had no real legal training. There is obviously a huge gap between a judge on the Supreme People's Court trained in legal issues in China and a judge trained overseas. The former judge may be drawn from the ranks of the army or the

42 For an excellent account of the recent judicial development in this field, *see* Timothy Webster, *Ambivalence and Activism: Employment Discrimination in China*, 44(3) Vand. J. Transnat'l L. (2011).

43 *See* Hualing & Cullen, *supra* note 35, at 28.

44 There are three other levels: 30 High People's Courts (*Gaoji renmin fayuan* 高級人民法院), which have authority in provinces, autonomous regions, and municipalities directly under the central government; 389 Intermediate People's Courts (*Zhongji renmin fayuan* 中級人民法院), which function at the prefecture level, with the municipalities catered for by courts at the level of provinces and autonomous regions; and, finally, more than 3,000 Basic People's Courts (*Jiceng renmin fayuan* 基層人民法院), which have authority at the district and county levels and are sometimes complemented by other People's Tribunals (*Renmin fating* 人民 法庭) regarding those counties that are geographically dispersed. Furthermore, there are more than a hundred specialist tribunals with authority in matters of fishing, maritime affairs, forestry, railways, and so on.

police or appointed by a local people's congress, and may continually confront problems of legitimacy vis-à-vis Party officials, a lack of resources, and the temptation of corruption, while the latter may maintain an awareness of international realities and a sense of belonging to a community of jurists who can exercise true power to interpret the law.[45]

In 1999, the Supreme People's Court adopted a first five-year reform plan aimed at enhancing the professionalism and independence of judges.[46] On October 18, 2001, the Court published a code of ethics, targeting, in particular, judicial corruption.[47] Finally, in October 2005, the Court unveiled its second five-year plan, one of whose highlights was to implement a process of centralized national review of capital punishment sentences.[48] Despite the commendable efforts of the Supreme People's Court, made more dynamic by the profile of Xiao Yang as its President, the Party's interference remained too strong for the acclaimed modernization to have a real effect.[49] This was sadly confirmed with the election, on March 16, 2008, of Wang Shengjun as the new President of the Supreme People's Court. Without any formal legal education, this native of Suzhou joined the Chinese Communist Party in 1972 and occupied various prestigious positions in the local communist apparatus until he became Deputy Secretary General of the Party Central Politics and Law Committee in 1993. Wang Shengjun also served as Deputy Director of the Central Committee for Comprehensive Management of Public Security from 2005 to 2008 and as a member of the 15th Party Central Commission for Discipline Inspection. With this change of presidency, the Supreme People's Court also modified its discourse, to the great confusion and dismay of the many "modern" judges who had anticipated the professionalization of the judiciary, which could eventually achieve independence from the Party-state. As stressed by Professor Jerome A. Cohen in one of his pertinent formulas: "In a series of mind-numbing ideological clichés, Mr. Wang emphasizes upholding party leadership and focusing the courts on economic development and social stability. For Mr. Wang [. . .] concerns for judicial fairness and justice must be interpreted in light of minyi, or 'public opinion.'"[50]

This return to the past not only brings disappointment to the legal profession, but also produces real worries about the future of an already uncertain judicial reform.[51] Clearly this

45 For a precise and rigorous history of the last 30 years of judicial reform, *see* STANLEY LUBMAN, BIRD IN A CAGE. LEGAL REFORM IN CHINA AFTER MAO (Stanford University Press, 1999).

46 *See Renmin Fayuan Wunian gaige Gangyao* (Five-Year Program of Reform).

47 *See* Li Yuwen, *Professional Ethics of Chinese Judges, A Rising Issues in the Landscape of Judicial Practice*, CHINA PERSPECTIVES (May–June 2003), http://chinaperspectives.revues.org/document274.html (last visited July 16, 2016).

48 *See Renmin Fayuan Dierge Wunian Gaige Gangyao* (Second Five-Year Program of Reform).

49 *See* Benjamin Liebman, *China's Courts: Restricted Reform*, COLUM. J. ASIAN L. (Fall 2007) and from the same author, *A populist threat to China's Courts*, in CHINESE JUSTICE: CIVIL DISPUTE RESOLUTION IN POST-REFORM CHINA (Mary Gallagher & Margaret Woo eds, Cambridge University Press, 2009).

50 *See* Jerome A Cohen, *Body Blow for the Judiciary*, SOUTH CHINA MORNING POST (October 18, 2008), http://www.scmp.com/article/656696/body-blow-judiciary (last visited July 16, 2016).

51 The Supreme People's Court is now facing a series of unprecedented turbulences. Huang Songyou, one of its Vice-Presidents and also a member of the Judicial Committee, has been detained by Party Central Commission for Discipline Inspection officials, and has been put under "shuanggui," a type of investigation. Huang oversaw the civil cases division and enforcement of the decisions of the Supreme People's Court and was famous for being in favor of the "constitutional" movement. In 2001, in the *Qi Yuling* decision, in which the Supreme People's Court instructed a plaintiff be granted relief by a lower court based on a violation of constitutional rights (in this case education), appeared as the first step towards the justiciability of the Constitution. Huang even briefly cited *Marbury v Madison*, as well as the German and Austrian experiences of constitutional courts. Nevertheless, this decision has never had the impact Chinese

is all a question of judicial independence. But how can this independence be assessed, and what type of progress can be made in terms of fairness – at a time when the new President of the Supreme People's Court calls for what is known in typical political terms as the "demystification" of the judicial process? Moreover, there is no institution equivalent to a kind of "high council for the judiciary," for example, and there is also absolutely no statutory guarantee of any judicial independence or impartiality. More specifically, the Standing Committee of the NPC Political Bureau seems to act as the body actually in charge of justice, through the establishment of a coordinating group on judicial reform (*sifa tizhi jizhi gaige* 司法體制機制改革). Through this group, and the Party's discipline inspection commissions, the entire judicial apparatus (prosecution, judges, ministry, and even the police) is subject to the Party.

The gagged lawyer

Other severe limitations to the RIL ambitions lie in the frequent and arbitrary repression of rights-defenders and the systematic promotion of mediation as the best alternative to judicial settlement.

As is too often demonstrated by the recent news, the professional work of lawyers receives insufficient protection, and a number of provisions tend to restrict the freedom of action of Chinese human rights defenders. Article 96 of the Criminal Procedure Law of the People's Republic of China[52] (Criminal Procedure Law) stipulates that lawyers accused of divulging state secrets who wish to seek outside help should first obtain permission from public security authorities. Already the concept of state secrets is defined so vaguely as to render rights-defenders vulnerable to such accusations. Article 306 of the Criminal Procedure Law, widely used to silence lawyers, deems some actions criminal by equating them with fabrication of evidence or perjury. And although the text of the Law on Lawyers has undergone recent changes, its direction and intention remain unclear.[53] Moreover, in 2008, a group of lawyers lobbying for the free election of the leadership for Beijing's Lawyers Association has seen its licenses suspended and its firm (Beijing Yitong Law Firm) forced to close for six months. The latest proposed amendments of the criminal procedure law do not go in the direction of better protection for rights-defenders. Largely commented, these amendments would

---

and foreign observers expected. Huang has been investigated over alleged involvement in an economic scandal in Guangdong that led to the detention of the senior provincial official Yang Xiancai in July 2008. *See* Vivian Wu, ***High Court Judge places under party investigation***, SOUTH CHINA MORNING POST (October 18, 2008), http://www.scmp.com/article/656782/high-court-judge-placed-under-party-investigation (last visited July 16, 2016).

An interesting new development took place in December 2008 when the Supreme People's Court had officially withdrawn or cancelled its 2001 "Reply" in the *Qi Yuling* case (*See* Supreme Court Notice of 18 December 2008). This might be part of an attack against Xiao Yang and its "liberal-western" legacy. Eventually, in August 2009, Huang was fired by the Supreme People's Court. It was the first time a judge of the Supreme People's Court was dismissed for suspected violations of the law and disciplinary code.

52 Zhōnghuá Rénmín Gònghéguó Xíngshì Sùsòng Fǎ (中华人民共和国刑事诉讼法) [Criminal Procedure Law of the People's Republic of China] (promulgated by the Standing Comm. Nat'l People's Cong., Lug. 7, 1979, effective January 1, 1997).

53 The Law on Lawyers has been amended by the Standing Committee of the National People's Congress of the People's Republic of China on October 28, 2007. These revisions afford more protection for the attorney-client relationship, raise legal ethics standards, allow solo practice, but maintain some ambiguities on the lawyer professional liability and status.

authorize the practice of enforced disappearance for political offenders and, thus potentially, rights-defenders challenging the regime.[54]

To this disenchantment, one needs to add the return of mediation as a tool to settle conflicts. Escalating disputes and the relative inability of the justice system to resolve them have aroused disillusionment in response to which Chinese authorities have again begun promoting their classic tool, mediation, now vested with the virtuous halo of socialist harmony. The recent adoption of the Provisions on the Negotiation and Mediation of Enterprise Labor Disputes,[55] which took effect on January 1, 2012, effectively illustrates this renewed trend.

These developments go against the commendable efforts to modernize and promote a Chinese legal system that is opening up rapidly to external influences. The restoration of norms, which occurs through legislative and procedural make-believe, hides an ambiguous attitude towards the law. Once again, this illusion of justice is based on the fiction of harmony and the need to discipline a society to better ensure its stability.

Conclusion: The perverse effect of justiciability – when democracy is kept at bay

The syncretic nature of China's legal system no longer evokes surprise. Although drawn from foreign rules and practices, China has synchronized these norms to better integrate them.[56] The Chinese RIL is one fascinating illustration of this ability to adapt and perpetuate a given system. In this context, one should examine the possible side effects of justiciability in an authoritarian state such as China. Far from challenging the regime, a manifestation of justiciability such as the Chinese RIL can also reinforce the existing political system by providing the leaders with breathing time and space. In this context, the synchronization undertaken by a socialist harmonious society, which is gradually reinventing China under the Party's watchful eye, is designed principally to stall for time. Using law as a powerful tool to discipline[57] society and prevent popular unrest, the socialist harmonious society adopts diversionary tactics in an effort to control a potentially troublesome political society.

Yet, these logical limitations and legitimate questions about the future and undesirable effects of the justiciability of economic and social rights in an authoritarian state should not overshadow two positive developments: the Chinese legislator and judiciary have taken socio-economic rights increasingly seriously, and the Chinese population has started to appropriate these new rights.

54 *See*, for instance, Jerome A. Cohen's comments in the *Asia Wall Street Journal* of December 13, 2011.

55 Qǐyè Láodòng Zhēngyì Xiéshāng Tiáojiě Guīdìng (企业劳动争议协商调解规定) [Provisions on the Negotiation and Mediation of Enterprise Labor Disputes] (promulgated by the Ministry of Human Resources and Social Security, November 30, 2011, effective January 1, 2012).

56 On the hopes and limitations of the internationalisation of Chinese law arising from the example of the WTO, *see* Leïla Choukroune, ***The Accession of China to the WTO and Legal reform: is China heading towards a rule of law through internationalisation without democracy?***, in La Chine et la démocratie [China and Democracy] 617–661 (Mireille Delmas-Marty & Pierre-Etienne Will eds, Fayard, 2007).

57 On the law of China's harmonious society, *see* Leïla Choukroune & Antoine Garapon, The Norms of Chinese Harmony: Disciplinary Rules as Social Stabilizer, 71 China Perspectives 36–49 (2007), http://search.informit.com.au/documentSummary;dn=685452095289424;res=IELHSS (last visited July 16, 2016), and Leïla Choukroune, "Harmonious Society" and the Law: an Epistemological Break? How China's Practice of International Law is Challenging Legal Theory, 13 (4) Ger. L.J. 497–510 (2012), www.germanlawjournal.com/pdfs/Vol13-No1/PDF_Vol_13_No_04_497–510_Articles_Choukroune.pdf (last visited July 16, 2016).

6 Law, Culture, and the Politics of Chinese Outward Foreign Investment**

*Valentina Sara Vadi**

Introduction

China has played an increasingly central role in international (economic) relations since its reform and opening-up policy beginning in 1978, triggering significant power shifts in the world economy.[1] China's mercantilist policy, which is characterized by compliance with international standards to attract foreign direct investment (FDI) and to gain access to overseas markets, and the pervasive role of the state in the market economy[2] has the potential to lead to an Asian Century[3] characterized by a multi-polar economy and the redistribution of political and economic power eastward.[4]

* The author wishes to thank Judy Carter, Paolo Davide Farah, Wolfgang Giernalczyk, Sungjin Kang, and Nikos Lavranos for helpful comments.

** It is part of the results of the Research Project on "*Current Trends of Chinese Law towards Non-Trade Concerns such as Sustainable Development and the Protection of Environment, Public Health, Food Safety, Cultural, Social and Economic Rights, Labor Rights and the Reduction of Poverty from the Perspective of International Law and WTO Law*" coordinated by Professor Paolo Davide Farah at gLAWcal – Global Law Initiatives for Sustainable Development (United Kingdom) and at West Virginia University John D. Rockefeller IV School of Policy and Politics, Department of Public Administration, in partnership with the Center of Advanced Studies on Contemporary China (CASCC) in Turin (Italy), Maastricht University Faculty of Law, Department of International and European Law and IGIR - Institute for Globalisation and International Regulation (Netherlands) and Tsinghua University, School of Law, Institute of Public international law and the Center for Research on Intellectual Property Law in Beijing (China). An early draft of this paper was presented at Conference Series "*China's Influence on Non-Trade Concerns in International Economic Law*", First Conference held at the Center of Advanced Studies on Contemporary China (CASCC) in Turin on November 23–24, 2011. This publication and the Conference Series were sponsored by China–EU School of Law (CESL) at the China University of Political Science and Law (CUPL). The activities of CESL at CUPL are supported by the European Union and the P.R. of China. The views expressed in this chapter are the author's only and do not necessarily reflect those of the EU or China.

1 Axel Berger, *The Politics of China's Investment Treaty-Making Program*, in THE POLITICS OF INTERNATIONAL ECONOMIC LAW 162 (Tomer Broude, Marc L. Busch, & Amelia Porges eds, Cambridge, 2011).

2 Jonathan Holslag, *China's New Mercantilism in Central Africa*, 5 AFR. & ASIAN STUD. 135–136 (2006). *See* Chapter 4 (Bonfanti) in this volume

3 Teemu Ruskola, *Where is Asia? When is Asia? Theorizing Comparative Law and International Law*, 44 U.C. DAVIS L. REV. (2011).

4 Kishan Khoday & Jonathan Bonnitcha, *Globalization and Inclusive Governance in China and India: Foreign Investment, Land Rights and Legal Empowerment of the Poor*, in SUSTAINABLE DEVELOPMENT IN WORLD INVESTMENT LAW 483, 484 (Marie-Claire Cordonier Segger, Markus Gehring & Andrew Newcombe eds, Kluwer Law International, 2011).

The history of outward foreign direct investment (OFDI) which flows from China "is short but spectacular."[5] According to the 2014 World Investment Report (WIR), China ranks among the top 20 investors in the world,[6] "has strengthened its position as one of the leading sources of FDI, and its outflows are expected to surpass its inflows within two years."[7] Chinese OFDI has evolved from an initial concentration on the development of natural resources to cover infrastructure, the mining industry (including metals and rare earth materials), manufacturing, finance, agriculture, forestry, and more. While most Chinese OFDI remains in Asia, which accounted for 61 per cent of Chinese OFDI at the end of 2013, China has become one of the most significant foreign investors in Latin America, which receives 16 per cent of Chinese OFDI.[8] China acts as a relatively small investor in Europe and Africa,[9] which received only 11 and 4 per cent of Chinese OFDI, respectively. Similarly, North America and Oceania received only 3 per cent and 5 per cent of Chinese OFDI, respectively.[10] The relevant figures may be an understatement.[11]

More than 90 per cent of Chinese OFDI comes from large state-owned enterprises (SOEs),[12] albeit private investors have become increasingly active players.[13] The public nature of most Chinese OFDI has raised concerns that strategy, rather than normal commercial considerations, governs such investments.[14] Chinese OFDI is supported by the government's firm commitment to cultivate relations with host states by signing bilateral investment treaties (BITs), providing aid, debt relief, and other forms of development assistance.[15] Thus, SOEs obtain a competitive advantage vis-à-vis other multinational corporations (MNCs), potentially undermining the ability of the latter to compete on a level playing field.[16] Political scientists have conceptualized Chinese investments as instruments of "soft power" in international relations.[17]

The emerging role of China as a capital exporter contributes to the current debate about the interplay between international investment law and non-economic issues. Concerns have arisen with regard to OFDI and its impact on the social, environmental, and cultural

5 Daniel H. Rosen & Thilo Hanemann, *China's Changing Outbound Foreign Direct Investment Profile: Drivers and Policy Implications*, Peterson Institute for International Economics Policy Brief 3, Washington (June 2009), at 3.

6 United Nations Conference on Trade and Development (UNCTAD), *2014 World Investment Report (WIR)*, xv.

7 *Id.* at 47.

8 *China Business Insights*, February 2013, at 10.

9 *See* Chapter 5 (Klaver & Trebilcock) in this volume

10 *Id.*

11 The statistics are based on information that Chinese companies submit during the registration and approval process. The primary official source for data on Chinese OFDI is the Annual Statistical Bulletin on China's Outward Direct Investment, which is compiled by the Chinese Ministry of Commerce (MOFCOM).

12 2009 Statistical Bulletin of China's Outward Foreign Investment.

13 Jing Gu, *China's Private Enterprises in Africa and the Implications for African Development*, 21 Eur. J. Dev. Res. 570, 570–587 (2009).

14 UNCTAD, *World Investment Report 2010: Investing in a Low Carbon Economy*, at 7.

15 David Zweig & Bi Jianhai, *China's Global Hunt for Energy*, 84 Foreign Aff. 25, 27 (2005).

16 *See* Chapter 4 (Bonfanti) in this volume.

17 Sheng Ding, The Dragon's Hidden Wings. How China Rises with its Soft Power (Lexington Books, 2008).

standards of the host state.[18] Can the Chinese BIT program promote sustainable development and/or include social and environmental standards?

This chapter adopts an international investment law perspective, focusing on the rise of Chinese BITs and exploring recent arbitrations under these treaties. At the same time, an attempt is made to achieve an interdisciplinary stance and to investigate the social, cultural, and environmental consequences of China's investment treaty–making program. In an effort to shed more light on China's FDI strategies and to answer the abovementioned question, this chapter proceeds as follows: first, it briefly defines foreign direct investment and examines the main features of international investment law and arbitration; second, it scrutinizes the recent proliferation of Chinese BITs and investor–state arbitrations under these treaties; and third, it discusses the political, social, and environmental implications of the rise of FDI and questions whether BITs can provide better regulation of FDI.

International investment law and arbitration

International investment law governs foreign direct investment, which is "the transfer of tangible or intangible assets from one country into another for the purpose of their use in that country to generate wealth under the total or partial control of the owner of the assets."[19] In the absence of a multilateral treaty, more than 1,300 investment treaties govern foreign investments and often provide foreign investors with direct access to international arbitration.[20] Investment treaties impart extensive protection to investors' rights in order to encourage FDI and foster economic development.[21] While investment treaties differ in their details, their scope and content have been standardized over the years, as negotiations have led to the exchange and refinement of different concepts.[22]

At the substantive level,[23] investment treaties typically define the scope and definition of FDI and establish protection against discrimination, fair and equitable treatment (FET), full protection and security, treatment no less favorable than required by customary international law, and assurances that the host country will honor its commitments regarding the investment – the so-called "umbrella clause". Investment treaties generally guarantee compensation in the event of nationalization, expropriation, or indirect expropriation, and clarify what level of compensation will be owed in such cases. A small number of investment treaties also include provisions prohibiting certain forms of performance requirements.[24]

18 *See* Chapters 22 (Germann), 23 (Creemers), and 24 (Kamperman Sanders) in this volume.

19 M. Sornarajah, The International Law on Foreign Investment 7 (Cambridge University Press, 2010).

20 Anthony Aust, Handbook of International Law 345 (Cambridge University Press, 2010).

21 The majority of economists and policy-makers in both developing and developed countries, *see* FDI as an engine for promoting economic growth and development. *See*, for instance, Jagdish Bhagwati, ***Why Multinationals Help Reduce Poverty***, 30 World Econ. 211–228 (2007); Vudayagiri N. Balasubramanyam, M. Salisu, & David Sapsford, ***Foreign Direct Investment and Growth: New Hypotheses and Evidence***, 8 J. Int'l Trade & Econ. Dev. 27, 27–40 (1999).

22 Campbell McLachlan et al., International Investment Arbitration 6 (Oxford University Press, 2007).

23 On the substantive standards of protection of foreign direct investment, *see* generally Standards of Investment Protection (August Reinisch ed., Oxford University Press, 2008).

24 *See* UNCTAD, Foreign Direct Investment and Performance Requirements: New Evidence from Selected Countries (2003).

At the procedural level, BITs provide investors direct access to an international arbitral tribunal.[25] This is a major novelty in international law, as customary international law does not incorporate such a mechanism; however, investor–state arbitration has become a standard feature in international investment treaties since the 1980s.[26] The rationale for internationalizing investor–state disputes lies in the assumed independence and impartiality of international arbitral tribunals in contrast to national dispute settlement procedures that are often perceived as biased or inadequate.[27] Contracting parties also use arbitration because of perceived advantages in confidentiality, speed, efficiency, and effectiveness.[28] The parties themselves select the members of the tribunal from a qualified group of law scholars or professionals. Unless agreed otherwise, arbitrators exercise independence and impartiality from the party that appointed them. Confidentiality is one of the main features of arbitral proceedings. The tribunal generally holds hearings *in camera*, and the submitted documents remain confidential in principle.[29] Final awards may not be published without the agreement of the parties.[30] Although efforts to make investment arbitration more transparent have been undertaken in various fora in recent years,[31] the lack of transparency may hamper efforts to track investment treaty disputes, monitor their frequency and settlement rate, and assess their policy implications.

Finally, awards rendered against host states are, in theory, readily enforceable against host-state property worldwide due to the widespread adoption of the New York[32] and Washington Conventions.[33] Under the New York Convention, the recognition and enforcement of an award may be refused only on limited grounds.[34] Arbitration under the ICSID rules is wholly exempted from the supervision of local courts, with awards subject only to an internal annulment process.[35] If arbitration takes place in a country other than the host state, there may be no capacity whatsoever for the host government to challenge the award in its own legal system.[36]

25 *See* Jan Paulsson, *Arbitration Without Privity*, 10 ICSID Rev. Foreign Inv. L. J. 232 (1995).

26 *See* David Sedlak, *ICSID's Resurgence in International Investment Arbitration: Can the Momentum Hold?*, 23 Penn St. Int'l L. R. 147 (2004).

27 *See* Andrew Newcombe & Lluis Paradell, Law and Practice of Investment Treaties 24 (Kluwer Law International, 2009).

28 *See* Ibrahim F. I. Shihata, *Towards a Greater Depoliticization of Investment Disputes: The Role of ICSID and MIGA* 1 ICSID Rev. Foreign Inv. L. J. 1, 4 (1986).

29 On transparency, see Andrea Bianchi and Anne Peters (eds.) *Transparency in International Law* (Cambridge University press 2013).

30 For instance, Article 34.5 of the UNCITRAL Rules (as revised in 2010, with new article 1, paragraph 4, as adopted in 2013) states that "the award may be made public with the consent of all parties."

31 For instance, the International Centre for Settlement of Investment Disputes (ICSID) requires public disclosure of dispute proceedings under its auspices. *See* Int'l Centre for the Settlement of Inv. Disputes [ICSID], *ICSID Convention, Regulations and Rules* 66 (2006), http://icsid.worldbank.org/ICSID/StaticFiles/basicdoc/CRR_English-final.pdf [hereinafter ICSID Regulations and Rules] Regulation 22(1).

32 United Nations Convention on the Recognition and Enforcement of Foreign Arbitral Awards, *opened for signature* June 10, 1958, 21 UST 2517, 330 UNTS 38 (entered into force June 7, 1959) [hereinafter New York Convention].

33 Convention on the Settlement of Investment Disputes between States and Nationals of other States, *opened for signature* March 18, 1965, 17 UST 1270, 575 UNTS 159 (entered into force October 14, 1966) [hereinafter Washington Convention or ICSID Convention].

34 New York Convention, *supra* note 32, art. 5.

35 Washington Convention, *supra* note 33, art. 52.

36 Luke Eric Peterson, *Bilateral Investment Treaties and Development Policy-Making*, 22 (International Institute for Sustainable Development, 2004).

Chinese bilateral investment treaties

The Chinese investment treaty–making program has become a key component of China's development policy. China has entered into 130 BITs – more than any other country except Germany.[37] In addition, China has signed nine free trade agreements (FTAs),[38] which include chapters providing for the protection of foreign investment.[39] While China currently negotiates a BIT with the United States (US),[40] the European Commission (EC) just closed a public consultation on the usefulness of an European Union (EU)–China BIT/FTA, and performed an impact assessment on such a deal.[41] In addition, China was designated a priority country in the EC's Communication on the Future European Investment Policy.[42] On the other hand, 26 EU Member States already have BITs with China. Chinese BITs are designed to attract FDI in its own territory and, increasingly, to protect Chinese investors abroad. Chinese BITs contain all the standard provisions found in other BITs, but also present unique features which reflect a country-specific evolution.

Three main phases illustrate the evolution of Chinese BITs. The first phase, from 1982 to 1998, was characterized by a restrictive model that stressed the regulation of inward FDI. Early Chinese BITs neither provided for national treatment, nor did they include investor–state arbitration. Although China began conceding investor–state arbitration in 1985, arbitration was usually limited to disputes concerning the amount of compensation owed to investors in the event of expropriation.[43] Similarly, when China joined ICSID in 1993, it filed a declaration stating that, "[p]ursuant to Article 25(4) of the Convention, the Chinese Government would only consider submitting to the jurisdiction of the International Center for the Settlement of Investment Disputes, disputes over compensation resulting from expropriation and nationalization."[44] Furthermore, China required investors to exhaust local remedies before resorting to investor–state arbitration.

The second phase followed the adoption of the 1998 "Going Out" policy encouraging OFDI.[45] Beginning in 1998, most standard provisions found in mainstream European BITs, including compulsory arbitration for investment disputes – albeit with limited national

37 *See* Guigo Wang, ***China's FTAs: Legal Characteristics and Implications***, Am. J. Int'l L. 493, 495 (2011). The List of China's BITs as well as most of these treaties are available at the UNCTAD website, http://investmentpolicyhub.unctad.org/IIA/CountryBits/42#iiaInnerMenu (last visited July 16, 2016).

38 *See* Chapter 28 (Di Masi) in this volume.

39 *See*, for instance, the Pakistan–China FTA (Chapter 9) (November 24, 2006); the New Zealand–China FTA (Chapter 11) (April 7, 2008); the Singapore–China FTA (Chapter 10) (October 23, 2008); and the Peru–China FTA (Chapter 10) (April 28, 2009). The full list of FTAs can be found at http://fta.mofcom.gov.cn/english/fta_qianshu.shtml (last visited July 16, 2016).

40 Warren H, Maruyama, Jonathan Stoel & Charles Rosenberg, ***Negotiating the U.S.-China Bilateral Investment Treaty: Investment Issues and Opportunities in the Twenty-First Century***, 7 Transnat'l Disp. Mgmt. 1 (2010). *See* Chapter 25 (Friedmann) in this volume.

41 The public consultation included an online questionnaire posted on its website asking about the need for an EU–China BIT and its potential impact on human rights and environmental regulation.

42 Communication from the Commission to the Council, the European Parliament, the European Economic and Social Committee and the Committee of the Regions: ***Towards a Comprehensive European International Investment Policy*** (July 7, 2010), http://trade.ec.europa.eu/doclib/docs/2011/may/tradoc_147884.pdf (last visited July 16, 2016) at 7.

43 *See* China–France BIT (1985) Article 8(3).

44 China's notification (January 7, 1993), available at the ICSID website, http://icsid.worldbank.org.

45 Axel Berger, ***supra*** note 1, at 171.

treatment – have worked their way into Chinese BITs.[46] The only restriction still required in this second generation of BITs is the so-called fork-in-the-road provision. Such a clause commands foreign investors to choose either a domestic court or an international arbitral tribunal in the event that a dispute arises. Once the investor has chosen either to go to court or apply for arbitration, the investor cannot change that final decision.[47] Such clauses aim to prevent multiple fora for the same set of facts.[48] It should be pointed out, however, that the Chinese practice is far from uniform. Some Chinese BITs negotiated after 1998 still do not refer to international investment arbitration.[49]

Finally, according to some authors, a third generation of China's BITs has emerged since 2008.[50] This third generation of BITs is characterized by effective dispute resolution provisions, but these BITs' more limited investment-protection language resembles the 2004 US model BIT.[51] Almost all FTAs joined by China call for investor–state arbitration.[52]

Dispute settlement: A Chinese way?

Several factors explain why, to date, there have been a very limited number of disputes under Chinese BITs. First, only recently have Chinese BITs promoted the use of investor–state arbitration for all types of investment disputes. Earlier Chinese BITs did not refer to dispute settlement mechanisms,[53] while others only went so far as to limit the scope of investment arbitration to the quantification of compensation for expropriation.[54] Because China used to be a capital importing country, it preferred to limit the scope of potential disputes with foreign investors and to maintain ample leeway for state maneuvering. It is not surprising then that China began granting unconditional access to arbitration in its BITs with developing countries because, in relation to those countries, China behaves as a capital exporting country aiming to secure its investments abroad.

Second, the scarcity of arbitrations under Chinese BITs so far must be considered in light of the more general paucity of arbitrations brought by Asian investors before investment arbitral tribunals.[55] For instance, only 8 per cent of ICSID investment disputes have involved Southern or Eastern Asia.[56] Asian investors' hesitation vis-à-vis international dispute

46 *Id.*, at 174.

47 *See* Jie Wang, *Investor-State Arbitration: Where Does China Stand?*, 32 SUFFOLK TRANSNAT'L L. REV. 493, 498 (2009).

48 UNCTAD, *Investor-State Disputes Arising From Investment Treaties: A Review* (2005), at 30.

49 Axel Berger, *supra* note 1, at 175.

50 NORAH GALLAGHER & WENHUA SHAN, CHINESE INVESTMENT TREATIES: POLICY AND PRACTICE 39 (Oxford International Arbitration Series, 2009).

51 *See* Elodie Dulac, *The Emerging Third Generation of Chinese Investment Treaties*, TRANSNAT'L DISP. MGMT 1, 3 (2010).

52 Guigo Wang, *supra* note 37, at 516. *See* Chapter 28 (Di Masi) in this volume

53 *See*, for instance, the China–Thailand BIT, signed on March 13, 1985 and entered into force on December 13, 1985.

54 *See*, for instance, the China–Poland BIT, signed on June 7, 1988 and entered into force on January 8, 1989, and the China–Italy BIT, Article 5 in conjunction with point 4 of the Protocol signed on January 28, 1985.

55 Luke Nottage & Romesh Weeramantry, *Investment Arbitration for Japan and Asia: Five Perspectives on Law and Practice* 3 (Sydney Centre for International Law Working Paper No 21, 2009).

56 ICSID, *The ICSID Caseload – Statistics*, Issue 1, 11 (2014).

settlement mechanisms may result from cultural factors based on Confucianism,[57] which emphasizes the principle of harmony. Dispute or conflict is despised because it disturbs harmony.[58] The reluctance by Chinese investors to commence arbitral proceedings may also depend on other factors such as cost–benefit analysis. Parties seeking to preserve their reputation and potential for future business deals may favor settlement over commencing arbitral proceedings.

Third, reportedly, a number of investment disputes have settled privately after one party files the arbitration but before the proceedings commence.[59] Chinese BITs commonly require a "cooling off" period of three or six months of amicable negotiation to settle the dispute before moved ahead with the arbitration. Only in cases that fail to settle may the investor submit its claim to a competent domestic court or to arbitration. For instance, the Multilateral Investment Guarantee Agency (MIGA)[60] has already mediated disputes between foreign investors and the Chinese government.[61] For instance, in 2005 a dispute which arose between a water company guaranteed by MIGA and a municipal authority in China settled under the auspices of MIGA.[62] Another dispute dealt with China's unilaterally reduced prices to certain, foreign, electric power producers. When an investor to which MIGA had issued a guarantee alerted MIGA about its difficulties, the agency stepped in. Negotiations between the investor and government representatives eventually yielded an agreement to resolve the conflict and avoid a claim by the investor.

Fourth, although public awareness of investment treaty law and arbitration may have grown during the past decade, the field remains relatively unknown. According to a survey conducted by Professor Shan in 2001, although most EU investors tried to investigate the legal framework before they invested in China, less than 50 per cent of them knew about the existence of BITs.[63] Similarly, Chinese companies do not appear to consider the availability of BITs when investing overseas.[64] However, companies are gradually becoming aware of investment treaty protection.[65] A 2008 survey illustrated that 63 per cent of investors expressed awareness of BITs.[66] As companies learn the rules of the game and familiarize themselves with how investor–state arbitration works, one can expect an increase of

57 Confucianism is a complex system of moral, social, political, and philosophical thought that has had tremendous influence on the culture and history of East Asia. Developed from the teachings of the Chinese philosopher Confucius (551–479 BC), Confucianism postulates the existence of a harmony extending throughout heaven and earth. For more details, see Paolo Davide Farah, *L'influenza della Concezione Confuciana sulla Costruzione del Sistema Giuridico e Politico Cinese*, in IDENTITA' EUROPEA E POLITICHE MIGRATORIE (Giovanni Bombelli and Bruno Montanari eds, Vita e Pensiero, 2008).

58 *See* Chaihark Hahm, *Law, Culture, and the Politics of Confucianism,* 16 COLUM. J. ASIAN L. 253 (2003).

59 Khoday & Bonnitcha, *supra* note 4, at 511.

60 Convention Establishing the Multilateral Investment Guarantee Agency (October 11,1985) 24 ILM 1605 (1985). MIGA promotes FDI by providing political risk insurance to investors and lenders against losses caused by noncommercial risks. China was a founding member of the MIGA Convention.

61 Monika C. E. Heymann, *International Law and the Settlement of Investment Disputes Relating to China,* 11 J. INT'L ECON. L. 507, 521 (2008).

62 *See* MIGA Protecting Investment in Water (June 2008), http://www.miga.org/documents/water.pdf (last visited July 16, 2016).

63 Wenhua Shan, *The International Law of EU Investment in China,* CHINESE J. INT'L L. 555, 557 (2002).

64 Nils Eliasson, *Investment Treaty Protection of Chinese Natural Resources Investments,* 7 TRANSNAT'L DISP. MGMT 1, 23 (2010).

65 *Id.*, at 24.

66 Wenhua Shan and Sheng Zhang, *FDI in China and the Role of Law: An Empirical Approach,* 12 J. WORLD INV. & TRADE 4 (2011).

arbitrations under Chinese BITs. Finally, because investment disputes settle under a variety of arbitral rules – not all of which provide for public disclosure of claims – there can be no accurate accounting of all such disputes.

Although few disputes have arisen from Chinese BITs so far, this may change soon. Notably, the first known award under a Chinese BIT adopted a relatively broad reading of a key dispute settlement provision in the treaty, suggesting that similar Chinese BITs may afford more extensive protection to foreign investments than many had previously assumed. In *Tza Yap Shum v Peru*,[67] the arbitral tribunal held that jurisdiction to hear a dispute involving the amount of compensation based on expropriation implied jurisdiction to determine whether expropriation had taken place in the first instance.[68] Like many of China's early BITs, the Peru–China BIT permits investors to seek arbitration only regarding the amount of compensation due in the event of expropriation. Mr. Tza argued that this limitation could be overcome by operation of the BIT's most-favored nation (MFN) clause, which requires the host state – in this case, Peru – to extend to the investor treatment no less favorable than that extended to investors from third-party states. As the Peru–Colombia BIT allows for investor–state arbitration for a broader category of claims, according to Mr. Tza, the MFN clause of the Peru–China BIT required Peru to extend to the claimant the right to arbitrate such claims. The tribunal rejected this argument because the BIT's dispute settlement provision explicitly permitted arbitration of claims other than expropriation claims only in accordance with a separate agreement between the parties, which had not been reached in the case at issue. Accordingly, the tribunal dismissed Mr. Tza's claims – with the exception of his expropriation claim – for lack of jurisdiction.[69]

With regard to the expropriation claim, however, the tribunal held that the word "involving" should be interpreted broadly in order to permit arbitration of claims concerning all aspects of expropriation, including the question of whether expropriation had occurred.[70] The tribunal noted that the BIT's dispute settlement provision contained a "fork-in-the-road" clause that required an investor to make a final and binding choice between submitting claims to domestic courts and submitting them to an arbitration tribunal. In the tribunal's view, forcing an investor to first submit a claim regarding the occurrence of expropriation to a domestic court would trigger the "fork-in-the-road" clause, effectively precluding any recourse to arbitration.[71] Preventing the question of whether expropriation had occurred from reaching arbitration would limit the practical utility of such BITs, and the result would not accord with the BITs' object and purpose.

The case may have significant implications for other investors, being that most early Chinese BITs contain dispute settlement provisions similar to the one in the Peru–China BIT. While the tribunal did not allow the investor to import a broader dispute resolution remedy by means of the MFN clause, it expanded the scope of the arbitral clause remarkably.

67 *Tza Yap Shum v Republic of Peru*, ICSID Case No. ARB/07/6, Decision on Jurisdiction (June 19, 2009). The tribunal consisted of Mr. Judd Kessler (President), Mr. Hernando Otero, and Professor Juan Fernández-Armesto.

68 *Id.*, ¶ 188.

69 *Id.*, ¶ 216.

70 *Id.*, ¶ 151.

71 *Id.*, ¶ 157.

If other arbitral tribunals follow this line of reasoning,[72] investors covered by older Chinese BITs could bring claims for expropriation to compulsory investor–state arbitration.[73]

The tribunal decided the case on the merits in August 2011.[74] The tribunal found that the Peruvian tax authorities' imposition of interim measures constituted an arbitrary taking – and thus an indirect expropriation – of Mr. Tza's investment. While the tribunal awarded compensation to the claimant, it rejected the claimant's request for moral damages. The tribunal ordered each party to split the costs evenly.[75]

Two other investor–state arbitrations that took place under Chinese BITs are *China Heilongjiang International et al. v Republic of Mongolia (China Heilongjiang)*[76] and *Ekran Berhad v People's Republic of China (Berhad)*.[77] *China Heilongjiang* involved two state-owned enterprise claimants in the strategic sector.[78] Due to the high degree of confidentiality that is a feature of the United Nations Commission on International Trade Law (UNCITRAL) Rules, little is known about this case. Reportedly, the facts of the dispute involve the cancellation of a mining license in the Tumurtei iron-ore mine in Mongolia.[79] Tumurtei is one of Mongolia's biggest iron-ore deposits, and, in the late 1990s, the state granted exploitation rights to a consortium of Mongolian and Chinese companies, assisted by a US Dollars (USD) 12.5 million preferential loan from the Chinese government.[80]

With regard to the *Berhad* case, which was suspended pursuant to the parties' agreement on July 22, 2011, the ICSID website mentions only that the case facts relate to "arts and culture facilities."[81] The dispute reportedly concerns the rights to a leasehold over land in the Chinese province of Hainan held by a subsidiary of Erkan Berhad, Sino Malaysia Art & Culture.[82] Allegedly, the local authorities in Hainan revoked the leasehold rights due to the company's failure to move forward with its development plans.[83] Nonetheless, due to a scarcity of information, it is unconfirmed whether the ICSID arbitration arose as a result of

72 There is no such thing as binding precedent in investment treaty arbitration. Nonetheless, prior tribunals' awards can have significant persuasive force. See Valentina Vadi, *Towards Arbitral Path Coherence & Judicial Borrowing: Persuasive Precedent in Investment Arbitration*, 5 Transnat'l Disp. Mgmt 1–16 (2008).

73 Wei Shen, *The Good, the Bad or the Ugly? A Critique of the Decision on Jurisdiction and Competence in Tza Yap Shum v. The Republic of Peru*, 10 Chinese J. Int'l L. 55, 94 (2011).

74 *Tza Yap Shum v Republic of Peru, supra* note 67, http://italaw.com/documents/TzaYapShumAward.pdf (last visited July 16, 2016).

75 *Id.*, ¶¶ 170, 218, 240, 252, 261–268, 279–280, 282–285, 292, and 302.

76 *China Heilongjiang International & Technical Cooperative Corp, Qinhuangdaoshi Qinlong International Industrial and Beijing Shougang Mining Investment v Republic of Mongolia*. This is an *ad hoc* arbitration under the UNCITRAL Arbitration Rules and the China–Mongolia BIT. The Permanent Court of Arbitration is providing administrative support in this arbitration. The members of the arbitral tribunal are Judge Peter Tomka (Presiding Arbitrator), Dr. Yas Banifatemi, and Mark Clodfelter, Esq. http://www.pca-cpa.org/showpage.asp?pag_id=1378 (last visited July 16, 2016).

77 *Ekran Berhad v People's Republic of China*, ICSID Case No. ARB/11/15 (May 24, 2011).

78 Eliasson, *supra* note 64, at 25.

79 Luke Eric Peterson, *Tribunal Chosen to Hear ad-Hoc Arbitration by Chinese Mining Investors against Republic of Mongolia*, Investment Arbitration Reporter (November 4, 2010).

80 *Genghis Khan's Legacy, Battle for Mongolia's Soul*, The Economist (December 19, 2006).

81 *See* http://icsid.worldbank.org/ICSID/FrontServlet (last visited July 16, 2016). *See* also *China Claim Over before it Begins?*, Global Arbitration Review briefing (August 5, 2011).

82 Luke Eric Peterson, *China is Sued for the First Time in an ICSID Arbitration; Malaysian Investor Had Rights to 900 Hectares of Land for Development in China*, Investment Arbitration Reporter (May 26, 2011), at 1.

83 *Id.*

the revoked land leases or due to some other investment.[84] While little is known about the details of the case, it would seem that the claimant filed for arbitration on the basis of the China–Malaysia BIT.[85] Once again, because an early Chinese BIT was at play, the investor could file an arbitral claim only for disputes "relating to the amount of compensation" and "any other disputes agreed upon by both parties." Assuming the claimant brought this case under this early Chinese BIT, the analogy with the *Tsa Yap Shum* case with regard to subject matter jurisdiction would be evident. On May 16, 2013, the parties filed a request for the discontinuance of the proceeding pursuant to ICSID Arbitration Rule 43(1). The Secretary General issued a procedural order, taking note of the discontinuance of the proceeding pursuant to ICSID Arbitration Rule 43(1). Other conflicts have arisen as well.[86]

Reconciling the Chinese investment treaty program with non-economic concerns

China's OFDI program has profoundly modified the investment landscape. Like other emerging economies, China has gone from a mere recipient of investment flows to a leading source of FDI among developing countries. One must examine this transformation in order to understand not only the emerging international economic order but also the adjustments in the global balance of power. While some scholars criticize Chinese OFDI as "wealth without conditionality,"[87] and contest the lax environmental and social standards by calling them forms of "neo-colonialism";[88] others emphasize that the "China factor" can lead to the economic development of the host state and contemplate whether China's model could constitute an alternative paradigm leading to economic growth.

Chinese OFDI can boost the economy of host countries by supplying additional and resilient capital flows. Over the past few decades, China has lifted hundreds of millions of its people out of poverty by combining state intervention with economic incentives.[89] Thus, Professor Brautigam argues that Chinese OFDI "mixes a hard-nosed but clear-eyed self-interest with the lessons of China's own successful development and of decades of failed aid projects [. . .]."[90] Brautigam adds that "in poor, resource-rich countries, which are often cursed rather than blessed by their mineral wealth, resource-backed infrastructure loans can act as an 'agency of restraint' and ensure that at least some of these countries' natural-resource wealth is spent on development investments."[91] Brautigam also stresses that the early stages of industrialization may bring pollution, low wages, and long workdays, but Chinese OFDI promises to provide host countries with employment opportunities,

84 *Id.*

85 The China–Malaysia BIT entered into force on March 31, 1990.

86 Luke Eric Peterson, *Chinese Financial Services Company Weighting Arbitration Claim Against Belgium in Dispute Over Collapsed Bank?*, INVESTMENT ARBITRATION REPORTER (June 29, 2009); *Sanum Investments Ltd v The Government of the Lao People's Democratic Republic*, Award on Jurisdiction, PCA Case No. 2013-13 (December 13, 2013).

87 Patrick Keenan, *Curse or Cure? China, Africa and Unconditioned Wealth*, 27 BERKELEY J. INT'L L. 83 (2009).

88 Peter Brookes, *Into Africa? China's Grab for Influence and Oil*, HERITAGE LECTURES (March 26, 2007).

89 *See* Chapter 7 (Klaver & Trebilcock) in this volume.

90 Deborah Brautigam, *Africa's Eastern Promise – What the West Can Learn from Chinese Investment in Africa*, FOREIGN AFF.,1 (January 5, 2010).

91 *Id.*, at 2.

technologies, and badly needed infrastructures.[92] Undeniably, as a source of capital, China can act as a growth engine, and increased Chinese OFDI, like any other FDI, may contribute to economic development, providing capital inflows, employment, infrastructures, and technology transfer.[93]

However, the activities of MNCs abroad have also aroused much controversy and many social, cultural, and environmental concerns.[94] Because coveted natural resources are often found in unruly states, Chinese companies have struck deals with governments that do not respect international regimes, resulting in frustration and ineffectiveness of the economic sanctions imposed on these states by the international community. On the one hand, China deems its relations with these countries to be matters of international affairs, claiming that business is business and that politics is separate.[95] On the other hand, China asserts its alleged respect for the host countries' sovereignty in choosing their own political systems and development models.[96] This approach, however, may affect "international standards of good governance,"[97] human rights, and the security interests of the international community.[98] For instance, while the United States and the European Union banned investments by their national companies in Myanmar,[99] in the past few years China has increasingly turned to major infrastructure projects to improve access to the country's natural resources. Among these projects, China has helped build railways, airports, roads, and pipelines used to transport natural resources to China.[100]

Host countries' rising gross domestic product (GDP) does not automatically place them on a path to sustainable development. Ensuring this outcome will require all of the relevant stakeholders – investors, home and host governments, financial institutions, and others – to examine and align their policies and activities. On the one hand, the host country must ensure that the current resource boom translates not only into continued economic growth but also sustainable growth.[101] The recipient states also have human rights obligations, and their ratification of BITs does not relieve them of their full range of responsibilities, including duties to guarantee that non-state actors observe human rights within their territories.[102]

On the other hand, if China wishes to become a great global power, it must take non-economic concerns into account. Are social, cultural, and environmental concerns compatible

92 *Id.*

93 *See* Chapter 11 (Cima) in this volume

94 OECD, *The Social Impact of Foreign Direct Investment*, Policy Brief, July 2008. For security concerns raised by Chinese investments, *see* David Zweig and Bi Jianhai, *China's Global Hunt for Energy*, 84 Foreign Aff. 25 (2005) and Timothy J. Keeler, *The United States Rejects Chinese Investment on National Security Grounds* (Mayer Brown, January 28, 2010), http://www.mayerbrown.com/publications/The-United-States-Rejects-Chinese-Investment-on-National-Security-Grounds-12–22–2009 (last visited July 16, 2016) . *See* Chapter 4 (Bonfanti) in this volume

95 David Zweig & Bi Jianhai, *China's Global Hunt for Energy*, in 84 Foreign Aff. 27, 32 (2005).

96 Denis M. Tull, *China's Engagement in Africa: Scope, Significance and Consequences*, 44 J. of Modern Afr. Stud. 459, 461 (2006).

97 *See* Chapter 2 (Farah) in this volume.

98 David Zweig & Bi Jianhai, *China's Global Hunt for Energy*, 84 Foreign Aff. 27, 38 (2005).

99 Burmese Freedom and Democracy Act of 2002 and Council Decision 2010/232/CFSP (OJ L 105, April 27, 2010, at 22).

100 Yan Pai, *Gli investimenti d'oro di Pechino in Birmania*, Internazionale 881 (January 21, 2011), at 24.

101 *See* Chapter 2 (Farah) in this volume.

102 Andrew Clapham, Human Rights Obligations of Non-State Actors 25 (Oxford, 2006). *See* Chapters 3 (Di Turi), 4 (Bonfanti), and 7 (Klaver & Trebilcock) in this volume.

with China's political structure? In abstract terms, they are.[103] While China is a mere signatory of the International Covenant on Civil and Political Rights (ICCPR),[104] it is a party to a number of human rights instruments, including the International Covenant on Economic, Social and Cultural Rights (ICESCR);[105] the Convention on the Elimination of All Forms of Discrimination against Women (CEDAW);[106] and the Convention on the Rights of the Child (CRC).[107] The Chinese Government additionally signed the Rio Declaration on Environment and Development.[108] However, the signature and ratification of these instruments does not necessarily assure compliance.

Chinese policy-makers have begun to discuss and draft rules for more responsible, overseas business conduct.[109] For instance, in 2008, the State-Owned Assets Supervision and Administration Commission of the State Council released the *Guide Opinion on the Social Responsibility Implementation for the State-Owned Enterprises Controlled by the Central Government*.[110] At present, the Ministry of Commerce and the Ministry of Environmental Protection (MEP) of the PRC are reportedly working on environmental guidelines for Chinese overseas projects.[111] In 2007, the Chinese government also initiated the green credit policy, directing Chinese banks to incorporate environmental performance into their credit assessments.[112] Even the Chinese MNCs "are starting to realize that they will have to pay attention to Corporate Social Responsibility as part of their effort to gain acceptability and build their brand."[113] Reportedly, some Chinese companies have adhered to the Global Compact;[114] however, it is still too early to tell whether Chinese MNCs will voluntarily follow these standards, and some skeptics suspect that China's exercise of Corporate Social Responsibility (CSR) is mere window dressing.[115] Furthermore, CSR

103 See Xiaohui We, *Human Rights: China's Historical Perspectives in Context*, 4 J. Hist. Int'l L. 335 (2002) and Leila Choukroune, *Nul Besoin d'imposer les droits de l'homme à la Chine, elle les a déjà integrés*, Le Monde (November 12, 2010).

104 International Covenant on Civil and Political Rights (ICCPR) (December 19, 1966), 999 UNTS 171, Can TS 1976 No. 47, 6 ILM 368 (entered into force March 23, 1976) [ICCPR]. China signed the ICCPR on October 5, 1998.

105 International Covenant on Economic, Social and Cultural Rights (ICESCR), opened for signature on December 16, 1966 and entered into force on 3 January 3, 1976, 993 UNTS 3. China signed the ICESCR on October 27, 1997 and ratified it on March 27, 2001.

106 Convention on the Elimination of All Forms of Discrimination against Women (CEDAW) (December 18, 1979), 19 ILM 33 (entered into force on September 3, 1981) [CEDAW].

107 Convention on the Rights of the Child (November 20, 1989), 1577 UNTS 3, 28 ILM 1456 (entered into force on September 2, 1990) [CRC]. *See* Chapter 3 (Di Turi) in this volume.

108 Declaration on Environment and Development, United Nations Conference on Environment and Development (UNCED) Rio de Janeiro, 1992, 31 ILM 874 (1992). *See* Chapters 9 (Ibrahim, Deleuil & Farah), 10 (Lemoine), 12 (He), and 14 (Peng) in this volume.

109 *See* generally Chapter 4 (Angelica Bonfanti) in this volume.

110 The Guide Opinion on the Social Responsibility Implementation by the Central-Government-Controlled State-Owned Enterprises, http://www.sasac.gov.cn/n1180/n1566/n259760/n264851/3621925.html (last visited July 16, 2016).

111 Rosen & Hanemann, *supra* note 5, at 17.

112 Li-Wen Lin, *Corporate Social Responsibility in China: Window Dressing or Structural Change?*, 28 Berkeley J. Int'l L. 64, 79 (2010).

113 *Going Global – CSR is Spreading around the World, but in Different Guises*, The Economist (January 17, 2008). *See* Chapter 4 (Bonfanti) in this volume.

114 Xiuli Han, *Environmental Regulation of Chinese Overseas Investment from the Perspective of China*, 11 J. World Inv. & Trade 375, 388 (2010).

115 Li-Wen Lin, *supra* note 112, at 64. *See* Chapter 4 (Bonfanti) in this volume.

remains a vague concept, which does not necessarily coincide with China's international obligations under human rights law.[116]

For instance, when Sinosteel Midwest Corp., a Chinese company wholly owned by the Chinese government, leased land with the intention to develop an iron mine on the site of Wilgie Mia in Australia, concerns arose with regard to the protection of indigenous cultural heritage.[117] Wilgie Mia was added to Australia's National Heritage List in 2011[118] because of its cultural significance to indigenous Australians, who extract ochre from the site for use in ceremonies, art, and healing practices.[119] Perhaps aware of the potential for damaging publicity, one of Sinosteel's chief operating officers stated that the company would not mine "some sites of very strong significance" and that it "[could not] afford to get this wrong."[120] It remains to be seen whether and how Sinosteel conserves Wilgie Mia as the project moves forward.

Integrating non-economic concerns into the text of investment treaties

De jure condendo, proposals have been made to insert specific provisions as a gateway to incorporating human rights issues into BITs.[121] Traditionally, BITs have been regarded as legal instruments to protect and promote investment by the capital exporting state, not to protect cultural, social, and environmental concerns. Accordingly, early Chinese BITs did "not contain explicit references to sustainable development, nor [did they] affirm the powers of local governments to enact non-discriminatory measures necessary to achieve environmental, developmental, or public health goals."[122]

Gallagher and Shan, nonetheless, presented a compelling case for China to adopt a more equitable model BIT to balance the interests of the investor and host states, arguing that a General Agreement on Tariffs and Trade (GATT) 1994 style exception clause should be applied to any government measures taken to protect environmental goods or public health. The authors also argued that, in addition to the existing clauses, the BITs should contain a clause that imposes corporate social responsibility.[123] Such drafting would promote socially, culturally, and environmentally responsible investment, and help avoid some unnecessary litigation. As it is well known, international human rights law applies directly to states, and, because most Chinese MNCs are public companies, in the event that they commit human rights violations, China itself could be held liable before international tribunals. By contrast, because foreign MNCs investing in China tend to be private companies, an international tribunal could not hold the MNCs' home country accountable for any violations of

116 *Id.*, at 74. *See* Chapter 4 (Bonfanti) in this volume.

117 Graham Lloyd, *Wilgie Mia Mine Site Will Test China's Iron Will*, The Australian (January 4, 2011).

118 Australia's National Heritage List, www.heritage.gov.au.

119 Graham Lloyd, *supra* note 117.

120 Stephen Sackur, *Australian Resources Key to Booming China*, BBC News (April 12, 2011).

121 *See generally* Barnali Choudhury, *Exception Provisions as a Gateway to Incorporating Human Rights Issues into International Investment Agreements*, SIEL Working Paper No 2010/13; Suzanne A. Spears, *The Quest for Policy Space in a New Generation of International Investment Agreements*, 13 J. Int'l Econ. L. 1037–1075 (2010).

122 Kodhay & Bonnitcha, *supra* note 4, at 511.

123 Gallagher & Shan, *supra* note 50, at 398–400.

environmental, cultural, and social standards in China.[124] Due to this inconsistency, and because China remains a capital importing country, the inclusion of environmental, cultural, and/or social standards within BITs will ultimately benefit China itself.[125] It is worth noting that as industrialized countries have become recipients of FDI, they have introduced more balanced language to their agreements.[126] For instance, the EU–South Korea FTA includes provisions establishing shared commitments and a framework for cooperation on trade and sustainable development.[127]

Interestingly, the architecture of more recent Chinese BITs has become more equitable. Eminent authors have highlighted that "there is some evidence that [China's and the United States'] BITs programs, despite their different histories, are, over the last couple of years, evolving towards common positions on a number of crucial provisions."[128] Accordingly, some authors presume that a third generation of Chinese BITs has emerged, presenting more balanced provisions than earlier Chinese BITs.[129] First, the preambles of recent Chinese BITs usually refer to "the prosperity of both states" and "mutual benefits."[130] Recent BITs with Trinidad and Tobago, Albania, and Guyana also recognize that hosts can promote and protect FDI "without relaxing health, safety, and environmental measures of general application."[131] The preamble of the FTA between China and New Zealand makes express reference to the parties' awareness that "economic development, social development, and environmental protection are interdependent and mutually reinforcing components of sustainable development and that closer economic partnership can play an important role in promoting sustainable development." Although, strictly speaking, preambles do not bind parties, they provide context to the agreement.

Second, as Dulac shows, almost all Chinese BITs contain the wording, "in accordance with the laws and regulations" of the host state, in their definition of investment.[132] Such phrasing may exclude illegal investments from the coverage of the treaty, and has particular significance with regard to those investments that do not fulfill the environmental, cultural, and social standards set by the host state. For instance, in the preamble of the Australia–China BIT, the parties acknowledge that "investments of nationals of one Contracting Party in the territory of the other Contracting Party would be made within the framework of laws of that other Contracting Party."[133]

Third, as Dulac points out, a number of recent Chinese BITs follow the 2004 US model BIT, whereby they incorporate express language to limit the possibility that regulation would be deemed to amount to indirect expropriation.[134] For instance, in the Annex on expropriation to China's FTA with New Zealand, it states that "[. . .] measures taken in the

124 *See* Chapter 4 (Bonfanti) in this volume.

125 *See* Chapter 25 (Friedmann) in this volume.

126 José E. Alvarez, *The Once and Future Foreign Investment Regime*, in LOOKING TO THE FUTURE: ESSAYS ON INTERNATIONAL LAW IN HONOUR OF W. MICHAEL REISMAN 628 (M. H. Arsanjani, R. D. Sloane & S. Wiessner eds, Martinus Nijhoff Publishers, 2010).

127 http://trade.ec.europa.eu/doclib/docs/2009/october/tradoc_145203.pdf (last visited July 16, 2016). *See* Chapter 28 (Di Masi) in this volume.

128 José E. Alvarez, *supra* note 126, at 634.

129 *See* Elodie Dulac, *supra* note 51.

130 GALLAGHER & SHAN, *supra* note 50, at 49.

131 *Id.*, at 50–51.

132 *Id.*, at 10.

133 Australia–China BIT, entered into force on July 11, 1988.

134 GALLAGHER & SHAN, *supra* note 50, at 15.

exercise of a state's regulatory powers as may be reasonably justified in the protection of the public welfare, including public health, safety, and the environment, shall not constitute an indirect expropriation."[135]

Finally, third-generation Chinese BITs routinely include exception clauses.[136] For instance, the China–ASEAN FTA incorporates general exceptions provisions based on Article XX of the GATT.[137] Article 200 of the China–New Zealand FTA incorporates Articles XX(b) and XX(g) of GATT and Article XIV(b) of the General Agreement on Trade in Services (GATS). Thus, the Chinese–New Zealand FTA, like the US 2004 Model, addresses comparable concerns with respect to labor and the environment.[138] These developments show that China has increasingly adopted a balanced approach to BITs that reflects its *status* as capital importer and exporter.

Conclusions

Departing from a planned socialist economy, China has adopted marked-based approaches, adapting them to its historical, cultural, and socio-political context. Only recently have international investment law scholars and practitioners focused their attention on China's rapid integration in mainstream international investment law and practice. While these scholars and practitioners have analyzed Chinese investment treaty law from a variety of perspectives, most of the legal interpretation has adopted a positivist stance. Little scholarly analysis has focused on the link between Chinese BITs and sustainable development.[139] This article's key question is whether or not Chinese BITs can provide a new paradigm and promote sustainable development. To address this inquiry, this chapter briefly examined the main characteristics of international investment law and scrutinized the primary features of Chinese BITs. After investigating the scarce use of investor–state arbitration under Chinese BITs, the chapter offered a critical assessment of the status quo and questioned whether Chinese BITs could include social and environmental standards. The chapter concluded that, since China has significant interests in both inward and outward foreign investment, it is in China's best interest to negotiate more equitable BITs.[140] In its most recent BITs, China seems to have embraced this balanced approach. Only time will tell if such level drafting can promote the respect of non-economic standards in practice.

135 Annex 13, para. 6 of China–New Zealand FTA.

136 Elodie Dulac, *supra* note 51, at 20.

137 China–ASEAN FTA, art. 16 (2009).

138 *See* Memorandum of Understanding on Labour Cooperation and Environment Cooperation Agreement, which is an integral part of the China–New Zealand FTA.

139 Kodhay & Bonnitcha, *supra* note 4, at 489.

140 Stephan Schill, *Tearing Down the Great Wall: The New Generation Investment Treaties of the People's Republic of China*, CARDOZO J. INT'L & COMP. L. 15 (2007).

7 Chinese Investment in Africa

Strengthening the Balance Sheet*

Mark Klaver and Michael Trebilcock

Introduction

Chinese investment in Africa has rapidly increased over the past two decades. This chapter seeks to explain the causes of Chinese foreign direct investment (FDI) in Africa; to analyze the benefits and drawbacks of Chinese FDI for African development; and to identify policies African states can choose so they can capitalize on Chinese FDI. To do so, this chapter makes the following arguments. Chinese investment in Africa is growing in part because the Chinese government actively promotes it. China's main motivation for investing in Africa is to access Africa's natural resources; but Chinese investors also seek market access in Africa and the West. Consequently, African economies are growing at unprecedented rates. However, Chinese investment in Africa is not unambiguously advantageous.

To redress the drawbacks of Chinese FDI, this chapter recommends African states promulgate a tax code through which Chinese FDI will develop Africa's manufacturing sector. Tax and fiscal policies should focus on infrastructure, education, and special economic zones. Ultimately, Chinese investment presents African states with a major opportunity for sustainable economic growth.

China's growing economic presence in Africa

China is the second-largest economy in the world. Its GDP exceeds US Dollars (USD) 2.25 trillion.[1] China's outward stock of FDI skyrocketed from under USD 100 million in the

* This chapter is part of the results of the Research Project on "*Current Trends of Chinese Law towards Non-Trade Concerns such as Sustainable Development and the Protection of Environment, Public Health, Food Safety, Cultural, Social and Economic Rights, Labor Rights and the Reduction of Poverty from the Perspective of International Law and WTO Law*" coordinated by Professor Paolo Davide Farah at gLAWcal – Global Law Initiatives for Sustainable Development (United Kingdom) and at West Virginia University John D. Rockefeller IV School of Policy and Politics, Department of Public Administration, in partnership with the Center of Advanced Studies on Contemporary China (CASCC) in Turin (Italy), Maastricht University Faculty of Law, Department of International and European Law and IGIR - Institute for Globalisation and International Regulation (Netherlands) and Tsinghua University, School of Law, Institute of Public international law and the Center for Research on Intellectual Property Law in Beijing (China). This publication and the Conference Series were sponsored by China–EU School of Law (CESL) at the China University of Political Science and Law (CUPL). The activities of CESL at CUPL are supported by the European Union and the P.R. of China.

1 Ali Zafar, *The Growing Relationship between China and Sub-Saharan Africa: Macroeconomic, Trade, Investment, and Aid Links*, 22(1) World Bank Res. Observer 103, 104 (2007).

1980s to USD 57.2 billion in 2005.[2] Of China's outward FDI, 14 per cent is in Sub-Saharan Africa (SSA).[3] China's stock of FDI in Africa in 2008 was USD 7.8 billion.[4] Chinese FDI flow in Africa is also growing rapidly. From USD 20 million a year in the early 1990s, it catapulted to $1 billion a year in 2006.[5] In fact, Chinese FDI in SSA grew faster than Chinese FDI in any other continent from 2003 to 2004 – rising over 300 per cent in SSA, in contrast to under 100 per cent in Asia, Latin America, and Europe.[6]

Chinese companies in Africa are also proliferating. From 2001 to 2007, the number of Chinese firms in Africa grew from 230 to 800.[7] Chinese investors are present in 48 African countries. More Chinese came to Africa in the past decade than Europeans in the past 400 years.

China is also Africa's largest trading partner.[8] This is a new relationship: China's share of Africa's trade surged from 0.8 per cent in 1996 to 11 per cent in 2009.[9] Trade between China and Africa grew 100-fold since 1990;[10] it has escalated at 30 per cent annually since 2000, from USD 7 billion in 2000 to USD 95 billion in 2008. In sum, China's escalating investment, corporate presence, and trade with Africa foretell the emergence of China as a primary economic actor on the continent.

The Chinese state's connection to FDI

The Chinese state is closely connected to Chinese FDI in Africa in four respects: law, finance, policy, and corporate control. On law, China has signed 28 bilateral investment treaties (BITs) with African states that seek to attract Chinese FDI.[11] Chinese–African BITs have standard liberal investment features. They define "investment" broadly, to include movable and immovable property, real estate, corporate shares, stocks, copyright, intellectual property rights, and royalties. Foreign investors have the right to fair and equitable treatment, most-favored nation rights, and national treatment. Investors are protected from expropriation and nationalization. Chinese–African BITs guarantee free transfer of funds related to investment. BITs also contain dispute settlement mechanisms for state–state and investor–state disputes. Thus, China encourages African states to establish a liberal investment climate through BITs.

On finance, the Chinese state provides major resource-backed loans to African states. China has concluded USD 14 billion in loan-for-resource deals in seven African countries.[12]

2 UNCTAD, Asian Foreign Direct Investment in Africa 52 (UNCTAD, 2007).

3 *The Chinese in Africa: Trying to pull together*, The Economist (April 20, 2011).

4 Richard Schiere & Peter Walkenhorst, ***Introduction: China's Increasing Engagement in Africa: Towards Stronger Trade, Investment and Development Cooperation***, 22(S1) Afr. Dev. Rev. 559, 559 (2010).

5 Ali Zafar, ***supra*** note 1, at 123.

6 *Never too late to scramble*, The Economist (October 26, 2006).

7 Deborah Brautigam, ***"Flying Geese" or "Hidden Dragon"? Chinese Business and African Industrial Development***, 4 (March 2007) (draft chapter, prepared for The Politics of Contemporary China-Africa Relations).

8 The Economist, ***supra*** note 3.

9 Stefaan Marysse & Sara Greenen, ***Win-win or Unequal Exchange? The Case of the Sino-Congolese Cooperation Agreements***, 47(3) J. Modern Afr. Stud. 77 (2009).

10 Deborah Brautigam, Farole Thomas & Tang Xiaoyang, ***China's Investment in African Special Economic Zones: Prospects, Challenges, and Opportunities*** (The World Bank, 2010).

11 UNCTAD, ***supra*** note 2, at 56.

12 Deborah Brautigam, ***Africa's Eastern Promise: What the West Can Learn From Chinese Investment in Africa***, Foreign Aff. (January 5, 2010).

The Chinese state also provides Chinese investors with easy access to finance in the form of inexpensive loans, equity, debt, and investment insurance. In its 2006 "Year in Africa", China pledged to institute a USD 5 billion development fund to encourage Chinese investments in Africa.

On policy, the Chinese state uses four policy mechanisms in its "Go Out" strategy to encourage Chinese companies to invest in Africa. First, according to *The Economist*, most loans and payments China provides to African states are "tied": the African state receiving Chinese loans must employ Chinese companies when spending those loans.[13] Second, China encourages outward FDI through tax incentives. Chinese enterprises that invest abroad are exempt from corporate income tax for five years. Third, China encourages FDI in Africa through state guidance. In 2005, the government opened the Chinese–African Chamber of Commerce to give guidance to Chinese investors in Africa. Fourth, China establishes Special Economic Zones (SEZs) in Africa to facilitate Chinese investment. SEZs are bounded geographic regions within states, where liberal investment regulations and lower taxes suspend more onerous nationwide economic policies. SEZs may receive ongoing support from foreign and domestic governments through low-cost loans to stimulate investment and infrastructure spending. China is one such government: it is establishing five SEZs in Africa – two in Nigeria, one in each of Ethiopia, Mauritius, and Zambia. In doing so, China promotes its model of economic development in Africa. During the 1980s, China sought FDI through duty-free export-processing zones in Shenzhen and other coastal cities. Consequently, China's exports grew 17 per cent a year on average for 30 years, lifting hundreds of millions of people out of poverty. Today, China has over 100 SEZs.

On corporate control, the Chinese state controls Chinese state-owned enterprises (SOEs) and many small- and medium-sized enterprises (SMEs) that invest in Africa. Through SOEs, the Chinese state is involved in many of Africa's largest deals in key sectors: oil, mining, infrastructure, and telecommunications. As for SMEs, *The Economist* explains that mainland Chinese business leaders "operate in the shadow" of China's ruling party.[14] Chinese banks investing in Africa are controlled by the government in Beijing.[15] In sum, the Chinese state is closely connected to Chinese FDI in Africa.

China's rationale for promoting outward FDI

The rationale for China's "Go Out" policy generally – not only in Africa – is two-fold. First, China aims to ascend the manufacturing value chain, so that exports of machinery and equipment overtake cheap consumer goods.[16] Thus China encourages mature industries like textiles to move offshore. Second, China aims to cultivate global corporations. China has designated approximately 180 companies to become major multinationals.[17] China selected 22 of its top 30 outward investors to be "corporate champions."[18]

13 The Economist, *supra* note 3.

14 *Chinese takeovers: What it feels like to be bought by a Chinese firm*, The Economist (November 11, 2010).

15 The Economist, *supra* note 3.

16 Deborah Brautigam, The Dragon's Gift: The Real Story of China in Africa 223 (Oxford University Press, 2009).

17 Chris Alden & Martyn Davies, *A Profile of the Operations of Chinese Multinationals in Africa*, 13(1) S. Afr. J. Int'l Aff. 86 (2006).

18 Dan Haglund, *In It for the Long Term? Governance and Learning among Chinese Investors in Zambia's Copper Sector*, 199 China Q. 627, 630 (September 2009).

China's primary motivation in Africa

China's primary motivation for investing in Africa is to acquire oil and minerals. In 2004, China became the world's second-largest consumer of petroleum, with total demand of 6.5 million barrels of oil per day.[19] The Middle East currently provides only 38 per cent of China's imported oil.[20] SSA has the world's second-largest oil reserves after the Middle East.[21] Thus China draws 30 per cent of its oil from Africa.[22] The number and size of Chinese–African oil deals indicate Chinese investment in Africa predominantly aims to secure access to oil.[23] China's motivation is further revealed by its investment and trade relationship with African states. Fifty per cent of China's FDI in Africa flows to three oil-rich countries: Sudan, Algeria, and Nigeria.[24] Out of the five leading African exporters to China, four sell virtually only oil to China – namely Angola, Sudan, Congo, and Equatorial Guinea.[25] Most other African economies have limited trade with China.[26] In fact, oil constitutes 71.1 per cent of China's imports from Africa.[27]

China also seeks African minerals. China's mineral demand is skyrocketing. China is the world's largest consumer of steel, copper, coal, platinum, and cement.[28] China's consumption of various base metals accounted for between 76 per cent and 100 per cent of the global rise in demand from 2000 to 2003.[29] Mining's share of Chinese investment in Africa is 29 per cent.[30] In sum, China FDI in Africa mainly seeks oil and minerals.

China's secondary motivation in Africa

Yet Chinese also invest in Africa to access markets. For non-SOE Chinese firms, access to local African markets is the primary motivation for investment.[31] The continent is a vast market for low-cost producers. But Chinese investment in Africa is also motivated by "tariff hopping." Chinese companies with global value chains set up manufacturing operations in Africa to overcome trade barriers in rich markets. They take advantage of the preferential market access that Western nations grant African states,[32] such as the United States' African Growth and Opportunity Act (AGOA) and the EU's Everything but Arms (EBA) initiative.[33]

19 Ali Zafar, *supra* note 1, at 119.

20 Michal Meidan, *China's Africa Policy: Business Now, Politics Later*, 30(4) Asian Persp. 77 (2006).

21 Linda Jakobson, *China's Diplomacy Toward Africa: Drivers and Constraints*, 9 Int'l Rel. Asia-Pacific 403, 410 (2009).

22 A Rockefeller Foundation Exploration China's Engagement in African Countries.

23 Ian Taylor, *China's Oil Diplomacy in Africa*, 82(5) Int'l Aff. 945 (2006).

24 Linda Jakobson, *supra* note 21, at 410.

25 Linda Jakobson, *supra* note 21. South Africa is the nation among the top five that is not a major oil exporter.

26 Schiere & Walkenhorst, *supra* note 4, at 559.

27 Linda Jakobson, *supra* note 21, at 410.

28 Ali Zafar, *supra* note 1 at 108.

29 Dan Haglund, *supra* note 18, at 550.

30 The Economist, *supra* note 3.

31 Marco Sanfilippo, *Chinese FDI to Africa: What is the Nexus with Foreign Economic Cooperation?*, 22(S2) Afr. Dev. Rev. 601 (2010).

32 *Id.*, at 601.

33 Raphael Kaplinsky & Mike Morris, *The Asian Drivers and SSA: Is There a Future for Export-oriented African Industrialisation?*, 32(11) World Econ. (2009), http://onlinelibrary.wiley.com/

Benefits of Chinese investment in Africa

Chinese investment in Africa is evidently self-interested, but it has expedited African economic growth. From 2000 to 2010, six of the world's ten fastest-growing economies were in SSA.[34] The world's fastest-growing economy was Angola, whose GDP growth in both 2006 and 2007 was 20 per cent.[35] Nigeria, Ethiopia, Chad, Mozambique, and Rwanda all had annual growth rates of 8 per cent or more.[36] The average growth rate of SSA over the decade was 5.7 per cent. This growth is creating a middle class in Africa. 60 million households in Africa have annual incomes above USD 3,000 at market exchange rates. According to *The Economist*, Africa's growth is primarily attributable to China's demand for African resources.[37] Seven factors explain how Chinese FDI causes Africa's unprecedented economic growth.

Commodity prices

First, Chinese demand for resources raises commodity prices and African revenues. From 2000 to 2005, international oil prices rose 89 per cent, mainly due to Chinese demand. Higher resource prices explain the impressive economic growth of oil exporters such as Angola, Gabon, Nigeria, and Sudan.[38] Angola's terms of trade – the ratio of export prices to import prices – grew from 86 in 2002 to 109 in 2005. China's burgeoning demand for metals has also led to the escalation of global metal prices. Between 2000 and 2005, aluminum prices rose 20 per cent and copper prices doubled; in 2003, nickel reached a 13-year high of USD 13 per pound; in 2004, zinc reached a seven-year high; platinum attained a 23-year high of USD 800 per oz; and from 2002 to 2007, gold prices rose by 60 per cent.[39] Consequently, Mauritania benefits from higher iron-ore prices; Mozambique from aluminum; South Africa from platinum; and Zambia from copper. China's impact on commodity prices is a leading cause of African economic growth. Overall, about one quarter of Africa's growth from 2000 to 2008 derived from higher revenues from natural resources.[40]

Capacity to extract

Second, many African countries lack the capacity to extract their own resources.[41] Chinese resource Transnational Corporations (TNCs), such as Sinopec and CNPC, are vertically integrated from exploration to production.[42] They bring the technological and human capacity to oversee all aspects of the resource extraction process. And they invest heavily in

doi/10.1111/j.1467–9701.2009.01253.x/abstract (last visited July 16, 2016). The US' African Growth and Opportunity Act (AGOA) provides trade preferences for quota- and duty-free entry to the US for textile and apparel goods from SSA countries. The EU's Everything but Arms (EBA) initiative grants duty-free and quota-free access to all imports from least developed countries, excluding armaments.

34 *Africa's Hopeful Economies: The Sun Shines Bright*, THE ECONOMIST (December 3, 2011).

35 *Rising Angola: Oil, glorious oil*, THE ECONOMIST (January 28, 2010).

36 *The struggle of the champions*, THE ECONOMIST (January 6, 2005).

37 *Id.*

38 Ali Zafar, *supra* note 1, at 109.

39 *Id.*, at 112.

40 *The Hopeful Continent: Africa Rising*, THE ECONOMIST (December 3, 2011).

41 Marysse & Greenen, *supra* note 9, at 375.

42 Ian Taylor, *supra* note 23, at 941.

Africa. Thus, Chinese investment raises African resource output, a primary cause of Africa's economic growth. For instance, copper production in Zambia doubled from 257 kilotons in 2000 to 561 kilotons in 2007.[43] As a leading investor in Zambian mining, China is largely responsible for Zambia's growing output.

Infrastructure

Third, China's contribution to African development is probably most significant in infrastructure. Alongside education, Africa's top priority for economic development is arguably infrastructure. The lack of adequate roads, ports, electricity, and water supplies significantly undermines the continent's competitiveness.

China's general approach to investment in Africa can be characterized as "resources-for-infrastructure." China provides financial assistance and funds construction projects in exchange for secure access to resources.[44] Thus, China's investment in African infrastructure totaled USD 11 billion in 2008, compared to USD 13.7 billion from the G8 countries combined.[45] Of private Chinese investment in Africa, 75 per cent is in construction.[46] Chinese companies are signing infrastructure deals worth USD 50 billion a year.[47] Consequently, *The Economist* proclaims "Angola feels like a gigantic building site."[48] Chinese FDI makes a major contribution to African infrastructure.

Manufacturing

Fourth, Chinese FDI has potential to develop Africa's manufacturing sector directly and indirectly. Directly, Chinese demand stimulates back-stream diversification.[49] African metals and machinery sectors are growing as Chinese construction projects seek African factories to produce cement, glass, brick, steel rods, and other building materials, in replacement of imports.[50]

Indirectly, Chinese SMEs can also improve African manufacturing. SMEs concentrate on manufacturing, construction, and service sectors. With the proliferation of Chinese SMEs in Africa, manufacturing's share of total Chinese investment in Africa has grown to 22 per cent, not far from mining at 29 per cent.[51] Chinese manufacturing SMEs can facilitate African industrialization in three ways. First, competition can promote productivity. Of course, too much competition can cause bankruptcy. But firms that persist through intensified competition by raising productivity often become global players. Second, African firms can improve productivity by imitating the technology, production methods, and marketing approaches of Chinese firms investing on the continent. Third, African companies can cultivate business ties with Chinese SMEs to improve manufacturing opportunities through

43 Dan Haglund, *supra* note 18, at 635.

44 Ali Zafar, *supra* note 1, at 120. *See* also Chapter 6 (Vadi) in this volume.

45 Richard Schiere, *Building Complementarities in Africa between Different Development Cooperation Modalities of Traditional Development Partners and China*, 22(S1) Afr. Dev. Rev. 615, 619 (2010).

46 The Economist, *supra* note 3.

47 *Id.*

48 The Economist, *supra* note 35.

49 Deborah Brautigam, Close Encounters: Chinese Business Networks as Industrial Catalysts in Sub-Saharan Africa, 102 Afr. Aff. 461 (2003).

50 Deborah Brautigam, *supra* note 16, at 224.

51 The Economist *supra* note 3.

consulting and input supply.[52] Consequently, labor productivity in Africa is growing at 2.7 per cent a year, above the United States' 2.3 per cent.[53]

Employment

Fifth, Chinese investment stimulates African employment. Chinese investors employ Africans for three main reasons. First, African labor is generally inexpensive. Second, the success of some Chinese investments in Africa depends on managers with local expertise. Third, Chinese firms placate local concerns by hiring, and listing subsidiaries, locally.[54] Accordingly, a World Bank study of Chinese exporting firms in Africa found that their workforce was 80 per cent African.[55] In Kenya, local employment represents 96 per cent of employment generated by Chinese FDI.

Market access

Sixth, China's open trade policy for Africa – which is part of Chinese–African economic relations – improves African access to China's market. In 2010, China approved zero-tariff treatment for 95 per cent of products from African least-developed countries (LDC).[56] Greater openness to China helped SSA to raise its merchandise trade-to-GDP ratio from 41 per cent in 1990 to 58 per cent in 2005.[57] SSA's annual export growth rate escalated from 4.4 per cent in 1998 to 12.5 per cent in 2004.[58] This export growth rate was 50 per cent higher than the global average.

Consumers

Seventh, Chinese FDI benefits African consumers in two ways. First, it lowers prices of manufactured goods and food. Chinese FDI has made basic goods such as shoes, radios, and chicken more affordable in Africa.[59] Second, Chinese FDI makes new products such as refrigerators and laundry machines available to African consumers in states with weak manufacturing sectors.

Drawbacks to Chinese investment in Africa

Despite these seven benefits, Chinese FDI is not unambiguously advantageous for African development. As a self-interested actor, China generally intends to neither hurt nor help Africa. African development can be a means to Chinese ends – resource acquisition and market access. But Chinese investment in Africa has three major drawbacks.

52 Deborah Brautigam, *supra* note 49, at 448.

53 *Africa's Hopeful Economies: The Sun Shines Bright,* The Economist (December 3, 2011).

54 Deborah Brautigam, *supra* note 49, at 448.

55 Deborah Brautigam, *supra* note 16, at 229.

56 Richard Schiere, *supra* note 45, at 622.

57 Raphael Kaplinsky & Mike Morris, *Do the Asian Drivers Undermine Export-Oriented Industrialization in SSA?* 4 (2007), http://asiandrivers.open.ac.uk/documents/Kaplinsky_Morris_WD_ADs_Special_Issue_April_07_final.pdf (last visited July 15, 2016).

58 Raphael Kaplinsky, *What Does the Rise of China Do for Industrialisation in Sub-Saharan Africa?*, 35(115) Rev. Afr.Pol. Econ. 5 (2008).

59 The Economist, *supra* note 3.

Low benefits, high costs

First, the costs of China's contribution to African infrastructure may exceed the benefits. On the benefits, much Chinese investment in African infrastructure is designed to facilitate natural resource exports to China.[60] Of course, Africa's accelerated growth needs resource exports. But infrastructure only related to resource extraction has limited benefits for African development. Chinese construction in Africa can also be shoddy.[61]

On the costs, African governments can pay too high a price in resources. The most striking example is the Congo–China Agreement of 2007.[62] The Congolese government signed a bilateral investment and trade agreement with Chinese SOEs, in which China's Eximbank gave Congo access to a USD 6.5 billion concessional loan to finance infrastructure projects.[63] Chinese companies would build or rehabilitate 3,500 km of tarred roads and 3,200 km of railways; and build 32 hospitals, 145 health centers, 2 universities, and 5,000 houses.[64] This was the biggest agreement China had signed in Africa. And the infrastructure is good for Congo. Yet the joint venture created to extract the resources may exploit the concession until depletion; and the agreement allows for continuous extraction over 30 years. Three points indicate the agreement is unfair for Congo. First, the market rate of the resources guaranteed through the deal amounts to between USD 39.7 and USD 83.6 billion; but Congo only receives USD 6.5 billion. Second, under the deal, no taxes are paid to the Congolese government in the "commercial stage". Congo will forego an estimated USD 20 billion in revenue through these tax exemptions. Third, the agreement will exhaust Congo's copper and cobalt reserves because quantities stipulated in the agreement represent 20 years of peak production. Chinese investment may deplete African resources and bring limited benefits for African infrastructure.

Few spillovers

Second, Chinese FDI transfers limited technology, skills, and employment to Africa. On technology, many of China's biggest projects in Africa rely on Chinese companies, due to tied loans and Chinese competitiveness. By not hiring African companies, Chinese investors limit technology transfer. On skills, many Chinese companies fail to transfer higher skills because they employ Chinese for managerial and technical positions.[65] And for short-term projects, many Chinese investors do not invest heavily to train African workers.[66] On employment, Chinese FDI makes a limited contribution. About 300,000 Chinese laborers are in Africa.[67] Chinese investors have ignited controversy for failing to hire more Africans, as in Zambia. Much anecdotal evidence also indicates unsafe conditions at Chinese mines throughout Africa.

60 Marysse & Greenen, *supra* note 9, at 388. *See* also Chapters 6 (Vadi) and 4 (Bonfanti) in this volume.
61 The Economist, *supra* note 3.
62 Marysse & Greenen, *supra* note 9, at 371.
63 *Id.*, at 16.
64 Marysse & Greenen, *supra* note 9, at 16.
65 Marco Sanfilippo, *supra* note 31, at 604.
66 Ali Zafar, *supra* note 1, at 124.
67 Linda Jakobson, *supra* note 21, at 414.

African deindustrialization

Third, Chinese FDI may deindustrialize Africa. Four factors indicate African manufacturing is already weak. First, its role in global and domestic economies is minimal. Africa's share of global manufacturing exports is under 1 per cent, even though 12 per cent of the world's population lives in Africa.[68] Manufacturing's share of SSA's GDP is only 3.3 per cent.[69] Second, manufacturing in Africa is nascent: the low-skilled industries of clothing and textiles accounted for 53 per cent of Africa's manufacturing exports in 2007.[70] Third, African manufacturing exports depend on trade preferences.[71] Excluding Mauritius and South Africa, 95 per cent of SSA exports to the US enter under AGOA.[72] Fourth, African manufacturing productivity is low; African goods are more expensive than similar Chinese ones.

Chinese FDI may further weaken African manufacturing by "pushing" and "pulling" African economies away from manufacturing and towards resource dependence. African economies are pushed to rely on resources when China out-competes them in manufacturing. China increased its clothing exports by 667 per cent from 1990 to 2005, to USD 74.2 billion. When MFA quotas were removed, China largely replaced African clothing and textile exports to the US.[73] Chinese competition drove many textile firms across Africa to bankruptcy.[74]Chinese demand for commodities also pulls African labor and capital towards resource extraction and away from manufacturing.[75] With China's rise between 1995 and 2005, oil and gas's share of SSA's exports grew from 31 per cent to 47 per cent.[76] Primary goods now account for 73 per cent of Africa's export revenues.[77] Commodity exports represent 30 per cent of Africa's GDP.[78]

The China–Africa relationship is now generally characterized by Africa exporting raw materials to China, which exports manufactured goods to Africa.[79] Chinese exports to SSA are almost exclusively manufactured products. SSA's trade surplus with China is due to resource exports: excluding oil and gas, SSA has a trade deficit with China, which grew from USD 13 billion to USD 20.9 billion between 1995 and 2005.[80]Due to Chinese competition and demand, African economies are increasingly resource-dependent.

68 Andy King, *Manufacturing in Africa: Adding Value for Economist Development*, Liberty Economics, Dumoe & Associates 5 (2010).

69 *Id.*, at 8.

70 African Economic Conference, *David v. Goliath: Mauritius facing up to China* 3 (2009), http://asian-drivers.open.ac.uk/Ancharaz%20Final.pdf (last visited July 16, 2016).

71 Kaplinsky & Morris, *supra* note 57.

72 African Economic Conference, *supra* note 70, at 11.

73 Raphael Kaplinsky, *supra* note 58.

74 Ali Zafar, *supra* note 1, at 121.

75 Ali Zafar, *supra* note 1, at 107.

76 Kaplinsky & Morris, *supra* note 57.

77 Denis M. Tull, *China's Engagement in Africa: Scope, Significance and Consequences,* 44(3) J. Modern Afr. Stud. 459, 471 (2006).

78 Paul Collier, The Plundered Planet: Why We Must – And How We Can – Manage Nature for Global Prosperity 42 (Oxford University Press, 2010).

79 Richard Schiere, *supra* note 45, at 619.

80 Kaplinsky & Morris, *supra* note 57, at 4.

The feasibility of tax reform

African policy-makers would be best advised to act urgently. In *The Dragon's Gift*, Deborah Brautigam emphasizes that China's economic activity in Africa is similar to Western economic activity in China in the past, and in Africa today.[81] However, Brautigam does not provide a concise list of policy prescriptions African governments can choose to capitalize on Chinese investment. This chapter fills that gap.

The policies prescribed here apply to Africa generally. The three drawbacks to Chinese investment may be more or less pronounced in different African states. And African states have varying levels of good governance. No policies are one-size-fits-all. But, ultimately, African states are likely to develop only through sustained economic growth via industrialization. This chapter suggests how.

For African states to enhance the seven benefits of Chinese FDI while diminishing the three drawbacks, African policy-makers must create an investment environment that makes African development a means for the ends of Chinese investors. Investor incentives are altered through regulation or taxation. This chapter recommends a stringent tax policy on Chinese investment in Africa. But first, the economic and legal arguments against a stringent tax code need rebutting.

The economic argument is that Africa needs low taxes to attract Chinese FDI. This contribution disagrees. African states can tax Chinese FDI substantially because China depends on African resources. In 1998, the Chinese Ministry of Defense stated that energy security is part of China's national security.[82] China draws 30 per cent of its oil from Africa.[83] Angola provides more oil to China than any other country. China's largest supplier of cobalt is Congo. China depends on Africa for diverse resources to sustain growth. Access to Africa's resources is integral to Chinese security. Thus when *The Economist* proclaims that Africa needs more self-confidence,[84] the continent can display this trait through a sense of certainty that Chinese FDI will bear more taxes to secure access to African resources.

As for legal arguments against higher taxes, BITs do not prohibit increasing taxes on future resource deals. This gives tax policy a significant advantage over regulatory conditions to foster development, many of which may breach profit repatriation rights and bans in BITs on local content, employment, and technology transfer requirements.[85] Africa has no legal impediments to taxing Chinese FDI to incentivize development.

The goal: Develop African manufacturing

This chapter contends that Africa's economic development is best achieved by cultivating Africa's manufacturing sector, for four reasons.[86] First, virtually every country that has experienced rapid growth over the past two centuries industrialized, progressing from agricultural and resource exporting; to low- and middle-technology manufacturing; on to high-tech

81 *Id.*, at 24.

82 Denis M.Tull, *supra* note 77, at 468.

83 A Rockefeller Foundation Exploration, *supra* note 22, at 6.

84 *The Heart of the Matter*, The Economist (May 11, 2000).

85 Peter Kragelund, *Knocking on a Wide-open Door: Chinese Investments in Africa* 8, http://gdex.dk/ofdi/24%20Kragelund%20Peter.pdf (last visited July 16, 2016).

86 Justin Yifu Lin, The Quest for Prosperity: How Developing Economies Can Take Off (Princeton University Press, 2012).

manufacturing and service industries. Second, natural resources deplete. Once resources are exhausted, African economies will have to rely on sustainable sectors such as manufacturing. Third, more profits and jobs are often generated through value-added processes than raw resource exports[87] Fourth, manufacturing exports diversify economies, reducing vulnerability to price shocks and Dutch disease – an appreciation of the currency due to resource exports.[88] Thus, this Chapter promotes an export-oriented manufacturing sector in Africa. Africa need not perpetually export raw materials and import manufactured goods.

Raising resource taxes

This chapter proposes a three-step tax policy to harness Chinese FDI for African development. First, African states should substantially increase taxes on resource deals with Chinese investors. Some African governments apply exceptionally low tax rates on resource profits. Instead, this chapter proposes a tax rate of 30 per cent on "ordinary profits" from resource investments, in line with many Western marginal corporate tax rates.

Ordinary profits are returns on investment – the capital, labor, and risk involved in extraction and production. Profit beyond returns on investment is "rent." When a resource is highly valued, firms that sell it make large profits often despite limited costs of extraction. Most oil profits are rent. The vast profitability of oil and mining firms largely reflects the high value of the assets they sell as opposed to returns on investment. Hence Paul Collier's characterization of rents as "excess profits."[89] Thus, this chapter proposes African states adopt a 99 per cent tax rate on resource rents. Chinese investors do not need resource rents to continue operations. As long as they receive much of their ordinary profit (returns on capital, labor, and risk) they will stay in business.

This proposal raises two problems. First, many national tax authorities lack capacity to distinguish ordinary profits from excess profits. To do so, they should hire specialist accountancy firms to audit firms' books. When Nigeria did so in 2004, it made a major windfall in back-payment.[90] Second, a "prisoner's dilemma" arises: each African state's individual self-interest is to lower taxes enough to attract Chinese investment away from other African states; but the collective interest of African states is to recoup higher revenues from Chinese resource investments. The optimal outcome requires African states to harmonize and commit to tax codes with high rates on resource investment. Preventing defection requires multilateral enforcement. The African Union's Economic Integration and Regional Cooperation Division is best suited for this role.

Savings and investment

Second, African states should save a substantial portion of revenue from resource taxes. Africa's savings rate is merely 20 per cent; developing Asia's is 40 per cent.[91] Africa's meager savings do not accumulate enough substitute assets for the eventual exhaustion of natural resources.

87 Andy King, *supra* note 68, at 7.
88 The Economist, *supra* note 6.
89 Paul Collier, *supra* note 78, at 88.
90 *Id.*
91 *Id.*, at 99.

This chapter recommends resource-rich African states put savings in sovereign wealth funds (SFW). With SWFs, resource revenues are earmarked for future generations, and the interest generated from investing in international capital markets becomes 'permanent income,' enabling spending in perpetuity. But this chapter does not advocate African states save 100 per cent of resource revenues. African states have low capital, which entails severe poverty. They should immediately spend some resource revenues on public investment. Public investment in infrastructure and education creates sustainable economic growth.

Thus the third step is for African states to spend some resource revenues to redress the three drawbacks of Chinese FDI, and to alter their tax codes to incentivize Chinese investors to redress these drawbacks themselves.

Infrastructure

To improve African infrastructure, the benefits of Chinese resource investment can be raised in two ways. First, Chinese firms that contribute to infrastructure not directly related to resource extraction should be taxed at lower rates than firms that construct infrastructure only to export resources. Second, the income derived from the latter firms should be spent on infrastructure projects unrelated to resource exports. As for those resource-for-infrastructure deals that do not provide taxable revenue, the amount of extraction rights Chinese investors acquire should correspond to their offers of infrastructure unrelated to resources.

On the costs of Chinese FDI, African states can prevent repetition of the Congolese resource-for-infrastructure deal through two steps. First, an open bidding process would reduce secrecy and allow investors besides China to present competitive resource-for-infrastructure proposals. Second, African states should hire professional valuation firms to explicitly determine the value of resources and what infrastructure matches it.

Employment and skills

To improve spillovers, African states can incentivize Chinese investors to employ and train Africans by reducing taxes on Chinese firms that have high portions of African employees or enter joint ventures with African firms. Chinese firms that fail to meet a local-hiring ratio should be subject to the original 30 per cent tax. The resultant tax revenue should fund education and training programs at universities and polytechnics for African workers, along with children's education.[92]

This chapter does not endorse a regulatory requirement that Chinese companies hire African employees, or subcontract some of their work to local firms, as in Angola and Congo. Chinese firms have encountered a shortage of skilled workers in Africa.[93] To require Chinese firms to hire under-skilled employees may deter investment. Instead, the drawback of Chinese firms employing Chinese workers can be addressed with tax incentives for Chinese firms to hire African workers, and by investing tax revenue in African education and training programs. Eventually, well-trained African workers will be an attractive labor pool for Chinese investors; and a well-educated African workforce will enable African firms to enter higher-skilled manufacturing and service sectors.

92 Raphael Kaplinsky, *supra* note 58, at 8.
93 UNCTAD, *supra* note 2, at 60.

SEZs

To prevent deindustrialization, Africa should establish more SEZs to improve its manufacturing sector. SEZs can foster export-oriented manufacturing in Africa in three ways. First, SEZs will attract manufacturing firms to Africa through tax-free, duty-free export-processing zones. Second, the concentration of manufacturing firms in SEZs will facilitate spillovers as firms learn, copy, and compete with each other.[94] Third, with SEZs, infrastructure is directed to economically productive regions first, which galvanizes national economic growth.

China is proof. In the 1980s, China sought FDI through duty-free export-processing zones in coastal cities. China's exports grew 17 per cent a year on average for 30 years,[95] lifting hundreds of millions out of poverty. Today, China has over 100 SEZs.

Conclusion

Chinese investment is changing Africa for the better. Through Chinese FDI, African states are gaining resource revenues, extraction-capacity, infrastructure, productivity, employment, market access, and new consumer products. Yet Chinese FDI is not unambiguously advantageous for Africa.[96] Chinese investors eagerly seek African resources and market access, sometimes bringing limited benefits and undermining Africa's industrialization. But Africa can keep the benefits of Chinese investment while redressing its drawbacks. African tax policies should develop the manufacturing sector by supporting infrastructure and education. Ultimately, Chinese investment presents Africa with a major opportunity for sustainable economic growth.

94 Brautigam, Thomas & Xiaoyang, *supra* note 10, at 2.

95 Ian Taylor & Yuhua Xiao, *A Case of Mistaken Identity: "China Inc." and Its "Imperialism" in Sub-Saharan Africa* 713 (2009), http://onlinelibrary.wiley.com/doi/10.1111/j.1943–0787.2009.01149.x/full (last visited July 16, 2016).

96 *See* also Chapters 6 (Vadi), 4 (Bonfanti), and 5 (Choukroune) in this volume.

Part II

Sustainable Development, Environmental Protection, and Climate Change*

* This Book Part II "Sustainable Development, Environmental Protection, and Climate Change" is participated by researchers funded by the Marie Curie IRSES of the European Union's Seventh Framework Programme (FP7/2007-2013) under REA grant agreement n° 269327 – Acronym of the Project: EPSEI (2011–2015) entitled "Evaluating Policies for Sustainable Energy Investments" within the results coordinated by gLAWcal – Global Law Initiatives for Sustainable Development (United Kingdom).

8 Soft, Complex, and Fragmented International Climate Change Practice

What Implications for International Trade Law?*

Francesco Sindico and Julie Gibson

Introduction

Climate change presents a global challenge because it affects all countries – albeit in different ways[1] – and because it requires efforts from all members of the international community – albeit with unique approaches.[2] The global nature of dealing with the increase in greenhouse gas (GHG) emissions and corresponding climate change necessitates, hence, an international response capable of uniting all countries. Has this happened? Is this likely to happen in the near future, or in the long term? And what are the implications if this collective action does not take place?

These questions will loom throughout this chapter, which has a twofold goal. First, it will highlight the trends in the development of the international climate change legal regime and of the overall international climate change efforts. For the purposes of this chapter, "international climate change legal regime" refers to that branch of international law that has developed in order to address climate change and that has as its two key primary sources the

* This chapter is part of the results of the Research Project on "*Current Trends of Chinese Law towards Non-Trade Concerns such as Sustainable Development and the Protection of Environment, Public Health, Food Safety, Cultural, Social and Economic Rights, Labor Rights and the Reduction of Poverty from the Perspective of International Law and WTO Law*" coordinated by Professor Paolo Davide Farah at gLAWcal – Global Law Initiatives for Sustainable Development (United Kingdom) and at West Virginia University John D. Rockefeller IV School of Policy and Politics, Department of Public Administration, in partnership with the Center of Advanced Studies on Contemporary China (CASCC) in Turin (Italy), Maastricht University Faculty of Law, Department of International and European Law and IGIR – Institute for Globalisation and International Regulation (Netherlands) and Tsinghua University, School of Law, Institute of Public international law and the Center for Research on Intellectual Property Law in Beijing (China). An early draft of this paper was presented at Conferences Series on "*China's Influence on Non-Trade Concerns in International Economic Law*", First Conference held at the Center of Advanced Studies on Contemporary China (CASCC) in Turin on November 23–24, 2011. This publication and the Conference Series were sponsored by China–EU School of Law (CESL) at the China University of Political Science and Law (CUPL). The activities of CESL at CUPL are supported by the European Union and the P.R. of China.

1 See how climate change affects different parts of the world in IPCC, *Fifth Assessment Report. Climate Change 2014: Impacts, Adaptation, and Vulnerability* (IPCC Working Group II Contribution to AR5, 2014).

2 At the heart of the international climate change legal regime there has always been the principle that some countries (developed) had a greater responsibility for climate change than other countries (developing). This has been enshrined in the principle of common but differentiated responsibilities, which can be found in art. 3.1 of the UNFCCC. For a detailed analysis of the common but differentiated responsibilities principle, *see* Chapters 9 (Ibrahim, Deleuil & Farah), 10 (Lemoine), and 11 (Cima) in this volume.

United Nations Framework Convention on Climate Change (UNFCCC)[3] and its Kyoto Protocol.[4] "International climate change efforts," on the other hand, refers to any kind of legal and policy instrument that States have adopted multilaterally, bilaterally, or unilaterally to address climate change. Within this chapter, we will sometimes refer to both of them as "international climate change practice." The second goal of this chapter is to discuss whether the trends, or characteristics, that identify current international climate change practice may lead to increased trade tensions between countries or, on the contrary, dampen such tensions.[5]

Accordingly, the chapter is divided into two main sections. Following the introduction, the second section analyzes the evolution of international climate change practice. The study concludes that the latter is becoming softer, more fragmented, and more complex. The third section focuses on the specific nature of the climate-trade relationship within the greater debate on trade and environment. It concludes that a softer, more fragmented, and more complex international climate change practice has already led to tangible interstate trade tensions in some cases (domestic policies supporting the deployment of renewable energy),[6] and could lead to conflict in other spheres (border adjustment measures and carbon trading). The last section draws some more general conclusions.

The evolution of international climate change practice

This section argues that three key trends can be identified in the development of international climate change practice: the prevalence of soft v hard commitments; an increasing fragmentation of international efforts in relation to climate change; and greater complexity within one specific instrument meant to make dealing with climate change more cost-effective – carbon trading, which, itself, is also becoming more fragmented.[7]

Soft v hard commitments

The debate about soft law and hard law in international law is not new in the literature.[8] Soft law may describe a legal instrument that is not legally binding,[9] while hard law usually refers to a document that bestows a mandatory obligation upon parties who have consented to such an obligation. The terminology becomes somewhat blurred, however, when one

3 United Nations Framework Convention on Climate Change, May 9, 1992, 31 ILM 822 (1992) [hereinafter UNFCCC].

4 Kyoto Protocol to the United Nations Framework Convention on Climate Change, December 10, 1997, 37 ILM 22 (1998) [hereinafter Kyoto Protocol]. *See* Chapter 10 (Lemoine) in this volume.

5 *See* Chapters 14 (Peng) and 11 (Cima) in this volume.

6 *See* Chapter 2 (Farah) and Chapter 11 (Cima) in this volume.

7 *See* Chapter 10 (Lemoine) in this volume.

8 *See* Pierre-Marie Dupuy, *Soft Law and the International Law of the Environment*, 12 MICH. J- INT'L L. 420, 420–35 (1990); Kenneth W. Abbott & Duncan Snidal, *Hard and Soft Law in International Governance*, 54(3) INT'L ORG. 421, 421 (2000); Francesco Sindico, *Soft Law and the Elusive Quest for Sustainable Global Governance*, 19(3) LEIDEN J. INT'L L. 829, 829–46 (2006); Jean d' Aspremont, *Softness in International Law: a Self-Serving Quest for New Legal Materials: a Rejoinder to Tony D'Amato*, 20(3) EUR. J. INT'L L. 911, 911–17 (2009).

9 Soft law is likely to appear whenever a key element of hard law, such as precision, obligation and delegation, is weakened; *See*, John J. Kirton & Michael J. Trebilcock, *Introduction: Hard Choices and Soft Law in Sustainable Global Governance, in* Hard Choices, Soft Law: Voluntary Standards In Global Trade, Environment And Social Governance 3, 3–20 (John J. Kirton & Michael J. Trebilcock eds., Ashgate Publication Ltd, 2004) & Chris Tollefson, *Indigenous Rights and Forest Certification in British Columbia, in* Hard Choices, Soft Law: Voluntary Standards In Global Trade, Environment And Social Governance at 93.

acknowledges that hard law can also generate soft commitments. This means that a treaty may well constitute a legally binding instrument, but because the parties drafted vague or unclear provisions, states are not really obliged to take specific actions and there is no way to control that the states have complied with such vague and imprecise obligations.[10] Is hard law better than soft law? The answer, as happens often, tends to be neither "yes" nor "no." More importantly, any answer depends on what, when, and where something is being regulated. Without hesitation, one can say that it is usually easier to reach agreement on soft law than hard law, and more countries tend to embrace soft law because they do not fear any penalties if they end up breaching it – if it can even be said that noncompliance with soft law amounts to a breach. The same can be said for soft commitments within hard law.

Applying this debate to the international climate change legal regime, and considering how the regime has developed since its inception, most key instruments arguably amount to hard law. This is definitely the case for the two key primary legal sources of the international climate change regime: the UNFCCC and its Kyoto Protocol. The latter not only serves as an example of hard law, but it also sets extremely clear targets that countries must achieve if they do not want to be found in noncompliance.[11] In other words, the Kyoto Protocol is hard law with hard commitments. The UNFCCC is, on the other hand, a legally binding agreement, but may be regarded as a framework agreement that sets out general objectives that states must pursue without prescribing detailed methods for states to fulfill those objectives.[12] In the mindset of the UNFCCC's drafters, the lack of specifics did not present a problem because the UNFCCC would have been complemented by other primary legal sources – namely protocols – that would have provided the necessary detail to deal adequately with climate change. This approach was rubber-stamped in the first Conference of the Parties (COP) of the UNFCCC in Berlin in 1995,[13] which paved the way for the Kyoto Protocol. The hard law approach should have steered the way forward for the post-2012 climate regime, since the Kyoto Protocol itself required negotiations to develop such a pathway.[14] However, we all know by now that this road has been, to say the least, a rough one leading to the agreement on the Doha Amendment to the Kyoto Protocol at COP 18,[15] which has not yet entered into force.

Moreover, it seems that, following the entry into force of the Kyoto Protocol in 2005, the international community has moved away from hard commitments to action on climate change and, in some cases, from hard law altogether. Three key events cumulatively lead me to this conclusion.

The first event was the adoption of the Bali Action Plan (BAP) in 2007. The BAP is a COP Decision,[16] which is arguably obligatory for UNFCCC Parties. Whether the BAP falls into the category of hard law depends on whether only primary international legal sources – for international environmental law purposes, Multilateral Environmental Agreements (MEAs) – should be considered hard law or whether also secondary international legal

10 *See* Jake Werksman, *Legal Symmetry and Legal Differentiation Under a Future Deal on Climate,* 10(6) CLIMATE POL. 672, 674–75 (2010).

11 Kyoto Protocol, art. 3.1. *See* Chapters 9 (Ibrahim, Deleuil & Farah) and 10 (Lemoine) in this volume.

12 UNFCCC, art. 2.

13 Decision 1/CP.1, *The Berlin Mandate: Review of the adequacy of Article 4, paragraph 2(a) and (b), of the Convention, including proposals related to a protocol and decisions on follow-up.*

14 Kyoto Protocol, art. 3.9.

15 Doha Amendment to the Kyoto Protocol, December 8, 2012, not yet in force.

16 Decision 1/CP.13, *Bali Action Plan.*

sources should be included. Should the latter be the case, COP decisions would amount to secondary legal sources within the international climate change regime and, as such, constitute hard law.[17] Notwithstanding its status, the BAP does not provide any specific obligations. In other words, it contains only soft commitments.

The second event that indicates a move towards a softer international climate change legal regime was the adoption of the Copenhagen Accord in 2009. This Accord is not a COP Decision, and, in fact, COP decisions have only taken note of it.[18] The Copenhagen Accord's unique nature has generated an interesting debate in the literature.[19] In this case, it seems quite clear that the Accord does not constitute hard law. Some would even argue that the Copenhagen Accord is not law at all,[20] but, in the same vain, some authors argue that if law is soft then it just is not law at all.[21] Whatever the nature of the Accord, what seems clear, once again, is the soft nature of the commitments provided therein. The Copenhagen Accord's system of pledges is not only soft, but also flexible and conditional,[22] muddling the debate even more.

The Durban Platform brought us closer to the current state of the international climate change regime.[23] It is a COP Decision, like the BAP. The Durban Platform did not establish any specific commitments, but it did launch negotiations for a future instrument, to take the form of "a protocol, another legal instrument or an agreed outcome with legal force under the Convention applicable to all Parties."[24] With no clarification over whether "legal force" would be binding upon parties[25] or whether it could therefore be assumed that such agreement would automatically also include hard commitments, the Durban Platform indicated that a further shift may arise during future international climate change negotiations. In the run-up to COP21 in Paris, it appeared that the Ad Hoc Working Group on the Durban Platform for Enhanced Action (ADP) negotiations were leading to a softer regime based on Intended Nationally Determined Contributions (INDCs) to be reviewed periodically in order to increase greenhouse gas abatement ambition. Negotiations also appeared to be linking INDCs with an again softer system of monitoring, reporting, and verification, which would ensure the much-needed transparency and accountability. A heavily "bracketed" text adopted

17 On the role of the COPs as rule makers *see* Robin Churchill & Geir Ulfstein, ***Autonomous Institutional Arrangements in Multilateral Environmental Agreements: A little-noticed Phenomenon in International Law***, 94(4) AM. J. INT'L L. 623, 623–59 (2000); Jutta Brunnée, ***COPing with Consent: Law-Making Under Multilateral Environmental Agreements***, 15 LEIDEN J. INT'L L. 1, 1–52 (2002).

18 Decision 2/CP.15, ***Copenhagen Accord***, 2010.

19 Some of the contributions within the debate over the Copenhagen Accord include Francesco Sindico, ***The Copenhagen Accord and the Future of the International Climate Change Regime***, 1(1) REVISTA CATALANA DE DRET AMBIENTAL 1, 1–24 (2010); Lavanya Rajamani, ***Neither Fish nor Fowl*** (Centre for Policy Research Climate Initiative Seminar 606, February 2010); Daniel Bodansky, ***The Copenhagen Climate Change Conference – A Post-Mortem***, 104 AM. J. INT'L L. 230, 230 (2010); Leonardo Massai, ***The Long Way to the Copenhagen Accord: Climate Change Negotiations in 2009***, 19(1) REV. EUR. CMTY. & INT'L ENVTL. L. 104, 104–21 (2010). On the future of international climate policy in the wake of Copenhagen, *see* Robert Falkner, Hannes Stephan & John Vogler, ***International Climate Policy after Copenhagen: Towards a 'Building Blocks' Approach***, 1(3) GLOBAL POL. 252, 252–62 (2010).

20 *See* Rajamani, ***supra*** note 19.

21 *See* D'Aspremont, ***supra*** note 8.

22 *See* example from pledges compiled by Sindico, ***supra*** note 19.

23 Decision 1 /CP.17, ***Establishment of an Ad Hoc Working Group on the Durban Platform for Enhanced Action***.

24 *Id.*, ¶ 2.

25 *See* Michael Grubb, ***Durban: The Darkest Hour?***, 11(6) CLIMATE POL. 1269, 1269–271 (2011).

in Lima, the Lima Call for Climate Action, set the stage for a very challenging year (2015) for the international community.[26]

As Paris drew closer general consensus emerged that in order to fulfil the mandate set by the ADP, the Paris Agreement would take the form of a treaty.[27] As adopted, the Paris Agreement[28] contains provisions regarding how states express consent to be bound[29], requirements for entry into force,[30] reservations, and mechanisms for withdrawal.[31] All of which are fitting with its legal form as a treaty.[32] Nonetheless, the Paris Agreement still contains a mix of both soft and hard commitments, shown through a series of "recommendations"[33] intermixed with harder obligations which states "shall" achieve.[34] A harder requirement is placed on Nationally Determined Contributions (NDCs), with states obligated to "prepare, communicate and maintain" NDCs that they intend to "achieve".[35] While it is important that the requirement is placed upon "each party" rather than the "parties" to which the majority of the Paris Agreements' provisions apply, an individual obligation on each state is not given. With a requirement only to 'pursue' rather than implement domestic measures, the provision represents an obligation of conduct, not result.[36] While it is certainly an ambitious and welcome text overall, a large number of provisions contained within the Paris Agreement take the form of recommendations, with relatively few binding legal obligations.[37] It is difficult to determine the extent to which the legal nature of the Paris Agreement will impact its effectiveness, ultimately the latter will be determined by the efficiency of monitoring, reporting and verification systems, making parties accountable for their NDCs.[38] However, whether soft or hard in nature, the Paris Agreement represents a comprehensive and historic

26 See Decision – /CP.20, *Lima Call for Climate Action* and for a commentary Lavanya Rajamani, *Lima Call For Climate Action' Progress Through Modest Victories and Tentative Agreements,* L(1) ECON. & POL. WKLY. 14, 14–17 (2015).

27 *See* D. Bodansky, *The Legal Character of the Paris Agreement*, REVIEW OF EUROPEAN, COMPARATIVE AND INTERNATIONAL ENVIRONMENTAL LAW, Forthcoming (March 22, 2016).

28 The resulting text from Paris, the "Paris Outcome" consists of the Paris Agreement, Paris Agreement (Paris 12 December 2015; not yet in force); UNFCCC, Decision 1/CP.21 (hereinafter 'Paris Agreement'), and the accompanying COP decision, 'Adoption of the Paris Agreement', UNFCCC/CP/2015/10/Add.1. For a general overview of the Paris Agreement see the special issues published in Climate Law (6.1–2, 2016). *See also* A. Savaresi, *The Paris Agreement: A New Beginning?*, 34 (1) JOURNAL OF ENERGY AND NATURAL RESOURCES LAW. 16, 16–26 (2016).

29 Paris Agreement, Article 20.

30 Entry into force requires acceptance by 55 states, representing 55% of global greenhouse gas emissions. *Id.*, Article 21

31 *Id.*, Articles 27 – 28.

32 The Paris Agreement constitutes a treaty within the meaning of the Vienna Convention on the Law of Treaties. Vienna Convention on the Law of Treaties (Vienna, 23 May 1969; in force 27 January 1980), Article 26.

33 For instance, most of the provisions detailing adaptation and means of implementation are in the form of recommendations, not legal obligations. See Paris Agreement, Articles 7–9.

34 For instance, Article 7.13 states "Continuous and enhanced international support shall be provided to developing country Parties for the implementation of paragraphs 7, 9 and 10 and 11 of this Article"; however as with a number of other provisions, although phrased in mandatory terms, the provision has no subject, therefore appears to be directed at parties generally.

35 Paris Agreement, Article 4.2.

36 *Id.*

37 *See* S Obertür & R Bodle, *Legal Form and Nature of the Paris Outcome,* 6 (1–2) CLIMATE LAW. 40, 40–57 (2016).

38 The main transparency framework for accountability is detailed within Article 13 of the Paris Agreement. While implementation and compliance mechanisms are provided within Article 15.

agreement to address climate change at a global level, signifying the greatest political will to combat climate change since the Kyoto Protocol.

In sum, what can be argued is that, currently, an international climate change regime with softer commitments has arisen. As previously mentioned, soft law and soft commitments usually result from a compromise for greater participation, and this seems to have happened in the development of the international climate change legal regime. In exchange for getting the United States (US) back at the negotiating table, and obtaining some sort of (soft) commitment from emerging developing countries, a softer regime has emerged with a lesser degree of ambition.[39] Unfortunately, due to the rapid negative effects of climate change, the international community does not have the luxury to wait for these soft commitments to materialize.[40]

Fragmentation

The second characteristic of the current international climate change legal regime is its increasing fragmentation.[41] Fragmentation has been a buzzword for some time now within the field of public international law,[42] with a related study forthcoming from the United Nations International Law Commission.[43] Without taking the time here to dwell on this debate, we shall emphasize that fragmentation can be understood in two ways. First, fragmentation can be seen as the development of rules for highly specific areas. In the climate change field, this would mean the development of *ad hoc* rules related to mitigation, adaptation, technology transfer, or, for even more specific areas such as the Clean Development Mechanism (CDM) or compliance.[44] How one understands fragmentation is not a concern if these rules are developed under a single overall legal framework. This has been the case until now with the UNFCCC supplying the overall legal framework that ties all these different areas together. In fact, the development of more specific rules through secondary legislation (COP decisions) is a positive characteristic of most MEAs.[45]

However, fragmentation can also be understood as a situation in which different rules govern similar cases. This kind of fragmentation is critical to the development of international efforts to deal with climate change. What we currently observe is that the international

39 *See* A.N. Kienast, *Consensus Behind Action: The Fate of the Paris Agreement in the United States of America*, 9 (4) Carbon and Climate Law Review. 314, 314–27 (2015).

40 IPCC, *supra* note 1.

41 *See* Chapter 2 (Farah) in this volume.

42 On fragmentation in Public International Law *see*, amongst many, Martti Koskenniemi & Paivi Lein, *Fragmentation of International Law? Postmodern Anxieties*, 15(3) Leiden J. Int'l L. 553, 553–79 (2002); Andreas Zimmermann & Rainer Hoffmann, Unity and Diversity in International Law. Proceedings of an International Symposium of the Kiel Walther Schucking Institute of International Law, November 4–7, 2004 (Duncker & Humboldt, 2006). On climate change and fragmentation *see* Harro van Asselt, Francesco Sindico & Michael A. Mehling, *Global Climate Change and the Fragmentation of International Law*, 30(4) L. & Policy 423, 423–49 (2008).

43 UN Doc. A/CN.4/L.682, *Fragmentation of International Law: Difficulties Arising from the Diversification and Expansion of International Law*, 2006.

44 *See* Chapters 10 (Lemoine), 11 (Cima), and 14 (Peng) in this volume.

45 *See* Werksman, *supra* note 10, at 674; Churchill & Ulfstein, *supra* note 17.

climate change legal regime has started to reflect a number of climate change–related regional, multilateral, and bilateral efforts. Again, this characteristic is not unique to climate change. The multilateral trading system, for example, seems to mirror the same process. The inability of the states to reach consensus during the Doha Round has led to a proliferation of regional and bilateral trade agreements, which seriously question the capacity of the World Trade Organization (WTO) to govern international trade properly.[46] Similarly, one can argue that the difficulties to reach a common agreement on a post-2012 international climate regime, and the differences on key principles that underpin the international climate change legal regime among primary players,[47] have led to a proliferation of regional, multilateral, and bilateral climate change efforts.

For example, the European Union (EU), despite its past leadership on climate change at the international level, has also taken bold unilateral measures both in relation to target-setting and to measures aimed at achieving those targets.[48] The decisions to include aviation in its Emissions Trading Scheme (ETS),[49] and the possibility to exclude offsets from emerging economies in the next commitment period of the EU ETS,[50] clearly demonstrate the EU regional approach to climate change. This approach, based on hard law and hard commitments, differs sharply from the one provided for, among others, the Asia-Pacific Partnership on Clean Development and Climate.[51] The latter brings together Canada, Australia, China, India, Japan, South Korea, and the United States, and it defines itself as a "public-private partnership," which tends to focus on projects concerning specific carbon-intensive sectors such as steel, cement, coal mining, or aluminum, to name a few.

46 *See* the concerns raised about fragmentation in the international trade regime in *The Future of the WTO, Addressing Institutional Challenges in the New Millennium*, Report by the Consultative Board to the former Director-General Supachai Panitchpakdi, 2005. An interesting example is the one of Bilateral Investment Treaties (BITs). Chapter 25 (Friedmann) in this volume deals with BITs in particular as far as social media, censorship, and market access in China are concerned. *See* also Chapter 2 (Farah) in this volume.

47 A key difference still exists on the role to be given to the principle of common but differentiated responsibilities within the international climate change legal regime. On this principle, *see* Lavanya Rajamani, Differential Treatment in International Environmental Law 1–254 (Oxford University Press, 2006). *See* Chapters 9 (Ibrahim, Deleuil & Farah) and 10 (Lemoine) in this volume.

48 *See* the 20 per cent emission reduction target by 2020 set in *Communication from the Commission to the European Parliament, the Council, the European Economic and Social Committee and the Committee of the Regions 20 20 by 2020 — Europe's Climate Change Opportunity*, COM (2008) 0030 final (January 23, 2008). This was more recently followed by the adoption of a 2030 policy framework on climate change and energy with a target of at least 40 per cent compared to 1990 levels. Communication from the Commission to the European Parliament, the Council, the European Economic and Social Committee and the Committee of the Regions, *A policy framework for climate and energy in the period from 2020 to 2030*, COM/2014/015 final.

49 Aviation has been included in the EU emission trading scheme as of January 1, 2012; *see* Press release IP/11/259, *Inclusion of Aviation in the EU ETS: Commission Publishes Historical Emissions Data on which Allocations will be Based* (March 7, 2011).

50 From May 2013, the EU will limit CDM eligibility for EU ETS compliance only for projects coming from Least Developed Countries. *See* Nina Chestney & Pete Harrison, EU Bans Disputed Carbon Offsets From May 2013 (January 21, 2011), http://www.reuters.com/article/2011/01/21/us-eu-offsets-climate-idUSTRE70K37L20110121 (last visited July 11, 2016).

51 For further information on the Asia-Pacific Partnership on Clean Development and Climate, *see* www.asiapacificpartnership.org/ (last visited July 11, 2016). *See* also Sylvia Karlsson-Vinkhuyzen & Harro van Asselt, *Introduction: Exploring and Explaining the Asia-Pacific Partnership on Clean Development and Climate*, 9(3) Int'l Envtl. Agreements: Pol., L. & Econ. 195, 195 (2009).

Hence, the Asia-Pacific Partnership on Clean Development and Climate pursues an approach based on soft law. As the Paris Agreement sees the international climate regime move towards increasing flexibility in the form of NDCs, it seems likely that fragmentation will only increase, as each state individually determines its own progression.

The fact that most states develop their own energy policies further fragments international climate change efforts. Many countries frame their efforts as energy security, based on two main pillars: security of supply and economic development.[52] The US energy security is axiomatic in this sense.[53] On the one hand, the Obama administration made it clear that it viewed green energy as one of the possible ways to restore the economy,[54] provided it created local jobs and opportunities. On the other hand, a push towards greener energy sources can be seen as a way to move away from oil and gas exports from instable regions. Both pillars may seem beneficial to climate change mitigation until a country realizes that it can rely further on conventional sources of energy (or semi-conventional) as shale gas in the US or oil sands (or tar sands) in Canada. When that happens, a country may achieve both security of supply and economic development without mitigating climate change. The clash between energy security and climate change policies is not only an issue in the US, it has also become a hot topic in the EU,[55] and is controversial in the emerging economies, where governments do not wish to switch entirely to low-carbon sources of energy if they have the capacity to secure their energy needs through fossil fuels.[56]

In sum, the presence of different climate policies and strategies between groups of countries alongside the international climate change legal regime, and the difficult relationship between energy security and climate change policies, are fragmenting international efforts to curb climate change.

Complexity

To some extent, a softer and more fragmented international climate change practice naturally results in greater complexity. This added level of complexity could be seen as the highest possible level within the international climate change legal regime, where the debates increasingly institutionalize each of the key areas – mitigation, adaptation, technology

52 Paolo Davide Farah & Piercarlo Rossi, ***National Energy Policies and Energy Security in the Context of Climate Change and Global Environmental Risks: A Theoretical Framework for Reconciling Domestic and International Law through a Multiscalar and Multilevel Approach,*** 20(6) Eur. Energy & Envtl. L. 232, 232–244 (2011).

53 *See* the Whitehouse, ***Blueprint for a Secure Energy Future,*** 2011, http://www.whitehouse.gov/sites/default/files/blueprint_secure_energy_future.pdf (last visited July 11, 2016).

54 According to the Whitehouse web site, President Obama would have maintained: "As we recover from this recession, the transition to clean energy has the potential to grow our economy and create millions of jobs – but only if we accelerate that transition. Only if we seize the moment."

55 *See* Camilla Adelle, Marc Pallemaerts & Joana Chiavari, ***Climate Change and Energy Security in Europe Policy Integration and its Limits*** (Swedish Institute for European Policy Studies 2009:4), http://www.ieep.eu/assets/435/ccenergy_sec_report.pdf (last visited July 11, 2016).

56 *See* for Brazil a policy brief from the Stockholm Environment Institute authored by M. Román and Marcus Carson according to which "Brazil tackles climate change and deforestation, but rapid growth, energy needs undermine progress," Mikael Roman & Marcus Carson, Shifting Ground: Brazil Tackles Climate Change and Deforestation, but Rapid Growth, Energy Needs Undermine Progress, Policy Brief (Stockholm Environment Institute, Dec, 2010), http://www.sei-international.org/mediamanager/documents/Publications/SEI-PolicyBrief-ShiftingGroundBrazil-2010.pdf (last visited July 11, 2016). Farah & Rossi, *supra* note 39, 52.

transfer, and finance.[57] The same can be seen for specific instruments aimed at tackling climate change, such as the CDM, and after the adoption of the Paris Agreement of the yet to be developed Internationally Transferred Mitigation Outcomes (ITMOs).[58]

The greater level of complexity in international climate change practice can also be seen in the framework of one specific instrument used by many countries to tackle climate change: emissions trading.[59] While the EU pioneered its use in the field of climate change within its EU ETS,[60] emission trading schemes have now mushroomed in different regional, bilateral, national, and subnational climate policies. New Zealand has its ETS,[61] Norway has had one for some time now,[62] the US has a number of schemes in place, both on the Eastern Coast (the Regional Greenhouse Gas Initiative)[63] and on the West Coast (developed by the California Air Resources Board),[64] and Japan runs a voluntary scheme,[65] amongst others.[66] Interestingly, not only have emission trading schemes arisen in developed countries, but emerging economies and developing countries have also started to look closely at this instrument. Mexico passed legislation,[67] which aims to launch its scheme in a few years, and China developed a number of pilot schemes in big cities.[68]

This means that we are witnessing a worldwide proliferation of emission trading schemes that do not necessarily have identical rules. In relation to this proliferation, complexity will increase for three reasons. First, while most schemes will follow similar procedures and mechanisms, there can be significant differences, for example in relation to auctioning or offsets. Second, in order to achieve a greater economy of scale, single emission trading schemes will seek to link with others such as the existing link between the California Air

57 *See* Chapters 10 (Lemoine) and 11 (Cima) in this volume.

58 *See* Chapter 14 (Peng) in this volume.

59 *See* Chapter 10 (Lemoine) in this volume.

60 Directive 2009/29/EC of the European Parliament and of the Council of April 23, 2009 amending Directive 2003/87/EC so as to improve and extend the greenhouse gas emission allowance trading scheme of the Community. Specific information about the EU ETS can be found at http://ec.europa.eu/clima/news/news_archives_en.htm#REGULATORY (last visited July 11, 2016).

61 Information about New Zealand's scheme is available at http://www.climatechange.govt.nz/emissions-trading-scheme/ (last visited July 11, 2016).

62 For an overview of Norway's scheme, *see* Christina Voigt, *Environmental Integrity and Non-Discrimination in the Norwegian Emissions Trading Scheme,* Rev. Eur. Cmty. & Int'l Envtl. L. 304, 304–11 (2009).

63 Further information on the Regional Greenhouse Gas Initiative is available at http://rggi.org/ (last visited July 11, 2016). *See* also Camilla Bausch & Sandra Cavalieri, *Allocation of Greenhouse Gas Allowances in the United States – A Northeastern Example,* 1(2) Carbon & Climate L. Rev. 129, 129–138 (2007).

64 Information on California's cap and trade program is available at http://www.arb.ca.gov/cc/capandtrade/capandtrade.htm (last visited July 11, 2016).

65 On Japan's climate policy, *see* Harro van Asselt, Norichika Kanie & Masahiko Iguchi, *Japan's Position In International Climate Policy: Navigating Between* Kyoto *And The* APP, 9(3) Int'l Envtl. Agreements: Pol., L. & Econ. 319, 319 (2009).

66 For a comprehensive list of Emissions Trading Systems operating around the world, see Emissions Trading Worldwide, International Carbon Action Partnership (ICAP), Status Report 2015, https://icapcarbonaction.com/images/StatusReport2015/ICAP_Report_2015_02_10_online_version.pdf (last visited July 12, 2016).

67 Point Carbon, *Mexico's SenateAapproves Climate Bill,* December 2011. *See* also Mexico's chapter in Michal Nachmany et al., *The GLOBE Climate Legislation Study: A Review of Climate Change Legislation in 66 Countries* (GLOBE International and the Grantham Research Institute, London School of Economics, 4th ed., 2014).

68 Point Carbon, *Guangdong Picks Exchange For Carbon Trading,* October 10, 2011 and SEI/FORES, *China's Carbon Emission Trading: An Overview of Current Development,* 2012. *See* Chapters 12 (He) and 14 (Peng) in this volume.

Resources Board and the system set up in Quebec, Canada.[69] The rules about linking,[70] although necessary to ensure certainty and economic efficiency, can increase the overall complexity of the current proliferation of emission trading schemes worldwide. Third, with the adoption of the Paris Agreement domestic emission trading schemes may be set to increase. ITMOs are likely to follow a soft law approach, produced from any type of scheme, and will not be subject to any framework structure by the COP.[71] The transfers are however required to "support sustainable development" and be consistent with UNFCCC guidance,[72] although once again, such guidance will likely be non-binding. As it currently stands their place within NDCs and within the overall framework of the international climate change regime is yet to be clarified.[73]

In sum, the more specialized the international climate change legal regime, the more complex it becomes because of its requisite institutionalization. Furthermore, a more fragmented international effort on climate change will inevitably lead to a more complex picture, as the proliferation of regional, national, and subnational emission trading schemes has shown.

We now move on to assess how a softer, more fragmented, and more complex international climate change legal regime, as well as the international community's overall effort, impacts the climate and trade debate.

Climate and trade

In this section, we will first explain the underlining tension between climate measures and trade liberalization, emphasizing that the tension stems from a more general debate involving trade and the environment. We will then move on to assess whether softer, more fragmented, and more complex international climate change practice may lead to more trade tensions.

Trade and the environment

The tension between measures aimed at mitigating climate change and trade rules is really just an element of the wider trade-environment debate. Environmental protection comes at a cost, and if some countries decide not to – or cannot – adopt similar stringent measures, they are perceived to have a competitive advantage over other countries that have instead adopted strong environmental protection measures. In such a scenario, countries fear that certain industries will relocate to those countries that have lower environmental standards. In the case of climate change, the fear is that if companies move to "climate

69 The link also foresees a joint auctioning scheme; *see* Release #14–50, March 6, 2014, *Québec and California Announce Plans for Joint Auction of Greenhouse Gas Emission Allowances*, http://www.arb.ca.gov/newsrel/newsrelease.php?id=625 (last visited July 11, 2016).

70 On linking, *see* Michael Mehling & Erik Haites, *Mechanisms for Linking Emissions Trading Schemes*, 9 Climate Pol. 169, 169–84 (2009).

71 A Marcu, Carbon Market Provisions in the Agreement (Article 6) CEPS Special Report, No. 128, January 2016. See also, T Jevnaker & J Wettestad, *Linked Carbon Markets: Silver Bullet, or Castle in the Air?*, 6 (1–2) Climate law.142, 142–51 (2016).

72 Paris Agreement, Article 6.2.

73 For greater detail on the implementation of Article 6 of the Paris Agreement, see IETA, A vision for the market provisions of the Paris Agreement 3-11 (May, 2016), http://www.ieta.org/resources/Resources/Position_Papers/2016/IETA_Article_6_Implementation_Paper_May2016.pdf (last visited July 12, 2016).

rogue" states, relocation will lead to two effects: carbon leakage and loss of competitiveness.[74] The former refers to the overall amount of greenhouse gas emissions that could occur if companies decide to install themselves where they are allowed to pollute more.[75] The latter is an economic – and political – concern according to which relocation will lead to job losses and economic stagnation in the country with higher climate standards.[76] The mantra goes that countries may decide to adopt climate-related trade measures in order to level the playing field and deal simultaneously with carbon leakage and competitiveness concerns. These measures may include, among others, border tax adjustments,[77] border adjustment measures linked to emission trading schemes,[78] and support measures for domestic carbon-intensive sectors.[79]

The relationship between trade and the environment had been a hot topic within the multilateral trading system even before the establishment of the WTO in 1994.[80] The debate is too complex to describe it adequately in this chapter,[81] but it is certainly worth mentioning the following points. First, the WTO legal system is based on the principle of non-discrimination, according to which countries cannot discriminate based on the nationality of the product or service.[82] Therefore, country-based trade bans almost always breach WTO law. Second, WTO

74 *See* Chapter 10 (Lemoine) in this volume.

75 On carbon leakage, *see* IPCC, *Climate Change 2007: Working Group III: Mitigation of Climate Change*, section 11.7.6: "Carbon leakage is defined as the increase in CO2 emissions outside the countries taking domestic mitigation action divided by the reduction in the emissions of these countries. It has been demonstrated that an increase in local fossil fuel prices resulting, for example, from mitigation policies may lead to the re-allocation of production to regions with less stringent mitigation rules (or with no rules at all), leading to higher emissions in those regions and therefore to carbon leakage."

76 *See* European Commission, McKinsey & Company & Ecofys, *EU ETS Review. Report on International Competitiveness* (2006). According to this study, the cost for a typical European cement production process will increase by 36.5 per cent due to CO_2 emissions trading; 93 per cent of this increase comes from direct emissions. *See* also Harro van Asselt & Frank Biermann, *European Emissions Trading and the International Competitiveness of Energy-intensive Industries: A Legal and Political Evaluation of Possible Supporting Measures,* 35 ENERGY POL. 497, 497–506 (2007).

77 *See* the 2006 French proposal debate by Jochem Wiers, *French Ideas on Climate and Trade Policies,* 2 CARBON & CLIMATE L. REV. 18, 18 (2008). More recently, the French government has come up with a similar suggestion, this time joined by the Italian government in a letter sent to the President of the Commission, Jose Manuel Barroso.

78 From the EU, *see* Directive 2009/29/EC, *supra* note 60, recital 25 and article 10b(1)(b). In past unadopted US climate change bills, similar climate-related trade measures were envisioned: see the Climate Security Act (2007), S. 2191, 110th Cong. 1st Sess, and the Lieberman–Warner Climate Security Act (2008), S. 3036, 110th Cong. 2nd Sess. On the compatibility of the EU and US suggested measures with the WTO *see* Francesco Sindico, *The EU and Carbon Leakage: How to Reconcile Border Adjustments with the WTO?,* 17 EUR. ENERGY & ENVTL. L. REV. 328, 328–40 (2008); and Francesco Sindico, *Climate and Trade in a Divided World: Can Measures Adopted in the North End Up Shaping Climate Change Legislative Frameworks in the South?,* in CLIMATE LAW AND DEVELOPING COUNTRIES: LEGAL AND POLICY CHALLENGES FOR THE WORLD COMMUNITY 361, 361–80 (Y. Le Bouthillier, H. McLeod-Kilmurray, B. Richardson & S. Wood eds, Edward Elgar, 2009).

79 These tend to include grandfathering of allowances to energy intensive sectors.

80 *See* Report of the Panel, *United States – Restrictions on Imports of Tuna* DS21/R (September 3, 1991).

81 On trade and environment *see*, amongst others, ERICH VRANES, TRADE AND THE ENVIRONMENT: FUNDAMENTAL ISSUES IN INTERNATIONAL LAW, WTO LAW AND LEGAL THEORY 9–172 (Oxford University Press, 2009).

82 General Agreement on Tariffs and Trade, October 30, 1947, 61 Stat. A-11, 55 UNTS 194 [hereinafter GATT], Articles I and III.

law tends not to distinguish how a specific product has been produced,[83] if such process does not leave a trace in the final product.[84] However, if the process and production method (PPM) determines something that a consumer within a specific marketplace values as an element that differentiates two products, such as the price or end use,[85] then such market products can be differentiated based on their process and production methods.[86] Third, while the WTO is, obviously, not an environmental agreement, it does acknowledge that, under certain circumstances, measures aimed at protecting the environment, which would otherwise be unlawful, can be considered compatible with the WTO.[87] Furthermore, the Marrakesh Agreement that established the WTO acknowledges that the organization must consider sustainable development as one of its primary goals.[88] Finally, negotiations within the multilateral trading system have also focused on the relationship between trade and the environment.[89] One of the agenda items of the Doha Mandate is the relationship between specific obligations in MEAs and the WTO.[90] While no final decision has been reached on this topic, there seems to be widespread consensus that trade measures that are clearly provided in MEAs will have priority over WTO rules, while unilateral measures will need to be assessed carefully to see whether they are compatible with WTO law and – should that not be the case – whether they fall under the above-mentioned environmental exceptions.

Applying this brief excursus on trade and environment to the climate and trade debate,[91] the first observation that can be made is that the international climate change legal regime does not provide for any specific trade measures. To the contrary, both the UNFCCC and the Kyoto Protocol adopt language that seems to support the idea that the international climate change

83 Like products and PPMs have been dealt with extensively in the literature. Two key papers are Steve Charnovitz, *The Law of Environmental "PPMs" in the WTO: Debunking the Myth of Illegality,* 27(1) YALE J. INT'L L. 59, 59–110 (2002); and Robert Howse & Donald Regan, *The Product/Process Distinction – An Illusory Basis for Disciplining "Unilateralism" in Trade Policy,* 11(2) EUR. J. INT'L L. 249, 249–289 (2000).

84 Report of the Panel, *United States – Restrictions on Imports of Tuna* supra note 80, ¶ 5.15.

85 *Report of the Working Party adopted on 2 December 1970* (Doc. L/3464), ¶ 18.

86 Appellate Body Report, *European Communities – Measures Affecting Asbestos and Asbestos-Containing Products (EC – Asbestos)*, WT/DS135/AB/R (March 12, 2001).

87 GATT Article XX provides that: "Subject to the requirement that such measures are not applied in a manner which would constitute a means of arbitrary or unjustifiable discrimination between countries where the same conditions prevail, or a disguised restriction on international trade, nothing in this Agreement shall be construed to prevent the adoption or enforcement by any contracting party of measures: b) necessary to protect human, animal or plant life or health; g) relating to the conservation of exhaustible natural resources if such measures are made effective in conjunction with restrictions on domestic production or consumption."

88 Marrakesh Agreement Establishing the World Trade Organization, April 15, 1994, 1867 UNTS 154. According to the preamble, "Recognizing that their relations in the field of trade and economic endeavour should be conducted with a view to raising standards of living, ensuring full employment and a large and steadily growing volume of real income and effective demand, and expanding the production of and trade in goods and services, while allowing for the optimal use of the world's resources in accordance with the objective of sustainable development, seeking both to protect and preserve the environment and to enhance the means for doing so in a manner consistent with their respective needs and concerns at different levels of economic development." *See* Chapter 2 (Farah) in this volume.

89 World Trade Organization, Ministerial Declaration of November 14, 2001, WT/MIN(01)/DEC/1, 41 I.L.M. 746 (2002) [hereinafter Doha Declaration], ¶¶ 31–33.

90 *Id.*, ¶ 31(i) launched negotiations on "the relationship between existing WTO rules and specific trade obligations set out in multilateral environmental agreements (MEAs)."

91 The academic literature on climate and trade cannot be fully quoted here. For a comprehensive analysis, *see* the special journal issue edited by Joost Pauwelyn & Francesco Sindico, *Climate Change in a Global Economy,* 2 CARBON & CLIMATE L. REV. (2008).

legal regime and the WTO should, and can, be mutually supportive.[92] The next sections will analyze whether the international climate change legal regime's direction, as well as more general international climate change efforts, will lead to increased trade tensions.

Old and new tensions

Countries with stronger climate change standards could react in two ways to a softer international climate change legal regime. On the one hand, they could react positively by appreciating that a softer regime brings together more key countries and, in particular, the largest GHG emitters (the US and emerging economies like China).[93] Should this be their perception, they would probably refrain from adopting border adjustment measures to level the playing field, since such measures would undermine the delicate political compromise that a softer regime has so rarely achieved. On the other hand, countries with allegedly high climate standards may consider a soft approach to climate change insufficient, and will ultimately harm the environment and, incidentally, their domestic economies. If this were the perception, carbon leakage and competitiveness concerns would prevail over international political compromise, and countries with stronger standards would likely impose climate-related border adjustment measures on their counterparts with lower standards.

Against this framework, it is interesting to note that developing countries are concerned that Annex I countries may decide at some point to adopt unilateral trade measures against them on climate change grounds.[94] This concern surfaced at the international climate change negotiations and it has found its way into the Cancún Agreements.[95] If eventually a COP

92 *See* UNFCCC, art. 3.5: "The Parties should cooperate to promote a supportive and open international economic system that would lead to sustainable economic growth and development in all Parties, particularly developing country Parties, thus enabling them better to address the problems of climate change. Measures taken to combat climate change, including unilateral ones, should not constitute a means of arbitrary or unjustifiable discrimination or a disguised restriction on international trade"; and Kyoto Protocol, preamble: "Being guided by Article 3 of the Convention."

93 *See* Chapters 12 (He), 13 (Li), and 14 (Peng) in this volume.

94 Countries Parties to the UNFCCC have been divided by the latter in different groups. Annex I countries represent mainly Organisation for Economic Cooperation and Development (OECD) countries, with the addition of Eastern European countries. The main difference is the different nature of commitments provided for in UNFCCC, art. 4 for Annex I and non-Annex I countries, with Annex I countries bearing most of the weight of climate change obligations, which was then confirmed by the top down approach present in the Kyoto Protocol. Non-Annex I countries include a very heterogeneous group of developing countries, which include major developing countries with emerging economies, but also Least Developed Countries and Small Island States. The rationale for the categorization of countries in Annex I and non-Annex I was to implement the principle of common but differentiated responsibilities and respective capabilities, but this is now questioned by the bottom-up approach first suggested in the Copenhagen Accord and then confirmed by the Cancún Agreements. The Durban COP Decision that launched the Ad Hoc Working Group on the Durban Platform for Enhanced Action did not mention the principle of common but differentiated responsibilities and respective capabilities, and the static approach has been abandoned within the Paris Agreement. In fact, the latter does not include any mention of the annex structure of the UNFCCC. Instead, the same core obligations apply to all countries, signifying a more flexible approach, which still accounts for changes in a country's circumstances and capacity.

95 Decision 1/CP.16, The Cancún Agreements: Outcome of the work of the Ad Hoc Working Group on Long-term Cooperative Action under the Convention, 2011, ¶ 90: "Reaffirms that the Parties should cooperate to promote a supportive and open international economic system that would lead to sustainable economic growth and development in all Parties, particularly developing country Parties, thus enabling them better to address the problems of climate change; ***measures taken to combat climate change, including unilateral ones, should not constitute a means of arbitrary or unjustifiable discrimination or a disguised restriction on international trade***" [emphasis added].

decision were to clearly prohibit unilateral climate-related trade measures, a softer regime could lead to less trade tensions. No such prohibition has been made under the Paris Agreement, with Parties allowed to fulfil their NDCs in whichever way best satisfies their individual priorities.[96] It is therefore possible that scope may be created for unilateral measures with trade implications.

Only time will tell if trade tensions will arise from the implementation of the Paris Agreement. However, a more fragmented international climate change practice has already led to tangible trade disputes. These have all originated from energy policies in different countries aimed at delivering environmental stewardship and economic development simultaneously, very much along the lines of the energy security climate change debate that has been mentioned in previous sections of this chapter.[97]

The first one of these cases saw Japan lodge a complaint against Canada,[98] which the EU later joined.[99] The Panel and later the Appellate Body were asked to decide over the allegedly WTO non-compatible law from one of Canada's provinces, Ontario, which would have adopted a feed-in tariff scheme aimed at fostering renewables. The scheme allegedly favored domestic producers through a domestic content requirement, making the measure a violation of the principle of non-discrimination, since it would have favored products and services based on their country of origin.[100] Both the Panel and Appellate Body ruled very much against Canada whose domestic content requirement was deemed to be WTO incompatible. A similar controversy has emerged between the US and China over the latter's regulations on wind energy,[101] and between China and a number of European countries.[102] More recently, the WTO's Dispute Settlement Body ruled that mandatory domestic content requirements contained within a solar power generation programme in India violated trade rules under both the GATT and the Agreement on Trade-Related Investment Measures.[103] As an integral part of its progression towards renewable energy, India has initiated the Jawaharlal Nehru National Solar Mission (JNNSM). The JNNSM represents a key component of India's commitment to abide by the Paris Agreement, demonstrating the clashing elements of the climate-trade debate. However, a clause requiring investors to use solar modules produced locally, as well as sourcing 30 percent of input locally, quickly came under fire with the WTO. The US challenged the provision, stating that it was protectionist in nature. The US argued that the discrimination was evident in the 90 percent fall American firms had

96 Paris Agreement, Article 4.2.

97 *See supra* in this Chapter.

98 Report of the Panel, *Canada – Certain Measures Affecting the Renewable Energy Generation Sector (Canada – Renewable Energy)*, WT/DS412/R (September 13, 2010) and Appellate Body Report, WT/DS412/AB/R (December 19, 2012).

99 Report of the Panel, *Canada – Measures Relating to the Feed-In Tariff Program (Canada – Feed-In Tariff Program)*, WT/DS426/R (December 19, 2012) and Appellate Body Report, WT/DS426/AB/R (May 6, 2013).

100 Luca Rubini, *The Subsidization of Renewable Energy in the WTO: Issues and Perspectives* (NCCR Trade Working Paper 32, 2011).

101 DS419, *China – Measures concerning wind power equipment. See* Chapter 11 (Cima) in this volume.

102 DS452, *European Union and certain Member States – Certain Measures Affecting the Renewable Energy Generation Sector.*

103 Panel Report, India-Certain Measures Relating to Solar Cells and Solar Modules, WT/DS456/R/ (Feb.24, 2016).

experienced in solar exports to India since the imposition of the clause.[104] The Panel ruled against the clause on the grounds of it being inconsistent with the national treatment obligation under GATT Article III:4.[105] These disputes demonstrate that energy security policies, when aimed at simultaneously boosting economic development, risk creating trade tensions with other WTO members wary about possible violations of the principle of non-discrimination.[106]

The final characteristic of international climate change efforts is its increasing complexity. This is particularly true for the current development of carbon trading epitomized by the proliferation of regional, national, and subnational emission trading schemes. Why should this lead to any trade tension? We wish to focus on one specific aspect of emission trading schemes that may, in the future, lead to a new type of climate-trade tensions: offsets.

Almost all emission trading schemes that are being developed provide for offsets, which allow participants in the scheme to invest elsewhere in green and sustainable projects from which they accrue credits that they can then use on their carbon market, either for trading or compliance purposes. Offsets should, theoretically, leverage sustainable development in the hosting country. However, the experience of the CDM within the international climate change legal regime has shown that either that is not always the case, or that it is inherently difficult to measure the success of projects from a sustainable development perspective. Some of the major criticisms of CDM projects have concerned, precisely, their lack of sustainability and overall geographical balance.[107] While market-based approaches such as emissions trading and the CDM were key features of the Kyoto Protocol, for the majority of the ADP negotiations it was unclear whether any market related language would be used within the Paris Agreement.

Surprisingly, the Paris Agreement contains an entire article on markets, without ever actually mentioning "markets" specifically.[108] As previously mentioned Article 6.2 states that countries can use and transfer "mitigation outcomes" to other countries, allowing for the linking of Emissions Trading Systems, using ITMOs, in order to deepen the targets set within NDCs.[109] As well as the requirement to promote sustainable development,[110] parties are also obliged to promote environmental integrity and transparency, suggesting that markets should consider wider environmental and social factors than simply the carbon being traded.[111] The measures are to be subject to "robust accounting rules", to avoid double counting.[112] However, with NDCs providing a heterogeneous platform, it is unclear how this will be implemented.

104 *See* Sahdev G, *Renewable Energy Subsidies: Reigniting the Clean Energy Trade Debate*, ORF Issue Brief, Issue No. 144 (June 2016), http://www.orfonline.org/wp-content/uploads/2016/06/ORF_Issue-Brief_144_Sahdev_Final.pdf (last visited July 12, 2016).

105 Panel Report, India-Certain Measures Relating to Solar Cells and Solar Modules, WT/DS456/R/ (Feb.24, 2016) para 8.3.

106 Farah & Rossi, *supra* note 52. *See also* ibid (footnote 3 in previous text addition)

107 *See* Christina Voigt, *Is the Clean Development Mechanism Sustainable? Some Critical Aspects,* 7(2) Sustainable Dev. L. & Pol. 15, 15–21 (2008); and Angus MacDonald, *Improving or Disproving Sustainable Development in the Clean Development Mechanism in the Midst of a Financial Crisis?,* 6(1) Law, Env't & Dev. J. 3, 3–19 (2010).

108 Paris Agreement, Article 6.

109 *Id.*, Article 6.2.

110 *Id.*

111 *Id.*

112 *Id.*

The Paris Agreement also establishes a new mechanism to "contribute to the mitigation of greenhouse gases and support sustainable development".[113] While the CDM is not mentioned within the text, the COP Decision contains details which suggest the mechanism will bear close resemblance to the CDM.[114] However unlike the CDM all countries will be able to generate and use offset credits. The mechanism has four key aims; to promote greenhouse gas mitigation while fostering sustainable development; to incentivise and facilitate participation in the mitigation of greenhouse gas emissions by public and private entities; to contribute to the reduction of emission levels in the host party which will benefit from mitigation activities resulting in emission reduction which can also be used by another party to fulfil its NDC; and to deliver overall mitigation in global emissions.[115] The new mechanism seems likely to extend beyond the project-based approach taken by the CDM, instead offering a broader range of support for new activities, policies and programmes, although this is yet to be determined.[116] Countries will be unable to use emissions reductions transferred to another country under the new mechanism to fulfil its NDC, again to avoid double counting.[117] Under the CDM the assessment of whether a project delivers sustainable development was left to the host country,[118] yet no universal sustainability standards were in place by which to make such assessment. It will be left to future UNFCCC meetings to flesh out the details of the new mechanism. It therefore remains to be seen whether the new mechanism will be subject to greater rules and restrictions than the CDM, and whether the problems encountered with the CDM can be resolved.[119]

Against this background, different emission trading schemes will probably produce slightly different rules regarding offsets. Some will favor offsets flowing from specific type of projects that are deemed more sustainable than others.[120] Other schemes may even consider banning credits accrued from projects based in specific countries, as is the case in the EU in its current ETS commitment period (2013–2020) for offsets coming from emerging economies.[121] This action would be taken in order to boost investment in projects in countries and regions of the world that have seen little, or no, investment until now.[122] Different rules on which offsets would be eligible in specific markets would need to be considered together with the desire to create economies of scale in the global carbon market by linking together different regional, national, and subnational emission trading schemes. If linking is not accompanied by clear rules on the reciprocal acceptance of credits, then trade tensions may arise. This could be the case if a country decides to allow credits from one emission

113 *Id.*, Article 6.4.

114 'Adoption of the Paris Agreement', UNFCCC/CP/2015/10/Add.1, para 38.

115 Paris Agreement, Article 6.4 (a) - (d).

116 Adoption of the Paris Agreement', UNFCCC/CP/2015/10/Add.1, para 37 (c).

117 Paris Agreement, Article 6.5.

118 Marrakech Accords (Decision 17/CP.7).

119 It can be noted that the COP Decision within the Paris Outcome states that Article 6.4 - the new mechanism - will be adopted with "experience gained with and lessons learned from existing mechanisms" 'Adoption of the Paris Agreement', UNFCCC/CP/2015/10/Add.1, para 37 (f).

120 This can be done through, for example, discounting; *see* Stefan Bakker et al., *The Future of the CDM: Same Same, but Differentiated?*, 11 Climate Pol. 752, 752–67 (2011); and Andrew Schatz, *Discounting the Clean Development Mechanism,* 20 Geo. Int'l Envtl. L. Rev. 703, 703 (2008).

121 See *supra* note 50.

122 As of July 2016, China was host to 3,764 registered projects (48.78 per cent of all registered projects), India was host to 1,618 (20.97 per cent), and Brazil to 339 (4.39 per cent). These three countries alone have attracted over half of all registered projects in the CDM pipeline.

trading scheme but not from another, based on sustainability grounds enshrined in the specific emission trading schemes rules on offsets.

Acknowledging that allowances and credits under the carbon trading provided for by the international climate change regime are neither goods nor services,[123] the same may not be the case for credits originating through regional, domestic, or subnational schemes. Should a dispute advance to a WTO Panel and a decision be reached holding that credits are subject to a trade transaction covered by the WTO agreements, then discrimination based on how that credit has been generated – in a more or less sustainable manner – would imply a differential treatment based on the process and production method. We have mentioned that such discrimination is allowed only if the process leaves a physical trace in the final product, if a consumer within a specific marketplace values the process as an element that differentiates two products, or if the measure can be saved as a general exception. All options would be difficult to pursue, and there is no guarantee that a country's measure banning offsets on sustainability grounds would be considered WTO-compatible. The best policy option in this case would be to focus on the link between different emission trading schemes and negotiate clear rules that will help avoid such trade tensions from happening in the first place.[124]

Conclusion

Two main conclusions can be drawn from the analysis in this chapter. First, three key features highlight the development of what has been defined as international climate change practice, which includes the international climate change legal regime, based on the UNFCCC, the Kyoto Protocol, and the legal architecture deriving from both leading to the Paris agreement, as well as other regional, bilateral, or national climate change efforts. The first characteristic is that international climate change has become "softer" and relies more heavily on soft commitments. Second, international climate change practice has become more "fragmented," with very different policies occasionally developing between key international players. Finally, both the international climate change legal regime and overall international climate change efforts lead to a much more "complex" web of legal and policy instruments and institutions. This is particularly true for emission trading.

The second main conclusion is that a softer, more fragmented, and more complex international climate change practice could potentially lead not only to increased climate and trade tensions, but also to novel types of problems. While the possibility that climate and trade may clash should not be overstated, it must be monitored carefully.

123 Most authors agree that they are "fundamentally government creations to facilitate compliance with international obligations"; *see* Annie Petsonk, *The Kyoto Protocol and the WTO: Integrating Greenhouse Gas Emissions Allowance Trading into the Global Marketplace,* 10 Duke Envtl. L. & Pol. F. 200, 200 (1999).

124 In order to avoid such trade tensions arising the design of domestic and regional linkages between carbon markets will have to pay close attention to the development and implementation of Article 6 of the Paris Agreement, see Carbon Pricing, The Paris Agreement's Key Ingredient, Joint paper by the Environmental Defense Fund (EDF) and the International Emissions Trading Association (IETA), April 2016, http://www.ieta.org/resources/Resources/Reports/Carbon_Pricing_The_Paris_Agreements_Key_Ingredient.pdf (last visited July 12, 2016)

9 The Principle of Common but Differentiated Responsibilities in the International Regime of Climate Change*

*Imad Ibrahim, Thomas Deleuil**, and Paolo Davide Farah*

"Preventing future calamity requires not only agreement but action. Governments and other responsible groups are usually accused of reacting to crises rather than foreseeing and preventing them. We have an opportunity here to show that experts, scientists, lawyers, and governments can foresee potentially catastrophic dangers, and prevent them from happening."[1] This abstract demonstrates the philosophy, issues and objectives of Multilateral Environmental Agreements (MEAs) adopted since the 1970s. Climate change has been described as "the most challenging environmental issue of our time,"[2] and one cannot help but associate this abstract with the construction of, what is called today, the climate regime. Following the process launched at the Rio Conference, the United Nations Framework Convention on Climate Change (UNFCCC)[3] was adopted in May 1992 and a protocol to the Convention followed in 1997: the Kyoto Protocol.[4]

* This chapter is part of the results of the Research Project on "*Current Trends of Chinese Law towards Non-Trade Concerns such as Sustainable Development and the Protection of Environment, Public Health, Food Safety, Cultural, Social and Economic Rights, Labor Rights and the Reduction of Poverty from the Perspective of International Law and WTO Law*" coordinated by Professor Paolo Davide Farah at gLAWcal – Global Law Initiatives for Sustainable Development (United Kingdom) and at West Virginia University John D. Rockefeller IV School of Policy and Politics, Department of Public Administration, in partnership with the Center of Advanced Studies on Contemporary China (CASCC) in Turin (Italy), Maastricht University Faculty of Law, Department of International and European Law and IGIR – Institute for Globalisation and International Regulation (Netherlands) and Tsinghua University, School of Law, Institute of Public International Law and the Center for Research on Intellectual Property Law in Beijing (China). An early draft of this paper was presented at Conferences Series on "*China's Influence on Non-Trade Concerns in International Economic Law*", First Conference held at the Center of Advanced Studies on Contemporary China (CASCC) in Turin on November 23–24, 2011. This publication and the Conference Series were sponsored by China–EU School of Law (CESL) at the China University of Political Science and Law (CUPL). The activities of CESL at CUPL are supported by the European Union and the P.R. of China.

** Thomas Deleuil was legal advisor on climate negotiations at the French Ministry of Foreign Affairs. However, the French Ministry of Foreign Affairs does not support or refute these opinions. They are to be considered as those of the author.

1 Dr. Mostafa K. Tolba (Executive Director of the United Nations Environment Programme), Address at the Conference of the Plenipotentiaries on the Protection of the Ozone Layer (March 18, 1985).

2 Jolene Lin, *Environmental Law and Policy in China – Responding to Climate Change*, in THE DEVELOPMENT OF THE CHINESE LEGAL SYSTEM: CHANGE AND CHALLENGES 295 (Guanghua Yu ed., Routledge, 2011).

3 United Nations Framework Convention on Climate Change, May 9, 1992, 1771 UNTS 107.

4 Kyoto Protocol to the United Nations Framework Convention on Climate Change, December 11, 1997, 2303 UNTS 148. For an analysis on the way China has reacted to these international documents on climate change, *see* Chapter 14 (Peng) in this volume.

Born with decolonization, differential treatment first appeared in international trade law in 1965 when it was adopted as Part IV of the World Trade Organization (WTO) General Agreement on Tariffs and Trade (GATT). Although the Doha Ministerial Declaration[5] reaffirmed it, the 1994 Marrakesh Accord did not give differential treatment much space. Meanwhile, however, it evolved quickly and became a milestone in international environmental law.[6] Indeed, acknowledging historical differences as well as disparities in economic and social development, "States [. . .] crafted a burden-sharing arrangement rooted in differential treatment"[7] in order to achieve a regime characterized by universality rather than uniformity.[8] This "*arrangement*" is deeply rooted in the philosophical notions of equity and fairness.[9] Adopted twenty years after the Stockholm Declaration, which had paved the way for differential treatment,[10] the Rio Declaration embodied the concept in its Principle 7:[11] "States have common but differentiated responsibilities. The developed countries acknowledge the responsibility that they bear in the international pursuit to sustainable development in view of the pressures their societies place on the global environment and of the technologies and financial resources they command."[12] One will notice the distinction between WTO law and environmental law on the specific issue of differential treatment.[13] In WTO law, there is a special and differentiated "treatment" for developing countries, while, under the Rio Convention, there are common but differentiated "responsibilities" for developed and developing countries. As a consequence, the Marrakesh Agreement enshrines "special and differential treatment" for developing countries with the idea to return, sooner or later, to the general rules of the Agreement – with an exception for the least-developed countries. Thus, WTO law establishes two different and parallel regimes but, normally, for a limited time. On the contrary, environmental law takes a more vertical approach, using a principle applicable to all Parties as a basis for differentiated legal obligations. Therefore, the different regimes are complementary and, it seems, without time limits.[14]

Back in 1992, in "common but differentiated responsibilities" (CBDRs), "*common*" meant that there is a universal responsibility to act for the benefit of "present and future generations."[15] Thus, common responsibilities embody both the notions of "common

5 World Trade Organization, Ministerial Declaration of November 14, 2001, WT/MIN(01)/DEC/1, 41 ILM 746 (2002) [hereinafter Doha Declaration], ¶44, http://www.wto.org/english/thewto_e/minist_e/min01_e/mindecl_e.htm (last visited July 6, 2016).

6 *See* Chapters 8 (Sindico & Gibson) and 10 (Lemoine) in this volume.

7 Lavanya Rajamani, Differential Treatment in International Environmental Law 8 (Oxford University Press, 2006).

8 Laurence Boisson de Chazournes, *Le Droit et l'Universalité de la Lutte Contre les Changements Climatiques*, Cahier Droit, Sciences et Technologies N°2 — Droit et Climat 23, 30 (2009). Our translation.

9 Amongst others, *see* Friedrich Solteau, Fairness in international climate change law and policy (Cambridge University Press, 2009).

10 Declaration of the United Nations Conference on the Human Environment, Stockholm, 1972, A/CONF.48/14/Rev.1 [hereinafter Stockholm Declaration].

11 The United Nations General Assembly had already worked on differential treatment at that time; *see* A/RES/44/228 UNGA (1989).

12 Declaration of the United Nations Conference on Environment and Development, Rio de Janeiro, 1992, A/CONF.151/26 (Vol. I) [hereinafter Rio Declaration].

13 *See* Chapter 8 (Sindico & Gibson) in this volume.

14 *See* Chapters 8 (Sindico & Gibson) and 10 (Lemoine) in this volume.

15 Stockholm Declaration Principle 1; Rio Declaration Principle 3.

concern" and "common heritage of humankind," two notions "as old as international environmental law itself."[16] In other words, environmental issues such as climate change have too much of a universal impact for the response to be "solely a matter of domestic jurisdiction."[17]

"*Differentiated*" was rather the core of the notion. It recognized that developed countries were primarily responsible – because of their industrial development – for the environment's current state and that they possess the technological and financial resources that will allow them to do so. Therefore, they were expected to play a greater role in addressing environmental concerns.[18]

As stated in the Rio Declaration, under the UNFCCC, differential treatment is expressed through the "common but differentiated responsibilities principle."[19] Nonetheless, the Convention does not perfectly integrate the Rio Declaration's definition of CBDRs. Indeed, when the Rio Declaration clearly refers to the historical contributions of developed countries to environment degradation as a basis of CBDRs, these only appear in the Preamble of the UNFCCC.[20] Article 3, paragraph 1 of the Convention only states, "the Parties should protect the climate system for the benefit of present and future generations of humankind, on the basis of equity and in accordance with their common but differentiated responsibilities and respective capabilities. Accordingly, the developed country Parties should take the lead in combating climate change and the adverse effects thereof." The last sentence refers only to the industrial countries' superior technological and financial capacities. For some, this language represents a clear victory for developed countries that did not want to include any reference to their contribution to environmental degradation in the Convention at the time when it was negotiated.[21] Beyond Article 3§1, which only states the CBDR principle, Article 4 of the Convention develops commitments that are set taking into account common but differentiated responsibilities, specific national and regional development priorities, objectives and circumstances. The fact that a country's contribution to environmental degradation holds increasingly less meaning for the climate regime is even more evident since, to determine whether or not a country will be subject to greenhouse gases (GHG) emissions quotas, economic development is the sole criterion.

CBDRs and the evolution of the climate regime

Negotiations at the 15th COP held in Copenhagen (2009) were difficult "for one thing, [because of] the continuing uncertainty about whether the United States [would] undertake serious action to curb its emissions [and] for another [because] Copenhagen negotiations have given serious attention to developing country emissions."[22] The question of the United

16 Rajamani, *supra* note 7, at 134.

17 Tuula Honkonen, The Common but Differentiated Responsibility Principle in Multilateral Environmental Agreements – Regulatory and Policy Aspects 2 (Wolters Kluwer, 2009).

18 Rio Declaration, Principle 7.

19 This is the most common name of CBDRs. However, the word "principle" is used with a general meaning, involving no legal nature whatsoever. *See* Laurence Boisson de Chazournes & Sandrine Maljean-Dubois, *Principes du Droit International de l'Environnement,* Juris Classeur Environnement et Développement Durable 1, 3 (2010).

20 UNFCCC Preamble ¶3.

21 Rajamani, *supra* note 7, at 137.

22 Daniel Bodansky, *The Copenhagen Climate Change Conference: A Post Mortem,* 104(2) Am. J. Int'l L. 230, 231–232 (2010).

States' commitments is not new, but in the recent years, developed countries have started to put the accent on 'common' responsibilities, asking emerging economies to take action to reduce their GHG emissions. Thus, for the United States, "developed and developing countries share common challenges in meeting all of their economic, social and environmental needs"[23] and "all countries have a common responsibility to take actions."[24] Meanwhile, Australia considers that "if key developed country mitigation commitments [. . .] were separated from commitments and actions relating to [. . .] advanced developing economies [. . .] it would be more difficult to assess comparability of effort."[25]

By contrast, emerging economies and other developing countries still emphasize "differentiated" responsibilities, asking developed country parties to keep leading the fight against climate change. Thus, for Brazil, "significant steps must be taken to promote, facilitate and finance the transfer of, access to and development of environmentally sound technologies and know-how, particularly from developed countries to developing countries."[26] Meanwhile, Bolivia calls "on developed countries to commit to deep emission reductions in order to advance the objective of avoiding dangerous anthropogenic interference with the climate system [. . .], to reflect their historical responsibility for the causes of climate change, and to respect the principles of equity and common but differentiated responsibilities."[27] It appears that the CBDR principle, which made it possible to create the international climate regime in the 1990s, contributed to post-2012 negotiation difficulties. The 2009 Copenhagen Accord[28] left "most substantive disagreements unresolved – in particular [. . .] the future of the Kyoto Protocol, the legal form and architecture of the future legal regime, and the nature and extent of differential treatment between developed and developing States."[29]

After the Copenhagen failure, the 2010 Cancún COP gave "*a new lease of life*"[30] to the climate regime. Still, the Cancún Agreements are characterized by the bottom-up/pledge and review approach that had been sketched in Copenhagen.[31] And yet, resulting from this

23 Subsidiary Body for Scientific and Technological Advice (SBSTA), *Views on Lessons Learned from the Mitigation Workshops Held to Date and on Future Work on Mitigation of Climate Change*, UN Doc. FCCC/SBST A/2005/MISC.12, 17 August 17, 2005, at 19.

24 Subsidiary Body for Implementation (SBI), *Review of the Financial Mechanism Referred to in Decision 6/CP.13*, 27, UN Doc. FCCC/SBI/2008/MISC. 3, May 9, 2008.

25 Ad Hoc Working Group on Further Commitments for Annex I Parties under the Kyoto Protocol (AWG-KP), *Views on the Legal Implications Arising from the work of the Ad Hoc Working Group on Further Commitments for Annex I Parties under the Kyoto Protocol, Pursuant to Article 3, Paragraph 9, of the Kyoto Protocol*, 3, UN Doc. FCCC/KP/AWG/2009/MISC.6/Add.2, March 26, 2009.

26 SBI, *Views on Elements for the Terms of Reference for the Review and Assessment of the Effectiveness of the Implementation of Article 4, Paragraph 1(c) and 5, of the Convention*, 4, UN Doc. FCCC/SBI/2008/MISC.1, March 17, 2008.

27 AWG-KP, *Further Views and Proposals Relating to a Proposal for Amendments to the Kyoto Protocol pursuant to its Article 3, paragraph 9, and a Text on Other Issues outlined in Document* FCCC/KP/AWG/2008/8, 45, UN Doc FCCC/KP/AWG/2009/MISC.8, May 6, 2009.

28 The Copenhagen Accord is attached to *Decision 2/CP.15, Copenhagen Accord*, UN Doc. FCCC/CP/2009/11/Add.1, 30 March 2010. It was only "taken note of" by the COP and still does not have any formal legal status.

29 Lavanya Rajamani, *The Making and Unmaking of the Copenhagen Accord*, 59(3) Int'l & Comp. L.Q. 842 (2011).

30 Lavanya Rajamani, *The Cancún Climate Agreements: Reading the Text, Subtext and Tea Leaves*, 60(2) Int'l & Comp. L.Q. 519 (2011).

31 *Decision 1/CP.16, The Cancún Agreements: Outcome of the Work of the Ad Hoc Working Group on Long-term Cooperative Action under the Convention*, UN Doc. FCCC/CP/2010/7/Add.1, Parts III and V, March 15, 2011.

new approach, the analysis of the pledges revealed an "increasing parallelism between the mitigation commitments and actions taken by developed and (some) developing countries."[32] After Cancún, the creation of the Ad Hoc Working Group on the Durban Platform for Enhanced Action in 2011 launched "a process to develop a protocol, another legal instrument or an agreed outcome with legal force under the Convention applicable to all Parties."[33] While not announcing the return to a "targets and timetables" approach as used in the Kyoto Protocol, and without establishing the legal form of the future agreement, the launch of this platform allowed, the continuation of the climate regime. The COP, which was held in Doha between November 26 and December 8, 2012, had the difficult task to create a positive dynamic around the Durban Platform to ensure the adoption of the future agreement before 2015 and to adopt a new commitment period for the Kyoto protocol.[34] However, one cannot help noticing that if the amendment to the Kyoto protocol was successfully adopted, no elements on a new binding agreement were sketched during the Qatari negotiations. The same thing can be said about the Warsaw (2013) decisions. Indeed, the COP only requested "the Ad Hoc Working Group on the Durban Platform for Enhanced Action to accelerate its development of a protocol, another legal instrument or an agreed outcome with legal force under the Convention applicable to all Parties in the context of decision 1/CP.17"[35] and tried to organize this acceleration. However, the Warsaw conference did call on countries to develop Intended Nationally Determined Contributions (INDC) that would be the basis of climate action under the agreement to be.[36] Ahead of COP 20, a climate change summit took place on September 23, 2014 at the United Nations (UN) headquarters in New York, United States. The conference had the objective of advancing political support for a climate change agreement in 2015.[37] Then, the 2014 Lima conference prepared the ground for a future binding climate change convention through the "Lima Call for Climate Action",[38] that was adopted and which also aimed at clarifying the process of submission of the INDCs.[39]

The hopes of reaching a climate change deal in Paris were further enhanced by the agreement made between the United States and China whereby both countries declared they would take unilateral actions to reduce their green gas emissions. The US announced they would reduce emissions up to 28 % by 2025 while China declared its intention to achieve the peaking of CO_2 emissions around 2030, to make best efforts to peak early, and to increase the share of non-fossil fuels in primary energy consumption to around 20% by

32 Rajamani, *supra* note 30, at 512.

33 *Decision 1/CP.17 Establishment of an Ad Hoc Working Group on the Durban Platform for Enhanced Action*, ¶ 2, UN Doc. FCCC/CP/2011/9/Add.1, March 15, 2012.

34 Sandrine Maljean-Dubois & Matthieu Wemaëre, *Les Résultats de la Conférence de Doha sur le Climat: un Processus de Négociation en Ordre de Marche, des Efforts Concrets de Réduction Insuffisants, Environnement et Développement Durable Revue mensuelle LexisNexis Jurisclasseur* 15 (February 2013).

35 *Decision 1/CP.19 Further advancing the Durban Platform*, ¶ 1, Doc. FCCC/CP/2013/10/Add.1, 2013, January 31, 2014.

36 Hermann Ott et al., Lima Climate Report- COP 20 Moves at Snails Pace on the Road to Paris 3 (Wuppertal Institute for Climate, Environment and Energy, Dec. 17, 2014).

37 Summary of Climate Summit 2014: 23 September 2014, 1–19 (Climate Summit Bulletin, Volume 172, Number 18, September. 26, 2014).

38 Decision 1/CP.20 Lima call for climate action, 2, UN Doc. FCCC/CP/2014/10/Add.1, March 15, 2012.

39 Summary of the Lima Climate Change Conference: 1–14 December 2014, 1–4 (Earth Negotiations Bulletin, Volume 12, Number 619, Dec. 16, 2014).

2030.[40] Both countries also agreed on combining their efforts for ensuring the adoption of a climate change convention by 2015.[41] The hard work done in 2014 and previous years led to the adoption of the Paris agreement in 2015[42], which addresses the necessary global actions that should be taken regarding climate change post 2020 and develops the new framework to do so.[43]

Through the last series of COP decisions, one thing clearly appears. Until 2009, CBDR was at the very center of attention, and the main issue of climate talks was how responsibilities should be distributed between State parties. However, while the first commitment period of the Kyoto Protocol came to an end, other issues such as the development of an International Mechanism for Loss and Damage associated with climate change impacts[44] appeared in the negotiations held in Doha, Warsaw, Lima and Paris. Although the CBDR principle still characterizes the regime, such new developments raise the question of its place and practice in the ongoing negotiations. Assessing this place will require one to study both the evolving role and understanding of the principle in the recent developments of the regime.

The role of CBDR in recent COP decisions

Since the very adoption of the UNFCCC, differentiated obligations have been at the core of the climate regime. Following the Convention, CBDR have shaped all the important texts of the regime.[45] One of the main objectives of the Bali Action Plan was indeed to develop "a shared vision for long-term cooperative action, including a long-term global goal for emission reductions, to achieve the ultimate objective of the Convention, in accordance with the provisions and principles of the Convention, in particular the principle of common but

40 U.S.-China Joint Announcement on Climate Change, Beijing, China (Nov. 12, 2014), https://www.whitehouse.gov/the-press-office/2014/11/11/us-china-joint-announcement-climate-change (last visited July 6, 2016).

41 The White House, Office of the Press Secretary, U.S.-China Joint Announcement on Climate Change, Beijing, China (Nov. 12, 2014), https://www.whitehouse.gov/the-press-office/2014/11/11/us-china-joint-announcement-climate-change (last visited July 6, 2016).

42 United Nations Framework Convention on Climate Change, Conference of the Parties Twenty-first Session, Paris, Nov. 30 to Dec. 11, 2015, Agenda item 4(b): Durban Platform for Enhanced Action (decision 1/CP.17), Adoption of a protocol, another legal instrument, or an agreed outcome with legal force under the Convention applicable to all Parties, Adoption of the Paris Agreement, Proposal by the President, Draft -/CP.21, FCCC/CP.2015/L.9, Distr.: Limited, Dec. 12, 2015.

43 European Parliament, Briefing, The Paris Agreement: A new framework for a global climate action 1-10 (Jan. 2016).

44 *Decision 2/CP.19 Warsaw International Mechanism For Loss and Damage Associated With Climate Change Impacts*, Doc. FCCC/CP/2013/10/Add.1 (January 31, 2014).

45 To quote only the most important texts, see: *Decision 1/CP.1, Berlin Mandate*, UN Doc. FCCC/CP/1995/7/Add.1, June 6, 1996; the Kyoto Protocol, *supra* note 4. *Decision 1/CP.8, Delhi Ministerial Declaration on Climate Change and Sustainable Development*, UN Doc. FCCC/CP/2002/7/Add.1, March 28, 2002; *Decision 1/CP.13, Bali Action Plan*, UN Doc. FCCC/CP/2007/6/Add.1, March 14, 2008; *Decision 2/CP.15, Copenhagen Accord*, UN Doc. FCCC/CP/2009/11/Add.1, March 30, 2010; *Decision 1/CP.16, The Cancún Agreements: Outcome of the Work of the Ad Hoc Working Group on Long-term Cooperative Action under the Convention*, *supra* note 31; *Decision 2/CP.17, Outcome of the Work of the Ad Hoc Working Group on Long-term Cooperative Action under the Convention*, UN Doc. FCCC/CP/2011/9/Add.1, March 15, 2012; *Decision 3/CP.17, Launching the Green Climate Fund*, UN Doc. FCCC/CP/2011/9/Add.1, March 15, 2012; *Decision 1/CP.18, Agreed outcome pursuant to the Bali Action Plan*, UN Doc. FCCC/CP/2012/8/Add.1, February 28, 2013.

differentiated responsibilities and respective capabilities."[46] Thus, in this decision and in many others, CBDR played its role as a philosophical and ethical basis for differentiated obligations that were designed to tackle climate change. As China said, the CBDR principle is "*a cornerstone of the system.*"[47]

However, the role of CBDR has evolved in new directions since the adoption of the Bali Action Plan. On substance, beyond the issue of carbon emissions, the regime had to deal with the growing challenge of adaptation and of loss and damages due to climate change. But besides, the last COPs have become more and more focused on the future of the climate regime itself, its goals and its institutions. The Cancún and Durban COPs have had to deal with the post-2012 question, the Doha COP has ensured the continuity of the Kyoto protocol, Warsaw and Lima COPs paved the road for the climate change agreement adopted in Paris and which organizes the post 2020 agenda. And yet, an analysis of the Durban decisions reveals changes in the practice of CBDR. For instance, Decision 1/CP.17 creating the Durban Platform makes no reference to the principle. It does refer to Decision 2/CP.17 and the Bali Action Plan, which both contain references to CBDR. Furthermore, the objective to develop "a protocol, another legal instrument or an agreed outcome with legal force under the Convention" does link the future text to the UNFCCC and, therefore, indirectly to CBDR. However, it is the first important decision that is not expressly built upon it when the Durban Platform is supposed to design the future regime. This evolution in the practice of CBDR is not limited to Decision 1/CP.17. Out of the 18 other decisions adopted in Durban, only Decision 2/CP.17 quotes CBDR, Article 3 and the principles of the Convention,[48] and Decision 3/CP.17 only refers to the latter.[49] Along with this decrease in the use of CBDR, references to other expressions of differential treatment – such as equity or special/national circumstances, priorities and needs – are more frequent in the Durban decisions than they were in the Cancún decisions. This is especially true for Decision 2/CP.17 and Decision 1/CP.16, which both deal with the outcome of the work of the Ad Hoc Working Group on Long-term Cooperative Action under the Convention. Similar observations can be made on the Doha decisions adopted at the COP 18. Thus, only two decisions contain the principle,[50] and, on the whole, there are only six references to CBDR and Article 3 in the Doha decisions, while there are 22 references to national circumstances, priorities and needs.

It is true that the agreed outcome of Decision 1/CP.18 should be negotiated pursuant to the Bali Action Plan and does, accordingly, enshrine the CBDR principle. For instance, Part I of the Decision focuses on "a shared vision for long-term cooperative action, including a long-term global goal for emission reductions, to achieve the ultimate objective of the Convention, in accordance with the provisions and principles of the Convention, in

46 *Decision 1/CP.13, Bali Action Plan, supra* note 45, ¶1(a).

47 SBI, *Procedures and Mechanisms relating to Compliance under the Kyoto Protocol*, 15, UN Doc. FCCC/SB/1999/MISC.12, September 22, 1999.

48 *Decision 2/CP.17, supra* note 45 at ¶¶ 8, 10, 17, 18, and 28.

49 *Decision 3/CP.17, Launching the Green Climate Fund*, UN Doc. FCCC/CP/2011/9/Add.1, ¶ 4 and Annex, March 15, 2012.

50 *Decision 1/CP.18 Agreed Outcome Pursuant to the Bali Action Plan*, UN Doc. FCCC/CP/2012/8/Add.1, February 28, 2013; *Decision 3/CP.18 Approaches to Address Loss and Damage Associated With Climate Change Impacts in Developing Countries that are Particularly Vulnerable to the Adverse Effects of Climate Change to Enhance Adaptive Capacity*, UN Doc. FCCC/CP/2012/8/Add.1, February 28, 2013.

particular the principle of common but differentiated responsibilities and respective capabilities." However, being largely turned towards the achievements of Bali, Decision 1/CP.18 was in fact bound to refer to CBDR and, far from being a new interpretation of this principle, the formulation of the Decision appears as almost a copy-and-paste of the Bali objectives. If this Decision does replace the CBDR principle and the debate on the setting of differentiated obligations at the center of the post-2020 negotiations, States' oppositions on the principle also live on. Thus, numerous developing countries have expressed concerns regarding the level of ambition on finance and mitigation in the same decision[51] when, at the same time, as they often did before, representatives of Canada, Japan, Switzerland and the United States expressed their concerns regarding the formulation of paragraph 2 of decision 1.CP/18 referring to equity and CBDR.[52] Decision 1/CP.18 shows that the impact of the fading of CBDR in COP decisions and the reference to less formal expressions of differential treatment should be nuanced. Indeed, the lack of mention in non-binding COP decisions does not affect the legal status of the principle, since it is still enshrined in the UNFCCC under which are adopted these decisions. Plus, some recent decisions do enshrine the principle. Thus, far from involving major consequences for the principle status in the regime, these differences should, at the most, be seen as changes in the practice of CBDR in COP decisions. However, this change has had consequences on the work of the Durban platform.

As such, decisions dealing with the advancement of the Durban Platform appear quite different. The Doha decision on the advancement of the Durban Platform does not refer directly to CBDR but only to "*the principles of the Convention*",[53] as does the decision of the 19th COP on the same topic.[54] Decision 2/CP.18 is much shorter than Decision 1/CP.18 and focuses mainly on institutional matters, sketching the different steps towards the adoption of the post-2020 agreement. Thus, Decision 2/CP.18 confirms the will of the COP to adopt a new legal instrument before 2015.[55] It states 2013 will be dedicated to the exploration of different "actions that can close the pre-2020 ambition gap with a view to identifying further activities for its plan of work in 2014 ensuring the highest possible mitigation efforts under the Convention."[56] Then, in 2014, the Durban Platform will develop a draft negotiating text "with a view to making available a negotiating text before May 2015."[57] On these points, the Doha COP has brought clarity and organization, so it is now easier to foresee the next steps of negotiation. These results constitute the basis of the Warsaw decision that requests the Platform to accelerate the development of the future climate agreement.[58]

Then, by opposition to Decision 1/CP.18, the Durban process is not linked with the Bali Action Plan. Doing so would have placed the ongoing negotiations under the shadow of a 2008 decision concerning a regime that still worked on a top-down approach with commitments to reduce emissions for developed countries and actions and assistance measures for

51 *Report of the Conference of the Parties on its eighteenth session, held in Doha from 26 November to 8 December 2012, Part One: Proceedings*, ¶ 73–77, UN Doc. FCCC/CP/2012/8, February 28, 2013.

52 *Id.*, ¶ 69.

53 *Decision 2/CP.18 Advancing the Durban Platform*, ¶ 7, UN Doc. FCCC/CP/2012/8/Add.1 February 28, 2013.

54 *Decision 1/CP.19 Further advancing the Durban Platform*, *supra* note 35.

55 *Decision 2/CP.18 Advancing the Durban Platform*, *supra* note 53, ¶ 4.

56 *Id.*, ¶ 5.

57 *Id.*, ¶ 9.

58 *Decision 1/CP.19 Further advancing the Durban Platform*, *supra* note 35, ¶¶ 1 and 2.

developing countries. It could have been interesting only if parties were willing to negotiate another Kyoto Protocol. However, the negotiating objectives of the parties were not the same than in 1997. Indeed, Decision 1/CMP.8 has developed the "Doha Amendment" to the Kyoto Protocol, to extend its application up to 2020.[59] And yet, only 66 parties have ratified it when 144 ratifications are necessary for the amendment to enter into force. And we already know that Canada, Japan, Russia or New Zealand will not take part in this extension. So even though it is "saved," the Kyoto Protocol has been marginalized and will definitely not bring the answer to climate change. Thus, the only body that had a clear objective for the future of climate change was the Durban Platform,[60] so it was important that negotiations avoid the precedent failures of the regime. Therefore, by distancing itself from the Bali Action Plan, the Platform appeared like an entirely new path for the regime and this created consensus.

At the Warsaw conference, the CBDR principle was not mentioned at all in any of the decisions made,[61] COP 19 however referred broadly to the "principles of the Convention".[62] It was still successful in creating a framework for the climate change agreement in 2015. Particular provisions, mainly the statement "in the context of adopting a protocol, another legal instrument or an agreed outcome with legal force under the Convention applicable to all Parties", reflected the compromise that had to be made as large emerging economies, in particular China and India, insisted on a division between countries on the basis of the CBDR.[63] This evolution in the use of CBDR culminated in 2014 when the traditional CBDR principle was given a new formula. Indeed, developing countries finally accepted to recognize that the vision of Rio in 1992 did not reflect the reality anymore. In order to reach that outcome, they had for the first time to compromise over the traditional concept as by 2014, the largest emitters also included emerging economies and several developing countries. Thus, the possibility of throwing all the responsibility on the developed states became unrealistic. Hence, a compromise was reached[64] and the concept of CBDR was transformed to "common but differentiated responsibilities and respective capabilities, in light of different national circumstances".[65] This new formula was mentioned for the first time in 2014 in the US-China joint Announcement on Climate Change[66] and then appeared in the COP 20 Lima decisions. According to the new principle, several requirements shall be taken into

59 *Decision 1/CMP.8 Amendment to the Kyoto Protocol pursuant to its Article 3, paragraph 9 (the Doha Amendment)*, ¶ 4, UN Doc. FCCC/KP/CMP/2012/13/Add.1, February 28, 2013.

60 *Decision 2/CP.17 Outcome of the Work of the Ad Hoc Working Group on Long-term Cooperative Action under the Convention*, *supra* note 45, ¶ 2.

61 United Nations Framework Convention on Climate Change, Warsaw Climate Change Conference (Nov. 2013), http://unfccc.int/meetings/warsaw_nov_2013/meeting/7649/php/view/decisions.php (last visited July 6, 2016).

62 Lavanya Rajamani, Differentiation in a 2015 Climate Agreement 1-2 (Center for Climate and Energy Solutions, June. 2015).

63 Claire Langley & Nathan Hultman, Climate Change Negotiations in Warsaw Result in a Timeline for an Agreement in 2015 (Nov. 27, 2013), http://www.brookings.edu/blogs/up-front/posts/2013/11/27-climate-change-warsaw-cop19-timeline-hultman (last visited July 6, 2016).

64 Cleo VerKuijl, Onwards and Upwards . . .? From Lima, to Geneva and Paris (Feb. 10, 2015), http://theverb.org/onwards-and-upwards-from-lima-to-geneva-and-paris/ (last visited July 6, 2016).

65 Michael Jacobs, Lima deal represents a fundamental change in global climate regime (Dec. 15, 2014), https://www.theguardian.com/environment/2014/dec/15/lima-deal-represents-a-fundamental-change-in-global-climate-regime (last visited July 6, 2016).

66 The White House, Office of the Press Secretary, *supra* note 41.

consideration when determining national emissions targets including: "past and present emissions, national GDP growth needs in addition to the capacity of the country to undertake mitigation and adaptation action".[67] COP 20 urged the adoption of climate change agreement in Paris taking into consideration the new established principle.[68] COP 21 included the new principle in the historical Paris Agreement. The principle was highlighted in article 2 (2) of the Agreement: "This Agreement will be implemented to reflect equity and the principle of common but differentiated responsibilities and respective capabilities, in the light of different national circumstances". Article 4 (3) also refers to the application of the principle when it comes to national determined contribution of each party: "Each Party's successive nationally determined contribution will represent a progression beyond the Party's then current nationally determined contribution and reflect its highest possible ambition, reflecting its common but differentiated responsibilities and respective capabilities, in the light of different national circumstances". Finally, article 4 (19) of the Agreement requests each party to apply the latter concept when formulating long term low greenhouse gas emission development strategies: "All Parties should strive to formulate and communicate long-term low greenhouse gas emission development strategies, mindful of Article 2 taking into account their common but differentiated responsibilities and respective capabilities, in the light of different national circumstances".[69]

The understanding of CBDR in recent COP decisions

All these examples show that climate decisions tend to refer more and more often to contextual norms of differentiation[70] based on general criteria such as national/special circumstances, priorities or needs rather than making direct references to CBDR. The principle was even modified to include a reference to national circumstances. The use of differential treatment through these expressions rather than principles is echoed in other MEAs like the Convention on Biological Diversity[71] and the UN Convention to Combat Desertification.[72] When CBDR allows developing differentiated obligations, these expressions usually set contextual norms, "which implies a norm that on its face provides identical treatment to all States [. . .] but the application of which requires (or at least permits) consideration of characteristics that might vary from country to country."[73] These contextual norms obtain a real success in international environmental negotiations because the consensus is easier to obtain on them than on true differentiated obligations. However, their generality can be an issue

67 Philip Lawn, Resolving the Climate Change Crisis: The Ecological Economics of Climate Change 562 (Springer, 2016).

68 European Parliament, Environment, Public Health and Food Safety, On the way to COP 21 in Paris 2 (Briefing, June. 2015).

69 Paris agreement, *supra* note 42. Annex of the Agreement, Art. 2 (2), 4 (3) & (19).

70 For the history of the expression, see Daniel Barstow Magraw, *Legal Treatment of Developing Countries: Differential, Contextual and Absolute Norms,* 1 CJIELP, 69–99 (1990).

71 *Convention on Biological Diversity*, Rio de Janeiro, June 5, 1992 (in force December 29, 1993), Article 6.

72 *United Nations Convention to Combat Desertification*, Paris, June 17, 1994 (in force December 26, 1996), Article 3d.

73 Werner Scholtz, *Different Countries, One Environment: A Critical Southern Discourse on the Common But Differentiated Responsibilities Principle*, 33 S. Afr. Y.B. of Int'l L. 114 (2008).

since they could result in divergent interpretations from State parties. Oppositions on their interpretation could restrict the effectiveness of MEAs.[74]

Moreover, this approach of differential treatment leads to putting the accent on States' capacities and needs. And yet, such an approach could involve a shift in the very concept of CBDR. It is true that "a particularly important aspect in the putting into operation of [differential treatment] is international assistance."[75] But if assistance represents an important part of differential treatment, capacities and needs cannot be the only things taken into account. Indeed, a conception of differential treatment that would focus only on capacities of States – and thus on assistance to strengthen such capacities – would not take into account parties' contribution to environmental degradation. The issue is of particular importance concerning emerging economies since such an approach would ignore their present massive contribution to environmental degradation to focus only on their lower level of development.[76] This would go directly against the current tendency of negotiations, that is, to ask emerging economies to take stronger commitments to tackle environmental degradation – a position shared by many developed and developing States. But above all, an interpretation of differential treatment that would ignore these countries' potential to pollute would not serve the environmental objectives set in MEAs, which differential treatment is supposed to help to reach.

Thus, the new formula of CBDR developed in 2014 seems like the best way forward for the climate regime to conciliate State parties' positions and reality with the Convention objectives. Emerging economies refuse to be assimilated with developed countries because their consumption levels per capita (and sometimes their GDP) are lower than those of developed countries.[77] Therefore, like developing countries, they ask to keep receiving assistance from developed countries to strengthen their capacities. However, they had to acknowledge the fact that they are today among the major polluters and that they need to take stronger action to reduce their pollution levels. With the path followed after the Durban COP to the adoption of the Paris Agreement,[78] the climate regime has started to develop this approach. However, each COP shows how many negotiating difficulties remain between States.

Because of its uniqueness, it seems certain that the CBDR principle will never disappear from international climate law. The whole regime has been built upon it, and parties are far too used to negotiating over it. It is definitely part of the fabric of climate law.

Yet, the CBDR principle is only an expression of differential treatment. Other expressions of differentiation are used in the climate regime and could take precedence in the future. It is parties' actual obligations that will matter to combat climate change. In order to do so, the climate regime must keep a balance between commitments and assistance. Indeed, although adaptation to climate change and assistance are truly important issues, one has to realize that

74 Duncan French, *Developing States and International Environmental Law: The Importance of Differentiated Responsibilities*, 49(1) INT'L & COMP. L.Q. 42 (2000).

75 Marie-Claire Cordonier Segger, Ashfaq Khalfan, Markus Gehring & Michelle Toering, *Prospects for Principles of International Sustainable Development Law after the WSSD: Common but Differentiated Responsibilities, Precaution and Participation*, 12(1) REV. EUR. COMMUNITIES & INT'L ENVTL. L. 58–59 (2003).

76 Duncan French, *supra* note 74, at 53–54; *see* also RAJAMANI, *supra* note 7, at 233–235.

77 Kristin Bartenstein, *De Stockholm à Copenhague: Genèse et Évolution des Responsabilités Communes Mais Différenciées dans le Droit International de l'Environnement*, 56(1) MCGILL L. J. 202 (2010).

78 *Decision 2/CP.17 Outcome of the Work of the Ad Hoc Working Group on Long-term Cooperative Action under the Convention*, *supra* note 45, ¶ 2.

the fight against climate degradation cannot be fought without commitments from stronger polluters to reduce their emissions. The notion of responsibility is central in CBDR but current contributions to climate change cannot be forgotten. COP 22 which will be held in Marrakesh between the 7th and 18th of November 2016, will constitute a new opportunity for developed/developing countries to further debate and enhance the latter principle in the light of the commitments/assistance balance that must be maintained.

10 The Kyoto Protocol: Carbon Pricing and Trade Prospects

The Clean Development Mechanism from the Perspective of the Developing Countries*

Marion Lemoine

Whatever their geographic origin from Earth, greenhouse gas (GHG) emissions have the same environmental impact. As such, the international community's response to climate change requires a strong interdependence between Northern and Southern States, and, based on this fact, the parties to the Kyoto Protocol[1] established the Clean Development Mechanism (CDM).[2] The CDM is the only mechanism under the Kyoto Protocol involving countries that are not subject to binding GHG emission caps by the Protocol – so-called non-Annex I countries.[3] The idea was to reward States and non-State actors for saving GHG emissions with carbon pricing.

States may no longer emit GHG emissions free of cost, and the exchange on the carbon market determines the price. In this context, the CDM allows industrialized countries to invest in low-carbon projects in developing countries, in order to reduce emissions in those territories and to help industrialized States fulfill their own emissions reduction commitments. The CDM relies on a multi-stage process for the assessment of projects and

* This chapter is part of the results of the Research Project on "*Current Trends of Chinese Law towards Non-Trade Concerns such as Sustainable Development and the Protection of Environment, Public Health, Food Safety, Cultural, Social and Economic Rights, Labor Rights and the Reduction of Poverty from the Perspective of International Law and WTO Law*" coordinated by Professor Paolo Davide Farah at gLAWcal – Global Law Initiatives for Sustainable Development (United Kingdom) and at West Virginia University John D. Rockefeller IV School of Policy and Politics, Department of Public Administration, in partnership with the Center of Advanced Studies on Contemporary China (CASCC) in Turin (Italy), Maastricht University Faculty of Law, Department of International and European Law and IGIR – Institute for Globalisation and International Regulation (Netherlands) and Tsinghua University, School of Law, Institute of Public International Law and the Center for Research on Intellectual Property Law in Beijing (China). An early draft of this chapter was presented at the Conferences Series on *"China's Influence on Non-Trade Concerns in International Economic Law"*, Second Conference held at Tsinghua University, School of Law on January 14–15, 2012. This publication and the Conference Series were sponsored by China–EU School of Law (CESL) at the China University of Political Science and Law (CUPL). The activities of CESL at CUPL are supported by the European Union and the People's Republic of China. The chapter was completed on January 2015 and does not report any following event.

1 Kyoto Protocol to the United Nations Framework Convention on Climate Change, December 11, 1997, 2303 UNTS 148.

2 To facilitate a prompt start of the CDM, COP 7 Decision allowed retroactive crediting for projects registered before December 31, 2005. These advance-crediting periods start prior to the date of registration, but not earlier than January 1, 2000 UNFCCC. Report to the Conference of the Parties on its seventh session. Part two: Action taken by the conference of the parties. United Nations Framework Convention on Climate Change, FCCC/CP/2001/13/Add2, Marrakesh.

3 *Annex I Countries of the UNFCCC* are the 34 most advanced economies in 1992. The so-called *Non-Annex I countries* are consequently all other States, generally considered as developing countries.

the resulting emission reductions. In delivering real, measurable, and additional emission reductions, CDM projects offer credits[4] of reduction that can be used by industrialized States in their own registry and contribute to the compliance of their quantified GHG emissions reduction targets[5] or be traded on the carbon market[6] – either on the regulatory market for Kyoto compliance or on the voluntary offset market. Once registered, a CDM project issues an amount of Certified Emission Reductions (CERs) corresponding to the verified emission reductions to the project participants through the CDM registry. Thus, if the CDM relies on economic support (trade of carbon credits), it serves non-trade objectives. Despite the success of this investment incentive, some developing countries, such as Bolivia and Venezuela, oppose market mechanisms. The critical countries question the environmental effectiveness of the CDM itself, since it does not reduce emissions but rather offsets the increase in emissions elsewhere. On the other hand, China requests that the members make developed countries' access to CDM depend on their individual commitment.

The aim of the CDM is not to act as the primary means to fulfill the Kyoto Protocol commitments but rather to complete the intern GHG emissions reductions with relocated GHG reductions. States participate in CDM projects on a voluntary basis. To supervise the project, the Conference of the Parties (COP) serving as the Meeting of the Parties (MOP) to the Kyoto Protocol provides authority over and guidance to the CDM. However, the CDM Executive Board (EB) carries out the daily supervision of the mechanism.[7]

The CDM strives to reach two goals: assisting developing countries to achieve sustainable development and to contribute to the convention's ultimate objective,[8] and making Annex I countries able to achieve their emission reduction targets cost-effectively. With 7,596 registered projects, the CDM has experienced extraordinary growth during the past six years, and the strong interest of numerous actors in its continuation makes it likely that it will persist beyond 2013. The CDM's importance at the economic level can be understood because, in addition to States, private firms may use the CDM. With 7,596 registered projects underway, participating parties expect to reduce 2,700,000 tons of GHG emissions by 2013.

Despite ever-growing uncertainty about the 2012–2020 period, the CDM shows a high degree of resilience, with additional projects consistently entering the pipeline and the CERs issuance on the rise. The majority of projects (74.53 per cent) occur in energy industries, while the second-largest category of projects tackles waste handling and disposal (10.92 per cent). The next two largest categories are agriculture (2.44 per cent) and avoided afforestation/reforestation (0.61 per cent).[9] Most of CDM projects focus on renewable energy. Nevertheless, many deficits in the CDM's ability to fulfill its goals are often pointed out. If the effectiveness of global environmental protection is not denied, the CDM consistently needs to improve the quality and quantity of its emissions reduction. The 2010 HFC_{23}

4 Hereafter *certified emission reduction*: CERs, CMP/2005/8/Add.1, at 7, ¶ 1.b.

5 Since Annex I countries have emission caps.

6 Linked with the third flexible mechanism of the Protocol, which is not project-based, the *Emissions Trading* allows Annex I States to exchange emissions reductions via a cap-and-trade system to meet their Kyoto Protocol targets (Article 17 of the Kyoto Protocol).

7 Parallel, the designated operational entities (DOEs) are firms and experts accredited by the EB to perform the tasks of validating, verifying, and certifying the CDM project activities throughout the CDM project cycle.

8 To limit the increasing GHG emissions to 2 per cent from 1991 to 2012.

9 UNFCCC, *Clean Development Mechanism* 21 (Executive Board Annual Report, 2013).

scandal[10] begs the question about the sustainability of 250 million tons of GHG and forced the EB of the CDM to block the issuance of all CERs for months. Beyond the environmental integrity of CDM emissions reduction, the parties regularly debate whether any individual project adds to the amount of GHG emissions reduction that would have occurred absent the project. The requirement of additionality foresees that CERs generated under the CDM will only be recognized when the reductions of GHG are made in addition to any that would occur in the absence of the certified project activity. Despite the increasing appropriateness of methodologies to control this additionality of emissions reduction, there is always debate about the reality of reduction. The equity of repartition of projects also raises controversies in the negotiations, as well as the guaranty of transparency, independence, and impartiality in the CDM decision-making process.

To assist developing countries with their adaptation to climate change, a *share of the proceeds* goes to cover administrative expenses, and 2 per cent of the CERs go to the Adaptation Fund.[11] This is the permanent part of the CDM contribution to developing countries' adaptation to climate change. The CDM remains a tool of mitigation. In this context, what extent do developing countries really benefit from CDM? The clear disparity in CDM projects' geographic distribution between developing countries leads to an understanding of the CDM's poor effectiveness in terms of sustainable development. In the absence of sustainable development, does CDM permit technology transfer to developing countries? Finally, what is the CDM future prospective from a developing country perspective?

Regional distribution of CDM projects: Who benefits from the CDM?

Article 12 of the Kyoto Protocol mandates that the CDM oversees emission reductions in projects carried out in developing States. But which States really benefit from those investments? The repartition of CDM projects is geographically unequal between regions of the world and among States. To understand this disparity, it is necessary to analyze the prominent role of emergent States in this repartition.

A clear disparity of CDM projects between regions

In October 2013, Asia and the Pacific benefited from almost 84.25 per cent of CDM projects, and Latin America and the Caribbean housed 12.72 per cent. With 71 projects, African States have only 2.40 per cent of total projects, and Eastern Europe profits from only 0.62 per cent. Africa's share of CDM projects spells clear underrepresentation, and 19 African States host no CDM projects at all.[12] The potential to host projects depends highly on the risk for

10 In June 2010, three NGOs (Noé21, CDM Watch, and Environmental Investigation Agency) highlighted the fact that some industries used HFC_{22}, a cooling gas to create HCF_{23} in order to destruct those tonnes of HFC_{23} and get credits for it; 200 millions tons of CO_2 are concerned, under 10 large projects. Falsifying GHG credits reinforces the need of objectivity of verification and evaluation on GHG economy. The EB has blocked all HFC_{23} issuance until early December 2010. Apparently this measure was sufficient in order to have actors still trust the system.

11 FCCC/CP/2001/13/Add2, Marrakesh, *supra*.

12 UNFCCC, *supra* note 9.

foreign investors. In this domain, investors see emergent States[13] as more secure than less economically dynamic States. In addition, the institutional and infrastructural capacity of States and domestic capital availability largely determine the investments flows.

The prominent role of emergent states

China profits from more than 50.59 per cent of CDM projects, India benefits from 19.60 per cent, Brazil 4.26 per cent, Mexico 2.53 per cent, and Malaysia has 1.94 per cent of all projects.[14] Besides the number of projects, the expected CERs by host States demonstrates additional disparities. China will reap 61.22 per cent of expected CDM tons of GHG reduction, India 13.38 per cent, and Brazil 6.42 per cent.[15] A limited number of projects exist in other developing countries, and even fewer projects have been launched in least-developed countries (LDCs). Today, 48 States have established a Designated National Authority (DNA) without hosting a single CDM project. It is obvious that China, India and Brazil monopolize the CDM projects, which remain unsatisfactory in their geographic distribution. China is clearly the main recipient of CDM classic multilateral projects. Do unilateral CDM projects offer another opportunity for other developing countries?

Besides the classic multilateral projects, we count some unilateral CDM projects, involving no foreign direct investment, but only the developing country initiative to reduce additional GHG emissions. Then, the developing country, with the approval of its DNA, can sell its CERs after certification directly to an industrialized country. Unilateral projects may be attractive for developing countries but represent, nevertheless, a high risk for investors. Because the host country also assumes more risk, the potential to carry out these unilateral CDM projects varies among developing countries. Finally, emergent States themselves benefit from this option as well. China and India can design and implement projects autonomously,[16] but most of the Sub-Saharan countries rely on foreign support. The EB focuses on regulatory changes in order to increasingly address those countries that are not presently the targets of foreign investors and support them in the design of local projects.

Although the majority of CDM projects take place in emergent States territories, it can be noted that the BASIC Group[17] does not have a common position concerning CDM. The individual interest of major States actors in CDM is most often defended. Thus, China and India assert very precise positions in negotiations, defending more directly their own interests shared with participating countries.[18]

At a political and normative level, the impact of the large benefits of CDM projects by China and India induce consequences.[19] The propositions of the main CDM actors largely

13 Emergent States is not a formal category of States under the UNFCCC, but have been progressively considered as a specific category, integrated to developing countries, following the call of differentiation by industrialized States, on the ground of economic criteria. "Emergent States," as regularly mentioned in COP Decisions, can also be called "advanced developing countries" or "major economies."

14 UNFCCC, *supra* note 9, at 4.

15 *Id.*, at 21.

16 *See* Chapter 14 (Peng) in this volume.

17 Brazil, China, India, South Africa, as a group, adopt a distinct position in the climate negotiations, serving both their national interests, as well as the common interests of the States in a similar socio-economic situation, still considered as developing countries according to the UNFCCC.

18 *See* Chapter 14 (Peng) in this volume.

19 *See* Chapter 14 (Peng) in this volume.

influence the formation of international norms related to the CDM by the EB and COP/MOP. Thus, the bottom-up approach of norm-making, based on best practices, reveals a mainly Chinese and Indian way of building CDM projects. Moreover, this element explains the few number of projects conducted in African States.

With the success of the CDM in emergent States, it is now quite sure that the CDM fulfills its environmental goal. However, it is less clear whether the CDM can reach its second goal: promoting sustainable development in developing countries.

The lack of effectiveness of sustainable development input, in favor of cost-effectiveness

According to its definition in the Kyoto Protocol,[20] the CDM should contribute to sustainable development in the host developing countries. This is also the first objective of the CDM and a procedural validation requirement of any project. Sustainable development, a principle of international law, encourages environmental protection, economic development, and social guaranties.[21] According to this principle, these elements should be coordinated and integrated.

Article 12, paragraph 2 of the Kyoto Protocol poses that: "The purpose of the [CDM] is to assist Parties not included in Annex I in achieving sustainable development." In practice, the procedural requirement grants developing countries the right to refuse a project in their territory if it does not contribute to national sustainable development policy. The DNA assesses a potential CDM project to determine whether it will assist the host country in achieving its sustainable development goals and to provide a letter of approval to participants in CDM projects.[22] This letter of approval must confirm that the project contributes to sustainable development in the State. The project is then submitted to the CDM EB to support its registration.[23]

What is the content of this sustainable development input within the CDM projects? Are developing countries effective beneficiaries of CDM projects in terms of sustainable development?

After analyzing registered projects as well as follow-up validations of CDM projects, we noted a homogeneous way of presenting the sustainable development piece of the project. Sustainable development is traditionally defined by its three dimensions: environmental, social, and economic inputs.[24] This paragraph aims not to qualify, as a jurist, the legal nature

20 Art. 12 of the Kyoto Protocol.

21 *See* Chapters 8 (Sindico) and 9 (Deleuil) in this volume.

22 On the definition of the balance between protection of national values and attraction of foreign investment, *see* Mariachiara Alberton, *The Designed National Authorities (DNA). Requirements, Models, Competences, Best Practices*, in Developing CDM Projects in the Western Balkans, Legal and Technical Issues Compared, Part 1 61–77 (Massimiliano Montini ed., Springer, 2010).

23 DNA, on the web site of the CDM, at the following address: http://cdm.unfccc.int/DNA/index.html?click=dna_forum (last visited July 8, 2014). It is interesting to see that on this institutional interface, DNA, sit mostly host countries, but especially African countries. DNA Statistics, CDM website, http://cdm.unfccc.int/Statistics/Registration/RegisteredDNAPieChart.html (last visited July 8, 2014).

24 The three pillars of sustainable development were recognized in the successive instruments adopted by UN Conferences. Initiated by the *Stockolm Declaration* in 1972, which link poverty and environmental pollution, the three pillars appear in the Bruntland Report, *Our common future*, and the Conference of Rio, in 1992, formally invited to integrate the three growth targets (environment, economic development, and social development).

of the principle of sustainable development but only to clarify its content, which is to favor the cooperation and integration of the three dimensions mentioned above. Within CDM practice, sustainable development is rarely ambitious. For the majority of partnerships, CDM projects tend to prefer the coupling of the environmental and developmental aspects. They seldom mention the social impacts. Some projects call upon another combination of elements: environment, economy, social impacts, and technology transfer.

Despite the central role of sustainable development defined by the Kyoto Protocol, the practice of CDM reveals a more descriptive and procedural role of sustainable development over an effective one. Even the most important CDM actors often mention the validation in terms of sustainable development only, without any precise instructions on how to implement it.[25] The implementation fields of sustainable development seem to rely more on the context and nature of the project, rather than the national sustainable development priorities. The sustainable dimension of projects is usually only marginally envisaged, without reference to international or national indicators of sustainable development. There is also no transposition of sustainable development criteria. Besides the GHG emission reduction, the projects rarely advance further environmental benefits. Several authors point out an inevitable trade-off between cheap emission reductions and sustainable development. The opinion of stakeholders, taken during the procedural part of the project, constitutes a good cursor of the progress and gaps of sustainable development. These opinions are published and often betray the project's negligence regarding complete sustainable development, although the real impact of these opinions is not evident.[26] Furthermore, the question concerning the project's sustainable development, posed to the consulted stakeholders, is often too general to generate a constructive criticism: "Does the CDM contribute yes or no to the sustainable development in the area?" The question's simplicity commonly results in generally positively answers without much elaboration. However, critics often point out the weak socio-economic impact on the local population and habitat (risk of noise pollution, destruction of the landscape, and so on).

The effective implementation of sustainable development through CDM remains one of its main problems.[27] It is argued that CERs from large-scale projects, particularly cost-effective projects with little or no sustainable development impact, are likely to dominate the market, whereas smaller projects, which are generally supposed to contribute more to sustainable development, are too expensive to carry out. The observer should not be surprised, since CDM projects are market-focused, and this market presents no clear sustainable development incentive. Apparently, the sustainable development input depends more on the nature of the project than on the actors involved.[28] Thus, projects reducing methane (CH_4)

25 For India and China, see Massimiliano Montini, *Sustainable Development and the Climate Change Regime* 45–46 (Sectorial Dimension of Sustainable Development, EUI Working Paper on Environmental Law 28, 2007).

26 Christina Voigt, Sustainable Development as a Principle of International Law, Resolving Conflicts between Climate Measures and WTO Law 36 (Martinus Nijhoff, 2009).

27 Christoph Sutter & Juan Carlos Parreño, *Does The Current Clean Development Mechanism (CDM) Deliver Its Sustainable Development Claim? An Analysis Of Officially Registered CDM Projects*, 84 Climatic Change 75–90 (2007). *See* also Tariq Banuri & Sujata Gupta, *The Clean Development Mechanism And Sustainable Development: An Economic Analysis*, in Implementation of the Kyoto Protocol: Opportunities and Pitfalls for Developing Countries 73–101 (Prodipto Ghosh ed., Asian Development Bank, 2000).

28 Karen H. Olsen & Jørgen Fenhann, *Sustainable Development Benefits Of Clean Development Mechanism Projects: A New Methodology For Sustainability Assessment Based On Text Analysis Of The Project Design Documents Submitted For Validation*, 36 Energy Pol. 2819–2830 (2008).

generally bring real sustainable development benefits compared to energy-efficiency projects.[29] The CH_4 projects often focus on discharge, and entail a certain type of land.

A recent study shows the trade-off between the sustainability and additionality of CDM projects. As far as Indian projects are concerned, the main determinant underlying this trade-off would be the type of the CDM projects. Thus, wind, hydro, and biomass projects would provide quite "high sustainable development benefits, but lack a strong likelihood of being additional. Energy efficiency and particularly HFC-23 projects, which are additional per definition, show a high probability of additionality, but are not as sustainable as the other kinds of projects."[30]

No impact evaluation is foreseen. International norms on the CDM do not envisage any control obligation of the sustainable development evolution during the project realization. As regards the specific CDM projects we analyzed, no participant envisaged any evaluation of sustainable development resulting from the project.[31] The mere fact that the DNA has accepted the project often satisfies the criteria. Developed States clearly view the CDM as a business opportunity or a way to comply with their obligations. On the other hand, many authors show that developing countries choose explicitly to put only marginal emphasis on securing the CDM's contribution to sustainable development.[32] Finally, the CDM is a tool to attract foreign investments.[33]

Does the CDM contribute to technology transfer?

Although not explicitly stated in the Kyoto Protocol, it seems that the CDM may benefit developing countries especially through technology transfer.[34] According to the words of the Marrakesh Agreements in 2001, the COP underlines that "CDM project activities should lead to transfer of environmentally safe and sound technology and know-how."[35] Since most CDM projects are renewable energy focused, developing countries may introduce many new technologies during their industrialization. Many Project Design Documents mention the technology transfer performed by the project since the CDM requires project participants to describe how the technology will be transferred.[36] Now, are the CDM projects true examples of technology transfer or a form of foreign direct investment? If foreign direct investment leads to the transfer of technological development, joint ventures

29 *Id.*

30 Johannes Alexeew, Linda Bergset, Kristin Meyer, Juliane Petersen, Lambert Schneider & Charlotte Unger, *An Analysis Of The Relationship Between The Additionality Of CDM Projects And Their Contribution To Sustainable Development,* 10 Int'l Envtl. Agreements 244 (2010).

31 Marion Lemoine, *The Clean Development Mechanism Of The Kyoto Protocol. A Vector Of Sustainable Development For The Mediterranean Basin?,* in Yvette Lazerri & Emmanuelle Moustier, Sustainable development in the Mediterranean area. A governance to be invented. Issues and Proposals 117–134 (Presses Universitaires d'Aix-Marseille, 2011).

32 Teresa Rindefjäll, Emma Lund & Johannes Stripple, *Wine, Fruit, And Emission Reductions: The CDM As Development Strategy In Chile,* 11 Int'l envtl. agreements 7–22 (2011).

33 *See* Chapter 6 (Vadi) in this volume.

34 Since industrialized countries invest financial and material means in the CDM project hosted by a developing country. On technology transfer issues, *see* Chapter 11 (Cima) in this volume.

35 COP, Decision 17/CP.7, 2001.

36 "A description of a project comprising the project purpose, a technical description of the project, including how technology will be transferred [. . .]," Decision 4/CMP. 1, Annex, Appendix B, ¶ 2.

between local actors and specialized technology suppliers from Annex I countries might lead to the transfer of technology capabilities.[37] Seen mostly as foreign investment, some authors interpret CDM in terms of technology transfer,[38] which can take the form of knowledge, equipment, or both.

While technology transfer has not been officially characterized so far, this qualification must be detailed in order to clarify the transfer of property rights attached. Contrary to that, some authors note that intellectual property rights barriers to the deployment of projects are low.[39] However, for this reason, developed and developing countries alike choose not to adopt this term to characterize their exchanges. To better understand the activity of developing countries in receiving technology transfers, it has been proven, by the example of China, that the "two key factors that affect the occurrence of technology transfer in China's CDM projects are CER income and the availability of local substitute technologies."[40] Both play a key role in the project owners' decision to adopt foreign technology. Depending on the procedures, technology diffusion effects and government policy, different degrees and forms of technology transfer can emerge. It has also been proven that "afforestation, biomass, energy, cement, fugitive gas, hydro, PFCs, and SF6, and reforestation projects are less likely than average to involve technology transfer while Energy Efficiency (Industry), HFCs, N_2O, Transportation and Wind projects are more likely than average to involve technology transfer."[41] Analyses reveal a general trend towards "lower rates of technology transfer for CDM projects as host country capacity increases, but the strength of this trend differs by country and project type."[42] China and India are the only two host States that make poor technology transfers. All other developing host countries benefit from a high technology transfer when CDM projects occur within their territory.[43] Consequently, the position in the negotiations of China and India and other developing countries cannot be characterized as homogenous.

Even if technology transfer was not a central question in the current commitment period for the CDM, today it has become inevitable. Kyoto non-compliance by Annex I States will directly impact the negotiating power of developing countries, especially China, India, and the BASIC States more generally. In fact, the growing importance of China and India in climate negotiations will link with the growing importance of other critical issues for those States, such as property rights and the potential of trade market access.[44]

37 *See* Chapter 11 (Cima) in this volume.

38 Erik Haites, Maosheng Duan & Stephen Seres, *Technology Transfer by CDM Projects,* 6 Climate Pol. 327–344 (2006).

39 Navraj S. Ghaleigh, *Barriers To Climate Technology Transfer – The Chimera Of Intellectual Property Rights,* 2 Carbon & Climate L. Rev. 233 (2011).

40 Bo Wang, *Can The CDM Bring Technology Transfer To Developing Countries? An Empirical Study Of Technology Transfer In China's CDM Projects* 20 (The Governance of Clean Development Working Paper 002, 2009).

41 UNFCCC, *The Contribution of the CDM under the Kyoto Protocol to Technology Transfer,* 43 (2010).

42 *Id.*, at 34.

43 *Id.*, at 44.

44 Sean Walsh, Huifang Tian, John Whalley & Manmohan Agarwal, *China And India's Participation In Global Climate Negotiations,* 11 Int'l Envtl. Agreements 272 (2011). *See* Chapter 14 (Peng) in this volume.

CDM and developing countries in the COP 21 perspective and beyond

On the road to the COP 21 in Paris in December 2015, the CDM, like other carbon markets, is in a stage of crucial transition. First, the lack of confidence in the CERs and the very low price of the quotas are central elements for considering its continuity. Since the European Union has decided to strictly limit the permissibility of international credits and ban them altogether starting in 2020, the future of the CDM is quite uncertain. Second, at the juridical and institutional level, the deep transformation of the Kyoto Protocol architecture raises serious questions concerning the continuity of the Kyoto Mechanisms beyond 2020. Third, the increasing risk of carbon leakage is a difficult reality that entails the role of the CDM as a motor of mitigation. After the COP 20 in Lima in 2014, the legal form,[45] as well as the content of the Paris agreement, is not yet defined. What would be the role of a carbon market in this agreement?[46] From the perspective of answering this question, the current development of the CDM in the 2012–2020 period is very interesting. Indeed, the institutional and normative governance of the CDM will certainly be taken as an example for setting the new market mechanism in the 2015 agreement and beyond.

More specifically, the EB's current review of the CDM Modalities and Procedures, started in 2012, could act as the basis of discussion for further market instruments. Current debates focus on the environmental integrity and governance of CDM, on the basis of the EB recommendation in 2013.[47] The link between the CDM and other market mechanisms is still to be defined in the post-2020 agreement. The proposition to include the private sector as well as LDCs in the decision-making process, debated in Lima, is still problematic. However, the inclusion of LDCs in the process could benefit the equal geographic repartition of CDM projects in the long term.

The UNFCCC Secretary has prepared a technical document[48] focusing on all main issues for the discussion in Lima. Main changes are at the CDM governance level. The equality of status between EB members and alternates could better the functioning, as well as the professionalization, of the Chair and Vice-Chair. Reinforcing the accountability of the Designated Operational Entities (DOEs) and shortening the period of accreditation has been fully considered, as proposed by Norway and Australia.[49] Reinforcing the role of the DOEs in terms of transparency and the rationalization and simplification of the project cycle (with standardized baseline) are the main issues in debate. The historical change could be to consider the CDM as an instrument building net mitigation for the developing countries, and not only for the industrialized States. The European Union has defended this position,[50] and it seems that in the context of the high level of decentralization of commitment since 2012 and this year in Lima, this option uniquely facilitates the survival of the CDM. This

45 Sandrine Maljean-Dubois, Matthieu Wemaëre & Thomas Spencer, *A comprehensive assessment of options for the legal form of the Paris Climate Agreement* (IDDRI Working Paper 15, 2014). *See* also Sebastian Oberthur, *Options for a Compliance Mechanism in a 2015 Climate Agreement*, 4 Climate L., 30–49 (2014).

46 A. Marcu, *The Role of Market Mechanisms in a Post-2020 Climate Change Agreement*,(CEPS Special Report, No 87, May 2014).

47 FCCC/SBI/2013/INF.1.

48 FCCC/TP/2014/1.

49 FCCC/SBI/2013/MISC.1; FCCC/SBI/2013/MISC.1/Add.1 (Australia).

50 CDM-EB78-AA-A01, Annex 1.

would be a radical change in the political role of the CDM in the negotiation. The EB adopted a technical note in this sense.[51]

In terms of the legal basis of the CDM existence, we should first preface that the CDM is a long-term mechanism that continues over time and is not tied to a specific commitment period. Although the Annex I parties negotiate their emissions targets on a commitment period by commitment period basis, the CDM could further apply to many aspects (registration of projects, issuance of CERs, approval of methodologies, and accreditation of DOEs). However, the CDM currently refers to the second commitment period of the Kyoto Protocol until 2020, since the first period of commitments of Annex I countries ended on December 31, 2012.[52] After 2020, what would be the legal basis for CDM investments?

The reality of the CDM's double objective could at this time determine the way the mechanism will survive, under or outside the Protocol. Formally, thanks to its second objective – assisting developing countries to achieve sustainable development – the CDM could continue on the basis of the UNFCCC, according to the common but differentiated responsibilities and the sustainable development principles,[53] that is to say, Non-Trade Concerns. Thanks to its first objective – assisting Annex I countries to meet their emission reduction commitments – it would be necessary to base the CDM on a new commitment text. From a practical perspective, with regards to the lack of effectiveness of the CDM's sustainable development goal, the *raison d'être* of the mechanism, that is to say the way of meeting the Annex I countries' obligations, will be discontinued.[54]

Many critics oppose a reform of the CDM. The nature of criticism varies depending on the type of developing State expressing it.

To address challenges to the future functioning and development of the CDM, the EB envisages improvements, such as the programmatic CDM,[55] the simplification of the procedures for projects in LDCs to achieve a better distribution of CDM projects, the review of the decisions to accept/refuse CDM projects or issue CERs,[56] and the launch of a new area of policy dialogue, inviting actors to voice their requirements for the better administration of the CDM[57] (although authors express their concerns about the independent, competent, and consistent composition of the decision-making appeals body).[58] Another initiative must be noted in terms of the broad participation with the CDM: the

51 CDM-EB78-AA-A01, Annex 1, https://cdm.unfccc.int/Meetings/MeetingInfo/DB/8B1HYWV6NFPMUCZ/view (last visited January 25, 2015).

52 For a large overview of post-2012 public policy perspectives for addressing climate change, *see* Daniel Bodansky, *W[h]ither the Kyoto Protocol? Durban and Beyond* 12 (Harvard Project on Climate Agreements, View Points, 2011). For the outcome of Cancun agreements, see Lavanya Rajamani, *The Cancun Climate Agreements: Reading the Text, Subtext and Tea Leaves,* 60 (2) Int'l & Comp. L.Q. 499–519 (2011).

53 *See* Chapter 7 (Deleuil) in this volume.

54 IISD, *Earth Negotiation Bulletin*, Vol. 12, No 521 (October 10, 2011) at 14.

55 COP/MOP, *Further guidance relating to the clean development mechanism*, FCCC/KP/CMP/2010/12/Add.2, Decision 3/CMP.6, March 15, 2011, at 3.

56 For the last developments of review process of EB decision, *see* EB 64 Report, CDM-EB-64, October 26, 2011, Annex IV.

57 Terms of Reference for the Policy Dialogue on the Clan Development Mechanism, CDM-EB-64, October 26, 2011, Annex I.

58 Ludger Giesberts, Alexander Sarac, & John Wunderlin, *The Institutional Design Of The CDM Appeals Body: Recent Developments And Key Considerations,* 2 Carbon & Climate L. Rev. 285–286 (2011).

DNA's forum[59] participates to share experiences and information between developing countries. The Copenhagen Summit also provides a loan scheme to support the development of CDM projects in countries with fewer than ten projects.[60] Those loans can cover the costs of the development of project-design documents and the costs of the project's validation and first verification. In the same sense, the EU, whose Emissions Trading Scheme is the main demand source for CDM offsets, privileges CERs issued from CDM LDCs projects. Beginning in 2013, the EU will also ban its companies from using credits to meet targets from CDM projects that are registered after 2012, unless those schemes are located in LDCs. Other kinds of partnerships may be concluded at the national level, such as in France, cdc climat, and proparco for Sub-Saharan African States and Mediterranean States.

In terms of the distribution of CDM projects, in Cancún many developing countries repeated their call for a reform of the CDM to help the poorest countries to benefit from CDM investments. Deeply attached to a legally binding agreement, developing countries brandish CDM as a threat. They refuse to guarantee the market mechanism's future in the negotiation unless rich States take on new legally binding emission targets. After Doha and Warsaw, during the debates in Lima in December 2014, Senegal said that CDM reform is critical for developing countries, particularly in Africa, noting that so far they have benefited very little from the mechanism.[61] However, the COP serving as the MOP to the Kyoto Protocol adopted a final decision on the CDM which does not change the perspective of its functioning with regards to the developing countries.[62] This only allows the validation by a DOE and the submission for approval by the EB of a monitoring plan at any time up to the first request for issuance of CERs for all scales of project activities and programs of activities.

What should be the future of the CDM from a developing country perspective? The question is often considered from an economic point of view.[63] First, the CDM could facilitate access to a project cycle for developing countries with few projects by reducing administrative and organizational constraints, such as reducing costs and delays in project registration and certification. Second, the current programmatic CDM could be extended, improving access to the entire mechanism for LDCs.[64] As such, differentiated approaches should be considered, which provide disadvantaged and vulnerable developing countries with preferential treatment under the CDM.[65] The common position of developing countries on the CDM has not changed since the COP 15. They do not want that CDM reforms lead them to accept mitigation and adaptation commitments.

59 Established by the EB of CDM.

60 *Guidelines And Modalities For Operationalization Of A Loan Scheme To Support The Development Of Clean Development Mechanism Project Activities In Countries With Fewer Than 10 Registered Clean Development Mechanism Project Activities*, FCCC/KP/CMP/2010/12/Add.2, Annex III, 13.

61 ENB, Summary of the Lima Climate Change Conference December 1–14, 2014, at 9.

62 FCCC/CP/CMP/2014/L.3.

63 Nhan T. Nguyen, Minh Ha-Duong, Sandra Greiner & Michael Mehling, *Improving the Clean Development Mechanism Post-2012: A Developing Country Perspective*, Carbon & Climate L. Rev. 13 (2010).

64 *Id.*, at 11.

65 Lambert Schneider, *Options to Enhance and Improve the Clean Development Mechanism (CDM)* (ETC/ACC Technical Paper, 2008), http://air-climate.eionet.europa.eu/docs//ETCACC_TP_2008_15_future_CDM.pdf (last visited July 8, 2014).

Conclusion

After having assessed the CDM's current functioning from a developing country perspective, the result is divergent. A few emergent States, especially China and India, receive the vast majority of CDM benefits. For other developing countries, the chance to host CDM projects is all the less when the State has not industrialized. Developing countries that host CDM projects benefit mainly in the economic sense. If the CDM GHG emission reductions claim great importance, other aspects of environmental protection significantly lack. The expected input of sustainable development has not nearly been fulfilled in practice, and technology transfer has been effective only in less industrialized States. Less ambitious than foreseen, the CDM is, however, quite efficient. In this context, developing countries use their central position in the CDM to put forward their expectations for achieving GHG emission mitigation. They have also made interesting propositions to increase non-trade aspects that could help improve the CDM and other market mechanisms in the 2015 agreement. However, the recent proposition to include the private sector in the decision-making process of CDM projects will certainly strengthen the role of emergent States in the CDM and weaken the role of other developing countries in the process.

11 The Role of Domestic Policies in Fostering Technology Transfer

Evidence from China*

Elena Cima

I Setting the framework: Climate change and the equity principle

In Chinese President Hu Jintao's speech on climate change delivered to the United Nations General Assembly on September 22, 2009, he expressed the following view:

> It is imperative to give full consideration to the development stage and basic needs of developing countries while we address climate change [. . .] Developed countries should take up their responsibility and provide new, additional, adequate, and predictable financial support to developing countries to enable them to have access to climate-friendly technologies.[1]

Many other developing countries[2] share this view, which clearly demonstrates that developing and least-developed nations tend to look at climate change as a North–South issue rather

* This chapter is part of the results of the Research Project on "*Current Trends of Chinese Law towards Non-Trade Concerns such as Sustainable Development and the Protection of Environment, Public Health, Food Safety, Cultural, Social and Economic Rights, Labor Rights and the Reduction of Poverty from the Perspective of International Law and WTO Law*" coordinated by Professor Paolo Davide Farah at gLAWcal – Global Law Initiatives for Sustainable Development (United Kingdom) and at West Virginia University John D. Rockefeller IV School of Policy and Politics, Department of Public Administration, in partnership with the Center of Advanced Studies on Contemporary China (CASCC) in Turin (Italy), Maastricht University Faculty of Law, Department of International and European Law and IGIR – Institute for Globalisation and International Regulation (Netherlands), and Tsinghua University, School of Law, Institute of Public International Law and the Center for Research on Intellectual Property Law in Beijing (China). An early draft of this chapter was presented at the Conferences Series on "*China's Influence on Non-Trade Concerns in International Economic Law*", Second Conference held at Tsinghua University, School of Law on January 14–15, 2012. This publication and the Conference Series were sponsored by China–EU School of Law (CESL) at the China University of Political Science and Law (CUPL). The activities of CESL at CUPL are supported by the European Union and the People's Republic of China.

1 *Hu Jintao's Speech on Climate Change*, New York Times (September 22, 2009).

2 Luiz Inácio Lula da Silva, former President of Brazil, addressing the general debate of the 64th session of the General Assembly at United Nations headquarters in New York stated: "*We are dismayed by the reluctance of developed countries to shoulder their share of the burden when it comes to fighting climate change. They cannot burden developing countries with tasks which are theirs alone*" (October 4, 2009). The same line is followed by countries like Indonesia and Kenya. The Indonesian government stressed that there is a widely recognized difference between the contribution of industrialized and developing nations to the global emissions of GHGs. As a consequence, industrialized countries need to take domestic action first and should also assist developing ones in implementing measures. The Kenyan position is very similar:

than simply as an environmental one. Several reasons underlie what we might call a "North–South Divide."[3] First of all, the climatic phenomena do not affect all regions of the world equally: the poorest countries and regions will suffer the most because they are least prepared to respond and react. Extreme poverty and weak infrastructure compound the problem that begins with geographical and climatic factors. Second, the international community should investigate each country's contribution to climate change. At present, countries who do not belong to the Organization for Economic Co-operation and Development (OECD)[4] discharge emissions which are higher than those registered in OECD countries.[5] Among the 20 countries that release the highest emissions, eight are developing ones; however, most developing countries – such as China, India, Brazil, and South Africa – have average per capita emissions remarkably lower than those in the developed world.[6] Moreover, we should remember that today's situation has developed since industrialization occurred in the eighteenth century[7] and is not merely the result of emissions released by human activities in the past few decades. It follows that we should take into account these "past" emissions, and, as a result, developing countries are blameworthy for only 23 per cent of them.[8] The continuous calls for developing nations to reduce their greenhouse gas (GHG) emissions substantiate the idea that the North deals with climate change and global warming by taking

according to the national plan, nations must act in concert to deal with environmental problems, but with due regard to equal but differentiated responsibilities.

3 For further reading on the North–South issue related to climate change policies, *see* ANIL AGARWAL & SUNITA NARAIN, GLOBAL WARMING IN AN UNEQUAL WORLD (Centre for Science and Environment, 1991); Henry Shue, *Equity in an International Agreement on Climate Change*, in EQUITY AND SOCIAL CONSIDERATIONS RELATED TO CLIMATE CHANGE (Richard S. Odingo et al. eds, ICIPE Science Press, 1995).

4 Most developing and least developed countries are not part of the Organization for Economic Co-operation and Development (OECD).

5 In 2010, non-OECD emissions exceeded OECD emissions by 38 per cent. In 2040, they are projected to exceed OECD emissions by about 127 per cent. OECD emissions increase by 0.2 per cent per year on average, while non-OECD emissions increase by an average of 1.9 per cent per year. Environmental Investigation Agency, *International Energy Outlook 2013*, at 7, 162, http://www.eia.gov/forecasts/ieo/pdf/0484%282013%29.pdf (last visited July 14, 2016).

6 According to the International Energy Agency (IEA) *World Energy Outlook*, in 2006, per-capita emissions in the United States amounted to 18.6 tonnes, followed by Russia with 11 tonnes, Japan with 9.5 tonnes, and the European Union with 8 tonnes. China's per-capita emissions were 4.3 tonnes (close to the global average, but 40 per cent of the level of the OECD), while in India they were 1.1 tonnes and a mere 0.9 tonnes in Africa. OECD/IEA, *World Energy Outlook 2008*, at 388, http://www.worldenergyoutlook.org/media/weowebsite/2008–1994/weo2008.pdf (last visited July 14, 2016). *See also* Environmental Investigation Agency, *International Energy Outlook 2008*, http://www.eia.gov/forecasts/archive/ieo08/index.html (last visited July 14, 2016). According to IEA projections, 2035 per-capita emissions in non-OECD countries will still be half of those of OECD countries. *See* OECD/IEA, *World Energy Outlook 2013*, http://www.worldenergyoutlook.org/publications/weo-2013/ (last visited July 14, 2016).

7 *See* JOYEETA GUPTA, THE CLIMATE CHANGE CONVENTION AND DEVELOPING COUNTRIES: FROM CONFLICT TO CONSENSUS? 75–98 (Kluwer Academic Publishers, 1994).

8 Hussein Abaza, Vesine Kulacoglu, Anne Olhoff, Benjamin Simmons, Robert Teh & Ludivine Tamiotti, *Trade and Climate Change. A Report by the United Nations Environment Programme and the World Trade Organization*, WTO Publications, World Trade Organization 2–24 (2009); UN IPCC Synthesis Report 2007, at 6; KEN CALDEIRA, MORGAN M. GRANGER, DENNIS D. BALDOCCHI, PETER G. BREWER & CHEN-TUN A. CHEN, GLOBAL CARBON CYCLE: INTEGRATING HUMANS, CLIMATE AND THE NATURAL WORLD 103–129 (Island Press, 2004); Michael R. Raupach, Gregg Marland, Philippe Ciais, Corinne Le Quéré, Josep G. Canadell, Gernot Klepper & Christopher B. Field, *Global And Regional Drivers of Accelerating CO_2 Emissions*, 104(24) PNAS (2007).

into account its own needs.[9] The political dialogue, which has focused on the "environment" without paying due attention to "development," offers further proof. The South has just started to experience industrialization: these countries are doing now what industrialized nations did a few centuries ago, and their actions constitute a vital and necessary step towards adequate economic and social development.

The current climate change debate focuses on finding ways to address this issue, and technology transfer certainly offers a huge potential to tackle the negative impacts of climate change. Given that most green technologies are developed in the North, their transfer to less-developed regions plays a crucial role in the current debate. Several obstacles interfere with this process, and the international community is seeking new mechanisms to facilitate the transfer. However, without denying the relevance of all these efforts at the international level, this chapter argues that the most effective way to address the ***real*** obstacles to technology transfer is to enact comprehensive domestic policies in the recipient country. The chapter further argues that only once these policies are in place will the mechanisms developed internationally be able to produce the positive effects they were designed to achieve.

The chapter is divided into three main sections. Section II, which provides an overview of the role played by technology transfer in developing countries, describes the main international rules governing the process, and identifies the obstacles that prevent the transfer from being as successful as it should. Section III analyzes the Chinese renewable energy market – especially the wind power industry – and the role of the government in the sector's growth. Finally, Section IV lays out the chapter's main argument, focusing on the role played by the enactment of domestic policies in facilitating the technology transfer process and enhancing the country's own domestic capacity, while Section V draws the final conclusions.

II The relevance of technology transfer in the climate change debate

The Intergovernmental Panel on Climate Change (IPCC)[10] defines technology transfer as:

> a broad set of processes covering the flows of know-how, experience, and equipment for mitigating and adapting to climate change amongst different stakeholders such as governments, private sector entities, financial institutions, non-governmental organizations (NGOs), and research/education institutions [. . .] The broad and inclusive term "transfer" encompasses diffusion of technologies and technology cooperation across

9 Julius K. Nyerere et al., The Challenge to the South: the Report of the South Commission 3 (Oxford University Press, 1990).

10 The IPCC (Intergovernmental Panel on Climate Change) was established in 1988 by the combined effort of the World Meteorological Organization (WMO) and the United Nations Environment Programme (UNEP). The main task of this scientific body is to provide the leading powers with a clear scientific view on the current state of climate change and its potential environmental and socio-economic consequences. It is open to all member countries of the United Nations (UN) and the WMO, and counts the participation of 195 countries so far. The IPCC released five Assessment Reports since 1990 – the first in 1990, and then in 1995, 2001, 2007, and 2014. The fifth assessment report consists of three Working Group (WG) reports and a Synthesis Report (SYR). All IPCC documents are available on the website of the IPCC, http://www.ipcc.ch/ (last visited July 14, 2016).

> and within countries. It covers technology transfer processes between developed countries, developing countries and countries with economies in transition, amongst developed countries, amongst developing countries, and amongst countries with economies in transition.[11]

Technology transfer may include two different aspects:[12] transfer of technology embodied in tangible physical assets or capital goods,[13] and transfer of the knowledge[14] and information inherent in any given technology or technological system.[15]

Numerous channels exist through which international technology transfer may occur, and the main ones are licensing and Foreign Direct Investment (FDIs).[16] A licensing contract may be a legal arrangement in which a company ("licensor") that has proprietary rights over a certain technology grants permission to another firm or individual ("licensee") to make use of that technology, under strict conditions delimited by the licensor. In return, the licensee agrees to pay royalties or provide other forms of compensation. FDI is, on the other hand, more complex. It takes place when an investor belonging to one country ("home country") acquires an asset in another country ("host country"), with the specific purpose of managing the asset (usually a business firm as well).[17]

As already mentioned in the introduction, given that most GHG-reducing technologies that may have the largest impact in the developing world originate in industrialized nations, the transfer of these technologies to developing countries represents a crucial component of the global effort to address climate change. As a matter of fact, technology transfer has become one of the main vehicles to enable developing and least-developed countries to participate in global efforts for climate change mitigation and adaptation while, at the same time, fostering their economic development.

11 IPCC Fourth Assessment Report: Climate Change 2007.

12 Martin Bell, *Technology Transfer To Transition Countries: Are There Lessons From The Experience Of The Post-War Industrializing Countries?*, in THE TECHNOLOGY OF TRANSITION: SCIENCE AND TECHNOLOGY POLICIES FOR TRANSITION COUNTRIES (David A. Dyker ed., Central European University Press, 1997).

13 K. Ramanathan, *An Analytical Framework For Technology Transfer*, in CONTEMPORARY ISSUES IN TECHNOLOGY TRANSFER (P. Gougeon & J. Gupa eds, ESKA, 1997).

14 Chapter 34 of Agenda 21 identifies this particular dimension of technology transfer: "Environmentally sound technologies are not just individual technologies, but a total system which include know-how, procedures, goods and services, and equipment as well as organizational and managerial procedures. This implies that when discussing transfer of technologies, the human resources development and local capacity-building aspects of technology choices [. . .] should also be addressed. Environmentally sound technologies should be compatible with nationally determined socio-economic, cultural and environmental priorities."

15 John S. Metcalfe, *Technology Systems And Technology Policy In An Evolutionary Framework*, 19 CAMBRIDGE J. ECON. (1995).

16 Other channels include trade in goods and services, since all exports bear some potential to transmit technological information. *See* Bernard M. Hoekman, Keith E. Maskus & Kamal Saggi, *Transfer of Technology to Developing Countries: Unilateral and Multilateral Policy Options* 3 (World Bank Policy Research Working Paper 3332, June 2004). *See* Chapter 10 (Lemoine) in this volume.

17 *See* Richard Blackhurst & Adrian Otten, *Trade and Foreign Direct Investment* 20–22 (World Trade Organization, Geneva 1996); for the methods to identify technology transfer in FDI, *see* Wilbut Chung, *Identifying Technology Transfer in Foreign Direct Investment: Influence of Industry Conditions and Investing Firms Motives*, 32 J. INT'L BUS. STUD. 214–215 (2001).

International framework for technology transfer

The relevance of technology transfer and the need to establish mechanisms to facilitate this process were taken into account in the main climate change agreements, namely the United Nations Framework Convention on Climate Change (UNFCCC)[18] and the Kyoto Protocol,[19] which established the "common but differentiated responsibilities" principle.[20] The latter developed from the application of the equity principle in public international law and the recognition that the needs and specific features of developing countries must be taken into account in the creation, interpretation and application of rules of international environmental law.[21] This principle was first established in the Rio Declaration as *Principle 7*:

> States shall co-operate in a spirit of global partnership to conserve, protect and restore the health and integrity of the Earth's ecosystem. In view of the different contribution to global environmental degradation, states have common but differentiated responsibilities. The developed countries acknowledge the responsibility that they bear in the international pursuit of sustainable development in view of the pressures their societies place on the global environment and of the technologies and financial resources they command.

The differentiated approach is then reflected in many other treaties,[22] and a similar language exists in the UNFCCC as well as in the Kyoto Protocol. In the Convention, it requires specific commitments only for developed country parties,[23] while in the Protocol it applies

18 UN Framework Convention on Climate Change, opened for signature May 9, 1992, 1771 UNTS 107, 31 ILM. 489 (entered into force March 21, 1994).

19 Kyoto Protocol to the United Nations Framework Convention on Climate Change, December 11, 1997, 2303 UNTS 148. The Protocol sets explicit emission targets for certain signatory countries: each of these countries was to reduce its GHG emissions so that its total emissions, when converted to a carbon-equivalent basis, did not exceed a specified percentage of its base period emissions. On the other hand, developing and least-developed countries were not addressed with any specific commitment, but could benefit from certain flexible mechanisms provided for in the Protocol and thus contribute to the global emission reduction. After the end of the first commitment period (2008–2012), the emission targets were reaffirmed for a second commitment period (2013–2020). *See* in general WORLD CLIMATE CHANGE: THE ROLE OF INTERNATIONAL LAW AND INSTITUTIONS (Ved P. Nanda ed., Westvlew Press, 1983); INTERNATIONAL LAW AND GLOBAL CLIMATE CHANGE (Robin Churchill and David Freestone eds, Graham & Trotman, 1991); VERHEYEN RODA, CLIMATE CHANGE DAMAGE AND INTERNATIONAL LAW: PREVENTION DUTIES AND STATE RESPONSIBILITIES (Martinus Nijhoff Publishers, 2005); FRIEDRICH SOLTAU, FAIRNESS IN INTERNATIONAL CLIMATE CHANGE LAW (Cambridge University Press, 2009). For an interesting and detailed analysis of these milestones in the Chinese perspective, *see* Chapters 8 (Sindico & Gibson), 10 (Lemoine), and 14 (Peng) in this volume.

20 For readings on the "common but differentiated responsibilities" principle, *see* PHILIPPE SANDS, PRINCIPLES OF INTERNATIONAL ENVIRONMENTAL LAW (Cambridge University Press, 2003). *See also* Chapter 9 (Ibrahim, Deleuil & Farah) in this volume.

21 PHILIPPE SANDS, *supra* note 20, at 285.

22 Examples are the 1972 London Convention (art. 11), the 1981 Abidjan Convention (art. 4(1)), the 1985 Vienna Convention (art. 2(2)), the 1976 Barcelona Convention (art. 11(3)), and the 1992 Biodiversity Convention (Preamble and art. 20(4)).

23 Article 4, where all the commitments are listed taking into account each country's "common but differentiated responsibilities" and "specific national and regional development priorities, objectives and circumstances" and art. 12, which establishes specific commitments which apply to developed countries only.

to OECD countries and sets different targets depending upon the states' historic contributions and current capabilities.[24]

Both the UNFCCC and the Kyoto Protocol recognize the potential key role of technology transfer. The ratification of the UNFCCC requires developed countries to assist developing ones with technology transfer. The Convention (Articles 4.1(c), 4.3 and 4.5) and the Protocol itself (Article 12) promote the transfer of technologies and know-how from developed to developing countries in order to facilitate their development in a sustainable way.[25] Article 4.5 of the UNFCCC states that "the developed country Parties and other developed Parties included in Annex II shall take all practicable steps to promote, facilitate, and finance, as appropriate, the transfer of, or access to, environmentally sound technologies and know-how to other Parties, particularly developing country Parties, to enable them to implement the provisions of the Convention." However, the Convention does not in any way specify the method and content of this commitment.[26] Similarly, the Protocol places the focus on the cooperation between industrialized and developing countries, in particular, through two of the three flexibility mechanisms[27] it provides – the Clean Development Mechanism (CDM) and Joint Implementation – but, as several developing countries including China have emphasized, it lacks a real technology transfer component, which it probably should have.

Obstacles to an effective transfer and the debate around the role of intellectual property protection

Traditionally, scholars have identified several barriers that make technology transfer to developing countries difficult.[28] These barriers include both *direct costs* – such as the payment of royalty fees necessary to secure access to technological information, the administrative costs for preparing and executing the transaction, as well as those resulting from the length of time agreed for the payment of fees – and *indirect costs* – related to imperfections in the technology market.[29] Such indirect costs exist because technology goods are heavily associated with a series of factors such as the monopolistic power granted to the technology owner, asymmetric information, and market restrictions.[30]

24 PHILIPPE SANDS, *supra* note 20, at 368–381.

25 CTI, *Methods for Climate Change Technology Transfer Needs Assessments and Implementing Activities – Developing and Transition Country Approaches and Experiences* (2002). *See* also Chapters 6 (Vadi) and 9 (Ibrahim, Deleuil & Farah) in this volume.

26 OECD/IEA, *Technology Without Borders: Case Studies of Successful Technology Transfer*, IEA Publications (2001), www.iea.org/papers/2001/ctifull.pdf (last visited July 14, 2016).

27 The Kyoto Protocol establishes three flexibility mechanisms – namely Emission Trading (ET), Joint Implementation (JI), and Clean Development Mechanism (CDM) – that have been conceived with the aim of providing countries with a flexible means by which they can meet their emission targets.

28 A number of authors analyze these barriers (asymmetric information, market power, and externalities) as such: *see* Hoekman, Maskus & Saggi, *supra* note 16, at 3–4.

29 The costs associated with technology transfer are considered by many authors to be mostly derived from inefficient markets for these specific goods: *see* Jack Hirshleifer, *On the Economics of Transfer Pricing*, 29 J. BUS. 172–179 (1956); EDWARD K.Y. CHEN, TRANSNATIONAL CORPORATIONS AND TECHNOLOGY TRANSFER TO DEVELOPING COUNTRIES 13–14 (Routledge, 1994).

30 As far as the first factor is concerned (monopolistic power), owners of new technologies typically have substantial market power, which creates a market distortion. As to the second factor (asymmetric information), it refers to the flaw flowing from the deficient knowledge of technology acquirers. Finally, market restriction encompass both FDI restriction and trade restrictive policies. *See* BERNARD H. HOEKMAN, GLOBAL INTEGRATION AND TECHNOLOGY TRANSFER 14 (World Bank Publications, 2006); Clem A. Tisdell,

In the complex process of transfer of technology, the role of intellectual property rights (IPR) protection has proven particularly contentious.[31] The debate is polarized between those who advocate for stronger IPR laws to encourage innovation on the one hand, and those calling for more IPR-related flexibilities to encourage access to key technologies by developing countries on the other. It is especially developing countries that claim IPRs should be eliminated and ask for flexibilities. The dichotomy is therefore once again North–South. A fundamental question this chapter addresses is whether IPRs are actually to be considered as a barrier.

Without denying the existence of all the aforementioned obstacles, I argue that – in the case of technology transfer to developing or least-developed countries – other issues should be addressed first, in order to facilitate an effective and sustainable transfer. First of all, weak legal systems and poor investment frameworks slow down the process and discourage foreign companies from investing and transferring their technology. Second, most least-developed countries are often not able to fully exploit or further develop the technology once they have gained access to it. This is the result of lack of know-how, appropriate education and relevant experience, investment in research and development (R&D) – which might not be feasible due to lack of access to capital – and lack of adequate infrastructure.[32] Thus, the lack of resources and absorptive capacity in developing countries impact both their ability to attract foreign technology and the likelihood that technologies will be developed domestically to meet their specific needs.[33]

III The role of domestic intervention in fostering technology transfer: Evidence from China

Despite the efforts at the international level to establish a mechanism aimed at facilitating technology transfer to developing countries, the specific obstacles I laid out in the previous section require a different kind of approach. In particular, I argue for the enactment of domestic policies focused on overcoming those obstacles. China represents an excellent example, given the remarkable growth of the country's renewable energy sector in the last decade and the extremely comprehensive strategy adopted by the Chinese government to facilitate such process. After briefly analyzing the expansion of the wind power industry in the People's Republic of China

---

Transfer Pricing, Technical and Productivity Change Within the Firm, 10 Managerial and Decision Economics (1989); Hoekman, Maskus & Saggi, *supra* note 16.

31 ICTSD, *Climate Change, Technology Transfer and Intellectual Property Rights,* ICTSD Background Paper, Trade and Climate Change Seminar, June 18–20, 2008, Copenhagen. A study by UNIDO states that "the results are far from definitive as a consequence. But while it would be premature to make strong claims on the basis of the limited evidence to date, the overall pattern of results justifies certain inferences," UNIDO (2006) 45.

32 Copenhagen Economics and The IPR Company, *Are IPR a Barrier to the Transfer of Climate Change Technology?* 29 (Copenhagen Economic Report, 2009). Andrzej Jasinski, *Barriers for Technology Transfer in Transitional Economies: Results of Empirical Studies* (Paper ID A089, School of Management, University of Warsaw, 2005). Jasinski notes that, in Poland, one of the main barriers to technology transfer is the lack of financial resources (together with other barriers such as an inefficient system supporting firms' innovation and R&D as well as the lack of innovative culture and mentality among the firms' employees).

33 Keith E. Maskus & Ruth L. Okediji, *Intellectual Property Rights and International Technology Transfer to Address Climate Change: Risks, Opportunities, and Policy Options* 5 (Int'l Center for Trade and Sustainable Dev., Intell. Prop. & Sustainable Dev. Series, Issue Paper No. 32, December 2010). *See* Matthew Burns, *A Sustainable Framework for International Green Technology Transfer,* 23(3) Colo. J. Int'l Envtl. L. & Pol'y. 405, 409 (2012).

(PRC), this section will explore the policies adopted by China to boost its renewable energy industry and foster inbound technology transfer flows, unraveling the deep causal connection between the two.

The growth of China's wins power sector

Among the top 10 wind turbine manufacturers by annual market share (installed capacity) in 2015,[34] five are Chinese companies – Goldwind, United Power, Mingyang, Envision, and CSIC Haizhuang. Despite the predominance of industrialized nations, non-OECD-based companies are climbing up the ranks, mainly through mergers and acquisitions.[35] However, as of today, China and India are probably the only developing countries with notable wind turbine manufacturing industries.[36]

Chinese manufacturer Goldwind aptly demonstrates the role of technology transfer as well as government intervention in this particular field. The company, established in 1986, is the leading Chinese wind turbine manufacturer, representing 18.9 per cent of domestic market share in 2014 and 12.5 per cent of the global market share in 2015.[37] The company initially purchased a license from Jacobs, a small German manufacturer, and then from GE Power. When China first entered the wind energy industry, international companies such as Vestas, GE Energy, and Gamesa produced about 65 per cent of the turbines that China purchased. However, as a result of the recently shaped "Buy Chinese" policy that favors local manufacturers, 70 low-cost local producers supply about 75 per cent of new wind turbines. In 2008, Goldwind completed the acquisition of Vensys and began to increase its R&D activities in Austria. As Vensys expanded its own wind turbine design and manufacturing partnerships around the world, Goldwind directly benefited from this extended knowledge base, which supplemented its own increasingly global expansions.[38] Moreover, the company's relationship with Vensys slowly changed as the Chinese company acquired a majority control of Vensys and gained full access to its technological know-how.[39]

Although several technology transfer models exist, most Chinese companies, including Goldwind, chose multiple licensing agreements with either well- or not-so-well-established firms. This type of agreement is characterized by the fact that it gathers the purchase of several licenses, so that the purchasing company has all the technology and technical knowledge it needs to start its activity – in this specific case, manufacturing wind turbines. These licensing agreements enabled Goldwind and other Chinese companies to acquire the necessary technology, and innovate accordingly.

34 *Navigant Consulting*. The shares in 2015 were divided as follows: Goldwind (China) 12.5%, Vestas (Denmark) 11.8%, GE (U.S.) 9.5%, Siemens (Germany) 8%, Gamesa (Spain) 5.4%, Enercon (Germany) 5%, United Power (China) 4.9%, Mingyang (China) 4.1%, Envision (China) 4%, CSIC Haizhuang (China) 3.4%, others (31.4%).

35 A good example is offered by the Indian company Suzlon. The company is Indian-owned and a key component of its strategy has been to acquire European technology companies, including Hansen International and AE-Rotor Techniek.

36 The same situation shows in other renewable energy sectors, especially as far as solar technologies are concerned.

37 Goldwind, *2013 Annual Report*, http://www.goldwindglobal.com/upload/files/201404/201404221722971.pdf (last visited July 14, 2016).

38 Joanna Lewis, *A Comparison of the Wind Power Technology Development Strategies of Chinese and Indian Firms* (Center for Resource Solutions Supported by the Energy Foundation, China Sustainable Energy Program, July 19, 2007).

39 Joanna Lewis, Green Innovation in China 133 (Columbia University Press, 2013).

China's strategy to facilitate technology transfer and boost the renewable energy sector

One of the main reasons underlying the incredible growth in China's use of renewable energy and deployment of technology transfer to innovate and develop is linked to government support. For example, relevant technologies for climate change mitigation are closely tied to energy-efficiency improvements, and the Chinese government has maintained long-standing policies and programs to promote greater efficiency in energy supply and end use, as well as the development of renewable and nuclear energy. Key to these efforts have been technology imports from developed countries.

This should not be surprising as China has been socialist since 1949, and the government has played a predominant role in the economy.[40] Despite the recent decline of government control, certain sectors, such as heavy industries, have remained largely state owned. Under the current government, the Chinese Communist Party (CCP) reserves the right to make broad decisions on economic priorities and policies, but the government apparatus, headed by the State Council, assumes the major burden of running the economy. The Chinese government has played such a paramount role even in the energy industry, doing so through various channels such as governmental plans, laws, regulations, and subsidies.

a) Governmental plans

Governmental plans – including the Five-Year National Development Plans – play a crucial role by designing the deployment and diffusion of specific technologies. The current 13th Five-Year Plan provides for targets of energy intensity by pledging to reduce emissions per unit of Gross Domestic Product (GDP) by 40 to 45 per cent by 2020 compared to 2005 levels. The first major measures were adopted as a result of the 11th Five-Year Plan, which set an initial 20 per cent reduction target of energy intensity per GDP.[41] To achieve the target, the government started the Top-1000 Enterprises Program,[42] which required the top 1,000 energy-consuming companies to reduce their energy intensity by various policy programs, including energy-efficiency diagnosis, reporting of energy consumption, voluntary agreements with the government, and energy-efficiency

40 Dwight Heald Perkins, Agricultural Development in China, 1368–1968 (Edinburgh University Press, 1969); Gang Zhao, Man and Land in Chinese History: an Economic analysis (Stanford University Press, 1986); William C. Kirby, State and Economy in Republican China: a Handbook for Scholars, Volume 1 (Harvard University Asia Center, 2000); Hui Wang & Theodore Huters, China's New Order: Society, Politics, and Economy in Transition (Harvard University Press, 2003); Christopher A. McNally, China's Emergent Political Economy: Capitalism in the Dragon's Lair (Routledge, 2008).

41 The Chinese Five-Year Plans are a series of economic development initiatives taken by the central government. This series started in 1953 with the first Plan. Among the main purposes of the 11th Five-Year Guideline are securing economic growth and economic structure, urbanizing the population, conserving energy and national resources, encouraging sound environmental practices, and improving education. Further information about the Plan can be found at the Government Web portal: http://www.gov.cn/english/special/115y_index.htm (last visited July 14, 2016). Further information on the 13th Five Year Plan can be found at http://www.apcoworldwide.com/docs/default-source/default-document-library/Thought-Leadership/13-five-year-plan-think-piece.pdf?sfvrsn=2 (last visited July 14, 2016).

42 Lynn price, Xuejun Wang & Yun Jiang, *China's Top-1000 Energy-Consuming Enterprises Program: Reducing Energy Consumption of the 1000 Largest Industrial Enterprises in China* (Lawrence Berkeley National Laboratory Report, 2008).

benchmarking efforts. The essential elements of such programs include the assessment of the energy-efficiency potential of the industrial facility as well as target-setting through a negotiated process. Participation by industries is motivated through the use of both incentives and disincentives. Supporting programs and policies – such as facility audits, assessments, benchmarking, monitoring, information dissemination, and financial incentives – all played an important role in assisting the participants in understanding and managing their energy use and GHG emissions in order to meet the target goals. In 2002, the Reform Policy was enacted, which was a plan for structural reform of the power industry.[43] In 2007, China introduced the National Climate Change Program, which outlined the steps that the government would take to meet the previously announced goals of improving energy efficiency by 20 per cent in 2010 (over the 2005 levels) and raising the proportion of renewable energy in the primary energy supply to 10 per cent by 2010, and other measures.[44]

b) Legal reforms

The history of Goldwind shows that one of the main reasons behind the shift from import of foreign products to local manufacturing lies in the systemic legal reforms promoted by the Chinese government. Since the beginning of the 1980s, China enacted several energy-related laws,[45] such as the 1997 Energy Conservation Law of the People's Republic of China (hereinafter Energy Conservation Law)[46] and the 2006 Renewable Energy Law of the People's Republic of China (hereinafter Renewable Energy Law).[47] The latter became effective on January 1, 2006. This law creates incentives and requirements for China to obtain 10 per cent of its energy from renewable sources by 2020. The government identifies "renewable energy" as the "*preferential area for energy development,*" and it sets some specific targets to be met by 2010 and 2020. The law mandates the establishment of a government fund to support the research and development of renewable-energy-related technologies and a smart power grid system. According to Article 32 of the Energy Conservation Law, the state shall, among other things, "encourage and support developing advanced energy conservation technologies [and] determine the key areas and directions in development of advanced energy conservation technologies." This framework regulates the market for energy, providing specific rules aimed at addressing its peculiar features. Chinese legal

43 The main tasks identified in the Reform Policy included the separation of plant and grid; restructuring of power regulatory bodies and establishment of the State Electricity Reform Commission (SERC); establishment of a competitive electricity market; implementation of power tariff reform; and formulation of environmental cost standards and surcharges for emissions.

44 *See* http://www.ccchina.gov.cn/WebSite/CCChina/UpFile/File188.pdf (last visited July 14, 2016).

45 Namely, in 1983, the Rural Energy Law was enacted; in 1984, the so-called Measures to Support Renewable Energy (wind farm development) were introduced. Later on, the Electric Power and Energy Conservation Law and the Energy Conservation Law came into force, respectively in 1995 and 1997. In 2000, the Renewable Portfolio Standard Models were introduced, followed by the Renewable Energy Law in 2006. For an analysis of Chinese legislation on energy and the environment, *see* Chapters 13 (Luo Li) and 14 (Peng) in this volume.

46 Zhōnghuá Rénmín Gònghéguó Jiéyuē Néngyuán Fǎ (2007 xiūdìng) (中华人民共和国节约能源法 (2007 修订) [Energy Conservation Law of the People's Republic of China (2007 Revision)] (promulgated by the Standing Comm. Nat'l People's Cong., October 28, 2007).

47 Zhōnghuá Rénmín Gònghéguó Kě Zàishēng Néngyuán Fǎ (2009 xiūdìng)(中华人民共和国可再生能源法 (2009 修订) [Renewable Energy Law of the People's Republic of China (2009 Revision)] (Promulgated by the Standing Comm. Nat'l People's Cong., December 26, 2009).

reforms did not stop at the environmental and energy sector: they completely changed the framework governing foreign investment and technology transfer itself. In particular, as far as the former is concerned, starting in 1979, the PRC has introduced many laws and regulations increasing the amount of legal incentives and protection aimed at attracting foreign investment. The 1979 Law of the People's Republic of China on Chinese-Foreign Equity Joint Venture (Equity Joint Venture Law),[48] the 1986 Law of the People's Republic of China on Foreign-Capital Enterprises (Law on Foreign-Capital Enterprises),[49] and the 2007 Enterprise Income Tax Law of the People's Republic of China[50] represent examples of the new framework introduced by the Chinese government to help the country attract foreign investment. Moreover, a number of environmentally friendly industrial processes and products have been labeled as 'encouraged,' thereby making them eligible for preferential policies. As to technology transfer *per se*, several provisions scattered within a number of laws govern this process. The most relevant include the 1985 Regulations of the People's Republic of China on the Administration of Technology Acquisition Contracts[51] and the Equity Joint Venture Law. In particular, Article 5 of the latter requires that "the technology or equipment contributed by any foreign party as investment shall be truly advanced and appropriate to China's needs,"[52] thus conditioning investment approval on the transfer of vital green technologies. Finally, the legal reforms undergone by the PRC involved the intellectual property system as well. In particular, as far as technologies are concerned, the first Patent Law of the People's Republic of China[53] was introduced in 1985 – and then amended in 1992, 2000, and 2008 – and it provided protection for investors willing to apply for patent rights in China.[54]

c) *Tax breaks and subsidies*

In the 1950s and 1960s, the state allocated a special fund to support the development of small hydropower sources by constructing water conservation works in rural areas to meet the demand for electricity. The following decade, the state offered subsidies to provide electricity to rural areas and extend biogas, fuel wood, and coal-saving technologies. With the reform of the rural economic system in 1978, the demand for electricity continued to increase. To meet this demand, the government reinforced financial and economic support

48 Zhonghua Renmin Gongheguo Zhongwai Hezi Jingying Giye Fa (中华人民共和国中外合资经营企业法) [Law of the People's Republic of China on Chinese-Foreign Equity Joint Ventures] (promulgated by the Standing Comm. Nat'l People's Cong., July 8, 1979, amended March 15, 2001).

49 Zhonghua Renmin Gongheguo Waizi Qiye Fa (中华人民共和国外资企业法) [Law of the People's Republic of China on Foreign-Capital Enterprises] (promulgated by the Nat'l People's Cong., April 12, 1986).

50 Zhonghua Renmin Gongheguo Qiye Suodeshui Fa (中华人民共和国企业所得税法) [Enterprise Income Tax Law of the People's Republic of China] (promulgated by the Nat'l People's Cong., March 16, 2007, effective January 1, 2008).

51 Zhonghua Renmin Gongheguo Jishu Yinjin Hetong Guanli Tiaoli (中华人民共和国技术引进合同管理条例) [Regulations of the People's Republic of China on the Administration of Technology Acquisition Contracts] (issued by the State Council May 24, 1985).

52 *Supra* note 48, article 5.

53 Zhonghua Renmin Gongheguo Zhuanli Fa (中华人民共和国专利法) [Patent Law of the People's Republic of China] (promulgated by the Standing Comm. Nat'l People's Cong., March 12, 1984, effective September 12, 1992).

54 Intellectual Property And TRIPS Compliance in China. Chinese And European Perspectives 12 (Paul Torremans, H. Shan & J. Erauw eds, Edward Elgar, 2007).

for small hydropower resources. In the 1990s, as a result of the particular emphasis on environmental protection, the government expanded its support to include wind power, solar energy, and biomass technologies. Instead of supply subsidies, government support shifted to tax reductions or exemptions, preferential pricing, and credit guarantees, among other types of assistance. These measures have contributed greatly to renewable energy development in China.

Tax breaks are specifically called for in Article 26 of the Renewable Energy Law: "The Government grants tax benefits to projects listed in the renewable energy industrial development guidance catalogue, and specific methods are to be prepared by the State Council."[55] Tax incentives might include investment tax incentives, production tax incentives, Value-Added Tax (VAT) reductions, reductions on import duty, property tax exemptions, tax reductions, and R&D tax credits. As way of example, a reduced Corporate Income Tax (CIT) rate of 15 per cent is given for qualified advanced and new technology enterprises in the fields of – among others – solar energy, wind energy, biomaterial energy, and geothermal energy, and 50 per cent refund of VAT is paid on the sale of wind power.[56]

IV Results of the analysis: The central role played by domestic policies in addressing the issue of technology transfer

The analysis of the development patterns of China's wind power industry led me to conclude that, despite the relevance of efforts and steps taken at the international level to facilitate and encourage technology transfer to developing countries, the key is domestic action: the creation of a strong legal structure and a suitable investment scenario in the host country is the main driver of technology transfer, while contributing to the country's development.

First, the model of technology transfer chosen by Chinese companies together with their foreign partners played a crucial role in China's success in acquiring foreign technology in a productive way. Foreign companies can pursue several options to enter the Chinese market: either form a joint venture with a Chinese partner or license the right to use a technology to a Chinese company.[57] Goldwind – as most Chinese companies in the sector – chose the latter.[58] Goldwind went a step further and started purchasing majority control of wind

55 Renewable Energy Law, *supra* note 47, Article 26.

56 KPMG, Taxes and Incentives for Renewable Energy, at 16 (2011), http://www.kpmg.com/Global/en/IssuesAndInsights/ArticlesPublications/Documents/Taxes-Incentives-Renewable-Energy-2011.pdf (last visited July 14, 2016).

57 The reasons why foreign companies might decide to establish a joint venture in China to manufacture wind turbines include the hope to benefit from lower costs, looser environmental and labor regulations, and preferential treatment offered by the central government.

58 Charles M. Perry & Robert L. Pfaltzgraff, Selling The Rope To Hang Capitalism?: The Debate On West-East Trade & Technology Transfer 231 (Pergamon-Brassey's, 1987); Denis Goulet, The Uncertain Promise: Value Conflicts in Technology Transfer 61 (New Horizons Press, 1989); Christian Ndubisi Madu, Strategic Planning In Technology Transfer To Less Developed Countries 3 (Quorum Books, 1992); Kamal Saggi, International Technology Transfer To Developing Countries 76 (Commonwealth Secretariat, 2004); Josef Drexl, Research Handbook On Intellectual Property And Competition Law 202 (Edward Elgar, 2008). Chinese companies are not the only ones with a strong preference for multiple licensing agreements. Indian companies tend to sign very similar agreements. The leading Indian wind turbine manufacturer Suzlon signed licensing agreements with several foreign companies – such as Sudwind, Aerpae, and Enron Wind – and then, building on the knowledge gained through these transfers, it later on formed many overseas subsidiaries. *See* Joanna Lewis, *supra* note 38, at 227.

turbine technology and components suppliers – for example with Vensys. This strategy further allows local companies to benefit from their own products and from the results of their research and development. The shift in Goldwind's strategy – from importer of foreign products to local manufacturer – was possible because of the combination of the company's new strategy, the new more-relaxed regulations on foreign investment and joint ventures by the central government, and foreign investors' growing confidence in the Chinese market.

In order to develop R&D and attract foreign direct investments (FDIs), the legal system needs to be strong and reliable from a foreign investor's point of view. In particular, the laws relating to joint ventures and foreign partnerships need to be amended in order for host countries to become suitable for foreign investment and subsequent transfer of technologies. As a matter of fact, well-established companies overseas may find it quite risky to transfer their technology to companies that could potentially become competitors. This is especially true when the transfer occurs between a developed and a less-developed country, where both labor and raw materials are cheaper. It should not be surprising then that foreign investment in China has positively increased with the country's transition to a market economy, which has been accomplished through, among others, the gradual relaxation of the legal framework governing the operations of foreign firms in China, including investment, ownership, partnership models, local content utilization, and technology transfer requirements.

Finally, the new Intellectual Property legal framework further contributed to fostering technology transfer. A robust patent system an efficient enforcement mechanism are prerequisites for both investment and technology transfer. Without patent protection, no business is comfortable in disclosing its technologies or investing in R&D. Patents create a safe environment in which business and further R&D may be conducted. Without adequate protection from leakage of new technical information, firms would be less willing to provide it on open technology markets.[59] Moreover, patents and trade secrets provide the legal basis for revealing the proprietary characteristics of technologies to subsidiaries and licensees, supporting the formation of contracts.

V Conclusions: The international trade law dimension

'Green' technology transfer is indeed a key component of a coherent global strategy aimed at addressing the negative effects of climate change. The international community is developing a number of mechanisms to encourage such transfer to developing countries, as it is

59 *See* KAMIL IDRIS, INTELLECTUAL PROPERTY: A POWER TOOL FOR ECONOMIC GROWTH 80 (World Intellectual Property Organization, 2003); Keith E. Maskus & Mohan Penubarti, *How Trade-Related are Intellectual Property Rights?*, 39 J. OF INT'L ECON. 227–248 (1995). For a comprehensive analysis of the role played by IPR protection in technology transfer models, *see* NAGESH KUMAR, GLOBALISATION, FOREIGN DIRECT INVESTMENT AND TECHNOLOGY TRANSFERS. IMPACT ON AND PROSPECTS FOR DEVELOPING COUNTRIES (Routledge, 1998); Nagesh Kumar, *Technology Generation and Technology Transfers in the World Economy: Recent Trends and Implications for Developing Countries,* 3 SCI., TECH. & SOC'Y 265–306 (1998); Dominique Foray, *Technology Transfer in the TRIPS Age: The Need for New Types of Partnerships Between the Leas Developed and Most Advanced Economies* 30 (ICTSD, 2008); Cameron Hutchison, *Does TRIPS Facilitate or Impede Climate Change Technology Transfer into Developing Countries?*, 3 U. OTTAWA L. & TECH. J. (2006); Yi Qian, *Do National Patent Laws Stimulate Domestic Innovation in a Global Patenting Environment? A Cross-Country Analysis of Pharmaceutical Patent Protection*, 1978–2002 89 REV. ECON. & STAT. 436–453 (2007); Hoekman, Maskus & Saggi, *supra* note 16; Phillip McCalman, *Reaping What You Sow: An Empirical Analysis of International Patent Harmonization,* 55 J. INT'L ECON. 161–186 (2001).

seen as a way to overcome the North–South division that characterizes the climate change debate. However, for these mechanisms to be effective, the receiving country needs to implement a cohesive strategy, designed to create the correct environment for technology transfer to flourish. The goal of this contribution was to highlight the role played by domestic policies in attracting foreign technologies and contributing to the creation of a suitable environment in developing countries, allowing them to build their domestic capacity and advance economically. In my conclusions, I want to turn to one final lesson that can be drawn from the Chinese experience: the importance of designing and implementing domestic policies keeping in mind international rules and obligations. The United States (US) challenged some of China's policies when, on October 15, 2010, the US Trade Representative (USTR) launched an investigation related to a variety of Chinese policies and practices affecting trade and investment in the wind power technology sector.[60] According to the USTR, a number of these policies directly violate the obligations China undertook when it joined the WTO in 2001. Even though China denied each one of the US' accusations,[61] this conflict clearly shows that even though the government support worked to boost China's energy sector, on the other hand, it is easy to cross the line and violate international rules. Thus, if it is true that government support is generally positive and should be incentivized in developing countries, the support must be regulated rather than unfettered. As the US–China case demonstrates, trade rules are deeply involved, and, therefore, a trade organization might be able to find solutions which take into account the trade-related aspects of a non-trade concern, such as renewable-energy technology transfer to deal with climate change.

If, on the one hand, China can be used as an example to follow when it comes to the way the legal framework has been transformed and investments have been prioritized, on the other, it shows how governments need to be careful when implementing their plans and programs and cannot overlook international rules and standards. Domestic policies can play a crucial role in advancing a country's technological development, and they will if they are integrated in the broader international legal framework each country is part of.

60 The USTR investigation was based on a petition filed on September 9, 2010 by the USW. C. Moyer, J. Wang & T. P. Stewart, on behalf of the United Steel, Paper and Forestry, Rubber, Manufacturing, Energy, Allied Industrial and Service Workers International Union, AFL-CIO CLC (USW), *China Policies Affecting Trade and Investment in Green Technology*, Petition for Relief under Section 301 of the Trade Act of 1974 as amended before the United States Trade Representative (USTR), Vol. 1 of 9: Petition and Exhibits s.1, September 9, 2010, at 208. As cited in Paolo Davide Farah & Piercarlo Rossi, *National Energy Policies and Energy Security in the Context of Climate Change and Global Environmental Risks: A Theoretical Framework for Reconciling Domestic and International Law through a Multiscalar and Multilevel Approach*, 20(6) Eur. Energy & Envtl. L. Rev. 232, 235–238 (2011). The text of the petition is available on the USTR website, at http://www.ustr.gov/about-us/press-office/reports-and-publications/2010/petition-chinas-policies-affecting-trade-and-inv. The United States have then requested a consultation to the WTO Dispute Settlement Body: *China – Measures concerning Wind Power Equipment*, WT/DS419.

61 S. Liu, Comment Provided on behalf of the Bureau of Fair Trade, Ministry of Commerce, China, *A Choice between Win-Win & Lose-Lose Scenarios*, Docket No. USTR-2010–0028, at 56.

12 China's Environmental Legislation and its Trend Towards Scientific Development*

Weidong He

Environmental protection in contemporary China

Since the advent of the "reform and opening-up" policy in the late 1970s, China's economy has developed rapidly and continuously, and its gross domestic product (GDP) has grown by an annual average of almost 10 per cent in the past 30 years.[1] However, the rapid development has created serious problems for China's environment because China's traditional model of economic development relies on exploitation of natural resources, pollution of the environment, ecological degradation, and energy consumption, which lead not only to air, water, and solid waste pollution, but also to severe ecological degeneration. The conflict between environmental protection and economic development is becoming ever more prominent.[2] A relative shortage of resources, a fragile ecological environment, and insufficient environmental capacity now hinder China's development.[3]

* This chapter is part of the results of the Research Project on "*Current Trends of Chinese Law towards Non-Trade Concerns such as Sustainable Development and the Protection of Environment, Public Health, Food Safety, Cultural, Social and Economic Rights, Labor Rights and the Reduction of Poverty from the Perspective of International Law and WTO Law*" coordinated by Professor Paolo Davide Farah at gLAWcal – Global Law Initiatives for Sustainable Development (United Kingdom) and at West Virginia University John D. Rockefeller IV School of Policy and Politics, Department of Public Administration, in partnership with the Center of Advanced Studies on Contemporary China (CASCC) in Turin (Italy), Maastricht University Faculty of Law, Department of International and European Law and IGIR – Institute for Globalisation and International Regulation (Netherlands), and Tsinghua University, School of Law, Institute of Public International Law and the Center for Research on Intellectual Property Law in Beijing (China). An early draft of this chapter was presented at the Conferences Series on "*China's Influence on Non-Trade Concerns in International Economic Law*", First Conference held at the Center of Advanced Studies on Contemporary China (CASCC) in Turin on November 23–24, 2011. This publication and the Conference Series were sponsored by China–EU School of Law (CESL) at the China University of Political Science and Law (CUPL). The activities of CESL at CUPL are supported by the European Union and the People's Republic of China.

1 Zhonghua Renmin Gongheguo Guojia Tongjiju [National Bureau of Statistics China], *Zhongguo Tongji Nianjian* [China Statistical Yearbook] 2010, http://www.stats.gov.cn/tjsj/ndsj/2010/indexch.htm (last visited July 13, 2016).

2 UNDP, Sustainable development and the environment (UNDP, 1991); FAO, Sustainable development and the environment: FAO policies and actions, Stockholm 1972–Rio 1992 (FAO, 1992); S. Bhatt, Environment protection and sustainable development (A.P.H. Pub. Corp., 2004).

3 Zhonghua Renmin Gongheguo Guowuyuan Xinwen Bangongshi [The Information Office of China's State Council], *Zhongguo De Huanjingbaohu (1996–2005)* [Environmental Protection in China (1996–2005) (white paper 2006), http://www.china.com.cn/chinese/huanjing/1230422.htm (last visited July 13, 2016).

Characteristics of China's environmental issues

China's environmental issues are closely related to rapid industrialization and economic development[4]

Following China's rapid industrialization and economic development, its environmental problems have intensified. From the 1970s to the 1980s, China's environmental problems mainly stemmed from point source pollution; in the 1990s, the demand for resources from economic and social development constantly increased, which deteriorated the Chinese environmental and ecological system each year. Many of the environmental problems that have haunted developed countries in different phases of their 100-year industrialization process have afflicted China simultaneously, thus making its environmental problems even more complex.[5] In the last 30 years, China has encountered, among others, industry pollution, urban pollution, acid rain, ecological degeneration, global climate change, biodiversity depletion, and Persistent Organic Pollutants (POPs).

Rapid economic growth has caused huge pollution emissions and resource consumption

As mentioned above, China's development has occurred based on the traditional pattern of "large consumption and large production." At the current technology level, this system, while producing a large number of inexpensive Chinese products for the rest of the world, also leads to extremely high rates of pollution and ecological degradation.

According to estimates, China's emissions of sulfur dioxide, ozone depleting substances (ODS), and carbon dioxide all top the world list. Chemical oxygen demand (COD) and nitrogen oxide emissions also rank among the highest positions.[6]

Environmental problems migrate from urban to rural areas, from developed areas to the western and central regions

Similar to the "pollute first, control later" development model that developed countries have followed, China focused on environmental protection only after it achieved a certain degree of economic development, even though China has always tried to avoid excessive pollution.[7] At first, environmental problems mostly distressed some of the more developed areas, such as the areas of the Zhujiang Delta, the Yangtze Delta, and some of the most developed cities in China. Thanks to targeted environmental protection measures, increased economic development, and ecological awareness, local governments gradually balanced the relationship between the environment and development. Some regions have even advocated

4 Kristen A. Day, China's environment and the challenge of sustainable development (Columbia University, 2005); Gang Chen, Politics of China's environmental protection: problems and progress (World Scientific Publishing, 2009); World Bank, China: air, land, and water: environmental priorities for a new millenium (The World Bank, 2001).

5 *Id.*

6 Zhongguo Huanjing Yu Fazhan Guoji Hezuo Weiyuanhui [China Council for International Cooperation on Environment and Development (CCICED)], *Zhongguo Huanjing Yu Fazhan De Zhanlve Zhuanxing* [Strategy Transformation of Environment and Development in China], http://www.bjelf.com/news/bencandy.php?fid=46&id=998 (last visited July 13, 2016).

7 *See* Chapter 2 (Farah) in this volume.

"prioritizing environmental protection during the development process," and, as a result, these coastal and developed areas have seen the environmental situation improve in recent years.[8] In the meantime, the facilities and projects that cause severe pollution have moved from developed provinces to undeveloped and rural areas, where environmental management remains lax. In these regions, environmental protection often yields to economic development, especially in the central and western parts of China, thus creating a grim situation of severe pollution and ecological degeneration.

Environmental protection in China

Following the development of the domestic economy and the international environmental movement, the Chinese government has paid more and more attention to environmental issues, at least at the Chinese national government level.[9] In order to promote coordinated development between the economy, society, and the environment, China has undertaken a series of measures aimed at environmental protection since the late 1970s. For example, the National People's Congress (NPC) Standing Committee promulgated the Environmental Protection Law of the People's Republic of China for trial implementation in 1979. China established environmental protection as one of two basic national policies in the Second National Environmental Protection Conference in 1983. In the 1980s, China promulgated and put into effect many policies, laws, and regulations concerning environmental protection. The Chinese government formulated the guiding principles of simultaneous planning, implementation, and development for economic, urban, rural, and environmental construction, and combining the economic returns with social effects and environmental benefits. The government also carried out three major policies: "prevention first and combining prevention with control," "polluter pays principle," and "intensifying environmental management." In the 1990s, especially after the United Nations Conference on Environment and Development in 1992, which made sustainable development the common strategy for development in the future, the Chinese government advanced several documents on environmental protection and development, such as the Ten Major Countermeasures in Connection With Enhancing Chinese Environment and Development, and China's Agenda 21—White Paper on China's Population, Environment, and Development in the XXI Century, clearly establishing sustainable development as China's overall strategy and action plan.[10] These measures clearly demonstrate that environmental protection has risen as a priority in China.

In the twenty-first century, the Chinese government, embracing scientific development as the guiding principle for environmental protection, has proposed building a resource-efficient, environmentally friendly society, including harmony between human beings and nature.[11] Key to implementing this plan is the three following transformations: first, moving from giving weight to economic growth over environmental protection to paying equal

8 For example, ShenZhen City (Guandong Province) requires urban development should follow the principles of environmental priorities: Shēnzhèn jīngjì tèqū huánjìng bǎohù tiáolì (深圳经济特区环境保护条例) [Regulations of Shenzhen Special Economic Zone on Environmental Protection] (adopted by the Standing Committee of the First Shenzhen Municipal People's Cong., September 16, 1994, revised March 3, 2000), Article 3.

9 *See* Chapters 8 (Sindico & Gibson), 9 (Ibrahim, Deleuil & Farah), and 10 (Lemoine) in this volume.

10 *See* Chapters 9 (Ibrahim, Deleuil & Farah) and 14 (Peng) in this volume.

11 *See* Chapters 2 (Farah) and 17 (Heurtebise) in this volume.

attention to both matters; second, progressing from the fact that environmental protection lags behind economic growth to enabling the former to keep pace with the latter; and finally, shifting from protecting the environment mainly by administrative means to resorting to a combination of legal, economic, technical, and administrative instruments, if necessary.[12] These three transformations are directional, strategic, and of historic nature, and symbolize a new milestone in the history of China's environmental protection development.[13]

Analysis of the causes of China's contemporary environmental issues

It is manifest that China's environmental issues relate to its pattern of development, which, in order to guarantee rapid economic growth, leads to the consumption of large quantities of natural resources and to the discharge of a great deal of pollutants. In essence, China's contemporary environmental problems mainly result from prioritizing economic development over environmental interests and from seeking individual gains instead of the common good. Since China opened to the outside world in 1978, it has made economic construction its central task. Government agencies at all levels pursue economic interests or GDP above other considerations. The traditional GDP, however, represents economic development only and does not account for the environment. The current performance evaluation and promotion mechanism system, which only considers economic benefits in the short term, forces government workers to overemphasize GDP growth, thus paying short shrift to environmental protection.

As a result of the development of the economy since the 1970s, the pressure on resources and the fragile environment has intensified. After decades of rapid but unsustainable economic growth, environmental issues have gradually become the shackles of economic development. Since China requires more resources to support its future development, more pollutants are discharged into the air, water, and soil. At present, the international community regards China as a kind of "black hole" of resources consumption. The grave environmental situation may impede further economic development and threatens people's property and lives, Chinese society, and the whole country.[14] From both international and domestic points of views, and also considering the factors of economic, social, and environmental development, China must correct its improper developmental model and balance the relationship between environmental protection and economic and social development. With this understanding, China has recently taken a series of legal, economic, and educational measures to alleviate its environmental protection issues.

In general, although environmental protection in China has made progress, the severity and complexity of China's environmental situation has not seen any dramatic changes. Environmental pollution and ecological deterioration remain very serious in some areas, and the environmental issue has become one of the most important factors hindering China's sustainable development.

12 Wen Jiabao, *Quanmian Luoshi Kexuefazhanguan, Jiakuai Jianshe Huanjing Youhaoxing* Shehui [Thoroughly Fulfilling the Scientific Outlook on Development, Accelerating the development of an environment-friendly society], Di Liu Ci Quanguo Huanjingbaohu Dahui [sixth national environmental protection conference] (2006), http://news.xinhuanet.com/newscenter/2006-04/23/content_4463242.htm (last visited July 13, 2016).

13 Guojia Huanjingbaohu Zongju [State Environmental Protection Administration], Zhongguo Huanjingbaohu Zhuangkuang Gongbao [Report on the State of the Environment in China] (2005), at 4.

14 *See* Chapter 17 (Heurtebise) in this volume.

China's environmental legal system

An overview of Chinese environmental legislation[15]

In the past 30 years, China's environmental legislation has grown from scattered attempts into a progressively complete system. Legislative approaches have changed from controlling point source pollution to controlling pollution within regions and drainage basins, shifted from pollutants concentration control to total emissions control, modified from emphasizing command and control instruments to market-based instruments and public participation, and gone from prohibiting people from discharging pollutants that exceed the stipulated standards to also taking into consideration emission trading as well. Thus, China's environmental regulations and rules have become increasingly comprehensive, strict, and comparable to international standards for environmental protection.[16]

In addition, legislation in other fields has paid greater attention to environmental protection. The 1978 revision of the Constitution of the People's Republic of China[17] requires that "the state must protect environment and nature resources. It must prevent and control pollution and other public nuisance."[18] For the first time, language about environmental protection appeared in the national basic law system, which provides the basis for environmental protection legislation. The national basic law system establishes the protection of natural resources and pollution prevention as two main components of environmental protection legislation, thus laying the basic framework for China's environmental law and its main content.

China's civil law system has promulgated provisions on, among other rights, an environmental property right, a lighting right, the right to a healthy life, and the right to damage relief. For example, the 1986 General Principles of Civil Law of the People's Republic of China[19] specified the obligation to compensate any direct loss caused by environmental pollution. The 2007 Property Law of the People's Republic of China[20] set up ownership rules for natural resources, and the 2009 Tort Law of the People's Republic of China[21] made specific provisions on liability for environmental pollution in chapter Eight, entitled

15 *See* Xiaoying Ma & Leonard Ortolano, Environmental regulation in China: institutions, enforcement, and compliance (Rowman & Littlefield Publishers, 2000); Phillip Stalley, Foreign Firms, Investment, and Environmental Regulation in the People's Republic of China (Stanford University Press, 2010); William P. Alford & Yuanyuan Shen, ***Limits of the Law in Addressing China's Environmental Dilemma,*** 16 Stanford Envtl. L. J.l 125 (1997); Stefanie Beyer, ***Environmental Law and Policy in the People's Republic of China,*** 5(1) Chinese J. Int'l L. 185–211 (2006); Michael Palmer, ***Environmental Regulation in the People's Republic of China: The Face of Domestic Law,*** 156 China Q. 788–808 (1998).

16 *Zhongguo De Huanjingbaohu Shi* [China's History of Environmental Protection] (June 1, 2010), http://bbs.sciencenet.cn/home.php?mod=space&uid=238437&do=blog&id=431203 (last visited July 13, 2016).

17 Zhōnghuá Rénmín Gònghéguó Xiànfǎ (Xianfa).

18 *Id.*, Article 11(3).

19 Zhōnghuá Rénmín Gònghéguó Mínfǎ Tōngzé (中华人民共和国民法通则) [General Principles of the Civil Law of the People's Republic of China] (promulgated by the Nat'l People's Cong., April 12, 1986, effective August 27, 2009).

20 Zhōnghuá Rénmín Gònghéguó Wùquánfǎ (中华人民共和国物权法) [Property Law of the People's Republic of China] (promulgated by the Nat'l People's Cong., March 16, 2007).

21 Zhōnghuá Rénmín Gònghéguó Qīnquán Zérèn fǎ (中华人民共和国侵权责任法) [Tort Law of the People's Republic of China] (promulgated by the Standing Comm. of the Nat'l People's Cong., December 26, 2009).

"Liability for Environmental Pollution." In 1997, the NPC amended the Criminal Law of the People's Republic of China,[22] into which a new section on "Crime of Impairing the Protection of the Environment and Resources" was added to chapter Six, defining the penalty for actions that cause environmental pollution and resource damage. In the field of administrative law, the 2003 Administrative License Law of the People's Republic of China[23] set general rules on administrative permits and special provisions concerning environmental permits. The 2005 Public Security Administration Punishments Law of the People's Republic of China[24] established the administrative punishment system to respond to violations of environmental regulations that do not constitute a criminal offense, such as producing, preserving, transporting, mailing, using, or disposing of dangerous substances. In addition, the government has promulgated many more provisions concerning environmental protection in other administrative regulations.

By the end of 2009, China had enacted over 30 laws in the environmental protection sector, for example, the Environmental Protection Law,[25] the Marine Environment Protection Law,[26] and the Energy Conservation Law.[27] Environmental protection law has become one of the fastest-growing sectors among all the law categories of China.[28]

Fundamental principles and institutions of the Chinese environmental legal system

The Chinese environmental legal system has established at least four fundamental principles and several important institutions, including environmental impact assessment, synchronous project design, construction and completion of safety and sanitation facilities, pollution discharge declaration and registration, pollution discharge fee, elimination or control of pollution within a prescribed period of time, control of levels of pollution and pollution discharge permissions, and legal mechanisms concerning the planning, ownership, permission, paid use, and energy conservation assessment of natural resources. Some of them are legal instruments applicable in both fields of pollution prevention and ecological preservation.

22 Zhōnghuá rénmín gònghéguó xíngshì sùsòng fǎ (中华人民共和国刑事诉讼法) [Criminal Procedure Law of the People's Republic of China] (promulgated by the Standing Comm. of Nat'l People's Cong., July 7, 1979, effective Jan 1, 1997).

23 Zhōnghuá Rénmín Gònghéguó Xíngzhèng Xǔkě fǎ (中华人民共和国行政许可法) [Administrative License Law of the People's Republic of China] (promulgated by the Standing Comm. of the Nat'l People's Cong., August 27, 2003).

24 Zhōnghuá Rénmín Gònghéguó Zhì'ān Guǎnlǐ Chǔfá Fǎ (中华人民共和国治安管理处罚法) [Public Security Administration Punishments Law of the People's Republic of China] (promulgated by the Standing Comm. of the Nat'l People's Cong., August 28, 2005).

25 Zhōnghuá Rénmín Gònghéguó Huánjìng Bǎohù Fǎ (中华人民共和国环境保护法) [Environmental Protection Law of the People's Republic of China] (promulgated by the Standing Comm. of the Nat'l People's Cong., December 26, 1989; and on 24 April 2014 the Standing Committee of China's National People's Congress (NPC), voted to adopt revisions to the Environment Protection Law of the People's Republic of China).

26 Zhōnghuá Rénmín Gònghéguó Hǎiyáng Huánjìng Bǎohù Fǎ (中华人民共和国海洋环境保护法) [Marine Environmental Protection Law of the People's Republic of China] (promulgated by the Standing Comm. Of the Nat'l People's Cong., August 23, 1982, amended December 28, 2013).

27 Zhonghua Renmin Gongheguo Jieyue Nengyuan Fa (中华人民共和国节约能源法) [Energy Conservation Law of the People's Republic of China] (promulgated by the Standing Comm. of Nat'l People's Cong., November 1, 1997).

28 Zhongguo Faxuehui [China Legal Association], *Zhongguo Fazhi Jianshe Niandu Baogao* [Annual Report on China's Legal Development Under Rule of Law], (Xinhua Chubanshe [Xinhua Press] (2010)). See Chapters 13 (Luo Li), 14 (Peng), and 15 (Huang) in this volume.

Principle of coordination of environmental protection and economic and social development

This principle aims at regulating and managing the economy, urbanization, and the environment at the same pace, thus unifying social, economic, and environmental interests. Although the principle is not identical to the sustainable development principle, it could be regarded as a kind of transformation of the latter in China.

Principle of prevention first

The principle's text directs the government to "put [. . .] prevention first, and combine it with remedial measures to curb environmental issues." This principle emphasizes prevention rather than remedial measures. Its objective is to integrate environmental protection into national economic development in order to control and manage the environment and its issues.[29]

Principle of environmental liability

The principle of environmental liability originates from the "polluter pays principle," according to which the discharger of pollutants shall pay discharge fees for eliminating and controlling the pollution caused.[30] The principle states that "the developer protects, the damager restores, the beneficiary compensates and the polluter pays." The legal basis of this principle is laid down in the Environmental Protection Law.[31]

Public participation principle

Environmental protection also calls for public participation.[32] In contemporary China, the form of public participation in environmental protection includes supervisory rights on verification of environmental protection publicity before a company goes public, rights of access to environmental information fulfilled through reviewing environmental status published at different levels, environmental rights of remedies advocated in all kinds of environmental litigations, environmental rights of participating in policy-making by way of motions submitted to a session of the NPC, and proposals to the National Committee of the Chinese People's Political Consultative Conference (CPPCC). After the Revised Environmental Protection Law came into force on January 1, 2015, environment public-interest litigation had become one of the most important form of public participation in China.

"Three synchronizations"

This principle stipulates that environmental protection measures involving construction, technological innovation, and urbanization projects must be designed, constructed, and implemented along with the main buildings under construction. It constituted one of three former environmental legal institutions in China's first stage of environmental legislation and has been a core feature of the Chinese environmental protection system for the last three decades.[33]

29 Stefanie Beyer, *supra* note 15, at 200–203.
30 Stefanie Beyer, *supra* note 15, at 203–204.
31 *Supra* note 25, Article. 28.
32 Stefanie Beyer, *supra* note 15, at 208–209. See also Chapter 13 (Huang) in this volume.
33 Stefanie Beyer, *supra* note 15, at 201.

Environmental impact assessments

Environmental impact assessments (EIAs) are used for new and expanding projects that have potential adverse effects on the environment. In other words, before any such project commences, EIA surveys are conducted and reports are produced regarding every phase from site selection to design, construction, and implementation. EIAs are regarded as one of the most effective instruments for pollution and ecological damage prevention. During the 1970s, China introduced the concept of EIAs in the form of a national policy. Almost all subsequent environmental legislation and natural resources conservation laws have adopted this tool.

Environment-related fees and taxes

This tool is designed to employ the principle of environmental liability, and refers to collecting fees and taxes from parties who exploit the environment and its natural resources, including both pollution charges and fees for resource consumption. For example, the government collects sulfur dioxide discharge fees from all related enterprises, public institutions, and private businesses. It further charges for the treatment of urban sewage, garbage, and hazardous waste, so as to promote the marketization and industrialization of pollution control. Not only does the government levy taxes on certain products of natural resources, but it also extends tax reduction or exemption to enterprises engaged in environmental protection, such as making comprehensive use of resources and producing equipment for environmental protection, as well as enterprises using waste water, gas, and residues as their primary production materials.

Environmental licenses and permits

Environmental licenses and permits are part of the most important preventive measures of management and supervision in environmental protection worldwide. Breach of environmental licenses or permits can give rise to civil and criminal liabilities, as well as to administrative fines. Although some newly promulgated or revised laws and regulations have confirmed this institutional tool, China's permit system remains in its early development stage. The Environmental Protection Law, regarded as the fundamental environmental law, does not contain provisions on this matter.

Environmental protection target responsibility

The environmental protection target responsibility system identifies scientific assessment indicators and integrates them into the comprehensive evaluation system for the performance of party and government officials. Under this system, fragmented environmental targets and tasks go to local government agencies at all levels that carry out their own targets. The inclusion of the examination mechanism for environmental management performance and mainstream environmental protection into the economic and social development evaluation system helps to achieve sustainable development.

Evaluation of the implementation of Chinese environmental laws

Although it is generally accepted that China has developed a comprehensive system of environmental legislation, there are still a lot of issues to be addressed.[34] For instance, in the

34 Alford & Shen, *supra* note 15.

Chinese environmental legal system, some areas remain uncovered, some contents are yet to be amended or revised, most parts of the major laws in the environmental protection field focus on pollution control rather than nature preservation, environmental regulations at the local level are relatively weaker than those at the national level, and the gap in the legislation level between the more advanced countries and China persists to a large degree. Moreover, even though China has successfully formulated environmental laws, it has not implemented them with the same degree of success.

Some Chinese environmental law researchers regard Chinese environmental legal institutions as "not very useful in controlling pollution and conserving the ecological system."[35]

On the one hand, the Chinese government has promulgated a lot of environmental rules and regulations, but, paradoxically, China's environmental situation has generally deteriorated. The major causes that contribute to the environmental legislation's poor effectiveness are mainly found in two fields: the legislation itself and its enforcement.[36] The vagueness, abstractness, and almost exhortative terms characteristic of Chinese law are the biggest problems of the environmental legislation:[37] "Significant elements of most major environmental measures seem more akin to policy statements and propositions of ideals than to laws."[38] Other deficiencies in the environmental legislative process relate to disputes and compromises among relevant departments, lack of coherence between regulations, lack of public participation, interference from external factors, and legislative abilities, just to name a few. The lack of more stringent enforcement mechanisms, interference from local government, and other factors inevitably result in the low effectiveness of China's environmental law enforcement.[39]

Suggestions for improving the implementation of environmental laws

To cope with the issues plaguing the effectiveness of China's environmental laws, the government could take some specific measures in both the areas of legislation and enforcement.[40] In the legislative field, China should take all necessary steps to enhance legislation technology, increase the operability of legal provisions, and provide more effective measures of law enforcement. China should also increase the severity of punishments for violations of regulations, timely revise and update laws and regulations, fill the legislative gaps, strengthen legislation on enforcement procedures, and encourage public participation. In the enforcement field, China should establish a scientific and rational environmental management system so as to coordinate the relationships between the relevant administrative departments. The government should also explore other effective channels, including employing public security and other law enforcement departments for environmental protection, and encouraging public participation in the supervision and management of environmental laws.[41]

35 Shaofei Li, *The Legal Issues Of The Rural Environmental Protection,* 11 Outlook Weekly 28 (2011). Or *see* http://www.lwgcw.com/NewsShow.aspx?newsId=21014 (last visited July 13, 2016).

36 Weidong He, Assessment on Effectiveness of Chinese Environmental Legislation (scientific research trends, December 10–17, 2010).

37 For further reasoning regarding these particularities also in other fields of the Chinese legislation, see Chapters 2 (Farah), 5 (Choukroune), 23 (Creemers), and 25 (Friedmann) in this volume.

38 Alford & Shen, *supra* note 15, at 135.

39 Weidong He, supra note 36.

40 *See* Chapter 13 (Luo Li) in this volume.

41 *See* Chapter 15 (Huang) in this volume.

Besides these measures, China could also stipulate specific, operational legal provisions to encourage public participation, give more exposure to environmental laws to enhance people's environmental awareness, and expand channels of public supervision and reporting to reduce environmental violations.

China and international environmental cooperation

Before the 1970s, China rarely participated in global environmental protection affairs. In the early 1970s, China regained its legal status in the United Nations and sent a delegation to participate in the first United Nations Conference on Human Environment (UNCHE). Since then, China has participated in international environmental activities. Starting from the 1980s, China gradually joined various international environmental cooperation activities, and actively participated in almost all the major global environmental conventions and regional environmental treaties in every field, including control of marine pollution, ozone depletion, persistent organic pollutants, hazardous waste, biodiversity conservation, biosecurity, climate change, and combating desertification.

The international environmental movement's influence on China's environmental legislation

On the basis of actively participating in the international environmental cooperation and in many international environmental convention negotiations, China has conscientiously performed its international environmental duties in accordance with the procedures prescribed by the conventions, and it has constantly strived to ensure the performance of its international environmental obligations through domestic legislation, national action programs, strong environmental law enforcement, and international cooperation. These efforts have caused China's environmental policies and environmental laws to incorporate international trends, which can be found in aspects of the development and revision of policies and regulations that are in keeping with the international environmental policies and treaty obligations.[42]

In January 1993, the Chinese government approved the *China's national phase-out of ozone-depleting substances program*, thus establishing the multilateral fund project management system for the implementation of the Montreal Protocol on Ozone Depleting Substances. On April 29, 1999, the NPC Standing Committee approved the newly revised Law of the Peoples Republic of China on the Prevention and Control of Atmospheric Pollution,[43] which clearly stipulates that "Units that produce or import ozone-layer-depleting substances must, within the time limit prescribed by the State, carry out the production and import in accordance with the quotas approved by competent administrative authorities under the State Council."[44] Whoever violates the provisions shall be fined not less than 20,000 Chinese Yuan (CNY) and not more than 200,000 CNY. Given serious circumstances, the competent

42 *See* Chapters 8 (Sindico & Gibson), 9 (Ibrahim, Deleuil & Farah), 10 (Lemoine), 11 (Cima), 14 (Peng), and 15 (Huang) in this volume.

43 Zhōnghuá Rénmín Gònghéguó Dàqì Wūrǎn Fangzhì Fǎ 2000 xiūdìng (中华人民共和国大气污染防治法 2000 修订) [Law of the People's Republic of China on the Prevention and Control of Atmospheric Pollution (2000 Revision)] (promulgated by the Standing Comm. of the Nat'l People's Cong., April 29, 2000).

44 *Id.*, Article 45.

administrative department under the State Council may revoke the production or import quotas. On August 29, 2015, the National People's Congress approved and released the updated version of the PRC Law on Air Pollution Prevention and Control.[45]

Its Article 85 stipulates that"The state shall encourage and support efforts to produce and use substitutes for ozone depleting substances (ODS), to gradually reduce and eventually stop the production and use of ozone-depleting substances. The state shall implement total emission control and quotas to manage the production, use, import and export of ozone depleting substances (ODS). The specific implementation method is developed by the State Council.

In order to conform with the Convention on Biological Diversity (CBD), China developed and implemented the China National Biosafety Framework, National Ecological Protection Plan, and National Biological Species Resources Protection and Utilization Plan, as well as other conservation plans and standards. China also amended certain laws and regulations to protect biological diversity, including the Law on the Entry and Exit Animal and Plant Quarantine,[46] Regulations on Wild Plants Protection,[47] Seed Law,[48] Regulations on Nature Reserves,[49] Regulations on Administration of Agricultural Genetically Modified Organisms Safety,[50] Regulations on Protection of New Varieties of Plants,[51] Forest law,[52] Marine Environmental Protection Law,[53] and Fisheries Law.[54] Thus, China has formed the basic legal system of the conservation of biological diversity.

In order to fulfill China's obligations to the Stockholm Convention on Persistent Organic Pollutants, and to effectively implement the control and management of POPs, the State Council approved the ***National Implementation Plan to fulfill Stockholm Convention*** in April 2007. The plan established national performance objectives, measures, and specific actions and the new version of the PRC Law on Air Pollution Prevention and Control (2015

45 Law of the People's Republic of China on the Prevention and Control of Atmospheric Pollution (2015 Revision) (promulgated by the Standing Comm. Of the Nat'l People's Cong., August 29, 2015).

46 Zhōnghuá Rénmín Gònghéguó Jìn Chūjìng Dòng Zhíwù Jiǎnyì Fǎ (中华人民共和国进出境动植物检疫法) [Law of the People's Republic of China on the Entry and Exit Animal and Plant Quarantine] (promulgated by the Standing Comm. of the Nat'l People's Cong., October 30, 1991)

47 Zhōnghuá Rénmín Gònghéguó Yěshēng Zhíwù Bǎohù Tiáolì (中华人民共和国野生植物保护条例) [Regulations of the People's Republic of China on Wild Plants Protection] (promulgated by the State Council, September 30, 1996).

48 Zhōnghuá Rénmín Gònghéguó Zhǒngzǐ Fǎ (中华人民共和国种子法) [The Seed Law of the People's Republic of China] (promulgated by the Standing Comm. Of the Nat'l People's Cong., July 8, 2000).

49 Zhōnghuá Rénmín Gònghéguó Zìrán Bǎohù Qū Tiáolì (中华人民共和国自然保护区条例) [Regulations of the People's Republic of China on Nature Reserves] (promulgated by the State Council, October 9, 1994, effective January 8, 2011).

50 Nóngyè Zhuǎnjīyīn Shēngwù Ānquán Guǎnlǐ Tiáolì (农业转基因生物安全管理条例) [Regulations on Administration of Agricultural Genetically Modified Organisms Safety] (promulgated by the State Council, May. 23, 2001, effective January 8, 2011).

51 Zhōnghuá Rénmín Gònghéguó Zhíwù Xīn Pǐnzhǒng Bǎohù Tiáolì (中华人民共和国植物新品种保护条例) [Regulation of the People's Republic of China on Protection of New Varieties of Plants] (promulgated by the State Council, March 20, 1997, effective March 1, 2013).

52 Zhōnghuá Rénmín Gònghéguó Sēnlín Fǎ (1998 Xiūzhèng) (中华人民共和国森林法 1998 修正) [Forest Law of the People's Republic of China 1998 Amendment] (promulgated by the Standing Comm. of the Nat'l People's Cong., April 29, 1998).

53 *Supra* note 26.

54 Zhōnghuá Rénmín Gònghéguó Yúyè Fǎ (中华人民共和国渔业法) [Fisheries Law of the People's Republic of China] (promulgated by the Standing Comm. of the Nat'l People's Cong., January 20, 1986, amended August 28, 2004).

Revision) at Article 79 stipulates that "Enterprises, institutions and other operators that discharge persistent organic pollutants into the atmosphere, as well as entities with waste combustion facilities shall, according to State regulations, adopt technologies and processes that reduce persistent organic pollutant emissions, and install purification devices to meet emission standards".

In order to fulfill China's obligations to the Convention on Climate Change, the State Council promulgated China's first climate change policy document – the *National Program on Climate Change* – a comprehensive exposition of China's climate change response prior to 2010.[55] China also utilizes the legislative process for energy conservation, renewable energy, recycling, and enhanced carbon sinks. In 2007, the NPC Standing Committee amended the Energy Conservation Law, stipulated that energy conservation plays a strategic role in China's economic and social development, expanded the adjustment range of the Law on Energy Conservation, and increased the requirements of building energy conservation, transportation energy saving, and public sectors' energy efficiency. Accordingly, the State Council revised and improved the Domestic Building Energy Conservation Regulations[56] and Energy Conservation Regulation for State-funded Institutions.[57] Moreover, to speed up the use of renewable energy and development, the NPC Standing Committee amended the Renewable Energy Law in December 2009.[58] In addition, the NPC Standing Committee has developed the Cleaner Production Promotion Law,[59] the Circular Economy Promotion Law,[60] and other laws to reduce pollution from the source. The State Council and relevant departments also developed a large number of related administrative regulations and departmental rules.

China's stand on participating in international environmental cooperation and the reasons behind it

China's cooperation with international environmental efforts stems from three basic positions: the first is sustainable development, that is, to respect other countries' choices of sustainable development models according to their domestic conditions and development processes and, on this basis, to encourage the relevant countries and regions to take concerted action to address global and regional environmental issues.[61] The second stand is international cooperation, that is, to strengthen international environmental technology and financial cooperation, to protect intellectual property, to eliminate communication barriers, to establish a reasonable transfer mechanism, to further eliminate the formation of trade

55 *See* Chapter 14 (Peng) in this volume.

56 Mínyòng Jiànzhú Jiénéng Tiáolì (民用建筑节能条例) [Regulation on Energy Conservation in Civil Buildings] (promulgated by the State Council, August 1, 2008).

57 Gōnggòng Jīgòu Jiénéng Tiáolì (公共机构节能条例) [Energy Conservation Regulation for State-funded Institutions] (promulgated by the State Council, August 1, 2008, effective October 1, 2008).

58 *See* Chapter 11 (Cima) in this volume.

59 Zhōnghuá Rénmín Gònghéguó Qīngjié Shēngchǎn Cùjìn Fǎ (中华人民共和国清洁生产促进法) [Law of the People's Republic of China on Promoting Clean Production] (promulgated by the Standing Comm. of the Nat'l People's Cong., June 29, 2002; amended Feb 29, 2012).

60 Zhōnghuá Rénmín Gònghéguó Xúnhuán Jīngjì Cùjìn Fǎ (中华人民共和国循环经济促进法) [Circular Economy Promotion Law of the People's Republic of China] (promulgated by the Standing Comm. Of the Nat'l People's Cong., August 29, 2008, effective January 1, 2009).

61 Ann Kent, Beyond compliance: China, international organizations, and global security 144–180 (NUS Press, 2009).

barriers due to high environmental standards, and to promote the simultaneous development of environmental protection and international trade.[62] On this basis, China will seek active cooperation with the global community on its environmental protection policies and sustainable development model. The third stand is differentiated responsibilities, that is, under the principle of "common but differentiated responsibilities," developed countries should shoulder more responsibility for global environmental protection.[63] Developing countries should continue to improve the quality of their economic growth, synergistically coordinate and promote environmental protection and economic development policies, and actively cooperate with the international community.

In the past 30 years, China has actively participated in negotiations on international environmental conventions and conscientiously implemented their regulations. Seeking the reasons for this behavior, one has to take two different aspects into consideration. First, the Chinese government has looked for opportunities to join international political and diplomatic activities, and the international community regards the problem of international environmental protection as one of the most important issues. Participation in environmental affairs creates a positive international image and promotes peaceful diplomatic ties. Therefore, the starting point for China's active participation in international environmental cooperation does not significantly differ from its participation in other international affairs. Second, domestic environmental problems have severely constrained China's economic and social development. The implementation of international environmental conventions helps to improve China's environmental technology, to strengthen the competence of its environmental law, and therefore facilitates the introduction of international funds and foreign technology investments.[64] The seriousness of environmental problems and the enormous international pressure make China's participation in international environmental cooperation appear flexible when compared with its participation in other areas of international affairs.[65]

From the trend of China's economic and social development, with increasingly severe problems related to natural resources and the environment and affecting the economic and social development of the country, with people's higher need for a comfortable and beautiful environment, as well as the ever-increasing international environmental protection external pressure, China made a significant decision, that is, to build an environment-friendly and resource-saving society. This strategy gradually starts from the top level of the government and moves to lower levels, and moves from the developed eastern regions to the less-developed western provinces and cities. In this context, one can foresee that in the next few years China's environmental legal system will make significant progress and, on the basis of a coordinated economic, social, and environmental development, will play an increasingly important role in the international environmental movement.

62 *See* Chapter 11 (Cima) in this volume.

63 For an analysis of this principle, *see* Chapter 9 (Ibrahim, Deleuil & Farah) in this volume. *See* also Chapters 10 (Lemoine) and 17 (Heurtebise) in this volume.

64 *See* Chapter 11 (Cima) in this volume.

65 This is manifest in the field of Global Climate Change Governance. *See* Chapter 14 (Peng) in this volume.

13 Research on the Reform of the Judicial Relief System for Environmental Disputes in China*

Luo Li

The reform of the judicial relief system for environmental disputes in China

Presently, China has developed a system of judicial relief for environmental disputes that integrates administrative litigation, criminal litigation, and civil litigation. This system has generated discernible positive effects in the implementation of punishing perpetrators, inhibiting environmental pollution and destruction, and providing relief to victims as well as other objectives.

Administrative litigation for environmental disputes

The development of administrative litigation for environmental disputes in China has had two stages. The first stage progressed in accordance with the trial phase of civil litigation procedure (prior to October 1, 1990). During this period, according to Article 3, paragraph 2 of the Civil Procedure Law of the People's Republic of China[1] (for trial implementation) (hereinafter Civil Procedure Law) now expired and the Supreme Court Notice on the Establishment of Administrative Tribunals, administrative cases for environmental disputes in China were accepted and heard by either civil or economic tribunals according to civil

* This chapter is part of the results of the Research Project on "*Current Trends of Chinese Law towards Non-Trade Concerns such as Sustainable Development and the Protection of Environment, Public Health, Food Safety, Cultural, Social and Economic Rights, Labor Rights and the Reduction of Poverty from the Perspective of International Law and WTO Law*" coordinated by Professor Paolo Davide Farah at gLAWcal – Global Law Initiatives for Sustainable Development (United Kingdom) and at West Virginia University John D. Rockefeller IV School of Policy and Politics, Department of Public Administration, in partnership with the Center of Advanced Studies on Contemporary China (CASCC) in Turin (Italy), Maastricht University Faculty of Law, Department of International and European Law and IGIR – Institute for Globalisation and International Regulation (Netherlands), and Tsinghua University, School of Law, Institute of Public International Law and the Center for Research on Intellectual Property Law in Beijing (China). An early draft of this chapter was presented at the Conferences Series on "*China's Influence on Non-Trade Concerns in International Economic Law*", First Conference held at the Center of Advanced Studies on Contemporary China (CASCC) in Turin on November 23–24, 2011. This publication and the Conference Series were sponsored by China–EU School of Law (CESL) at the China University of Political Science and Law (CUPL). The activities of CESL at CUPL are supported by the European Union and the People's Republic of China.

1 Zhōnghuá Rénmín Gònghéguó Mínshì Sùsòng Fǎ (Shìxíng) (中华人民共和国民事诉讼法 (试行) [Civil Procedure Law of the People's Republic of China (For Trial Implementation)] (promulgated by the Standing Comm. of the Nat'l People's Cong., March 8, 1982).

procedure. The second stage unfolded in accordance with the trial phase of administrative litigation procedure (October 1, 1990, onwards). According to Article 11 of the Administrative Procedure Law of the People's Republic of China[2] (hereinafter Administrative Procedure Law) if citizens, legal persons, and other organizations refuse to accept the specific administrative actions of Article 11, they can bring an administrative lawsuit. Following the implementation of the Administrative Procedural Law, there has been a noticeable rising trend in China's environmental administrative litigation cases.[3]

Civil procedure for environmental disputes

Following the development process of China's judicial institutions, civil proceedings for environmental disputes took place in various judicial tribunals, including economic tribunals. Chongqing Municipal Intermediate People's Court established the first national economic division in February 1979. On July 1, 1979, the regulations for establishing economic tribunals within Supreme People's Courts, Higher People's Courts, and Intermediate People's Courts of provincial cities, provinces, autonomous regions, and cities (which were approved by the Second Meeting of the Fifth National People's Congress), created the legal basis for the formation of economic tribunals and the development of economic administrative judgments. Following the implementation of the Organic Law of the People's Court of the People's Republic of China[4] (January 1, 1980), the Higher People's Courts in some provinces, municipalities, and autonomous regions and the Intermediate People's Court in some areas began to institute economic tribunals one by one.

According to the needs of local economic trial practice, the Supreme People's Court promulgated the *Preliminary Views of the Supreme People's Court Economic Tribunals on the Scope of People's Court Economic Tribunals' Case* (hereinafter, *Preliminary Views*), which clearly stipulate that the economic tribunals of the People's Court may temporarily accept three types of cases: economic disputes, economic crimes, and economic cases involving foreign interests. Among them, "disputes regarding environmental protection" belong to "economic disputes," and "cases [involving] major accidents where factories, mining, [and] construction companies have major responsibilities" belong to " economic crimes."[5]

According to the Highest People's Court Explanations of the *Preliminary views on the range of acceptable cases for the economic division of the People's Court*,[6] the phrase, "disputes regarding environmental protection," refers to disputes between the environmental protection authorities that implement environmental protection laws and decrees and other companies or institutions as well as disputes between the parties that request

2 Zhōnghuá Rénmín Gònghéguó Xíngzhèng Sùsòng Fǎ (中华人民共和国行政诉讼法) [Administrative Procedure Law of the People's Republic of China] (promulgated by Nat'l People's Cong., April 4, 1989).

3 Luo Li, *Zhongguo Huanjing Jiufen Sifa Jiuji Tujing Yanjiu* [*Research About The Judicial Remedy For China's Environmental Disputes*], 1 Faxue jiazhi [Law Science Magazine] 102 (2009).

4 Zhōnghuá Rénmín Gònghéguó Rénmín Fǎyuàn Zǔzhī Fǎ (中华人民共和国人民法院组织法) [Organic Law of the People's Courts of the People's Republic of China] (promulgated by the Standing Comm. Of the Nat'l People's Cong., July 5, 1979, effective January 1, 1980).

5 *Zuigao Renmin Fayuan Jingji Shenpanting Guanyu Renmin Fayuan Jingji Shenpan ting Shouan Fanwei de Chubu Yijian* [*The Supreme People's Court. the Preliminary Views of the Supreme People's Court Economic Tribunals on the Scope of People's Court Economic Tribunals' Case*] (August 8, 1980).

6 *Id*.

reparation for environmental damages and the parties responsible for the same damages. From this definition, one can see that the characteristics of "disputes regarding environmental protection" lead us to classifying them as civil cases. However, the Explanations lack more detailed instructions regarding "cases [involving] major accidents where factories, mining, [and] construction companies have major responsibilities." Since these disputes may cause environmental pollution or devastation, any such harm is to be treated as an "economic crime" and is thus to be heard by an economic division in accordance with civil procedure.

From this point of view, one can see that there are cases where judicial relief for environmental disputes presents an integration of civil, administrative, and criminal characteristics. For example, economic disputes that belong to the "disputes regarding environmental protection" category, or economic crimes that led to economic pollution or devastation because they "[involve] major accidents where factories, mining, [and] construction companies have major responsibilities," are usually assigned to economic divisions in accordance with civil procedure.

In the second stage, civil divisions hear the cases. During the reform of the court's trial organization, the Supreme People's Court made the decision in early August 2000 to build a large civil structure and improve the criminal, civil, and administrative trial system, thereby making the classification of the People's Courts' responsibilities clearer and more scientifically sound.[7] An important reform concerned the establishment of trial divisions, which cancelled the original economic divisions and established four civil tribunals that act as the first senate of civil trials on special hearings of marriage and family-type cases, personal rights, and real estate disputes; the second senate of civil trials on contract and infringement disputes between legal persons and other economic organizations; the third senate of civil trials on copyrights and trademark privileges, patents, technology contracts, and other intellectual property cases; and the fourth senate of civil trials on maritime cases. One can therefore see that the second senate usually accepts civil cases regarding environmental disputes, while the fourth senate hears maritime disputes.[8]

Criminal litigation

Criminal procedures for environmental disputes in China experienced two developmental stages. The first preceded the revised Criminal Law of the People's Republic of China[9] (hereinafter Criminal Law) in 1997. During this period, some relevant regulations could also be found in China's substantive legislation. For example, in *the* Environmental Protection Law of the People's Republic of China[10] (for Trial Implementation), Article 32 clearly required that the leaders, direct persons liable, and other persons causing serious

7 *See* Luo Li, *supra* note 3, at 103.

8 Zhu Mingshan, *Zai Zuigao Renmin Fayuan Jigou Gaige Xinwen Fabuhui shangde Jianghua* [*The speech of the vice president of the Supreme People's Court at the Supreme People's Court of institutional reform news conference*], RENMIN FAYUAN BAO [PEOPLE'S COURT DAILY] (August 9, 2000).

9 Zhōng Zhōnghuá Rénmín Gònghéguó Xíngfǎ (97 Xiūdìng) (中华人民共和国刑法 97 修订) [Criminal Law of the People's Republic of China (97 Revision)] (promulgated by the Nat'l People's Cong., March 14, 1997).

10 Zhōnghuá Rénmín Gònghéguó Huánjìng Bǎohù Fǎ (中华人民共和国环境保护法) [Environmental Protection Law of the People's Republic of China] (promulgated by the Standing Comm. Of the Nat'l People's Cong., December 26, 1989).

environmental pollution or damage leading to casualties or heavy losses of public or private property in farming, forestry, animal husbandry, sideline production, and fishery, should bear administrative, economic, or even criminal responsibility. Article 114 of the revised Criminal Law clearly provided that if any staff member or worker of a factory, mine, forestry center, construction enterprise, or other enterprise or institution disobeys management and violates the rules and regulations or forces workers to work in a hazardous manner in violation of the rules and thereby causes a serious accident involving injury, death, or other serious consequences, he or she shall be sentenced to fixed-term imprisonment of up to three years of criminal detention; if the circumstances are especially flagrant, he or she shall be sentenced to fixed-term imprisonment of not less than three years and not more than seven years. According to Article 115, if anyone violates the regulations concerning the handling of explosive, inflammable, radioactive, poisonous, or corrosive materials and thereby causes a serious accident during the production, storage, transportation, or use of those materials, he or she shall be sentenced to fixed-term imprisonment of up to three years of criminal detention; if the consequences are especially serious, he or she shall be sentenced to fixed-term imprisonment of not less than three years and not more than seven years.

The second stage materialized with the revision of the *Criminal Law* in 1997. In order to increase the penalties for environmental crimes and use stricter legal means to protect the ecological environment, Section 6, "Crimes of Undermining Protection of Environmental Resources," made the serious pollution of the land, air, water, forests, and other natural resources a criminal offense. Section 6 clearly defined different types of environmental crimes such as "serious environmental pollution accident," "disposal of solid waste imported," "unauthorized imports of solid waste," "illegal fishing for aquatic products," "illegal hunting, killing of endangered wildlife," "illegal acquisition, transporting, and selling rare and endangered wildlife," "illegal occupation of agricultural land," "illegal mining," "destructive mining," "illegal logging and destruction of precious trees," "illegal felling of trees," "illegal denudation," "illegal deforestation," and "illicit acquisition, felling and deforestation."[11] Amendment VIII to the Criminal Law was the first step towards improving Articles 338 and 343.[12] These rules play an important role in protecting environmental resources.

11 *See* Luo Li, *supra* note 3, at 103.

12 *Zhonghua Renmin Gongheguo Xingfa Xiuzhengan(八) [Amendment (VIII) to the Criminal Law of the People's Republic of China]*. Article 46: Article 338 is amended as: "Whoever, in violation of the state provisions, discharges, dumps or disposes of any radioactive waste, any waste containing pathogens of any infectious disease, any poisonous substance or any other hazardous substance, which has caused serious environmental pollution, shall be sentenced to imprisonment of not more than 3 years or criminal detention and/or a fine; or if there are especially serious consequences, be sentenced to imprisonment of not less than 3 years but not more than 7 years and a fine." Article 47, Paragraph 1 of Article 343 is amended as: "Whoever, in violation of the Mineral Resources Law, engages in mining without a mining permit, enters a mining area under state planning, a mining area of great value to the national economy or a mining area of any other person to engage in mining without approval, or engages in mining of a special mineral which is subject to protective excavation according to the state provisions without approval shall be sentenced to imprisonment of not more than 3 years, criminal detention or control and/or a fine if the circumstances are serious; or if the circumstances are especially serious, be sentenced to imprisonment of not less than 3 years but not more than 7 years and a fine."

The recent development of the judicial relief system for environmental disputes in China

The trend of establishing trial divisions of environmental protection and environmental protection courts

On November 20, 2007, the Intermediate People's Court in Guiyang City established the first environmental protection trial division in China.[13] According to the regulations of the trial division, the court's jurisdiction includes water resources protection of the "two lakes, one bank" area (which includes the Hongfeng lake and the Baihua and Aha Reservoirs), the protection of water and soil in the Guiyang area, sewage infringement, forest protection, compensation for damages, environmental public interest litigation, and other types of first and second instances of civil, administrative, criminal, and related enforcement cases. In accordance with the designated jurisdiction decision transmitted by the High Court, the trial division oversees the protection of water resources, management, infringement, and other civil, administrative, and related cases of first instance outside the "two lakes, one bank" area of Guiyang City. The environmental protection court's primary responsibility is to handle cases regarding water resources protection involving the "two lakes, one bank" area, sewage infringement of the water, soil, and forest protection in Guiyang City, compensation for damages, environmental public interest litigation, and other types of first and second instances of civil, administrative, criminal, and related enforcement cases based on the following designated jurisdiction decision transmitted by the High Court and Court; and also involves "two lakes, one bank" area protection of water resources, management, and infringement of civil and administrative cases of first instance, and related enforcement cases.[14]

Having this example of the first trial division, other Chinese cities have successively set up trial divisions and courts for environmental protection. On May 5, 2008, the Intermediate People's Court in Wuxi City (Jiangsu Province) announced the establishment of its environmental protection trial division – the second such division in China. Following the formation of the environmental protection trial division, the Wuxi municipal district area – Yixing District, Jiangyin District, Binhu District, Xishan District, and Huishan District's grassroots courts – also formally established the Environmental Protection Collegiate Bench. The environmental protection trial division in Wuxi City pledged that the Case Filing Chamber and environmental protection court would directly examine common environmental protection cases from the day of application and that they would register the cases meeting the conditions of acceptance and hearing the same day. The trial division further implemented a "No Holiday system" affecting evidence collection, preservation, the opening of a court

13 Li Chengsi & Zhang Jun, *Yudao Wuran Shigu Yingruhe Weiquan Huanbao Fating Nengfou Zoudeyuan?* [*How To Defend Rights Involving Pollution Accidents – How Long Will Environmental Protection Tribunal Can Exist?*], Zhongguo Huan Jing Bao [China Environmental News] (July 28, 2009).

14 Luo Hua Shan & Wang TaiShi, *Guiyang Chengli Huanjing Baohu Shenpanting he Huanjing Baohu Fating* [*The Establishment Of Environmental Tribunals And Environmental Protection In Guiyang*], Guizhou ri Bao [Guizhou Daily] (November 21, 2007). After the Yuxi Intermediate People's Court in Yunnan Province established its environmental protection trial division on December 18, 2008, the Chengjiang County Court in Yuxi City, the Tonghai court, and other courts also followed by establishing their own environmental protection trial divisions. *Yuxishi Renmin Jianchayuan Gongzuo Baogao* [People's procuratorate work report in Yuxi City], http://www.yxzf.gov.cn/fy/fydt/xw/2010/570953.shtml (last visited July 13, 2016).

session, and other trial activities to ensure speedy trials. This system ensures that environmental protection cases can be carried out 24 hours a day; every means is employed to increase the effectiveness of enforcement: they implement a brand new three-in-one "criminal, civil and administrative" trial mode for environmental protection cases, and they provide legal advice, legal aid, and other comprehensive services on environmental protection.[15] On November 24, 2008, the Wuxi Intermediate People's Court and the People's Procuratorate in Jiangsu Province also jointly issued the Trial Regulations on Environmental Civil Public Interest Litigation Cases, which clearly stipulate the People's Procuratorate's main responsibilities to prosecute cases regarding environmental welfare on behalf of the public, stipulate the accepted range of environmental public interest litigation cases, and set out rules on its own support and supervision to the prosecution.

On December 11, 2008, the Kunming Intermediate People's Court formally established the environmental protection trial division. At the same time, led by the Politics and Law Committee of the Kunming Municipal Party Committee, the Kunming Intermediate Court, and the Procuratorate, the Public Security Bureau and the Kunming Environmental Protection Agency jointly issued *Implementation Opinions on the Establishment of Coordination Mechanism on Environmental Law Enforcement* (hereinafter *Opinions*). The *Opinions* make clear that the Kunming Intermediate People's Court establishes environmental protection trial divisions, adopts a "four-in-one" trial and implementation mode for criminal, civil, and administrative cases involving environmental protection, and explores the environmental public interest litigation and environmental pollution litigation across administrative regions.

The *Opinions* also stipulate that in cases of environmental public interest litigation, the procuratorial organ, the environmental law enforcement agencies, and relevant social organizations are responsible for litigating before the People's Court, including collecting evidence and bearing the burden of proof. As such, the environmental protection administrative enforcement authority identifies the environmental pollution accident, and entrusts other qualified institutions to assess the consequences and provide the necessary technical support for the environmental public interest litigation. In the realm of grassroots courts, the specialized collegiate bench presently hears criminal, civil, and administrative cases involving environmental protection. Once it gains substantial experience, however, the environmental protection court will take centralized control of environmental protection cases.[16]

Beijing's first trial division for environmental protection was established in the court of Yanqing County in November 2010. It adopted the acceptance model of combining civil, administrative, and criminal cases and focuses on tort cases for environmental pollution.[17]

15 *Wuxishi Zongji Renmin Fayuan* [*Intermediate People's Court Of Wuxi City, The First Establishment of Environmental Protection Judicial Tribunal in Wuxi Court and "Four Commitments' To The Public*], Fazhi wuxi Zhong He Xin Xi Wang [The Legal System Integrated Information Network Of Wuxi] (May 23, 2008).

16 *Huanjing Gongyi Susong Poke Er Chu "Lianghuyiku"Daxiang Diyiqiang* [*Environmental Public Interest Litigation Hatched "Two Lakes and One Bank' and Fired the First Shot*], Zhongguo Huna Jing Bao [China Environmental News] (December 30, 2008).

17 Liu Shaoren, *Minshi Xingzheng Xingshi Anjian "Sanheyi" Jingcheng Sheli Shoujia Huanbao Fating* [*Beijing's First Court for Environmental Protection, Integrating Civil, Administrative and Criminal Cases*], Zhongguo Huna Jing Bao [China's Environmental News] (November 15, 2010).

The development of environmental public interest litigation

According to Article 108 of the Civil Procedure Law and Article 41 of the Administrative Procedure Law, the plaintiff of civil or administrative proceedings must be a citizen, legal person, or other organization who has a direct stake in the case or whose legitimate rights are, or could be, infringed by specific administrative acts, and the provisions on the plaintiff's qualification in China's current legislation preclude the existence of environmental public interest litigation.[18]

To overcome the shortcomings of the current legislation in China, Guiyang City, Wuxi City, Kunming City, and other cities have successively formulated local laws and regulations that provide a legal basis for the development of environmental public interest litigation. Just as the *Provisions on the accepted scope of environmental protection trial division of Guiyang Intermediate People's Court and environmental protection court of Qingzhen People's Court*, the *Provisions on the promotion of ecological civilization in Guiyang*, the *Implementation Stipulation on the handling of environmental public interest litigation cases in civil trial*, the *Implementation Opinions on the establishment of law enforcement coordination mechanism for environmental protection*, and so on, all clearly confirm that, for environmental public interest, the procuratorial organs, the environmental protection management agencies, and the public interest organizations, have the plaintiff qualification to bring the environmental public interest litigation.

Since 2007, several environmental protection trial divisions and courts of Guiyang City, Wuxi City, Kunming City, and other cities have accepted and heard a variety of typical environmental public interest cases. These cases not only achieved the goal of protecting the environmental public interest, but also showed that local procuratorial organs, administrative departments of environmental protection, and environmental protection community organizations can effectively prosecute environmental public interest litigations, thus gathering abundant experience for the legislation of the environmental public interest litigation system in China.

The significance of the establishment of environmental trial divisions

In today's China, with its increasingly serious environmental situation and the difficulty in solving environmental disputes, the significance of establishing environmental protection trial divisions lies in its bold breakthrough in China's current legislation. The breakthrough involves a number of different aspects, such as China's current trial methods, the provisions on the jurisdiction of courts and the manner of accepting cases, and judgment method. It has thus promoted the development of the judicial relief system for environmental disputes in China.[19]

18 *See* Chapters 12 (He) and 15 (Huang) in this volume.

19 Luo Li, *Kankyou Saiban:Tyugoku No Kankyou Hogo Senmon Houtei To Koueki Sosyou No Arata Na Tenkai* [*The New Development of China's Environmental Protection Trial Division and Public Interest Litigation*], in TYUGOKU KANKYO HANDO BUKKU 2011–2012 NENHAN [CHINA ENVIRONMENTAL HANDBOOK 2011–2012] 113–20 (Sososha Japan, 2011).

Proposals for improving judicial relief for environmental disputes in China

The improvement of relevant legislation

The inadequate legislation of procedural law is not conducive to thoroughly solve environmental problems

Environment is defined as the sum of natural and artificial factors that influence human survival and development.[20] The survival and development of human beings depends on the health of the environment, so care for the environment is in the common interest of mankind, both current and future.[21] For China, a healthy environment serves as the premise for economic development and a comfortable life for the general public. Therefore, environmental protection directly benefits the country's well-being and leads to the enjoyment of beautiful, comfortable surroundings for the public at large.[22] However, under China's current Article 108 of the Civil Procedure Law or Article 41 of the Administrative Procedure Law, if injured parties – whether private individuals or the government – do not meet the conditions set by the aforementioned laws, if they do not have direct interest in the case but have instead been indirect victims of environmental pollution, or if the public interest has been damaged by environmental contamination, there are no means to protect their rights from illegal behaviors, nor of protecting the public environmental interest, in general. As a result, China lacks an effective way to protect the environment and the environmental interests of the general public. Therefore, improving the legislation behind procedural law and clearly regulating environmental public interest litigation is a pressing matter.[23]

China should revise its Civil Procedure Law and its Administrative Procedure Law as soon as possible and clearly stipulate provisions for the environmental public welfare litigation system, the plaintiff qualifications for instituting environmental public welfare proceedings, the distributive rules guiding the plaintiff and defendant's burden of proof in environmental public welfare lawsuits, the obligation that administrative authorities read reports in advance in order to prevent the public from abusing the right of appeal, etc. Such reforms would help provide the legal basis for the successful development of environmental public interest litigation in China.[24]

20 *Supra* note 10, at Article 2. "Environment", as used in this law, refers to the total body of all natural elements and artificially transformed natural elements affecting human existence and development, which includes the atmosphere, water, seas, land, minerals, forests, grasslands, wildlife, natural and human remains, nature reserves, historic sites and scenic spots, and urban and rural areas. *See* also Chapters 2 (Farah), 9 (Ibrahim, Deleuil & Farah), 12 (He), and 17 (Heurtebise) in this volume.

21 Patricia Birnie & Alan Boyle, International law and the Environment 97–99 (2nd ed. Oxford University Press, 2002); Keman Baslar, The Concept of the Common Heritage of Mankind in International Law 306 (Martinus Nijhoff Publishers, 1998).

22 *See* Chapter 36 (Nie) in this volume.

23 On the general concepts of public interest litigations, and more specifically related to labour rights, please *see* Chapter 5 (Choukroune) in this volume. On public interest litigations related to consumer rights please, *see* Chapter 32 (Hu), and on consumer law *see* in general Chapters 30 (Rossi) and 31 (Prasad) in this volume.

24 Luo Li, *supra* note 3, at 105. *See* also Chapters 12 (He) and 15 (Huang) in this volume.

The inadequate legislation of substantive law is not conducive to the smooth development of judicial relief for environmental disputes

Under the prevailing legislation in China, legal provisions concerning environmental protection in civil, administrative, and criminal legislation operate together to build the environmental responsibility system in which the perpetrator bears the responsibilities for polluting or damaging the environment. This type of substantive law provides the legal basis for the Chinese People's Courts to prosecute perpetrators with civil, administrative, or criminal responsibilities. Therefore, from the perspective of substantive law, the improvement of civil, criminal, and administrative legislation would lead to the unimpeded development of judicial relief for environmental disputes in China.[25]

The improvement of the judgment system

In terms of judicial practice, the establishment and operation of the environmental trial division of the Guiyang Intermediate People's Court and the Wuxi Intermediate People's Court has accelerated the punitive process for environmental pollution or destruction, keeping law-infringing behaviors in check and providing more timely relief to the victims. Therefore, on the basis of improving substantive and procedural law, China should proceed by combining the needs of the environmental judicial courts, promptly summarizing and displaying the experience of successful pilot projects, and solving the urgent problems during the process of establishing and operating environmental trial divisions, such as the legal prerequisites for establishing them and their specific trial rules, in order to realize in full their positive effects.

Improving environmental trial teams

In order to fully provide the benefits of judicial relief for environmental disputes, China should pay attention to strengthening the links between related legislation on judicial relief for environmental disputes and, meanwhile, raise the professional knowledge level of judges on hearing environmental disputes by centralizing training and importing environmental law professionals. It should also seek to improve the level of the judges' trial knowledge and ability within the field of environmental law in order to fully realize impartiality in the judicial system.[26] Especially after courts in certain Chinese cities began establishing environmental trial divisions one after the other, the People's Court earnestly started building a team of judges with specialized knowledge in environmental law, which is essential for correctly understanding and enforcing the law, realizing the environmental trial divisions' functions, and achieving their real objectives.[27]

25 Wang Jin, *Zhongguo de Huanjing Gongyi Susong: Heshi Neng Fuchu Shuimian?* [*China's Environmental Public Interest Litigation: When will it Emerge?*], 6 SHIJIE HUAN JING [WORLD ENVIRONMENT] 18–21 (2006).

26 Lu Zhong mei, *Lun Huanjing Jiufen de Sifa Jiuji* [*On the Judicatory Relief of Disputes*], 4 HUAZHONG KEJI DAXUE XUEBAO (SHEHUI KEXUE BAN) [JOURNAL OF HUAZHONG UNIVERSITY OF SCIENCE AND TECHNOLOGY (SOCIAL SCIENCE EDITION)] 46 (2004).

27 Luo Li, *supra* note 3, at 105. For example, since 2001, the Research and Service Center on Environment and Resources Law in China University of Political Science and Law has provided free training for 6 years to 262 lawyers, 189 judges, and 21 officials of environmental and administrative law around the country. The Center has established a nationwide network of environmental lawyers. The author believes that training activities, which are held by the Research and Environmental Resources Law Center in China University of Political Science and Law, play an active role in enhancing the quality of Chinese environmental law and judges' technology and skills.

14 The Impact of the Kyoto Protocol and UNFCCC on Chinese Law and the Consequential Reforms to Fight Climate Change*

Carla Peng

Introduction

Since the 1970s and the rise of environmental consciousness, especially after China's accession to the World Trade Organization (WTO), China has become part of the international environmental community. The development of international environmental law greatly promoted the process of domestic environmental policy- and lawmaking. Much of international environmental law is concerned with regulating environmental problems, providing common standards and practices for prevention or control of pollution, and promoting conservation and the sustainable use of environmental resources and energy.[1] However, national environmental legislation primarily depends on each country's level of economic development, legal culture, and national interests.[2]

* This chapter is part of the results of the Research Project on "*Current Trends of Chinese Law towards Non-Trade Concerns such as Sustainable Development and the Protection of Environment, Public Health, Food Safety, Cultural, Social and Economic Rights, Labor Rights and the Reduction of Poverty from the Perspective of International Law and WTO Law*" coordinated by Professor Paolo Davide Farah at gLAWcal – Global Law Initiatives for Sustainable Development (United Kingdom) and at West Virginia University John D. Rockefeller IV School of Policy and Politics, Department of Public Administration, in partnership with the Center of Advanced Studies on Contemporary China (CASCC) in Turin (Italy), Maastricht University Faculty of Law, Department of International and European Law and IGIR – Institute for Globalisation and International Regulation (Netherlands), and Tsinghua University, School of Law, Institute of Public International Law and the Center for Research on Intellectual Property Law in Beijing (China). An early draft of this chapter was presented at the Conferences Series on "*China's Influence on Non-Trade Concerns in International Economic Law*", First Conference held at the Center of Advanced Studies on Contemporary China (CASCC) in Turin on November 23–24, 2011. This publication and the Conference Series were sponsored by China–EU School of Law (CESL) at the China University of Political Science and Law (CUPL). The activities of CESL at CUPL are supported by the European Union and the People's Republic of China.

1 Edith Brown Weiss, Environmental change and international law: new challenges and dimensions (United Nations University Press, 1992); Philippe Sands, Greening international law (Earthscan, 1993); Philippe Sands, Richard Tarasofsky & Mary Weiss, Principles of international environmental law (Manchester University Press ND, 1994); Laurence Boisson De Chazournes, Ethique emvironnementale et droit international (Ed. scientifica, 2003); Philippe Sands & Paolo Galizzi, Documents in international environmental law (Cambridge University Press, 2004). *See* also Chapters 8 (Sindico & Gibson), 9 (Ibrahim, Deleuil & Farah), 10 (Lemoine), and 11 (Cima) in this volume.

2 *See* Chapters 2 (Farah), 5 (Choukroune), 6 (Vadi), 12 (He), 15 (Huang), 17 (Heurtebise), 22 (Germann), 23 (Creemers), and 25 (Friedmann) in this volume.

As one of the major international environmental issues, climate change plays a direct role in national energy security and affects the strategy for national economic growth.[3] By implementing the United Nations Framework Convention on Climate Change (UNFCCC) and the Kyoto Protocol, China has made great legislative achievements, but its legal system continues to face serious problems: incomplete climate and energy policies, lack of supporting regulations, and difficulties in implementation and enforcement. China must complete its transition to a low-carbon economy and has to seek a new reform breakthrough.

The establishment of the Chinese climate and energy institution

National Coordination Committee on Climate Change

On May 29, 1998, the Chinese government signed the Kyoto Protocol, which was then approved on September 3, 2002. On February 16, 2005, the Kyoto Protocol came into effect.[4] After signing the Protocol, China established the National Coordination Committee on Climate Change (NCCCC), which presently comprises 17 ministries and agencies. The NCCCC oversees the formulation and coordination of China's climate change–related policies and measures, providing guidance for central and local governments' responses to climate change. Beginning in 2001, the NCCCC compiled the Initial National Communication on Climate Change of the People's Republic of China and presented the report to the UNFCCC at the tenth session of the Conference of the Parties (COP10) in December 2004. To effectively address climate change, the Chinese government established the National Leading Committee on Climate Change in June 2007, which was based on the NCCCC. Former Premier Wen Jiabao served as its leader, and 20 ministries and government sectors are involved. In July 2013, the State Council made an adjustment to the composition and personnel of the National Leading Group for Addressing Climate Change, with Premier Li Keqiang acting as group leader and several functional departments being added. China has established a basic management system and working mechanism for addressing climate change in which the National Leading Group for Addressing Climate Change plays a leadership role, the National Development and Reform Commission is responsible for centralized administration, and tasks are assigned to relevant departments and local governments with widespread public participation as well.[5]

3 Gu Dejin, *Cong Ba Li Dao Ge Ben Ha Gen: Qi Hou Bian Hua Tan Pan De Yuan Ze He Tai Shi* [*Progress And Principle Of Negotiating On Climate Change: The Road From Bali To Copenhagen*], Kin Ming Li Gong Da Xue Xue Bao (She Hui Ke Xue Ban) [Journal Of Kunming University of Science and Technology (Social Sciences Edition)] 9 (2009).

4 Zhuang Guiyang & Chen Yin, Guo Ji Qi Hou Zhi Du Yu Zhong Guo [International Climate Regime and China] 33–41 (Shijie Zhishi Publishing House, 2005).

5 Zhong Guo Ying Dui Qi Hou Bian Hua De Zheng Ce Yu Xing Dong 2013 (English Edition) [China's Policies and Actions For Addressing Climate Change, White Paper of the Information Office of the State Council, China's Cabinet, 2013] 5–6.

National Energy Commission

In January 2010, China's State Council set up the National Energy Commission (NEC) with Premier Wen Jiabao as its head to step up strategic policy-making and coordination. The commission is responsible for drafting national energy development plans, reviewing energy security and major energy issues, and coordinating domestic energy development and international cooperation. It is composed of 21 members from various government agencies. In 2013, the State Council issued the Circular on Adjusting the Composition and Personnel of the National Energy Commission, with Premier Li Keqiang as director and Vice Premier Zhang Gaoli serving as deputy director. This is currently the highest Chinese energy institution.[6]

The process of Chinese climate and energy legislation

Whether, and to what degree, a country is concerned about a low-carbon economy will directly determine the success or failure of its transformation to such. According to the *Initial National Communication on Climate Change of the People's Republic of China*, "China's total GHG emissions in 1994 [were] 4,060 million tons of CO_2 equivalent (3,650 million tons of net emissions), of which 3,070 million tons of CO_2, 730 million tons of CO_2 equivalent (tCO_2e) of CH_4 and 260 million tCO_2e of N_2O. According to tentative estimates by Chinese experts, China's total GHG emission in 2004 [were] about 6,100 tCO_2e (5,600 million tons of net emissions), of which 5,050 million tons of CO_2, 720 million tCO_2e of CH_4 and 330 million tCO_2e of N_2O. From 1994 to 2004, the annual average growth rate of GHG emissions [was] around 4%, and the share of CO_2 in total GHG emissions increased from 76% to 83%."[7] China's primary energy mix is coal-based. The communication stated that:

> In 2005, the primary energy production in China was 2,061 Mtce, of which raw coal accounted for as high as 76.4 per cent. For the same year, China's total primary energy consumption was 2,233 Mtce, among which, the share of coal was 68.9 per cent, oil 21.0 per cent, and natural gas, hydropower, nuclear power, wind power and solar energy 10.1 per cent; while the shares of coal, oil, and natural gas, hydropower and nuclear power in the world primary energy consumption were 27.8 per cent, 36.4 per cent and 35.8 per cent, respectively. Because of the coal-dominated energy mix, CO_2 emission intensity of China's energy consumption [was] relatively high.[8]

In 2011, China's carbon emissions reached 80 million tons, accounting for a quarter of the total global emissions, more than 50 per cent of US emissions. From 2005 to 2011, China was responsible for 60 per cent of the world's increase in CO_2 emissions. China's per capita CO_2 emissions have reached six tons, exceeding the world average per capita emissions, and by 2020 China's per capita emissions are expected to exceed those

6 *See* National Energy Commission, http://www.nea.gov.cn/gjnyw/ (last visited July 16, 2016).

7 Zhong Guo Ying Dui Qi Hou Bian Hua Guo Jia Fang An [China National Climate Change Program] (June 4, 2007) (English Edition) 6, http://www.ccchina.gov.cn/WebSite/CCChina/UpFile/File188.pdf (last visited July 16, 2016).

8 *Supra* note 7, at 15.

registered in the EU.[9] China's distribution of resources and energy is characterized by "rich coal, oil-poor, less gas." Since the restructuring of energy depends on the available resources, high technical innovation and numerous financial investments will lead to energy efficiency. The coal-based energy resources and consumption structure has not fundamentally changed in China for many years. The Chinese government has paid attention to this problem and passed a series of measures to reduce energy consumption and develop new energy sources.

UNFCCC period (before 2000)

Before the early 1970s, scientists from different countries had carried out limited systematic research on climate change issues. In 1972, a UN Conference on the Human Environment was held in Stockholm to promote awareness of potential climate change and related issues.[10] In 1988, the World Meteorological Organization (WMO) and the United Nations Environment Programme (UNEP) jointly established the Intergovernmental Panel on Climate Change (IPCC), and the First Climate Change Assessment Report was issued in 1990. During the same year, the UN General Assembly established an Intergovernmental Negotiation Committee (INC) to broker a Framework Convention on Climate Change. The IPCC released five Assessment Reports since 1990 – the first in 1990, and then in 1995, 2001, 2007, and 2014.[11] The IPCC's First Assessment Report was the main scientific basis for the INC's work. The Member States signed the UNFCCC at the Earth Summit in Rio de Janeiro in June 1992.

Without any doubt, the UNFCCC is one of the most far-reaching international legal documents in the domain of international environmental development, but it does not include any specific provisions to solve the greenhouse gas (GHG) emissions issue: it is too general, and it lacks specific dispositions aimed at clarifying developed countries' commitments. Discussions on the adequacy of commitments at COP-1 resulted in the adoption of "The Berlin Mandate."[12] The Parties called for negotiations on a protocol or other legal instruments to begin. This negotiation round ended with COP-3 in 1997, which adopted the Kyoto Protocol. Although the UNFCCC has no direct impact on the Kyoto mechanisms, it established the objectives and basic principles, which ultimately led to the opening of the Kyoto Protocol agenda.

Throughout the process of establishing the UNFCCC, China's domestic energy policy was not in line with the international climate and energy regime. Prior to this period, the National People's Congress (NPC) Standing Committee promulgated the Mineral Resources Law of the People's Republic of China[13] in 1986. During the 1990s, along with the accelerated

9 Xue JinJun & Zhao ZhongXiu (eds), Zhong Guo Di Tan Jing Ji Fa Zhan Bao Gao (2014) [Annual Report On China's Low-Carbon Economy Development (2014)], 3–4 (Social Sciences Academic Press, 2014).

10 *See* Chapters 8 (Sindico & Gibson) and 17 (Heurtebise) in this volume.

11 The fifth assessment report consists of three Working Group (WG) reports and a Synthesis Report (SYR). All IPCC documents are available on the website of the IPCC, http://www.ipcc.ch/ (last visited July 16, 2016).

12 COP-1 established an open-ended Ad Hoc Group on the Berlin Mandate (AGBM) through decision FCCC/CP/1995/7/Add.1/ Decision 1/CP.1. In this decision, known as the "Berlin Mandate," the COP agreed to begin a process to strengthen the commitments on the part of industrialized countries to reduce greenhouse gas emissions beyond the year 2000 through the adoption of a protocol or other legal instrument. *See* http://unfccc.int/resource/docs/cop1/07a01.pdf (last visited July 16, 2016).

13 Zhōnghuá Rénmín Gònghéguó Kuàngchǎn Zīyuán Fǎ (中华人民共和国矿产资源法) [Mineral Resources Law Of The People's Republic Of China] (Promulgated By The Standing Comm. Nat'l People's Cong., March 19, 1986).

process of China's economic legislation, the NPC constructed three energy-related laws, that is the Electricity Power Law[14] (1995), the Coal Industry Law[15] (1996, amended in 2011 and 2013), and the Energy Conservation Law[16] (1997, amended in 2007 and 2016).

Kyoto period (2000–2007)

In the twenty-first century, while the socialist market economic system had already been established, energy policy progressed considerably. For purposes of national economic and social development, China proposed, in the Tenth Five-Year Plan (2001–2005),[17] to adhere to resource development and energy conservation, where the latter aims to improve the efficiency of resource use and achieve a sustainable development strategy. China also emphasized the need to actively develop wind, solar, and geothermal energy as well as other renewable energy sources, to promote energy saving, and to ensure a comprehensive use of clean technology. In its Eleventh Five-Year Plan (2006–2010),[18] China underscored the goals of energy consumption reduction and renewable energy use. In 2004, the State Council adopted a *Draft Mid- and Long-term Energy Development Plan* (2004–2020) in its national strategic plan.[19] The National Development and Reform Commission further issued the first Chinese *Special Plan for Energy Efficiency* in 2004.[20] In August 2005, the State Council issued a *Circular on the Important Work on the Establishment of Resources Conservation Society*[21] and *Opinions on Speeding-Up of Recycling Economy.*[22] In December 2005, it also released the decision on the issuance and implementation of the provisions on the promotion

14 Zhōnghuá Rénmín Gònghéguó Diànlì Fǎ (中华人民共和国电力法) [Electric Power Law Of The People's Republic Of China] (Promulgated By The Standing Comm. Nat'l People's Cong., December 28, 1995).

15 Zhōnghuá Rénmín Gònghéguó Méitàn Fǎ (中华人民共和国煤炭法) [Coal Industry Law Of The People's Republic Of China] (Promulgated By The Standing Comm. Nat'l People's Cong., August 29, 1996, amended April 22, 2011 and June 29, 2013).

16 Zhonghua Renmin Gongheguo Jieyue Nengyuan Fa (中华人民共和国节约能源法) [Energy Conservation Law of the People's Republic of China] (promulgated by the Standing Comm. Nat'l People's Cong., November 1, 1997, amended October 28, 2007 and July 2, 2016).

17 Zhong Guo Guo Min Jing Ji He She Hui Fa Zhan Shi Wu Gui Hua Gang Yao [China's National Economic and Social Development in the 10th Five-Year Plan] (2001–2005), http://www.people.com.cn/GB/shizheng/16/20010318/419582.html (last visited July 16, 2016).

18 Zhong Guo Guo Min Jing Ji He She Hui Fa Zhan Shi Yi Wu Gui Hua Gang Yao [China's National Economy and Social Development in the 11th Five-Year Plan] (2006–2010), http://www.gov.cn/ztzl/2006–03/16/content_228841.htm (last visited July 16, 2016).

19 On June 30, 2004, Premier Wen Jiabao chaired the State Council executive meeting in which the State Council discussed and approved in principle Mid- and Long-Term Energy Development Plans (2004–2020) (the draft) [Neng yuan zhong chang qi fa zhan gui hua gang yao (cao an)], http://news.xinhuanet.com/zhengfu/2004–07/01/content_1559228.htm (last visited July 16, 2016).

20 Jie Neng Zhong Chang Qi Zhuan Xiang Gui Hua [Mid- and Long-term Energy-Saving Special Plan] (2004), *see* JIE YUE NENG YUAN FA XIU DING QI CAO ZU [DRAFTING GROUP OF ENERGY CONSERVATION LAW] ZHONG HUA REN MIN GONG HE GUO JIE YUE NENG YUAN FA SHI YI [THE INTERPRETATION OF ENERGY CONSERVATION LAW OF P.R.C] 185 (Pekin University Press, 2008).

21 Guo Wu Yuan Guan Yu Zuo Hao Jian She Jie Yue Xing She Hui Jin Qi Zhong Dian Gong Zuo De Tong Zhi [Circular on the Important Work on the Establishment of Resources Conservation Society], http://www.gov.cn/zwgk/2005–09/08/content_30265.htm (last visited July 16, 2016).

22 Guo Wu Yuan Guan Yu Jia Kuai Fa Zhan Xun Huan Jing Ji De Ruo Gan Yi Jian [Opinions on Speeding-Up of Recycling Economy], http://www.gov.cn/zwgk/2005–09/08/content_30305.htm (last visited July 16, 2016).

of a transiting industrial structure.[23] In August 2006, the State Council issued a decision on energy efficiency.[24] These official documents provide policies and legal safeguards for improving China's capacity construction to respond to climate change.

In February 2005, the NPC deliberated and adopted the Renewable Energy Law of the People's Republic of China,[25] which specifies the government's responsibilities and obligations, lists enterprises and consumers in the development and use of renewable energy, and provides guidelines on domestic energy consumption goals, rules on the production and transmission of electricity from renewable energy sources, regulation of prices, allocation of costs, special funds, and tax preferential treatment. In October 2005, the government promulgated the Regulation about Measures for Operation and Management of Clean Development Mechanism Projects[26] (now expired, replaced by 2011 revised edition).

Bali to Copenhagen (2007–2009)

At the Bali conference, the participants made significant progress towards pushing developing countries' action, and China started to feel mounting international pressure. In order to comply with its obligation to implement the UNFCCC and the Kyoto Protocol, China adopted its National Climate Change Program in 2007 and, in 2008, issued *China's Policies and Actions for Addressing Climate Change*, a governmental white paper, which specifically provides the basic principles, main tasks, and policy measures to be implemented in 2010. According to these two documents, China's efforts to confront climate change shall adhere to the following principles: a sustainable framework to address climate change; common but differentiated responsibilities;[27] taking simultaneous mitigation and adaptation measures;[28] relying on innovation and technology transfer; and public participation and international cooperation.[29] China subsequently established governmental agencies to coordinate policies on climate change and adopted a series of policies and measures to respond to climate change.

On May 20, 2009, the Chinese Government issued the official document, *China's Position on the Copenhagen Climate Change Conference-Implementation of The Bali Roadmap*,[30] and reaffirmed once again its adhesion to the common but differentiated

23 Cu Jin Chan Ye Jie Gou Tiao Zheng Zan Xing Gui Ding De Jue Ding [The decision on the issuance and implementation of the provisions on the promotion of transiting industrial structure], http://www.gov.cn/zwgk/2005-12/21/content_133214.htm (last visited July 16, 2016).

24 Guan yu jia qiang jie neng gong zuo de jue ding [The decision on energy efficiency] (2006), *see* Jie Yue Neng Yuan Fa Xiu Ding Qi Cao Zu, *supra* note 20.

25 Zhōnghuá Rénmín Gònghéguó Kě Zàishēng Néngyuán Fǎ (中华人民共和国可再生能源法) [Renewable Energy Law of the People's Republic of China] (Promulgated By The Standing Comm. Nat'l People's Cong., February 28, 2005, amended December 6, 2009).

26 Qīngjié Fāzhǎn Jīzhì Xiàngmù Yùnxíng Guǎnlǐ Bànfǎ (清洁发展机制项目运行管理办法) [Measures for the Operation and Management of Clean Development Mechanism Projects] (Issued by the Technology, State Development and Reform Comm., October 12, 2005, expired, effective August 3, 2011).

27 *See* Philippe Sands, Principles of International Environmental Law (Cambridge University Press, 2003); Tuula Honkonen, The Common but Differentiated Responsibility Principle in Multilateral Environmental Agreements – Regulatory and Policy Aspects (Wolters Kluwer, 2009); Lavanya Rajamani, Differential Treatment in International Environmental Law 8 (Oxford University Press, 2006).

28 For an overview of both mitigation and adaptation strategies, *see* UN IPCC Second Assessment Report: Climate Change 1995 (SAR).

29 *See* Chapters 8 (Sindico & Gibson), 9 (Ibrahim, Deleuil & Farah), and 10 (Lemoine) in this volume.

30 China's Position on the Copenhagen Climate Change Conference-Implementation of The BALI Roadmap, http://en.ndrc.gov.cn/newsrelease/200905/t20090521_280382.html (last visited July 16, 2016).

responsibilities principle. On the eve of the Copenhagen Conference, the Chinese Government firmly expressed its support to the 15th COP of the UNFCCC, and its willingness to support the global reduction of GHG under the conditions that it secure its right to development and not abandon national interests. On November 25, 2009, during a meeting presided by Premier Wen Jiabao, the State Council decided that GHG emissions for each unit of GDP shall be reduced by 40 to 50 per cent by 2050, an ambitious goal by any standard.

Two years after a Senior Fellow of the Chinese Academy of Science proposed to make a climate change law during the National People's Political Consultation Conference in 2007, the Chairperson of the Environmental and Resources Committee of the NPC presented the draft Resolution of the Standing Committee of the National People's Congress on the Active Response to Climate Change. The draft Resolution demonstrated that legislation on climate change should be regarded as critical to the development of a socialist legal system with Chinese characteristics. The draft Resolution called for strict enforcement of all relevant laws and close supervision of their implementation. The NPC's Standing Committee adopted the Energy Conservation Law Amendment[31] on 28 October 2007 and the Renewable Energy Law Amendment[32] on 26 December 2009.

Post-Copenhagen period (2009–2012)[33]

The Copenhagen COP-15 in 2009 marked an important turning point for China. With media coverage and under tremendous public pressure, the Chinese Government realized that, as one of the world's major emerging economies, it had to actively participate in international climate negotiations and begin to change its international role from that of "spectator" to "participant," rebuilding its global image as a responsible country. With this in mind, the Chinese government made a solemn commitment to develop a low-carbon economy and has taken a number of initiatives to support its development and deal with climate change. During a United Nations talk on climate change in October 2010, China's top climate change official called on all parties to seek the largest amount of common ground. While developed and developing countries remained divided on many issues, the talks helped rebuild mutual trust and increase each country's sense of shared responsibility. At the Durban Climate Change Conference in December 2011, the leader of the Chinese delegation stated for the first time that China would conditionally agree to participate in a legally binding treaty on climate change after 2020. China's conditions included:

31 Zhōnghuá Rénmín Gònghéguó Jiéyuē Néngyuán Fǎ (2007 xiūdìng) (中华人民共和国节约能源法 (2007 修订) [Energy Conservation Law of the People's Republic of China (2007 Revision)] (promulgated by the Standing Comm. Nat'l People's Cong., October 28, 2007).

32 Zhōnghuá Rénmín Gònghéguó Kě Zàishēng Néngyuán Fǎ (2009 xiūdìng) (中华人民共和国可再生能源法 (2009 修订) [Renewable Energy Law of the People's Republic of China (2009 Revision)] (Promulgated By The Standing Comm. Nat'l People's Cong., December 26, 2009).

33 Warwick. J. McKibbin & Peter. J. Wilcoxen, Climate Change Policy after Kyoto. Blueprint for a Realistic Approach (Brookings Institution Press, 2002); Niklas Höhne, What is Next after the Kyoto Protocol? Assessment of Options for International Climate Policy post 2012, 116–137 (Techne Press, 2006).

> new carbon-cutting pledges by rich nations in the second commitment period under the Kyoto Protocol; fast launch of the Green Climate Fund agreed on in Cancun under a supervisory regime; implementing the consensus of adaptation; technology transfer, transparency, capability building and other points agreed upon in the former conferences as well as appraising developed countries' commitment during the first period of the Kyoto Protocol.[34]

The State Council's Information Office first published *China's Policies and Actions for Addressing Climate Change* in 2008 but later released an updated version on November 22, 2011. According to the white paper,[35] China will cope with climate change in 11 major areas during 2011–2015, to achieve its announced targets. During these years, China would strengthen the legal system and strategic planning, accelerate economic restructuring, optimize energy mix, and develop clean energy to fulfill its goals. China aims to reduce its carbon dioxide emission per-unit GDP by 17 per cent by 2015 and energy consumption per-unit GDP by 16 per cent compared with that in 2010. The white paper further states that:

> China will continue to implement key energy-conservation projects, vigorously develop a circular economy, steadily launch low-carbon pilot projects, gradually establish a carbon emissions trading market, and enhance the capacity of carbon sinks to cope with climate change. Efforts will also be made to enhance the capacity of adaptation to climate change and strengthen capacity building, as well as carrying out all-directional international cooperation on climate change.[36]

The white paper noted that China disclosed its overall strategy for energy conservation, emission reduction and GHG emission control in the Comprehensive Work Plan for Energy Conservation and Emission Reduction during 2011–2015 and the Work Plan for Greenhouse Gas Emission Control this year. In 2011 the Twelfth Five-Year Plan (2011–2015)[37] clearly proposed a domestic emission trade scheme for 2011–2015. In July 2011 the National Development and Reform Commission announced a pilot carbon emissions trading project. The pilot cities include Beijing, Shanghai, Tianjin, Chongqing, Hubei Province, and Guangdong Province.

Discussion about passing a climate change law has continued since 2007. In March 2011, the National Development and Reform Commission began to collect public comments and suggestions for a Climate Change Law draft, and it issued the amendments to Measures for Operation and Management of Clean Development Mechanism Projects in September 2011. According to the State Council's 2011 Legislation Program, laws on soil management, atmosphere pollution prevention and control, mineral resources, and forest were

34 *China Sets Conditions on Binding Climate Change Commitment After 2020*, http://news.xinhuanet.com/english/china/2011-12/06/c_131290906.htm (last visited July 16, 2016).

35 China's Policies and Actions for Addressing Climate Change (2011), http://www.ccchina.gov.cn/WebSite/CCChina/UpFile/File1148.pdf (last visited July 16, 2016).

36 China to cope with climate change in 11 major aspects, http://www.china.org.cn/environment/2011-11/22/content_23980862.htm (last visited July 16, 2016).

37 Zhong Guo Guo Min Jing Ji He She Hui Fa Zhan Shi Er Wu Gui Hua Gang Yao [China's national economic and social development in the 12th Five-Year Plan] (2011–2015), http://www.gov.cn/2011lh/content_1825838.htm (last visited July 16, 2016).

added to the revised list; laws on energy and atomic energy law remained in the updated draft.

Post-2012 period: Paris and beyond

Since 2012, with a high sense of responsibility, China has continued to play an increasingly constructive role in international climate change negotiations, as its international role shifted from mere "participant" to active "promoter." In the process of building consensus among all parties, China has made a positive contribution towards the creation of a fair and reasonable international mechanism for addressing climate change. In 2012, the COP-18 was held in Doha, the capital city of Qatar, and in November 2012 the National Development and Reform Commission issued *China's Policies and Actions for Addressing Climate Change (2012)*. The latter stated China's Basic Positions and Stand on Participation in the Doha 2012 UN Climate Change Conference. China maintained that the Doha Climate Change Conference should give priority to the implementation of the consensus reached among all parties. In the first place, the key to the successful accomplishment of the negotiations on the Bali Road Map would be the establishment of a legally binding second commitment period of the Kyoto Protocol and its guaranteed timely implementation. Developed countries should take genuine actions to fulfill their promises to take the lead in reducing emissions and provide funding and technology to developing countries.[38] Following the joint efforts of China and other developing countries, the Doha Climate Change Conference achieved a balanced package of results, accomplished the Bali Road Map negotiations, finalized arrangements for international action to fight climate change before 2020, worked out a plan for negotiations within the Durban Climate Change Conference framework, determined principles governing further actions after 2020, maintained the effectiveness of the United Nations multilateral negotiations progress, and boosted confidence in international cooperation to address climate change.[39]

In November 2013, the National Development and Reform Commission issued *China's Policies and Actions for Addressing Climate Change (2013)*. This white paper stated the priority at the 2013 Warsaw Conference as taking concrete actions to implement the results of the Bali Road Map negotiations, such as mitigation, adaptation, funding, technology, reviews, and transparency, pushing all parties to swiftly ratify the amendment to the second commitment period of the Kyoto Protocol, continuing to discuss relative unsolved issues under the protocol, and fulfilling the agreements and promises made during the previous conferences. Developed countries should fulfill their emission cuts, funding and technology transfer pledges as well as scale up efforts with action before 2020.[40] Chinese Vice Premier Zhang Gaoli reiterated that China has committed to actively promote energy conservation, low-carbon development and ecological construction, and has achieved remarkable results. China committed to ensuring the realization of 2020 carbon intensity by 40–45 per cent compared to 2005, and to working together with all parties concerned to help secure that

38 Zhong Guo Ying Dui Qi Hou Bian Hua De Zheng Ce Yu Xing Dong 2012(English Edition) [China's Policies and Actions For Addressing Climate Change 2012] at 26.

39 Zhong Guo Ying Dui Qi Hou Bian Hua De Zheng Ce Yu Xing Dong 2013 (English Edition) [China's Policies and Actions For Addressing Climate Change 2013], at 54.

40 *Ibid.*, at 57–58.

the 2015 Paris conference will result in an agreement as scheduled, based on the principles of "common but differentiated responsibilities" and openness and transparency, broad participation, and negotiated consensus.

The 18th Chinese Communist Party (CCP) National Congress held in November 2012 set forth that in the face of increasing constraints on resources, severe environmental pollution, and a deteriorating ecosystem, it would be essential to raise the country's ecological awareness. The report of the Congress noted for the first time the need for China to prioritize ecological development and incorporate it into the "five in one" arrangement for socialism with Chinese characteristics with a focus on promoting green, cyclical, and low-carbon development, and therefore increasing the role played by climate change in China's overall economic and social strategy.[41]

In order to fully prepare for the COP21 Paris conference, the Chinese government began a series of bilateral climate negotiations in early 2015, which led to the signing of the Joint Statement on Climate Change between the Government of the People's Republic of China and the Government of the Republic of India[42] as well as the Joint Statement on Climate Change between the Government of the People's Republic of China and the Government of the Federative Republic of Brazil[43] on May 15th and May 19th respectively.

Since November 2014, President Barack Obama and President Xi Jinping made a historic Joint Announcement on Climate Change[44], underscoring both countries' intentions to achieve a long term transition to low-carbon economies. On June 23, 2015, the Report of the U.S.-China Climate Change Working Group to the 7th Round of the Strategic and Economic Dialogue was published. The post-2020 climate targets announced by President Obama and President Xi are part of the longer term effort to facilitate the transition to low-carbon economies, taking into consideration the global temperature goal of 2 °C. Eight action initiatives covering major sectors of the economy, including Heavy-Duty and Other Vehicles, Smart Grids, Carbon Capture, Utilization and Storage, Energy Efficiency in Buildings and Industry, Collecting and Managing Greenhouse Gas Emissions Data, Climate Change and Forests, Climate-Smart/Low-Carbon Cities, and Industrial Boilers Efficiency and Fuel Switching were launched in 2013[45].

41 Since 2012, the Chinese government has continued to promote low-carbon pilot projects in 29 selected provinces and cities and pushed forward carbon emissions trading pilot programs. Among them, the pilot programs for carbon emission trading have witnessed positive progress. On the basis of the local pilot programs, China plans to launch a national emissions trading scheme in 2017. The National Development and Reform Commission (NDRC) has drafted a national management rule that would provide the legal backbone for the scheme. It is foreseeable that China's national emissions trading scheme will play an important role in the future international carbon market.

42 Joint Statement on Climate Change between the Government of the People's Republic of China and the Government of the Republic of India (May 15, 2015), http://en.ccchina.gov.cn/archiver/ccchinaen/UpFile/Files/Default/20150518100423412162.pdf (Last visited July 13, 2016).

43 Joint Statement on Climate Change between the Government of the People's Republic of China and the Government of the Federative Republic of Brazil (May 19, 2015), http://en.ccchina.gov.cn/archiver/ccchinaen/UpFile/Files/Default/20150521102001198192.pdf (Last visited July 13, 2016).

44 U.S.-China Joint Announcement on Climate Change (Nov 12, 2014), https://www.whitehouse.gov/the-press-office/2014/11/11/us-china-joint-announcement-climate-change (Last visited July 13, 2016).

45 Report of the U.S.-China Climate Change Working Group to the 7th Round of the Strategic and Economic Dialogue (June 23, 2015), http://en.ccchina.gov.cn/archiver/ccchinaen/UpFile/Files/Default/20150629094252876092.pdf (Last visited July 13, 2016).

On June 29th, 2015, China–EU Joint Statement on Climate Change has been signed, the two sides recalled the need to urgently enhance global climate action to ensure the full, effective and sustained implementation of the Convention, up to and beyond 2020, in light of the latest and best available scientific information, bearing in mind the limitation of the global average temperature to 2 degrees Celsius above pre-industrial levels. The two sides noted their respective announcements of enhanced climate actions by 2030, as the intended nationally determined contributions by China on one side and by the EU and its Member States on the other side towards achieving the objective of the Convention are set out in its Article 2.[46]

China submitted INDC on June 30th, 2015, which noted that "*Based on its national circumstances, development stage, sustainable development strategy and international responsibility, China has nationally determined its actions by 2030 as follows:*

- *To achieve the peaking of carbon dioxide emissions around 2030 and making best efforts to peak early;*
- *To lower carbon dioxide emissions per unit of GDP by 60% to 65% from the 2005 level;*
- *To increase the share of non-fossil fuels in primary energy consumption to around 20%; and*
- *To increase the forest stock volume by around 4.5 billion cubic meters on the 2005 level.*"[47]

On the occasion of President Xi's Visit to Washington, D.C., U.S. - China Joint Presidential Statement on Climate Change was published in September 2015, the two sides recognized that Parties' mitigation efforts are crucial steps in a longer-range effort needed to transition to green and low-carbon economies and that they should move in the direction of greater ambition over time. Both sides stressed the importance of adaptation; they reaffirmed that, in the context of meaningful mitigation actions and transparency on implementation, developed countries committed to a goal of mobilizing jointly USD 100 billion a year by 2020 to address the needs of developing countries and that this funding would come from a wide variety of sources, public and private, bilateral and multilateral, including alternative sources of finance. China planned to start in 2017 its national emission trading system, covering key industry sectors such as iron and steel, power generation, chemicals, building materials, paper-making, and nonferrous metals. The United States reaffirmed its $3 billion pledge to the Green Climate Fund (GCF) and China announced that it will make available ¥20 billion for setting up the China South-South Climate Cooperation Fund to support other developing countries to combat climate change, including to enhance their capacity to access GCF funds.[48] In November 2015, the National Development and Reform Commission issued China's Policies and Actions for Addressing Climate Change (2015), the white paper reiterated China's INDC target.[49]

After the adoption of the Paris climate agreement in December 2015, the 195 countries that signed the Paris climate agreement agreed to review national climate pledges every five years to limit global warming to "well below 2C" and "pursue efforts" to hold it to 1.5C

46 China–EU Joint Statement on Climate Change (June 29, 2015), http://en.ccchina.gov.cn/archiver/ccchinaen/UpFile/Files/Default/20150630160147006208.pdf (Last visited July 13, 2016).

47 China's INDC (June 30, 2015), http://www.ccchina.gov.cn/archiver/ccchinaen/UpFile/Files/Default/20150701085931838916.pdf (Last visited July 13, 2016).

48 U.S.-China Joint Presidential Statement on Climate Change (Sep 25, 2015), https://www.whitehouse.gov/the-press-office/2015/09/25/us-china-joint-presidential-statement-climate-change (Last visited July 13, 2016).

49 China's Policies and Actions for Addressing Climate Change (2015), http://en.ccchina.gov.cn/archiver/ccchinaen/UpFile/Files/Default/20151120095849657206.pdf (Last visited July 13, 2016).

within this century. China has revealed that it may strengthen its climate targets, in response to an earlier peak in carbon emission. It would "implement and enhance" its climate strategy in its 13th five-year plan released in March 2016.

In Washington D.C., on March 31st, 2016, the latest China-U.S. Joint Presidential Statement on Climate Change have been issued. The two sides recognized that the Paris Agreement marked a global commitment to tackling climate change and a strong signal of the need for a swift transition to low-carbon, climate-resilient economies. To accelerate clean energy innovation and deployment, the two sides would work together to implement the goals of the Mission Innovation initiative announced at the Paris conference and carry forward the work of the Clean Energy Ministerial. They supported a successful G-20 Summit in Hangzhou in September 2016, including strong climate and clean energy outcomes, and called on the G-20 countries to engage constructively in international cooperation on energy and climate change.[50] Chinese Vice Premier Zhang Gaoli signed the Paris agreement in New York on April 22nd, 2016.

Since the signing of the Paris agreement, China has been taking on an unprecedentedly active role in fulfilling its responsibility in promoting international climatic awareness. To be more specific, such endeavor has demonstrated its unique trait of "constructivism", which comes from its ambition to attain the position of the rule stipulator in the arena of international climatic change regulation to some extent.

The motivation behind Chinese climate and energy legislation

The pressure from international climate negotiations and the exposure to foreign countries' legislation greatly informed Chinese legislators and jurists' research. As can be seen from Table 14.1, since the approval of the Kyoto Protocol in 2002, the Chinese government has accelerated its climate and energy legislation process.

Table 14.1 The timetable of China's climate and energy legislation

	Launch	*Adoption*	*Revision*
Electric Power Law	–	1995	–
Coal Law	–	1996	2011 2013
Energy Conservation Law	–	1997	2007, 2016
Renewable Energy Law	2003	2005	2009
Energy Law	2005	–	–
Petroleum and Natural Gas Law	2005 2009	–	–
Atomic Energy Law	1984 1998 2008 2011	–	–
Climate Change Law	2011	–	–
Nuclear Safety Law	2013	–	–

Source: compiled by author

50 China-U.S. Joint Presidential Statement on Climate Change (Mar 31, 2016), http://en.ccchina.gov.cn/Detail.aspx?newsId=59854&TId=98 (Last visited July 13, 2016).

International climate negotiation and China's new role

With the evolution of international climate negotiations, according to the common but different responsibility principle,[51] all countries were divided into three groups: Annex II parties (countries that were part of the OECD in 1992, meaning mainly industrialized countries); Annex I parties (all countries in Annex II and economies in transition); and Non-Annex I parties. In particular, Annex I includes all those countries subjected to "specific commitments," which means that developed countries take the lead in emission reduction commitments. Developing countries with low economic levels and technical capacities do not have an obligation to reduce emissions.

The Kyoto Protocol designed three market mechanisms to help developed countries reduce the costs of fulfilling their emission reduction commitments. The Clean Development Mechanism (CDM) in Article 12 of the Kyoto Protocol aims to assist Non–Annex I parties (developing countries) in achieving sustainable development.[52] The CDM assists Annex I parties (industrialized countries) in achieving compliance with their quantified emission limitation and reduction commitments under Article 3 of the Kyoto Protocol and contributes to the UNFCCC's ultimate objective, that is, to reduce GHG emissions to a "safe" level.[53] Within the current Kyoto Protocol framework, China, as a developing country, does not bear any GHG emission reduction commitments, but it has nonetheless promoted sustainable development through the financial and technical transfer obtained from participating in CDM projects. China has a clear competitive advantage in the international CDM market in the short term, which is the primary reason why the Chinese government approved the UNFCCC and the Kyoto Protocol. However, since 2007, when China became the first GHG emitting country in the world, its role has changed. Beijing evidently feels tremendous pressure from international communities. Since the Copenhagen Conference, China and the United States have become two of the major players in the international climate negotiations, and China's role continues to grow alongside its surging economic might. As a result, China must prepare to bear GHG emission reduction commitments in the future.

The tendency of national climate and energy legislation

To address climate change, both developed and developing countries have adopted special domestic legislations. As far as the European Union (EU) is concerned, the European Commission proposed a strategy for the implementation of the Kyoto Protocol, which strongly focuses on domestic action to achieve the goal of reducing GHG emissions by 8 per cent.[54] Immediately afterwards, in March 2000, the Commission launched the European Program on Climate Change.[55] The EU Emissions Trading System (EU ETS) is the cornerstone of the EU's policy to confront climate change and it is fundamental to reducing GHG

51 *See* Chapter 9 (Ibrahim, Deleuil & Farah) in this volume.

52 Three Market Mechanisms: Clean Development Mechanism (Article 12), Joint Implementation (Article 6) and Emissions Trading (Article 17) of Kyoto Protocol.

53 Deborah Stowell, Climate Trading, Development of Greenhouse Gas Markets 64–65 (Palgrave Macmillan, 1st ed., 2005).

54 Sandrine Maljean-Dubois & Mathieu Wemaere, La diplomatie climatique: les enjeux d'un regime international du climat 267–268 (Editions A. Pedone, 1st edn, 2010).

55 *Ibid.*

emissions in a cost-effective manner. On October 23, 2001, the Commission proposed a directive that would establish a scheme for GHG emission allowance trading, and the European Parliament and Council adopted Directive 2003/87/EC nearly two years later. The Council later adopted the Climate Energy Package on April 6, 2009, which aims to put emissions trajectories on the right track and achieve the "20-20–20" objectives by 2020. Those objectives are namely 20 per cent reduction of GHG emissions, 20 per cent renewable energy of final energy consumption, and 20 per cent improvement to energy efficiency.[56] The European Parliament and the Council subsequently amended Directive 2003/87/EC, which became Directive 2009/29/EC, so as to improve and extend the GHG emission allowance trading scheme. Currently, the EU ETS is the most successful and influential carbon market practice. In October 2014, EU leaders agreed to cut GHG emissions within the Union to at least 40 per cent below their 1990 levels by 2030. The deal was aimed at countering climate change and setting an example. The package agreed to at the 2014 EU summit also requires renewable energy to provide at least 27 per cent of the EU's energy needs, and demands an increase in energy efficiency of at least 27 per cent in the next 16 years.

To reach the goals set by the Kyoto Protocol, the UK began to collect climate change taxes in 2001, established the first carbon trading system in the world, and became the first country to implement the cap-and-trade system for GHG in 2002. The UK adopted the Climate Change Act on 26 November 2008 and the UK Low Carbon Transition Plan on 15 July 2009.[57] The United Kingdom (UK) and other EU members – such as Germany, France, and Spain – also tackled climate change issues with provisions in related legislation on renewable energy, electricity, and recycling economy. In France, the Grenelle de l'Environnement adopted the National Program against Climate Change (Programme national de lutte contre le changement climatique). Following the Grenelle conference, a law was issued on August 3, 2009, and a second law was issued on July 12, 2010 in the wake of the second Grenelle. The whole "Grenelle de l'Environment" Law, a total of 57 articles, is divided into four parts: climate change (including reducing the energy consumption of buildings, urban planning, transport, energy, and sustainable development studies); biodiversity (including wildlife diversity preservation, water resources, agriculture, and marine and coastal management); environmental, health and waste avoidance (including environment and health, waste, management, information, and education) and overseas territories' provisions. Germany adopted the Renewable Energy Law in 2000 and then modified it in 2004, 2008 and 2011. The Combined Heat and Power Law took effect in 2002, the Energy Conservation Law was enacted in 2005, and the Renewable Energy Heating Law was adopted in 2008.[58]

The legislative practices of other states further promote the process of China's climate and energy lawmaking. In 1998, two years after the Kyoto Protocol was adopted, Japan passed the Law Concerning the Promotion of the Measures to Cope with Global Warming, which was later modified in 2002, 2005 and 2008.[59] On 13 January 2010, the President of South

56 *Ibid.*, at 266–277.

57 Li Yanfang, *Ge Guo Ying Dui Qi Hou Bian Hua Li Fa Bi Jiao Ji Qi Dui Zhong Guo De Qi Shi* [*Legislations to Cope with Climate Change: A Comparative Study and its Enlightenment to China*], Zhong Guo Ren Min Da Xue Xue Bao [Journal of Renmin University of China] 59 (2010).

58 *Ibid.*, at 60.

59 *Ibid.*, at 61.

Korea, Lee Myung-bak, signed the Basic Law on Low Carbon and Green Growth.[60] The Climate Change Act of 2009 took effect in the Philippines on 23 October 2009.[61] After declining to join the Kyoto Protocol for several years, the US, under the Obama Administration, took an active position towards climate change issues, and made new energy and green economy the centerpieces of a plan to boost economic development. The US House of Representatives adopted the Clean Energy and Security Act in June 2009.[62] Following these and other acts of foreign legislatures, the NPC began to research and draft its own climate change law. At the same time, it has accelerated the review process of other related laws. In significant ways, the framework structure, content, instrument and mechanism of all climate change and energy-related laws refer to these foreign legislative experiences.

The requirement of integrity in the Chinese climate and energy legal system

Climate change facts and projections weigh heavily on China's strategic ambitions and priorities. China's National Climate Change Program of 2007 clearly notes that "Studies indicate that climate change has caused some impacts on China, such as sea level rise in the coastal areas, glacial retreat in northwest area, the earlier arrival of spring phenophase. It will also bring about significant impacts on China's natural ecosystems and social economic system in the future."[63] For example, "the glacier area in the northwestern China shrunk by 21 per cent and the thickness of frozen earth in Qinghai-Tibet Plateau reduced a maximum of 4–5 meters in recent 50 years."[64] In addition, "climate change has already caused the changes of water resources distribution over China. There is evidence for an increase in frequency of hydrological extreme events, such as drought in North and flood in South."[65] Although many of the impacts of climate change remain uncertain, the effects have been more clearly shown in some places, like northwestern China, than in other regions. Therefore, it is necessary to construct a complete climate and energy legal system. The requirement of integrity in the legal system became the key reason for lawmaking. The system integrity means that, in the situation of A, B, and C, three laws form a complete "legal system" or "legislative Group," while in the presence of A and B, and in the lack of C, C's draft is based on the consideration of a complete legal system.[66] China's climate[67] and energy[68] legal system frameworks are explained in Tables 14.2 and 14.3.

Tables 14.2 and 14.3 show that although China has a relatively complete legal system framework to address climate change, it still lacks two basic laws, that is, an energy law and a climate change law, as well as some others. For example, because of the rising

60 *Ibid.*, at 62.
61 *Ibid.*, at 62.
62 *Ibid.*, at 61.
63 *Supra* note 7, at 14.
64 *Supra* note 7, at 17.
65 *Supra* note 7, at 17–18.
66 Yeh Jiunn-Rong, Huai Jing Zheng Ce Yu Fa Lv [Environment Policy and Law] 103–104 (2nd ed. Yuan-Chao Publishing, 2010).
67 Li Yanfang, *Lun Zhong Guo Ying Dui Qi Hou Bian Hua Fa Lv Ti Xi De Jian Li* [*On the Establishment of Legal System of China's Reaction to Climate Change*], Zhong Guo Zheng Fa Da Xue Xue Bao [Journal of China University of Political Science and Law] 81–84 (2010).
68 Ye Rongshi & Wu Zhonghu, Zhong Guo Neng Yuan Fa Lv Ti Xi Yan Jiu [China's Energy Legal System Research] 25–32 (China Power Publishing House, 2006).

Table 14.2 China's energy legal system framework

Basic law	*Sector law*
Energy Law (No)	Coal Law Electricity Power Law Petroleum and Natural Gas Law (No) Atomic Energy Law (No)/ Nuclear Safety Law (No) Renewable Energy Law Energy Conservation Law Energy Public Utilities Law (No)

Source: compiled by author

Table 14.3 China's climate legal system framework

Basic law	*Mitigation legislation*	*Adaptation legislation*
Climate Change Law (No)	Energy Conservation Law Renewable Energy Law Clean Production Promotion Law Recycling Economy Law Environmental Impact Assessment Law Population and Family Planning Law Forest Law	Agriculture Law Grassland Law Fisheries Law Land Management Law Desert Prevention and Transformation Law Water and Soil Conservation Law Water Law Water Pollution Prevention and Control Law Flood Control Law Marine Environment Protection Law Sea Areas Use Management Law Forest Law

Source: compiled by author

domestic pressure caused by its energy and resources supply, and the serious environmental pollution and ecological disruption, China makes efforts to improve its energy structure, energy efficiency, and ecological environment protection. For these purposes, China adopted the Energy Conservation Law,[69] the Renewable Energy Law,[70] the Circular Economy Promotion Law,[71] the Law on Promoting Clean Production,[72]

69 *Supra* note 16.

70 *Supra* note 25.

71 Zhōnghuá Rénmín Gònghéguó Xúnhuán Jīngjì Cùjìn Fǎ (中华人民共和国循环经济促进法) [Circular Economy Promotion Law of the People's Republic of China] (promulgated by the Standing Comm. Of the Nat'l People's Cong., August 29, 2008, effective January 1, 2009).

72 Zhōnghuá Rénmín Gònghéguó Qīngjié Shēngchǎn Cùjìn Fǎ (中华人民共和国清洁生产促进法) [Law of the People's Republic of China on Promoting Clean Production] (promulgated by the Standing Comm. Of the Nat'l People's Cong., June 29, 2002).

the Forest Law,[73] the Grassland Law,[74] and other energy and environmental laws that mitigate the effects of climate change. Although these laws address climate change issues independently, China must urgently coordinate, integrate, and systematize them.

The shortcoming of Chinese climate and energy legislation

An incomplete climate and energy legal system

With regards to climate change and energy, China's main shortcoming is an incomplete legal system. As mentioned above, the system lacks two basic laws, a climate change law and an energy law. There are four different views on whether China needs a separate law addressing climate change issues. The first view holds that China should make a law specifically addressing climate change issues; the second view holds that China should include a special chapter addressing climate change issues in an energy law because it is difficult to make a law specifically addressing climate change issues and also because the NPC is already drafting an energy law; the third view holds that China should mitigate and adapt to climate change by making and revising relevant laws; and the fourth view holds that China should include legal provisions addressing global and regional climate change in the Law on the Prevention and Control of Atmospheric Pollution.[75] After much discussion, and motivated by the integrity of China's legal system, the National Development and Reform Commission launched the draft work for a separate climate change law.

The Chinese legal system still lacks an energy law even though the Commission began to draft one in 2005. However, the NPC has yet to pass it, partially because it is extremely difficult to break the "monopoly" interest from traditional interest groups. The government launched draft work of an atomic law three times, in 1984, 1994, and 2008, but each attempt failed for reasons such as government institutional reform, the impact of the Fukushima nuclear accident, and intense media and public pressure. Draft work on the Atomic Law was launched for the fourth time in 2011, but, in the State Council Legislation Plan 2011, it remained on the list of legislation to be strengthened rather than completed.

Although the Chinese Government has adopted or modified a series of climate and energy-related laws, the legal system remains incomplete. On the one hand, some laws still need to be drafted in their entirety, while, on the other hand, many existing laws should be modified to better address the present situation. The drafting of the Climate Change Law has only just begun, and the draft and modification processes of these laws will take years.

73 Zhōnghuá Rénmín Gònghéguó Sēnlín Fǎ (1998 Xiūzhèng) (中华人民共和国森林法 1998 修正) [Forest Law of the People's Republic of China 1998 Amendment] (promulgated by the Standing Comm. Of the Nat'l People's Cong., April 29, 1998).

74 Zhōnghuá Rénmín Gònghéguó Cǎoyuán Fǎ (中华人民共和国草原法) [Grassland Law of the People's Republic of China] (Promulgated By The Standing Comm. Nat'l People's Cong., June 18, 1985, amended December 28, 2002 and June 26, 2013).

75 Zhōnghuá Rénmín Gònghéguó Dàqì Wūrǎn Fangzhì Fǎ (2000 xiūdìng) (中华人民共和国大气污染防治法 (2000 修订) [Law of the People's Republic of China on the Prevention and Control of Atmospheric Pollution (2000 Revision)] (promulgated by the Standing Comm. Of the Nat'l People's Cong., April 29, 2000).

Lack of supporting regulations

The second shortcoming of China's legal system is the lack of supporting regulations, which means that climate and energy-related laws are often stipulated in vain because of lack of operability.[76] As a result of international pressure, the drafting of some laws, such as the Climate Change Law, aims at the function of declaration. However, for purposes of implementation, other laws need to be reformulated in line with the State Council supporting regulations and administration institution rules. For example, the supporting regulations for the Energy Conservation Law[77] and Renewable Energy Law[78] are still being written. This lack of operability inhibits the effective implementation of all the aforementioned laws.

Difficulty of implementation

The third shortcoming of the Chinese legal system is the fact that implementing laws is extremely difficult. Under heavy pressure following the post-2012 climate negotiations, China put forward legislation and reform proposals; however, that is not the end of the story. While foreign legislation provides a rich example for China regime's design, it does not act as a simple solution since the legislator must consider the domestic market environment, state of technology, and other elements. Therefore, the effectiveness of the implementation remains quite unsatisfactory.

Conclusion

With its strong economic growth, China has created an economic miracle, but paid heavy costs. According to Chinese economist Chi Fulin, China has reached a historical turning point, where its new policy leads to justice and sustainable development. During the past 30 years of the economic system reform launched by the Third Plenary Session of the 11th Central Committee in 1978, China has undergone three transitions. The first one is characterized by an export-oriented model, the second one is characterized by an investment-driven model, and the third one is characterized by the so-called economic growth theories centered on GDP.[79] For many years, China has relied on massive investment and heavy energy and environmental resources consumption to foster high-speed economic growth, which has resulted in the formation of high carbon emission levels and excessively intolerable pollution. Today, facing high development risks and the need to build a sustainable society, China must start a fourth transition to a low-carbon economy that reforms its destructive policies.

The UNFCCC, the Kyoto Protocol, and the Bali Roadmap exempt China from bearing the mandatory GHG emission reduction commitments since it is a developing country, yet, in 2007, it overtook the US as the largest global emitter of GHGs. According to the World Meteorological Organization, China's emissions amount to 69 million tons, accounting for

76 *See* also Chapter 12 (He). For further reasoning regarding these particular aspects also in other fields of the Chinese legislation, *see* Chapters 23 (Creemers), 5 (Choukroune), and 25 (Friedmann) in this volume.

77 *Supra* note 16.

78 *Supra* note 25.

79 Chi Fulin, Change of China's Development Models at the Crossroads 6–46 (Wuzhou Chuanbo Publishing House, 2010).

22 per cent of the world's emissions in 2008.[80] However, while new statistics show that China's carbon emissions reached 80 million tons, accounting for a quarter of total global emissions in 2011,[81] experts predict that by 2020 China's emissions will reach nearly 100 million tons, accounting for 33 per cent of the world's total.[82] The prevailing opinions from the international community state that since China is the fastest-growing economy and the most populous country in the world, its actions against climate change will determine the success or failure of global emissions reduction. Due to the need for development model transition and because of pressure from the international community, the Chinese government has taken a lot of measures and has gradually strengthened and reformed its legal system to address climate change.

Although China is the most populous emerging country, it is also the global leader of GHG emissions and seriously contributes towards environmental pollution. Despite international influence on the Chinese government's policy-making and legislative processes, the climate and energy aspects of its legal system remain incomplete: its legislation is still not operational, its legal enforcement continues to face obstacles, and domestic legislation evolves weakly and slowly. The government has made some great legislative achievements, but China is still a poor country with a considerable poor population, and therefore economic development and social equity drive the Chinese government. On the one hand, it is important that China bears more responsibility in proportion to its growing international role. On the other hand, under the common but differentiated responsibilities principle, developed countries should help China strengthen its capacity construction through financial mechanisms and technology transfers. The next reform to address climate change in China still has a long way to go, but this reform will have a great influence on the world.

80 Wang Yigang, Ge Xin'an & Shao Shiyang, Tan Pan Fang Jiao Yi Zhi Du De Zhong Guo Dao Lu: Guo Ji Shi Jian Yu Zhong Guo Ying Yong [China's Pathway towards Carbon Emissions Trading Scheme: International Experience & China's Practices] 7 (Economy & Management Publishing House, 2011).

81 *Supra*, note 9.

82 *Ibid.*

15 The Development of NGOs in China

A Case Study on their Involvement with Climate Change*

Zhixiong Huang

The period of economic reform of the People's Republic of China (PRC) started in 1978 and accelerated the rapid development of non-governmental organizations (NGOs) in contemporary China. Taking the field of climate change as a case study, this chapter explores how Chinese NGOs adapt and develop over time. After introducing the terminology and development of NGOs in China, the chapter examines the general involvement of Chinese NGOs in the field of climate change, and more specifically at the Copenhagen Climate Change Conference. The chapter will then discuss how the role of Chinese NGOs in this field can be enhanced, before reaching its conclusions.

Introduction: NGOs – terminology and development in China

It should be noted that, in China, NGOs have their own path of development, and even their own terminology. An introduction of this general background should serve as a starting point for understanding their role and structure.

Terminology

While Western countries and some developing countries have embraced the term "NGOs," several phrases with "Chinese characteristics" have been developed to refer to such organizations in China. Officially, the Chinese government used the term "social groups" (*shehui tuanti*) before 1998, and shifted to the term "civil organizations" (*minjian zuzhi*) when the State Council changed the name of the bureau in charge of those organizations

* This chapter is part of the results of the Research Project on "*Current Trends of Chinese Law towards Non-Trade Concerns such as Sustainable Development and the Protection of Environment, Public Health, Food Safety, Cultural, Social and Economic Rights, Labor Rights and the Reduction of Poverty from the Perspective of International Law and WTO Law*" coordinated by Professor Paolo Davide Farah at gLAWcal – Global Law Initiatives for Sustainable Development (United Kingdom) and at West Virginia University John D. Rockefeller IV School of Policy and Politics, Department of Public Administration, in partnership with the Center of Advanced Studies on Contemporary China (CASCC) in Turin (Italy), Maastricht University Faculty of Law, Department of International and European Law and IGIR – Institute for Globalisation and International Regulation (Netherlands), and Tsinghua University, School of Law, Institute of Public International Law and the Center for Research on Intellectual Property Law in Beijing (China). This publication and the Conference Series were sponsored by China–EU School of Law (CESL) at the China University of Political Science and Law (CUPL). The activities of CESL at CUPL are supported by the European Union and the People's Republic of China.

from "Social Groups Administration Bureau" to "Civil Organizations Administration Bureau" (under the Ministry of Civil Affairs) in 1998. In recent years, the government has increasingly adopted the term "social organizations" (*shehui tuanti*), although the name of the Civil Organization Administration Bureau remains unchanged. In addition to these official terms, some scholars have favored the phrase "non-profit organizations" (*fei yingli zuzhi*).[1]

Several reasons explain why the term "NGOs" has not been popular in China. According to one author, besides the general ignorance about the NGO sector within China and more broadly about the role NGOs play in development, there is also the fear that the phrase, non-governmental (*fei zhengfu*), might imply that the government has no role to play (*wu zhengfu*, implying anarchism), or that such organizations might be anti-government (*fan zhengfu*).[2] As this chapter will demonstrate, the relationship between NGOs and the Chinese state – which is inevitably complicated and sensitive – has always been essential in understanding their development. Furthermore, this tension affects the very naming of such organizations.

However, despite the existence of the abovementioned phrases, some circles still prefer to use the term NGOs. The Chinese Ministry of Foreign Affairs, for example, which is responsible for managing international NGOs (INGOs) in China, refers to such organizations as NGOs.[3] Most scholars of international relations and international law, probably due to a higher level of internationalization, also favor the term NGOs. Even among scholars and practitioners of social studies, the term NGOs is sometimes used.[4]

In this chapter, the term NGOs will appear interchangeably together with the abovementioned phrases, which are officially and unofficially adopted in China. Unless otherwise indicated, "Chinese NGOs" does not include INGOs operating in China through their offices, branches, or projects.

Development

Before China's economic reform and opening-up in 1978, only a handful of "social groups" under strict state control (which can be better referred to as "governmental NGOs" or "GONGOs"), such as the Youth Union, the Women's Union, and some academic groups were allowed to operate in China. Since 1978, NGOs developed rapidly in terms of both their numbers and their role in society. According to the Ministry of Civil Affairs, by the end of 2001 there were 129,000 registered social organizations in China, and that number

1 *See* Wang Ming & Jia Xijin, *Zhongguo Feiyingli Zuzhi: Dingyi, Fazhan Yu Zhengce Jianyi* [*China's Non-Profit Organizations: Definition, Development, and Policy Suggestions*], in QUANQIUHUA XIA DE SHEHUI BIANQIAN YU FEI ZHENGFU ZUZHI [SOCIAL TRANSITION IN THE CONTEXT OF GLOBALIZATION] 251, 251–261 (Shanghai People's Publisher, 2003).

2 *See* Tony Saich, *Negotiating the State: The Development of Social Organizations in China*, 161 CHINA Q. 124 (2000).

3 Assistant Minister Cheng Guoping, Address at the Inaugural Session of the Seminar on "Non-governmental Organizations in the Context of Globalization" (August 27, 2010); Assistant Minister Cheng Guoping, Address at the 2011 New Year Reception for NGOs (January 12, 2011).

4 For example, in 1998, a research center at Qinghua University with close links to the Chinese Ministry of Civil Affairs (especially its Civil Organizations Administration Bureau that manages this sector) chose to name itself "NGO Research Center." Tony Saich, *supra* note 2.

reached 664,800 by the first quarter of 2016.[5] The current total number of NGOs significantly exceeds that number. For reasons that will be discussed below, numerous unregistered (and hence at least technically "illegal") organizations operate in China.

Meanwhile, NGOs play an increasingly important role within society.[6] For example, in May 2008, after a deadly earthquake struck in Wenchuan, Sichuan Province, at least 231 NGOs went to Sichuan and formed effective networks to provide disaster relief, while many more NGOs directed fundraising and relief efforts in other parts of the country. The government and society widely acknowledged their contribution.[7] During the 2008 Olympic Games, held in Beijing, NGOs had an almost ubiquitous presence. In recognition of their role, the Organizing Committee of the Beijing Olympics invited members of two NGOs, Friends of the Earth and Earth Village, to act as environmental advisors for the Olympics. The Committee, in partnership with various NGOs, also carried out a large number of public educational activities in the field of environmental protection.[8] This led Mr. Li Xueju, former Minister of Civil Affairs, to make the following comment:

> It's time to correctly understand the relationship between social organizations and the modernization of our country. Social Organizations are one of the major forces in the construction and management of society. Their functions cannot be replaced by the government and business sector. We should integrate the construction of social organizations into the overall modernization of our country consistently with its economic and social development, thus making the most of their positive role.[9]

What, then, accounts for the rapid development of NGOs in China in the past three decades? In short, this can be explained by China's rapid social transformation as a result of its economic reform and opening-up.

While the state was deemed omnipotent during the pre-reform era, economic reforms in the 1980s, especially the transition to a "socialism market economy" started in 1992, contributed to the separation between state and society, thus opening new spaces for the development of NGOs.[10] Step by step, the state realized that it was no longer possible for it to take care of everything in the country. Thus, since the mid 1990s, the government reformed itself with the aim of achieving a "small government, large society," which led to the "retreat" of the government from many fields, and, as a result, the NGOs began to fill

5 Chinese Ministry of Civil Affairs, *2001 Nian Minzheng Shiye Fazhan Tongji* Gongbao [*2001 Statistics on the Development of Civil Affairs*] (March 20, 2002), http://cws.mca.gov.cn/article/tjkb/200711/20071100003707.shtml (last visited July 15, 2016); Wang Sibei, Quanguo jing Minzheng Bumen Yifa Dengji de Shehui Zuzhi Shuliang da 66.84 wan [The number of Social Organizations Lawfully Registered by the Civil Administration Department in China Reached 664,800] (May 1, 2016), http://news.cctv.com/2016/05/01/ARTIYa66zXNhT77e5sen4SL0160501.shtml (last visited July 10, 2016).

6 On civil society movements, *see* Chapter 5 (Choukroune) in this volume.

7 *See* Wang Hui, *NGO de Jiti Liangxiang: Dizhen zhong de NGO Lianhe Xingdong* [*Collective Appearance of NGOs-Joint Actions of NGOs in the Earthquake*] (November 25, 2008), http://www.chinadevelopmentbrief.org.cn/qikanarticleview.php?id=888&page=0 (last visited July 15, 2016).

8 Li Miaoran, Xibu Minzu Diqu Huanjing Baohu Feizhengfu Zuzhi Yanjiu- Jiyu Zhili Lilun de Shijiao [Research on the Environmental Organizations in Western Minority Regions – From the Perspective Theory of Governance] 33 (Zhongguo Shehui Kexue Chubanshe, 2011).

9 Li Xueju, *Chongfen Fahui Shehui Zuzhi zai Goujian Hexie Shehui zhong de Zuoyong* [*Fully Utilize the Role of Social Organizations in the Construction of a Harmonious Society*].

10 *See* Guobing Yang, *Environmental NGOs and Institutional Dynamics in China,* 181 China Q. 46, 47 (2005).

the gap.[11] In the new wave of government reforms that started in 2008, Shenzhen, a city in southern China regarded as the pioneer of China's economic reform since 1978, reportedly reorganized its bureaus such that social organizations took control of 80 per cent of the functions previously assumed by the government.[12]

The idea of human rights and public participation also played an important role in the development of NGOs, especially the "bottom-up" grassroots organizations.[13] Thus, the development of NGOs since the 1980s benefited enormously from the changing state–society relationship. However, this is not to say that, nowadays, the state no longer controls the society or fields where NGOs work – such as poverty reduction or environmental protection. To the contrary, the state profoundly influences the fields where NGOs operate, even those fields where they operate with relative ease, as well as the way those NGOs function. Government control over the operation of NGOs is best illustrated by the principle of "double responsibility" for the registration and administration of NGOs, which was established by the Regulation on the Registration and Administration of Social Groups,[14] promulgated by the State Council in 1989 (and amended in 1998). According to this principle, the establishment of an NGO requires the consent of both the bureau responsible for the registration and administration – that is, the Civil Organizations Administration Bureau – and an "operational management bureau," which agrees to take care of the operation of the NGOs concerned. Due to the potential political risks for the two bureaus (especially for the latter bureau), the regulation imposes an extremely high threshold for the registration and operation of NGOs.[15]

It seems fair to say, however, that the increasing participation of NGOs in society is an inevitable trend in contemporary China. Not surprisingly, the 13rd Five-Year Plan for National Economic and Social Development (2016–2020), which was based on advice by the Central Committee of the Chinese Communist Party (CCP) in 2015 and adopted by the National People's Congress (NPC) on March 16, 2016, devoted one section to "Exploring the role of Social Organizations." Among other goals, the plan foresees "improving the management system for social organizations, forming a modern system for social organizations featuring division between government and society, clearly established rights and responsibilities, and autonomy according to the law."[16] In line with this idea, several provinces, including Guangdong and Hainan, have already begun to reform and ease the requirements for the registration of NGOs, which will pave the way for their further development.[17]

11 Ming & Xijin, *supra* note 1, at 268–269.

12 Zhou Yuanchun, *Zhengfu Zhanghao Duo, Shehui Zuzhi Huahao Jiang* [*The Government Steers the Boat while Social Organizations Row the Boat*] (September 22, 2011), http://www.sznews.com/zhuanti/content/2011-09/22/content_6103578.htm (last visited July 15, 2016).

13 For example, China Civil Climate Action Network (CCAN) and similar NGOs to be introduced below.

14 Shèhuì Tuántǐ Dēngjì Guǎnlǐ Tiáolì (社会团体登记管理条例) [Regulation on Registration and Administration of Social Organizations] (Promulgated by the State Council, October, 25, 1998).

15 For a discussion of the principle of "double responsibility," *see* Wu Yuzhang, Minjian Zuzhi de Fali Sikao [The Legal Thinking on NGOs in China] 94–118 (Shehui Kexue Wenxian Chubanshe, 2010).

16 *See* Xinhua News Agency, *Zhonghua Renmin Gonghe Guo Guomin Jingji he Shehui Fazhan di Shisan ge Wunian Guihua Gangyao [Outline of the 13th Five-Year Plan for National Economic and Social Development of the People's Republic of China*] (March 17, 2011), http://news.xinhuanet.com/politics/2016lh/2016-03/17/c_1118366322.htm (last visited July 12, 2016).

17 Huang Xiaohua et al., *Xuexi Jiejian Guangdong Jingyan, Wosheng Yunniang Fangkuan Shehui Zuzhi Dengji Tiaojian* [*Learning from the Experience of Guangdong, Our Province is about to Loosen the Requirements for the Registration of Social Organizations*].

NGOs in the field of climate change: An overview

Internationally, NGOs have participated in the deliberations on climate change for many years, and have played an important role in the negotiation of the United Nations Framework Convention on Climate Change (UNFCCC) and its Kyoto Protocol.[18] In China, NGOs have entered the field of climate change relatively recently. Friends of Nature (FON) was founded as China's first nature conservation organization in 1993, and several other organizations emerged in the late 1990s, mainly focused on public education campaigns for nature conservation. Gradually, such organizations began to devote some of their efforts to climate-related issues. To date, most of the NGOs in the field of climate change define themselves as environmental NGOs, and they represent the mainstream voice in the debate. However, as climate change relates closely to economic and social development, some development and industrial NGOs also joined the field, complementing the perspective of environmental organizations. Development NGOs view climate change not only as an environmental issue, but also an economic and political issue. Industrial NGOs initially emphasized the uncertainties surrounding climate change and resisted constraints on the use of fossil energies; however, since the adoption of the Kyoto Protocol, they increasingly embraced the goal of mitigating climate change and explored the opportunities for new energy industries and adaptive technologies.[19] They have different interests and concerns, but they also provide cooperation and mutual support.

Throughout the ongoing climate change debate, Chinese NGOs have faced several major obstacles. The first obstacle is the attitude of the Chinese government, since it initially considered climate change to be a sensitive political issue. Prior to the mid 2000s, NGOs had to frame their climate-related activities as energy-saving campaigns. Following the shift in China's governmental approach towards climate politics, however, several NGOs reframed some of their activities as climate protection campaigns.[20] Today, NGOs express more confidence in their interactions with the government. One example is the participation of NGOs in the debate on China's future legislation on climate change. In September 2011, the 12 member organizations and four organizations that have observer status in the China Civil Climate Action Network (CCAN) joined hands to prepare a 13-page *Proposal from Chinese Civil Society on China's Climate Change Legislation*, with detailed proposals on the objectives, basic principles, and contents of the future legislation. They submitted the Proposal to the government and also made it available on the Internet.[21] However, unlike some of their counterparts in foreign countries, Chinese NGOs tend to avoid taking confrontational

18 *See* Michele M. Betsill, *Environmental NGOs and the Kyoto Protocol Negotiations: 1995–1997*, in NGO Diplomacy: The Influence of Nongovernmental Organizations in International Environmental Negotiations 43, 43–66 (Michele M. Betsill & Elisabeth Corell eds, 2008). *See* also Chapters 8 (Sindico & Gibson), 9 (Ibrahim, Deleuil & Farah), 10 (Lemoine), 11 (Cima), and 14 (Peng) in this volume.

19 Lan Yuxin et al., *Quanqiu Qihou Bianhua Yingdui yu NGO Canyu: Guoji Jingyan Jiejian* [*Responding to Global Climate Change and the Participation of NGOs: Exploring International Experiences*, 5 Zhongguo Fei Yingli Pinglun [China Nonprofit Review] 87, 90–91 (2010). *See* also Chapters 10 (Lemoine) and 11 (Cima) in this volume.

20 *See* Miriam Schroeder, *The Construction of China's Climate Politics: Transnational NGOs and the Spiral Model of International Relations,* 21 Cambridge R. Int'l Aff. 505, 513–517 (2008).

21 CCAN, Zhongguo Minjian Zuzhi Guanyu Zhongguo Yingdui Qihou Bianhua Lifa de Jianyi (Zhonggao) [Proposal from Chinese Civil Society on China's Climate Change Legislation (final draft)], http://www.c-can.cn/zh-hans/node/677 (last visited July 16, 2016).

and aggressive approaches in their communication with the government. Rather, they carefully extend constructive efforts and cooperation.

Chinese NGOs are also restricted by their limited expertise in the climate change field, which involves complex natural and social science problems that produce uncertainties and controversies. The large majority of Chinese NGOs working on climate change arose from related fields such as environmental protection and development, and few of them specialize in climate change. Without sufficient knowledge in the field, these NGOs struggle to effectively lobby the government and mobilize the public. To overcome this obstacle and bolster their expertise, NGOs have adopted several strategies, including forming networks or coalitions within which to share knowledge. Two major networks of NGOs have emerged since 2007: CCAN, previously mentioned, and the China Youth Climate Action Network (CYCAN).[22] Networks also strengthen the NGOs' voice in the media and in their communication with the government. Thus, collective activities in the form of networks, which are now common practice, marked a new developmental stage for NGOs in the field of climate change.

Over time, Chinese NGOs also developed transnational linkage to enhance their expertise. Since the 1990s, Chinese NGOs have cooperated with Greenpeace and other INGOs on climate-related activities, such as funding, joint campaigns, publications, statements, and exchange visits. Communication between INGOs enables Chinese NGOs to broaden their international perspective on climate change and access the rich resources (including funding and expertise) of INGOs. Such transnational linkage has facilitated the Chinese NGOs' involvement in international climate negotiations since 2007, which will be discussed in the next section.

Chinese NGOs actively use the media,[23] publicizing their own research materials and conducting educational campaigns to raise public awareness about climate change. Most NGOs still prefer to frame their activities in the context of energy-saving because they feel that they can more easily transfer their message to the public.[24] The "26 Degree Campaign" aptly demonstrates how Chinese NGOs have worked together to raise consumers' awareness of climate change and influence individual behavior. Six Chinese NGO's initiated the campaign in the summer of 2004 by asking public and private enterprises, as well as individuals, to set their air conditioners to a maximum of 26 degrees. The campaign has realized a savings of 350,000 to 550,000 tons of CO_2, and it led to the State Council's "***[. . .] announcement about strictly implementing the standard of temperature control in air conditioners in public buildings***," which the NGOs celebrated as a result of their campaign.[25]

Chinese NGOs in the Copenhagen Summit

Chinese NGOs first joined the international climate negotiations in 2007. In July of that year, eight Chinese, as well as international, NGOs jointly launched the "Chinese Civil Society's Response to Climate Change: Consensus and Strategies" Project. On December 20, 2007,

22 CCAN was jointly launched by eight organizations in 2007, and its official website is http://www.c-can.cn/; CYCAN was jointly launched by seven youth environmental organizations in August 2007, and its official website is http://www.cycan.org/.

23 On media and cultural issues, *see* Chapters 22 (Germann), 23 (Creemers), 242 (Kamperman Sanders), and 25 (Friedmann) in this volume.

24 Miriam Schroeder, *supra* note 20, at 517.

25 *Id.*

the coalition published its first joint position paper, *A Warming China: Thoughts and Actions for the Chinese Civil Society*, which was released at Oxfam International's side event at the 13th session of the Conference of Parties serving as the Meeting of Parties to UNCCFC (COP/MOP 13) in Bali in December 2007.[26] This not only marked the first time that Chinese NGOs participated in an international climate conference, but also became the first occasion on which Chinese NGOs strategically attempted to influence such negotiations.

The COP/MOP 15 held in Copenhagen, which aimed to reach a post-2012 international climate agreement to replace the Kyoto Protocol, brought even closer engagement of Chinese NGOs in the negotiation process.[27] Representatives of Chinese NGOs, such as CYCAN, CCAN, and the Society of Entrepreneurs and Ecology (SEE), went to Copenhagen. Several proposals were released during the conference, such as *Our Future-Youth Climate Proposal* by CYCAN, *2009 China Civil Society Climate Change Position Paper* by the "Chinese Civil Society's Response to Climate Change: Consensus and Strategies" Project, *Chinese Scholars Copenhagen Summit Proposal* by several academic groups, and the *Chinese Entrepreneurs Copenhagen Declaration* by SEE.[28] CCAN alone sent eight representatives, the largest delegation among all Chinese NGOs, and worked hard to boost its expertise on climate change. In Copenhagen, CCAN's members divided their tasks based on the different topics in order to follow the negotiation strategies of the major participants, and then met to analyze the progress every day.[29] CCAN was also one of the most active organizations during the conference. Its delegation members organized one side event, presented a speech at another, and organized eight other events (including two meetings with officials from China and abroad, three dialogues with foreign and Chinese Hong Kong youth groups, and three shows to express their appeals). Altogether, there were 61 pieces of media coverage (51 by Chinese media and 10 by international media) on the activities of CYCAN.[30] Notably, they had a dialogue with high-level government officials including China's chief climate negotiator, Dr. Xie Zhenhua. All these activities show that Chinese NGOs definitely had some influence in Copenhagen.

Before Copenhagen, such a collective presence of Chinese NGOs at major international conferences never happened. Why, then, did these NGOs go to Copenhagen?

First of all, climate change is a global issue that cannot be solved without effective actions at the global level. Chinese NGOs, like their counterparts in other countries, must influence their own governments in addition to other governments around the world. The Copenhagen Summit provided an excellent opportunity in this regard. Meanwhile, it also allowed Chinese NGOs to inform foreign governments and public about the situation in China – what has been achieved and what are the challenges ahead in reducing greenhouse gases.

26 Friend of Nature et al., *A Warming China: Thoughts and Actions for the Chinese Civil Society*, http://www.oxfam.org.hk/content/98/content_3529tc.pdf (last visited July 16, 2016).

27 *See* Chapters 12 (He) and 14 (Peng) in this volume.

28 Lai Yulin, *Zhengce Changyi Lianmeng yu Guoji Tanpan: Zhongguo Feizhengfu Zuzhi Yingdui Gebenhagen Dahui de Zhuzhang yu Huodong* [*Advocacy Coalitions and International Negotiations: The Stance and Activities of Chinese NGOs in the Copenhagen Conference*], 3 Waijiao Pinglun [Foreign Affairs Review] 72, 76 (2011).

29 Yao Yao, *Gebenhagen Qihou Fenghui: Quanqiu Zhengzhi Boyi zhong de Zhongguo Guanshangmin* [*Copenhagen Climate Summit: Chinese Officials, Businessmen, and Civil Society in the Global Political Gaming*], 1 Wenhua Zongheng [Culture Review] 48, 52 (2010).

30 Lai Yulin, *supra* note 28, at 80.

Of course, participation in such international conferences also helps these NGOs in several ways. In the words of a Chinese NGO representative in Bali COP/MOP 13, this is "a good method for NGOs to get international exposure, which in turn might increase their national reputation and status vis-à-vis the government."[31] In their proposal released in Copenhagen, the NGOs made several demands to the Chinese government (albeit in a rather general way), including taking a leading role in the climate negotiation, strengthening domestic implementation of climate actions, and broadening public participation in the climate debate.[32] In a sense, this reflects the NGOs strategy to "negotiate the state" in an international context.[33]

International conferences also provide Chinese NGOs with the chance to learn from foreign NGOs, to gain experience, and to expand transnational linkage. All these benefits are essential to increase the expertise and global perspective of Chinese NGOs. Yet, for several reasons, Chinese NGOs exhibit modest overall influence at best. For example, in the two meetings with Dr. Xie Zhenhua and three climate experts in the Chinese government delegation, respectively, members of CYCAN, due to their limited knowledge about climate change, could only raise questions and receive answers from the officials, but they did not have the capacity to make their own points and influence the officials.[34] In their proposals released in Copenhagen, Chinese NGOs did make some demands to the Chinese government as well as on foreign countries, yet almost all these demands contained general principles void of any detail. Most likely, their limited expertise on climate change prevented them from further articulating their demands.

To some extent, political considerations also explain the performance of Chinese NGOs. For example, a group of Chinese youth representatives (mainly members of the CYCAN), together with an American youth delegation, planned to issue a Sino-US Youth Joint Declaration on Climate Change before the closure of the summit, highlighting the joint responsibility of the governments and youth in the two countries to counter climate change. The declaration neared completion after days of careful preparation, but the Chinese youth eventually made the painful decision to give up. There is no indication that Chinese officials exerted pressure over CYCAN, but it is clear that as the international pressure on the Chinese government mounted at that time, CYCAN did not want to create "any trouble" for the Chinese government and did not want other countries to misinterpret the declaration.[35] In general, Chinese NGOs adopt refrain from aggressive strategies, especially vis-à-vis the Chinese government.

After the failure of the Copenhagen Summit, Chinese NGOs continued to actively participate in the COP/MOP 16 in Cancún during December 2010 and later events. As "newcomers" to such events, Chinese NGOs have a lot to learn about how to influence the governments and general public and to solidify their own expertise. Chinese NGOs have begun to get involved in "NGO diplomacy," and to exercise their voices in major

31 Miriam Schroeder, *supra* note 20, at 519. *See* also Chapter 2 (Farah) in this volume.

32 *See* Friend of Nature et al., *2009 China Civil Society Climate Change Position Paper*, http://www.c-can.cn/zh-hans/node/494 (last visited July 16, 2016).

33 I am borrowing the phrase "negotiate the state" from Tony Saich. *See* Tony Saich, *supra* note 2, at 124–141.

34 Lai Yulin, *supra* note 28, at 80.

35 Meng Si, *Zhongmei Qingnian Qihou Bianhua Xuanyan Weihe Yaozhe* [*The Death of the Sino-US Youth Joint Declaration on Climate Change*] (April 14, 2010), http://www.chinadialogue.net/article/show/single/ch/3568 (last visited July 16, 2016).

international negotiations.[36] The signal is clear: Chinese society, as distinct from the government, has begun to make its own diplomatic appeals.

Towards a greater role for NGOs

Climate change is an area where, on the one hand, NGO participation is particularly needed (as it involves actions of the society at large), and, on the other hand, its political sensitivity and technical complexity may produce substantial obstacles to the participation of NGOs (especially those from developing countries). China's unique situation as both the largest developing country and one of the largest greenhouse gas emitting countries in the world would seemingly provide an additional obstacle to Chinese NGOs' involvement in China's climate politics. Thus, it is no wonder that Chinese NGOs entered the field of climate change relatively late. Yet, as international consensus about the need to mitigate climate change continues to increase, the stimulus for Chinese NGOs to get involved also escalates. Judging from the domestic and international presence of Chinese NGOs, climate change has now become one of the most dynamic areas for Chinese NGOs.[37]

Politically, the Chinese government has accepted more and more NGO advocacy on climate-related issues. The Chinese government has realized that "dealing with climate change requires changes in the traditional ways of production and consumption, and the participation of the whole of society," and is endeavoring to "foster a social atmosphere in which the enterprises and the public participate on a voluntary basis under the guidance of the government, and raise enterprises' awareness of corporate social responsibility and the public's awareness of the necessity of care for the global environment."[38] This vision promises a greater role for these NGOs in the future. Indeed, the NGOs in this field conduct activities in accordance with China's national interest. The strength and influence of Chinese NGOs does not currently match China's international status as an emerging power. For the Chinese government, taking a more accepting stance towards NGOs is but the first step. In the coming years, the government must offer more targeted and coordinated support for NGO activities at the local, national, and international levels. For example, in their proposals released in Copenhagen, several NGOs expressed the hope that civil society could be integrated into the design and implementation of China's climate change policies.[39] It is important for the government to ensure that the inputs of NGOs will be well received.

In terms of expertise in climate-related advocacy, Chinese NGOs have made great leaps forward and gained invaluable experiences in the past years. In comparing the two China Civil Society Climate Change Position Papers released in 2007 and 2009, respectively, one can see that the latter is substantially more specific, targeted, and professional. In fact, NGOs understand that such expertise is critical for their survival and development. Meanwhile, they express more confidence about their future. CCAN, for example, has set the ambitious goal

36 For the concept of NGO diplomacy, *see* Michele M. Betsill & Elisabeth Corell, *Introduction to NGO Diplomacy*, in Betsill & Corell, *supra* note 18, at 2–3.

37 *See* also Chapter 2 (Farah) in this volume.

38 The State Council Information Office, *White Paper: China's Policies and Actions on Climate Change* (October 29, 2008), http://www.china.org.cn/government/news/2008-10/29/content_16681689.htm (last visited July 16, 2016).

39 *See* Friend of Nature et al., *supra* note 32.

to "become a leading civil society think tank on climate change issues" by 2016.[40] However, this is also a great challenge. Above all, NGOs in this field must increase their level of specialization so as to enhance their expertise and effectiveness. They also need to find ways to establish closer links with competent research institutions and scholars in the field, to cooperate more advantageously with INGOs, and to interact with the government in a more constructive way. Some Chinese government officials have made the point that most NGOs remain incapable of providing policy suggestions to the government in line with China's unique situation. So, if NGOs can devise a greenhouse gases emission program based on the principles of development and equity proposed by the Chinese government, it will be of great value and will enormously increase their influence.[41]

Conclusions

Since 1978, China has undergone a rapid and profound social transition. The gradual formation of a Chinese "society" created a unique opportunity for the development of NGOs in China. In a sense, NGOs witnessed the changing state–society relationship in China. Thus, the case study of Chinese NGOs in the field of climate change provides an interesting example in this regard.

Compared with NGOs in Western countries, Chinese NGOs are still in their infancy. CYCAN's "questions–answers" style meetings with Chinese officials in Copenhagen, as previously mentioned, exemplifies that in many ways Chinese NGOs are indeed "students" – before the government as well as before the international community. While they try hard to broaden their international perspective and develop their expertise on many complicated issues such as climate change, the government's policies may easily affect them, as the model of "small government, large society" has not yet formed. From another angle, though, a virtuous cycle is gradually emerging. The extensive space for the operation of NGOs as a result of China's reform and opening-up has never existed before, and NGOs now have greater influence on China's political environment and social life. Looking into the future, Chinese NGOs will play a more important role in the continuing social transition and modernization of China.

40 CCAN, Zhongguo Minjian Qihou Bianhua Xingdong Wangluo Xuanchuan Shouce [Brochure of the CCAN].

41 Lai Yulin, *supra* note 28, at 84–85.

16 A Comparison Between Shale Gas in China and Unconventional Fuel Development in the United States: Water, Environmental Protection and Sustainable Development**

Paolo Davide Farah and Riccardo Tremolada*

Introduction

China is believed to have the world's largest exploitable reserves of shale gas, however, several legal, regulatory, environmental, and investment-related hurdles will likely restrain its exploitation. China's capacity to face these hurdles successfully and produce commercial shale gas will have a crucial impact on the regional gas market and on China's energy

* Earlier drafts of this chapter were circulated in September 2013 as a gLAWcal Working Paper and in December 2013 as a FEEM Working Paper and presented at Colloquium on Environmental Scholarship 2013, Vermont Law School (USA), at the faculty workshops held at University of Amsterdam Law School 2013 (Netherlands), at West Virginia University, Eberly College of Arts and Sciences, Department of Public Administration and College of Law (USA), at the Ninth Annual General Conference of the European China Law Studies Association (ECLS), "Making, Enforcing and Accessing the Law" held at Chinese University of Hong Kong, Faculty of Law, Hong Kong, November 15–16, 2014, at the International Conference "Managing the Globalization of Sanitation and Water Services: 'Blue Gold' Regulatory and Economic Challenges", organized by The Chinese University of Hong Kong, Faculty of Law, in cooperation with Maastricht University, Faculty of Law, University of Sydney, School of Economics, University of Leeds, Business School, British Institute of International and Comparative Law held at the Chinese University of Hong Kong (CUHK), Faculty of Law, Hong Kong, March 23–24, 2015, at the faculty workshops and lectures at Chinese University of Hong Kong Faculty of Law, Hong Kong, March 25, 2015, at University of Macau, Faculty of Law, and at Fundação Rui Cunha in Macao, March 25–26, 2015. A special thanks should be addressed to the participants in the abovementioned events as well as Nicholas Ashford (MIT), Sachin Desai, Fernando Dias Simões (University of Macau, Faculty of Law), Sam Kalen (University of Wyoming College of Law), Rebecca Purdom (Vermont Law School), Siu Tip Lam (Vermont Law School), Sharon Jacobs (University of Colorado Law School and Harvard Law School), Andreas Kotsakis (Oxford Brookes University Law School), Melissa Scanlan (Vermont Law School), Brad Mank (University of Cincinnati Law School), Julien Chaisse (Chinese University of Hong Kong), Bryan Mercurio (Chinese University of Hong Kong), Anatole Boute (Chinese University of Hong Kong), Yuhong Zhao (Chinese University of Hong Kong), and Laurence Boisson de Chazournes (University of Geneva), David Zaring (University of Pennsylvania, Wharton School), Weitong Zheng (University of Florida, Levin College of Law), and Pamela Bookman (Temple University Beasley School of Law) for their questions and comments.

** This article is part of the West Virginia University Energy Institute and Multi-Disciplinary Center for Shale Gas Utilization (WV, USA). The research leading to these results received funding from the People Programme (Marie Curie Actions) of the European Union's Seventh Framework Programme (FP7/2007–2013) under REA grant agreement n°269327 Acronym of the Project: EPSEI (2011–2015) entitled "Evaluating Policies for Sustainable Energy Investments: Towards an Integrated Approach on National and International Stage". The article is the result of the joint research of the authors, as shown in the Introduction and Conclusions. Paolo Davide Farah focused on the sections entitled "Chinese institutional and regulatory framework", "Environmental considerations: Focus on water resources management," and "Comparative analysis with the United States' previous experience: A model of development for the unconventional gas market?" and Riccardo Tremolada on the sections entitled "The revolutionary role of shale gas through the prism of China's energy mix: The growth of a new industry," and "The prospects for shale gas in China between regulatory interventions and new geopolitical balances". An extended version of this paper was previously published in the *Brooklyn Journal of International Law*, Volume 41, Issue 2, 2016.

mix, as Beijing strives to meet growing energy demand, and, at the same time, maintain a certain level of resource autonomy by decreasing its reliance on imported oil and coal. The development of the unconventional natural gas extractive industry would also provide China with further negotiating power to obtain more advantageously priced gas.

This article, which adopts a comparative perspective, underlines the trends taken from unconventional fuel development in the United States, emphasizing their potential application to China in light of recently signed product-sharing agreements between qualified foreign investors and China. The wide range of regulatory and enforcement problems in this matter are increased by an extremely limited liberalization of gas prices, lack of technological development, and barriers to market access curbing access to resource extraction for private investors. This study analyzes the legal tools that can play a role in shale gas development while assessing the new legal and fiscal policies that should either be crafted or reinforced. It also examines the institutional settings' fragmentation and conflicts, highlighting how processes and outcomes are indeed path dependent. These issues are exacerbated by many concerns. One such concern is related to the risk of water pollution deriving from mismanaged drilling and fracturing. Another concern is the absence of adequate predictive evaluation regulatory instruments and industry standards, entailing consequences for social stability and environmental degradation, which are inconsistent with the purposes of sustainable development. Moreover, the possibilities of cooperation and coordination (including through U.S.-China common initiatives), and the role of transparency and disclosure of environmental data are assessed.

The significant growth in the production of natural gas from shale formations constitutes one of the most relevant developments in the energy sector. This growth was made possible by the reduction of production costs and overcoming of technological barriers. Recent advances in fracturing (also known as 'fracking') and horizontal drilling technologies have led to a dramatic increase in shale gas production in the United States, which has resulted in energy experts describing shale gas as a "bridge fuel" to carbon-free renewable resources as the United States' primary source of energy.[1] The U.S. Energy Information Administration (IEA) estimates a 49 percent growth in global marketed energy consumption by 2035.[2] Unconventional fossil fuel energy resources will grow approximately 4.9 percent per year up to 2035.[3]

1 On the strategic relevance of shale gas in the United States, see Howard Rogers, *Shale Gas – the Unfolding Story*, 27 (1) Oxford Rev. Econ. Pol'y 117–143 (2011). Steffen Jenner & Alberto J. Lamadrid, *Shale Gas vs. Coal: Policy Implications from Environmental Impact Comparisons of Shale Gas, Conventional Gas, and Coal on Air, Water, and Land in the United States*, 53 Energy Pol'y 442–453 (2013). An interesting comparative analysis between shale gas development in China and the United States has been carried out by Joshua Harvey and Yang Min in the framework of the Vermont Law School – China Partnership for *Environmental Law. See* in particular, Joshua Harvey & Yang Min, *The Unconventional Promise and Problems of Shale Gas Development in the US and China: A Comparative Study*, VLA-China Partnership Envt'l L. 1, 1 (2011).

2 That is, compared to a 2007 pre-recession baseline. The Energy Information Administration predicts that unconventional fossil fuel energy resources will grow at approximately 4.9 percent per year until 2035. U.S. Energy Info. Admin., *International Energy Outlook 2010*, DOE/EIA-0484(2010), 1–9 (July 2010).

3 *See* generally Stephen A. Holditch, *The Increasing Role of Unconventional Reservoirs in the Future of Oil and Gas Business*, 55(11) J. Petroleum Tech. 34, 34 (2003) (defining conventional reservoirs of oil and gas as "*those that can be produced at economic flow rates and that will produce economic volumes of oil and gas without large stimulation treatments or any special recovery process*," whereas he defines unconventional reservoirs of oil and gas as those "*that cannot be produced at economic flowrates or that does not produce economic volumes of oil and gas without assistance from massive stimulation treatments or special recovery processes and technologies*").

Furthermore, shale formations are found in almost every region of the globe; thus the potential for shale gas development is of great relevance.[4]

Although shale gas represents a revolutionary element in the global energy framework, several regulatory and environmental concerns related to its extraction and production processes have been raised, in particular about the use of hydraulic fracturing fluids and the consequential risk of drinking water contamination.[5] As the "shale gas revolution" taking place in the United States has highlighted, human health and environmental concerns continue to dog shale gas development.[6] In that respect, given the global scope of its potential, it is crucial to ensure that the development of shale gas resources will be carried out in an environmentally sound manner.[7]

China is aware of the importance of unconventional gas as a carbon-friendly energy source and pivotal element in achieving the country's future energy and environmental objectives. As it is the country with the largest increase in greenhouse gas ("GHG") emissions, China's capacity to substitute coal with cheaper gas as its primary electricity generating fuel has the potential to represent a huge step towards global warming mitigation.[8] However, China lacks comprehensive legal instruments capable of addressing the potential environmental hazards of shale gas extraction and suffers from a weak enforcement of environmental laws and regulations.[9]

This article begins with the section "The revolutionary role of shale gas through the prism of China's energy mix: The growth of a new industry" examining the implications of shale gas on the world's energy market and its relevance regarding energy security, the recent vast increase in shale gas production and its potential for China's energy mix and supply. In the following section, "Chinese institutional and regulatory framework", the article investigates the current Chinese regulatory framework, which lacks cohesive and satisfactory provisions regarding shale gas extraction. Specifically, this section will examine the institutional shortcomings that hinder effective enforcement of environmental provisions, the pricing and fiscal regime, and the current

4 Christophe McGlade, Jamie Speirs & Steve Sorrell, *Unconventional Gas – A Review of Regional and Global Resource Estimates,* 55 Energy 571–584 (2013).

5 Hydraulic fracturing implies the high-pressure injection of millions of gallons of water-based hydraulic fracturing fluids to increase the permeability of the rock by holding the fractures open. Fracturing fluid is a mixture of about 90 per cent water, 9.5 per cent sand, and 0.5 per cent of other chemical additives. *See* generally Environmental Protection Agency, *Hydraulic Fracturing Research Study* 2010.

6 Stephen G. Osborn et al., *Methane Contamination of Drinking Water Accompanying Gas-Well Drilling and Hydraulic Fracturing,* 108(20) Proceedings of the National Academy of Sciences 8172–8176 (2011); David M. Kargbo, Ron G. Wilhelm & David J. Campbell, *Natural Gas Plays in the Marcellus Shale: Challenges and Potential Opportunities,* 44(15) Envtl. Sci. & Tech. 5679–5684 (2010); Charles W. Schmidt, *Blind Rush? Shale Gas Boom Proceeds Amid Human Health Questions,* 119(8) Envtl. Health Perspectives (2011); Robert W. Howarth, Anthony Ingraffea & Terry Engelder, *Natural Gas: Should Fracking Stop?,* Nature 271–275 (2011).

7 *See* Hannah Wiseman, *Untested Waters: The Rise of Hydraulic Fracturing in Oil and Gas Production and the Need to Revisit Regulation,* 20 Fordham Envtl. L. Rev. 115, 116 (2009); Eleanor Stephenson, Alexander Doukas & Karena Shaw, *Greenwashing Gas: Might a "Transition Fuel" Label Legitimize Carbon-intensive Natural Gas Development?,* 46 Energy Pol'y 452–459 (2012).

8 Choi Ieng Chu, Bikram Chatterjee & Alistair Brown, *The Current Status of Greenhouse Gas Reporting by Chinese Companies: A Test of Legitimacy Theory,* 28(2) Managerial Auditing J. 114–139 (2013); Mingde Cao, *Greenhouse Gas Emission Reduction,* 43(1) Envtl. Pol'y & L. 52 (2013); Zhu Liu et al., *Uncovering China's Greenhouse Gas Emission From Regional and Sectorial Perspectives,* Energy (2012); Lorraine Sugar, Christopher Kennedy & Edward Leman, *Greenhouse Gas Emissions From Chinese Cities,* 16(4) J. Indus. Ecol. 552–563 (2012); Hong Huo et al., *Projection of Energy Use and Greenhouse Gas Emissions by Motor Vehicles in China: Policy Options and Impacts,* 43 Energy Pol'y 37–48 (2012).

9 *See infra* for a discussion about Chinese institutional and regulatory framework.

barriers to foreign investments access to the Chinese energy market, which strongly counters China's need for technology and know-how. This analysis points out that there are no Chinese laws that explicitly tackle the environmental risks of the fracking process.

The section "Environmental considerations: Focus on water resources management" discusses critical concerns about fresh water management vis-à-vis unconventional gas.[10] These two natural resources have come to be complexly linked because the extraction, treatment, and distribution of fresh water entails considerable energy, while the production of fossil fuel energy involves fresh water.

The ensuing section, "Comparative analysis with the United States' previous experience: A model of development for the unconventional gas market?", discusses the similarities between China and the United States regarding shale gas. Shale gas is a pivotal element for the energy future of both countries, where energy security, energy efficiency, and environmental concerns are deeply intertwined. Their regulatory frameworks are not completely dissimilar, as both have far-reaching federal or central laws enforced by designated agencies. Furthermore, both countries exhibit a gap between the formulation of federal/central law and their enforcement at the local level. The similarities between the U.S. and Chinese energy systems allow for the drawing of parallels, which could be beneficial to the Chinese shale gas industry. In that perspective, this article argues that the current applicable Chinese legal framework is neither sufficient nor satisfactory, given what is at stake. In particular, it questions how shale gas can represent a transitional fuel to renewable energy resources.

In the last section, "The prospects for shale gas in China between regulatory interventions and new geopolitical balances", we discuss how shale gas radically impacts supply and demand of the world's energy mix and market, how new geopolitical factors must be assessed, how economic and demographic growth will increase pressure on global energy supplies, and as a result, how all fuel sources will have to be exploited. This article concludes that a comprehensive legal and regulatory change is necessary in order to foster an environmentally sound development of the shale gas sector in China. This change would be conducive to the need to increase energy security, to achieve the country's future energy and environmental objectives, and to ensure beneficial economic growth and social development.

The revolutionary role of shale gas through the prism of China's energy mix: The growth of a new industry

The potential for shale gas development is currently being explored in several countries.[11] Shale gas is found in unconventional reservoirs, from which natural gas is extracted from the low permeable source rock itself using a combination of techniques such as hydraulic fracturing[12] and horizontal drilling,[13] which create fissures in the rock allowing the gas to flow more easily through it. In addition to shale gas resources, there are other types of unconventional gas

10 For a wider debate on the carbon footprint of unconventional gas, see Robert H. Abrams & Noah D. Hall, *Framing Water Policy in a Carbon Affected and Carbon Constrained Environment*, 50 Nat. Resources J. 3, 7 (2010).

11 Shale gas development is currently being explored in several countries, and shale gas reserves have been identified in some European countries and in Algeria, Libya, Morocco, Tunisia, South Africa, Argentina, Brazil, Bolivia, Chile, Colombia, Mexico, Paraguay, Uruguay, Venezuela, India, and Pakistan, as well as in China. There are 137 exploratory drilling operations are currently underway in China and in parts of South America, particularly Argentina.

12 For a definition of "hydraulic fracturing", see *supra* note 5.

13 Horizontal drilling involves drilling a vertical well to the desired depth and then drilling laterally to access a larger portion of the reservoir. George King, *Hydraulic Fracturing 101: What Every Representative, Environmentalist, Regulator, Reporter, Investor, University Researcher, Neighbor and Engineer Should Know about Estimating Frac Risk and Improving Frac Performance in Unconventional Gas and Oil Wells*, SPE Hydraulic Fracturing Technology Conference (Feb. 6–8, 2012).

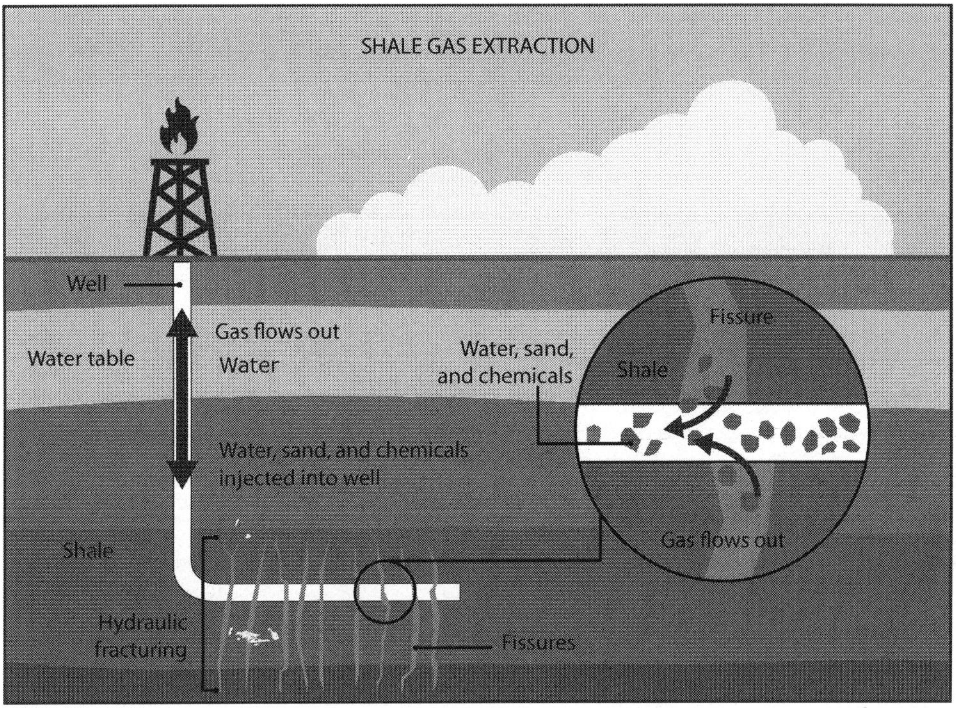

Figure 16.1 Illustrative diagram of fracking and horizontal drilling operations

reservoirs: tight gas[14] and coal bed methane ("CBM").[15] That said, the present article focuses on shale gas due to recent enormous increase in shale gas production and its potential for China's energy mix and supply.[16]

A transition toward a more sustainable future?

Shale gas is widely referred to as a "bridge fuel," implying its capability to eventually replace hydrocarbons with carbon-free renewable resources as our primary source of

14 Tight gas refers to natural gas that is trapped in sandstones. For the significance of this energy source in China, see Dai Jinxini, Ni Yunyan & Wu Xiaoqi, *Tight Gas in China and Its Significance in Exploration and Exploitation*, 39(3) Petroleum Exploration & Dev. 277–284 (2012).

15 CBM is a natural gas that is produced from coal seams, which act as the source and reservoir for the natural gas. China's focus has historically been on CBM, but recently its focus has shifted towards developing its shale gas resources. Yumin Lv, Dazhen Tang, Hao Xu & Haohan Luo, *Production Characteristics and the Key Factors in High-Rank Coalbed Methane Fields: A Case Study on the Fanzhuang Block, Southern Qinshui Basin, China*, 96 Int'l J. Coal Geology 93–108 (2012). The term "unconventional gas" is used herein to indicate shale gas, which has been acknowledged as the most promising unconventional gas.

16 China's potential unconventional gas reservoirs are significant, although many still need to be exactly estimated. The political support of shale gas is also relevant, and the Chinese Ministry of Land and Resources (MLR) announced "a strategic goal of reaching a production target of 15–30 BCM (billion cubic meters) by 2020." *See* International Energy Agency, *Medium-term Oil & Gas Markets* 185 (2010). To achieve this goal, China will have, *inter alia*, to acquire fracking technology and expertise. In that sense, the state-owned company Sinopec has already launched a dialogue with international oil companies in furtherance of this goal. What is more, in November 2009, China and the United States signed a Memorandum of Understanding ("MoU") to jointly cooperate in assessing China's shale gas resources and foster investments in this sector. *See* International Energy Agency, *Medium-Term Oil & Gas Markets* 185–188 (2010).

energy.[17] This concept acknowledges that renewable resources cannot replace hydrocarbons as our primary generating fuel in the near term, and that, while shale gas remains a hydrocarbon, it has less detrimental consequences on the environment than other fossil fuels.[18] In that respect, it appears that at the moment, renewable resources are less cost-competitive than fossil fuels, in particular natural gas.[19]

Moreover, in addition to their high costs, renewable resources present further downsides, including the need for installing thousands of miles of new transmission lines requiring onerous investments and burdensome regulatory approvals. With the European Union and the United States examining ways to develop electricity projects that use renewable resources to generate electricity and to market the electricity produced by such projects, it appears that they mainly rely on the continued availability of federal and state subsidies and state renewable resource portfolio mandates.[20] Given the ongoing global financial recession. However, those subsidies and mandates are unlikely to be granted in the future. Rather, many EU countries have already either reduced or eliminated those subsidies.[21]

On the other hand, replacement of coal with natural gas, including shale gas, as a generating fuel reduces emissions of carbon dioxide. Hence, the expression "bridge fuel" reflects the expectation of many policy-makers that we can achieve mitigation of climate change in the near term by replacing coal with natural gas, while eventually entirely replacing all hydrocarbons with carbon-free renewable resources in the longer term.[22] Clearly the practicality of

17 See Noam Lior, ***Sustainable Energy Development with Some Game-Changers***, 40 Energy 3, 4 (2012). *See generally* Hanna Mäkinen, ***Shale Gas–a Game Changer in the Global Energy Play***, 1 Baltic rim economies (2010); Amy Myers Jaffe, ***Shale Gas Will Rock the World***, Wall Street Journal (May 10, 2010); Paul Stevens, The 'Shale Gas Revolution': Hype and Reality (Royal Institute for International Affairs/ Chatham House, 2010); Noam Lior, ***Sustainable Energy Development with Some Game-Changers***, 40(1) Energy 3–18 (2012); Martin Wolf, ***Prepare for a Golden Age of Gas***, Financial Times, February 22 (2012).

18 See generally Stevens, ***supra*** note 17.

19 It costs two to five times as much to generate electricity through the use of renewable resources such as solar and wind as through use of gas. Furthermore, given that most renewables can generate electricity exclusively on an intermittent basis, a unit of electricity generated through the use of a renewable resource is worth only about 25 percent as much as a unit of electricity generated through the use of gas. Paul L. Joskow, ***Comparing the Costs of Intermittent and Dispatchable Electricity Generating Technologies***, 100(3) Am. Econ. Rev.: Papers & Proceedings 238–241 (2011), http://web.mit.edu/ceepr/www/publications/reprints/Reprint_231_WC.pdf (last visited Aug 8, 2016); Paolo Davide Farah & Elena Cima, ***Energy Trade and the WTO: Implications for Renewable Energy and the OPEC Cartel***, 16 (3) J. Int'l Econ. L. 707–740 (2013).

20 Manuel Frondel et al., ***Economic Impacts From The Promotion Of Renewable Energy Technologies: The German Experience***, 38(8) Energy Pol'y 4048–4056 (2010); Richard Schmalensee, ***Evaluating Policies To Increase Electricity Generation From Renewable Energy***, 6(1) Rev. Envtl. Econ. & Pol'y 45–64 (2012); Richard Schmalensee, ***Evaluating Policies to Increase the Generation of Electricity from Renewable Energy*** (2011); Mark A. Delucchi & Mark Z. Jacobson, ***Providing All Global Energy with Wind, Water, and Solar Power, Part II: Reliability, System and Transmission Costs, and Policies***, 39(3) Energy Pol'y 1170–1190 (2011); Keith Williges, Johan Lilliestam & Anthony Patt, ***Making Concentrated Solar Power Competitive with Coal: the Costs of a European Feed-In Tariff***, 38(6) Energy Pol'y 3089–3097 (2010); Paul Lehmann & Erik Gawel, ***Why Should Support Schemes for Renewable Electricity Complement the EU Emissions Trading Scheme***, Energy Pol'y (2012).

21 For instance, Portugal and Spain took the extraordinary decision of reneging on the long-term commitments they made to renewable resource projects by retroactively eliminating their subsidies. This way, the two Iberian countries saved many billions of Euros in the efforts to avoid defaulting on their sovereign debt.

22 Richard J. Pierce, Jr., ***Natural Gas: A Long Bridge to a Promising Destination***, 32 Utah Envtl. L. Rev. 245 (2012). *See* also Daniel P. Schrag, ***Is Shale Gas Good for Climate Change?***, 141(2) Dædalus, the Journal of the American Academy of Arts & Sciences (2012). On the other hand, unconventional

this scenario is dependent on the ability to take adequate measures to guarantee society that hydraulic fracturing of shale basins can be carried out with low environmental costs.

China is likely to benefit greatly from shale gas. The International Energy Agency (IEA) predicts that China will consume more gas than the entire EU by 2035.[23] As it is the country with the largest source of greenhouse gas emissions and the largest source of increase in GHG emissions, China's capacity to substitute coal with cheaper gas as its primary electricity-generating fuel has the potential to represent a huge step towards global warming mitigation.[24]

However, relying on shale gas introduces the risk of neglecting investments in renewable energies. Some critics say that the industry's focus on developing shale gas and other unconventional sources is diverting attention and capital from the development of renewables because low-cost power is generated from copious natural gas supplies, which could frustrate the economic viability of wind, solar, and geothermal projects, and eventually delay the shift to renewable energies by many years.[25] Indeed, in the United States, shale gas as a source of low-priced electric power created a more difficult competitive environment for new wind projects.[26] Similarly, the IEA suggests that the effect of falling gas prices due to increased shale gas development could hamper the viability of low-carbon alternatives.[27] Nevertheless, it is important to bear in mind that it is not certain that gas prices will remain low if shale gas must meet tighter regulatory criteria. Additionally, the ultimate price competitor in the power sector is not gas, but coal (and, for base load capacity, nuclear and hydropower). On this point, Jenner and Lamadrid remark that "the crucial challenge in order to achieve grid parity is to meet the coal price. This objective can be approached from two sides: increased cost-effectiveness of renewable energies and storage solutions by further technological innovation; or internalization of the cost of carbon into the price of coal. Both ways are relatively independent from the shale gas issue."[28] In other words, "shale gas holds the

---

natural gas production is noted for its potential for significantly large quantities of methane leakage, which is a potent greenhouse gas. During oil and gas production processes, fugitive methane emissions are most commonly leaked or intentionally vented at the wellhead, and from pipes and valves. Merisha Enoe, Yan He & Erica Pohnan, *Lessons Learned: A Path toward Responsible Development of China's Shale Gas Resources*, NAT. RESOURCES DEF. COUNS. 6 (2012). Arguing that dynamic governance innovation can facilitate climate-energy-water balancing to address natural gas governance gaps: Elizabeth Burleson, *Climate Change and Natural Gas Dynamic Governance*, 63 (4) CASE W. RES. L. REV. (2013).

23 International Energy Agency, *Are We Entering a Golden Age of Gas?* 8 (World Energy Outlook, 2011).

24 For a scientific perspective on the fact that a significant part of recent global warming is driven by the accumulation of anthropogenically derived greenhouse active gases in the Earth's atmosphere, see JOHN DODSONN, *Introduction*, in CHANGING CLIMATES, EARTH SYSTEMS AND SOCIETY xix (John Dodson ed., Springer, 2010).

25 In light of the great potential for investments in carbon markets, renewable energy sources and low carbon technologies, it clearly appears that international investment, renewables, and climate change are interdependent concepts. On this point, *see* Kate Miles, *International Investment Law and Climate Change: Issues in the Transition to a Low Carbon World*, Society of International Economic Law (SIEL) Inaugural Conference (July 2, 2008), http://ssrn.com/abstract=1154588 (last visited Aug 8, 2016).

26 *See generally* DANIEL YERGIN, THE QUEST: ENERGY SECURITY AND THE REMAKING OF THE MODERN WORLD (2011).

27 This was confirmed by the chief economist of the International Energy Agency (IEA), Fatih Birol, who stated that "if gas prices come down, that would put a lot of pressure on governments to review their existing renewable energy support policies [. . .] We may see many renewable energy projects put on the shelf." Fiona Harvey, Natural Gas is No Climate Change 'Panacea', Warns IEA, THE GUARDIAN (June 6, 2011), http://www.theguardian.com/environment/2011/jun/06/natural-gas-climate-change-no-panacea (last visited Aug 8, 2016).

28 S. Jenner & A. J. Lamadrid, *supra* note 1, at 17. On the internalization of the cost of carbon into the price of coal, see generally, David M. Driesen, *Putting a Price on Carbon: The Metaphor*, 44 ENVTL. L. 695 (2014); David M. Driesen, *The Limits of Pricing Carbon*, 4 CLIMATE L. 107 (2014).

potential to smoothen the transition to an age of renewable energies but we must be aware of the potential of low gas prices to cause temporarily a spike."[29]

Extreme reliance on natural gas would equally frustrate the efforts to maintain fuel mix diversity in the power sector, leaving ratepayers, utilities, and the economy as a whole vulnerable to the hazards of commodity price volatility. In that sense, substitution of natural gas for other fossil fuel cannot be the exclusive means to tackle GHG emissions and climate change, given that natural gas is itself a fossil fuel. Further complementary actions are then needed in order to have a reasonable chance of meeting climate goals.[30] To this end, low-carbon investments, renewable energy deployment, carbon capture and storage technologies, and energy efficient measures must be prioritized in the international energy governance agenda. Another critical step in the right direction would be the establishment of a carbon tax that would allow negative externalities related to fossil fuels not to be priced by society.[31] Finally, further actions would require the development of a real-time pricing mechanism for electricity[32] and the reduction of direct releases of methane into the atmosphere during the extraction process. Emissions of methane are mainly caused by 'flowback' of the water forced into the rock formation during fracking, and by leaks in processing and during transportation.[33] Recent studies suggest that these losses can be limited by the use of best technology, but cannot be completely avoided.[34] In that respect, it is crucial to measure precisely the GHG emissions from both natural gas production and consumption to minimize emissions reductions along the entire natural gas value chain.[35] As technologies for producing shale gas continue to advance and the industry grows in scale, wider collaboration on research and development issues is required among governmental agencies and international energy governance institutions.

In light of the aforesaid, a growing body of scientific research questions how shale gas could ever be a transitional fuel that is able to shift society from its current overreliance on fossil fuels to a greater use of sustainable renewable energy, given its carbon intensity and the level of investment needed.[36] Furthermore, shale gas would most likely involve costly regulation.

29 *Id.*

30 Instead of being thought of as competitors, however, natural gas and renewable energy sources should be seen as complementary, not competitive, components of the power sector. Natural gas plants can quickly scale up or down their electricity production and so can act as an effective hedge against the intermittency of renewables. The Center for Climate and Energy Solutions (C2ES), *Leveraging Natural Gas to Reduce Greenhouse Gas Emissions, Summary Report* (June 2013), http://www.c2es.org/publications/leveraging-natural-gas-reduce-greenhouse-gas-emissions (last visited Aug 8, 2016).

31 William D. Nordhaus, *To Tax or Not to Tax: Alternative Approaches to Slowing Global Warming*, 1(1) Rev. Envtl. Econ. Pol'y 26–44 (2007); Liang Qiao-Mei, Ying Fan & Yi-Ming Wei, *Carbon Taxation Policy in China: How to Protect Energy-and Trade-Intensive Sectors?*, 29(2) J. Pol'y Modeling 311–333 (2007).

32 Mark G. Lijesen, *The Real-Time Price Elasticity of Electricity*, 29(2) Energy Econ. 249–258 (2007); Stephen P. Holland and Erin T. Mansur, *Is Real-Time Pricing Green? The Environmental Impacts of Electricity Demand Variance*, 90(3) Rev. Econ. & Stat. 550–561 (2008); Hunt Allcott, *Rethinking Real-Time Electricity Pricing*, 33(4) Resource & Energy Econ. 820–842 (2011).

33 CTR, For Climate & Energy Solutions, *supra* note 30, at 22.

34 Recent scientific research indicates that relying on shale gas could in fact be as harmful to the climate as reliance on coal. Robert W. Howarth, Renee Santoro & Anthony Ingraffea, *Methane and the Greenhouse-Gas Footprint of Natural Gas from Shale Formations*, 106(4) Climatic Change 679–690 (2011).

35 Indeed, natural gas is not carbon-free. On the contrary, it releases emissions by its combustion. Moreover, it contains methane (CH_4), a potent greenhouse gas, whose release during production, transmission, and distribution may offset the beneficial climate outcome of shale gas use.

36 On this point, Nobuo Tanaka, executive director of the International Energy Agency (IEA), stated: "While natural gas is the cleanest fossil fuel, it is still a fossil fuel. Its increased use could muscle out low

Provided that natural and shale gas prices remain low, there will be fewer inducements to invest in greener sources. Hence, in order to satisfy their carbon reduction targets, there is a risk that governments could force the energy industry to make these investments through regulation, which would greatly augment costs across the entire oil and gas industry, and result in repercussions on highly cost-sensitive shale gas investments, projects and operations.

China's stake in the shale gas saga

Shale gas is already revolutionizing the world energy markets and industry. Vast deposits are being discovered throughout the world. China is aware of the role of unconventional gas as a carbon-friendly energy source and pivotal element in achieving the country's future energy and environmental objectives: increasing energy security, decreasing GHG emissions,[37] and ameliorating domestic air quality while simultaneously empowering the country to persevere a beneficial economic growth and social development.[38] A 2013 assessment of international shale gas resources issued by the U.S. IEA[39] estimated technically recoverable shale gas resources in China at 1115 trillion cubic feet,[40] nearly 50 percent more than resources in the United States.[41] In reality, China's national oil companies have already commenced shale gas exploratory drilling with the technical and financial assistance of joint ventures with multinational companies such as Total, BP, and Royal Dutch Shell.[42] The rigid structure of China's state-controlled oil and gas industry hampers efforts to exploit reserves since the current

carbon fuels such as renewables [. . .] an expansion of gas use alone is no panacea for climate change." *See* Fiona Harvey, *supra* note 24. Indeed, according to studies carried out by the IEA, the development of the shale gas industry would put our CO_2 emissions on a "trajectory consistent with a probable temperature rise of more than 3.5 degrees Celsius in the long term." International Energy Agency (IEA), May 2012, *Golden Rules for a Golden Age of Gas*, May 2009, at 91, http://www.worldenergyoutlook.org/goldenrules/ (last visited Aug 8, 2016).

37 According to the Kyoto Protocol's emission reduction obligations, the Chinese government announced on November 25, 2009 that China's unit GDP CO_2 emissions in 2020 compared with that in 2005 will decrease by 40 per cent to 45 per cent. Margret Kim and Robert Jones, China's Energy Security and the Climate Change Conundrum, 19(3) Nat. Resources & Env't 3 (2005); Deng Haifeng, *Legal Interactive Mechanism on Climate Change: A Comparative Study of China and U.S. Experiences*, 8 US-China L. Rev. 431, 431–444 (2011); Paul Howard, *Harmony in China's Climate Change Policy*, in Climate Change and Growth in Asia (Edward Elgar, 2011).

38 For a prediction of Chinese energy consumption and carbon dioxide emissions in a scenario of the all-inclusive well-off society in 2020, *see* Wei Lu and Yitai Ma, *Image of Energy Consumption of Well Off Society in China*, 45 Energy Conversion & Mgmt. 1357–1367 (2004). On the relationship between economic growth and social development, *see* in general Gheorhe H. Popescu, *The Social Evolution of China's Economic Growth*, 1 Contemp. Readings in Law and Social Justice 88–93 (2013).

39 The EIA is an independent arm of the U.S. DOE.

40 U.S. Energy Info. Admin., Technically Recoverable Shale Oil and Shale Gas Resources: An Assessment of 137 Shale Formations in 41 Countries Outside the United States 6 (2013). *See* also Li Shizhen, *The Status of World Shale Gas Exploration and Development and Implications for China*, 6 Geological Bulletin 918–924 (2010) (in Chinese).

41 China has an estimated 1,115 Tcf of risked, technically recoverable shale gas, mainly in marine- and lacustrine-deposited source rock shales of the Sichuan (626 Tcf), Tarim (216 Tcf), Junggar (36 Tcf), and Songliao (16 Tcf) basins. Additional risked, technically recoverable shale gas resources totaling 222 Tcf exist in the smaller, structurally more complex Yangtze Platform and the Jianghan and Subei basins. Shale gas leasing and exploration drilling are already underway in China, primarily in the Sichuan Basin and Yangtze Platform areas and led by PetroChina, Sinopec, and Shell, and the government has set an ambitious but probable unachievable target for shale gas production of 5.8 to 9.7 Bcfd by 2020. *See* McGlade, Speirs & Sorrell, *supra* note 4.

42 *Id.*

absence of competition between the three state-owned energy giants (CNPC, Sinopec, and PetroChina) is not conducive to a fair allocation of resources. In that sense, the country's current energy regulation is characterized by an overregulation of the energy market, a fragmented system of regulation, and insufficient environmental regulation.[43] Moreover, numerous Chinese investments into North American shale basins illustrates Beijing's concrete commitment to exploring the potential of shale gas resources, as China is exponentially building its shale gas capacity in order to achieve energy security and influence in the world's gas pricing regimes.[44] What emerges is a growing Chinese engagement in international relations in order to guarantee a steady energy supply for its ever-increasing domestic needs.[45] At the moment, natural gas demand continues to exceed supply, making China a net importer; but, at the same time, domestic production has been burgeoning,[46] increasing the share of natural gas in total energy requirements from 2 percent to 4 percent, and expected to reach 10 percent by 2020.[47]

However, after assessing the development of the shale gas industry in China, one can see that the current applicable legal framework is neither sufficient nor satisfactory, given what is at stake. China must still adequately delineate a policy framework regarding energy regulation and physical infrastructures, pricing mechanisms, as well as management of environmental risks that may be connected to the development of its unconventional gas resources. The exploitation of natural reserves is a strategic sector for national security and, in that sense, is highly sensitive to political influences and extremely prone to State intervention. The central government firmly controls shale gas blocks by granting exploration rights and organizing auctions. The first round of tendering for shale gas exploration rights in June 2011 was held in the form of an invitation tender, and only State- and province-controlled oil and gas enterprises were able to bid on the gas drilling projects, namely, China National Off-shore Oil Corporation (CNOOC), Sinopec, PetroChina, Yanchang Petroleum, China

43 Xin Qiu & Honglin Li, *Energy Regulation and Legislation in China*, 42 ENVTL. L. REP. 10678 (2012).

44 Globally, States engage in multilateral or bilateral inter-State relations to pursue energy security, while building up extensive reserves that inevitably impact on the world's oil and gas supply. Paolo Davide Farah & Piercarlo Rossi, *National Energy Policies and Energy Security in the Context of Climate Change and Global Environmental Risks: A Theoretical Framework for Reconciling Domestic and International Law through a Multiscalar and Multilevel Approach*, 20(6) EUR. ENERGY & ENVTL. L. REV. 232–234 (2011); Rafael Leal-Arcas & Andrew Filis, *The Fragmented Governance of the Global Energy Economy: A Legal-Institutional Analysis*, 6(4) J. WORLD ENERGY L. & BUS. 1–58 (2013).

45 Andreas Goldthau, *Energy Diplomacy in Trade and Investment in Oil and Gas*, in GLOBAL ENERGY GOVERNANCE: THE NEW RULES OF THE GAME 25–47 (Brookings Institution Press, 2010).

46 China augmented natural gas domestic production from 27.2 billion cubic meters (bcm) in 2001 (approximately 106 percent of domestic consumption) to 94.5 bcm in 2010 (approximately 89 percent of domestic consumption). Given the continuingly increasing domestic need, China is also implementing its energy infrastructure network. In that respect, the 4,200-km West-to-East pipeline was built to transport gas from Xinjiang Province in the west to Shanghai, and the TransAsian pipeline was opened in 2009 to bring gas from Turkmenistan to China. Moreover, four LNG receiving terminals were brought online, allowing LNG to meet some 10 per cent of Chinese gas demand. A few more LNG receiving terminals are under construction. *See* McGlade, Speirs & Sorrell, *supra* note 4; Ruud Weijermars & Crispian McCredie, *Assessing Shale Gas Potential*, PETROLEUM REV. (October 2011).

47 Boqiang Lin and Ting Wang, *Forecasting Natural Gas Supply in China: Production Peak and Import Trends*, ENERGY POL'Y (2012); Guy C. K. Leung, *China's Energy Security: Perception and Reality*, 39(3) ENERGY POL'Y 1330–1337 (2011); OIL AND GAS RESOURCES IN CHINA: A ROADMAP TO 2050 (Guangding Liu, Changchun Yang & Tianyao Hao eds, Spring Science & Business Media, 2011); Junchen Li et al., *Forecasting the Growth of China's Natural Gas Consumption*, 36(3) ENERGY 1380–1385 (2011).

United Coalbed Methane Corporation, and Henan CBM.[48] The exclusion of foreign companies from being eligible to obtain production licenses was possibly aimed at retaining control over the scope of investments and the production ratio. The second round of tendering was held in October 2012 and it opened bidding to state-owned enterprises in other industries as well as privately-held Chinese investment entities (Sinochem and Zhenhua Oil) in order to foster greater competition and innovativeness in the infant shale gas industry.[49] However, the Chinese government still has enormous leeway in deciding which enterprises can access its shale gas industry, and the entry of non-state Chinese companies will not change this situation given that these entities continue to rely on cooperation with State-controlled PetroChina, which owns and runs the national transmission network.[50] Nevertheless, foreign companies are not able to bid or act independently for either extraction or infrastructure projects, as they are merely allowed to operate under approved joint ventures with Chinese firms. Domestic companies apply for permits to explore and develop sites, after which they can enter into partnerships with foreign investors.[51]

State-owned enterprises such as CNPC and CNOOC can acquire specific technical skills by investing in North American companies of shale gas and establishing joint ventures. For instance, Shell and CNPC have joined in digging more than thirty gas wells in Middle Sichuan Province, and discovered shale gas in Fushun-Yongchuan Block, which is considered the first commercial shale gas project in China.[52] The two companies signed the first production-sharing agreement approved for foreign involvement in the shale gas sector.[53] Usually foreign oil and gas companies seek to join product sharing agreements ("PSAs"), which represent the classic form of contracting of oil and gas resources. Similarly, Statoil, ConocoPhillips, BP, Chevron, and Exxon Mobil have entered into joint study agreements with Chinese national oil companies and they are likely to transform their agreements into PSAs later on.[54]

In a PSA, an international oil company is more of a partner in the venture and shares in the resulting oil as well as control of the operation either directly or through a joint-operation body. PSAs can be beneficial to governments of countries that lack the expertise and capital to exploit their natural resources and wish to attract foreign companies to do so. An international oil company usually shares the resulting profits and oil/gas, but is obligated to pay not only royalties but also income tax on its share. An alternative method to approaching the market is to acquire or enter into a cooperation agreement with a local oil or gas field service provider.

The principal technique to foster production and use of unconventional natural gas is through government-set goals and mandates, which State-run entities, with some participation from private companies, pursue with projects and adequate investments. The vast participation in the aforementioned tenders reflects the market enthusiasm concerning the potential of the shale gas industry. However, lack of experience will carry relevant hindrances

48 U.S. Energy Info. Admin., China – International Energy Data and Analysis (May 14, 2015).

49 Cameron McKenna, *Shale Gas: Legal Developments in Some Key Jurisdictions Across the Globe*, Lexology (Dec. 5, 2011).

50 Christina Larson, *China's Shale-Gas Potential and Peril*, Bloomberg Business Week (April 18, 2013).

51 KPMG, Global Energy Institute, Shale Gas: Global. M&A Trends, KPMG International, May 2012.

52 Chinese Nat'l Petrol. Corp, Unconventional Oil & Gas Resources, http://www.cnpc.com.cn/en/umconventional/common_index.shtml (last visited Aug 8, 2016).

53 Shell committed to contributing at least $1 billion each year for the joint venture to fund exploration. *Shell Plans to Spend $1 Billion a Year on China Gas*, Bloomberg News (Mar. 28, 2013).

54 Edwin Lee, *Shale Gas in China: How Far From Dream to Reality?*, Lexology (June 3, 2013).

on shale gas exploitation in China. Lack of technology, equipment, market and transportation networks, coupled with blind investment and over-exploitation, are the common challenges to economic development in China. Furthermore, a great number of enterprises entering the market at once might cause excessive production capacity, industrial structure imbalance, and uncontrolled environmental pollution. Additionally, the concerns related to land availability, lack of supply chains, and foundation facilities, will bring more challenges to shale gas exploitation in China.

It remains to be seen what the implications will be in terms of environmental costs. Shale gas is obtained through hydraulic fracturing, a controversial extracting technology which creates, as highlighted by the shale gas boom that took place in the United States,[55] critical environmental threats, namely contamination of freshwater aquifers by fracturing fluids and depletion of local water supplies. In China, these obstacles to the mature development of the country's unconventional gas reserves are augmented by two deeply intertwined hurdles: the absence of a comprehensive legal framework specifically addressing the potential environmental hazards of shale gas production, and weak enforcement of relevant laws and regulations. Acknowledging the importance of shale gas as a bridging source of energy in the shift from fossil fuels to clean energy, the primary need is to minimize environmental damages related to the process of shale gas extraction and achieve the goal of extracting shale gas in an environmentally responsible way, which is mainly a matter of regulation and enforcement. In the last decade, the United States has taken the lead in exploration, development, technology, production, and export of shale gas. Consequentially the U.S. experience could be helpful for other countries, such as China, which wish to develop their own shale gas industries.

Chinese institutional and regulatory framework

The current Chinese regulatory framework lacks cohesive and satisfactory provisions regarding shale gas extraction and its related environmental concerns. There appears to be a generalized absence of cohesiveness of the energy-resources system, which is characterized by institutional fragmentation and conflicts of interest among a plethora of entities. The Chinese legal system features a tripartite structure: the National People's Committee passes laws; the State Council passes regulations; various ministries create rules, and departments within the ministries create other legislative documents. In the context of shale gas production, the Ministry of Environmental Protection (MEP) plays a fundamental role as it is responsible for enforcing environmental laws through its provincial and municipal subsidiaries. Another fundamental body is the National Development and Reform Commission (NDRC), which oversees the National Energy Administration and sets broad environmental standards and long-term goals, regulated and enforced through provincial and municipal-level branches of the Ministry of Environmental Protection.[56]

55 Pulitzer Prize–winning energy author Daniel Yergin remarks how quickly natural gas from shale formations joined the energy mix in the United States: "Shale gas really has been a revolution that's happened extremely rapidly [. . .] It's gone from being virtually none of our natural gas production to about 30 percent of our total natural gas production." DANIEL YERGIN, THE QUEST: ENERGY SECURITY AND THE REMAKING OF THE MODERN WORLD (Penguin, 2011). *See* Wiseman, *supra* note 7; Angela C. Cupas, *The Not-So-Safe Drinking Water Act: Why We Must Regulate Hydraulic Fracturing at the Federal Level*, 33 WILLIAM & MARY ENVTL. L. & POL'Y REV. 605 (2009).

56 ALBERT CHEN, AN INTRODUCTION TO THE LEGAL SYSTEM OF THE PEOPLE'S REPUBLIC OF CHINA (Lexis/Nexis, 2004).

Regulation of the shale gas industry in China

Regulation of the shale gas industry is horizontally fragmented and jointly undertaken by at least six authorities at the ministerial level, including the NDRC, Ministry of Land Resources (MLR), Ministry of Finance (MOF), Ministry of Environmental Protection (MEP), Ministry of Science and Technology (MOST), and the State Administration of Taxation (SAT). The presence of many regulators carries the risks of conflict and makes the allocation of competences unclear. What appears to emerge from an initial analysis is that the NDRC is in charge of shale gas industrial policies and planning, which covers targets, transportation, consumption, and pricing.[57] MLR is responsible for public tenders of shale gas blocks and the setting of thresholds for entry.[58] MOF and SAT jointly determine tax incentives, such as grants and preferential fiscal policies.[59] MOST works on improving and developing technologies for the peculiar Chinese geological environment, while MEP has a strategic relevance as supervisor and sets minimum standards for underground and surface water protection, wastewater treatment and recycling, air pollution, and protection of species of animals and plants.[60]

There are currently no Chinese laws that explicitly tackle the environmental risks of the fracking process; moreover, although shale gas development is part of China's current Five-Year Strategic Plan, the Chinese government has not passed legislation or provided any guidance for shale gas exploration, market application, and strategic planning.[61] Despite this, several existing laws, if broadly interpreted, might be applied, although they are neither exclusively concerned nor purposely drafted to deal with shale gas. In particular, the most pertinent law regarding shale gas production and its potential environmental perils is the Water Pollution Prevention and Control Law (WPPCL),[62] which sets central and local water standards to which local governments must adapt their regulations within a "cooperative federalism" framework.[63] This legal tool provides a number of measures aimed at protecting drinking water[64] and forbidding the construction of drainage outlets in specific areas. Article 38 of the Water Law lays down that "protective measures shall be taken [. . .] while constructing underground engineering facilities or carrying out underground prospecting, mining, and other underground activities."[65] The expression "*other underground activities*" certainly includes the fracturing process. Furthermore, the Water Law prohibits the discharge of a number of chemicals usually used in American fracturing fluids,[66] while allowed pollutant discharges are capped at fixed amounts.[67]

57 Lee, *supra* note 54.

58 *Id.*

59 *Id.*

60 *Id.*

61 For text in English of the Energy and Climate Goals of China's 12th Five-Year Plan, see Joanna Lewis, Pew Ctr. on Glob. Climate Change, Energy and Climate Goals of China's 12th Five-Year Plan (Mar. 2011).

62 Law on Prevention and Control of Water Pollution (promulgated by the Standing Comm. Nat'l People's Cong., May 11, 1984, amended Feb. 28, 2008). Another law that could come into play in this context is the Water and Soil Conservation Law. On this point see, Nengye Liu, People's Republic of China: Water and Soil Conservation Law, 1 Iucn Acad. Envtl. L. E-Journal 69–74 (2012).

63 Elizabeth Burleson, *Cooperative Federalism and Hydraulic Fracturing: A Human Right to a Clean Environment,* 22 Cornell J.L. & Pub. Pol'y 289 (2013), http://ssrn.com/abstract=2007234 (last visited Aug 8, 2016).

64 Law on Prevention and Control of Water Pollution, supra note 62, art. 56.

65 *Id.*, art. 38.

66 Such as "any oil, acid, or alkaline solutions or highly toxic liquid waste" or "any highly toxic soluble waste residue containing mercury, cadmium, arsenic, chromium, lead, cyanide, etc." *Id.*, Articles 29, 31.

67 *Id.*, art. 18.

Although the Water Law constitutes a fundamental tool in relation to the issues analyzed in this chapter, its coverage is still limited. While it requires that the State establish and improve compensation mechanisms for the ecological protection of the water environment in drinking water source areas and reservoirs by instruments such as payment of transfers, no supporting laws and regulations currently exist.[68] Furthermore, the WPPCL contains some ambiguous provisions and lacks any definition of the authority of the local governments, creating a vacuum that negatively affects the effectiveness of the regulatory framework.[69] The WPPCL permits the governments of provinces, autonomous regions, and municipalities to establish their own standards for items not set by a central body, and includes strong punitive measures to be imposed upon violators who can be fined and ordered to remediate the damage they have caused.[70] In particular, in the amended WPPCL promulgated in February 2008 and effective on June 1, 2008, stricter penalties against violators have been added to enhance law enforcement.[71] Nevertheless, without detailed guidelines for implementing the law, effective enforcement of those stricter penalties remains unfulfilled.

Other relevant legal instruments are the Mineral Resources Law[72] and the Regulations of the People's Republic of China on Sino-foreign Cooperation in the Exploitation of Continental Petroleum Resources.[73] The former outlines a unified regional registration regime for the exploration of mineral resources, and is thus applicable to shale gas exploitation.[74] To obtain permission for exploration and extraction of minerals, a production plan must be submitted for approval by the Department of Geology and Mineral resources. However, the qualifying criteria for approval are quite vague and the law does not specifically define them.[75] On the other hand, the Regulations of the People's Republic of China on Sino-foreign Cooperation in the Exploitation of Continental Petroleum Resources targets the types of partnerships currently spreading in the exploration and production of unconventional gas.[76] The problem appears to be that there are potentially applicable domestic and regional laws but inadequate mechanisms for their implementation.

68 Research Handbook On Chinese Environmental Law 72 (Tianbao Qin ed., 2015).

69 On the authority of local governments on environmental issues in China, see Alex Wang, *The Search for Sustainable Legitimacy: Environmental Law and Bureaucracy in China*, 37 Harv. Envtl. L. Rev. 365 (2013).

70 Law on Prevention and Control of Water Pollution, *supra* note 62, art. 13.

71 Jingyun Li & Jingjing Liu, Quest for Clean Water: China's Newly Amended Water Pollution Control Law, Wilson Ctr. (July 7, 2009).

72 P.R.C. Law on Mineral Resources (promulgated by Order No. 36 of the President of the People's Republic of China, Mar. 19, 1986, effective Aug. 29, 1996).

73 Regulations of the People's Republic of China on the Exploitation of On-shore Petroleum Resources in Cooperation with Foreign Enterprises (promulgated by Decree No. 317 of the State Council of the People's Republic of China, Sept. 23, 2001, effective Sept. 23, 2001).

74 P.R.C. Law on Mineral Resources, *supra* note 72, art. 16.

75 The qualifying criteria for approval require adherence to: "qualifications prescribed by the State, and the department in charge of examination and approval shall, in accordance with law and relevant State regulations examine the enterprise's mining area, its mining design or mining plan, production and technological conditions and safety and environmental protection measures." *Id.*, art. 15.

76 In particular, Article 13 states: "To cooperate in the exploitation of on-shore resources, the Chinese petroleum companies and the foreign enterprise must enter into a contract. Unless laws, regulations or the contract specifies otherwise, the foreign enterprise entering into the contract (hereinafter referred to as the 'foreign contractor") solely shall provide the investment for the exploration, be responsible for the exploration operations and bear all exploration risks. After the discovery of an oil (gas) field with commercial exploitation value, the foreign contractor and the Chinese petroleum companies shall jointly invest in cooperative development. The foreign contractor shall undertake the development and production operations, until production operations are taken over by Chinese petroleum companies as stipulated in the contract." Regulations of the People's Republic of China on Exploitation of On-shore Petroleum

As for environmental law, despite the efforts made by China to craft a comprehensive environmental legal framework over the past thirty years, implementation in practice has been notoriously poor.[77] Nevertheless, during China's 11th Five-Year Plan period (2006–2010), bureaucrats started taking innovative action on environmental protection and energy efficiency, setting high-priority, quantitative pollution reduction and energy efficiency performance targets that were assigned to governors, mayors, county magistrates, and State-owned enterprise leaders in every corner of China's massive bureaucracy. This new perspective derived from the prioritization of environmental protection through the 'cadre evaluation system', i.e. China's system for top-down bureaucratic personnel evaluation.[78] As Alex L. Wang remarked, this evaluation framework is part of a far-reaching political strategy to limit risks on the party-state's hold on power.[79] In this vein, cadre evaluation system fostered the use of environmental protection as an instrument for promoting the essential elements of China's 'performance legitimacy', namely, sustained economic growth and social stability.[80] This shows how decentered the role of law in Chinese governance still is, and stresses the primary role of hierarchical structures and bureaucratic plan targets.[81] Consequentially, Chinese leaders have relied mainly on top-down party-state bureaucratic mandates to drive performance of new environmental goals. At the same time, the cadre evaluation system represents an effort to promote (although haltingly) environmental values as a new source of legitimacy in line with the Hu-Wen rubric of a 'harmonious society' as a programmatic response to concerns about declining State legitimacy.[82]

Resources in Cooperation with Foreign Enterprises, art. 13. Lianyong Feng et al., *Developmental Features of the Chinese Petroleum Industry in Recent Years, in* THE CHINESE OIL INDUSTRY: HISTORY AND FUTURE 17, 36–37 (Lianyong Feng et al eds., Springer, 2013).

77 A leading Chinese environmental law scholar stated: "*China's green laws are useless.*" Jin Wang, *China's Green Laws are Useless* (September 23, 2010), http://www.chinadialogue.net/article/show/single/en/3831 (last visited Aug 8, 2016).

78 Wang, *supra* note 69, at 368, n. 13 ("'Cadres,' simply put, are party-state bureaucrats, which in the Chinese system include bureaucrats in State agencies and bureaus, state-owned enterprise workers, and staff in a range of other state institutions.").

79 *Id.*, at 370.

80 *Id.*

81 Wang remarks: "Bureaucratic mandates sit at the core of China's governance apparatus, leading the way. Despite years of official rhetoric on the development of Chinese rule of law, laws and regulations remain secondary. And their implementation is heavily influenced by whether they support or conflict with senior bureaucratic mandates. As a practical matter, to understand Chinese governance we must understand this relationship between targets and law." *Id.* at 372; *see also* Carl Minzner, *China's Turn Against Law*, 59 AM. J. COMP. *L.* 935, 949 (2011).

82 In the early 2000s, China's leadership spurred an internal debate on how to strengthen China's regime's legitimacy. The debate mirrored concerns about the limits of regime legitimacy mainly relying on economic performance and highlighted the need for "an ongoing shift from growth-centered performance to a post-growth mode of legitimation that incorporated social equality, justice, and welfare." Bruce Gilley & Heike Holbig, *The Debate on Party Legitimacy in China: a Mixed Quantitative/Qualitative Analysis*, 18(59) J. CONTEMP. CHINA 339 (March 1, 2009). On February 19, 2005, former Chinese President Hu Jintao stressed the importance of developing the capacity to create a "harmonious socialist society", such as a society based on democracy and rule of law, fairness and justice, honesty and friendliness, full of vigor, and a harmonious relationship between humans and nature. *See* Hu Jintao, *Building a Harmonious Society Important Task for CPC*, PEOPLE'S DAILY ONLINE (February 21, 2005). *See* Paolo Davide Farah, *Five Years of China's WTO Membership. EU and US Perspectives about China's Compliance with Transparency Commitments and the Transitional Review Mechanism*, 33 (3) LEGAL ISSUES OF ECONOMIC INTEGRATION, 263–304 (2006). Furthermore, the report to the 18th National Congress of the Communist Party of China stresses the importance of ecological civilization as a key element for the well-being of the Chinese people and the future of the country. The report also develops the concept of "Beautiful China", introducing a notion of development that emphasizes the strategic relevance of environmental protection even when

On more general terms, it can be said that there are two generations of Chinese 'environmental' laws: the first focused on economic development, the second on environmental protection. This parallels the general shift in US legislation as well, from pre-1960s laws to the new laws enacted from the 1960s through the 1980s.[83] The traditional Chinese environmental laws,[84] focused on the development and use of natural resources by humans rather than the relationship between humans and nature,[85] whose ethical basis is to be found in the deep-rooted concept of "harmonious nature."[86] These laws do not emphasize the prevention of environmental pollution, rather focusing on remediation and passive reactions and

---

this could be in contrast with energy security and economic development. Bruce Gilley and Heike Holbig argue that the Hu-Wen harmonious society represented a "programmatic solution to China's 'performance dilemma' and an innovative model of political legitimation." *Id.* On this point *see* Resolution on Strengthening the Construction of the Party's Governing Capacity, approved by the 4th plenary session of the 16th CCP Central Committee (September 16–19, 2004), translated in *Quarterly Chronicle and Documentation,* 180 CHINA Q. 1123, 1153–71 (2004), http://www.people.com.cn/GB/shizheng/1026/2809350.html (last visited Aug 8, 2016). The performance dilemma is the risk that autocratic rulers face undermining their own power if reforms that generate good economic performance lead to demands for greater political participation and democracy.

83 Christopher L. Bell et al., *Government Institutes, in* ENVIRONMENTAL LAW HANDBOOK (21d ed., Thomas F. P. Sullivan ed., 2011); Brittany Dunton, *Recent Developments in Environmental Law,* 26 TUL. ENVTL. L.J. 147, 166–175 (2012); Lisa Heinzerling, *New Directions in Environmental Law: A Climate of Possibility,* 35 HARV. ENVTL. L. REV. 263, 266–68 (2011); Linda K. Breggin et al., *Trends in Environmental Law Scholarship 2008–2012,* 43 ENVTL. L. REV. 10643 (2012); Amy J. Wildermuth, *Next Step: The Integration of Energy Law and Environmental Law,* 31 UTAH ENVTL. L. REV. 369, 380 (2011); Donald N. Zillman, *Evolution of Modern Energy Law: a Personal Retrospective,* 30 J. ENERGY & NAT. RESOURCES L. 485, 489–94 (2012); J. B. Ruhl, *Climate Change Adaptation and the Structural Transformation of Environmental Law,* 40 ENVTL. L. 343 (2010); VED P. NANDA & GEORGE ROCK PRING, INTERNATIONAL ENVIRONMENTAL LAW AND POLICY FOR THE 21ST CENTURY (2d ed., Martinus Nijhoff, 2012); R. Daniel Kelemen & David Vogel, *Trading Places: The Role of the United States and the European Union in International Environmental Politics,* 43 COMP. POL. STUD. 427 (2010).

84 These laws include the Prevention and Control Atmospheric Pollution Act, the Prevention and Control of Water Pollution Act, the Prevention and Control of Solid Wastes Act, the Prevention and Control of Prevention from Environmental Noise Act, and the Prevention and Control of Radioactive Pollution Act. P.R.C. Law on the Prevention and Control of Atmospheric Pollution (promulgated by the President of the People's Republic of China, Apr. 29, 2000, effective Sept. 1, 2000) art. 1.; P.R.C. Law on the Prevention and Control of Water Pollution (promulgated by Standing Comm. Nat'l People's Cong., Feb. 28, 2008, effective June 1, 2008) art. 1.; P.R.C. Law on the Prevention and Control of Envtl. Pollution by Solid Wastes (promulgated by Standing Comm. Nat'l People's Cong., Dec. 29, 2004, effective Apr. 1, 2005) art. 1.; P.R.C. Law on the Prevention and Control of Pollution From Envtl. Noise (promulgated by Standing Comm. Nat'l People's Cong., Oct. 29, 1996, effective Mar. 1, 1997) art. 1.; P.R.C. Law on Prevention and Control of Radioactive Pollution (promulgated by Standing Comm. Nat'l People's Cong., Jun. 28, 2003, effective Oct. 1, 2003) art. 1. *See also* Mingde Cao, *Fundamental Principles of Ecological Law,* 39 (2002) U.WUHAN INT'L L. REV. 39 (2002).

85 Mingde points out that China's environmental and energy law and policy before 2000 was built upon the ethical basis of a narrow anthropocentrism, whose concept for legislation and tenet embodied the natural concept of utilitarianism. Mingde Cao, *The Current and Future Trends in Chinese Environmental and Energy Law and Policy,* 18 PACE INT'L L. REV. 253 (2006), http://digitalcommons.pace.edu/pilr/vol18/iss1/9 (last visited Aug 8, 2016).

86 Mingde Cao remarks that the concept of "harmonious nature" has a deep cultural root in China's traditional culture and it should be inherited and applied to today's environmental challenges. In that respect, Confucianism developed the principles of "nature and human beings understand each other", and of "nature and human beings combined into one." Regarding the relationship between humans and nature, Taoism preached noninterference and adaptation with the course of natural events. In the same vein, Buddhism advocated the right of natural life forms other than humans to exist. Mingde Cao & Yi-xiang Xu, *The Formulation of Chinese Civil Code and the Protection of Ecology,* 4 XIAN DAI FAXUE [Mod. L. Sci.] 13 (2003); *see also* PAOLO D. FARAH, *L'influenza della concezione confuciana sulla costruzione del sistema giuridico e politico cinese* [The Influence of Confucianism in the Construction of the Chinese Juridical

eventually resulting in the danger of disharmony and frictions in the relationship between humans and nature. Conversely, the newest generation of Chinese environmental laws emphasizes the purpose of achieving harmony with nature and its conservation, rather than stressing economic growth. That said, recent Chinese environmental laws are substantially different from the earlier legal instruments as they foster on the recycling economy and regulate clean processes of production,[87] focusing on minimizing pollution from the very beginning through all the production processes.

In the context of shale gas environmental hazards, two legal instruments come into play: the 2003 Law of the People's Republic of China on the Promotion of Clean Production,[88] and the 2002 Law of the People's Republic of China on Environment Impact Assessment.[89] The former specifically addresses pollution from oil and gas production, requiring that operators and subcontractors involved in petroleum production "protect fishery resources and other natural resources and prevent the environment, including the air, sea, rivers, lakes and land, from being polluted or damaged" through respect of international standards and best practices.[90] On the other hand, the 2002 Law on Environment Impact Assessment fosters a predictive evaluation policy on the environmental impact that may occur due to the implementation of building projects and planning. This regime is thus consistent with the purposes of sustainable development[91] and the principle of environmental law of "pollution prevention first"[92].

---

and Political System], *in* IDENTITÀ EUROPEA E POLITICHE MIGRATORIE 193–226 (Giovanni Bombelli & Bruno Montanari eds., 2008).

87 "Clean production" is understood as a new industrial mode featuring technical plausibility, economic rationality and eco-efficiency, which is at the core of realizing a hazardless industry, for example, production is organized in accordance with ecological principles, and raw materials are recycled in a closed cycle.

88 Law on the Promotion of Clean Production (promulgated by the Standing Comm. Nat'l People's Cong. June 29, 2002, effective January 1, 2003), 2003 – Order of the President of the People's Republic of China No. 72, as revised pursuant to the Decision of the Standing Committee of the National People's Congress on Revising the "Law of the People's Republic of China on Promotion of Cleaner Production" promulgated on February 29, 2012 – Order of the President of the People's Republic of China No. 54.

89 Jesse L. Moorman & Zhang Ge, *Promoting and Strengthening Public Participation in China's Environmental Impact Assessment Process: Comparing China's EIA Law and U.S. NEPA*, 8 VT. J. ENVTL. L. 278 (2006–2007).

90 An indicative case study on enforcement is the benzene chemical spill of 2005 in the Junhgua River. Weili Duan et al., *The Situation of Hazardous Chemical Accidents in China between 2000 and 2006*, 186(2) J. HAZARDOUS MATERIALS 1489–1494 (2011). Jane Qiu, *China to Spend Billions Cleaning Up Groundwater*, 334(6057) SCI. 745 (2011). Xiao Yong Wang et al., *Water Pollution Emergencies in China: Actualities, Prevention and Response*, 159 ADVANCED MATERIALS RESEARCH 589–594 (2011).

91 This concept of "sustainable development" stems from the concept that individuals should respect and care for the community of life, recognize that all beings are interdependent and that every form of life has value regardless of its worth to human beings. *See* Nicholas A. Robinson, *Enforcing Environmental Norms: Diplomatic and Judicial Approaches*, 26 HASTINGS INT'L & COMP. L. REV. 387, 387–389 (2003); As Chapin Folke, and Kofinas remarked: "social–ecological sustainability requires that society's economy and other human activities not exceed the capacity of ecosystems to provide services, which, in turn, is constrained by the planet's life-support system." F. Stuart Chapin III, Carl Folke & Gary P. Kofinas, *A Framework for Understanding Change*, in PRINCIPLES OF ECOSYSTEM STEWARDSHIP: RESILIENCE-BASED NATURAL RESOURCE MANAGEMENT IN A CHANGING WORLD 6 (F. Stuart Chapin III, Carl Folke & Gary P. Kofinas eds, Springer, 2009). *See* also Doug M. Brown, *Market and Exchange in Premodern Economies*, in ENCYCLOPEDIA OF POLITICAL ECONOMY 84–88 (Philip Anthony O'Hara ed., Routledge, 2001).

92 On this principle, *see* James E. Hickey Jr & Vern R. Walker, *Refining the Precautionary Principle in International Environmental Law*, 14 VA. ENVTL. L.J. 423 (1994); and NICOLAS DE SADELEER, ENVIRONMENTAL PRINCIPLES: FROM POLITICAL SLOGANS TO LEGAL RULES (Oxford University Press, 2002).

Potential regulations, policies, and protections for hydraulic fracturing

As a result, it would be advisable for jurisdictions in which hydraulic fracturing techniques are employed to first have gas companies to conduct a thorough environmental impact assessment.[93] The shale gas drilling process can lead to land subsidence and earth vibrations, carrying with it civil liability for the oil operators who need to implement protective measures with a view of damage prevention.[94] If damage to protected interests- such as property, life, or environment- occurs, compensation takes the form of restoration of the conditions as they existed before the damage occurred. In this regard, the liability regime established by the Chinese Civil Code, mining, and environmental legislation is applicable to any damage resulting from shale gas exploration and production activities. Moreover, Chinese lawmakers should also adopt, and effectively enact, legislation requiring water sampling near proposed well sites and a minimum liability insurance coverage for bodily injury and property damage caused by well operations.[95] Regarding the crucial value of assessment, Hannah Wiseman maintains that the assessment process is necessarily multifactorial and contingent, consequentially determining whether optimal regulation occurs at the state, regional, or national level is contingent on being able to assess accurately the risks associated with resource development.[96]

China undoubtedly has a number of laws that are able to guarantee the protection of its water supplies in the fracking process. Nonetheless, due to the general nontechnical content of environmental laws and the lack of risk assessment, they could be described as merely vague policy commitments rather than substantive, enforceable legal instruments. Several Chinese extraction laws could be relevant regarding shale gas production. However, they shape an inconsistent and fragmented combination of regulations addressing other nontraditional extractive industries and government directives on extraction.[97] For instance, the Chinese policy on unconventional gas development and production partially reflects regulatory solutions adopted for methane extraction from coal seams (Coalbed Methane or CBM).[98] This would entail a series of import duty' reductions or exemptions for technological imports that are used for shale gas exploration, exemptions from the payment of exploration and extraction rights, and also production subsidies.[99] The government is actually

93 The EIA should be topped by a seismological impact assessment on the geological impact of shale gas operations on the stability of earth at or near the well sites.

94 Environmental and Social Risk Briefing Oil & Gas, (BARCLAYS, Mar. 2015).

95 *See* the adopted legislation in Ohio on this point, Senate Bill 315, Ohio Department of Natural Resources, Division of Oil and Gas.

96 Wiseman, *supra* note 7.

97 In particular, regulations crafted by the Ministry of Environmental Protection deal with issues related to emissions standards, surface draining systems, and restriction on gas emission in the environment. Moreover, regulations developed by the Ministry of Land and Resources outline the national policy on fees and royalties from mining prospects and other fiscal related concerns, while standard price-sharing contracts require international energy enterprises to share large portions of their output with the government besides paying corporate taxes on profits. Finally, land rights and control of shale acreage are also tackled by regulations issued by the Ministry of Land and Resources and not directly by national oil companies.

98 The CBM is a methane gas that is extracted from the coal seams existing in some geological fields' subsoil. Dameng Yu, Yuanjiang Yang, Qi Liu & Huang Wenhui, *A Review on Studies of Coalbed Methane Reservoirs in China,* 1 GEOLOGICAL SCI. & TECH. INFORMATION 13 (2001); Qin Yong, *Advances and Reviews on Research of Coalbed Gas Geology in China,* 3 GEOLOGICAL J. CHINA UNIVERSITIES 2 (2003).

99 In this context, one must also evaluate whether the WTO Agreement on Subsidies and Countervailing Measures' (ASCM's) rules, especially Articles III and I that define the Agreement's sphere of application

already referring to the policy developed for the CBM as a starting point to draft a policy related to shale gas,[100] especially regarding the environmental approach developed in the CBM area.[101] With regard to international cooperation policies, CBM exploration from foreign companies must happen pursuant to domestic laws regulating onshore oil resources in order to ensure a minimum standard of environmental protection, which should be enhanced in the shale gas field as well.[102]

The CBM legislation can set an example also with regard to the fiscal policy applied for energy companies involved in the unconventional gas production cycle. For example, every energy company operating in the CBM industry obtains a full refund of value-added tax.[103] Similarly, the equipment and instrumentation required for exploration and developing operations are free of duties, import taxes, and value-added tax.[104] Less onerous business income taxations are desirable as well. With regard to this, the Chinese government set the business income tax for independent national companies operating in the CBM industry at the favorable rate of 25 percent starting from 2008.[105] Likewise, domestic energy companies cooperating with foreign companies in the CBM industry benefit from a preferential fiscal policy, under which they are exempted from paying income taxes for two years starting from the first income-accruing year. This mechanism might allow energy companies to face the very high unconventional gas production initial costs, therefore fostering investments and technological progress.

Given that the costs related to producing shale gas in China are higher than conventional gas, a subsidy policy is advisable in order to allow companies join the sector. This technique has already been implemented by the MOF regarding energy companies involved in the CBM sector in China, which are entitled to a financial allowance of 0.02 renminbi per cubic meter when the gas is exploited locally, sold for domestic use or used as a raw material for chemical

---

and subject, find a match in the energy sector. For an in-depth analysis of subsidies regulation within the WTO legislation, *see*, in addition to the cited volumes and note 20, P. F. J. Macrory, A. E. Appleton & M. G. Plummer, The World Trade Organization: Legal, Economic and Political Analysis 687–734 (Springer, 2005); J. Waincymer, WTO Litigation: Procedural Aspects of Formal Dispute Settlement 765–769 (Cameron May, 2002); R. K. Gupta, Anti-Dumping and Countervailing Measures: the Complete Reference (Sage, 1996); M. J. Trebilcock & R. Howse, The Regulation of International Trade 268–273 (Routledge, 2005); A. O. Sykes, *The Economics of WTO Rules on Subsidies and Countervailing Measures* (John M. Olin Law & Economics Working Paper No. 186, Chicago, May 2003). *See* also V. Di Comite, Le sovvenzioni e le Misure Compensative nell'Organizzazione Mondiale del Commercio (Wolters Kluwer Italia, 2009); M. Orlandi, *La disciplina delle sovvenzioni concesse dagli Stati nella normativa OMC*, in Quaderni di Studi Europei. I Sussidi e gli Aiuti di Stato (Giuffrè, 2002).

100 Don Kun Luo et al., *Economic Evaluation Based Policy Analysis for Coalbed Methane Industry in China*, 36 Energy 360 (2011).

101 Specifically, in July 2008 the Ministry of Environmental Protection issued the Emission Standard of CBM/CMM regarding new mines and surface drainage systems.

102 Technology development in the shale gas exploration and exploitation field should be encouraged by the Chinese government as it already did in the 1983 National Programme on Research of Essential Technologies, through which the government incentivized the development of technologies related to CBM exploration and development. Baizhan Li & Runming Yao, *Urbanisation and its Impact on Building Energy Consumption and Efficiency in China*, 34 Renewable Energy 1994 (2009). The development of innovative technologies in natural gas and oil exploration has been fostered also by the Mid-term and Long-term Scientific and Technological Programme (2006–2020). Fourth Globelics Conference in Mexico City, *Report by Shulin Gu et al. on China's System and Vision of Innovation: Analysis of the National Medium- and Long-term Science and Technology Development Plan for 2006–2020* (Sept. 22–24, 2008).

103 Jane Nakano, David Pumphrey, Robert Price, JRS. & Molly A. Watson, Prospects for Shale Gas Development in Asia Examining Potentials and Challenges in China and India 7 (2012).

104 *Id.*

105 *Id.*

processes.[106] To that end, the Chinese government has introduced some subsidies for the shale gas industry development, offering mining enterprises operating in the sector an allowance of 0.4 renminbi per cubic meter from 2012 to 2015, which is twice the amount provided for the CBM sector, though it has been observed that the allowance's short duration is not enough to draw foreign investments.[107] Also, pursuant to the Foreign Investment Industrial Guidance Catalogue (effective since January 30, 2012), foreign investments in the shale gas sector are subsumed under the "promotional" investment category, which allows foreign investors to form joint ventures – including contractual ones – with their Chinese partners.[108] Furthermore, equipment and technologies imported for the exploration and development of the shale gas industry that are earmarked for that specific use and are not producible in China are free of duties and customs tariffs.[109]

Environmental considerations: Focus on water resources management

There are existing critical concerns about the fresh water management in relation to unconventional gas.[110] These two natural resources have come to be complexly associated because the extraction, treatment, and distribution of fresh water entails considerable energy, while the production of fossil fuel energy involves fresh water.[111] Water concerns associated with unconventional fossil fuel extraction and production are augmented by the growing demand from an increasing population and the influence of climate change on the hydrologic cycle.[112] Shale gas is a relatively clean and efficient burning fuel with the potential to lower carbon emissions. Nevertheless, risks remain and shale gas's greater role in the world's overall energy mix has met with fierce opposition due to environmental concerns over the hydraulic

106 Sino Gas & Energy, Developing Chinese Unconventional Gas Assets, Presentation to dbAccess China Conference 2014, at 17.

107 *Id.*

108 Norton Rose Fulbright, Shale Gas Handbook 53 (2013). *See* Catalogue of Encouraged Foreign Investment Industries, section II. Mining and Quarrying Industries: "(6) Prospecting and exploitation of such conventional oil resources as oil shale, oil sand, heavy oil and super heavy oil (limited to equity joint venture and contractual joint venture) . . . (9) Prospecting and exploitation of unconventional natural gas resources such as shale gas and submarine natural gas hydrate (limited to equity joint venture and contractual joint venture)." Ministry of Commerce People's Republic Of China, Catalogue for the Guidance of Foreign Investment Industries (Amended in 2011) (Feb. 21, 2012), http://english.mofcom.gov.cn/article/policyrelease/aaa/201203/20120308027837.shtml (last visited Aug. 8, 2016).

109 Desheng Hu & Shengqing Xu, *Opportunity, Challenges and Policy Choices for China on the Development of Shale Gas*, 60 Energy Pol'y 21, 21–26 (2013). In the same sense, *see* the new Foreign Investment Industrial Guidance Catalogue draft, the consultations of which closed on December 3, 2014.

110 A wider debate exists on the carbon footprint of unconventional gas, *see* Robert H. Abrams & Noah D. Hall, *Framing Water Policy in a Carbon Affected and Carbon Constrained Environment*, 50 Nat. Resources J. 39 (2010).

111 As remarked by scholar Paula J. Schauwecker, "Water consumption and oil consumption are on a precariously parallel course." Paula J. Schauwecker, *Oil and Water: Fueling Questions*, 24 Nat. Resources & Env't 46, 47 (2009).

112 Robert E. Beck, *Current Water Issues in Oil and Gas Development and Production: Will Water Control What Energy We Have?*, 49 Washburn L.J. 423, 424 (2009–2010). Becks remarks that there are no fresh water alternatives, and water cannot be replaced. Consequentially, given the overlap between energy and water, both lawmakers and the scientists must account for these interconnections as they model and manage the hydrologic cycle.

fracturing technology and its potential to cause environmental harm,[113] due to its shallower deposits, greater permeability, and more-superficial formations.

Fracking involves drilling a well bore into the reservoir rock formation and then forcing water, sand, and chemicals into the well at high pressure to create fractures or fissures in the rock. Once the fracture is open, the released gas flows out of the fractures and into the well bore. In addition to shale gas, the process has recently been applied to extract gas from coal seam and tight sand deposits.[114]

These considerations mean that the extent to which shale gas will be a larger element of the energy mix will depend on balancing environmental protection against economic growth. Some U.S. states and some EU countries, such as France, have already banned or imposed moratoria[115] on hydraulic fracturing due to environmental concerns[116] in attempts to harmonize environmental risks with energy security benefits. Conversely, China may opt for accepting greater environmental risks in order to bolster shale gas production and thus satisfy growing domestic energy demands, as well as create new jobs that full-scale production would generate, in particular for low-skilled workers.[117] However, bearing in mind the relevant geological factors, infrastructure challenges, and environmental hazards, it is one thing to find shale gas, and another to obtain commercially viable production from it.

As the creation of fracking fluid entails mixing millions of gallons of fresh water with thousands of gallons of chemicals,[118] it is crucial to assess how harmful the fracking process might be to the environment.[119] First, hydraulic fracturing is supposedly responsible for a number

113 The focus of this study on the environmental aspects related to shale gas exploration and extraction should not make us oblivious of the other issues that may impact the development of global unconventional gas resources: fiscal conditions, landowner acceptance, interference from local authorities, pipeline and infrastructure issues, availability of technology, equipment and skilled labor force, and gas players' experience. Susan L. Sakmar, *The Global Shale Gas Initiative: Will the United States Be the Role Model for the Development of Shale Gas Around the World?,* 33(2) Houston J. Intl. L. 369 (2011).

114 Nahed Taher, Bandar Al-Hajja, Energy and Environment in Saudi Arabia: Concerns & Opportunities 139 (Springer, 2013).

115 Moratoria represents a precautionary measure par excellence. Arie Trouwborst, Precautionary rights and duties of States 129 (Martinus Nijhoff Publishers, 2006). *See* also Jeffrey C. King, *Selected Re-Emerging and Emerging Trends in Oil and Gas Law as Result of Production from Shale Formations,* 18 Texas Wesleyan L. Rev. 1, 3 (2011); Thomas Swartz, *Hydraulic Fracturing: Risks and Risk Management,* 26 Nat. Resources & Env't 30, 30 (2011).

116 The French Senate approved a ban on fracking in June 2011, as a result of the extensive public protests. However, fracking is still permitted for scientific testing. *See* Ruven Fleming, *Shale Gas-a Comparison of European Moratoria,* 1 Eur. Energy & Envtl. L. Rev. 12–32 (2013).

117 In the US, the shale gas industry has created 600,000 new jobs. Secretary of Energy Advisory Board ("The Deutch Committee"), Shale Gas Subcommittee 90 Day Report, August 18, 2011, at 1, 5. *See* also Thomas C. Kinnaman *The Economic Impact of Shale Gas Extraction: A Review of Existing Studies,* 70(7) Ecological Econ. 1243–1249 (2011).

118 The EPA reports that hazardous fluids employed in fracking are often injected into shale formations at high volumes (a maximum average of 150,000 gallons per well, and a minimum average of 57,500 gallons per well). United States Envtl. Prot. Agency, *Final Report on Evaluation of Impacts to Underground Sources of Drinking Water by Hydraulic Fracturing of Coalbed Methane Reservoirs* 3–11 (June 2004) [hereinafter EPA 2004].

119 On the risks related to shale gas development, *see* generally Mark Zoback, Saya Kitasei, & Brad Copithorne, Addressing The Environmental Risks from Shale Gas Development (World Watch Institute, 2010); Elizabeth Burleson, *Cooperative Federalism and Hydraulic Fracturing: A Human Right to a Clean Environment,* 22 Cornell J. L. & Pub. Pol'y 289 (2012). On the potential health hazards, *see* Michelle Bamberger & Robert E. Oswald, *Impacts of Gas Drilling on Human and Animal Health,* 22(1) New Solutions, A Journal of Environmental and Occupational Health Policy 57–77 (2012).

of incidences of seismic activity such as minor earthquakes and tremors. These seismic activities seem to be caused by either the fracking process itself or the injection of fracking wastewater into wells.[120] So far, there has been a more than four-fold increase in earthquakes of magnitude 3.0 and greater in the central United States since 2008, that are 'almost certainly' caused by fracking activities.[121] Similarly, in April and May 2011, shale gas exploratory drilling has been suspended in Lancashire, UK, following two earthquakes with magnitudes of 1.5 and 2.3.[122] A consequent report commissioned by the Cuadrilla Resources Ltd.,[123] the British company exploring for natural shale gas in the Bowland Basin in Lancashire, indicated that "it is highly probable that the hydraulic fracturing of Cuadrilla's Preese Hall-1 well did trigger a number of minor seismic events."[124] This of course has relevant implications for local residential and infrastructure damage. Seismic activity could also impact on a well's integrity and cause further underground water contamination, as it could create leakages and new fractures, besides deforming well casings. Seismic activities can break or shear well casings as well, which is particularly dangerous in earthquake zones. This means that even if technical precautions to block off sensitive upper-level groundwater zones are taken, damaged casing will result in leaks, especially under pressure environments. Moreover, Sichuan province, where most of the Chinese shale gas is located, is a region extremely prone to earthquakes; for example, the 2008 Great Sichuan Earthquake resulted in 69,195 deaths and over 18,300 missing.[125]

In addition to the risks related to seismic activities, principal concerns include groundwater contamination with fracking chemicals,[126] gasification,[127] water usage risks, surface water and soil risks spills, and blow-outs. Conversely, environmentalists argue that, although hydraulic fracturing is believed to be less water-intensive than nuclear and coal, it is unlikely

120 Zoback, *supra* note 119, at 9.

121 Ajay Makan, *Fracking Water Linked to Earthquakes,* FINANCIAL TIMES (April 14, 2012), http://www.ft.com/intl/cms/s/0/e268a268-84f6-11e1-a3c5-00144feab49a.html#axzz2gMxH4mz3 (last visited Aug 8, 2016).

122 C. A. Green, P. Styles & B.J. Baptie, *Preese Hall Shale Gas Fracturing: Review and Recommendation for Induced Seismic Mitigation* 1 (Induced Seismicity Mitigation Report, Department of Energy & Climate Change, 2012).

123 Dep't of Energy and Climate Change (DECC), Fracking UK Shale: Understanding Earthquake Risk 5 (2014).

124 Cuadrilla Resources, Press Release Geomechanical Study, Cuadrilla Resources (Feb. 11, 2011) http://www.cuadrillaresources.com/news/cuadrilla-news/article/pressrelease-geomechanical-study/ (last visited Aug 8, 2016).

125 Xinglin Lei et al., *A Detailed View Of The Injection-Induced Seismicity in a Natural Gas Reservoir in Zigong, southwestern Sichuan Basin, China,* 118(8) J. GEOPHYSICAL RESEARCH: SOLID EARTH 4296–4311 (2013); Michael Esposito, *Water Issues Set the Pace for Fracking Regulations and Global Shale Gas Extraction,* 22 TUL. J. INT'L & COMP. L. 167–213 (2013); Nicola Jones, *Wastewater Injection Cracks Open Quake Concerns,* 6.5 NATURE GEOSCIENCE 329–329 (2013); William L. Ellsworth, *Injection-Induced Earthquakes,* 341(6142) SCI. (2013); Bob Weinhold, *Energy Development Linked with Earthquakes,* 120(10) ENVTL. HEALTH PERSPECTIVES 388 (2012); Thomas W. Merrill, *Four Questions about Fracking,* 63(4) CASE WESTERN RESERVE LAW REVIEW 971 (2013).

126 Currently China does not have a regulatory framework aimed at ensuring that wastewater injection into underground wells will not endanger groundwater. These regulations would ensure that wastewater injection into underground wells, including injection of hazardous wastewater produced from hydraulic fracturing, does not menace local water supplies. Lan Nan, *Legal Tools for Groundwater Protection: Insights from International Experience,* 8 CHINA J. NAT. RESOURCES ECON. 33–43 (2011) (in Chinese).

127 When gas migrates into groundwater, the build-up of pressure due to gasification may lead to tremors or explosions. Aquifer gasification due to shale gas development has been cited as a potential cause for recent minor seismic activity in the United Kingdom, though these claims are largely unproven at this point and are being investigated. *See* KPMG Global Energy Institute, *supra* note 51.

that it will replace either energy source.[128] Rather, shale gas development carries the danger of creating an additional demand for water. Shortage of water is one of the most crucial issues facing shale gas development in China, as water is a fundamental element in the fracking process. In the shale gas–rich Sichuan Basin, this is a primary concern due to the province's agricultural legacy that furnishes the country with roughly 7 percent of its rice, wheat, and other grains.[129] There are three possible outcomes for the water used during fracking: (1) it can be extracted, recycled, and used again; (2) it can be left inside of the shale deposit; or (3) it can be extracted and stored on or off site or treated for other uses.[130]

The use of recycled water for hydraulic operations is highly advisable, given the intense residential and industrial demand for water in Sichuan and water scarcity concerns in Xinjiang.[131] Regulations should also consider the possibility of establishing a closed-loop system of energy production, using mine drainage water from coal production (after having neutralized and removed heavy metals), thus integrating industrial ecology practices into the fracking process. However, this practice should only be implemented after groundwater regulations are strengthened, and after China has gained substantial experience in minimizing pollution from fracturing operations, while also ensuring the proper disposal of the heavy-metal waste products from treating these industrial water sources.[132]

Water is an especially urgent issue for China as its per capita availability of drinking water is very low, and water resources are not well distributed through the country.[133] Diverging water supplies from the agriculture to shale gas production could be catastrophic, in particular if the contaminated water also pollutes farmlands. Conversely, for other shale gas basins in Tarim, Xinjiang, and Inner Mongolia, the scarcity of water is aggravated by the arid and hot climate. Shale gas exploration and production would thus require water to be carried from other parts of the country, which would unsustainably raise costs and impact the environment. Furthermore, climate change and China's rapid economic development have led to an increase in industrial and agricultural water consumption, while areas of desertification are expanding, deteriorating the ecological environment which is already overexploited.[134] In China, water

128 Bridget R. Scanlon, Ian Duncan & Robert C Reedy, *Drought and the Water–Energy Nexus*, TEXAS ENVTL. RESOURCES LETT. 8 (2013); J. P. Nicot & B. R. Scanlon, *Water Use for Shale-Gas Production in Texas*, US ENVTL. SCI. TECH. 46 3580–6 (2012); I. J. Laurenzi & G. R. Jersey, *Life Cycle Greenhouse Gas Emissions and Freshwater Consumption of Marcellus Shale Gas,* ENVTL. SCI. TECH. 4896–4903 (2013).

129 Joel Kirkland, *China Begins to Tap Its Shale Gas, Despite Daunting Technological, Environmental Hurdles*, N.Y. TIMES, (Oct. 14, 2011), http://www.nytimes.com/cwire/2011/10/14/14climatewire-china-begins-to-tapits-shale-gas-despite-da-95706.html?pagewanted=all (last visited Aug 8, 2016).

130 Deweese, *supra* note 92, at 19. Schauwecker, *supra* note 86, at 47. Gas drillers are experimenting with new technologies and methods empowering them to be more effective at recycling fracking water. See the use of "mobile heated distillation units" by Devon Energy Corporation as an example of emerging efficiencies. *See* Laura C. Reeder, *Creating a Legal Framework for Regulation of Natural Gas Extraction from the Marcellus Shale Formation*, 34WM. &MARY ENVT'L L. & POL'Y REV. 999, 1013 (2010).

131 Zmarak Shalizi, *Addressing China's Growing Water Shortages and Associated Social and Environmental Consequences* 6 (World Bank, Policy Res. Working Paper No. 3895, 2006), http://papers.ssrn.com/sol3/papers.cfm?abstract_id=923238.

132 For example, in November 2011, the Pennsylvania Department of Environmental Protection released a statement encouraging the oil and gas industry to utilize recycled mine drainage water in hydraulic fracturing. Pennsylvania Department of Environmental Protection, *DEP Effort Encourages Oil and Gas Industry to Use Mine Drainage Water,* November 18, 2011,: http://www.portal.state.pa.us/portal/server.pt/community/newsroom/14287?id=19161&typeid=1 (last visited Aug 8, 2016).

133 *See* Chapter 21 (Soprano) in this volume.

134 On desertification and water management in China, *see* CI LONGJUN, DESERTIFICATION AND ITS CONTROL IN CHINA (Springer-Verlag, 2010). There is clearly a tension between economic self-sufficiency in

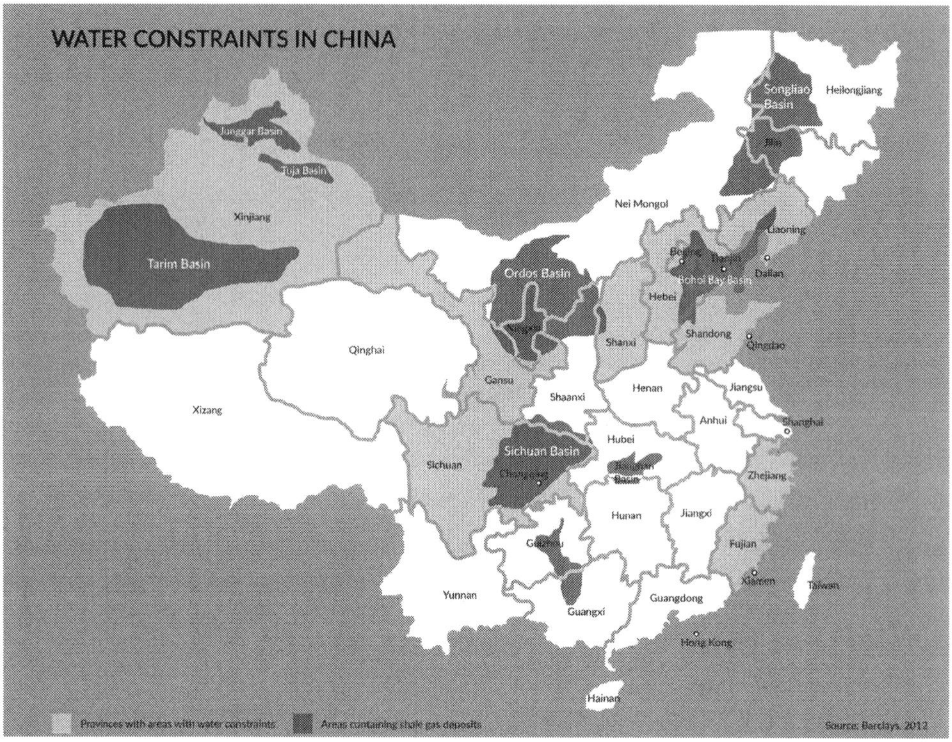

Figure 16.2 China shale resource and water stress map

Source: map replicated from "Natural Gas Weekly Kaleidoscope," Barclay's Capital Commodities Research (November 16, 2010)

availability for hydraulic fracturing may significantly reduce the prospective for national shale development in certain areas. Figure 16.2 draws attention to these potential water scarcity issues in China, which are likely to make the costs of shale development exorbitant.

Implementation and enforcement of energy and environmental laws: Fragmentation of competences

China's poor law enforcement has undermined the efficacy of past efforts. In particular, China features a highly fragmented water resources management system. Horizontally, several institutions are involved at every level of government. At the central level, the National People's Congress and the State Council enact laws and administrative regulations and

agriculture and in energy. Mark Harvey & Sarah Pilgrim, *The New Competition for Land: Food, Energy, and Climate Change*, 36 Food Policy (2011). Jörg Friedrichs, *Global Energy Crunch: How Different Parts of the World Would React to a Peak Oil Scenario*, 38(8) Energy Pol'y 4562–4569 (2010).

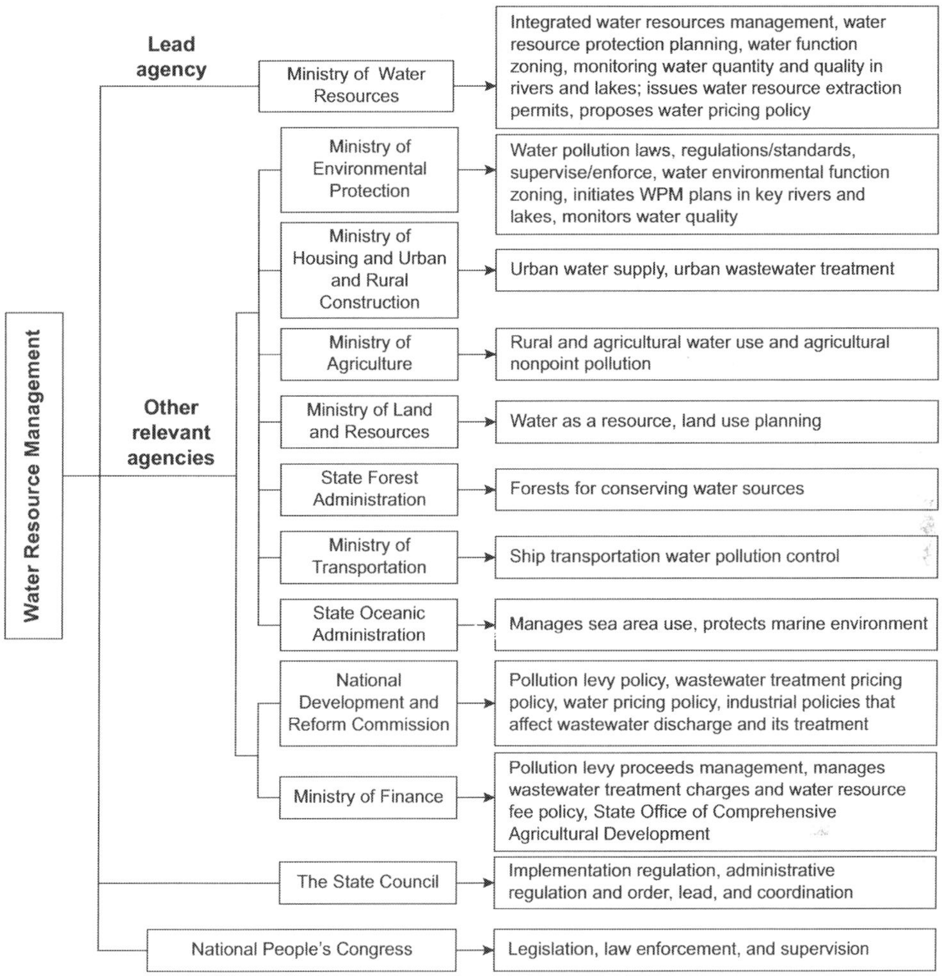

Figure 16.3 Water management competences allocation in China

Source: Xie, Jian; Liebenthal, Andres; Warford, Jeremy J., *Addressing China's Water Scarcity: A Synthesis of Recommendations for Selected Water Resource Management Issues*, 2008, World Bank Publications.

supervise their local implementation and enforcement. Additionally, several ministries and authorities are responsible in different ways in water management.[135]

135 The Ministry of Water Resources, which is a leading agency for integrated water resources management, water resource protection planning, water function zoning, and monitoring water quantity and quality in rivers and lakes, issues water resource extraction permits and proposes water pricing policy; the Ministry of Environmental Protection, specifically competent for water pollution laws, regulations, and standards supervision and enforcement, and monitoring of water quality; the Ministry of Housing and Urban and Rural Construction; the Ministry of Agriculture; the Ministry of Land and Resources; the State Forest Administration; the Ministry of Transportation; the State Oceanic Administration; the National Development and Reform Commission; and the Ministry of Finance. A common expression to describe the current system is that "nine dragons" manage the water. *See* JIAN XIE, ADDRESSING CHINA'S

This unwieldy regime carries the risks of creating both overlaps and friction in responsibility, as the lines of demarcation between institutional jurisdictions and competences are not always clear. Even the responsibility for water pollution prevention and control, which should be a fundamental step in the shale gas extraction process, is distributed to different governmental bodies. Vertically, the water management regime features a similar fragmentation, and relies on unclear administrative boundaries linked to different levels of government. Finally, the political friction and information asymmetry between central and local governments block more meaningful cohesive action. The absence of an overarching energy law causes overlaps and contentious bureaucratic infighting that have a detrimental effect on the ability to face long-term energy challenges. In fact, not just the water management but the energy governance as a whole has been decentralized during the course of several rounds of administrative reorganizations, dispersing and scattering the country's decentralized energy authority among parallel central ministries.[136]

It remains to be seen what the implications will be for shale gas industry expansion in China, whether this fragmentation will further hamper its development or whether these challenges will be adequately met by a more integrated system, inspired, for instance, by the water resources management systems of France and the United Kingdom.[137] Given the fact that in China levels of pollution from industry and agriculture are dangerously high, shale gas should be developed and extracted relying on a regulatory and institutional framework capable of reducing any related environmental hazards, striking a balance between energy security benefits and environmental costs, in order to guarantee the right to water universally.[138]

Water Scarcity 30 (World Bank Publications, 2009); Jiang Yong, *China's Water Scarcity,* 90(11) J. Envtl. Mgmt. 3185–3196 (2009). Wang Xinbo, *Water Governance in China: The Failure of a Top-Down Approach,* in The Water Revolution: Practical Solutions to Water Scarcity (Barun Mitra, Kendra Okonski & Mohit Satyanand eds, 2006); Yan Feng, He Daming & Beth Kinne, *Water Resources Administration Institution in China,* 8(4) Water Pol'y 291–301 (2006).

136 Bo Kong, Governing China's Energy in the Context of Global Governance, 2 Global Pol'y, Special Issue 51–65 (2011).

137 Those water resources management systems specifically aim at ensuring the security of water supplies, protecting ecological resources of the water environment, and improving the efficiency of local water supply and wastewater treatment. Those regulatory objectives are achieved through different instruments, ***inter alia***, consensual agreements among all stakeholders and technical advice. The financial resources originated from water pricing and the enforcement of the consumer-pays principle for quantitative management and the polluter-pays principle for pollution control. *Id.*

138 Recognition of the right to water has been debated in a number of international law *fora*. The right to water is a crucial element in the work of the Human Rights Council, the U.N. General Assembly, many scholars, and nongovernmental organizations (NGOs). In September 2010, a resolution adopted by consensus by the Human Rights Council affirmed that the right to water and sanitation is recognized in existing international law. *See* Human Rights Council Res. 15/L.14, U.N. Doc. A/HRC/15/L.14 (Sept. 24, 2010). In 2010, China voted in favor of a U.N. General Assembly resolution recognizing the right to water as a human right. G.A. Res. 64/292, The Human Right to Water and Sanitation (Aug. 3, 2010). This Resolution acknowledges that clean drinking water and sanitation are integral to the realization of all human rights. Accordingly, the right to water imposes a burden on China to develop new policies and rules to ensure safe drinking water for its population. However, the resolution does not have a legally binding effect, and is generally regarded as a soft law legal instrument. The vote in favor of the U.N. General Assembly resolution is an important first step, but China should pursue formal recognition of the right to water in international and domestic laws in order to grant its citizens legal entitlement against the state in case of serious interferences with the enjoyment of the right to water, which requires the state to adopt, inter alia, effective legislation to restrain third parties from polluting

The recognition of such a right would be a first desirable step, but should be followed by effective policy implementation and enforcement.[139]

Many factors contributed to the currently weak enforcement of environmental regulations of China. The breakthrough of shale gas exploration and production in China is undermined by the country's unsatisfactory record on environmental enforcement, which jeopardizes the capacity of existing laws to prevent and minimize the downsides of hydraulic fracturing.[140] China relies on a multilevel system of authority based on the central supervision of local governments to guarantee adequate legal enforcement. Environmental regulations are accordingly enforced at the local level through central government Regional Supervision Centers ("RSCs") and local governments' Environmental Protection Bureaus, which are responsible for supervising the implementation of central laws, investigating major pollution events, coordinating and settling trans-boundary environmental disputes, and receiving and responding to complaints.[141] However, the efficiency of the government RSCs is weakened by several constraints. The RSCs are extremely underfunded, which results in weak governmental enforcement capacity, and are financed by local governments, causing conflicts of interest, corruption, and complicity.[142] Moreover, the RSCs lack enforcement authority over local government Environmental Protection Bureaus. To overcome these hindrances, the RSC's role should be reinforced by providing specific legal tools and conferring to the centers more adequate funding and greater powers.

Transparency and disclosure about fracking activities: evaluating the Chinese and U.S. approaches

Other factors not limited to the area of water pollution control and prevention contribute to current weak law enforcement in China. In particular, the existing legal instruments lack enforcement mechanisms and procedures, namely supervision, monitoring, reporting, and

water resources. Jade Harsha, *Conflicts and Dilemma of Human Right to Water*, 100 CURRENT SCI. 1178, 1778 (2011). It is nevertheless uncertain what incentives China has to take such a step, and whether this scenario is plausible at all. In fact in China new regulations have been adopted to protect the environment, but lack of control and enforcement measures remains a crucial problem. Recognition of the right to water within the national political and legal systems by way of legislative implementation would constitute a step in the right direction, but it should be accompanied by monitoring and enforcement measures. The right to water is not recognized at the constitutional level in China. Article 9 of the Constitution of the People's Republic of China [*Zhonghua Renmin Gongheguo Xianfa, Di Jiu Tiao*] states that "mineral resources, waters, forests, mountains, grassland, unreclaimed land, beaches and other natural resources are owned by the State, that is, by the whole people, with the exception of the forests, mountains, grasslands, unclaimed land, and beaches that are owned by collectivities in accordance with the law. The State ensures the rational use of natural resources and protects rare animals and plants. The appropriation or damage of natural resources by any organization or individual by whatever means is prohibited". As previously mentioned, provisions on supply and sanitation are included in secondary resources, *inter alia*, the Law of the People's Republic of China on Prevention and Control of Water Pollution the Water, *see infra* note 49. William C. Jones, *The Constitution of the People's Republic of China*, 63 WASHINGTON U. L. Q. 707 (1985), http://digitalcommons.law.wustl.edu/lawreview/vol63/iss4/4 (last visited Aug 8, 2016)

139 Peter Gleick, *China and Water*, in THE WORLD'S WATER 2008–2009: THE BIENNAL REPORT ON FRESHWATER RESOURCES 432 (Peter H. Gleick, Heather Cooley & Mari Morikawa eds, Island Press, 2008).

140 *See generally* Alex Wang, *The Search for Sustainable Legitimacy: Environmental Law and Bureaucracy in China*, 37 HARV. ENVTL. L. REV. 365, 429 (2013).

141 Scott Moore, *Commentary: Shifting Power in Central-Local Environmental Governance in China: The Regional Supervision Centers*, 11 China Env't Series 188, 188 (2011).

142 *Id.*, at 191.

evaluation. The enforcement of environmental laws could be improved through legal instruments that facilitate access of the general public to information and statistics in order to foster a positive feedback mechanism which could exercise greater pressure on local or central government to enforce existing regulations.[143]

These transparency measures have already contributed to filling the gap between central and regional regulations for the oil industry in both the United States and China. In 1986, the United States adopted the Emergency Planning and Community Right to Know Act (EPCRA),[144] which fosters and promotes emergency preparedness by asking local and federal governments to publicize precise information about the presence of potential chemical risks.[145] Similarly, the Environmental Protection Agency's (EPA) Toxics Release Inventory ("TRI")[146] maintains a searchable database of toxic chemical releases and waste management activities whose aim is to inform and guide policy decisions of local communities and federal government, enhancing participatory mechanisms. However, U.S. shale gas companies are not required by federal law to disclose the chemicals being used for hydraulic fracturing. Although to date, eleven states have passed laws or rules requiring drilling companies to reveal some, though not all, of the chemicals they use. The U.S. Groundwater Protection Council and Department of Energy (DOE) have also developed a web-based national registry called "FracFocus," which allows the public to access information, on a well-by-well basis, on chemical constituents used in hydraulic fracturing.[147] Moreover, in some states, such as Texas[148] and Colorado,[149] disclosure on FracFocus is a mandatory legislative requirement. The case against mandating the disclosure of hydraulic fracturing chemicals is that "[t]he specific make-up of the chemicals used in fracturing in particular is considered proprietary information and should be protected."[150] Conversely, it should be kept in mind that considerable knowledge gaps about the effects of hydraulic fracturing on water, hence public health, still exist.

143 Ma Jun, *Public Disclosure in China: Fighting Pollution with Open Information*, CHIAN DIALOGUE (December 13, 2010), https://www.chinadialogue.net/article/show/single/en/4001-The-power-of-public-disclosure (last visited Aug 8, 2016).

144 Emergency Planning and Community Right-to-know Act (EPCRA) Code of Federal Regulations, 40 CFR Parts 355, 370, and 372. The Emergency Planning and Community Right-to-Know Act: Section 313 Release and Other Waste Management Reporting Requirements. Environmental Protection Agency publication EPA 260/K-01–001, February 2001.

145 EPCRA §§ 311–12 (2011).

146 TRI was established in 1986 by the Emergency Planning and Community Right-to-Know Act (EPCRA). In 1990, Congress passed the Pollution Prevention Act (PPA), which required that facilities report additional data on waste management and source reduction activities under TRI. The TRI-specific sections of these two laws are section 313 of the EPCRA and section 6607 of the PPA. *Toxic Release Inventory Program*, UNITED STATES ENVTL. PROT. AGENCY, http://www.epa.gov/toxics-release-inventory-triprogram (last revised Aug 8, 2016).

147 On the role of FracFocus and its implications, see generally Leah A. Dundon, Mark Abkowitz & Janey Camp, *The Real Value of FracFocus as a Regulatory Tool: A National Survey of State Regulators*, 87 ENERGY POL'Y 496 (2015); Katherine Konschnik & Archana Dayalu, *Hydraulic Fracturing Chemicals Reporting: Analysis of Available Data and Recommendations for Policymakers*, 88 ENERGY POL'Y 504, 504 (2016).

148 The Texas legislature enacted legislation in mid-2011 that directed the Texas Railroad Commission (which regulates oil and gas activity in Texas) to draft regulations that require companies to disclose fracturing fluid composition on a well-by-well basis by posting information on FracFocus. The Commission complied with the directive, enacting such regulations in December 2011. *See* TEX. NAT. RES. CODE ANN. § 91.851(a)(1)(A) (West 2012). 75; TEX. ADMIN. CODE § 3.29 (2012).

149 COLO. CODE REGS. § 404-1:205A (2012).

150 Wes Deweese, *supra* note 92, at 11.

One embryonic tendency in the United States is that shale gas operators are starting to voluntarily publish the chemicals employed in the hydraulic fracturing processes. For instance, Aubrey McClendon (President and Chief Executive Officer of Chesapeake Energy) and John Pinkerton (Chairman and Chief Executive Officer of Range Resources Inc.) have specified that their companies will make publicly available the list of chemicals used.[151] In 2009, in regards to legislative responses, the Fracturing Responsibility and Awareness of Chemicals Act (FRAC Act) was proposed in attempts to close the loophole exempting companies drilling for natural gas from disclosing the chemicals involved in fracking operations that would normally be required under federal clean water laws. An attempt was made to introduce the FRAC Act in 2009, and on March 15, 2011, U.S. Representatives Diana DeGette and Jared Polis reintroduced it to Congress. Congress had not yet passed either of the FRAC Act bills. This bill was reassigned as number S. 785 to a congressional committee on March 18, 2015, which will consider the bill before possibly sending it on to the House or Senate as a whole. In 2009, in regards to legislative responses, the Fracturing Responsibility and Awareness of Chemicals Act (FRAC Act) was proposed in attempts to close the loophole exempting companies drilling for natural gas from disclosing the chemicals involved in fracking operations that would normally be required under federal clean water laws.[152] An attempt was made to introduce the FRAC Act in 2009, and on March 15, 2011, U.S. Representatives Diana DeGette and Jared Polis reintroduced it to Congress.[153] Congress had not yet passed either of the FRAC Act bills. This bill was reassigned as number S. 785 to a congressional committee on March 18, 2015, which will consider the bill before possibly sending it on to the House or Senate as a whole.[154]

In China, transparency initiatives are growing in order to tackle information shortcomings. The Water Law[155] requires the environmental protection administration departments of the local people's governments to periodically disclose pollution quantity control targets.[156] This legal tool also requires the environmental protection administration department of the State Council and local governments to 'name and shame' local governments[157] who fail to meet their quantity control targets.[158] The first ministry-level disclosure law is the Measures on Open Environmental Information (for Trial Implementation) was passed on February 8, 2007 by the Ministry of Environmental Protection in order to foster public

151 *Id.* at 12–13; *see also* Timothy Gardner & Sarah N. Lynch, *Despite Probe, SEC Says Not Regulating Fracking*, REUTERS (Sept. 15, 2011), http://www.reuters.com/article/2011/09/15/us-usasec-frackingidUSTRE78E5NK20110915 (last revised Aug 8, 2016).

152 On the FRAC Act, see generally SUSAN L. SAKMAR, ENERGY FOR THE 21ST CENTURY: OPPORTUNITIES AND CHALLENGES FOR LIQUEFIED NATURAL GAS (LNG) 316 (Edward Elgar Pub, 2013).

153 David O. Williams, DeGette, Polis Once Again Introduce FRAC Act to Bring Federal Oversight to Gas Fracking, COLO. INDEP. (Mar. 15, 2011), http://coloradoindependent.com/79273/degettepolis-once-againintroduce-frac-act-to-bring-federal-oversight-to-gas-fracking (last visited Aug 8, 2016).

154 Fracturing Responsibility and Awareness of Chemicals (FRAC) Act, S.785, https://www.govtrack.us/congress/bills/114/s785

155 *See* P.R.C. Law on Prevention and Control of Water Pollution, *supra* note 49.

156 *Id.*, Article 19.

157 Even before the Water Law was approved, some laws fostering transparency and public participation had been adopted, such as the Clean Production Law of 2003, which required emissions and other environmental data. Furthermore, the *Environmental Impact Assessment Law* of 2003 requires partial public disclosure of the environmental impact assessments completed for permit applications.

158 *Id.*

participation in fighting pollution.[159] The measures require companies to timely and accurately disclose their environmental information[160] and promote citizens' involvement, in that "citizens, legal persons and other organizations" are allowed to "ask environmental protection departments to obtain government environmental information."[161]

Despite the progresses made by Chinese local governments regarding transparency and disclosure of environmental information, relevant differences among provinces and regions remain. In particular, the disclosure of the environmental impact by large energy companies is limited and, because the companies are big taxpayers, the government generally sits by when they refuse to disclose their environmental information. Another hurdle is related to the normative nature of these regulations, which do not usually impose environmental disclosure requirements on enterprises as mandatory, but merely encourage companies to take their own initiative in providing the information.

Environmental disclosure and transparency directly affect social acceptance, which is a key element for the long-run success of shale gas development, as previous North American experience shows.[162] It is crucial to developing mutual-trust and mutual-benefit relations between the shale gas industry and local communities. This would minimize the social risk for the developer while involving the community in the decision-making process, and ensuring tangible and equitable benefits from the project. In this vein, strong transparency initiatives and mandatory disclosure of environmental information represents a crucial step towards safer regulation of shale gas development and a better enforcement of domestic environmental laws.

Comparative analysis with the United States' previous experience: A model of development for the unconventional gas market?

Although there are clear differences between China and the United States in the context of shale gas, further analysis reveals important similarities. Shale gas is a pivotal factor for the future of energy in both countries, where energy security, energy efficiency, and environmental concerns are deeply intertwined. These two countries strive to guarantee greater energy security by boosting domestic resources.[163] Additionally, their regulatory frameworks

159 Measures on Open Environmental Information (for Trial Implementation). Adopted by the State Environmental Protection Administration of China on February 8, 2007; Effective May 1, 2008.

160 Article 4: "Environmental protection departments shall observe the principles of justice, fairness, convenience to the people and objectivity and disclose government environmental information promptly and accurately. Enterprises shall disclose enterprise environmental information promptly and accurately under the principle of combining voluntary disclosure with mandatory disclosure". *Id.*

161 *Id.*, Article 5.

162 On this point, see Eleanor Bayley, *Conflict Sensitivity of the Shale Gas Industry*, NEWCLIMATEFORPEACE.ORG, (Sept. 17, 2015), https://www.newclimateforpeace.org/blog/nrm-and-conflict-%E2%80%93-conflict-sensitivity-shale-gas-industry (last visited Aug 8, 2016). Bayley states: "Where there is a lack of disclosure from companies over policies and plans for meeting environmental standards and strong opposition from environmental groups, coupled with only nascent independent research and analysis on the environmental impacts of fracking and strong national and international anti-fracking campaigns can result in mis-information, thus clouding effective discussion and contributing to company-community misunderstanding and conflict." *Id.*

163 *See generally* Int'l Energy Agency, *World Energy Outlook Special Report: Energy and Climate Change* (2015), https://www.iea.org/publications/freepublications/publication/weo-2015-special-report-energy-climate-change.html (last visited Aug 8, 2016).

share similarities, as both have far-reaching federal or central laws enforced by designated agencies. Furthermore, both countries exhibit a gap between the formulation of federal or central law and their enforcement at the local level. These similarities between the U.S. and Chinese energy systems allow for drawing parallels that could be beneficial to the Chinese shale gas industry.[164]

For the purposes of this article, it is useful to analyze the factors that allowed the United States to trigger what is called the "shale revolution".[165] Shale gas industry development has deeply altered the U.S. energy scenario, allowing the transition from energy shortage to energy abundance, and the country – globally at the top of the list for energy consumption – could soon become the main hydrocarbon producer.[166] Shale gas is already influencing global energy relationships by replacing oil in the new global energy balance, and its impact will be even clearer when its export starts in 2017.[167] In the United States there are many liquified natural gas ("LNG") platforms, which originally were built to import gas but are now being converted for shale gas export, if possible towards Europe, India, and China. This shift aimed to widen the political and commercial sphere of influence of the United States in global energy safety and related geopolitical relationships, as well as for reducing the near Russian and Middle Eastern monopoly in the natural gas industry.[168] The shale gas revolution has altered hydrocarbon production economic assets in the United States, reducing dependency on imports and strengthening the domestic manufacturing sector, thanks to reduced energy costs.[169] It is therefore useful to analyze the factors that have influenced U.S. policies on unconventional gas.

164 However, the two countries have different geological characteristics. In particular, hydraulic fracturing in China is much more geographically challenging than in the US, mainly because Chinese shale gas is found in much rougher and deeper terrain than US shale gas, which is usually within two to six kilometers deep, whereas in China some key deposits are found six kilometers deep. Hence the expertise derived from the US shale industry may not be directly functional to China as it would demand more experienced staff, supplementary equipment, technological innovation, and augmented costs. Additionally, the quality of the shale rock and gas in China is also different than the US as it is more difficult to be fractured and contains much more non-hydrocarbon gasses, which means that Chinese shale gas is of a lower quality, and consequentially may be costly in the long term as China may be compelled to define ways in which to render the gas more usable. Liu Honglin, *The Drilling and Completion Technology of Shale Gas and It's Status Reservoir Stimulation Technology in Foreign, and Our Adaptive Analysis*, SENIOR SYMPOSIUM OF NATIONAL OIL AND GAS WELL ENGINEERING SCIENTIFIC RESEARCH PROGRESS AND DRILLING ENGINEERING TECHNOLOGY (2009) (in Chinese).

165 STEVENS, *supra* note 17.

166 Mary Lashley Barcella & David Hobbs, *Fueling North America's Energy Future*, THE WALL STREET JOURNAL (March 10, 2010), at A10. *See* also John Deutch, *The Good News about Gas-The Natural Gas Revolution and Its Consequences*, 90 FOREIGN AFFAIRS 82 (2011); John Deutch, *The US Natural-Gas Boom Will Transform the World*, THE WALL STREET JOURNAL (August 14, 2012). As a consequence of the shale gas revolution, the North American gas basin, currently estimable at 3,000–4,000 billion cubic feet, could bear current energy consumption for more than 100 years. *See* DANIEL YERGIN, *supra* note 26, at 332.

167 Cuckoo Paul, *Will Shale Gas Trigger a New World Order?* (Aug. 5, 2013), http://forbesindia.com/blog/businessstrategy/will-shale-gas-trigger-a-new-world-order/#ixzz3xo2MwosF (last visited Aug 8, 2016).

168 James T. Jensen, Presentation to the Paris Energy Club: LNG Exports from North America: How Competitive Are They Likely to Be? (May 4, 2012).

169 Starting in 2007, the increase in domestic gas production has led to a significant gas surplus that demand could not completely absorb. As has been observed by the US Energy Information Agency in its 2013 Annual Outlook on Energy: "The US Energy Information Agency [. . .] forecasts that natural gas production in the United States will grow from 23 billions of cubic feet in 2011 to 33.1 billions of cubic feet in 2040, with a 44% increase. Almost the entirety of this increase in domestic natural gas production is due to the forecast boost in shale gas production, that will switch from 7.8 billions of cubic feet in

Shale gas industry development in the United States has greatly benefited from the regulatory regime that developed on the basis of the pattern of "cooperative federalism."[170] The entire process is governed by complex state and federal agencies that deal, respectively, with drilling operations and the monitoring of water treatment and disposal activities. Despite this division of competences, in practice the federal government has delegated a considerable portion of its powers to the states that provide for identical or better standards than the minimum ones set at the federal level. As a consequence, at the state level, shale gas regulation varies widely, depending on the specific interest and on political assessments in relation to the extraction of this resource.[171] Due to this wide regulatory fragmentation, federal minimum standards have often been ignored or applied with a wide margin of discretion

2011 to 16.7 billions of cubic feet in 2040." *What Is Shale Gas and Why Is It Important?*, US Energy Info. Admin. (December 5, 2012). In 2000, shale gas represented only 1 per cent of the US natural gas demand. David Brooks, *Shale Gas Revolution*, NEW YORK TIMES (November 3, 2011). In 2012, its percentage has increased to 30 per cent. *See* US Energy Info. Admin., Doe/Eia-0383, *Annual Energy Outlook 2013 With Projections To 2040*, 9–10 (2013). The most important incentive to increasing natural gas demand in the United States has been the electrical production achieved by replacing coal-powered plants or by increasing the existent production capacity. At the same time, exports have the potential to facilitate demand development and make the natural gas sector more competitive. Finally, an increase in gas demand could be engendered by a series of factors, such as the use of natural gas vehicles, electricity production, and gas demand for industrial purposes. K. W. Costello, *Exploiting the* Abundance *of* U.S. Shale Gas: Overcoming Obstacles to Fuel witching *and* Expanding *the* Gas Distribution System, 34(2) ENERGY L. J. VOL., 541, 543 (2013).

170 Francis Gradijan, *State Regulations, Litigation, and Hydraulic Fracturing*, 7 ENVTL. & ENERGY L. & POL'Y J. 47, 47 (2012).

171 For example, New York requires a comprehensive environmental impact assessment, an application to gain the permission to start drilling, and a preventive procedure plan. In Texas, drilling permission is granted easily, provided that every project presented is accompanied by an environmental impact assessment. On the different state regulations in the United States, see in general David H. Getches, *Groundwater Quality Protection: Setting a National Goal for State and Federal Programs*, 65 CHI.-KENT L. REV. 387, 410 (1989); Mark A. Latham, *The BP Deepwater Horizon: A Cautionary Tale for Ccs, Hydrofracking, Geoengineering and Other Emerging Technologies With Environmental and Human Health Risks*, 36 WM. & MARY ENVTL. L. & POL'Y 31, 56 (2011); Hannah Wiseman, *Fracturing Regulation Applied*, 22 DUKE ENVTL. L. & POL'Y F. 361, 361 (2012). Such differentiation among state legislations becomes evident through analysis of regulation of the "Marcellus" shale gas field, where every state involved executes different regulatory frameworks, while complying with federal principles, which only set minimum requirements for fracking activities. More specifically, noxious waste and toxic chemical transportation are governed by federal transport acts. The Clean Water Act prohibits the release of pollutants in a watercourse without specific authorization. Clean Water Act, 33 U.S.C. § 1251 et seq. (1971). Federal law lays down various forms of liability for the pollution of sites intended to be used for well drilling, in compliance with the Safe Drinking Water Act (SDWA), aiming at "protecting public health and regulating the supply of drinkable water at the national level." Safe Drinking Water Act, Pub. L. 93-523, 88 Stat. 1660 (1974). Similarly, the EPA has the task to issue regulations regarding fluid introduction in the subsoil, so as to protect potable subterranean aquifers. Until 1997, the EPA interpreted the definition of "subterranean introduction" contained in Section 300 of the SDWA as not applying to the subterranean storage of fluids, and excluding oil and natural gas extraction techniques, including fracking. 42 U.S.C. § 300h(d); Cupas, supra note 47, at 605–06. This interpretation was overruled in *Legal Environmental Assistance Foundation v. U.S. EPA*, 118 F.3d 1467 (11th Cir. 1997), where the Eleventh Circuit Court of Appeals stated that the SDWA interpretation followed by the EPA was wrong, and that fracking had to be considered included in the definition of "subterranean introduction," and therefore subject to regulation. Despite this decision, in 2005, Congress amended Section 300(d) of the SDWA in order specifically to exclude fracking. For an overview of the connection between the Safe Drinking Water Act and fracking, see Keith B. Hall, *Regulation of Hydraulic Fracturing Under the Safe Drinking*

according to the political line of the concerned state.[172] Standardization over this differentiated approach from state to state is desirable, especially for the regulation of environmental matters.[173]

Water Act, 19 Buff. Envtl. L.J. 1 (2012); Holly A. Vandrovee, *The Fight Over Fracking: Recent Hydraulic Fracturing Litigation in Texas*, 74 Tex. B.J. 390, 391 (2011).

172 This differentiated approach is clear in the recovery and disposal of fracturing fluid. For example, New York chose to endorse the precautionary principle, while Ohio and West Virginia adopted a non-intervention policy, and are promoting shale gas development and exploitation through a minimal regulation. *See generally, e.g.*, Hannah Wiseman, (presented 2012, March). State and Local Regulation of Shale Oil and Gas Development: Adaptation, Experimentation, or Chaos? Presentation at Conference on Federalism and Energy in the United States, Searle Center, Northwestern University Law School, Chicago, IL. (National). Here, it is useful to refer to the fundamental aspects of the precautionary principle. This principle has been developed first in the environmental policy area. Already the Ministerial Declaration of the Second International Conference on the Protection of the North Sea (1987) states: "in order to protect the North Sea from possibly damaging effects of the most dangerous substances, a precautionary approach is necessary which may require action to control inputs of such substances even before a causal link has been established by absolutely clear scientific evidence." Second International Conference on the Protection of the North Sea, Ministerial Declaration (1987), http://www.vliz.be/imisdocs/publications/140155.pdf. Later, during the Third International Conference on the Protection of the North Sea (1990), a new Ministerial Declaration clarified the previous one: "Participating governments will continue to apply the precautionary principle, that is to take action to avoid potentially damaging impacts of substances that are persistent, toxic and liable to bioaccumulate even where there is no scientific evidence to prove a causal link between emissions and effects." Third International Conference on the Protection of the North Sea, Ministerial Declaration (1990), www.vliz.be/imisdocs/publications/140228.pdf (last visited Aug 8, 2016). Finally, the principle has been specifically legitimized in Principle 15 of the Rio Declaration: "In order to protect the environment, the precautionary approach shall be widely applied by States according to their capabilities. Where there are threats of serious or irreversible damage, lack of full scientific certainty shall not be used as a reason for postponing cost-effective measures to prevent environmental degradation." U.N. Conference on Environment and Development, *Rio Declaration on Environment and Development*, U.N. Doc. A/CONF.151/26 (Vol. I) (Aug. 12, 1992). The principle was later recalled in similar terms in the Preamble of the Convention on Biodiversity (1992), in Article 3 (Principles) of the Convention on Climate Change (1992), and in the Paris Convention for the Protection of the Marine Environment of the North-East Atlantic (September 1992). The principles that should inspire recourse to the precautionary principle are the following: (i) implementation of the principle should be founded on the most complete scientific assessment possible, which determines at every moment the degree of scientific uncertainty; (ii) any decision on whether to act under the precautionary principle should be preceded by an assessment of the risk and of the potential consequences of not acting; and (iii) as soon as the results of the scientific assessments and/or of the risk assessment are available, all the stakeholders should have the chance to participate in the evaluation of the various foreseeable actions with the greatest possible transparency. See Cordini Giovanni - Fois Paolo - Marchisio Sergio, Diritto ambientale. Profili internazionali europei e comparati, 2008, Giappichelli; Mariachiara Alberton, La quantificazione e la riparazione del danno ambientale nel diritto internazionale e dell'Unione Europea. 2008, Giuffrè.

173 Schauwecker reaffirms that the EPA has the duty, pursuant to the Water Use Efficiency and Conservation Research Act of 2009 (H.R. 631 (111th)), to manage the risks linked to fracking, as this legislation "imposes on the US Environmental Protection Agency the drafting of a research and development programme that fosters water efficiency and conservation." Schauwecker, *supra* note 86, at 47. Deweese affirms that by far state regulation has proved to be ready and effective, and that the Congress' efforts to connect fracking to the SDWA will only hold back further industrial development of this fundamental resource. Dewesee, *supra* note 92. *See also* Cameron Jefferies, *Unconventional Bridges Over Troubled Water: Lessons to Be Learned from the Canadian Oil Sands as the United States Moves to Develop the Natural Gas of the Marcellus Shale Play*, 33 Energy L.J. 75, 75 (2012).

A. *Pricing and fiscal regime*

In 1978 the United States implemented the Natural Gas Policy Act (NGPA),[174] which entailed gradual removal of price controls and supplied economic subsidies for the development of new natural gas sources, including for gas obtained from unconventional sources. Previously, the maximum price for interstate natural gas was set at a level that was artificially lower than the equilibrium price that would have arisen from free competition in the marketplace.[175] This rate regulation produced an increase in demand and a tightening in supply, with consequent repercussions on natural gas stocks and on production.[176] Moreover, the NGPA contained advantageous conditions for unconventional gas also in the light of the very high extraction costs involved.[177] This partial natural gas price deregulation constituted a critical advantage for the development of these natural resources.

Turning to natural gas tariff regulation in China, the lack of a national agency responsible for pricing creates uncertainties in potential investors. The Chinese pricing regime for natural gas is a mosaic of different market and administered prices, set according to a number of factors.[178] The Twelfth Five-Year Plan (2011–2015) foresees a doubling of the output of gas-fired power plants and an increase in the consumption of natural gas by households.[179] This is the reason the price of natural gas is kept at an artificially depressed level that is lower than the international market price. The consequent gap with domestic prices forces Chinese firms to import gas at a loss, significantly reducing the potential relevance of natural gas. The current government intervention and

174 Natural Gas *Policy Act* (NGPA), 15 US Code § 3301. On this matter *see* Richard Greer Morgan & Martha Priddy Patterson, *Natural Gas Policy Act of 1978: Four Years of Practice and Two Years to Make Perfect, The*, 71 Ky. L. J. 105 (1982); Joseph P. Tomain, *The Dominant Model of United States Energy Policy*, 61 U. Colo. L. Rev. 355 (1990); Rodney L. Brown, Jr., *Legislative History of the Natural Gas Policy Act: Title I*, 59 Tex. L. Rev. 101 (1980).

175 *See generally* Kevin L. Ward, *Preemption Survives Deregulation of Natural Gas: Transcontinental Gas Pipe Line Corp. v. State Oil and Gas Board of Mississippi*, 22 TULSA L. J. 639, 639 (1986).

176 After the oil embargo in 1973 and the following "energy crisis" in 1979, the US government fostered a large number of projects, including the strengthening and expansion of research and development projects linked to energy sources, which were later salvaged with the creation of the Department of Energy (DOE), and to which has been given the task of identifying and best defining the respective responsibilities and competences of all federal energy plans and research and development plans. It should be noted that the first oil crisis, coincident with the embargo put into effect by the Arab countries in 1973, resulted from the hostilities which arose between Arab countries and Israel during the Yom Kippur War – the fourth and last of the Israeli-Arab conflicts. In fact, for the first time in history, an oil-exporting country decided to use oil as a real weapon of war. Oil prices increased by 70 per cent, reaching $5.11 per barrel. In addition to the price increase, an embargo was announced, and production fell by 5 per cent in the first month, continuing with equal reductions during each month following. "Towards the United States the embargo was total, as a reaction to the support it gave to Israel. The second oil crisis resulting from the Iranian revolution, took place between 1978 and 1979. Iran stopped its production, and the consequent oil shortage, which at first was balanced by a production increase by other OPEC members, started to be widely felt, as Iran was globally the second largest oil-producing country." Paolo Davide Farah & Elena Cima, *Energy Trade and the WTO: Implications for Renewable Energy and the OPEC Cartel*, 16(3) J. Int'l Econ. L. (2013).

177 15 U.S.C. § 3301 (1978).

178 For a comparative analysis of the US gas pricing regime, *see* Boriss Siliverstovs, Guillaume L'Hégaret, Anne Neumann & Christian von Hirschhausen, *International Market Integration for Natural Gas? A Cointegration Analysis of Prices in Europe, North America and Japan*, 27(4) Energy Econ. 603–615 (2005).

179 China's Twelfth Five-Year Plan, *supra* note 62.

monopoly energy prices neither reflect the scarcity of resources nor demand in the market. Furthermore, price distortions are not conducive to the effectiveness of market mechanisms and the allocation of resources, since energy prices are detached from the market, which forces the government to subsidize certain energy industries, worsening the financial burden.[180] Today, China's gas pricing is a cost-plus regime that is disciplined throughout the entire value chain.[181] It has undergone some changes as the economy moves towards a market-based economy. In spite of this, it essentially follows a fixed-price model, and a market-based pricing mechanism has yet to be developed.

As a result, price and regulatory reform are much needed. Experimental price mechanisms have already been implemented, starting in December 2011, in the province of Guangdong and in the Guangxi region, where gas prices are no longer kept artificially lower than the market price levels, but are instead connected to the market price of fuel oil and liquefied petroleum gas imported to Shanghai, which is a Chinese hub for gas trading and consumption.[182] This trial reform overhauls the old pricing formation and moves towards an oil-indexation mechanism. The final objective is to liberalize the wellhead price and establish a market-based pricing regime. It will rely on the concept of oil indexation to determine the gas price. By connecting the price of domestic natural gas with the international price of its competing fuel, the oil-indexed price formula will mirror international market fundamentals and demand. Eventually the wellhead price will no longer be subject to government-administered price, but will be set on a market basis.[183] The cost-plus regime does not provide the fundamental price signal that a market economy requires. A clear price signal is essential to reflect the market value of natural resources, to indicate the market trend, and to guide investment decisions. The low domestic price creates disincentives to upstream companies form investing in exploration and production, thus hindering the development of conventional and unconventional reserves.[184] Furthermore, the current Chinese shale gas

180 National People Congress of China, Twelfth Five-Year Plan (2011–2015), (March 2011), http://www.britishchamber.cn/content/chinas-twelfthfive-year-plan-2011–2015-full-english-version (last visited Aug 8, 2016). Zhu Yi, Zhongguo Nengyuan Shichang Xianzhuang Fenxi: Jianlun *Zhongguo Nengyuan Shichang Guojihua* [*Chinese Situation of Energy Market: Discussion on the Internationalization of China's Energy Market*], 8 ZHEJIANG JINGJI [ZHEJIANG ECON.] 17 (2004).

181 Cost-plus pricing entails that, in accordance with the value chain, the pricing formation flows from the price set by the government for the upstream producer to the midstream pipeline operator and them to the end user. YI CHEN, DEVELOPMENT STRATEGIES OF THE CHINESE NATURAL GAS MARKET 19 (2013).

182 OXFORD INST. FOR ENERGY STUD., THE DEVELOPMENT OF CHINESE GAS PRICING: DRIVERS, CHALLENGES, AND IMPLICATIONS FOR DEMAND 9 (Registered Charity No. 286084, 2014) http://www.oxfordenergy.org/wpcms/wpcontent/uploads/2014/07/NG-89.pdf (Aug 8, 2016).

183 *Id.* at 22–24.

184 *Id.* at 22. Preferential pricing has already been adopted in other unconventional gas resources that present higher extraction costs as compared to conventional resources; reasonably these regimes could be extended to shale gas production. In particular, the government has implemented several preferential policies to support Coalbed Methane and coalmine methane extraction and commercialization. CHINA GREENTECH INITIATIVE, UNCONVENTIONAL GAS IN CHINA 8 (2011), http://www.chinagoabroad.com/sites/v2/files/v1_attachments/2012/04/CGTI2011-CCE-WS1-Unconventional-Gas.pdf (last visited Aug 8, 2016). Other policies include exemption from corporate tax for the first two years of production and a reduction of 50 per cent for the following three years, exemption from mining rights fees, royalty fees, value-added tax (VAT), and feed-in-tariffs for Coalbed Methane and coalmine methane-fired power. *Id.*

exploration and exploitation framework should be improved also in relation to the tax system, which is a critical element in investment development and in the fostering of efficient resource use.

The current Chinese shale gas regulatory framework should be enhanced in two particular sectors, namely the fiscal and pricing regimes, which are key elements in fostering needed investments and promoting efficient use of resources. Under China's production-sharing contracts, international energy companies must share a percentage of their profits with the government or government-owned companies, in addition to paying corporate taxes on gains.[185] This creates a deterrent for overseas investors in a high-risk activity such as shale gas exploration and production. Conversely, the U.S. regulatory regime based on royalties requires energy firms to merely pay a portion of project revenues and corporate taxes on gains.

Other factors were also important in U.S. shale gas development. First, in the 2000s, natural gas prices were particularly high.[186] This allowed companies to realize significant profit margins from drilling shale gas wells. The prospect of high profit margins pushed existing energy enterprises and new entrants to invest heavily in shale gas plays, which eventually pushed down natural gas prices.[187]

B. Barriers to entry and consequences on competition in the gas market

The barriers for entry for small and large firms into the American shale gas industry were much lower than in China as individual companies were able to lease or acquire land to explore. The North American market structure also played a decisive role in development of the shale gas industry, which is undoubtedly one of the most capital-intensive industries. It follows that small natural gas firms do not have the financial capacity and technical know-how to make substantial venture investments in technology. Indeed, in the United States it was large, independent natural gas firms that significantly invested in the early stage of shale gas development. Conversely, the major oil firms, although having the capacity, considered shale gas less appealing as an investment than conventional oil and gas. The capital market's role was fundamental in this context, and contributed to pushing the shale gas boom forward by providing natural gas firms with copious capital to drill, and it also eased many transactions in which larger oil and gas enterprises bought out smaller firms committed to shale gas drilling.[188]

In China, however, the central government exerts power firmly on shale gas blocks by organizing auctions or granting exploration rights.[189] This scheme creates various barriers to entry for overseas small and large firms into the domestic shale gas industry,[190] because in order to take part

185 *See generally* Erica Downs, *Who's Afraid of China's National Oil Companies?*, *in* Energy Security: Economics, Politics, Strategies and Implications (2010).

186 Zhongmin Wang & Alan Krupnick, *US Shale Gas Development What Led to the Boom?*, Resources for the Future, May 2013, at 10, http://www.rff.org/files/sharepoint/WorkImages/Download/RFF-IB-13-04.pdf (last visited Aug 8, 2016).

187 *Id.*

188 *Id.*, at 11.

189 *Id.*, at 10.

190 In the first auction, held in June 2011, only state-owned companies were admitted to compete. This auction stimulated a feeble response, as only six companies put in bids for four blocks, and only two blocks were eventually awarded. A second auction was organized in October 2012, collecting 152 bids for twenty blocks. CSIS, *China Awards More Shale Gas Blocks Although Much Remains to be Seen* (Jan. 23, 2013), http://csis.org/publication/chinaawards-more-shale-gas-blocks-although-much-remains-be-seen (last visited Aug 8, 2016).

in auctions, firms had to be either Chinese or Chinese-held joint-venture companies, and they needed to have an extremely elevated minimum value.[191] In particular, the approval system for foreign investments in the mineral industry, embracing any underground activities, is subject to both foreign capital and industry access approval mechanisms.[192] The former implies a multi-tiered administrative approval system according to which authorities of different levels exercise different powers over different industrial categories and total investment amounts. As for industry access, China enforces an authorization scheme for the exploration and exploitation of underground natural resources. Specifically, the investor must apply for registration, hold an exploitation or explorations license, and gain the right of exploration and exploitation.[193]

As one might expect, such a burdensome policy for foreign investments in the Chinese mineral industry is far from conducive to shale gas production. Joint ventures between domestic and foreign companies through both inbound and outbound investments for extraction technology and potentially for infrastructure development seem to be the best strategy in this early stage of the shale gas industry. Obviously, Chinese restrictions on foreign investments constitute a relevant barrier. As explained above, prior to January 30, 2012, exploration and exploitation of shale gas in China could only be carried out by Chinese state-owned companies. However, according to the revised Foreign Investment Industry Guidance Catalog, shale gas foreign investments are included in the "encouraged" category of the catalog, allowing foreign investors to form with their Chinese partners Sino-foreign joint ventures and Sino-foreign contractual (cooperative) joint ventures.[194] Additionally, an MLR Circular issued on October 26, 2012 reaffirms that private Chinese oil companies may also explore for and exploit shale gas, including by way of creating joint ventures with foreign companies. The regulations do not specify a maximum percentage equity shareholding that a foreign company is permitted to hold in such a joint venture; however, the MLR's public bidding invitation terms require that the Chinese party must have a majority ownership.[195] Furthermore, investors will likely wait to see what shale gas pricing policies and government support mechanisms are put in place before actually investing in Chinese shale gas, as uncertainty and regulatory changes might have detrimental effects on them.[196]

191 Enterprises are required to invest at least RMB 30,000 ($4747 USD) per square meter annually, three times the minimum amount for crude oil exploration. Additionally, the second shale gas tender, launched in 2012, required bidding companies to have 300 million yuan ($47.4 million USD) in registered capital. Ministry of Land & Res. of the People's Republic of China, *Shale Gas Tender Submission Announcement*, RFFF.ORG (May 17, 2012), http://www.rff.org/files/sharepoint/WorkImages/Download/RFF-IB-13-04.pdf (in Chinese) (last visited Aug 8, 2016). While a high market entry threshold may defeat China's goal of attracting diversified investment and fostering competition, this practice may lessen environmental risks, as in China small and medium-sized companies are more difficult to regulate and have less financial and technical ability to adopt best practices. *See* Enoe et al., *supra* note 19.

192 Chinese Acad. of Land & Res. Econ., Dep't of Sci. & Tech. & Int'l Cooperation of the Ministry of Land & Res., A Guide to Investment in China's Mineral Industry 13 (2012), http://www.chinaminingtj.org/en/document/A_Guide_to_Investment_in_China's_Mineral_Industry(2012).pdf (last visited Aug 8, 2016).

193 *See generally id.*

194 *See Catalogue of Encouraged Foreign Investment Industries*, Ministry Comm. People's Republic China II(6), II(9) (Feb. 21, 2012), *translation at* http://english.mofcom.gov.cn/article/policyrelease/aaa/201203/20120308027837.shtml (last visited Aug 8, 2016).

195 Dina Yin, Zhao Yan, *Shale Gas and CBM Companies to Pay* VAT, China L. Insight (June 28, 2013), http://www.chinalawinsight.com/2013/06/articles/fdi/shale-gas-and-cbmcompanies-to-pay-vat/ (last visited Aug 8, 2016).

196 *See* KPMG Global Energy Institute, *supra* note 51, at 11.

In this context, it should be pointed out that the absence of competition in the energy market generates an unfair allocation of resources. In fact, in 2001 China joined the World Trade Organization (WTO), and consequentially must increase competitiveness of state-owned energy companies while restraining national control over energy companies.[197] At the moment, there is no actual competition between the three major Chinese oil companies, as they have the same, single shareholder, i.e., the State-owned Assets Supervision and Administration Commission of the State Council ("SASAC"). Indeed, there is no competition in either the upstream or downstream energy sectors, as they feature market monopolies and administrative price guides,[198] regardless of the fact that both the Twelfth Five-Year Plan (2011–2015) and the 2012 Energy White Paper call for the introduction of private capital and market mechanisms, which would terminate the current energy monopoly that exacerbates lack of supervision and inefficiency.[199] The only way China could improve its future energy policy is by converting non-market mechanisms to market mechanisms, adopting a modern corporate system for energy companies, and changing the governmental management system from strict controls to limited supervision.[200] Another aspect that has certainly advanced the growth in shale gas development in the United States is its distinctive market structure for gas transportation. In particular, "ownership of transportation capacity rights is unbundled from ownership of the pipeline itself."[201] This makes it possible for many of the small producers that first ventured into shale to access the market through a competitive bid for pipeline capacity. This is an inherent problem affecting market access in China, where pipeline capacity is bundled to facility ownership, and large incumbent state-owned enterprises dominate the entire transportation infrastructure.

C. *Mineral rights ownership regulation*

Another fundamental element of the present comparative analysis is the land and mineral rights ownership regime. In the United States, shale gas development has taken place mainly on private land.[202] Private land ownership allowed natural gas firms a way to ensure

197 As a condition for joining the WTO, China agreed to reduce tariffs on all imported goods, and to open to foreign investors. In return, China has benefited the Most Favored Nation treatment and reciprocal rights for trade and investment. *See* Paolo Davide Farah, *supra* note 64. In addition, China agreed on the establishment and enforcement of a stronger intellectual property rights regime. Paolo Davide Farah & Elena Cima, ***China's Participation in the World Trade Organization: Trade in Goods, Services, Intellectual Property Rights and Trasparency Issues***, in El comercio con China. Oportunidades empresariales, incertidumbres jurídicas 83–121 (Aurelio Lopez-Tarruella Martinez ed., Castellano | Tirant lo Blanch S.L, 2010).

198 In practice, China National Petroleum Corporation (CNPC), the Sinopec Group, and China National Offshore Oil Corporation (CNOOC) possess the absolute majority of the exploration blocks, despite the fact that the 1998 Mineral Resources Exploration Block Regulation stipulates that 25,000 unit blocks are the maximum features in exploration projects of oil and gas. Chen Shou Hai, ***Woguo Tianranqi Chanye de Longduan Ji Falv Guizhi [Legal Regulation of Monopoly in China's Natural Gas Industry]*** in Nengyuan Yanjiu Baogao [Energy Law Research Report] 336 (Law Press China, 2012).

199 The National Energy 12th Five-Year Plan calls for a reform of energy mix, advocates for a rationalization of energy-pricing mechanisms to encourage private capital to invest in the field of energy, and fosters the granting of propriety to encourage technological progress and to progress in the innovation of scientific and technical equipment. In the same vein, the 2012 Energy White Paper promotes a sustainable use of energy through the establishment of a market mechanism in energy pricing, and the creation of interconnected institutional mechanisms. Text available at http://www.gov.cn/english/official/2012-10/24/content_2250497.htm (last visited Aug 8, 2016).

200 Ni Jian Ming, *Guojia Nengyuan Anquan Baogao [National Energy Security Report]* 329–330 (2005).

201 Kenneth B. Medlock Et Al., Shale Gas and U.S. National Security 14 (Baker Institute Policy Report 49 on Shale Gas and U.S. National Security, 2011).

202 Wang & Krupnick, *supra* note 181.

reasonable returns from their early investments in technology innovations through acquiring land, proving its potential and then selling it. Private mineral rights ownership creates a constituency favoring drilling and helps restrain the temptation of governments to raise revenues through shale gas drilling.[203] China has auctioned off drilling blocks and has required a certain minimum investment to develop auctioned blocks within a certain period of time.[204] In theory, this should force firms to drill, but it is not clear whether this mechanism would offer a sufficient incentive to innovate. On the other hand, private land ownership carries the risk that some speculating energy companies may rent large areas of land without making appropriate investments. In China, below-ground mineral rights are owned by the State. State ownership can back operators piecing together contiguous blocks of land, achieving a more efficient and unhindered exploitation of a play. Moreover, the government can lease the drilling rights at below-market rates if it wishes to.

A further element to be analyzed is the legal regime concerning water rights regulation in the United States.[205] A mineral lease to a shale gas operator generally comprises the details of what consumption the operator can make of water on the surface of the property, and the specific lease terms will govern the relationship between the surface fee owner and mineral rights holder.[206] Customarily, these contracts allow water to be employed for operating on the premises and the owner or operator can use a reasonable quantity of water so long as other riparian rights holders are not prejudiced in their use.[207] In fact, the reasonable-use doctrine renders "virtually all uses of water made upon the land from which it is extracted [. . .] 'reasonable,' even if they more or less deplete the supply to the harm of neighbors, unless the purpose is malicious or the water is simply wasted."[208] Some states comprising the Marcellus Shale, namely New York and Ohio, have implemented a "regulated riparian" pattern to deal with these unclear provisions.[209] Conversely, Pennsylvania and West Virginia depend heavily on the common law regulatory precedents, and have yet to pass permitting procedures.[210]

D. *Pipeline Network*

Moreover, in the United States, an extensive and sophisticated network of natural gas pipelines existed before shale gas became a major gas resource. Fundamental in this context was the

203 *Id.* at 10.

204 U.S. Energy Info. Admin., *China: International Energy Data and Analysis*, at 20 (May 14, 2015), https://www.eia.gov/beta/international/analysis_includes/countries_long/China/china.pdf (last visited Aug 8, 2016).

205 The water rights regulation in the United States is derived from the English "riparian" rights regime. Accordingly, landowners adjacent to waterways gain water rights to that waterway as an appurtenant feature of land ownership. The specific rights that landowners gain depend on the type of water in question. The rights are designed to address the following water resources: (i) "diffused surface water" (such as rainwater); (ii) traditional stream, river, and lake surface water; (iii) groundwater that flows in "well-defined subterranean streams"; and (iv) "percolating groundwater". For an overview on this point, *see* R. Timothy Weston, *Harmonizing Management of Ground and Surface Water Use under Eastern Water Law Regimes*, 11 U. Denv. Water L. Rev. 239 (2007–2008).

206 Cameron Jefferies, *Unconventional Bridges Over Troubled Water - Lessons to be Learned from the Canadian Oil Sands as the United States Moves to Develop the Natural Gas of the Marcellus Shale Play*, 33 ENERGY L.J. 75, 100 (2012).

207 *Id.*, at 100.

208 *Id.*, at 250.

209 *Id.*, at 255.

210 *Id.*, at 250–59.

policy of open access to interstate natural gas pipelines (as well as storage facilities) resulting from a series of Federal Energy Regulatory Commission (FERC) orders in the 1980s and early 1990s.[211] In the following years, significant technological advances enabled a surge in investment in the production of shale gas, which determined a surge in supply coupled with strong demand driven by sustainable low natural gas prices.[212] This constituted an exciting opportunity for energy infrastructure providers. Today, infrastructure investors benefit from attractive opportunities, relatively stable low-risk cash flows underpinned by long-term contracts and growth perspectives stemming from the need for expanded pipeline capacity. This scenario has increased the potential for attractive returns and represents a crucial case for investment in energy infrastructure across the gas supply chain. In the United States, investors rely on provisions of pipeline infrastructure that are generally predicated on stable, fee-based revenues, largely insulated from direct commodity price exposure. Additionally, more than half of the top midstream pipeline enterprises have adopted a 'master-limited partnership' structure as an effective alternative to a corporate structure.[213] This partnership model does not pay corporate tax, which has contributed to promoting investment in the shale gas industry.[214]

Although China has a considerable reserve estimate, the development of shale gas as a key element of the country's energy mix may be undermined by the lack of adequate physical infrastructure, mainly gas pipelines for transport and delivery. Large-scale pipelines will have to be built to manage the capacity of targeted output and to transport the product from the major gas fields, which could be challenging for smaller exploration and production firms.[215] In particular, there is no integrated national gas grid, and most of China's infrastructures were constructed to transport its most important fuel, coal.[216] Currently all principal gas transmission lines are owned by the state,[217] and new pipelines are needed. Developing transportation and storage facilities is crucial for shale gas expansion, and even though much still needs to be done, China plans to build 14,400 miles of new gas pipelines between 2010 and 2016 to

211 *See* in particular, FERC 1985 Order No. 436, the Natural Gas Wellhead Decontrol Act (NGWDA) passed by Congress in 1989, and FERC 1992 Order No. 636. Richard J. Pierce, *Reconsidering the Roles of Regulation and Competition in the Natural Gas Industry,* HARV. L. REV. 345–385 (1983).

212 *See generally* Dan Alger & Michael Toman, *Market-Based Regulation of Natural Gas Pipelines*, 2.3 J. REG. ECON. 263, 263 (1990); Harry G. Broadman & Joseph P. Kalt, *How Natural Is Monopoly? The Case of Bypass in Natural Gas Distribution Markets,* 6 YALE J. REG. 181, 184 (1989).

213 Maquarie Inv. Mgmt., *US Shale Gas: A Good News Pipeline* 2 (2012), https://www.macquarie.com.au/dafiles/Internet/mgl/au/mfg/mim/docs/miminsight/mim-insight-apr12-shalegas.pdf?v=1 (last visited Aug 8, 2016); *Conoco Eyeing Chinese Shale Despite Block Exits,* ENERGY CHINA FORUM (May 28, 2015), http://www.shalegaschinasummit.com/News_Show.asp?pid=9156 (last visited Aug 8, 2016).

214 *Id.*

215 *See* KPMG Global Energy Institute, *supra* note 51, at 10.

216 45 percent of domestic railway capacity is devoted to coal transport. On the coal sector in China, *see* Mou Dunguo & Zhi Li, *A Spatial Analysis of China's Coal Flow,* 48 ENERGY POL'Y 358–368 (2012); Richard Heinberg & David Fridley, *The End of Cheap Coal,* 468(7322) NAT. 367–369 (2010); Wang Bing, *An Imbalanced Development of Coal and Electricity Industries in China,* 35(10) ENERGY POL'Y 4959–4968 (2007); Lin Bo-qiang & Jiang-hua Liu, *Estimating Coal Production Peak and Trends of Coal Imports in China,* 38(1) ENERGY POL'Y 512–519 (2010).

217 Currently, CNPC essentially monopolizes pipeline construction and operations in China. It owns and operates 90 per cent of pipelines. Whether CNPC would allow for shale gas transport by the third party via their pipelines still needs to be seen, since it has no legal obligation to do so. *See* Guo-Hua Shi, You-Yin Jing, Song-Ling Wang & Xu-Tao Zhang, *Development Status of Liquefied Natural Gas Industry in China,* 38 (11) ENERGY POL'Y 7457–7465 (2010).

reinforce the current 21,000-mile network.[218] In addition, China will need to construct or reinforce infrastructures that can safely dispose of the contaminated material used to fracture the shale rock, thus protecting the environment. Energy expert Diana Ngo stresses that these factors are important because they will reduce costs caused by environmental damage occurring in the future.[219] Additionally, these precautionary steps will also help China exponentially speed up their well-development timeline (for instance, PetroChina took a lengthy period of eleven months to complete the country's first horizontal well).[220]

E. *The politics of shale: Grounds for international cooperation*

Shale gas development has deeply modified the energy scenario in the United States from a status of shortage to that of plenty. Already the world's biggest energy consumer, the United States may soon become the largest producer of hydrocarbons.[221] As a consequence of the shale gas revolution, North America's natural gas base, now estimated at 3400 trillion cubic feet, could provide for current levels of consumption for over one-hundred years.[222] Shale gas, replacing oil as the principal agent of a new global energetic equilibrium, is already transforming global energy relations, and the impact will be more evident when gas exports begin (the first LNG exports are expected to start around 2017).[223] There are several LNG terminals located in the US, originally constructed to import gas, which are now looking to start exporting from the US, possibly to Europe, India, and China, as a way to extend their

218 On January 23, 2013 the State Council issued the notice of the Energy 12th Five-Year Plan stressing that, due to the instability of marine energy transportation, China will develop on-shore pipeline constructions for oil and gas transportation, which should reduce energy supply security threats. Enhancing transportation and storage facilities would help to expand shale gas development. Furthermore, some parts of the shale-gas-rich provinces have existing pipeline networks, but small-scale LNG and compressed natural gas technologies may be necessary to boost the early stage of shale gas development in China. At the moment, the 4,200-km West-East Pipeline links the Tarim and Ordos Basins to markets in the Shanghai area. The second West-East Pipeline was completed in June 2011, although several sub-lines remain to be completed. A recently completed 1,700-km gas pipeline carries Sichuan Province gas to Hubei, Anhui, Jiangxi, Jiangsu, and Zhejiang Provinces, and Shanghai. Jane Nakano, David Pumphrey, Robert Price, Jr. & Molly A. Watson, Prospects for Shale Gas Development in Asia Examining Potentials and Challenges in China and India 7–12 (2012), http://csis.org/files/publication/120911_Nakano_ProspectsShaleGas_Web.pdf (last visited Aug 8, 2016).

219 Diana Ngo, *3 Reasons Why Shale Gas is a Pipe Dream in China- Part I*, Energy in Asia (May 11, 2012), http://energyinasiablog.com/2012/05/ (last visited Aug 8, 2016). By the same author, *Why China Lags Behind the U.S. in Shale Gas Development*, Energy in Asia (January 15, 2013), http://energyinasiablog.com/2013/01/15/why-china-lags-behind-us-shale-gas-development/ (last visited Aug 8, 2016).

220 *Id.*

221 Much of the credit for the technological advancements that allowed the shale gas development is owed to the members of the Mitchell Energy shale gas team, in particular to the late George Mitchell (1919–2013), who worked to refine shale technologies despite harsh criticism, especially in the Barnett shale formation of northern Texas. Hydraulic fracturing has been so successful that energy experts have called this the "most significant energy innovation so far of this century." Mary Lashley Barcella & David Hobbs, *Fueling North America's Energy Future*, Wall St. J., Mar. 10, 2010, at A10; *see also The Good News About Gas: The Natural Gas Revolution and its Consequences, supra* note 128; *The US Natural-Gas Boom Will Transform the World, supra* note 128.

222 *See* Yergin, *supra* note 26, at 332.

223 Keith Johnson & Ben Lefebvre, *U.S. Approves Expanded Gas Exports*, Wall St. J. (May 18, 2013, 11:18 AM), http://www.wsj.com/articles/SB10001424127887324767004578489130300876450 (last visited Aug 8, 2016).

sphere of influence, while reducing the dominance of the Middle East and Russia in the gas sector. The shale gas revolution has modified the economics of oil and gas production in the United States, reducing dependence on imported oil and gas supplies and reinforcing domestic manufacturing through lower energy costs.

Over the last decade, the political attitude towards shale gas has been changing, and more consideration is given to concerns regarding shale's potential detrimental effects on the environment, and in particular water sources. Accordingly, the Obama administration plans to enforce more stringent controls over drillers by forcing them to seize emissions of determined air pollutants from new wells beginning in 2015.[224] The rapid development of shale gas in the United States has nevertheless stoked environmental controversy and debate. The suitability of taking the US regulatory framework as a model scheme remains debatable because the United States is experiencing difficulties with environmental aspects related to shale gas extraction,[225] in particular given the complex barriers that developing countries such as China are facing in this sector. Nevertheless, it is likely that a comparative analysis might contribute to resolving some of these issues.

Large-scale production of shale gas in the US is already transforming the worldwide dynamics of the gas industry. The rapid growth of this new resource created a global surplus of LNG, whose rapid buildup coincided with the emergence of shale gas as a new supply source.[226] Until 2010, the US was supposed to represent the greatest LNG market due to a projected domestic shortfall. Conversely, shale gas increase may transform the US into an LNG exporter, leaving much LNG in search of a market that will be only partially absorbed by growing Asia. This over-supply of LNG determined wider competition among gas suppliers and reduced prices. It is also modifying the economic and political equilibrium stemming from a new, wider geopolitical impact of the global gas market, which is engendering new gas competition.[227] As shale gas expands globally, we should assess the possible consequences of price development in relation to the potential establishment of an Organization of Gas Exporting Countries (OGEC), stemming from the Gas Exporting Countries Forum (GECF), a gas-exporting countries recurrent forum with headquarters in Doha, Qatar (which is the main gas supplier to Europe, after Russia).[228] In particular, if gas prices further

224 In President Barack Obama's March 30, 2011 energy proposal, he pointed out that shale gas could play a large role in US energy policy, particularly with mitigation of its environmental impacts: "Recent technology and operational improvements in extracting natural gas resources, particularly shale gas, have increased gas drilling activities nationally and led to significantly higher natural gas production estimates for decades to come. The Administration is taking steps to address these [environmental] concerns and ensure that natural gas production proceeds in a safe and responsible manner." White House Office of the Press Secretary, ***Remarks by the President on America's Energy Security***, White House (Mar. 30, 2011), https://www.whitehouse.gov/the-press-office/2011/03/30/remarks-presidentamericas- energy-security (last visited Aug 8, 2016). *See generally Jody Freeman, **Climate and Energy Policy in the Obama Administration***, 30 Pace Envtl. L. Rev. 375, 375 (2012).

225 *See* Reeder, ***supra*** note 101 (describing the complex legal obstacles inherent to shale gas development).

226 In the United States, the surplus of domestic gas production is partly due to the mismatches between LNG project start-ups and the completion of LNG tanker construction combined with the expiry of charter agreements for older tankers as a result of production declines in older projects. *See* Paul Stevens, ***supra*** note 16, at 21.

227 *See* Daniel Yergin, ***supra*** note 47, at 335.

228 Int'l Energy Agency, Key World Energy Statistics 13 (2015), https://www.iea.org/publications/freepublications/publication/key-worldenergy-statistics-2015.html (last visited Aug 8, 2016).

lower reducing exporters' revenues, this would constitute an incentive for an OGEC to take the lead and defend falling prices.[229] It remains to be seen to what extent the GECF will develop into an OGEC. It is not clear how such a cartel would fix the gas price, possibly enacting price-fixing mechanisms or imposing production quantitative restrictions. In reality, traded gas is often subject to long-term contracts which feature rigid pricing terms supported by international commercial provisions. As one might expect, government interference in pricing terms would amount to a breach of such agreements, triggering international arbitration in order to settle the contractual dispute.

On a different level, U.S. President Barack Obama and the former Chinese General Secretary Hu Jintao acknowledged the relevance of fostering cooperation in shale gas development by establishing a Global Shale Gas Resource Initiative (GSGI) in November 2009. This agreement provides U.S. assistance to assess, develop, and promote investment in shale gas reserves, and to help develop operational best practices and effective environmental safeguards.[230] The goal of the GSGI is to assist countries seeking to develop their own unconventional gas resources while balancing energy security and environmental concerns.[231] So far, partnerships have been arranged with India, Poland, and China. Chinese State-owned gas producers have entered into major transactions with large international players to develop shale gas reserves in China and to exploit shale gas reserves in Western Canada and the United States.[232]

Whether the GSGI can provide a regulatory model to develop unconventional natural gas resources in an environmentally sensitive manner remains to be seen. In that respect, appropriateness of the U.S. legal framework as a model scheme is still debatable, given the problem that shale gas is creating in the United States, especially in relation to the environment. While good progress on the exploration and development aspects of this agreement has been made, environmental cooperation is still lacking. This is in part due to the fact that the United States is still struggling to design the most adequate domestic regulatory framework for safeguards. Environmental protection is not the priority for either side, as they do not want to jeopardize the potential of China's shale gas by firmly pursuing environmental protection. At the same time, U.S. energy companies engaged in these bilateral exploration and development projects aim at exchanging assessment and extraction technology for Chinese commercial market access. On the other side, China strives to transfer technology from the United States, which often implies intellectual property rights concerns.[233]

229 *See* Paul Stevens, ***supra*** note 15, at 23, remarking that this was precisely the mechanism that led to the creation of OPEC in 1960. *See* also Farah & Cima, ***supra*** note 17.

230 *See* Melanie Hart & Daniel J. Weiss, *Making Fracking Safe in the East and West, Environmental Safeguards on Shale Gas Production Needed as China Begins Development* (Center for American Progress, October 2011).

231 David L. Goldwyn, *Briefing*, Global Shale Gas Initiative Conference (August 24, 2010).

232 *See* KPMG Global Energy Institute, ***supra*** note 51, at 11.

233 *Zhong Mei Ye Yan Qi He Zuo: Ge You Suo Tu [China-United States Shale Gas Coopeation: Each Side Has its Own Plans]*, Zhongguo Huagong Bao (China Chemical Industry News), June 8, 2010; Clifford M. Gross, *The Growth of China's Technology Transfer Industry over The Next Decade: Implications for Global Markets*, J. Tech. Transfer 1–32 (2012); Arnaud De La Tour, Matthieu Glachant & Yann Ménière, *Innovation and International Technology Transfer: The Case of The Chinese Photovoltaic Industry*, 39(2) Energy Pol'y 761–770 (2011); Bo Wang, *Can CDM Bring Technology Transfer To China?—An Empirical Study Of Technology Transfer In China's CDM Projects*, 38(5) Energy Pol'y 2572–2585 (2010); Bronwyn H. Hall & Christian Helmers, *The Role Of Patent Protection In (Clean/Green) Technology Transfer*, No. 16323 National Bureau of Economic Research (2010); David G. Ockwell et al., *Intellectual Property Rights And Low Carbon Technology Transfer: Conflicting Discourses Of Diffusion And Development*, 20(4)

Almost all fracking technology and experience are owned by U.S. companies, and China needs to learn from them in order to develop its own shale gas services and industries. To this end, Chinese oil companies have already started investing in the U.S. shale market. Namely, CNOOC has joined with Chesapeake Energy on production ventures,[234] and Sinopec partnered with Devon Energy in a similar deal.[235] These agreements were minority interests in actual gas production, and constituted investments to export fracking know-how and technologies through participation in the exploration and production team.[236] However, the way China will overcome the technology and experience barriers is still open to debate. U.S. techniques are not very mature, and may fail to answer China's know-how needs. Also, Chinese shale gas is found in deeper reserves, while shale gas in the United States is mostly distributed in plains and hidden shallowly.[237] The hidden depth and the peculiar geological context make the exploitation much more challenging. Moreover, given that China's ultimate goal is to achieve and maintain energy security by developing its domestic natural resources, it cannot exclusively bid on U.S. technology and expertise. Accordingly, it will continue to invest in major foreign energy companies (as happened with Chesapeake Energy and Devon Energy), and then it will import early models of hydraulic fracturing in order to develop its own domestic model of fracking technology by reverse engineering the technology.[238]

US companies have a strong interest in supporting bilateral environmental protection efforts, as a shale gas environmental accident in China would not only affect the Chinese economy, but it would also augment opposition to fracking in the United States.[239]

Global Envtl. Change 729–738 (2010); Rasmus Lema & Adrian Lema, *Technology Transfer? The Rise Of China And India In Green Technology Sectors,* 2(1) Innovation & Dev. 23–44 (2012).

234 Joe Carroll & Benjamin Haas, *Sinopec's U.S. Shale Deal Struck at Two-Thirds' Discount*, Bloomberg Bus. Week, (Feb. 26, 2013, 4:03 PM), http://www.bloomberg.com/news/articles/2013-02-25/sinopec-to-buychesapeake-oil-and-gas-assets-for-1-02-billion (last visited Aug 8, 2016).

235 Angel Gonzalez & Ryan Dezember, *Sinopec Enters U.S. Shale*, Wall St. J. (Jan. 4, 2012), http://www.wsj.com/articles/SB10001424052970203550304577138493192325500 (last visited Aug 8, 2016).

236 Chesapeake Energy concluded a deal that transferred 33 per cent of its license rights in the US to CNOOC in exchange for Chinese financial support necessary to guarantee continued operations on the Chesapeake-owned sites. Energy expert Elias Hinckley underlines that the price of fracking technologies and extraction expertise is going to rise in the US as Chinese firms bid to take possession of the necessary technology and expertise to hasten their own shale gas revolution. Hinckley remarks: "How significant the technology and expertise price increases will be remains to be seen, but the Chinese appetite, and the likely pace of acquisition over the next few years will likely have a material impact not just on service and technology, but also on the cost of production here in the US." Elias Hinckley, *The Road to Chinese Shale Gas Goes Through the U.S.*, http://www.energytrendsinsider.com/2012/12/12/the-road-to-chinese-shale-gas-goes-through-the-u-s/ (last visited Aug 8, 2016).

237 Wang & Krupnick, *supra* note 181.

238 Diana Ngo notes that historically this procedure has been done by the Chinese in the nuclear reactor technology field, where China brought in models from the US' Westinghouse and France's Areva nuclear reactor technologies. Through these partnerships, China was able to reverse engineer and create their own versions of nuclear reactors (albeit less efficient) that are now being sold to developing countries. *See* Diana Ngo, *supra* note 157.

239 As happened following the Fukushima nuclear meltdown in Japan, which increased US and European opposition to nuclear power: Bettina B. F. Wittneben, *The Impact of the Fukushima Nuclear Accident on European Energy Policy,* 15(1) Envtl. Sci. & Pol'y 1–3 (2012); Howard L. Hall, *Fukushima Daiichi: Implications for Carbon-free Energy, Nuclear Nonproliferation, and Community Resilience,* 7(3) Integrated Envtl. Assessment & Mgmt. 406–408 (2011). On Germany's nuclear energy phaseout, *see* Jahn Detlef & Sebastian Korolczuk, *German Exceptionalism: the End of Nuclear Energy in Germany!,* 21(1) Envtl. Politics 159–164 (2012).

Moreover, if China does not comply with best practices in capturing GHG, shale gas development will increase China's emissions instead of reducing them. Further efforts are needed to guarantee that China optimizes the advantages from shale gas development, that is to say, decreasing oil imports and pollution, while reducing the environmental hazards. Within the U.S.–China bilateral cooperation on shale gas development, a collaborative dialogue has already commenced, engaging governments, non-governmental organizations, the private sector, researchers, and academia. This exchange should be reinforced, and China should focus on importing and developing environmentally friendly technologies, best practices, and a comprehensive regulatory framework to foster safe and secure exploitation of its shale gas resources.

The prospects for shale gas in China between regulatory interventions and new geopolitical balances

As shale gas radically impacts on supply and demand of the world's energy mix and market, new geopolitical factors must be assessed taking into account that, as far as China is concerned, economic and demographic growth will increase pressure on global energy supplies, and thus all fuel sources will have to be exploited.[240] China has historically depended on fuel imports from politically sensitive regions, restraining its foreign policy options.[241] This predominant dependence on foreign energy poses different risks: disruptions to its imported energy, sustained and extremely volatile energy prices, and a clash between China's foreign policy interests and its overseas energy interests.[242] Copious shale gas production can help the country acquire security of energy supply, which could lead to a dramatic and radical change in its relationships with other nations. The emergence of this new resource in North America is already changing the dynamics of the global gas business and energy geopolitics, demonstrating that the gas market is truly global.[243]

Indeed, the energy market is currently affected by a substantial excess of production. The principal cause of this surplus consists in the mass production of shale gas from the United States, which is now closer to the goal of energy independence. Energy demand cannot absorb this excess in resources produced, particularly as demand has decreased because of the current global economic recession, especially in Europe. In other words, U.S. investment

240 Globally, the shale gas revolution will also have important geopolitical consequences, for instance reducing Europe's overdependence on its two present dominant gas suppliers, Qatar and Russia.

241 In light of the absence of a sustainable supply of conventional fossil energy and excessively rapid growth of demand for energy, Chinese energy external dependence is still high. On this point, Zha Daojiong points out the relevance of energy efficiency measures, remarking that "Dependence on foreign sources of energy supply is in itself a threat to China's energy security; the key threat is the ever-growing consumption without significant improvement in energy efficiency." Zha Daojiong, *China's Energy Security: Domestic and International Issues*, 48(1) Survival 179–190 (2006).

242 *See* Bo Kong, *supra* note 106.

243 Shale gas can be a strategic tool to deter a strengthening of the political risk the global oil market currently faces while reducing "*U.S. and Chinese dependence on Middle East natural gas supplies, lowering the incentives for geopolitical and commercial competition between the two largest consuming countries and providing both countries with new opportunities to diversify their energy supply*". Medlock, *supra* note 158, at 13.

in the industry of fracking is bearing fruit for which there is excess supply of oil and gas in a time in history when the global economy is struggling to recover.[244]

The excess of production has caused a collapse in oil prices and natural gas, which, however, has not been followed by an effort by Organization of the Petroleum Exporting Countries (OPEC) to cut production. International experts in the energy market are trying to understand the reasons behind this strategy. One hypothesis, which sees in the failure to cut production by OPEC an attempt to exclude from the market competition of U.S. shale gas, is far-fetched. Indeed, hydrocarbons extracted from shale rock in the United States produce income at prices between $40 and $115, implying that if OPEC could keep crude oil at $70 per barrel, competition of shale gas in the U.S. would be strongly affected.[245] Such a pricing strategy would slow the development of the new generation of Western mining technologies that are slowly eroding the bargaining and geopolitical power of the members of OPEC.[246] Protracted low prices would produce a financial return which would defeat the costly investment required for starting the production of shale gas, and would create further instability. From a different perspective, shale gas can be a strategic tool to discourage the rise of the political risk that the global oil market is facing, while reducing "dependence on the US and Chinese natural gas reserves of the Middle East, limiting the incentives for geopolitical competition and trade between the two main consuming countries and providing both new opportunities to diversify their energy reserves."[247]

In the light of the analysis above, some essential elements of potential Chinese shale gas development have to be pointed out. First, there is a need to design a comprehensive and conducive regulatory environment, legally implemented, which would take into consideration the environmental hazards related to shale gas exploration and production. Shale gas production in China is in its infancy, and a sound regulatory system is required to assure long-term exploitation. Overarching effective unitary regulation would reduce the uncertainty in the gas market and foster future investments offering attractive terms to private investors.[248] Second, China needs to tackle the unsatisfactory record of environmental enforcement which jeopardizes the capacity of existing laws to prevent the downside of hydraulic fracturing. This can be accomplished through adoption of transparency initiatives and mandatory disclosure of environmental information. This would also help reduce the friction between Beijing's concerns over energy security and the opposition by reluctant local communities preoccupied with the environmental costs of shale gas exploration and extraction. Infrastructure development and technology transfer are equally needed, and the

244 See Leonardo Maugeri, *Troppa offerta di greggio e non c'è il coraggio ditagliare la produzione [Too Much Supply of Crude Oil and There is Not the Courage to Cut Production]*, Repubblica.it (Nov. 29, 2014), http://www.repubblica.it/economia/2014/11/29/news/leonardo_maugeri_troppa_offerta_di_greggio_e_non_c_il_coraggio_di_tagliare_la_produzione-101702664/?refresh_ce (last visited Aug 8, 2016).

245 On oil price data, see Arthur Berman, *Why the Oil Price Collapse is U.S. Shale's Fault*, Oil Price (Apr. 6, 2015), http://oilprice.com/Energy/Oil-Prices/Why-The-Oil-Price-Collapse-Is-U.S.- Shales-Fault.html (Aug 8, 2016).

246 In this vein, *see* Federico Fubini, Petrolio, *tutti contro tutti così la strategia saudita indebolisce Usa e Russia* [Oil-for-All as the Saudi Strategy Weakens the US and Russia], Repubblica.it (Nov. 29, 2014), http://www.repubblica.it/economia/2014/11/29/news/petrolio_tutti_contro_tutti_cos_la_strategia_saudita_indebolisce_usa_e_russia-101679458/ (last visited Aug 8, 2016).

247 Medlock, *supra* note 158, at 13.

248 On the other hand, rigid environmental legislation could inhibit shale gas exploration. This environmentally friendly over-regulation, however, does not appear to be likely to develop in China.

previous experience of the United States in this sector can be of great help to the Chinese shale gas industry. As part of this strategy, China's Ministry of Resources has invited some major oil and gas companies to pitch for shale gas exploration work, granting licenses for exploration in western China.[249]

The Chinese national political climate for shale gas appears to be positive as well. In March 2012, the first five-year shale gas development plan for the period 2011–2015 was jointly released by the NDRC, the MOF, the Ministry of Land and Resources, and the National Agency of Energy. It called for development of a policy framework for the regulation of the country's shale gas sector, and it ambitiously estimated that production will reach 80 billion cubic feet in 2020 from production at the time of zero.[250] In this vein, according to the plan, China will develop projects for the "assessment for shale and confirming the current reserve estimates."[251] A National Shale Gas Development Program has been adopted, in which great importance is given to research and development for technology, exploration, and development of shale gas in light of the Thirteenth Five Year Plan (2016–2020), which will greatly emphasize the importance of exploring unconventional and alternative energy sources. As long as China is pursuing joint ventures with foreign enterprises to acquire know-how in shale gas exploration and extraction, it seems probable that the Chinese leadership will continue to encourage shale gas commercial exploitation. An actual shale gas market is expected to develop over an extended period of time; and although government support appears sound, it is hard to foresee how the market will shape until major policy decisions on pricing, infrastructure development, and competition have been announced.

It is in this context of uncertainty that we should see the agreement signed in May 2014, in Shanghai by China and Russia (or rather, by the two state-owned energy companies Gazprom and China National Petroleum Corporation – CNPC). It is a thirty-year agreement that is binding on Russia to provide to China 38 billion cubic meters of gas per year starting in 2018.[252] The still uncertain forecasts for exploitation of unconventional gas necessitate an increase in imports of natural gas. Following the agreement, China will be able to take advantage of an additional supply to meet its growing demand for natural gas, and thus face the need to reduce the supply of coal in national energy demand, currently equal to two-thirds of it.[253]

Conclusions

In conclusion, successful and adequate shale gas development in China would meet domestic demand, and this new resource may grant China stronger bargaining power with gas exporters on price and other matters, narrowing the gap between North American and Asian natural gas prices. The strategic significance of China in the shale gas revolution is undeniable in

249 KPMG Global Energy Institute, *supra* note 51, at 11.

250 "Development Plan for Shale Gas (2011–2015) (Fa Gai Neng Yuan (2012) No. 612)" (页岩气发展规划(2011–2015) (发改能源(2012) 612号)).

251 *Id.*

252 James Paton & Aibing Guo, Russia, *China Add to $400 Billion Gas Deal With Accord*, Bloomberg Bus. Week, (Nov. 10, 2014), http://www.bloomberg.com/news/articles/2014-11-10/russia-china-add-to-400-billion-gas-deal-with-accord (last visited Aug 8, 2016).

253 On the agreement, *see* Richard Weitz, *The Russia-China Gas Deal: Implications and Ramifications*, World Affairs (September/October 2014).

light of the current rise of energy prices and struggle for reducing harmful emissions in order to contain climate change. It remains to be seen whether this “bridge fuel” will be a viable resource, capable of contributing to greater energy security, while being developed in an environmentally sound manner in a country with a $12 trillion USD economy that is deeply involved in the global economy.

Part III

Fundamental Rights and Cultural Diversity*

* This Book Part III "Fundamental Rights and Cultural Diversity" is participated by researchers funded by the Marie Curie IRSES of the European Union's Seventh Framework Programme (FP7/2007–2013) under REA grant agreement n° 317767 – Acronym of the Project: LIBEAC (2013–2016) entitled "Liberalism in Between Europe And China" within the results coordinated by gLAWcal - Global Law Initiatives for Sustainable Development (United Kingdom).

17 Understanding Non-Trade Concerns Through Comparative Chinese and European Philosophy of Law*

Jean Yves Heurtebise

Global governance paradoxes: Non-Trade Concerns, human rights and WTO

In 2004, the former Director-General of the World Trade Organization (WTO) from 2005 to 2013, Pascal Lamy, vividly framed the paradoxes of global governance caught between the contradictory exigencies of power and legitimacy. Because of the globalized nature of the contemporary capitalistic production of goods and services, all nations link into a growing web of monetary and human flux. If the power to regulate such a world economy lies in international institutions – such as the WTO, the International Monetary Fund (IMF), and the United Nations (UN) – on the other hand, historically speaking, legitimacy belongs to nation-states in which democracy as a political institution has emerged during the nineteenth century. Nation-states are legitimate institutions without economic power, whereas international institutions are powerful institutions deprived of democratic legitimacy.[1] Pascal

* This chapter is part of the results of the Research Project on "*Current Trends of Chinese Law towards Non-Trade Concerns such as Sustainable Development and the Protection of Environment, Public Health, Food Safety, Cultural, Social and Economic Rights, Labor Rights and the Reduction of Poverty from the Perspective of International Law and WTO Law*" coordinated by Professor Paolo Davide Farah at gLAWcal – Global Law Initiatives for Sustainable Development (United Kingdom) and at West Virginia University John D. Rockefeller IV School of Policy and Politics, Department of Public Administration, in partnership with the Center of Advanced Studies on Contemporary China (CASCC) in Turin (Italy), Maastricht University Faculty of Law, Department of International and European Law and IGIR – Institute for Globalisation and International Regulation (Netherlands), and Tsinghua University, School of Law, Institute of Public International Law and the Center for Research on Intellectual Property Law in Beijing (China). An early draft of this chapter was presented at the Conferences Series on "*China's Influence on Non-Trade Concerns in International Economic Law*", First Conference held at the Center of Advanced Studies on Contemporary China (CASCC) in Turin on November 23–24, 2011. This publication and the Conference Series were sponsored by China–EU School of Law (CESL) at the China University of Political Science and Law (CUPL). The activities of CESL at CUPL are supported by the European Union and the People's Republic of China.

1 Thomas D. Zweifel, International Organizations and Democracy: Accountability, Politics, and Power 14 (Lynne Rienner Publishers, 2006): "There are three possible reactions to this democratic deficit of international institutions. First we can decry how undemocratic international institutions are and urge caution in their use. Second, we can reject international organization on the grounds that democracy and international relations are two incompatible concepts [. . .]. Hence the third response: we can decry the lack of democracy of international institutions, but push for their reform and democratization."

Lamy proposed to resolve this paradox by transferring the capital of legitimacy from nation-states to the institutions of global governance.[2]

However, the transfer of legitimacy from nation-states to international institutions implies not only a democratization of the decisional processes of those institutions, but the integration of ethical principles into the applications and implementations of their resolutions as well. According to a point that Ernst-Ulrich Petersmann made unambiguously about the WTO:

> in order to remain democratically acceptable, global integration law – in the WTO for example – must pursue not only "economic efficiency" but also "democratic legitimacy" and "social justice" as defined by human rights. Otherwise citizens will rightly challenge the democratic and social legitimacy of integration law if it pursues economic welfare without regard to human rights [. . .].[3]

As Paolo Davide Farah noted, the challenge at stake for the WTO involves more than a single revision of internal management and the opening of decision processes (such as democratization). It implies an integration of ethical principles framing international trade as well.[4]

It is precisely in this framework that the concept of Non-Trade Concerns (NTCs) comes to the fore of the discussions in international law about WTO regulations. NTCs, mentioned in Article 20 of the Agreement on Agriculture (AoA) negotiated during the Uruguay Round of the General Agreement on Tariffs and Trade (GATT) – which came into force on January 1, 1995 with the creation of the WTO – implies the existence of objectives other than free trade. NTCs can be seen as the proper means to address the aforementioned necessity of pursuing economic welfare with regard to fundamental rights. As noted by James R. Simpson and Thomas J. Schoenbaum, "The excesses of globalization can be managed only by paying adequate attention to what are termed 'Non-Trade Concerns' (NTCs) [. . .]. A balance must be struck in the WTO between liberalization on the one hand, and NTCs on the other."[5] According to Simpson and Schoenbaum, if we do not find this balance between economic and non-economic concerns and the international community ignores NTCs, the Doha negotiations are very likely to fail.

The achievement of the Doha Development Round depends on the difficult task of conciliating the egos of each nation. The challenge brought by NTCs is even greater in the sense that it not only requires overcoming national selfishness, but it also calls for universal recognition of some fundamental rights, implying the constitution of a legal–ethical platform, potentially superseding national sovereignties and bridging cultural differences.

2 Pascal Lamy, La Démocratie-Monde – Pour une Autre Gouvernance Globale 20 (Seuil, 2004): "la globalisation des enjeux, pour le meilleur et pour le pire, rend chaque jour plus nécessaire l'organisation d'un pouvoir politique mondial, à la fois légitime et efficace, c'est-à-dire démocratique."

3 Ernst-Ulrich Petersmann, *Time for a United Nations "Global Compact" for Integrating Human Rights into the Law of Worldwide Organizations: Lessons from European Integration*, **13**(3) Eur. J. Int'l L. 621–650 (2002).

4 Paolo Davide Farah, *Influence Des Considérations "Autres Que D'ordre Commercial" En Droit International Et OMC Sur Les Transformations De La Loi Chinoise: Une Perspective Européenne*, Market Economy, Rights, Freedoms and Commun Values in Europe and Asia, Europe-Asia International Conference, University Paul Verlaine-Metz, Metz, France, March 18, 2011.

5 James R. Simpson & Thomas J. Schoenbaum, *Non-Trade Concerns in WTO Trade Negotiations: Legal and Legitimate Reasons for Revising the "Box" System?*, Paper presented at the International Conference, *Agricultural Policy Reform and the WTO: Where are we heading?*, Capri (Italy), June 23–26, 2003.

Understanding NTCs from the viewpoint of comparative philosophy of law

To help understand the conceptual basis of this problem, a historical and multicultural *mise en perspective* will be proposed. The fact that questions about NTCs are raised in the specific context of China's role in international trade and global governance calls for a comparative perspective on Chinese and Western legal cultures.

The natural law v positive law debate: Legality and legitimacy

The understanding of the connection between legitimacy and legality, between the notion of justice and the actuality of law, is a pivotal issue within the field of the philosophy of law. Logically speaking, in terms of concepts, the philosophical debate tackles the issue of knowing whether the Augustinian proposition, "*lex iniusta non est lex*,"[6] has any legal meaning. Traditionally, positivist legalism and natural law theory disagree on this issue. For legal positivists, the primary goal of the law is to be obeyed and followed; it has a coercive function directed at establishing social order.[7] Just or unjust is defined within the scope of the law, and the aforementioned proposition brings no more meaning than saying that the "law is too iniquitous to be applied or obeyed."[8] On the other hand, for natural law theorists, law does not only aim to combine the commanding power with the legal leverage to fulfill its managerial task, but moreover, to provide an authorized frame of actions to which even the commanding power itself is bound.[9] In this respect, the *just or unjust* character of the law does not come from its inscription in a legal text, but from the common acceptance by a human group, respectively to its own cultural standards, of what kind of behaviors and actions are to be called *just or unjust*. On one hand, the law prescribes what is *just*; on the other, the law should be framed with reference to what is *just*. From a legalist positivist point of view, the validity of the law is implied by its existence in a functional social structure; from a naturalist point of view, the validity of the law depends on its extrajudicial existence within the field of norms. Matthew Grellette interestingly proposed to overcome the limits of both the legal positivist and the naturalist conception of law by using the naturalist idea of a distinction between validity and existence of the law itself, while defining its validity in legal – rather than normative – terms. In other words, its validity does not come from mere legal enforcement but rather from the respect of fundamental constitutional principles.[10]

Historical perspective: Natural law, positive law – their emergence and overcoming

Historically speaking, the inception of this debate in modern Europe dates back to Saint Thomas Aquinas' interpretation of Aristotle's *Politics*. According to Saint Thomas Aquinas,

6 Augustine of Hippo, City of God 987 (Penguin, 2003), translated by Henry Bettenson.

7 Hans Kelsen, General Theory of Law and State 19 (Harvard University Press, 1945), translated by Anders Wedberg.

8 Herbert Lionel Adolphus Hart, The Concept of Law 204 (Clarendon Press, 1961).

9 Lon L. Fuller, The Morality of Law 210–16 (Yale University Press, 1969).

10 Matthew Grellette, *Legal Positivism and the Separation of Existence and Validity*, 23(1),Ratio Juris 22–40 (2010). The author refers to the Canadian Constitution Act, s. 52(1): "The Constitution of Canada is the supreme law of Canada, and any law that is inconsistent with the provisions of the Constitution is, to the extent of the inconsistency, of no force or effect."

law is "an ordinance of reason for the common good of a [complete] community, promulgated by the person or body responsible for looking after that community."[11] In terms of natural law, if "positive law [is] the creature of the sovereign," nevertheless "all sovereigns [are] subject to natural law, and their enactments in conflict therewith [are] simply void."[12] However, in the context of English civil wars, Hobbes stated the supremacy of the authority of the sovereign to dictate the law, developing the idea of a radical discontinuity between nature and society. Law cannot come from nature since natural law will lead to the war of all against all. In order to escape from the state of nature, men have to abandon their mutually incompatible desire to act as they wish, and relinquish it to follow the unique rule of the state: they have to "reduce all their wills, by plurality of voices, unto one will" to which they "owe peace and defense."[13] Positive law is nothing but the expression of the will of the sovereign power.[14] There is no moral power outside social law that could nullify the actions of the sovereign and weaken or counterbalance the sovereignty of the state.

The opposition between natural law and positive law will be "resolved" by the constitutionalist movement and through the concept of the "rule of law." Contending against Hobbes's royalist conception of an absolute power given to the ruler to impose order in the name of the rule by law, Locke argued that, "the institutors [should] retain extensive and constant control over the government."[15] This control of power was obtained through the separation of legislative and executive powers and the preeminence given to the former:[16] "in all cases, whilst the government subsists, the legislature is the supreme power."[17] The Lockean conception of law will be instrumental for US constitutionalists. James Madison, in his collective work with Alexander Hamilton and John Jay – *The Federalist Papers* – referred to a dual step of law-governance: "In framing a government which is to be administered by men over men, the great difficulty lies in this: you must first enable the government to control the governed; and in the next place oblige it to control itself."[18] This dual step actually articulates the difference between the rule *by* law and the rule *of* law: the rule by law refers to the control by the government over the governed while the rule of law refers to the control over the governance of the government.[19] From Saint Thomas Aquinas to Bracton, the morality of natural law referred to the spiritual power of the Catholic Church – precisely from which Hobbes tried to free the sovereign. In this perspective, the constitution of the "rule of law," establishing a legal counter-power within the state with the independence of the judiciary, equates to the secularization and institutionalization of moral reason by which natural law theorists evaluate the legitimacy of legality. The legitimacy of law is not outside the realm of legality, but it flows from its function being not to control the people, but rather the rulers.

11 John Finnis, Aquinas: Moral, Political and Legal Theory 255 (Oxford University Press, 1998).

12 Roscoe Pound, *Common Law and Legislation*, 21(6) Harv. L. Rev. 383–407 (1908).

13 Thomas Hobbes, Leviathan 120 (Cambridge University Press, 1991).

14 *Id*., at 197.

15 Catherine Valcke, *Civil Disobedience and the Rule of Law – A Lockean Insight*, in The Rule of Law 45–62 (I. Shapiro ed., New York University Press, 1994).

16 Michael P. Zuckert, *Hobbes, Locke and the Problem of the Rule of Law*, in Hobbes on Law 517–536 (Claire Finkelstein ed., Ashgate, 2005).

17 John Locke, Two Treatises of Government II 150 (Cambridge University Press, 1967).

18 James Madison, *The Federalist No. 51. The Structure of the Government Must Furnish the Proper Checks and Balances Between the Different Departments*, Independent Journal (Wednesday, February 6, 1788).

19 Eric W. Orts, *Positive Law and Systemic Legitimacy: A Comment on Hart and Habermas*, 6(3) Ratio Juris 245–278 (1993).

Comparative perspective: Confucian and Legalist visions of law

If we turn now to the Chinese cultural context, we could say that, *mutatis mutandis*, the debate between "Confucians" and "Legalists" in antique China somewhat echoes the one between natural law theorists and legal positivists in contemporary Europe.[20]

If "Confucians" and "Legalists" are put into inverted commas it is because, notwithstanding the usage of such generic terms by non-specialists of Chinese philosophy, Chinese philosophy scholars have prevented us from the danger of such conventional labeling. Theodore de Bary evidenced that "Confucianism" is not a static set of notions, but rather a dynamic process greatly varying not only over time – Classical Confucianism of Confucius and Mencius, Neo-Confucianism of Zhu Xi and Wang Yang-ming, New Confucianism of the twentieth century – but also over space – China, Japan, Korea, and so on.[21] Similarly, Paul R. Goldin[22] criticizes the habit, taken from Sima Tan (d. 110 BC), of dividing Chinese philosophy into six schools, one of them being called "*fajia*," which can be translated as the school of the method (for ruling state) or the school of law, and to which Graham referred as the "*amoral science of statecraft*."[23] Therefore, we will limit ourselves to the "Confucianism" of Confucius and the "Legalism" of Shang Yang.

This being said, we will follow Scott Cook in saying that the main debate that arose during the period was the one between the Confucians and the Legalists concerning "whether the primary means of motivating the populace and bringing order to society should lie in education through ritual, music, and moral suasion, or through the use of punishments, rewards, and other relatively more coercive and practical measures."[24] The contentious point between Confucius and Shang Yang is about the use of punishments and rewards to control people's behavior. For Confucius, morality should prevail since the impulse to do good – for example, to follow informal social rules – should come from within, so that human actions can be trustworthy.[25] For Shang Yang, relying on morality implies introducing a subjective criterion whose conformity to morality depends on the approval of moral censors, in general, and Confucians, in particular. Only laws can represent an objective, universal, transparent, and predictable rule of behavior.[26] Therefore, Confucians were closer to the concept of natural law (provided that the term "law" is understood in a non-positivist but anthropological

20 Paolo Davide Farah, *L'influenza Della Concezione Confuciana Sulla Costruzione Del Sistema Giuridico E Politico Cinese*, in IDENTITÀ EUROPEA E POLITICHE MIGRATORIE 193–226 (Giovanni Bombelli & Bruno Montanari eds, Vita e Pensiero, 2008).

21 William Theodore de Bary, *The Trouble with Confucianism*, in THE TANNER LECTURES FOR ON HUMAN VALUES, VOL. X 131–184 (Cambridge University Press, 2011).

22 Paul R. Goldin, *Persistent Misconceptions About Chinese "Legalism"*, 38(1) J. CHINESE PHIL. 88–104 (March 2011).

23 ANGUS C. GRAHAM, DISPUTERS OF THE TAO 267–292 (Open Court, 1989).

24 Scott Cook, *The Use and Abuse of History in Early China*, 18(1) XUN ZI TO LÜSHI CHUNQIU, ASIA MAJOR (THIRD SERIES) 45–73 (2005).

25 JAMES LEGGE, THE LIFE AND TEACHING OF CONFUCIUS 122 (J.B. Lippincott & Co. 1., 1867): "If the people be led by laws, and uniformity sought to be given them by punishments, they will try to avoid the punishment, but have no sense of shame. If they be led by virtue, and uniformity sought to be given them by the rules of propriety, they will have the sense of shame, and moreover will become good" (Confucius, *Analects*, 2.3, §§1–2).

26 J.J.L. DUYVENDAK, THE BOOK OF LORD SHANG 170 (Arthur Probsthain, 1928): "Nowadays, if you wish to stimulate the multitude of people to make them do what even filial sons and loyal ministers dislike doing, I think it is useless unless you compel them by means of punishments, and stimulate them by means of rewards."

way):[27] social order should emerge from the informal institutionalization of ethical behaviors. Similarly, "Legalists" were closer to the understanding of positive law,[28] since they view the law as bearing the sole legitimate authority.[29] Obviously, Confucians and Legalists were not fighting only about words and concepts, but were striving also to obtain a position of influence within the government. Actually, during the Qin Dynasty (from 221 to 207 BC), when the Legalist thinking prevailed and dominated the imperial agenda, not only were books of Mozi and Confucius burned, but hundreds of scholars were buried alive. Confucians and Legalists did not use the same strategy to be well accepted at court. Confucians tried to educate the aristocracy to bind them morally and symbolically to the Emperor. Legalists, more radically, wanted to help the Emperor get rid of the aristocracy so as to have direct leverage on the peasant masses.

Historically speaking, as Jacques Gernet noted,[30] the influence of the Legalists on the elaboration of the administrative legal basis of the Chinese Empire can be compared to the influence of legal positivists on the elaboration of Monarchic States in Europe. However, and this is the point we aimed to raise, if one can find, ***mutatis mutandis***, the equivalent of European "natural law theorists" in Chinese "Confucians," and that of European "legal positivists" in Chinese "Legalists" (though it is of course a debated point),[31] what *cannot* be found in China[32] is the synthesis between natural law and positive law, whose result is the emergence of the concept of the "rule of law" and the establishment of institutional means – constitution, independence of justice, and elections – in relation to which the rulers can be held accountable for their actions. The consequence of this conceptual cavity can be seen today in the difficulties China faces when it comes to formulating a concept of the rule *of* law entailing a clear distinction from the rule *by* law.

The 2004 UN Secretary-General's report about the rule of law and transnational justice provides a contemporary definition of the rule of law: "[The rule of law] refers to a principle of governance in which all persons, institutions and entities, public and private, including the state itself, are accountable to laws that are publicly promulgated, equally enforced and independently adjudicated, and which are consistent with international human rights norms and standards."[33] However, the definition of the rule of law proposed by the Chinese delegate in the General Assembly Sixth Committee's debate in 2007 showed striking dissimilarities: "the

27 Lon L. Fuller, The Morality of Law 23 (Yale University Press, 1969): "The conventional concept of law as a body of rules derived from the statutes and court decisions – reflecting a theory of the ultimate source of law in the will of the lawmaker ('the state') – is wholly inadequate to support a study of a transnational legal culture." Paolo Davide Farah, ***supra*** note 20.

28 Randall P. Peerenboom, Law and Morality in Ancient China: The Silk Manuscripts of Huang-Lao (State University of New York Press, 1993).

29 J. J. L. Duyvendak, ***supra*** note 26: "Law is the authoritative principle for the people, and is the basis of government; it is what shapes the people."

30 Jacques Gernet, L'Intelligence de la Chine (Gallimard, 1994).

31 Kenneth Winston, ***The Internal Morality of Chinese Legalism***, Sing. J. Legal Stud. 313–47 (2005).

32 *See* Henrique Schneider, ***Legalism: Chinese-Style Constitutionalism?***, 38(1) J. Chinese Phil. 46–63 (March 2011); in this recent paper, Henrique Schneider argued that Legalism could be understood in the framework of constitutionalism. However, not only is there nothing like a provision for a constitution defended by Han Fei, but, moreover, there is no real complete independence of the law: a) the law is viewed as a guarantee against bad rulers more than as a means to control rulers in general; and b) the law is viewed as a tool provided to the Emperor to control not only the people but also the officials.

33 Report of the Secretary-General, ***The Rule of Law and Transitional Justice in Conflict and Post-Conflict Societies***, UN Doc. S/2004/616, ¶ 6.

rule of law [is] a universal goal for all nations and the effective instrument for establishing and maintaining social order, promoting social justice and achieving social progress."[34] What precisely constitutes the essence of the rule of law – such as accountability – is omitted, with international human rights and norms being engulfed by this omission. Instead it claims a top-down definition of law – in line with a patriarchal representation of power: maintaining order while providing care – which is the very signature of the rule *by* law. Due to divergent past cultural histories and different present strategies of power in Europe and China, the same words can refer to opposite concepts. Without acknowledging this, numerous misunderstandings can become a serious obstacle to the elaboration of international law.[35]

NTCs and the new rule of law: An international challenge for global governance

Within this comparative philosophical framework, we can understand the challenge raised by NTCs and fundamental rights, regarding the usual conceptions of law in Europe and in China as well as their consequence for global governance.

The contemporaneous emergence of NTCs and fundamental rights implies a complete rewriting of the traditional debate between natural and positive law. On the one hand, this development overcomes the scope and limits of the legal positivists' conception of law, since it no longer refers to the legal system of one sovereign state. Fundamental rights are aimed at defending human groups and people, whatever the context of their national inscription as citizens. On the other hand, it also surmounts the role and function attributed to law in a naturalist perspective, where the ethical principles funding the legitimacy of legality are rooted in human reason. If NTCs imply a right given to human groups to dispose of public goods,[36] the reference to "public goods" also embraces environmental sustainability.[37] Thus, Henry Shue's definition of subsistence rights established a link between freedom from want, in general, one of the four fundamental freedoms,[38] and the right for *secure* food and *unpolluted* water, in particular.[39]

34 UN Doc. A/C.6/62/SR.14 (2007), ¶ 35.

35 World Bank, *The Rule of Law as a Goal for Development Policy*, http://web.worldbank.org/WBSITE/EXTERNAL/TOPICS/EXTLAWJUSTINST/0,,contentMDK:20763583~menuPK:1989584~pagePK:210058~piPK:210062~theSitePK:1974062,00.html (last visited July 14, 2016): "Policymakers need to be clear about what they mean by the rule of law because answers to many of the questions they are interested in – whether 'rule of law' facilitates economic development and whether democracy is a necessary precondition for rule of law, to cite just two examples – depend crucially on what definition of the rule of law is being used."

36 Simpson & Schoenbaum, *supra* note 5: "It seems reasonable that all citizens can, and should, have an interest in assuring that they have an input in deciding how, and in what form, the public goods related to agriculture are used and maintained for future generations. That is one of every person's fundamental rights."

37 UNIDO, Public Goods for Economic Development 9 (United Nations Industrial Development Organization, 2009): "The provision of public goods is a key element of the quality of life and environmental sustainability [. . .] Because of the characteristics of public goods, the market alone is often unable to ensure their efficient provision."

38 Franklin D. Roosevelt, *State of the Union Message to Congress, January 11, 1944*, in The Public Papers & Addresses of Franklin Delano Roosevelt vol. XIII (Samuel Rosennman ed., Harper, 1950).

39 Henry Shue, Basic Rights: Subsistence, Affluence, and U.S. Foreign Policy 23 (Princeton University Press, 1980): "Subsistence, or minimal economic security, which is more controversial than physical security, can also be shown to be as well justified for treatment as a basic right as physical security is. By minimal economic security, or subsistence, I mean unpolluted air, unpolluted water, adequate clothing, adequate shelter, and minimal preventive public health care."

Fundamental rights, overcoming both natural and positive law categories, imply a revision of the concept of rule of law which via the integration of NTCs into WTO rules may open the path to the universalization of constitutionalism. However, on this specific point, Ernst-Ulrich Petersmann's ideas[40] must be qualified with regard to Philip Alston's critics.[41] Ernst-Ulrich Petersmann assumed that "as freedom for hunger and economic welfare are preconditions for the enjoyment of many other human rights, the WTO guarantees of economic liberties and of welfare-increasing cooperation across frontiers serve important human rights functions."[42] The misleading element in Petersmann's appealing proposition comes from the fact that it inverts the cause and the goal, the impulse and the frame. It is not because freedom from hunger is recognized as a human right that WTO law application incorporates its universal recognition. Rather, it should be stated that the right to food as well as social rights serve as *regulatory ideas* (in the Kantian sense) to frame the extension of WTO rules. Actualizing such a shift from the globalization of liberalism purported to be conductive of human rights to constitutionalizing fundamental rights to frame worldwide market operations shall be the objective of including NTCs in WTO rules. Since constitutionalism means not only the universalization of general rules but also the establishment of legal counter-powers, NTCs based on fundamental rights could give the economic global governance the moral legitimacy it needs, provided that an international agreement is reached.

For such an international agreement, China's commitment is needed. However, as it is also the case for human rights and environmental protection,[43] developing countries often treat NTCs with suspicion, as a tool possibly used by Western countries to weigh on their internal policies. China's reluctance to embrace NTCs could be explained by the difficulties of Chinese scholars and officials to reconcile rule *by* law and state sovereignty with rule *of* law and international accountability. China's potential acceptation of NTCs also relates to her legal history and culture. Since Asian cultural conception of rights is focused on economic security and human safety rather than on individual liberty,[44] China could naturally accept notions such as the right to food and freedom from want. Therefore, the debate on NTCs within the frame of WTO agreements could be a unique occasion for China to take the lead on these issues. Nevertheless, at the same time, China must accept that her sovereignty may be challenged by universal norms. Thus, China must choose between universalizing the Asian cultural conception of rights, while opening to the international exigencies of the rule *of* law, to co-create a world economy based on NTCs, or preserving her integrity in the name of the rule *by* law in order to profit from an unsustainable mode of development.

40 Ernst-Ulrich Petersmann, *Human Rights In European And Global Integration Law: Principles For Constitutionalizing The World Economy*, in European Integration and International Co-ordination 338, 340 (Bogdandy, Mavroidis & Mény eds, Kluwer, 2002).

41 Philip Alston, Resisting The Merger And Acquisition Of Human Rights By Trade Law: A Reply To Petersmann, 13(4) Eur. J. Int'l L. 815–84 (2002).

42 Ernst-Ulrich Petersmann, *From "Negative" To "Positive" Integration In The WTO: Time For "Mainstreaming Human Rights" Into WTO Law?*, 37 Common Mkt. L. Rev. 1363–1382 (2000).

43 Han Sung-Joo, *Forward & Asian Values: An Asset or a Liability, in* Changing Values in Asia: Their Impact on Governance and Development 3, 9 (Han Sung-Joo ed., Japan Center for International Exchange, 2003): "to many Asian leaders, Western concern for areas such as human rights and the environment is often seen as unwarranted interference at best and as revealing ulterior motives at worst."

44 Hyakudai Sakamoto, *Foundations of East Asian Bioethics*, 6 Eubios J. Asian & Int'l Bioethics 31–32 (1996): "First of all, in many countries in Asia and Southeast Asia, the sense of human rights is very weak and foreign, and they have no theoretical background for the concept of human rights. Rather they are concerned with overcoming starvation and poverty, not by means of promoting human rights but by increasing national wealth and mutual aid."

18 The Right to Food in International Law and WTO Law

An Appraisal*

Flavia Zorzi Giustiniani

The international law framework

The origins of the right to food as a universal human right can be traced back to the renowned "Four Freedoms Speech," given by United States (US) President Franklyn Delano Roosevelt on January 6, 1941 before the US Congress. In his speech, Roosevelt outlined a vision of the world based on four fundamental freedoms: freedom of speech and expression, freedom of worship, freedom from want, and freedom from fear.[1] Freedom from want was thus regarded in the same way as political freedoms and freedom from fear, a *sine qua non* condition for the safeguard of human dignity.

The 1948 Universal Declaration of Human Rights, directly inspired by the Rooseveltian formula, affirms the right of everyone to a standard of living that should be adequate for the health and well-being of themselves and of their family, including, in the first place, food.[2] An analogous provision was also incorporated in the United Nations (UN) International Covenant on Economic, Social and Cultural Rights (ICESCR), whose Article 11 recognizes "the fundamental right of everyone to be free from hunger."[3] Article 11 thus enshrines two distinct components of the right to food: the right to food security[4] and the "fundamental"

* This chapter is part of the results of the Research Project on "*Current Trends of Chinese Law towards Non-Trade Concerns such as Sustainable Development and the Protection of Environment, Public Health, Food Safety, Cultural, Social and Economic Rights, Labor Rights and the Reduction of Poverty from the Perspective of International Law and WTO Law*", coordinated by Professor Paolo Davide Farah at gLAWcal – Global Law Initiatives for Sustainable Development (United Kingdom) and at West Virginia University John D. Rockefeller IV School of Policy and Politics, Department of Public Administration, in partnership with the Center of Advanced Studies on Contemporary China (CASCC) in Turin (Italy), Maastricht University Faculty of Law, Department of International and European Law and IGIR – Institute for Globalisation and International Regulation (Netherlands), and Tsinghua University, School of Law, Institute of Public International Law and the Center for Research on Intellectual Property Law in Beijing (China). An early draft of this chapter was presented at the Conferences Series on "*China's Influence on Non-Trade Concerns in International Economic Law*", First Conference held at the Center of Advanced Studies on Contemporary China (CASCC) in Turin on November 23–24, 2011. This publication and the Conference Series were sponsored by China–EU School of Law (CESL) at the China University of Political Science and Law (CUPL). The activities of CESL at CUPL are supported by the European Union and the People's Republic of China.

1 Franklin D. Roosevelt, Address to Congress: The "Four Freedoms" (January 6, 1941).

2 *See* Universal Declaration of Human Rights, GA Res. 217 (III) A, UN Doc. A/RES/217(III) (December 10, 1948), Article 25.1.

3 See International Covenant on Economic, Social and Cultural Rights, GA Res. 2200A (XXI), 21 UN GAOR Supp. No. 16 , UN Doc. A/6316 (1966), 993 UNTS 3, at 49 (January 3, 1976), Article 11.2.

4 Regarding food security, *see* generally Chapter 20 (Simpson) in this volume.

right to be free from hunger[5] – the only ICESCR right to be qualified as "fundamental." While the former right must be realized progressively and its implementation is conditioned by the extent of resources available to each state party, the latter represents the core component of the right to food and as such must be immediately and wholly implemented even in times of disasters.[6]

Espousing Amartya Sen's well-known analysis of food security, the Committee on Economic, Social, and Cultural Rights (CESCR), in its General Comment 12, affirmed that the right to food implies, at the very least, the availability of food in sufficient quantity and quality and sustainable accessibility for people to care for themselves and their own food needs.[7] The CESCR then articulated three levels of state obligations arising under Article 11. States ought to do the following: *respect* people's existing access to adequate food by abstaining from adopting measures that may result in disrupting it; *protect* the right to food by taking steps to prevent non-state actors from engaging in similar interference; and *fulfill* the right to food by facilitating people's access to food and directly *providing* food to those unable to provide for themselves.[8] The right to food is thus mainly conceived as the right to feed oneself in dignity, and not the right to be fed (except in extreme circumstances).[9]

Other international instruments of universal reach also recognize the right to food. In particular, the Convention on the Rights of the Child requires states parties to combat malnutrition and to provide adequate and nutritious food, as well as to supply material support to nutrition programs.[10] Moreover, at the regional level, the African,[11] European,[12] and Inter-American[13] human rights systems all protect the right to food.

5 Regarding the Chinese situation, *see* Chapter 19 (Ning) in this volume.

6 Committee on Economic, Social and Cultural Rights, General Comment 12, The Right to Adequate Food, UN doc. E/C.12/1999/5, ¶ 6.

7 *Id.* As a matter of fact, Sen argued that "starvation is the characteristic of some people not having enough food to eat. It is not the characteristic of there being not enough food. While the latter can be a cause of the former, it is but one of many possible causes." *See* AMARTYA SEN, POVERTY AND FAMINES. AN ESSAY ON ENTITLEMENT AND DEPRIVATION 1 (Oxford University Press, 1981).

8 Committee on Economic, Social and Cultural Rights, *supra* note 6, ¶ 15.

9 These three levels of obligations have subsequently been accepted by the states in the FAO Voluntary Guidelines to support the progressive realization of the right to adequate food in the context of national food security, adopted by the 127th Session of the FAO Council, November 2004.

10 *See* Convention on the Rights of the Child, GA Res. 44/25, annex, 44 UN GAOR Supp. No. 49, at 167, UN Doc. A/44/49 (September 2, 1990), Articles 24.2 (c), 27.3. *See* also Convention Relating to the Status of Refugees, 189 UNTS 150 (April 22, 1954), Articles 20, 23; Convention on the Elimination of All Forms of Discrimination against Women, GA Res. 34/180, 34 UN GAOR Supp. No. 46, at 193, UN Doc. A/34/46 (September 3, 1981), Articles 12, 14; Indigenous and Tribal People Convention, 72 ILO Official Bull. 59, (September 5, 1991), Articles 14, 19; International Convention on the Protection and Promotion of the Rights and Dignity of Persons with Disabilities, GA Res. 61/106, Annex I, UN GAOR, 61st Sess., Supp. No. 49, at 65, UN Doc. A/61/49 (2006) (May 3, 2008), Article 28.

11 African Charter on the Rights and Welfare of the Child, OAU Doc. CAB/LEG/24.9/49 (1990) (November 29, 1999), Articles 14, 20; The African Charter on Human and Peoples' Rights ("Banjul Charter") does not contain an explicit recognition of the right to food, but it includes other rights, in particular the right to health, which can be interpreted as protecting the former (cf. African Commission on Human and Peoples' Rights, *SERAC v Nigeria*, 2001). *See* African Charter on Human and Peoples' Rights, OAU Doc. CAB/LEG/67/3 rev. 5, 21 I.L.M. 58 (1982) (October 21, 1986).

12 As for the Banjul Charter, the European Social Charter does not explicitly recognize the right to food, which nonetheless can easily fall within the scope of other rights (*See* Articles 4.1, 12, 13, 19).

13 *See* Article 12 of the 1988 Additional Protocol to the American Convention on Human Rights in the Area of Economic, Social, and Cultural Rights ("Protocol of San Salvador").

In addition to human rights treaties, international humanitarian law also protects the right to food.[14] While this right is not expressly mentioned, several provisions of the 1949 Geneva Conventions and of the 1977 Additional Protocols convey their *raison d'être* by ensuring that people are not denied access to food and are adequately fed. In this respect, the main rules prohibit starvation as a method of warfare[15] and require, during times of war or conflict, that the belligerents adequately supply the civilian population *inter alia* with foodstuffs.[16] The said rules must be respected both by states and non-state actors alike and – like all humanitarian law provisions – are non-derogable and must be implemented immediately (not progressively). They can hence be considered as complementary to human rights food-related provisions in times of armed conflict[17] and guarantee the immediate applicability of both the right to be free from hunger and the right to adequate food within the same context.

This brief study reveals that the right to food is firmly and widely established in international treaty law. Additionally, it is routinely reaffirmed in a plethora of soft law instruments such as General Assembly resolutions. The foundational nature of this right explains its wide recognition.[18] As it was most clearly stated by the CESCR, the right to food is one of the core human rights that are an indispensable precondition to the enjoyment of all other rights. Taken together, these factors strongly militate in favor of the customary status of this right.[19]

WTO law and the Agreement on Agriculture

Despite the importance of the right to food, no World Trade Organization (WTO) agreement seeks to regulate, nor even mentions, it. Nevertheless, these instruments have serious implications for its realization. In particular, the Agreement on Agriculture (AoA), which regulates the import and export of food and agricultural products, plays a vital role.[20] Because agriculture constitutes the main source of livelihood in most countries of the world, agricultural trade has a huge impact on the right to food. Moreover, recent food crises have shown that the great majority of the world's hungry people live in rural areas and, ironically, are food producers.[21] This paradox reveals that the current multilateral trading system for

14 International humanitarian law (IHL) – also known as the law of war or the law of armed conflict – is a set of rules and principles which limits the use of violence in times of armed conflict. Its objectives are twofold: to protect persons who are not, or are no longer, directly engaged in hostilities (wounded, shipwrecked, prisoners of war, and civilians) and to regulate the conduct of hostilities, in particular setting limits on methods and means of warfare. As it applies only in the exceptional circumstance of armed conflict, no derogations are allowed.

15 Protocol I, Article 54(1); Protocol II, Article 14.

16 Articles 3, 23, 55, 59 IV Geneva Convention; Articles 69–70 Protocol I; Article 18 Protocol II.

17 *See* Jelena Pejic, *The Right To Food In Situations Of Armed Conflict: The Legal Framework,* 83/844 Int'l Rev. Red Cross 1097 (2001).

18 Committee on Economic, Social and Cultural Rights, *supra* note 6, ¶ 4.

19 *See* Special Rapporteur on the Right to Food, *Report of the Special Rapporteur on the right to food, delivered to the General Assembly,* UN Doc. A/63/278 (October 21, 2008), ¶ 10.

20 *See* generally Chapter 20 (Simpson) in this volume.

21 Commission on Human Rights, *The Right to Food,* Report of the Special Rapporteur on the right to food, Mr. Jean Ziegler, E/CN.4/2006/44 (March 16, 2006), ¶ 4; Olivier De Schutter, *International Trade In Agriculture And The Right To Food, Dialogue On Globalization,* Occasional Paper No. 46, 39 (November 2009). See WTO, UN Rapporteur and WTO Head Debate the Impact of Trade on Hunger, http://www.wto.org/english/forums_e/debates_e/debate14_summary_e.htm (last visited July 17, 2016) ("This is where the food crisis is. It is small farmers driven towards the cities, unable to live off their fields, relegated to subsistence farming because prices are not sufficiently profitable").

agriculture, as regulated by the AoA, does not guarantee people's access to food but rather, in its actual implementation, has impaired such a right.

The AoA was reached at the end of the Uruguay Round in 1994,[22] and aimed to initiate a process of liberalization in agricultural trade. It consists of three pillars, dealing respectively with market access, domestic support, and export subsidies. With a view towards increasing market access for agricultural products, WTO members committed to convert quantitative restrictions into tariffs and subsequently reduce the latter.[23] Under the second pillar, they agreed to reduce their levels of domestic support for agricultural production and to abstain from introducing new support measures. Finally, the third pillar mandated the reduction of export subsidies and prohibited the introduction of new ones.

In anticipation of the negative effects that the Least-Developed Countries (LDCs) and Net Food-Importing Developing Countries (NFIDCs) would experience from trade liberalization, Article 16 of the AoA provides that developed countries shall take the measures envisaged in the Marrakesh Decision.[24] This Decision established four response mechanisms to assist LDCs and NFIDCs in addressing the fluctuation in prices on the world markets. However, the Decision has failed because it has never been adequately implemented and suffers from the absence of an enforcement mechanism.[25] Article 5 of the AoA also contains a safeguard clause, which allows for temporary protection in case of a sudden rise in imports or fall in world prices. The application of these special safeguards, however, was conditioned on the addition of tariffs to non-tariff barriers, which most developing countries historically did not use.

As previously noted, the AoA does not mention the right to food but, instead, refers to food security. The Preamble of the Agreement in fact includes food security among the Non-Trade Concerns (NTCs) that WTO members should consider. However, the AoA does not define NTCs, and it remains unclear how they fit within the Agreement.[26] In particular, it is open to debate whether states can invoke NTCs in order to protect or support domestic agriculture and what happens if they are violated.[27] Article 20 only provides for NTCs to be taken into account in the ongoing WTO agricultural reform process.

22 *See* Agreement on Agriculture, April 15, 1994, Marrakesh Agreement Establishing the World Trade Organization, Annex 5, 1869 UNTS 410 [hereinafter AoA].

23 Tariffs in fact were seen as more predictable and transparent, and therefore easier to negotiate down in the future. *See* Mitsuo Matshshita, Thomas J. Schoenbaum & Petros C. Mavroidis, The World Trade Organization: Law, Practice, and Policy 136 (Oxford University Press, 2003).

24 WTO Uruguay Round, ***Decision on Measures Concerning the Possible Negative Effects of the Reform Programme on Least-Developed and Net Food-Importing Developing Countries*** (April 15, 1994) [hereinafter Marrakesh Decision].

25 Melaku G. Desta, ***Food Security and International Trade Law: An Appraisal of the World Trade Organization Approach,*** 35 J. World Trade 455 (2001).

26 Nonetheless, a widely accepted definition of food security is given in the first paragraph of the World Food Summit Plan of Action: "food security exists when all people, at all times, have physical, social[,] and economic access to sufficient, safe[,] and nutritious food that meets their dietary needs and food preferences for an active and healthy life" (FAO, ***Rome Declaration on World Food Security***, Food World Summit November 13–17, 1996), http://www.fao.org/docrep/003/w3613e/w3613e00.HTM (last visited July 17, 2016). Enjoyment of food security can thus be considered a key component of the right to food.

27 *See* Kevin R. Gray, ***Right To Food Principles Vis À Vis Rules Governing International Trade***, Research Paper (Center for International Development at Harvard University, 2003) at 24. Gray correctly argues that "[t]he combination of these non-trade concerns provides substantive support for members to take measures to protect citizens' right to food and ensure its fulfilment. However, the emerging disciplines on

As a whole, the AoA, despite incorporating a special and differential treatment for developing countries,[28] favors developed countries disproportionately. The majority of the latter already had tariffs and export subsidies in place and, while they are theoretically bound to reduce trade-distorting domestic support, have utilized the numerous exceptions envisaged under the second pillar to maintain their protectionist measures.[29] As a consequence, many agricultural products continue to trade at prices well below the production cost, with devastating effects for the local production in developing countries. At the same time, products exported from developing countries still face high tariffs on the markets of Organization for Economic Cooperation and Development (OECD) states, where they have to compete with subsidized food. The dirty manipulation of tariffs has resulted in increased market protection in the industrialized world,[30] substantially betraying the AoA's stated objective – the creation of a fair and market-oriented agricultural trading system.[31]

In 2001, the Doha Declaration committed WTO members to comprehensive negotiations aimed at substantially reducing trade-distorting measures and establishing a special and differential treatment for developing countries.[32] Nevertheless, the Doha Round talks are currently stalled because of a blatant disagreement among the North and South over domestic support and, more fundamentally, over how they can ensure that trade in food does not undermine food security.[33]

Reconciling WTO trade rules with the right to food

The negative impact that WTO obligations, and in particular those deriving from the AoA, have on the right to food is not inevitable. In principle, WTO and human rights obligations are not incompatible. As it is well known, the Agreement establishing the WTO envisages that states should conduct their trade relations with a view towards raising standards of living,[34] and the AoA endeavors to establish a "fair" agricultural trading system.[35] Nonetheless, trade differs from human rights in that it focuses on averages and aggregates, while the latter concerns individuals. It can thus well be said that "at the level of abstract objectives, the liberalization of trade of agriculture and the right to food are complementary and international trade can even support the realization of the right. Yet, conflicts and tensions may

---

tariffs, domestic support and export subsidies under the AoA have limited the range of policy interventions to guarantee such right."

28 AoA, Article 15.

29 *See* AoA, Article 6(1), which refers to criteria for exceptions, listed in Article 6 as well as Annex 2.

30 Melaku G. Desta, *Legal Issues in International Agricultural Trade: The Evolution of the WTO Agreement on Agriculture from Its Uruguay Origins to its Post-Hong Kong Directions* 8 (FAO Legal Paper Online No. 55, 2006).

31 Agreement on Agriculture, *supra* note 22, Preamble, ¶ 2. *See* Carmen G. Gonzalez, *Institutionalizing Inequality: The WTO Agreement On Agriculture, Food Security, And Developing Countries*, 27(2) COLUM. J. ENVTL. L. 457 (2002).

32 World Trade Organization, Ministerial Declaration of November 14, 2001,WT/MIN(01)/DEC/1, 41 ILM 746 (2002) ¶ 13 [hereinafter Doha Declaration].

33 In particular, discussions are stumbling on the trade-distorting impacts of various forms of domestic support provided by developed countries to their farmers, and on the special safeguard measure which several developing countries demand to include in the AoA (*see* UN Doc. A/63/278, ¶ 16).

34 Marrakesh Agreement Establishing the World Trade Organization, April 15, 1994, 1867 UNTS 154, Preamble, ¶ 1 [hereinafter Marrakesh Agreement].

35 AoA, Preamble, ¶ 2.

arise at [the] implementation level."[36] To avoid such conflicts, the UN Special Rapporteur on the right to food, Olivier De Schutter, in his report of his mission to the WTO propounded an approach to international trade based on the right to food. In his view, trade liberalization in agriculture should aim to enhance the welfare of the most vulnerable and food insecure, such as, in particular, small-scale farmers.[37]

The protection of the right to food in the context of international trade is complicated by the presence of a multiplicity of non-state actors, in particular Transnational Corporations (TNCs) and international organizations – such as the WTO, the International Monetary Fund (IMF), and the World Bank – whose behavior directly or indirectly hampers the enjoyment of such a right. While efforts in recent times have focused on establishing criteria for holding these non-state actors accountable, this should not overshadow the responsibilities of states, which are still the main subjects of international law and the primary duty bearers under the international human rights regime.[38]

As far as TNCs are concerned, the obligation to protect the right to food requires host states to adopt measures to ensure that the former do not deprive individuals of their access to adequate food.[39] The host state has primary responsibility for the protection of human rights within its territory and should therefore negotiate human rights–compatible arrangements with TNCs. Additionally, human rights obligations are posed on home states. The due diligence principle indeed requires the latter to prevent, to the extent possible, foreseeable violations by those corporations over which they can exert some degree of authority.[40] An effective measure, in this respect, would be the enactment of domestic legislation with extraterritorial effects,[41] but also other initiatives proposed by De Schutter, such as the imposition of transparency or reporting requirements and preconditions for access to export credits, could be interesting.[42] In addition to the all-encompassing obligations posed on a state within its jurisdiction, the general principle of international cooperation would seem to require, as a minimum, that *all* states do not contribute to human rights violations in other countries.[43]

36 Kerstin Mechlem, *Harmonizing Trade In Agriculture And Human Rights: Options For The Integration Of The Right To Food Into The Agreement On Agriculture,* 10 Max Planck Y.B. UN L. 165 (2006).

37 Human Rights Council, *Report of the Special Rapporteur on the right to food*, Olivier de Schutter. Addendum. Mission to the World Trade Organization (June 25, 2008), A/HRC/10/5/Add.2 ¶47 (February 4, 2009).

38 In particular, numerous codes of conduct have been developed at the international level to strengthen human rights accountability of TNCs, such as the OECD Guidelines for Multinational Enterprises (OECD 2000) and the *Norms on the Responsibilities of Transnational Corporations and Other Business Enterprises with Regard to Human Rights*, adopted by the Sub-Commission on the Promotion and Protection of Human Rights in 2003. Ultimately, however, these efforts have not yielded the expected results. *See* Emeka Duruigbo, *Corporate Accountability and Liability for International Human Rights Abuses,* 6 Nw. U. J. Int'l Hum. Rts. 243–47 (2008).

39 Accordingly, the UN Special Rapporteur on the Right to Food recommended that WTO members "adequately regulate private actors over which the State may exercise an influence, in discharge of their obligation to protect the right to food."

40 *See* 1997 Maastricht Guidelines on Violation of Economic, Social and Cultural Rights, section 18; Surya Deva, *Acting Extraterritorially to Tame Multinational Corporations for Human Rights Violations: Who Should "Bell the Cat,"* 5 Melb. J. Int'l L. 49 (2004); Smita Narula, *The Right to Food: Holding Global Actors Accountable Under International Law,* 44 Colum. J. Transnat'l L. 691, 764–766 (2006).

41 Smita Narula, *Reclaiming The Right To Food As A Normative Response To The Global Food Crisis,* 13 Yale Hum. Rts. & Dev. L. J. 418–19 (2011).

42 Human Rights Council, *supra* note 37, ¶ 46.

43 Federica Donati & Margret Vidar, *International Legal Dimensions Of The Right To Food*, in Global Obligations For The Right To Food 67 (G. Kent ed., Rowman & Littlefield Publishers, 2008). It is

States must comply with the obligations to protect, respect, and fulfill the right to food even in the context of international organizations such as the WTO. This means that states members should refrain from supporting any WTO measure or decision that could harm the enjoyment of the right to food.[44] By virtue of their primacy, human rights should prevail over other international obligations.[45] Nevertheless, the ostensible primacy of human rights obligations, in general, is not adequately supported by enforcement mechanisms, especially at the global level. This problem is particularly acute for economic and social rights whose justiciability is still rather weak, although improving.[46] In contrast, violations of WTO trade rules are sanctioned by a judicial organ – the Dispute Settlement Body – and, as a last resort, by retaliatory measures adopted by the complainant party. As a consequence, in the case of a conflict between human rights and trade obligations, WTO members are obviously inclined to give preference to the latter.

In order to overcome this state of affairs, De Schutter has called on member states to define their positions in trade negotiations in accordance with national strategies for the realization of the right to food and always conduct human rights impact assessments of trade agreements.[47] Additionally, he has advocated that member states fully implement the Marrakesh Decision and establish an effective monitoring mechanism, capable of ensuring its implementation.[48] These recommendations, if enacted, would contribute to the effective reconciliation of trade rules with the right to food. Moreover, the current stall in the Doha Round negotiations shows that only a radical change in the existing trade system, which seriously takes account of, ***inter alia***, the food security needs of developing countries, could guarantee the attainment of the AoA's objective – a fair agricultural trade market – and ultimately the survival of the system itself.

---

worth recalling that the CESCR in its General Comment 12 affirmed as follows: "In the spirit of article 56 of the Charter of the United Nations, the specific provisions contained in articles 11, 2.1, and 23 of the Covenant and the Rome Declaration of the World Food Summit, States parties should recognize the essential role of international cooperation and comply with their commitment to take joint and separate action to achieve the full realization of the right to adequate food. In implementing this commitment, States parties should take steps to respect the enjoyment of the right to food in other countries, to protect that right, to facilitate access to food and to provide the necessary aid when required. States parties should, in international agreements whenever relevant, ensure that the right to adequate food is given due attention and consider the development of further international legal instruments to that end" (CESCR, General Comment 12, ¶ 36).

44 Fons Coomans, *Application of the International Covenant of Economic, Social and Cultural Rights in the framework of international organisations,* MAX PLANCK Y.B. UN L. 365 (2007).

45 "Arguably, the universal recognition of the inalienable character of the essential core of human rights implies recognition of the legal primacy of their inalienable core *vis-à-vis* governmental and intergovernmental limitations that are arbitrary or 'unnecessary' for protecting other human rights." *See* Ernst-Ulrich Petersmann, *Time for a United Nations 'Global Compact' for Integrating Human Rights into the Law of Wordwide Organizations: Lessons from European Integration,* EUR. J. INT'L L. 634 (2002).

46 The adoption of the Optional Protocol to the ICESCR, in December 2008, represents important progress in this respect (Optional Protocol to the International Covenant on Economic, Social and Cultural Rights, GA Res. 63/117, UN Doc. A/RES/63/117 (December 10, 2008). *See* Human Rights Council, *Report of the Special Rapporteur on the right to food,* Jean Ziegler, A/HRC/7/5 (January 10, 2008), ¶¶ 66–68.

47 Human Rights Council, *supra* note 37, ¶ 50.

48 *Ibid.*

19 The Right to Food in China

Cultural Foundation, Present and Future**

*Libiao Ning**

The right to food is a human right stipulated in The Universal Declaration of Human Rights[1] and The International Covenant on Economic, Social and Cultural Rights.[2] It advocates that all human beings are entitled to food that is adequate to satisfy their needs, does not contain toxic substances, and is culturally acceptable.[3] Even if the right to food did not attract global attention when it was first introduced, it subsequently became the focus of many international *fora* about human rights due to the global grain crisis.[4] Like many other countries, China has taken measures and made remarkable progress to guarantee and protect this right. This chapter analyzes the cultural basis behind ensuring the right to food, the government's political inclination to protect it, relevant progress, and existing problems, and will conclude with some proposals for its improved protection.

The cultural basis for the protection of the right to food

Even if the concept of human rights has been imported from Western countries – and therefore we cannot find the correspondent word in ancient Chinese writings – we cannot

* The author wishes to thank Paolo Davide Farah for helpful comments on an earlier draft. The usual disclaimer applies.

** This chapter is part of the results of the Research Project on "*Current Trends of Chinese Law towards Non-Trade Concerns such as Sustainable Development and the Protection of Environment, Public Health, Food Safety, Cultural, Social and Economic Rights, Labor Rights and the Reduction of Poverty from the Perspective of International Law and WTO Law*", coordinated by Professor Paolo Davide Farah at gLAWcal – Global Law Initiatives for Sustainable Development (United Kingdom) and at West Virginia University John D. Rockefeller IV School of Policy and Politics, Department of Public Administration, in partnership with the Center of Advanced Studies on Contemporary China (CASCC) in Turin (Italy), Maastricht University Faculty of Law, Department of International and European Law and IGIR – Institute for Globalisation and International Regulation (Netherlands), and Tsinghua University, School of Law, Institute of Public International Law and the Center for Research on Intellectual Property Law in Beijing (China). An early draft of this chapter was presented at the Conferences Series on "*China's Influence on Non-Trade Concerns in International Economic Law*", Second Conference held at Tsinghua University, School of Law on January 14–15, 2012. This publication and the Conference Series were sponsored by China–EU School of Law (CESL) at the China University of Political Science and Law (CUPL). The activities of CESL at CUPL are supported by the European Union and the People's Republic of China.

1 Universal Declaration of Human Rights, GA Res. 217 (III) A, U.N. Doc. A/RES/217(III) (December 10, 1948).

2 International Covenant on Economic, Social and Cultural Rights, GA Res. 2200A (XXI), 21 UN GAOR Supp. No. 16 , UN Doc. A/6316 (1966), 993 UNTS 3, at 49 (January 3, 1976).

3 *See* Chapter 18 (Zorzi Giustiniani) in this volume.

4 *See* Chapters 18 (Zorzi Giustiniani) and 20 (Simpson) in this volume.

conclude that human rights principles are incompatible with Chinese traditional culture.[5] In fact, "*Ren*" (benevolence) in traditional Chinese culture lays a cultural foundation for human rights, especially for the right to food. As the most important category in ethics, *Ren* not only embodies the moral norm of interpersonal relationships, but also the ethics of the relation between state and person.

In regards to interpersonal relationships, Confucius (551–479 BC), founder of the Confucian philosophy, advocated that "the benevolent loves the people" and "those who want to succeed must help others succeed, those who want to be developed must develop others first."[6] The essence of "the benevolent loves the people" coincides with the principles of human rights: respecting human beings and caring for the underprivileged. In fact, Doctor Zhang Pengchun, who played a crucial role in drafting The Universal Declaration of Human Rights, made constant efforts to introduce Confucian benevolence to the Declaration.[7]

As for the relation between state and person, *Ren* elaborated on that which is most important between the people, the state, and its ruler. During the Western Zhou Dynasty (1046–771 BC), some people insisted that "people are the foundation of a country, and the country is in peace when the foundation is stable."[8] In the Warring States Period (475–221 BC), Mencius (372–289 BC), a great Confucian philosopher, believed that people are the most important element in a state, next come the state, and the least important is the ruler himself.[9] Xunzi (313–238 BC), another great Confucian philosopher from the Warring States Period, insisted that Heaven did not make the people for the ruler, but made the ruler for the people;[10] he also conceived of the ruler like a boat and the people like the water, the same water that buoys the boat and swallows it.[11] Jia yi (200–168 BC), a famous politician in the Western Han Dynasty (202 BC – AD 9), also held that the people are the base of good governance.[12]

Besides the abovementioned principles, *Ren* strongly advocates the protection of people's livelihoods. During the Western Zhou Dynasty, it was believed that the state should "advocate morality and protect the people." Confucius, the most famous advocate of *Ren*, thought that the state should feed the people and make them wealthy, and that the ruler should bring benefits to the people by all means.[13] He also insisted that "[s]trong military power, adequate food and trust from the people are the three important conditions for governance," and that "sufficient food is more crucial than military power."[14] On the basis of Confucius's thoughts, Mencius explained how to guarantee people's livelihood. In his opinion, people require a steady income and properties for society to find stability and prosper. Thus, the

5 *See* Chapters 2 (Farah), 17 (Heurtebise) in this volume; *see* also Paolo Davide Farah, *L'influenza Della Concezione Confuciana Sulla Costruzione Del Sistema Giuridico E Politico Cinese (The Influence of Confucianism in the Construction of the Chinese Juridical and Political System)*, in IDENTITÀ EUROPEA E POLITICHE MIGRATORIE 193–226 (Giovanni Bombelli e Bruno Montanari eds, Vita e Pensiero, 2008).

6 Confucius, *Yōng Yě* [*Yong Ye*], in Lún Yǔ [THE ANALECTS OF CONFUCIUS].

7 Lú Jiànpíng, *Zhāng Péngchūn Hé Shìjiè Rénquán Xuānyán [Zhang Pengchun And The Universal Declaration Of Human Rights]*, Nánfāng Zhōumò [SOUTHERN WEEKEND] (December 24, 2008), http://www.infzm.com/content/21637 (last visited August 1, 2016).

8 *Wǔzǐ Zhī Gē* [Song of Five Sons], in Shàng Shū.

9 Mencius, *Jìn Xīn Xià [Jin Xin. Part Two]*, in Mèng Zǐ [the Works of Mencius].

10 Xún Zǐ, *Dà Lüè [Great Stratagem]*, in Xún Zǐ, [the Works of Xuncius].

11 Xún Zǐ, *Wáng Zhì [System of Kings]*, in Xún Zǐ, [the Works of Xuncius]

12 iă Yí, *Dà Zhèng Shàng [Great Politics]*, in Xīn Shū [New Book].

13 Confucius, *Yáo Yuē* [*What Yao Said*], in Lún Yǔ [THE ANALECTS OF CONFUCIUS].

14 Confucius, *Yán Yuān* [*Yan Yuan*], in Lún Yǔ, THE ANALECTS OF CONFUCIUS].

ruler should bestow wealth on the people, enabling them to take care of their parents and raise their children, so that they will have abundant food in years of good harvests, and they can survive when famine strikes.[15] As for the amount of property necessary to guarantee people's livelihood, people should have at least five *Mu* of land on which the mulberry trees grow, so that 50-year-old people can have enough clothing; livestock should be raised at the proper time, so that 70-year-old people have meat to eat; if farming could continue uninterrupted by the government during the farming season, a family of eight people will not starve.[16] Moreover, Mencius explored the connection between food security and the kingcraft. He maintained that the elderly should have adequate food and clothing; common people should not starve or suffer from the cold.[17] Mencius's opinions were widely adopted by later generations. During the later Qin Dynasty (221–206 BC), Li Shiqi told Liu Bang, who became the first emperor of the Western Han Dynasty, that people are what matters most to the king and that food is what matters most to the people.[18]

Mencius' and Xunzi's thought about the relation between the king and the people is similar to the idea of human rights. Moreover, Confucius's attitude towards sufficient food and Li Shiqi's elaboration on the relation between food security and kingcraft both provide a cultural basis for the right to food. However, even if both *Ren* and the notion of human rights equally attach great value to the security of the people, especially to food security, *Ren* and benevolent governance depend exclusively on the morality and good conscience of the ruler, without an effective power restraint system. Although the concept of food security can be traced throughout Chinese history, and food relief was distributed to selected groups of people in need over the course of many dynasties, food security could only amount to reflective interest, and thus it cannot qualify as a kind of human right.

China's political inclination and relative policy and laws to protect the right to food

Political inclination to protect the right to food

Ren was not carried away by the waves of time. On the contrary, it was not only included as an essential point in the Three People's Principles proposed by Sun Yat-sen,[19] but it also became an important part of the governance idea of the Communist Party of China (CPC). Since the reform and opening-up in 1978, with the class struggle gradually receding, traditional thoughts about people's livelihood was brought new vitality through the combination of contemporary constitutionality and the notion of human rights. The protection of people's livelihood has always been a crucial focus in the documents published by the Central Committee of the CPC the work reports of the State Council, and the guidelines for national economic and social development.

15 Mencius, *Liáng Huì Wáng [King Hui of Liang]*, in Mèng Zǐ [The Works Of Mencius].

16 *Id.*

17 *Id.*

18 Bān Gù, *Lì Lù Zhū Liú Shūsūn Zhuàn [Li Lu Zhu Liu and Shusun's biography]*, in Hàn Shū.

19 The Three People's Principles is a theory for constructing modrn state and society proposed by Sun Yat-sen (1866–1925), who was the great leader of the Revolution 1911. The Three People's Principles include nationalism, democracy, and people's livelihood.

The Constitution of the CPC stipulates that "the chief criterion and general starting point for all our work should be whether it promotes the growth of the productive forces in a socialist society, increases the overall strength of the socialist state and raises living standards."[20] Besides the Constitution of the CPC, work reports of the CPC's Central Committee also show concern for people's livelihood. For example, in the work report of the 12th National Congress of the CPC, General Secretary Hu Yaobang emphasized that a basic principle of the national economic work is to feed the people and build the country, and its main objective is to improve people's lives in the next 20 years. In the work report of the 14th National Congress of the CPC, General Secretary Jiang Zemin stated that the beneficial effect on people's living conditions is the criteria to evaluate all the work, and that the reform and opening-up during the 1990s aimed to improve people's lives. The 15th National Congress of the CPC stressed that improving people's lives is the ultimate goal of economic development. In the work report of the 17th National Congress of the CPC, General Secretary Hu Jintao pointed out that the party and the country should aim to build a well-off society by 2020, and it is in the interest of all people throughout the country. We are also requred in the report to the 18th National Congress of the Communist Party of China to ensure the goal of completing the buiding of a moderately prosperous society in all aspepcts by 2020. In the Bulletin of the fifth Plenary Session of the 18th CPC Central Committee, It was required to guarantee basic livelihood and realize all the people step into the well-off society together.

In addition to the documents issued by the Central Committee of the CPC, the protection of people's livelihood also became an important topic in the Report on the Work of the Government and outline of national economic and social development after the reform and opening-up policy in 1978. For instance, Premier Wen Jiabao laid more emphasis on people's livelihood in the Report on the Work of the Government, which was drafted in the 4th Session of the Standing Committee of the 11th National People's Congress. In this report, he declared that the country should "accelerate progress in all social programs and significantly improve people's lives," and that "ensuring adequate food for 1.3 billion Chinese people is always a top priority and we must never treat this issue lightly." He continued: "We have the confidence and the ability to handle this important matter well," and "[w]e should work tirelessly to ensure everyone has access to old-age care, medical treatment, and housing."[21] It was pionted out in the work report of the 4th session of the 12th national People's Congress in 2016 that the government should speed up the agricultural structural adjustment, strengthen agricultural basic surport and reinforce the construction of farmland. It was also required in the Outline of the 13th Five-Year Plan for Economic and Social Development of the People's Republic Of China to ensure the basic livelihood of the people, and constantly improve people's living standard, realize all the people together into a well-off society in an all-round way.Further more, we should strenthen poverty alleviation, steadily implementate of rural poverty population no sorrow of food and clothing, reinforce food safety supervision and endeavor to safeguard food safety.

What is even more noteworthy is that the 2009–2010 National Human Rights Action Plan and the 2012–2015 National Human Rights Action Plan also fully expressed the wish

20 Zhōngguó Gòngchǎndǎng Zhāngchéng [The Constitution of Chinese Communist Party], http://cpc.people.com.cn/GB/64156/65682/4475081.html (last visited August 1, 2016).

21 Wēn Jiābǎo, *2011 Nián Zhèngfǔ Gōngzuò Bàogào [Report on the Work of the Government in 2011]*, http://www.china.com.cn/policy/txt/2011-03/16/content_22150608_3.htm (last visited August 1, 2016).

to protect the people's livelihood. They replaced some customary expressions on livelihood with the phrase of the rights of basic standards of living. The 2010–2011 National Human Rights Action Plan clearly expresses the Chinese government's political inclination to protect the rights that guarantee a basic standard of living, including the right to food. As China's first human rights plan of action, it calls on the government to continue to take effective measures promoting urban and rural residents' income levels, especially for low- and middle-income citizens, and to improve the system of subsistence allowances. In order to feed and clothe the poor, the government is trying its best to increase the national income level. Furthermore, this plan requires improving the level of social security, improving the standard of urban and rural basic cost of living allowance, expanding the coverage of social welfare insurance programs, and raising the basic old-age fund of welfare insurance. In addition, it includes improving the "five-guarantee" supporting system in order to assure the people's basic living conditions and, finally, implementing relief measures for vagrants and beggars in the cities, and establishing the temporary relief system completely.

Policies to protect the right to food

China has expressed its political will to guarantee people's livelihood in the documents of the Central Committee of the CPC, the government work reports, and the outline of China's economical and social development. It has also established a series of policies to guarantee people's livelihood and to realize the right to food. These policies can be classified into the following types according to their contents.

(1) Policies encouraging the national grain production

The Chinese government has always considered grain production a top priority because it is fundamental to the right to food. Since the reform and opening-up policy in 1978, the government implemented the household contract responsibility system in rural areas on the basis of land connective ownership because the collective ownership model did not benefit farmers. As a result, farmers boosted grain production. Towards the end of the twentieth century, farmers in some areas abandoned their land because of falling grain prices and overwork. The government put into effect targeted measures to ensure grain production, such as canceling the agricultural tax in 2006 and raising the price of grain; establishing many agricultural subsidies which boosted farmers' efficiency; and increasing the transferred payments to the counties producing grain, oil, plants, and pigs, widening the scope of the existing subsidies.

(2) Policies enhancing the purchasing power over food

Food purchasing power can be enhanced mainly by increasing income, reducing burdens, and improving social security.[22] The Chinese government has increased income by raising the employment rate and increasing the lowest salary, the farmers' salary, and the salary of workers in urban and rural areas. In order to lighten burdens, the government canceled the agricultural tax, and rescinded tuition and fees for nine-year compulsory education. In regards to social welfare, China reformed the system to ensure a minimum standard of living for urban and rural residents, the rural cooperative medical system, the basic livelihood

22 *See* Chapter 20 (Simpson) in this volume.

insurance "five-guarantees" system for the household,[23] and the pension insurance. These systems can support the underprivileged economically and enhance their purchasing power and the quality of their food consumption, promoting the realization of the right to food.

(3) *Policies improving nutrition*

In 1995, China launched the public nutrition improvement project with the Asian Development Bank and the United Nation Children's Fund. Since then, it has carried out extensive research, propaganda, and training on public nutrition. In 1996, China composed the "China Plan of Action for Nutrition Improvement," which established the goal of nutrition improvement from 1996 to 2000. In 2001, China drafted the Food and Nutrition Development Program (2001–2010), which provides that "accelerating food development, improving the dietary structure and promoting the people's health are urgent requirements for improving the quality of the whole nation and a major task for the socialist modernization of our country."[24] In addition, it established the principles of harmonious development between food production and consumption; balance between resource utilization and protection of food and between food quality and security and health management; and optimization of structure and disease prevention. Additionally, it specifies goals for per capita nutrient intake and food intake for 2010, and requires the continuation and regulation of the implementation of the National Nutrition Improvement Plan, National Soybean Plan, National School Milk Scheme, and so on. Under the influence of the program, the working group of "National Public Nutrition Improvement Project" established the fortification of food with nutrients as the entry point to improve the national nutritional and health conditions, including the addition of Vitamin A to edible oil, nutrients to flour, Ferrum (Fe) to soy, and nutrients to baby food. All these measures produced an evident effect on improving the country's nutritional level. It is particularly noteworthy that China has implemented the Program of Improving Nutrition of Rural Compulsory Education Students since the fall of 2011. This program requires the central government to invest 16 billion CNY (Chinese Yuan) per year to carry out an experiment, which aims to subsidize nutritious meals for 26 million rural compulsory students in designated, high-concentration poor areas according to a standard of 3 CNY per day. Furthermore, the central government encourages the local government to conduct experiments of nutrition improvement especially in poor regions, ethnic minority regions, and old revolutionary base areas.

(4) *Policies guaranteeing food safety*

In order to let people "*buy easily, eat without worries and use comfortably*,"[25] the Chinese government developed an in-depth food safety supervision system, strictly applied standards for product quality and safety, implemented a rigorous access system for the food market, a product quality traceability system, a recall system, and a food safety monitoring system. In order to effectively complete the work on food safety, the Chinese government founded the National

23 The five-guarantee system was adopted for childless and helpless old folks, according to which they are provided with food, clothing, medical care, housing, and burial expenses.

24 *Zhōngguó Shíwù Yǔ Yíngyǎng Fāzhǎn Gāngyào (2001–2010) [The Food and Nutrition Development Program of China (2001–2010)]*, http://news.xinhuanet.com/zhengfu/2001-12/06/content_151092.htm (last visited August 1, 2016).

25 Wēn Jiābǎo, *2009 Nián Zhèngfǔ Gōngzuò Bàogào [Report on the Work of the Government in 2009]*, http://www.gov.cn/test/2009-03/16/content_1260221_3.htm (last visited August 1, 2016).

Food Safety Committee in 2010. The committee is led by the Vice Premier of the State Council, with the participation of many persons in charge of the ministries and commissions of the State Council. The committee has presently carried out many successful programs.

Legal guarantees for the right to food in China

Since laws codify social regulations backed by the coercive power of the state, using the law to protect human rights has become a current trend. Like many other countries, in recent years China has reinforced the protection of human rights by law. As for the right to food, nowadays a complex system including the Constitution, laws, and regulations not only protects grain production and circulation, but also secures the right to food in natural calamities and for the disadvantaged. Moreover, it safeguards food safety and food cultural acceptability.

The constitution

According to the text of the Constitution of the People's Republic of China[26] (Constitution), the right to food is not explicitly expressed as a fundamental right. However, certain Constitutional provisions still protect the right to food to some extent. First, Article 33 requires "respecting and guaranteeing human rights and respecting human dignity and basic rights."[27] Consequently, as one of the human rights stipulated by the International Bill of Rights, the right to food should be protected by the Constitution. Second, Article 14 requires that "the state gradually improve the material and cultural life of the people and establish a social security system adequate for the level of economic development."[28] Since food is necessary for daily life and the social security system helps realize the right to food, Article 14 indirectly protects this right. Third, Article 45 stipulates that all "[c]itizens of the People's Republic of China have the right to material assistance from the state and society when they are old, ill or disabled. The state develops the social insurance, social relief and medical and health services that are required to enable citizens to enjoy this right."[29] Because food assistance is the component of the right to material assistance, Article 45 also lays a solid foundation to protect the right to food of the old, ill, or disabled.

Laws and regulations

Apart from its Constitution, China has many laws and regulations to protect the right to food, and they can be divided into the following groups.

(1) LAWS AND REGULATIONS TO PROTECT FOOD PRODUCTION AND DISTRIBUTION

As China's most important law to protect grain production, the 1993 Agriculture Law of the People's Republic of China[30] amended in 2002 and 2012 (Agriculture Law) aims to

26 Zhōnghuá Rénmín Gōnghégūo Xīan Fǎ (中华人民共和国宪法) (1982) [The Constitution of the People's Republic of China (1982)].

27 *Id.*, Article 33.

28 *Id.*, Article 14.

29 *Id.*, Article 45.

30 Zhōnghuá Rénmín Gònghéguó Nóngyè Fǎ (中华人民共和国农业法) [Agriculture Law of the People's Republic of China] (Promulgated by the Standing Comm. Nat'l People's Cong., July 2, 1993, revised December 28, 2002, amended December 28, 2012).

safeguard agricultural production as well as farmers' rights. In order to fulfill this purpose, it clearly defines the management system for rural production, circulation and processing of agricultural products, food security, farmers' rights protection, law enforcement supervision, and legal responsibility. In terms of food security, chapter 5, entitled "Food security," not only sets the rules for ensuring a steady increase in food production, but also contains the regulations of the farmland protection system as well as protection of basic farmland.[31] Meanwhile, it also calls for the establishment of a protective price system for grain products, an early warning system for food security and a grain risk fund system. In addition to the Agriculture Law, China has also drafted the 1999 Law of Land Administration of the People's Republic of China[32] (Law of Land Administration) and the 1994 Basic Farmland Protection Regulations[33] to preserve arable land. The Law of Land Administration makes it clear that urban land belongs to the state, and suburban and rural land is owned collectively. It also established the planning and licensing systems of land use and the farmland protection system, thus strictly controlling the act of turning farmland into non-arable land. In terms of food distribution and food market management, the State Council passed regulations such as the 2003 Regulations on Administration of Central Grain Reserves[34] and the 2004 Grain Circulation Management Regulations.[35] The former provides the rules for setting up a central grain reserve in response to major natural disasters and emergencies, in order to stabilize the grain market. The central grain reserve is required to implement a vertical management system, while the local governments and relevant departments should provide assistance. The China Grain Reserves Corporation takes full responsibility for the operation and management of the central grain reserves. In addition, this law clearly defines the procedures for the planning, storage, and use of the central grain reserves. The Grain Circulation Management Regulations articulate the qualifications required to be a food operator, the grain market macro-control system, and the legal responsibilities connected with it. Furthermore, the Regulations also require the country to establish an emergency food fund system as well as a grain risk system.

(2) LAWS AND REGULATIONS ON FOOD SAFETY

China promulgated the Food Hygiene Law of the People's Republic of China[36] in 1995, the Agricultural Genetically Modified Organisms Safety Control Regulations[37] in 2001, and

31 *See* Chapter 20 (Simpson) in this volume.

32 Zhōnghuá Rénmín Gònghéguó Tǔdì Guǎnlǐ Fǎ (1998 xiūdìng) (中华人民共和国土地管理法 (1998 修订) [Land Administration Law of the People's Republic of China (1998 Revision)] (Promulgated by the Standing Comm. Nat'l People's Cong., August 29, 1999, effective January 1, 1999, amended August 28, 2004)

33 Jīběn Nóngtián Bǎohù Tiáolì (基本农田保护条例) [Regulations on the Protection of Basic Farmland] (promulgated by the State Council August 18, 1994, expired).

34 Zhōngyāng Chúbèiliáng Guǎnlǐ Tiáolì (中央储备粮管理条例) [Regulations on Administration of Central Grain Reserves] (promulgated by the State Council, August 15, 2003).

35 Liángshi Líutōng Guǎnlǐ Tiáolì (粮食流通管理条例) [Grain Circulation Management Regulations] (promulgated by the State Council, May 19, 2004).

36 Zhōnghuá Rénmín Gònghéguó Shípǐn Wèishēng Fǎ (中华人民共和国食品卫生法) [Food Hygiene Law of the People's Republic of China] (Promulgated by the Standing Comm. Nat'l People's Cong., October 30, 1995, expired).

37 Nóngyè Zhuǎnjīyīn Shēngwù Ānquán Guǎnlǐ Tiáolì (农业转基因生物安全管理条例) [Regulations on Administration of Agricultural Genetically Modified Organisms Safety] (promulgated by the State Council, May 23, 2001, effective January 8, 2011).

the Agricultural Product Quality Safety Law of the People's Republic of China[38] in 2006. Although these laws help protect people's rights, many serious issues regarding food safety remain. Consequently, the Standing Committee of the National People's Congress (NPC) promulgated the Food Safety Law[39] in 2009, and the State Council subsequently developed the Implementing Rules for the Food Safety Law.[40] Both laws contain provisions on the monitoring and evaluation of food safety risks, standards, supervision, legal responsibilities, and so on.[41]

In order to build a solid foundation for effectively controlling infringing behaviors in the field of food safety, Amendment VIII to the Criminal Law of the People's Republic of China[42] (Criminal Law), which was promulgated in 2011, also increased the efforts to crack down on criminal acts that violate food safety. Compared with former Articles 143 and 144 of the Criminal Law, the revised articles added "other grave circumstances" as a constituting condition of the crime, besides serious harm to human health. In addition, Amendment VIII canceled the upper limit of fine penalty in Articles 143 and 144. Moreover, Amendment VIII regulated the criminal responsibilities of supervisors. According to the revised Article 408 of the Criminal Law:

> [a] State functionary with food safety supervision and management duties shall be sentenced to fixed-term imprisonment of not more than five years of criminal detention if he/she abuses his/her powers or neglects his/her duties, thus causing a major food safety accident or resulting in other serious consequences. If especially serious consequences are caused, he/she shall be sentenced to fixed-term imprisonment of not less than five years but not more than ten years. Any person who commits the aforementioned crime and engages in malpractice for personal gain shall be subject to a heavier punishment.[43]

Moreover, Food Safety Law of the People's Republic of China was amended and passed in 2015, it is called the most strict food-safety law in Chinese history. In this law,the unified supervision has replaced segmented supervision, and the food safety risk management and legal liability has been strengthened.

(3) LAWS AND REGULATIONS TO GUARANTEE FOOD ASSISTANCE IN DISASTERS

Nowadays, China pays more attention to food security issues brought about by disasters. In order to provide effective prevention and relief, China promulgated various laws and

38 Zhōnghuá Rénmín Gònghéguó Nóngchǎnpǐn Zhí Liàng Ānquán Fǎ (中华人民共和国农产品质量安全法) [Agricultural Product Quality Safety Law of the People's Republic of China] (Promulgated by the Standing Comm. Nat'l People's Cong., April 29, 2006).

39 Zhōnghuá Rénmín Gònghéguó Shípǐn Ānquán Fǎ (中华人民共和国食品安全法) [Food Safety Law of the People's Republic of China] (Promulgated by the Standing Comm. Nat'l People's Cong., February 28, 2009).

40 Zhōnghuá Rénmín Gònghéguó Shípǐn Ānquán Fǎ Shíshī Tiáolì (中华人民共和国食品安全法实施条例) [Regulation on the Implementation of the Food Safety Law of the People's Republic of China] (promulgated by the State Council July 20, 2009)

41 *See* Chapter 27 (Prevost) in this volume.

42 Zhōnghuá Rénmín Gònghéguó Xíngfǎ Xiūzhèng Àn (bā) (中华人民共和国刑法修正案(八) [Amendment (VIII) to the Criminal Law of the People's Republic of China]] (Promulgated by the Standing Comm. Nat'l People's Cong., February 25, 2011).

43 *Id.*

regulations to guarantee provisions following calamities. For instance, according to Article 38 of the Grain Reserve Regulations of the Central Government,[44] people can use the central grain reserves in case of natural disasters. Similarly, in Articles 31 and 32 of the Central Grain Circulation Management Regulations,[45] the Chinese government also requires an emergency mechanism to monitor grain products. Furthermore, Article 47 of the Flood Control Law of the People's Republic of China[46] requires that:

> [a]fter the occurrence of floods and water logging, the people's government should organize the relevant departments and units to ensure the relief work in the disaster area in respect to the supply of relief materials, public security, necessary health care and immunization, resumption of classes, resumption of production and rebuilding of homes as well as repairing of various engineering structures destroyed in floods within its jurisdiction.[47]

According to Article 73 of the Law of the People's Republic of China on Protecting Against and Mitigating Earthquake Disasters,[48] government departments in quake-hit areas at all levels shall mobilize people from all sectors of society to provide services such as medical assistance, shelter arrangements, psychological aid, and so on. Furthermore, Article 62 also provides that government at the county level has the responsibility to supervise drinkable water, food sanitation, and monitor the epidemic situation. In addition, the Emergency Response Law[49] states that government "may" adopt one or more emergency measures listed in the regulations during the aftermath of a disaster. Paragraph 7 of Article 49 guarantees the supply of food, drinkable water, and fuel. Besides the aforementioned laws and regulations, the Regulation on the Relief of Natural Disasters,[50] which was promulgated on July 8, 2010, clearly defines some regulations for the preparation of emergency relief, disaster assistance, management of relief funds and emergency supplies, and related legal liability. Disasters that meet the conditions established by this regulation trigger immediate emergency responses by the government at the county level or its comprehensive emergency mechanism. Thus, relief funds and materials such as provisions, clothes, temporary shelter, medical care, and post-disaster reconstruction aid shall be arranged in order to guarantee the basic livelihood of the people in the disaster-stricken areas.

44 *Supra* note 35, Article 38.

45 *Supra* note 36, Articles 31, 32.

46 Zhōnghuá Rénmín Gònghéguó Fánghóng Fǎ (中华人民共和国防洪法) [Flood Control Law of the People's Republic of China] (Promulgated by the Standing Comm. Nat'l People's Cong., August 29, 1997, revised July 15, 2005).

47 *Id.*, Article 47.

48 Zhōnghuá Rénmín Gònghéguó Fángzhèn Jiǎnzāi Fǎ (2008 xiūdìng) (中华人民共和国防震减灾法(2008 修订) [Law of the People's Republic of China on Protecting Against and Mitigating Earthquake Disasters (2008 Revision)] (Promulgated by the Standing Comm. Nat'l People's Cong., December 27, 2008).

49 Zhōnghuá Rénmín Gònghéguó Tú Fā Shìjiàn Yìngduì Fǎ (中华人民共和国突发事件应对法) [Emergency Response Law of the People's Republic of China] (Promulgated by the Standing Comm. Nat'l People's Cong., August 30, 2007).

50 Zìrán Zāihài Jiùzhù Tiáolì (自然灾害救助条例) [Regulation on the Relief of Natural Disasters] (Promulgated by the State Council, July 8, 2010).

(4) LAWS AND REGULATIONS TO GUARANTEE CULTURAL ACCEPTABILITY OF FOOD

Since cultural acceptability of food belongs to the category of human dignity, it is closely connected with dietary folkways and customs, especially dietary taboos; therefore, regulations that protect dignity and customs form the legal basis for such law. For instance, Article 38 of the Constitution states that "the personal dignity of citizens of the People's Republic of China is inviolable."[51] Article 14 of the Law of the People's Republic of China on the Protection of Consumer Rights and Interests[52] provides that "[a] consumer shall, when purchasing or using a commodity or receiving a service, have the right that human dignity, national customs and traditions be respected."[53] Article 52 of the Prison Law of the People's Republic of China[54] provides that "considerations shall be given to the special habits and customs of prisoners of minority ethnic groups."[55] In addition, several provinces have passed regulations on the management of halal food, which create a legal basis for protecting the traditions and customs of Islamic culture.

(5) LAWS AND REGULATIONS TO GUARANTEE THE RIGHT TO FOOD FOR UNPRIVILEGED GROUPS

Nowadays, laws protecting the right to food of unprivileged groups are mainly regulations promulgated by the State Council, including the Regulations on the Lowest Life Guarantees of Urban Residents[56] in 1999, the Regulations on the Work of Providing Five Guarantees[57] in 2006, and the Measures for the Administration of Relief for Vagrants and Beggars without Assured Living Sources in Cities[58] in 2003. Among these regulations, the Regulations on the Lowest Life Guarantees of Urban Residents provide that urban residents whose average family income falls below the minimum living standard will receive basic living allowances. In addition, the Regulations of Rural Five Guarantees regulated the social security for rural households with "five guarantees." Finally, the Measures for Administration of Public Relief for Vagrants and Beggars without Any Assured Living Source in Cities require that city governments above the county level should set up relief stations to provide temporal accommodation for the homeless, including food and clothing.

51 *Supra* note 27, Article 38.

52 Zhōnghuá Rénmín Gònghéguó Xiāofèi Zhě Quányì Bǎohù Fǎ (中华人民共和国消费者权益保护法) [Law of the People's Republic of China on Protection of Consumer Rights and Interests] (Promulgated by the Standing Comm. Nat'l People's Cong., October 31, 1993, amended October 25, 2013). *See* Chapters 30 (Rossi), 31 (Prasad), and 32 (Hu) in this volume.

53 *Id.*, Article 14.

54 Zhōnghuá Rénmín Gònghéguó Jiānyù Fǎ (中华人民共和国监狱法) [Prison Law of the People's Republic of China] (Promulgated by the Standing Comm. Nat'l People's Cong., December 29, 1994, amended October 26, 2012).

55 *Id.*, Article 52.

56 Chéngshì Jūmín Zuìdī Shēnghuó Bǎozhàng Tiáolì (城市居民最低生活保障条例) [Regulations on the Lowest Life Guarantees of Urban Residents] (Promulgated by the State Council, September 28, 1999).

57 Chéngshì Shēnghuó Wúzhuó De Liúlàng Qǐtǎo Rényuán Jiùzhù Guǎnlǐ Bànfǎ (城市生活无着的流浪乞讨人员救助管理办法) [Measures for the Administration of Relief for Vagrants and Beggars without Assured Living Sources in Cities] (Promulgated by the State Council, June 20, 2003).

58 Nóngcūn Wǔ Bǎo Gòngyǎng Gōngzuò Tiáolì (农村五保供养工作条例) [Regulations on the Work of Providing Five Guarantees] (Promulgated by the State Council, January 21, 2006).

The present situation of the right to food in China

Progress in the realization of the right to food in China

In contemporary China, political inclinations and related regulations gave a powerful impetus to the realization of the right to food. With the rapid development of the national economy since China adopted the reform and opening-up policy in 1978, remarkable progress has been made, particularly in the following aspects.

First, with the distinct improvement in the total output of grain, the per capita quota of grain rapidly increased, equaling 319 kg per capita in 1978.[59] The total grain output of China grew from 113 million tons in 1949 to 304.765 million tons in 1978. Resulting from continuous growth of grain output in China, the total grain output in China reached 60702.6 million tons in 1949,almost 6 times of that in 1949, and the per capita quota in 2014 amounted to 445 kg.[60]

Second, food consumption expenditures of citizens experienced significant growth. For instance, food expenditures of urban residents in China increased from 2,709.6 CNY in 2004 to 6,311.9 CNY in 2013. Furthermore, the increase in food expenditures not only happened in high-income and middle-income groups, but also in low-income groups. Within the low-income groups, food expenditures of households demonstrating financial difficulties also rose significantly. For example, food expenditures in the lowest income groups increased from 1,417.76 CNY in 2004 to 3310.41 CNY in 2012. In regards to rural citizens, the food expenditures of households dealing with financial difficulties increased from 694.3722 CNY in 2004 to 1620.32 CNY in 2012, and cash expenses climbed from 326.4964 CNY in 2004 to 1173.21 CNY in 2012.[61]

Third, citizens' food consumption patterns also radically changed. Consumption patterns showed a trend towards diversification among the residents. In proportion to other products, the share of grain products declined since all "staple food[s]" experienced a gradual reduction. The per capita annual purchases of major foods nationwide decreased from 238.80 kg in 1990 to 141.0 kg in 2014, and poultry increased from 1.73 kg to 8.0 kg in 2014. Some food products, which were regarded as "non-staple foodstuff[s]" in the past, have steadily gained more prominence. In addition, the demand for meat, water, and dairy products has surged. For example, the per capita consumption of meat swelled from 16.64 kg in 1990 to 20.00 kg in 2014; the per capita consumption of aquatic products increased from 6.53 kg in 1990 to 10.8 kg in 2014.[62] It may be obvious to conclude that since the 1978 reform, food consumption patterns in China have migrated from staple foodstuffs to non-staple foodstuffs and from being relatively one-dimensional to a diversified menu. It seems that food consumption patterns have evolved from having a full meal to having a good meal and from overcoming hunger to obtaining nutritional balance.

59 *See* Chapter 20 (Simpson) in this volume.

60 Zhōngguó Tǒngjī Niánjiàn 2015 [Chinese Statistical Yearbook in 2015], http://www.stats.gov.cn/tjsj/ndsj/2015/indexch.htm (last visited July 8, 2016).

61 Zhōngguó Tǒngjī Niánjiàn 2014 [Chinese Statistical Yearbook in 2005], http://www.stats.gov.cn/tjsj/ndsj/2014/indexch.htm(last visited November 16, 2014).

62 Zhōngguó Tǒngjī Niánjiàn 2015 [Chinese Statistical Yearbook in 2015], http://www.stats.gov.cn/tjsj/ndsj/2015/indexch.htm (last visited July 8, 2016).

Problems in the realization of the right to food

China has indeed made some progress in the realization of the right to food. Having solved the issue of food shortage, however, does not mean the country does not have any more problems concerning the right to food. Here are some of the main issues on the right to food in China.

Imbalance in the realization of the right to food

Imbalance presents a serious problem to the realization of the right to food. Owing to the urban–rural dual structure of distribution and social security, tremendous differences between urban and rural areas threaten the effective realization of the right to food. According to the grain quota system, prior to the reform and opening policy in 1978, urban residents had the right to obtain food rations, while rural residents had only the right to obtain surplus grain after compulsory purchase. Consequently, the realization of the right to food for rural residents was in greater danger in case of natural disasters. During the famine from 1959 to 1961, for example, the great majority of people that died lived in rural areas.[63] After the reform in 1978, despite the abolition of the grain quota system partial to urban citizens, the capability of the resident in rural areas to realize the right to food is still weaker than the urban resident, particularly the backwardness of the social security system. Generally speaking, food consumption and nutritional levels in the countryside fall below the ones registered in cities. Despite a higher consumption of cereals, rural residents show a lower consumption level of beans, proteins, meat products, etc.[64] Urban residents also absorb more micronutrients than rural citizens, such as proteins, fat, vitamin E, Potassium, Sodium, Calcium, Zinc, and Ferrum, even though they have a lower overall caloric intake.[65]

In addition, food expenditures differed drastically between urban and rural areas. In 2009, the average food expenditures of urban households in the highest income amounted to 10,323.06 CNY; urban households in the lowest income spent 3,310.41 CNY, and urban households in the poor income allocated only 2,979.29 CNY to food. Food consumption per annum for urban residents in the highest-income households exceeded by three and a half times that of urban households demonstrating poor income. Furthermore, food consumption of the highest-income households in rural areas was 3,622.70 CNY, and one of the lowest-income households spent only 1,620.32 CNY, meaning the former spent 2.2 times more on food than the latter.[66]

Food and malnutrition problems of disadvantaged groups

Amartya Sen, winner of the Nobel Prize in Economics (2004), maintains that, in the analysis of world hunger, the total quantity of food is an uncertain economic variable that is hard to define. Faced with a shortage of food, some live in hunger while others often enjoy a full

63 *Lín Yìfū, Zàilùn Zhìdù Jìshù Yǔ Zhōngguó Nóngyè Fāzhǎn,* [*Second Discussion of Rules,Teconology and Devlopment of the Agriculture in China*] 267 (Peking University Press, 2010).

64 *Zhōngguó Wèishēng Hé Jìhuà Shēngyù Tǒngjì Niánjiàn 2013* [*Chinese Statistical Yearbook on Hygiene and Family Planning in 2013*].

65 *Zhōngguō Weìshēng Tǒngjī Niánjiàn 2008 [Chinese Statistical Yearbook on Hygiene in 2008].*

66 Zhōngguó Tǒngjī Niánjiàn 2013 [Chinese Statistical Yearbook in 2013], http://www.stats.gov.cn/tjsj/ndsj/2010/indexch.htm (last visited November 16, 2014).

meal.[67] Therefore, the increase of the supply quantity and per capita consumption of food alone does not necessarily mean that China has solved its problem of hunger and malnutrition. Furthermore, the hunger and malnutrition problems of disadvantaged groups present the most serious issues. According to the poverty standard in 2009, which defined poverty as income under 1,196 CNY per year, China's poverty-stricken population decreased from 40.07 million in 2009 to 26.88 million in 2010.[68] Since the poverty standard merely equaled the lowest living standard of 2,100 calories a day, hunger and malnutrition persistently threaten disadvantaged and impoverished people.

According to World Health Organization (WHO) statistics, the stunted rate of children under 5 years was 20.7 per cent during 1990 to 1999, and it decreased to 9.4 per cent from 2007 to 2010. The rate of underweight children under 5 years was 12.6 per cent from 1990 to 1995, and it decreased to 3.4 per cent from 2007 to 2014.[69] Compared with other developing countries, the rate of children demonstrating slow growth or underweight was relatively low; however, with such an immense population, the total number of children in China with physical growth problems now ranks among the highest in the world. Besides the malnutrition problems of children under five years of age, the nutritional status of school-aged children presents another matter for concern. Although the nutrition condition has improved remarkably since 2005 because of the implementation of nutrition improvement programs, we cannot deny that some disadvantaged people still suffer from malnutrition.

Food safety problems

Food safety problems are also a crucial issue in modern China. Due to some actors' thirst for profits and defects in the supervision system, crimes in the food safety area have increased in recent years. This trend appears mainly in the following aspects. First, food industry members used illegal additives that are dangerous to people's health, such as the Sanlu milk powder scandal in 2008. Some milk powders, including Sanlu, were found to contain a chemical called melamine, which can greatly damage infants' health.[70] Second, other producers made food with illegal ingredients that are harmful to people's health or failed the health inspections. In March 2011, for example, police in Haining, Zhejiang Province discovered an extraordinary case of illegal cooking oil, which was refined from recycled food and called Di Gou oil. According to the police report, the case involved 32 suspects from 14 provinces.[71] In addition to these two cases, there are also other issues regarding food safety,[72] such as food packed with harmful materials and sales of expired food products.

67 Amartya Sen, Poverty and Famine 188 (Commercial Press, 2004). Translated by Wang Yu, Wang Wen.

68 *Lǐ Yúnlóng, Jiǎnhuǎn Nóngcūn Pínkùn, Bǎozhàng Shēngcúnquán Hé Fāzhǎnquán [Alleviating rural poverty, ensuring the right to subsistence and development]*, in *Zhōngguó Rénquán Shìyè Fāzhǎn Bàogào Dìyīhào 2011 Nián* [The Report for Human Rights Development No. 1] 58 (Li Junru ed., Social Sciences Academic Press, 2011).

69 World Health Organization, *Statistics of World Health in 2010*, at 103; and World Health Organization, *Statistics of World Health in 2014*, at 118 World Health Organization, *Statistics of World Health in 2015*, at 102.

70 *Sānlu Nǎifěn Shìjiàn Huígù [Looking Back on San Lu Milk Incident]* (January 2, 2009), http://news.xinhuanet.com/fortune/2009-01/02/content_10590633.htm (last visited August 1, 2016).

71 *Liú Zīqiàn, Hé Jiǎngyǒng, Zhōngguó Shǒucì Pòhuò Dìgōuyou Zhìshòu Ànjiàn, Jiē Hēisè Lìyì Liàn [China detected recycled cooking oil case the first time]* (September 27, 2011), http://www.chinanews.com/jk/2011/09-27/3356877.shtml (last visited August 1, 2016).

72 *See* Chapter 27 (Prevost) in this volume.

Consequently, all of the cases above not only seriously damaged people's health and weakened their sense of security as consumers,[73] but also obstructed the realization of the right to food.

The future of the right to food in China

The above analysis of the status quo manifests that China has made great progress in protecting the right to food. However, some inadequacies still exist. In order to perform the obligations prescribed by the Constitution and international laws, as well as successfully build an all-around well-off society, China should take the right to food more seriously. The following measures may be taken.

First, stick to the strategic principles of basing the right to food on the fight against poverty. Poverty is the most important factor that constrains the realization of the right to food. To some extent, the level of implementation of the right to food flows from the realization of the same right for the population who lives below the poverty line. This is a case of the "Barrel Principle," which means that the barrel's capacity to hold water does not depend on its longest plank, but on its shortest one. Therefore, the state of human rights throughout a country depends on the degree to which the government upholds the right for its socially disadvantaged groups. Since the fight against poverty leads to the realization of the right to food in China, the government should undoubtedly adopt poverty alleviation as its central strategy.

In order to follow a strategy based on fighting poverty, China should first raise the poverty line. The 1,196 CNY poverty line implemented in 2008 not only falls below the prevailing international standards, but also falls short of the expectations of most poor people. Besides, this standard can only meet the minimum requirement of 2,100 calories a day, and is hardly able to cover any other basic needs.[74] At the Central Conference on Poverty Alleviation of 2011, Premier Wen Jiabao declared that the government would raise the poverty line to 2,300 CNY, which would undoubtedly contribute to the protection of the right to food. However, a significant disparity remains between the 2,300 CNY benchmark and the international standard. In my view, China should adopt the internationally accepted poverty line. In addition to raising the poverty line, China must put capacity-building at the core of its strategy to realize the right to food, since it is only when people have a decent opportunity to become self-supporting that they may live with dignity.[75] The basic concept of the right to food should not be to provide for people, but to enable people to provide for themselves. The state only bears the obligation to provide for those who do not have the ability to support themselves. From this point of view, in order to adhere to the anti-poverty strategy, China must strive for capacity-building and improve people's ability to obtain food through education, skills training, expansion of employment, and other means.

Second, modify the legislation concerning the right to food. At the constitutional level, China can incorporate this right into the fundamental rights system. To be specific, add the right to an adequate standard of living to Article 45 of the Constitution, that is, to create

73 *See* Chapter 32 (Hu) in this volume.

74 *See* Chapter 20 (Simpson) in this volume.

75 George Kent, Freedom From Want: The Human Right to Adequate Food 4 (Georgetown University Press, 2005).

one section stipulating that everyone is entitled to an adequate standard of living, including food, housing, and drinking water. At the level of laws and regulations, China should primarily strengthen the legislation on the following three aspects. First, on the aspect of nutrition, the Nutrition Act, which is currently being drafted, should be completed expeditiously. In order to further improve the nutritional status of the Chinese people, the government should pass the act as soon as possible. However, the Nutrition Act should not only focus on the establishment of a nutritional standard, but also make clear the groups of people who should receive primary protection. Furthermore, the government's obligations and specific initiatives concerning nutritional guarantees should be clearly expressed. Second, China should strengthen the social security legislation. The implementation of basic living standards based on dual standards for urban and rural areas has created a state of imbalance in the realization of the right to food. Therefore, China should establish a unified regulation of basic living standards as soon as possible. Finally, China should draw up a unified Disaster Relief Act. Although the country has already issued many laws aiming to guarantee the right to food during natural disasters, most of them do not have a unified standard. For example, the Emergency Response Law stipulates that the governments "may" take some measures, including guaranteeing provisions, while other laws generally direct that the government "should" do it. Such legislative discrepancies undoubtedly impede enforcement of the law. Therefore, it is necessary to establish a natural disaster relief law with a unified standard. Although the Regulation on the Relief of Natural Disasters issued in 2010 unified all the natural disaster relief provisions, it is just an administrative regulation promulgated by the State Council, which is weaker than law. For this reason, in order to strengthen the protection of human rights during natural disasters, China has to pass a Natural Disasters Relief Law with a unified standard based on the Regulation on the Relief of Natural Disasters.

Third, enhance law enforcement. The most severe problem China faces today in establishing the rule of law is not creating the law, but enforcing it. Therefore, the realization of the right to food depends on the government's resolute enforcement of the law, especially in the field of food security and farmland protection. Even though the legal system of food security in China has already reached a stage of completion, the reality of the right to food shows that food security problems persist and remain difficult to solve. In this case, China should complete its supervision system of food safety incidents, thereby implementing strict control over food quality. Meanwhile, the government should make full use of its supervision capacity over society to set up a monitoring system with the joint power of both the state organs and the public. As for farmland protection, the problem of illegal occupation of farmlands arises periodically, particularly due to the rapid development of urbanization, the overheating of the real estate market and the reality of land-based finance. The government should therefore strictly enforce the law in the department of land management to prevent the farmlands from disappearing.

Last but not least, provide unimpeded access to justice. The judicial system is the last line of defense, so one can say that access to the judicial system means access to justice. Therefore, providing the people with unimpeded access to the courts is an essential means of guaranteeing the right to food. Judging from the experience in practice, judicial cases related to the right to food usually require the government to fulfill its obligation to protect, or deal with food safety disputes between consumers, and producers or dealers. In the cases where the government should perform its obligations, the abstract administrative action cannot be brought within judicial procedures, and the counterparts of the non-specific administrative action body cannot initiate legal proceedings, due to the restrictions on the plaintiffs' qualification and current range of accepted cases directed by the Administrative Procedural Law. This weakens the effect of the judicial system's supervision of the right to food. Therefore, China has to enlarge the range of cases accepted by administrative proceedings, loosen the restrictions on the plaintiffs' qualifications, and perfect the system of administrative proceedings for the public interest. In the food safety cases concerned with disputes between consumers and food producers or dealers, the characteristics of the cases and the economic disparity between the parties should be taken into consideration, in order to guarantee the consumers' rights and interests concerning the burden of proof, legal proceedings, and litigation costs; this way, food safety incidents can be reduced or eliminated.

In conclusion, human rights are the basic rights of every citizen, and protecting them is the common undertaking of all mankind. China has already expressed its strong political will to fulfill the right to food. Meanwhile, the policies and laws China formulated have played a positive role in realizing the right to food. However, although much has been achieved, some problems still exist, and China must dispassionately deal with this reality in order to better meet the obligations called for by the right to food. This is not only the requirement of China's human rights principles written in the Constitution, but also China's obligation under international law, and the legitimate basis of the Chinese Communist Party's ruling position.

20 Projections of China's Food Security to 2030

Obligations as an Agricultural Superpower*

James R. Simpson

Introduction

China, with one-fifth of the world's population and rapidly rising incomes, is a country which has naturally been open to speculation about its ability to feed itself over the next few decades. The nation's population is projected to grow to 1.44 billion in 2020, and 1.48 billion in 2030. It will begin to decline after that. Simultaneously, per capita income growth will lead to greater demand for animal and aqua products, thus resulting in expanded animal feedstuffs requirements.

A myriad of articles has appeared in recent years expressing serious concerns about the world's ability to feed itself, fueled by the hefty spikes in crop and retail food prices. China is a primary focus with a number of pundits forecasting the need for the country to drastically increase maize imports primarily due to absolutely unrealistic short-term growth in consumption of livestock products. The whole issue has been blown way out of proportion by the well-known Mr. Lester Brown, President of Earth Policy Institute, who has recycled his 1995 book (*Who Will Feed China? Wake-Up Call for a Small Planet*) with the argument that a prosperous China will be a hungry China that devours the world's food supply. To him "Beijing is losing a long battle to feed its growing population on its own [. . .] Just as China is America's banker, America could become China's farmer [. . .] The evidence of China's plight is clear."[1]

It is concluded that these pundits are guilty of using "back-of-the envelope, kneejerk thinking." In contrast, the science-based research presented in this chapter reveals that

* This chapter is part of the results of the Research Project on "*Current Trends of Chinese Law towards Non-Trade Concerns such as Sustainable Development and the Protection of Environment, Public Health, Food Safety, Cultural, Social and Economic Rights, Labor Rights and the Reduction of Poverty from the Perspective of International Law and WTO Law*", coordinated by Professor Paolo Davide Farah at gLAWcal – Global Law Initiatives for Sustainable Development (United Kingdom) and at West Virginia University John D. Rockefeller IV School of Policy and Politics, Department of Public Administration, in partnership with the Center of Advanced Studies on Contemporary China (CASCC) in Turin (Italy), Maastricht University Faculty of Law, Department of International and European Law and IGIR – Institute for Globalisation and International Regulation (Netherlands), and Tsinghua University, School of Law, Institute of Public International Law and the Center for Research on Intellectual Property Law in Beijing (China). This publication and the Conference Series were sponsored by China–EU School of Law (CESL) at the China University of Political Science and Law (CUPL). The activities of CESL at CUPL are supported by the European Union and the People's Republic of China.

1 Lester R. Brown, *Can the United States Feed China?*, Washington Post (March 13, 2011), http://www.washingtonpost.com/wp-dyn/content/article/2011/03/11/AR2011031106993.html (last visited July 16, 2016).

technically, despite human population growth and changes in diet, China will be able to maintain its current level of being essentially self-sufficient in animal feedstuffs, animal and aquaculture products, and other foods for humans. The research method from which projections are derived is calculation of all animal and aquaculture feedstuffs requirements and availabilities on the basis of metabolizable energy (ME) and crude protein (CP). Crops contain both energy and protein, and animals require both as well. Projections are based on medium scenario crop yield increases and per capita consumption projections derived from a robust economy in which growth rates moderate over time.[2] Constraints on China's natural resources are taken into account, and the great potential biotechnology will probably have on crop production worldwide is only conservatively factored in. It can be expected there will be years in which feedstuffs imports will likely be needed and other years of surpluses due to climatic variations and other factors such as commodity price fluctuations. Human consumption of food from sources other than livestock products (such as crop co-products for example) is taken into consideration in the modeling.

China has emerged from *developing country* status into *newly industrialized country* status. Its agricultural sector has improved dramatically in harmony with the general economy and it is projected that it will achieve superpower status as the nation morphs into an *economically developed country*. The compelling question that constitutes the last section of this chapter is how China will utilize its agricultural powerhouse for achieving the calls for "balance" in agricultural trade by many developing nations – and also by economically developed ones that are substantial food importers. China's approach to food security, which is essentially based on "rights" is examined in the context of international covenants and what that implies for its future obligations to alleviating concerns and tensions about the use and abuse of agricultural trade.

Consumption of animal and aqua products

Per capita projections of demand were primarily derived from cross country analysis and evaluation of other projections. Beef is a high-growth meat commodity, as per capita consumption (and production) is projected to double from 4.3 kg in 2006–2008 (termed 2007 hereafter) to 7.5 kg in 2030 (Table 20.1). Poultry also doubles, from 11.6 kg to 20.0 kg in that same period. Pork, already quite high, grows very little, from 34.2 kg to 38.0 kg. China's per capita meat and aqua product consumption is projected to grow from 79.1 kg to 100 kg in 2030. As a comparison, the totals in 2007 were 96 kg in Argentina, 100 in Germany, 107 in Japan, 105 in the United Kingdom (UK), and 146 in the United States (US) (data not shown).[3]

Production of animal and aqua products from 1989–1991 to 2030 is provided in Table 20.2: Total production of meat and aqua products increases 38 per cent in the 23 years

2 Income, on a PPP basis, is projected by the author to grow from USD 9,550 in 2007, to USD 24,950 in 3030 (growth rate 8 per cent 2007–2015, 7 per cent 2015–2020, and 5 per cent 2020–2030). In comparison, it was USD 34,099 for Japan in 2008 and USD 46,716 in the United States. *See* James R. Simpson, *Can China Continue to Feed its Population?*, FEEDSTUFFS 1 (September 27, 2010).

3 Detailed data and results, published in a three part series in *Feedstuffs*, the Weekly Newspaper for Agribusiness, *Can China Feed its Population?* 1 (September 27, 2010); *Land Use, Production to Shape China's Future* 1 (October 4, 2010); and *Feedstuffs Play Key Role in China's Food Needs* 16 (October 11, 2010), http://www.jamesrsimpson.com. Historical data are from the Food and Agriculture Organization of the United Nations (FAO), and available at www.faostat.fao.org/ (last visited July 16, 2016).

Table 20.1 Projections of per capita supply of animal and aqua products, China, economy robust, 2007 to 2030

Item	Compound annual growth rate (pct)			Per capita projections (kg)			
	2007–2015	2015–2020	2020–2030	2007	2015	2020	2030
Beef and veal	3.07	3.40	1.44	4.32	5.50	6.50	7.50
Pork	0.66	0.55	0.27	34.15	36.00	37.00	38.00
Mutton, lamb, and goat	-0.19	0.70	0.17	2.84	2.80	2.90	2.95
Mutton and lamb	-0.06	0.66	0.32	1.51	1.50	1.55	1.60
Goat meat	-0.34	0.76	0.00	1.34	1.30	1.35	1.35
Buffalo meat	0.27	-4.78	-6.70	0.23	0.23	0.18	0.09
Total red meat	0.87	0.90	0.41	41.54	44.53	46.58	48.54
Poultry meat	1.47	4.24	2.26	11.56	13.00	16.00	20.00
Total meat	1.01	1.70	0.91	53.10	57.53	62.58	68.54
Aqua products (cultivated)	0.93	1.39	0.65	26.00	28.00	30.00	32.00
Total meat and aqua products	0.98	1.60	0.83	79.10	85.53	92.58	100.54
Milk							
Cow	-0.67	3.71	2.92	25.86	25.00	30.00	40.00
Goat meat	-1.08	0.00	0.00	0.20	0.18	0.18	0.18
Buffalo meat	-2.24	-2.33	-1.33	0.22	0.18	0.16	0.14
Eggs, hen	-0.03	0.18	0.03	16.34	16.30	16.45	16.50

Source: Simpson, modeling results

Table 20.2 Total production of animal and aqua products, China, economy robust, 1989–1991 to 2030 (1,000 MT)

Item	1989–1991	1994–1996	1999–2001	2006–2008	2015	2020	2030
Beef and veal	1,167.7	3,054.7	4,745.5	5,730.4	7,681.5	9,316.1	10,994.8
Pork	24,061.9	33,009.7	40,768.7	46,244.0	50,640.4	53,357.8	56,009.4
Mutton, lamb, and goat	1,070.6	1,681.9	2,642.7	3,759.4	3,889.9	4,133.3	4,299.3
Mutton and lamb	550.7	893.3	1,445.3	1,972.0	2,065.9	2,191.1	2,314.1
Goat meat	519.9	788.6	1,197.3	1,787.4	1,824.1	1,942.2	1,985.3
Buffalo meat	165.1	274.6	368.8	300.8	313.2	252.6	129.5

(*Continued*)

Table 20.2 (Continued)

Item	*1989–1991*	*1994–1996*	*1999–2001*	*2006–2008*	*2015*	*2020*	*2030*
Total red meat	26,465.4	38,021.0	48,525.6	56,034.5	62,524.9	67,059.7	71,433.0
Poultry meat	3,863.4	8,213.9	12,324.5	15,045.8	17,850.7	22,630.4	29,026.0
Total meat	30,328.8	46,234.9	60,850.1	71,080.3	80,375.6	89,690.1	100,459.0
Aqua products (cultivated)	6,078.0	13,531.0	22,269.7	29,484.6	32,000.0	35,000.0	38,000.0
Total meat and aqua products	36,406.8	59,765.9	83,119.8	100,564.9	112,375.6	124,690.1	138,459.0
Milk							
Cow	4,411.4	6,090.2	8,915.9	34,561.8	35,097.5	43,182.0	58,852.0
Goat meat	1,906.7	2,200.0	2,643.3	2,883.3	2,566.9	1,971.7	950.0
Buffalo meat	162.6	192.4	232.5	262.4	252.7	259.1	264.8
Eggs, hen	6,700.6	13,912.0	18,858.5	21,839.2	22,883.6	23,678.1	24,276.5

Source: Simpson, modeling results

from 2007 to 2030. Beef and veal production increases 92 per cent, from 5.7 million tons to 11.0 million tons during that 23-year projection period.

Animal productivity improvement

The remarkable growth recorded in China's livestock product production is projected to continue for the foreseeable future, primarily because there is still great latitude for further progress in production efficiency and productivity, as they are still quite low. A multitude of technical aspects were taken into account in the modeling to project animal numbers and feedstuffs requirements. Pigs, for example, are quite complicated, involving 65 variables in the program such as whether they are backyard or commercial, number born per litter, number of litters per year, energy and protein changes by weights, time on feed by stage of feeding, just to give a sampling of the information needed to explain and project technological changes in production. Poultry, in particular, are equally as complex.

Pigs also provide a good example of the impact technology adoption can have on production. In 1990, only 67 kg of pork was produced per pig in inventory (Table 20.3). By 2007, it had reached 106 kg, and is projected at 137 kg by 2030. In comparison, the average in 2007 was 129 kg in Japan, 150 kg in the UK, and 158 kg in the US. Offtake rates – the percentage of pigs going to slaughter compared to inventory – in China are projected to increase from 139 per cent in 2007 to 170 per cent in 2030. As a point of reference, rates for the above three other countries in 2007 were 167 kg, 191 kg, and 172 kg, respectively.

Table 20.3 Production per head of inventory, China, economy robust, 1989–1991 to 2030

Item	*1989–1991*	*1994–1996*	*1999–2001*	*2006–2008*	*2015*	*2020*	*2030*
	(Kg of meat per head of inventory)						
Sheep	4.9	7.5	11.2	13.6	12.7	13.1	13.8
Goats	5.4	6.2	8.2	12.4	10.8	10.8	11.1
Cattle	14.7	31.5	46.3	60.2	65.6	78.8	95.8
Buffalo	7.7	11.9	16.3	13.2	16.1	17.6	19.5
Pigs	66.7	80.8	94.6	105.7	112.9	122.4	136.5
Poultry	1.5	2.1	2.8	2.7	2.9	3.6	5.0
Chickens	1.3	1.8	2.4	2.4	2.7	3.5	5.1
	(Kg of milk per head of inventory)						
Goats	1.7	1.5	1.6	1.8	1.5	1.4	1.5
Milk cows	1,563.6	1,543.8	1,836.7	2,776.9	3,600.0	5,000.0	6,500.0
Buffalo	89.0	95.5	116.6	126.3	132.0	137.5	143.0
	(Kg of eggs per chicken hen in inventory)						
Eggs	8.7	10.2	9.9	9.1	10.7	14.0	16.2

Source: Simpson, modeling results

It is important to realize that productivity will continue to increase in other countries over the next two decades covered in the projections. With proper policy formulation, China will benefit from those changes as well as adoption of nationally developed technology and structural changes. The point is that accuracy in projections about China's agriculture depends on a good understanding of its agricultural structure, recognition that China's agriculture is a dynamic industry and not a static one, and that in most respects it is more like European agriculture than that of its East Asian neighbors to which it is often, and misleadingly, compared.

Cattle are particularly important in determining whether China can feed itself, because total beef production will have to double in order to meet increased demand. Most cattle in China are found in the cropping areas rather than on rangelands. Originally, they were mainly used for draft and transport, with milk and beef as by-products from aged animals that had to be culled. As the rural areas have begun to mechanize and national per capita incomes have increased, demand for beef has also grown so that a true beef industry is quickly emerging in which cows are kept primarily for calf production in both cropping and grassland areas. A variety of growing and fattening operations have sprung up, but US style feedlots will not come into being in the foreseeable future.[4]

Productivity is increasing rapidly in China's cattle industry. In 2007, production per head of inventory was 60 kg, up dramatically from 15 kg in 1990. It is projected to reach 79 kg by 2020 and 96 kg in 2030. The projections are quite reasonable for, by comparison, in 2007 Germany recorded 93kg, the UK 84 kg, and the US 125 kg.

4 *See* Beef in China: Agribusiness Opportunities and Challenges (John W. Longworth, Colin G. Brown & Scott A. Waldron eds, University of Queensland Press, 2001).

Animal inventory projections

Historical data and projections on livestock inventory are given in Table 20.4. Review of them is very instructive, for they reveal the impact from technology adoption and structural change. As an example, despite total production continuing to grow, inventories of pigs and poultry are projected to grow moderately until 2015 and then decline slightly as those industries continue shifting to large-scale technologically advanced enterprises that will also expand their adoption of productivity enhancing technologies. Growth in milk consumption has received considerable attention, with speculation that the number of milk cows and attendant feed-stuffs requirements will have to increase dramatically. Just the opposite is most likely, as the milk industry is a nascent one with yield per cow at just 2,800 kg in 2007. It is projected to grow to 6,500 kg in 2030 with the outcome that, while considerable growth in numbers is projected to 2015, dairy cow inventory is calculated to remain at about 9 million head through 2030. The projected decline in non-bovine work animal numbers from 18 million

Table 20.4 Livestock inventory, China, economy robust, 1989–1991 to 2030

Item	*1989–1991*	*1994–1996*	*1999–2001*	*2006–2008*	*2015*	*2020*	*2030*
	(1,000 Head)						
Non-bovine work animals							
Asses	11,128	10,853	9,378	7,409	4,498	2,423	694
Goats	470	360	330	258	129	69	20
Horses	10,338	10,025	8,889	7,141	4,994	4,080	3,509
Mules	5,417	5,480	4,647	3,337	2,127	1,414	767
Total, non-bovine	27,353	26,718	23,244	18,145	11,748	7,986	4,989
Cattle							
Milk cows	2,821	3,945	4,854	12,446	9,749	8,636	9,054
Draft/beef	76,463	93,029	97,611	82,745	107,358	109,537	105,770
Total cattle	79,284	96,974	102,465	95,191	117,107	118,173	114,824
Buffalo	21,412	23,028	22,678	22,831	19,446	14,340	6,644
Total cattle, buffalo	100,696	120,002	125,143	118,022	136,553	132,513	121,467
Total, large animals	128,049	146,720	148,387	136,167	148,301	140,500	126,457
Sheep	112,299	118,919	129,491	144,597	162,678	167,609	167,450
Goats	95,615	126,432	146,672	144,674	169,649	180,635	178,274
Total small ruminants	207,913	245,350	276,164	289,271	332,328	348,244	345,724
Pigs							
Commercial				188,055	246,779	305,152	348,713
Backyard				249,282	201,910	130,779	61,538
Total pigs	360,543	408,782	430,848	437,337	448,689	435,931	410,250
	(Million birds)						
Total poultry	2,556	3,920	4,407	5,568	7,923	8,055	7,533

Source: Simpson, modeling results

head in 2007 to 5 million head in 2030 will free up considerable feedstuffs resources for other animals. The bottom line: focus on technological change and adoption.

Feedstuffs utilization and production

The research method from which projections are derived is calculation of all animal and aquaculture feedstuffs requirements and availabilities on the basis of metabolizable energy and crude protein. Crops contain both energy and protein. For example, maize (corn) contains 3.4 Mcal of energy per kg and 8.6 per cent protein. Soybeans contain 3.3 Mcal and have 38 per cent protein.[5] The dynamics of changes in human diets and animal and aquaculture productivity can be appreciated by noting that cattle accounted for about 26 per cent of all ME, and 14 per cent of CP requirements by animals and aquaculture in China in 2007 (data not shown). These proportions are projected to increase to 36 and 20 per cent, respectively, by 2030. Pigs have been, by far, the largest user of feedstuffs, accounting for 32 per cent of ME and 41 per cent of CP in 2007. Those proportions are projected to decline to 25 and 27 per cent in 2030. Importantly, aquaculture accounts for nearly a fifth of China's protein use, and rapid growth in this value-added export-oriented industry is a major reason for soybean imports increasing so rapidly. Nutrition, particularly type of feedstuffs, is central to understanding the extent to which China can meet the great increases projected in livestock and aquaculture to meet changes in demand for them.

Each country feeds its animals according to resource availabilities, tastes and preferences, food safety desires, and comparative advantage in production of feedstuffs. This is a key point to understand and project China's livestock structure. For example, Americans have come to believe that large-scale feedlot type grain-fed beef is the standard for quality and production cost-effectiveness. Consequently, they believe that China will inexorably move towards such a system and, since China's grain production capacity is in doubt, substantial feedstuffs imports will thus be required. This is unlikely to happen, as the Australians Longworth, Brown, and Waldron have pointed out.[6] The issue is a very important one and should be a major focal point of agricultural policy planning because a relatively small change in cattle inventory has a large impact on feedstuffs requirements. Cattle are ruminants and thus crop residues are quite suitable for them.

Contrary to popular thinking, just 29 per cent of energy-based feedstuffs availabilities were derived from principal crop sources – which essentially means harvested grains or seed heads fed directly to livestock – in 2007. That proportion will increase marginally to 31 per cent by 2030 as the industry and economy mature, still leaving 69 per cent from other sources. By-products such as brewers' distilled grains, brans from processing, and silage

5 A major problem with trade models about China is that, apart from lack of rigor regarding technological change, the wide variety of feedstuffs utilized is not considered. Another problem is that, because they are price-based, their relevance is lost after a few years. The results provided in this chapter are based on a model especially developed for long-term projections of animal inventories, feedstuffs requirements, and feedstuffs availabilities. Originally constructed by Simpson in the late 1980s and early 1990s (*see* James Simpson, Xu Cheng & Akira Miyazaki, China's Livestock and Related Agriculture: Projections to 2025 (CAB International, 1994)), this non-deterministic simulation spread sheet programmed model has been greatly revised and updated several times since then. Suffice it to say that the program is very large and complicated, with more than 5,000 lines of spread sheet program, 800 variables, and more than 2,200 parameters, and success in various previous projections lends credence to reliability of results.

6 *Supra* note 4.

accounted for 21 per cent and are expected to grow to 26 per cent in 2030. Most important is that crop residues are the largest proportion, 38 per cent in 2007, declining to 33 per cent as the economy matures. Protein sources are significantly different since by-products (such as soybean meal from processing soybeans for oil) accounted for 48 per cent of them in 2007, increasing to 51 per cent in 2030. Crop residues are also an important source, 28 and 26 per cent for those two periods, respectively.

Crop yields

Crops were divided into two types for projections, major and minor. Ten, chosen as major crops, account for about two-thirds of sown (harvested) area (Table 20.5). Yield growth rates for the ten were ascertained by evaluating six factors that affect them; fertilizer, land reclamation, irrigation, seed variety, soil improvement, and "other", which includes management, mechanization, etc., as well as natural resource conditions in China, and international yields and conditions. Yield growth rates for the 24 minor crops for which published data are available (data not shown) were determined by evaluation of past growth rates, domestic and international demand and markets, and technology adoption by farmers and international yields. Sown areas for each were set by consideration of past growth rates, comparison of the impact on total production by yield increases and probable demand for them.

China's yields in the major crops are generally lower than in most economically developed countries, with the exception of cotton and wheat. For example, maize yield in the United States averaged 9,491 kg in 2007, while in China it was 44 per cent less, 6,674 kg. Maize yields in China grew a relatively slow 1.0 per cent annually from 2000–2007 but are projected to grow an average of 2.1 per cent annually over the next 20 years. However, even at that rate the yield would only reach 8,701 kg, 8 per cent below the US yield in 2007. The point is that comparison of the yield projections for 2030 among the ten major crops with five other countries in 2007 reveal projections for China are very conservative considering the potential for yield increases due to advances in biotechnology and agricultural restructuring.

Land use

Land reclamation and structural production improvement led to sown (harvested) area remaining about the same between 2000 and 2007 (about 155 million ha) despite considerable cultivated land having been converted to non-agricultural uses (data not shown). Sown area is projected to increase slightly to 2015, and then decline at an accelerated rate to 153 million ha in 2030. The multiple crop index, meaning the number of times cropland is used annually, grew from 1.17 in 1995, to 1.22 in 2000, and 1.28 in 2007. Clearly, there will come a time when the index can no longer rise. A conservative path was followed, with the index only projected to increase to 1.32 by 2030. The result is cultivated cropland needed to attain the projected crop production could decline from 121.8 million ha in 2007, to 116.2 million ha in 2030, a reasonable amount considering conversion of land to non-agricultural uses.

The implications of the sown/cultivated area analysis are that, as irrigation water becomes scarcer placing greater constraints on crop yield growth, it will be imperative that crop research and extension continue to be expanded, and technology adoption accelerated, if China is to meet increased demand for food and animal feedstuffs. In particular, given the projected shortfall in protein, it would appear that research should be focused on oilseed

Table 20.5 Growth rate in technology and adoption, and yield per hectare of major crops, China economy robust, 1994–1996 to 2030 and comparison with other countries

	Seed cotton	*Maize*	*Rape seed*	*Paddy rice*	*Sorghum*	*Soybean*	*Wheat*	*Barley*	*Triticale*	*Ground nuts*
Growth rate in technology										
Compound annual growth rate yield in per cent										
1994–96 to 2006–08	–0.21	0.67	2.59	0.54	0.66	–0.57	2.24	2.75	–9.33	1.50
1999–2001 to 2006–08	1.81	1.00	1.59	0.22	3.12	–0.42	1.64	2.10	–9.76	0.73
2006–08 to 2015	1.00	2.05	1.50	1.20	1.45	1.30	1.55	1.65	1.45	1.45
2015 to 2020	0.90	2.05	1.40	1.20	1.00	2.10	1.20	1.50	1.40	0.90
2020 to 2030	0.50	2.25	1.00	0.45	1.00	2.25	0.95	1.00	1.40	0.55
Yield per hectare										
1994–1996	1,500	4,939	1,359	6,018	4,314	1,722	3,567	2,696	3,077	2,682
1999–2001	1,179	4,748	1,528	6,250	3,230	1,690	3,830	2,910	3,257	2,938
2006–2008	1,462	5,350	1,847	6,418	4,670	1,608	4,654	3,734	950	3,206
2015	1,583	6,293	2,081	7,061	5,240	1,782	5,264	4,256	1,065	3,597
2020	1,656	6,965	2,231	7,495	5,507	1,978	5,587	4,585	1,142	3,762
2030	1,741	8,701	2,464	7,839	6,084	2,471	6,141	5,065	1,313	3,974
Per cent										
Increase 2006–2008 to 2030										
Total	19.0	62.6	33.4	22.1	30.3	53.7	31.9	35.6	38.2	24.0
Compound annual	0.8	2.1	1.3	0.9	1.2	1.9	1.2	1.3	1.4	0.9
Kg										
Yield per ha 2006–2008										
China	1,462	5,350	1,847	6,418	4,670	1,608	4,654	3,734	950	3,206
Argentina	0	6,674	1,446	6,816	4,709	2,824	2,473	3,409	0	2,554
Germany	3,749	9,096	3,644	0	0	1,000	7,416	5,809	5,637	0
Japan	0	2,556	1,306	6,445	0	1,630	4,093	3,472	0	2,283
United Kingdom	0	0	3,227	0	0	0	7,847	5,850	4,276	0
United States	2,318	9,491	1,445	7,832	4,064	2,746	2,778	3,311	0	3,519

Source: Simpson, modeling results

crops and adjustments in planting them, and expanded use of crop residues rather than energy-oriented grain crops.

The projections of total production of cereal crops, following the People's Republic of China (PRC) definition, are for expansion from 463 million tons in 2007 to 559 million tons in 2020, and 629 million tons in 2030. Coarse grains are projected to grow from 163 million tons in 2007 to 268 million tons by 2030 (using the international and USDA definition of coarse grains). Oilseed crop production, following the PRC definition, is projected to grow from 27 million tons in 2007, to just 32 million tons in 2030, a 19 per cent increase, unless there is some policy to shift more resources into additional oilseed crop production to meet projected protein shortfalls. There was a slight decline in oilseed production from 2000 to 2007.

Crop production, trade, and crop residues

China produced 14.6 million tons of soybeans in 2007 and had net imports of 31.5 million tons, resulting in total consumption of 46 million tons. Production in 2015 is projected to be 16.4 million tons, net imports in the model were specified at 39.6 million tons, from which the additional soybean equivalents are calculated to be 8.7 million tons. Soybean equivalent imports are calculated to be 57.8 million tons in 2020, and 55.4 million tons in 2030.

Energy is an entirely different story. China produced 156.7 million tons of maize in 2007, and had just 843 tons of net imports. It is projected that production will be 187.3 million tons in 2015, and that imports will be a net 1.0 million tons. That projection is verified by the calculated energy surplus being equivalent to a whopping 30.1 million tons of maize. Something has to happen to that surplus, but what? Most of it will be in the form of crop residues, so market forces are one likely mitigating factor. Unneeded stover can be burned, used as fuel and, as increasingly researched in pilot projects, converted into biofuels. Government policy is particularly critical since the maize equivalent surplus – provided there are no major use changes – is projected to double five years later in 2020, to 62 million tons, and to reach 98 million tons in 2030.

Crop residues, part of what are known as non-conventional feed resources (NCFR), really are the heart of understanding animal feedstuffs use in China. Most of the more minor NCFR such as processing waste from canning fruit are included in the by-products category in the modeling. Residues, a major source of both energy and protein,[7] were calculated to have accounted for 38 per cent of ME and 28 per cent of CP availabilities as feedstuffs (in effect, utilization, fed to animals) in 2007. Among them, wheat accounted for 16 per cent, rice 18 per cent (from straw) and maize (stover) 36 per cent for a total of 70 per cent of protein from all residues. Other residues include vines, roots and tubers, other field crops, vegetables, tree crops, and non-crop sources.

In 2007, 947 million tons of roughages were produced in China, of which 417 million tons, 44 per cent, were fed to animals. The remainder was burned in the field, used as fuel, and for making cellulosic products such as paper. The proportions of roughages produced are projected to change over time. For example, in 2007 vines, straw, and stover accounted

7 Maize stover contains 1.9 Mcal per kg. It can be increased 30 per cent to 2.5 Mcal by treating it to improve quality and palatability. It contains 5.4 per cent protein, which can be increased 50 per cent to 8.0 per cent with treatment, about the same as maize grain. China has a large program for treatment of crop residues. About one-fifth of all maize stover is treated.

for 83 per cent of roughages, and silage 17 per cent. It is projected that by 2030, silage will account for 27 per cent of the total.

China as an agricultural superpower

The long-term, science-based research on China presented in this chapter reveals a very different scenario than that expressed by pundits described in this chapter. For example, since 1995, China has become a significant net exporter of cereals in most years. It has been a major net corn exporter for the past two decades, with relatively minor imports of 3 million MT in 1995, and about 1 million MT in 2009 and 2010. China logged net exports of 15 million MT in 2002 and 8 million in 2003 and 2007. It has been a net wheat exporter several of the past years and is a regular rice exporter.

A main message in this chapter is that China's crop and animal productivity is still quite low. Mr. Brown and others act as though technology is standing still. But the reality is that the impact of biotechnology, combined with institutional and farm management change, will provide for dramatic increases in yields that will lift China's crop production significantly higher than the ones presented in this chapter. For example, globally, Pioneer Hi-bred is targeting a 40 per cent yield increase in corn and soybeans over the next 10 years. Monsanto projects doubling of corn and soybean yields by 2030. Monsanto and China are taking steps to launch drought-resistant corn, and China – as a leader in biotechnology – has an array of genetically modified crops awaiting government approval.

So what about water?[8] Of potential concern is that the dry North China Plain has become China's grain belt, relying heavily on groundwater; and that urban sprawl is occupying productive farmland and taking water from agriculture which in China, as in the rest of the world, is economically one of the lowest value uses of water. Yet here, too, productivity has come to the rescue, and is likely to continue to do so. Total agricultural water use has fallen from 392 billion cbm in 1997 to about 360 billion cbm at present. At the same time, China's farmers are getting more crop per drop, with water productivity (the amount of crop per ton of water) increasing at a rate of 2.67 per cent per year over the past two decades. There is still great potential for saving water as it becomes scarcer, even if this rate of productivity slows.

One factor in China's favor is its commitment to putting funds into agricultural and water research and extension – widely recognized as critical to maintaining productivity and competitiveness. Add to this major investments in water infrastructure, such as the south to north canal. China seeks to continue producing 95 per cent of its own food, despite its commitments to expanding free trade in agriculture under the World Trade Organization (WTO). We see no reason that China's agricultural superpower status will change in the foreseeable future. Indeed, it makes as much sense to pose the question whether China can afford to feed the United States.

China's rights and obligations regarding agriculture and food

Regardless of how the WTO negotiations on the Doha Development Agenda (DDA) of multilateral trade negotiations turn out, the crucial issues at stake are part of the larger

8 Thanks for this section go to Shaofeng Jia, Chair of the Water and Land Resource Department of the Institute of Geographical Sciences and Natural Resources Research, Chinese Academy of Sciences, and James E. Nickum, a China specialist, Secretary-General of the International Water Resources Association, and Editor-in-Chief of *Water International*.

controversy over management of globalization so that domestic and international social and political stability will be improved. This is the overriding issue of our time, and agricultural trade can be viewed as a philosophical heart of the matter. The social concerns and tensions arising from this process must not be overlooked. This is what is meant by calls for "balance" by many developing nations – and by economically developed countries that are substantial net food importers. China's use of its superpower status is a case in point.

The excesses of globalization regarding food and agriculture can be managed only by paying adequate attention to what are termed "Non-Trade Concerns" (NTCs), and those concerns then taken into account in regional and bilateral negotiations as well as international ones.[9] To some, including many trade theorists and net food exporting countries, NTCs are simply trade protectionism in disguise. China's approach to food security, which is essentially based on "rights" to a very high level of nationally determined self-sufficiency ratio, is a case in point. To others, particularly economically developed net food-importing countries exemplified by the G-10 Group at risk of basically losing their agricultural sector (the other two are manufacturing and services) under heavy trade liberalization, it truly is a major issue that cannot be made without careful consideration of long-term consequences.[10] The issues on NTCs in the Doha Round are not perused now.[11] Rather, the issue that forms a central part of obligations China will, and should face, as it moves from Newly Industrialized Country (NIC) status to Developed Country status, is what I term "trade prisoner risk."

Japan serves as a useful example of why China must recognize its obligations for *fair and equitable treatment* of trade partners set forth in the Preamble of the Doha Agenda's precursor, the Uruguay Round of Agricultural Trade Negotiations, as its agricultural superpower status grows. Japan's food self-sufficiency rate is now 40 per cent. Its production costs are so high that any meaningful reduction in tariffs of rice, dairy, and other commodities would result in a 15–20 per cent level. In essence, it would essentially lose its agricultural sector and much of its food subsector.

Economic efficiency is a value, and it is a good value. However, ethically and legally it should be balanced against other values, and it should not violate human rights. The concept that "peoples" and countries, regardless of whether they are rich or poor, have a right to use their natural resources in the way they feel best meets their needs, desires, and values serves

9 Non-Trade Concerns and specific issues such as multifunctionality, non-economic values, and rights to self-determination in production and consumption of food are taken up in-depth in ***Non-Trade Concerns in WTO Agricultural Trade Negotiations: Conflict Resolution in the Doha Development Agenda***, Special Issue, INT'L J. AGRIC. RESOURCES, GOVERNANCE & ECOLOGY (James R. Simpson ed., 2005). Contact the editor at jamesrsimpson@gmail.com.

10 Article 13 of the Doha Development Agenda Ministerial Declaration states: "We agree that special and differential treatment for developing countries shall be an integral element of all elements of the negotiations [. . .]." Further, "we take note of the non-trade concerns reflected in the negotiating proposals submitted by the Members and confirm that non-trade concerns will be taken into account in the negotiations as provided for in the Agreement on Agriculture." It is important to realize that in addition to developing countries like China, the mandate covers economically developed countries such as those in the so-called G-10 group (Iceland, Israel, Japan, South Korea, Liechtenstein, Norway, Switzerland, and Taiwan, plus Mauritius. Bulgaria had been a member but withdrew before it joined the EU). See World Trade Organization, Ministerial Declaration of 14 November 2001, WT/MIN(01)/DEC/1, 41 I.L.M. 746 (2002) [hereinafter Doha Declaration].

11 *See* also James R. Simpson & Thomas J. Schoenbaum, ***Non-Trade Concerns in WTO Trade Negotiations: Legal and Legitimate Reasons for Revising the "Box" System***, 3/4 INT'L J. AGRIC. RESOURCES, GOVERNANCE & ECOLOGY 399–410 (2003).

as the basis for the G-10's argument that they have the right to reserve for *special treatment* certain "sensitive" and "special" agricultural products.

There are several international covenants such as The Universal Declaration of Human Rights,[12] and a later document promulgated by the United Nations called the International Covenant on Economic, Social and Cultural Rights[13] (ICESCR) that provide a human rights framework for NTCs related to food and agriculture. It was brought into effect in 1966 and, as of July 2014, had 162 parties (paradoxically, China signed the agreement while six other countries, notably the United States, signed the agreement in 1977 but did not ratify it.). Several sections pertain to food strategies by G-10 countries. Article 1 states: "All peoples have the right of self-determination. By virtue of that right they freely determine their political status and freely pursue their economic, social and cultural development. All Peoples may, for their own ends, freely dispose of their natural wealth and resources without prejudice to any obligations arising out of international economic cooperation, based upon the principle of mutual benefit, and international law. In no case may a people be deprived of its own means of subsistence."[14]

There is also Article 6, which says: "The States Parties to the present Covenant recognize the right to work, which includes the right of everyone to the opportunity to gain his living by work which he freely chooses or accepts, and will take appropriate steps to safeguard this right."[15] Common sense says improvement of economic welfare through international trade shifts will lead to losers in some countries and gainers in others. But this is different than imposition of regulations worldwide that could eventually emasculate a whole sector of a country's economy, or at least most of it.

Article 11 deals specifically with food by saying: "The States Parties to the present covenant recognize the right of everyone to an adequate standard of living for himself and his family, including adequate food, clothing and housing, and to the continuous improvement of living conditions."[16] Certainly the term "continuous improvement of living conditions" must include the right to a nationally decided level of domestic food production (as China does) as part of living a stress-free life. This aspect is further reinforced in Article 11, which also exhorts States Parties to take into account "the problems of both food-importing and food-exporting countries, to ensure an equitable distribution of food supplies in relation to need."[17] This article should be enough to show that a "true level playing field" (a term often used by the agricultural exporting countries bent on drastic market opening measures) should include, for example, the right for countries to set the minimum domestic food production levels they want as an integral part of fair and equitable agricultural trade rules.

So, what about Japan's trade prisoner risk – and conceptually that of other countries in the Asian region in a decade or two in relation to China?[18] Japan's cost of Japonica rice

12 Universal Declaration of Human Rights, GA Res. 217 (III) A, UN Doc. A/RES/217(III) (December 10, 1948).

13 International Covenant on Economic, Social and Cultural Rights, GA Res. 2200A (XXI), 21 UN GAOR Supp. No. 16 , UN Doc. A/6316 (1966), 993 UNTS 3, at 49, (January 3, 1976).

14 *Ibid.*, Article 1.

15 *Ibid.*, Article 6.

16 *Ibid.*, Article 11.

17 *Ibid.*

18 Consider ASEAN (the Association of Southeast Asian Nations), which consists of 10 member states. There is much effort focusing on better integration of it with what is known as ASEAN Plus Three Countries (China, Japan, and South Korea).

production is six times greater than in China.[19] Japan's milk production cost is US Dollars (USD) 0.62 per kg compared with USD 0.16 per kg on a medium-size farm in Jilin Province near the Sea of Japan.[20] If tariff levels are set too low, Japan will have crossed a bridge with no return and they will be a prisoner to one system. While loss of human, capital, and other resources is an integral aspect of "trade prisoner risk," a very real problem is the potential for disruptions in exports of specialized commodities and products such as Japonica rice, as well as a whole host of foods not traded internationally, or which may ultimately only be available from a neighboring country specializing in it. For example, what happens if the producing country suddenly becomes bellicose with the other and halts food shipments, or shuts off exports due to production problems, as in the case of the 2010 wheat crisis?

The point of all this is that food and agricultural commodities are not immune to use as weapons, deterrents and threats in policy application. In effect, with its technical and infrastructure development in agricultural and food production, China will increasingly have the power to influence trade decisions and leverage that power as it develops economically. The reality is that simply relying on it to be a "good neighbor" or "to do the right thing and be nice" is unrealistic, as is the case of most countries. The solution to its obligations as an agricultural superpower is to fight for the right of all countries to identify "special" and "sensitive" commodities to protect their agricultural and food security just as China has and will, in all likelihood, continue to do. China's economic and social development confer on it the obligation – as an agricultural superpower – to accept leadership in assuring that globalization does not lead to trade-prisoner risks by a nation regardless of size, level of economic development, or structure of its agricultural sector.

19 Shoichi Ito, Mark W. Rosegrant & Mercedita C. Agcoaoili-Sombilla, *Quality and Production Cost Oriented Measurement of International Competitiveness – Is U.S. Rice Feasible in the Japanese Market?* (Paper presented at the 1995 Southern Agricultural Economics Association Meeting, January 30 – February 1, 1995).

20 James R. Simpson. *Future of the Dairy Industries in China, Japan and the United States: Conflict Resolution in the Doha Round of WTO Agricultural trade Negotiations* (Afrasian Centre for Peace and Development Studies, Ryukoku University, Kyoto Japan, Working Paper Series No. 1, 2005). As audacious as it might seem, but a perfect example of technological development is that conceptually fresh fluid milk slurry can be flown to Tokyo for recombining with water competitive or cheaper than the same product transported there from domestic production areas.

21 China and the Recognition and Protection of the Human Right to Water**

*Roberto Soprano**

Introduction

Water is becoming increasingly a source of concern for China. Its per capita availability of drinking water is very low, and water resources are not well distributed throughout the country. They are mainly concentrated in Southern China and in Tibet, while in Northern China groundwater is being depleted. In addition, pollution has led to the deterioration of the quality of surface and ground water, aggravating existing water shortages.

The transformation of China's economy from agriculture-based to industry-based has caused a rapid shift of the geography of water demand. The relocation of a significant percentage of the population from rural to urban areas has a deep impact on the quantity and quality of water available, in particular for rural areas, as well as on water policies throughout the whole country.

The recognition and protection of a right to water has been debated in several international law fora. The Human Rights Council[1] and the United Nations (UN) General Assembly, as well as many scholars and non-governmental organizations (NGOs), have started to

* I am extremely grateful to Prof. Paolo Davide Farah for the helpful comments and suggestions. The author gratefully acknowledges the contribution of Imad Ibrahim (gLAWcal – Global Law Initiatives for Sustainable Development) for his research assistance. All errors, of course, remain mine.

** This chapter is part of the results of the Research Project on "*Current Trends of Chinese Law towards Non-Trade Concerns such as Sustainable Development and the Protection of Environment, Public Health, Food Safety, Cultural, Social and Economic Rights, Labor Rights and the Reduction of Poverty from the Perspective of International Law and WTO Law*", coordinated by Professor Paolo Davide Farah at gLAWcal – Global Law Initiatives for Sustainable Development (United Kingdom) and at West Virginia University John D. Rockefeller IV School of Policy and Politics, Department of Public Administration, in partnership with the Center of Advanced Studies on Contemporary China (CASCC) in Turin (Italy), Maastricht University Faculty of Law, Department of International and European Law and IGIR – Institute for Globalisation and International Regulation (Netherlands), and Tsinghua University, School of Law, Institute of Public International Law and the Center for Research on Intellectual Property Law in Beijing (China). An early draft of this chapter was presented at the Conferences Series on "*China's Influence on Non-Trade Concerns in International Economic Law*", First Conference held at the Center of Advanced Studies on Contemporary China (CASCC) in Turin on November 23–24, 2011. This publication and the Conference Series were sponsored by China–EU School of Law (CESL) at the China University of Political Science and Law (CUPL). The activities of CESL at CUPL are supported by the European Union and the People's Republic of China.

1 The Human Rights Council is an intergovernmental body within the UN system and is responsible for strengthening the promotion and protection of human rights around the globe. The Council was created by the UN General Assembly Resolution 60/251, UN Doc. A/RES/60/251 (March 15, 2006) with the aim of addressing situations of human rights violations and make recommendations on them.

focus on the right to water. In 2010, China voted in favor of a UN General Assembly resolution to recognize the right to water as a human right. Like all other human rights, the right to water contains both rights and duties. It thus provides rights to Chinese citizens to have access to water and obliges the People's Republic of China (PRC) to take all necessary measures to implement such right. Accordingly, the right to water imposes a burden on China to develop new policies and rules to supply and ensure safe drinking water for its population, which might have an impact on current water diversion projects.

This chapter aims to describe China's attitude towards the protection of the human right to water, in particular by preventing pollution to ensure access to safe drinking water and by guaranteeing the "equal" enjoyment or exercise of this right in urban and rural areas.

The right to water and China

The lack or contamination of water is the greatest cause of human death in the world.[2] More than 1.1 billion people do not have access to drinking water, and more than 2.4 billion people suffer from different forms of illness caused by contaminated water. Water scarcity also presents a problem in China.[3] Approximately a quarter of its territory is classified as desert, in many areas groundwater is overexploited, and most of the rivers are too polluted to provide the 1.3 billion Chinese people with adequate supplies of freshwater.[4] Although total water flows from all surface and underground sources, in 2010 China[5] ranked sixth in the world behind Brazil, Russia, Canada, Indonesia, and the US; on an annual per capita basis, China's water flow ranks as one of the lowest.[6] As reported in World Bank studies, "China's per capita availability of water is exceedingly low, suggesting the potential for water stress as demand for usable water rises with growth in population and in per capita incomes."[7]

According to the data of a World Health Organization (WHO)/UNICEF Joint Monitoring Program for Water Supply and Sanitation, access to improved water sources for the

2 Lindsay Knight, The Right to Water 6 (World Health Organization, 2003).

3 As noted by Shalizi, using the per capita definition of the UNDP, UNEP, World Bank, WRI China should be classified as water stressed by 2010 at the current rate of population growth. Using the classification of the International Water Management Institute, China currently uses 44 per cent of its water and is still within the "comfortable" water use margin, but its use of water is projected to exceed 60 per cent by 2028, putting it in the "environmentally overexploited" category. Thus, by either definition, China will face a potentially serious water management problem in the coming decades. Zmarak Shalizi, ***Addressing China's Growing Water Shortages and Associated Social and Environmental Consequences***, 5 (World Bank Policy Research Working Paper No. 3895, 2006). *See* also, Todd Johnson, Feng Liu & Richard S. Newfarmer, Clear Water, Blue Skies: China's Environment in the New Century 87–102 (World Bank Publications, 1997).

4 Keith Schneider et al., *China, Tibet, and the Strategic Power of Water* (May 8, 2008), http://www.circleofblue.org/waternews/2008/world/china-tibet-and-the-strategic-power-of-water/ (last visited July 3, 2016).

5 Food and Agriculture Organization of the United Nations, China, Water Resources, http://www.fao.org/nr/water/aquastat/countries_regions/Profile_segments/CHN-WR_eng.stm (last visited July 3, 2016).

6 Zmarak Shalizi, *supra* note 3, at 4.

7 China's per capita naturally available water per annum is one-third of the average of the developing countries (7,762 m^3/person), one-fourth of the world average (8,549 m^3/person), and almost one-fifth of the US average (10,332 m^3/person). The UNDP, UNEP, World Bank, and the World Resources Institute define "water stress" on a per capita basis as annual water availability of 2,000 m^3/person or less. In this framework "water scarcity" is defined as 1,000 m^3/person or less. *Ibid.*

Chinese population has increased significantly in the past two decades.[8] Thanks to the 1990–2008 investments, which followed the country's economic growth, a high number of Chinese people gained access to improved water sources; however, increased fecal contamination and growing industrial and agricultural chemical pollution continued to make some water unsafe for drinking.[9] China experiences inefficiencies in water resources management and gross pollution "to the point that vast stretches of rivers are dead and dying, lakes are cesspools of waste, groundwater aquifers are over-pumped and unsustainably consumed, uncounted species of aquatic life have been driven to extinction, and direct adverse impacts on both human and ecosystem health are widespread and growing."[10] In addition, water conditions and availability in urban and rural areas in China differ significantly.[11] Ninety-six per cent of urban inhabitants have access to a piped water supply, while only 76 per cent of rural inhabitants enjoy similar conditions.[12] The recent development of the recognition of the right to water in international law may have a positive impact on water access for the Chinese population; however, the shift of the international regime alone will not solve China's water problems.

In recent times, scholars, officials, and practitioners have debated about the existence in international law of a human right to water, but not until the last few years did international organizations start to take action.[13] In June 2010, the UN General Assembly adopted a resolution formally recognizing the right to water and sanitation.[14] General Assembly

8 UNICEF and WHO, Joint Monitoring Program for Water Supply and Sanitation: Estimates for the use of Improved Sanitation Facilities, updated March 2010, China and Estimates for the use of Improved Water Facilities, updated March 2010, http://www.wssinfo.org/ (last visited July 3, 2016).

9 Ministry of Water Resources, *China to Invest US$303 billon in Water Projects*, (January 21, 2011), http://www.china.org.cn/china/2011-01/21/content_21793211.htm (last visited July 3, 2016) and *China to Spend 12b Yuan on Tibet's Water Projects*, China Daily (August 16, 2011), http://www.chinadaily.com.cn/bizchina/2011-08/16/content_13124732.htm (last visited July 3, 2016). Jeffrey Hays, *Water Pollution in China* (2008). *See* also, Gang Chen, Politics of China's Environmental Protection: Problems and Progress 1–6 (World Scientific, 2009). *See* Chapter 12 (He) in this volume.

10 Peter Gleick, *China and Water*, in The World's Water 2008–2009: The Biennial Report on Freshwater Resources 432 (Peter H. Gleick, Heather Cooley & Mari Morikawa, eds, 2008). *See* also, Liang Chao, *Experts Warn of Water Crisis*, China Daily (April 20, 2005), http://www.chinadaily.com.cn/english/doc/2005-04/20/content_435724.htm (last visited July 3, 2016).

11 Availability in the North is about a quarter of that in the South, 757 m^3/person vs. 3,208 m^3/person, respectively, and a tenth of the world average. The 757 m^3/person in the North in 2003 qualifies the North as a whole as an area of "water scarcity," which is a condition worse than "water stress." Yet the North is a very large area. It is home to roughly 42 per cent of China's population in 2003, that is, 538 million people (greater than the total population in Europe or in Latin America), with access to only 14 per cent of China's water resources. Zmarak Shalizi, *supra* note 3, at 5. *See* also, Jian Xie, Addressing China's Water Scarcity: Recommendations for Selected Water Resource Management Issues 9–24 (World Bank Publications, 2009).

12 Zmarak Shalizi, *supra* note 3, at 5.

13 Peter Gleick, *The Human Right to Water,* 1 Water Pol. 487, 487–503 (1998); Helen Greatrex, *The Human Right to Water* in Human Rights Research (Paul Morris and Helen Greatrex eds, Victoria University, Wellington, 2004); Erik B. Bluemel, *The Implications of Formulating a Human Right to Water*, 31 Ecology L. Q. 957, 957–1005 (2004); Dinara Ziganshina, *Rethinking the Concept of the Human Right to Water,* 6 Santa Clara J. Int'l L. 113, 113–128 (2008); Stephen C. McCaffrey, *The Human Right to Water*, in Fresh Water and International Economic Law 96 (Edith Brown Weiss, Laurence Boisson de Chazournes & Nathalie Bernasconi-Ostrewalder eds, Oxford University Press, 2005); Stephen C. McCaffrey, *Human Right to Water: Domestic and International Implications,* 5 Geo. Int'l Envtl. L. Rev. 1, 1–12 (1992).

14 *The Human Right to Water and Sanitation,*GA Res. 64/292, UN Doc. A/RES/64/292 (August 3, 2010). *See* also, General Assembly press release, *General Assembly Adopts Resolution Recognizing Access*

Resolution 64/292 acknowledges that clean drinking water and sanitation are integral to the realization of all human rights. In September 2010, the Human Rights Council adopted a resolution by consensus affirming that existing international law recognizes the right to water and sanitation.[15] However, the resolutions of the UN Human Rights Council and the General Assembly are forms of soft law and thus do not have binding effects.

Under existing binding law, water considerations are relevant to the supply of water to children, women, prisoners, and civilians during wartime. Article 14 of the Convention on the Elimination of All Forms of Discrimination against Women sets forth that States Parties shall guarantee to women the right to enjoy adequate living conditions, particularly in relation to housing, sanitation, electricity, and water supply.[16] According to the Convention on the Rights of the Child, States Parties shall take adequate measures to combat diseases and malnutrition, including within the framework of primary health care, through, ***inter alia***, the application of readily available technology and through the provision of adequate nutritious foods and clean drinking water.[17] Article 127 of the Geneva Convention (IV) sets forth that "the Detaining Power shall supply internees during transfer with drinking water."[18] However, these treaties create rights which are tailored and limited to specific subjects and are not addressed to all human beings.[19]

Even in the alleged absence of an explicit recognition of a human right to water in international law, it is unreasonable to conclude that international law does not protect access to drinking water.[20] Certain articles of the International Covenant on Economic, Social and

---

to Clean Water, Sanitation as Human Right, by Recorded Vote of 122 in Favour, None against, 41 Abstentions, Doc. GA/10967, July 28, 2010.

15 *Human Rights and Access to Safe Drinking Water and Sanitation*, UN Doc. A/HRC/15/L.14 (September 30, 2010).

16 *Convention on the Elimination of All Forms of Discrimination against Women*, GA Res. 34/180, 34 UN GAOR Supp. No. 46, at 193, UN Doc. A/34/46 (September 3, 1981), Article 14 ¶ 2(*h*). China signed it on July 17, 1980 and ratified it on November 4, 1980.

17 Convention on the Rights of the Child, GA res. 44/25, annex, 44 UN GAOR Supp. No. 49, at 167, UN Doc. A/44/49 (September 2, 1990), Article 24 ¶ 2(*c*). China signed it on August 29, 1990 and ratified it on March 2, 1992.

18 Geneva Convention relative to the Treatment of Prisoners of War arts. 20, 26, 29, and 46, August 12, 1949, 75 UNTS 135. *See* also Geneva Convention relative to the Protection of Civilian Persons in Time of War, arts. 85, 89, and 127, August 12, 1949, 75 UNTS 287. Additional Protocol I, arts. 54 and 55 (June 8, 1977); Additional Protocol II, arts. 5 and 14, (June 8, 1977).

19 The right to water is mentioned in other documents, including: the preamble of the Mar Del Plata Action Plan of the United Nations Water Conference (United Nations Water Conference, Mar del Plata, March 14–25, 1977, *Mar Del Plata Action Plan*, UN Doc. E/CONF.70/29). Paragraph 18.47 of Agenda 21, United Nations Conference on Environment and Development, Rio de Janeiro, Brazil, June 3–14, 1992, *Rio Declaration on Environment and Development*, UN Doc. A/CONF.151/26/Rev.1 (Vol. I), Annex II (August 12, 1992); Principle No. 3 of the Dublin Statement on Water and Sustainable Development (International Conference on Water and the Environment, Dublin, January 26–31, 1992, *Dublin Statement on Water and Sustainable Development*, UN Doc. A/CONF.151/PC/112); Principle No. 2 of the Programme of Action of the United Nations International Conference on Population and Development, Cairo, September 5–13, 1994, UN Doc. A/CONF.17/13 (chap. I), Res. I, Annex. Paragraphs 5 and 19 of the Recommendation Rec (2001)14 of the Committee of Ministers to Member States on the European Charter on Water Resources. Resolution 2002/6 of the United Nations Sub-Commission on the Promotion and Protection of Human Rights on the promotion of the realization of the right to drinking water.

20 Although the human right to water specifically addresses access to water for personal and domestic use, water is required for a range of different purposes and to realize many of the Covenant rights. For instance, water is necessary to produce food (right to adequate food) and ensure environmental hygiene (right to health). Water is essential for securing livelihoods (right to gain a living by work) and enjoying

Cultural Rights (ICESCR), a binding agreement to which China is party, implicitly recognize a right to water.[21] According to General Comment No. 15, the right to water constitutes an element of the right to adequate living standards and the right to food and health.[22] General Comment No. 15 is a non-binding but authoritative interpretation of Articles 11 and 12 of the ICESCR, issued by the Committee on Economic, Social and Cultural Rights in 2002, according to which the human right to water entitles everyone to sufficient, safe, acceptable, physically accessible, and affordable water for personal and domestic use.[23] Thus, Chinese citizens hold a right to have access to water, which must be adequate, in terms of "availability,"[24] "quality,"[25] and "accessibility,"[26] for human dignity, life, and health in a non-discriminatory manner. In addition to having access to water for personal and domestic use, they also hold the right to have access to water for agricultural purposes, which are necessary to realize the right to food.[27]

The right to water and the obligations for the People's Republic of China

Like any other right, the right to water imposes on States Parties various obligations. In particular, it imposes three types of specific legal obligations: the obligations to *respect*, *protect*, and *fulfill*.[28]

---

certain cultural practices (right to take part in cultural life). Substantive Issues Arising in the Implementation of the International Covenant on Economic, Social and Cultural Rights, General Comment No. 15, UN ESCOR Comm. On Econ., Soc. & Cultural Rights, 29th Sess., Agenda Item 3, UN Doc. E/C.12/2002/11 (2002) [hereinafter General Comment No. 15], ¶ 6.

21 International Covenant on Economic, Social and Cultural Rights, GA Res. 2200A (XXI), 21 UN GAOR Supp. No. 16 , UN Doc. A/6316 (1966), 993 UNTS 3, at 49 (January 3, 1976). China signed it on October 27, 1997 and ratified it March 27, 2001. *See* Chapters 5 (Choukroune), 18 (Zorzi), and 19 (Ning) in this volume.

22 Dinara Ziganshina, *supra* note 13.

23 The right to water contains both freedoms and entitlements. The freedoms include the right to maintain access to existing water supplies necessary for the right to water, and the right to be free from interference, such as the right to be free from arbitrary disconnections or contamination of water supplies. By contrast, the entitlements include the right to a system of water supply and management that provides equality of opportunity for people to enjoy the right to water. General Comment No. 15, ¶ 10.

24 Water supply for each person must be sufficient and continuous for personal and domestic use including drinking, personal sanitation, washing of clothes, food preparation, personal, and household hygiene. The quantity of water available for each person should correspond to World Health Organization (WHO) guidelines. *Ibid.* ¶ 12(a).

25 Water must be safe, and thus free from micro-organisms, chemical substances, and radiological hazards that constitute a threat to a person's health. Furthermore, water should be of an acceptable color, odor, and taste for each personal or domestic use. *Ibid.* ¶ 12(b).

26 Water and water facilities and services have to be accessible to everyone without discrimination, within the jurisdiction of the State party. Water, and adequate water facilities and services, must be the following: a) *physically accessible* (water, and adequate water facilities and services, must be within safe physical reach for all sections of the population) b) *economically accessible* (affordable for all); c) *non-discriminatory* (accessible to all, including the most vulnerable or marginalized sections of the population); and d) *information accessible* (which includes the right to seek, receive and impart information concerning water issues). *Ibid.* ¶ 12(c).

27 *Ibid.* ¶ 7. *See* Chapters 18 (Zorzi Giustiniani), 19 (Ning), and 20 (Simpson) in this volume.

28 General legal obligations mainly require States to guarantee that the right will be exercised without discrimination and take steps towards the full realization of article 11, ¶¶ 1, and 12 ICESCR. General Comment No. 15, ¶¶ 17–19.

The first obligation – to *respect* – requires parties to refrain from interfering directly or indirectly with the enjoyment of the right to water. As reported in General Comment No. 15, this entails, ***inter alia,*** refraining from engaging in any practice or activity that denies or limits "equal" access to adequate water.[29] Thus, one of the main objectives of the right to water is to ensure that States provide "equal" opportunity for people to enjoy the right, such as by avoiding differential treatment between rural and urban areas.[30] This duty should also be read together with one of the nine "core obligations" which take immediate effect and requires States Parties to guarantee "equitable" distribution of all available water facilities and services.[31]

The obligation to *respect* is of particular concern to China and its water-diverting projects. China relies on large infrastructure projects to divert water from one region to another because the north and, in particular, the highly populated urban areas have limited water access. A recent project intending to provide water to northern areas – the so-called South-North Water Diversion Project – plans to divert around six trillion gallons of water from the south each year at a cost of 62 billion US dollars (USD).[32] The project calls for the construction of three artificial channels that would transport water from the Yangtze River, which flows through a southern region that is increasingly afflicted by droughts.[33] According to *The New York Times*, it is China's most ambitious attempt to subjugate nature.[34]

The South-North Water Diversion Project has been under consideration for over half a century, but because concerns about its cost and complexity had taken priority since its formulation, environmental concerns have only recently surfaced.[35] If, on the one hand, the

29 General Comment No. 15, ¶¶ 23–24.

30 *See*, for instance, General Comment No. 15, ¶¶ 10, 14, 16(c), 37 (f).

31 Core obligations in relation to the right to water which are of immediate effect: a) to ensure access to the minimum essential amount of water, that is sufficient and safe for personal and domestic use to prevent diseases; b) to ensure the right of access to water and water facilities and services on a non-discriminatory basis, especially for disadvantaged or marginalized groups; c) to ensure physical access to water facilities or services that provide sufficient, safe, and regular water; that have a sufficient number of water outlets to avoid prohibitive waiting times; and that are at a reasonable distance from the household; d) to ensure personal security is not threatened when having to physically access water; e) to ensure equitable distribution of all available water facilities and services; f) to adopt and implement a national water strategy and plan of action addressing the whole population; the strategy and plan of action should be devised, and periodically reviewed, on the basis of a participatory and transparent process; it should include methods, such as right to water indicators and benchmarks, by which progress can be closely monitored; the process by which the strategy and plan of action are devised, as well as their content, shall give particular attention to all disadvantaged or marginalized groups; g) to monitor the extent of the realization, or the non-realization, of the right to water; h) to adopt relatively low-cost targeted water programs to protect vulnerable and marginalized groups; i) to take measures to prevent, treat and control diseases linked to water, in particular ensuring access to adequate sanitation. General Comment No. 15, ¶ 37.

32 Jennifer Huang McBeath & Jerry McBeath, Environmental Change and Food Security in China 77 (Springer, 2010).

33 James E. Nickum, *The Status of the South to North Water Transfer Plans in China* (Additional Paper of the 2006 Human Development Report, 2006), http://hdr.undp.org/en/content/status-south-north-water-transfer-plans-china (last visited July 3, 2016). As noted by Nickum, South-North Water Transfer refers to three sets of diversions, the Eastern, Middle, and Western routes, each serving separate areas, with the exception of the coastal city of Tianjin, which will receive water from both the Eastern and Middle routes. The Eastern and Middle routes will pass under the Huang He, while the West routes will directly replenish the Huang.

34 Edward Wong, *Plan for China's Water Crisis Spurs Concern*, New York Times (June 1, 2011), http://www.nytimes.com/2011/06/02/world/asia/02water.html?_r=0 (last visited July 3, 2016).

35 Mao uttered: "Water in the south is abundant, water in the north scarce. If possible, it would be fine to borrow a little." *Ibid.*

project could help provide water to the cities' growing population, on the other hand, it would sacrifice the well-being of farmers in the province. Put another way, to quench the thirst of richer urban communities, the government would reduce the water supply to rural people, resulting in unequal water access for Chinese citizens.

To prepare for the new project, the Chinese government has relocated local villagers to other regions. According to official estimates, the project will displace between 300,000 and 400,000 people, mostly along the Middle Route.[36] In addition, in 2014 estimated costs rose to USD (US Dollars) 79.4 billion and may make it one of the most expensive civil engineering undertakings in history.[37]

The project will also have an adverse impact on water flows from other rivers, such as the Han River, essential to farming and industrial production as well as to energy policies, cultural relics, and regional ecosystems. Moreover, the right to water is strictly linked to the right to food, and, by depriving southern rural regions of the water they need, the government will reduce the possibility to source water for agriculture and food production.[38] In fact, water transfer started to occur since 2014 from Danjiangkou reservoir located on the border between Hubei and Henan provinces (Insert footnote: Huw Pohlner, Can China's South-North Water Transfer project and industry co-exist (Oct. 20, 2015), https://www.thethirdpole.net/2015/10/20/can-chinas-south-north-water-transfer-project-and-industry-co-exist/ (last visited July 3, 2016) to the capital and other cities. (Insert footnote: Codi Kozacek, Photo Slideshow: China Completes Second Line of South-North Water Transfer Project (Jan. 8, 2015), http://www.circleofblue.org/2015/world/photo-slideshow-china-completes-second-line-south-north-water-transfer/ (last visited July 3, 2016). Yet, several Chinese cities are not using the water due to the lack of infrastructure such as pumping stations and processing plants while others are still trying to figure out how to charge users for the consumption of the latter (Insert footnote: Te-Ping Chen, Cities in China's North Resist Tapping Water Piped From South (Apr. 23, 2015), http://www.wsj.com/articles/cities-in-chinas-north-resist-tapping-water-piped-from-south-1429781402 (last visited July 3, 2016).

Mutatis mutandis, similar concerns arose in relation to the planned diversion project to transfer water from the Tibetan Plateau to China's eastern cities. This new project will likely affect access to water in Tibet, intensify "domestic" (Tibet–China) frictions, and raise disputes with other neighboring countries such as India.[39]

The second obligation – to *protect* – requires States Parties to prevent third parties from interfering in any way with their citizens' enjoyment of the right to water. The obligation includes, *inter alia*, adopting the necessary and effective legislative measures, for example, to restrain third parties from polluting and inequitably extracting from water resources, including natural sources, wells, and other water distribution systems. The core obligations

36 James E. Nickum, *supra* note 33.

37 Gordon G. Chang, *China's Water Crisis Made Worse by Policy Failures*, (January 8, 2014) http://www.worldaffairsjournal.org/blog/gordon-g-chang/china%E2%80%99s-water-crisis-made-worse-policy-failures (last visited July 3, 2016).

38 Lester R. Brown, *Worsening Water Shortages Threaten China's Food Security* (October 4, 2001), http://www.earth-policy.org/plan_b_updates/2001/update1 (last visited July 3, 2016). *See* Chapters 19 (Ning) and 20 (Simpson) in this volume.

39 *The difficult relationship between India and China over the Brahmaputra River*, Asia News (July 11, 2011), http://www.asianews.it/news-en/The-difficult-relationship-between-India-and-China-over-the-Brahmaputra-River-22066.html (last visited July 3, 2016).

described in General Comment No. 15 also include the duty of the state to take measures to prevent and control diseases linked to water consumption.[40]

The obligation to ***protect*** has particular importance for China since it requires states to take all necessary measures to protect sources of freshwater, in particular, from pollution. China has some of the world's worst water pollution caused primarily by industrial waste, chemical fertilizers, and raw sewage.[41] According to scientific studies, about one-third of water from industrial waste and around 90 per cent of household sewage in China is released into rivers and lakes without treatment. Around 80 per cent of China's cities have no sewage treatment facilities and few have plans to build any.

New regulations seek to protect the environment, but lack of control and the absence of enforcement measures remain a huge problem, hampering the realization of the right.[42] It is not by chance that General Comment No. 15 lists, among several examples of violations of the obligation to protect, the failure to enforce relevant laws to prevent the contamination of water.[43]

The third obligation – to *fulfill* – is divided into the obligations to facilitate, promote, and provide. The obligation to *facilitate* requires States to take positive measures to assist individuals and communities to enjoy the right while the obligation to ***promote*** obliges States Parties to take steps to ensure that there is appropriate education concerning the hygienic use of water, protection of water sources, and methods to minimize water wastage. The obligation to ***provide*** obliges the States to provide the right when individuals or a group are unable, for reasons beyond their control, to realize that right for themselves by the means at their disposal.[44]

More generally, the obligation to *fulfill* requires States Parties to adopt necessary measures directed towards the full realization of the right to water. These measures should include the recognition of the right to water within the national political and legal systems, preferably by way of legislative implementation, adopting a national water strategy and plan of action to realize this right. These measures should also facilitate improved and sustainable access to water, particularly in rural and deprived urban areas.

China does not recognize the right to water at the constitutional level.[45] The Chinese Constitution establishes that the State shall ensure the rational use of natural resources and prohibits any organization or individual from damaging natural resources by whatever

40 General Comment No. 15, ¶ 37(e).

41 Greenpeace, *Water Pollution: the Dirty China Story* (October 13, 2009), http://www.greenpeace.org//eastasia/news/stories/toxics/2009/silent-giants-news/ (last visited July 3, 2016).

42 Jian Xie, ***supra*** note 11, at 121; The World Bank, ***Water Pollution Emergencies in China Prevention and Response*** (June 2007), available on the World Bank Website: http://siteresources.worldbank.org/INTEAPREGTOPENVIRONMENT/Resources/Water_Pollution_Emergency_Final_EN.pdf (last visited July 3, 2016). *See* Chapter 12 (He) in this volume.

43 General Comment No. 15, ¶ 44(b).

44 *Ibid.* ¶ 25.

45 Xianfa art. 9 (1982): mineral resources, waters, forests, mountains, grassland, unclaimed land, beaches, and other natural resources are owned by the State, that is, by the whole people, with the exception of the forests, mountains, grassland, unclaimed land, and beaches that are owned by collectives in accordance with the law. The State ensures the rational use of natural resources and protects rare animals and plants. The appropriation or damage of natural resources by any organization or individual by whatever means is prohibited.

means. Secondary sources, ***inter alia***, the 2002 Water Law of the People's Republic of China, provide provisions on water supply and sanitation.[46]

Recognizing the right to water in domestic law is the first step in the proper direction, but it should be accompanied by monitoring and enforcement measures – in particular for pollution related issues – which are indispensable conditions to realize the right. While debates about the adequacy of China's environmental standards continue, there is little dispute that enforcement of existing water-quality and monitoring laws has been grossly inadequate.[47] In 2007, ***China Daily*** noted that China needs "more severe rules and penalties to change business as usual including stopping discharged waste water from further polluting our rivers, oceans and underground water supplies."[48]

Recently, China has made huge investments in the water sector, mostly in sanitation, and the central government has also called for foreign investment.[49] According to a World Bank report, during 1991–2005, a total of USD 54 billion was invested in urban water supply and sanitation, equivalent to USD 3.7 billion per year, and investments have continued in more recent times.[50] However, most of these investments aim to enhance water and sanitation in urban areas, thus exacerbating the inequality of treatment between rural and urban residents.[51]

Conclusion

Several issues challenge water supply and sanitation in China. Rapid urbanization, disparities between urban and rural areas, scarcity, contamination, and pollution of water resources pose serious concerns for the government. In the recent past, China has invested intensively in the water sector, in particular, during the 11th Five-Year Plan (2006–2010).[52] In past decades, access to services, wastewater treatment, and the creation of water and wastewater utilities have increased and helped ameliorate the living conditions of Chinese citizens. However, as evidenced in data collected by WHO and UNICEF, millions of Chinese people still do not have access to improved water sources and sanitation.

46 Zhōnghuá Rénmín Gònghéguó Shuǐ Fǎ (2002 xiūdìng) (中华人民共和国水法(2002修订) [Water Law of the People's Republic of China (2002 Revision)] (Promulgated by the Standing Comm. Nat'l People's Cong., August 29, 2002). *See* also Zhōnghuá Rénmín Gònghéguó Shuǐ Wūrǎn Fángzhì Fǎ (2008 xiūdìng) (中华人民共和国水污染防治法(2008修订) [Water Pollution Prevention and Control Law of the People's Republic of China (2008 Revision)] (Promulgated by the Standing Comm. Nat'l People's Cong., February 28, 2008) and Zhōnghuá Rénmín Gònghéguó Shuǐtǔ Bǎochí Fǎ (2010 xiūdìng) (中华人民共和国水土保持法(2010修订) [Water and Soil Conservation Law of the People's Republic of China (2010 Revision)] (Promulgated by the Standing Comm. Nat'l People's Cong., December 25, 2010). *See* the website of the Ministry of Water Resources of the People Republic of China at http://www.mwr.gov.cn/english/laws.html (last visited July 3, 2016).

47 Peter Gleick, ***supra*** note 13, at 92. *See* Chapters 12 (He) and 13 (Luo Li) in this volume.

48 China Daily (February 28, 2007).

49 Lijin Zhing & Tao Fu, *BOT Applied in Chinese Wastewater Sector* (paper presented on ADB workshop on Sanitation and Wastewater Management: The Way Forward, Malina, February 2007).

50 Greg Browder et al., Stepping Up – Improving the Performance of China's Urban Water Utilities 108 (World Bank Publications, 2007).

51 Jonhatan Watts, *100 Chinese Cities Face Water Crisis, Says Minister,* The Guardian (June 8, 2005), https://www.theguardian.com/world/2005/jun/08/china.jonathanwatts (last visited July 3, 2016).

52 In the 12th Five-Year Plan, water crisis is recognized. The plan focuses on the construction of water conservation structures, irrigation, rivers/lakes pollution: http://chinawaterrisk.org/regulations/water-policy/12th-five-year-plan/#sthash.yYDt7UoJ.dpuf (last visited July 3, 2016).

The inequality of treatment between rural and urban populations is one of the main concerns that the Chinese authorities should take into consideration while drafting water policies. The transformation of the Chinese economy from agriculture to industry-based has led to rapid urbanization. Water services in cities across China were not equipped to provide water to the growing population, and the government became more reluctant to invest in rural areas. Current investment in projects that divert water from poorer to richer areas has created inequitable treatment and led to increasing political discontent.

Ensuring access to water also requires huge efforts to protect the environment. Most rivers, lakes, and underground water reserves are polluted by urban, industrial, and agricultural wastes dumped into freshwater sources. Protecting these water resources would entail investments in water and waste treatments as well as enhanced controls and law enforcement actions to supervise the respect of domestic laws.

The positive attitude towards the recognition of the right to water demonstrated by China when it voted in favor of the General Assembly resolution in 2010 was a step in the right direction but, on its own, does not solve China's water problems. China should be aware that a formal recognition of the right to water in international and domestic laws would increase the burden on the State to ensure the protection of this right. China could potentially face serious repercussions due to legal empowerment bestowed on citizens by the right since they might be entitled to bring legal actions against the State.[53] The denial of this right might exacerbate domestic malcontent. In addition, Non-Governmental Organizations, governments, and international organizations may have further arguments to criticize China for human rights violations.

In conclusion, China's awareness of its water scarcity problems has moved the government to invest widely in the sector, although the investments have been disproportionate between rural and urban areas. In order to comply with international obligations and realize the right to water, China must rethink its policies and projects to reduce the inequitable access to water and make further efforts to diminish the pollution of water resources to provide safe drinking water for people in urban and rural areas.

53 Harsha, *Conflicts and Dilemma of Human Right to Water*, 12 Current Science 1178, 1178 (2011).

22 China Meets Hollywood at WTO: Janus' Faces of Freedom

Standards of Right and Wrong Between National and International Moralities*

Christophe Germann

Implementing the UNESCO convention on cultural diversity

In the Natural History Museum of Geneva, the city which hosts the World Trade Organization (WTO), there is a living turtle that has two heads. The name of this attraction is Janus, the god of beginnings and transitions in Roman mythology. Janus the god is depicted as a two-faced divinity who looks to both the future and the past.[1]

China ratified the UNESCO Convention on the diversity of cultural expressions of 2005 ("UNESCO Convention") a year after its adoption.[2] Then Culture Minister Sun Jiazheng stated that ratification would allow China to protect its cultures and promote the development of a cultural industry that would help reverse an imbalance in trade of cultural goods and services.[3]

Pursuant to Article 3, the UNESCO Convention "shall apply to the policies and measures adopted by the Parties related to the protection and promotion of the diversity of cultural expressions."[4] The scope of this treaty must be construed in combination with Articles 1 and 2, which define its objectives and guiding principles. Article 4 paragraph 3 provides a definition of "cultural expressions" that are "those expressions that result from the creativity of individuals, groups and societies, and that have cultural content."[5] Pursuant to paragraph 2

* Ph.D. (University of Berne), DEA Master in Law (University of Geneva), pro bono lecturer at the Université populaire de Genève (international law and relations, European law); formerly visiting scholar at the Law Schools of the University of Oxford and Birkbeck College, University of London (2011), Max Weber Fellow, European University Institute, and FNS/Marie Curie visiting post doctoral fellow at the Universities of Yale and Cambridge; attorney at law in Geneva. Contact: www.germann-avocats.com

1 For pictures of Janus the turtle, *see* www.odditycentral.com/pics/janus-the-two-headed-turtle.html (last visited July 16, 2016).

2 The UNESCO Convention On The Protection And Promotion Of The Diversity Of Cultural Expressions entered into force in March 2007 following its ratification by 30 countries. The text of the UNESCO Convention, its operational guidelines, and related information can be consulted at www.unesco.org/culture/en/diversity/convention (last visited July 16, 2016). UNESCO Convention On The Protection And Promotion Of The Diversity Of Cultural Expressions, October 20, 2005, 45 ILM.269 [hereinafter UNESCO Convention].

3 *China ratifies UNESCO convention on protecting cultural diversity,* People's Daily Online (December 29, 2006). For an analysis from the European perspective, *see* Delia Ferri, *An Investigation on the (Desirable) Role of Cultural Diversity in the EU-China Partnership,* in Europe, India and China: Strategic Partners in a Changing World (F. Snyder ed., Bruylant, 2008).

4 UNESCO Convention, Article 3.

5 UNESCO Convention, Article 4.3.

of the same provision, "cultural content" refers to "the symbolic meaning, artistic dimension, and cultural values that originate from or express cultural identities."[6]

The UNESCO Convention has notably the objective to protect and promote the diversity of cultural expressions, to create the conditions for cultures to flourish and to freely interact in a mutually beneficial manner, and to encourage dialogue among cultures with a view to ensuring wider and balanced cultural exchanges in the world in favor of intercultural respect and a culture of peace (Article 1(a)–(c)).[7]

The mechanism underlying the UNESCO Convention can be described as a "limited free pass," empowering its Parties with the "sovereign right" to formulate and implement cultural policies and to adopt measures to protect and promote the diversity of cultural expressions and to strengthen international cooperation to achieve the purposes of this treaty (Articles 5 and 6). This right is subject to the respect for human rights and fundamental freedoms pursuant to Article 2.1 that recalls that "cultural diversity can be protected and promoted only if human rights and fundamental freedoms, such as freedom of expression, information, and communication, as well as the ability of individuals to choose cultural expressions, are guaranteed."[8] As a consequence, Article 2.2 limits the scope of the Parties' sovereignty in cultural matters by requiring compliance with the Charter of the United Nations (UN) and the principles of international law.

The principle of international solidarity and cooperation, as articulated in Article 2.4 of the UNESCO Convention, arguably prescribes that states overcome a narrow and introverted understanding of the concept of sovereignty. International solidarity and cooperation should aim to enable countries, especially developing and least-developed economies, to create and strengthen their means of cultural expressions and cultural industries that are either nascent or established. The same interpretation should also apply to the principles of equitable access, openness, and balance (Articles 2.7 and 2.8). These principles stress that "equitable access to a rich and diversified range of cultural expressions from all over the

6 UNESCO Convention, Article 4.2.

7 For an introduction to the UNESCO Convention, *see* Ivan Bernier, *The Unesco Convention on the Protection and Promotion of the Diversity of Cultural Expressions: A Cultural Instrument at the Junction of Law and Politics* (2008), http://www.diversite-culturelle.qc.ca/index.php?id=133&L=1 (last visited July 16, 2016), and, from the same author, *Trade and Culture,* in THE WORLD TRADE ORGANIZATION: LEGAL, ECONOMIC AND POLITICAL ANALYSIS, vol II, 747 (P. Macrory, A. Appleton & M. Plummer eds, Springer Science & Business Media, 2005); LA CONVENTION DE L'UNESCO SUR LA DIVERSITÉ CULTURELLE, UMRDC ACTES DU COLLOQUE 18–19 JUIN 2008 (Hélène Ruiz Fabri ed., Ed. de la Société de Législation Comparée, 2010). On the rationale of law and policies aimed at protecting and promoting cultural diversity from an European angle, see A. Von Bogdandy, *The European Union as Situation, Executive, And Promoter Of The International Law of Cultural Diversity – Elements Of A Beautiful Friendship,* 19(2) EUR. J. INT'L L. 241–275 (2008); Gabriel N. Toggenburg, *Unity in Diversity: Searching for the Regional Dimension in the Context of a Someway Foggy Constitutional Credo,* in AN EVER MORE COMPLEX UNION 27–56 (Roberto Toniatti, Marco Dani & Francesco Palermo eds, Nomos, 2004); Bruno de Witte, *The Value of Cultural Diversity in European Union Law,* in PROTECTION OF CULTURAL DIVERSITY FROM A EUROPEAN AND INTERNATIONAL PERSPECTIVE (Schneider H. and Van den Bossche P. eds, Intersentia, 2008); Craufurd Smith R., *From Heritage Conservation To European Identity: Article 151 EC And The Multifaceted Nature Of Community Cultural Policy,* EUR. L. REV. (1/2007); DELIA FERRI, LA COSTITUZIONE CULTURALE DELL'UNIONE EUROPEA (CEDAM, 2008). On the notion of "diversity management," *see* Daniel Thürer, *Minorities and majorities: managing diversity,* 15(5) SCHWEIZERISCHE ZEITSCHRIFT FÜR INTERNATIONALES UND EUROPÄISCHES RECHT 659–663 (2005); Janina W. Dacyl and Charles Westin, *Governance of Cultural Diversity,* in CEIFO (Stockholm University Publications, 2000).

8 UNESCO Convention, Article 2.1.

world and access of cultures to the means of expressions and dissemination constitute important elements for enhancing cultural diversity and encouraging mutual understanding."[9]

The UNESCO Convention acknowledges that states should seek to appropriately promote openness to other cultures of the world, when they adopt measures to support the diversity of cultural expressions. The principles of equitable access, openness, and balance thus further restrict the powers of the Parties in matters of cultural policies. Article 7, which expresses the legal essence of the UNESCO Convention, articulates these principles on a more operational level. Pursuant to this core provision, the Parties shall endeavor to create in their territory an environment that encourages individuals and social groups to create, produce, disseminate, distribute, and have access to their own cultural expressions, as well as to diverse cultural expressions from within their territory and from other countries of the world. The Parties shall also endeavor to "recognize the important contribution of artists, others involved in the creative process, cultural communities, and organizations that support their work, and their central role in nurturing the diversity of cultural expressions."[10] In other words, Parties shall contribute to empowering individuals and social groups to create cultural expressions, and to have access to the diversity of these expressions. Very importantly, the Parties should consider artists and others involved in the creative process as key contributors to the diversity of cultural expressions.

The right of sovereignty for cultural matters is highly problematic when it applies to authoritarian regimes. Such regimes tend to use and abuse the power vested in sovereignty, and ignore its limitations requiring compliance with human rights and fundamental freedoms. A recent example illustrates this issue in the field of freedom of expression: the jury of the international film festival of Venice awarded in 2011 one of the most prestigious prizes, the Golden Lion for the best director, to Cai Shangjun from China for his film *Ren Shan Ren Hai* ("*People Mountain People Sea*"). According to the French newspaper *Le Monde*, the Chinese authorities censored on several occasions this film, which depicts work conditions in coal mines.[11]

In this chapter, I submit that the promotion of cultural diversity combined with the freedom of expression in authoritarian regimes as well as in developing and least-developed countries requires from liberal democracies and developed economies a change of paradigm in international law on intellectual property protection.[12] In the absence of other capable and potent international fora, the WTO could play a pivotal role in the elaboration and implementation of new rules aimed at materializing equitable access, openness, and balance. Cultural diversity and trade liberalization share these goals: there is no equitable trade without cultural diversity and, vice versa, there is no cultural diversity without equitable trade – "equitable trade" being understood here as trade that is compliant with the principles of equitable access, openness, and balance in conformity with Articles 2.7 and 2.8 of the UNESCO Convention. So far, however, the WTO has not succeeded in doing so, although

9 UNESCO Convention, Article 2.7.

10 UNESCO Convention, Article 7.

11 *La Mostra de Venise couronne "Faust" du Russe Alexandre Sokourov* (September 11, 2011), www.lemonde.fr (last visited July 16, 2016).

12 On the interface between trade and culture law, compare also Tomer Broude, *Conflict and Complementarity in Trade, Cultural Diversity and Intellectual Property Rights,* Asian J. WTO & Int'l Health L. & Pol. 345 (2/2007); Mira Burri-Nenova, *Trade and Culture: Making the WTO Legal Framework Conducive to Cultural Considerations,* Manchester J. Int'l Econ. L. 3 (5/2008); by the same author, *Trade and Culture in International Law: Paths to (Re)conciliation,* J. World Trade 49 (1/2010).

it has achieved some honorable results in other areas involving Non-Trade Concerns (NTCs), such as access to essential medicines.[13] The litigation between the United States and China on cultural goods and services under the General Agreement on Tariffs and Trade (GATT),[14] General Agreement on Trade in Services (GATS)[15] and the Agreement on Trade-Related Aspects of Intellectual Property Rights (TRIPS),[16] that I shall briefly address in the second part of this contribution in the light of newer disputes, illustrates some of the causes for this failure. As a solution to the issues raised by this case study, I shall introduce the idea of variable geometry for the duration of copyright protection as a novel remedy against excessive intellectual property protection eroding and damaging both cultural diversity and equitable trade.[17]

The strength of trade law and the weakness of culture law

The UNESCO Convention, as it was adopted in 2005, is full of provisions containing vague terms and concepts that can be interpreted in many different ways, or that even conflict with each other. Moreover, it does not have a dispute settlement system with an efficient sanction mechanism, which could produce precise, concrete, and binding interpretations of its terms and concepts in order to make its rules more predictable and transparent. The Parties, therefore, do not have an incentive to clarify and develop this law through litigation.[18] The history of certain treaties dealing with intellectual property protection illustrates this shortcoming. For several decades, there was no significant international case law related to the treaties administered by the World Intellectual Property Organization (WIPO), such as the Berne Convention and the Paris Convention. This situation changed dramatically when these treaties were partially incorporated into the TRIPS Agreement. Since the TRIPS Agreement entered into force in 1995 and thus became enforceable through the WTO dispute settlement system, it has generated a number of cases which have provided a better understanding and, consequently, a more effectively binding interpretation of the rules at stake. The UNESCO Convention, therefore, faces trade regulations that are generally clearer

13 *See* Chapters 35 (Watal) and 37 (Spigarelli & Filippetti) in this volume.

14 General Agreement on Tariffs and Trade, October 30, 1947, 61 Stat. A-11, 55 UNTS 194 [hereinafter GATT].

15 General Agreement on Trade in Services, April 15, 1994, Marrakesh Agreement Establishing the World Trade Organization, Annex 1B, 1869 UNTS 183, 33 ILM 1167 (1994) [hereinafter GATS].

16 Agreement on Trade Related Aspects of Intellectual Property Rights, April 15, 1994, Marrakesh Agreement Establishing the World Trade Organization, Annex 1C, 1869 UNTS 299, 33 ILM 1197 (1994) [hereinafter TRIPS Agreement].

17 This contribution provides an analysis based on the Study for the European Parliament ***Implementing the UNESCO Convention of 2005 on the Diversity of Cultural Expressions in the European Union*** that the author conducted with a multidisciplinary research team in 2010 and that is available at www.diversitystudy.eu (last visited July 16, 2016). See also the author's working paper ***The Puzzle of a Muzzle: Copyright, Culture and Censorship,*** in Weblog of the Journal of Intellectual Property Law and Practice, http://jiplp.blogspot.com/2011/07/puzzle-of-muzzle-copyright-culture-and.html (last visited July 16, 2016).

18 UNESCO's Convention on the Protection and Promotion of the Diversity of Cultural Expressions: Making It Work (Nina Obuljen and Joost Smiers eds, Culturelink, 2006); Tania Voon, Cultural Products and the World Trade Organization (Cambridge University Press, 2007), and more generally Joost Pauwelyn, Conflict of Norms in Public International Law: How WTO Law Relates to Other Rules of International Law (Cambridge University Press, 2003).

and more effective. Due to these systemic discrepancies, it is very likely that WTO law will continue to prevail over the rules of the UNESCO Convention.

In contrast to the initial GATT of 1948 and to WTO law since 1995, one may not expect that the UNESCO law on the diversity of cultural expressions will substantially develop in a binding way in the near future; that is, unless civil society becomes a driving force that pushes its governments towards improvement of the current pitfalls. If civil society does not take appropriate initiative, and instead remains passive, this instrument will likely remain a dead letter that does not generate its own case law and stays largely irrelevant with respect to the realities of most culture-concerned stakeholders.[19]

While the WTO considers itself as an organization driven by its member countries, the reality is that these countries are generally themselves driven by their own private import- and export-related interests. Culture-concerned pressure groups in most jurisdictions do not have the same bargaining power as trade concerned lobbyists. The rules of the UNESCO Convention will, thus, not put governments under the same compliance pressure as WTO law. This situation is worsened by the fact that if the UNESCO Convention enters into conflict with WTO law, the latter will generally prevail over the former. As a consequence, culture-concerned stakeholders have no incentive to make use of the UNESCO Convention and invoke its toothless legal remedies. Therefore, in terms of implementation and enforcement, the playing field between trade and culture concerns in the area of those industries that condition cultural diversity is presently not level. This conclusion certainly applies to the film industry as well as to the music and book industries.[20]

Intellectual property, cultural discrimination, and marketing

The TRIPS agreement harmonizes, to a large extent, national intellectual property law among WTO Members. As an important side effect, it reinforces corporate power concentrated in oligopolies from largely uniform cultural affiliations that dominate the market of cultural goods and services without providing commensurate checks and balances due to the lack of effective competition law addressing the specifics of cultural industries on the national, regional, and international levels.[21] In other words, the TRIPS agreement imposes relatively high standards of intellectual property protection on the basis of the WTO fundamental principles of National Treatment (NT) and Most Favored Nation (MFN) treatment, without any multilateral requirement to legislate on competition aimed at counterbalancing excessive owners' rights. Since the costs of implementing intellectual property laws and regulations are already high for economically weak countries, these economies generally cannot afford the additional significant costs of national competition law as well.

19 *See* video contribution by Jan Aart Scholte on the role of civil society, in STUDY FOR THE EUROPEAN PARLIAMENT ON THE IMPLEMENTATION OF THE 2005 UNESCO CONVENTION ON THE PROTECTION AND PROMOTION OF THE DIVERSITY OF CULTURAL EXPRESSIONS, Section "Stakeholders Dialogue" at www.diversitystudy.eu (last visited July 16, 2016).

20 For a further analysis, compare Tania Voon, *The UNESCO Convention and the WTO: promoting dialogue on the legal relationship, Study Paper 3B*, in STUDY FOR THE EUROPEAN PARLIAMENT ON THE IMPLEMENTATION OF THE 2005 UNESCO CONVENTION ON THE PROTECTION AND PROMOTION OF THE DIVERSITY OF CULTURAL EXPRESSIONS, long version of the Study, *supra* note 19, at 165.

21 *See* Fiona Macmillan, *Copyright And Corporate Power*, in COPYRIGHT IN THE CULTURAL INDUSTRIES (Ruth Towse ed., Edward Elgar, 2002).

There is scarce research so far on the interactions between international trade rules and state intervention aimed at protecting and promoting the diversity of cultural expressions on one side, and intellectual property and competition laws on the other. For the time being, the discussion on culture and trade mainly focuses on GATT and GATS, the WTO agreements on trade in goods and services. However, WTO Members must also comply with the minimum standards of intellectual property protection as provided in the TRIPS Agreement, the third pillar of the WTO. This instrument offers a specific approach to deal with the relationship between trade and NTCs, which should be further explored in the context of protecting and promoting cultural diversity from the legal angle.[22] In this context, one must stress that intellectual property protection not only produces positive effects on the diversity of cultural expressions, but can also be a threat.

In the cultural sector, most stakeholders currently focus their concerns on the rules of GATT and GATS addressing progressive liberalization in the field of trade in goods and services. In contrast, so far, the TRIPS Agreement has not attracted these stakeholders' attention to the extent that it deserves. There is today a wide consensus to consider excessive patent protection as potentially detrimental to public health policies in developing and least-developed countries.[23] In the area of cultural policies, however, the misleading dogma still prevails that the stronger copyright and trademark protection is, the better it is for culture in general, and the diversity of cultural expressions in particular.

The widespread perception of the value of intellectual property protection among culture-concerned stakeholders focuses on economic rights: copyright and related rights fuel an essential source of revenue that insures the economic existence of creators, producers, and distributors of cultural goods and services. While this understanding is correct on the micro level, it neglects the fact that on the macro level, copyright and other relevant forms of intellectual property rights are the main instruments to secure investments for the marketing (advertisement) of cultural goods and services and, as such, the main tool for highly concentrated corporations to dominate the relevant markets. On the dark side of this regime, the system may exclude and thereby muzzle creators and producers whose works do not enjoy competitive marketing. The prevailing system thereby silences them.

Disproportionately high standards of intellectual property protection give the incentive to disburse excessive expenditures in advertising for cultural expressions intended for mass consumption. They are the primary means for market domination, and such market domination is a most effective tool to culturally discriminate. Copyright and related intellectual property rights protect, for instance, 40 million US Dollars (USD) of creative activities and 60 million USD of marketing on average, per Hollywood film produced each year. This reality is detrimental to the creation, production, and dissemination of films, books, music, and other cultural expressions that do not enjoy comparable investments in advertisement to attract the public's attention. In other words, excessive copyright, trademark, and trade name protection generally contributes to marginalizing and excluding contents and aesthetics that are culturally different from the economically dominant ones. They do not enjoy competitive marketing power even when they have the same or more consumer appeal. A few top corporate decision makers in the film, book, and music industries dispose of highly concentrated power to allocate marketing resources, and, more often than not, they use and

22 Compare Thomas Cottier & Christophe Germann, *Commentary at the Preamble, art. 1 to 8 et 40 TRIPS*, in Concise International and European IP Law – TRIPS, Paris Convention, European Enforcement and Transfer of Technology (Thomas Cottier et al. eds, Kluwer Law International, 2014).

23 *See* Chapters 31 (Prasad), 35 (Watal), and 36 (Nie) in this volume.

abuse this power to culturally discriminate. They can and do impose their cultural preferences around the world, and silence all the rest. They are a privately driven censorship apparatus in democratic market economies. Whereas the Chinese government officially censors Cai Shangjun's *People Mountain People Sea* via its public institutions, the diktat from those corporations that dominate the markets through excessive intellectual property protection achieves similar results in the Western world.[24]

A new deal: Variable geometry for copyright duration

Policy and law makers, who reject both public and private censorship, should consider redesigning some aspects of copyright and related intellectual property rights protection in such a way that these rights become more workable for individual creators and small and medium-sized producers. This means developing new safeguards against cultural discrimination resulting from the abuse of dominant positions in the market. This domination is essentially tributary to exorbitant levels of intellectual property standards that protect predatory advertising.

Intellectual property rights can grant providers of cultural expressions an indispensable independence from public power, that is the states, their bureaucracies, and the experts on their payroll. This is a lesson to be learned in the European Union (EU) especially. It is equally applicable to liberal and authoritarian regimes as well as to wealthy and developing economies. This argument runs against a complete abolition of intellectual property protection as proposed by certain scholars, most prominently by Joost Smiers.[25] The task ahead consists of limiting the risks of abuses of private power resulting in systematic cultural discrimination by way of a better-balanced intellectual property regime.

The combined effects of the market power caused by excessive intellectual property protection on one side, and some rich democracies' covert control of contents by way of "selective" state aid on the other side, are highly damaging to the freedom of expression. Accordingly, creators, producers, and the public who refuse either diktat need protection.[26]

Variable geometry in copyright duration could solve this problem: the higher the marketing investments, the shorter the duration of copyright protection. In other words, the works with modest advertising shall keep the full term of copyright protection (70 years after the author's death), whereas the protection for works enjoying high investments in publicity shall endure fewer years. As a consequence, a great diversity of small and medium-sized fish will flourish while large sharks are kept at a safe distance.

24 For a more detailed analysis, *see* Christophe Germann, ***Intellectual Property And Competition, Study Paper 2B***, in Study for the European Parliament on the Implementation of the 2005 UNESCO Convention on the Protection and Promotion of the Diversity of Cultural Expressions, long version of the Study, *supra* note 19, at 85. *See* Chapters 23 (Creemers), 24 (Kamperman Sanders), and 25 (Friedmann) in this volume.

25 Joost Smiers & Marieke van Schijndel, Imagine There Is No Copyright And No Cultural Conglomerates Too . . . Better For Artists, Diversity And The Economy (2010), http://networkcultures.org/_uploads/tod/TOD4_nocopyright.pdf (last visited July 16, 2016).

26 On the pitfalls of so-called "selective" state aid, *see* Christophe Germann, ***The "Rougemarine Dilemma": How Much Trust Does A State Deserve When It Subsidises Cultural Goods And Services?*** (European University Institute, Max Weber Working Paper), http://cadmus.iue.it/dspace/handle/1814/9027 (last visited July 16, 2016). For an analysis of the South Korean approach based on quantitative restrictions for the film industry, *see* Won-Mog Choi, ***Screen Quota and Cultural Diversity: Debates in Korea-US FTA Talks and Convention on Cultural Diversity***, 2(2) Asian J. WTO & Int'l Health L. & Pol. (2007).

Variable geometry could provide strong disincentives for exorbitant investments in marketing that damage the diversity of cultural expressions and provide commensurate incentives for reasonable investments in marketing, to the greater benefit of consumers. Tax measures to be adopted at the national level shall compliment the system and, in particular, prevent circumvention via trademark protection or similar means.

Further developing and eventually implementing this idea could achieve a level playing field for talents and contents from all cultures by imposing a repellent against exclusionary marketing practices that muzzle creativity and expressions from diverse cultural origins. It will be instrumental for the full realization of genuine freedom of speech, and will open frontiers and remove unjustifiable obstacles to equitable trade.[27]

Last but not least, this idea is also likely to reinforce the legitimacy of the copyright system and, thus, bring about the most effective way to fight piracy. OECD figures indicate that international trade in counterfeit and pirated products could have amounted up to 200 billion USD in 2005. This estimate is larger than the national GDPs of about 150 economies based on World Bank data for that year. It does not include domestically produced and consumed counterfeit and pirated products and the volume of pirated digital goods and services being distributed via the Internet. If these items were also accounted for, the total magnitude of counterfeiting and piracy worldwide could well be several hundred billion USD more per year.[28] For major corporations from the Western world that are dependent on intellectual property protection, the effectiveness of enforcement of legislation aimed at fighting piracy appears to be of crucial importance.

If we rely on these statistical figures, piracy and counterfeiting appear to be a serious problem for developed countries that is not likely to be solved without effective cooperation from developing countries and least-developed countries. An incentive for such cooperation could result from promoting cultural diversity in exchange for fighting piracy: developed economies would start to effectively implement the access rights under Article 7 of the UNESCO Convention for cultural goods and services from developing and least-developed countries. In turn, the latter countries would actually benefit from the international intellectual property regime and, accordingly, start to enforce it in their own territories. Under this scenario, cultural diversity promises to provide new gains for all parties.

Three discourses on culture and trade from "identity" to "diversity"

We can observe three generations of discourses on policies and rules of law that are relevant to the scope of the UNESCO Convention.

Historically, the first generation of discourse was based on a predominantly ethnocentric understanding that focused on the protection and promotion of the concept of "cultural identity." With the spectacular reinforcement of the multilateral trading system in the last decade of the twentieth century, culture-concerned stakeholders in various jurisdictions became aware of their need to join forces in order to meet new challenges. The WTO agreements entered into force in 1995. During the negotiations that led to the formation of these

27 For a critical discussion of these proposals, *see* the video contribution by Fiona Macmillan, in Study for the European Parliament on the Implementation of the 2005 UNESCO Convention on the Protection and Promotion of the Diversity of Cultural Expressions, ***supra*** note 19.

28 OECD, ***The economic impact of counterfeiting and piracy***, Paris, 2007.

treaties, these stakeholders failed to impose a so-called cultural exception. This exception would have carved out cultural regulation from the scope of the regulation on the progressive liberalization of trade in goods and services (GATT and GATS), and on trade-related aspects of intellectual property rights (TRIPS).[29]

The success in terms of predictability and enforceability of WTO law essentially resulted from a radical change of the dispute settlement mechanism that applied to the GATT from 1948 to 1994. This new reality arguably contributed to a shift of strategy among culture-concerned stakeholders, ushering in a second generation of discourses revolving around the concept of "cultural diversity." These stakeholders reacted to the imminent threat by calling for, and contributing to, the elaboration of new law. This process started with soft law in the form of a declaration on cultural diversity adopted in 2000 under the auspices of the Council of Europe. This was followed by a similar declaration at the UNESCO Convention in 2001, and by more binding law through the UNESCO Convention of 2005. Although a variety of discourses on cultural diversity started much earlier, new multilateral trade regulation gave them the momentum to be translated into increasingly well-articulated norms of law.[30]

At present, we perceive an emerging third generation of legal and policy-related ideas and initiatives on cultural diversity. This impending era presents the opportunity to welcome new allies for the cultural cause who are concerned about the protection of human rights, fundamental freedoms, minorities' rights, and even the early prevention of certain crimes against humanity – in particular ethnic cleansing. The considerable value of the UNESCO Convention resides in its potential to offer inspiration and guidance for a future legal framework that can manage the sources of tensions within countries and regions that flow from the diversity not only of cultural expressions, but also from the diversity of other forms of human expressions. Such a new development beyond a strictly cultural focus would stress the diversity of "human expressions" that would include not only "cultural expressions" in the sense of the legal definition provided under the UNESCO Convention, but also other types of expressions such as religious, ethnic, political, social, economic, and more generally ideological as well as intellectual expressions.[31]

The European Commission considers that "the implementation of the UNESCO Convention within the EU is not a strict legislative activity as such but rather the pursuit of policy developments, both in internal and external policies, which might take the form of legislative

29 Christophe Germann, Diversité culturelle et libre-échange à la lumière du cinéma (Helbing Lichtenhahn, 2008); compare also Michael Hahn, *A Clash of Cultures? The UNESCO Diversity Convention and International Trade Law*, J. Int'l Econ. L. 515 (3/2006).

30 *See* generally Serge Regourd, L'exception culturelle (Presses Universitaires de France, 2003), and by the same author, *De L'exception A La Diversité Culturelle*, in Problèmes Politiques Et Sociaux 904 (La Documentation française, 2004). Compare also R. Craufurd Smith, *The UNESCO Convention on the Protection and Promotion of the Diversity of Cultural Expressions: Building a New World Information and Communication order?*, Int'l J. Comm. 24 (1/2007); Alan Couder, *The UNESCO Convention on Cultural Diversity: Treacherous Treaty or Compassionate Compact?*, 18 Policy Papers on Transnational Economic Law 1 (2005); Rolf H. Weber, *Cultural Diversity and International Trade – Taking Stock and Looking Ahead*, in The World Trade Organization and Trade in Services (K. Alexander & M. Andenas eds, Martinus Nijhoff Publishers, 2008).

31 On the scope of the UNESCO Convention, *see* Study for the European Parliament on the Implementation of the 2005 UNESCO Convention on the Protection and Promotion of the Diversity of Cultural Expressions, long version, *supra* note 19, at 48.

action in specific instances."[32] This understanding presents the opportunity for new creative thinking in political and legal terms beyond a mere static and formalistic approach. The UNESCO Convention has the great potential to mobilize, inspire, and stimulate law- and policy-makers in search of innovative solutions to address their constituencies' core societal concerns pertaining to questions of identities and diversity of human expressions.

In the European Agenda for Culture, the European Commission calls for "mainstreaming culture in all relevant policies" on the basis of the Treaty's cultural clause (point 4.4): "With regard to the external dimension, particular attention is paid to multi-intercultural and inter-religious dialogue, promoting understanding between the EU and international partners and reaching out increasingly to a broader audience in partner countries. In this context, education and particularly human rights education play a significant role."[33] The relationships, for example, between Tibet and China, or Palestine and Israel, exemplify the urgency to further examine such an avenue in depth. The protection and promotion of the diversity of cultural expressions, in compliance with human rights and fundamental freedoms, can deliver a road map to the elaboration of novel international law aimed at protecting and promoting human diversity and the early prevention of certain crimes against humanity, including crimes against human diversity.[34]

United States versus China at the WTO

Shortly after China's ratification of the UNESCO Convention, the US initiated two WTO dispute settlement procedures against China regarding cultural industries or, in Hollywood jargon, "entertainment" industries. Lobbyists from the Motion Picture Association of America (MPAA), which represents the oligopoly of the major Hollywood film companies, and from like-minded trade organizations successfully pressured the US administration to take these actions. Interestingly and relevant for the purpose of this contribution, essential aspects of the litigation between China and the US appeared to be at the crossroads between censorship, intellectual property protection, and international trade in cultural goods and services.[35]

In the first case, the US alleged violations of the TRIPS Agreement, *inter alia*, in relation to the denial of copyright and related rights protection and enforcement of creative works of authorship, sound recordings, and performances that have not been authorized for

32 *See* EU Commission's reply to question 4 of the Regional Organisations Survey, in Study for the European Parliament on the Implementation of the 2005 UNESCO Convention on the Protection and Promotion of the Diversity of Cultural Expressions, *supra* note 19.

33 "Mainstreaming culture," according to point 4.4 of the European Agenda for Culture, means, "integrating culture in all relevant policies" pursuant to Article 167 para. 4 TFEU ("Intégration de la culture dans toutes les politiques pertinentes" or "Einbeziehung der Kultur in andere betroffene Politikbereiche"). Article 167 para. 4 TFEU (ex Article 151 TEC) obliges the Union to take cultural aspects into account in its action under other provisions of the Treaties, particularly in order to respect and to promote the diversity of its cultures. Since the entry into force of the Lisbon Treaty, this obligation is reinforced by Article 22 of the Charter of Fundamental Rights of the European Union. Pursuant to this provision, the Union shall respect cultural, religious, and linguistic diversity.

34 Study for the European Parliament on the Implementation of the 2005 UNESCO Convention on the Protection and Promotion of the Diversity of Cultural Expressions, long version, *supra* note 19, at 27, and video contribution by Ben Kiernan on the early prevention of "cultural genocide", in *Ibid.*, Section "Stakeholders Dialogue" at www.diversitystudy.eu (last visited July 16, 2016).

35 *See* Chapters 23 (Creemers), 24 (Kamperman Sanders), and 25 (Friedmann) in this volume.

publication or distribution within China.[36] This claim addressed the issue of censorship and its effect on copyright protection. China referred to the Berne Convention for the Protection of Literary and Artistic Works to justify a right of censorship in relation to copyright, in particular to Article 17.[37]

The first sentence of Article 4 of the Copyright Law of the People's Republic of China[38] (hereinafter Copyright Law) provided that works the publication and/or dissemination of which are prohibited by law shall not be protected by this law.[39] The US claimed that this article denies legal protection to certain categories of works, in particular works that were censored, and that it denies the authors of such works of the broad set of rights enumerated in Article 10 of the Copyright Law, which largely encompasses the rights contemplated by the provisions of the Berne Convention (1971).[40]

China responded that, like many other countries in the world, it bans the publication and dissemination of works consisting entirely of unconstitutional or immoral content. Moreover, China argued that public censorship renders private enforcement unnecessary, that such censorship enforces prohibitions on content seriously, and that this removes banned content from the public domain more securely than would be possible through copyright enforcement.[41] The Panel concluded that copyright and government censorship address different rights and interests: "Copyright protects private rights, as reflected in the fourth recital of the preamble to the TRIPS Agreement, whilst government censorship addresses public interests."[42]

The Panel found that Article 4(1) denies the protection of Article 10 to certain works, including those of WTO Members' nationals. The Panel considered that evidence originating from China's Supreme Court supported its interpretation of the meaning of the provision at stake.[43] The Panel concluded that, notwithstanding the fact that the rights of China

36 Panel Report, *China – Measures Affecting the Protection and Enforcement of Intellectual Property Rights*, para. 7.120, WT/DS362/R (January 26, 2009) [hereinafter *China – Intellectual Property* Rights]. *See* also summary at www.wto.org/english/tratop_e/dispu_e/cases_e/ds362_e.htm (last visited July 16, 2016).

37 Article 17 states that the provisions of the Berne Convention "cannot in any way affect the right of the Government of each country of the Union to permit, to control, or to prohibit, by legislation or regulation, the circulation, presentation, or exhibition of any work or production in regard to which the competent authority may find it necessary to exercise that right."

38 Zhōnghuá Rénmín Gònghéguó Zhùzuòquán Fǎ (2010 xiūzhèng) (中华人民共和国著作权法(2010修正) [Copyright Law of the People's Republic of China (2010 Amendment)] (Promulgated by the Standing Comm. Nat'l People's Cong., February 26, 2010).

39 The Panel Report refers to the first sentence of Article 4 as "Article 4(1)" for ease of reference, although the original version does not use paragraph numbers within that Article.

40 Panel Report, *China – Intellectual Property Rights, supra* note 36, para. 7.16, referring to the United States' first written submission, paras 217–219.

41 China's rebuttal submission, paras 273 and 318. Furthermore, the authors of works who are denied protection of the Copyright Law do not benefit from the remedies specified in Articles 46 and 47 of the Copyright Law. Consequently, the authors of such works do not enjoy the minimum rights that are "specially granted" by the Berne Convention, inconsistently with Article 5(1) of that Convention.

42 Panel Report, *China – Intellectual Property Rights, supra* note 36, para. 7.135.

43 Panel Report, *China – Intellectual Property Rights, supra* note 36, paras 7.50–7.52. The United States submitted a letter sent from the Supreme People's Court to a provincial Higher People's Court during that case, which the Supreme People's Court reissued in 2000. This letter, from China's highest judicial body, is instructive in the interpretation of Article 4(1) of the Copyright Law. That case concerned a book, the publication of which violated administrative regulations but the content of which did not violate any laws. In the letter, the Court ruled that it was correct for the courts of the first and second instances to

to control content was recognized by Article 17 of the Berne Convention, Article 4(1) of the Copyright Law was inconsistent with Article 5(1) of the Berne Convention, as incorporated by Article 9.1 of the TRIPS Agreement.[44]

In the second case, the Panel considered a complaint by the US concerning a series of Chinese measures regulating activities related to the importation and distribution of reading materials, audiovisual home entertainment products, sound recordings, and film for theatrical release that all qualified as "cultural goods and services" under the legal definition contained in the UNESCO Convention.[45] The US claimed that some of the Chinese measures violated trading rights commitments undertaken by China, notably by restricting the right to import the goods at stake into China to Chinese state-owned enterprises (SOEs).[46] The US thus alleged that these measures were inconsistent with provisions under GATT 1994 and GATS as well as with specific obligations under China's accession protocol.[47] The Panel ruled in favor of the US, and the Appellate Body upheld this decision.[48]

In its defense, China submitted that cultural goods and services share a unique nature. They do not merely satisfy a commercial need, but are "vectors of identity, values, and meaning" playing an essential role in the evolution and definition of aspects such as societal features, values, ways of living together, ethics, and behaviors.[49] China argued that there is a link between cultural goods and the protection of public morals, asserting that cultural goods have a major impact on societal and individual morals as emphasized in the UNESCO Convention. China submitted that the state has a vital interest in imposing a high level of protection of public morals through an appropriate content review mechanism that prohibits

provide protection under the Copyright Law to the book at issue for the following reason: "The Inside Story was originally published in the magazine *Yanhuang Chunqiu* (1994, No. 2). In May of the same year, the United Front Department of the Sichuan Provincial Communist Party Committee reviewed the book and approved its publication. Nothing was found in the text of the Inside Story to violate any laws. Therefore, it is correct for the courts of the first and second instances to provide it protection under the *Copyright Law*." The Panel found that the Supreme People's Court letter confirms that Article 4(1) of the Copyright Law denies copyright protection and clarifies that Article 4(1) applies where the publication and/or dissemination of a work is prohibited due to its content.

44 Panel Report, *China – Intellectual Property Rights, supra* note 36, para. 7.139.

45 For a detailed analysis of this case, *see* Tania Voon, *China – Measures Affecting Trading Rights and Distribution Services for Certain Publications and Audiovisual Entertainment Products,* 4 Am. J. Int'l L. 710 (2009).

46 WTO Ministerial Conference, *Report of the Working Party on the Accession of China*, WT/MIN(01)/3 (November 10, 2001); WTO Ministerial Conference, Accession of the People's Republic of China: Decision of November 10, 2001, WT/L/432 (November 23, 2001). China accepted the Protocol on the Accession of the People's Republic of China (annexed to the Decision of November 10, 2001) on November 11, 2001 and, in accordance with its terms, became a WTO Member on December 11, 2001: WTO Director-General Mike Moore, Protocol on Accession of the People's Republic of China Done at Doha on November 10, 2001: Notification of Acceptance, Entry into Force, WLI/100 (November 20, 2001).

47 Article XVI and/or Article XVII of GATS and Article III:4 of GATT 1994. See Panel Report, *China – Measures Affecting Trading Rights and Distribution Services for Certain Publications and Audiovisual Entertainment Products*, WT/DS363/R, para. 3.1 (August 12, 2009), and Appellate Body Report, WT/DS363/AB/R, para. 2 (December 21, 2009) [hereinafter *China – Publications and Audiovisual Products*].

48 Appellate Body Report, *China – Publications and Audiovisual Products, supra* note 47, paras 5, 10, and 414. Panel Report, *China – Publications and Audiovisual Products*, paras 8.1–8.2.

49 Article 8 of the UNESCO Declaration and Article 1(g) of the UNESCO Convention. *See* WTO Panel Report, *China – Publications and Audiovisual Products, supra* note 47, paras 4.89, 4.276 and 7.751.

any cultural goods with content that could have a negative impact on public morals.[50] China, thus, defended its regulations as necessary to protect public morals, and fully justified its contention under Article XX(a) of the GATT and its *chapeau*.[51]

While the Panel adopted an open interpretation of "public morals" as culturally and socially oriented, it concluded that China's regulations were not "necessary" to protect public morals within the meaning of Article XX(a).[52] Accordingly, the Panel made its decision on the grounds of technical compliance with GATT regarding the necessity of China's regulations. On appeal, China requested the Appellate Body to be "mindful" of the "specific nature of cultural goods," although without success.[53]

In contrast to the first case on TRIPS, in which China did not invoke any arguments based on the protection and promotion of the diversity of cultural expressions, it should be highlighted that the Panel and Appellate Body did not use the word "censorship" at all in the second case. In other words, the parties did not make any link between cultural diversity and intellectual property in the first case, and avoided discussing inconsistencies between censorship and cultural diversity in the second.

Panem et circenses: Desirable new international law on trade and culture

There is momentum today to further analyze this case law in the light of the disputes initiated by Canada and Norway against the EU over seal products and the discussion about the right to regulate NTCs. Before the recent settlement of these disputes by the Appellate Body's reports of May 22, 2014,[54] Howse and Langille (2012) argued the case for an open debate on law and policy related to moral concerns that WTO Members raise against trade liberalization as follows:

> If the WTO were to allow countries to justify trade restrictive measures through moral rationales, countries would be able to make the reasons for their actions explicit. Therefore, an authoritarian country wishing to curtail the freedom of speech of its people could use this rationale explicitly, stating that, under the political morality of that country, this was why the measure was adopted. This would bring potentially unsavory political viewpoints to light, and would open them up to contestation.[55]

50 This "negative" content could include violence, pornography, and any content that China deems as posing a threat to Chinese culture and traditional values. *See* also Chapter 25 (Friedmann) in this volume.

51 To address the meaning of the concept of "public morals" as it appears in Article XX(a), the Panel adopted the same interpretation of the expression as it is used in Article XIV of the GATS and given in *US – Gambling*, at paras 4.109, 4.276, 7.714 and 7.753. The *chapeau* is the introductory paragraph of Article XX. It contains general requirements that must be satisfied by a measure in order to comply with it.

52 WTO Panel Report, *China – Publications and Audiovisual Products*, *supra* note 47, para. 7.759. *See* also Chapters 24 (Kamperman Sanders) and 25 (Friedmann) in this volume.

53 Lucia Bellucci and Roberto Soprano, *Study Paper 3A: The WTO System and the implementation of the UNESCO Convention: two case studies*, in Study for the European Parliament on the Implementation of the 2005 UNESCO Convention on the Protection and Promotion of the Diversity of Cultural Expressions, long version of the Study, *supra* note 19, at 159.

54 Reports of the Appellate Body, *European Communities-Measures Prohibiting the Importation and Marketing of Seal Products*, WT/DS400/AB/R and WT/DS401/AB/R [hereinafter *EC – Seal Products AB*].

55 Robert Howse & Joanna Langille, *Permitting Pluralism: The Seal Products Dispute And Why The WTO Should Permit Trade Restrictions Justified By Non-Instrumental Moral Values*, 37(2) Yale J. Int'l L. (2012).

In its reports on the Seal Products dispute, the Appellate Body recalled the Panel's observation that "moral concern regarding the protection of animals is a value of high importance in the European Union (5.203)."[56] In this context, the Panel also referred to the statement by the panel in *China – Publications and Audiovisual Products* that the protection of public morals "ranks among the most important values or interests pursued by members as a matter of public policy."[57]

The Panel concluded in its reports that the evidence presented by the European Union, taken as a whole, illustrates "standards of right and wrong conduct maintained by or on behalf of [the European Union]" concerning seal welfare (5.203). It observed that ascertaining the precise content and scope of morality in a given society may not be an easy task. It quoted the panel in *US – Gambling* according to which "Members should be given some scope to define and apply for themselves the concepts of 'public morals' in their respective territories, according to their own systems and scales of values." The Panel was eventually persuaded in the instant cases that the evidence as a whole sufficiently demonstrated that animal welfare is an issue of ethical or moral nature in the European Union: "International doctrines and measures of a similar nature in other WTO Members [. . .] illustrate that animal welfare is a matter of ethical responsibility for human beings in general."

The Dispute Settlement Body of the WTO was thus confronted in the *Seal Products* case with questions of "international morality" to which I shall return below. First, however, I wish to observe that interestingly and relevant for the purposes of this contribution, the *Seal Products* reports also dealt with the diversity of cultural expressions.

The European Union submitted that the objective of the EU Seal Regime is "to address the moral concerns of the EU public with regard to the welfare of seals" (7.367, with further references): "Those concerns arise from the fact that seal products may have been obtained from animals killed in a way that causes them excessive pain, distress, fear, or other forms of suffering." The European Union asserted further that "contributing to the welfare of seals by reducing the number of seals killed in an inhumane way" can be regarded as being simultaneously a legitimate objective on its own and one of the instruments to achieve the first, broader and overarching, objective of addressing public moral concerns on seal welfare. In addition, the Panel recalled that the initiative to introduce a measure governing trade in seal products in the European Union originates in the 2006 "Declaration of the European Parliament on banning seal products in the European Union" (Parliament Declaration). In its preamble, the Parliament Declaration referenced, ***inter alia***, an observation that a certain proportion of seals hunted may have been skinned while still conscious. According to the Panel, although the Parliament Declaration did not explicitly elaborate on the specific reasons for the initiative to ban seal products, a list of points contained in the preamble suggests a connection between the Declaration and seal welfare. This Declaration also stated that "this regulation should not have an impact on traditional Inuit seal hunting." (7.391)

The latter concern led the EU to introduce a so-called Inuit Community (IC) exception that Canada and Norway used to challenge the European seals regime. Canada argued inconsistency with the IC exception, stating in particular that the European Union's defined objective is not legitimate because it is based on an arbitrary and unjustifiable distinction between "commercial" and "non-commercial" hunts (7.412). Canada argued further that

56 *Supra* note 54, para. 7.632.

57 AB Reports – *Seal Products*, fn 1261 to 5.203, referring to the Panel Reports – *Seal Products*, fn 972 to 7.632 quoting the Panel Report, *China – Publications and Audiovisual Products*, para. 7.817.

the EU Seal Regime, under the IC category, contains trade-restrictive requirements with no rational connection to the objectives of animal welfare and public concerns regarding animal welfare, which in fact undermine those objectives.

As for Norway, it would accept that addressing a public moral relating to seal welfare was *a priori* legitimate (7.413), but that a distinction based on the alleged "commercial" and "non-commercial" seal hunts was illegitimate "because it discriminates in favour of particular communities."

The European Union replied to these objections that, "in light of the 'unique' situation in which Inuit and indigenous communities find themselves, it would have been 'morally wrong' for the EU legislator to prohibit the placing on the market of seal products resulting from the hunts traditionally conducted by those communities." In essence, for the European Union, seal hunts conducted for the subsistence of Inuit and indigenous communities benefit from an "inherent legitimacy" that "overrides the general concerns over the killing methods for purely commercial motives." The European Union stressed that its regulatory approach on seal products, in particular regarding the IC exception, was in line with a consistent body of international law echoing the legitimacy of protecting the interests of Inuit and indigenous communities, and that the European Union is bound by these international legal instruments (7.254).

The Panel said it understood the EU's justification of the distinction between commercial and IC hunts to rest on two premises: First, if the objective of the IC exception is found to be legitimate, then, *a fortiori*, the regulatory distinction should also be considered "legitimate". Second, highlighting the alleged uniqueness of IC hunts, the European Union argues that IC hunts, which are conducted for the "subsistence" of Inuit and indigenous communities, benefit from an "inherent legitimacy" that "overrides the general concerns over the killing methods for purely commercial motives." According to the European Union, therefore, the purpose of the hunt distinguishes IC hunts from commercial hunts and justifies any risk of suffering inflicted upon seals as a result of the hunts conducted by those communities (7.278): "The European Union explains further that, because the subsistence of the Inuit and other indigenous communities and the preservation of their cultural identity provide benefits to humans, from a moral point of view, this outweighs the risk of suffering inflicted upon seals as a result of the hunts conducted by those communities."

Although the EU replied, *inter alia*, with arguments related to cultural expressions, it did not invoke the UNESCO Convention on cultural diversity.[58] This was unfortunate, especially in view of the fact that the three parties, the European Union and her opponents, Canada and Norway, are parties to this treaty.

In its preamble, the UNESCO Convention affirms that cultural diversity:

- is a defining characteristic of humanity;
- expresses its consciousness that cultural diversity forms a common heritage of humanity and should be cherished and preserved for the benefit of all;
- recognizes the importance of traditional knowledge as a source of intangible and material wealth, and in particular the knowledge systems of indigenous peoples, and

58 *See* European Union's first written submission, paras 270–272; second written submission, paras 223–224 and fn 245 citing UN Department of Economic and Social Affairs, "State of the World's Indigenous People", ST/ESA/328 (2009), at 10. This report focuses primarily on the Convention on biological diversity (CBD) and only superficially mentions the UNESCO Convention while briefly criticizing it in an arguably unfounded manner (at 222).

its positive contribution to sustainable development, as well as the need for its adequate protection and promotion;

- recognizes the need to take measures to protect the diversity of cultural expressions, including their contents, especially in situations where cultural expressions may be threatened by the possibility of extinction or serious impairment;
- recognizes that the diversity of cultural expressions, including traditional cultural expressions, is an important factor that allows individuals and peoples to express and to share with others their ideas and values;
- takes into account the importance of the vitality of cultures, including for persons belonging to minorities and indigenous peoples, as manifested in their freedom to create, disseminate, and distribute their traditional cultural expressions and to have access thereto, so as to benefit them for their own development;
- and is being convinced that cultural activities, goods, and services have both an economic and a cultural nature, because they convey identities, values, and meanings, and must therefore not be treated as solely having commercial value.

Last but not least, Article 7, para. 1(a) of the UNESCO Convention would also have been of relevance for the Inuit exception since it provides that Parties shall endeavor to create in their territory an environment which encourages individuals and social groups to create, produce, disseminate, distribute, and have access to their own cultural expressions, paying due attention to the special circumstances and needs of women as well as various social groups, including persons belonging to minorities and indigenous peoples.

Canada did not contest the unique characteristics of IC hunts before the panel. In fact, Canada acknowledged that, regardless of hunting methods, the Inuit hunt itself is traditional and a fundamental element of Inuit culture and society. For example, Canada stated that the purpose of the Canadian Inuit hunt today is not materially different from the hunt 1,000 years ago, although the emergence of a monetized society and new technologies has caused the Canadian Inuit to commercialize some output to generate income (7.281). However, Canada disagreed with the European Union on whether the purpose of IC hunts ("subsistence" purpose) and the purpose of commercial hunts ("primarily or exclusively commercial reasons") can strictly be distinguishable as asserted by the European Union. Canada argued, ***inter alia***, that the "subsistence" purpose of IC hunts can equally be used to describe the Canadian east coast seal hunt (commercial hunts).

The Panel concluded that "while IC hunts may also have a commercial aspect, we are persuaded that the subsistence aspect of IC hunts, combined with the identity of the hunter as Inuit, has significance for their culture and tradition as well as for their livelihood. To that extent, the primary purpose of IC hunts is distinguishable from that of commercial hunts" (7.289; footnote omitted). Furthermore, the Panel became persuaded by the European Union's explanation that "the primary purpose of IC hunts, namely to preserve the tradition and culture of Inuit and to sustain their livelihood, is distinguishable from that of commercial hunts, and justifies the IC distinction, which protects IC interests." It did not find, however, that the rationale or the cause of the distinction can be linked to the alleged "standard of the EU public's morality" in general (7.300).

In order to determine the objective of the EU Seal Regime, the Panel examined whether the evidence as a whole shows (a) the existence of the EU public's concerns on seal welfare and/or any other concerns or issues that the European Union seeks to address; and, (b) the connection between such concerns, if proven to exist, and the "public morals" (i.e. standards of right or wrong) as defined and applied within the European Union (7.403 with reference to 7.383).

As regards the first question, the Panel concluded that the text and legislative history of the measure established the existence of the EU public's concerns on seal welfare. As to the second question, namely, whether the concerns at issue fall within the scope of "public morals" in the European Union, in view of the Panel's determination that IC interests do not constitute an objective of the EU Seal Regime, it found it unnecessary to determine whether such interests are "articulations of the same standard of morality" governing the public concerns on seal welfare as claimed by the European Union. Thus, the Panel confined its task to assessing whether the public concerns on seal welfare are anchored in the morality of European societies, and found that the legislative history of the measure suggests a link between the public concerns on seal welfare and an ethical or moral consideration (7.404 and 7.405).

Eventually, it is worth noting that, in support of its position that the stated objective is legitimate, the European Union also referred to various measures on animal welfare and seal products adopted by other WTO Members as well as international instruments on animal welfare. However, the Panel concluded with respect to this argument that it did not need to determine whether "these examples as such exhibit the existence of a global social norm ('a universal value' according to the European Union) on animal welfare in general or seal welfare in particular." Nevertheless, these various actions concerning animal welfare at the international as well as national levels suggested in the Panel's view that "animal welfare is a globally recognized issue" (7.420).

As Wu recalled in a comment on the *US – Gambling* case, it was unclear prior to that dispute whether the public morals clause should be interpreted statically or dynamically: "Static interpreters would limit the exception to the scope of public morals as understood by the drafters in 1947. Dynamic interpreters, in contrast, would argue that the scope can expand over time as new issues of public morality emerge."[59] The Panel in the *Gambling* case endorsed a dynamic interpretation of public morals, that the Appellate Body confirmed, by stating that "the content of [public morals] can vary in time and space, depending upon a range of factors, including prevailing social, cultural, ethical, and religious values." This case, however, did not address the basic definitional question: which morals are "public morals" as opposed to those that are simply shared by a group of individuals? Wu further noted that both a universalist and a unilateralist approach to this question would pose potential problems:

> If one were to require that morals be near-universal before being considered a 'public moral', then the set of morals that would actually qualify might be so limited as to render the exceptions clause effectively useless. [. . .] On the other hand, allowing states to unilaterally define their 'public morals' would also entail certain problems. The main threat is that, left unconstrained, states will abuse the exception to pass a large number of trade restrictions under the guise of protecting public morals.[60]

59 Mark Wu, *Free Trade and the Protection of Public Morals: An Analysis of the Newly Emerging Public Morals Clause Doctrine,* Yale J. Int'l L. 231 (2008), with further references.

60 Mark Wu, *Free Trade and the Protection of Public Morals: An Analysis of the Newly Emerging Public Morals Clause Doctrine,* Yale J. Int'l L. 231, 232 (2008), footnotes omitted.

In his classic introduction to the study of international relations, Edward Hallett Carr submitted an intellectually stimulating definition of "international morality":

> International politics are always power politics; for it is impossible to eliminate power from them. But that is only part of the story. The fact that national propaganda everywhere so eagerly cloaks itself in ideologies of a professedly international character proves the existence of an international stock of common ideas, however limited and however weakly held, to which appeal can be made, and of a belief that these common ideas stand somehow in the scale of values above national interests. This stock of common ideas is what we mean by international morality.[61]

Carr affirmed in this context that power over opinion cannot be dissociated from military and economic power, and that power over opinion, which is a necessary part of all power, can never be absolute.

Coming back to the US/Hollywood versus China case, we can observe that many forms of cultural expressions as defined by the UNESCO Convention on Cultural Diversity arguably qualify as "national propaganda". As a consequence, it seems to make sense to understand an essential part of that treaty, in particular its Article 7 para. 1(b), as a form codification of "international morality" to restrain the power and law of the stronger state over opinion: Parties shall endeavor to create in their territory an environment which encourages individuals and social groups to have access to diverse cultural expressions from within their territory as well as from other countries of the world.

Several third parties' submissions to the dispute on cultural goods and services challenged China's invocation of the UNESCO Convention. Pursuant to Korea, for example, reference to the UNESCO Convention on cultural diversity failed to support the proposition offered by China: "Not only the Cultural Diversity Convention itself precludes a situation where the convention is somehow used as a ground to justify alleged violations of the WTO Agreements, but also relevant provisions of the DSU explicitly prohibits a panel from accepting such an argument." Such statements clearly illustrate poor knowledge of the contents of the UNESCO Convention and of its impact on other treaties. As a matter of fact, those countries that are parties to this treaty can require that China respect its provisions. Such respect includes compliance with human rights and fundamental freedoms that are relevant for the protection and promotion of the diversity of cultural expressions, notably the freedom of expression, as expressly mentioned in Article 2.1. As a consequence, if the public morals exception under the applicable WTO agreements would have been interpreted by the Panel and the Appellate Body in a consistent way with China's commitment under the UNESCO Convention, these instances could not reasonably have ruled that the public morals exception under the WTO agreements authorizes control of content that violates the freedom of expression. Thus, if the US were a party to the UNESCO Convention, it could have successfully challenged China's good faith in claiming that most of the rights to control content provided under the relevant Chinese legislation are clearly inconsistent with this treaty, and that they should be assessed and sanctioned under the principle of estoppel ("*venire contra*

61 Edward Hallett Carr, The Twenty Years Crisis, 1919–1939, An Introduction to the Study of International Relations 141, 145 (Harper Perennial, 1946; reprint 2001).

proprium factum").[62] This strategy, however, would have put the driving forces behind these disputes at risk of backfire; the Hollywood oligopoly could sooner or later have faced the claim that these industries, largely thanks to US economic and military power, themselves also practice censorship of a private kind that is equally inconsistent with the UNESCO Convention, particularly with its Article 7. However, in this constellation, China or the EU would have quite a harder time invoking the UNESCO Convention to protect and promote freedom of expression since the US is not party to this treaty. The EU is well advised to remember this reality in the context of its current negotiations with the US on a bilateral free trade agreement.[63]

For the time being, the US remains the ideologically dominating power worldwide in terms of the strength and influence of its "entertainment" industries. This country seeks the highest standards of intellectual property protection in order to enable its content industries to impose their films, music, and books worldwide as a sustainable instrument of "power over opinion," in Carr's understanding. China, on the other hand, became a very strong player particularly in financial markets in recent years. As an aspiring economic superpower, China is not only steadily reinforcing its military role, but it is also seeking to win the ideological and cultural battle as well, one day soon.[64]

For third parties, such as European countries, Brazil, or India and other non-authoritarian states, the TRIPS case should spread awareness that both the US and China censor content in their own unique ways: China via the state machinery and the US via intellectual

62 This approach arguably provides also a solution to Pauwelyn's suggestion that the WTO could contribute, with the right litigation strategies, in "translating restrictions on freedom of speech, opinions or ideas into restrictions on the free movement of goods or services, including openly contesting that some content censored by China has little, if anything, to do with 'public morals' [. . .]," adding that "to the extent that prying open markets can pry open minds, here is an area where free trade and free speech can be mutually reinforcing." Joost Pauwelyn, *Squaring free trade in culture with Chinese censorship: the WTO Appellate Body report on China – audiovisuals*, Melb. J. Int'l L. (2010). On the principle of estoppel, see *Temple of Preah Vihear (Cambodia v Thailand)*, [1962] ICJ Rep. 6, 32–3: "[. . .] the principle operates to prevent a State contesting before that Court a situation contrary to a clear and unequivocal representation previously made by it to another state, either expressly or impliedly, on which representation that other State was, in the circumstances, entitled to rely and in fact did rely, and as a result that other State has been prejudiced or the State making it has secured some benefit or advantage for itself." Compare also Chan, *Acquiescence/Estoppel in International Boundaries: Temple of Preah Vihear Revisited*, Chinese J. Int'l L. 3 (2004), 421; MacGibbon, *Estoppel in International Law*, Int'l & Comp. L.Q. 7 (1958), 468; Ovchar, *Estoppel in the Jurisprudence of the ICJ, A principle promoting stability threatens to undermine it*, Bond L. Rev. 6–1 , Vol. 21 (2009), Contribution 5; Gaillard, *L'interdiction de se contredire au détriment d'autrui comme principe général du droit du commerce international (le principe de l'estoppel dans quelques sentences arbitrales récentes)*, Rev. d. Arb. (1985), 241.

63 *See* Christophe Germann, *Ce que M. Barroso aurait dû dire à son collègue Barack Obama*, Le Temps (November 12, 2013) (English translation at www.worldmeets.us with search words: Europe's Price for Trade Talks Must Be End to U.S. Impunity, Le Temps, Switzerland).

64 Compare Carr, *supra* at 133 on censorship from private sources in the age of cultural industries: "The problem of power over opinion in its modern mass form has been created by development in economic and military technique – by the substitution of mass production industries for individual craftsmanship and of the conscript citizen army for the volunteer professional force. [. . .] The problem is one which no modern government ignores. In appearance, the attitude adopted towards it by democracies and by totalitarian states is diametrically opposed. Democracies purport to follow mass opinion; totalitarian states set a standard an enforce conformity to it. In practice, the contrast is less clear cut. Totalitarian states, in determining their policy, profess to express the will of the masses; and the profession is not wholly vain. Democracies, or the groups which control them, are not altogether innocent of the arts of moulding and directing mass opinion."

property-induced marketing power insuring market domination that causes systematic cultural discrimination wherever local competitors do not enjoy similar advertisement force. US major content industries arguably use excessive levels of copyright and trademark protection as the most effective way to covertly muzzle alien content in order to better propagate their own *Weltanschauung* wrapped in entertainment and culture for mass consumption.

Panem et circenses – give the people *bread and games* to distract them from critical dissent – that was the way the emperors and the ruling classes of ancient Rome kept their constituencies under control. Today, the case law on gambling, entertainment, and animal welfare related to the public moral exception of the WTO agreements reveals both the existing insufficiencies and the potential for improvement of this body of law. As a consequence, desirable development of international law on culture and trade should duly consider Janus' two faces of the freedom of expression, and its equally twofold negation by public and private censorship. Indeed, very much is at stake when law and policies on cultural diversity meet those on international trade, because genuine freedom of expression is essential to a functioning democracy, and because a functioning democracy can be of existential value for a great many people, as Amartya Sen, who witnessed the Bengal famine of 1943 as a child, recalled in his *The Idea of Justice:*

> The prevalence of famines, which had been a persistent feature of the long history of the British Indian Empire, ended abruptly with the establishment of a democracy after independence. Despite China's greater success than India's in many economic fields, China – unlike independent India – did have a huge famine, indeed the largest famine in recorded history, in 1958–61, with a mortality count estimated at close to 30 million. Though the famine raged for three years, the government was not pressed to change its disastrous policies: there was, in China, no parliament open for critical dissent, no opposition party and no free press. [. . .] The direct penalties of famine are borne only by the suffering public and not by the ruling government. The rulers never starve. However, when a government is accountable to the public, and when there is free news-reporting and uncensored public criticism, then the government too has an excellent incentive to do its best to eradicated famines.[65]

The core value of the UNESCO Convention on cultural diversity arguably resides in its potential to challenge power over opinion to bring about changes of normative normalities through international morality without recourse to military or economic power.

In this context, I agree with Carr that, in the long run, military and economic power cannot exist in isolation of power over opinion:

> If, however, it is utopian to ignore the element of power, it is an unreal kind of realism which ignores the element of morality in any world order. Just as within the state every government, though it needs power as a basis of its authority, also needs the moral basis of the consent of the governed, so an international order cannot be based on power alone, for the simple reason that mankind will in the long run always revolt against naked power. Any international order presupposes a substantial measure of general consent. [. . .] Power goes far to create the morality convenient to itself, and coercion is a fruitful source of consent. But when all these reserves have been made, it remains true that a new international order and a new international harmony can be built up

65 Amartya Sen, The Idea of Justice 342–343 (Belknap Press, 2010).

> only on the basis of an ascendancy which is generally accepted as tolerant and unoppressive or, at any rate, as preferable to any practical alternative.[66]

Power over opinion requires popularity of morality underlying such power. The international order today structures the relationship between human groups and individuals essentially in relation to power, wealth, and popularity. It uses for these purposes a monopoly of violence in matters of power, a monopoly by property (or ownership) in matters of wealth, and a monopoly on human expressions in matters of popularity, including, but not limited to cultural expressions. The United States for example arguably upholds her current hegemony in the world by way of three clusters that I shall metaphorically coin "WashWallWood": Washington, its political heart (power); Wall Street, its financial capital (wealth); and Hollywood, its culture and entertainment sanctuary (popularity). The state, defined by Max Weber as the holder of the legitimate monopoly of violence, ensures the monopoly by property by way of its monopoly of violence. The state either holds itself the monopoly by property (e.g. communism) or guarantees it to private actors (e.g. capitalism). Most states provide today a mix between these two basic forms of exercise of the monopoly by property (e.g. China currently practices some political and economic hybrids between state capitalism and liberal communism). Some states have insufficient monopoly of violence (e.g. Somalia) while others abuse it (e.g. North Korea, Syria, and Eritrea). States that are labeled as "emerging, developing or least-developed economies" suffer from inequalities resulting from the exercise of the monopoly by property. These inequalities are related to the distribution of wealth and can be either homegrown or caused by unfair trade with wealthier states, or both. These inequalities in the distribution of wealth in turn condition inequalities in the distribution of popularity. Popularity requires resources of power and wealth and vice-versa: power requires wealth and popularity, whereas wealth requires power and popularity. Furthermore, differences and variations among states are conditioned by the political regimes in force that range from consensus in more liberal states to diktat in more authoritarian ones. In domestic affairs, rather liberal states will tend to dispose of their monopoly of force to protect the monopoly by property of qualifying private actors. More authoritarian states, in contrast, will tend to capture the monopoly by property in order to reinforce their own monopoly of force and, more often than not, the monopoly by property of their ruling classes. In their international relations, all states will tend to assert both monopolies vis-à-vis third states on the basis of the principle of sovereignty and related immunity. In times of crisis or of other drastic changes of ***normative normalities*** such as revolutions, popularity can escape both monopolization of force and monopolization by property. Outside such situations, however, popularity is normally induced and determined by both power resulting from the monopoly of force and wealth from the monopoly by property.[67]

In the WTO cases of the US versus China as well as Canada and Norway versus the EU that were analyzed above, we can observe both absurd uses and equally absurd non-uses of the UNESCO Convention on Cultural Diversity, respectively. This could be explained by the mere fact that the parties to these disputes considered this treaty to be a useless tool, due to its lack of an effective dispute settlement mechanism. In the future, however, it must be expected that the increasing impact of the multilateral and bilateral trading systems on

66 Carr, *op. cit.*, at 235,

67 Christophe Germann, *Menschliche Vielfalt im Lichte der Friedensförderung – Cosmopolis unter einem Schleier des Unwissens um Gruppenzugehörigkeit*, ARCHIVES FOR PHILOSOPHY OF LAW AND SOCIAL PHILOSOPHY 2/2015.

NTCs will cause a greater focus on the so-called "public morals exception" in most walks of life affected by international economic law and policy. In such scenarios, if an unrestrained recourse to national standards of right and wrong shall be avoided for the reasons that Wu recalled, the time has come to employ the concept of an "international morality" as a legal alternative to both national and allegedly "universalist" public morals. I argue that the UNESCO Convention on Cultural Diversity can play a key role in delivering concrete meanings to such a concept.

The WTO Dispute Settlement Body, which today offers one of the most effective mechanisms of settling international litigations, will be increasingly confronted with questions of standards of right and wrong related to NTCs. In such situations, it will have to substantially contribute to elaborate, develop, and articulate a new concept of international morality.

Like the god Janus, who gave his name to the two-headed turtle of Geneva, international morality is a spirit of beginnings and transitions that looks to the past and the future with a view to both challenge existing and create new normative normalities beyond the power of the ephemeral stronger state. The most noble effect of international trade is precisely about questioning and, as the case may be, disturbing monopolies, be they monopolies of violence, by property, or on human expressions. In this light, international morality will be about achieving a fairer distribution and exercise of power, wealth, and popularity among nations.

23 Cultural Products and the WTO

China's Domestic Censorship and Media Control Policies*

Rogier Creemers

In December 2009, the World Trade Organization (WTO) Appellate Body circulated its report in the landmark case, *China – Publications and Audiovisual Products.*[1] This was the first WTO case involving trade in cultural products with regards to China, and may have serious implications for both the development of WTO law and Chinese media regulation. The case dealt with China's market access regime for a range of cultural products, including cinematic films, audiovisual products, and publications. In a number of areas, the Appellate Body found that China violated WTO law by prohibiting foreign investment in certain sectors; introducing State discretion into licensing processes, where China had committed to granting trading rights in a non-discretionary manner; limiting foreign participation in media enterprises; and treating domestic and foreign enterprises differently in regards to sector access.[2]

This case has provoked its fair share of controversy. Some have criticized the Appellate Body for failing to interpret the trading rights provisions in their systemic context, in the light of their object and purpose, and hence to contribute to the expansion of the WTO's trade liberalization doctrine.[3] Such critics condemn the decision for having taken little regard

* This chapter is part of the results of the Research Project on "*Current Trends of Chinese Law towards Non-Trade Concerns such as Sustainable Development and the Protection of Environment, Public Health, Food Safety, Cultural, Social and Economic Rights, Labor Rights and the Reduction of Poverty from the Perspective of International Law and WTO Law*", coordinated by Professor Paolo Davide Farah at gLAWcal – Global Law Initiatives for Sustainable Development (United Kingdom) and at West Virginia University John D. Rockefeller IV School of Policy and Politics, Department of Public Administration, in partnership with the Center of Advanced Studies on Contemporary China (CASCC) in Turin (Italy), Maastricht University Faculty of Law, Department of International and European Law and IGIR – Institute for Globalisation and International Regulation (Netherlands), and Tsinghua University, School of Law, Institute of Public International Law and the Center for Research on Intellectual Property Law in Beijing (China). An early draft of this chapter was presented at the Conferences Series on "*China's Influence on Non-Trade Concerns in International Economic Law*", Third Conference held at Maastricht University, Faculty of Law on January 19–20, 2012. This publication and the Conference Series were sponsored by China–EU School of Law (CESL) at the China University of Political Science and Law (CUPL). The activities of CESL at CUPL are supported by the European Union and the People's Republic of China.

1 Appellate Body Report, *China – Measures Affecting Trading Rights and Distribution Services for Certain Publications and Audiovisual Entertainment Products*, WT/DS363/AB/R (December 21, 2009) [hereinafter *China – Publications and Audiovisual Products*].

2 For a detailed overview of the case, *see* Tania Voon, *China – Publications and Audiovisual Products,* 103 Am. J. Int'l L. 710–715 (2009). *See* Chapters 24 (Kamperman Sanders) and 25 (Friedmann) in this volume.

3 Julia Qin, *Pushing the Limit of Global Governance,* 10 Chinese J. Int'l L. 271–322 (2011).

for its political and social ramifications.[4] Doubts exist about China's ability and willingness to implement the Appellate Body's findings, and fears that the United States' (US) tactic to force market access for cultural products through the international trade arena may lead to accusations of cultural imperialism.[5] Other observers, however, praise the Panel and Appellate Body for their flexibility in dealing with the sensitive nature of the case.[6]

Divergent conceptions of cultural products and their role in international trade lie at the center of this dispute. For the US, cultural products – and audiovisual media in particular – are tradable commodities produced by private actors. Audiovisual media is a significant export industry, which contributes about 13 trillion dollars to the US trade balance, according to industry figures, and which has considerable political clout through sector organizations such as the Motion Pictures Association of America (MPAA) and the International Intellectual Property Association (IIPA).[7] In a single-party state like China, media plays a much more sensitive political role, and the Party-State has made it a priority to maintain control over the public debate. The government expects that media products will not detract from its political messages, at a minimum, and will preferably contribute to them. This objective requires mechanisms by which the Party-State can influence which products are produced, imported, and distributed, and control their entrance to the market, in order to maximize public exposure to the political message.[8]

This chapter aims to explain the nexus between media control and international trade. Understanding how the censorship system operates makes it possible to better gauge the impact of international trade law – and *China – Publications and Audiovisual Products* in particular – on this important aspect of Chinese domestic regulation. The chapter consists of three parts. In the first part, I will outline the relevant actors and structures controlling Chinese media. In the second part, I will analyze the tensions between this media control regime and the expectations of the international trade regimes, paying particular attention to the *China – Publications and Audiovisual Products* dispute, mentioned above. Finally, in the last part, I will sketch the current state of the field, and outline possible future scenarios.

The domestic media control regime

As indicated above, the media plays a crucial role in Chinese politics, and is closely monitored by a complex web of institutional, Party-political, and regulatory measures. At the central level, the State Administration of Radio, Film and Television (SARFT), the General Administration of Press and Publications (GAPP), and the Ministry of Culture collectively govern the media sphere. As their names indicate, these agencies cover different media sectors, but their administrative divisions clash whenever the agencies' responsibilities overlap. These structures are replicated at the provincial level and at lower levels, although, in the latter case, these departments are often amalgamated into broad cultural offices. In principle, one of these departments supervises every media enterprise, and the departments can take

4 *Id.*

5 Elanor A. Mangin, *Market Access in China – Publications and Audiovisual Materials: A Moral Victory With a Silver Lining*, 25 Berkeley Tech. L. J. 279–310 (2010).

6 Jingxia Shi & Weidong Chen, *The "Specificity" of Cultural Products versus the "Generality" of Trade Obligations* (Yale Law School Student Scholarship Papers, Paper 104, 2010), at 41.

7 MPAA, *The Economic Contribution of the Motion Picture & Television Industry to the United States* (2010).

8 See Chapters 24 (Kamperman Sanders) and 25 (Friedmann) in this volume.

administrative action against both media enterprises and the individuals within them. Also, within the scope of their functional and geographical jurisdictions, all departments have the power to draft their own administrative regulations.

The State governance structure is complemented by Party structures, which mirror the hierarchy of the State structure and develop media policy. The Party structures also wield significant power over both State institutions and media enterprises. At the top level, the Party's Central Propaganda Department (CPD) gathers the most important policy-makers in the media and communications field. For example, the SARFT and GAPP directors and the Minister of Culture act as vice-chairpersons of the CPD, and the head of China Central Television (CCTV) also participates as a CPD member. Again, this structure is replicated at lower levels. Furthermore, through the Organization Departments, the Party controls the appointment and promotions of cadres throughout the media sphere, including State institutions and media enterprises. All media distribution and broadcast enterprises must have a Party Committee, where it is implied that the Party Secretary outranks management. As a result, the incentives for making a career in the media sector include implementing Party policy, not only professional or governmental objectives.[9]

This dual-command structure is visible in the way policies and regulations are made and implemented.[10] The CPD and relevant State Council departments jointly formulate top-level policy plans and list policy objectives. Administrative authorities then issue policy opinions and regulations on the basis of the plans, while the Party maintains *ad hoc* control over individual enterprises and departments. Media regulations consist of three levels. The highest level are management regulations (管理条例 *guanli tiaoli*), promulgated by the State Council. In the field of entertainment, such regulations exist for television, film, and audiovisual publications, among others. The relevant administrations are responsible for developing concrete rules and measures (规定 *guiding* and 办法 *banfa*), which further concretize specific aspects of the management regulations. For example, SARFT pronounced rules on topics as various as on-demand radio and television broadcasts,[11] film script filing,[12] and standardizing selection-type television program.[13] The lowest level consists of notices and circulars. These *ad hoc* administrative instructions deal with issues that arise, handle individual instances of violations, or amend standards and procedures. This structure is problematic in itself because it is difficult to track the current state of law at any given time since different documents may contradict each other, while some documents may not remain valid.[14]

This regulatory structure aims to maximize administrative control, rather than lay down basic and commonly applicable legal principles. Among all the laws, only the Copyright

9 For a comprehensive evaluation of the CPD's powers and functions, *see* Anne-Marie Brady, *Guiding Hand: The Role of the CCP Central Propaganda Department in the Current Era,* 3 Westminster Papers in Communication and Culture 58–77 (2006).

10 A collection of translated Chinese media regulations is available on the author's web site.

11 SARFT, 2004.

12 SARFT, 2005.

13 SARFT, 2007. This refers to competitions where the public participates in voting, such as Hunan Television's Super Girl (超级女声 *chaoji nüsheng).*

14 Similar problems appear in other policy areas, such as food safety. World Health China Representative Henk Bekedam was quoted as stating that "food regulations and standards have been developed in an ad hoc way without the benefit of a basic food law," as more than a dozen governmental agencies cover food safety. Nicholas Zamisky, *Who's Monitoring Chinese Food Exports*?, Wall Street Journal (April13, 2007).

Law[15] and the Advertising Law,[16] as well as some sections of the Criminal Law of the People's Republic of China,[17] deal with the media.[18] Hence, the administrative bodies maintain the power to interpret the regulations, amend them, and rule on violations of them, except where the latter involve suspected criminal activities. Neither the National People's Congress nor the civil courts get involved.

Substantively, most regulations deal with sector access and content regulation. In other words, the regulations aim to control, mainly through licensing, who may enter the sector, who may invest in the sector, and what they are allowed to produce. For example, before a film screens in a theater, both the script and the final cut require approval, and if the film addresses significant historical or revolutionary themes, it must undergo specific expert appraisal. In addition, the film-production company, distribution company, and cinemas must obtain licenses. In cases of noncompliance, administrative authorities may revoke licenses, meaning they can effectively remove enterprises from the marketplace. Furthermore, regulations are often drafted in such a manner as to maximize discretion for intervention whenever the administrative authorities deem necessary.[19] For example, SARFT has sole discretion to revoke the license of any previously approved film or television program. Also, the licensing authorities may request any document they like before making a licensing decision.

Over time, it has become increasingly necessary for the Party-State to balance political control with other objectives. One reason market mechanisms were introduced into the media sector was to relieve the government of the financial burden of issuing propaganda. The government realized that making media economically viable would allow it to function more effectively as a propaganda tool, but this has come with increasing incentives for media actors to push the boundaries of acceptability and to create products aimed at large audiences, rather than pleasing propaganda departments. Since the early 1990s, a number of measures have rationalized the number of media entities,[20] restructured the media market,[21] and created cross-sector subsidy mechanisms within the cultural sphere.[22]

As a result, increasing importance was attached to the cultural industries as a new locus of economic growth. In 2001, the government invested efforts to transform a number of State-owned entities from public-service work units (事业单位 *shiye danwei*) into enterprises

15 Zhōnghuá Rénmín Gònghéguó Zhùzuòquán Fǎ (2010 xiūzhèng) (中华人民共和国著作权法(2010修正) [Copyright Law of the People's Republic of China (2010 Amendment)] (Promulgated by the Standing Comm. Nat'l People's Cong., February 26, 2010).

16 Zhōnghuá Rénmín Gònghéguó Guǎnggào Fǎ (中华人民共和国广告法) [Advertising Law of the People's Republic of China] (Promulgated by the Standing Comm. Nat'l People's Cong., October 27, 1994).

17 Zhōng Zhōnghuá Rénmín Gònghéguó Xíngfǎ (97 Xiūdìng) (中华人民共和国刑法 97修订) [Criminal Law of the People's Republic of China (97 Revision)] (promulgated by the Nat'l People's Cong., March 14, 1997).

18 The Copyright Law regulates the rights of individual authors, the Advertising Law provides for minimum standards as to advertising content and display, and the Criminal Law criminalizes certain forms of copyright infringement, trade in prohibited media and certain types of expression.

19 *See* Chapter 25 (Friedmann) in this volume.

20 *Guanyu wenhua shiye ruogan jingji zhengce yijian baogao [Report Concerning Some Economic Policy Opinions for Cultural Undertakings*] (1991), *Zhonggong zhongyang bangongting, guowuyuan bangongting guanyu yasuo zhengdun yinxiang danwei de tongzhi [Central Committee Secretariat, State Council Secretariat Notice Concerning Compression and Rectification of Audiovisual Work Units]* (1991).

21 Referred to in *Guanyu jinyibu shenhua dianyingye gaige de ruogan yijian [Some Opinions Concerning Further Deepening Film Sector Reform]* (2000).

22 *Guanyu zhichi wenhua shiye fazhan ruogan jingji zhengce de tongzhi [Notice Concerning Some Economic Policies Supporting the Cultural Sector Development]* (2000).

based on market principles (企业单位 *qiye danwei*),[23] separating the media industry in public-service and commercial sectors. This division became entrenched in the 2002 16th Party Congress, which identified the development of the cultural industries as one of the most vital national tasks,[24] opening the door for deeper structural reforms. In 2006, a broad development plan for the cultural sector outlined key objectives for the development of theoretical and ideological construction, public cultural services, news undertakings, the cultural industry, cultural innovation, national cultural protection, foreign-related cultural exchange, and training of talented staff.[25] Among others, private capital groups were permitted to invest in some links of the cultural value chain,[26] special industry parks were set up for valuable industries such as cartoons and computer games,[27] and support was instituted for the export of cultural products.[28] The 2007 17th Party Congress confirmed that cultural industries had become one of the key development areas since China wanted to move up the value chain.[29] China considered these industries to have high technological content and added-value, as well as low pollution. The industries were also considered to be significant to "strengthening socialist culture construction, satisfying the masses' spiritual culture needs, stimulating integrated development of economy and society, and enlarging the international competitiveness and influence of Chinese culture and strengthening State culture soft power."[30] However, control over the cultural industries still remains crucial to the political project of the Chinese Communist Party (CCP).[31]

Throughout the cultural industry modernization process, the Party-State has aimed to maintain final control over media, even as it relaxed certain access controls. It permitted private investment in less crucial activities, such as art performance troupes, cultural venues, film technology development, and cultural agencies, as well as printing and optical disc reproduction. The government permitted minority participation in certain State-Owned Enterprises (SOEs), but it prohibited investment aimed at "establishing and operating news agencies, newspaper and periodical companies, publishers, radio stations, television stations, radio and television broadcast platforms, relay stations, radio and television satellites, satellite sending and receiving stations, microwave stations, monitoring stations, cable television transmission backbone networks, etc." In addition, the Party-State has taken action so that:

> [private investments] may not use information networks to launch audiovisual program services as well as operation of news websites, etc., may not engage in newspaper and

23 For a broader analysis of this shift, *see* Yuezhi Zhao, Communication in China: Political Economy, Power and Conflict (Rowman & Littlefield College Publishing, 2009).

24 Desmond Hui, *From Cultural to Creative Industries: Strategies for Chaoyang District, Beijing*, 9 Int'l J. Cultural Stud. 317–331 (2006).

25 *Guojia "shiyi wu" shiqi wenhua fazhan guihua gangyao [Outline of the National "11th Five-Year Plan" Period Cultural Development Plan]* (2006).

26 *Guanyu fei gongyou ziben jinru wenhua chanye de ruogan jueding [Some Decisions Concerning Non-Public Capital Entering the Cultural Industry]* (2005).

27 *Guanyu tuidong woguo dongman chanye fazhan de ruogan yijian [Some Opinions Concerning Promoting Our Country's Cartoon Industry Development]* (2006).

28 *Wenhua chanpin he fuwu chukou zhidao mulu [Cultural Products and Services Export Guidance Catalogue]* (2007).

29 *See* Michael Keane, Created in China: The New Great Leap Forward (Routledge, 2007).

30 *Guowuyuan bangonting guanyu cujin dianying chanye fanrong fazhan de zhidao yijian [State Council Secretariat Guiding Opinions Concerning Stimulating Flourishing and Development of the Film Industry]* (2010).

31 *See* Chapters 22 (Germann) and 25 (Friedmann) in this volume.

> periodical layout, radio and television channels and programming, and may not engage in import operations of cultural products such as books and periodicals, film and television programs, finished audiovisual products, etc.; and may not enter into State-owned cultural relic museums.[32]

Administrative entities have maintained licensing power over all distribution and broadcast activities and retain the discretion to withdraw already-approved works from the market.

All development plans indicate that the cultural sector must serve the people and serve Socialism by integrating social and economic benefit; however, the plans indicate that social effects must take first priority. To a certain degree, cultural development intends to improve the cultural sector's propaganda role by making propaganda messages more attractive and deepening societal penetration.[33] Upgrading cinema infrastructure, especially in the countryside, has been one of the key policy goals in the media industry for the last decade. The Party has always considered films as one of the most important propaganda tools,[34] and has recently increased its investment in supporting "main melody" (主旋律 *zhuxuanlü*) films, such as *Founding of a Republic* (建国大业 *jianguo daye*), *Great Beginnings of the New Revival* (建党大业 *jiandang daye*), and *Confucius* (孔子 *Kongzi*). These films are much more complex and expensive than the basic propaganda pieces of the 1980s and 1990s, but, within the context of increasing marketization, the Party-State must make its message much more attractive for audiences.

International trade commitments and the WTO disputes

The idea of cultural industries strongly impacts trade relations; however, Chinese media policy does not include the importation of foreign media products. While the 2009 Cultural Industries Promotion Plan provides strategies to attract foreign capital and trained personnel to Chinese cultural industries, it does not once mention the importation of foreign cultural products. Similarly, the 2005 Five-Year Plan provides for the expansion of Chinese cultural industries into foreign markets, which requires the expertise of foreign cultural experts and joint Sino-Foreign cultural projects, but it does not refer once to the importation of foreign cultural products.

As with private capital, the Chinese leadership's attitude towards foreign media enterprises remains ambiguous. On the one hand, China would like to acquire foreign operators' skills, know-how, and technology, but also use them to gain a foothold for Chinese media abroad. On the other hand, China aims to minimize the inflow of foreign media for both political and economic reasons. Politically speaking, the conservative media departments take the view that foreign products often are morally debased, featuring licentious sexual and violent content.[35] Also, the Chinese nationalist narrative fosters the idea of the Party's role in bringing China back to the leading ranks of the international scene, after a long period of national

32 *Some Decisions Concerning Non-Public Capital Entering the Cultural Industry* (2005).

33 For example, a number of measures are especially taken to expand media coverage into the countryside and into urban communities.

34 Yingchi Chu, *The Consumption of Cinema in Contemporary China*, in MEDIA IN CHINA, CONSUMPTION, CONTENT AND CRISIS 44 (Stephanie Hemelryk Donald et al. eds, Routledge, 2002).

35 Wendy Su, *Resisting Cultural Imperialism Or Welcoming Cultural Globalization? China's Extensive Debate On Hollywood Cinema From 1994 To 2007*, 21(2) ASIAN J. COMM. 186–201 (2011).

humiliation by the Japanese, the British, and the Americans.[36] From this point of view, foreign media serve as a tool for foreign cultural imperialism and weaken the Chinese nation. This sentiment is reflected in China's sensitivity to portrayals of Chinese characters in films.[37] The diagnosis that foreign support for domestic underground media was one of the main causal factors leading to the collapse of the Soviet Union further reinforces this.[38] Illustratively, during the retrenchment following the 1989 Tiananmen Massacre, the government prohibited the screening of foreign laser discs and feature films.[39] Lastly, China remains wary of the impact of US culture on Chinese society.

Economically speaking, China's domestic media sector has not achieved the strength to withstand an onslaught from the large foreign conglomerates. For example, although Chinese theaters import only 20 foreign movies per year on a revenue-sharing basis, they bring in a disproportionally large share of the revenue.[40] In 2010, Chinese theaters screened 24 foreign and 526 domestic films, but the foreign films accounted for around 45 per cent of box office income. Within the region, the contrasting examples of Taiwan and Korea also seem to support this argument. Taiwan had a system of film quotas, which it gradually lowered throughout the 1990s and eventually abolished upon its entry into the WTO. The ensuing Hollywood invasion greatly damaged the Taiwanese film industry, and by 2001, foreign films claimed 96 per cent of exhibition revenues.[41] This evolution also hit Hong Kong's cinema hard because Taiwan was one of the major export markets for films from Hong Kong. Korea, on the other hand, retains film quotas in place, requiring that theaters reserve 73 days per year to screen Korean films.[42] Many observers believe that this policy has sparked the Korean film sector's resurgence. Between 1996 and 2005, Korean box office intake tripled, while Hollywood's market share fell by half, from 77 per cent to 38 per cent.[43]

Hence, given the impossibility to govern the production of foreign media works, China seeks to strictly control the importation, broadcast, and distribution of these works. These measures mostly echo those taken to command the domestic media. As with domestic works, the government required foreign works to undergo content examination procedures. To keep this manageable, it limited import rights to a relatively small number of state-owned companies, which perform a preliminary content examination before official submission.

36 For a broad analysis of this discourse pattern, *see* William Callahan, China: The Pessoptimist Nation (Oxford University Press, 2008).

37 For example, the film, *Pirates of the Caribbean 3*, had to be edited for Chinese theatres, removing a significant amount of screen time of the Chinese pirate character, Sao Feng. *China Censors "Cut" Pirates Film*, BBC (June 12, 2007), http://news.bbc.co.uk/2/hi/entertainment/6744245.stm (last visited July 22, 2016).

38 David Shambaugh, China's Communist Party: Atrophy and Adaptation (University of California Press, 2008).

39 *Guanyu tingzhi jinkou he bofang jiguang shipan (gushipian) de tongzhi [Notice Concerning Stopping Import and Screening of Laser Discs (Feature Films)]* (1990).

40 China made this commitment in its GATS schedule, and doubled the previous quota of 10 films per year that was established in 1994. These quotas are not always enforced to the letter. In 2010, Chinese cinemas screened 24 foreign films on a revenue-sharing basis. People's Republic of China, Schedule of Specific Commitments, GATS/SC/135 (2002) [hereinafter Services Schedule].

41 Yingjin Zhang, Chinese National Cinema 294 (Routledge, 2004).

42 Although Hollywood pressure is present here as well. Jinhee Choi, The South Korean Film Renaissance: Local Hitmakers, Global Provocateurs 1–2 (Wesleyan University Press, 2010).

43 *Id.*

Sino-foreign co-productions, even if not intended for broadcast in China, are also subject to Chinese content requirements.[44] The government also restricted foreign investment to those areas that required technology and expertise, and, furthermore, implemented a screening quota. Apart from the cinema film quota referred to above, the government capped foreign television programming at 20 per cent of broadcasting time, and 15 per cent during the prime time "Golden Hours," from 18:00 until 22:00.[45]

At the same time, the Chinese leadership has shown its intent to import foreign technology and know-how, including cinema technology. In October 2000, the Ministry of Culture, the Ministry of Foreign Trade and Cooperation (MOFTEC) and SARFT permitted foreign investors to finance Chinese theaters, subject to a number of conditions. Foreign capital flowed through a joint venture,[46] limited to minority participation and a duration of 30 years. The joint venture could not use the brand name of a foreign media or cinema company. Furthermore, any such undertaking would be subject to the catchall provision, "conforming to local cultural facility deployment and planning,"[47] and an administrative approval process by the three Ministry-level entities involved. These Regulations were revised in 2003. Although the government raised the required registered capital from 1 million Chinese Yuan (CNY) to 6 million, it dropped the naming restrictions, and allowed foreign participation up to 75 per cent in a number of pilot cities (Beijing, Shanghai, Guangzhou, Chengdu, Xi'an, Wuhan, and Nanjing). However, the push to attract more foreign expertise and capital into the cinema sector backfired. Chinese audiences and Western business culture did not mix well, resulting in staff conflicts and communication issues between Western and Chinese sides. By 2005, the joint projects ended, and Chinese-majority ownership became the norm again.[48] Ironically, China's aim to maintain control over foreigners can lead it to condone foreign activities in China that, in principle, violate regulations, as long as these enterprises maintain friendly relations with the leadership.[49]

In order to maintain as free a hand as possible over the media sector following its WTO accession, China has tried to screen the media from its WTO commitments. In its GATS (General Agreement on Trade in Services) schedule,[50] it expressly excluded audiovisual sector subsidies from the horizontal commitments. It also restricted market access to foreign services suppliers, thereby establishing audiovisual product distribution joint ventures (with the exception of motion pictures) and minority participation in the construction or

44 *Zhongwai hezuo zhizuo dianshiju (luxiangpian) guanli guiding [Sino-foreign Television Drama (Video) Co-Production Management Regulations]* (2004).

45 *Foreign Television Programme Import and Broadcast Regulations* (1994).

46 *Waishang touzi dianyingyuan zanxing guiding [Foreign Cinema Investment Regulations, Article 3]* (2002). Minority investment in cinemas was one of the two GATS commitments that China made in its WTO Services Schedule.

47 *Id.*, Article 4(1).

48 Anthony Y. H. Fung, Global Capital, Local Culture: Transnational Media Corporations in China 73–78 (Peter Lang Publishing, 2008).

49 *Id.*, at 70 *et seq.*

50 General Agreement on Trade in Services, April 15, 1994, Marrakesh Agreement Establishing the World Trade Organization, Annex 1B, 1869 UNTS 183, 33 ILM 1167 (1994) [hereinafter GATS]. A GATS Services Schedule lists the sectors in which a WTO Member guarantees market access and national treatment to other Member States. Hence, where a sector is not explicitly mentioned in a Schedule, GATS discipline in principle does not apply. On GATS commitments, *see* Chapter 25 (Friedmann) in this volume.

renovation of cinemas. It further implemented the twenty-film quota.[51] As *China – Publications and Audiovisual Products* demonstrated, China was not entirely successful in completely insulating the cultural sector from its WTO obligations. In part, communication difficulties between MOFTEC[52] and the media regulators led to insufficient attention to detail during the trade negotiations.[53] However, the more important question remains: how does the case impact Chinese media governance?

Two important aspects help to understand the impact of WTO decisions, in general. First, we should look at the substantive impact of the decisions. Second, we must analyze the political dimension of implementation and retaliation. Substantively speaking, the *China – Publications and Audiovisual Products* decision has relatively little impact.[54] Foreign enterprises must have the right to import audiovisual works and to hold majority participation in audiovisual distribution enterprises, with the exceptions of films. Given the complex web of media control measures and the Party's overarching influence, the leadership still employs a range of tools to keep unwanted films and television programs off the market. At the political level, remedies are limited to retaliatory tariffs the US can impose on Chinese products. Such tariffs are difficult to calculate and may damage US economic interests, reducing the US incentive to press for them. Nonetheless, China desires to be seen as a State willing to abide by international trade rules. Consequently, at least for the time being, China has opted for taking a narrow interpretation of the aforementioned Dispute Settlement Body (DSB) decision,[55] and the US has not initiated sanction procedures, even though China has missed the implementation deadline.[56] However, the US may have recently switched tack. In October 2011, the US Trade Representative (USTR) filed a request for information about the procedural aspects of China's Internet censorship.[57] Depending on China's response, another WTO case may emerge, severely testing China's commitment to the rule of law in international trade.

Conclusion

The Chinese media regime is fundamentally a domestic affair intended to maintain political control over the public debate. Government-implemented foreign-related trade measures are simply an extension of similar measures aimed at domestic non-State actors. While the leadership allows some trade in cultural goods and services, it is determined to retain final

51 Services Schedule, ¶ D.

52 The Ministry of Foreign Trade and Economic Cooperation, the predecessor of the current Ministry of Commerce (MOFCOM).

53 Shi & Chen, *supra* note 6, at 41.

54 *See* Chapter 24 (Kamperman Sanders) in this volume.

55 *See*, for example, the revision of the *Regulations on the Administration of Audio and Video Products* in 2011: Yīnxiàng Zhìpǐn Guǎnlǐ Tiáolì (2011 xiūdìng) (音像制品管理条例(2011修订) [Regulations on the Administration of Audio and Video Products] (promulgated by the State Council, March 19, 2011).

56 The deadline for implementation was March 2011. Although the USTR issued a statement of regret that China missed the deadline, the US has not made any overt moves. Meanwhile, China has provided the DSB with monthly reports reiterating its commitment to implement the AB's findings, but stating that China's domestic situation has presented implementation difficulties. Doug Palmer, *US says China missed copyright goods deadline*, Reuters (March 21, 2011), http://www.reuters.com/article/2011/03/21/industry-us-usa-china-piracy-idUSTRE72K5F720110321 (last visited July 22, 2016). The summary of the *China – Publications and Audiovisual Products* dispute can be found at http://www.wto.org/english/tratop_e/dispu_e/cases_e/ds363_e.htm (last visited July 22, 2016).

57 USTR, *United States Seeks Detailed Information on China's Internet Restrictions* (October 20, 2011).

discretion and control over the sector. Given the fundamental importance of this power to the CCP's survival and the perpetuation of the single-party system, it seems unlikely that the leadership will voluntarily relinquish even parts of the regime any time soon. In other words, foreign media conglomerates that want to enter the Chinese market will need to find strategies to work with the leadership and to accept that they will remain subject to the volatile Chinese political environment.

This does not mean that the Party-State is all-powerful. Increasingly, citizens use digital technology to communicate and consume media products outside of the State's reach. Growing numbers of citizens have turned away from the main melody films and television programs, which are often described as boring, in favor of more interesting forms of entertainment. Media piracy has created channels for audiences to watch foreign films and television shows that would not otherwise be available. Hence, it seems that the leadership has diverted the pressure for liberalization into a broadly accepted black market, at the expense of foreign rights holders and domestic producers, who must compete with cheap or free pirated works, as a result. In the future, this tension may drive change in the Chinese media regime, where pressure via the international trade regimes seems to be non-productive or even counterproductive.

24 Trade in Audiovisuals – the Case of China*

Anselm Kamperman Sanders

Introduction

Protection of cultural diversity has long been a concern of European Union (EU) Member States.[1] This is expressed in screen quotas and subsidies to support European audiovisual industries.[2] The practice is often described as a covert way to maintain trade barriers to stem the dominant inflow of media products from the United States (US). The US has increasingly objected to these practices, and has made it an express issue in its trade negotiations with Korea.[3] Europe, meanwhile, is committed to the protection of cultural diversity through its accession to the UNESCO Convention on the Protection and Promotion of the Diversity of Cultural Expressions,[4] and finds itself in the opposite camp to the US on this issue.

* This chapter is part of the results of the Research Project on "*Current Trends of Chinese Law towards Non-Trade Concerns such as Sustainable Development and the Protection of Environment, Public Health, Food Safety, Cultural, Social and Economic Rights, Labor Rights and the Reduction of Poverty from the Perspective of International Law and WTO Law*", coordinated by Professor Paolo Davide Farah at gLAWcal – Global Law Initiatives for Sustainable Development (United Kingdom) and at West Virginia University John D. Rockefeller IV School of Policy and Politics, Department of Public Administration, in partnership with the Center of Advanced Studies on Contemporary China (CASCC) in Turin (Italy), Maastricht University Faculty of Law, Department of International and European Law and IGIR – Institute for Globalisation and International Regulation (Netherlands), and Tsinghua University, School of Law, Institute of Public International Law and the Center for Research on Intellectual Property Law in Beijing (China). An early draft of this chapter was presented at the Conferences Series on "*China's Influence on Non-Trade Concerns in International Economic Law*", Third Conference held at Maastricht University, Faculty of Law on January 19–20, 2012. This publication and the Conference Series were sponsored by China–EU School of Law (CESL) at the China University of Political Science and Law (CUPL). The activities of CESL at CUPL are supported by the European Union and the People's Republic of China.

1 Lothar Ehring, *Article IV of the GATT: An Obsolete Provision or Still a Basis for Cultural Policy?*, in TRADE AND COMPETITION LAW IN THE EU AND BEYOND 96 (Inge Govaere, Reinhard Quick and Marco Broncker eds, Edward Elgar, 2011).

2 Directive 2010/13/EU of the European Parliament and of the Council of 10 March 2010 on the coordination of certain provisions laid down by law, regulation or administrative action in Member States concerning the provision of audiovisual media services (Audiovisual Media Services Directive), 2010 O.J. (L 95).

3 Won-Mog Cho, *Screen Quota and Cultural Diversity: Debates in Korea-US FTA Talks and Convention on Cultural Diversity,* 2 ASIAN J. WTO & INT'L HEALTH L. & POL. 267 (2007); *see* also Kim Tae-jong, *Korean Culture Industry Feels The FTA*, http://www.bilaterals.org/spip.php?article7885&lang=en (last visited July 8, 2016). *See* also http://www.bilaterals.org/spip.php?article6299&lang=en and http://www.bilaterals.org/spip.php?article5028&lang=en (last visited July 8, 2016).

4 UNESCO Convention On The Protection And Promotion Of The Diversity Of Cultural Expressions, October 20, 2005, 45 ILM 269 [hereinafter UNESCO Convention]. *See* Chapter 22 (Germann) in this volume.

At the Second Plenary Meeting of the Sixth Plenum of the 17th Central Committee on October 18, 2011, former Chinese President Hu Jintao called for the members of the Chinese Communist Party (CCP) to fight hostile international powers and meet the cultural demands of the people.[5] According to Hu Jintao, "[h]ostile international powers are strengthening their efforts to Westernize and divide us." In response, China is to spend 45 billion Chinese Yuan (CNY) to expand its overseas media, including an international edition of the CCP-influenced newspaper, *China Daily*.[6] Inside China itself, examples of the state exercising control over the media are manifold, from blatant censorship[7] to curbing culturally undesirable material from being broad- or webcast.[8] This chapter explores the way in which trade in cultural works has led to discussions on Non-Trade Concerns in the context of free trade agreements and World Trade Organization (WTO) obligations.[9] It concludes that in China there is a convergence of measures that are all subservient to the desire to exercise full political and cultural control over the media market.[10] It is, however, questionable whether the moral exception argument raised successfully by China to defend its policies will be sustainable in the long run.

The WTO and China

After the WTO Appellate Body declared a number of Chinese measures in the field of audio-visuals to be in breach of the General Agreement on Tariffs and Trade (GATT)[11] and the General Agreement on Trade in Services (GATS),[12] it seems as though the Chinese government has stepped up its efforts to retain control over its domestic media in increasingly militant fashion. The dispute was part of a two-pronged attack of the US in relation to Chinese media law and policy. The WTO adopted two panel reports: *China – Intellectual Property Rights*[13] and *China – Publications and Audiovisual Products.*[14]

5 Hu Jintao, *Jiandingbuyi zou Zhongguo tese shehuizhuyi wenhua fazhan daolu, nuli jianshe shehuizhuyi wenhua daguo* [*Resolutely Follow the Cultural Development Path of Socialism with Chinese Characteristics, Work to Build a Socialist Strong Culture Country*], published in Communist Party journal *Qiushi* (Seeking Truth) 2012, available in translation at http://chinacopyrightandmedia.wordpress.com/2012/01/04/hu-jintaos-article-in-qiushi-magazine-translated/ (last visited July 8, 2016).

6 Peter Simpson, *Chinese President Hu Jintao warns of cultural warfare from West*, The Telegraph (January 2, 2012), http://www.telegraph.co.uk/news/worldnews/asia/china/8988195/Chinese-President-Hu-Jintao-warns-of-cultural-warfare-from-West.html (last visited July 20, 2014).

7 Council on Foreign Relations, *Media Censorship in China*, http://www.cfr.org/china/media-censorship-china/p11515 (last visited July 8, 2016).

8 Ben Blanchard, *China claims success in curbing racy entertainment,* Reuters (January 4, 2012), http://www.reuters.com/article/2012/01/04/us-china-television-regulator-idUSTRE8030UC20120104 (last visited July 8, 2016). *See* also Chapter 23 (Creemers) in this volume.

9 *See* in this light also the UNESCO Convention, *supra* note 4. *See* also Chapter 22 (Germann) in this volume.

10 *See* Chapter 23 (Creemers) in this volume.

11 General Agreement on Tariffs and Trade, October 30, 1947, 61 Stat. A-11, 55 UNTS 194 [hereinafter GATT].

12 General Agreement on Trade in Services, April 15, 1994, Marrakesh Agreement Establishing the World Trade Organization, Annex 1B, 1869 UNTS 183, 33 ILM 1167 (1994) [hereinafter GATS].

13 Panel Report, *China – Measures Affecting the Protection and Enforcement of Intellectual Property Rights*, ¶ 7.120, WT/DS362/R (January 26, 2009) [hereinafter *China – Intellectual Property Rights*]. *See* also Rogier Creemers, *The Effects of WTO Case DS362 on Audiovisual Media Piracy in China,* 31(11) Eur. Intell. Prop. Rev. 568 (2009).

14 Panel Report, *China – Measures Affecting Trading Rights and Distribution Services for Certain Publications and Audiovisual Entertainment Products*, WT/DS363/R, ¶ 3.1 (August 12, 2009), and Appellate

The former concerned four main issues that the US considered to be in breach of the Agreement on Trade-Related Aspects of Intellectual Property Rights[15] (TRIPS): thresholds for criminal prosecution; scope and coverage of criminal prosecution; legislation non-compliant to TRIPS and Berne minimum standards; and the disposal of confiscated goods by Chinese customs authorities. The claim concerning minimum copyright standards focused on Article 4 of the Copyright Law of the People's Republic of China (hereinafter Copyright Law), which denies copyright protection to works not approved for circulation in the Chinese market.[16] The approval process, conducted by the State Administration for Radio, Film and Television (SARFT) not only results in frequent censorship but, furthermore, results in a quota of 20 foreign films allowed on the market per annum. This practice of creating scarcity, in itself, fosters a demand for pirated products.

In this dispute, the Panel upheld the complaint because the Chinese legislation could be construed as denying copyright protection to a large class of works. The Panel held that China was in breach of its obligations under Article 5(2) of the Berne Convention and, therefore, also under Article 9(1) of the TRIPS Agreement.[17] However, this decision reaffirmed China's right to suppress the distribution of copyright works on the basis of the Berne Convention itself, thus recognizing the right of states to censor in general.[18] As such, the panel made clear that the denial of copyright protection is something entirely different from suppressing the distribution (censoring) of copyrighted works. It can be argued, in fact, that the denial of copyright protection altogether makes it impossible for rights holders to act against infringers in a market that is rife with piracy of audiovisual works.[19] The government has since brought the Copyright Law in line with the WTO panel decision.[20]

China managed to keep the upper hand in the issue on criminal thresholds. This issue revolved around the question of how many infringing copies would have to be found in order to hold that the infringer had acted on a commercial scale, as defined in Article 61 of the TRIPS Agreement. The scale of activity may elevate the trader of such items from a mere

Body Report, WT/DS363/AB/R, ¶ 2 (December 21, 2009) [hereinafter *China – Publications and Audiovisual Products*]. *See* Paola Conconi & Joost Pauwelyn, *Trading Cultures: Appellate Body Report on China – Audiovisuals* 10(1) World Trade Rev. 95 (2011); *see* also Chapters 22 (Germann), 23 (Creemers), and 25 (Friedmann) in this volume.

15 Agreement on Trade-Related Aspects of Intellectual Property Rights, April 15, 1994, Marrakesh Agreement Establishing the World Trade Organization, Annex 1C, 1869 UNTS 299, 33 ILM 1197 (1994) [hereinafter TRIPS Agreement].

16 Zhōnghuá Rénmín Gònghéguó Zhùzuòquán Fǎ (2010 xiūzhèng) (中华人民共和国著作权法(2010修正) [Copyright Law of the People's Republic of China (2010 Amendment)] (Promulgated by the Standing Comm. Nat'l People's Cong., February 26, 2010).

17 Article 9(1) TRIPS, implementing Article 5(1) of the Berne Convention: "Authors shall enjoy, in respect of works for which they are protected under this Convention, in countries of the Union other than the country of origin, the rights which their respective laws do now or may hereafter grant to their nationals, as well as the rights specially granted by this Convention."

18 Article 9(1) TRIPS, implementing Article 17 Berne Convention: "The provisions of this Convention cannot in any way affect the right of the Government of each country of the Union to permit, to control, or to prohibit, by legislation or regulation, the circulation, presentation, or exhibition of any work or production in regard to which the competent authority may find it necessary to exercise that right."

19 Rogier Creemers, *Explaining Audiovisual Media Piracy in China* (Maastricht University PhD, February 2, 2012).

20 Hao Dong & Minkang Gu, *Copyrightable or Not: A Review of The Chinese Provision "Illegal Works" Targeted by WTO DS362 and Suggestions for Legal Reform,* 4(2) Asian J. WTO & In'l Health L. & Pol. 335 (2009).

infringer to a counterfeiter or pirate, in which case criminal sanctions may be imposed, rather than civil sanctions only. The panel held that the US did not convincingly prove that the contested thresholds impacted the commercial marketplace. It then stated that the threshold for criminal enforcement covering activities on a commercial scale is set at "counterfeiting or piracy carried on at the magnitude or extent of typical or usual commercial activity with respect to a given product in a given market."[21]

China – Publications and Audiovisual Products mainly concerned market access for media products. The primary issue raised by the US dealt with trading rights that confer the right to import foreign films upon certain Chinese companies only. The second contentious issue was that, according to the US, certain measures affecting distribution services for media publications present an unfair trade barrier for American service providers wishing to enter the Chinese market. Examples of products include the following: a) reading materials such as books, periodicals, and electronic publications; b) audiovisual home-entertainment products such as DVDs; c) sound recordings; and d) films for theatrical release. Once again, the issue of SARFT approval was relevant here.[22] Given the low number of foreign works admitted to the Chinese market annually, it can be argued that the restricted inflow artificially creates a demand for pirated products. Whether distributed by physical carriers or through online platforms, the dissemination of foreign audiovisual content often transpires through an intimate marriage of activities of professional pirates and fans who provide the subtitles for such foreign works.[23] The widespread practice of online distribution of "fan-subs" that can be superimposed on the digital file of an audiovisual work makes foreign movie content legible and accessible for the Chinese domestic market.

The US complaint, however, focused on the fact that only a limited number of state-approved enterprises may engage in the importation, clearance, and distribution of films in China. These importers are responsible for ensuring compliance with the censorship laws as well. China argued that its regulatory regime for films for theatrical release was akin to regulating services: "films for theatrical release are not goods because they are exploited through a series of services; because the commercial value of films for theatrical release lies in the revenue generated by these services; and because the delivery materials containing the content of films are mere accessories of such services and have no commercial value of their own."[24] The Appellate Body rejected this position, concluding that, although services are involved, a physical carrier will ultimately and inevitably engage in an act of importation. Consequently, this dispute has both GATS and GATT components, and the measures must be tested cumulatively regarding their compliance.[25]

China further invoked the GATT Article XX(a) exception related to public morals in relation to several of its restrictions on trading rights. On this basis, China asserted that it censors works of art only when they contravene "public morals."[26] According to China, this position

21 Panel Report on *China – Intellectual Property Rights, supra* note 13, ¶ 131.

22 *See* Chapter 23 (Creemers) in this volume.

23 Nathaniel T. Noda, *Copyrights Retold: How Interpretive Rights Foster Creativity and Justify Fan-Based Activities,* 57 J. Copyright Soc'y USA 987 (2010); see also Tianxiang He, Copyright, Fan Generated Contents, and Open Society in China: Towards and Open Innovation Mechanism of Copyrighted Contents with Fans (Maastricht University PhD, July 1, 2016).

24 Appellate Body Report, *China – Publications and Audiovisual Products, supra* note 14, ¶173.

25 On the GATS issues, *see* Chapter 25 (Friedmann) in this volume.

26 On the application of Article XX GATT *see* Peter van den Bossche, The Law and Policy of the World Trade Organization 614 (Cambridge University Press, 2008). As far as the "public morals" argument is concerned, *see* Chapter 22 (Germann) in this volume.

extends to any work that "injures the national glory," "undermines the solidarity of the nationalities," "propagates evil cults or superstition," "destroys social stability," or "jeopardizes social morality or fine cultural traditions of the nationalities."[27] Referring to the UNESCO Universal Declaration on Cultural Diversity, China argued that its restrictions on cultural goods were necessary to prevent the dissemination of cultural goods whose content would negatively impact public morals in China. It may be that such measures help ensure cultural diversity, but it is questionable whether trade-restrictive discriminatory measures against foreign undertakings can be justified by their promotion of cultural diversity, let alone their protection of public morals. The Appellate Body held, therefore, that China may not restrict trading rights on a discriminatory basis.

However, the Appellate Body found that China's obligations to grant the right to trade without discrimination did not deprive it of the right to regulate trade consistent with the WTO Agreement. This seemingly overarching principle that Article XX GATT may provide exceptions to the GATT obligations extending to other WTO Agreements remains an issue that will require further elaboration in the future.[28] What is clear now, however, is that the Chinese public authorities are entitled to censor. The quotas on foreign movies also remain in place, even though it is not entirely clear whether these measures are Article XX GATT–compliant alternatives to the ones that were found to be in violation of WTO obligations, namely those, where government-approved importers were responsible for censorship.

Media quotas

As to the application of restrictions in the trade of cultural goods, some literature suggests that trade restrictions – such as quotas – can promote social welfare. This is specifically the case in relation to goods where production occurs using return-to-scale technologies, and where consumers value some cultural goods highly, while others are valued relatively uniformly.[29] When applied to Hollywood versus domestic production, it is easy to see that while some cultural goods can be and are appreciated globally, others are appreciated solely within smaller cultural communities or by groups who speak a specific language. The same can be said for television programs, print media and literature, yet relatively identical high fixed costs of production would sometimes force producers to sell enough units at relatively low marginal costs. Price differentiation between these two types of production, however, is only possible within a relatively narrow margin. While global media products may be sold in multiple markets, domestic cultural works may not be exported in the same manner. This would lead to lower than optimal production of domestic cultural works and consequentially to the loss of welfare. Cultural identity would also be affected.

Still, the question is whether the government should promote domestic production through subsidies or whether it should protect consumers by limiting their access to foreign works. A study on naming patterns in France concludes that since exposure to foreign media leads to a mere five per cent change in naming patterns towards foreign names, the

27 Appellate Body Report, *China – Publications and Audiovisual Products, supra* note 14, ¶ 7.760.

28 *See* Conconi & Pauwelyn, *supra* note 14, at 103–106.

29 Patrick Francois and Tanguy van Ypersele, *On the Protection of Cultural Goods,* 56(2) J. Int'l Econ. 359 (2002).

negative effects on domestic cultural diversity may be exaggerated.[30] Regarding consumption, however, it has been shown that trade liberalization affects the diversity of consumption patterns where cultural works are concerned.[31] This is due to network externalities, where the individual's desire to share experiences with others, thus forging a cultural identity, affects the consumption pattern of cultural works. As such, social media, like iTunes, Ping, or Facebook-Spotify setups, play an increasingly important role in steering consumption patterns, benefiting global cultural products over domestic or sub-cultural ones. Yet, in this context, the loss of diversity in cultural identity flows from consumers' tendency to gravitate towards larger, common cultural identities. Furthermore, it seems that generational transmission from parents to children also reinforces this process.[32] Deviation from a common identity has become costly under trade liberalization and will become increasingly so in the age of globalization. Therefore, the challenge of safeguarding cultural diversity and meeting the obligations of the UNESCO Convention on the Protection and Promotion of the Diversity of Cultural Expressions lies in protecting global, regional, national, indigenous, and personal cultural identities,[33] where the individual is capable of connecting to multiple identities that he or she can share with others. Given the nature of the market for audiovisual media, as outlined above, market interference may be legitimate.[34]

Article IV GATT 1947–1994

GATT Article IV contains a *lex specialis* providing the conditions for domestic quotas on cinematographic screenings of films.[35] Since screen quotas operate in a discriminatory fashion, they can only be legitimate if certain conditions are met: a) quotas must be allocated per theater on an annual basis in the form of a specified minimum proportion of the total screen time actually utilized, and b) screen time must not be allocated among foreign sources of supply, except for a case of quota allocation for films of specified origin that does not increase the quota level above the level that existed prior to GATT.[36] In addition, GATT mandated that screen quotas must be subject to negotiation for their limitation, liberalization, or elimination.[37] GATT Article IV does not amount to a general cultural exception, nor would it justify import restrictions or subsidies. In fact, these latter types of measures may not be appropriate at all. As Ehring argues:

> the underlying policy objectives of Article IV, allowing Members to protect their film industries by reversing to them a share of the domestic market through screen quotas,

30 Anne-Célia Disdier, Keith Head & Thierry Mayer, *Exposure to Foreign Media Changes in Cultural Traits: Evidence from Naming Patterns in France,* 80 J. INT'L ECON. 226 (2010).

31 Eckhard Janeba, *International Trade and Consumption Network Externalities,* 51 EUR. ECON. REV. 781 (2007).

32 Jacques Olivier, Mathias Thoening & Thierry Verdier, *Globalization and the Dynamics of Cultural Identity,* 76(2) J. INT'L ECON. 356 (2008).

33 *See* Chapter 17 (Heurtebise) in this volume.

34 On the interface between trade and culture *see* PETER VAN DEN BOSSCHE, *supra* note 26, at 29–31. *See* also Chapter 22 (Germann) in this volume.

35 Lothar Ehring, *supra* note 1, at 110–18.

36 GATT 1994 Article IV(a), (b), (c).

37 GATT 1994 Article IV(d).

> explains the departure from the standard GATT structure: import tariffs, structurally the preferred and permitted form of protection, would not be able effectively to protect the domestic industry in case of films. The ineffectiveness of tariffs results not only from the possibility to show foreign films from physical media that have been manufactured domestically or otherwise to show foreign films without the importation of a dutiable product. It is also because a single exposed film can be shown many times, whereas import tariffs are imposed only once on each imported product, be it ad valorem terms or a specific amount.[38]

GATS stipulates national treatment and market access obligations as specific commitments,[39] meaning that although screen quotas may be legitimate where they act as barriers to trade in services, only Member States foregoing, reducing, or eliminating Article IV GATT privileges through commitments to unlimited market access and national treatment in audiovisual services or exemptions from most-favored-nation treatment will be affected.[40] It can even be argued that technological change since the drafting of the provision in 1947 has been such that under GATT 1994, quotas for films shown on television are covered, but whether this also extends to, for example, webcasting is debatable.

When it comes to other forms of cultural products on physical carriers – such as Blu-Ray or books – the likely coverage by Article IV GATT is even more remote. For this reason, many states have endorsed the UNESCO Convention on the Protection and Promotion of the Diversity of Cultural Expressions, which in Article 5 recognizes the sovereign right of states to formulate and implement cultural policies and to adopt measures to protect and promote the diversity of cultural expressions.[41] This ambition does not find favor with the US, which has not signed the Convention because it wishes to liberalize cultural services in the WTO and through Free Trade Agreements.

In *China – Publications and Audiovisual Products,* China invoked the GATT Article XX(a) exception related to public morals in order to bolster its argument in favor of protecting cultural identity. Whichever way the protection of cultural diversity is presented, it presumes not only the preservation and promotion of existing cultures, but also the reception of others, whether domestic or foreign, traditional or new. A state can therefore frame its legitimate measures to protect or promote one cultural identity in the context of redressing balance where balance was absent or lost. However, cultural identity and the protection of public morals do not necessarily correspond. As Conconi and Pauwelyn state, "[w]hen it comes to China's censorship it is far from clear whether or not it is related to public morals, let alone culture. Moreover, even to the extent that it is related to culture, further examination would be needed to see whether any of China's measures are welfare enhancing."[42] In the immediate future, the *China – Publications and Audiovisual Products* case is not likely to affect the Chinese market for importation and distribution of media content in a major way, but neither is the public morals argument likely to succeed in the

38 Lothar Ehring, *supra* note 1, at 110.

39 GATS, Part III.

40 Tania Voon, Cultural Products and the World Trade Organization 11 (Cambridge University Press, 2007).

41 *See* also Chapter 22 (Germann) in this volume.

42 *See* Conconi & Pauwelyn, *supra* note 14, at 116.

"fight against hostile international powers to meet the cultural demands of the people,"[43] as announced by Hu Jintao.

Standards

China's policies for setting domestic standards for Information and Communication Technologies (ICT) and distribution services indicates that the Chinese government and state-controlled conglomerates will acquire increasing control. In this respect, China's efforts to become as strong a player in setting standards as it plays in creating ICT technology are remarkable.[44] China sets and uses its own standards – in telecoms, DVD, and other ICT industries – to control access to the Chinese market and to offer an alternative to standards dominated by non-Chinese multinational players. As in the discussion about Microsoft's standard Office Open XML (OOXML) and the competing OpenDocument Format (ODF) standard before it, the future development of the Chinese Uniform Office Format (UOF) will be monitored much more closely from the perspective of international trade than from a more domestic need for the inclusion of Chinese language and character functionality.[45] The newly announced and AVS codecs-based China Blue High Definition (CBHD) standard[46] can easily be seen as a powerful alternative for the state authorities' direct control over media. The recent announcements of patent pooling by Chinese firms in the smartphone sector to fend off foreign right holders also demonstrates a defensive strategy favoring domestic industry only and will thus be subject to scrutiny by China's trading partners.[47]

The WTO Agreement on Technical Barriers to Trade[48] (TBT) deals with the possibility that standards may have protectionist effects, even if they do not intend to. The TBT Agreement addresses a limited class of measures[49] – namely technical regulations (product characteristics or their related processes and production methods), standards (a document approved by a recognized body, that provides common and repeated use, rules, guidelines, or characteristics for products or related processes and production methods, with which compliance is not mandatory), and conformity assessment procedures (any procedure used, directly or indirectly, to determine that relevant requirements in technical regulations or standards are fulfilled).[50] Technical regulations have played a role in three disputes only,

43 *See* Hu Jintao, ***supra*** note 5.

44 *See* James P. Popkin and Partha Iyengar, IT and the East: How China and India Are Altering the Future of Technology and Innovation (Harvard Business School Press, 2007).

45 *See* Anselm Kamperman Sanders, ***Standards Setting in the ICT Industry – IP or Competition Law? A Comparative Perspective***, in Os 10 Anos de Investigação do CIJE – Estudos Jurídico-Económicos 103 (G. Teixeira & A. Carvalho eds, Coimbra, Almedina, 2011).

46 CBHD is based on the AVS audio and video standard. CBHD's developers, the Optical Memory National Engineering Research Center (OMNERC) of Tshingua University, stated that the new format should cut piracy rates as well as royalty payments for foreign patents.

47 *E. Yen & S. Shen, **China Market: Handset Makers Form Alliance To Counter Possible Patent Infringement Lawsuits***, Digitimes (December 30, 2011), http://www.digitimes.com/ (last visited July 8, 2016); see also Matt Heckman, The Strategic Use of Patents in Standardization in relation to US, European and Chinese Competition Law (Maastricht University PhD, April 22, 2016).

48 Agreement on Technical Barriers to Trade, April 15, 1994, Marrakesh Agreement Establishing the World Trade Organization, Annex 1A, 1867 UNTS 187.

49 *See* in this respect, Appellate Body Report, ***European Communities – Measures Affecting Asbestos and Products Containing Asbestos***, ¶ 80, WT/DS135/AB/R (March 12, 2001).

50 *See* Annexes 1.1, 1.2, and 1.3 to the TBT Agreement for their definitions.

and, so far, no case law addresses standards and conformity assessment procedures under the TBT Agreement.[51] Similarly, no case law has yet addressed how the TBT Agreement may in itself focus on ensuring that standards do not become barriers to trade.[52] As illustrated in *China – Publications and Audiovisual Products*, non-standards cases may also prompt discussion about the media market's larger structure if foreign companies feel excluded from shaping market access frameworks.

Conclusion

If the Panel Reports in *China – Intellectual Property Rights* and *China – Publications and Audiovisual Products* have made anything clear, it is that the underlying issue is the quest for control over access to the Chinese market, where standards-setting, regulation of (online) distribution, screen quotas, and intellectual property enforcement converge and are all subservient to the desire to exercise full political and cultural control over the media market. So far, however, China's cocktail of policies provides a mixed bag of results, none of them very positive, except perhaps for the protection of vested domestic commercial and maybe also political interests. The lack of intellectual property enforcement results in piracy, favoring the unauthorized domestic production of works. Measures limiting the importation of foreign works furthermore foster demand for foreign works. Domestic standards-setting has the potential to cut out foreign manufacturers, and screen quotas, even though permissible, do nothing to stem the Chinese people's desire to access a culturally diverse media offering.

All that remains then is the public morals argument and the call for the protection of national cultural identity. Although much can be said to support such notions, protection of cultural diversity equally calls for policies ensuring that a plurality of cultural content is similarly safeguarded. So far, the results demonstrate visible favoritism for domestic state-controlled enterprises, where control over (online) distribution services and technologies seems to be the latest step to ensure that both economic and political authority remains in the hands of Chinese domestic and state-controlled entities. New disputes in relation to the control exercised over imports and distribution services, or even the technical fabric of dissemination of media that is favoring domestic players, seem inevitable. Given the intricate complexities of WTO law, it remains to be seen whether China's trading partners can take the Chinese policy cocktail to task and, if so, whether it leads to meaningful results.

51 *Supra* note 49. *See* Appellate Body Report, *European Communities – Trade Descriptions on Sardines*, WT/DS231/AB/R (September 26, 2002) and Panel Report, *European Communities – Protection of Trademarks and Geographical Indications for Agricultural Products and Foodstuffs*, WT/DS174/ R (March 15, 2005).

52 *See* in this respect World Trade Report 2005: *Exploring the links between trade, standards and the WTO* (WTO, 2007).

25 Rise and Demise of US Social Media in China

A Touchstone of WTO and BIT Regulations*

Danny Friedmann

Introduction

From 2007 to 2010, China added more Internet users than there are people in the United States (US). This high growth, in combination with a low saturation level, makes China the most promising market in the world for companies that want to provide Internet services. However, China has restricted foreign social media,[1] including Facebook, Twitter, and YouTube, by either blocking the sites or making access so erratic or slow that discouraged Internet users shun them. A publication of the Chinese Communist Party (CCP) explained the ban of Facebook[2] by pointing out that after the deadly riots in Xinjiang Uyghur Autonomous Region, the Xinjiang independence movement[3] used Facebook as a medium.

* This chapter is part of the results of the Research Project on "*Current Trends of Chinese Law towards Non-Trade Concerns such as Sustainable Development and the Protection of Environment, Public Health, Food Safety, Cultural, Social and Economic Rights, Labor Rights and the Reduction of Poverty from the Perspective of International Law and WTO Law*" coordinated by Professor Paolo Davide Farah at gLAWcal – Global Law Initiatives for Sustainable Development (United Kingdom) and at West Virginia University John D. Rockefeller IV School of Policy and Politics, Department of Public Administration, in partnership with the Center of Advanced Studies on Contemporary China (CASCC) in Turin (Italy), Maastricht University Faculty of Law, Department of International and European Law and IGIR – Institute for Globalisation and International Regulation (Netherlands), and Tsinghua University, School of Law, Institute of Public International Law and the Center for Research on Intellectual Property Law in Beijing (China). An early draft of this chapter was presented at the Conferences Series on "*China's Influence on Non-Trade Concerns in International Economic Law*", Third Conference held at Maastricht University, Faculty of Law on January 19–20, 2012. This publication and the Conference Series were sponsored by China–EU School of Law (CESL) at the China University of Political Science and Law (CUPL). The activities of CESL at CUPL are supported by the European Union and the People's Republic of China.

1 Social media, also known as Web 2.0 applications, have in common that they are based on user-generated content, which is communicated to a network of users.

2 Facebook was initially blocked periodically following the riots that started in Tibet on March 10, 2008. Aw Guo, *UPDATE: facebook.com is completely blocked in China then* (July 2, 2008), http://www.ifgogo.com/94/facebook-blocked-in-china/ (last visited July 16, 2016). As of July 2, 2009, Facebook was either blocked or the access was made very slow. See in the comment section Facebook users commenting on the status of Facebook in different parts of China. Jeremy Goldkorn, *Facebook blocked in China*, (July 2, 2008), http://www.danwei.org/net_nanny_follies/facebook_blocked_in_china.php#comments (last visited July 16, 2016).

3 The People's Daily Online mentions a survey taken by Huaqiu.com, a site under the auspices of the Chinese Communist Party, on July 8, 2009. According to the survey, 80 per cent of the netizens said that Facebook should be punished for being a medium for the Xinjiang independence movement. *80 percent of netizens agree China should punish Facebook*, People's Daily Online (July 10, 2009), http://english.people.com.cn/90001/90776/90882/6697993.html (last visited July 16, 2016).

The CCP then banned Twitter just before the 20th anniversary of the Tiananmen Square crackdown.[4] A graph demonstrating when YouTube was accessible and blocked[5] corresponds with sensitive political events in China.[6]

Since foreign social media sites have been banned, three Chinese social media sites, all listed in the New York Stock Exchange or NASDAQ, are thriving, partly because Chinese social media does not face foreign competition within the domestic market.[7] However, doing business in China remains difficult for them as well since they have to abide by ever more stringent censorship regulations. Until China's Gini Coefficient for income inequality drops significantly, China's leaders deem the risk of social unrest so substantial that they will insist on the sophisticated and extensive forms of censorship.

After banning foreign social media, the Chinese government reached the conclusion that Chinese social media is an indispensable tool to monitor the thoughts of millions of Chinese people. Therefore, rather than ban Chinese social media, the CCP decided to tame it, especially after witnessing the prominent role social media played during the Arab Spring and following the collision of two bullet trains in Wenzhou. In the latter case, millions of Chinese vented their criticism about how the government allegedly short-changed safety measures in favor of economic progress. This made the Chinese government realize that in order to guide the public, it should not only intercept the information that it deems harmful but revise it into wholesome information as well.

Following the CCP Secretary's visit in Beijing to the offices of "Chinese Twitter" called Sina Weibo in September 2011, the government announced that false and harmful information on social media must be squelched and the socialist core value system and advanced culture should be spread. Sina Weibo reacted to the high-profile official's visit by establishing a group of ten anti-rumor leagues that monitor, verify, and clarify false information.[8] Simultaneously, the government is considering a requirement that users provide their real name when registering with social media sites.

Although China has obligations to the global community via international treaties, the freedom of expression provisions in both the Universal Declaration of Human Rights and the International Covenant on Civil and Political Rights are not equipped to help foreign

4 Tania Branigan, *China blocks Twitter, Flickr and Hotmail ahead of Tiananmen anniversary*, THE GUARDIAN (June 2, 2009), http://www.guardian.co.uk/technology/2009/jun/02/twitter-china (last visited July 16, 2016).

5 HerdictWeb, demonstrates the dynamic of giving access to and blocking YouTube using a graph, HerdictWeb, Berkman Center for Internet & Society (undated), http://www.herdict.org/explore/indepth;jsessionid=84FD049D1295D9630E636DB54A014981#!fs=2071&fc=CN (last visited July 16, 2016).

6 Schwankert suspected that China blocked YouTube because of the upcoming Communist Party Congress in 2007. Steven Schwankert, *YouTube blocked in China; Flickr, Blogspot restored*, INFO WORLD (October 18, 2007), http://www.infoworld.com/d/security-central/youtube-blocked-in-china-flickr-blogspot-restored-351 (last visited July 16, 2016).

7 In this chapter the author will use the three most popular Chinese social media companies as examples: social network site RenRen, microblog Sina Weibo, and video-sharing site Youku. For an overall view of the Chinese social mediascape, *see* P. Candace Miles & J. Barratt Deans, *A Framework For Understanding Social Media Trends In China* (The 11th International DSI and APDSI Joint Meeting, Taipei, Taiwan, July 12–16, 2011, http://iceb.nccu.edu.tw/proceedings/APDSI/2011/web/session/aframeworkforunderstandingsocialmediatrends.pdf (last visited July 16, 2016).

8 David Bandurski, *China Tackles The Messy World Of Microblogs* (China Media Project, HKU, August 11, 2011), http://cmp.hku.hk/2011/08/11/14706/ (last visited July 29, 2014). *See* also Qin Xue, Li Jing & Xiao Yu, *Sina Has No License?*, NTD, video on YouTube, http://www.youtube.com/watch?v=lRsemhfGdpU (last visited July 16, 2016).

companies gain access to the Chinese market.[9] However, these companies could lobby their home country's government to bring the case to the World Trade Organization (WTO), which includes a binding dispute resolution system.

In order to achieve its Herculean goal of lifting millions of people out of poverty, China considers its WTO membership of paramount importance. Therefore, China gives its undivided attention to each country that brings a case against it at the WTO. Two cases in particular, one regarding Chinese censorship[10] and the other concerning market access in China,[11] are relevant because they demonstrate that a country cannot disregard WTO treaty law.[12] Foreign companies may be able to more effectively gain uncensored access to the Chinese market, or due compensation, if their home country has signed a Bilateral Investment Treaties (BIT).[13] These companies can reap the benefit of suing China directly via a transnational tribunal. The General Principles of Civil Law of the People's Republic of China[14] recognizes the supremacy of international treaties concluded by or acceded to by China, which apply to the law in civil relations with foreigners.[15]

This chapter is divided into three sections. The first section investigates whether the home countries of foreign social media companies can invoke the provisions of the General Agreement on Trade in Services (GATS) to ensure that China grants these companies market access.[16] The second section explores whether another country may use a BIT to oblige China to meet its commitments and give foreign social-media companies market access. The third section provides an explanation about why China does not welcome influential foreign social-media companies, even if they are willing to censor their content. Finally, the chapter ends with some conclusions.

9 The Universal Declaration of Human Rights is not really universal. It has no signatories. Therefore, it is not binding to any country. Besides, only the predecessor of the People's Republic of China proclaimed the Declaration in 1948. It is to the successor state's discretion what to do with the Declaration. China did sign the International Covenant on Civil Political Rights (ICCPR) in 1998; however, China can easily base its defense of censorship on the exceptions of Article 19.3(a) ICCPR: reputation of others and (b) protection of national security or public order. Furthermore, the ICCPR has no enforcement mechanism.

10 Panel Report, *China – Measures Affecting the Protection and Enforcement of Intellectual Property Rights*, ¶ 7.120, WT/DS362/R (January 26, 2009) [hereinafter *China – Intellectual Property* Rights]. *See* the summary at http://www.wto.org/english/tratop_e/dispu_e/cases_e/ds362_e.htm (last visited July 16, 2016).

11 Panel Report, *China – Measures Affecting Trading Rights and Distribution Services for Certain Publications and Audiovisual Entertainment Products*, WT/DS363/R (August 12, 2009), and Appellate Body Report, WT/DS363/AB/R (December 21, 2009) [hereinafter *China – Publications and Audiovisual Products*]. *See* the summary at http://www.wto.org/english/tratop_e/dispu_e/cases_e/ds363_e.htm (last visited July 16, 2016).

12 *See* Chapters 22 (Germann), 23 (Creemers), and 24 (Kamperman Sanders) in this volume.

13 For an analysis of Bilateral Investment Agreements *see* BRYAN MERCURIO, BILATERAL AND REGIONAL TRADE AGREEMENTS: COMMENTARY AND ANALYSIS (Simon Lester ed., Cambridge University Press, 2009).

14 Zhōnghuá Rénmín Gònghéguó Mínfǎ Tōngzé (中华人民共和国民法通则) [General Principles of the Civil Law of the People's Republic of China] (promulgated by the Nat'l People's Cong., April 12, 1986, effective August 27, 2009).

15 *Id.*, Article 142.

16 General Agreement on Trade in Services, April 15, 1994, Marrakesh Agreement Establishing the World Trade Organization, Annex 1B, 1869 UNTS 183, 33 ILM 1167 (1994) [hereinafter GATS], http://www.worldtradelaw.net/uragreements/gats.pdf (last visited July 16, 2016).

China's GATS commitment

This chapter will examine whether social media can be classified as a service. If this is the case, to what degree does China have an obligation to allow market access to foreign providers of this service based on international treaties?

China automatically became a member of the GATS[17] when it acceded to the Agreement Establishing the WTO on December 11, 2001. The GATS contains two kinds of commitments: a) a positive list of commitments concerning market access;[18] and b) national treatment in specifically designated sectors which are disclosed in schedules of specific commitments per Member, and general obligations which apply directly to all Members.

Providing the Internet is a telecommunication service

China's GATS commitments towards social media are not directly transparent because China's schedule of commitments does not explicitly describe them. However, China's commitments become clear when one examines its taxonomy.

Taxonomy of social media in China: ((((social media services) Internet information service) value-added telecommunication) telecommunication)

China regulates Internet services – including social media services – as a form of telecommunication.[19] The Regulation on Telecommunications of the People's Republic of China[20] (Regulation on Telecommunications) gives a broad definition of telecommunications: "the use of wired or wireless electromagnetic systems, or photoelectric systems, to transmit, emit or receive speech, text, data, graphics, or any other form of information."[21] In addition, the Regulation on Telecommunications makes a distinction[22] between basic telecommunications services, which include Internet service and other public data transmission services, and value-added telecommunications services,[23] which include electronic mail services, online database hosting and sorting, online data processing and trading processes, Internet connection services, and Internet information services. Social media services are a subcategory of Internet information services.

17 *Id.*

18 In contrast to the exceptions in the commitments of the General Agreement on Tariffs and Trade (GATT) 1994.

19 Michael Aldrich & Gaston Fernandez, *A practical insight to cross-border Telecommunication Laws and Regulations*, The International Legal Guide to: Telecommunications Laws and Regulations Ch. 13 (2010), http://www.iclg.co.uk/khadmin/Publications/pdf/3093.pdf (last visited July 16, 2016).

20 Zhōnghuá Rénmín Gònghéguó Diànxìn Tiáolì (中华人民共和国电信条例) [Regulation on Telecommunications of the People's Republic of China] (promulgated by the State Council, September 25, 2000), http://www.lawinfochina.com/display.aspx?lib=law&id=1667 (last visited July 16, 2016).

21 *Id.*, Article 2, ¶ 2.

22 *Id.*, Article 8 and Appendix: Catalogue of Telecommunications Business.

23 Hu Ling, *Shaping the virtual state: Internet regulation (1994–2009)*, (Dissertation, University of Hong Kong, May 2011), http://hub.hku.hk/handle/10722/141945 (last visited July 16, 2016).

What value-added telecommunication services obligations of GATS are relevant for social media in China?

One can distinguish the GATS provisions that are relevant to the value-added telecommunication services. The Uruguay Round negotiations, in which China did not participate, led to specific commitments for value-added services, the GATS Annex on Telecommunications and the general rules of GATS.[24] It seems a bit arbitrary to categorize Internet content providers – including social media – within the category of value-added telecommunication services; however, if one makes this categorization, he or she must consider that, although the Internet existed since the 1960s, the medium only became mainstream in 1989 when Berners-Lee's invention of the World Wide Web popularized it.[25] As a result, the Uruguay Round negotiators could not foresee the impact the medium would have on society. This claim applies *a fortiori* to social media, such as Facebook, Youku, and Twitter, which were launched in February 2004, February 2005, and July 2006, respectively. Nonetheless, Hindley and Lee-Makiyama point to the *Online Gambling*[26] and *Audiovisuals*[27] cases in which the WTO dispute settlement bodies adopted the principle of interpreting provisions in a technology neutral way.[28]

Schedule of commitments

Since 1995, all new countries acceding to the WTO must make market access commitments and provide exemptions in a number of service sectors. Following negotiations with WTO Members, China formed a schedule of commitments[29] in different service sectors, including the telecommunication sector.[30] As of December 11, 2001, China has permitted foreign-service suppliers to establish joint ventures – with a maximum foreign share of 40 per cent – in Beijing, Shanghai, and Guangzhou since social media sites fall within the category of value-added telecommunication services. A year later, China granted access to foreign suppliers in 17 cities[31] with a maximum foreign share of 49 per cent. As of December 11, 2003, China allowed foreign suppliers to establish joint ventures nationwide, with a maximum foreign share of 50 per cent.[32]

24 Uruguay Round between 1986 and 1994.

25 World Wide Web, a system of interlinked hypertext documents accessed via the Internet.

26 Panel Report, *United States – Measures Affecting the Cross-Border Supply of Gambling and Betting Services*, WT/DS285/R, ¶ 6.281 (November 10, 2004) [hereinafter *US – Gambling*].

27 *China – Publications and Audiovisual Products*, *supra* note 11, ¶ 396–397, WT/DS363/AB/R (December 21, 2009).

28 Brian Hindley & Hosuk Lee-Makiyama, *Protectionism Online: Internet Censorship and International Trade Law* 10 (ECIPE Working Paper, No. 12, 2009), http://www.ecipe.org/publications/ecipe-working-papers/protectionism-online-internet-censorship-and-international-trade-law (last visited July 16, 2016).

29 General Agreement on Trade in Services, *supra* note 16, Article XX: Schedules of Specific Commitments.

30 A summary of Implementing GATS Commitments in Main Service Sectors, World Bank: http://siteresources.worldbank.org/INTRANETTRADE/Resources/WBI-Training/288464–1139428366112/SummaryOfTheOpeningProgressOfMainServiceSectors.pdf (last visited July 16, 2016).

31 Beijing, Shanghai, Guangzhou, Chengdu, Chongqing, Dalian, Fuzhou, Hangzhou, Nanjing, Ningbo, Qingdao, Shenyang, Shenzhen, Taiyuan, Xiamen, Xi'an, and Wuhan.

32 Robert Lewis, *New Telecom Enterprise Regulations: The Door is Opened, but MII Still Keeping the Gate*, China Law & Practice (February 2002), http://www.chinalawandpractice.com/Article/1693772/

GATS Annex on Telecommunications

The GATS Annex on Telecommunications[33] is an integral part of GATS. Article 5 guarantees that all kinds of services, including value-added telecommunication services, can access and make use of the public telecommunications transport networks and services. The provision ensures that value-added service providers, including those providing social media, can benefit from the WTO Member's schedule of commitments if they do not have their own network to transport their services.

GATS general commitments

China clearly has the obligation to apply the general provisions of GATS to the regulation of Internet information services. Of these general provisions, we will review transparency, domestic regulation, and national treatment.

Article 3:1 GATS prescribes that each Member shall publish all relevant measures by the time of their entry into force, except in emergency situations. Although the Article does not define emergency situations, it may be interpreted narrowly since the clause is an exception. The deadly uproar in Xinjiang Uygur Autonomous Region might qualify as an emergency situation in contrast to the news reports following the high-speed train accident in Wenzhou in July 2011.[34] China does not accept that this provision may be reduced to a list of prohibited words, and it has only made these ever-changing lists available to those entities – including Internet content providers such as social media – that are responsible/liable for censoring the Internet. The government does not permit these entities to share the content of the lists with the public.

As already stated, social media can be classified as value-added telecommunication services and as Internet information services. Article 57 of the Regulation on Telecommunications and Article 15 of the Measures on the Administration of Internet Information Services, respectively, sum up what kind of information cannot be produced, copied, published, or transmitted via the telecommunication or via the Internet. The dual-classification creates a lot of overlap and stimulates an expansive and opaque form of self-censorship. As a result, companies censor themselves more broadly, just to be on the safe side and avoid liability. According to Hu, three different categories of prohibited expressions can be determined in both provisions: a) harmful content or politically sensitive content, which are enforced strictly; b) obscenity, violence, and gambling, which are not so strictly enforced; and c) piracy, privacy, and parody, which can be used to prohibit some speech using copyright instead of invoking the information security law.[35]

Channel/9949/New-Telecom-Enterprise-Regulations-The-Door-is-Opened-but-MII-Still-Keeping-the-Gate.html (last visited July 16, 2016).

33 Annex on Telecommunications, http://www.wto.org/english/tratop_e/serv_e/12-tel_e.htm (last visited July 16, 2016).

34 Following ethnic riots in Xinjiang Uyghur Autonomous Region in July 2009, China cut off the Internet, text messaging, and international phone service for half a year. After that period, the Internet and phone service was restored, but with severe limitations, e.g. people have a limited number of text messages they can send, no access to non-Chinese websites, and even limited access to Chinese websites. Rebecca MacKinnon, *China's Internet Censorship and Controls: The Context of Google's Approach in China*, in China's Internet: Staking Digital Ground (China Rights Forum, Human Rights in China, No. 2, 2010), http://www.hrichina.org/en/content/3248 (last visited July 16, 2016).

35 Hu Ling, *supra* note 23, at 35.

One intrinsic goal of Chinese censorship is to hide what information is censored. It may be impossible for a normal Internet user to determine whether a site has been blocked or whether there is merely a technical problem because an Internet browser either receives a technical error message or the connection speed decreases to such a low level that the site becomes *de facto* inaccessible. Article 3:2 GATS states that if the publication of these measures is not practicable, they should be made otherwise publicly available. However, one can imagine the government's fears that publishing such a list could spark its own social unrest.

Article VI GATS consists of Domestic Regulation. Article 4:2(a) obliges Members to pass legislation that institutes an independent, objective, and impartial review of administrative decisions affecting trade, "as soon as practicable." More importantly, Article 6:2(b) states that Members with a constitutional structure incompatible with Article 6:2(a) are not obliged to comply. However, in its Protocol of Accession to the WTO, China committed to establishing review procedures that include the opportunity for appeal, without penalty, by individuals or enterprises affected by any administrative action subject to review.[36] Furthermore, if the initial right of appeal is directed at an administrative body, the individual(s) or enterprise(s) shall have the opportunity in all cases to instead choose to appeal the decision to a judicial body. Notice of the decision on appeal shall be given to the appellant, and the reasons for such decision shall be provided in writing. The appellant shall also be informed of any right to further appeal. However, China does not grant the right to sue the government for censorship. Nonetheless, an individual from Shanghai successfully filed a lawsuit against China Telecom because it censored his website.[37]

Article 17:1 GATS states the crucial national treatment principle. Within the specific schedule of commitments for the value-added telecommunication services, China must treat each foreign, value-added service provider the same as it treats domestic ones. However, in practice, China arguably acts inconsistently with this commitment. RenRen is a direct clone of Facebook.[38] The same can be said for Youku in relation to YouTube. Sina Weibo presents a more complicated analysis because although it might have started out as a copycat of Twitter, it has arguably developed into a more innovative platform. In regard to the services and the service providers, the "likeness" of the services between the three pairs of social media is extremely similar.[39] At present, no law impedes foreign companies from participating in a joint venture and gaining access to provide social media services nationwide in China as long as they do not exceed a 50 per cent share. Encouraged by the market access case, which was based on national treatment Article XVII GATS, the US or the European Union (EU) could consider bringing a case against China at the WTO.[40] Bringing a case to the WTO seems like a better option than classifying Internet censorship as a barrier to trade to be dealt

36 Protocol of Accession to the World Trade Organization of the People's Republic of China, Section I:2(D), WT/L/432:2, http://www.wto.org/english/thewto_e/acc_e/completeacc_e.htm (last visited July 16, 2016).

37 Jeremy Goldkorn, *Suing the Net Nanny*, DANWEI (May 28, 2007), http://www.danwei.org/media_regulation/suing_the_net_nanny.php (last visited July 29, 2014); Yetaai, *A practical lawsuit against China Internet censorship* (May 9, 2007), http://yetaai.blogspot.com/2007/05/practical-lawsuit-against-china.html (last visited July 16, 2016).

38 *See* DAVILS KIRKPATRICK, THE FACEBOOK EFFECT: THE INSIDE STORY OF THE COMPANY THAT IS CONNECTING THE WORLD 171 (Simon & Schuster, 2010).

39 Mireille Cossy, *Determining "Likeness" Under The GATS: Squaring The Circle?* (Staff Working Paper ERSD-2006–08, September 2006), http://www.wto.org/english/res_e/reser_e/ersd200608_e.pdf (last visited July 16, 2016).

40 *Supra* note 11.

with during trade negotiations, as some have suggested, but such legal actions could result in trade retaliation.[41]

China's BIT commitments

Countries sign BITs in order to protect their respective companies' investments in the host country against damages caused by violations of substantive and procedural provisions contained in the treaty. The great advantage of BITs for companies that invest abroad is that they obtain direct legal personality under international law,[42] whereas under the WTO system, companies must lobby their home government to bring a claim against the host government.

China has signed BITs with 130 countries.[43] Despite several negotiations, China and the US have not been able to agree on the contents of a BIT yet, so, thus far, the banned US social media sites cannot rely on BIT protection. As China has opened its economy throughout the last 30 years, it has received large amounts of foreign investment inflows. Because China primarily acted as the host country for investments, it generally drafted restrictive BITs in its own interest.[44] In one respect, China has been rather liberal: it has acknowledged investor–state arbitration since 1985, even before it signed the Convention of the International Centre for Settlement of Investment Disputes (ICSID)[45] in 1990. Chen argues that the ICSID Convention is not in China's interest since China receives a lot of foreign direct investment (FDI)[46] inflows, and the country is going through a transitional phase.[47] Since 1998, China's FDI outflows have become more significant, although it is still a net-FDI country.[48] China started to invest especially in developing countries.[49] Therefore, it wants stronger protection for its investments, which suggests that China would be more inclined to sign liberal BITs.[50] Berger writes that the main difference found in liberal BITs is the degree to which they protect investments already in the pre-establishment phase, for

41 A discussion on trade retaliations can be found in Bryan Mercurio, *Retaliatory Trade Measures in the WTO Dispute Settlement Understanding: Are There Really Alternatives?*, in TRADE DISPUTES AND THE DISPUTES SETTLEMENT UNDERSTANDING OF THE WTO; AN INTERDISCIPLINARY ASSESSMENT 397–442 (James Hartigan ed., Emerald/Elsevier, 2009). *See* Chapter 24 (Kamperman Sanders) in this volume.

42 On multinational corporations and international law, *see* Chapter 4 (Bonfanti) in this volume.

43 *See* http://www.unctad.org/sections/dite_pcbb/docs/bits_china.pdf (last visited July 16, 2016).

44 *See* Chapters 4 (Bonfanti), 6 (Vadi), and 7 (Klaver & Trebilcock) in this volume.

45 Convention on the Settlement of Investment Disputes between States and Nationals of Other States, 17 UST 1270, entered into force October 14, 1966, http://icsid.worldbank.org/ICSID/StaticFiles/basicdoc/CRR_English-final.pdf (last visited July 16, 2016).

46 Definition of the World Bank: Foreign direct investment is the net inflow of investment to acquire a lasting management interest of at least 10 per cent of the voting stock, in an enterprise operating in an economy other than that of an investor. Foreign direct investment, net inflows (BoP, current USD), World Bank, http://data.worldbank.org/indicator/BX.KLT.DINV.CD.WD (last visited July 16, 2016).

47 An Chen, *Distinguishing Two Types of Countries and Properly Granting Differential Reciprocity Treatment. Re-comments on the Four Safeguards in Sino-Foreign BITs Not to be Hastily and Completely Dismantled*, 8(6) J. WORLD INV. & TRADE 771–795 (2007).

48 More about China's outbound investments can be found in Julien Chaisse, *International Investment Treaties and China Outbound Investments*, in CHINA OUTBOUND INVESTMENTS – GUIDE TO LAW AND PRACTICE 213–234 (Lutz-Christian Wolff ed., Kluwer, 2011).

49 *See* Chapters 2 (Farah), 4 (Bonfanti), 5 (Choukroune), 6 (Vadi), and 7 (Klaver & Trebilcock) in this volume.

50 Alex Berger, *China's New Bilateral Investment Treaty Programme: Substance, Rational and Implications for International Investment Law Making* 7, ASIL IELIG 2008 Biennial Conference "The Politics of International Economic Law: The Next Four Years," Washington, D.C., November 14–15, 2008.

example before the host country's authorities have admitted the FDI project in accordance with national laws and regulations.[51] In principle, a country needs to sign only one liberal BIT in order to liberalize the BITs it signed earlier, as a result of the most favored nation (MFN) provisions it agreed to previously.

If the Sino-German BIT[52] is any indication of what China would like to see in a BIT with the US, opinions differ about the application of the national treatment[53] and MFN principles.[54] In the Sino-German BIT protocol,[55] which is integral to the Sino-German BIT, the nondiscrimination provisions clearly do not apply to existing nonconforming measures. So, in the unlikely scenario that the US and China would sign a BIT under these conditions, it would not help US companies that have already invested in providing social media services in China. Another condition in the Sino-German BIT is that measures that must be taken for reasons of public security and order, public health, or morality shall not be deemed "treatment less favorable" as in the meaning of the nondiscrimination provisions.[56] This condition, which gives China much leeway, will make the investments by German companies that want to provide social media in China very uncertain.

Why social media in China stay Chinese

As one can read in the first section of this chapter, based on the GATS and China's special schedule of commitments, China should grant market access to social media sites that are 50 per cent or less foreign owned. In this section, we will review the instrumental objectives of Chinese social media, and answer the following question: why does China not want any influential foreign social media to be active in the domestic market, even if it is willing to censor its content, just as many foreign Internet sites are already doing?[57]

For example, Facebook launched a Chinese language version of its site in 2008, but China banned the US social network site a year later. CEO Mark Zuckerberg visited China twice to see whether he could establish a joint venture with a Chinese firm. Zuckerberg has stated clearly that Facebook is willing to abide by China's censorship policy.[58] Unfortunately for

51 *Id.*, at 4.

52 Agreement between the People's Republic of China and the Federal Republic of Germany on the Encouragement and Reciprocal Protection of Investments (December 1, 2003), http://tradeinservices.mofcom.gov.cn/en/b/2003-12-01/29421.shtml (last visited July 16, 2016).

53 *Id.*, Article 3(2).

54 *Id.*, Article 3(3).

55 *Id.*, Article 3.

56 *Id.*, Article 4(a).

57 MSN has censored bloggers in China since 2005. *Microsoft censors bloggers*, BBC News (June 14, 2011), http://news.bbc.co.uk/2/hi/technology/4088702.stm (last visited July 16, 2016). Yahoo.cn was considered one of the strictest censors in China, according to Reporters Without Borders. Eli Milchman, *Yahoo "Strictest" Censor in China*, Wired (June 15, 2006), http://archive.wired.com/politics/onlinerights/news/2006/06/71166 (last visited July 16, 2016). Google censored in China from 2005 until 2010. Google also filed for a US patent application for a location-based censoring methodology. Danny Friedmann, *Paradoxes, Google and China – How Censorship Can Harm and Intellectual Property Can Harness Innovation*, in Google And The Law: Empirical Approaches to Legal Aspects of Knowledge-Economy Business Models (Aurelio Lopez-Tarruella, ed., Springer Science & Business Media, 2012), http://ssrn.com/abstract=1885267 (last visited July 16, 2016).

58 Jason Kincaid, *Mark Zuckerberg On Facebook's Strategy For China (And His Wardrobe)*, TC (October 16, 2010), http://techcrunch.com/2010/10/16/mark-zuckerberg-on-facebooks-strategy-for-china-and-his-wardrobe/ (last visited July 16, 2016).

Facebook, *Businessweek* published a story in which it is said that, "Zuckerberg believes Facebook can be an agent of change in China, as it has been in countries such as Egypt and Tunisia."[59] Whether true or not, this statement is unlikely to charm the Chinese government and may stoke its fears.

The Chinese government realized that social media plays a crucial role within the media-mix offered to the public.[60] Following the Wenzhou train accident, it became known that a quarter-billion people had watched more TV online than offline and got as much news from Chinese social media than Chinese mainstream, such as state-controlled media.[61]

When China opened up to the outside world, especially after it acceded to the WTO, it was anticipated that globalization would become more powerful and that nationalism would lose importance. Decentralization would become more prominent than centralization. It was also expected that the playing field for foreign companies that wanted to operate in China would be leveled. Tuinstra argues that China acceded to the WTO to use the treaty as a vehicle to regain the power it lost during decentralization efforts.[62] Also, many thought that social media would bring freedom of expression. However, it has become increasingly clear that China uses social media to control its people, going beyond mere censorship.[63] Moreover, China wants to use social media to spread propaganda, monitor public opinion, and use nationalism as a soft power tool to counter foreign cultural influences. The Chinese government may also intend – or welcome the collateral effect – to breed national champions, insulated from foreign competition.

China's instrumental use of social media

China's top propaganda chief urged microblogging services, such as Sina Weibo, to serve the work of the CCP and the nation. Further, microblogging services should popularize sciences, advance culture and project social morality. In general, the Chinese government intends to use social media to support the CCP's political integrity, guide and elevate the people to social morality, and maintain social cohesion and harmony. Social media also function as society's safety valves since, for example, people can vent their frustrations about local corrupt bureaucrats. The Chinese government further monitors public opinion trends in real time and tries to respond with calculated actions and policies. This could be interpreted as an embryonic form of direct democracy. In foreign affairs, the Chinese government sometimes uses the voice of the people, when aligned with its own strategic objectives. Sometimes it whips up nationalist sentiments, and sometimes it curbs them.[64] The Chinese government actively promotes socialist culture to resist the invasion of foreign cultures and enhance national identity and solidarity.[65]

59 Unfortunately for Facebook, Businessweek published a story in which it is said that, "Zuckerberg believes Facebook can be an agent for change in China, as it has been in countries such as Egypt and Tunesia." Brad Stone, Why Facebook Needs Sheryl Sandberg, Bloomberg (May 12, 2011), http://www.bloomberg.com/news/articles/2011-05-12/why-facebook-needs-sheryl-sandberg (last visited July 12, 2016).

60 *See* Chapters 22 (Germann), 23 (Creemers), and 24 (Kamperman Sanders) in this volume.

61 Bill Bishop, *China's Internet: The Invisible Birdcage,* China Economic Quarterly (September 2010), http://digicha.com/index.php/2011/02/chinas-internet-the-invisible-birdcage/ (last visited July 16, 2016).

62 Fons Tuinstra, Beijing's Secret WTO Agenda, 2003. See Chapter 2 (Farah) in this volume.

63 *See* Chapter 24 (Kamperman Sanders) in this volume.

64 Hu Ling, *supra* note 23, at 38.

65 Hu Ling, *supra* note 23, at 35, footnote 4. *See* Kang Xiaoguang, China Returns 328–329 (Bafang Wenhua Chuangzuoshi, 2008).

In addition to controlling content that may potentially damage socialist morale, there might be another underlying economic reason for withholding market access from foreign competition or it might be a welcome collateral effect of censorship. Limiting foreign competition may enable national companies to flourish, such as RenRen, Sina Weibo, and Youku, and these companies may eventually prosper in the global market.[66] According to Brahm, one of the Chinese government's major objectives is to use the WTO to prepare these local champions for the international arena.[67] US social media that the Chinese government has excluded from China must be frustrated that Chinese social media, funded through US stock exchanges, could grow into national champions in China. These companies take advantage of the economies of scale to develop innovations, which allow them to compete with US social media outside China.

Why foreign companies are not suitable instruments for the Chinese government

If history is any guide, the Chinese government wants social media sites not just to censor, but also to help catch transgressors. However, asking foreign companies' cooperation may cross the line. The public relations backfire to companies such as Yahoo, which released information leading to the arrest of at least two subscribers, supports this view. Moreover, foreign governments could export their legislation to companies doing business abroad, including in China. US representative Christopher Smith drafted the Global Online Freedom Act (GOFA), which makes it a crime if US companies share personal information with any government that practices censorship; however, the bill has not yet passed into law despite its proposal in 2007 and 2009. Another point of concern is that the asymmetric quality of information between Chinese and foreign social media users would become too obvious and embarrassing. An English version of Sina Weibo will soon launch, and the company will censor content using the Chinese standard, even outside China.[68] In short, foreign companies remain dependent on their home government's wishes and cannot rely on China.

After a WTO or BIT victory

Even though a claimant may win a WTO case against China for acting inconsistently with its GATS commitments, the result would not guarantee that foreign social media could establish themselves in China successfully. Because the responsibility for social media companies is divided among many ministries, each can independently raise a barrier.[69] Obtaining the required licenses would be time-consuming and costly, if not impossible. Even the Chinese company Sina Weibo needed 11 licenses, and Sina has exceptional "guan xi,"

66 *See* Chapter 24 (Kamperman Sanders) in this volume.

67 China After WTO 222 (L. J. Brahm ed., China Intercontinental Press, 2002).

68 The English version of Sina Weibo will be filtered in the same way as in China. According to a Sina spokesperson: "Sina will continue to comply with Chinese regulations." This could mean that Chinese censorship will be exported outside China. Owen Fletcher, *Sina Weibo: Competition for Twitter*, China Real Time Report, Wall Street Journal (June 8, 2011), http://blogs.wsj.com/chinarealtime/2011/06/08/sina-weibo-competition-for-twitter/ (last avisited July 29, 2014).

69 *See* Chapter 23 (Creemers) in this volume.

meaning good relations with government officials, which are crucial for doing business in China.[70] According to the *Decision of the State Council on Establishing Administrative License for the Administrative Examination and Approval Items Really Necessary To Be Retained*, the following licenses are needed :[71]

- Telecommunication and information service business license (Ministry of Information Industry),
- Value-added telecommunication business license (Ministry of Information Industry),
- BBS license (Ministry of Information Industry),
- Internet news license (State Council Information Office) and Internet education service license (Ministry of Education),
- Internet health information service license (Ministry of Health),
- Internet medicine information service license (State Drug Administration),
- Advertisement business license (State Administration for Industry and Commerce),
- Internet publishing license (General Administration of Press and Publication),
- Internet culture business license (Ministry of Culture), and
- Online video license (State Administration of Radio Film and Television).

Besides these licenses, the government often forces Chinese Internet companies to sign mandatory "self discipline" pledges.[72] If a company does not obtain all the required licenses and does not comply with additional legislation, which might not be transparent, the government may easily prevent a company from doing business in China.

Conclusions

Following the social unrest in the western provinces of China, and given the role social media played in aggregating and distributing news about these events, China decided to ban the three most influential foreign social media sites: Facebook, Twitter, and YouTube. The government took action only after RenRen, Sina Weibo, and Youku – clones of the respective banned social media sites – were up and running since they could, at least partially, fill the void. Notably, these three Chinese social media companies became national champions with financial help from the US stock exchanges.

After the Arab Spring and the Wenzhou train collision, the Chinese government realized that social media, acting as an outlet for public opinion, could allow it to monitor the thoughts of millions of Chinese people, in real time. The government started to develop a program to not only censor and restrict social media information, but also to monitor and influence it. High CCP officials pressured social media sites to guide the masses towards socialist values, promote coherence and solidarity, and squelch rumors.

70 Niva Elkin-Koren & Eli M. Salzberger, Law, Economics and Cyberspace: The Effects of Cyberspace on the Economic Analysis of Law (Edward Elgar, 2003). See also Chapter 2 (Farah) in this volume.

71 Guówùyuàn Duì Què Xū Bǎoliú De Xíngzhèng Shěnpī Xiàngmù Shè Dìng Xíngzhèng Xǔkě De Juédìng (国务院对确需保留的行政审批项目设定行政许可的决定) [Decision of the State Council on Establishing Administrative License for the Administrative Examination and Approval Items Really Necessary To Be Retained] (Issued by the State Council, June 29, 2004, effective July 1, 2004, revised in 2009). http://www.lawinfochina.com/display.aspx?lib=law&id=4429 (last visited July 16, 2016).

72 Bill Bishop, *supra* note 60.

Although the Chinese government's policy is a gross violation of the freedom of expression protected by human rights treaties, these treaties are either toothless or irrelevant to China and cannot be used to force open the Chinese market. What remains are the WTO and BIT regulations.

Bringing a case against China before the WTO is promising; however, aggrieved companies must lobby their home government because they cannot bring the case directly themselves. Social media may be classified as value-added telecommunication services, and China has GATS commitments that require it to grant nationwide market access to foreign companies that have a share of 50 per cent or less, via a joint venture. However, despite the fact that some social media companies might be willing to abide by Chinese censorship rules, the government has banned Facebook, Twitter, and YouTube. Therefore, it can be argued that China has violated the market access national treatment provision.

This legal remark leaves us with its practical implication. It is questionable whether a foreign social media company would agree to spearhead a WTO case against China. By doing so, the company would explicitly expose its willingness to contribute to Chinese censorship policy. Making a case against China might force the country to fulfill its legal obligations. On the other hand, China might resort to non-legal tactics, such as slowing down traffic to its site(s) or making online access erratic, to prevent the western social media from competing on equal footing.

As an alternative, foreign companies from home countries that have signed a BIT with China can bring a direct claim against it at a transnational tribunal. However, US companies cannot access this route because, thus far, China and the US have not agreed on any text for a BIT. German companies, however, can make use of the Sino-German BIT. German companies that invested in China after the treaty took effect could, in principle, sue China if they are banned. In response, China could invoke the protocol to the BIT that provides an interpretation about how the national treatment principle should be applied. If China takes measures based on public security, social order, and morality, these measures would not amount to "less-favorable" national treatment. As a result, doing business in China is likewise uncertain for German companies that want to provide social media services. After availing itself of a BIT, a victorious company might still need to address practical trade barriers.

The Chinese government uses social media as an instrument to censor and guide its population, and it does not trust foreign companies to control its people accordingly. Therefore, even if a company wins a WTO or BIT case, the government may still make market access *de facto* impossible. In addition to overcoming slow and erratic access to their websites, social media companies must obtain 11 licenses, each available at different departments. This could be another formidable tool to guarantee that social media in China stays Chinese.

26 Can Trade Restrictions be Justified by Moral Values? Revisiting the Seals Disputes through a Law and Economics Analysis**

*Julien Chaisse and Xinjie Luan**

Introduction

The high-profile World Trade Organization (WTO) dispute on the European Union's seal import ban has captivated the attention of the international community for over five years. In 2009, Canada requested World Trade Organization (WTO) consultations with the European Union (EU) on the EU seal products ban under the Seal Ban Regulation (SBR) and subsequent amendments, replacements, extensions, implementing measures, and other related measures,[1] and a panel was later established that issued a report in November 2013.[2] This Panel report was appealed, and the WTO's Appellate Body reached a subsequent decision in June 2014.[3] This chapter intends to revisit the dispute from a legal and economics perspective. Instead of commenting on the merits of the WTO decisions, this

* The authors would like to thank Paolo Davide Farah, Bryan Mercurio, David Wilmshurt, and Mu-Hsiang Yu for comments and suggestions on earlier drafts of this chapter. They would also like to thank Haweni Bedada, who provided research assistance. The views expressed by the authors here are personal. This chapter is sponsored by "Standardization and Intellectual Property Management–Key. Universities Research Institute in Humanities and Social Sciences, Zhejiang Province, China."

** This chapter is part of the results of the Research Project on "Current Trends of Chinese Law towards Non-Trade Concerns such as Sustainable Development and the Protection of Environment, Public Health, Food Safety, Cultural, Social and Economic Rights, Labor Rights and the Reduction of Poverty from the Perspective of International Law and WTO Law" coordinated by Professor Paolo Davide Farah at gLAWcal – Global Law Initiatives for Sustainable Development (United Kingdom) and at West Virginia University John D. Rockefeller IV School of Policy and Politics, Department of Public Administration, in partnership with the Center of Advanced Studies on Contemporary China (CASCC) in Turin (Italy), Maastricht University Faculty of Law, Department of International and European Law and IGIR – Institute for Globalisation and International Regulation (Netherlands), and Tsinghua University, School of Law, Institute of Public International Law and the Center for Research on Intellectual Property Law in Beijing (China). This publication and the Conference Series were sponsored by China–EU School of Law (CESL) at the China University of Political Science and Law (CUPL). The activities of CESL at CUPL are supported by the European Union and the People's Republic of China.

1 Request for Consultations by Canada, *European Communities – Measures Prohibiting the Importation and Marketing of Seal Products*, WT/DS400/1 (November 4, 2009). Following the complaint lodged by Canada, Norway also requested consultation with the EC concerning the EC seal regime. *See* Request for Consultations by Norway, *European Communities – Measures Prohibiting the Import and Marketing of Seal Products*, WT/DS401/1 (November 10, 2009).

2 Panel Report, *European Communities – Measures Prohibiting the Importation and Marketing of Seal Products*, WT/DS400/R; WT/DS401/R (November 25, 2013).

3 Appellate Body Report, *European Communities – Measures Prohibiting the Importation and Marketing of Seal Products*, WT/DS400/AB/R, WT/DS401/AB/R (May 22, 2014).

chapter returns to the facts and the law and provides a new analysis of the dispute with a view to shed light on some of the arguments that were ignored by the WTO organs. The structure of the chapter is as follows. We first present Canada's specific complaints. In Canada's view, the SBR aims to prohibit the importation and marketing in the customs territory of the EU of all seal products, and it "appears to be inconsistent with the EU obligations under the 1994 General Agreement on Tariffs and Trade[4] (GATT) and the Agreement on Technical Barriers to Trade[5] (TBT)."[6] Canada's request for consultations is linked to an existing dispute over bans by Belgium and the Netherlands on seal products, also initiated by Canada.[7] Canada hopes that "all issues related to seal bans in Europe will be resolved through the new consultations."[8] We then expound on the specific contentions between the EU and Canada; the concerns raised by Canada are trade-related, while the EU focuses on the issue of cruelty to animals. The material reasons why the EU bans seal products are also discussed thoroughly in this section. Against this background, we consider the implications of "public morals" and the optimal instrument for protection of public morals concerning the dispute over the EU's SBR. Finally, the chapter examines the differences between the risk assessment mechanisms in the Agreement on Technical Barriers to Trade and the Agreement on the Application of Sanitary and Phytosanitary Measures (SPS Agreement).[9] In conclusion, the chapter predicts the outcome of the dispute between Canada and the EU.

Analysis of Canada's complaints

Seal hunting is an important part of Canada's cultural heritage and is a way of life for the Inuit and other residents of Atlantic Canada, Quebec, and the Far North.[10] More importantly, the right of indigenous peoples to secure their livelihood by hunting is recognized by the United Nations Declaration on the Rights of Indigenous Peoples.[11] Canada's Department of Fisheries and Oceans (DFO) has asserted that seal hunting provides important seasonal income and food to this group.[12] The income of indigenous peoples from

4 General Agreement on Tariffs and Trade, October 30, 1947, 61 Stat. A-11, 55 UNTS 194 [hereinafter GATT].

5 Agreement on Technical Barriers to Trade, April 15, 1994, Marrakesh Agreement Establishing the World Trade Organization, Annex 1A, 1868 UNTS 120 [hereinafter TBT Agreement].

6 Request for Consultations by Canada, *supra* note 1.

7 Regarding the Belgian legislation in particular, *see* Robert Galantucci, *Compassionate Consumerism Within the GATT Regime, Can Belgium's Ban on Seal Products Imports Be Justified Under Article XX*, 39(2) California Western Int'l L. J. 281–312 (2009).

8 ICTSD, *Canada Launches WTO Complaint over EU Seal Ban*, Bridges Weekly Trade News Digest (November 4, 2009), http://ictsd.org/i/news/bridgesweekly/58533/ (last visited July 16, 2016).

9 Agreement on Sanitary and Phytosanitary Measures, April 15, 1994, Marrakesh Agreement Establishing the World Trade Organization, Annex 1A, 1867 UNTS 493 [hereinafter SPS Agreement].

10 ICTSD, *Canada, Norway Launch WTO Complaint over EU Seal Ban* Bridges Trade BioRes, November 13, 2009, at 3.

11 UN General Assembly, *United Nations Declaration on the Rights of Indigenous Peoples,* October 2, 2007, A/RES/61/295.

12 Dep't of Fisheries and Oceans ("DFO") of Canada, *Overview of the Atlantic Seal Hunt 2006–2010*, para. 2 [hereinafter *Overview of Atlantic Seal Hunt*]. *See* also Julien Chaisse & Luan Xinjie, *Preliminary Comments on the WTO Seals Products Dispute – Traditional Hunting, Public Morals and Technical Barriers to Trade*, 22(1) Colo. Nat. Resources Energy & Envtl L. Rev. 79–121 (2010).

sealing represents between 25 and 35 per cent of their total annual income.[13] It would therefore be extremely difficult for the Canadian authorities to end seal hunting in Canada.[14]

The commercial benefits of seal hunting have long been recognized in Canada. Commercial seal hunting in Canada's Arctic waters is attested to have occurred at least as early as the sixteenth century.[15] About one-third of Canadian seal products are exported to the market of the EU. Whereas Canada has laid great stress on its concern for conservation, parading its commitment to the sustainable use of seal resources, the EU has deplored the use of inhumane and cruel seal hunting methods. Against this background,[16] the European Parliament issued a Declaration banning seal products in the European Union (the Declaration) in September 2006. The Declaration called for a full ban on all trade in harp and hooded seal products, apart from limited products from traditional Inuit community hunting.[17] On September 16, 2009, the European Parliament and the Council of the EU adopted Regulation No. 1007/2009 on trade in seal products (the Seal Ban Regulation or SBR) to ban the import, export, and sale of all seal products.[18] The SBR has been in force since November 20, 2009, and its Article 3 – titled "Conditions for placing on the market" – took effect on August 20, 2010.[19]

Like many other WTO Agreements, the TBT Agreement stipulates the principles of both Most Favored Nation (MFN) and National Treatment. Both principles are set out in Article 2.1 of the TBT Agreement, which requires that "in respect of their technical regulations, products imported from the territory of any Member be accorded treatment no less favorable than that accorded to like products of national origin"[20] (National Treatment), and that the products of the territory of any contracting party imported into the territory of any other contracting party shall be accorded treatment no less favorable than that accorded "to like products originating in any other country"[21] (Most-Favored Nation). This provision is in line with GATT Articles I:1 – which requires Member States to accord equal treatment to all their trading partners, provided they are also members of the Organization –[22] and III on National Treatment.

13 DFO of Canada, *Socio-economic Importance of the Seal Hunt* [hereinafter *Socio-economic Importance of the Seal Hunt*]. *See* also Chaisse & Xinjie, *supra* note 12.

14 *See* for example Robert Galantucci, *supra* note 7, at 284–85.

15 *Overview of Atlantic Seal Hunt*, *supra* note 12, para. 2.

16 Bans on seal products have a long history under the EU import regime since it was already prohibited by a directive adopted by the EU in 1983. *See* Maurizio Gambardella, *European Union Ban on Seal Products: Some Customs and WTO Open Questions*, Global Trade & Customs J. 145 (April 2010).

17 *See* Declaration on Banning Seal Products in the European Union, para. H.1.

18 Council Regulation 1007/2009, Article 3, 2009 O.J. (L 286).

19 On the EU decision-making process, *see* Julien Chaisse, *Adapting the European Community Legal Structure to the International Trade*, Eur. Bus. L. Rev. 1615–1621 (November–December 2006).

20 TBT Agreement, Article 2.1.

21 *Id.*

22 Article I:1 reads as follows: "With respect to customs duties and charges of any kind imposed on or in connection with importation or exportation or imposed on the international transfer of payments for imports or exports, and with respect to the method of levying such duties and charges, and ***with respect to all rules and formalities in connection with importation and exportation***, and with respect to all matters referred to in paragraphs 2 and 4 of Article III, any advantage, favour, privilege or immunity granted by any contracting party to any product originating in or destined for any other country shall be accorded immediately and unconditionally to the like product originating in or destined for the territories of all other contracting parties" (emphasis added).

Another fundamental provision of the GATT is that of Article XI:1, on the "elimination of quantitative restrictions."[23] According to Article XI:1 – as well as Article 4.2 of the Agreement on Agriculture (AoA)[24] – it is clear that a full ban on imports can be treated as one kind of quantitative restriction and such restrictions shall not be prepared, adopted, or applied in any manner.

Canada requested the Panel to rule on all these claims: whether the EU's SBR conflicts with the principles of MFN treatment, national treatment, or the elimination of quantitative restrictions, according to GATT Articles I, III, and XI; TBT Article 2.1; and AoA Article 4.2.

The most-favored nation principle

The MFN principle – as well as the one of national treatment – is designed to prevent discrimination against a particular region or country. We will now explain that the EU's SBR does no such thing, thus ruling out a possible violation of such principle.

First of all, the SBR defines both "seal" and "seal product."[25] "Seals" are defined as specimens of all species of pinnipeds; and "seal product" means all products, either processed or unprocessed, deriving or obtained from seals, including meat, oil, blubber, organs, raw fur skins and fur skins, tanned or dressed, including fur skins assembled in plates, crosses and similar forms, and articles made from fur skins.[26] As the SBR does not define "seal" and "seal product" based on geographical factors, and its provisions apply to all sea products from all countries, the SBR cannot reasonably be held to discriminate against a particular region or country.

"Inuit exceptions" to the total ban contained in the SBR are contentious since they seem to conflict with the principle of MFN treatment. It is well known that the Inuit and other aboriginal communities have a traditional sealing culture, and their seal products may be traded for cultural, educational, or ceremonial purposes.[27] In effect, the Inuit exception demonstrates that the EU respects the culture, tradition, and subsistence lifestyle of Inuit and other aboriginal communities. Those who object to the Inuit exception aim not to eliminate it but rather to extend that preference to other areas and countries, subject to the restrictions of the SBR on trade in seal products. Therefore, it is not clear that the Inuit exception violates the principle of MFN treatment. If the exception were put aside, then a ban on trade in seal products, applied equally to all EU Member States and third parties, would certainly not be discriminatory.

23 Article XI:1 of the GATT reads: "No prohibitions or restrictions other than duties, taxes or other charges, whether made effective through quotas, import or export licenses or other measures, shall be instituted or maintained by any contracting party on the importation of any product of the territory of any other contracting party or on the exportation or sale for export of any product destined for the territory of any other contracting party."

24 According to Article 4.2 of the AoA, "Members shall not maintain, resort to, or revert to any measures of the kind which have been required to be converted into ordinary customs duties." Agreement on Agriculture, April 15, 1994, Marrakesh Agreement Establishing the World Trade Organization, Annex 5, 1869 UNTS 410 [hereinafter AoA].

25 Seal Ban Regulation, *supra* note 18, at Article 2.

26 *Id.*

27 *Canada-EU Vote Could Lead to Tight Ban on Seal Products*, Res. Ctr. for the Rights of Indigenous Peoples, http://www.galdu.org/web/index.php?odas=3730&giella1=eng (last updated March 3, 2009; last visited July 16, 2016).

The principle of national treatment

As to the national treatment, the preamble of the SBR states that "in order to ensure that the harmonized rules provided for in this Regulation are fully effective, those rules should apply not only to seal products originating from the Community, but also to those introduced into the Community from third countries."[28]

Compared to the principle of general National Treatment provided by Article 2.1 of the TBT Agreement and Article III:4 of the GATT 1994, the national treatment here can be called "adverse national treatment," meaning that seal products either originating in the EU or exported from third countries are granted identical, non-preferential treatment. Even so, this provision *per se* complies with the principle of national treatment.

Elimination of quantitative restrictions

As mentioned above, a full ban on seal products can be treated as one kind of quantitative restriction. That is certainly the thrust of the SBR. For instance, Article 3 of the SBR stipulates that seal products can only be placed on the EU market in a very few exceptional circumstances.[29] This provision is inconsistent with the principle of "elimination of quantitative restrictions" under GATT 1994 and the Agreement on Agriculture.[30] The issue of "protection of public morals" was not included in the request for consultations and is unlikely to be considered in any subsequent request for the establishment of a panel. Therefore, in the SBR dispute, the WTO Panel cannot assess the "protection of public morals" as a "general exception" under Article XX of the GATT 1994.[31] As a result, the provisions for the "elimination of quantitative restrictions" will work against the EU.

The principle of avoidance of unnecessary obstacles to trade

The principle of avoidance of unnecessary obstacles to trade is enshrined in Article 2.2 of the TBT Agreement, which requires technical regulations not to be "more trade-restrictive than necessary to fulfill a legitimate objective," and such legitimate objectives include – among others – "national security requirements; the prevention of deceptive practices;

28 Seal Ban Regulation, *supra* note 18, Preamble (13).

29 Article 3.1: "The placing on the market of seal products shall be allowed only where the seal products result from hunts traditionally conducted by Inuit and other indigenous communities and contribute to their subsistence [. . .] 2. By way of derogation from paragraph 1: (a) The import of seal products shall also be allowed where it is of an occasional nature and consists exclusively of goods for the personal use of travellers or their families. The nature and quantity of such goods shall not be such as to indicate that they are being imported for commercial reasons; (b) The placing on the market of seal products shall also be allowed where the seal products result from by-products of hunting that is regulated by national law and conducted for the sole purpose of the sustainable management of marine resources. Such placing on the market shall be allowed only on a non-profit basis. The nature and quantity of the seal products shall not be such as to indicate that they are being placed on the market for commercial reasons." Seal Ban Regulation, *supra* note 18, at Article 3.

30 GATT, *supra* note 4, at Article XI:1; AoA, *supra* note 24, at Article 4.2.

31 In a nutshell, GATT Article XX (b) recognizes certain protective measures "necessary to protect human, animal, or plant life or health," as long as these measures are not applied in a manner which would constitute a means of arbitrary or unjustifiable discrimination between countries where the same conditions prevail, or a disguised restriction on international trade. The general purpose of Article XX is reviewed in the following paragraphs.

protection of human health or safety, animal or plant life or health, or the environment." Is the outright ban on seal products in the EU more trade-restrictive than necessary to fulfill the objective of forbidding cruel sealing in Canada? Can the full ban be replaced by less-trade-restrictive labeling requirements? In the EU's view, "given the conditions in which seal hunting occurs, consistent verification and control of hunters' compliance with animal welfare requirements is not feasible in practice or, at least, is very difficult to achieve in an effective way."[32] In other words, poor weather conditions make effective monitoring and enforcement by the EU's responsible authorities virtually impossible. It is well recognized, however, that the management of origin is at the core of the labeling system. Logically, the EU has no alternative but to impose a full ban on trade in seal products with a limited exemption for Inuit and other aboriginal communities.[33]

It is not clear whether implementing labeling requirements would have been sufficient to end cruel and inhumane sealing methods.[34] In any case, the provisions complained of by Canada are not those that primarily concern the EU, and which it intends to resolve under the SBR. As a result, this dispute will inevitably proceed to the succeeding panel procedures under the Dispute Settlement Understanding (DSU).

Points of contention between the EU and Canada

Canada lodged a complaint challenging the EU's ban on the trade, import, production, and marketing of seal products.[35] Predictably, the Canadian complaint avoids the issue of the cruelty involved in hunting seals. This issue, however, is at the heart of the EU's concerns, and was the main motivation for its decision to introduce the SBR.

The issue of cruelty raised by the EU

The SBR objective is "the elimination of obstacles to the functioning of the internal market by harmonizing national bans concerning the trade in seal products at [the] Community level."[36] The rationale behind the EU decision to ban seal products was clearly set out in the preamble 1 to the SBR which aims at banning "all cruel hunting methods which do not guarantee the instantaneous death, without suffering, of the animals, to prohibit the stunning of animals with instruments such as hakapiks, bludgeons and guns, and to promote initiatives aimed at prohibiting trade in seal products."[37]

By banning the import of Canadian seal products, the EU seeks to demonstrate its distaste for the cruel methods used in commercial seal hunting in Canada. The SBR represents an important first step by the EU towards the ultimate goal of the elimination of large-scale

32 Seal Ban Regulation, *supra* note 18, Preamble (11).

33 Indeed, in 2008, rapporteur Diana Wallis MEP proposed an alternative labeling scheme, but her alternative was rejected by fellow MEPs on the Parliament's internal market committee. Jennifer Rankin, *MEPs Approve Ban on Trade in Seal Products*, EUROPEANVOICE.COM (May 5, 2009), http://www.europeanvoice.com/article/2009/05/meps-approve-ban-on-trade-in-seal-products/64783.aspx (last visited July 16, 2016).

34 This is the key point of the SBR dispute, and Section 6 of this paper, *infra*, considers this issue in more detail.

35 *See supra* Introduction..

36 Seal Ban Regulation, *supra* note 18, Preamble (21).

37 Seal Ban Regulation, *supra* note 18, Preamble (1).

commercial seal hunting. In this respect, the EU has aligned itself with the United States and Mexico, who have also banned all trade in marine mammal products.

The economic value of commercial seal hunting

On August 1, 2008, the Canadian DFO stated: "While the value of the seal hunt may appear negligible to some, it is tremendously valuable to those individuals who use it as a source of income at a time of year when economic opportunities are limited in many remote, coastal communities."[38] A bit further in the same document, Canadian DFO underscored that "[m]ost sealers are fishers who participate in other fisheries. The seal hunt provides them with the income needed to pay expenses such as insurance and fishing gear."[39]

The Canadian government's concern for the maintenance and development of its sealing industry seems to be based on the considerations that "[r]emote fishing communities offer few employment opportunities" and "[m]any sealers would be forced to leave their homes if unable to hunt seals."[40] Sealing can provide for more than 6,000 sealers from Canada's rural communities with "as much as 35 per cent of a sealer's annual income," or approximately 15,750 Euros.[41] The Canadian government seems indifferent to the argument that "[g]lobal markets for seal products are fast closing, and an end is now in sight for Canada's commercial seal hunt."[42] Canada's commercial seal hunt has been described as "the world's largest slaughter of marine mammals."[43]

A report from the Canadian DFO entitled *Public Views on Commercial Hunting and Current Federal Seal Hunting Policy* was released on February 23, 2005.[44] This report released the results of a national survey conducted as part of the Ipsos-Reid Express Poll, a weekly omnibus poll of 1,000 Canadian adults nationwide.[45] It is apparent that Canada treated the survey as providing statistically reliable results for every major region of Canada.[46] It seems to be true that a large majority of Canadians support seal hunting. However, what should be mentioned is that 39 per cent opposed Canada's current seal hunting policy, regardless of the qualification of humane hunting.[47] It is presumable that more Canadians would have opposed commercial seal hunting in Canada had it not been for the "humane hunting" qualification to the questions asked in the questionnaire.

In contrast to Canada's general support for sealing, public opinion polls conducted in two EU Member States in the same year showed high levels of opposition to commercial seal hunting.[48]

38 *Socio-economic Importance of the Seal Hunt, supra* note 13, at 1.
39 *Id.*
40 DFO of Canada, *The Canadian Seal Hunt – A Way of Life. See* also Chaisse & Xinjie, *supra* note 12.
41 *Id.*
42 The Humane Society of the United States, *European Parliament Resolution to Ban Harp and Hooded Seal Products Achieves Historic Record Number of Signatories*, September 18, 2006.
43 *Id.*
44 DFO of Canada, *Public Views on Commercial Hunting and Current Federal Seal Hunting Policy*, (February 23, 2005) [hereinafter *Public Views*].
45 *Id.*
46 *Overview of Atlantic Seal Hunt, supra* note 12, para. 6.5.4.
47 *Id.*
48 For example, according to an Opinion Research Business poll conducted for Respect for Animals in November 2005, 79 per cent of United Kingdom residents believed that the annual Canadian seal hunt should be stopped, and 73 per cent supported an import ban on seal products.[48] In the Netherlands, a

The issue of humaneness

Compared with the detailed Objective-Based Fisheries Management (OBFM)[49] approach, relatively little space is given in the existing Management Plan to make the Canadian seal hunt more humane.[50] However, the Plan does invoke the provisions with respect to humane hunting methods in the Canadian Marine Mammal Regulations (MMR).[51]

Canada also amended its legislation on hunting practices in 2003 to establish "a clearer determination of death before bleeding and skinning," and defined such a determination as that recommended by the Canadian Veterinary Medical Association (CVMA).[52] In 2005, the Independent Veterinarians' Working Group (IVWG) on the Canadian Seal Hunt examined seal hunting methods and made recommendations to further improve humaneness in the hunt as detailed below.[53]

"Humaneness" is commonly defined as "the quality of compassion or consideration for others (people or animals)."[54] It is difficult to discern this quality in the methods used in large-scale commercial sealing. Even though seals are supposedly given a fast death in bulk, they may still suffer pain, distress, and fear. It is also difficult to see how this kind of hunting avoids the abuse and exploitation of animals, which is at the heart of the philosophy of animal welfare.[55] Respect for the principle of humaneness underlies the EU's SBR, which is conceptualized as an animal welfare measure.

Canada has also accused the EU of using misleading information supplied by interest groups. A study conducted by well-respected veterinarians found that the number of seals killed by inhumane methods accounted for less than two per cent of the total catch.[56] Furthermore, the Canadian authorities "are constantly working on ensuring that all seals are killed as humanely as possible."[57]

---

remarkable 95 per cent of respondents polled considered the Canadian commercial seal hunt to be unacceptable, and 92 per cent supported a Netherlands ban on the trade in seal products. Humane Soc'y Int'l (Canada), *Fast Facts on Canada's Commercial Seal Slaughter* (February 25, 2006), http://www.hsi.org/world/canada/work/protect_seals/research/seal_hunt_facts.html (last visited July 16, 2016).

49 Canada uses an Objective-Based Fisheries Management (OBFM) approach to manage the seal population in the interests of a market-based hunt. As far as the OBFM approach for harp seals is concerned, it specifically sets out the applicable conditions of certain management measures in accordance with the seal population.

50 *Overview of Atlantic Seal Hunt*, *supra* note 12, para. 6.3.

51 Section 8 of the MMR stipulates that persons can only dispatch marine mammals in a manner designed to do so quickly. The MMR also stipulates that seals may be killed only by the use of high-powered rifles, shotguns firing slugs, clubs, and hakapiks. Further requirements pertaining to the size, weight, muzzle velocity, and gauge of weapon are specified in subsection 28(1) of the MMR.

52 *Id.*

53 *Id.*

54 *Humaneness*, The Free Dictionary.

55 In the Saunders Comprehensive Veterinary Dictionary, animal welfare is defined as "the avoidance of abuse and exploitation of animals by humans by maintaining appropriate standards of accommodation, feeding and general care, the prevention and treatment of disease and the assurance of freedom from harassment, and unnecessary discomfort and pain." *Animal Welfare*, The Free Dictionary, *citing* Saunders Comprehensive Veterinary Dictionary (3rd ed. 2007).

56 Greenland Dep't of Fisheries, Hunting & Agric., Management and Utilization of Seals in Greenland 15 (November 2006).

57 *Id.*

WTO general exceptions

In the practice of WTO law, Article XX of the GATT 1994 is one of the most important provisions. It justifies deviations from other rules, in particular, but not exclusively, from the principle of national treatment and from the prohibition of quantitative restrictions. Article XX is composed of two distinct parts: First, it contains an enumeration of specific motives and conditions for restricting trade, listed in paragraphs (a) through (j). Not all of them are of equal practical importance. The critical provisions which are frequently invoked in practice – as WTO Members have become increasingly concerned with environmental and human health issues as well as with the protection of intellectual property rights – refer to measures necessary to protect human, animal, or plant life and health (paragraph b), measures necessary to secure compliance with laws relating to the protection of patents, trademarks and copyrights, and the prevention of deceptive practices (paragraph d), and measures relating to the conservation of exhaustible natural resources (paragraph g). Moreover, protection of public morals is provided for (paragraph a). This latter paragraph may gain, along with banning imports from prison labor (paragraph e), increased importance in relation to the protection of human rights. These paragraphs are examined in detail in this chapter. Second, Article XX contains a general provision, the so-called *chapeau*, which applies in addition to the specific motives.

In state practice, the motives and policies relating to the protection of the environment and of human, plant, and animal health are of particular importance. However, this chapter focuses on paragraph (a), which protects the public morals at the center of the Seals dispute.

Public morals as key legal issue

Undoubtedly, the main goal of the EU's SBR is the protection of public morals, including animal welfare. The meaning and scope of this term has yet to be explored in practice. It has mainly been invoked in state practice to restrict the importation or exportation of products banned under religious rules, in particular alcoholic beverages and meat. Similarly, restrictions of pornographic products operate under this provision.[58] However, the provision has never been brought before a GATT 1947 or WTO panel. It is of particular significance in the context of increasing linkage of trade and human rights because it may serve as a basis of trade restrictions motivated by human rights considerations.[59]

The SBR's protection of public morals incorporated in the Declaration is evident in two aspects: a) the Inuit exception, and b) the elimination of inhumane seal hunting practices.

As we said at the outset of this chapter, the initial document proposing to prepare, adopt, and apply the SBR is the Declaration. The Declaration is a crucial step in obtaining legislation concerning a seal products ban. As a programmatic document, the Declaration's proposed SBR should not impose a restriction on traditional Inuit seal hunting. Considering that "the hunt is an integral part of the culture and identity of the members of the Inuit society, and as such is recognized by the United Nations Declaration on the Rights of Indigenous Peoples," the SBR provides an exemption for seal products harvested by Inuit and

58 *See* Hoe Lim, *Trade and Human Rights: What's at Issue?*, 35(2) J. World Trade 275, 283–5, 447 (2001).

59 *See* Simon Lester et al., *World Trade Law: Text, Materials and Commentary* 389–90 (Hart Publishing, 2008).

other aboriginal hunters.[60] That is to say, the seal products from Inuit and other indigenous communities are permitted in European markets.

Regardless, public opinion in the EU is hostile to seal hunting in any form. Yet, a moody and sentimental – rather than a data-driven – argument inevitably leaves a loophole. Furthermore, there is a different viewpoint even in the EU that the Declaration concerning a seal hunt ban will not achieve the animal welfare considerations intended by its authors.[61]

The GATT 1994 makes it possible for a country to impose quantitative restrictions on trade for "protecting public morals" and/or "protecting human, animal or plant life or health."[62] However, in order to justify the sealing ban on the grounds of the protection of public morals and animal welfare, it must be shown that the outright bans are all "necessary" to achieve the protection aims, which is not the case here. The EU position lacks an objective rationale that is required to justify the ban.

A labeling system might offer an alternative to an outright ban, and it would probably be less offensive in the eyes of the WTO Dispute Settlement Body (DSB) than a total ban. However, a labeling system would be difficult to implement effectively because consistent verification and control of hunters' compliance with animal welfare requirements under the EU labeling system "is not feasible in practice or, at least, is very difficult to achieve in an effective way."[63] Most commercial seal hunting takes place outside the EU, in Greenland, Namibia, Canada, and Russia, and is therefore difficult for the EU to monitor. Although a stringent ban on all trade in seals and pinnipeds (such as sea lions and walruses) would be more effective than the labeling option, it is unlikely to succeed given the difficulties the EU would face in monitoring seal hunting. The EU would find it difficult to decide whether a labeling scheme would impose fewer restrictions on the trade in seal products than a total ban. Generally speaking, labeling is a relatively modest instrument and indirectly impinges upon seal hunting practices through market demand and consumer pressure.

Finally, there is no guarantee that EU consumers would respond as desired to the introduction of a labeling scheme. EU consumers might indeed decide only to buy products originating from seals that were dispatched in a humane manner as opposed to those seal products that do not meet the "humaneness standard." However, they might equally well decide to shun all seal products.[64] As a result, a labeling system cannot be considered as a sufficient and satisfactory alternative to the ban that remains the only way for the EU to achieve its goal. It is therefore fair to conclude that an import ban – such as the one imposed by the EU – is a "necessary" measure when it comes to protecting public morals – or "protecting human, animal, or plant life or health."

Furthermore, Article XX contains a general provision, the so-called *chapeau*, which applies in addition to the specific motives. According to consistent GATT 1947 and WTO practice,

60 Seal Ban Regulation, *supra* note 18, Preamble, para. 14.

61 *Report on the Proposal for a Regulation of the European Parliament and of the Council Concerning Trade in Seals Products*, at 17.

62 GATT 1994, *supra* note 4, at Article XX.

63 Seal Ban Regulation, *supra* note 18, Preamble, para. 11.

64 On May 4, 2009, the Humane Society International (HSUS) stated that millions of Europeans, Members of European Parliament (MEPs), and a Qualified Majority of EU Member States "all agree the only way to stop the cruelty is to stop these [seal] products from being placed on the EU market," and the HSUS called for the MEPs' vote on the plenary session for a strong prohibition on seal product trade with a slogan: "MEPs! Make History: Stop the Trade. End the Cruelty." For details, see *Ban the Cruel Seal Trade*, Humane Soc'y Int'l (May 4, 2009).

the correct interpretation and application of Article XX of the GATT 1994 follows a two-step examination. First, it is to be determined whether the policy pursued by the Member with the adoption of the measure in question falls within the range of policies and motives enumerated in paragraphs (a) through (j) and is consistent with the paragraphs' requirements. Second, the measure needs to be applied in conformity with the *chapeau* of the Article.[65] The *chapeau* sets out the general test which, in addition to the requirements stipulated in the respective paragraphs, needs to be fulfilled by a measure in order to justify a violation of another provision of the GATT 1994. As long as the exceptions set forth in the paragraphs were interpreted narrowly, the chapeau was of little relevance. When this changed at the dawn of the WTO, the provision became operationally important.

Complexity of the assessment of risk

The dispute between the EU and Canada on the banning of seal products deals with a complex issue of risk assessment. Risk assessment is used to "characterize the nature and magnitude of health risks to humans – residents, workers, recreational visitors – and ecological receptors – birds, fish, wildlife."[66] Thus, risk assessment is primarily a rational scientific basis for regulatory action, supported by scientific evidence. Logically, it should not serve as a policy exercise involving social value judgments of political bodies.[67] However, assessing the sufficiency of scientific evidence "is not a simply scientific task but it also has a normative dimension where judgments of the experts reflecting their attitude toward particular risks (less or more cautious) and values of their community play an important role."[68] It seems that the factor of social value judgments has also soaked into the risk assessment of both the EU and Canada.

As we will demonstrate, the different procedures under the TBT and SPS Risk Assessments tend to work in Canada's favor. Risk assessments always incorporate four steps: hazard identification, hazard characterization, exposure assessment, and risk characterization.[69] The importance of risk assessment in the dispute over the EU's SBR lies in the requirement that the implementation of the SBR must have regard for the results of the EU's risk assessment.[70] Conducting a risk assessment, particularly in the inhospitable arctic weather of

65 The Appellate Body first stated this two-tier analysis in the *US – Gasoline* case.

66 *Basic Information on Risk Assessment*, U.S. Envtl. Protection Agency (last updated August 19, 2010).

67 The Appellate Body rejected the Panel's view that risk assessment is not a "policy" exercise involving social value judgments made by political bodies. For details, *see* Appellate Body Report, *European Communities – Measures Concerning Meat and Meat Products*, XI: A, WT/DS26/AB/R, WT/DS48/AB/R (January 16, 1998) (adopted February 13, 1998).

68 *See* Lukasz Gruszczynski, *SPS Measures Adopted in Case of Insufficiency of Scientific Evidence – Where Do We Stand after EC-Biotech Products Case?*, in 2 Essays on the Future of the World Trade Organization – The WTO Judicial System: Contributions And Challenges 91, 139 (Julien Chaisse & Tiziano Balmelli eds, Editions interuniversitaires suisses – Edis, 2008).

69 Codex Alimentarius Commission, Joint Food & Agric. Org. [FAO]/World Health Org. [WHO] Food Standards Program, *Working Principles for Risk Analysis for Food Safety for Application by Governments*, at 5, CAC/GL 62–2007 (1st ed. 2007). For a discussion of the risk analysis process, *see* Lukasz Gruszczynski, *Risk Management Policies under the WTO Agreement on the Application of Sanitary and Phytosanitary Measures*, 3 Asian J. WTO & Int'l Health L. & Pol'y 261, 267–68 (2008).

70 Article 5.1 of the Agreement on Sanitary and Phytosanitary Measures reads as follows: "Members shall ensure that their sanitary or phytosanitary measures are based on an assessment, as appropriate to the circumstances, of the risks to human, animal or plant life or health, taking into account risk assessment techniques developed by the relevant international organizations."

northern Canada, is a difficult process for the EU, and even for the Canadian government; yet, such an assessment of risks is necessary to define the scope of the issue under dispute and the possible options open to both parties.

Divergence of risk assessment regimes under the TBT and SPS Agreements

Risk assessment under the TBT Agreement (TBT-RA) differs somewhat from that under the SPS Agreement (SPS-RA), even though the SPS-RA was "negotiated in the Uruguay Round as a companion to the TBT Agreement."[71]

Article 2.2 of the TBT Agreement deals with the issue of risk assessment related to technical regulations, which provides that in assessing "the risks of non-fulfillment" of a legitimate objective such as national security requirements, the prevention of deceptive practices, protection of human health or safety, animal or plant life or health, or the environment, the "relevant elements of consideration are, *inter alia*: available scientific and technical information, related processing technology or intended end-uses of products."[72] Pursuant to this provision, the risks refer to those materially created by the defendant – the EU in the seal products dispute – who does not fulfill one or more of these legitimate objectives in the preparation, adoption, or application of technical regulations.[73] Of course, the risks assessed under the TBT-RA originate *pro forma* from the imperfect technical regulations.

By contrast, according to the definition of the SPS-RA, if a member adopts and operates a more restrictive measure not conforming to a corresponding international standard, the member is held to conduct a risk assessment and to base the measure on sufficient scientific evidence (with the exception of the precautionary principle).[74] The SPS-RA, by definition, means:

> the evaluation of the likelihood of entry, establishment or spread of *a pest or disease* within the territory of an importing Member according to the sanitary or phytosanitary measures which might be applied, and of the associated potential biological and economic consequences; or the evaluation of the potential for adverse effects on human or animal health arising from the presence of additives, contaminants, toxins or disease-causing organisms in food, beverages or feedstuffs.[75]

Obviously, the risks under the SPS Agreement are those that the technical regulations are designed to eliminate. However, Article 2.2 of the TBT Agreement further stipulates that "[i]n assessing such risks, relevant elements of consideration are, *inter alia*: *available*

71 Ichiro Araki, *China and the Agreement on Technical Barriers to Trade*, RIETI Discussion Paper Series 02-E-008 4, (July 2002).

72 SPS Agreement, *supra* note 9, Article 2.2.

73 *Id.*

74 Article 3.3 of the SPS Agreement states the following: "Members may introduce or maintain sanitary or phytosanitary measures which result in a higher level of sanitary or phytosanitary protection than would be achieved by measures based on the relevant international standards, guidelines or recommendations, if there is a scientific justification, or as a consequence of the level of sanitary or phytosanitary protection a Member determines to be appropriate in accordance with the relevant provisions of paragraphs 1 through 8 of Article 5."

75 SPS Agreement, *supra* note 9, Annex A (emphasis added).

scientific and technical information, related processing technology or intended end-uses of products."[76] This provision is at least in partial compliance with the basic principle set forth in Article 2.2 of the SPS Agreement, according to which "Members shall ensure that any sanitary or phytosanitary measure is applied only to the extent necessary to protect human, animal or plant life or health, is based on scientific principles and is not maintained without *sufficient scientific evidence,* except as provided for in paragraph 7 of Article 5."[77]

That is to say, all WTO Members must establish SPS measures on the basis of an appropriate assessment of the actual risks involved, and in the assessment of risks, account should be taken of available scientific evidence, relevant processes and production methods, relevant ecologic and environmental conditions, and so on.[78]

It is thus clear that both kinds of risk assessment under the SPS and TBT Agreements seem to follow the same principles but actually diverge in the purpose they are serving.

Risk assessment based on scientific evidence

A risk assessment, whether for a TBT measure or for a SPS measure, must be based on sufficient scientific evidence.[79] In other words, the assessment of risks, particularly risks dealing with sensitive ecosystems and biodiversity, is the first step for the related task force to prepare, adopt, and adapt a TBT or SPS regulation.

In certain cases, only by enforcing a full ban based on available scientific evidence can the aims of protecting natural environment, biodiversity, and/or public morals be achieved. Nevertheless, "basing on scientific evidence" *per se* is an abstract and ongoing concept. Indeed, a hot debate over scientific evidence arises in the SBR dispute. In Canada's opinion, a lack of scientific information in the EU's *de facto*, ill-formed assessment of risks makes the EU's arguments for implementing the SBR untenable.

Concluding remarks

The EU introduced the SBR in order to demonstrate its distaste for the seal hunting methods employed in the Canadian commercial seal hunt. Canada has responded with a pure free trade defense, accusing the EU of violating regulations on MFN treatment, national treatment, elimination of quantitative restrictions, and avoidance of unnecessary obstacles to trade. In so doing, the Canadian government has merely availed itself of its legal rights.

However, the procedures used have allowed Canada, as the complainant, to narrow the focus of the debate to certain technical aspects of trade policy. That is to say, Canada merely put emphasis on the EU's SBR being in breach of Articles 2.1 and 2.2 of the TBT Agreement; Articles I:1, III:4 and XI:1 of GATT 1994; and Article 4.2 of the AoA.

76 TBT Agreement, *supra* note 5, Article 2.2 (emphasis added).

77 SPS Agreement, *supra* note 9, Article 2.2. For a commentary, *see* Andrew T. F. Lang, *Provisional Measures Under Article 5.7 of the WTO's Agreement on Sanitary and Phytosanitary Measures: Some Criticisms of the Jurisprudence So Far* (London Sch. of Econ. Legal Studies Working Paper No. 11/2008, November 11, 2008) (emphasis added).

78 *See* Caroline E. Foster, *Precaution, Scientific Development and Scientific Uncertainty Under the WTO Agreement on Sanitary and Phytosanitary Measures,* 18 Rev. Eur. Cmty. & Int'l Envtl. L. 50, 51–52 (2009).

79 *Id.*, at 54.

As a result, the arguably wider issue, the European assertion of the "cruel" commercial seal hunt in Canada, is likely to drop out of sight as the dispute resolution methods are pursued. There are two fundamental reasons why the EU is unlikely to prevail in the dispute with Canada: a) the partial sympathy mechanism and exclusion mechanism in the consultation and panel procedures under the current DSM of the WTO are flawed because in effect they permit the complainant (Canada) to control the agenda;[80] and b) the different procedures under the TBT-RA and the SPS-RA also tend to work in Canada's favor.

Putting an end to the seal hunting methods employed in Canada will be a difficult process. Sealing, in the eyes of many people, is inherently inhumane, and the only satisfactory long-term solution is its complete abolition. Short-term alternatives include measures like the EU's SBR, and a labeling system that allows consumers to choose whether to buy seal products that originate from Canada and other countries widely perceived to use cruel hunting methods.

80 It is up to Canada to decide which matters to bring forward in its request for consultations, while the EU is required merely to "accord sympathetic consideration to and afford adequate opportunity for consultation" (Article 4.2). Under this kind of partial "sympathy" mechanism, the key issues of cruelty and inhumaneness in the Canadian seal hunt, which form the justification for the EU's SBR, can be excluded from the consultations under the current WTO DSM, and the EU has no opportunity to adjust or supplement the issues proposed by the complainant. Also, in the absence of a mutually agreed upon solution to the SBR dispute in the consultations between the EU and Canada, Canada – rather than the EU – is entitled to request the establishment of a panel. Canada also has the discretion to determine the scope of the matters to be addressed by the panel, which it must list in the request for the establishment of the panel. Complainants are unlikely to include matters prejudicial to themselves in such cases. The EU's stance counts for little, even though the EU is convinced that its SBR is justified by public morals, animal welfare, and environmental concerns.

Part IV

Public Health, Product and Food Safety, Consumer Protection

27 Health Protection Measures as Barriers to EU Exports to China in the Framework of the WTO Agreement on the Application of Sanitary and Phytosanitary Measures*

Denise Prévost

Introduction

A significant Non-Trade Concern that often conflicts with trade liberalization objectives is the goal of health protection. Regulations that aim to protect the health of humans, animals, or plants against food-borne risks or risks from pests or diseases of plants and animals may create considerable market access barriers. They are a particular concern for European Union (EU) exporters of food and agricultural products that wish to have access to the Chinese market, but are confronted with regulations establishing requirements for the purpose of health protection.

These regulations, termed sanitary and phytosanitary (SPS) measures, may impose requirements for food or agricultural products[1] – such as requirements regarding permissible additives in processed foods – or for the production processes through which these products are made – such as hygiene requirements for abattoirs. Examples of SPS restrictions for access to the Chinese market are its 'zero-tolerance' limit for the salmonella bacterium in

* This chapter is based on the following previous publication by the same author: *Food Safety in China: Implications of Accession to the WTO*, 1 China Perspectives 39–47 (2012). The author gratefully acknowledges the contribution of Imad Ibrahim (gLAWcal – Global Law Initiatives for Sustainable Development) for his research assistance.

This chapter is part of the results of the Research Project on "*Current Trends of Chinese Law towards Non-Trade Concerns such as Sustainable Development and the Protection of Environment, Public Health, Food Safety, Cultural, Social and Economic Rights, Labor Rights and the Reduction of Poverty from the Perspective of International Law and WTO Law*", coordinated by Professor Paolo Davide Farah at gLAWcal – Global Law Initiatives for Sustainable Development (United Kingdom) and at West Virginia University John D. Rockefeller IV School of Policy and Politics, Department of Public Administration, in partnership with the Center of Advanced Studies on Contemporary China (CASCC) in Turin (Italy), Maastricht University Faculty of Law, Department of International and European Law and IGIR – Institute for Globalisation and International Regulation (Netherlands), and Tsinghua University, School of Law, Institute of Public International Law and the Center for Research on Intellectual Property Law in Beijing (China). An early draft of this chapter was presented at the Conferences Series on "*China's Influence on Non-Trade Concerns in International Economic Law*", Third Conference held at Maastricht University, Faculty of Law on January 19–20, 2012. This publication and the Conference Series were sponsored by China–EU School of Law (CESL) at the China University of Political Science and Law (CUPL). The activities of CESL at CUPL are supported by the European Union and the People's Republic of China.

1 On agricultural security, please *see* Chapters 19 (Ning) and 20 (Simpson) in this volume; on the right to food, *see* Chapters 18 (Zorzi Giustiniani), 19 (Ning), and 20 (Simpson) in this volume.

imported poultry meat,[2] its bans on animal products in response to outbreaks of bovine spongiform encephalopathy and H1N1 influenza, and its maximum residue levels (MRLs) for certain heavy metals and veterinary drugs.[3]

SPS measures are usually accompanied by rules regarding conformity assessment procedures, which are control mechanisms to check compliance with the relevant requirements. These may take various forms, such as certification systems, random sampling and testing procedures, systems for prior approval of additives, and pre-shipment inspections. They may be imposed on products within the domestic market – for example, requirements regarding veterinary inspections of cattle within the national territory – or on products crossing borders, at the time of either importation or exportation.[4] Examples of conformity assessment requirements in China include those of entry/exit inspection on SPS grounds, which is required for products listed in the Catalogue of Entry-Exit Commodities Subject to Inspection and Quarantine,[5] and of certification of the disease-free status of imported dairy products.[6]

The potential restrictive effect of such SPS measures on market access for imported agri-food products is clear. It is therefore interesting to examine the rules of the World Trade Organization (WTO) that discipline the trade-restrictive effect of such health regulations and the accompanying conformity assessment procedures. These disciplines appear primarily in the Agreement on the Application of Sanitary and Phytosanitary Measures (SPS Agreement).[7] This agreement aims at balancing the need to liberalize agri-food trade with the right of WTO Members to address health risks posed by food or feed and from pests and diseases of plants and animals.[8]

The SPS Agreement will therefore be examined to establish the extent to which it permits China to pursue its Non-Trade Concerns in the area of food safety, as well as plant and animal health, and how far the limits it imposes reach. This will also determine the possibilities for the EU to pursue its trade interests by using the rules of the SPS Agreement to challenge China's SPS measures. Before doing so, it is, however, essential to understand the principal objective of the SPS Agreement as a tool to balance the competing interests of trade liberalization and health protection. This matter will be addressed first, in order to provide the context within which the following discussion should be understood.

2 United States Trade Representative, *2015 Report To Congress on China's WTO Compliance,* December 2015 at 113.

3 *Id.* at 114. Regarding other SPS restrictions put in place by the Chinese Government following other health scandals, *see* also Chapters 19 (Ning), 29 (Gruszczynski, Ötvös & Farah), and 32 (Hu) in this volume.

4 One example of conformity assessment at the time of exportation is the requirement by the importing country of export certificates. Horton notes that export certificates serve to show that a supplier meets certain requirements and are based on the expectation that the certifying body (either a government authority or officially recognized non-governmental organization) will conduct inspections or tests to substantiate the accuracy of the information on the certificate. Linda R. Horton, *Food from Developing Countries: Steps to Improve Compliance,* 53 Food & Drug L. J. 139, 147 (1998).

5 Trade Policy Review Body, *Trade Policy Review–China: Report by the Secretariat, Revision,* WT/TPR/S/230/Rev.1 (July 5, 2010) Part III, para. 51. More recently *see* Trade Policy Review Body, *Trade Policy Review–China: Report by the Secretariat,* WT/TPR/S/300 (May 2014) para. 3.80.

6 United States Trade Representative, *supra* note 2, at 81.

7 Agreement on the application of Sanitary and Phytosanitary Measures, April 15, 1994, Marrakesh Agreement Establishing the World Trade Organization, Annex 1A, 1867 UNTS 493.

8 Other WTO Agreements contain provisions that address different measures that might result in trade barriers. An example is the Agreement on Technical Barriers to Trade (TBT). For an analysis of the relationship between the SPS and the TBT Agreements, *see* Chapter 29 (Gruszczynski, Ötvös & Farah) in this volume.

Balancing role of the SPS Agreement

Both trade liberalization and health protection measures pursue important societal objectives, namely economic growth and development, through the earning of foreign revenue and the protection of the life and health of humans, animals, and plants, respectively. However, these two objectives are often in conflict with one another.

On the one hand, traded products, particularly in the food and agricultural sector, can introduce health risks to the importing region, such as the spread of insect pests hosted by imported fruit or vegetables, the transfer of infectious animal diseases carried by imported animals or animal products, and food safety risks from inadequate standards in the production, processing, or transportation of food imports. These risks are ever-increasing due to the changing nature of traded agri-food products. The growing demand for processed food products creates more possibilities for contamination at various stages of the processing chain. Risks are compounded by the use of new technologies in agriculture and food processing, such as pesticides, additives, irradiation, and genetic modification. Further, there is growing trade in fresh and perishable products, which are more vulnerable to infection by pests and pathogens than traditionally traded, bulk agricultural commodities, such as dried grains and pulses. States thus need to take protective measures to respond to citizens' demands for food safety and to ensure the health of their own agricultural sectors.[9]

On the other hand, the SPS measures that importing states take to protect health in their territories from such risks are likely to act as significant barriers to market access for exporting countries, thereby reducing their export earnings and affecting rural livelihoods. SPS requirements thus have an important impact on exports in the agricultural sector – including both primary and processed products. In addition, states could misuse SPS requirements for protectionist purposes, thereby undermining the gradual gains in the liberalization of agricultural trade pursued under the WTO Agreement on Agriculture (AoA).[10] It is notable that regulators encounter pressure from domestic agriculture and food industry lobbies in the face of increased competition due to progress in agricultural liberalization. The first hard-won steps towards liberalizing this traditionally protected sector and the subsequent ongoing agricultural trade liberalization mandated by the AoA,[11] the subject of torturous and now stalled negotiations in the context of the Doha Round of trade negotiations,[12] aim to break down traditional protections – tariffs, export subsidies, and domestic support – shielding domestic producers from competition. The agricultural industry therefore lobbies regulators

9 *See* Chapter 19 (Ning) in this volume.

10 Agreement on Agriculture, April 15, 1994, Marrakesh Agreement Establishing the World Trade Organization, Annex 1A, 1867 UNTS 410 [Not reproduced in ILM] [hereinafter AoA]. The AoA is among the agreements resulting from the Uruguay Round of trade negotiations. It takes the first steps towards liberalizing the agricultural sector, which is traditionally among the most protected sectors in international trade. The AoA imposes disciplines on traditional barriers to trade in this sector, namely tariffs, domestic support, and export subsidies. These disciplines could be undermined if complementary rules were not in place to prevent the use of regulatory requirements for disguised protectionist purposes.

11 AoA, *Id.*, Article 20.

12 World Trade Organization, Ministerial Declaration of 14 November 2001, WT/MIN(01)/DEC/1, 41 I.L.M. 746 (2002) paras 13–14 [hereinafter Doha Declaration]. The work program set out in the Doha Declaration with regard to agriculture aims at substantial improvements in market access; reductions, with a view to phasing out, of export subsidies; and substantial reductions in trade-distorting domestic support. In the WTO Ministerial Conference in Nairobi in December 2015, WTO Members agreed to abolish export subsidies on agricultural products. Ministerial Conference, Export Competition, Ministerial Decision of December 19, 2015 WT/MIN(15)/45, WT/L/980.

to institute non-tariff barriers to trade in the form of SPS regulations to replace these traditional forms of protection.

While the potential conflict between SPS measures and trade is not a new phenomenon, the exponential increase in the speed and diversity of traded agri-food products in the last 50 years, and the accompanying proliferation of health risks and SPS measures to address them, has meant that the international trade regime, embodied in the rules of the WTO, has had to find new ways of mediating this conflict. The SPS Agreement reflects a negotiated balance between the competing goals of the liberalization of agri-food trade and the protection of health by national governments. In examining the rules of the SPS Agreement and their implications for China–EU trade, this balancing objective must be kept in mind.

China's SPS measures as barriers to EU exports

The main infrastructure that makes up the SPS regime of China is composed of the State Food and Drug Administration, which supervises food safety; the Ministries of Agriculture and Health; and the State Administration of Industry and Commerce, which provides specific supervision of agricultural and processed food products.[13] The primary legislation on SPS protection in China consists of the Agricultural Product Quality and Safety Law,[14] the Law on the Entry and Exit of Animals and Plant Quarantine,[15] the Law on Animal Disease Prevention,[16] the Law on Import and Export Commodity Inspection,[17] the Law on Frontier Health and Quarantine,[18] together with the implementing regulations and rules.[19] Following the food safety scandal resulting from melamine contamination of infant formula in 2008,[20] China revised its food safety regime. A new Food Safety Law[21] entered into force on June 1, 2009, triggering the promulgation of unified national food safety standards.[22] The latter

13 Trade Policy Review Body, *supra* note 5.

14 Zhōnghuá Rénmín Gònghéguó Nóngchǎnpǐn Zhí Liàng Ānquán Fǎ (中华人民共和国农产品质量安全法) [Agricultural Product Quality Safety Law of the People's Republic of China] (Promulgated by the Standing Comm. Nat'l People's Cong., April 29, 2006).

15 Zhōnghuá Rénmín Gònghéguó Jìn Chūjìng Dòng Zhíwù Jiǎnyì Fǎ (中华人民共和国进出境动植物检疫法) [Law of the People's Republic of China on the Entry and Exit Animal and Plant Quarantine] (Promulgated by the Standing Comm. Of the Nat'l People's Cong., October 30, 1991).

16 Zhōnghuá Rénmín Gònghéguó Dòngwù Fángyì Fǎ (2013 xiūzhèng) (中华人民共和国动物防疫法(2013修正)) [Animal Epidemic Prevention Law of the People's Republic of China (2013 Amendment)] (Promulgated by the Standing Comm. Nat'l People's Cong., June 29, 2013).

17 Zhōnghuá Rénmín Gònghéguó Jìn Chūkǒu Shāngpǐn Jiǎnyàn Fǎ (2013 xiūzhèng) (中华人民共和国进出口商品检验法(2013修正) [Law of the People's Republic of China on Import and Export Commodity Inspection (2013 Amendment)] (Promulgated by the Standing Comm. Nat'l People's Cong., June 29, 2013).

18 Zhōnghuá Rénmín Gònghéguó Guójìng Wèishēng Jiǎnyì Fǎ (2007 xiūzhèng) (中华人民共和国国境卫生检疫法(2007修正) [Frontier Health and Quarantine Law of the People's Republic of China (2007 Amendment)] (Promulgated by the Standing Comm. Nat'l People's Cong., December 29, 2007).

19 Other relevant laws are the Zhonghua Renmin Gongheguo Chanpin Zhiliang Fa (2000 Xiuzheng) [Product Quality Law of the People's Republic of China (2000 amendment)] and Zhonghua Renmin Gongheguo Xiaofeizhe Quanli Baohu Fa (1993) [Law of the People's Republic of China on the Protection of Consumer Rights and Interests (1993)].

20 For a detailed analysis of the melamine case, *see* Xiaofang Pei, Annuradha Tandon, Anton Alldrick & Liana Giorgi, *The China Melamine Milk Scandal and its Implications for Food Safety Regulation*, 36 (3) Food Pol. 412–420 (2001). *See* Chapter 19 (Ning) in this volume.

21 Zhōnghuá Rénmín Gònghéguó Shípǐn Ānquán Fǎ (中华人民共和国食品安全法) [Food Safety Law of the People's Republic of China] (Promulgated by the Standing Comm. Nat'l People's Cong., February 28, 2009).

22 In the second half of 2013, the Chinese Government launched the revision process for the Food Safety Law in order to review its experiences from the past four years. The draft has been published for comments.

regulation was amended on April 24, 2015 and its implementation occurred on October 1, of the same year.[23]

In acceding to the WTO in December 2001, China was bound to all WTO obligations to promote the elimination or reduction of trade barriers, including those contained in the SPS Agreement.[24] Beijing has made significant progress in reforming its trade policy to comply with its WTO obligations. Nevertheless, several SPS barriers to trade remain in place, as demonstrated by the concerns raised by WTO Members during the recent reviews of China's trade policies,[25] and by EU commercial operators in the Chinese market.[26] It is useful to assess these barriers in terms of the obligations laid down by the SPS Agreement. This section will therefore focus on those disciplines of the SPS Agreement of relevance to the aspects of China's SPS regime that lead to trade concerns for the EU and its exporters.

Harmonization

International rules establishing trade-related and scientific requirements for national SPS regulatory measures are insufficient to achieve full trade liberalization. Their disciplining effect has clear limits on the sovereign right of national governments to protect the health of their societies against SPS risks, as recognized by the SPS Agreement. While requiring that SPS measures be science-based, non-discriminatory, and applied only to the extent necessary to protect health, the SPS Agreement leaves much room for Members to make policy choices regarding the level of protection they wish to ensure within their territories. These choices reflect particular conditions in each Member, including consumer preferences,[27] economic considerations, and industry interests. The measures Members impose to achieve their chosen level of protection therefore also diverge.

However, differences in SPS measures can act as significant trade barriers since exporters must adjust their products or production processes to satisfy the requirements of their various export

23 Food Safety Law of the People's Republic of China as amended on April 24, 2015. USDA Foreign Agriculture Service, China's Food Safety Law (2015), http://gain.fas.usda.gov/Recent%20GAIN%20Publications/Amended%20Food%20Safety%20Law%20of%20China_Beijing_China%20-%20Peoples%20Republic%20of_5-18-2015.pdf (last visited July 6, 2016).

24 China's WTO obligations are those contained in the WTO Agreement, including all its Annexes, as well as the Protocol of Accession of China to the WTO (WT/L/432), and the incorporated paragraphs of its Working Party Report (WT/ACC/CHN/49).

25 The WTO administers a Trade Policy Review Mechanism, which conducts periodic reviews of the trade policies of all Members, in the context of which the WTO Secretariat and the reviewed Member submit reports that are discussed in a meeting of the Trade Policy Review Body. Other Members may submit questions and concerns, and the reviewed Member may respond. The latest Trade Policy Review of China that is publically available was conducted in 2014, and the reports are to be found in WTO documents WT/TPR/S/300 and WT/TPR/300. In addition, Section 18 of the Protocol of Accession of China establishes the Transitional Review Mechanism for China. It provides for eight years of annual reviews of China's trade policies, concluding with a final review in the tenth year. The reviews were conducted by the 16 subsidiary bodies of the WTO with a mandate in the specific area of China's WTO commitments. These bodies reported to the relevant WTO specialized council, which in turn reported to the General Council at the end of each year. The final review took place in October 2011. Regarding the Transitional Review Mechanism for China, *see also* Paolo Davide Farah, *Five Years of China's WTO Membership: EU and US Perspectives on China's Compliance with Transparency Commitments and the Transitional Review Mechanism,* 33 Legal Issues of Economic Integration 263–304 (2006).

26 The recent report of the EU Chamber of Commerce in China reflects these concerns. *See* European Union Chamber of Commerce in China (European Business in China Position Paper 2014/15) 139–150.

27 *See* Chapters 28 (Di Masi), 30 (Rossi), 31 (Prasad), and 32 (Hu) in this volume.

markets, thereby reducing economies of scale. The promotion of the harmonization of SPS regulations at the international level has emerged in response to this problem. As the WTO is not a regulatory body with norm-setting capacity in the area of health, it cannot itself set the international standards to be used as benchmarks. The SPS Agreement therefore encourages WTO Members to harmonize their SPS requirements with the standards developed by the existing authoritative international bodies in the area of food safety, animal health, and plant health.[28] These are the Codex Alimentarius Commission (CAC)[29] for food safety standards, the Secretariat of the International Plant Protection Convention (IPPC) for plant health standards, and the World Animal Health Organization, previously called the International Office for Epizootics (OIE), for animal health issues.[30] SPS measures that conform to international standards are granted a safe harbor from challenge by means of a presumption of consistency with the obligations of the SPS Agreement and the GATT 1994.[31] If Members choose to apply measures reflecting a higher level of protection than those embodied in existing international standards, a scientific justification is needed in the form of a risk assessment.[32]

The EU has pointed out that China's SPS measures to address risks from H1N1 (swine flu), bovine spongiform encephalitis (BSE or mad cow disease), and several plant health risks, do not conform to the standards set by the relevant international standard-setting organizations referred to in the SPS Agreement.[33] For example, the OIE has listed which bovine products can be safely traded, regardless of the BSE status of the exporting country, including deboned skeletal muscle meat from cattle. The OIE has also classified 25 EU Member States as "controlled risk" or "negligible risk." Despite these international standards, China continued to ban beef and other bovine products from the EU.[34] This situation changed in 2014, when China allowed the export of live cattle from Romania, and in 2015 Hungary was granted permission to export live cattle beef to the country.[35] Subsequently, the Chinese authorities lifted the ban that was imposed on bovine and ovine products from Denmark, France, Germany and United Kingdom in 2016.[36] Similarly, China persistently imposed additional trade requirements on live pigs from EU Member States in response to the H1N1 influenza pandemic. These requirements take the form of requirements of disease-free areas that export live pigs to China. However, in both cases China did not provide adequate

28 SPS Agreement, Article 3.

29 The Codex Alimentarius Commission was established as a joint body of the UN Food and Agriculture Organization (FAO) and the World Health Organization (WHO) in 1963. It has the mandate to develop food standards, guidelines and related texts. It operates under the Joint FAO/WHO Food Standards Programme that aims to protect the health of the consumers and ensure fair practices in food trade. *See* further www.codexalimentarius.net (last visited July 6, 2016).

30 SPS Agreement Annex A.3 (a)–(e).

31 SPS Agreement Article 3.2.

32 SPS Agreement Articles 3.3 and 5.1.

33 Committee on Sanitary and Phytosanitary Measures, *Transitional Review Mechanism Pursuant to Paragraph 18 of the Protocol on The Accession of the People's Republic of China ("China"), Questions from the European Communities to China concerning Sanitary and Phytosanitary Measures*, G/SPS/W/262, paras 11, 15 (October 6, 2011).

34 This matter is reported in Committee on Sanitary and Phytosanitary Measures, *Summary of the Meeting of 28 June, Note by the Secretariat*, G/SPS/R/71, para. 4.33 (August 23, 2013).

35 European Commission, SPS: Sanitary and Phytosanitary Issues, China – SPS- Longstanding ban on EU Bovine/Ovine and products thereof (Feb. 11, 2016), http://madb.europa.eu/madb//sps_barriers_details.htm?barrier_id=040039&version=10 (last visited July 6, 2016).

36 Farminguk, China lifts its import ban on bovine and ovine products from UK and others (June. 4, 2016), http://www.farminguk.com/News/China-lifts-its-import-ban-on-bovine-and-ovine-products-from-UK-and-others_42002.html (last visited July 6, 2016).

scientific justification for these stricter measures. If no such justification exists, this behavior would violate the SPS Agreement.

In the same vein, in 2011 the EU Chamber of Commerce noted that, with respect to food additives, China's Hygiene Standards for Uses of Food Additives include less than half of the additives approved for food use by the Codex Alimentarius Commission, indicating that the Chinese legislation is lagging behind the development in international standards.[37] This resulted in unjustified barriers to EU exports.[38] In 2014, a new National Safety Standard for Uses of Food Additives was issued by the Chinese authorities.[39]

An example of a trade conflict between China and the EU in the area of harmonization of SPS requirements that was resolved in line with the SPS Agreement is certainly worth examining.[40] This dispute related to the Chinese regulation on wood packaging material,[41] which imposed important discrepancies from the relevant IPPC standard (ISPM 15). In April 2002, following the regular detection of large numbers of pests by the inspection and quarantine authorities of China in wood packaging material from the EU, China took emergency measures to prevent the introduction of dangerous wood pests, and to protect its environment, forestry, and tourism resources. The EU made considerable efforts to address China's concerns, and it encouraged China to bring its requirements into conformity with the IPPC standard promptly. In June 2003, the EU reported that it had adopted the IPPC standard and that China had committed to do the same.

Scientific justification

The SPS Agreement uses the essential tool of science to distinguish between measures that aim at health protection and those that are disguised forms of protectionism. The centrality of science to the operation of the SPS Agreement is irrefutable – it is the scale on which the competing values of health protection and trade liberalization are balanced. Requiring a scientific basis for SPS measures can be seen as an attempt to ensure rational, science-based decision-making in national SPS regulations, thereby preventing private-interest capture of the regulatory process.[42] In particular, in situations where harmonization is not possible due to the lack of relevant international standards, or is not feasible due to differences in national conditions or policy preferences, science operates to generate rational regulatory choices.[43]

37 European Union Chamber of Commerce in China, *European Business in China Position Paper, 2010/11*, at 168. In the most recent position paper (*supra* note 26, 144) the EU Chamber of Commerce notes that certain additives face difficulty in obtaining a production licence as there is no standard for those types of products.

38 This issue was also raised by the EU in the context of the TRM. *See* Committee on Sanitary and Phytosanitary Measures, *Transitional Review Mechanism Pursuant to Paragraph 18 of the Protocol on The Accession of the People's Republic of China ("China"), Questions from the European Communities to China concerning Sanitary and Phytosanitary Measures*, G/SPS/W/262 (October 6, 2011).

39 National Food Safety Standards for Uses of Food Additives, USDA Foreign Agricultural Service, Chinese Standards for Food Additives – GB2760- 2015 (4/28/2015), http://gain.fas.usda.gov/Recent%20GAIN%20Publications/Standard%20for%20Food%20Additive%20Use%20-%20GB2760-2015_Beijing_China%20-%20Peoples%20Republic%20of_4-28-2015.pdf (last visited July 6, 2016).

40 This issue is described in Committee on Sanitary and Phytosanitary Measures, *Specific Trade Concerns – Note by the Secretariat*, G/SPS/GEN/204/Rev.8/Add.2 (March 1, 2011), item 143.

41 Notified as G/SPS/N/CHN/14.

42 Robert Howse, *Democracy, Science, and Free Trade: Risk Regulation on Trial at the World Trade Organization*, 98 Mich. L. Rev. 2329 (2000).

43 As noted by Jacqueline Peel, "the very fact of having to take a risk assessment into account and respond to its findings could have the salutary effect of forcing national regulators 'to articulate objectives, to assess means, and to rationalize results,' a substantial improvement for the regulatory processes of many

To give effect to this objective, the SPS Agreement requires that SPS measures be based on scientific principles and not be maintained without sufficient scientific evidence[44] – except in the case of provisional measures taken in situations of insufficiency of science.[45] This obligation is further fleshed out through the requirements that SPS measures be "based on" a risk assessment as appropriate to the circumstances,[46] and be adapted to the SPS conditions of the region where the product originates.[47]

These disciplines facilitate efforts to regain market access, which has been denied without a good scientifically founded reason. For example, in 2007, the EU successfully relied on the requirement of scientific justification in the SPS Agreement to challenge China's import restrictions on animal products due to alleged dioxin contamination.[48] These restrictions were imposed following an isolated incident in January 2006, after which all possibly affected products had promptly been recalled. Although all other WTO Members withdrew their trade restrictions, China maintained its ban, and the EU raised its concerns before the SPS Committee. The EU requested China to remove the ban or provide a scientific justification for its maintenance. Technical consultations between the EU and China followed and resulted in a removal of the ban in October 2007.

More recently, an example of constructive cooperation to resolve a concern regarding the lack of scientific basis for a trade-restrictive measure has arisen.[49] The EU has repeatedly raised its concerns regarding China's import ban on spirits and wine exceeding the temporary maximum level it laid down for phthalates, while in the process of conducting a risk assessment. China reported that AQSIQ had been monitoring phthalates in imported spirits since January 2013, and that in some of those spirits, it had discovered phthalate levels that exceeded the temporary maximum levels put in place during the period for conducting a risk assessment. The EU indicated its willingness to share scientific information to help China in this process. China established expert panels to conduct risk assessments on phthalates in food, and an EU–China workshop on risk assessments for phthalates in food was held on April 17, 2013. China indicated that it would continue to work with the EU to resolve the matter.

nations." *See* Jacqueline Peel, ***Risk Regulation under the WTO SPS Agreement: Science as an International Normative Yardstick?*** 57 (Jean Monnet Working Paper 02/04, NYU School of Law, New York, June 2004), http://www.jeanmonnetprogram.org/archive/papers/04/040201.pdf (last visited July 6, 2016). The citation referred to by Peel comes from Henrik Horn & Joseph H. H. Weiler, ***European Communities – Trade Description of Sardines: Textualism and Its Discontent,*** in 1 The WTO case law of 2002: The American Law Institute reporter's studies 248–275 (Cambridge University Press, 2005).

44 SPS Agreement, Article 2.2.

45 SPS Agreement, Article 5.7.

46 SPS Agreement, Article 5.1. What is meant by a risk assessment is set out in Annex A.4 of the SPS Agreement.

47 SPS Agreement, Article 6. In assessing the SPS characteristics of a region, Members must 'take into account, inter alia, the level of prevalence of specific diseases or pests, the existence of eradication or control programmes, and appropriate criteria or guidelines which may be developed by the relevant international organizations'.

48 Information regarding this issue is provided in Committee on Sanitary and Phytosanitary Measures, ***supra*** note 40, item 246.

49 This matter is reported in Committee on Sanitary and Phytosanitary Measures, ***Summary of the Meeting of 28 June, Note by the Secretariat,*** G/SPS/R/71, paras 4.29–4.30 (August 23, 2013).

The latter issue was resolved in 2016 as the temporary ban on imports of spirits was removed.[50] Concerns regarding lack of scientific justification have been raised repeatedly by the EU with regard to the ban imposed by China in February 2014 on imports of swine and swine products from all EU Member States. This ban was introduced in response to African Swine Flu outbreaks, and maintained despite the fact that the EU has provided information on the strict control, surveillance and monitoring measures in place to prevent the spread of the disease to other regions in the EU and thus to allow trade in swine products to resume safely. The EU requested several times that China provide a risk assessment justifying the EU-wide ban and the non-recognition of the EU zoning measures, but China responded that it still needed to assess the EU measures.[51] Similar unresolved issues concerning the lack of adaptation to regional conditions have been raised at the most recent SPS Committee meeting by the EU with regard to China's EU-wide restrictions on bovine imports due to concerns regarding the Schmallenberg virus, and on poultry products due to concerns with regard to highly pathogenic avian influenza.[52]

Another example of a Chinese SPS measure affecting EU exports that appears to lack a scientific basis is the limitation of the level of yeast in cheese to a maximum of 50 cfu/g. In other markets where cheese consumption has a longer history, it is recognized that yeast in cheese poses no safety concern and no maximum limit is needed.[53] Thus, the measure would appear not to be based on a risk assessment, as required by the SPS Agreement. The EU could therefore rely on the scientific disciplines of the SPS Agreement to raise its concerns regarding this trade restriction.

Undue trade restrictiveness

While the SPS Agreement defers to the right of WTO Members to choose for themselves the level of SPS protection they deem appropriate ensuring within their territories,[54] it monitors the choice of SPS measure to achieve this level of protection. In particular, Members are obliged to ensure that their SPS measures are no more trade-restrictive than required to achieve their appropriate level of SPS protection, taking into account technical and economic feasibility.[55] In several instances, WTO Members have questioned the conformity of China's SPS regime with this obligation.

For example, the EU has raised doubts as to the compatibility of the chapters on imports and exports in China's 2009 Food Safety Law with the requirement of least-trade-restrictiveness. The EU noted the vagueness on how different procedures will work in practice and was concerned that these may delay the processing of imports or cause trade disruptions.[56] If alternative, less-trade-restrictive measures are available that achieve the requisite level of

50 European Commission, EU Market Access Flash Note, China lifts its temporary restrictions on imports of spirits (May. 20, 2016), http://trade.ec.europa.eu/doclib/docs/2016/may/tradoc_154575.pdf & http://madb.europa.eu/madb/news.htm (last visited July 6, 2016).

51 See Committee on Sanitary and Phytosanitary Measures, Report of the Meeting of 14–16 October 2015, G/SPS/R/81, (January. 4, 2016), at 22.

52 WTO Secretariat, New Trade Concerns Reviews by WTO Committee on Food Safety and Animal/Plant Health, News Item (March. 16-17, 2016).

53 European Union Chamber of Commerce in China, *supra* note 37, at 170.

54 SPS Agreement, Annex A.5.

55 SPS Agreement, Article 5.6.

56 Committee on Sanitary and Phytosanitary Measures, *supra* note 34, para. 14.

protection from food safety risks, then the relevant chapters would be in violation of the SPS Agreement.

One of the most important trade-restrictive measures facing agri-food exporters to China is the requirement of a Quarantine Inspection Permit (QIP) before a contract may be signed for these exports to be purchased.[57] China's State Administration of Quality Supervision, Inspection and Quarantine (SAQSIQ) has discretion to annul QIPs without prior notification or explanation, creating unpredictability for exporters. Further, the delays in granting QIPs have led to shipments of agricultural products arriving in Chinese ports of entry without QIPs, resulting in delays in product discharge and unnecessary costs for demurrage for Chinese purchasers.[58] QIPs are granted for limited periods (and can be extended from three months to six months), which lock purchasers into a tight window in which to purchase, transport, and discharge cargoes.[59] It may be questioned whether these QIP requirements are the least trade-restrictive means to achieve China's SPS objectives.

Another example is the "zero-tolerance" standard imposed by China for pathogens in food – such as salmonella and listeria – which has led to several foreign meat and poultry facilities being "delisted," meaning the government has removed them from the list of facilities authorized to export to China. This measure can be seen as unduly trade-restrictive because zero tolerance often sets an unattainable and excessively strict standard since certain pathogen levels are unavoidable, and do not pose risks to consumers.[60]

Transparency and adaptation period

An important, and perhaps underestimated, aspect of the SPS Agreement is its insistence on transparency of SPS measures.[61] The significance of transparency disciplines relates to two main aspects.

First, transparency generates what can be called *ex ante* effects. Exporters of food and agricultural products are affected by regulatory decisions taken in foreign jurisdictions, yet they traditionally cannot participate in the decision-making process. Foreign regulators take into account national priorities and interests when making SPS decisions. This raises the problem which Robert Keohane has called the "external accountability gap,"[62] which describes the situation that arises in a globalizing world where the impact of a state's actions no longer coincides with its jurisdiction but goes beyond it, affecting the lives of persons outside it. Imposing *ex ante* transparency obligations on regulating countries ensures that exporting countries are informed of proposed new or amended SPS measures and that

57 United States Trade Representative, *supra* note 2, at 81.

58 Emerging Markets Group & Development Solutions, *Study on the Future Opportunities and Challenges of EU-China Trade and Investment Relations* 21 (Study 6: Agriculture, Study Commissioned by the European Commission, February 2007).

59 United States Trade Representative, *supra* note 2, at 117.

60 United States Trade Representative, *supra* note 2, at 113. *See* also Emerging Markets Group & Development Solutions, *supra* note 58, at 20. *See* also Chapters 30 (Rossi) and 32 (Hu) in this volume.

61 For a useful analysis of China's compliance with its transparency commitments under WTO law in general, *see* Paolo Davide Farah, *Five Years of China's WTO Membership: EU and US Perspectives on China's Compliance with Transparency Commitments and the Transitional Review Mechanism*, 33 LEGAL ISSUES OF ECONOMIC INTEGRATION 263–304 (2006).

62 Robert Keohane, *Global Governance and Democratic Accountability*, in TAMING GLOBALIZATION: FRONTIERS OF GOVERNANCE 141 (David Held & Mathias Koenig-Archibugi eds, Polity, 2003).

affected foreign traders have the opportunity, through their governments, to raise concerns regarding these proposals, thus playing a role in the regulatory process.

The second important aspect of transparency lies in its *ex post* effects. An important hurdle to exporters of food and agricultural products is the paucity of information that is available regarding the SPS measures that they must comply with in their export markets. SPS measures are often complex and subject to change, giving exporters no certainty that their products will have access to the markets of the country of destination. Obtaining necessary information regarding the SPS measures they have to comply with is often a costly and burdensome process for exporters. Therefore, transparency obligations requiring publication of adopted SPS measures are crucial in facilitating market access for exports from Members since they greatly reduce the cost and difficulty of obtaining information on their trading partners' SPS measures.

Not only is the *ex post* effect of transparency important for traders, but it is also essential in enabling WTO Members to exercise their rights and police the implementation of the SPS Agreement obligations.[63] Information regarding the existence, content and scientific basis of SPS measures makes it possible for Members, whose exporters are faced with SPS barriers to trade, to determine whether they have legal grounds to challenge these measures based on the SPS Agreement. It also makes it possible for traders to be well informed of the SPS measures affecting their exports and to lobby their governments to take action in this regard. Consequently, Members can try to resolve their trade concerns in bilateral discussions with the relevant Member,[64] in multilateral discussions at SPS Committee meetings, or in formal dispute settlement proceedings.

For these reasons, the SPS Agreement has rules in place to promote transparency in SPS regulation.[65] These rules require not only that Members promptly publish adopted SPS regulations, with the provision of a reasonable period between the regulation's publication and entry into force for other Members to adapt to the new requirements, but also that Members provide notice of draft SPS legislation at an early stage as well as a comment period. Copies of the draft legislation must be provided upon request.

The EU has complained that China has not fulfilled its obligation to exercise transparency towards its trading partners while developing its SPS legislation.[66] Although China has issued a vast number of SPS notifications[67] of draft legislation since its accession in 2001[68] – the

63 Scott refers to this as the "all-important accountability function" of transparency, which operates to enable other Members to evaluate and contest proposed SPS regulations. Joanne Scott, *The WTO Agreement on Sanitary and Phytosanitary Measures: A Commentary*, in Oxford Commentaries on the GATT/WTO Agreements 192–193 (Oxford University Press, 2007).

64 Wolfe notes that the WTO Secretariat "knows that the real reason many experts attend [SPS] Committee meetings is to hold private unrecorded bilateral meetings with each other." Robert Wolfe, *See You in Geneva? Legal (Mis)Representations of the Trading System*, 11 Eur. J. Int'l Relations 339, 353 (2005).

65 They are contained in Article 7, Annex B and Article 5.8 of the SPS Agreement.

66 Committee on Sanitary and Phytosanitary Measures, *supra* note 34, para. 4.

67 See for instance, Committee on Sanitary and Phytosanitary Measures, – Notification – China – Food Nutritional Fortifier Magnesium Gluconate, G/SPS/N/CHN/1042 (Jan 29, 2016), at 1–2 & Committee on Sanitary and Phytosanitary Measures – Notification – China – Food Nutritional Fortifier 5'-Cytidylic Acid, G/SPS/N/CHN/1043 (Jan 29, 2016), at 1–2.

68 By October 2015, China had submitted 1115 regular notifications; second only to the United States which had submitted 2695 such notifications. See Committee on Sanitary and Phytosanitary Measures, *Overview regarding the Level of Implementation of the Transparency Provisions of the SPS Agreement, Note by the Secretariat*, G/SPS/GEN/804/Rev.8 (October 6, 2015).

EU notes that in practice, access to China's SPS legislation as well as possibilities to comment on the draft legislation remains limited. This is because China has not made its SPS regulations available in one or more WTO languages, despite its accession commitment to do so.[69] In addition, according to the EU, it is not always clear whether China takes the comments given by its trading partners into account before it finalizes its SPS regulations. Finally, the EU has pointed out that China must comply with the obligation to allow a reasonable adaptation period between the publication of an SPS regulation and its entry into force.[70]

The following example illustrates China's failure to comply with the transparency obligations of the SPS Agreement. On June 1, 2009, China's then-new Food Safety Law and the Regulation on the Implementation of the Food Safety Law entered into force. However, China failed to issue notice of both this new legislation and its implementing regulations prior to implementation. Furthermore, China did not provide a "reasonable adaptation period" to allow time for other Members to adapt to the new requirements, as the SPS Agreement requires between the publication of a SPS regulation and its entry into force.[71] Such lack of transparency acts as a formidable barrier to market access and is subject to challenge under the rules of the SPS Agreement.

Undue delays

In order to ensure that their SPS requirements are complied with, Members usually have control, inspection, and approval procedures in place. If these procedures are complex, lengthy, or costly, they may effectively restrict market access, especially in the case of perishable products. Therefore, the SPS Agreement contains detailed rules on control, inspection, and approval procedures, which broadly aim at ensuring that such procedures are not more lengthy and burdensome than is reasonable and necessary and that they do not discriminate against imports.[72] Whether a procedural delay is "unreasonable" depends, according to the panel in the *EC – Biotech Products* case,[73] not on the length of the delay but on whether there is a legitimate reason or justification for it. Members applying approval procedures must be allowed to take the time reasonably needed to ensure with adequate confidence that their SPS requirements are complied with.

The EU has noted that slow progress of negotiations of SPS protocols and slow progress for inspections impose considerable market access restrictions for EU exports to China, especially for meat, fruit, and vegetables.[74] In particular, the EU has raised concerns that China's approach to audit and inspection, which deviates from the standard laid down by the Codex Alimentarius Commission, results in unjustified delays. In the absence of an adequate justification for such procedural delays, the measures may be challenged under the rules of the SPS Agreement.[75]

69 See the *Report of the Working Party on the Accession of the People's Republic of China*, para. 334.

70 Committee on Sanitary and Phytosanitary Measures, *supra* note 34, para. 6.

71 Committee on Sanitary and Phytosanitary Measures, *supra* note 34, para. 13.

72 SPS Agreement, Article 8 and Annex C.

73 Panel Report, *EC–Measures Affecting the Approval and Marketing of Biotech Products*, WT/DS291/R paras 7.1496–1498 and 7.1511–1530 (September 29, 2006).

74 Committee on Sanitary and Phytosanitary Measures, *supra* note 34, para. 16.

75 *Id.*, para. 17.

Conclusion

The current proliferation of health protection measures in China, on the one hand, and the great advancements in trade liberalization brought about by China's accession to the WTO, on the other, mean that the interaction between the two policy areas of trade and health has assumed critical importance for China. The SPS Agreement strives to achieve a balance between the trade and health objectives of WTO Members. As such, it sets the limits within which China may exercise its sovereign right to take measures to protect health within its territory and to achieve the level of health protection it deems appropriate.

These limits promote rationality in SPS regulation and prevent restrictions that are based on unfounded fears or are a response to protectionist pressures from the domestic industry. Exporting WTO Members, such as the EU, may rely on the disciplines of the SPS Agreement to challenge SPS restrictions implemented by other Members, either through raising their concerns in the multilateral forum of the SPS Committee or, as a last resort, by bringing a dispute under the WTO dispute settlement mechanism. They may also use the trade policy review mechanism (and until recently the transitional review mechanism for China) to highlight their concerns.

To date, China's SPS measures have been the subject of discussions in all these fora except for the dispute settlement mechanism. Members, including the EU, have worked to find constructive solutions to the problems raised rather than seek adjudicative solutions. The EU has noted China's significant efforts to reform its SPS regime in line with its obligations under the SPS Agreement, and has recognized that China has increased these efforts as trade grows.[76]

China has a formidable task before it to conform its SPS regime to the requirements of the SPS Agreement. It must give effect to its health objectives in a manner that respects the disciplines laid down in this Agreement – a sometimes costly and administratively burdensome task. However, it should not be forgotten that at the same time China can, and does, use the same Agreement to challenge the trade restrictions imposed by its trading partners in the form of SPS requirements.[77] It is through its careful balance between trade and health concerns that the SPS Agreement serves the interests of all WTO Members.

76 *Id.*, para. 3.

77 In 2009, China initiated a WTO dispute settlement proceeding against the United States in respect of restrictions on its poultry exports. The WTO Panel found the US measure in violation of the SPS Agreement, and recommended its withdrawal. The US did not appeal this decision. *See* Panel Report, *United States – Certain Measures Affecting Imports of Poultry from China*, WT/DS392/R, (October 25, 2010).

28 SPS, Public Health, and Environmental Provisions in East Asia RTAs

ASEAN and China**

*Lorenzo Di Masi**

Introduction

The regulation of international trade follows two different modalities. On the one hand, world trade is regulated multilaterally within the framework of the World Trade Organization (WTO). On the other hand, during the last 15 years there has been an incredible proliferation of Regional Trade Agreements (RTAs), also known as preferential trade agreements (PTAs). According to the most recent statistic data published by the WTO, as of July 1, 2016, 635 RTAs have been notified to the GATT/WTO. At the same date, 423 agreements were already in force. The main goal of PTAs is to establish a higher degree of economic integration and trade liberalization among the participant countries than the one that has already been achieved by the same countries within the WTO legal system.[1]

The traditional economic approaches to PTAs have focused mainly on two aspects. A first approach, which can be defined as "static analysis," moves from the assumption that these agreements mainly deal with reciprocal tariff cuts and border measures and studies the trade diversion and trade creation effects.[2] A second approach, which is commonly defined as

* The author wishes to thank Prof. Paolo Davide Farah for the invitation to contribute to the present book. The views adopted in the present article represent the personal opinions of the author and not the position of Crowell & Moring LLP.

** This chapter is part of the results of the Research Project on "*Current Trends of Chinese Law towards Non-Trade Concerns such as Sustainable Development and the Protection of Environment, Public Health, Food Safety, Cultural, Social and Economic Rights, Labor Rights and the Reduction of Poverty from the Perspective of International Law and WTO Law*", coordinated by Professor Paolo Davide Farah at gLAWcal – Global Law Initiatives for Sustainable Development (United Kingdom) and at West Virginia University John D. Rockefeller IV School of Policy and Politics, Department of Public Administration, in partnership with the Center of Advanced Studies on Contemporary China (CASCC) in Turin (Italy), Maastricht University Faculty of Law, Department of International and European Law and IGIR – Institute for Globalisation and International Regulation (Netherlands), and Tsinghua University, School of Law, Institute of Public International Law and the Center for Research on Intellectual Property Law in Beijing (China). An early draft of this chapter was presented at the Conferences Series on "*China's Influence on Non-Trade Concerns in International Economic Law*", First Conference held at the Center of Advanced Studies on Contemporary China (CASCC) in Turin on November 23–24, 2011. This publication and the Conference Series were sponsored by China–EU School of Law (CESL) at the China University of Political Science and Law (CUPL). The activities of CESL at CUPL are supported by the European Union and the People's Republic of China.

1 WTO, *Regional Trade Agreements,* http://www.wto.org/english/tratop_e/region_e/region_e.htm (last visited July 21, 2016).

2 The static analysis of PTAs has been pioneered by economist Jacob Viner. In extreme synthesis, according to Viner, PTAs can both divert trade from an efficient to an inefficient source of production (therefore

"dynamic time path analysis," inquires the impact of PTAs over time. This method concentrates on the alternative of PTAs being stumbling blocks or stepping stones to multilateral trade liberalization through rounds of negotiations within the WTO.[3] In more recent times, economic and legal studies have moved away from these arguments and turned their attention to the presence of "deep commitments" within PTAs. The expression "deep commitments" indicates a wide range of provisions in RTAs covering areas that are different from tariff cuts and other border measures.[4] Recently signed agreements include bilateral or regional commitments on competition policies, foreign direct investments, intellectual property rights, telecommunications, labor, and environmental standards. Deep commitments are often referred to as WTO *plus* or WTO *extra* obligations. Following the definitions given by Horn, Mavroidis, and Sapir,[5] the WTO *plus* category corresponds to those provisions in PTAs that come under the current mandate of the WTO, where the parties undertake bilateral commitments going beyond those they have accepted at the multilateral level. An example would be a further liberalization of trade in services that goes beyond the rules of the General Agreement on Trade in Services[6] (GATS *plus*). By contrast, the WTO *extra* category includes those PTAs provisions on sectors that lie outside the current WTO mandate. An example would be an arrangement on labor standards. Some of these WTO *extra* and WTO *plus* obligations deal with Non-Trade Concerns (NTCs). Consider, for instance, environmental and labor regulations or other commitments on SPS (Sanitary and Phytosanitary) measures, public health, and food safety, which are often found in PTAs.

This chapter inquires about the presence of NTCs, WTO *plus*, and WTO *extra* provisions in the Association of South-East Asian Nations (ASEAN) and China's RTAs, in order to evaluate their possible contribution to the evolution of international economic law in a

having a negative impact on the economies of their participants) and create trade through a shift from an inefficient to and efficient production source. Jacob Viner, The Custom Union Issue (The Carnegie Endowment for International Peace, 1950).

3 According to the stumbling blocks theory, members of an FTA or of a customs union become self-satisfied with their agreements and show little interest in expanding it to other nations or in carrying on multilateral talks. Most important, the proliferation of PTAs has created a "spaghetti bowl," an intricate web of multiple tariff rates and different rules of origin. The result of several rules of origins is legal complexity, which increases the transaction costs of engaging in international trade. Complying with the significant paper burden required by these rules is a significant business cost, especially in terms of expedition of trades. On the stumbling blocks theory, *see* Jagdish Bhagwati & Arvind Panagariya, *Preferential Trading Areas And Multilateralism – Strangers, Friends, or Foes*, in The Economics of Preferential Trade Agreements (Bhagwati & Panagariya eds, Aei Press, 1996). The stepping stones argument, often referred to as "competitive liberalization" or "domino effect" is based on the fact that each wave of regionalism that occurred in recent history has tended to coincide with significant advances in GATT negotiations. For instance, some argue that the Uruguay Round benefited from the second wave or regionalism of the 1980s. The Uruguay Round, launched in 1986 after several failed attempts, had a negotiating mandate on services, intellectual property, and investments, that is to say, on those areas that had already been included in regional agreements concluded in those years, for example NAFTA. On this point, *see* in general John Ravenhill, *Regionalism*, in Global Political Economy 140 (Ravenhill eds, Oxford University Press, 2006).

4 For a detailed analysis of the reasons that have brought to the inclusion of deep commitments in RTAs, *see* WTO, *World Trade Report 2011, The WTO and Preferential Trade Agreements: from Coexistence to Coherence* 105 (2011).

5 Henrik Horn, Petros C. Mavroidis & Andrè Sapir, *Beyond the WTO? An Anatomy of EU and US Preferential Trade Agreements*, CEPR Discussion Paper No. DP7317 (2009).

6 General Agreement on Trade in Services, April 15, 1994, Marrakesh Agreement Establishing the World Trade Organization, Annex 1B, 1869 UNTS 183, 33 ILM 1167 (1994) [hereinafter GATS].

"sustainable development oriented" direction. More specifically, this attempt represents an innovative approach with respect to the greatest part of the existing literature on Chinese and ASEAN RTAs, that, as it will be discussed later on, focuses rather on the reasons justifying RTAs than on their actual content. The work is structured as follows. It first discusses the reasons that have led China and ASEAN to pursue an intensive regional policy during the last ten years. It then focuses on regional provision in the areas of SPS measures, public health, and environmental protection. Eventually, some conclusions will be drawn.

China and ASEAN Regional Trade Agreements

China's Regional Trade Agreements

As of July 16, 2016, the People's Republic of China (PRC) entered into 14 free trade agreements (FTAs). Following the 2003 Closer Economic Partnership Agreements (CEPAs) with Hong Kong and Macau, the Chinese government has signed FTAs with ASEAN (2004), Chile (2005), Pakistan (2006), New Zealand (2008), Singapore (2008), Peru (2009), Costa Rica (2010), Iceland (2013), Switzerland (2013), Australia and South Korea (2014). Negotiations have been launched for the conclusion of trade agreements with the Gulf Cooperation Council (GCC), Norway, Japan, Sri Lanka, Maldives and Georgia, as well for an upgrade of the China–ASEAN FTA. In addition, China is taking part to the negotiations of the Regional Comprehensive Economic Partnership (RCEP), a trade agreement plan between the ASEAN countries, Korea, Australia, New Zealand and India. Moreover, FTAs with India, Moldova, Fiji, Nepal and Colombia are currently under consideration.[7] The new wave of Chinese RTAs is certainly striking, especially if one considers that China has not been a very active member on the international scene until the early 1990s.[8]

According to the Chinese Government, PTAs represent "a new platform to further opening up to the outside and speeding up domestic reforms, an effective approach to integrate into [the] global economy and strengthen economic cooperation with other economies, as well as particularly an important supplement to the multilateral trading system."[9]

The relevant studies on the topic have shown four main reasons beyond China's FTAs strategy.[10] First, economic considerations play a primary role. Trade statistics show that

7 *See* China's FTAs Network, *China's Free Trade Agreements*, http://fta.mofcom.gov.cn/english/fta_qianshu.shtml (last visited July 17, 2016)

8 On this point, *see* Jun Zhao & Timothy Webster, *Taking Stock: China's First Decade of Free Trade*, 33 U. Penn. J. Int'l L. 65, 80 (2011) and Henry Gao, *The RTA Strategy of China: A Critical Visit*, in Challenges to Multilateral Trade: The Impact of Bilateral Preferential and Regional Agreements 52–64 (Ross Buckly, Vai Io Lo & Laurence Boulle eds, Kluwer Law International, 2008). Since the early 1990s, China has become a more active player in the region. Besides the good relationship established with ASEAN, China has also joined the Asia-Pacific Economic Cooperation (APEC) and has started a military and strategic cooperation with Central Asian countries since 1992 in the Framework of the Shanghai Cooperation Organization.

9 China's FTAs Network, *supra* note 7.

10 For reasons of space, not all the relevant literature on the topic can be properly reviewed. In particular, a growing scholarship that studies PTAs from the point of view of domestic politics, showing the various Chinese internal forces that are in favor and against trade liberalization, deserves at least a separate mention. *See* Yang Jang, *China's Pursuit Of Free Trade Agreements: Is China Exceptional?*, 17 Rev. Int'l Pol. Econ. 238–261 (2010) and Ka Zeng, *Multilateral versus Bilateral and Regional Trade Liberalization: Explaining China's Pursuit of Free Trade Agreements (FTA)*, 19 J. Contemp. China 635–652 (2010).

Chinese FTAs have enormously increased bilateral trade with the other signing country. In other words, FTAs are incredible tools to improve market access conditions and enhance the investments environment.[11] Second, China needs constant access to natural resources to maintain the economic growth rates registered in the past three years. For this reasons, an FTA has already been concluded with Chile, a country rich of copper, and Peru and Australia, which has huge mineral resources too, while other FTAs are under negotiation with other natural gas and oil suppliers, like Norway, and the Gulf Cooperation Council.[12]

Third, FTAs are often signed for strategic reasons. For a long time, China has been considered as a threat by its neighbors that were worried to see their markets invaded by cheap imports. In order to ease up these concerns, China has started to negotiate FTAs in the region. The China–ASEAN FTA (CAFTA) – which is now the third-largest preferential area in the world, second only to the European Union (EU) and NAFTA – was negotiated also with the intent to prove to south-east Asian nations that China did not represent a danger, but rather a reliable trading partner.[13] Moreover, by strengthening the relationships with its neighbors – Pakistan, ASEAN, but also New Zealand and Australia – China is striving to become the leading power in the Asia-Pacific region at the expense of Japan and the United States (US).[14]

Fourth, as it is well known, the WTO does not consider China as a full-market economy. More specifically, China's Protocol of Accession to the WTO contains some extremely restrictive provisions, especially with regard to dumping and subsidies.[15] For this reason, China has inserted the recognition of its market economy status as a preliminary condition for the conclusion of FTAs. The recognition of this new status in RTAs can be regarded as a necessary step towards a future *reshaping* of the condition of accession of China to the WTO.[16]

It is also important to note that China has shown a high degree of flexibility in the negotiation of its FTAs.[17] China, unlike the US and often also the EU, does not adopt a strict model for all its RTAs, but it rather prefers to tailor the agreements to the specific expectations and

11 Guiguo Wang, *China's FTAs: Legal Characteristics and Implications,* 105 Am. J. Int'l L. 493, 505–506 (2011).

12 *Ibid.*, at 507.

13 Timothy Webster, *Bilateral Regionalism, Paradoxes of East Asian Integration,* 25 Berkeley J. Int'l L. 434, 445, 457 (2007); Jiangyu Wang, *China's Regional Trade Agreements: the Law, Geopolitics and impact on the Multilateral trading System,* 8 Sing. Y.B. Int'l L. 109, 131 (2004). The author also argues that the first Chinese FTAs concluded with Macau and Hong Kong are functional to integrate the economies – eventually also Taiwan – in order to create the *Greater China Economic Circle.* As a matter of fact, an agreement between the Association for the relations among China and Taiwan has been recently notified to the WTO.

14 Wang, *supra* note 13, at 131; Wang, *supra* note 11, at 499.

15 *See* WTO, *Protocol of Accession of the People's Republic Of China,* WT/L/432 (November 23, 2011), Articles 10 and 15. Note, however, that, despite the strictness of these anti-dumping commitments, China is trying to improve its burdensome position also at the multilateral level. The WTO Appellate Body ruling in favor of China in the *EC – Fasteners* Case is certainly proof. *See* Appellate Body Report, *European Communities – Definitive anti-Dumping Measures On Certain Iron Or Steel Fasteners From China,* WT/DS397/AB/R (July 15, 2011).

16 On the "reshaping" of rules, *see* Wang, *supra* note 11, at 508–511; Zhao & Webster, *supra* note 8, at 113. *See* also Paolo Davide Farah, *Five Years of China's WTO Membership. EU and US Perspectives about China's Compliance with Transparency Commitments and the Transitional Review Mechanism,* 33(3) Legal Issues of Economic Integration, 263, 263–304 (2006).

17 Webster, *supra* note 13, at 457; Wang, *supra* note 11, at 498–499; Zhao & Webster, *supra* note 8, at 110; Claude Barfield, *The Dragon Stirs: China's Trade Policy for Asia and the World,* 24 Arizona J. Int'l & Comp. L. 93, 110 (2007).

needs of the participating countries. For example, CAFTA was negotiated step-by-step and annex-by-annex since ASEAN wanted the FTA to enter into force gradually. Conversely, the Chilean 121-articles-long FTA was designed to enter into force as a unique block.

To conclude, some scholars have noted that Chinese FTAs are "comprehensive" in the sense that they set rules on all the main aspects of bilateral trade.[18] Chinese FTAs often include provisions on rules of origin, customs procedure, SPS measures, technical barriers to trade, trade remedies, investments, trade in services, movement of natural persons, intellectual property, environment, labor, and dispute settlement. Moreover, the percentage of goods that are liberalized through PTAs is impressive. The CAFTA, for examples, rules on the liberalization of 90 per cent of goods, while the Chile–China FTA will progressively eliminate tariffs on 97 per cent of the tariff lines by 2017. Similarly, the China–Hong Kong CEPA liberalizes 18 services sectors.

In sum, Chinese FTAs are characterized by geopolitical and strategic – in addition to mere economic – rationales (for example, resources and the run for regional leadership), by flexibility in the negotiations and by comprehensiveness. In our opinion, as it will be shown later, the importance played by geopolitical and economic considerations affects the space granted – within Chinese PTAs – to non-trade issues.

ASEAN Regional Trade Agreements

The ASEAN has a long tradition of regionalism in trade. The ASEAN Free Trade Area (AFTA) dates back to 1992. Since then, ASEAN has entered into five other Free Trade Agreements: with China (CAFTA 2004), Japan (AJFTA 2008), India (AIFTA 2009), Australia–New Zealand (AANZFTA 2009), and Korea (KAFTA 2009). Negotiations are currently ongoing for an FTA with Hong Kong as well as for the conclusion of the RCEP. The main reasons behind ASEAN PTAs are analyzed below.[19]

First, ASEAN Regional Trade Agreements are concluded for economic reasons, in particular, in order to enhance market access.[20] For instance, the AFTA Common Effective Preferential Tariff (CEPT) plan has eliminated 99 per cent of tariff lines for intra ASEAN trade. Similarly, as noted previously, CAFTA has enormously increased the trade between its constituents. Market access is also guaranteed by uniform rules on investments, as in the ASEAN–Australia–New Zealand FTA.[21]

18 *See* Wang, *supra* note 11, at 498. A different interpretation is offered by Zeng who argues on the contrary that Chinese PTAs are "of a low quality, characterized by a low level of legal obligation." *See* Ka Zeng, *supra* note 10, at 638. *See* also Agata Antkiewitcz & John Whalley, *China's New Regional Trade Agreements,* 28 World Econ. 1539, 1554 (2005).

19 *See* United Nations Policy Department, *The Great Maze: Regional and Bilateral Free Trade Agreements in Asia, Asia-Pacific Trade and Investment Initiative* (2005); Rahul Sen, *New Regionalism in Asia: A Comparative Analysis of Emerging Regional and Bilateral Trading Agreements involving ASEAN, China and India,* 40 J. World Trade 553 (2006). Useful indications to the understanding of ASEAN RTAs can be found in Joon Lian Wan, *ASEAN's Regional Trade Agreements,* Presentation to the WTO/ESCAP Regional Seminar on WTO and Regional Trade Agreements for Asian Economies, July 2011. A recent study of ASEAN RTAs can be found in David Kleimann, *Beyond Market Access? The Anatomy of ASEAN's Preferential Trade Agreements,* 48 J. World Trade 629 (2014). For a more general introduction to Asian FTAs, *see* Rahul Sen, Free trade agreements in Southeast Asia (Institute of Southeast Asian Studies, 2004).

20 For a detailed analysis on this point *see* Kleimann, *supra* note 19, at 636.

21 *See* ASEAN–Australia–New Zealand FTA, Chapter 11, http://rtais.wto.org/rtadocs/713/TOA/English/Combined%20ECFA%20Text.pdf (last visited July 19, 2016). The agreement can be regarded as the most comprehensive among ASEAN PTAs.

Second, it is interesting to note that ASEAN has exclusively entered into PTAs with the other great economies of the Asian-Pacific region. Thus, again, strategic considerations play a crucial role. ASEAN intends to remain in good economic relationships with other leading states and at the same time reaffirm its centrality in the region through FTA negotiations with the EU and the US.

Third, and most important, ASEAN FTAs are concluded in order to elevate the socio-economic development of ASEAN Member States (AMS). The prominence of the achievement of social development through economic integration is enshrined in the *ASEAN Economic Community Blueprint* and the *Socio-Cultural Community Blueprint* contained in the *Roadmap for an ASEAN Community 2009–2015*. More specifically, the *Socio-Cultural Community Blueprint* lists, among the main strategic objectives, the enhancement of food safety, the accessibility of health care, the promotion of better working conditions, and environmental sustainability.[22] As it will be shown later, all these objectives are effectively pursued through the inclusion of specific provisions in PTAs.

Two other aspects should be highlighted in order to conclude the analysis of ASEAN FTAs. In the first instance, many AMS are conducting their own parallel PTAs in addition to the one carried out by the organization. In other words, AMS remain free to conclude PTAs with third countries. Singapore, for instance, has been particularly active and has signed many FTAs, notably with the US, EFTA, Korea, China, Japan, and the EU. Although this topic goes beyond the scope of this chapter, the presence of overlapping RTAs between ASEAN and its Member States can lead to problems of compatibility.[23]

In the second instance, ASEAN methods of negotiations deserve a short separate analysis. ASEAN FTAs are negotiated either by a *sequential approach* or a *single undertaking approach*.[24] The sequential approach implies the negotiation of a Framework Agreement on Comprehensive Economic Cooperation, which is the basis for future agreements for trade in goods, services, and investments. CAFTA, the ASEAN–Korea FTA, and ASEAN–India FTA were negotiated using this approach. Through this method, the comprehensiveness of the agreement is slowly achieved over the years. On the other hand, the single undertaking approach implies one single negotiation of a comprehensive agreement covering goods, services, and investments. The Japan–ASEAN FTA and the ASEAN–Australia–New Zealand FTA were concluded as single undertakings. Like China, ASEAN shows great flexibility in the negotiations processes. The areas covered by ASEAN PTAs are analogous to those recalled while discussing China.

In sum, the ASEAN way to Regional Trade Agreements is characterized not only by economic and strategic rationales, but also by the political will to use RTAs in order to promote social development.

22 *See* ASEAN, *Roadmap for an ASEAN Community 2009–2015*, at 67, http://www.aseansec.org/publications/RoadmapASEANCommunity.pdf (last visited July 18, 2016).

23 Rahul Sen, *supra* note 19, at 562. For an overview of the reasons leading AMS to negotiate parallel PTAs with countries that have already entered in other agreements with ASEAN, *see* also Kleimann, *supra* note 19.

24 Joon Lian Wan, *supra* note 19.

Comparing ASEAN and China's approach to food safety, public health, and environmental protection in Regional Trade Agreements

The following subsections enquire about ASEAN and China NTC provisions in the areas of food safety (sanitary and phytosanitary measures), public health (in particular access to medical treatment), and environmental protection. The present chapter does not include an analysis of China-Korea FTA and China Australia FTA.

SPS measures in RTAs between consolidation of the WTO SPS Agreement and further evolutions

With the exception of the CEPAs concluded between China, Hong Kong, and Macau, every other Chinese and ASEAN PTA explicitly regulates the issue of sanitary and phytosanitary measures. The centrality of SPS chapters in East Asian RTAs responds to precise motivations. In the case of ASEAN, as mentioned in the previous comment on the main features of its RTAs, the insertion of SPS measures seems to be justified at the light of the importance given to food security by the *Socio-Cultural Community Blueprint*. In particular, the blueprint states that appropriate actions should be taken by the organization to "harmonize national food safety regulations with internationally-accepted standard, including quarantine and inspection procedures for the movement of plants, animals, and their products," and "strengthen the cooperation with regional and international institutions including private organizations to secure food for the region."[25] In the case of China, in the absence of official documents on the point, it is possible only to make suggestions.[26] In addition to the obvious importance that food safety rules have for an economy that is an active exporter of food products, it may be claimed that it is in China's best interest to work for the implementation of clear rules in order to avoid litigation of food issues in front of the WTO judiciary bodies. As a matter of fact, as it is well known, China has been already involved in disputes involving SPS standards against other WTO Members.[27]

As China and ASEAN's SPS chapters do not differ with regards to their structure and the depth of their obligations, their characteristic traces are summarized here below.

First, most of the chapters start by listing their objectives. SPS chapters are usually directed to facilitate trade among the parties while protecting human, animal, or plant life, strengthen the cooperation among the parties in order to implement regional rules in accordance with the WTO SPS Agreement, assure that SPS measures do not constitute an arbitral and unjustified distortion of trade, promote greater transparency in the understanding of each party's national standards, exchange information in case of notification of new measures, and establish joint committees in charge of monitoring the implementation of the agreement.

Second, in line with the objects of these chapters, in many RTAs the contracting parties reaffirm the main rights and obligations under the WTO SPS Agreement.[28] For instance, it often happens that states agree to work for the strict implementation of WTO SPS provisions

25 Roadmap for an ASEAN Community 2009–2015, *supra* note 22, at 73.

26 *See* Chapter 27 (Prevost) in this volume.

27 *See* for instance Panel Report, *United States – Certain Measures Affecting Imports of Poultry from China*, WT/DS392 (September 29, 2010).

28 Agreement on Sanitary and Phytosanitary Measures, April 15, 1994, Marrakesh Agreement Establishing the World Trade Organization, Annex 1A, 1867 UNTS 493 [hereinafter SPS Agreement].

such as harmonization of standards, harmonization of risk assessment procedures, transparency, and adaptation to regional conditions.[29] The presence of such "consolidation" rules should not be underestimated. The existence of such rules strengthens the argument that the SPS Agreement is currently implemented through a binary system. Of course, the respect of the SPS Agreement is granted by the presence of an efficient multilateral dispute resolution mechanism. This mechanism, however, represents only the first component of the system. The second part is constituted by bilateral and regional agreements in which states reaffirm their obligations under the SPS Agreement and establish cooperation activities to assure the respect of such obligations. From this point of view, PTAs can be regarded as stepping stones of the multilateral trading system.

Third, Chinese and ASEAN SPS chapters are not only about "consolidation" rules. On the contrary, in many cases, East Asian RTAs create new rules, which go beyond those established by the WTO Agreement.[30] For instance, there are provisions setting detailed procedures for the management of emergency situations (such as food crisis and pests) and change of status of pest-free zones.[31] Moreover, some agreements provide for dispute settlement mechanisms in case disagreements arise in the application of SPS measures.[32]

In sum, the existing synergy between regional rules "consolidating" the SPS Agreement and new SPS *plus* provisions should be positively welcomed. As noted above, "consolidation" rules contribute to the creation of a variable geometry system for the implementation of the SPS Agreement. Moreover, the drafting of new SPS rules constitutes a positive evolution of international trade law towards higher standards of protection in the field of food security. Nevertheless, it should be verified if and how these regional SPS commitments are implemented into domestic legislation and if and how the institutional apparatus built around these treaties effectively works. For instance, the real functioning of the bilateral Joint Committees in charge of implementing the regional SPS rules deserves a careful and separate analysis.

The protection of public health

The second subsection enquires about the protection of health in China and ASEAN RTAs. While the agreements regulating trade in goods do not contain provisions on public health, the analysis of preferential services' schedules may reveal interesting results. The positive effects of health services' liberalization can be easily understood. For instance, granting the possibility to build hospitals or permitting the access of medical professionals can greatly improve the welfare of the Chinese and ASEAN population. Moving from these considerations, a question should be posed. Do ASEAN and Chinese regional commitments offer a greater liberalization of health services than in the WTO framework? In other words, do RTAs create GATS *plus* commitments in the area of health services? In order to evaluate the impact of service liberalization on NTC, the WTO GATS commitments of China and the ASEAN countries in the areas of health (sector 1.A.h of the WTO schedule of commitments)

29 *See* SPS Agreement, Articles 3, 5, and 7. *See* for instance Articles 84 AFTA, 5 AANZFTA, 32–33 China–Pakistan FTA, 57 China–Chile FTA, 49–54 China–Singapore FTA, 79–81 China–New Zealand FTA, and 86–88 China–Peru FTA.

30 For an overview of SPS *plus* provisions in ASEAN FTAs *see* Kleimann, *supra* note 19, at 664–665.

31 ASEAN FTA at Article 83.

32 *See* China–Peru FTA at Article 91 and ASEAN–Australia–New Zealand, Chapter 7, Article 9.

and medical services (sector 2 of the WTO schedule of commitments) were compared to the commitments undertaken by the same states at a regional level, especially with regard to the third mode of supply (commercial presence).[33] The results of the study are exposed as it follows.

Studies have shown how the level of liberalization of health services in ASEAN is already relatively high.[34] The analysis of ASEAN PTAs seems to confirm the aforementioned trend with the relevant addition that, in some cases, the specific regional commitments undertaken by AMS go beyond the multilateral ones. For example, Indonesia, Malaysia, and Singapore somehow improved through PTAs the degree of liberalization of health services.[35]

The study of the same service sectors in Chinese RTAs reveals a partially different reality. The greatest part of the agreements in which China has entered into does not present GATS *plus* obligations in the area of health services.[36] A partial explanation can be found in the fact that the multilateral commitments in sector 1.A.h (medical services) are already relatively elevated.[37] Interestingly, in the recent China–Australia FTA, China has decided to grant the possibility for Australian companies to establish wholly-owned hospitals in China.[38]

The data show a higher level of liberalization of health services in ASEAN PTAs than in Chinese ones. The reasons for such a difference could be that ASEAN PTAs are signed not only for economic and strategic reasons but also to promote social development. Notably,

33 For the multilateral commitments of ASEAN Member States and China, *see* WTO *List of Services Commitments and Article II Exemptions*, http://www.wto.org/english/tratop_e/serv_e/serv_commitments_e.htm (last visited July 16, 2016). The regional services' commitments are annexes to the main body of the treaty. All the treaties are published by WTO, *List of all RTAs*, http://rtais.wto.org/UI/PublicAllRTAList.aspx (last visited July 16, 2016). For a general overview on service commitments in Chinese RTAs, *see* Heng Wang, *China, Free Trade Agreements and WTO Law: a Perspective on the Trade in Services* (European University Institute Max Weber Programme Working Papers, 2011).

34 On the liberalization of health services in ASEAN, *see* an excellent paper by Philippa Dee, Services liberalization towards an ASEAN Economic Community, in TOWARDS A COMPETITIVE ASEAN SINGLE MARKET: SECTORAL ANALYSIS (S. Urata and M. Okabe eds, ERIA Research Project Report, 2011). *See* also Philippa Dee & Huong Dinh, *Barriers to Trade in Health and Financial Services in ASEAN* (2009). In the first paper, the author argues that the level of liberalization in medical professional services is relatively high, while there are still significant barriers to the possibility of foreign suppliers to establish health services in AMS (*see* Philippa Dee, at 51–59).

35 More specifically, Indonesia and Singapore, who did not insert any specific commitment in the field of health services in their WTO lists, negotiated specific obligations in their AANZFTA, CAFTA, and KAFTA services' schedules. Malaysia's preferential health services schedules increase by 10 per cent of the foreign shareholding quota of foreign corporations (from 30 per cent to 40 per cent) under mode 3. The complete schedules are available at http://www.aseansec.org/4920.htm (last visited July 16, 2016).

36 *See* China–Singapore FTA and China–Hong Kong CEPA.

37 *See* WTO, *Sector Specific Commitments of China-Professional Services*, http://tsdb.wto.org/simplesearch.aspx (last visited July 16, 2016). Moreover, it is interesting to note that important national sanitary reforms were undertaken by the Chinese government in 2014, as an attempt to ameliorate the conditions to accessibility to health care. As part of this general reform, China seems to be committed to open the heath services' market to foreign enterprises. *See, inter alia*, James A. C. Sinclair, *China's Healthcare Reform – Reform plans promise significant change, but what does that mean for foreign healthcare players?*, http://www.chinabusinessreview.com/chinas-healthcare-reform/ (last visited July 16, 2016).

38 *See* China–Australia FTA, *Understanding the Agreement – Factsheet on Services*, http://www.dfat.gov.au/trade/agreements/chafta/fact-sheets/Pages/understanding-the-agreement.aspx (last visited July 16, 2016). China's GATS schedules provide that "foreign solely-owned hospital or clinics (i.e. foreign-capital enterprises) are not permitted, but foreigners are permitted to establish equity joint venture or contractual joint venture hospitals or clinics with Chinese partners with a quantitative limitation in line with China's needs."

public health is one of ASEAN's highest priorities as stated, once again, by the *Socio-Cultural Community Blueprint*. ASEAN Members should take actions "to promote investment in primary health care infrastructure, in a rational manner and likewise ensure adequate financing and social protection for the poor and marginalized populations for better access to services."[39] Conversely, China seems to be more interested in the use of PTAs for strategic purposes and to foster its exports rather than as means to support development.

Environmental protection

Whereas international environmental protection is usually granted through specific agreements, the increasingly higher impact of trade on the environment has triggered the insertion of environmental chapters within PTAs. Following the example set by US FTAs, ASEAN and China have also started to dedicate some space to environmental provisions in their RTAs.

China, in particular, has concluded Environmental Cooperation Side Agreements (ECSD) with New Zealand and Chile. In general, the level of commitments established by these agreements is not very high. The main obligation set by these treaties is a generic request made to the parties to "respect the sovereign rights of each country to set its own policies and national priorities and to set, administer, and enforce its own environmental laws and regulations."[40] There is no express obligation that invites the parties to join multilateral environmental agreements (MEAs) or to conform their legislation to internationally recognized standards. In addition to the "enforce your own law" provision, China agrees to start cooperation activities with its trading partners in the "areas of environmental management, environmental remediation, nature conservation, and technologies (including systems and processes) for environmental benefit."[41] Cooperation activities may include the exchange of expertise and information as well as the organization of joint study groups and seminars.

As far as ASEAN FTAs are concerned, no special environmental arrangements have been negotiated so far. The protection of the environment is sporadically recalled in technical barriers to trade (TBT) provisions.[42]

The liberalization of environmental services (Sector 6 of the WTO schedule of commitments) deserves at least a brief comment. The comparison between the multilateral and regional schedule of commitments of ASEAN Member States indicates that few GATS *plus* obligations exist in their PTAs. Relevant examples in this sense are the Philippines and Thailand.[43] In Chinese PTAs, most environmental services are liberalized, with the exclusion of environmental quality monitoring and pollution-source inspection services. Surprisingly, in

39 Roadmap for an ASEAN Community 2009–2015, *supra* note 22, at 74–75.

40 China-New Zealand Environmental Cooperation Side Agreement, Article 1, para. 1.

41 *Ibid.* at Article 2, para. 2.

42 *See* for instance Article 2, para. 2 of Chapter 6 of AANZFTA and Article 44, para. 3 and Article 53 of AJFTA.

43 *See* for instance the Philippines schedule of commitments in AANZFTA and AKFTA, where some additional commitments to the one made in the multilateral forum exist for sewerage services. As for Thailand, see again the AANZFTA and AKFTA schedules of commitments where some slightly wider obligations exist, especially under mode 4.

all the relevant sub-sectors of some RTAs, China permits companies wishing to supply services under mode 3 (commercial presence) to be entirely owned by foreign investors.[44]

While ASEAN attention to environmental protection is justified by the same arguments used while discussing public health,[45] China's approach to environmental protection deserves more attention. Why is China, one of the world's greatest polluters, inserting environmental commitments in its PTAs? Actually, the Chinese attitude regarding environmental protection has radically changed in the last years. The attention dedicated by the 11th Five Year Plan (2006–2011) to the construction of an eco-friendly society was already really high. The 12th Five Year Plan (2011–2015) is even more striking; environmental protection is one of the three key themes of the plan, together with economic restructuring and social equality.[46] Environmental protection continues to play an important role also under the 13th Five Year Plan (2016–2020). More specifically, China is committed to adopt a green development model by reducing carbon emissions and continuing to develop alternative energy sources. The new Chinese consciousness of the importance of environmental protection has probably influenced the inclusion of new provisions in RTAs. In this sense, the cooperation activities already started by China in ECSDs can be deemed as the first steps towards the inclusion of deeper and more comprehensive environmental standards in PTAs.

Conclusions

The empirical analysis of NTCs provisions in China and ASEAN RTAs presents both light and shadow. On the one hand, it may be argued that regional rules do not offer elevated standards of protection for NTCs. In effect, regional commitments do not set deep and enforceable obligations, as they usually call on the states to establish mere cooperation activities (*see* China's environmental agreements). On the other hand, SPS chapters and, to a certain extent, GATS *plus* provisions in the areas of public health and environmental services can make RTAs a powerful means to safeguard NTCs as long as a real implementation of obligations occurs at the national level. In addition to these considerations, it must be noted that, in general, ASEAN uses PTAs to promote social development more than China.

Despite the correctness of these observations, China's efforts towards the inclusion of NTCs should be appreciated. China seems interested to conform its national and international policies to the ideal of sustainable development. Important indications in this sense are offered by the central role of environmental protection in recent Five-Year plans.

The future avenues of ASEAN and Chinese PTAs are difficult to foresee. ASEAN future FTAs' efforts seem to be focused mainly on further integrating its member States in the

44 *See* China–New Zealand FTA, China–Singapore FTA, China–Chile FTA and China–Switzerland FTA. The complete text of the schedule of commitments is available at http://fta.mofcom.gov.cn/english/index.shtml.

45 Roadmap for an ASEAN Community 2009–2015, *supra* note 22, at 80.

46 *See* the 12th Five-Year Plan (2011–2015), unofficial translation by the Delegation of the European Union in China, http://cbi.typepad.com/china_direct/2011/05/chinas-twelfth-five-new-plan-the-full-english-version.html (last visited July 16, 2016). A summary of the 13th Five-Year Plan is available at http://www.china-un.org/eng/zt/China123456/ (last visited July 18, 2016). See also the summary prepared by APCO, 'China's 13thFive Year Plan' available at http://www.apcoworldwide.com/docs/default-source/default-document-library/Thought-Leadership/13-five-year-plan-think-piece.pdf?sfvrsn=2 (last visited July 21, 2016).

global economy and on the removal of non-tariff barriers to trade.[47] Against this background, it cannot however be excluded that social development will continue to play an important role in ASEAN upcoming RTAs plans. The situation of China is more unpredictable. The Chinese government has always entered into PTAs for geopolitical and economic reasons. This fact would explain the only partial attention given to sustainable development issues in Chinese RTAs. Whether this behavior is going to change in future FTAs is hard to say. However, the traditional Chinese flexibility in carrying on negotiations, combined with the fact that sustainable development is becoming an essential part of the country's economic planning, leaves open the possibility of new unexpected scenarios.

47 These priorities are spelled out in the new strategic document published by the ASEAN Secretariat and entitled 'Asean 2025: forging ahead together', http://www.asean.org/storage/2015/12/ASEAN-2025-Forging-Ahead-Together-final.pdf (last visited June 21, 2016), at 64 and 79.

29 Product Safety in the Framework of the WTO Agreement on Technical Barriers to Trade*

Lukasz Gruszczynski, Tivadar Ötvös, and Paolo Davide Farah

Introduction

In recent decades, the problem of product safety has become one of the main issues on the agendas of national regulators. All developed states and an increasing number of developing countries have adopted various comprehensive legal frameworks that detail specific safety requirements for industrial as well as agricultural goods. An example of such activities is the system for registration, evaluation, authorization, and restriction of chemical substances adopted by the European Union (EU) – the so-called REACH Regulation.[1]

Despite all the efforts, product safety scandals still occur. They relate not only to food products – such as melamine in dogs' pet food (2007) or in milk and infants' formulas (2008), both imported from China – but also to industrial goods.[2] For example, in 2007, the United States Consumer Product Safety Commission ordered a recall of 967,000 toys – mainly Sesame Street toys – produced in China by Mattel's Fisher Price, because some of their parts were coated with lead-based paint.[3] Two years later, another recall in the United States (US) covered 5.2 million Toyota cars with a problem related to accelerator pedals that

* This chapter is part of the results of the Research Project on "*Current Trends of Chinese Law towards Non-Trade Concerns such as Sustainable Development and the Protection of Environment, Public Health, Food Safety, Cultural, Social and Economic Rights, Labor Rights and the Reduction of Poverty from the Perspective of International Law and WTO Law*", coordinated by Professor Paolo Davide Farah at gLAWcal – Global Law Initiatives for Sustainable Development (United Kingdom) and at West Virginia University John D. Rockefeller IV School of Policy and Politics, Department of Public Administration, in partnership with the Center of Advanced Studies on Contemporary China (CASCC) in Turin (Italy), Maastricht University Faculty of Law, Department of International and European Law and IGIR – Institute for Globalisation and International Regulation (Netherlands), and Tsinghua University, School of Law, Institute of Public International Law and the Center for Research on Intellectual Property Law in Beijing (China). An early draft of this chapter was presented at the Conferences Series on "*China's Influence on Non-Trade Concerns in International Economic Law*", Third Conference held at Maastricht University, Faculty of Law on January 19–20, 2012. This publication and the Conference Series were sponsored by China–EU School of Law (CESL) at the China University of Political Science and Law (CUPL). The activities of CESL at CUPL are supported by the European Union and the People's Republic of China. The chapter reflects the TBT case law as of June 2016.

1 Regulation (EC) No. 1907/2006 of the European Parliament and of the Council of 18 December 2006 concerning the Registration, Evaluation, Authorisation and Restriction of Chemicals (REACH), OJ. L. 396, December 30, 2006, at 1–849.

2 For an analysis of product-safety related scandals in China, *see* Chapters 19 (Ning), 27 (Prevost), and 32 (Hu) in this volume.

3 *Notification of the US Consumer Product Safety Commission,* http://www.cpsc.gov/cpscpub/prerel/prhtml07/07257.html (last visited June 30, 2016).

tended to jam. The press reported 34 deaths in Toyota vehicles that may have been attributable to this defect.[4]

While product safety standards normally serve a legitimate interest of human and animal health protection, they can also constitute a serious barrier to trade.[5] As a consequence of the subsequent rounds of liberalization – including the one initiated in Uruguay – custom tariffs for industrial goods have been considerably reduced. Yet the benefits of trade liberalization could be easily undermined by the creation of internal barriers, which limit the access of foreign goods to national markets and/or considerably increase the costs of such access. In some instances, such internal barriers, including product safety rules, are motivated more by protectionism than real health concerns. A still debated example of such a controversial safety regulation (though more related to the specific Sanitary and Phytosanitary Measures due to its scientific basis – see the part regarding the applicability of the TBT agreement) could be the issue of banning the import of meat coming from animals given the feed additive ractopamine in several WTO Member States. Although limits have been established[6] and discussed by the SPS Committee several times[7], countries e.g. Russia, China among others still apply a "zero tolerance" regarding the access of such products on their market. The lift of these bans are currently under consideration[8], though their further application might lead to the use of the WTO Dispute Settlement Mechanism by the exporters such as the USA.[9] In other cases, national regulators may adopt technical standards that are irrational from the technical point of view or do not properly take into account their impact on exporting countries. It is a known fact that governments, when preparing safety standards, tend to be most responsive to the concerns of domestic industries. The World Trade Organization (WTO) law attempts to tackle these types of problems with the Agreement on Technical Barriers to Trade[10] (TBT Agreement) specifically designed to address national technical barriers to trade, including product safety requirements.

4 Peter Valdes-Dapena, *Toyota recalls top 5.3 million vehicles*, http://money.cnn.com/2010/01/27/autos/toyota_recall_expanded/index.htm (last visited June 30, 2016).

5 For similar considerations about the WTO SPS Agreement, *see* Chapter 27 (Prevost) in this volume.

6 See the international standards set by the *Codex Alimentarius Commission* based on the risk assessment of the Joint FAO/WHO Expert Committee on Food Additives (JECFA) creating guidelines for nations to use in developing national legislative provisions to provide consumers safe and wholesome food products. *Discussion On Ractopamine in Codex and in The Joint FAO/WHO Expert Committee on Food Additives (JECFA)* (April 26, 2012), http://www.fao.org/fileadmin/user_upload/agns/pdf/Ractopamine_info_sheet_Codex-JECFA_rev_26April2012__2_.pdf (last visited June 30, 2016). See also H. Bottemiller, *Codex Adopts Ractopamine Limits for Beef and Pork* (July 6, 2012), http://www.foodsafetynews.com/2012/07/codex-votes-69-67-to-advance-ractopamine-limits-for-beef-and-pork/#.V3Tj51efRok (last visited June 30, 2016).

7 WTO, *Committee Debates Pros and Cons of Standard for Lean Meat Additive* (June 30 & July 1, 2011), https://www.wto.org/english/news_e/news11_e/sps_30jun11_e.htm (last visited June 30, 2016).

8 DTN's Washington Insider, *A New Food Safety Scandal* (February 5, 2016), https://www.dtnpf.com/agriculture/web/ag/perspectives/columns/washington-insider/article/2016/05/02/new-food-safety-scandal (last visited June 30, 2016).

9 Related concerns have been raised in front of the SPS Committee during the meeting in March 2016 by the EU (against China) and Brazil (against the EU). See e.g. WTO, *New Trade Concerns Reviewed by WTO Committee on Food Safety and Animal/Plant Health*, (Mar 16 & 17, 2016), https://www.wto.org/english/news_e/news16_e/sps_16mar16_e.htm (last visited June 30, 2016); T. J. Centner, J. C. Alvey & A. M. Stelzleni, Beta Agonists in Livestock Feed: Status, Health Concerns, and International Trade, 92 (9) J Animal Science. 4234, 4234-240 (2014).

10 Agreement on Technical Barriers to Trade, April 15, 1994, Marrakesh Agreement Establishing the World Trade Organization, Annex 1A, 1868 UNTS 120 [hereinafter TBT Agreement].

The problem of product safety standards is particularly relevant for China. First, owing to the size of its economy and export – for example, it produces about 80 per cent of the toys worldwide, the majority of them for export – China is constantly confronted with various safety requirements in different jurisdictions, some of them probably being disguised protectionism. Second, due to the size of its export and relatively poor record in terms of product safety, China is frequently subject to restrictions based on human health concerns. Recent examples include the 2007 recall of toys due to excessive levels of lead, the 2009 recall of drop-side cribs due to entrapment and suffocation hazards, and the 2011 recall of infant girls' sandals due to a choking hazard. In the US alone, authorities issued 220 recalls of Chinese products in 2010[11] (but note that the number of recalls dropped from 348 in 2008). Third, China has progressively increased its own regulatory activities regarding product safety on its domestic market, but exporters have criticized some of these developments.[12]

This chapter discusses the basic obligations for national product safety regulations imposed by the TBT Agreement, and gives a general picture of the rules on technical standards that are applicable in the relations between China and its trading partners. The first section defines the scope of the agreement, while the second analyzes its specific requirements relevant to domestic product safety regulations. The last section concludes with some general observations on the functioning of the agreement. Due to the space limitations, this chapter should be regarded more as an introduction than a comprehensive analysis of existing legal obligations.

From the previous reasoning, it is evident that this chapter defines product safety rules quite broadly. They include provisions that aim at eliminating particular health risks – for example, by prohibiting particular chemical substances in some or all products – as well as provisions aimed at limiting their extent – for example, by setting specific thresholds for nicotine in cigarettes or by requiring certain safety devices in cars. In the second instance, a regulator may accept, for other reasons, a certain level of risk connected with the use of a product. Product safety rules also include informational requirements imposed on sellers or producers, such as various labeling obligations requiring them to disclose the composition of a product, provide instructions on its safe use, or indicate specific risks related to such use.

TBT Agreement: Defining its applicability

The TBT Agreement is one of the treaties adopted as a result of the Uruguay Round trade negotiations and currently constitutes a part of the WTO legal system. The aim of the agreement, as pronounced in its preamble, is to ensure that technical standards do not create unnecessary obstacles to international trade.[13] At the same time, the agreement recognizes that no WTO Member should be prevented from taking measures which are necessary for, among other things, the protection of human life or health at the levels it considers appropriate. This pronouncement is not absolute, since such measures cannot be applied in a manner that would constitute a means of arbitrary or unjustifiable discrimination or a

11 *U.S. official: Quality of Chinese products greatly improved* (August 8, 2011), http://news.xinhuanet.com/english2010/china/2011-08/08/c_131036551.htm (last visited June 30, 2016).

12 *See* TBT Committee, *Minutes of the Meeting March 24–25 2011, Note by the Secretariat*, G/TBT/M/53 (May 26, 2011).

13 TBT Agreement, Preamble, recital No. 10.

disguised restriction on international trade.[14] In other words, the agreement aims to limit the negative impact that national technical barriers may have on international trade, without however constraining Members from choosing whatever regulatory goals they deem appropriate. Consequently, it is concerned more with the design and rationality of specific measures than the reasonableness of the political choices that underlie them.

The TBT Agreement applies to those national measures that can be characterized as technical standards. This broad category is divided into three separate groups, each of them being subject to a distinctive – although similar – set of rules. In particular, the agreement distinguishes between technical regulations, standards, and conformity assessment procedures. The first group is defined as mandatory provisions that determine product characteristics or their related processes and production methods. This may concern not only the physical features of a product, but also relate to terminology, packaging, or labeling requirements for products or their production methods.[15] Standards are understood as documents, approved by a recognized body, which set specific rules, guidelines, or characteristics for products or production methods. However, contrary to technical regulations, standards are of a voluntary nature[16] and their fulfillment is not a formal condition for placing a product on the market.[17] Conformity assessment procedures are practices "used, directly or indirectly, to determine that relevant requirements in technical regulations or standards are fulfilled."[18] In other words, such procedures are applied to guarantee the effective implementation of substantive requirements (whether mandatory or voluntary).

The most important category for the purposes of this chapter is technical regulations. In the contemporary world, the problem of product safety is predominantly addressed through norms that are of a mandatory nature, issued either directly by governments or by special public agencies. Standards, on the other hand, are more concerned with ensuring the quality of products – such as their ability to fulfill the customer's needs and expectations – or the technical compatibility of different devices, other than their safety.[19] This difference results from the assumption that all goods available on the market should be safe in the first place, while the question of their quality is left, in principle, to market operators (and constitutes an important element of competitive advantage). As mentioned above, conformity-assessment procedures are of an ancillary nature. They do not impose any substantive product safety requirements – for example, as to the chemical composition or specific production method – but regulate the processes that are used to ensure that a product meets certain requirements. Again, due to the limited size of this contribution, this category is not discussed here. Moreover, since product safety standards are adopted primarily at the national

14 *Id.*, recital No. 6.

15 *Id.*, Annex 1(1).

16 *Id.*, Annex 1(2).

17 Note, however, that in practice standards may have a serious impact on trade. If economic operators on the market (including ultimate consumers) require compliance with such standards, failure to observe them may actually foreclose a market to outsiders. *See* Peter Van den Bossche, The Law and Policy of the World Trade Organization. Text, Cases and Materials 807 (Cambridge University Press, 2010).

18 TBT Agreement, Annex 1(3).

19 There are also, of course, standards that address safety issues. A good example is the US Standard Specification for Volatile N-Nitrosamine Levels in Rubber Nipples on Pacifiers (ASTM F1313–90). Safety standards may also aim for a higher level of protection than that provided by mandatory technical regulations. Nevertheless, technical regulations remain the most important category when it comes to product safety.

(central) level, the TBT provisions relating to local and non-governmental bodies are also left outside of this analysis.

Technical standards should be conceptually distinguished from sanitary and phytosanitary (SPS) measures.[20] The latter category refers to those measures that are adopted in order to address certain specific risks, based on scientific principles and tangible scientific results[21] including risks to human life or health connected with foods and beverages. Even though SPS measures are a type of technical standards, owing to their specificity, they are controlled exclusively by the SPS Agreement,[22] and the two agreements remain mutually exclusive.[23] It is the type of measure, which determines whether it is covered by the TBT Agreement, but the purpose of the measure is relevant when determining whether a measure is subject to the SPS Agreement.[24] As a result, national food and feed-safety measures, including labeling, can be analyzed only under the SPS Agreement. Note, however, that this does not mean that the TBT Agreement is only relevant for industrial products (as far as their safety is concerned). It also applies to those agricultural goods that, although intended for human consumption, cannot be classified as food or beverages. A good example is tobacco and its derivatives (for example, snuff).[25]

Specific product safety requirements

As previously mentioned, the TBT Agreement recognizes that WTO Members have the right to adopt and enforce technical regulations relating to product safety which are aimed at any level of protection deemed appropriate by that Member. Hence, the WTO does not require its Members to lower standards or to give a preference to trade over health concerns. Having said that, Members are expected to observe a number of principles established by the agreement. Below is an overview of these requirements.

Definition of a technical regulation

WTO case law has identified three criteria that need to be met in order to qualify a specific national measure as a technical regulation.[26]

20 For a detailed analysis of SPS measures related to product safety as well as to public health concerns, *see* Chapter 27 (Prevost) in this volume.

21 Christiane R. Conrad, *PPMs, the EC-Biotech Dispute and Applicability of the SPS Agreement: Are the Panel's Findings Built on Shaky Ground?*, Research Paper No. 8-06, International Law Forum of the Hebrew University of Jerusalem Law Faculty (August, 2006), http://ssrn.com/abstract=920742 (last visited June 30, 2016). See also Article 2.2 of the Agreement on Sanitary and Phytosanitary Measures, April 15, 1994, Marrakesh Agreement Establishing the World Trade Organization, Annex 1A, 1867 UNTS 493.

22 Agreement on Sanitary and Phytosanitary Measures, *supra note* 21.

23 WTO case law provides a very interesting analysis of the relationship between those two agreements. For example, the panel in *EC – Biotech Products* held that a single measure can serve two distinctive (SPS and TBT) purposes; in such a case, the SPS and TBT aspects of a measure should be examined separately under the respective agreement. *See* Panel Report, *European Communities – Measures Affecting the Approval and Marketing of Biotech Products*, WT/DS291/R, WT/DS292/R, WT/DS293/R, Corr.1 and Add.1, 2, 3, 4, 5, 6, 7, 8 and 9, ¶¶ 7.165–67 (November 21, 2006).

24 WTO, *Understanding the WTO Agreement on Sanitary and Phytosanitary Measures* (May 1998), https://www.wto.org/english/tratop_e/sps_e/spsund_e.htm (last visited June 30, 2016).

25 In fact, one of the recent TBT disputes relates to the ban on the importation and marketing of clove cigarettes, instituted by the US. *See* Panel Report, *United States – Measures Affecting the Production and Sale of Clove Cigarettes,* WT/DS406/R (September 2, 2011) [hereinafter *US – Clove Cigarettes*].

26 The WTO Agreements Series, Technical Barriers to Trade 14 (World Trade Organization, 2014).

First, it must target one or more characteristics of a product (such as composition, flammability, shape, and hardness), which may be expressed either as a positive obligation (a product must have a specific attribute) or a negative prohibition (a product cannot have a certain feature). Typical product safety rules will include: a) requirements relating to specific shapes and sizes of toys intended for small children (in order to prevent swallowing); b) prohibition of certain specific chemical substances in products (to prevent allergenic reactions or development of cancer); and c) requirements concerning the flammability of fabrics. Product safety rules may also prescribe information characteristics related to products, such as means of identification (e.g. safety labels providing specific instructions).

Second, a technical regulation needs to be of a mandatory character, meaning that compliance with it is compulsory and does not depend on the decision of a specific market player. As noted above, the majority of national safety rules easily satisfy this condition.

Third, it must specify the product coverage – for example, products or group of products – that fall within its ambit. This coverage may be explicitly expressed – such as toys for children below the age of three – or more indirect – like a general ban on the use of asbestos fibers.[27]

National treatment and most-favored nation principles

Article 2.1 of the TBT Agreement provides a variation of two traditional GATT principles: most-favored nation and national treatment. In particular, it requires WTO Members, insofar as technical regulations are concerned, to accord no less favorable treatment to imported products as compared to like domestic products or such products imported from any other Member. An example of a measure that would violate the above obligation would be a law prohibiting, on safety grounds, the presence of specific chemical substances (such as benzyl cyanide) in toys imported from one specific country (such as China), without imposing such a restriction on domestic toys or toys coming from other WTO Members. Naturally, real-life cases are much more complex than this.

A crucial issue in the context of Article 2.1 is determining when two products can be regarded as "like." This was recently addressed in *US – Clove Cigarettes*, where the panel analyzed a very specific type of product safety measure. The case concerned the US ban on the production and sale of flavored cigarettes (including clove cigarettes), with the exception of menthol versions. The aim of this prohibition was to reduce youth smoking by eliminating cigarettes that, by masking the regular taste of tobacco (which may be unpleasant for beginners), are particularly appealing to young people. Indonesia claimed, among other things, that the ban was discriminatory (Article 2.1) when compared to menthol-flavored cigarettes, as well as unnecessary (Article 2.2.). The standard approach to "likeness," under Article III:4 of the GATT 1994, which served as a model for the TBT provision, is to examine the competitive relation between the products under consideration. In doing so, four elements are normally considered: a) the property, nature, and quality of products (physical characteristics), which also include the existence of health risks; b) the end-uses of the products; c) consumer tastes and habits; and d) the tariff classification of products under examination.[28] Although the panel considered each of these elements, in the end it did not rely on

27 *See* Appellate Body Report, *European Communities – Measures Affecting Asbestos and Asbestos-Containing Products*, WT/DS135/AB/R ¶¶ 66–70 (April 5, 2001) [hereinafter *EC – Asbestos*]. *See* also Appellate Body Report, *European Communities – Trade Description of Sardines*, WT/DS231/AB/R ¶ 176 (October 23, 2002) [hereinafter *EC – Sardines*].

28 Appellate Body Report, *EC – Asbestos*, *supra* note 27, ¶¶ 101 and 113.

the competition-based approach to make its determination of the substitutability of the products under consideration. According to the panel, the analysis of likeness under Article 2.1 of the TBT Agreement needed to take into account the regulatory objective sought by the US (reduction of youth smoking).[29] In particular, the objective was deemed to affect the determination of what are relevant physical characteristics, as well as consumer tastes and habits. Ultimately, the panel found that clove and menthol cigarettes had to be regarded as like products (despite some physical differences and only partial substitutability). It looked at the properties of the two products, but also gave some additional weight to the fact that both contain an additive which produces a distinguishing flavor that reduces the harshness of tobacco (which goes to the heart of the objective underlying the US measure).[30] Similarly, when assessing consumer tastes, it chose young smokers and those susceptible to becoming smokers as a reference group (rather than smokers in general), identifying the foregoing as the target group of the US regulation.[31]

This type of analysis was labeled elsewhere as a regulatory context test. Thus, "what matters is not the positioning of those [products] in relation to each other within the market ('competition test'), but rather the factual support for the government's distinction between the two when taking regulatory action ('regulatory context test')."[32]

The consequences of such an approach may be potentially far-reaching. Two products may be physically quite different but pose the same risk that a particular domestic measure seeks to reduce or eliminate (for example, risk of cancer resulting from exposure to a chemical substance that may be present in different products). Hence, they may be determined to be "like." The opposite situation is also possible. Two products that on their face look very like – such as plastic and aluminum cups – can be nevertheless regarded as different in the context of a measure regulating specific end use – for example, whether they can be used safely in microwave ovens.[33] Thus, Article 2.1 may be read as containing a consistency requirement that obliges WTO Members to address similar regulatory situations (such as the same type of risk) in a coherent fashion. This resembles the obligation of Article 5.5 of the SPS Agreement, which also calls for relative consistency when regulating the same or similar SPS risks.[34] Yet, it remains to be seen, considering the lack of textual basis in the TBT Agreement, what are the limits of the panel's new approach.

29 Panel Report, *US – Clove Cigarettes, supra* note 25, ¶ 7.119. The panel based its finding on the absence of an equivalent provision to Article III:1 in the TBT Agreement and the differences in the textual context (such as a TBT preambular statement that no Member should be prevented from taking measures necessary for the protection of human health). The Appellate Body adopted its final Report on April 4, 2012, upholding the findings of the Panel (WT/DS406/AB/R).

30 *Id.*, ¶ 7.175.

31 *Id.*, ¶ 7.214. Note, however, that in another TBT case, the Appellate Body instructed panels to rely on the traditional GATT test of competitive relation stating that regarding competitiveness "[t]he relevant question is . . . whether "[t]he governmental intervention [i.e. the measure itself] affects the conditions under which like goods, domestic and imported, compete in the market within a Member's territory". – See Appellate Body Report, *United States – Measures Concerning The Importation, Marketing And Sale Of Tuna And Tuna Products*, WT/DS381/AB/RW (April 14, 2015) [hereinafter USA-Tuna and Tuna Products].

32 Nicholas DiMascio & Joost Pauwelyn, *Nondiscrimination in Trade and Investment Treaties: Worlds Apart or Two Sides of the Same Coin?*, 102(1) Am. J. Int'l L. 48, 81 (2008).

33 Panel Report, *US – Clove Cigarettes, supra* note 25, ¶ 7.245.

34 *See* generally, Lukasz Gruszczynski, Regulating Health and Environmental Risks under WTO Law. A Critical Analysis of the SPS Agreement 230–42 (Oxford University Press, 2010).

As far as less-favorable treatment is concerned, it is necessary to compare whole groups of like products (for example, imported v. domestic).[35] It is not enough to find simply that some imported products are treated less favorably than some domestic products. Second, a panel needs to enquire whether less-favorable treatment can be explained by factors or circumstances ***unrelated to the foreign origin of the product*** (if so, there will be no violation of Article 2.1). This was not the case in *US – Clove Cigarettes*, where the panel found that the main reason for excluding menthol cigarettes (like domestic products) was the potential costs that might be incurred by the United States. In other words, menthol cigarettes were excluded not because they were not a type of cigarette with a characterizing flavor that appeals to youth, but because of the domestic costs of banning them.[36] In sum, the 'competition test' based on the GATT 1994 (Article I:1 and III:4), and the 'regulatory context test' according to Article 2.1 of the TBT can be adequately considered in particular cases – within the same one, if the compliant points out inconsistency with both of the provisions of GATT and TBT.[37] On the other hand, when it comes to the relation of Article 2.1 of TBT and Article XX and its chapeau of GATT 1994, an independent consistency analysis of the object technical regulation needs to be carried out considering the specific terms and requirements of both WTO regulations.[38]

Necessity of technical regulations

The TBT Agreement prohibits the adoption of technical requirements with a view to or with the effect of creating unnecessary obstacles to international trade. As a consequence, technical regulations cannot be more trade-restrictive than is necessary in order to fulfill a legitimate societal objective (Article 2.2). The second part of the article ("technical regulations shall not be more trade-restrictive than necessary to fulfill a legitimate objective") elaborates on this requirement by setting up "a mechanism to determine what would be an 'unnecessary' obstacle to trade."[39] When assessing necessity, one also needs to take into account risks that may otherwise materialize.

The TBT Agreement enumerates various legitimate objectives that include, among other things, protection of human health and safety. Product safety regulations will qualify here – depending on the specific design of measures – as related to human health, human safety, or both. Note, however, that the list provided in Article 2.2 is not exhaustive and other regulatory goals may also be included.

The examination process to determine whether a technical regulation is more trade-restrictive than necessary to fulfill a legitimate objective consists of weighing a series of

35 Panel Report, *US – Clove Cigarettes, supra* note 25, ¶¶ 7.273–5, following the approach taken by the Appellate Body in *EC – Asbestos* (*see* ¶ 100). *Nota bene*, the comparison might focus on a single imported product's domestic treatment compared to all the other like products on a particular market, when it comes to applying the 'competition test' – See Appellate Body Report, *USA – Tuna and Tuna Products, supra note* 31.

36 Panel Report, *US – Clove Cigarettes, supra* note 25, ¶ 7.289.

37 See Appellate Body Report, USA – Tuna and Tuna Products, *supra note* 31.

38 See Appellate Body Report, European Communities — Measures Prohibiting the Importation and Marketing of Seal Products, WT/DS400/AB/R; WT/DS401/AB/R ¶¶ 5.3.4.3 (May 22, 2014) [hereinafter EC – Seal Products].

39 WTO: Technical Barriers and SPS Measures, Max Planck Commentaries on World Trade Law 218 (Rüdiger Wolfrum, Peter-Tobias Stoll & Anja Seibert-Fohr eds, Koninklijke Brill NV, 2007). *See* also Panel Report, *US – Clove Cigarettes, supra* note 25, ¶ 7.330.

factors, such as a measure's contribution to the attainment of the objectives pursued, the importance of the values at stake, and the restrictive impact of a measure on international trade.[40] The contribution to the attainment of objectives should be material, meaning that there needs to be a genuine relationship between the objective pursued and the measure (and not merely a marginal or incidental connection). The WTO case law also recognizes that protection of human health and safety is one of the most vital and important values.[41] This factor is significant and, in the case of product safety regulations, will usually weigh heavily in favor of the national measure under consideration. As far as the impact on trade is concerned, a strict ban will weigh against a measure, while milder restrictions – such as warning labels – may be easier to justify.

As a second step in the analysis, a preliminarily justified measure needs to be compared with possible alternatives. The aim of this determination is to establish whether there are less-restrictive measures that could provide an equivalent result (for example, assure the same level of health protection as the original measure).[42] One has to remember that only the means, not the regulatory objectives, are examined in this step. Consequently, a WTO Member cannot be forced to adopt a lower level of protection in order to minimize negative trade effects. This was well-captured by the panel in US – Clove Cigarettes when it explained that, "if an alternative means of achieving the objective [. . .] would involve greater 'risks of non-fulfillment,' this may not be a legitimate alternative", as well as in the EC – Seal Products, where the Appellate Body stated that, "in order to qualify as a "genuine alternative", the proposed measure must be not only less trade restrictive than the original measure at issue, but should also "preserve for the responding Member its right to achieve its desired level of protection with respect to the objective pursued."[43]

As a part of both examinations (necessity in the strict sense and the existence of alternatives), one has to consider available scientific evidence, technical information, and the intended end-uses of a specific product. This means that a measure that e.g. aims at the protection of human health and safety needs to be backed up with sufficient scientific evidence that demonstrates the existence of a genuine risk related to the product, and supports a finding that a regulation will be effective in reducing such a risk ("the complaining Member bears the burden of identifying possible alternatives to the measure at issue that the responding Member could have taken").[44] This does not go as far as the requirement of a scientific risk assessment provided by the SPS Agreement, but a mere discussion of potential health effects that falls short of rigorous scientific discourse would most likely be deemed insufficient.

In TBT practice, it is Article 2.2 that generates the majority of controversies. Lately for example the EU has raised concerns against South Africa regarding the requirement for seven different health warnings to be rotated during a twelve-month cycle, considering it an excessive burden and a potential technical barrier to trade, especially for small and medium

40 *See* Appellate Body Report, *Korea – Measures Affecting Imports of Fresh, Chilled and Frozen Beef*, WT/DS161/AB/R, WT/DS169/AB/R ¶ 164 (January 10, 2001); Panel Report, *US – Clove Cigarettes*, *supra* note 25, ¶ 7.379.

41 *See* Appellate Body, *Brazil – Measures Affecting Imports of Retreated Tyres*, WT/DS332/AB/R, ¶ 144 (December 17, 2007).

42 Panel Report, *US – Clove Cigarettes*, *supra* note 25, ¶¶ 7.418–9.

43 *Id.*, ¶ 7.424; Appellate Body Report, *EC – Seal Products*, *supra* note 37, ¶¶ 5.3.3.6..

44 Appellate Body Report, *EC – Seal Products*, *supra* note 37.

enterprises. The EU at the same time asked to share scientific evidence on the relationship between these new requirements and the fulfillment of a legitimate objective (e.g. protection of human health) by reducing the harmful consumption of alcoholic beverages.[45] Similar concerns are being constantly raised and discussed on regular TBT Committee meetings, the point of which is to resolve the issues directly between the Member States without DSM involvement (See further below).[46]

The TBT agreement and international standards

The TBT Agreement promotes the international harmonization of technical regulations, "(d)esiring [. . .] to encourage the development of [. . .] international standards and conformity assessment systems."[47] This approach rests on the assumption that harmonized rules will facilitate international trade by allowing companies to benefit from economies of scale – offering a single product that complies with a uniform set of technical standards in the various national markets[48] – and reducing the costs of regulatory compliance borne by the enterprises in different jurisdictions. These would include, for example, information costs (such as costs of learning about different regulatory requirements) and conformity assessment costs (such as costs of demonstrating compliance with different requirements of various jurisdictions).[49]

To this end, Article 2.4 provides that, when relevant international standards exist, WTO Members are obliged to use them as a basis for their technical regulations. Again, this obligation is not absolute – departure is possible if such standards would be an ineffective or inappropriate means for the fulfillment of legitimate objectives pursued by a Member (for example, because of varying climatic or geographical factors or fundamental technological problems). Interestingly, in the context of the TBT Agreement not only are adopted standards relevant, but the drafts of standards are pertinent if their completion is imminent.[50] One of the panels also explained that when examining a national measure under Article 2.4, the term "ineffective" should be understood as relating to the

45 TBT Committee, *Minutes of the Meeting 09–10 March 2016, Note by the Secretariat*, G/TBT/M/68, ¶ 2.2.2.3 (May 12, 2016).

46 Solutions require understanding the complaint and cooperation between the Member States in order to better understand domestic national regulations and their background reasons. See e.g.: Indonesia complaining about a Chinese policy "requiring exporters to submit custom clearance documents, such as phytosanitary certificates, quality certificates from government, SPPSNI (Chinese translation version) or SPPSNI (Indonesian/English bilingual version). In addition, the required documentation was costly and lengthy to complete. Indonesia recalled Article 2.2 of the TBT Agreement, which stated that Members shall ensure that technical regulations should not be prepared, adopted or applied with a view to or with the effect of creating unnecessary obstacle to international trade." The problems is currently being resolved between all the involved states via collaboration in order clarify the compliance of the particular policy with WTO rules. – TBT Committee, *Minutes of the Meeting 17–18 June 2015, Note by the Secretariat*, G/TBT/M/66 (September 17, 2015).

47 TBT Agreement, Recital No. 4.

48 Alan Sykes, *The (Limited) Role of Regulatory Harmonization in International Goods and Services Markets*, 2 J. Int'l Econ. L. 49, 55 (1999).

49 *Id.*, at 55–56.

50 Again this differs from the SPS Agreement, where the adoption of a standard is a condition *sine qua non* for its formal relevance.

results of the means employed, while "inappropriate" relates to the nature of the means employed.[51]

WTO case law has clarified that the obligation to base technical regulations on international standards implies a rather strong relationship between such regulations and standards.[52] Yet, some flexibility remains since the "basis for" test does not call for full conformity. At the same time, it is clear that the requirement indicates a substantive relationship between a standard and technical regulation. The fact that a WTO Member took a standard into consideration when enacting its regulation is definitely not sufficient.[53] In the context of product safety measures, it is also important to note that neither the TBT Agreement nor the case law enunciates whether a measure, in order to be considered as "based on," needs to reflect the same level of protection as that provided by a relevant standard. The language of the TBT Agreement seems more permissive in this regard than its SPS counterpart. Consequently, in principle one should not exclude the possibility that a measure may be still regarded as "based on" even if it aims for a different level of protection.

In case of a dispute, the burden of proof with respect to all the conditions enumerated above is on the complaining party.[54] This is the same approach as adopted under the SPS Agreement, where a complainant must make a *prima facie* case of inconsistency with standard-related provisions (Articles 3.1 and 3.3).

In order to encourage WTO Members to use international standards, Article 2.5 provides a rebuttable presumption of consistency with Article 2.2 ("presumed not to create an unnecessary obstacle to international trade"). A Member may take advantage of this presumption if two conditions are met: a technical regulation is adopted and applied in order to attain one of the legitimate objectives indicated by the agreement; and it simultaneously conforms to ("is in accordance with") relevant international standards. As mentioned above, human health and safety are explicitly identified in Article 2.2, so product safety regulations in principle can benefit from the presumption. As far as the second condition is concerned, note that it goes beyond a simple requirement to base measures on such standards. Consequently, a finding of compliance with Article 2.4 is not a finding that a particular measure does not create an unnecessary obstacle to international trade. On the other hand, since Article 2.5 provides for a higher threshold, conformity will also imply that a measure is based on international standards as required by Article 2.4.

Contrary to the SPS Agreement, TBT provisions do not enumerate specific organizations whose standards are relevant in its context. The agreement only refers to international (standardizing) bodies or systems and defines them vaguely as bodies or systems whose membership is open to the relevant bodies of at least all Members (thus, the list is open-ended).[55] Elaborating on this provision, the TBT Committee proposed a set of principles that should be followed when developing and adopting such standards.[56] These include transparency of

51 Panel Report, *EC – Sardines*, *supra* note 27, ¶ 7.116.

52 Appellate Body Report, *EC – Sardines*, *supra* note 27, ¶ 245.

53 *See* also Lukasz Gruszczynski, *supra* note 34, at 96–101 (discussing this requirement in the context of the SPS Agreement).

54 Appellate Body Report, *EC – Sardines*, *supra* note 27, ¶ 277.

55 TBT Agreement, Annex 1(4).

56 TBT Committee, *Decision of the Committee on Principles for the Development of International Standards, Guides and Recommendations with Relation to Article 2, 5 and Annex 3 of the Agreement*, G/TBT/1/

the standard-setting processes, open membership of the international standardizing bodies (on a non-discriminatory basis), impartiality in the process of developing standards, effectiveness and relevance for national regulatory needs, and coherence. Although it is not possible to precisely identify all product safety standard-setting organizations, two entities are the most important: the International Electro technical Commission (IEC), and the International Organization for Standardization (ISO).[57] China is a full member of both organizations. Standards adopted under the auspices of the World Health Organization may also be relevant.

Transparency

An important part of the TBT Agreement is dedicated to the improvement of transparency in the process of adopting technical regulations.[58] Members are expected to publish both a draft of a proposed regulation and its final version (Articles 2.9.1 and 2.11) and guarantee a reasonable *vacatio legis* (Article 2.14). This obligation is supplemented with notification requirements. According to Article 2.9.2–4, WTO Members need to notify (via the WTO Secretariat) other Members of any anticipated technical regulations, providing information on their content, product coverage, objectives, and rationale for such regulation, and grant other Members a reasonable period of time to make comments. The transparency obligations, however, are not absolute. They arise only if two conditions are met: a) there is no relevant international standard or the proposed technical regulation does not conform to such a standard; and b) the proposed technical regulation may have a significant effect on international trade. There is also a special simplified procedure for urgent matters relating, among other things, to health and safety (Article 2.10).

All notifications can subsequently become a subject for discussion in the TBT Committee, where WTO Members may formally raise their specific concerns. Interestingly, proposed product safety regulations have become the most important category of official notifications. For example, in 2015, there were 1989 national notifications of new or previously changed measures.[59] Not surprisingly, the next category also occupies first place when it comes to the discussions in the TBT Committee – between 1995 and 2015, 231 specific trade concerns (STC) related to human health and safety have been raised and deliberated upon at the meetings of the Committee (more than 40 per cent of the overall total).[60] The most STCs in general have been raised by the European Union, while China is currently the second among countries most frequently being subject to STCs.[61]

Rev.8, at 26–29. Note that the legal status of a decision of the TBT Committee remains uncertain. Although formally they are not binding, they may be relevant in the process of interpretation of the TBT provisions. For a more extensive discussion in the context of the SPS Committee, *see* Lukasz Gruszczynski, *supra* note 34, at 45–47.

57 It is estimated that the ISO and IEC together produce approximately 85 per cent of all international standards. *See* WTO, *World Trade Report 2005, Exploring the Limits between Trade, Standards and WTO* 76 (2005).

58 *See* Chapter 27 (Prevost) in this volume.

59 WTO, *Annual Report 2016 – Implementation and Monitoring* at 63, https://www.wto.org/english/res_e/booksp_e/anrep_e/anrep16_chap5_e.pdf (Last visited July 5, 2016).

60 TBT Committee, *Twenty-First Annual Review of the Implementation and Operation of the TBT Agreement, Note by the Secretariat*, G/TBT/38/Rev.1 (March 24, 2016), at 20.

61 China is second behind Ecuador, the country, against which record of 25 new STCs have been raised in 2015. See Id., 16.

Concluding remarks

The TBT Agreement constitutes an important part of the WTO legal regime, and it may be seen as an effort by the Members to further the objectives of GATT 1994. As far as product safety rules are concerned, the agreement clearly recognizes that no country should be prevented from taking measures necessary for the protection of human health and safety. At the same time, Members are expected to observe some specific requirements when enacting and applying technical standards. The agreement not only repeats some of the traditional principles of international trade law (sometimes rephrasing them), but also introduces a number of novelties as compared to the GATT 1994 regime (for example, harmonization and equivalence). From the domestic point of view, these rules are particularly important when it comes to product safety requirements, which are normally regarded as technical regulations.

Surprisingly, for a long time the TBT Agreement was somewhat unappreciated by Members. TBT disputes were rare, particularly in comparison to disputes under the SPS Agreement. As a consequence, the scope of Members' obligations and rights flowing from TBT provisions was uncertain. This obviously affected the predictability of the whole system and additionally discouraged Members from initiating disputes under the agreement (and could also have a chilling effect with respect on the adoption of some national measures). It was only 2011 that witnessed a proliferation of TBT controversies and led to decisions of the WTO dispute settlement bodies.[62] This increase should be welcomed because the incoming reports shed (and will shed) light on the normative content of the TBT provisions. One of the most interesting developments in the case law is probably the "regulatory context test" under Article 2.1, which requires taking into account the objective of a domestic measure in a "like products" analysis.

In contrast, the TBT Agreement, so far, has probably been more successful as a dispute prevention mechanism. In this context, the central role is played by the TBT Committee, which provides a convenient platform for discussions among WTO Members. Practice shows that countries tend to take into consideration concerns raised by other Members, which obviously reduces the potential for future trade disputes. The technical nature of the discussion also allows the TBT Committee and its Members to depoliticize (at least in some cases) trade controversies. The EU REACH Regulation, a comprehensive product safety measure, may serve as a good example. Its initial draft was heavily criticized by a number of WTO Members, including China, which saw the new EU law as constituting a serious trade barrier to its industry. In response to this criticism, the EU introduced a number of changes and launched different initiatives to help its trading partners adapt to the new legal framework (such as publication of guidance materials, provision of technical assistance, or initiation of other forms of capacity-building for industry from developing countries).[63] Although a number of concerns still remain, the regulation in its present form appears to be more adapted to the expectations of other WTO Members.

62 These are: *US – Clove Cigarettes*, *US – Tuna and Tuna Products*, *United States – Certain Country of Origin Labelling (COOL) Requirements*.

63 *See* Lukasz Gruszczynski, *Chemicals (REACH)*, in RESEARCH HANDBOOK ON THE TBT AGREEMENT (Michael Trebilcock & Tracey Epps eds, Edward Elgar, 2013).

30 Non-Trade Concerns and Consumer Protection in China

Surrounding Issues*

Piercarlo Rossi

Consumerism and international trade: Interactions between two global phenomena

Most countries, including the People's Republic of China (PRC), regulate consumer protection; however, diversified sets of rules concerning different areas of law exist in each jurisdiction: contract and tort law, administrative regulations for goods and services provided to consumers, criminal liability of companies for the misconduct of their agents towards consumers, as well as procedural rules aimed at promoting access to justice for individual consumers and the organizations that represent them, and at entrusting administrative authorities with the task of educating consumers. Those rules that govern the relationship between the distribution of goods and services, on the one hand, and citizens' rights, on the other, may be based on several other justifications in addition to consumer protection. Two phenomena support the idea that many legal orders have enacted a consolidated consumer law, autonomous from other legal disciplines.

The first phenomenon concerns what has been called a change in the contract design. The internationalization of trade and liberalization of national economies have fostered the worldwide spread of the adhesion contract model to mass transactions. This model of contractual relationship is characterized by several parties beyond the business seller and final buyer, regardless of the nationality of either. These parties include sellers, intermediaries, and service providers throughout every step of the supply chain, from the producer to the end consumer. Moreover, every market may have several competitors within and without the same supply chain. On the one hand, through the influence of the main international trade players, primarily multinational companies and their lawyers, new types of

* This chapter is part of the results of the Research Project on "*Current Trends of Chinese Law towards Non-Trade Concerns such as Sustainable Development and the Protection of Environment, Public Health, Food Safety, Cultural, Social and Economic Rights, Labor Rights and the Reduction of Poverty from the Perspective of International Law and WTO Law*", coordinated by Professor Paolo Davide Farah at gLAWcal – Global Law Initiatives for Sustainable Development (United Kingdom) and at West Virginia University John D. Rockefeller IV School of Policy and Politics, Department of Public Administration, in partnership with the Center of Advanced Studies on Contemporary China (CASCC) in Turin (Italy), Maastricht University Faculty of Law, Department of International and European Law and IGIR – Institute for Globalisation and International Regulation (Netherlands), and Tsinghua University, School of Law, Institute of Public International Law and the Center for Research on Intellectual Property Law in Beijing (China). This publication and the Conference Series were sponsored by China–EU School of Law (CESL) at the China University of Political Science and Law (CUPL). The activities of CESL at CUPL are supported by the European Union and the People's Republic of China.

contracts are spreading, which are based on principles and practices transcending national laws and regulations, and whose identification and administration is devolved to organizations – such as international arbitration chambers – which do not fall under any individual country's jurisdiction.[1] This *lex mercatoria* wields a persuasive power on national legislation because of the growing interdependence between firms' strategies and domestic economic sectors involved in those activities. On the other hand, national jurisdictions try to restore the balance of contractual relationships in order to protect further interests. These might include citizens' welfare and protection of competition, which, from a domestic point of view, is often equivalent to the protection of domestic firms' productivity against the potential misconduct of foreign firms as well as foreign products that do not meet safety standards.[2]

The second phenomenon is a social movement, so-called consumerism, which developed in the twentieth century in the United States (US) and then spread to other countries. Consumerism "seek[s] to augment the rights and power of the buyers in relation to the sellers,"[3] where the latter are seen as the industrial persons who operate within the distribution of standardized goods and services.[4] The *Consumer Union*, born in the 1910s, gained attention by bringing issues related to misleading advertising, standardized contracts, and defective products before the US courts,[5] and these issues further influenced the US debate on regulatory policies aimed at consumer protection.[6] After the Second World War, the movement spread to Europe and, in 1947, the first consumer union was created in Denmark. Subsequently, France,[7] Germany,[8] Spain,[9] Sweden,[10] and the United Kingdom,[11] as well as

1 *See* The Practice of Transnational Law (Klaus P. Berger ed., The Hague, 2001); Filip de Ly, International Business Law and Lex Mercatoria (Emerald Group Publishing Limited, 1992).

2 Therefore, modern contract theory stands between contractual freedom and public policy. As for the European debate, *see* C. Joerges & G. Brüggemeier, *Europäisierung des Vertrags- und Haftungsrechts*, in Gemeinsames Privatrecht in der Europäischen Gemeinschaft 233 (P. C. Müller-Graff ed., Baden-Baden, 1993).

3 *See* Philip Kotler, *What Consumerism Means for the Marketers*, Harv. Bus. Rev. 35 (May–June 1972). *See* Consumerism: The Eternal Triangle 67 (Barbara B. Murray ed., Goodyear Publishing, 1972).

4 For a detailed analysis of this issue, *see* the divergent opinions of Daniel Miller, Material Culture and Mass Consumption (Wiley-Blackwell, 1987); Don Slater, Consumer Culture and Modernity (Polity, 1998); The Business of Consumption: Environmental Ethics and the Global Economy (Laura Westra & Patricia H. Werhane eds, Rowman & Littlefield, 1998).

5 *See* Robert N. Mayer, The Consumer Movement: Guardians of the Marketplace (Twayne Publishers, 1989); Norman I. Silber, Test and Protest: The Influence of Consumers Union (Holmes & Meier, 1983).

6 *See* Lizabeth Cohen, A Consumer Republic: The Politics of Mass Consumption in Postwar America (Random House Digital, 2003).

7 The *Loi Scrivener* (January 23, 1978) established information rights and consumer protection. Gunnar Trumbull, Consumer Capitalism: Politics, Product Markets, and Firm Strategy in France and Germany (Cornell University Press, 2006).

8 The 1976 *Allgemeinen Geschäftsbedingungen Gesetz* created general conditions of contract.

9 In 1978, a constitutional provision (Article 51) expressly provided for the protection of consumers. *See* The Politics of Consumption: Material Culture and Citizenship in Europe and America (M. Daunton & M. Hilton eds, Berg Publishers, 2001).

10 In 1971, the *Ombudsman* was created in Sweden, becoming the model for the ombudsmen adopted in other jurisdictions.

11 The government passed the 1974 Consumer Credit Act and the 1977 Unfair Contract Terms Act. *See* Matthew Hilton, Consumerism in Twentieth-Century Britain: The Search for a Historical Movement (Cambridge University Press, 2003).

some South American countries,[12] adopted legislative and administrative measures related to consumer protection. The movement then went global, and consumer unions started to appear throughout the world. Recently, the unions have broadened the notion of the consumer itself, including not only buyers but workers as well, since they participate in mass-production processes.[13]

The "global" success of open markets and consumerism leads us to consider the laws and regulations adopted in different jurisdictions under the profile of consumer protection, within the parameters provided for by the two aforementioned phenomena.[14] However, if we analyze the provisions aimed at protecting consumers in the different jurisdictions from a strictly legal point of view, we see a quite uniform tendency when it comes to identifying those contractual and economic relationships that make consumers more vulnerable in the abstract. Nonetheless, as far as the remedies available to protect consumers, several discrepancies still remain.[15] These situations mainly relate to disproportionate bargaining power in favor of entrepreneurs conducting mass transactions, information asymmetry – presumably against consumers, especially when it comes to specific contractual terms – as well as imperfections in the production/distribution chain of goods and services for final consumers.

In the legal literature, there are not consistent doctrines concerning the balance between provisions aimed at protecting competition and markets and those solely designed to protect consumers. The main differences appear between those provisions that accept only a limitation to the freedom of contract in order to overcome the information asymmetry and those that promote a large limitation of the freedom of contract in order to compensate for the economic disadvantages of consumers against corporations.

Given these differences, it is of great interest to analyze how consumer protection laws may create an exception to the principles of international free trade, if not an obstacle. It is clear that inadequate consumer protection laws will likely lead to distorted competition because those players who take advantage of price competition at the expense of quality will

12 The 1975 Mexican federal regulation is the oldest one. We can also include, among others, the 1990 Brazilian Consumer Protection Code, the 1990 Ecuadorian Law of Consumer Protection, and the 1992 Venezuelan Consumer Protection Act. *See* Robert G. Vaughn, *Consumer Protection in South America,* 17 HASTINGS INT'L & COMP. L. REV. 275 (1994).

13 The development of the consumer movement was not, and is still not, happening without crises or contrasts due to the existence of many different views. For an overview, *see* MICHAEL PERTSCHUK, REVOLT AGAINST REGULATION: THE RISE AND PAUSE OF THE CONSUMER MOVEMENT (Berkeley, 1982); STEVEN MILES, CONSUMERISM – AS A WAY OF LIFE (Sage, 1998); CONSUMERS AGAINST CAPITALISM? CONSUMER COOPERATION IN EUROPE, NORTH AMERICA AND JAPAN, 1840–1990 (Ellen Furlough & Carl Strikwerda eds, Rowman & Littlefield, 1999).

14 *See* Allison Coleman, *Trends in the Development of Consumer Protection Law,* 5(1) INT'L J. CONSUMER STUD. 63 (2007). The idea of a one-and-only concept of consumer protection is widespread among international organizations officials as well as among non-governmental organizations activists. *See* AKIRA IRIYE, GLOBAL COMMUNITY: THE ROLE OF INTERNATIONAL ORGANIZATIONS IN THE MAKING OF THE CONTEMPORARY WORLD (University of California Press, 2002).

15 Not even the regulatory initiatives of those European countries that first supported consumer demands have ever been coordinated on this matter, which is why consumer protection was later harmonized through Community actions. Some jurisdictions prefer an administrative control approach (which may be either under government control, such as the British Fair Trading, or independent, like the Swedish system); other jurisdictions opt for a general legal framework, while other options include a hybrid of these two main approaches or even self-regulation in the hands of economic players. Moreover, a country can opt either for a different approach, according to the relevant sector (as happens in the French system), or for a horizontal approach (like in the German system).

tend to marginalize those who adopt higher standards. From a domestic perspective, market welfare increasingly tends to connect competition and consumer protection; the rules on unfair competition are the most obvious example. However, it is not clear whether this reasoning applies to the international context, where the authorities that regulate the market operate from different countries, and it is not always easy to assess whether rules aimed at consumer protection are actually designed to favor consumers rather than national businesses over foreign competitors,[16] playing with an equal, or maybe even superior, quality-price ratio. The Chinese example of this matter is extremely helpful.

Consumer law in China

The introduction to the provisions aimed at consumer protection in China correlates, at least as far the first provisions are concerned, to the country's transition towards a socialist market economy. The PRC used legal reforms to progressively transform the economy in order to attract foreign investment and foster economic growth.[17] After the PRC's accession to the World Trade Organization (WTO) in 2001, the consumer market entered a new phase, which required the government to review its laws and policies: it was necessary to protect, on the one hand, foreign consumers through the export of safe products and, on the other, Chinese consumers against business strategies and contractual relationships with foreign companies. Chinese laws on product quality[18] were mostly considered inadequate by the US and the European Union (EU) to protect their consumers, especially for food and toys.[19] At the same time, the PRC often discussed the public perception about the inadequacy of Chinese laws to protect even its own consumers.[20]

16 For a description of how the general exceptions of Art. XX of the GATT can be often misused as justifications for disguised restrictions on international trade in violation of the WTO core principles, *see* Chapter 2 (Farah) in this volume. Regarding public health as a potential tool for protectionist purposes, *see* Chapters 27 (Prevost) and 28 (Di Masi) in this volume. For similar considerations regarding products safety and technical standards as serious barriers to trade rather than rational and legitimate instruments for the protection of human and animal health, *see* Chapter 28 (Gruszczynski, Ötvös & Farah) in this volume. For an analysis of how measures aimed at protecting the environment and addressing climate change might as well become disguised restrictions on trade, *see* Chapter 8 (Sindico & Gibson) in this volume.

17 *See* Dorothy J. Solinger, *Economic Reform via Reformulation in China: Where do Rightist Ideas come from?*, 21(9) Asian Survey (1981). *See* also Paolo Davide Farah, *Five Years of China's WTO Membership: EU and US Perspectives on China's Compliance with Transparency Commitments and the Transitional Review Mechanism,* 33 Legal Issues of Econ. Integration 263–304 (2006).

18 *See* Chapter 32 (Hu) in this volume.

19 In August 2007, the State Office for the Quality and Technologic Supervision adopted two regulations to recall certain food products as well as toys from the market. Such regulations try to better define the concept of defective products, based on the definition given by the 1993 Product Quality Law, as well as strengthen the inspection system and the control by independent experts. The adoption of progressively stricter regimes in the US, with the 2008 Consumer Safety Improvement Act, and in the EU, with Directive 2009/48/CE, affected China, which reacted by adopting a number of regulations consistent with such higher standards. As it regards the quality of Chinese products, as well as food and toys scandals that occurred in China, *see* Chapters 19 (Ning), 27 (Prevost), 29 (Gruszczynski, Ötvös & Farah), and 32 (Hu) in this volume.

20 One of the cases that most influenced national public opinion was raised by a number of Chinese citizens who, after buying certain defective Toshiba products, obtained assistance but were not refunded, while in the US consumers managed to reach an extrajudicial settlement for compensation. *See* Mary Ip, *Consumer Protection in China: An Examination of the Toshiba Notebook Case from an Australian Perspective,*

In the transition from a planned to a market economy, the progressively adopted provisions reflected the relationship between industrial production, fixed contracts, and consumer protection in very distinct ways. As a result, the PRC created a broad array of remedies, which encompass civil and criminal law, as well as civil, administrative, and criminal procedural law. Relevant provisions exist at the national, regional, and provincial levels, in both laws and regulations. The PRC passed the 1993 Law of the People's Republic of China on Protection of Consumer Rights and Interests[21] and the 1993 Product Quality Law[22] (revised in 2000) as part of the legislative reform of financial relationships. Other reforms inspired general rules like the 1986 General Principles of the Civil Law[23] and the 1999 Contract Law,[24] as well as those of sectoral rules, whose design changed over time, such as the 1982 Trademark Law[25] (revised in 1993 and 2013), the 1984 Patent Law[26] (revised in 1993, 2000, and 2008), the 1990 Copyright Law,[27] the 1993 Anti-Unfair Competition law,[28] and the 1994 Advertising Law.[29] In addition, since 1993, the PRC has adopted many laws concerning companies, banks, and State-Owned Enterprises (SOEs).[30]

The 1993 Law of Protection of Consumer Rights and Interests and the Product Quality Law were adopted during a phase characterized by a growing attention towards western models according to the instrumentalistic approach, aimed at increasing China's international credibility. Therefore, such approach is no longer limited to the regulation of the economy in relation to foreign countries, as it was in the 1980s. At the same time, these two laws address issues arising from the growth of the domestic market as well as from the need to protect Chinese consumers by channeling the growing awareness of their rights in a way

2(1) Asian J. Comp. L. (2007), at Art. 5. For a description of the legal protection granted to consumers in developing countries from an Asian perspective, *see* also Chapter 31 (Prasad) in this volume.

21 Zhōnghuá Rénmín Gònghéguó Xiāofèi Zhě Quányì Bǎohù Fǎ (中华人民共和国消费者权益保护法) [Law of the People's Republic of China on Protection of Consumer Rights and Interests] (Promulgated by the Standing Comm. Nat'l People's Cong., October 31, 1993, amended October 25, 2013).

22 Zhōnghuá Rénmín Gònghéguó Chǎnpǐn Zhí Liáng Fǎ (中华人民共和国产品质量法) [Product Quality Law of the People's Republic of China] (Promulgated by the Standing Comm. Nat'l People's Cong., February 22, 1993, effective September 1, 2000, amended in 2000).

23 Zhōnghuá Rénmín Gònghéguó Mínfǎ Tōngzé (中华人民共和国民法通则) [General Principles of the Civil Law of the People's Republic of China] (promulgated by the Nat'l People's Cong., April 12, 1986, effective August 27, 2009).

24 Zhōnghuá Rénmín Gònghéguó Hétóng Fǎ (中华人民共和国合同法) [Contract Law of the People's Republic of China] (Promulgated by the Nat'l People's Cong., March 15, 1999).

25 Zhōnghuá Rénmín Gònghéguó Shāngbiāo Fǎ (2013 Xiūzhèng) (中华人民共和国商标法 (2013修正) [Trademark Law of the People's Republic of China (2013 Amendment)] (Promulgated by the Standing Comm. Nat'l People's Cong., August 30, 2013).

26 Zhōnghuá Rénmín Gònghéguó Zhuānlì Fǎ (2008 Xiūzhèng) (中华人民共和国专利法 (2008修正) [Patent Law of the People's Republic of China (2008 Amendment)] (Promulgated by the Standing Comm. Nat'l People's Cong., December 27, 2008).

27 Zhōnghuá Rénmín Gònghéguó Zhùzuòquán Fǎ (2010 Xiūzhèng) (中华人民共和国著作权法 (2010 修正) [Copyright Law of the People's Republic of China (2010 Amendment)] (Promulgated by the Standing Comm. Nat'l People's Cong., February 26, 2010).

28 Zhōnghuá Rénmín Gònghéguó Fǎn Bú Zhèngdàng Jìngzhēng Fǎ (中华人民共和国反不正当竞争法) [Anti-Unfair Competition Law of the People's Republic of China] (Promulgated by the Standing Comm. Nat'l People's Cong., September 2, 1993).

29 Zhōnghuá Rénmín Gònghéguó Guǎnggào Fǎ (中华人民共和国广告法) [Advertising Law of the People's Republic of China] (Promulgated by the Standing Comm. Nat'l People's Cong., October 27, 1994).

30 *See* Eugene Clark, ***Consumer law and economic development in the PRC: overview and brief commentary,*** 4 Canberra L. Rev. 125 (1997).

that allows their harmonic expression, together with the government's overall objectives for the economic and social development of the country.[31] The Product Quality Law is far more specific and underwent a major revision in 2000, followed by minor improvements starting in 2002.[32] It relates to an extremely important aspect of the Chinese economy: the under-determination of the provisions of the Product Quality Law could have had serious consequences for the sale of Chinese products.

Therefore, the Chinese government decided to conform to the major disciplines found in other jurisdictions, in order to facilitate access to foreign markets.[33] With an eye to international trade barriers, based on Non-Trade Concerns (NTCs), it is interesting to see how Chinese laws actually function. As a matter of fact, the Product Quality Law is the result of the compromise between two different legal inspirations, the oldest of which is strictly Chinese. Until the mid-1980s, problems related to product quality were solved through the adoption of technical disciplines, often at the administrative level, aimed at the standardization, supervision, and authorization of a variety of industrial products.[34] The sectoral nature of these measures belonged to the planned economy,[35] and they did not link quality control to the economic effects caused by the manufacturer of shoddy goods. Obviously, the government's aim to maintain high productivity levels together with the fact that manufacturers belong to the public sector did not encourage the introduction of a liability system for producers.

The situation changed during the second phase of the consumer revolution, when the government decided to adopt a regulation introducing a liability system for industrial producers. Article 122 of the 1986 General Principles of the Civil Law sets out the general principles of liability for both producers and sellers, when a substandard product causes damage to property or persons.[36] However, since Article 122 applies in combination with the Product Quality Law, it is important to understand the scope of Articles 40 and 46 of the Product Quality Law. Article 40 (contractual liability) states that the parties shall agree upon the standard of quality, while Article 46 (torts) requires that the parties not consider the defect if the product meets national standards and standards of public business, when available.[37] Obviously, the fulfillment of legal obligations represents an exemption in other jurisdictions as well. However, the frequent use of standards has actually created a problem for the PRC because of the prolific standardization criteria adopted previously. Too many standards have persisted, without update, at different levels of the Chinese state structure.

31 For similar reasoning, *see* Chapter 31 (Prasad) in this volume.

32 *See* Gary Zhao, *Chinese Product Liability Law: Can China Build Another Great Wall to Protect Its Consumers?*, 1 Wash. U. Global Stud. L. Rev. 581 (2002).

33 *See* Han Li, *The Product Quality Law in China: A Proper Balance between Consumers and Producers?*, J. Chinese & Comp. L. 1 (2003).

34 Edward J. Epstein, *Tortious Liability for Defective Products in the People's Republic of China*, J. Chinese L. 285 (1988). For an analysis of the strategies that justify standardization, *see* Katharina Pistor, *The Standardization of Law and Its Effect on Developing Economies*, 50(1) Am. J. Comp. L. 97 (2002).

35 *See* Frederick R. Burke, *The Administrative Law of Standardization in the PRC*, 1 J. Chinese L. 271 (1987).

36 *See* Donald B. King & Gao Tong, Consumer Protection in China: Translations, Developments, and Recommendations 45 (Littleton, 1991).

37 This situation did not change with the adoption of a broader framework for product liability introduced by the 2009 Tort Liability Law of the People's Republic of China, which specifically did not change the sector regulations.

Analyzing the other provisions of the Product Quality Law, we can see that it is not a harmonious conjugation of a public regulatory system of product safety with a private system of responsibility,[38] but rather a mere combination of the two systems, without identification of the areas of influence and overlap. The lack of a liability regime for independent certifiers of product safety (Article 14) clearly illustrates the problem. Although the 2000 amendments to the Product Quality Law addressed this oversight and rearranged the competent authorities, the issue remains that the public inspectorate that monitors manufacturers lacks the necessary staff to compensate for the producers' poor knowledge of technical specifications.[39]

Non-Trade Concerns and consumer protection in China: The relationship between law and economy

Consumer protection can also be found in sectoral legislation, such as consumer credit, investment services, and private insurance, where it is possible to identify needs addressing different types of interests.[40] As far as China is concerned, it may be useful, rather than dwelling on individual disciplines, to look at the national economic regulation as a whole, since it is where legal policies that might sacrifice consumer protection in favor of other interests originate.

The relationship between market and State is not only influenced by its economic development stage or its laws, such as in the field of consumer protection. As a matter of fact, the counterbalance between consumers and businesses, as well as State enterprises, depends on the country's leading socio-economic policy.[41]

Perhaps, one of the shortcomings of the study of legal reforms concerning the Chinese market is the tendency to attribute all the observed phenomena to one single explanatory scheme, according to which there exists a set of rules. For example, because consumer protection laws are widespread among advanced economies, emerging countries, like China, should simply adapt. It is argued that because globalization applies external pressure on national enterprises and the national authorities responsible for monitoring the market, the international market will eventually regulate the national state, rather than simple national regulation of the market. Therefore, international rules on consumer protection will ultimately and inevitably prevail since Chinese consumers will demand the same standards that

38 *See* Susan Rose-Ackerman, *Tort Law as a Regulatory System: Regulation and the Law of Torts,* 81 American Economic Review, Paper and Proceedings 54 (1991); Steven Shavell, *Liability for Harm versus Regulation of Safety,* 13 J. Legal Stud. 357 (1984); Paul Burrows, *Consumer Safety Under Products Liability and Duty to Disclose,* 12 Int'l Rev. L. & Econ. 457 (1992).

39 Actually, beyond the law, in the field of product quality, many authorities exist at different levels of the national hierarchy. The problem was raised especially as far as food safety is concerned. *See* Waikeung Tam & Dali Yang, *Food Safety and the Development of Regulatory Institutions in China*, 4 Asian Perspective 5 (2005).

40 On the other hand, the legislation on direct selling is exclusively designed for consumer protection. On August 23, 2005, the Administration of Direct Selling Regulation was adopted and entered into force on December 1, 2005. At the same time, a regulation prohibiting pyramid selling was also adopted. A sale is directed towards a consumer when it takes place away from a fixed retail location. Since 1998, Chinese authorities had prohibited both domestic and foreign firms from "direct selling," as a reaction to the frauds that took place through the "pyramid scheme." Financial requirements, such as deposits as well as professional requirements were then introduced for direct selling.

41 *See* Wladyslaw B. Sztyber, *Market and State in Times of Globalisation,* 12 Eur. J. L. & Econ. 145 (2001).

the government itself will finally adopt, in order to compete with not only international products but the best legal systems as well.[42]

Apart from the fact that there is no agreement on the parameters of efficiency and distributive justice to assess the best standards and rules, these remarks do not take sufficiently into account the specific features of the Asian region China belongs to.[43]

China evaluates the competitive advantage of certain sectors not only based on the economic structures of the US and EU, but also on China's Asian neighbors, its local competitors. First of all, considering the geographical distribution of the world's population rather than per capita income, the East Asian region appears a substantially more promising consumer market than advanced Western economies. Moreover, foreign investors and consumers may prefer China's Asian neighbors if their regulatory frameworks generate higher standards of safety and reliability. Finally, one should not underestimate the cultural element, at least for those neighboring countries that were most influenced by Chinese thought.[44]

Undoubtedly, consumer law could be one of those areas where political rhetoric can justify certain choices by stressing the fact that those choices do not reflect the government's will but rather the necessity to satisfy unique, widespread cultural needs. For example, one could argue that the structure created for consumer protection through the China Consumers' Association (CCA) reflects the traditional Chinese spirit, which prefers that the government coordinate, at least to some extent, certain individual initiatives in order to pursue the public interest. Lacking any external evaluation criteria with respect to the political debate, and given the impossibility of any historical counterevidence, it is only by an evaluation of the effectiveness of CCA instruments that we can discuss the ability to reform the protection system.[45]

A move towards a bottom-up system of aggregating consumers' concerns, provided with effective injunctive powers, might be inadvisable because of China's diversity. It could lead to counterproductive consequences.

We can therefore study the legal policies pursued by China and its neighbors as well as consumer behavior throughout Asia, which can be determined by certain aspects of their state structures and economic development patterns, but also by broader cultural aspects.[46] The relationship between the regulation of consumer protection and the underlying social fabric has not developed equally in all Asian systems. Nevertheless, we can identify some common features shared by different Asian countries as far as both legal policies and social awareness are concerned.[47]

If we limit our analysis to the mutual influence on respective legal frameworks, it is possible to see that China belongs to a group of consumer protection models that grows in "circles" of increasing intensity. The first circle includes Taiwan, Singapore, and South Korea; the

42 *See* David K. Round & Zeljka Sporer, *Globalisation And Consumer Protection In East Asia: Is It A Zero Sum Game?*, Asian-Pacific Economic Literature 39 (2003).

43 *See* Chapter 31 (Prasad) in this volume.

44 *See*, on the necessity of avoiding easy generalizations at the cultural level, Chailhark Hahm, *Law, Culture, and the Politics of Confucianism,* 16 Colum. J. Asian L. 253 (2003). *See* also Chapter 6 (Vadi) in this volume.

45 On the effectiveness of remedies, *see* Gary Zhao, *supra* note 32, at 584.

46 Broadly speaking, consumers' lifestyle and culture deeply influence each other, as shown by Mike Featherstone, *Life Style and Consumer Culture,* 4(1) Theory, Culture, and Society 55 (1987). However, we are here dealing with a quite broader concept of culture: *see* Culture and Privilege in Capitalist Asia (M. Pinches ed., London, Routledge, 1999); Consumption in Asia: Lifestyles and identities (B. H. Chua ed., London, Routledge, 2000).

47 *See* Takao Tanase, *Global Markets and the Evolution of Law in China and Japan,* 27 Michigan J. Int'l L. 873 (2006).

second one includes all other emerging Asian countries, such as Thailand; the third and final circle groups advanced economies in the area, such as Japan, Australia, and New Zealand. On the other hand, in the field of consumer protection, the relationships between Russia and neighboring Central Asian countries are rather negligible. In the circle of greatest intensity, we should also include the administrative area of Hong Kong; the latter, because of legal developments prior to reunification, provides alternative legislative models to those existing in the motherland, even though it does not operate outside Hong Kong.[48] The neighboring countries, which have mostly adopted the models from advanced economies, affect China not so much in the way consumer protection laws are drafted, but rather in the way they are enforced, where these countries represent the comparative basis for China.

In China, provisions contained in a single law, such as the 1993 Anti-Unfair Competition Law, may cover aspects of unfair commercial practices which can only be executed by entrepreneurs, such as the case of blatant imitation of other people's products, or even aspects which, though harmful to consumers, do not create any real protection, such as the case of misleading advertising.

Moreover, the Chinese legal framework is fragmented into many different legal acts: in the field of misleading advertising, for example, there is, in addition to the aforementioned 1993 Anti-Unfair Competition Law, the 1994 Advertisement Law, which has a mixed approach. On the one hand, it establishes the rules of conduct for market operators and, on the other, maintains an authorization system based on technical and administrative standards.[49]

Unfair commercial practices are constantly evolving. Therefore, we should not rule out the possibility of future harmonization, in the Asian area of Chinese interest, of the modalities for the identification and prosecution of those actors engaging in practices harmful to consumers. At the moment, the problem mainly relates to Hong Kong, where many registered companies operate in a way that harms consumers living in mainland China, exploiting the lack of effective communication between the agencies responsible for consumer protection in China and Hong Kong.[50]

A growing number of scholars see cross-border cooperation to protect consumers as one of those issues that will promote regionalization in Asia within the context of globalization.[51] Nonetheless, in conclusion, we should probably stress one last aspect. The growing interdependence of national economies makes the ineffectiveness, within a jurisdiction, of control methods and remedies extremely dangerous for consumers in other jurisdictions. Similarly, social concerns related to NTCs might be treated differently within the WTO, compared to the EU or countries like China, considering the different underlying relationships between law and economy.

48 Already in 1988, the special zones of Shenzhen and Shanghai had introduced elements of the Hong Kong system: for example, in terms of negotiable instruments, it was noted that the *consideration* (daijia) to support the holder's title had been surreptitiously introduced, although most reforms adopted in China so far mainly looked at civil law. *See* Edward Epstein, *China's Legal Reforms*, in CHINA REVIEW 24 (H. C. Kuan & M. Brousseau eds, Hong Kong, Chinese University Press 1991).

49 *See* Gao Zhihong, *The Evolution of Chinese Advertising Law: A Historical Review*, 8(1) ADVER. & SOC'Y REV. (2007).

50 The Hong Kong Consumer Council was established in 1974 to meet temporary needs and was later turned into a permanent body. It is a governmental body, and it represents consumer interests and promotes consumer information. Therefore, it is not able to act quickly in relation to unfair commercial practices that might emerge from society.

51 *See* REGIONALIZATION IN A GLOBALIZING WORLD: A COMPARATIVE PERSPECTIVE ON FORMS, ACTORS, AND PROCESSESS (M. Schulz, F. Soderbaum & J. Ojendal eds, Zed Books, 2001).

31 Legal Protection of Consumers in Developing Countries

An Asian Perspective*

A. Rajendra Prasad

Consumers exist throughout the globe but encounter distinct problems depending on their country of residence. Diverse problems afflict each country; however, consumers in developing nations generally have the least protection. In most developed countries, stringent government policies, active consumer groups, responsible traders, effective laws, and vigilant judicial institutions contribute to healthy consumerism. In developing countries, to the contrary, social, economic, political, and legal problems undermine the issues faced by consumers. For a long time, they have been the most neglected group in most developing countries. As a matter of fact, consumer problems represent society's problems as a whole, including harsh realities and issues of human dignity.[1] The legal protection of consumers depends upon the milieu in which they live. In the developing world, problems experienced by consumers are manifold, surpassing the simple issue of buying and consuming.

The first part of this chapter outlines the problems of developing countries as far as consumer protection is concerned, with reference to non-trade issues. The second part highlights global trade and consumer interests in developing countries with special reference to India and China. The third part deals with the legislative attempts of various Asian countries to protect consumers' interests. The fourth and final part explores consumer protection through the Indian experience, which triggered a new legal revolution in India with informal dispute resolution.

* This chapter is part of the results of the Research Project on "*Current Trends of Chinese Law towards Non-Trade Concerns such as Sustainable Development and the Protection of Environment, Public Health, Food Safety, Cultural, Social and Economic Rights, Labor Rights and the Reduction of Poverty from the Perspective of International Law and WTO Law*", coordinated by Professor Paolo Davide Farah at gLAWcal – Global Law Initiatives for Sustainable Development (United Kingdom) and at West Virginia University John D. Rockefeller IV School of Policy and Politics, Department of Public Administration, in partnership with the Center of Advanced Studies on Contemporary China (CASCC) in Turin (Italy), Maastricht University Faculty of Law, Department of International and European Law and IGIR – Institute for Globalisation and International Regulation (Netherlands), and Tsinghua University, School of Law, Institute of Public International Law and the Center for Research on Intellectual Property Law in Beijing (China). This publication and the Conference Series were sponsored by China–EU School of Law (CESL) at the China University of Political Science and Law (CUPL). The activities of CESL at CUPL are supported by the European Union and the People's Republic of China.

1 *See* Chapter 17 (Heurtebise) in this volume.

Consumers in developing countries and causes for legal deprivation with reference to non-trade issues

About 80 per cent of the world's population lives in developing countries, popularly called the Third World during the 1970s and 1980s,[2] "marked by low income and high poverty, high unemployment and low education."[3] The economic strength of a country is judged in terms of its development. According to a report of the United Nations Development Programme (UNDP), trade fosters development,[4] and development leads to growth. In the process of market-related growth, both developed and developing economies should consider the legal necessity to protect consumers, who are the ultimate targets of all economic decisions. It is rightly remarked that "[t]rade can and will take place with and in a society that does not observe the rule of law, but that society will have to pay a price for not observing the rule of law."[5] However, the strength of any legal framework depends on the rights of consumers, who act as the partners and promoters of trade. In fact, consumers are weakened by the problems that developing countries confront in the process of governance. The following are some of the factors that impair the enforcement of basic consumer rights in matters of non-trade issues in the developing world.

Consumers in developing countries are not economically strong enough to assert their rights.[6] Poverty deprives the developing world's consumers of free choice and forces them to accept unfair conditions. "Poverty" can be defined as the inability to attain a minimal standard of living[7] or in terms of the deprivation of sufficient consumption.[8] Despite these attempts to define poverty, it is a complex concept and cannot be marked by a single indicator. Any attempt to define it should take into account several criteria such as income, assets, education, nutrition, class or caste, and access to certain public services.[9] These indicators are very important from a consumer's perspective.

Nearly half of the developing world's poor, and nearly half of those in extreme poverty, live in South Asia. About one-third of the population of Sub-Saharan Africa is poor, and Middle Eastern and North African countries have the new highest poverty rates. They are followed by Latin America, the Caribbean, and East Asia.[10] Despite some Asian countries that are well developed, like Japan and South Korea, many failings explain the widespread poverty throughout Asia:[11] population growth, caste discrimination, inadequate provisions for education, insufficient medicine, and problems of land ownership. The poor suffer from

2 The countries that are lagging behind in matters of their growth are labeled "third world." Perhaps the most appropriate terms to use are "developed" and "developing." *See* John Cole, Development and Underdevelopment: A Profile of the Third World 5 (Routledge, 1987).

3 Joseph E. Stiglitz, Making Globalization Work 26 (W.W. Norton & Company, 2006).

4 UNDP, Human Development Report 9 (2005).

5 Lord Woolf, The Pursuit of Justice 410 (Christopher Campbell-Holt ed., Oxford University Press, 2008).

6 On the legal empowerment, *see* Chapter 5 (Choukroune) in this volume.

7 Gerald M. Meier & James E. Rauch, Leading Issues in Economic Development 18 (7th ed., Oxford University Press, 2004).

8 IFAD, *Rural Poverty Report 2001 – The Challenge of Ending Rural Poverty,* at 19.

9 Jacques Loup, Can the Third World Survive? 110 (John Hopkins University Press, 1983).

10 Meier & Rauch, *supra* note 7, at 19.

11 *World Poverty – A look at Causes and Solutions* (October 2, 2011), http://world-poverty.org/povertyinasia.aspx (last visited July 18, 2016).

the most severe effects of poverty, and "often lack adequate food and shelter,[12] education and health, deprivations that keep them from leading the kind of life that everyone values. They also face extreme vulnerability to ill health, economic dislocation, and natural disasters. And they are often exposed to ill treatment by institutions of the state and society and are powerless to influence key decisions affecting their lives."[13] The weight of poverty falls most heavily on certain social groups, such as women and children. Women account for 70 per cent of the world's poor, and children[14] are routinely deprived of adequate nutrition, health care, and education.[15] More than 98 per cent of the children who die each year live in poor countries.[16] Those living in poverty are denied access to services[17] and excluded from participating in decision-making processes while they are the victims of all sorts of exploitation.

In most developing societies, poverty is the root cause for social inequality.[18] Most developing countries are economically weak and inherited frail social infrastructures as an outcome of the colonial experience.[19] The incidence of poverty among socially disadvantaged groups such as ethnic groups and minorities like the indigenous peoples in Bolivia, Ecuador, Guatemala, Mexico, and Peru, as well as the scheduled castes in India, is exceedingly high.[20] Distributive justice is needed in matters of economic and social development. Pandit Jawaharlal Nehru, First Prime Minster of India, once said that "[i]f there is no proper distribution, no proper social justice, there will be conflicts on an enormous scale."[21] Poor consumers are no exception to social conflicts, and it is generally understood that "high levels of inequality will affect social cohesion and lead to problems such as increasing crime and violence."[22]

One of the major problems faced by developing countries in matters of legal protection is access to justice. The term "Access to Justice" is used to mean "improving the availability of fair, efficient, and meaningful justice for all courts users."[23] Consumers in some countries fail to approach the courts because of a "lack of legal information about dispute resolution options."[24] Moreover, court systems in many developing countries are poorly funded and

12 On the right to food, *see* Chapters 18 (Zorzi Giustiniani), 19 (Ning), and 20 (Simpson) in this volume. On the right to water, *see* Chapter 20 (Soprano) in this volume.

13 World Bank, ***World Development Report – Attacking Poverty*** 1 (2000/2001).

14 Regarding the legislation adopted by the Chinese government in favor of children, *see* Chapter 19 (Ning) in this volume.

15 MEIER & RAUCH, ***supra*** note 7.

16 UNDP, ***supra*** note 4 at 24.

17 Francesca Dagnino, ***Expanding Access to Justice in Africa: Experiences and Perspectives, in*** JUSTICE FOR THE POOR: PERSPECTIVES ON ACCELERATING ACCESS 419, 422 (Ayesha Kadwani Dias & Gita Honwana Welch eds, Oxford University Press, 2011).

18 Some economists argue that poverty is not the same as inequality, *see* MEIER & RAUCH, ***supra*** note 7.

19 Shrawan Kumar Singh, ***Globalisation and Developing Countries: Some Critical Issues***, in LIBERALIZATION IN INDIA: THE ROAD AHEAD 192, 200 (V.S. Jafa ed., New Century Publications, 2001).

20 MEIER & RAUCH, ***supra*** note 7.

21 ATTAR CHAND, NEHRU AND NEW ECONOMIC ORDER – ECONOMIC JUSTICE AND REGIONAL DEVELOPMENT Vol. II 67 (H.K. Pub. & Distributors, 1990).

22 Anup Shah, ***Causes of Poverty*** (October 22, 2011), http://www.globalissues.org/issue/2/causes-of-poverty (last visited July 18, 2016).

23 Interim Report on Access to Justice Initiatives in the Trial Court, 7(January 8, 2010).

24 Ayesha Kadwani Dias & Gita Honwana Welch, ***Introduction,*** in JUSTICE FOR THE POOR: PERSPECTIVE ON ACCELERATING ACCESS xv, xvi (Ayesha Kadwani Dias & Gita Honwana Welch eds, Oxford University Press, 2011).

equipped, and mechanisms for enforcing judgments are often weak.[25] It is recognized worldwide that delay, cost, and complexities constitute the main threat to the civil justice system. For many, especially the poor, access to courts may still be a last resort.[26] Interestingly, in the last 20 years, the courts of a number of countries "dramatically expanded the circumstances in which the poor and oppressed sectors of society can approach them."[27] For example, Public Interest Litigation (PIL)[28] is an innovation of Indian judicial liberalism that has transformed the rule of standing. The courts of several other countries including Bangladesh, Pakistan, and Sri Lanka soon followed.[29] It is true that "lack of access to justice limits the effectiveness of poverty reduction and democratic governance programs by limiting participation, transparency and accountability."[30]

Globalization may bring some of the following new institutional innovations to society: market, trade and finance, communication and media, technology and science, migration, and intercultural transactions.[31] In the Millennium Declaration,[32] governments agreed that globalization, which is "driving ever-increasing interaction among the world's people," should act as a positive force for all.[33] From a consumer's point of view, it has already provided greater access to international markets, meaning wider choice, which is one of the basic consumer rights. For instance, one can buy an Indian mango in the United States and an American apple in India. At the global level, a simple integrated system for an effective dispute redressal mechanism, which is approachable and accessible to all, remains absent. There is a necessity to think about the legal interests of "individuals" rather than of the "State." It is certainly true that "world problems need to be brought down to the level of individuals, the actual people who are the 'disinherited'."[34]

The world's population explosion is the root cause for many problems because the increasing number of consumers naturally disturbs economic activities. It is said that if the "population were to multiply unhindered at the existing rate, there would be so many people living by 3700 AD that the weight of humanity would be greater than the weight of the planet itself!"[35] It is interesting to note that, at present, 60 per cent of people above 60 years old live in developing societies. By the third decade of the twenty-first century, this figure will rise to 70 per cent.[36] However, India has the advantage of a relatively large size of working-age population. On the other hand, some East Asian countries, like Japan, South Korea, and China, are experiencing a decline in the number of young people, which forecasts a shortage

25 World Bank, *supra* note 13, at 104.

26 CHRI's Millennium Report – *Human Rights and Poverty Eradication – A Talisman for the Commonwealth* 78 (2001).

27 *Id.*, at 79.

28 On Public Interest Litigation in China, *see* Chapter 3 (Choukroune) in this volume.

29 *Id.*

30 UNDP, Access to Justice, Practice Note 3 (March 9, 2004), http://www.unrol.org/files/Access%20to%20Justice_Practice%20Note.pdf (last visited July 16, 2016).

31 Yogendra Singh, Cultural Change in India: Identity and Globalization 50 (Rawat Publications, 2002).

32 UN General Assembly, United Nations Millennium Declaration, GA Res. 55/2 (September 18, 2000).

33 Human Development Report, 12 (2004).

34 John Hill, The Disinherited – Social and Economic Problems in the Undeveloped Countries 30 (Benn, 1970).

35 *Id.*, at 48.

36 CHRI's Millennium Report, *supra* note 26, at 14.

of young and energetic human capital in near future, which will have an adverse effect on their economies, indirectly affecting the interests of consumers.

Most developing countries also face problems of corruption in their governance. Corrupt governments often deprive the poor of their rights and deny them access to economic and social welfare.[37] It is pertinent to note that most Asian societies prioritize values over material development,[38] and the concept of consumer protection is no exception.

Global trade and consumers' interests in developing countries, with special reference to India and China

It is universally recognized that all countries, particularly developing countries, must integrate with the world economy since it is considered an engine of economic growth. In the era of globalization, developing countries realized the importance of the multilateral trading system and have shown a keen interest to accede to the World Trade Organization (WTO) in order to participate in free and fair trade.[39] One of the key objectives of the WTO is to help developing countries benefit fully from global trading. Developing countries immensely benefit from rule-based and multilateral trading liberalization; however, in the process, they must safeguard the interest of consumers, the promoters of trade. From the consumers' point of view, globalization has given access to new products and markets. Multinational Corporations (MNCs) enter into the markets equipped with global market strategies that present tough competition to domestic entrepreneurs. Of course, the MNCs create competitive environments that lead to comparative advantages.[40] It is rightly said that, "[t]here is a broad consensus that consumers should welcome competition – in a competitive environment, firms are compelled not only to produce desirable goods and services in the most efficient manner, but also to allocate them at the right quality and price if they are to survive. Competition policy is therefore of benefit to consumers in promoting competitive or 'fair' markets [. . .]."[41] The benefits of globalization outdo the disadvantages, and now nearly all countries favor global trade via the WTO. Globalization has raised many consumer issues, and the WTO is expected to play a dominant role in safeguarding them.[42] Some of the areas in need of protection, especially in the developing world, include the following: health, environment, social standards, preservation of biodiversity, genetic engineering applications, intellectual property rights, food security,[43] and unfair trade practices.[44]

37 *Id.*, at 29.

38 Subodh Dhawan, *Value-based Societies*, YOJANA 33 (2008).

39 Regarding the accession to the WTO as an important tool to foster liberalization and to promote free and fair trade, *see* Chapter 2 (Farah) in this volume.

40 On Multinational Corporations and the key role played by corporate social responsibility and corporate accountability to balance both competitiveness and fair trade, *see* Chapter 4 (Bonfanti) in this volume.

41 Consumer Policy and Multilateral Competition Frameworks: A Consumers International Discussion Paper 2003, 7 (January 10, 2012), http://www.wto.org/english/tratop_e/dda_e/symp03_ci_disc_paper.pdf (last visited July 18, 2016).

42 Regarding Multinational Corporations and the risks for the host country connected to Foreign Direct Investments, *see* Chapters 6 (Vadi) and 7 (Klaver & Trebilcock) in this volume.

43 For an analysis of food security issues, *see* Chapters 20 (Simpson), and 19 (Ning) in this volume.

44 On health protection, environment, and social standards, see the contributions of this section of the book such as Chapters 27 (Prévost) and 32 (Hu). On intellectual property rights and other related matters affecting the civil society including also the category of the consumers, *see* Chapters 34 (Feng, Shu & Zhang), and 36 (Nie).

Undoubtedly, developing countries play a crucial role in the global trading system; a number of developing countries rank in the list of top 20 exporters. In fact, the accession to the WTO by China[45] and India, large and emerging economies, greatly strengthened the world economy since they are major trading nations. India is a founding member of the General Agreement on Tariff and Trade (GATT) and WTO. India and China recently emerged as leaders in global trade relations,[46] and it is aptly said that, "China has emerged as a leading destination for foreign direct investment, and India is emerging as a leading destination for outsourcing of business processes by global investors."[47] By its accession, China, the second-largest economy in the world, is expected to bear international trade obligations for global prosperity. The role of China and India in the WTO is commendable in the sense that their participation in the multilateral trading system and the economic reforms which they implemented, as developing countries, makes them economically sound to face the challenges of the recent global economic crisis.

India and China exhibit several similarities on the economic front such as developing their foreign economic relations to promote their own economic growth, large domestic markets, and so on. Referring to China's economic capabilities, it is observed, "China is dependent on foreign capital and foreign markets. But China has also emerged as a world economic power, a center of world manufacturing. It has accumulated vast foreign exchange reserves, and gained considerable financial leverage-increasingly over the dollar. It is more aggressively seeking markets in the third world and exporting capital beyond it borders."[48] Chinese scholars attribute "India's sustainable growth and development [. . .] to many factors such as relatively high investment efficiency, dynamic private enterprise, a relatively healthy financial system and a young labor force with sizeable educated segment."[49] The advantages of these countries help them withstand global economic imbalances: "Asia continues to perform well, with China and India leading the world growth rates during the crisis, in spite of the global contagion."[50]

On the recent occasion marking China's ten years of accession to the WTO, Pascal Lamy, Director-General of the WTO remarked that "China has been and should remain important for the WTO. The WTO has been and should remain important for China."[51] Trade growth and consumers' interests are inseparable in the sense that increased trade strengthens the economy, and a robust economy enables the people (consumers) to acquire comfortable living conditions. Effective economic policies, impressive trade growth, and a strong legal

45 Paolo Davide Farah, *Five Years of China's WTO Membership: EU and US Perspectives on China's Compliance with Transparency Commitments and the Transitional Review Mechanism*, 33 Legal Issues of Econ. Integration 263–304 (2006).

46 Emilian Kavalski, India and Central Asia: The International Relations of a Rising Power (I.B. Tauris, 2009).

47 Rajalaxmi Kamath, *China and India: What Do Their Business Firms Have to Say, in* Economic Reforms in India and China: Emerging Issues and Challenges 191 (B. Sudhakara Reddy ed., Sage Publications India Pvt. Ltd., 2009).

48 Raymond Lotta, *China's Rise in the World Economy,* XLIV (8) Econo.& Pol. Wkly 29, 33 (2009).

49 Yang Dali and Zhao Hong, *The Rise of India: China's Perspectives and Responses, in* Socio-Political and Economic Challenges in South Asia 47, 53 (Tan Tai Yong, ed., Sage Publications India Pvt. Ltd, 2009).

50 Y. V. Reddy, Global Crisis, Recession and Uneven Recovery 54 (Orient Black Swan Pvt. Ltd., 2011).

51 Pascal Lamy, *A new chapter in China's reform and opening* (January 11, 2012), http://www.wto.org/english/news_e/sppl_e/sppl211_e.htm (last visited July 18, 2016).

framework mark a nation's well-being.[52] All three factors characterize the economies of India and China, and, having gained the strength to confront global economic challenges, they now have the responsibility to strive for an international legal framework, with the support of international institutions, that protects the interests of global consumers.[53]

Some Asian laws on consumer protection

Asia, the world's largest continent, is home to more than 60 per cent of the world's current population, and, by 2030, is expected to represent the largest group of consumers in the world. Consumer protection is the subject of concern in most Asian countries, and governments have enacted necessary legislation to protect consumers' interests. Some Asian consumer protection laws, such as those of the Philippines and Turkey, are comprehensive to include all the different problems faced by consumers. Most Asian countries realized the need to provide consumers with simple, speedy, and inexpensive justice and included built-in dispute settlement mechanisms in their consumer protection laws. Some Asian countries recognized only the rights of consumers, while others, interestingly, specified their responsibilities too. Notably, legal measures to protect consumers in most Asian countries were initiated following international pressure imposed by the United Nations Guidelines on Consumer Protection in 1985. On the contrary, consumer movements in developed countries were well advanced by then. The growth of trade unionism and the introduction of socialist ideas contributed to the development of the consumer movement in the United Kingdom, while in the United States, the evolution of the modern consumer movement stemmed from several literary works.[54] However, consumer movements in developing countries, particularly Asian countries, grew out of the bedrock of the fight against exploitation by mighty traders, socio-economic conditions, and the legal deficiencies of consumer protection. In course of time, most Asian legal systems extended legal protection to their consumers. An outline of some major Asian laws on consumer protection will be now presented.

China has enacted stringent laws to protect the interests of consumers.[55] It enacted the 1994 Law on Protection of Consumer Rights and Interests[56] (amended in 2013) to protect the lawful rights and interests of consumers, and to promote sound development of the socialist market economy. Declaring that the protection of consumers' rights and interests is the common responsibility of the whole society, operators shall, in providing consumers with commodities or services, fulfill their obligations in accordance with the provisions of the 1993 Product Quality Law of the People's Republic of China,[57] (amended

52 Gianmaria Ajani, *Legal Change and Economic Performance: An Assessment*, *in* Asian Constitutionalism in Transition: A Comparative Perspective 281–305 (Groppi Tania, Piergigli Valeria & Rinello Angelo eds, Giuffré Editore, 2008).

53 The necessity for an international legal framework is not limited to the interests of global consumers, but it is true also for all the other Non-Trade Concerns.

54 Such literary works include Upton Sinclair's *The Jungle*, which depicted the deplorable conditions in the Chicago meat packing industry as well the unstinted efforts of Ralph Nader.

55 *See* Chapters 30 (Rossi) and 32 (Hu) in this volume.

56 Zhōnghuá Rénmín Gònghéguó Xiāofèi Zhě Quányì Bǎohù Fǎ (中华人民共和国消费者权益保护法) [Law of the People's Republic of China on Protection of Consumer Rights and Interests] (Promulgated by the Standing Comm. Nat'l People's Cong., October 31, 1993, amended October 25, 2013).

57 Zhōnghuá Rénmín Gònghéguó Chǎnpǐn Zhí Liáng Fǎ (中华人民共和国产品质量法) [Product Quality Law of the People's Republic of China] (Promulgated by the Standing Comm. Nat'l People's Cong., February 22, 1993, effective September 1, 2000, amended in 2000). *See* Chapter 32 (Hu) in this volume.

in 2000) and other relevant laws and regulations. The Japan 2000 Consumer Contract Act protects the utmost interests of consumers by imposing a duty on business operators to draft clauses in consumer contracts to ensure the rights and duties of consumers. Consumer rights and the general duties of business are embodied in the 2005 Consumer Fundamental Act of Japan. The Consumer Protection Act, B.E.2522 (1979) in Thailand, which recognizes many consumers' rights, provides consumers with effective protection against defective goods and deficiencies of services. Singapore passed the Consumer Protection (Fair Trading) Act 2003 to protect consumers against unfair practices. Courts, including Small Claims Tribunals, have the power to decide cases under the Act, which was amended in 2008. The Consumer Protection Act of Philippines R.A.7394 (1992) is comprehensive legislation that protects the best interests of consumers from various problems. The highlight of this legislation is the appointment of arbitration officers. The 2003 Sri Lanka's Consumer Affairs Authority Act is intended to establish a Consumer Affairs Authority (CAA) and to provide for better protection of consumers through the regulation of trade and prices of goods and services and to protect traders and manufacturers against unfair and restrictive trade practices. In Maldives, the government passed the 1996 Consumer Protection Act to protect consumers' rights, and states that traders and service providers shall not, while trading or providing a service, engage in any unfair or discriminatory practice. Pakistan's capital passed the Islamabad Consumer Protection Act in 1995 to promote and protect the interests of consumers, and it became a model for the provinces to follow. The Act prohibits false advertisements, and the hallmark of the legislation is the establishment of a Consumer Protection Council with wide powers. The 1999 Consumer Protection Act in Indonesia guarantees the rights of consumers; the Act prohibits unfair or deceptive practices and regulates the use of standard clauses in consumer agreements. The Nepalese Consumer Protection Act, 2054 (1998), protects consumers from irregularities concerning the quality, quantity, and prices of consumer goods or services. In India, the Consumer Protection Act was passed in 1986 to provide easy access to consumer justice.

Some consumer groups or Non-Governmental Organizations (NGOs) work to protect consumers' rights in developing countries. In China, the China Consumers' Association (CCA) is a registered national organization funded by government subvention and donations that protects consumer interests by supervising the quality of commodities and services.[58] The Consumers Union of Japan (CUJ) is a politically and financially independent NGO founded in April 1969 as Japan's first nationwide grassroots consumer organization. It was officially certified as a nonprofit organization in 2006. The Consumer Association of Singapore (CASE) is an NGO launched to protect and promote consumers' interests through the spread of information and education; it also advocates the importance of fair and ethical trade practices. In India, the consumer movement became a significant phenomenon in the 1990s, and today many consumer groups work to protect consumers' rights and promote consumer education throughout India.[59]

58 China Society for Human Rights Studies, *Protecting the Rights and Interests of Consumers* (October 19, 2011), http://www.humanrights-china.org/zt/protectinginterestsofconsumers/200602006310144400.htm (last visited July 18, 2016).

59 *See* generally, D. N. Saraf, Law of Consumer Protection in India (N. M.Tripathi Pvt. Ltd. 1990); A. Rajendra Prasad, *Historical Evolution of Consumer Protection in India: A Bird's Eye View,* 11(3) J. Tex. Consumer L. 132 (2008).

Consumer protection and the Indian experience

In India, the consumer jurisprudence dates back centuries, but the consumer movement originated recently.[60] In ancient India, during the *Vedic* period,[61] consumer protection was an issue of great importance.

Consumers in India differ from consumers in other systems because the Indian society consists of a heterogeneous group based on different social, geographical, and economic considerations. The culture and social unity of India has long been recognized in studies on caste, family, and rural communities – the three basic social institutions in India.[62] It has been estimated that there are 2,000 or 3,000 castes (or sub-castes, as they are sometimes called),[63] 4,635 communities, and 325 languages spoken by various communities in India. There are commonalities of cultural traits, rituals, beliefs, and customs.[64] Interestingly, the majority of consumers in India are rural since "India is the land of villages."[65] It is common in villages to organize "weekly markets" (*Shandis*) where rural consumers are exploited.

Indian consumers have great institutional support to resolve their disputes. Contrary to the traditional justice system, the present consumer law in India provides a flexible dispute settlement mechanism. The 1986 Consumer Protection Act grants access to consumer justice. A group of consumers having a common interest can file a case, and a three-tier dispute settlement mechanism is constituted at the district, state, and national levels to resolve the disputes with informal procedures that require a case to be disposed of within a set period of time. The Supreme Court of India hears the final appeal, if any. In short, the present consumer law has undoubtedly considered the economic and social realities of consumers and attempted to provide simple consumer justice. In addition to this legal remedy, "*Lokadalats*" (People's Courts) in India were constituted under the 1987 Legal Service Authority Act to enable parties to settle amicably, and "Permanent *Lokadalats*" were established to entertain general complaints against the public utility services. A new legal effort seeks to constitute "*Gramanyayalayas*" at the village level to provide "instant" justice at the local level, particularly in rural India. A separate Ministry of Consumer Affairs protects consumer interests at the national level and initiates programs to promote consumer education among millions of ignorant and indifferent consumers.

The number of pending cases in different consumer courts in India indicates the public support for the informal dispute settlement mechanism under the Consumer Protection Act. As of July 17, 2016, the total number of cases pending in different consumer fora in India was 395,261.[66] What more is needed to confirm the consumers' faith in the present consumer dispute resolution system in developing countries like India?

60 Gurjeet Singh, *The Problem of Consumer Protection in India: A Historical Perspective,* 3 Consumer Prot. Rep. 704, 719 (1994).

61 5,000 BC to 2,500 BC.

62 Yogendra Singh, *supra* note 31, at 43.

63 Marc Galanter, Competing Equalities – Law and the Backward Classes in India 8 (Oxford, 1984).

64 Yogendra Singh, *supra* note 31, at 46.

65 L. S. S O' Malley, India's Social Heritage 100 (International Publications Service, 1976).

66 National Consumer Disputes Redressal Commission – Statistics, http://ncdrc.nic.in/ (last visited July 17, 2016). There were 10,354 cases pending in the National Commission; 98,389 in State Commissions; and 286,518 in District Fora.

Conclusions

Consumers in developing countries face many problems, but the governments have initiated legal measures to protect consumers' rights. Poverty presents a particular challenge to developing countries, but too often the governments deprive the poor of access to all benefits. Social inequality also afflicts developing countries, denying equal opportunities to all, and gender discrimination makes women consumers more vulnerable to all types of exploitation. Generally, market mechanisms reflect the consumption culture of a particular community and the cultural influences of consumers' behavior. Consumers in developing countries find it difficult to access traditional courts for various reasons even though access to justice is a basic human right.

In the era of globalization, global trade has the capacity to strengthen developing countries economically, and WTO accession may generate further trade flow. China and India have greatly benefited from the multilateral trading system and emerged as global leaders in the world economy. In addition to its objective to promote global trade, the WTO has undertaken the responsibility to protect the general interests of global consumers. As important emerging economies with newfound power, India and China should adjust their trade and economic policies to maximize their influence for the good. It is true that consumers have gained access to the global market without effective access to a global legal network. However, consumer law ends up being nothing but a legal exercise without social relevance. Asian countries enacted laws taking into account consumers' economic and social problems, and some of these laws effectively provide various legal remedies to consumers. For example, Indian consumer law, which is based on ancient legal foundations, has taken note of contemporary society and introduced a flexible legal mechanism to make the regime more consumer-friendly. Irrespective of legal protection, Indian society attaches great importance to its value system(s), like any Asian society, and therefore, it has incorporated these values as part of consumer education. India advocates "*vasudhaiva kutumbakam*" ("the whole world is one family") to inculcate a global spirit among all consumers.

32 From Remedy of Damage to Risk Prevention

An Analysis of the New Legislative Implications of the Chapter on "Product Liability" in China's Tort Liability Law from the Perspective of Consumer Protection*

Junhong Hu

Introduction

The Tort Law of the People's Republic of China,[1] (hereinafter Tort Law) which was enacted on December 26, 2009 and came into effect on July 1, 2010, provides for "Product Liability" in a particular chapter as a special kind of tort liability. Article 45 provides that "[w]here the defect of a product endangers the personal or property safety of another person, the victim shall be entitled to require the producer or seller to assume the tort liabilities by removing the obstruction or eliminating the danger." Article 46 stipulates that "[w]here any defect of a product is found after the product is put into circulation, the producer or seller shall promptly take appropriate remedial measures such as warning and recall. The producer or seller who causes any damage by failing to take remedial measures in a timely manner or by taking insufficient or ineffective measures shall assume the tort liability." These two provisions reflect the trend of modern tort liability laws, which emphasize taking preventive action against damages before they happen, thus embodying renewed legislative principles. This chapter will analyze the significance of these new legislative concepts based on the following aspects: a) the normative framework of product liability before the enactment of the Tort Law; b) the system of product liability and the legal regulations of product

* This chapter is part of the results of the Research Project on "*Current Trends of Chinese Law towards Non-Trade Concerns such as Sustainable Development and the Protection of Environment, Public Health, Food Safety, Cultural, Social and Economic Rights, Labor Rights and the Reduction of Poverty from the Perspective of International Law and WTO Law*", coordinated by Professor Paolo Davide Farah at gLAWcal – Global Law Initiatives for Sustainable Development (United Kingdom) and at West Virginia University John D. Rockefeller IV School of Policy and Politics, Department of Public Administration, in partnership with the Center of Advanced Studies on Contemporary China (CASCC) in Turin (Italy), Maastricht University Faculty of Law, Department of International and European Law and IGIR – Institute for Globalisation and International Regulation (Netherlands), and Tsinghua University, School of Law, Institute of Public International Law and the Center for Research on Intellectual Property Law in Beijing (China). An early draft of this chapter was presented at the Conferences Series on "*China's Influence on Non-Trade Concerns in International Economic Law*", Second Conference held at Tsinghua University, School of Law on January 14–15, 2012. This publication and the Conference Series were sponsored by China–EU School of Law (CESL) at the China University of Political Science and Law (CUPL). The activities of CESL at CUPL are supported by the European Union and the People's Republic of China.

1 Zhōnghuá Rénmín Gònghéguó Qīnquán Zérèn fǎ (中华人民共和国侵权责任法) [Tort Law of the People's Republic of China] (promulgated by the Standing Comm. Of the Nat'l People's Cong., December 26, 2009).

safety; c) legal loopholes revealed in product safety accidents; and d) the Tort Law's innovation of product liability regulations.

The normative framework of product liability before the enactment of the Tort Law

It was not until recently that China began to address the issue of product safety and established the product liability system.[2] In addition, no specific law exclusively regulates product liability, and related provisions can only be found in legislation pertaining to other legal fields and different time periods.

The earliest provisions about civil liabilities of producers and sellers date back to the General Principles of the Civil Law, passed in 1986, in which Article 122[3] adopts the concept of "substandard" product instead of "defective" product, which is generally used in the system of products liability. The original legislative purpose was to establish an objective principle of culpability that could be used to impose tort liability on the producers of defective products.[4]

Subsequently, the 1993 Product Quality Law[5] and the Law of Protection of Consumer Rights and Interests[6] both contain relevant provisions on product liability. "The products present defects" test, which appears in Article 40 of Chapter VII in the Law of Protection of Consumer Rights and Interests, shapes one of the nine conditions in which sellers should assume civil responsibility; together with Article 40, Article 35 further defines the practical measures consumers can adopt to protect their rights and interests in case of damage caused by defective products.

More systematic provisions on product liability appear in the Product Quality Law enacted almost at the same time (February 22, 1993, and revised on July 8, 2000). Articles 41 to 46 of Chapter IV "Compensation for Damage" stipulate that if a producer's defective product causes physical injury to a person or damage to property, he shall be liable for compensation (Article 41, clause 1). The law also defines the circumstances where a producer shall not be liable for compensation (Article 41, clause 2); joint liability of producers and sellers (Article 43); a range of damage compensation (Article 44); the limitation period for bringing a compensation claim for the damage (Article 45); and the definition of defective product (Article 46).

2 Regarding product safety in general, *see* Chapter 29 (Gruszczyński, Ötvös & Farah) in this volume. On consumer protection in Asian countries including China, *see* Chapters 30 (Rossi) and 31 (Prasad) in this volume.

3 Zhōnghuá Rénmín Gònghéguó Mínfǎ Tōngzé (中华人民共和国民法通则) [General Principles of the Civil Law of the People's Republic of China] (promulgated by the Nat'l People's Cong., April 12, 1986, effective August 27, 2009), Art. 122, "If a substandard product causes property damage or physical injury to others, the manufacturer or seller shall bear civil liability according to the law. If the transporter or storekeeper is responsible for the matter, the manufacturer or seller shall have the right to demand compensation for its losses."

4 China's academic field usually considers it as no fault liability or strict liability, which means that the subjective fault is not a necessity for liability. *See* LIANG HUIXING, ZHONGGUO MINSHI LIFA PINGLUN: MINFA, WUQUANFA, QINQUAN ZERENFA [CHINESE CIVIL LEGISLATION COMMENTS: CIVIL LAW, PROPERTY LAW, THE TORT LIABILITY LAW] 285 (Falü Chubanshe, 2010); Liang Huixing, *Zhongguo Chanpin Zeren Fa: Jianlun Jiamaoweilie zhi Genyuan ji Duice* [*Chinese product liability law: Concurrently on the fake root and countermeasure*], 1 FAXUE [LAW SCIENCE] 38 (2001).

5 Zhōnghuá Rénmín Gònghéguó Chǎnpǐn Zhí Liáng Fǎ (中华人民共和国产品质量法) [Product Quality Law of the People's Republic of China] (Promulgated by the Standing Comm. Nat'l People's Cong., February 22, 1993, effective September 1, 2000, amended in 2000).

6 Zhōnghuá Rénmín Gònghéguó Xiāofèi Zhě Quányì Bǎohù Fǎ (中华人民共和国消费者权益保护法) [Law of the People's Republic of China on Protection of Consumer Rights and Interests] (Promulgated by the Standing Comm. Nat'l People's Cong., October 31, 1993, amended October 25, 2013).

In recent years, the government has passed some laws aimed at products belonging to specific departments, such as the Agricultural Products Quality Safety Law (2006)[7] and the Food Safety Law (2009).[8] Compensation liability caused by substandard agricultural products or food is stipulated in their "legal liability" sections.[9]

The system of product liability and the legal regulations of product safety

Legal definition of product safety and related legal regulations

The current laws regulating product quality often refer to the distinct concepts of product quality and product safety,[10] without providing specific definitions. The product quality requirements set out in Article 26 of the Product Quality Law can be considered as an explanation of the concept of product quality: a) constituting no unreasonable threats to personal or property safety, and conforming to the national or industry standards for protecting human health, personal, and property safety, where such standards exist; b) possessing the properties required for its use; the directions stating their functional defects, however, should not be considered relevant to the concept of product quality; and c) conforming to the quality standards marked on the product, on its package and samples, and in its directions.

Some European scholars believe that the concept of product quality has a very broad definition without an absolute meaning in the legal field, while the academic world is inclined to define it as a product's whole nature and character, including its function, usage, and quality.[11] Scholars further divide the concept of product quality into compulsory quality and competitive quality. Compulsory quality means the safety of the product itself, which means that the product presents no defect or unreasonable danger.[12] Competitive quality, on the other hand, includes essential quality and promised quality. Essential quality means that a product possesses certain functions that make it suitable for sale, the lack of which would definitely constitute a defect;[13] the promised quality is the quality and character that a product should have according to the express or implied contract. Different from the essential quality, the promised quality restricts sellers only when it is adopted in express or implied contracts in addition to the general and specific property and character of the product.[14]

It is evident that compulsory quality, essential quality, and promised quality, respectively, correspond to the product quality requirements articulated in clauses 1, 2 and 3 of Article 26 of China's Product Quality Law. Hereby we can conclude that the concept of product quality

7 Zhōnghuá Rénmín Gònghéguó Nóngchǎnpǐn Zhí Liàng Ānquán Fǎ (中华人民共和国农产品质量安全法) [Agricultural Product Quality Safety Law of the People's Republic of China] (Promulgated by the Standing Comm. Nat'l People's Cong., April 29, 2006).

8 Zhōnghuá Rénmín Gònghéguó Shípǐn Ānquán Fǎ (中华人民共和国食品安全法) [Food Safety Law of the People's Republic of China] (Promulgated by the Standing Comm. Nat'l People's Cong., February 28, 2009).

9 Agricultural Products Quality Safety Law, Art. 54 and Food Safety Law, Art. 96.

10 Such as the Product Quality Law, the Agricultural Products Quality Safety Law and the Food Safety Law.

11 Massimo C. Bianca, *La Vendita e a Permuta,* in Trattato di Diritto Civile Italiano, founded by F.Vassalli, VII, I, 887 (Torino 1993).

12 Elena Bellisario, *Lo Stralcio Delle Disposizioni Sulle Certificazioni Di Qualità Dal Codice Del Consumo: Un'occasione Mancata,* 1 Europa e diritto privato 1064 (2005).

13 Massimo C. Bianca, *supra* note 11, at 296–297, 890–891.

14 Massimo C. Bianca, *supra* note 11, at 298–299, 890.

contains the concept of product safety because the product's safety is a basic mandatory requirement of product quality, indicating the absence of defects and unreasonable danger.

The European Union (EU) regulates product compulsory quality, which is product safety, through the Product Safety Law (EU Council Directive 95 of 2001 Concerning Product Comprehensive Safety) and the Product Liability Law (EU Council Directive 374 of 1985 Concerning Defective Product Compensation Liability). The difference between the Product Safety Law and the Product Liability Law is that the former mostly concerns the sellers' and country's obligation to prevent damage when a product is unsafe but has not yet caused actual harm, thus emphasizing the function of preventive protection. The latter, on the other hand, focuses on liability sharing and compensation after damage has taken place, thus providing *ex post* protection.

Compared with the EU legislation, Chinese legal regulations on product safety mainly focused on protection *ex post*, while lacking a systematic regulation performing the function of preventive protection, especially prior to the enactment of the Tort Law.[15]

The legislative model of China's product liability regulations and its function among product safety regulations

As mentioned above, there is no specific law that exclusively regulates product liability in China. Related provisions were mainly contained in Chapter IV of the Product Quality Law (Articles 41 to 46) before the Tort Law was enacted. This law follows China's legislative convention that there is no distinction between public and civil law, where the same law can regulate both aspects of a single phenomenon. Chapter II "Supervision over Product Quality," Chapter III "Liability and Obligation of Producers and Sellers in Respect of Product Quality," and Chapter V "Penalty Provisions," all belong to public law, which functions as administrative law and intends to regulate sellers' behavior. Chapter IV "Compensation for Damage," however, can be categorized as civil law, which intends to provide protection for victims (including consumers).[16]

This comprehensive legislative model reflects the purpose of trying to establish a system that is centered on quality administration, focused on *ex ante* supervision, and makes punishment and compensation *ex post* subsidiary methods.[17] According to this model, the target of product quality and safety is achieved when the product's quality meets the national and industry standards concerning the safety of people's health and property.[18] Therefore, the Product Quality Law stipulates that the national product quality supervision department shall carry out random supervision inspections as the main method of implementation.[19] The national inspections determine the product's quality based on national, industry, and local standards, other product regulations, as well as the producer's express standard or quality guarantee.[20] The objects randomly inspected may be harmful to people's health, safety or property, including important industrial products that may negatively affect the national welfare and people's livelihood, and products that consumers and other organizations deem

15 For provisions on product safety with preventive nature, please refer to Section IV.

16 Liang Huixing, *supra* note 4, at 88.

17 B. Sun, *Thoughts of Perfection of the Law on Product Liability in China*, 6 Tribune of Political Science and Law 99 (2001).

18 Product Quality Law, *supra* note 5, Art. 13.

19 Product Quality Law, *supra* note 5, Art. 15.

20 *Guojia Chanpin Zhiliang Jiandu Choucha Guanli Banfa [National Supervision Selective Examination of Product Quality Management Approach]*, Art. 7.

faulty.[21] The department will deal with faulty products according to two methods, depending on whether their quality is generally substandard or if they present serious problems.[22]

Based on the current legal framework of product quality and safety, besides the aforementioned inspections and the administrative penalties carried out by the government, the producers or sellers should bear civil responsibility for the damage caused. In addition, the product liability regime provides civil remedies such as compensation for the victims injured by defective products.[23] Furthermore, China's legislation also adopted criminal liability as a viable method to ensure product safety.[24] The Chinese laws on product liability and the provisions on product quality in China's criminal laws both belong to the category of remedies and sanctions *ex post*.[25]

Legal loopholes revealed in product safety accidents

Scholars have noted that China has enacted strict laws on product safety, including administrative laws on product supervision and punishment and tough civil and criminal laws on product liability. Nevertheless, consumer safety cases in which serious damage occurs constantly arise. Since the 2000 revision of the Product Quality Law, which systematically regulates product liability, to the enactment of the Tort Law, two major product safety accidents transpired: the Fuyang milk powder accident in 2003 and the melamine milk powder accident in 2008. A careful analysis of both may be helpful to perfect the legal system.[26]

Fuyang milk powder accident[27]

The following discussion is based on three cases (of many) reported in the news.

Case One: In the first months of 2002, the State Administration of Quality Supervision Inspection and Quarantine published a list of substandard infants' milk powder products and their producers. Fuyang Sainuo Dairy Limited, which was established by Lin Shiming and Chen Yuequan on January 15, 2001, was included in the list, in addition to its Junma milk powder. Later in 2003, however, these two people registered another brand called Jiyuan with

21 Product Quality Law, *supra* note 5, Arts 15, 22.

22 Product Quality Law, *supra* note 5, Arts 17, 49.

23 Han Ch, *Anquan Shijiao xia de Chanpin Zhiling Jiandu* [*Product Quality Supervision from Aspect of Safety*], Huadong Zhengfa Xueyuan Xuebao [Journal of East China University of Politics and Law] 195 (2005).

24 Zhōng Zhōnghuá Rénmín Gònghéguó Xíngfǎ (97 Xiūdìng) (中华人民共和国刑法 97 修订) [Criminal Law of the People's Republic of China (97 Revision)] (promulgated by the Nat'l People's Cong., March 14, 1997), Chapter III, Section 1, *Shengchan Jiamao Weilie Shangpin Zui* [*Crime of Producing or Selling Fake or Inferior Commodities*].

25 Liang Huixing, *supra* note 4, at 90.

26 For further analysis about the food safety accidents in China, *see* Chapters 19 (Ning), 27 (Prévost), and 29 (Gruszczyński, Ötvös & Farah) in this volume.

27 According to the State Council's investigation of the Fuyang milk powder incident, the number of Fuyang infants born after March 1, 2003 who had inferior milk powder and suffered malnutrition amounts to 229 people. There were a total of 12 people who died because of malnutrition due to the consumption of inferior milk powder. Throughout the incident, lawless producers partially replaced milk powder with starch, sucrose, and other cheap raw food material, and added milk flavor additive to produce inferior milk powder. The necessary elements for infant growth such as protein, fat, vitamin, and mineral content were far lower than the national standards. Infants who took such inferior milk powder for a long time suffered malnutrition, growth retardation, decreased immunity, other diseases, and even death. According to the investigation, Fuyang tracked down and seized 55 kinds of unqualified milk powder involving a total of more than 40 enterprises from 10 provinces, autonomous regions, and municipalities directly under the central government.

the Fuyang Commerce and Industry Bureau, and continued producing faulty milk powder. Some of the infants who had drunk such milk were affected by serious cases of malnutrition.

Case Two: The daughter of Wang Bencheng, a farmer in the town of Funan, died from drinking milk made by Le Zichun milk powder. The local Bureau of Quality Supervision tests of a sample showed that the proteins contained in the milk powder were less than half of the national standard while the coli group exceeded the permitted quota by six times. Having paid a monetary penalty, the producer left Funan; however, stores throughout China continued to sell the milk powder that led to the girl's death.

Case Three: Another farmer from Funan, Yang Chengjun, took his four-month-old baby to have a physical examination on June 27, 2003 because he wanted to prove that it was Yang Guang Beibei milk powder bought from Fu Yang Xing Yuan Wine Limited that directly caused his child's malnutrition. Subsequently, he sued the Fu Yang Commerce and Industry Bureau. The 12315 Center of Consumers' Claims carried out an investigation, obtained evidence, and eventually proved that the milk powder was indeed substandard. After mediation, Xing Yuang Limited agreed to pay 80 per cent of the total medical bills Yang had paid to restore his child's health, 5,489.76 Chinese Yuan (CNY). Plaintiff Yang agreed to pay the remaining 20 per cent, equivalent to 1,372.44 CNY, himself. As part of the mediation contract, the parties agreed that neither would bring further claims related to the case against the other.

These three cases demonstrate that the Product Quality Law cannot fully protect people's health and personal safety *ex ante* by random inspection.[28] First, the necessary coordination is absent between the quality supervision departments at different levels and between the departments and the Commerce and Industry Bureau. As a result, they cannot properly share information about unsafe products obtained by such inspections. Second, the law does not confer to the competent authorities the power to restrict or forbid the circulation of unsafe products; the competent departments can only deal with individual cases based upon victims' claims, and they only have the power to order punishment or compensation *ex post*. Third, the laws do not require producers or sellers to recall, warn, or provide information concerning unsafe products, especially after their circulation and use by consumers.

Melamine milk powder accident[29]

Five years later, the melamine milk powder accident confirmed once again the necessity for the law to require producers and sellers to recall unsafe products. The outbreak struck in December 2007 when consumers began complaining to the San Lu Group that some infants who had drunk the milk powder produced by the group showed red deposit in their urine, in addition to other symptoms. On May 17, 2008, San Lu's Customer Service provided a written report on the situation to the group's leaders. On May 20, it was confirmed that the

28 Feng Ch, *Zhuisu Fuyang Liezhi Naifen Shijian* [*Tracking the Fuyang incident of inferior milk powder*], *Fuyang Leizhi Naifen Shijian zhong de Xingzheng Bumen Biaoxian Huifang*, [*The Fuyang incident of inferior milk powder in the executive branch performance playback*], ZHONGGUO QINNIANBAO [CHINA YOUTH] (April 24, 2004), at A5.

29 During the melamine outbreak in September 2008, in order to increase protein content in milk powder, lawbreaking cow farmers factitiously added melamine, a poisonous chemical, to fresh milk. Consequently, 290,000 infants suffered from nephrolith at different stages, and 6 of them died from it. The State Quality Inspection Administration subsequently conducted an urgent inspection on infant milk powder, and the result demonstrated that 69 patches of products from 22 companies contained melamine.

non-protein nitrogen contained in the infant series of milk powder was 1.5 to 6 times higher than the one present in the same kind of product produced in China and abroad, and it was extremely possible that there was melamine in it. On July 24, 16 batches of infant milk powder were sent to the Hebei Entry-Exit Inspection and Quarantine Bureau Center to be tested, and the results confirmed that 15 batches of the milk powder samples contained melamine. The group's leaders convened the same day, and decided to seal all products in stock and test them for melamine. They agreed to recall all milk powder containing an excess of 10 mg of melamine per kg of powder; however, they would continue to sell milk powder with a smaller ratio of melamine until the government forbade it. In addition, they sent the rejected milk containing melamine to a subordinate company to make fluid milk.[30] After the faulty product started circulating, the company neglected consumers' safety complaints and failed to take immediate remedial measures, such as to warn consumers or recall the product. The resulting serious accidents therefore amounted to a large-scale violation of the public's health and safety rights.

The painful price paid following this accident finally inspired renewed legislative principles. The government concluded that its focus on punishment and compensation after the damage caused by defective products, the method in place before the adoption of the Tort Law, would not protect the public's rights to health and life. The government realized that it should instead emphasize preventive protection of civil rights from the dangerous sources of unsafe products.

Tort Liability Law's innovation of the product liability regulations

The renewed legislative principles

Chapter V "Product Liability" of the Tort Law includes seven articles (Articles 41 to Article 47). Articles 41, 42, and 43 follow Articles 41 to 43 of the Product Quality Law, reaffirming the main subjects of product liability – producers and sellers should bear distinct responsibilities according to different principles, the strict liability principle and the fault principle, but should share joint liability. Article 44 further emphasizes the contents of Article 122 of the General Principles of the Civil Law – for example, producers and sellers should bear responsibility when transporters, storekeepers, or third parties cause a product to become defective. The innovations in Articles 45 and 46 give potential infringers the right to remove obstacles and eliminate dangers caused by defective products before actual damage occurs. Furthermore, producers and sellers should issue warnings or recalls without delay and bear the corresponding obligations to remove obstacles and eliminate dangers. Article 47 establishes punitive damages for whomever, though clearly knowing about a product's defect, continues to produce or sell such product, and causes the death of a person or any serious damage to his or her health.

Articles 45 and 46 of the chapter on Product Liability show that the legislators began to favor regulations that encouraged preventive protection instead of *ex post* compensation for individual cases. Such renewed legislative principles provide infringees with protection of a preventive nature, and will thus keep the damage to a minimum. As for the civil rights listed in Article 3 of the Tort Law, their *ex post* nature merely affirms the right to claim damages after

30 Chen L, Chanpin Zeren [The Product Liability] 59–72 (Fazhi Chubanshe, 2010).

a violation, basically only providing for economic or material compensation. On the contrary, preventive remedies emphasize the infringee's rights to life and health. From a societal viewpoint, preventive measures no doubt serve a higher purpose compared to *ex post* remedies.

From renewed legislative principles to practical regulations

China's product safety regime, as mentioned above, lacks the functions of preventive protection and systemic regulation, while the Law of Protection of Consumer Rights and Interests includes relevant principles. Clause 1 of Article 18, for example, states "[b]usiness operators shall guarantee that the commodities and services they supply meet the requirements for personal or property safety." These terms regulate all business operators, regardless of whether they are producers, suppliers, or sellers, and regardless of what stage they are in when providing a product or a service. However, even with these broad regulations stipulating compulsory requirements about business operators' safety, there are no more-specific legal safety requirements for products or services.

Clause 2 of Article 18 requires business operators to warn consumers about products or services that present potential danger to people's health or property. In addition, according to clause 3 of Article 18, operators should immediately report to the competent administrative department and to consumers, and then take the required preventive measures. However, the government has not regulated the timing and content of the information to be reported, together with what specific measures operators should take.

The Food Safety Law, which was hastily introduced after the abovementioned product safety accidents, codifies the system of food recall and safety information reporting. Based on regulations concerning defective automobile product recall management, provisions on the administration of food recall, children's toy recall management, and drug recall management, the Defective Product Recall Management Regulations (draft)[31] began to solicit opinions from the public since April 8, 2009.

The Tort Law reaffirms the producers' and sellers' duty to issue warnings about or recall unsafe products in circulation. However, the other requirements still need further implementation, such as inspections after product circulation, and analysis and organization of consumers' complaints, statistics, and reports of product accidents. The clarification and enhancement of business operators' duties, together with more business awareness, not only are beneficial to the protection of people's rights to life and health, but will also achieve the same effect as strict product liability.

31 Quexian Chanpin Zhaohui Guanli Tiaoli (caoan) [Defective Product Recall Management Regulations (draft)].

33 Tort Liability for the Compensation of Damages Caused by Dangerous Substances in China*

Nadia Coggiola

Introduction

It is well known that China is facing high levels of pollution, although scholars have only recently turned their attention to the impact of environmental pollution on health. Whoever had the chance to interview a few Chinese university professors, government representatives, and NGO activists on the issue of the compensation of damages caused by environmental pollution, could easily infer that the problem is at the same time pressing and ignored.[1] What is also stricking is the contrast between the comprehensive Chinese legislation on the compensation for tortious damages and the poor litigation records on the compensation for damages caused by exposure to dangerous substances.

This chapter is devoted to understanding the reasons and meanings of the discrepancies between the formal declarations written on paper and the actual operating rules. In these investigation, we shall adhere to the idea that Chinese law could only be grasped by inquiring how formal rules are actually implemented in the Chinese courts and in society. Therefore, we shall not limit our research to the narrow borders of Chinese black-letter laws and regulations, but, instead, we shall try to ascertain whether and how these laws and regulations are applied to actual cases and to understand how formal legislation is actually implemented by Chinese legal and non-legal institutions.

The period of time taken into consideration is starting from the last wave of enactments of laws and regulations concerning the compensation of tortious damages, that is to say, the end of the last century, to the present. This investigation will show how much and how frequently the implementation of the provisions of laws and regulations regarding damages

* This chapter was written when I was EU Commission Marie Curie Fellow at Tsinghua University School of Law, THCEREL – Center for Environmental, Natural Resources & Energy Law in Beijing (China).

The research leading to these results has received funding from the People Programme (Marie Curie Actions) of the European Union's Seventh Framework Programme (FP7/2007–2013) under REA grant agreement n° 269327 Acronym of the Project: EPSEI (2011–2015) entitled "Evaluating Policies for Sustainable Energy Investments: Towards an Integrated Approach on National and International Stage", coordinated by University of Turin – Dipartimento di Giurisprudenza. I am grateful to Professors Gianmaria Ajani and Michele Graziadei of Università di Torino (Italy) and Paolo Davide Farah of West Virginia University (USA) for the opportunity they offered me to participate in the project. I am also deeply indebted to Dr. Jinrong Huang, Institute of Law, Chinese Academy of Social Sciences, for the help in my research in Beijing and Xiaoqian Hu, Harvard Law School, Harvard University, for the insightful comments of the first drafts of this article. Obviously, all the errors and mistakes are mine.

1 Some significant interviews on the subject are in file with the author.

created by dangerous substances is hindered by a number of obstacles, which are rooted in the inextricable connection between Chinese traditional culture and the present political and social system.

Notwithstanding the recent economic development, traditional patterns of thinking about morality and law as a punishment are in fact still prevailing in Chinese society, as well as the idea that law is a political and administrative tool used to maintain social order.[2] The organization of the administrative and judicial systems, the pervading presence of the political local powers, and the need to preserve social stability contribute, as we will see, to this stalemate situation, hampering the implementation of the laws and regulations that should be used to compensate for the damages suffered by the victims of dangerous substances.

China has made undeniable efforts to build an efficient system of tortious compensation by enacting laws and regulations providing for a comprehensive discipline on the subject. However, notwithstanding these efforts, in cases of damages caused by the exposure to dangerous substances, the Chinese system of tortious compensation unfortunately often seems more apt to protect the interests of the powerful parties over the generally weaker and damaged ones. The system also seems more aimed at preserving social stability and the political status quo than to compensate tortious damages. In such cases, the effectiveness of the laws and regulations on the compensation of tortious damages is in fact often subordinated to contingent non-legal considerations.

The judicial hurdles to the compensation of damages caused by dangerous substances

From a theoretical point of view, the provisions contained in the Chinese laws aimed to compensate for damages suffered as a consequence of exposure to dangerous substances could easily guarantee, at least in many cases, an effective compensation for the injured persons.

First of all, the new Tort Law of the People's Republic of China (Tort Law),[3] enacted in 2009 and entered into force July 1, 2010, provides general and special rules on the compensation of torts, on the basis of fault and no-fault principles of liability. The general provision contained in Article 2 states that the tortfeasor is liable for the infringement of "civil rights and interests"; these include, among others, the right to life, the right to health, and other personal and property rights and interests. This liability is for fault, unless otherwise provided (Article 6). With regard to the amount of the compensation, Article 16 states that, in cases of personal injuries:

> the tortfeasor shall compensate the victim for the reasonable costs and expenses for treatment and rehabilitation, such as medical treatment expenses, nursing fees and travel expenses, as well as the lost wages. If the victim suffers any disability, the tortfeasor shall also pay the costs of disability assistance equipment for the living of the victim and the

2 Janfu Chen, Chinese law: Context and Transformation 19 (Brill Nijhoff, 2008); Paul A. Barresi, *The Chinese Legal Tradition as a Cultural Constraint on the Westernization of Chinese Environmental Law and Policy*, 30 Pace Envtl. L. Rev. 1156 (2013).

3 Zhōnghuá Rénmín Gònghéguó Qīnquán Zérèn fǎ (中华人民共和国侵权责任法) [Tort Law of the People's Republic of China] (promulgated by the Standing Comm. Of the Nat'l People's Cong., December 26, 2009).

disability indemnity. If it causes the death of the victim, the tortfeasor shall also pay the funeral service fees and the death compensation.

Compensation for the serious mental distress suffered by the victim could also be requested, as well the damages inflicted on the property rights (Articles 19, 20, and 22), while Article 18 provides that, in case of the death of the victim, the tortfeasor shall pay the compensation to the close relatives and reimburse the expenses for medical treatment, funeral service, and other expenses incurred on the victim's behalf. Where the exposure to dangerous substances was instead caused by environmental pollution, Articles 65 through 68 could be applied, as they are exclusively devoted to the liability of the tortfeasor for environmental pollution on the basis of a no-fault system that excludes the polluter liability only when they can prove that they are not liable or that there is not a causal relationship between their conduct and the harm.

Liability for environmental pollution is also provided for by other laws, such as Article 124 of the General Principles of Civil Law of the People's Republic of China of 1986,[4] for damages caused to others in violation of state provisions for environmental protection and the prevention of pollution, and Article 41 of the 1989 version of the Environmental Protection Law,[5] which provided that the unit that had caused excessive environmental pollution was obliged to eliminate it and compensate the unit or individual that suffered direct losses. Other special laws contain similar provisions on the compensation for damages created by pollution, such as the 1984 Law on the People's Republic of China on the Prevention and Control of Water Pollution,[6] the 1995 Law on Prevention and Control of Environmental Pollution by Solid Waste,[7] and the 2000 Law on Prevention and Control of Atmospheric Pollution.[8]

Although these rules seem clear and explicitly provide a civil liability for damages, they actually do not provide compensation in most of the cases.

First of all, Chinese laws are sometimes not prescriptive and imperative rules but, rather, as in the case of environmental laws, policy statements and declarations of ideals, which need to be implemented by other laws and regulations.[9] However, those same implementation

4 Zhōnghuá Rénmín Gònghéguó Mínfǎ Tōngzé (中华人民共和国民法通则) [General Principles of the Civil Law of the People's Republic of China] (promulgated by the Nat'l People's Cong., April 12, 1986, effective August 27, 2009).

5 Zhōnghuá Rénmín Gònghéguó Huánjìng Bǎohù Fǎ (中华人民共和国环境保护法) [Environmental Protection Law of the People's Republic of China] (promulgated by the Standing Comm. Of the Nat'l People's Cong., December 26, 1989). That article was cancelled by the revised version of the Environmental Protection Law, entered into force on January 1, 2015. On the issue, read the Final Considerations.

6 Zhōnghuá Rénmín Gònghéguó Shuǐ Wūrǎn Fángzhì Fǎ (2008 xiūdìng) (中华人民共和国水污染防治法(2008修订) [Water Pollution Prevention and Control Law of the People's Republic of China (2008 Revision)] (Promulgated by the Standing Comm. Nat'l People's Cong., February 28, 2008).

7 Zhōnghuá Rénmín Gònghéguó Gùtǐ Fèiwù Wūrǎn Huánjìng Fángzhì Fǎ (2013 Xiūzhèng) (中华人民共和国固体废物污染环境防治法(2013修正) [Law of the People's Republic of China on the Prevention and Control of Environmental Pollution by Solid Wastes] (Promulgated by the Standing Comm. Nat'l People's Cong., June 29, 2013)

8 Zhōnghuá Rénmín Gònghéguó Dàqì Wūrǎn Fangzhì Fǎ (2000 xiūdìng) (中华人民共和国大气污染防治法(2000修订)) [Law of the People's Republic of China on the Prevention and Control of Atmospheric Pollution (2000 Revision)] (promulgated by the Standing Comm. Of the Nat'l People's Cong., April 29, 2000).

9 William P. Alford & Yuanyuan Shen, *Limits of the Law in Addressing China's Environmental Dilemma*, 16 Stan. Envtl. L.J. 125, 135 (1997).

rules and regulations are often mere duplications of the general rule, which provide no guidance to the interpreters and leave disproportionate interpretative discretion to governmental officials. Environmental laws are in fact characterized by the frequent use of the verb "should" (*ying/yinggai*) rather than of the stronger "shall" (*bixu*) or "must" (*dei*), which suggests a completely different meaning of the provisions contained in the laws. Moreover, the vagueness of the environmental laws is accrued by the lack of clear definitions of the terms used and by the poor case law,[10] also due to the lack of a centralized repository of court decisions. In fact, it must be pointed out that, although in the Chinese legal system the decisions of the courts never have the force of a precedent as in common law systems, they could nevertheless provide guidance on the implementation of law and interpretation to lawyers and judges, as often is the case in civil law countries. The practical consequence of this situation is that in some cases, articles that could be read by Western jurists as clearly prescriptive provisions ready for direct implementation are instead understood by Chinese scholars as mere principles of law, waiting for the enactment of further laws and regulations to become effective. Unfortunately, several environmental and tort laws are still waiting for these implementation laws and regulations.

The generality and vagueness of these kinds of Chinese laws probably adhere to the Chinese guidelines for legislative drafters, which dictate that primary legislation should be both "general" and "flexible". These rules were approved by Mao in the 1950s and are justified by the idea that a general and flexible national legislation can best be implemented throughout the country and be adapted to local conditions.[11] Some of these laws are still operative today. In fact, the characteristics of generality and flexibility enable political control, subordinating legislation to policy and leaving space for its instrumental use by the Chinese Communist Party (CCP). Therefore, Chinese legislation could sometimes appear as deprived of an independent life since it was always dependent on the Party's authoritative political directives and makeshift regulations and from the control the same Party exercises over Chinese bureaucracy.[12]

This muddled situation is further complicated by the contradictory and conflicting attitude of the CCP towards the issue of law enforcement, either on general principles or in specific cases. In fact, the Party is conscious that law enforcement is a highly problematic issue, as the failure to enforce national laws is detrimental to the central government's powers and its legitimacy, and, therefore, the Party actively promotes actions to enforce the national laws. On the other hand, it would prefer not to deal directly with actually enforcing the national laws because the local governments directly fund the judges and courts and the central government probably fears the possible outcomes of an independent judicial system in certain sensitive fields.[13]

10 Stefanie Beyer, *Environmental Law and Policy in the People's Republic of China*, 5(1) Chinese J. Int'l L. 185, 205–206 (2006).

11 Perry Keller, *Sources of Order in Chinese Law*, 42 Am. J. Comp. L. 711, 749–752 (1994).

12 Stanley Lubman, Bird in a Cage. Legal Reform in China After Mao 130–288 (Stanford University Press, 1999); Randall Peerenboom, China's long march toward rule of law (Cambridge University Press, 2002); Scott Tanner, The Politics of Law-Making in China (Clarendon Press, 1999).

13 Randall Peerenboom, *Law Enforcement and the Legal Profession in China*, in Implementation of Law in the People's Republic of China 125, 128–129 (J. Chen, Y. Li, & J.M. Otto eds, Martinus Nijhoff, 2002); Benjamin Van Rooij, *Implementing Chinese Environmental Law Through Enforcement*, in Implementation of Law in the People's Republic of China, *supra*, at 149. For a contrary opinion, *see* Zhu

Legislative powers and jurisdictions are fragmented and ill-defined, and under the formal hierarchy lies a range of competing and confused national and local legislative powers. As for administrative rule-making, administrative authorities enjoy large discretion in enforcing laws and enacting local rules that they use extensively.[14] The same absence of a substantially respected hierarchy applies to the interpretation of law, as interpretative powers are shared by different and often contrasting authorities[15]

Another problem resides in the judiciary system itself. After the previous decades of dismantling, the judiciary began rebuilding in 1979, but is today often still plagued by poorly trained judges. The enforcement of the court decisions can also often be difficult.[16] Chinese courts do not enjoy the powers and independence that a system would derive from a tradition of enforcement of the principle of judicial independence. In fact, they are considered as administrative agencies whose duty is to pursue the governmental policy, and not a separate branch of State power. The procedures used are often not transparent or straightforward, but to the contrary, they are intertwined in a web of personal and official relationships and are balanced among the parties.[17] Besides the provisions of the laws and the legal procedures, the outcome of the dispute could be determined by many other factors.

Among these factors are the possible contacts among the parties, the local government, the judges, and other protagonists. These contacts sometimes follow the rules of the traditional *guanxi*, which is an established and respected tradition of doing business through reciprocal favors and gifts based on personal relationships, either in the private or public sector. Although *guanxi* is regarded as respectful in China, where it interferes with the application of the law it can produce a judicial decision that is far from the prescriptions of the law.[18]

The relationship between local government and the judiciary is another source of common distortion of the courts' decisions, as the local government often interferes in court judgments. This is especially true when the defendants are, as in cases of polluting industries, the major taxpayers and, therefore, supporters of local economies, or when the same local government is a major shareholder of the defendant industry. The income produced by the industries is generally reputed by local governments to be a more important asset than the environmental or general health protection; in these cases, the local government can find itself in conflict with central government decisions or policies, especially, as it often happens, when public officers are evaluated by their superiors on the basis of economic growth statistics, without taking into consideration other factors.[19]

Suli, *The Party and the Courts*, in JUDICIAL INDEPENDENCE IN CHINA 52 (R. Peerenboom ed., Cambridge University Press, 2010).

14 STANLEY LUBMAN, *supra* note 12, at 138–147; Douglas B. Grob, *Legalizing the Local State* in CIVIL DISPUTE RESOLUTION IN CONTEMPORARY CHINA 91 (M.Y.K. Woo & M.E. Gallagher eds, Cambridge University Press, 2011).

15 Perry Keller, *supra* note 11, at 741–742; JANFU CHEN, *supra* note 2, at 198–203.

16 ELIZABETH ECONOMY, THE RIVER RUNS BLACK 112 (Cornell University Press, 2004); YUWEN LI, THE JUDICIAL SYSTEM AND REFORM IN POST-MAO CHINA STUMBLING TOWARDS JUSTICE (Routledge, 2014).

17 Vincent R. Johnson, *The Rule of Law and Enforcement of China Tort Law*, 34 T. JEFFERSON L. REV. 43, 88–92 (2011).

18 STANLEY LUBMAN, *supra* note 12, at 113–114, 278–280; Ling Li, *Corruption in China's Courts*, in JUDICIAL INDEPENDENCE IN CHINA, *supra* note 13, at 196.

19 C. Wang, *Chinese Environmental Law Enforcement: Current Deficiencies and Suggested Reforms*, 8 VT. J. ENVTL. L. 161, 172 (2007); Benjamin Van Rooij, *The People's Regulation: Citizens and Implementation of Law in China*, 25 COLUMB. J. ASIAN L. 116, 128–134, 162–163 (2012).

The power of local governments must not be undervalued, as economic reforms deeply changed the allocation of powers in favor of local governments. The relationship between local governments and local enterprises is so close that local governments have acquired a large degree of economic and political independence and are apparently quite insensitive to every reform effort for centralization.[20] It could, therefore, happen that because of the pressures from the local government, grassroots judges misapply the law, rather preferring to adjudicate on the basis of the substantial outcome of the case because of fears of complaints or social instability.

The independence of judges is also jeopardized by a responsibility system, which can sanction them for a wide range of behaviors, contrary to ethics or duty, or for a simple legal error. Party authorities are generally responsible for the evaluation of judges in these cases and, therefore, it is not uncommon that lower Chinese courts judges resort to a practice called *qingshi*, consisting in the solicitation of the advice of a higher court to avoid "incorrect" decisions, especially in more sensitive cases, where conformity to the policy directive is more convenient for the judge.[21] We must not forget that under the Chinese institutional framework, only the independence of courts and adjudicative committees is (formally) recognized, not that of judges, who are usually treated as an ordinary state functionary.[22]

Moreover, the high costs of litigation, which include a "case acceptance fee" that can vary from 0.5 to 4 per cent of the compensation requested by the defendant and the "litigation costs" that could be levied at the discretion of the court, can easily discourage the poorer and weaker parties and become a source of abuse.[23]

Despite these problems and, as we shall see later, the large recourse to non-judicial means, the number of judicial cases for injuries compensation is increasing. Among these compensation cases we can find some "pollution compensation cases" (*wuran sunhai peichang anjian*), that is to say, cases for the compensation of damages to property or health caused by environmental pollution.[24]

In those cases, the petitioners encountered a series of juridical hurdles. For example, although Article 41 of the Environmental Protection Law clearly provided a strict liability system for the polluters, who could be held liable for damages when (also lawfully) discharged wastewaters or emitted air pollutants or caused other environmental pollution if it is proved that such (even lawful) acts caused any harm,[25] this principle of strict liability has not been fully accepted by the enterprises, administrative bodies, and some courts. These bodies would in fact rather prefer to support the idea that the discharge of pollutants in compliance

20 Stanley Lubman, *supra* note 12, at 103–110.

21 Zhuoyan Xie, *Petition and Judicial Integrity*, 2(1) J. Pol'y & L. 24, 25–27 (2009); Carl Minzner, *Judicial Disciplinary Systems for Incorrectly Decided Cases*, in Civil Dispute Resolution in Contemporary China, *supra* note 14, at 58.

22 Stephanie Balme, *Local Courts in Western China, The Quest for Independence and Dignity*, in Judicial Independence in China, *supra* note 13, at 154, 162.

23 C. Wang, *supra* note 19, at 207.

24 Kathinka Fürst, Access to Justice in Environmental Disputes: Opportunities and Obstacles for Chinese Pollution Victims (unpublished thesis, University of Oslo, 2008); Robert V. Percival, *China's "Green Leap Forward" Toward Global Environmental Leadership*, 12 Vt. J. Envtl. L. 633, 641 (2010–2011); Rachel E. Stern, Environmental Litigation in China (Cambridge University Press, 2013).

25 *See* Depei Han, Textbook on Environmental Protection Law (Law Publishing Company, 2005); Ke Zhou, Ecological Environmental Law (Chinese Law Book Company, 2001).

with the state standards or permit limits did not constitute a source of civil liability, even where environmental harm was caused.[26]

To wipe away those uncertainties, the former Environmental Protection Agency (now State Environmental Protection Administration) in 1991 issued the Reply on Deciding the Compensation Liability for Environmental Pollution, which has binding effect on the implementation of the Environmental Protection Law upon all the environmental protection bureaus. That provision clearly stated that environmental damages can be compensated when the polluter caused environmental harm and the claimants suffered damages because of that harm, notwithstanding the existence of a fault of the defendant or of a discharge of pollutants exceeding the established limits.

Shortly after, the Supreme People's Court's 1992 *Opinion on Several Issues in Applying the Civil Procedure Law of the People's Republic of China*, stated at Article 74 that "in action for compensation as a result of environmental pollution, if the defendant objects to the tortuous allegations of the plaintiff, the defendant bears the burden of proof."[27] The same Supreme People's Court in 2001 issued the *Several Provisions on the Evidence of Civil Litigation* (also translated as Judicial Interpretations on Evidence), and Article 4 states that "if the litigation of environmental damage compensation is caused by the environmental pollution, then the injurer shall bear the burden of proof of the statutory exemptions and the fact that there is no causation between his act and the damages."[28]

Last, Articles 65 and 66 of the Tort Law, respectively, state that "[w]here any harm is caused by environmental pollution, the polluter shall assume the tort liability" and that "[w]here any dispute arises over an environmental pollution, the polluter shall assume the burden to prove that it should not be liable or its liability could be mitigated under certain circumstances as provided for by law or to prove that there is no causation between its conduct and the harm."

The sequence of the statements indicates that there has been a progressive shift from a strict liability system, where the defendant is liable notwithstanding their lack of fault, but where causation must be proved by the petitioners, to a system where causation between the pollution and the damage could be presumed, unless the defendant proves the contrary.

These statements, repeated in different provisions over 20 years, also incontrovertibly tell us that the rule providing that "in environmental cases the polluters are liable for the compensation of the injuries unless they prove they are not responsible for the damages occurred" was not easily implemented in China.

In fact, although the rules provide for a strict liability system in environmental pollution cases, it is still quite common for Chinese courts to require plaintiffs to demonstrate the liability of the defendant, with the inevitable and frequent consequence of dismissing the claimant's petition because of the inability to prove the defendant's responsibility, either under the negligence or the causal profile.[29]

26 On this issue, *see* Theory and Practice of Environmental Dispute Resolution 127 (Canfa Wang ed., China University of Political Science and Law Press, 2002).

27 Translation by Yuhong Zhao, *Environmental Dispute Resolution in China*, 16(2) J. Envtl. L. 157, 181 (2004).

28 Translation by C. Wang, *supra*, note 19, at 162.

29 C. Wang, *supra* note 19, at 205; Rachel E. Stern, *supra* note 24.

One recent example is a case concerning the chromium pollution of the river Nam Pam by a local factory near the Xing Long Village in Yunnan, which caused the death of the villagers' goats. The discharge of the polluting substances in the river was stopped in 2011, but in July 2013, the Public Participation Project Coordinator of Friends of Nature, the NGO that was assisting the villagers, affimed in an interview that only the compensation of the expenses for cleaning the water and soil was under discussion in front of the court. On the contrary, when one of the villagers, living near the river, sued the factory to ask for compensation for the damages caused by the cancer he had developed and that he affirmed was the consequence of the chromium pollution, the court refused to grant him the compensation, affirming that he was not able to prove that his cancer was actually caused by the chromium pollution.

The main problem for petitioners is showing the causal link between the pollution and the damages. Chinese courts show great deference to reports from official or certified authorities, assessing the damages or the causal link, but those official reports can be very costly or can be influenced, as some environmental advocates and scholars claim, by the more powerful polluters. Moreover, as judges are unable to independently evaluate scientific reports and use scientific uncertainty criteria in legal cases, they usually completely rely upon official reports.[30] But this latter problem is also shared, as we all know, by Western jurisdictions, as the famous *Daubert* case reminds us.[31]

Nonetheless, there are also cases where the defendant was asked to prove he was not liable for the damages. Probably one of the first cases was *Sun Youli et al. v Qianan Diyi Zaozhichang et al.*,[32] which concerned damages to 18 fish and shellfish farmers. A claim was brought because the discharge of an excessive amount of wastewater from nine pulp factories and chemical plants caused the death of the fish and shellfish. In that case, the Tianjin Maritime Court held the defendants jointly and severally liable for the damages suffered by the farmers, although the same court held that the only enterprise that had complied with the legal limits on waste had to pay the compensation of the damages caused, but that it should not be jointly and severally liable with the other defendants.

On this last point it should be observed that Chinese law provides, at Article 130 of the General Principles of Civil Law, the joint and several liability of the defendants where two or more persons infringe another person's rights, causing damages. However, Chinese courts seldom apply this principle of law, as they generally prefer to apportion the liability among the different defendants.[33]

Moreover, the opposite (and less favorable to petitioners) principle of several liability was chosen for the cases where the damages were caused by environmental pollution. Article 67 of the Tort Liability Law provides in fact that "[w]here the environmental pollution is caused by two or more polluters, the seriousness of liability of each polluter shall be determined according to the type of pollutant, volume of emission and other factors."

That choice of the several liability rule in cases of multiple polluters probably traces its rationale to the presumption that the polluters do not have a joint intent and that the

30 Adam Moser & Tseming Yang, *Environmental Tort Litigation in China*, 41(10) ENVIRONMENTAL LAW INSTITUTE 10895, 10898–10899 (2011).

31 *Daubert v Merrel Down Pharmaceutical*, 727 F. Supp. 570 (S.D. Cal. 1989), *aff'd*, 951 F.2d 1128 (9th Cir. 1991), *vacated*, 509 U.S. 579 (1993).

32 Hebei, 2002 and 2003.

33 Yuhong Zhao, *supra* note 27, at 179–185.

pollution is caused by independent conduct, although the application of joint and several liability in those cases where the polluters collaborated in causing the pollution is not excluded.

Similarly, in the notorious case *Zhang Changjian et al. v Pingnan Rongping Chemical Plant*,[34] the judges stated that the defendant's liability was a no-fault liability and that it was his duty to prove he was not responsible for the injuries.

In that case, although the defendant proved that the factory's equipment was modern and, according to the Provincial Environmental Protection Bureau inspection, its air and water emissions were in accordance with the required standards, the court stated that he was liable for the damages because they were caused by the pollution from his factory. In the opinion of the judges:

> [i]n accordance with the "Supreme People's Court Certain Regulations Regarding Evidence in Civil Litigation" [. . .], the polluter has the burden to raise evidence to show the lack of causal connection between his behavior and the harmful result [. . .] So, [. . .] whether or not pollutant discharges meet standards is not the criteria by which we determine whether liability attaches to a polluting unit.

Since the defendant was not able to prove that he had not caused the harm to the crops, bamboo, fruit trees, and timber strands or that another nearby factory caused the harm, as he alleged, he was therefore held liable to pay compensation for the damages.

Although the court refused to order the defendant compensate for the "emotional damages" claimed by the petitioners, and the actual compensation for the material losses was modest, this decision was heralded as an important step in the implementation of environmental laws and was selected as one of the "ten most influential Chinese lawsuits of 2005".[35]

During an interview, Professor Wang Canfa suggested that this courageous decision was largely the fruitful consequence of both the specialized environmental training received by the judge of the case by the Center for Legal Assistance to Pollution Victims[36] and the presence of experienced environmental litigators acting on behalf of the petitioners. Therefore, this decision should be considered as an exception to the, by now standard, rules on the liability of the polluters in cases of damages caused by environmental pollution.

The extrajudicial hurdles to the compensation of damages caused by dangerous substances

Extrajudicial obstacles also hinder the compensation for the damages caused by dangerous substances.

First of all, it should be remembered that some scholars have suggested that the traditional Chinese approach to the environment is historically characterized by an antagonistic relationship between man and nature, stemming from the anthropocentric Confucian belief that man should exploit nature to his own advantage. That attitude was subsequently and firmly

34 Pingnan Interm. People's Ct., Fujian Provincial High People's Ct., 2005

35 Fa Zhi Ri Bao "2005 Zhong Guo Shi Da Ying Xiang Xing Su Song" Ping Xuan Jie Xiao (Legal Daily "2005 China Ten Most Significant Impact Litigations" Selection Announcement), XINHUA, January 1, 2006.

36 *See* http://clapv.org/english_lvshi/.

reasserted by Mao and, according to the same scholars, still permeates Chinese society, which is generally unwilling to consider damages such as those caused by environmental pollution as compensable damages.[37]

Moreover, non-judicial methods of resolution are largely used in China. Among these non-judicial methods of resolution we can first mention the procedures of conciliation, which may occur between the litigants either before or during judicial[38] or administrative procedures. If the conciliation occurs before the judicial or administrative procedure, it does not need to be approved or reviewed by third parties, while if the litigants conciliate during the procedure, the act of conciliation must be approved by the judicial or administrative body.[39] The results of these conciliations can often be unfavorable to the injured litigants in environmental cases, most likely because of the disparities in bargaining powers, the lack of external bindings on the conciliation outcome, and the possibility in disputing it.[40]

Although conciliation procedures are quite common, they do not reach the massive diffusion of mediation, a traditional extrajudicial dispute resolving method that differs from conciliation because it is conducted by a third party, which helps the parties achieve an acceptable settlement without any official authority to impose on them a final decision. In spite of its unofficial appearance, mediation is actually endowed of all the characters of authority. More precisely, depending on who is leading it, it can be distinguished in People's mediation, administrative mediation, and judicial mediation.

In cases of People's mediation, the mediator is a person without administrative or judicial functions, generally the People's Mediation Committees of the Resident's Committee of urban areas or of the Villager's Committees in rural areas, which resolve civil disputes (supposedly) in accordance with the law.[41] Economical and fast, if signed or chopped by the disputing parties, it is treated as a civil agreement that cannot be modified or repudiated, but can only be disputed in court, and can be enforced by the People's Courts for its performance. However, its content often suffers from the limited legal abilities and incentives of the mediators.[42] It is generally suitable for resolving certain tortious cases, such as cases about nuisances generated by manufacturing and/or operation processes between township or community enterprises, solely owned workshops and stalls, and their neighboring residents.[43] Although the recourse to People's Mediation appears to be less used in more modern and affluent contexts and among more educated people, it nonetheless remains largely used by certain categories of people in the countryside and small towns. Because of the large popularity of People's mediation, the Chinese government still continues to rely on and take advantage of this instrument, which reinforces its power and control over the

37 Judith Shapiro, Mao's War Against Nature (2001); Roda Muschkat, *Contextualizing Environmental Human Rights*, 26 Pace Envtl. L. Rev. 119, 149 (Cambridge University Press, 2009).

38 In force of Article 51 of the Civil Procedure Law. Zhōnghuá Rénmín Gònghéguó Mínshì Sùsòng Fǎ (Shìxíng) (中华人民共和国民事诉讼法(试行) [Civil Procedure Law of the People's Republic of China (For Trial Implementation)] (promulgated by the Standing Comm. of the Nat'l People's Cong., March 8, 1982).

39 Supreme People's Court interpretation of the Civil Procedure Law (1992), Article 191.

40 Yuhong Zhao, *supra* note 27, at 160–161.

41 Civil Procedure Law, *supra* note 38, Article 16.

42 Yuhong Zhao, *supra* note 27, at 162–164.

43 Canfa Wang, *Preliminary Study of Environmental Dispute Resolution in China*, in Theory and Practice of Environmental Dispute Resolution 12 (C. Wang ed., China University of Political Science and Law Press, 2002).

people and reduces litigation costs.[44] But we should not forget that this large recourse to mediation leaves room for the application of criteria that are not drawn from the law and could be highly sensitive to the individual personal powers and social position of the litigants.[45]

The competent department of administrative bodies can also perform the task of mediation. Administrative mediation is not considered an administrative act; therefore, it is less constraining on the parties who, after the administrative mediation, can still file suit against each other or the same settlement before the People's Courts. The Environmental Protection Bureaus (EPBs) have always been very active in settling disputes concerning environmental cases, and the administrative bodies are generally quite efficient in such cases because of their knowledge and investigative powers.[46]

Lastly, we must cite judicial mediation, which has been practiced in Chinese civil courts since the late 1930s[47] and was formally institutionalized in 1982 with the Civil Procedure Law of the People's Republic of China.[48] Judges generally give prominence to mediation when adjudicating matters. One reason for this is that due to the current policies of the Supreme People's Court, the court's performance is assessed on the basis of the percentage of mediations in comparison with their total caseload. However, these settlement agreements must be voluntarily reached by the parties and must comply with the law. Judicial mediation can be carried out either before or during the trial, and in appellate procedures, it has binding authority on the parties. Once they reach an agreement, it can be enforced by the courts if one of the parties fails to perform its obligations. Judicial mediation is extensively used in China, for a number of reasons.

Some scholars suggest that many Chinese judges believe that mediation is their primary duty before adjudication. Therefore, judicial mediation is not always a voluntary choice of the parties, but rather a proposal and a "warm" suggestion of the judges, if not actually a judicial imposition.[49] The superimposition of the mediator and adjudicator roles in the same judge clearly is not without practical consequences, as there could be flairs in the judgments, the lack of formal procedural requirements can entail substantial injustices, and mediation could be used by lower court judges as a means to avoid the application of a positive law they do not know well enough.[50]

The powers given to judges with the mediation instrument is well known by the Chinese government, which shows swinging attitudes towards it and uses it as a tool of its political and social interests. In fact, following the Court Reform 5 Years Plan commencing in 1999, promoting judicial efficiency and justice by the improvement of judges' professionalism, procedural justice reform, and the introduction of adversarial proceedings, there had been a steady decline of judicial mediation cases, especially in urban courts and major coastal cities,

44 Benjamin L. Read & Ethan Michelson, *Mediating the Mediation Debate*, 52 (5) J. Conflict Resol. 737, 755 (2008).

45 Aris Chan & Geoffrey Crothall, *Is It Worth Going to Court?*, 5 J. Comp. L. 281, 307–309 (2010).

46 Xiaoying Ma & Leonard Ortolano, Environmental Regulation in China (Rowman and Littlefield Publishers, 2000); Yuhong Zhao, *supra* note 27, at 164–170.

47 Richard Cullen & Fu Hualing, *From Mediatory to Adjudicatory Justice: The Limits of Civil Justice Reform in China*, in Civil Dispute Resolution in Contemporary China, *supra* note 14, at 25; Zeng Xianyi, *Mediation in China – Past and Present*, 17 A.P.L.R. 1 (2009).

48 *Supra* note 38.

49 Carl Minzner, *China's Turn Against Law*, 59 (4) Am. J. Comp. L. 935, 959 (2011).

50 Yuhong Zhao, *supra* note 27, at 170–175.

although their number remained relatively high in county courts and small cities. This trend did not last for long. After the judicial reform was first halted and then partially reversed due to an increase of social conflicts and the number of petitions directed to the central authorities in Beijing against the court decisions in the early 2000s, court mediation resurged and has since slowly but steadily grown.

Different interpretations have been given by scholars of Chinese law to this resurgence: someone saw it as a sign of the failure of the ideals lying under the Courts Reform Plan, and the victory of the political system and its power.[51] Others affirmed it should be interpreted as "a part of broader reconsideration of role of law, lawyers, courts, and adjudication,"[52] while others affirmed that it has instead become the weapon used by judges to defend themselves from the always larger use unsatisfied petitioners make of the *xinfang* system against courts' decisions, as judicial mediation is less likely to be the object of petitions and letters and is more fitting to the political emphasis on an "harmonious society".[53]

This large recourse to judicial mediation is not without consequences, as it entails problematic judicial behaviors, affects judges' decisions and their handling of cases, and is a short-term solution guided by the emergence situation, which does not bring any actual social stability or meaningful long-term institutional change.[54]

The preference for non-judicial systems can also be clearly observed in cases of damages caused by dangerous substances. For example, frequently the compensation for personal damages caused by pollution is directly asked of the same polluters, but the request of compensation is filed in the government offices and not with the polluters, although the government offices do not take part in the settlement of the dispute between the injured parties and polluters. Apparently, this procedure, named *xìnfǎng tiáo lì*, could sometimes guarantee a larger compensation to the injured party than a judicial decision, and requires a lower level of proof.

An example of this kind of dispute resolution is a recent case in which five breeders of crabs in the town of Gu, in Anhui Province, affirmed that the pollution of the river Nan Tuo, which flows along two towns, caused the death of their crabs. The local environmental agency found that the river water exceeded some of the prescribed limits, but a meeting coordinated by the Environmental Protection Department of Anhui Province found no connection between the data of the water and the death of the crabs. Nevertheless, the breeders were compensated by the two municipalities, following an agreement reached with the supervision of the same Environmental Protection Department of Anhui Province.[55]

According to the literature, *xinfang* is a petition directly made to higher-level bodies, called *xinfang bureaus*, which are outside of formal legal institutions but at the same time formally established, and which draw their power directly from that of the CCP and its individual officials. *Xinfang* bureaus have a capillary diffusion in China, as they can be found in almost all Chinese government organs, including courts, local government offices, and

51 Cullen & Hualing, *supra* note 47, at 39–54.

52 Carl Minzner, *supra* note 49, at 937.

53 Benjamin Liebman, *A Populist Threat to China's Courts?*, in CIVIL DISPUTE RESOLUTION IN CONTEMPORARY CHINA, *supra* note 14, at 269, 303–306.

54 Benjamin Van Rooij, *supra* note 19, at 169–171.

55 The case is available at http://www.aepb.gov.cn/pages/Aepb11_ShowNews.aspx?NewsID=89915 (last visited July 14, 2016).

Party committees.[56] Born to resolve political problems, *xinfang* has gradually evolved into a system of assistance, which is more of a multipurpose political governance tool rather than an institution of popularized justice based on legal norms. The resort to petitioning practices and *xinfang* bureaus is much more common in the Chinese experience than the pleading in front of a court, even if the contemporary recourse to both remedies is not uncommon.[57] People make use of the petition system either because they have no confidence in the independence and impartiality of the judicial system or because they want to influence it. Moreover, many provincial *xinfang* regulations oblige courts to hear a wide range of petitions along with their judicial duties, so expanding their powers outside of the provisions of the law. Therefore, courts can be approached by petitioners before, during, and after judicial hearings on the same issues, and the judiciary and *xinfang* bureau functions can easily overlap.[58]

As mentioned before, notwithstanding the Courts Reform Plan, the number of petitions filed with the central authorities in Beijing against court decisions had greatly increased in the early 2000s because the reform of the Chinese judicial system did not meet the goals it pursued and the probably amplified expectations of the citizens.[59] In fact, the *xinfan* system of petitions and letters can be used by litigants to pressure courts to rule in their favor or to alter court decisions because Chinese courts are extremely sensitive to populist pressure as a consequence of the political concerns about social stability and the increased strains put on them. A delicate and contradictory situation is created by the lack of petitioners' confidence in the law and in the courts, along with their high expectations from the law and the courts, joined with the political concerns in social stability, and the pressures from party officials. The courts are asked to deal with this situation. Pressures on courts are sometimes so high that they may be called to change their opinion in the case, rehear the case, pay compensation to quiet petitioners, ignore the letter of the law, or even consider cases without any legal basis.[60]

This pervasive and massive use of *xinfang* is encouraged by the Chinese government, which instrumentally uses it to avoid social unrest, although it delegitimizes the Chinese courts' authority through the invalidation of their decisions.[61]

Final considerations

Notwithstanding a legislative framework that would be able to formally compensate the damages suffered by the petitioners injured by dangerous substances, the Chinese judicial system is currently unable to attain reasonable levels of protection of the rights of the harmed parties and to ascertain compensation for their damages.

As discussed above, this inability is partly due to technical problems related to the way Chinese courts and laws operate, and is partly the consequence of the influence of social and

56 Stanley Lubman, *supra* note 14, at 40ff.; Yongshun Cai, *Managed Participation in China*, 119 Pol. Sci. Q. 425, 431–432 (2004).

57 Zhuoyan Xie, *supra* note 21; Carl F. Minzner, *Xinfang: An Alternative to Formal Chinese Legal Institutions*, 42 Stan. J. Int'l L. 103, 105–107 (2006).

58 Carl Minzner, *supra* note 57, at 126–139.

59 Cullen & Hualing, *supra* note 47, at 44–46.

60 Nanping Liu, *A Vulnerable Justice: Finality of Civil Judgment in China*, 13 Colum. J.A.L. 35 (1999); Benjamin Van Rooij, *supra* note 19, at 169–217.

61 Carl Minzner, *supra* note 57, at 107; Benjamin Liebman, *supra* note 53, at 306.

political considerations over the implementation of legislative provisions. In fact, courts are not always independent enough from external pressures, either from local governments, industry owners, or the same petitioners, and judges may not always possess the capacity or juridical knowledge to adjudicate solely on the basis of the existing legislation. Moreover, laws could still be waiting for their implementing regulations, or their interpretation could be unclear or disputed.

Although the central government is often seriously trying to build an efficient system of tortious damages compensation, as this would fulfill its aims of legislative consistency, centralized administration, and protection of the injured parties, its purposes often clash with the local governments' interests, which would rather preserve their major sources of economic financing and power. Moreover, it must be remembered that, especially if the number of injured parties grow, the compensation for the damages that are the consequence of dangerous substances could become, in the Chinese system, a possible source of social unrest. Hence, the strong need for a delicate balance of interests and powers in such cases.

This fragile situation should not, in my opinion, be detrimental to the right to compensation for those injured by the dangerous substances. It is impossible to ignore that the continued extensive use of dangerous substances in unsafe and uncontrolled conditions will entail in the near future a relevant increase in the number of cases of damages in China, with inevitable serious social and economic consequences.

The Western experience in analogous cases could be a warning. In fact, as it is widely known, the uncontrolled use in Western countries of different dangerous substances in the past two centuries has caused a relevant increase in cases of injuries to goods and persons, with high social and economic losses. The search for the appropriate compensation remedies to these problems has endured for many years, and is still continuing. The solutions found are different, depending on the countries, and not always satisfactory. Certainly, all of them are rather expensive for all parties involved.

In cases such as the ones listed above, the major problem is in finding a satisfactory compromise among industrial production, economic growth, and protection of the harmed parties. As long as China wants to grow economically without imposing too harsh of a burden on a large part of its population, a solution should be found in a short time, as China can still successfully avoid some of the Western countries' mistakes. The Chinese government is certainly aware of these problems, as we can easily infer from the entry into force, on January 1, 2015, of the revised Environmental Protection Law, which tackles some of these problematic issues.

The amended version of the law strengthens the companies' and individuals' liability for preventing and controlling pollution, provides more severe punishments in cases of violation, gives more responsibilities to local governments in the control and enforcement of environmental protection rules, and establishes a system of environmental public interest litigation. Moreover, with regards to the issue of the compensation of the damages caused by environmental pollution, Article 41 of the former version of the law is now replaced by the new Article 64, which provides that those who cause damages due to environmental pollution and ecological destruction shall bear tort liability in accordance with the provisions of the Tort Liability Law. Shortly after, on January 6, 2015, the Supreme People's Court issued its ***Interpretation on Several Issues Regarding the Application of Law in Public Interest Environmental Civil Litigation***. These provisions, which try to facilitate the access of public litigation in environmental civil cases, could provide a solution to some of the problems highlighted in this article, permitting certain NGOs to file a case in a court different from the local court where the pollution occurred; enabling injured private parties to take advantage of the NGO's action and reducing the costs of the litigation; providing that the damages paid by the polluters are to be put in a pool of money, which should be used to compensate all the injured parties; requiring the control of the settlements of the cases, to avoid that it is the consequence of the intimidation of the polluter or local government on the petitioners; and, lastly, putting on the polluter the onus of the probation of all the information concerning the pollution and providing that the same courts could investigate the facts of the case and allow the hearing of experts.

The first positive outcomes of this legislation could maybe be glimpsed in the recent successful case *Taizhou City Environmental Protection Association v Jiangsu Changlong Agrochemical Co. Ltd Higher*, discussed in front of the People's Court of the Jiangsu Province,[62] which severely fined six companies, sued by a local NGO, for the environmental pollution they caused.

Nonetheless, the Chinese judicial and social system is complex, and it is difficult to make easy predictions on the actual impact of the revised Environmental Protection Law and of the Supreme People's Court *Interpretation* on the lives of Chinese people. Therefore, currently, we can only sit and wait.

62 Report on the case available at http://www.nytimes.com/2015/01/01/world/asia/chinese-court-orders-6-companies-to-pay-26-million-for-polluting.html?_r=0 (last visited July 14, 2016).

34 The Protection of Biotechnological Innovation by Patent in the United States, Europe, France, and China

A Comparative Study from the Perspective of the TRIPS Agreement*

Shujie Feng, Xin Shu, and Ningning Zhang

Biotechnology consists of modern scientific and technological development; as with most new sectors, it brings new problems in various fields, including science, technology, ethics, economy, and law. Legislators need to find a way to effectively regulate biotechnology so that the public can benefit from its development, enterprises can grow their business in related industries, and morality and *ordre public* are not disturbed. Among all the problems raised by biotechnology, the patentability of biotechnological inventions remains one of the most important. As a satisfactory solution has not yet been found, the legal regime for biotechnology is in constant flux. It is in this context that the Agreement on Trade-Related Aspects of Intellectual Property Rights[1] (TRIPS Agreement) tries to carry out an international harmonization of national laws among all World Trade Organization (WTO) members. Since all WTO members experience different levels of technological and economic development and since they do not share the same moral or ethical rules, divergences are unavoidable in political and legal fields. We will first analyze the obligations of WTO members under the TRIPS Agreement and then examine their implementation in the United States (US), the European Patent Office (EPO), the European Union (EU), France, and China.

* This chapter is part of the results of the Research Project on "*Current Trends of Chinese Law towards Non-Trade Concerns such as Sustainable Development and the Protection of Environment, Public Health, Food Safety, Cultural, Social and Economic Rights, Labor Rights and the Reduction of Poverty from the Perspective of International Law and WTO Law*", coordinated by Professor Paolo Davide Farah at gLAWcal – Global Law Initiatives for Sustainable Development (United Kingdom) and at West Virginia University John D. Rockefeller IV School of Policy and Politics, Department of Public Administration, in partnership with the Center of Advanced Studies on Contemporary China (CASCC) in Turin (Italy), Maastricht University Faculty of Law, Department of International and European Law and IGIR – Institute for Globalisation and International Regulation (Netherlands), and Tsinghua University, School of Law, Institute of Public International Law and the Center for Research on Intellectual Property Law in Beijing (China). An early draft of this chapter was presented at the Conferences Series on "*China's Influence on Non-Trade Concerns in International Economic Law*", Second Conference held at Tsinghua University, School of Law on January 14–15, 2012. This publication and the Conference Series were sponsored by China–EU School of Law (CESL) at the China University of Political Science and Law (CUPL). The activities of CESL at CUPL are supported by the European Union and the People's Republic of China.

1 Agreement on Trade-Related Aspects of Intellectual Property Rights, April 15, 1994, Marrakesh Agreement Establishing the World Trade Organization, Annex 1C, 1869 UNTS 299, 33 ILM 1197 (1994) [hereinafter TRIPS Agreement].

Obligations on the protection of biotechnological inventions under the TRIPS agreement

Given the serious disagreements between countries during the negotiations and drafting of WTO agreements at the start of the 1990s,[2] the TRIPS Agreement has only one provision on biotechnological inventions.[3] Article 27.3(b)[4] provides for items that may be excluded from patentability and items that may be protected: on the one hand, members can exclude from patentability plants, animals, and processes which are mainly biological; on the other hand, they must protect microorganisms, non-biological processes, microbiological processes, and plant varieties with patents, an efficient *sui generis* system,[5] or by a combination of both methods. Although apparently clear, this measure remains ambiguous because of the lack of definitions concerning the terms used, especially the terms "plants," "animals," "microorganisms," "mainly biological processes," "non-biological processes," "microbiological processes," and "efficient *sui generis* system."

Since most international documents contain some ambiguity, it is widely accepted that those equivocal issues leave room for flexibility to the contracting members. This flexibility is as reasonable as necessary for WTO members to adapt their intellectual property rights (IPR) legislation to their economic and technological development requirements. However, ambiguity and flexibility also produce legal insecurity, which may harm international IPR protection as well as international trade.[6]

The WTO members' implementation of these obligations encountered several problems, mainly of ethical, technical, and politico-economic nature.

Ethical problems

Article 27.2[7] of the TRIPS Agreement allows WTO Members to exclude from patentability inventions contrary to ***ordre public*** or morality.[8] This provision constitutes a general principle, but its application to the case of biotechnological inventions requires detailed rules.

2 TRIPS, GATT (General Agreement on Tariffs and Trade) and GATS (General Agreement on Trade of Services) are the three pillar sectorial agreements of the WTO. They are the result of the Uruguay Round multilateral trade negotiation that ended in 1994 and led to the establishment of the WTO itself.

3 *See* generally NUNO PIRES DE CARVALHO, THE TRIPS REGIME OF PATENT RIGHTS (Kluwer Law International, 2002); DUNCAN MATTHEWS, GLOBALISING INTELLECTUAL PROPERTY RIGHTS: THE TRIPS AGREEMENT (Routledge, 2002); INTELLECTUAL PROPERTY AND INTERNATIONAL TRADE: THE TRIPS AGREEMENT (Carlos M. Correa, and Abdulqawi A. Yusuf, eds, Kluwer Law International, 1998); Lawrence R. Helfer, ***Intellectual Property Rights in Plant Varieties*** 33–54 (FAO, 2004); John Worthy, ***Intellectual Property Protection after GATT,*** 16 EUR. INTELLECTUAL PROPERTY REV. (1994).

4 This article provides: "Members may also exclude from patentability: (a) diagnostic, therapeutic and surgical methods for the treatment of humans or animals; (b) plants and animals other than micro-organisms, and essentially biological processes for the production of plants or animals other than non-biological and microbiological processes. However, Members shall provide for the protection of plant varieties either by patents or by an effective sui generis system or by any combination thereof. The provisions of this subparagraph shall be reviewed four years after the date of entry into force of the WTO Agreement."

5 *See* HANS MORTEN HAUGEN, THE RIGHT TO FOOD AND THE TRIPS AGREEMENT 255–285 (Martinus Nijhoff Publishers, 2007).

6 For an analysis of the level of discretion available to WTO members as well as to members of other treaties or conventions, *see* Lawrence R. Helfer, ***supra*** note 4, at 65–82.

7 It provides: "Members may exclude from patentability inventions, the prevention within their territory of the commercial exploitation of which is necessary to protect ordre public or morality, including to protect human, animal or plant life or health or to avoid serious prejudice to the environment, provided that such exclusion is not made merely because the exploitation is prohibited by their law."

8 NUNO PIRES DE CARVALHO, ***supra*** note 4, at 207.

Among all biotechnological inventions, the main ethical problems arise for those innovations related to the human body and animals.

In the name of *ordre public* and morality, US, EU, French, and Chinese laws strictly prohibit the following from patentability: a) human cloning technologies; b) technologies for the modification of the human genome; c) the use of human embryos for industrial or commercial purposes; and d) technologies for the genetic modification of animals which cause suffering to them without substantial medical utility for human beings or animals.[9] Based on these provisions, it can be observed that respect for human dignity constitutes a primary element of the notions of *ordre public* and morality, which has and shall have a universal value. It is in this spirit that governments and scientific associations have conducted international campaigns against the cloning of human beings. However, even if the prohibition of cruelty to animals and respect for their identity also form part of the content of morality, it is not an imperative rule. Every country can weigh the benefit to human beings against the suffering of animals, and if the former significantly outweighs the latter, the law permits genetic modifications of animals as well as patenting thereof.[10] The memories of protests against the use of animals for medical experiments remains fresh; however, the supporters of these ideas do not constitute the majority of society, which makes it impossible to qualify these convictions as moral rules for general application.

In addition to having made genetic modification of animals morally acceptable, the interests and needs of humanity have also made acceptable certain technologies related to the modification of the human body. It is for this reason that the EU (via Directive 98/44) and US accept the patentability of elements isolated from the human body or otherwise produced by a technical process, including the sequence or the partial sequence of a gene, even if the element's structure is identical to that of a natural element. In this international climate, following bilateral negotiations, China modeled its legislation after the US and EU. Since the TRIPS Agreement leaves WTO members leeway to evaluate potential violations of the *ordre public* or morality, the conformity of the European and Chinese legislation with this agreement cannot be doubted.

However, the issues regarding the patentability of elements isolated from the human body or otherwise produced by processes are worthy of consideration. In China, unfortunately, the ethical issues stemming from the patentability of biological elements have not generated enough public debate, which can be explained by the general public's lack of knowledge and civil society's detachment from the legislative activities.[11] The discussion among an elite group of intellectuals produces only limited influence on the Chinese authorities, who are more interested in economic and scientific development in the context of globalization.

9 Though there were difficulties in the application of Directive 98/44/CE in France, the provisions in Article 6.2 of the Directive have been introduced into French law without problems. *See* also Chapter 36 (Nie) in this volume.

10 *See Ex parte Allen* case (2 U.S.P.Q.2d (BNA) 1425 (Bd. Pat. App. & Interferences 1987)) before USPTO, *Harvard Mouse* case (T 19/90, October 3, 1990, *JO OEB* 1990, at 476. *PIBD* 1991, n°494, III, p. 96) before EPO and 3.1.2 Chapter I Part II of the Guidelines for Examination of Chinese Patent Office.

11 Yongnian Zheng & Joseph Fewsmith, China's Opening Society: The Non-State Sector and Governance (Routledge, 2008). On the importance of the civil society participation not only to the legislative activities, but on the entire legal system including access to justice, public interest litigations, monitoring, and accountability of the action of the governments and enterprises, *see* Chapters 2 (Farah), 3 (Di Turi), 4 (Bonfanti), 5 (Choukroune), 6 (Vadi), 12 (He), 15 (Huang), 19 (Ning), 30 (Rossi), 31 (Prasad), and 32 (Hu) in this volume.

At the EU level and national level of France, the patentability of subject matter related to the human body was the center of debate in both society and the parliaments. Led by its economic policies, the EU settled the issues regarding *ordre public* and morality by resorting to the difference between natural and artificial states to which elements of the human body belong and to the degree of human intervention in their discovery or production. In the authors' opinion, this difference is relevant, to a certain extent, for the distinction between discovery and invention, but does not resolve ethical problems because, according to our view, there is no difference between a gene in its natural state and one made by a human being, since both of them carry genetic information belonging to a person. It is true that granting a patent on these elements does not result in the ownership of a gene or of a human body; however, one cannot deny the fact that the genetic information of a person is thus made the incorporeal property of another person or company. This constitutes a kind of damage to the dignity of the human source or carrier of the gene. In addition, EPO, EU (via Directive 98/44), and Chinese law[12] declare that genes are essentially chemical materials; however, this characterization does not contradict the fact that genes are at the same time biological materials. The qualification of human genes as chemical materials is just a method to bypass the ethical problems that nonetheless remain. How can one deny the existence of genetic information carried by genes, which is moreover the key element of the invention concerned? How can one explain the use of chemical patents in the field of biology? In our view, the patentability of an element of the human body, regardless of it being in its natural state or produced by a human being, constitutes direct damage to the dignity of the person concerned and indirect damage to the dignity of humanity as a whole. It is this spirit of protection of human rights and dignity that one can view the provisions of Article L.611–18 of the Intellectual Property Code (CPI) in French law.

How can we then evaluate the application of Article 27.2 of the TRIPS Agreement in these countries? As we have said, the evaluation of the violation of *ordre public* or morality falls within the competence of legislators, patent offices, and national judges; the WTO has only marginal control over the respect of the conditions provided in Article 27.2 of the TRIPS Agreement. Under the provisions of this article,[13] if the French law excludes from patentability elements of the human body isolated or otherwise produced by a process, it shall simultaneously forbid or limit the commercialization of these elements.[14] In fact, the French law satisfies this condition because the Civil Code provides for a principle of non-commercialization of human body elements.[15] Therefore, if the French law, seen from this point of view, is not in conformity with EU Directive 98/44, it is totally in conformity with the TRIPS Agreement.[16]

12 Biotechnological inventions are regulated by section 9, Chapter X, Part II of the *Shencha Zhinan* [Guidelines for Examination] which is the chapter entitled *Guanyu Huaxue Lingyu Zhuanli Shenqing Shencha de Yuogan Guiding* [Provisions on the Examination of Inventions in the Chemical Field].

13 Article 27.2 of the TRIPs Agreement provides that "Members may exclude from patentability inventions, *the prevention within their territory of the commercial exploitation of which is necessary* to protect ordre public or morality" [emphasis added].

14 Nuno Pires de Carvalho, *supra* note 4, at 211.

15 *See* Law No. 94–653 of July 29, 1994 regarding respect of the human body.

16 On the contrary, if one day France is obligated to modify its law to accept explicitly the patentability of Article 27.2 of the TRIPs Agreement, it is up to the French to articulate the definition of public morality for its society.

Likewise, both the EU and French laws are in conformity with the TRIPS Agreement, but the French law could be, at the same time, not in conformity with the EU law. The difference between the French and EU laws has its origin in the fact that *EU morality*, in the sense of Directive 98/44, differs from French morality. From this point of view, one can observe that the WTO law facilitates the harmonization of its members' laws in an appropriate manner, while the EU law imposed harmonization, since it forced one kind of morality on all its Member States.

Technical problems

Plant and animal inventions

From a technical point of view, the key issue in this field consists of the adaptation of common patent law for biotechnological inventions. Because of the particular characteristics of these types of inventions compared to classical inventions in mechanical, physical, or chemical fields,[17] the common patent law is considered unsuitable for the protection of biotechnological inventions. That is why both the EPO and French law have excluded from patentability animal and plant varieties. The particular interests of industries and the common interests of society, however, make the protection of biotechnology necessary; that is why France has created the *sui generis* regime of Plant Variety Certificate (PVC), based on the Convention for the Protection of New Varieties of Plants (UPOV Convention). The EU and China have also adopted the PVC model.[18]

Contrary to expectations, the existence of the PVC regime later became the reason to exclude plant varieties from patentability in order to avoid overlapping protections. Thus, it is not the inappropriate nature of patent law when applied to biotechnology that explains the exclusion of plant innovation from patentability. *A contrario*, plant varieties should have been patentable if there was no PVC regime. The case law of the EPO and the promulgation of EU Directive 98/44 confirm this conclusion since they accept the patentability of plant and animal inventions except those excluded explicitly by the texts of the European Patent Convention (EPC) and the Directive. If one recalls the initial reason for this exclusion, one could deduce that the terms "animal races" and "plant varieties" have been chosen to designate all plant and animal inventions, whatever may be their taxonomic classification. However, times have changed. In fact, the case law of the EPO as well as Directive 98/44, which consolidated the former into a legal text, has reversed Article 53(b) of the EPC as much as possible. This point presents an unsettled technical problem: if the existence of the PVC regime is the reason why plant varieties are excluded from patentability, why is there no such *sui generis* regime for animals, like an *Animal Race Certificate*? Moreover, if plant and animal

17 It concerns especially the appreciation of novelty, inventive steps, and the description of biotechnological inventions.

18 Convention for the Protection of Plant Varieties. The UPOV has 63 members as of November 24, 2006, but before 1992 it was accepted by only 20 members. *See* HANS MORTEN HAUGEN, *supra* note 6, at 84–85, 256; GEERTRUI VAN OVERWALLE, THE LEGAL PROTECTION OF BIOTECHNOLOGICAL INVENTIONS IN EUROPE AND IN THE UNITED STATES: CURRENT FRAMEWORK AND FUTURE DEVELOPMENTS (University Press, 1997); Lawrence R. Helfer, *supra* note 4, at 21–32; NUNO PIRES DE CARVALHO, *supra* note 34 at 218–222; Jim Chen, *Diversity and Deadlock: Transcending Conventional Wisdom on the Relationship between Biological Diversity and Intellectual Property*, 31(10) ENVTL. L. REP. 625 (2001); John Linarelli, *Treaty Governance, Intellectual Property and Biodiversity*, 6 ENVTL. L. REV.21–38 (2004).

inventions other than plant varieties and animal races are patentable, why should only plant varieties and animal races be excluded, since common patents are applicable to them? Thus, if one cannot justify this different treatment, the patentability of plant varieties[19] and animal races should be accepted.

Taking a different approach, Chinese law excludes all plant and animal inventions from patentability, whatever may be their taxonomic classification. This is explicitly permitted by the TRIPS Agreement if the terms *plant* and *animal* in Article 27.3(b) are to be interpreted by their broader definition, as they should.

Whatever the ethical or technical reasons, the TRIPS Agreement leaves to WTO members the decision to exclude or include biotechnological inventions in their patent laws in view of the worldwide divergences. However, TRIPS Article 1.1 permits its members to put into place stronger protection of IPR than that provided for in this Agreement.[20] The Agreement shall then shall apply in a systemic spirit, which is even in the primary logic of law. That is why we wish to point out that plant and animal inventions could be excluded from or included in patent law according to the TRIPS Agreement, but there shall be no discordance in theory and in practice.

Plant varieties

The TRIPS Agreement imposes on WTO members the obligation to efficiently protect plant varieties; however, it leaves them some freedom of choice in regards to the protection method. The EU, France, and China have all chosen to protect these types of inventions through the *sui generis* regime of PVC, which follows the model of the UPOV Convention. Though the 1978 UPOV Convention forbids overlapping protection by patent and PVC, the 1991 UPOV version permits it. However, the EU, France, and China opted for protection through the PVC only.[21] It remains to be seen if this regime constitutes an efficient protection of plant varieties; the answer depends on the criteria that one chooses to judge.

Some WTO members dispute whether the UPOV Convention represents the only choice for an efficient *sui generis* system,[22] and the US has even indicated that specific criteria exist for evaluating the efficiency of this system.[23] In fact, the obligation regarding an *efficient sui generis regime* under the TRIPS Agreement deals only with results, and the WTO members have complete freedom of choice regarding the implementation method. However, most WTO members regard the UPOV Convention as an important reference in this respect, and any divergence stems from the differences between the 1991 and 1978 versions. Developed countries – especially the EU – consider that the balance between rights and obligations in the 1991 version is favorable to all countries, while developing

19 The prohibition of overlapping protections by patent and PVC by UPOV 1978 has already been deleted in the 1991 version of the Convention.

20 Article 1.1 reads as follows: "[. . .] Members may, but shall not be obliged to, implement in their law more extensive protection than is required by this Agreement, provided that such protection does not contravene the provisions of this Agreement." *See* Daniel Gervais, The TRIPS Agreement, Drafting History and Analysis 86 (Sweet & Maxwell, 2nd ed., 2003).

21 There are, after all, in EPO and in France exceptional cases in which a patent of genetic engineering includes a series of plant products, whatever may be their taxonomic classification. Therefore, it is possible that PVC and a patent simultaneously protect the same variety.

22 IP/C/W/369, at 11–12.

23 United States, IP/C/W/209.

countries prefer the 1978 version because they think it leaves more flexibility to Contracting Parties to take into account different national strategies. In fact, the most notable difference between the two versions lies in the regulation of exceptions regarding preferential policies for farmers.

When compared to the 1978 version of the UPOV Convention, which does not treat the exceptions regarding farmers, the 1991 version provides conditions for the application of farmers' rights. According to Article 15(2) of the 1991 version, farmers' rights shall be applied within reasonable limits and under the condition of safeguarding the PVC holders' legitimate interests. As Nuno Pires de Carvalho indicated, this provision is similar to the one present in Article 30 of the TRIPS Agreement.[24] If the *sui generis* regime also is to be in line with the principle of balance between rights and obligations present in Articles 7 and 30 of the TRIPS Agreement, it seems that the aforementioned conditions are necessary for the protection of the PVC holders' legitimate rights. However, under the *sui generis* regime, the level of protection for plant varieties can be inferior to that for patents since the subject matter of this regime is of considerable interest for agricultural development and food security.[25] As a consequence, the fundamental interests of farmers shall also be taken into account, which is in the spirit of TRIPS Article 8.1.[26] Even if agricultural development and food security constitute a legitimate objective for farmers' rights, the principle of proportionality[27] should still be respected. This means that farmers' rights shall be permitted only to the extent necessary to achieve their legitimate objective. From this point of view, Article 15(2) of the 1991 UPOV Convention could logically become the reference point for the evaluation of the efficiency of the *sui generis* regime.

In order to implement Article 15(2) of the 1991 UPOV Convention, the second and third paragraphs of Article 14 of Community Regulation 2100/94 and especially Regulation 1768/95 provide conditions for the application of farmers' rights. EU law limits the application of farmers' rights to certain categories of plant varieties that are considered important for food security, and exempts small farmers from paying licensing fees. Under French law, no exception outside of the compulsory licensing system is provided for, but we can predict that the French law will move closer to the EU law on this point. Meanwhile, Chinese law has integrated the provisions of the 1978 UPOV Convention, making the conditions for the application of farmers' rights more flexible. Chinese law allows farmers to use seeds

24 Article 30 of TRIPs reads as follows "Members may provide limited exceptions to the exclusive rights conferred by a patent, provided that such exceptions do not unreasonably conflict with a normal exploitation of the patent and do not unreasonably prejudice the legitimate interests of the patent owner, taking account of the legitimate interests of third parties." Nuno Pires de Carvalho, *supra* at 180 (2002).

25 On agricultural development, food security, and the related matters of the right to food, *see* Chapters 18 (Zorzi Giustiniani) and 20 (Simpson) in this volume; for a focus on China, *see* Chapter 19 (Ning) in this volume.

26 Article 8.1 of the TRIPs Agreement provides that: "Members may, in formulating or amending their laws and regulations, adopt measures necessary to protect public health and nutrition and to promote the public interest in sectors of vital importance to their socio-economic and technological development, provided that such measures are consistent with the provisions of this Agreement."

27 Article 2.2 of Regulation 1768/95/CE goes in this direction which provides that: "The legitimate interests shall not be considered to be safeguarded if one or more of these interests are adversely affected without account being taken of the need to maintain a reasonable balance between all of them, or of the need for proportionality between the purpose of the relevant condition and the actual effect of the implementation thereof."

obtained from their own harvest for reproduction purposes.[28] Farmers are also exempted from paying royalties to PVC holders. In view of Article 15(2) of the 1991 UPOV Convention, and in comparison to the EU law, Chinese law needs to define the notion of farmers by excluding agricultural companies and to limit the application of farmers' rights only to categories of plant varieties important to food security and national agricultural development.

Distinction between discovery and invention

The most relevant impact that biotechnology has had on patent law is that the patentability of certain subject matters obscures the distinction between discovery and invention. In order to adapt patent law to the protection of biotechnological inventions, the US, the EU, France, and China have accepted the patenting of biological materials in isolation from their natural environment, even if they existed in their natural state. One can observe that the involvement of artificial manipulation and the possible concrete applications of the materials constitute two essential criteria for the qualification of an invention; in our opinion, however, these criteria do not seem to be justified.

In fact, a discovery can involve as much human intervention as an invention, and the object of discovery can become a critical element for an invention. In other words, one can distinguish the step of discovery from the use of the discovered object. The first step qualifies as discovery, and the second constitutes an invention of application. Hence, we think the US, EU, and Chinese laws have combined these two steps into one and thus transposed the human efforts at the stage of discovery to the stage of conception, which relaxed the criteria for classifying the stage of invention in the sense of patentability. Alternatively, these laws transported the criteria of industrial application of the second step to the first step of discovery in order to make the discovery meet the condition of patentability; either way, this amounts to an unjustified technical choice in law. Otherwise, if it is the discovery's value that has created the need for protection, the patent should protect not only biological discoveries, but also those in other technological areas whose creation or process is of critical use to this discovery. However, if adopted, this rule would cause a revolution within the patent regime, which cannot be accepted.

If ethical and technical considerations have led France to refuse the patentability of biological materials isolated from their natural environments, the reasons behind the patentability of these elements in the US, the EU, and China are rather of an economic and political nature.

When compared to exceptions to patentability in the name of *ordre public* or morality, exceptions based on technical reasons often appear thin or disappear altogether. The exceptions concerning biotechnology serve as a clear example. Given the evolution of patent law, the PVC *sui generis* system is no longer necessary to protect plant innovation, and technical problems are not able to prevent patent law from following economic policies oriented by economic and industrial interests.

28 Zhōnghuá Rénmín Gònghéguó Zhíwù Xīn Pǐnzhǒng Bǎohù Tiáolì (中华人民共和国植物新品种保护条例) [Regulation of the People's Republic of China on Protection of New Varieties of Plants] (promulgated by the State Council, March 20, 1997, effective March 1, 2013), Article 10. This provision allows a broader and satisfactory application of the right to food in China, *see* Chapter 19 (Ning) in this volume.

Politico-economic problems

Due to the importance of biotechnology for public health, agro-alimentation, the environment, and many industries, all countries have adopted economic policies favorable to the technological and industrial development of this field.[29] However, they have not adopted the same policies concerning the protection of biotechnological innovations by industrial property law because the legal regime can either positively or negatively affect technological development. This effect depends on the level of technological and industrial development of each specific field in an individual country. Strong protection of IPRs would hinder the development of a country which is not advanced in the field because certain big foreign companies would dominate the technology market and domestic companies would have to pay excessively during their developing period.[30] On the contrary, weak protection of IPRs would deter the technological development of a country where domestic companies have the capacity to compete against foreign companies.

Given its high level of technological and economic development in the field of biotechnology, the EU and France are sure that the US' efficient protection of IPRs has greatly contributed to its success in this field.[31] In order to reinforce their competitiveness in research and commerce, the European Commission and the French government have decided to provide better legal protection for biotechnological innovations. In this aspect, the European Commission is more advanced than France because French economic policies have been moderated by the country's ethical considerations as witnessed by the debates concerning the implementation of the Community Directive 98/44 into French law.

If the high level of technological and economic development justifies widespread protection of biotechnological innovations in the EU and in France, the gap between China and the EU or France should have resulted in a different Chinese economic policy in this field. Since the application of an open-door policy and the domestic reforms, which took place 30 years ago, China has accumulated substantial experience with research and development in the field of biotechnology. Engineers and enterprises are making progress towards launching China's future development; however, the country has not yet achieved independent development capacity in this field. For now, most Chinese-made products remain imitations of products developed by foreign companies, and Chinese enterprises have made only limited innovations themselves.[32] Given the current state of affairs, the Chinese government excluded from patentability all innovations related to plants and animals, while accepting the patentability of genes and DNA sequences. In our opinion, the Chinese government should have excluded all these elements from patentability in order to prevent foreign

29 On issues related to technology transfer, *see* Chapter 11 (Cima) in this volume. Technological and industrial development legislations in the field of public health, agro-alimentation, and the environment can be often used to discriminate against foreign companies and favor domestic production, *see* Chapters 8 (Sindico & Gibson), 9 (Ibrahim, Deleuil & Farah), 11 (Cima), 27 (Prévost), and 29 (Gruszczynski, Ötvös & Farah) in this volume.

30 *See* Chapters 4 (Bonfanti), 11 (Cima), 35 (Watal), and 36 (Nie) in this volume.

31 Hélène Gaumont-Prat, ***Brevetabilité Of Vivant: Animal Et Humain, Inventions Biotechnologiques Et Contexte Socio-Juridique***, 4240(41) Juris-classeur 11 (2006).

32 *See* Guojia Fazhan He Gaige Weiyuanhui Gaojishu Si & Zhongguo Shengwu Gongcheng Xuehui (Bureau of Hi-technology of National Development and Reform Commission and Chinese Academy of Biotechnology), ***Zhongguo Shengwu Chanye Fazhan Baogao 2010*** [***Annual Report on the Development of Biotechnological Industries in China 2010***], Huaxue Gongye Chubanshe [Chemistry industry press] (2011). *See* also Chapter 36 (Nie) in this volume.

companies from dominating genetic resources,[33] which can otherwise be justified by the theory of the distinction between discovery and invention.

Comparative evaluation of TRIPS implementation in the field of biotechnology

On the basis of a comparative study, we can also draw a conclusion about the related provisions in Articles 27.2 and 27.3 of the TRIPS Agreement.

First, WTO members shall benefit from leeway in the implementation of TRIPS Articles 27.2 and 27.3. Since it is not possible to give common criteria for the application of *ordre public* or morality in all societies of WTO members who have different history, culture, ethics, morality, and legal systems,[34] conformity of national laws with the TRIPS Agreement can only be conducted on a case-by-case basis. Moreover, national patent offices and judges are better suited than WTO Panels or the Appellate Body of the WTO dispute settlement system to evaluate an offense to *ordre public* or morality. Nonetheless, this does not deny the competence of the Panel to exercise control over the proportionality of national measures. Furthermore, since no consensus exists on the definition of "plants," "animals," "microorganisms," "essentially biological processes," and "efficient *sui generis* regime" for the protection of plant varieties, WTO members shall also benefit from a certain degree of liberty in this regard. Precisely, plants and animals should be understood in a broad sense, which leaves free choice to WTO members to make patentable (or not) such subject matters. As far as the *sui generis* regime for protection of plant varieties is concerned, it seems the 1991 UPOV Convention will become an important reference point in the appreciation of the efficiency of the regime, whatsoever the intention of the members, especially concerning farmers' rights. In our opinion, this privilege is absolutely necessary for developing countries and for global food security[35] and, as a consequence, shall be maintained in either the *sui generis* system or in the patent law. However, at the same time, this privilege shall also be limited to the extent necessary for development.[36] Finally, taking into account the leeway that the TRIPS Agreement leaves to WTO members, it is not necessary to give uniform criteria for the application of the aforementioned terms. On one hand, despite the lack of definitions for the terms mentioned above, Article 27.3 of the TRIPS Agreement prescribes what shall be protected and what may be excluded from patentability; on the other hand, the absence of definitions should not obstruct the national application of TRIPS provisions.

Second, on the future negotiation and revision of Articles 27.2 and 27.3 of the TRIPS Agreement, we foresee that it shall always include certain exceptions for objectives such as the protection of *ordre public* and morality as well as the life and health of persons and animals, the preservation of plants, the respect of human dignity, the protection of the environment, and food security. Facing the tendency of developed countries to enlarge the field of patent protection, if we delete the provisions of Article 27.2 from the TRIPS Agreement, the influence of comparative law and bilateral pressure will make developing countries adopt

33 *See* also Chapter 36 (Nie) in this volume.

34 On the concepts of culture and ethics and how these elements affect the perceptions, borders, and definition of morality and legal systems, *see* Chapters 6 (Vadi) and 17 (Heurtebise) in this volume.

35 For further reasoning on these matters, *see* Chapters 19 (Ning), and 20 (Simpson) in this volume.

36 *See* Chapter 2 (Farah) in this volume.

the same patent regimes as developed countries, though this might not be their intention.[37] As far as exceptions in the field of plant and animal inventions are concerned, it seems that the only possible basis is the provision in Article 27.2 concerning *ordre public* and morality. However, from an economic point of view, taking into account the unequal technological and economic development among WTO members, the TRIPS Agreement shall leave them sufficient flexibility to adapt their patent laws to their national economic policies. Otherwise, since it seems that the *sui generis* regime for the protection of plant varieties will not replace the patent regime in the short term, farmers' privileges shall be permitted for food security as well as development purposes.[38]

37 *See* Chapter 4 (Bonfanti) in this volume.

38 We can and shall assimilate these privileges with the exceptions to patent rights under Articles 8 and 30 of the TRIPs Agreement.

35 Public Health, Intellectual Property Rights, and Developing Countries' Access to Medicines**

*Jayashree Watal**

Introduction: Why is the subject of IPRs and access to medicines important? Contextualizing it[1]

Many would consider the right to have access to essential medicines as being an integral part of the right to health.[2] The question that arises is: which medicines are essential? Are these those medicines that are on the World Health Organization (WHO) list of essential medicines,[3] or those that are on the national lists, or those that are the most important medicines needed to treat diseases that contribute most to disease around the world? Among such causes, should the focus be on communicable diseases only or can epidemics be also of the non-communicable kind?

Finding a balance in the protection of intellectual property rights (IPRs) between the short-term interest in maximizing access to medical technologies and the long-term interest in promoting creativity and innovation is important at the national level.[4] This task has been made more difficult at the international level on account of international IPR treaties that

* This chapter is written in the author's personal capacity and does not engage the responsibility of the WTO Secretariat or WTO Members either individually or jointly.

** This chapter is part of the results of the Research Project on "*Current Trends of Chinese Law towards Non-Trade Concerns such as Sustainable Development and the Protection of Environment, Public Health, Food Safety, Cultural, Social and Economic Rights, Labor Rights and the Reduction of Poverty from the Perspective of International Law and WTO Law*", coordinated by Professor Paolo Davide Farah at gLAWcal – Global Law Initiatives for Sustainable Development (United Kingdom) and at West Virginia University John D. Rockefeller IV School of Policy and Politics, Department of Public Administration, in partnership with the Center of Advanced Studies on Contemporary China (CASCC) in Turin (Italy), Maastricht University Faculty of Law, Department of International and European Law and IGIR – Institute for Globalisation and International Regulation (Netherlands), and Tsinghua University, School of Law, Institute of Public International Law and the Center for Research on Intellectual Property Law in Beijing (China). This publication and the Conference Series were sponsored by China–EU School of Law (CESL) at the China University of Political Science and Law (CUPL). The activities of CESL at CUPL are supported by the European Union and the People's Republic of China.

1 Much of this chapter is drawn from my chapter *WTO, IPRs and Access to Medicines*, in HEALTHY IPRS (Meir Pugatch, ed., Stockholm Network, 2007), http://www.stockholm-network.org/downloads/publications/Healthy_IPRs.pdf (last visited July 16, 2016).

2 *See* factsheet on the *Right to Health*, http://www.ohchr.org/Documents/Publications/Factsheet31.pdf (last visited July 16, 2016).

3 http://www.who.int/medicines/publications/essentialmedicines/en/ (last visited July 16, 2016).

4 For an overview of the relationship between health and intellectual property rights, *see* HIROKO YAMANE, INTERPRETING TRIPS: GLOBALISATION OF INTELLECTUAL PROPERTY RIGHTS AND ACCESS TO MEDICINES (Hart, 2011).

may not take account of differing levels of economic, technological, and social development. Perhaps nowhere do these issues excite stronger feelings than in regard to pharmaceutical patents, where tension between the need to provide incentives for research and development into new medicines and the need to make existing medicines as widely available as possible can be acute.

TRIPS provisions relevant to public health: Relevance of public health in TRIPS negotiations; end results

The negotiators of the World Trade Organization (WTO) Agreement on Trade-Related Aspects of Intellectual Property Rights[5] (TRIPS) attempted to find an appropriate balance both within the Agreement and within the single undertaking that incorporated the results of the Uruguay Round. Even if not all developing countries participated in these negotiations in equal measure, it would be fair to say that the developing countries' perspective was represented.[6] As it is widely acknowledged, the TRIPS Agreement, in an effort to strike a proper balance between the differing interests of the participating countries, provides for significant flexibility in the protection to be given. This flexibility, which went considerably further than some of the ***demandeurs*** in the negotiations would have liked and were achieving in bilateral agreements at the time, resulted from a compromise achieved through negotiation by developing countries acting collectively and making issue-based alliances in a multilateral context.[7] In addition to the provisions entitled "Objectives" (Article 7) and "Principles" (Article 8), developing-country negotiators influenced several of the flexibilities in the provisions relevant for pharmaceutical inventions, such as those relating to exhaustion of IPRs, compulsory licenses, and government use of patents and minimal requirements for test data.

Although many aspects of the TRIPS Agreement could potentially bear on access to medicines, such as trademarks, copyright, industrial design, and enforcement of IPRs,[8] the focus of this chapter is on the sections on patents and the protection of undisclosed information.

The TRIPS Agreement requires Member countries to make patents available for all inventions – whether products or processes – in all fields of technology, subject to the normal tests of novelty, inventiveness, and industrial applicability. It also requires that patents be available and patent rights enjoyable without discrimination as to the place of invention, field of technology, or whether products are imported or locally produced (Article 27.1). Thus, no longer is it possible for Members to exclude entire sectors of technology – such as pharmaceuticals or chemicals – from the grant of patents or to discriminate against such patents once these are granted.

5 Agreement on Trade-Related Aspects of Intellectual Property Rights, April 15, 1994, Marrakesh Agreement Establishing the World Trade Organization, Annex 1C, 1869 UNTS 299, 33 ILM 1197 (1994) [hereinafter TRIPS Agreement].

6 The author was India's negotiator during 1989–1990 when the TRIPS Agreement was largely drafted.

7 For an overview of the TRIPS Agreement, *see* Jayashree Watal, Intellectual Property Rights in the WTO and Developing Countries Chapter II (Kluwer Law International, 2001).

8 For instance, the brand name of the medicine (either originator or generic) could be protected under trademarks; the inserts that accompany the medicine could contain copyrighted material; and the packaging could be the subject of industrial design protection. Similarly, the issue of enforcement of IPRs so as to eliminate counterfeit medicines in the market should be at the heart of the debate on public health.

There are three permissible exclusions from patent grant even where the inventions meet the criteria for patentability. One is for inventions contrary to *ordre public* or morality, which explicitly includes inventions that are dangerous to human, animal, and plant life or health, or that seriously prejudice the environment.[9] The use of this exclusion is subject to the conditions that the commercial exploitation of the invention must also be prevented and that this prevention must be necessary for the protection of *ordre public* or morality (Article 27.2). This means that if a Member decides to exclude certain types of inventions from patent grant – for example, processes of human cloning – it cannot then allow the commercial exploitation of these inventions in its territory.

The second exclusion is for inventions that are diagnostic, therapeutic, and surgical methods for the treatment of humans or animals (Article 27.3(a)). For example, an eye surgeon who invents a novel, more effective method of removing cataracts may not be granted a patent if a country opts to incorporate this option in its law. Some may argue that such methods of treatment are not industrially applicable and therefore not patentable in any event. However, since this may not be very clear and also since industrial applicability is treated as synonymous with utility under the TRIPS Agreement (footnote 5), the negotiators considered it useful to make explicit such exclusion.

The final exclusion is for inventions that are plants and animals (other than microorganisms) and essentially biological processes for the production of plants or animals (other than non-biological and microbiological processes).[10] However, any country excluding plant varieties from patent protection must provide an effective *sui generis* system of protection. Moreover, the whole provision was made subject to review four years after the Agreement comes into force (Article 27.3(b)).

A product patent must confer the following exclusive rights on the right holder: making, using, offering for sale, selling, and importing the patented product. Process patent protection must give exclusive rights not only over use of the process but also over products obtained directly by the process. Patent owners shall also have the right to assign, or transfer by succession, the patent, and to conclude licensing contracts (Article 28). The exclusive right of importation must be read with Article 6 on the exhaustion of IPRs, which obliges only non-discrimination in the application of the regime and excludes this subject from the WTO dispute settlement processes.

Members may provide limited exceptions to the exclusive rights conferred by a patent, provided that such exceptions do not unreasonably conflict with a normal exploitation of the patent and do not unreasonably prejudice the legitimate interests of the patent owner, taking into account the legitimate interests of third parties (Article 30). This provision has been the subject of a dispute settlement decision in the WTO wherein the act of using the patented pharmaceutical invention to obtain regulatory approvals for marketing was considered to be a permissible exception.[11] Finally, the term of protection available shall be at least a period of 20 years counted from the filing date (Article 33).

9 For a further reasoning on the concept of *ordre public* and morality which excludes the patentability of certain inventions, *see* Chapter 34 (Feng, Shu & Zhang) in this volume.

10 For a deeper analysis on the protection of biotechnology innovation by patent, *see* Chapter 34 (Feng, Shu & Zhang) in this volume.

11 Report of the Panel, *Canada – Patent Protection for Pharmaceutical Products*, WT/DS114/R (March 17, 2000).

Members shall require that an applicant for a patent shall disclose the invention in a manner sufficiently clear and complete for the invention to be carried out by a person skilled in the art. Members may require the applicant to indicate the best mode for carrying out the invention known to the inventor at the filing date or, where priority is claimed, at the priority date of the application (Article 29.1). If the subject matter of a patent is a process for obtaining a product, the judicial authorities shall have the authority to order the defendant to prove that the process to obtain an identical product is different from the patented process, where certain conditions indicating a likelihood that the protected process was used are met (Article 34).

Compulsory licensing and government use without the authorization of the right holder are allowed without any restriction on grounds, but they are subject to conditions aimed at protecting the legitimate interests of the right holder. Mainly contained in Article 31, these conditions include the obligation – as a general rule – not to grant such licenses unless an unsuccessful attempt has been made to acquire a voluntary license on reasonable terms and conditions within a reasonable period of time. The requirement to pay remuneration that is adequate in the circumstances of each case – taking into account the economic value of the license – must also be observed, as must a requirement that decisions be subject to judicial or other independent review by a distinct higher authority. Another important condition is that such use must be made predominantly to supply the domestic market. Some of these conditions are relaxed in the case of public noncommercial use and when compulsory licenses are employed to remedy practices that have been established as anticompetitive by a legal process or in cases of emergency. A common misconception is that Article 31 restricts the grounds of compulsory licenses to national emergencies or extreme cases of urgency, which is not the case and was subsequently clarified, as discussed below, in a later WTO instrument.

The TRIPS Agreement also contains provisions to protect undisclosed information. The Agreement requires that a person lawfully in control of such information must have the possibility of preventing it from being disclosed to, acquired by, or used by others without his or her consent in a manner contrary to honest commercial practices. "*Manner contrary to honest commercial practices*" includes breach of contract, breach of confidence and inducement to breach, as well as the acquisition of undisclosed information by third parties who knew, or were grossly negligent in failing to know, that such practices were involved in the acquisition (Article 39.2). In addition, undisclosed test data and other data that governments require to be submitted as a condition of approving the marketing of pharmaceutical or agricultural chemical products that use new chemical entities must be protected against unfair commercial use where the generation of such data has involved considerable effort. Members must also protect such data against disclosure, except where necessary to protect the public, or unless steps are taken to ensure that the data are protected against unfair commercial use (Article 39.3). While market exclusivity for the originator of such test data is not explicitly required, Members cannot meet their obligation to protect such data against unfair commercial use simply by protecting it against disclosure. In the run up to the Doha ministerial meeting in 2001, some Members expressed their view in the TRIPS Council that the most effective way to implement Article 39.3 was through market exclusivity, while others disputed this.[12]

12 Some of these views are reflected in document IP/C/M/31 which reproduces Members' statements in the TRIPS Council made on June 20, 2001 in the special discussion on intellectual property and access to medicines.

Doha declaration of the TRIPS Agreement and public health: What did it say, what did it change, why is it important?

The Doha Declaration on the TRIPS Agreement and Public Health[13] was a political response to concerns about the possible implications of the TRIPS Agreement for public health, in particular access to patented medicines. As mentioned earlier, the TRIPS Agreement allows countries to take various kinds of measures to qualify or limit IP rights, including for public health purposes, notably in respect of early working (Article 30), parallel imports (Article 6), and compulsory licensing (Article 31). However, some doubts had arisen as to whether the flexibility in the TRIPS Agreement was sufficient to ensure that it supported public health. It was unclear whether the TRIPS Agreement promoted affordable access to existing medicines while supporting research and development into new ones.

The Declaration responds to these concerns in a number of ways. First, it emphasizes that the TRIPS Agreement does not and should not prevent Members from taking measures to protect public health. It reaffirms the right of Members to use, to the full, the provisions of the TRIPS Agreement that provide flexibility for this purpose. Through these important declarations, all WTO Members have signaled that they will not seek to prevent other Members from using these provisions.

Second, the Declaration makes it clear that the TRIPS Agreement should be interpreted and implemented in a way that supports WTO Members' right to protect public health and, in particular, to promote access to medicines for all. Further, it highlights the importance of the objectives and principles of the TRIPS Agreement regarding the interpretation of its provisions. These statements thus provide important guidance to both individual Members and, in the event of disputes, WTO dispute settlement bodies.

Third, the Declaration clarifies some of the flexibilities contained in the TRIPS Agreement. It makes it clear that each Member is free to determine the grounds upon which compulsory licenses are granted. This is a useful corrective to views often expressed in some quarters that some form of emergency is a precondition for compulsory licensing. The TRIPS Agreement does refer to national emergencies or other circumstances of extreme urgency in connection with compulsory licensing, but this is only to indicate that, in these circumstances, the usual condition that an effort must first be made to seek a voluntary license does not apply. The Declaration makes it clear that each Member has the right to determine what constitutes "a national emergency or other circumstances of extreme urgency."[14] It also declares that public health crises, including those relating to HIV/AIDS, tuberculosis, malaria, and other epidemics, can represent such circumstances.

In regard to the exhaustion of intellectual property rights, which is linked to a Member's right to permit parallel imports, the TRIPS Agreement states that a Member's practices in this area cannot be challenged under the WTO dispute settlement system.[15] The Declaration makes it clear that the effect of the provisions in the TRIPS Agreement on exhaustion is to leave each Member free to establish its own regime without challenge – subject to the general TRIPS provisions that prohibit discrimination on the basis of the nationality of persons.

13 World Trade Organization, Ministerial Declaration of 14 November 2001, WT/MIN(01)/DEC/1, 41 ILM 746 (2002) [hereinafter Doha Declaration].

14 Language taken from Article 31(b) of the TRIPS Agreement.

15 On the exhaustion of the intellectual property rights, *see* Chapter 34 (Feng, Shu & Zhang) in this volume.

In regard to the least-developed country (LDC) Members of the WTO, the Declaration agrees to provide them with an extension of their transition period from January 2006 until January 2016, for protecting and enforcing patents and rights in undisclosed information with respect to pharmaceutical products. This was given legal effect through a Decision of the TRIPS Council that extended the transition period for least-developed countries until January 1, 2016[16] and another Decision of the General Council that waived the exclusive marketing rights provisions of Article 70.9[17] for the same period. In 2005, the TRIPS Council extended the time given for these countries to implement other provisions of the TRIPS Agreement to July 2013.[18]

While emphasizing the flexibility in the TRIPS Agreement to take measures to promote access to medicines, the Declaration also recognizes the importance of IP protection for developing new medicines and reaffirms the commitments of WTO Members in the TRIPS Agreement.

The so-called "Paragraph 6 Decision": Why was this necessary? What did it change and how does it work? Will it work when required?

In paragraph 6, the Doha Declaration recognized the problem of countries with insufficient or no manufacturing capacities in the pharmaceutical sector in making effective use of compulsory licensing. Such countries could, under normal TRIPS rules, import under a compulsory license since there is no special problem with Members issuing compulsory licenses for importation as well as for domestic production. The problem, however, was whether sources of supply from generic producers in other countries to meet such demand would be available, particularly given Article 31(f) of the TRIPS Agreement, according to which production under a compulsory license in those other countries must be "predominantly for the supply of the domestic market of the Member." The problems facing countries with insufficient capacities in the pharmaceutical sector in accessing sources of supply were expected to increase as some countries with important generic industries were coming under an obligation to provide patent protection for pharmaceutical products as from 2005.

In order to solve this problem, the WTO General Council adopted on August 30, 2003, a Decision[19] that waives in certain circumstances Article 31(f) and (h) of the TRIPS Agreement. This Decision was adopted in the light of a Chairman's statement[20] that sets out several key shared understandings of Members on how the Decision would be interpreted and implemented. The Decision covers any patented pharmaceutical products, or pharmaceutical products manufactured through a patented process, needed to address public health problems recognized in paragraph 1 of the Doha Declaration on the TRIPS Agreement and Public Health, including active ingredients necessary for their manufacture and diagnostic kits needed for their use. The Decision grants three waivers from the obligations set out in subparagraphs (f) and (h) of Article 31 of the TRIPS Agreement with

16 Document IP/C/25 – June 2002.
17 Document WT/L/478 – July 2002.
18 Document IP/C/40.
19 Documents WT/L/540 and Corr.1.
20 Contained in paragraph 29 of document WT/GC/M/82.

respect to pharmaceutical products, subject to certain conditions. The three waivers are the following:

- A waiver of the obligation of an exporting Member under Article 31(f) of the TRIPS Agreement to the extent necessary for the purposes of production and export of the needed pharmaceutical products to those countries that do not have sufficient capacity to manufacture them. This waiver is subject to certain conditions to ensure transparency in the operation of the system and that only countries with insufficient domestic capacity import under it, and to provide for safeguards against the diversion of products to markets for which they are not intended;
- A waiver of the obligation under Article 31(h) of the TRIPS Agreement on the importing country to provide adequate remuneration to the right holder in situations where remuneration in accordance with Article 31(h) is being paid in the exporting Member for the same products. The purpose of this waiver is to avoid double remuneration of the patent owner for the same product consignment; and
- A waiver of the obligation under Article 31(f) of the TRIPS Agreement on any developing or least-developed country that is party to a regional trade arrangement at least half of the current membership of which is made up of countries presently on the United Nations list of LDCs. The purpose of this waiver is to enable such countries to better harness economies of scale for the purposes of enhancing purchasing power for, and facilitating the local production of, pharmaceutical products.

The aforementioned Chairman's statement was designed to meet the concerns of those who feared that the Decision was too open-ended and might be abused to undermine the benefits of the patent system. It recognizes that the Paragraph 6 system set out in the Decision should be used in good faith to protect public health and not to pursue industrial or commercial policy objectives. It addresses some concerns relating to the risk of diversion, and it sets out ways in which any differences arising from the implementation of the system can be settled expeditiously and adequately. The Decision also records that the 33 most advanced countries have agreed to opt-out of the system as importers, including since their accession to the European Union (EU) the ten new EU Member States.[21] In addition, 11 other Members have agreed to only use the system as importers in situations of national emergency or other circumstances of extreme urgency.[22]

The Decision went into effect on August 30, 2003. So far, there has been one use of the system by Rwanda, which sought import of antiretroviral drugs from a generic company in Canada. Notifications made to the WTO to use the system, and other useful information, is available on the WTO website.[23] There are a number of reasons of a transitional nature that can explain the lack of further use of the system so far. One is that WTO Members, especially those exporting under the system, usually have to amend primary legislation in

21 The Czech Republic, Cyprus, Estonia, Hungary, Latvia, Lithuania, Malta, Poland, the Slovak Republic, and Slovenia.

22 Hong Kong, Israel, Korea, Kuwait, Macao, Mexico, Qatar, Singapore, Chinese Taipei, Turkey, and the United Arab Emirates. This also makes it clear that the system need not only be used by others in case of an emergency situation.

23 Notifications about the use of the system will be accessible through a dedicated webpage on the WTO website: http://www.wto.org/english/tratop_e/trips_e/public_health_e.htm (last visited July 16, 2016).

order to be able to use the additional flexibility. This inevitably takes time. As of 2011, several Members have modified their laws/regulations to enable exports under their legislation, for example Canada, Norway, India, the European Union, and Korea.[24] A second reason is that there is no need to use the system to import drugs from non-patent sources. Most important drugs currently on patent elsewhere are still available from such sources since some countries that are significant suppliers of generic drugs like India only started providing product patent protection for pharmaceutical products since the beginning of 2005. This is true for all first-line antiretrovirals and some second-line drugs for the treatment of HIV/AIDS. A third point is that, as is well known, a compulsory licensing system can have a great effect in influencing prices even if the system is never used. We have seen, since the Doha Declaration on the TRIPS Agreement and Public Health was agreed in 2001 and the additional TRIPS flexibility agreed in 2003, a large reduction in the prices of many important pharmaceuticals, such as antiretrovirals to treat HIV/AIDS sold to poorer countries. Although much of the price reduction is due to competition from Indian generic producers, and more importantly the volume discounts obtained because of the large influx of financing of the purchase of these medicines, countries have also had the confidence to use or threaten to use TRIPS flexibilities.

The protocol amending the TRIPS agreement: How was this achieved – when will it enter into force?

Paragraph 11 of the August 2003 Decision called for the TRIPS Council to prepare an amendment based, where appropriate, on the Decision that would replace its provisions. Agreement on such an amendment was reached on December 6, 2005, when the General Council adopted a Protocol amending the TRIPS Agreement and submitted it to WTO Members for acceptance. In substance, the amendment tracks the August 2003 text. After about two years of negotiation exploring various options, the Decision on the amendment was also taken in the light of a rereading by the General Council Chairman of the statement of August 2003. The Protocol will enter into force upon acceptance by two-thirds of the Members. To date, 52 Members, counting the EU as one, have accepted the amendment.[25] The waiver provisions of the August 2003 Decision remain applicable until the date on which the amendment takes effect for a Member.

Conclusion: Has the problem of IP and access to medicines been solved? What does the future hold?

The WTO is often portrayed by its detractors as a club for rich countries meant to perpetuate their world dominance. The TRIPS Agreement, particularly with its obligation to provide patents for pharmaceuticals, is often cited as an example of this. However, a plain reading of the Agreement and of the subsequent WTO instruments relating to public health shows that a balance has been sought between the interests of right holders and those of users of intellectual property rights, including patents. It is up to Members to use the flexibilities offered to them in the TRIPS Agreement as well as the additional flexibility

24 *See* http://www.wto.org/english/tratop_e/trips_e/par6laws_e.htm (last visited July 16, 2016).

25 The latest list can be obtained from http://www.wto.org/english/tratop_e/trips_e/amendment_e.htm (last visited July 16, 2016).

to obtain patented medicines from other WTO Members given in subsequent instruments to obtain more affordable access to patented medicines. Those choosing to do so need not fear any challenge under the WTO dispute settlement mechanism. Would this alone, however, solve the access to medicines/medical technologies problem? One study shows that improving access to medicines requires several other factors such as political will, funding, domestic health-care capacity, procurement strategies, and differential pricing or voluntary licensing by originator companies.[26] The fundamental question is whether lower and lower prices should be an end in itself or whether affordability should be balanced with availability of both existing medicines and new innovative medicines in the future. If the latter seems a more realistic goal, innovators (and generics) should be allowed to make reasonable profits.

26 *See* Tim Wilsdon et al., *Evidence to Access to Medicines for the treatment of HIV/AIDS* (2011), http://www.ifpma.org/fileadmin/content/Publication/2011/CRA_Access_to_Essential_Medicines_HIV-AIDS_October2011.pdf (last visited July 16, 2016).

36 The Relationship between the TRIPS Agreement and the Convention on Biological Diversity (CBD)

Intellectual Property and Genetic Resources, Traditional Knowledge, and Folk Protection *from a Chinese Perspective**

Jianqiang Nie

Introduction

The progress of science and technology, especially biotechnologies,[1] contributes to the domestic and transnational exploitation and use of genetic resources (GR), traditional knowledge (TK), and traditional cultural expressions (TCE). Frequent exploitation gives rise to legal questions concerning access and utilization of GR, TK, and TCE, and benefit-sharing between the exploiter/user and holder/beneficiary of the GR, TK, and TCE. These issues relate to sovereignty, human rights, safety, cultural diversity, intangible cultural heritage, biodiversity, and intellectual property (IP).

The international community has adopted a number of international legal instruments to regulate the transnational activities relating to the exploitation and use of GR, TK, and TCE.

* The research for this chapter has been funded by the research project for humanities and social science "Several Significant Legal Issues Relating to the 21st International Intellectual Property System", which was approved by Chinese Ministry of Education (07JJD820163), and the project "Reconstructing International Intellectual Property System under the Notion of Harmonious World" (approved by China's National Social Science Fund 2008 (08BFX083)). Many thanks go to PhD candidates Wang Meng, Zhao Li, and Xiao Shenggao for their collection of documents and materials.

This chapter is part of the results of the Research Project on "Current Trends of Chinese Law towards Non-Trade Concerns such as Sustainable Development and the Protection of Environment, Public Health, Food Safety, Cultural, Social and Economic Rights, Labor Rights and the Reduction of Poverty from the Perspective of International Law and WTO Law", coordinated by Professor Paolo Davide Farah at gLAWcal – Global Law Initiatives for Sustainable Development (United Kingdom) and at West Virginia University John D. Rockefeller IV School of Policy and Politics, Department of Public Administration, in partnership with the Center of Advanced Studies on Contemporary China (CASCC) in Turin (Italy), Maastricht University Faculty of Law, Department of International and European Law and IGIR – Institute for Globalisation and International Regulation (Netherlands), and Tsinghua University, School of Law, Institute of Public International Law and the Center for Research on Intellectual Property Law in Beijing (China). This publication and the Conference Series were sponsored by China–EU School of Law (CESL) at the China University of Political Science and Law (CUPL). The activities of CESL at CUPL are supported by the European Union and the People's Republic of China.

1 On the protection of biotechnological innovation by patent, *see* Chapter 34 (Feng, Shu & Zhang) in this volume.

The Convention on Biological Diversity (1992)[2] (CBD), for example, establishes for the field of biological diversity the principles of state sovereignty rights,[3] prior-informed consent, access,[4] and fair, equitable benefit-sharing.[5] The Bonn Guidelines on Access to Genetic Resources and Fair and Equitable Sharing of the Benefits Arising out of their Utilization (2002)[6] (Bonn Guidelines) and the Nagoya Protocol on Access to Genetic Resources and the Fair and Equitable Sharing of Benefits (2010)[7] (Nagoya Protocol) have further implemented these principles,[8] thus forming the CBD system in respect to the protection of GR and TK.

The 1994 Agreement on Trade-Related Aspects of Intellectual Property Rights[9] (TRIPS Agreement) standardizes international rules on the protection of copyright and related rights, trademark, geographic indication, industrial design, patent, integrated circuit layout, and undisclosed information from the perspective of the protection of private IP rights. These rules, particularly the provisions of Article 27.3(b) – which relate to the patentability of microorganisms and non-biological and microbiological processes for the production of plants, animals, and plant varieties – may have significant effects on the exploitation and use of GR, TK, and TCE, as well as related inventions or innovations.[10]

Other international instruments further protect GR, TK, and TCE from the perspectives of safety,[11] indigenous and local people's rights,[12] food and agriculture related genetic resources and farmers' rights,[13] new plant varieties,[14] cultural diversity,[15] and intangible cultural heritage.[16] However, these international instruments are independent of each other, and their jurisdictions do not intersect. The international rules related to GR, TK, and TCE

2 Convention on Biological Diversity, June 5, 1992, 1760 UNTS 79, 31 ILM 818.
3 CBD, *supra* note 2, Article 15(1).
4 CBD, *supra* note 2, Article 15(5).
5 CBD, *supra* note 2, Article 1. On the precautionary principle, the respect of biological diversity, equitable benefit-sharing, *see* Chapters 9 (Ibrahim, Deleuil & Farah) and 10 (Lemoine) in this volume.
6 The Bonn Guidelines were adopted in 2002.
7 Nagoya Protocol on Access to Genetic Resources and the Fair and Equitable Sharing of Benefits Arising from Their Utilization to the Convention on Biological Diversity, October 29, 2010, (hereinafter Nagoya Protocol), http://www.cbd.int/cop10/doc/ (last visited July 13, 2016).
8 Nagoya Protocol, *supra* note 7, Articles 5, 6, and 7.
9 Agreement on Trade-Related Aspects of Intellectual Property Rights, April 15, 1994, Marrakesh Agreement Establishing the World Trade Organization, Annex 1C, 1869 UNTS 299, 33 ILM 1197 (1994) [hereinafter TRIPS Agreement].
10 TRIPS Agreement, *supra* note 9, Article 27.3(b). On the patentability of microorganisms and non-biological and microbiological processes for the production of plants or animals, *see* Chapter 34 (Feng, Shu & Zhang) in this volume.
11 Cartagena Protocol on Biosafety to the Convention on Biological Diversity, January 29, 2000, 2226 UNTS 208, 39 ILM 1027 (hereinafter Cartagena Protocol).
12 United Nations Declaration on the Rights of Indigenous People, September 12, 2007, A/61/L.67/Annex, Articles 11, 26, 31.
13 International Treaty on Plant Genetic Resources for Food and Agriculture, November 3, 2001, U.N.T.S. 2400, Article 9.2.
14 The International Convention for the Protection of New Varieties of Plants (1961, 1972, 1978, 1991), 815 UNTS 89.
15 Convention for the Protection of Cultural Property in the Event of Armed Conflict, May 14, 1954, 249 UNTS 240. *See* in general Chapters 4 (Bonfanti), 6 (Vadi), and 19 (Ning) in this volume. On another perspective regarding cultural diversities, *see* Chapters 22 (Germann), 23 (Creemers), 24 (Kamperman Sanders), and 25 (Friedmann) in this volume.
16 Convention for Safeguarding of the Intangible Cultural Heritage, October 17, 2003, 2368 UNTS 1.

are fragmentary. On the one hand, the scope of IP protection is broadening, the internationalization and standardization of IP protection is accelerating, and the mechanism for settling IP disputes is strengthening; on the other hand, international regulations relating to GR, TK, and TCE protection are not well developed. The most prominent issue is that these regulations are not integrated into or coordinated with international IP regulations; they are disconnected or mismatched. Some developed countries only emphasize IP protection and do not care about protecting GR, TK, and TCE, especially where they have no comparative advantages. The biopirates and the pirates of traditional cultures took advantage of the *lacunae* under the international regulations and have been unlawfully or unjustifiably granted IP rights over GR, TK, and TCE.

In 2000, the World Intellectual Property Organization (WIPO) established an Intergovernmental Committee on Intellectual Property and Genetic Resources, Traditional Knowledge and Folklore (IGC) to coordinate international cooperation and negotiation on intellectual property and GR, TK, and TCE,[17] and drafted articles on the protection of genetic resources, traditional knowledge, and traditional cultural expressions (the GR draft, the TK draft, and the TCE draft). Furthermore, in October 2011, the WIPO General Assembly adopted the Matters Concerning the Intergovernmental Committee on Intellectual Property and Genetic Resources, Traditional Knowledge and Folklore[18] (WIPO IGC Matters 2011).

China has rich resources in terms of biological diversity, GR, TK, and TCE (or Folklore). At the same time, China's biological diversity is greatly threatened, its genetic resources are disappearing, its traditional knowledge is being lost, and its traditional cultural expressions are being exploited by cultural pirates.[19] In the 1980s and 1990s, the Chinese government started to protect GR through environmental and natural resources legislation.[20] Only after the year 2000, China introduced GR and TK protection into its IP legislation[21] and began to explicitly protect crop- and livestock-related GR by law.[22] As regards TCE (or folklore) protection, in the 1950s China started to rescue and compile the folklores from the perspective of protecting its cultural heritage,[23] and provided some protection for the collectors and providers of the folklore.[24] China's *Copyright Law (2010 Revision)*[25] states that: "[C]opyright

17 WO/GA/26/6.

18 WO/GA/40/7.

19 The Biological Diversity Protection Strategies and Action Plan (2011–2030) of the People's Republic of China.

20 On the protection of the environment and the natural resources in China, *see* Chapters 12 (He) and 14 (Peng) in this volume.

21 Article 16 of the Trademark Law of the People's Republic of China (2013 Revision), Articles 5.2 and 26.5 of the Patent Law of the People's Republic of China (2008). *See* also Chapter 34 (Feng, Shu & Zhang) in this volume.

22 Examples are the Seed Law of the People's Republic of China (2015 Revision) and the Animal and Husbandry Law of the People's Republic of China (2015 Revision).

23 Since 1979, China's Ministry of Culture, the State Ethnic Affairs Commission, China's Federation of Literatures, and the Chinese Musicians Association have collected and compiled ten volumes of folk works, including "Chinese Folk Songs," "Chinese Folk Opera and Music," and "Chinese Folk Dancing."

24 Trial Provisional Regulations on Protection of Copyright Relating to Books and Journals (1984), issued by China's Ministry of Culture. The Regulations are expired.

25 Zhōnghuá Rénmín Gònghéguó Zhùzuòquán Fǎ (2010 xiūzhèng) (中华人民共和国著作权法(2010修正) [Copyright Law of the People's Republic of China (2010 Amendment)] (Promulgated by the Standing Comm. Nat'l People's Cong., February 26, 2010).

protection of folklore shall be enacted by the State Council separately." In 1997, the State Council enacted the Regulations on Protection of Traditional Arts and Crafts,[26] which prescribe special legal protection for traditional arts and crafts. On February 25, 2011, the Standing Committee of the National People's Congress – China's national legislative body – promulgated its Intangible Cultural Heritage Law,[27] which protects folklore from the perspective of intangible cultural heritage. Several local legislations have further strengthened the protection of traditional national folklore. For example, Yunnan Province passed its Regulations on Protection of National Traditional Folk Culture[28] on May 26, 2000, which was the first local legislation of its kind in China.

This chapter will make the legal protection of intellectual property and GR, TK, and TCE in China its starting point, refer to the relevant international regulations, and explore from China's perspective the relationship between IP and GR, TK, and TCE. The chapter mainly investigates two issues: a) how to clarify legal requirements or conditions under IP legislations to prevent the unlawful or unjustifiable approval or grant of IP rights over GR, TK, or TCE, or, in other words, the aspect of defensive protection; and b) how to make use of the IP legal system to protect GR, TK, or TCE, such as the aspect of affirmative or positive protection.

Intellectual property and genetic resources

The expression "Genetic Resources" (GR) indicates any material of plant, animal, microbial, or other origin containing functional units of heredity that have actual or potential value.[29] This definition is adopted by the Chinese Implementation Rules of Patent Law (2010).[30] The outer shell of GR is the substance they are made of, while their contents are their hereditary information, the material thus being the carrier of the information. GR may produce considerable effects on ecological, economic, social, hereditary, technological, cultural, and security aspects, and can be characterized as valuable, hereditary, and distinctively associated. These features contribute to the complexity and special nature of the legal protection of GR.[31]

Even if many laws relate to GR protection, no law can provide full protection to all GR. For instance, property law may regulate the outer shell of GR – their material – but cannot protect the hereditary information; IP laws mainly govern innovative or distinctive

26 Chuántǒng Gōngyì Měishù Bǎohù Tiáolì (传统工艺美术保护条例) [Regulations on Protection of Traditional Arts and Crafts] (Issued by the State Council, May 20, 1997, effective July 18, 2013).

27 Zhōnghuá Rénmín Gònghéguó Fēi Wùzhí Wénhuà Yíchǎn Fǎ (中华人民共和国非物质文化遗产法) [Intangible Cultural Heritage Law of the People's Republic of China] (Promulgated by the Standing Comm. Nat'l People's Cong., February 25, 2011).

28 Yúnnánshěng Mínzú Mínjiān Wénhuà Bǎohù Tiáolì (云南省民族民间传统文化保护条例) [Regulations on Protection of National Traditional Folk Culture] (promulgated by the Standing Comm. Of Yunnan Provincial People's Cong., May 26, 2000).

29 CBD, *supra* note 2, Article 2.

30 Zhōnghuá Rénmín Gònghéguó Zhuānlì Fǎ Shíshī Xìzé (2010 xiūdìng) (中华人民共和国专利法实施细则(2010修订) [Detailed Rules for the Implementation of the Patent Law of the People's Republic of China (2010 Revision)] (Issued by the State Council, September 1, 2010), Article 26(1).

31 *See* also Pu Li, Yichuan Ziyuan Yu Xiangguan Chuantong Zhishi De Minfa Baohu Yanjiu [Studies on Civil Protection of Genetic Resources and Related Traditional Knowledge] 16–20 (Renmin Fayuan Chubanshe, 2009).

information, so it is doubtful whether those laws can deal with hereditary information;[32] ecological law (or environmental law) deal with the externalities of exploitation or the use of GR from the perspective of public law, but is in a difficult position when dealing with internal issues such as the cost and benefit relating to the exploitation, use, and protection of GR or, in other words, the private right and duty issues relating to them.

In China, there is no specific GR law *per se*. Different types of GR are protected under different legislations which focus mainly on administrative matters concerning identification, collection, sorting, and registration of GR, and application and approval procedures relating to collection, import and export, transaction, production, operation, and use of GR. These legislations involve issues such as the protection of the environment,[33] resources,[34] animals and plants,[35] traditional Chinese medicine,[36] human rights,[37] safety,[38] and intellectual property.[39] There are both public law stipulations and private rights protection; both domestic and foreign factors are involved in GR administration.[40] However, current Chinese legislation emphasizes administration rather than private rights protection. As regards the administrative approval of GR, different categories of GR have been prescribed with different

32 *See,* in this sense, Chapter 34 (Feng, Shu & Zhang) in this volume.

33 Zhōnghuá Rénmín Gònghéguó Huánjìng Bǎohù Fǎ (中华人民共和国环境保护法) [Environmental Protection Law of the People's Republic of China] (promulgated by the Standing Comm. Of the Nat'l People's Cong., December 26, 1989). Zhōnghuá Rénmín Gònghéguó Hǎiyáng Huánjìng Bǎohù Fǎ (中华人民共和国海洋环境保护法) [Marine Environmental Protection Law of the People's Republic of China] (promulgated by the Standing Comm. Of the Nat'l People's Cong., August 23, 1982, amended December 28, 2013).

34 Zhōnghuá Rénmín Gònghéguó Zhǒngzǐ Fǎ (中华人民共和国种子法) [The Seed Law of the People's Republic of China] (promulgated by the Standing Comm. Of the Nat'l People's Cong., July 8, 2000, amended Nov. 4, 2015). Zhōnghuá Rénmín Gònghéguó Xùmù Fǎ (中华人民共和国畜牧法) [Animal Husbandry Law of the People's Republic of China] (Promulgated by the Standing Comm. Nat'l People's Cong., December 29, 2009, amended April 24, 2015).

35 Zhōnghuá Rénmín Gònghéguó Yěshēng Zhíwù Bǎohù Tiáolì (中华人民共和国野生植物保护条例) [Regulations of the People's Republic of China on Wild Plants Protection] (promulgated by the State Council, September 30, 1996).

36 Zhōnghuá Rénmín Gònghéguó Yěshēng Yàocái Zīyuán Bǎohù Guǎnlǐ Tiáolì (1987) (中华人民共和国野生药材资源保护管理条例(1987) [Administrative Regulations on Protection of Wild Medicinal Resources of the People's Republic of China (1987)] (promulgated by the State Council, October 30, 1987)

37 Zhōnghuá Rénmín Gònghéguó Rénlèi Yíchuán Zīyuán Guǎnlǐ Zànxíng Bànfǎ (1998) (中华人民共和国人类遗传资源管理暂行办法(1998) [Provisional Rules on Administration of Human Genetic Resources of the People's Republic of China (1998)] (promulgated by the State Council, December 8, 1998)

38 Nóngyè Zhuǎnjīyīn Shēngwù Ānquán Guǎnlǐ Tiáolì (农业转基因生物安全管理条例) [Regulations on Administration of Agricultural Genetically Modified Organisms Safety] (Issued by the State Council, May 23, 2001, amended January 8, 2011).

39 Zhōnghuá Rénmín Gònghéguó Shāngbiāo Fǎ (2013 Xiūzhèng) (中华人民共和国商标法(2013修正) [Trademark Law of the People's Republic of China (2013 Amendment)] (Promulgated by the Standing Comm. Nat'l People's Cong., August 30, 2013), Articles 3 and 16; Zhōnghuá Rénmín Gònghéguó Zhuānlì Fǎ (2008 Xiūzhèng) (中华人民共和国专利法(2008修正) [Patent Law of the People's Republic of China (2008 Amendment)] (Promulgated by the Standing Comm. Nat'l People's Cong., December 27, 2008), Articles 5.2 and 26.5.

40 Zhōnghuá Rénmín Gònghéguó Chù Qín Yíchuán Zīyuán Jìn Chūjìng Hé Duìwài Hézuò Yánjiū Lìyòng Shěnpī Bànfǎ (中华人民共和国畜禽遗传资源进出境和对外合作研究利用审批办法) [Measures of the People's Republic of China for the Examination and Approval of Entry & Exit and the Foreign Cooperative Research on the Application of Genetic Resources of Livestock and Poultry] (Issued by the State Council, August 28, 2008).

procedures and requirements. The legislations are disconnected, mismatched, or not well-coordinated, and relevant provisions are fragmentary.

The Chinese National Guidelines for Intellectual Property Strategy (2008) (Chinese IP Strategy) proclaim the need to:

> improve systems relating to protection, development and utilization of GR, prevent loss of GR and its inappropriate use [. . .] [t]o coordinate interest relations among preservation, exploitation and utilization of GR, to establish a reasonable mechanism concerning GR access and benefit sharing [. . .] [and to s]afeguard the right of prior-informed consent enjoyed by GR suppliers.[41]

With respect to the interrelationship between IP, GR, and trademarks, geographical indications (GI), or geographical origin marks can provide some protection for distinctive or special GR-related geographical origins.[42] The relationship between patent and GR protection involves two aspects: a) whether the patent system can be adopted to protect GR (positive approach), and b) how to prevent the unlawful or unjustifiable patent grant or approval over GR via prescribing legal requirements or conditions under patent law (defensive protection).

GR contain hereditary information; the subject matter of patent protection is also a kind of information. The two are similar in this respect. However, GR is the hereditary information whereas the subject matter of patents is the creative information; the two are different by nature. Hereditary information exists naturally within the human body, plants, and microorganisms without innovation. It should be ascribed as "scientific discovery" under Article 25(1)(i) of the Patent Law of People's Republic of China (2008), and thus cannot be granted patent except when otherwise provided.[43] However, the dividing line between scientific discovery and invention seems to have been blurred by the United States Supreme Court's ruling in the case *Diamond v Chakrabarty*. Some biopirates took advantage of the flexible interpretation of patentability, and were unlawfully or unjustifiably granted IP rights over GR.[44]

According to the Chinese Patent Law, an invention relating to GR shall be granted a patent where the invention fits the requirements of novelty, inventive step, and utility, and is accordingly protected by the patent law.[45] A new plant variety may be protected under the Chinese Regulations on Protection of New Plant Variety (1997) if it possesses novelty, distinctness, consistency, stability, and it is duly named.[46] However, where a GR invention

41 Paragraph 33 of the National Strategy of the People's Republic of China for Intellectual Property (2008).

42 Chen Zongbo & Zhou Yulin, *Lun Yichuan Ziyuan de Xianxing Zhishi Chanquan Baohu Moshi* [*On Current Intellectual Property Protection Model Relating to Genetic Resources*], SHEHUI KEXUEJIA [SOCIAL SCIENTIST] 90 (April 2010); Yang Yuanbin, *Yichuan Ziyuan de Zhishi Chanquan Baohu Fenxi* [*Analysis of Protection of Genetic Resources in Perspective of Intellectual Property*], 4 XUESHU LUNTAN [ACADEMIC FORUM] 23 (2005).

43 Zhuānlì Shěnchá Zhǐnán (2010 xiūdìng) (专利审查指南2010修订) [Patent Examination Guidelines (2010 Revision)] (Issued by the State Intellectual Property Office, January 21, 2010), Paragraph 9.1.2.2, Chapter 10, Part II.

44 For example, Monsanto's patent on wild bean genetic resources originated near Shanghai in 2000, and the Curcuma Longa patent case.

45 Article 22(1) of the Patent Law of the People's Republic of China, *supra* note 39.

46 Zhōnghuá Rénmín Gònghéguó Zhíwù Xīn Pǐnzhǒng Bǎohù Tiáolì (中华人民共和国植物新品种保护条例) [Regulation of the People's Republic of China on Protection of New Varieties of Plants] (promulgated by the State Council, March 20, 1997, amended March 1, 2013), Article 2.

belongs to state of the art[47] and has no novelty, creative step or utility, no patent shall be granted; if the new plant variety does not conform to the requirements under the aforementioned Regulations, no new plant variety right shall be approved.

Although the patent law cannot protect GR directly by granting patent rights over them, they may be protected indirectly by disclosure of the origin of the GR, and protected defensively by prevention of unlawful access and use of the genetic material.[48] The disclosure of the origins of the GR has been prescribed under the Chinese Patent Law. Article 26(5) provides that "for an invention based on genetic resources, the applicant shall state direct source and original source of the genetic resources in the application documents. If the applicant is not able to state the original source, it or he shall state reasons." The Implementation Rules of Patent Law (2010) further state that "when applying for a patent for an invention based on GR, the applicant shall explain in his claims and fill out the form prescribed by the Patent Administrative Authorities of the State Council."[49] The disclosure of the origin of the GR is a mandatory formal requirement in the application. Although the disclosure does not affect the three substantive requirements of novelty, inventive step, and utility,[50] where the disclosure does not comply with the requirements of the regulations, the patent application may be rejected.[51]

General provisions relating to GR protection have also been provided for under the Chinese Patent Law. It provides that "a patent shall not be granted to an invention which is based on genetic resources if the access or utilization of said genetic resources is in violation of any Chinese law or administrative regulation."[52] The Implementation Rules of Patent Law have further clarified the provision under Article 26(1): "[A]n invention based on genetic resources means the invention has utilized the genetic function of the GR."[53] The Guidelines for Patent Examination (2010) explain that "an invention-creation using the hereditary function of the genetic resources refers to, for example, isolating, analyzing and/or processing the functional units of heredity to develop the invention-creation and to realize the value of the genetic resources," and "access or use of the genetic resources is not consistent with the provisions of the laws and administrative regulations" means the access or use of the generic resources has not been approved by the relevant administrative departments or licensed by the relevant right holder.[54] This formal explanation is merely from the

47 Article 22.5 of the Patent Law of the People's Republic of China, *supra* note 39.

48 Zhang Qingkui Deng, *Yichuan Ziyuan Jiqi Laiyuan Zhidu Yanjiu* [*Studies on Genetic Resources and Its Disclosure System*], Zhuanlifa Yanjiu [Studies on Patent Law] 475–532 (2008).

49 Zhōnghuá Rénmín Gònghéguó Zhuānlì Fǎ Shíshī Xìzé (2010 xiūdìng) (中华人民共和国专利法实施细则2010修订) [Detailed Rules for the Implementation of the Patent Law of the People's Republic of China (2010 Revision)] (Issued by the State Council, January 9, 2010), Article 26(2).

50 A scholar suggested that genetic resources and traditional knowledge should be introduced into patent law and taken into consideration in the process of patent application, review, and objection to determine whether to grant or maintain the patent, *see* Yang Hong, *Zhuanli Zhidu yu Yichuan Ziyuan Chuantong Zhishi de Falu Baohu* [*Patent System and Legal Protection of Genetic Resources and Traditional Knowledge*], Zhuanlifa Yanjiu [Studies on Patent Law] (2006).

51 Paragraph 5.3, Chapter 1, Part I of the Guidelines for Patent Examination of the People's Republic of China, *supra* note 43.

52 Article 5.2 of the Patent Law of the People's Republic of China, *supra* note 39.

53 Article 26.1 of the Implementation Rules of the Patent Law of the People's Republic of China (2010 Revision), *supra* note 49.

54 Paragraph 3.2, Chapter 1, Part II of the Guidelines for Patent Examination of the People's Republic of China (2010), *supra* note 43.

perspective of patent application review rather than from the perspective of substantive and procedural laws; in regards to whether access and use of the GR violate Chinese laws or administrative regulations on prior-informed consent and fair and justified benefit-sharing principles, there are no clear explanations.

GR protection is incorporated into the Chinese Patent Law by the provisions on the disclosure of the origin of the GR and the prevention of grant of patent from unlawful access or use. The patent system is coordinated with GR protection, and GR is protected defensively under the Patent Law. Nevertheless, the defensive protection of GR is limited because the defensive approach cannot deal with all the legal issues relating to their access and use. The protection of GR needs a new legal mechanism such as a law on the protection of genetic resources outside of the current IP system.[55] The new legal mechanism should mainly deal with legal issues relating to the hereditary information of GR rather than the material that carries them, and be within the scope of the information law.

GR and its related TK are the result of generations of inheritance, evolution, and development of their holders or beneficiaries – in particular, the relevant indigenous and local people. GR and TK are their spiritual and cultural identities or symbols that may have multiple values and pursuits, and are regulated and maintained by their traditions or customs. The law on the protection of GR should respect those traditions and customs, take into account all their special characteristics, and establish the right over genetic resources based on the concept of collectively enjoyed – in particular, by minorities or local people – exclusive rights.[56] The law may adopt the model of both rights protection and administrative regulations. The rights protection approach establishes collective exclusive rights so as to raise awareness and initiatives of the holders or beneficiaries to protect their GR and relevant TK. The administrative regulations, on the other hand, seek to set forth uniform administrative measures relating to the access and use of GR and categorize them as prohibited, restricted, and non-restricted so as to exercise authoritative power and professional competence over their administration; in addition, they also seek to consolidate and improve the rules relating to prior-informed consent access and fair and equitable benefit-sharing[57] or, in other words, a model combination of private and public law.[58] The model may contribute to the

55 Zheng Jingrong & Chen Bo, *Shengwu yu Yichuan Ziyuan Quan de Quanli Shuxing jiqi Lifa Moshi Tanxi* [*Analysis on the Rights and Legislation Model Relating to Biological and Genetic Resources*], 4 BEIJING HUAGONG DAXUE XUEBAO (SHEHUI KEXUE BAN) [JOURNAL OF BEIJING CHEMICAL UNIVERSITY (SOCIAL SCIENCE EDITION)] 4–9 (2009); Chen Zongbo & Zhou Yulin, *Lun Yichuan Ziyuan de Xianxing Zhishi Chanquan Baohu Moshi* [*On Current Intellectual Property Protection Model Relating to Genetic Resources*], SHEHUI KEXUEJIA [SOCIAL SCIENTIST] 90 (April 2010).

56 Yang Ming, *Qianxi Yichuan Ziyuan Quan de Zhidu Goujian* [*Analysis on Institutional Construction Relating to Rights over Genetic Resources*], 1 HUAZHONG KEJI DAXUE XUEBAO (SHEHUI KEXUE BAN) [JOURNAL OF HUANGZHONG UNIVERSITY FOR SCIENCE AND TECHNOLOGY (SOCIAL SCIENCE EDITION)] 47–49 (2006); Yan Yonghe, *Yichuan Ziyuan Caichan Quan Falu Luoji Quanshi: Yi Shengwu Duoyangxing Gongyue Wei Zhongxin* [*Explanations of Genetic Resources Property Rights from the Perspective of Legal Logic: Centering on CBD*], 1 JINAN XUEBAO (ZHEXUE SHEKE BAN) [JOURNAL OF JINAN UNIVERSITY (PHILOSOPHY AND SOCIAL SCIENCE EDITION)] 66–70 (2010).

57 Both Article 8 of the Chinese Seed Law and Article 16 of the Chinese Animal and Husbandry Law have provided for administrative approval requirements relating to access and use of genetic resources, but have few provisions on prior-informed consent and benefit-sharing.

58 Luo Xiaoxia, *Yichuan Ziyuan Baohu de Lifa Moshi Tantao* [*Research on Legislation Model Relating to Genetic Resources Protection*], HEBEI FAXUE [HEBEI LEGAL STUDIES] 110–112 (September 2011).

coordination with patent application reviews, to clarify administrative regulations on GR and be in parallel with GR international legislations.

Finally, a cooperation or coordination mechanism should be established between the patent authorities and GR administrative organs to decide whether access to them, their use, and the inventions based on them are in violation of Chinese laws and administrative regulations. For example, the patent authorities could review whether the disclosure of the origin of the GR is in compliance with patent laws, whereas the GR administrative organs could determine whether the access to the GR is consistent with the prior-informed consent principle, and their use compatible with the fair equitable benefit-sharing principle. They should cooperate and coordinate with each other to improve GR-related patent application review and GR legal protection.

In international law, the legal status of GR is clarified under the CBD,[59] namely GR are under the jurisdiction of state sovereignty, and the parties bound by the CBD have the responsibility to protect and use GR in a sustainable way. The CBD has rejected the view that GR are "common heritage of humankind,"[60] and has further provided that access and use of GR shall be based on the principles of prior-informed consent and fair and equitable benefit-sharing. However, these provisions have not been integrated into or coordinated with the TRIPS Agreement.[61] The TRIPS Agreement and the CBD are independent of each other under international law and have no cross-jurisdiction. The uncoordinated positions or disparities relating to GR protection under the CBD and the TRIPS Agreement may cause adverse effects on GR protection.[62]

A cooperative mechanism should also be established between intellectual property and GR protection, in particular between the CBD and WTO, especially to coordinate Article 27 of the TRIPS Agreement with the CBD and the Nagoya Protocol. Article 8 of the TRIPS Agreement may be revised to include provisions on the protection of biodiversity; Article 27.2 of the TRIPS Agreement may be modified to explicitly provide that patent applications may be rejected or patents may be withdrawn where the access and use of the GR are unlawful or they do not conform to the principles of prior-informed consent and fair and equitable benefit-sharing or to the requirements relating to disclosure of GR origin. These revisions may contribute to the uniformity and predictability of IP, GR, and TK protection. It is also necessary to accelerate negotiation of the treaties (multilateral, regional, or bilateral) on IP and GR to prevent the misuse or abuse of GR and to prevent inventions based on unlawful access and use of GR from being granted patents. In addition, developing countries may use the flexibilities under Article 27.3(b) of the TRIPS Agreement to consolidate and strengthen their domestic GR and TK protection.

59 *See* in general Chapter 9 (Ibrahim, Deleuil & Farah) in this volume.

60 Chinese scholar Pu Li defined genetic resources as "common concerns of humankind," *see supra* note 31, at 24–33; Zhong Xiaoyong, Yichuan Ziyuan De Huoqu He Huiyi Yu Zhisgi Chanquan [Access and Benefit Sharing of Genetic Resources and Intellectual Property] 34 (Zhishi Chanquan Chubanshe, 2007).

61 The legal regime for biotechnology is still in a formation period and a satisfactory solution has not yet been found. The TRIPs Agreement tries to carry out an international harmonization of national laws in all the WTO members. For a deeper analysis, *see* Chapter 34 (Feng, Shu & Zhang) in this volume.

62 Article 16.5 of the CBD provides that: "The Contracting Parties, recognizing that patents and other intellectual property rights may have an influence on the implementation of this Convention, shall cooperate in this regard subject to national legislation and international law in order to ensure that such rights are supportive of and do not run counter to its objectives."

Intellectual property and traditional knowledge

The term "traditional knowledge" (TK) refers in general to the know-how, skills, innovations, practices, teachings, and learning resulting from intellectual activity and developed within a traditional context.[63] TK in a broad sense may include TCE and even GR. TK can be characterized as being intellectual, traditional, collective, distinctively associated, cultural, and to a certain extent publicly known[64] (in this context TK can be categorized as TK in the both the public and nonpublic domains).[65] These features determine the special nature of the legal protection of TK.

Although China is very rich in traditional knowledge resources, Chinese TK has been subject to pirating and has been facing heavy losses.[66] There are several provisions under the Chinese Intangible Cultural Heritage Law (2011),[67] the Regulations on the protection of Chinese medicine, intellectual property legislations, and unfair competition laws relating to the protection of TK,[68] but China has no law on the protection of traditional knowledge *per se* and cannot provide for its full protection. The Chinese IP Strategy put forward a plan to establish a sound system for the protection of TK; to support the organization and passing down of TK to further its development; and to strengthen the coordination mechanism for the administration, protection and utilization of traditional arts.[69] The Chinese State Intellectual Property Office (SIPO) published its *Working Plans for National Traditional Knowledge Property Protection (Trial)* in October 2009, which suggested that China explore new mechanisms, channels, approaches, and measures at the national and local levels as well as strengthen the protection of traditional knowledge property rights.

With respect to the interrelationship between IP and TK protection, the first question is whether TK is the eligible subject matter of IP. The "intellectual" nature of TK is the same as the nature of the subject matter of IP, and should be qualified as such[70] and protectable

63 WIPO IGC Matters 2011 Annex B at 5 WO/GA/40/7.

64 One Chinese scholar argued from the perspective of a legal relationship that TK possesses the following features: the right holders are multiple, the subject matter of TK is publicly known, and TK is potentially valuable. *See* YAN YONGHE, LUN CHUANTONG ZHISHI DE ZHISHI CHANQUAN BAOHU [STUDIES ON INTELLECTUAL PROPERTY PROTECTION OF TRADITIONAL KNOWLEDGE] 26–28 (Falu Chubanshe, 2006). *See* in general Chapters 4 (Bonfanti), 6 (Vadi), 17 (Heurtebise), and 22 (Germann) in this volume.

65 Chen Zhicheng, *Chuantong Zhishi Falu Baohu* [*Legal Protection of Traditional Knowledge*], Zhongguo Zhengfa Daxue Boshi Lunwen [Chinese University of Politics and Law, Doctoral Thesis] 150–151 (2009).

66 Chinese Biological Diversity Protection Strategies and Action Plan (2011–2030). *See* also Lu Zhiyao, *Guizhousheng Qian Dongnan Chuantong Zhishi Baohu Anli Yanjiu* [*Case Studies on Traditional Knowledge in Southeast Region of Guizhou Province*], ZHONGYANG MINZU DAXUE [CENTRAL UNIVERSITY OF ALL NATIONALITIES] (2011); Zhao Fuwei, *Minzu Yiyao Chuantong Zhishi Chuancheng dui Huiyi Fenxiang de Yingxiang* [*The Impacts of Transmission of Traditional Knowledge Relating to National Medicines on Benefit Sharing*], ZHONGYANG MINZU DAXUE [CENTRAL UNIVERSITY OF ALL NATIONALITIES] (2008).

67 Article 2.1(3) of Intangible Cultural Heritage Law of the People's Republic of China, *supra* note 27.

68 Zhōnghuá Rénmín Gònghéguó Zhōng Yīyào Tiáolì (中华人民共和国中医药条例) [Regulation of the People's Republic of China on Traditional Chinese Medicines] (Issued by the State Council, April 7, 2003), Articles 23, 24(2), 24(3), 28. Zhōnghuá Rénmín Gònghéguó Fǎn Bú Zhèngdàng Jìngzhēng Fǎ (中华人民共和国反不正当竞争法) [Anti-Unfair Competition Law of the People's Republic of China] (Promulgated by the Standing Comm. Nat'l People's Cong., September 2, 1993).

69 Paragraph 34 of the National Strategy of the People's Republic of China for Intellectual Property (2008), *supra* note 41.

70 Zheng Chengsi, *Chuantong Zhishi yu Lianglei Zhishi Chanquan Baohu* [*Traditional Knowledge and Two Types of Intellectual Property Protection*], 2 ZHISHI CHANQUAN [INTELLECTUAL PROPERTY] 5 (2002).

under IP.[71] Some other features of TK – except for being "publicly known," which may affect patents on TK – such as being traditional, collective, distinctively associated, and cultural will not, in principle, hinder IP protection.

Intellectual property laws such as trademark laws may provide TK with some form of protection.[72] For instance, the Chinese Trademark Law may, on the one hand, defensively prevent TK-related geographical indications from being registered improperly as trademark or used as trademark;[73] on the other hand, right holders may affirmatively register TK-related geographical indications as collective trademark or certification trademark under the trademark law and be protected accordingly.[74] TK-related geographical indications may also be protected under the Chinese Regulations on Protection of Geographical Indications Products (2005).[75] Some forms of TK, such as traditional arts, traditional recipes, and exclusive, unique techniques and secret prescriptions handed down in the family from generation to generation, which are not disclosed to the public or are only known in closed circles, can be protected by trade secret laws. TK may also be protected under the Anti-Unfair Competition Law.[76]

The critical issue is whether TK can be protected by patent law. TK embraces the nature of intellectual result, and it should be qualified as the subject matter of a patent if it conforms with the requirements of novelty, inventive step, and utility under the patent law. The TK's other features, such as being traditional, collective, distinctively associated, and cultural, may not constitute barriers to the TK's patent application and approval. The only challenging factor is constituted by the "publicly known" TK. Because those TKs are publicly known, they may not be considered novel[77] and state of the art, thus being disqualified from being granted a patent.[78]

Whether non–publicly known TKs or secret TKs[79] are novel depends on the interpretation of the term "novelty." If the term "novelty" is construed as prior to the date of application, and the TK is not publicly used or known outside of its traditional context and relevant

71 Gu Zuxue, *Lun Chuantong Zhishi de Ke Zhishi Chanquan Xing* [*On Intellectual Property Protection on Traditional Knowledge*], 2 Xiamen Daxue Xuebao (Zhexue Sheke Ban) [Journal of Xiamen University (Philosophy and Social Science Edition)] 12–16 (2006).

72 Zang Xiaoli, *Chuantong Zhishi de Falu Baohu Wenti Yanjiu* [*Studies on Legal Protection of Traditional Knowledge*], Zhongyang Minzu Daxue Boshi Lunwen [Central University of All Nationalities Doctoral Thesis 2006] at 40. Xu Jiali, Chuantong Zhishi de Liyong yu Zhishi Chanquan de Baohu [*Use of Traditional Knowledge and Intellectual Property Protection*], 6 Zhongguo Faxue [China Legal Studies] 116 (2005).

73 Article 16 of the Trademark Law of the People's Republic of China, *supra* note 39.

74 Article 3 of Trademark Law of the People's Republic of China, *supra* note 39.

75 Zhōnghuá Rénfín Gònghéguó Dìlǐ Biāozhì Chǎnpǐn Bǎohù Guīdìng (2005) Dì 2 Tiáo (中华人民共和国地理标志产品保护规定 (2005) 第2条 [Article 2 of the Regulation of the People's Republic of China on Protection of Geographical Indication Products (2005)] (promulgated by the State Council, May 16, 2005).

76 Article 5 of the Anti-Unfair Competition Law of the People's Republic of China, *supra* note 68.

77 One scholar argued to use "business novelty" under Article 6 of the Convention on Protection of New Plant Varieties as the base of the novelty relating to traditional knowledge. *See* Tu Lu, *Lun Chuantong Zhishi de Ke Zhishi Chanquan Xing* [*On Intellectual Property Protection of Traditional Knowledge*], Xibei Daxue [Northwest University] (2009).

78 Zang Xiaoli, *supra* note 72, at 38–40.

79 The secret TK is the knowledge that is kept secret by the beneficiary group and is not shared, and has not been shared, by those outside of the beneficiary group, WIPO/Genetic Resources and Traditional Knowledge F/IC/19/5.

local communities or traditional indigenous groups, the TK may have novelty. However, the lax interpretation of "novelty" may produce negative effects on the strictness and unity of the patent system and the quality of patents. Protection of secret TK may need to employ another type of right rather than the patent right.

The Patent Law may nevertheless provide some defensive protection for TK or for inventions based on it (including GR-related TK) where the access and use of the TK is in violation of laws or regulations. For those publicly known TK, they are considered state of the art and disqualified from being patentable (in this context there is a need to require documentation on TK on the one hand and, on the other hand, to establish absolute global criteria relating to novelty for TK patent applications). For those non–publicly known TK, provisions relating to the compulsory disclosure of their origin, the prior-informed consent of their access, and the fair equitable benefit-sharing on their use may be put forth to prevent improperly granting or exercising patent rights over TK or GR-related TK. Article 5(2) of the Chinese Patent Law could be revised to include the provision, "patent shall not be granted to an invention based on genetic resources and/or traditional knowledge where the access or utilization of said genetic resources and/or traditional knowledge is in violation of any law or administrative regulation."

Nevertheless, the defensive protection of TK is limited. The current IP laws cannot provide full protection for TK access, exploitation, and use. Furthermore, due to the special features of TK, the current IP system, and the Patent Law in particular – which is incentive-oriented, private property–emphasized, and regulated according to term of protection – may not fit TK protection. TK protection may need to create a special *sui generis* legal mechanism such as a traditional intellectual property rights (TIPR) protection mechanism under the framework of the IP system. The TIPR mechanism should take account of all characteristics of TK, and be built upon the principles of respect for traditions, collectively enjoyed exclusive rights, generational equity, development orientation, interest balance, and absence of time limit. Furthermore, the qualifications of TK protection should be different from those of current IP. They should not only reflect the "intellectual" nature of TK, but also embody its other features such as being distinctively associated, its collectiveness, social value, and cultural identities.[80]

As regards the nature of traditional intellectual property rights, it is argued whether the right should be a "private right,"[81] an "exclusive right,"[82] or rather a "social right."[83] These three rights are not, in fact, contradictory to each other. TIPR is a mixture of those three rights and can be defined as a special exclusive right collectively enjoyed by indigenous or local people or other beneficiaries. "Special" shows that the qualifications of TK protection are different from those of current IP; "collectively enjoyed" is determined by the collective nature of TK; "exclusive right" means that only those indigenous people or local communities or other beneficiaries can enjoy those rights. Because TK possesses the features

80 In some cases the "not widely known" and "non-obviousness" should also be taken into consideration, see Article 1.2 of WIPO (Draft Articles on Traditional Knowledge), WO/GA/40/7 Annex B, at 5.

81 Gu Zuxue, Jiyu TRIPS Kuangjia Xia Baohu Chuantong Zhishi de Zhengdang Xing [*The Justification of Protection of Traditional Knowledge under TRIPS Framework*], 7 Shidai Faxue [Times Jurisprudence] 137–138 (2006).

82 Zhang Dong, *Chuantong Zhishi Baohu Lifa Quxiang Chuyi* [*Discussion on Legislation Protection of Traditional Knowledge*], 4 Zhishi Chanquan [Intellectual Property] 76–77 (2011).

83 Zhou Fang, Chuantong Zhishi Falu Baohu Yanjiu [Studies on Protection of Traditional Knowledge] 24–28 (Zhishi Chanquan Chubanshe, 2011).

of "traditional values and cultural identities," the contents, limitations, and exceptions of the TIPR mechanism should accommodate those sociological factors.

The TIPR includes moral rights such as to respect, conserve, and maintain TK, and to ensure that the use of traditional knowledge respects the cultural norms and practices of the holders,[84] and economic rights such as benefit-sharing.[85] The TIPR may also include defensive rights and affirmative rights.[86] A part of the defensive rights may be realized by the current intellectual property laws; the affirmative rights, however, cannot be realized the same way and need to be implemented under the new TK protection mechanism.

With respect to the protection model, there are four suggestions, namely the "IP model,"[87] the "special exclusive right model,"[88] the "basic law model,"[89] and the "differentiation model."[90] These four models emphasize different aspects of TK protection, and they are complementary rather than contradictory. As discussed above, the TIPR is a collectively enjoyed exclusive right; accordingly, the TIPR protection mechanism should be based on the same concept. TIPR protection may adopt the IP framework, differentiate publicly known TK from non–publicly known TK, prescribe collectively enjoyed exclusive rights, and enact a *sui generis* TK protection law that covers objectives and principles, subject matter of protection, beneficiaries of protection, scope of protection, exceptions and limitations of protection, administration of rights, formalities, and terms of protection. In the context of Chinese traditional IP right protection, in addition to putting forth those exclusive rights, the administration of rights should be improved, administrative regulations on TK access and use should be strengthened, and capacity-building of indigenous people and local communities relating to TK protection should be emphasized.

Intellectual property and traditional cultural expressions

TCE or folklore is any form of artistic expression, tangible or intangible, in which traditional culture and knowledge are embodied.[91] TCE possess the features of being diverse, intellectual, traditional, collective, cultural, and distinctively associated.[92] These features contribute to the complex legal protection of TCE, including laws on cultural diversity, human rights, intangible cultural heritage, and IP.[93] However, none of these laws can provide full and consistent protection for TCE.

84 WIPO IGC Matters 2011, Annex B, at 11, WO/GA/40/7.
85 Article 8(j) of the CBD.
86 WIPO IGC Matters 2011, Annex B, at 11, WO/GA/40/7.
87 Ding Liying, Chuantong Zhishi Baohu De Quanli Sheji He Zhidu Goujian [Rights Design and Institutional Setting Relating to Protection of Traditional Knowledge] 39–43 (Falu Chubanshe, 2009).
88 Zhang Dong, *supra* note 82, at 76–77.
89 Zhou Fang, *supra* note 83, at 235.
90 Chen Zhicheng, supra note 65, at 150–151.
91 WIPO IGC Matters 2011, Annex A, at 4, WO/GA/40/7.
92 One scholar put forward that folklore contains the following features: it is collectively created and individually transmitted; tradition is at times stable and at times changing; information is local and culture is open; and embodiment is tangible and information is invisible, Zhang Geng, Minjian Wenxue Yishu De Zhishi Chanquan Baohu Yanjiu [Studies on Intellectual Property Protection of Folklore] 18–25 (Falu Chubanshe, 2007).
93 For other perspectives on cultural diversity, human rights, and intangible cultural and intellectual property, *see* Chapters 6 (Vadi), 17 (Heurtebise), 22 (Germann), 23 (Creemers), 24 (Kamperman Sanders), and 25 (Friedmann) in this volume.

China, accordingly, adopted several forms of laws to protect TCE, such as the Constitution of the People's Republic of China,[94] the Intellectual Property Law, administrative and local regulations, and, in particular, the Intangible Cultural Heritage Law.[95] The Chinese Law on Intangible Cultural Heritage, enacted in 2011, applies to several forms of TCE protection. The scope of the "intangible cultural heritage" under the Law is consistent with the forms of TCE.[96] All the preservation measures relating to identification, recording and filing of the Law on Intangible Cultural Heritage, and the protective measures concerning inheritance, transmission, and dissemination of intangible cultural heritage,[97] and the rights and legitimate interests[98] provided under the Law are equally applicable to TCE.

It should be noted that Article 44 of the Law on Intangible Cultural Heritage provides that "where intellectual property rights are involved in the use of intangible cultural heritage, the provisions of the relevant IP laws and administrative regulations shall apply; where any other law or administrative regulation provides otherwise for the protection of traditional medicine, traditional arts and crafts, etc., such provisions shall prevail."[99] These provisions indicate that the Law on Intangible Cultural Heritage cannot deal with intellectual property issues relating to intangible cultural heritage (including TCE), and where there are conflicts between the Law on Intangible Cultural Heritage and other legal provisions or administrative regulations relating to the protection of some specified forms of intangible cultural heritage, such as traditional medicine and traditional arts and crafts, the other legal provisions or regulations shall prevail.

However, both the Regulations on Chinese Traditional Medicine and the Regulations on Traditional Arts and Crafts (1997) emphasize administrative measures rather than private rights protection. For instance, under the Regulations on Traditional Arts and Crafts (1997), only one provision touches on rights (for example, the great Master of Arts and Crafts has the right to carve his name on his works).[100] All other provisions are non-proprietary administrative measures (for example, the title of Great Master of Arts and Crafts of China may be awarded to a person who has been engaged in the creation of traditional arts and crafts for a long time),[101] and awards will be given to units and individuals who made outstanding contributions to the passing down, protection, and development of traditional arts and crafts.[102]

With respect to the interrelationship between intellectual property and TCE protection, it is interesting to note that one of the features of TCE is its "intellectual" nature; this indicates that TCE may be qualified as the subject matter of IP rights. Copyright, trademarks, and geographical indications are all able to provide limited protection for TCE. For instance, some forms of

94 Xianfa, Articles 4.4 and 119 (1982) (China).

95 In 2006, China ratified the UNESCO Convention on the diversity of cultural expression. According to the Culture Minister Sun Jianzheng, ratification would have allowed China to protect its culture and promote the development of a cultural industry; *see* in this sense Chapter 22 (Germann) in this volume.

96 Article 2 of Intangible Cultural Heritage Law of the People's Republic of China, *supra* note 27.

97 Article 3 of Intangible Cultural Heritage Law of the People's Republic of China, *supra* note 27.

98 Article 5 of Intangible Cultural Heritage Law of the People's Republic of China, *supra* note 27.

99 Article 44 of Intangible Cultural Heritage Law of the People's Republic of China, *supra* note 27.

100 Article 13(2) of the Regulations of the People's Republic of China on Protection of Traditional Arts and Crafts, *supra* note 26.

101 Article 12 of the Regulations of the People's Republic of China on Protection of Traditional Arts and Crafts, *supra* note 26.

102 Article 19 of the Regulations of the People's Republic of China on Protection of Traditional Arts and Crafts, *supra* note 26.

TCE are identical or similar to the forms of "work" (in Chinese, "*zuopin*") provided for under the Chinese Copyright Law, and may accordingly qualify for its protection if they fit its concept of "work."[103] Some TCE-related geographical origins can be recognized as geographical indications[104] and be protected under the Chinese Trademark Law either via defensive means[105] or affirmative means where the geographical indications can be registered as collective or certification trademark.[106] Some forms of TCE-related geographically original products can also apply for geographically original product mark protection,[107] and the Unfair Competition Law can be applied where the use of TCE involves competition relationships.[108]

Nevertheless, except for its "intellectual" nature, TCEs have other features such as being traditional, collective, cultural, and distinctively associated. The current intellectual property legal system appears to be in a difficult position to accommodate all features of TCE, and cannot provide full protection to all its forms. Scholars suggest that the modern IP system is built upon the concepts of modernity and private rights. It is essentially different from TCE, which embodies tradition, collectiveness, and cultural identities, and is distinctively associated. Modern IP may not match TCE protection; using current IP institutions to protect TCE may produce inconsistent and incomplete results. The modern copyright law is not fit to be employed for TCE protection.[109] The protection of TCE needs to create a special mechanism outside of the IP framework.

However, it may be argued that TCE possess the nature of being "intellectual," the same as the nature of the subject matter of IP. Furthermore, the IP system itself is an open and evolutionary system. In this context, the IP system is not, in principle, contradictory to TCE protection. The IP system as a framework could be adapted to the protection of TCE[110] via a restructuring focused on allowing for the accommodation of its special features. A *sui generis* TCE legal protection mechanism may be established, such as a traditional copyright law.

With regard to creating a new *sui generis* TCE protection mechanism, scholars have suggested that the criterion of originality of "work" under copyright law should be modified and the concept of authorship should be adapted to include collective authorship, for the purpose of fitting the specialty of traditional cultural expressions.[111] The originality of TCE is, however, a dynamic process that includes continuity, evolution, and updating. It is not

103 Article 3 of the Copyright Law of the People's Republic of China, *supra* note 25.

104 Article 16(1) of the Chinese Trademark Law provides "*geographical indications mentioned in the preceding paragraph are indications which identify a good as originating in a region, where a given quality, reputation or other characteristic of the goods is essentially attributable to its natural or human factors.*"

105 Article 16(2) of the Chinese Trademark Law states: "*Where a trademark contains or consists of a geographical indication with respect to goods not originating in the place indicated, misleading the public as to the true place of origin, the registration shall be refused and the use of the mark shall be prohibited. But for those which have obtained registration bona fides shall continue to be valid.*"

106 Article 3 of the Trademark Law of the People's Republic of China, *supra* note 39.

107 Zhōnghuá Rénín Gònghéguó Dìlǐ Biāozhì Chǎnpǐn Bǎohù Guīdìng (2005) Dì 2 Tiáo (中华人民共和国地理标志产品保护规定 (2005) 第2条 [Article 2 of the Regulation of the People's Republic of China on Protection of Geographical Indication Products (2005)] (promulgated by the State Council, May 16, 2005). *Supra* note 75.

108 Article 5 of the Anti-Unfair Competition Law of the People's Republic of China, *supra* note 68.

109 Huang Yuye, Woguo Minjian Wenxue Yishu de Tebie Quanli Baohu Moshi [*Chinese Special Rights Model Relating to Protection of Folklore*], 8 FAXUE [LEGAL STUDIES] 122–125 (2009).

110 Yang Hong, Minjian Wenyi Tebie Zhishi Chanquan Baohu de Guoji Lifa Shijian Yanjiu [*Studies on International Legislations on Special Intellectual Property Protection of Folklore*], Huadong Zhengfa Daxue Boshi Lunwen [East China University of Politics and Law, Doctoral Thesis 2010] at 29–40.

111 GUAN YUYING, ZHISHI CHANQUAN SHIYAN ZHONG DE MINJIAN WENYI BAOHU [PROTECTION OF FOLKLORE IN THE VIEW OF INTELLECTUAL PROPERTY] (Falu Chubanshe, 2006).

easy to determine the originality of TCE, in particular those oral TCE that are difficult to identify. In this context, the originality of TCE may be either presumed to exist unless proven otherwise, or it may be replaced with the criteria of "distinctness" and "association" with regard to protection of TCE. Distinctness means that the TCE is different and special, whereas association indicates the close relationship between the TCE and the indigenous people or the traditional local cultural community.

On account of these features of TCE, the *sui generis* TCE protection legislation should emphasize not only the proprietary aspect of TCE but also its intrinsic values. The legislation should further recognize and respect TCE, preserve cultural diversity, promote cultural exchanges and innovation, and contribute to sustainable development.

Due to TCE being diverse, collective, and distinctively associated, the right holders or beneficiaries should be diversified. The right should be collectively enjoyed by indigenous peoples/communities and local communities, families, nations, or any national entity that develops, uses, holds, and maintains the cultural expressions, and has distinctive association with the TCE.[112] In addition, transmitters, collectors, and adapters should also be taken into consideration. It needs to keep balance of all interests and coordinate all rights between the State, indigenous or local communities (minorities), transmitters, collectors, adapters, and other derivative works.[113]

In respect to the protection model, China has a tradition of strong administration, and may easily adopt administrative measures to deal with the protection of TCE. However, public administration may also exhibit bureaucratic problems such as being incentive-driven, corrupt, and having low efficiency. With TCE rights enacted by law, TCE holders or beneficiaries can exercise their rights, protect their interests, and contribute to their development. The exclusive rights over TCE include economic and moral rights. The Chinese Law on Intangible Cultural Heritage has provided for some moral rights such as, "to conduct an intangible cultural heritage investigation, the investigator shall obtain the consent of the respondents, respect their customs and shall not impair their legitimate rights and interests" and "both the intangible cultural heritage forms and connotations shall be respected in their usage. The intangible cultural heritage shall not be used in the form of distortion, derogation, etc."[114] However, economic rights have not been fully clarified under the Law on Intangible Cultural Heritage or other legislations. The *sui generis* TCE legislation could make reference to the WIPO Draft Articles on Traditional Cultural Expressions in order to prescribe further from both a defensive perspective and an affirmative one, for both economic and moral rights.[115]

In addition, the special protection mechanism should also pay attention to the exceptions and limitations to its scope, balance private rights and public interest, provide for both right protection and administrative regulations, adopt a collective management system, and realize a harmonious relationship between the preservation, transmission, and development of TCE.

Conclusion

In general, GR, TK, and TCE are traditional, cultural, distinctively associated, and to some extent publicly known. These features indicate that legal protection of GR, TK, and TCE is a complex matter, which not only relates to property value – especially intellectual property – but

112 WIPO Draft Articles on Protection of Traditional Cultural Expressions WO/GA/40/7, Annex A, at 6.
113 Paragraph 35 of the National Strategy of the People's Republic of China for Intellectual Property (2008), *supra* note 41.
114 Articles 5, 16 of Intangible Cultural Heritage Law of the People's Republic of China, *supra* note 27.
115 WIPO IGC Matters 2011, Annex A at 9, WO/GA/40/7.

also has other non-property concerns such as indigenous people's rights, safety, biodiversity, cultural diversity, and development. In this context, intellectual property as exclusive private rights may provide partial protection for GR, TK, and TCE, especially from a defensive perspective, to preclude the grant of improper intellectual property rights to unauthorized parties, and to prevent misappropriation and misuse of GR, TK, and TCE.

Nevertheless, due to the special features of GR, the current intellectual property system cannot provide full and consistent protection. GR protection may need to establish a special legal mechanism such as a law on the protection of genetic resources outside of the intellectual property system. However, with respect to the protection of TK and TCE, a *sui generis* legal mechanism could be created under the intellectual property framework because both TK and TCE possess the nature of "intellectual," which shares the same nature as the subject matter of IP. TK may be protected via traditional intellectual property rights and TCE by traditional copyright law.

Either the law on protection of genetic resources, the traditional intellectual property right law, or traditional copyright law should take account of the special features of GR, TK, and TCE, in particular their collectiveness and cultural value, in addition to keeping the interests of all stakeholders (right holders or beneficiaries) in balance. These rights are collectively enjoyed exclusive rights that include economic and moral rights. Exceptions or limitations to them should be prescribed so as to safeguard public interest and their fair use. Both rights protection and administrative regulations are necessary. With respect to the protection of GR, TK, and TCE, a harmonious relationship should be established between modern property rights and indigenous people's traditions and customs, and between the preservation, exploitation, utilization, and sustainable development of GR, TK, and TCE.

For the purpose of establishing a new property rights concept in China, where there is no tradition of private property rights, the theoretical foundation of property rights concerning GR, TK, and TCE protection needs to be well-expounded and convincingly explained. This issue would present a challenging and, at the same time, interesting research subject in the future.

37 Grasping Knowledge in Emerging Markets

Is This the Case of Western Pharmaceutical Companies in China?**

*Francesca Spigarelli and Andrea Filippetti**

Introduction

The traditional theory highlights the emerging issues related to the infringement of intellectual property rights of indigenous people by foreign multinational enterprises (MNE). By settling their branches in the developing world, MNEs are able to capture traditional knowledge, register patents based on such principles and incorporate them into their products.[1] The industrialized countries win in this game.

What is the situation for China in the pharmaceutical sector, as for the Traditional Chinese Medicine (TCM) and the growing presence in the country of foreign pharmaceutical companies?

Analyzing the Chinese context, this type of exploitation of traditional knowledge seems to have no place, for several reasons. Although China ranks among the emerging economies, it does not seem a developing country. In terms of economic growth, China holds many records in the world: from production, to exports, to import and foreign direct investments (FDI). China's economic development model is outward-oriented: attracting FDI and pushing exports to leverage domestic growth. In any case, China can take advantage of an internal market of over 1.4 million people. Domestic consumption, in the future, could be the driver of a dynamic and long-lasting economic growth. China is self-sufficient and, in this

* We would like to thank Paolo Davide Farah for having the idea and proposing us to work on this new topic and for his helpful suggestions, ideas and contribution on an earlier draft of the chapter. The authors also thank Alberto Rossi, ItalyChina Foundation, for data provided to support the study.

** This chapter is part of the results of the Research Project on "Current Trends of Chinese Law towards Non-Trade Concerns such as Sustainable Development and the Protection of Environment, Public Health, Food Safety, Cultural, Social and Economic Rights, Labor Rights and the Reduction of Poverty from the Perspective of International Law and WTO Law", coordinated by Professor Paolo Davide Farah at gLAWcal – Global Law Initiatives for Sustainable Development (United Kingdom) and at West Virginia University John D. Rockefeller IV School of Policy and Politics, Department of Public Administration, in partnership with the Center of Advanced Studies on Contemporary China (CASCC) in Turin (Italy), Maastricht University Faculty of Law, Department of International and European Law and IGIR – Institute for Globalisation and International Regulation (Netherlands) and Tsinghua University, School of Law, Institute of Public International Law and the Center for Research on Intellectual Property Law in Beijing (China). This publication and the Conference Series were sponsored by China–EU School of Law (CESL) at the China University of Political Science and Law (CUPL). The activities of CESL at CUPL are supported by the European Union and the People's Republic of China.

1 Paolo Davide Farah & Riccardo Tremolada, *Conflict between Intellectual Property Rights and Human Rights: A Case Study on Intangible Cultural Heritage*, 94 (1) Oregon L. Rev. (2015); Paolo Davide Farah & Riccardo Tremolada, *Diritti di Proprietà Intellettuale, Diritti Umani e Patrimonio Culturale Immateriale*, 2(1) Rivista di Diritto Industriale 21–47 (2014).

perspective, it could manage pharmaceutical sector development and the traditional medicine market as well. China may be able to produce the products required to meet the needs of its population regardless of the foreign pharmaceutical companies.

In this context, however, it is important to understand how the Chinese government should act to foster internationalization and strengthen the position of Chinese companies within the pharmaceutical sector. Is it appropriate that the Chinese government invests and strengthens the pharmaceutical companies, through appropriate policies and economic structures, so that they remain independent enough to take advantage of the development of the internal market and of the protection of the rights related to TCM? Which is the best solution to protect the interests of the Chinese population in the pharmaceutical sector?

These topics are addressed in this chapter. The chapter is divided into three parts. First, we outline the characteristics of the Chinese economic growth. In the second part, we analyze the domestic pharmaceutical market and its level of penetration by foreign multinational companies. Finally, we describe the situation of the TCM sector, to evaluate the actual position of Chinese as well as of foreign companies. Some final remarks close the work

Is China an emerging market?

The classification of China among developing countries is inappropriate when analyzing macroeconomic data on production and on the level of openness of the economy abroad.

In terms of economic growth, in 2010 China overtook Japan's total gross domestic product (GDP). Thanks also to the effects of the financial crisis, which has folded the industrialized economies to a larger extent, the growth rates of GDP are extraordinary.

In the external accounts, many astonishing results have been achieved. China has gained the leading position among world exporters, at the expense of Germany. China has further increased its share of total goods sold: in 2013 it controlled 11.74 per cent of exports worldwide. With regard to imports, China has been growing at an exceptional rate (7 per cent in 2013), and is now the second largest global importer of goods (10.32 per cent of world import in 2013).[2]

These data are a direct consequence of the policy pursued by the government, over the past 30 years, to stimulate the internal development and to project the country into the world economy. The fundamental directions of growth have been guided by an outward-looking philosophy, aiming to attract foreign investment, to acquire knowledge, to upgrade technology and skills and to produce consistent flows of products to be exported. Exports and FDI have become the key levers of development.

Just with respect to FDI, few records have been reached recently. China is, from 2009, the second most important destination for foreign investment flows, after the US. FDI inflows reached USD 124 billion at the end of 2013.[3]

The huge inflow of capital and knowledge has allowed China to move from an agricultural peripheral country to the "factory of the world". Its production capacity is able to satisfy the needs of major companies worldwide. More than 470 of the 500 largest companies in the world have a presence in China and are not just looking for low cost of production but also increasingly technological excellence and high quality standards.[4]

2 http://stat.wto.org/CountryProfile/WSDBCountryPFView.aspx?Country=CN& (last visited July 14, 2016).

3 UNCTAD.

4 Wenley Ding, *The World's Top Choice. China Remains The Most Popular Destination for Foreign Direct Investment*, 38 Beijing Review (September 23, 2010).

FDI and exports led to the accumulation of large quantities of foreign exchange reserves, such as to create pressure on the exchange rate.[5] To solve the imbalances "in the national accounts" generated by this exceptional growth, as well as to elevate the role of China among the global economy, the Chinese government has begun, starting in the late 1970s, a second policy, inspired by a different "dimension" of internationalization.

The Go Global strategy, formally encouraged by the 11th Five-Year Plan, aims to stimulate and encourage domestic firms to expand into international markets, through both greenfield investments and acquisitions.[6] From 2000 onwards, approval procedures to go abroad have been simplified, and increasing financial support has been provided to Chinese companies, as well as consulting, legal and administrative help. The results are huge: from annual investment flows out of just over USD 2 billion until 2000, total outward FDI flows have reached USD 101 billion in 2013.[7]

The Ministry of Foreign Trade reported that at the end of 2009 about 12,000 investors had launched more than 13,000 business activities abroad, in over 177 countries. Also thanks to the anti-crisis stimulus measures, with a package of over 586 billion dollars,[8] China has jumped to sixth place among global investors to cash flows.

Overall, data confirm the effectiveness of the measures taken by the government to change the role and position of China in the world. By adopting a strong international vocation (opened to foreign investments and to investments abroad as well), China has changed its internal market. A deep modernization of both the domestic demand and the supply has been achieved.

On the demand side, consumption patterns are evolving rapidly; styles and standards of living are more and more similar to the Western ones. This is why China is becoming a market outlet for Western companies.

On the supply side, the production structure is constantly improving, inspired by industrialized countries. Producing in China today is no longer synonymous with low labor cost, but also of quality and advanced technology. The infrastructure has been radically reprogrammed, to serve the industry and the mobility of people.

The Chinese pharmaceutical market

The economic developments of China are also reflected in the pharmaceutical field. The Chinese pharmaceutical market is becoming increasingly attractive to Western firms, as it is considered one of the world's most promising emerging pharmaceutical markets.[9]

Economic growth, aging population, urbanization and health system reforms are affecting consumption.[10]

5 Simon Rabinovitch, *China's Foreign Reserves Climb by $153bn*, Financial Times (July 12, 2011), http://www.ft.com/intl/cms/s/0/13c382e6-ac59–11e0-bac9–00144feabdc0.html#axzz3ZCMWAeDf (last visited July 14, 2016).

6 Paola Bellabona & Francesca Spigarelli, *Moving from Open Door to Go Global: China Goes on the World Stage*, 1 Int'l J. Chinese Culture & Mgmt. (2007).

7 Unctad, http://unctad.org/en/pages/DIAE/World%20Investment%20Report/Annex-Tables.aspx (last visited July 14, 2016).

8 Ariana Eunjung Cha & Maureen Fan, *China Unveils $586 Billion Stimulus Plan*, Washington Post Foreign Service (November 10, 2008), http://www.washingtonpost.com/wp-dyn/content/article/2008/11/09/AR2008110900701.html (last visited July 14, 2016).

9 Business Monitor International Ltd, *China Pharmaceuticals & Healthcare Report Q3 2011. Executive Summary.*

10 ICE, *Il Mercato Cinese dei Prodotti Chimici*, Market Report 2009, at 1.

The population of China has achieved an increased sensitivity on health-care services and products. Due to the increasing longevity of people, new lifestyle and environment pollution, key chronic diseases are booming.[11] Confidence and trust in Western medical treatment are spreading quickly.

From the institutional side, in 2009, the government launched new plans for a massive expansion of the national health care coverage, as part of the anti-crisis fiscal stimulus package,[12] aiming for near-universal health coverage.[13] By 2020, China is planned to have a basic health care system providing "safe, effective, convenient and affordable" health services to urban and rural residents, according to the *Guidelines on Deepening the Reform of Health-care System* document.[14] The 12th Five-Year Plan (2011–2016) has also put strong attention on health care and pharmaceutical industries.[15]

As a result, some interesting trends can be highlighted. The Chinese pharmaceuticals market grew by 17 per cent in 2010, reaching a value of USD 25.7 billion and accounting for 18.6 per cent of the Asia-Pacific pharmaceuticals market. In 2011, Chinese market growth was forecasted at 25–27 per cent. China is expected to increase expenditure on health care from 4.7 per cent of GDP to 6–7 per cent in the next years. Even the global financial crisis has not compromised the expenditure boom: at the moment, China is the world's third-largest pharmaceutical market.[16] but it should become the second-largest by 2020, behind only the United States.

Foreign pharma companies in China

Western pharmaceutical companies are becoming more and more interested in China, both as a destination market and as a key pole for research and production purposes.[17] The industry is highly fragmented and with intensive competition; 10 per cent of the market is in the hands of three companies: Yangtze River Pharmaceutical Group (3.6 per cent of the market's value), AstraZeneca PLC (3.4 per cent) and Pfizer Inc. (3.0 per cent).[18] A short company profile of the main pharmaceutical companies operating in China is provided in Box 1.

11 Jan-Willem Eleveld, *China and the New Harbingers of Change,* IMS 2011, http://www.imshealth.com/deployedfiles/ims/Global/Content/Innovation/Powering%20Client%20Transformation/Emerging%20Markets/IMS_Harberingers_of_Change.pdf (last visited July 14, 2016).

12 In 2009, "On Apr. 7, the State Council announced China will spend $124 billion over the next three years widening insurance coverage to include many more of China's hundreds of millions of rural residents, as well as building thousands of community health-care centers to provide a range of basic services, including expanded access to drugs and vaccinations." *See* http://www.businessweek.com/globalbiz/content/nov2009/gb20091113_520982.htm (last visited July 14, 2016).

13 Shaun Rein, *Health-Care Reform, China Style,* Bloomberg Businessweek (August 21, 2009), http://www.businessweek.com/globalbiz/content/aug2009/gb20090821_005732.htm (last visited July 14, 2016); RDPAC, *RDPAC Response to China's Pharmaceutical Policy Reform in the context of China's Healthcare System Reform* (2008).

14 Ye Yuan & Guocheng Jiang, *China Unveils Health-Care Reform Guidelines,* Xinhua (April 6, 2009), http://news.xinhuanet.com/english/2009-04/06/content_11138643.htm (last visited July 14, 2016).

15 Tung Ariel, *Alliances Form in Growing Pharmaceutical Market,* China Daily (August 3, 2011).

16 IMS, *Strategies for emerging markets: 7 keys to the Kingdom,* 30(8) Pharmaceutical Executives (2010), http://www.imshealth.com/deployedfiles/ims/Global/Content/Innovation/Powering%20Client%20Transformation/Emerging%20Markets/emerging_markets_seven_keys_to_kingdom.pdf (last visited July 14, 2016).

17 Francesca Spigarelli & H. Wei, *The Chinese Pharmaceutical Market: Driving Forces and Emerging Trends,* 3 L'Industria, 503–528 (2014).

18 Datamonitor, *Pharmaceuticals in China,* ref. 0099–0372–2010 (2010), at 2.

Box 1. Major pharmaceutical players in the Chinese market

Yangtze River Pharmaceutical Group consists of more than 20 core subsidiary companies, engaged in the development, manufacture and commercialization of both Chinese traditional medicines and on modern medicines.[19] The group, based in the Jiangsu province, was established in 1971. It employs around 5,000 people. In the TCM segment, it has worked with five universities to create the Nanjing Hailing National Engineering Research Center for TCM Manufacturing Technology. Since 2000, the company has exported to Hong Kong, Southeastern Asia, South America, Eastern Europe, and Africa. Its international business has focused on TCM products and plant extracts, and active pharmaceutical ingredients for Western pharma drugs.[20]

AstraZeneca is one of the two major Western companies operating in China. The group is focused on the discovery, development, manufacturing and marketing of prescription pharmaceuticals and biological products for the therapeutics areas including cardiovascular, gastrointestinal, infection, neuroscience, oncology, respiratory and inflammation. Main manufacturing facilities are in the UK, Sweden, the US, Australia, France, Italy, Japan and Puerto Rico. Bulk drug production is concentrated in the UK, Sweden and France. Manufacturing operations for biological products are developed in the US, the UK and the Netherlands. The company has a worldwide sales and marketing network. In the majority of key markets such as the US, Europe and Japan, the company sells through wholly-owned local marketing companies. In other markets, it sells through distributors or local representative offices.[21]

Pfizer is the world's largest biopharmaceutical company, in terms of market share. The company is engaged in the discovery, development, manufacture and marketing of branded prescription small-molecule and biologic medicines, vaccines, nutritional and consumer health products. The company operates in more than 150 countries, with manufacturing plants in 81 locations. The majority of R&D centers are in North America and the UK.[22] As for China, the company has six manufacturing facilities in the country, as well as two research centers. In 2010, Pfizer became the first multinational company "to reach the billion-dollar sales mark in human prescription pharmaceuticals sales in China."[23]

GlaxoSmithKline (GSK) is a global health care company specialized in the discovery, development, manufacturing and marketing of pharmaceutical and consumer health-related products. The company has operations in over 120 countries, with products being sold in more than 150 countries. Its principal R&D facilities are located in the UK, the US, Japan, Italy, Spain and Belgium. Its products are manufactured in about 40 countries. The major markets for the company's products are the US, the UK, France, Germany, Italy and Spain.[24]

The *Northeast Pharmaceutical Group Company Limited* (NEPG) has an increasingly important role in the Chinese market, as a domestic firm. It is a large pharmaceutical enterprise, mainly covering active pharmaceutical ingredients, bio-fermentation, traditional Chinese and Western medicinal preparations and micro-ecological substances.[25]

19 Datamonitor, *Pharmaceuticals in China*, ref. 0099–0372 (2009), at 16.
20 Datamonitor, *supra* note 18, at 31, 32.
21 Datamonitor, *supra* note 18, at 16–18.
22 *Id.*, at 27–30.
23 Pizfer, Our Impact Annual Review 2010, http://www.pfizer.com/files/annualreport/2010/review2010_globalopportunities.pdf (last visited July 14, 2016)
24 Datamonitor, *supra* note 18, at 21–25.
25 *Id.*, at 26.

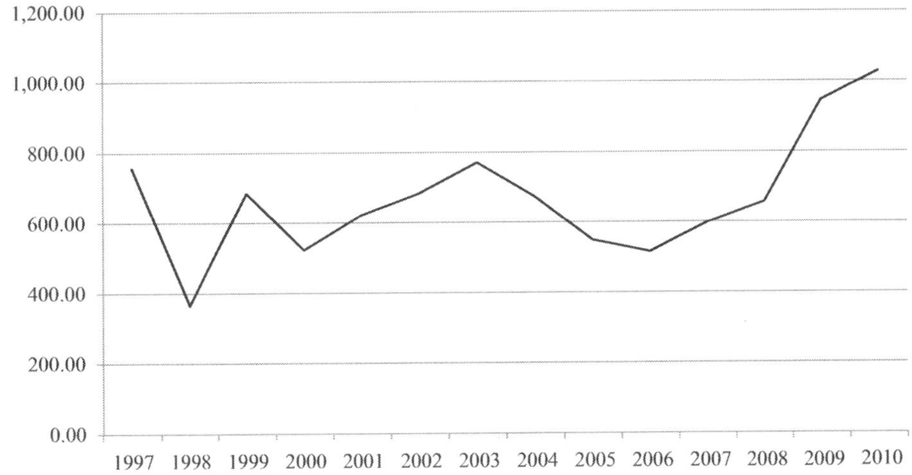

Figure 37.1 FDI in China in the medical and pharmaceutical product sector (data in millions USD)
Source: own calculation on data provided by CeSif, Fondazione Italia Cina – Ceic

Even if the presence in the Chinese market is considered as a high-risk, time-consuming and expensive choice, compared to other emerging markets locations, the increasing amount of foreign FDI in China is a proof of the attractiveness of the Chinese market for Western pharmaceutical companies. From 2000 to 2010, investments nearly doubled (*see* Figure 37.1).

The interest in the Chinese market can be related to several factors.

China is, first of all, a promising outlet market. Internal consumptions are increasing thanks to improved life standards and new behaviors, as well as a consequence of several active promotion policies promoted by the government.[26]

New health care behavior includes a change in attitude towards TCM. Especially in the case of life-saving drugs, Chinese people tend to prefer more and more Western medicines. From an industry perspective, even if generics are the most relevant products in terms of sales (61.4 per cent of the market share in 2009), new kinds of products are expected to gain market shares. Data on imports confirm the strong expansion of Western products: a 195 per cent increase of the value of flows from 2006 to 2010. At the same time, exports flows are also gaining momentum (135 per cent increase over the same period). *See* Figure 37.2.

China is also a strategic logistic base. Western companies located in China have the possibility to establish an effective platform from which it is very easy and convenient to explore and serve the whole Asian area.

Several provinces in China are, indeed, good areas to delocalize the production of raw materials. During the last decades, China has been gaining huge competitive advantages both for economic and for legal motives. Environmental legislation and safety laws do not allow efficient and operative fermentation and chemical plants in Europe and the US.

26 Spigarelli Wei, *supra* note 17.

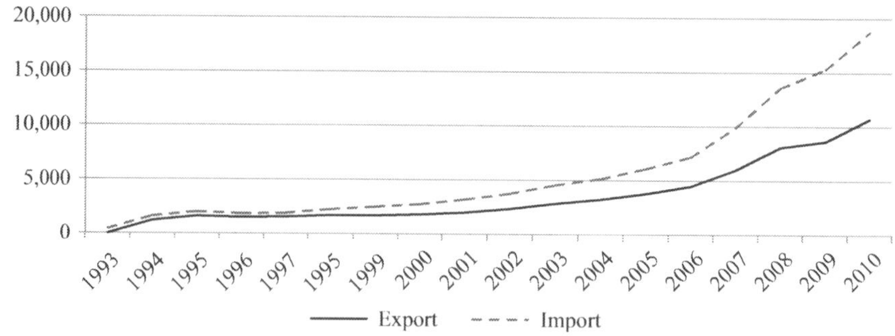

Figure 37.2 Import and export trade in the medical and pharmaceutical product sector (data in millions USD)

Source: own calculation on data provided by CeSif, Fondazione Italia Cina – Ceic

Therefore, antibiotics, cephalosporin and other chemical substances have been produced in China where the costs, as well as the legal implications, are not an issue.

The booming delocalization choices of Western firms are also the result of a process of internationalization of production in China that started right after the launch of the Open-Door Policy by the Chinese government. Thanks to the favorable conditions offered by the Chinese government, in key provinces, multinational corporations built industrial plants for fermentation in northern China, mostly for the production of basic products for antibiotics. After consolidation of its internal industrial base, China became a global leader for the production of base materials. Exports flows of raw materials produced in China are directed to home countries of Western pharmaceutical multinationals, which re-import them to finalize the production of medicines.

Looking at more recent trends, China is engaged in a "new revolution", as clearly highlighted by the 12th Five-Year Plan: the country is investing to become the frontier to develop R&D–intensive industries. This trend is reflected also in the pharmaceutical sector. As shown in Box 2, key champions in the global industry have settled research centers in China. The whole geographical distribution of the value chain is changing. R&D centers take care of basic programs in the Western home markets. Also, the whole process of introducing new drugs is carried out in the Western pharmaceutical firms' countries of origin, mostly to comply with severe rules for trials in Europe and the US.[27] Implementation and applied research phases are performed in China in highly qualified R&D centers to which drug improvement, trials and market extension activities are sometimes outsourced. In-house or external R&D centers in China can benefit from talented Chinese researchers and cooperation with leading universities.[28]

27 "The globalisation process of industry-sponsored clinical trials is growing. More and more study sites are located outside North America and Europe, especially phase III trials. From the latest analysis, there are now more phase II-III trial sites in the rest of the world (ROW) than Europe; 27.0% versus 24.6%, respectively. [. . .] The major emerging regions are still Eastern Europe, Asia and Latin America." *See* Johan Karlberg & Marjorie Speers, *Reviewing Clinical Trials: A Guide for the Ethics Committee* 58 (2010), http://media.pfizer.com/files/research/research_clinical_trials/ethics_committee_guide.pdf (last visited July 14, 2016).

28 Tung Ariel, *supra* note 15.

Box 2. Major Western pharmaceutical R&D centers in China

AstraZeneca

Innovation Center China (ICC) opened its lab facilities in Zhangjiang Hi-tech Park in October 2007. ICC's presence is traced back to the announcement, in May 2006, of a large USD 100 million R&D investment in China. The initial concentration is on cancer through the development of knowledge about Chinese patients, biomarkers and genetics. Researchers at the facility work on the identification, development and validation of new biomarkers. The center also draws on the extensive alternative compound resources of AstraZeneca to analyze and select suitable drugs for Chinese patients. These also provide useful data for further decision-making in clinical trials.[29]

Merck Serono

Merck Serono has established a global R&D center in Beijing, supported by a four year investment of $225 million USD. The center, which will eventually house 200 employees, will be the fourth major R&D center for the company.[30]

Novartis

In 2009, Novartis announced its five-year plans to invest USD 1.25 billion in its two Chinese R&D centers. In 2007, the Novartis Institute of BioMedical Research was opened in Shanghai.[31] Two years later, another center was established in Changshu, near Shanghai, to develop and manufacture active pharmaceutical ingredients (API). In March 2011, Novartis expanded its presence in the Chinese vaccine market by acquiring an 85 per cent stake in Zhejiang Tianyuan Bio-Pharmaceutical Co Ltd., one of the largest private vaccine companies in China.[32]

Pfizer

Pfizer recently has been undertaking a series of initiatives in China to tap into the expertise of Chinese academics and professionals. The aim is to enhance its capabilities in the research and development field. Pfizer has grown its workforce at its Shanghai R&D center to 342 from the 14 hired in 2005, when the center was established. After Shanghai, in 2010 Pfizer completed a greenfield scientific center in Wuhan in China's mid-west region, in the Biolake Science Park.

Roche

Roche has established the R&D Centre China LTD (RRDCC) in 2004 in Zhangjiang Hi-Tech Park in Shanghai, for pharmaceutical R&D, employing about 100 people.[33] The group also controls the following entities in China: Roche Holding Shanghai, Roche Diagnostics (Shanghai) Limited, Shanghai Roche Pharmaceuticals Limited.

29 *See* in general http://en.astrazeneca.com.
30 *See* in general http://seekingalpha.com.
31 *See* http://www.businessweek.com/globalbiz/content/nov2009/gb2009113_520982.htm (last visited July 14, 2016), ***supra*** note 12.
32 Tung Ariel, ***supra*** note 15.
33 Laurie Burkitt, ***Roche Boosts Presence in China***, WALL STREET JOURNAL (September 8, 2010).

The patent surge in China

The increasing role played by China in the global arena is also witnessed in patents data. Overall, patent applications and patents granted have been steadily growing in China over the last decade. This is due to three main factors: (1) an increase in the endogenous production of innovation and technology;[34] (2) an increase in the foreign direct investment in China in technology-intensive industries; and (3) an effect of institutional reforms in the Chinese intellectual property system (Hu and Jefferson, 2009).[35]

The United States and China reached record-level patent-filing activity via WIPO in 2013, as the number of annual international patent applications surpassed 200,000 for the first time. The total number of filings under WIPO's Patent and Cooperation Treaty (PCT) applications filed in 2013 amounted to 205,300 – equal to 5.1 per cent growth compared with 2012. The United States had double–digit growth in PCT filings and together with China accounted for 56 per cent and 29 per cent of the total PCT growth, respectively. China surpassed Germany to become the third-largest user of the PCT system, with Japan as the second-highest user. Figure 37.3, showing the number of patent applications filed with major patent offices in the world, is quite revealing.

Within an international environment increasingly interconnected in terms of technology, the pharmaceutical industry plays an important role. Figure 37.4 shows patent applications filed under the PCT in the pharmaceuticals industry in the period 2001–2011. It is easy to see that China, along with Korea, had a remarkable surge in patents related to the pharmaceutical sector. However, it should be noted that in absolute terms, China has filed 664 patents in the pharmaceutical industry in 2011, compared to 4,165 of the United States.

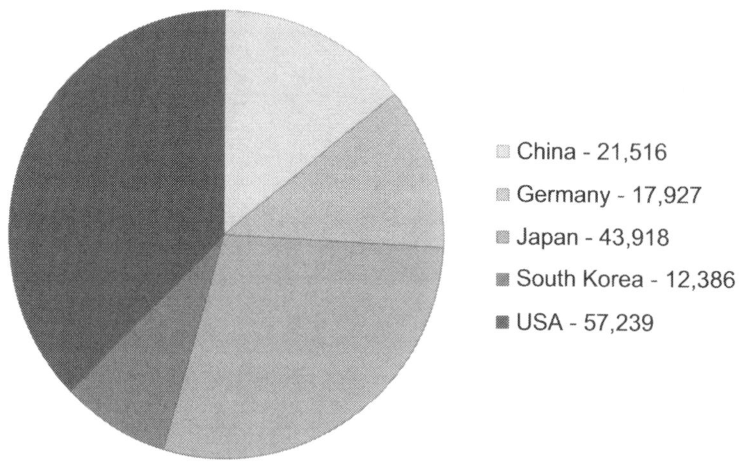

Figure 37.3 Top PCT applicants in 2013
Source: authors' calculations on WIPO data

34 Andrea Filippetti & Antonio Peyrache, *The Patterns of Technological Capabilities of Countries: A Dual Approach Using Composite Indicator and Data Envelopment Analysis,* 37(7) World Dev. (2011).

35 Hu, A. G. and Jefferson, G. H. (2009) 'A Great Wall of Patents: What Is behind China's Recent Patent Explosion?', *Journal of Development Economics*, 90, 57–68.

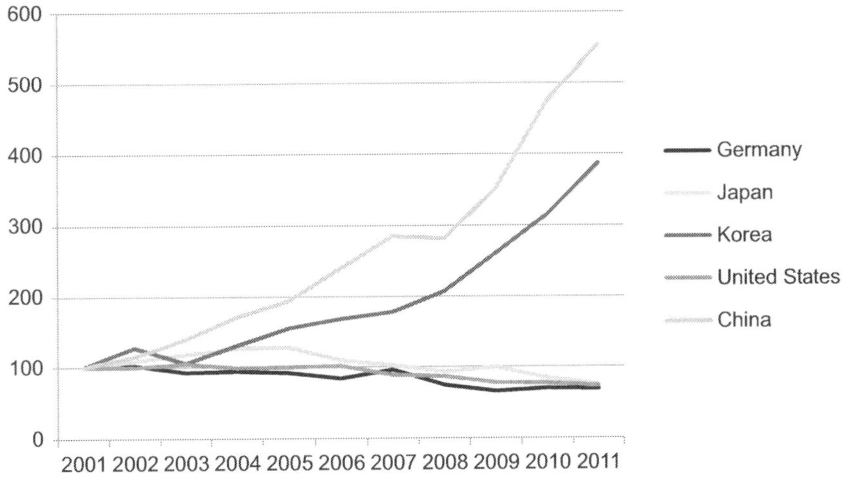

Figure 37.4 Patent applications filed under the PCT – pharmaceuticals industry (2001–2011)
Source: authors' calculations on WIPO data

Since the TRIPS Agreement in 1995, Big Pharma has been a relentless advocate for stronger and more-harmonized patent regimes across the world.[36] Several empirical studies have shown that while on average patents are not regarded as an effective tool to protect innovation, this is indeed the case regarding the pharmaceutical sector.[37] This is also reflected in the great deal of controversy raised by pharmaceutical multinational corporations with respect to the TRIPS compliance, mainly in large emerging economies such as India, Brazil and South Africa.[38]

China arises as a key actor in this case. In the world ranking of total patent applications in the pharmaceutical field, in the period 2003–2007, China is second with 43,508 applications, after the United States (102,133). Japan and Germany follow with 27,685 and 22,203, respectively. Figure 37.5 shows the relative importance of the pharmaceutical sector compared to other hi-tech sectors in China and certain other countries in the period 2003–2007. It reveals how in China patent applications in the pharmaceutical sector have the higher share.

Figure 37.6 displays the granted patents in the Chinese Patent Office in pharmaceutical-related technological class, divided by domestic and foreign, in the period 2003–2009. The

36 Peter Drahos, *Global Property Rights in Information: The Story of TRIPS and the GATT,* 11(1) PROMETHEUS 6–19 (1995); Daniele Archibugi, & Andrea Filippetti, *The Globalization of Intellectual Property Rights: Four Learned Lessons and Four Thesis,* 1(2) J. GLOBAL POL'Y 137–149 (2010); SUSAN K. SELL, PRIVATE POWER, PUBLIC LAW. THE GLOBALIZATION OF INTELLECTUAL PROPERTY RIGHTS (Cambridge University Press, 2003).

37 Wesley M. Cohen, Richard R. Nelson & John P. Walsh. *Protecting their Intellectual Assets: Appropriability Conditions and Why US Manufacturing Firms Patent (or not)* (NBER Working Paper 7552, 2000).

38 PETER DRAHOS & RUTH MAYNE, GLOBAL INTELLECTUAL PROPERTY RIGHTS. KNOWLEDGE, ACCESS AND DEVELOPMENT (Oxfam, Palgrave MacMillan, 2002); Jerome H. Reichman, *Securing Compliance with the TRIPS Agreement after US v India,* 1(4) J. INT'L ECON. L. 585–601 (1998).

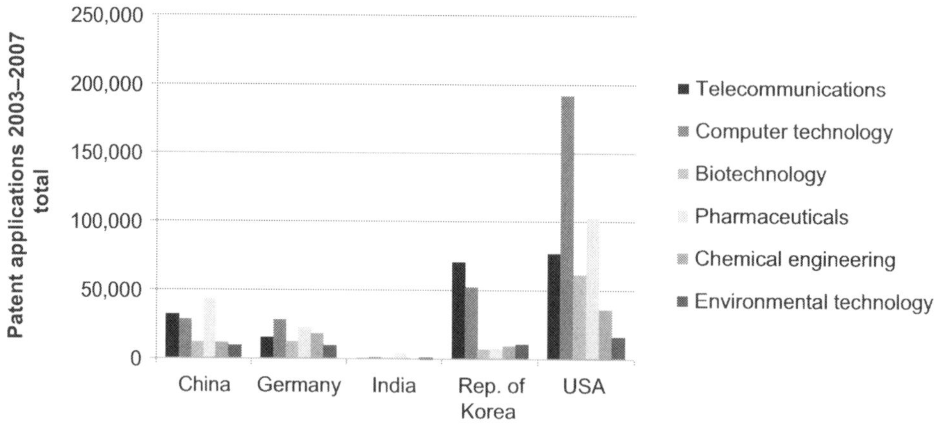

Figure 37.5 Patent applications in hi-tech sectors and country of origin: 2003–2007 total (selected countries)

Source: authors' calculations on WIPO data

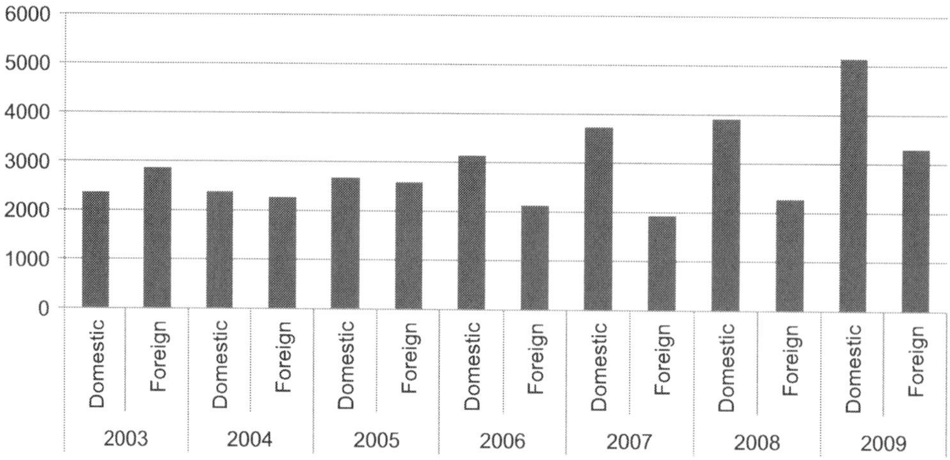

Figure 37.6 Granted patents in the Chinese Patent Office in pharmaceutical-related technological class

Source: authors' calculations on WIPO data

Note: Pharmaceutical-related technological class patents are obtained using a concordance between the International Patent Classification (IPC) used by the European Patent Office (EPO) and the International Standard Industrial Classification of All Economic Activities; biotech-related patents are not included.

chart reveals an interesting trend. While in 2003 the number of foreign patents granted exceeded domestic patents, since 2006 the trend has been inverted. In 2009, the number of patents granted to domestic companies in China was 5,148, in comparison to the 3,305 patents granted to foreign applicants. This reveals an increase in the endogenous capacity of delivering technological innovation by the domestic industry in the pharmaceutical sector.

In addition, it can also be interpreted as the absence of a process of intellectual property colonization.

The traditional Chinese knowledge: An asset to acquire in China?

Considering the surge of FDI in China, it is interesting to consider whether part of the interest of key Western pharmaceutical companies is related to TCM.

The use of alternative or holistic medicines has increased significantly in recent years within the general public.[39] Annual global trade in herbal medicine has surpassed USD 40 billion, with an annual growth rate of 10 per cent.[40]

Chinese companies do not have a primary role in this market. China had nearly 4,700 herbal medicine companies by the end of 2010, with annual output worth 1.2 trillion CNY (USD 186.5 billion).

As for the internal Chinese market for TCM, TCM represents around two-thirds of drug sales in China, but figures are changing rapidly, due to the competition of the conventional drug industry. The sector is fragmented, with the top 10 TCM companies accounting for 14 per cent of total market share. Local companies, including many state-owned enterprises, dominate the internal Chinese market.[41]

Most of China's herbal medicine firms have a weak internationalization propensity.[42] As a consequence, only a small portion of the global TCM market is controlled by Chinese firms.[43]

Partnership and alliances with Western companies could help Chinese companies focused on TCM products enter the international market. They lack competencies on how to position and promote their products, as well as on how to protect their intellectual property rights.[44]

The Chinese State Intellectual Property Office reported that since 1985, more than 68,000 TCM patents were registered. Over 66,000 of them were from domestic applicants.[45] At the same time, China has applied for 3,000 TCM patents in foreign countries, but foreign countries applied for more than 10,000 TCM patents in China.

Big pharmaceutical players have not a significant "place" in this market yet. Consider that GlaxoSmithKline registered in 1997 a TCM patent on "a pharmaceutical composition for the prevention and treatment of gastrointestinal diseases, and its preparation method,"[46] while Roche has registered two TCM patents: on "the use of erythropoietin and iron

39 Datamonitor, *supra* note 18, at 15.

40 Zhang Zhao, *Meeting the EU Formula to Market Herbal Medicines*, China Daily (August 10, 2011).

41 Price Waterhouse Coopers (PWC), Investing in China's Pharmaceutical Industry – 2nd Edition (2009), at 4, http://www.pwc.com/gx/en/pharma-life-sciences/investing-china (last visited July 14, 2016).

42 Zhang Zhao, *supra* note 38.

43 Spigarelli & Wei, *supra* note 17.

44 *Id.* The case of European market is significant. It is the world's second-largest market for herbal medicine, after China. The position of Chinese companies is neglectable. Consider that after the European directive in 2004, regulating herbal medicines, a company must demonstrate that a herbal medicine has been in use for at least 30 years, including 15 years in the EU. "It must also get a certificate that it meets standards for quality and safety. In the seven years following adoption of the regulation, none of the 350 newly authorized herbal medicines came from China.

45 Jingjing H., *TCM growing pains*, Global Times (October 22, 2010).

46 *See* http://chmp.cnipr.cn/englishversion/help/help.html (last visited July 14, 2016).

preparations for producing pharmaceutical combination preparations for treating rheumatic diseases" and the other on "hedgelog protein medicinal composition and its use/a protein solution and its use." Other important Western players do not appear in the database of TCM patents.

Concluding remarks

The position and role of China in international trade and investment flows are so strong and crucial that China cannot be considered as a developing economy anymore. The ability to attract inward FDI is currently beyond the cost benefits related to labor. China is considered a key country because it is a large export market. Huge availability of incentives and facilities for research, innovation and collaborations with centers of excellence are pushing Western companies to invest in China.

These factors are attracting major players in the pharmaceutical market in China: they can have access to a rapidly growing market to sell Western products. In parallel, the possibility to cooperate with excellent R&D institutions and to set up plants to carry out experiments and tests are fueling interest in the Chinese market. The study and the acquisition of distinctive skills related to TCM do not seem strategic, currently, for Western companies. In this sense, some considerations can be made in relation to non-trade issues and concerns.

One of the issues raised by those opposing the establishment of a global regime of intellectual property established by the TRIPS Agreement is the risk of a new colonization based on intellectual property. That is, advanced countries filing patents in foreign countries in order to prevent domestic companies from developing competitive technologies. With some caution, we can claim that there is no evidence of this process in this specific sector. The increase in foreign patents in the pharmaceutical industry suggests the presence of an interesting scientific and technological environment for foreign firms. This is consistent with our results on the dynamics of FDI. Yet, the remarkable pace of domestic patent growth reveals the success of domestic companies to carry out technological innovation themselves. These findings are also in line with those related to traditional Chinese medicine.

Index